THE CONCISE
ROGET'S
International
Thesaurus®

THE CONCISE
ROGET'S
International
Thesaurus®

Fifth Edition

Edited by
Robert L. Chapman

HarperPaperbacks
A Division of HarperCollinsPublishers

HarperPaperbacks   *A Division of* HarperCollins*Publishers*
10 East 53rd Street, New York, N.Y. 10022

First HarperPaperbacks printing: May 1994

Printed in the United States of America

HarperPaperbacks and colophon are trademarks of HarperCollins*Publishers*

20

Contents

Tracking down words in this way is the most obvious and direct use of the thesaurus. The notes that follow explain some of the other ways in which the unique features of *Roget's International Thesaurus®* will help you to solve a word problem.

The thesaurus is a device for finding specific words or phrases for general ideas. A dictionary will tell you many things about a word—spelling, pronunciation, meaning and origins. You use a thesaurus when you have an idea but do not know, or cannot remember, the word or phrase that expresses it best or when you want a more accurate or effective way of saying what you mean. A thesaurus gives you possibilities and you choose the one that you think is best. The range of possibilities includes not only meaning as we usually think of it, but the special sense and force given by nonformal words and phrases (slang and informal), of which many are included and labeled.

Roget's International Thesaurus® is a more efficient word-finder because it has a structure especially designed to stimulate thought and help you organize your ideas. The backbone of this structure is the ingenious overall arrangement of the large categories. The plan is outlined in the "Synopsis of Categories," which begins on page xvii. To make good use of the thesaurus's structure all you need to remember is that it contains many sequences of closely related categories. Beginning at 48, for example, you will see HEARING, DEAFNESS, SOUND, SILENCE, FAINTNESS OF SOUND, LOUDNESS, etc., a procession of similar, contrasting and opposing concepts, all dealing with the perception and quality of sounds. So, when you are not quite satisfied with what you find in one place, glance at nearby categories too; it may be that your original intention was not the best. If you are having trouble framing a thought in a positive way, you may find that it can be more effectively expressed negatively. Seeing related terms, and antonyms, often opens up lines of thought and chains of association that had not occurred to you.

You will have already noticed that the large categories of ideas are numbered in sequence; there are 1073 of them in this edition of *Roget's International Thesaurus®*. Within each category the terms are presented in short paragraphs, and these are also numbered. References from the index to the text are made with two-part numbers such as 247.4, the first part being the number of the category, the second the number of the paragraph within that category. This system, unique to this book, makes for quick and easy pinpointing of the place where you will find the words you need.

The terms within a category are organized also by part of speech, in this order: nouns, verbs, adjectives, adverbs, prepositions, conjunctions, and interjections. This grouping by parts of speech is another aspect of the usefulness of *Roget's International Thesaurus®*. When you are casting about for a way of saying something, rather than looking for a specific word, do not limit your search to the narrow area of the category suggested by the index reference, but examine the offerings in all parts of speech.

There is a further refinement of word arrangement. The sequence of terms within a paragraph, far from being random, is determined by close, semantic relationships. The words closest in meaning are offered in clusters or "domains" that are set off with semicolons; the semicolon signals a slight change in sense or application. A close examination of the groupings will make you aware of the fine distinctions between synonyms, and you will soon recognize that few words are exactly interchangeable. As a help in focusing on the *right* word, terms with special uses—foreign terms and technical terms—are identified by labels in angle brackets.

Cross references are an important feature of the text. They suggest additional meanings of the words you are examining. Notice also that the paragraphs of text are highlighted with terms in boldface type. The bold words are those most commonly used for the idea at hand.

"Word elements" such as prefixes, suffixes, and combining forms, are listed when helpful after the final text paragraph of the category, and before any word lists.

The use of an appropriate quotation often enlivens one's prose. Here again, *Roget's International Thesaurus*® can help you, for it contains thousands of such quotes on scores of subjects. Another bonus of the thesaurus is its dozens of word lists. These contain the names of specific things—animals, poisonous plants, measurements, architectural ornaments—few of which have synonyms. The lists can save you many excursions to specialized reference books.

Thus, *Roget's International Thesaurus*® can help you in countless ways to improve your writing and speech and to enrich your active vocabulary. But you should remember the caution that very few words are true synonyms and use the thesaurus in conjunction with a good dictionary whenever a selected word or phrase is new to you.

Acknowledgments

A work of this scope is only possible through the combined effort of many people. We wish to particularly acknowledge the superior work of Dr. Robert L. Chapman, who reorganized, rethought and rewrote this edition, and to Eugene Ehrlich who oversaw the abridgment.

Computer technology has made working with the technical aspects of the book more efficient. We wish to thank George Alexander for his valuable contributions. Our thanks for the editorial contributions of Andrea Sargent, Mary Kay Linge, Jill Korey, Kenneth Wright, Joe Ford, Ruth Koenisberg, Pamela Marshall, Dave Prout, Ellen Zucker, Frank Gribbon and Edward Mansour.

A special thanks to John Day, supervisor of reference production, who oversaw the complexity of turning the many discs and printouts during the various stages of development into final discs for composition. Our thanks to his staff: Douglas Elam, Elaine Verriest, Celeste Bantz, Ryon Fleming, Jim Hornfischer, Dorian Yeager, and Craig Young. Our appreciation to C. Linda Dingler for the new design; to Dianne Pinkowitz, Joseph Montebello and Helen Moore. And last, we wish to acknowledge the valuable contributions of Mark Liberman and Ken Church of Bell Labs.

How to Use This Book

Roget's International Thesaurus® is a true thesaurus, following the principles of Dr. Peter Mark Roget's great original. It has a text of about 230,000 words and phrases, arranged in categories by their meanings, and a comprehensive index.

The search for a word that you need is a simple process that begins in the index. Suppose that you want a word to describe something that first occurred in the past:

1. In the index, look up the word first and pick the subentry closest to the meaning you want.

2. Follow its number into the text and you will find a whole paragraph of adjectives for things "previous" or "prior."

---

firmament 1070.2

first
 n baseball 745.1
 first ever 817.3
 adj leading 165.3
 front 216.10
 chief 249.14
 preceding 813.4
 beginning 817.15
 foremost 817.17
 previous 833.4
 novel 840.11
 adv before 216.12
 preferably 371.28
 firstly 817.18
first aid 91.14
first base 745.1
first-born
 n senior 304.5
 adj older 841.19
first-class
 superlative 249.13
 first-rate 998.17

---

833 PREVIOUSNESS

NOUNS 1 previousness, earliness 844, **antecedence** *or* antecedency, priority, **anteriority, precedence** *or* precedency 813, precession; *status quo ante* <L>, previous *or* prior state, earlier state; preexistence; **anticipation,** predating, antedating; antedate; **past time** 836

2 antecedent, precedent, premise; forerunner, **precursor** 815, ancestor

VERBS 3 be prior, be before *or* early *or* earlier, come on the scene *or* appear earlier, **precede, antecede, forerun,** come *or* go before, set a precedent; **herald,** usher in, proclaim, announce; **anticipate,** antedate, predate; **preexist**

ADJS 4 previous, prior, early 844.7, **earlier,** *ci-devant* *or* *ci-dessus* <Fr>, **former,** fore, prime, first, **preceding** 165.3, foregoing, above, anterior, **anticipatory,** antecedent; **preexistent;** older, elder, senior

Acknowledgments

A work of this scope is only possible through the combined effort of many people. We wish to particularly acknowledge the superior work of Dr. Robert L. Chapman, who reorganized, rethought and rewrote this edition, and to Eugene Ehrlich who oversaw the abridgment.

Computer technology has made working with the technical aspects of the book more efficient. We wish to thank George Alexander for his valuable contributions. Our thanks for the editorial contributions of Andrea Sargent, Mary Kay Linge, Jill Korey, Kenneth Wright, Joe Ford, Ruth Koenisberg, Pamela Marshall, Dave Prout, Ellen Zucker, Frank Gribbon and Edward Mansour.

A special thanks to John Day, supervisor of reference production, who oversaw the complexity of turning the many discs and printouts during the various stages of development into final discs for composition. Our thanks to his staff: Douglas Elam, Elaine Verriest, Celeste Bantz, Ryon Fleming, Jim Hornfischer, Dorian Yeager, and Craig Young. Our appreciation to C. Linda Dingler for the new design; to Dianne Pinkowitz, Joseph Montebello and Helen Moore. And last, we wish to acknowledge the valuable contributions of Mark Liberman and Ken Church of Bell Labs.

Peter Roget's Preface to the First Edition
(1852)

It is now nearly fifty years since I first projected a system of verbal classification similar to that on which the present work is founded. Conceiving that such a compilation might help to supply my own deficiencies, I had, in the year 1805, completed a classed catalog of words on a small scale, but on the same principle, and nearly in the same form, as the Thesaurus now published. I had often during that long interval found this little collection, scanty and imperfect as it was, of much use to me in literary composition, and often contemplated its extension and improvement; but a sense of the magnitude of the task, amidst a multitude of other avocations, deterred me from the attempt. Since my retirement from the duties of Secretary of the Royal Society, however, finding myself possessed of more leisure, and believing that a repertory of which I had myself experienced the advantage might, when amplified, prove useful to others, I resolved to embark in an undertaking which, for the last three or four years, has given me incessant occupation, and has, indeed, imposed upon me an amount of labor very much greater than I had anticipated. Notwithstanding all the pains I have bestowed on its execution, I am fully aware of its numerous deficiencies and imperfections, and of its falling far short of the degree of excellence that might be attained. But, in a work of this nature, where perfection is placed at so great a distance, I have thought it best to limit my ambition to that moderate share of merit which it may claim in its present form; trusting to the indulgence of those for whose benefit it is intended, and to the candor of critics who, while they find it easy to detect faults, can at the same time duly appreciate difficulties.

P. M. ROGET

April 29, 1852

Foreword

by Robert L. Chapman

Apart from rigorous updating and the addition of thirty new categories, the chief innovation of this fifth edition is a rearrangement of the classes and categories into which Dr. Roget organized our verbal universe. This was undertaken gingerly, since Roget's scheme had held its own for nearly a century and a half, and one hesitates to tamper with the work of a master.

Nevertheless, my own reflection and the comments of some users have convinced me that the recasting is justified. Dr. Roget wished, as he said in his original Introduction, "to obtain the greatest amount of practical utility." That should be the aim of all lexicography. Hence he adopted principles of order which seemed "the simplest and most natural, and which would not require, either for their comprehension or application, any disciplined acumen, or depth of metaphysical or antiquarian lore."

At this distance from his intellectual milieu, Roget's scheme no longer seems simple and natural. It reflects a Platonic view of the cosmos, combined with an Aristotelian marshaling of concepts. By "Platonic" I mean that he orders things as though abstract ideas exist in some supraterrestrial realm, and are made temporal and physical as they descend to Earth. By "Aristotelian" I mean that he proceeds by strict logic.

However respectable this cosmos and its deployment may be philosophically, it does not coincide with the way most people now apprehend the universe. Casting about for a more fitting arrangement, I chose what I call a "developmental–existential" scheme, which can be examined in the "Synopsis of Categories." The notion has been to make the arrangement analogous with the development of the human individual and the human race. It is more associational and durational than logical. This seems to me "the simplest and most natural" array in the mind of our own time.

I wish to acknowledge the help of Charles Courtney, a philosopher at Drew University, and of George Miller, a cognitive psychologist at Princeton, for hearing and counseling me as I thought about the new arrangement. Dr. Donald Kent, who provides the biographical account of his fellow physician Peter Mark Roget, has also given ear to my perplexities.

This edition has benefited enormously from access to the natural-language corpora at AT&T Bell Laboratories, Murray Hill, New Jersey. In particular my thanks go to Mark Liberman and Ken Church of the Labs.

My editor Carol Cohen has been as always the mainstay of the enterprise.

And I reassert with added earnestness my debt to the library of Drew University; and to my wife Sarah, companion of my labors and the one I have most wanted to please.

Synopsis of Categories

996 Importance
997 Unimpor-
   tance

998 Goodness
999 Badness
1000 Bane
1001 Perfection
1002 Imperfection
1003 Blemish
1004 Mediocrity

1005 Danger
1006 Safety
1007 Protection
1008 Refuge

1009 Prosperity
1010 Adversity
1011 Hindrance
1012 Difficulty
1013 Facility
1014 Ugliness
1015 Beauty

Class Fifteen:
SCIENCE AND
TECHNOLOGY

1016 Mathematics
1017 Physics
1018 Heat
1019 Heating
1020 Fuel
1021 Incom-
    bustibility
1022 Cold
1023 Refrigeration

1024 Light
1025 Light Source
1026 Darkness,
    Dimness
1027 Shade
1028 Transparency
1029 Semitrans-
    parency
1030 Opaqueness

1031 Electricity,
    Magnetism
1032 Electronics
1033 Radio
1034 Television
1035 Radar, Radio-
    locators
1036 Radiation,
    Radioactivity
1037 Nuclear
    Physics
1038 Mechanics
1039 Tools,
    Machinery
1040 Automation
1041 Computer
    Science

1042 Friction
1043 Density
1044 Hardness,
    Rigidity
1045 Softness,
    Pliancy
1046 Elasticity
1047 Toughness
1048 Brittleness,
    Fragility

1049 Powderiness,
    Crumbliness
1050 Materiality
1051 Immateriality
1052 Materials
1053 Inorganic
    Matter
1054 Oils, Lubri-
    cants
1055 Resins, Gums
1056 Minerals,
    Metals
1057 Rock
1058 Chemistry,
    Chemicals

1059 Liquidity
1060 Semiliquidity
1061 Pulpiness
1062 Liquefaction
1063 Moisture
1064 Dryness
1065 Vapor, Gas
1066 Biology
1067 Agriculture
1068 Animal
    Husbandry

1069 Earth
    Science
1070 The Universe,
    Astronomy
1071 The Environ-
    ment
1072 Rocketry,
    Missilery
1073 Space Travel

Abbreviations Used in This Book

ADJS	adjective(s)	Eng	England, English
ADVS	adverb(s)	etc	etcetera
Anon	anonymous	fem	feminine
Arab	Arabic	Fr	French
Austral	Australian	Ger	German
Brazil Pg	Brazilian Portuguese	Gk	Greek
Brit	British	gram	grammar
Can	Canadian	Heb	Hebrew
Can Fr	Canadian French	Hind	Hindustani
		Hung	Hungarian
Chin	Chinese	Ir	Irish
CIS	Commonwealth of Independent States	Ital	Italian
		L	Latin
		masc	masculine
Cz	Czechoslovakian	N	North, Northern
Dan	Danish	Norw	Norwegian
E	East, Eastern	Pg	Portuguese
		PHRS	phrase(s)

pl	plural	Sp	Spanish
Pol	Polish	Sp Amer	Spanish
Russ	Russian		American
S	South,	Swah	Swahili
	Southern	Swed	Swedish
Scots	Scottish	Turk	Turkish
sing	singular	UN	United Nations
Skt	Sanskrit	US	United States

1 BIRTH

NOUNS **1 birth,** genesis, **nativity,** nascency, **childbirth, childbearing, having a baby, giving birth, birthing,** parturition, the stork <nonformal>; **confinement,** lying-in, being brought to bed, **childbed; labor,** travail, birth throes *or* pangs; **delivery,** blessed event <nonformal>; *t*he Nativity; multiparity; **hatching;** littering, whelping, farrowing

VERBS **2 be born,** have birth, come forth, issue forth, see the light of day, come into the world; **hatch;** be illegitimate *or* born out of wedlock, have the bar sinister; be born on the wrong side of the blanket, come in through a side door <nonformal>

3 give birth, bear, bear *or* have young, **have; have a baby,** bear a child; drop, cast, throw, pup, whelp, kitten, foal, calve, fawn, lamb, yean, farrow, litter; lie in, be confined, labor, travail

ADJS **4 born,** given birth; **hatched;** cast, dropped, whelped, foaled, calved, etc; née; newborn; stillborn; **bearing,** giving birth

2 THE BODY

NOUNS **1 body,** the person, carcass, anatomy, frame, bodily *or* corporal *or* corporeal entity, physical self, physical *or* bodily structure, physique, soma; organism, organic complex; the material *or* physical part

2 the skeleton, the bones, one's bones, framework, bony framework, endoskeleton; axial skeleton, appendicular skeleton, visceral skeleton; rib cage; skeletology; cartilage

3 the muscles, myon, voluntary muscle, involuntary muscle; **musculature,** physique; **connective tissue,** connectivum; cartilage

4 the skin, skin, dermis, **epidermis,** scarfskin, ecderon; hypodermis, hypoderma; dermis, derma, corium, true skin, cutis,

cutis vera <L>; epithelium, pavement epithelium; endothelium; mesoderm; endoderm, entoderm; blastoderm; ectoderm, epiblast, ectoblast; enderon; connective tissue

5 <castoff skin> slough, cast, desquamation, exuviae

6 membrane; eardrum; mucous membrane; velum; peritoneum; meninges; hymen *or* maidenhead

7 member, appendage, external organ; head, noggin *and* noodle <both nonformal>; **arm;** forearm; wrist; elbow; upper arm, biceps; **leg,** limb, shank, gam *and* pin <both nonformal>, legs, wheels <nonformal>, cnemis; ankle, tarsus; calf; knee; thigh, ham; popliteal space; **hand,** paw <nonformal>; **foot,** dog *and* puppy <both nonformal>

8 teeth, dentition, ivories <nonformal>; periodontal tissue, alveolar ridge; **tooth,** fang, tusk

9 eye, visual organ, organ of vision, oculus, optic, **orb,** peeper <nonformal>; clear eyes, bright eyes, starry orbs; saucer eyes, banjo eyes <nonformal>, popeyes, goggle eyes; naked eye, unassisted *or* unaided eye

10 ear, auditory apparatus; external ear, **outer ear;** auricle, pinna; cauliflower ear; concha, conch, shell; ear lobe, lobe, lobule; auditory canal, acoustic *or* auditory meatus; **middle ear; inner ear**

11 genitals, genitalia, sex organs, reproductive organs, pudenda, private parts, privy parts, privates meat <nonformal>; **crotch,** pubic region, perineum, pelvis; **male organs; penis, phallus;** gonads; **testes, testicles,** balls *and* nuts *and* rocks *and* ballocks *and* family jewels <all nonformal>; spermary; scrotum, bag *and* basket <both nonformal>; **female organs; vulva,** cunt <nonformal>; **vagina;** clitoris; labia, labia majora, labia minora, lips, nymphae; cervix; ovary; uterus, womb; secondary sex characteristic, pubic hair, beard, breasts

12 **nervous system, nerves,** central nervous system, peripheral nervous system; autonomic nervous system; sympathetic *or* thoracolumbar nervous system, parasympathetic *or* craniosacral nervous system; **nerve; neuron; synapse; ganglion; spinal cord**

13 **brain,** encephalon

14 **viscera, vitals, internal organs, insides, innards** <nonformal>, inwards, internals, thoracic viscera, abdominal viscera; inner mechanism, works <nonformal>; peritoneum, peritoneal cavity; **guts** *and* kishkes *and* giblets <all nonformal>; **heart,** ticker *and* pump <both nonformal>, endocardium; **lung, lungs; liver;** gallbladder; spleen; pancreas; **kidney, kidneys**

15 **digestion,** ingestion, assimilation, absorption; primary digestion, secondary digestion; predigestion; salivary digestion, gastric *or* peptic digestion, pancreatic digestion, intestinal digestion; digestive system, alimentary canal, gastrointestinal tract; salivary glands, gastric glands, liver, pancreas; digestive secretions, saliva, gastric juice, pancreatic juice, intestinal juice, bile

16 <digestive system> mouth, maw, salivary glands; gullet, crop, craw, **throat,** pharynx; esophagus, gorge; **abdomen; stomach, belly** <nonformal>, **midriff, paunch; intestine, intestines,** entrails, **bowels; appendix**

17 <nonformal terms> goozle, guzzle; tum, tummy, tum-tum, breadbasket, **gut,** bulge, fallen chest <nonformal>, corporation, spare tire, bay window, **pot,** potbelly, potgut, beerbelly, German *or* Milwaukee goiter, pusgut, swagbelly; **guts,** tripes, stuffings

18 **metabolism,** metabolic process, tissue change; basal metabolism, acid-base metabolism, energy metabolism; **anabolism; catabolism**

19 **breathing, respiration,** aspiration, **inspiration, inhalation; expiration, exhalation;** insufflation, exsufflation; **breath,** wind, breath of air; pant, puff; wheeze, asthmatic wheeze; broken wind; gasp, gulp; snoring, snore, stertor; sniff, sniffle, snuff, snuffle; sigh, suspiration; sneeze, sternutation; cough, hack; hiccup; **artificial respiration,** kiss of life, mouth-to-mouth resuscitation

20 <respiratory system> **lungs; windpipe, trachea**

21 **duct, vessel,** canal, passage; vasculature, vascularity, vascularization; vas, meatus; thoracic duct, lymphatic; **blood vessel; artery; vein; capillary**

22 <body fluids> humor, **lymph,** chyle; rheum; serous fluid, serum; **pus, matter,** purulence; suppuration; ichor, sanies; discharge; **phlegm,** snot <nonformal>; **saliva, spit** <nonformal>; **urine, piss** <nonformal>; **perspiration, sweat** <nonformal>; **tear,** teardrop, lachryma; **milk,** mother's milk, colostrum, lactation

23 **blood,** whole blood, lifeblood, venous blood, arterial blood, **gore;** ichor, humor; grume; **serum,** blood serum; **plasma; blood cell** *or* **corpuscle,** hemocyte; **red corpuscle** *or* **blood cell,** erythrocyte; **white corpuscle** *or* **blood cell,** leukocyte, blood platelet; **hemoglobin;** blood pressure; circulation; **blood group** *or* **type; Rh factor** *or* Rhesus factor; antigen, antibody, isoantibody, globulin; opsonin; blood grouping; blood count, blood picture

ADJS 24 **skeleton, skeletal; bone,** osteal; **bony,** osseous, ossiferous; ossicular; ossified; **spinal,** myelic; **muscle, muscular,** myoid; cartilage, cartilaginous

25 **cutaneous,** cuticular; skinlike, skinny; skin-deep; **epidermal,** epidermic, ecderonic; hypoder-

mic, hypodermal, subcutaneous; dermal, dermic; ectodermal, ectodermic; endermic, endermatic; cortical; epicarpal; testaceous; membranous

26 eye, optic, ophthalmic; visual; **ear,** otic; aural

27 genital; phallic, penile, penial; testicular; scrotal; spermatic, seminal; vulvar, vulval; vaginal; clitoral; cervical; ovarian; uterine

28 nerve, neural; brain, cerebral, cerebellar

29 digestive; stomachal, stomachic, abdominal; ventral, celiac, **gastric,** ventricular; big-bellied 257.18; **metabolic,** basal metabolic, anabolic, catabolic; assimilative, dissimilative

30 respiratory, breathing; inspiratory, expiratory; nasal, rhinal; bronchial, tracheal; **lung,** pulmonary, pulmonic, pneumonic; puffing, huffing, snorting, wheezing, wheezy, asthmatic, stertorous, snoring, panting, heaving; sniffy, sniffly, sniffling, snuffy, snuffly, snuffling; sneezy, sternutative, sternutatory, errhine

31 circulatory, vascular, vascularized; vasiform; venous, veinal, venose; capillary; arterial, aortic; **blood,** hematal, hematic; bloody, gory, sanguinary; lymphatic, rheumy, humoral, phlegmy, ichorous, serous, sanious; chylific, chylifactive, chylifactory; **pussy,** purulent, suppurated *or* suppurating, suppurative; teary, tearing, tearlike, **lachrymal,** lacrimatory

3 HAIR

NOUNS **1 hairiness, shagginess,** hirsuteness, pilosity, fuzziness, frizziness, **furriness,** downiness, fluffiness, woolliness, fleeciness, bristliness, stubbliness, burrheadedness, mopheadedness, shockheadedness; crinosity, hispidity, villosity; hypertrichosis, pilosis, pilosism

2 hair, pile, **fur** 4.2, coat, pelt, **fleece,** wool, camel's hair, horse-hair; **mane;** shag, tousled *or* matted hair, **mat of hair;** pubescence, pubes, pubic hair; hairlet, villus, capillament, cilium, ciliolum 271.1; seta, setula; bristle 288.3

3 gray hair, grizzle, silver *or* silvery hair, white hair, salt-and-pepper hair *or* beard, graying temples

4 head of hair, head, crine; **crop,** crop of hair, mat, elflock, **thatch,** mop, **shock,** shag, fleece, **mane; locks, tresses,** crowning glory, helmet of hair

5 lock, tress; flowing locks, flowing tresses; **curl, ringlet;** earlock, *payess* <Yiddish>; lovelock; frizz, frizzle; crimp; ponytail

6 tuft, flock, fleck; forelock, widow's peak, fetlock, cowlick; **bang, bangs,** fringe

7 braid, plait, twist; **pigtail,** rat's-tail *or* rat-tail, tail; **queue,** cue; coil, knot; topknot, scalplock, pig-tail; bun, chignon; widow's peak

8 beard, whiskers; beaver <nonformal>; full beard, chin whiskers, side whiskers; **side-burns,** burnsides, **muttonchops; goatee,** tuft; imperial, **Vandyke,** spade beard; adolescent beard, pappus, down, peach fuzz, **stub-ble,** bristles, five o'clock shadow

9 <plant beard> awn, brush, arista, pile, pappus

10 <animal and insect whiskers> tactile process, tactile hair, **feeler, antenna,** vibrissa; barb, barbel, barbule; cat whisker

11 mustache, mustachio, soup-strainer <nonformal>, tooth-brush, handle bars *or* handlebar mustache, walrus mustache, tash <nonformal>

12 eyelashes, lashes, cilia; **eye-brows,** brows

13 false hair, switch, fall, chignon, rat <nonformal>

14 wig, peruke, toupee, hairpiece, rug *and* divot *and* doormat <all nonformal>; **periwig**

15 hairdo, hairstyle, haircut, coif-fure, coif, headdress; wave; marcel, marcel wave; **perma-nent,** permanent wave; home permanent; cold wave

16 **feather, plume,** pinion; **quill;**
pinfeather; contour feather,
penna, down feather, plume
feather, plumule; filoplume;
hackle; scapular; **crest,** tuft,
topknot; panache

17 <parts of feathers> quill, cal-
amus, barrel; barb, shaft,
barbule, barbicel, cilium, filament, filamentule

18 **plumage, feathers,** feather,
feathering; contour feathers;
breast feathers; hackle; flight
feathers; remiges, primaries, sec-
ondaries, tertiaries; covert,
tectrices; speculum, wing bay

19 **down, fluff,** flue, floss, **fuzz,
fur,** pile; eiderdown, eider;
swansdown; thistledown; lint

VERBS 20 grow *or* sprout hair;
whisker, **bewhisker**

21 **feather, fledge,** feather out;
sprout wings

22 cut *or* dress the hair, trim, **barber, coiffure,** coif, style *or* shape
the hair; pompadour; wave, marcel; process, conk; **bob, shingle**

ADJS 23 **hairlike,** trichoid, capillary; filamentous, filamentary,
filiform; bristlelike 288.10

24 **hairy, hirsute,** barbigerous,
crinose, crinite, pubescent; pi-
lose, pilous, pileous; **furry,**
furred; villous; villose; ciliate, cirrose; hispid, hispidulous; **woolly,
fleecy,** lanate, lanated, flocky,
flocculent, floccose; woolly-
headed, woolly-haired, ulo-
trichous; bushy, tufty, **shaggy,**
shagged; matted, tomentose;
mopheaded, burrheaded, shock-
headed, unshorn; **bristly** 288.9;
fuzzy

25 **bearded,** whiskered, whiskery,
bewhiskered, barbate, barbigerous; mustached *or* mustach-
ioed; awned, awny, pappose;
goateed; unshaved, **unshaven;**
stubbled, stubbly

26 **wigged,** periwigged, peruked,
toupeed

27 **feathery, plumy;** hirsute; feath-
erlike, plumelike, pinnate, pennate; **downy,** fluffy, nappy, velvety, peachy, fuzzy, flossy, furry

28 **feathered, plumaged,** flighted,
pinioned, plumed, pennate, plu-
mate, plumose

29 **tufted, crested,** topknotted

4 CLOTHING MATERIALS

NOUNS 1 **material, fabric, cloth,
textile,** textile fabric, texture, tissue, stuff, weave, weft, woof, web,
material, goods, drapery; napery, table linen, felt; silk; lace; rag,
rags

2 **fur, pelt, hide,** fell, fleece, vair
<heraldry>; imitation fur, fake
fur, synthetic fur; furring; peltry,
skins; **leather,** rawhide; imitation
leather, leather paper, leatherette

5 CLOTHING

NOUNS 1 **clothing, clothes, apparel, wear, wearing apparel,
daywear, dress,** dressing, **raiment,** garmenture, **garb, attire,
array,** habit, habiliment, fashion,
style 578.1, guise, **costume,** costumery, gear, toilette, trim;
vestment, vesture, investment,
investiture; **garments,** robes,
robing, rags <nonformal>, drapery, finery, feathers; toggery *or*
togs *or* **duds** *or* threads <all non-
formal>, sportswear; work
clothes, fatigues; linen; mens-
wear, men's clothing, womens-
wear, women's clothing; uni-
sex clothing, uniwear, gender-
crossing clothing; gender bender

2 **wardrobe,** furnishings, things,
accouterments, trappings; **outfit,**
livery, harness, caparison; turnout *and* getup *and* rig *and* rig-out
<all nonformal>; wedding
clothes, bridal outfit, trousseau

3 **garment,** vestment, vesture,
robe, frock, gown, rag <nonfor-
mal>, togs *and* duds <both
nonformal>

4 **ready-mades,** ready-to-wear,
store *or* store-bought clothes
<nonformal>

5 **rags, tatters,** secondhand
clothes, old clothes; worn clothes,
hand-me-downs *and* reach-me-
downs <both nonformal>; slops

6 **suit,** suit of clothes, **frock,** dress,

rig <nonformal>, **costume, habit,** bib and tucker <nonformal>

7 uniform, livery, monkey suit <nonformal>

8 mufti, civilian dress or clothes, **civvies** and cits <both nonformal>, plain clothes

9 costume, costumery, character dress; outfit and getup and rig <all nonformal>; masquerade, disguise; tights, leotards; ballet skirt, tutu; motley, cap and bells; buskin, sock

10 finery, frippery, fancy dress, fine or full feather <nonformal>; **best clothes,** best bib and tucker <nonformal>; **Sunday best** and Sunday clothes and Sunday-go-to-meeting clothes and Sunday-go-to-meetings <all nonformal>, **glad rags** <nonformal>, party dress

11 formal dress, formals, **evening dress, full dress,** dress clothes, evening wear, white tie and tails, **soup-and-fish** <nonformal>; dinner clothes; dress suit, full-dress suit, tails <nonformal>; tuxedo, tux <nonformal>; **regalia,** court dress; dress uniform, full-dress uniform, special full-dress uniform, social full-dress uniform; whites <nonformal>, dress whites; evening gown, dinner dress or gown

12 cloak, overgarment

13 outerwear; coat, jacket; overcoat, great-coat, **topcoat,** surcoat; **rainwear;** rain gear, raincoat, slicker, rainsuit, foul weather gear

14 waistcoat, weskit <nonformal>, **vest;** down vest

15 shirt, waist, **shirtwaist,** linen, sark and shift <both nonformal>; **blouse,** bodice, corsage; dickey; sweater

16 dress, gown, frock; skirt

17 apron; pinafore, bib, tucker; smock

18 pants, trousers, pair of trousers or pants, **breeches,** britches <nonformal>, **pantaloons,** jeans, slacks

19 waistband, belt 280.3; **sash,** cummerbund; **loincloth,** breechcloth or breechclout, waistcloth, **G-string,** loinguard, dhoti, moocha; **diaper,** dydee <nonformal>

20 dishabille, déshabillé <Fr>, **undress,** something more comfortable; **negligee; wrap,** wrapper; sport clothes, playwear, leisure-wear, **casual clothes** or **dress,** fling-on clothes

21 nightwear, night clothes; **nightdress, nightgown, nightie** <nonformal>, bedgown; nightshirt; **pajamas,** pj's <nonformal>; sleepers

22 underclothes, underclothing, undergarments, bodywear, **underwear, undies** <nonformal>, skivvies, body clothes, smallclothes, unmentionables <nonformal>, **lingerie, linen,** underlinen; flannels, woolens

23 corset, stays, foundation garment, corselet; **girdle,** undergirdle, panty girdle; garter belt

24 brassiere, bra <nonformal>, bandeau, underbodice; falsies <nonformal>

25 headdress, headgear, headwear, headclothes, headtire; **millinery;** headpiece, **chapeau, cap, hat;** lid <nonformal>; headcloth, **kerchief,** coverchief; **handkerchief**

26 veil, veiling, veiler; yashmak <Turk>, chador <Iranian>; mantilla

27 footwear, footgear; **shoes, boots;** clodhoppers and gunboats and waffle-stompers and shitkickers <all nonformal>; wooden shoes, sabots, pattens

28 hosiery, hose, stockings; socks

29 swimwear; bathing suit, swim suit, swimming suit, tank suit, tank top, two-piece suit; **trunks;** bikini, string bikini or string, thong; wet suit

30 children's wear; rompers, jumpers; creepers; layette, baby clothes, infantwear, infants' wear, baby linen; swaddling clothes, swaddle

31 garment making, **tailoring; dressmaking, the rag trade** <nonformal>, **Seventh Avenue, the garment industry; millinery,** hatmaking, hatting; **shoemaking,** bootmaking, **cobbling;** habilimentation

32 clothier, haberdasher, outfitter; costumier, costumer; glover; hosier; furrier; dry goods dealer

33 garmentmaker, garmentworker, needleworker; cutter, stitcher, finisher

34 tailor, tailoress; fitter; busheler, bushelman; furrier, cloakmaker

35 dressmaker, modiste, *couturière* or *couturier* <both Fr>; seamstress 741.2

36 hatter, hatmaker, **milliner**

37 shoemaker, bootmaker, booter, **cobbler**

VERBS **38 clothe,** enclothe, **dress, garb, attire,** tire, array, **apparel,** raiment, garment, habilitate, **tog** *and* tog out <both nonformal>, dud <nonformal>, robe, enrobe, invest, endue, **deck,** bedeck, dight, rag out *or* up <nonformal>; drape, bedrape; wrap, enwrap, lap, envelop, sheathe, shroud, enshroud; wrap *or* bundle *or* muffle up; swathe, swaddle

39 cloak, mantle; coat, jacket; gown, frock; breech; shirt; **hat,** coif, bonnet, cap, hood; boot, shoe; stocking, sock

40 outfit; equip, **accouter,** uniform, caparison, rig, rig out *or* up, fit, **fit out,** turn out, **costume,** habit, suit; **tailor,** tailor-make, make to order; order, bespeak

41 dress up, get up, doll *or* **spruce up** <nonformal>, **primp** *and* prink *and* prank <all nonformal>, gussy up <nonformal>, spiff *or* fancy *or* slick up <nonformal>, pretty up <nonformal>, deck out *or* up, trick out *or* up, tog out *or* up <nonformal>, rag out *or* up <nonformal>, fig out *or* up <nonformal>; titivate; overdress; put on the dog *or* style <nonformal>; **dress down,** underdress

42 don, put on, slip on *or* into, get

on *or* into, try on, assume, dress in; change; suit up

43 wear, have on, be dressed in, affect, sport <nonformal>

ADJS **44 clothing; dress,** vestiary, sartorial; **clothed, clad, dressed, attired, togged** <nonformal>, tired, arrayed, **garbed,** garmented, habited, habilimented, decked, bedecked, decked-out, turned-out, tricked-out, riggedout, vested, vestmented, robed, gowned, raimented, **appareled,** invested, endued, liveried, uniformed; **costumed,** in costume, cloaked, mantled, disguised; trousered, pantalooned; coifed, capped, bonneted, hatted, hooded; **shod,** shoed, booted

45 dressed up, dolled *or* **spruced up** <nonformal>; spiffed *or* fancied *or* slicked up <nonformal>, gussied up <nonformal>; spruce, dressed to advantage, dressed to the nines, dressed *or* fit to kill <nonformal>; in Sunday best, in one's best bib and tucker <nonformal>, in fine *or* high feather; in full dress, in full feather, in white tie and tails, in tails; **well-dressed, chic,** *soigné* <Fr>, stylish, modish, wellturned, well turned-out; **dressy; overdressed; underdressed,** casual, casually dressed

46 in dishabille, *en déshabillé* <Fr>, **in negligee; casual,** nonformal, sporty

47 tailored, custom-made, bespoke <Brit>; ready-made, storebought *and* off-the-rack <both nonformal>, ready-to-wear; vestmental; sartorial

6 UNCLOTHING

NOUNS **1 unclothing,** divestment, divestiture, divesture; **removal; stripping,** denudement, denudation; baring, stripping *or* laying bare, uncovering, **exposure,** exposing; indecent exposure, exhibitionism, flashing <nonformal>; decortication, excoriation; desquamation, exfoliation; exuviation, ecdysis

2 disrobing, undressing, disrobement, unclothing; uncasing, discasing; shedding, molting, peeling; striptease

3 nudity, nakedness, bareness; **the nude, the altogether** *and* **the buff** <both nonformal>, **the raw** <nonformal>; state of nature, **birthday suit** <nonformal>; not a stitch, not a stitch to one's name *or* back; full-frontal nudity; décolleté, décolletage, toplessness; nudism, naturism, gymnosophy; nudist, naturist, gymnosophist; stripper, stripteaser, ecdysiast

4 hairlessness, baldness, acomia, alopecia; beardlessness, bald-headedness *or* -patedness; baldhead, baldpate, baldy <nonformal>; shaving, tonsure, depilation; hair remover, depilatory

VERBS **5 divest, strip, strip away, remove; uncover,** uncloak, unveil, **expose,** lay open, bare, lay *or* strip bare, **denude,** denudate; fleece, shear; pluck

6 take off, remove, doff, douse <nonformal>, off with, put off, slip *or* step out of, slip off, slough off, cast off, throw off, drop; unwrap, undo

7 undress, unclothe, undrape, ungarment, unapparel, unarray, disarray; **disrobe;** unsheathe, discase, uncase; **strip,** strip to the buff <nonformal>, do a striptease

8 peel, pare, skin, strip, flay, excoriate, decorticate, bark; scalp

9 husk, hull, pod, **shell,** shuck

10 shed, cast, throw off, **slough, molt,** slough off, exuviate

11 scale, flake, scale *or* flake off, desquamate, exfoliate

ADJS **12 divested, stripped, bared,** denuded, denudated, **exposed, uncovered,** stripped *or* laid bare, unveiled, showing; unsheathed, discased, uncased

13 unclad, undressed, unclothed, unattired, disrobed, ungarmented, undraped, ungarbed, unrobed, unapparaled, uncased;

clothesless, garbless, garmentless, raimentless; half-clothed, underclothed, *en déshabillé* <Fr>, in dishabille, nudish; low-necked, low-cut, décolleté, strapless, topless; **seminude,** scantily clad

14 naked, nude; bare, peeled, raw <nonformal>, **in the raw** <nonformal>, in a state of nature, in nature's garb; in one's birthday suit, **in the buff** *and* in native buff *and* stripped to the buff *and* **in the altogether** <all nonformal>, with nothing on, without a stitch, without a stitch to one's name *or* on one's back; **stark-naked,** bare-ass <nonformal>, bare as the back of one's hand, naked as the day one was born, naked as a jaybird <nonformal>; nudist, naturistic, gymnosophical

15 barefoot, barefooted, unshod; discalced, discalceate

16 bare-ankled, bare-armed, barebacked, bare-breasted, topless, bare-chested, bare-faced, barehanded, bare-headed, barekneed, bare-legged, bare-necked, bare-throated

17 hairless, depilous; **bald,** acomous; bald as a coot, bald as an egg; **bald-headed,** bald-pated, tonsured; **beardless,** whiskerless, shaven, clean-shaven, smooth-shaven, smooth-faced; smooth, glabrous

18 exuvial, sloughy; desquamative, exfoliatory; denudant *or* denudatory

ADVS **19** nakedly, barely, baldly

7 NUTRITION

NOUNS **1 nutrition, nourishment,** nourishing, feeding, nurture; alimentation; **food** *or* **nutritive value, food intake;** food chain *or* cycle

2 nutritiousness, nutritiveness, **digestibility,** assimilability; healthfulness

3 nutrient, nutritive, **nutriment** 10.3, food; nutrilite, growth factor, growth regulator; **natural food,** health food; roughage, fiber

4 **vitamin,** vitamin complex; provitamin, provitamin A *or* carotene

5 **carbohydrate,** carbo *or* carbs <nonformal>, simple carbohydrate, complex carbohydrate; hydroxy aldehyde, hydroxy ketone, saccharide, monosaccharide, disaccharide, trisaccharide, polysaccharide *or* polysaccharose; **sugar; starch**

6 **protein** *or* proteid, simple protein, conjugated protein; **amino acid,** essential amino acid; peptide, dipeptide, polypeptide, etc

7 **fat,** glyceride, **lipid,** lipoid; fatty acid; steroid, sterol; **cholesterol;** triglyceride; **lipoprotein,** high-density lipoprotein *or* HDL, low-density lipoprotein *or* LDL; polyunsaturated fat

8 **digestion,** ingestion, assimilation, absorption

9 **digestant,** digester, digestive; pepsin; **enzyme**

10 **metabolism,** basal metabolism, acid-base metabolism, energy metabolism; **anabolism,** assimilation; **catabolism,** disassimilation

11 **diet, dieting,** dietary; dietetics; **regimen,** regime; bland diet; soft diet, pap, spoon food *or* meat, spoon victuals <nonformal>

12 vitaminization, **fortification, enrichment,** restoration

13 **nutritionist, dietitian,** vitaminologist, enzymologist

14 <science of nutrition> **dietetics,** dietotherapeutics, dietotherapy; vitaminology; enzymology

VERBS 15 **nourish,** feed, sustain, nurture; **sustain,** strengthen

16 **digest, assimilate,** absorb; metabolize; predigest

17 **diet,** go on a diet; watch one's weight *or* calories, count calories

18 vitaminize, **fortify, enrich,** restore

ADJS 19 **nutritious,** nutritive, nutrient, **nourishing,** alimentary, alimental; digestible, assimilable

20 **digestive,** assimilative; peptic

21 **dietary,** dietetic; regiminal

8 EATING

NOUNS 1 **eating, feeding, dining,** messing; the nosebag <nonformal>; ingestion, consumption, deglutition; **tasting,** relishing, savoring; **gourmet eating** *or* **dining,** fine dining, gourmandise; nibbling, pecking, licking, **munching;** snacking; **devouring,** gobbling, wolfing, **gorging, overeating,** gluttony, overconsumption; **chewing,** mastication, manducation, rumination; **feasting, regaling,** regalement; **appetite, hunger** 100.7; nutrition 7; **dieting** 7.11; gluttony 672; carnivorism, carnivorousness, carnivority; herbivorism, herbivority, herbivorousness, grazing, browsing, cropping, pasturing, pasture, vegetarianism, phytophagy; omnivorism, omnivorousness, pantophagy; cannibalism, anthropophagy; omophagia *or* omophagy

2 **bite, morsel, taste,** swallow; mouthful, gob <nonformal>; a nibble, a bite, munchies; cud, quid; bolus; **chew,** chaw <nonformal>; nip, nibble; munch; gnash; champ, chomp <nonformal>; snap

3 **drinking,** imbibing, imbibition, potation; lapping, slipping, tasting, nipping; quaffing, gulping, swigging <nonformal>, swilling *and* guzzling <both nonformal>, pulling <nonformal>; compotation, symposium; drunkenness 88.1,3

4 **drink,** potation, potion, libation; draft, dram, drench, **swig** <nonformal>, swill *and* guzzle <both nonformal>, quaff, **sip,** sup, suck, tot, bumper, snort *and* slug <both nonformal>, pull <nonformal>, lap, gulp, slurp <nonformal>; nip, peg; beverage

5 **meal, repast,** feed *and* sit-down <both nonformal>, mess, spread <nonformal>, table, board, meat; **refreshment,** refection, regale-

ment, entertainment, treat; frozen meal, meal pack
6 <meals> **breakfast**, continental breakfast, English breakfast; **brunch** <nonformal>; **lunch, luncheon**, tiffin, hot luncheon; **tea,** teatime, high tea, cream tea; **dinner; supper;** buffet supper *or* lunch; box lunch; take-out; precooked frozen meal, TV dinner; **picnic, cookout,** alfresco meal, **barbecue,** fish fry, clambake, wiener roast *or* wienie roast; coffee break, tea break
7 **light meal, refreshments,** light repast, light lunch, spot of lunch <nonformal>, collation, **snack** *and* nosh <both nonformal>, **bite** <nonformal>
8 **hearty meal, full meal,** healthy meal, large *or* substantial meal, heavy meal, **square meal,** man-sized meal, large order; three squares
9 **feast, banquet,** festal board; lavish *or* Lucullan feast; blow *or* blowout <nonformal>, groaning board
10 **serving,** service; **portion, helping,** help; second helping; **course;** dish, plate; entree, entremets; dessert; cover, place
11 <manner of service> service, table service, counter service, self-service, curb service, take-out service; table d'hôte, ordinary; à la carte; cover; cover charge; American plan, European plan
12 **tableware,** dining utensils; **silverware,** silver, silver plate, stainless-steel ware; **flatware,** flat silver; hollow ware; **cutlery,** knives, forks, spoons; tablespoon, teaspoon; chopsticks; **dishware, china, dishes,** plates, cups, glasses, saucers, bowls, finger-bowls; **dish,** salad dish, fruit dish, dessert dish; **bowl,** cereal bowl, fruit bowl, punchbowl; **tea service, tea set,** tea things, tea strainer, tea-caddy, tea-cozy
13 **table linen, napery,** tablecloth, table cover, table-mat, table pad; **napkin, table napkin**
14 **menu, bill of fare,** carte

15 **gastronomy,** gastronomics, gastrology, **epicurism,** epicureanism
16 **eater,** feeder, consumer, devourer; **diner,** luncher; picnicker; mouth, hungry mouth; diner-out, eater-out; boarder, board-and-roomer; **gourmet,** gastronome, epicure, gourmand, connoisseur of food *or* wine, bon vivant, high liver, Lucullus, Brillat-Savarin; **glutton,** overeater, pig <nonformal>, gourmand; omnivore, pantophagist; **flesh-eater, meat-eater, carnivore,** omophagist, predacean; **man-eater, cannibal; vegetarian,** lactovegetarian, fruitarian, plant-eater, **herbivore,** phytophagan, phytophage; grass-eater, graminivore; grain-eater, granivore; gourmand, trencherman, **glutton** 672.3
17 **restaurant,** eating place, eating house, dining room; eatery *and* beanery *and* hashery *and* hash house *and* greasy spoon <all nonformal>; **fast-food restaurant,** hamburger joint <nonformal>; *trattoria* <Ital>; **lunchroom,** luncheonette; **café; tearoom,** *bistro* <Fr>; **coffeehouse,** coffeeroom, **coffee shop,** coffee bar, coffeepot <nonformal>; **tea shop,** tearoom, tea-garden, teahouse; pub, tavern; chop-house; **grill,** grillroom; cookshop; buffet, smorgasbord; **lunch counter,** quick-lunch counter; hot-dog stand, hamburger stand, drive-in restaurant, drive-in; **snack bar;** milk bar; sushi bar; juice bar; raw bar; pizzeria; **cafeteria,** automat; mess hall, dining hall; canteen; cookhouse, cookshack, lunch wagon, chuck wagon; **diner,** dog wagon <nonformal>; **kitchen** 11.3
VERBS 18 **feed, dine,** wine and dine, mess; nibble, snack, graze <nonformal>; satisfy, gratify; regale; bread, meat; board, sustain; pasture, put out to pasture, graze, grass; forage, fodder; provision 385.9
19 **nourish, nurture,** nutrify, aliment, foster; **nurse, suckle,**

lactate, breast-feed, wet-nurse, dry-nurse; fatten, fatten up, stuff, force-feed

20 eat, feed, fare, take, partake, partake of, break bread, break one's fast; refresh *or* entertain the inner man, feed one's face *and* put on the feed bag <both nonformal>, fall to, pitch in <nonformal>; **taste,** relish, savor; hunger 100.19; **diet,** go on a diet, watch one's weight, count calories

21 dine, dinner; **sup,** breakfast; lunch; picnic, cook out; **eat out, dine out;** board; mess with, break bread with

22 devour, swallow, ingest, **consume,** take in, tuck in *or* away *and* tuck into <all nonformal>, down, take down, get down, put away <nonformal>; **eat up;** dispatch *or* dispose of *and* get away with <all nonformal>; surround *and* put oneself outside of <both nonformal>

23 gobble, gulp, bolt, wolf, gobble *or* gulp *or* bolt *or* wolf down

24 feast, banquet, regale; eat heartily, have a good appetite, eat up, lick the platter *or* plate, do oneself proud <nonformal>, do one's duty, do justice to, polish the platter, put it away <nonformal>

25 stuff, gorge 672.4, pig out <nonformal>, engorge, glut, guttle, cram, eat one's fill, stuff *or* gorge oneself, gluttonize

26 pick, peck <nonformal>, **nibble; snack** <nonformal>, nosh <nonformal>; pick at, peck at <nonformal>, eat like a bird, show no appetite

27 chew, chew up, chaw <nonformal>, bite into; **masticate,** manducate; ruminate, chew the cud; **bite,** grind, champ, chomp <nonformal>; **munch;** gnash; nibble, **gnaw;** mouth, mumble; gum

28 feed on *or* **upon, feast on** *or* **upon,** batten upon, fatten on *or* upon; prey on *or* upon, live on *or* upon, pasture on, browse, graze, crop

29 drink, drink in, **imbibe,** wet one's whistle <nonformal>; **quaff, sip, sup,** bib, swig *and* swill *and* guzzle *and* pull <all nonformal>; **suck,** suckle, suck in *or* up; drink off *or* up, toss off *or* down, drain the cup; wash down; **toast,** drink to, pledge; tipple, **booze** 88.23

30 lap up, sponge *or* soak up, lick, lap, slurp <nonformal>

ADJS **31 eating, feeding, gastronomical, dining,** mensal, commensal, prandial, postprandial, preprandial; **nourishing, nutritious** 7.19; **dietetic; omnivorous,** pantophagous, **gluttonous** 672.6; **flesh-eating, meat-eating, carnivorous,** omophagous, predacious; **man-eating, cannibal,** cannibalistic; insect-eating, insectivorous; vegetable-eating, **vegetarian,** lactovegetarian, fruitarian; plant-eating, **herbivorous,** phytivorous, phytophagous; grass-eating, graminivorous; grain-eating, granivorous

32 chewing, masticatory, manducatory; ruminant, ruminating, cud-chewing

33 edible, eatable, comestible, gustable, esculent; kosher; **palatable,** succulent, **delicious,** dainty, savory; **fine, fancy, gourmet**

34 drinkable, potable

9 REFRESHMENT

NOUNS **1 refreshment,** refection, refreshing, **bracing, exhilaration, stimulation,** enlivenment, vivification, **invigoration,** reinvigoration, reanimation, revival, revivification, revivescence *or* revivescency, renewal, recreation; regalement, regale; **tonic,** bracer, breath of fresh air, pick-me-up *and* a shot in the arm *and* an upper <all nonformal>; cordial

VERBS **2 refresh, freshen,** refreshen, freshen up, fresh up <nonformal>; **revive,** revivify, **reinvigorate,** reanimate; **exhilarate, stimulate, invigor-**

ate, fortify, enliven, liven up, animate, vivify, quicken, brisk, brisken; brace, **brace up,** buck up *and* pick up <both nonformal>, perk up *and* chirk up <both nonformal>, set up, set on one's legs *or* feet <nonformal>; renew one's strength, put *or* breathe new life into, give a breath of fresh air, give a shot in the arm <nonformal>; renew, recreate, charge *or* recharge one's batteries <nonformal>; **regale, cheer,** refresh the inner man

ADJS **3 refreshing,** refreshful, **fresh,** brisk, crisp, crispy, zesty, zestful, **bracing, tonic,** cordial; analeptic; **exhilarating, stimulating, stimulative, stimulatory, invigorating,** rousing, energizing; regaling, cheering

4 refreshed, restored, invigorated, exhilarated, stimulated, energized, recharged, animated, reanimated, **revived,** renewed, recreated

5 unwearied, untired, unfatigued, unexhausted

10 FOOD

NOUNS **1 food,** foodstuff, food and drink, sustenance, kitchen stuff, victualage, **comestibles, edibles,** eatables, viands, **cuisine;** soul food; fast food, junk food; **fare,** cheer, creature comfort; provision, provender; meat <old>, bread, daily bread, bread and butter; health food; board, table, feast 8.9, spread <nonformal>

2 <nonformal terms> **grub,** grubbery, **eats, chow,** chuck, grits, groceries, the nosebag, scarf *or* scoff, tuck, victuals *or* vittles

3 nutriment, nourishment, nurture; pabulum, pap; aliment, alimentation; **refreshment,** refection; **sustenance,** support, keep

4 feed, fodder, provender; forage, pasture, eatage, pasturage; grain; corn, oats, barley, wheat; meal, bran, chop; **hay,** timothy, clover, straw; ensilage, silage; chicken feed, scratch, scratch feed, mash; slops, swill; pet food, dog food, cat food; bird seed

5 provisions, groceries, provender, supplies, stores, larder, food supply; fresh foods, canned foods, frozen foods, dehydrated foods, precooked foods; commissariat, commissary, grocery

6 rations, board, meals, mess, allowance, allotment, food allotment; emergency rations; K ration, C ration, field rations

7 dish 11.1, culinary preparation *or* concoction; cover, **course** 8.10; casserole; grill, broil, boil, roast, fry; **main dish, entrée,** *pièce de résistance* <Fr>, culinary masterpiece, dish fit for a king; side dish

8 delicacy, dainty, goody <nonformal>, treat, kickshaw, **tidbit,** titbit; **morsel,** choice morsel; savory; dessert; ambrosia, nectar, cate, manna

9 appetizer, whet, *apéritif* <Fr>; foretaste, *antipasto* <Ital>; **hors d'oeuvre;** smorgasbord; canapé **dip,** guacamole, salsa, clam dip, cheese dip, hummus; falafel; rumaki; zakuska; **pickle,** sour pickle, dill pickle, cornichon

10 soup, *potage* <Fr>, *zuppa* or *minestra* <both Ital>

11 stew, olla, olio; meat stew; Irish stew, mulligan stew *or* mulligan <nonformal>; goulash, Hungarian goulash; ragout; salmi; *bouillabaisse* <Fr>, *paella* <Catalan>, oyster stew, chowder; fricassee; curry**12 meat,** flesh, red meat; butcher's meat; **cut of meat;** game; venison; **roast,** joint; pot roast; barbecue, boiled meat; forcemeat; mincemeat, mince; hash; jugged hare; pemmican, jerky; sausage meat, scrapple; aspic

13 beef; roast beef; hamburger, ground beef; corned beef, bully *or* bully beef; dried beef; chipped beef; salt beef; jerky; pastrami; beef extract, beef tea, bouillon; suet

14 veal; veal cutlet; breast of veal;

fricandeau; calf's head; calf's liver; sweetbread; calf's brains

15 mutton; muttonchop; **lamb**; breast of lamb; leg of lamb, leg of mutton; saddle of mutton; baked sheep's head

16 pork, pig, pigmeat <nonformal>

17 steak, beefsteak

18 chop, cutlet; pork chop; mutton chop, Saratoga chop; veal cutlet, veal chop, *Wiener schnitzel* <Ger>

19 <variety meats> kidneys; heart; brains; liver; gizzard; tongue; sweetbread <thymus>; beef bread <pancreas>; tripe <stomach>; marrow; cockscomb; chitterlings *or* chitlins <intestines>; prairie *or* mountain oyster <testis>; haslet, giblets

20 sausage, *saucisson* <Fr>, *Wurst* <Ger>; *pâté* <Fr>

21 fowl, bird, edible bird

22 <parts of foul> leg, drumstick

23 fish, *poisson* <Fr>; seafood; finnan haddie; kipper, kippered salmon *or* herring, gravlax; smoked salmon, lox, nova <nonformal>; smoked herring, red herring; fish eggs, roe, caviar; ceviche, sushi; squid, calamari; flatfish, sole, lemon sole, Dover sole, flounder, fluke, dab, sand-dab

24 shellfish; **mollusc,** snail, *escargot* <Fr>

25 eggs; fried eggs; boiled eggs; coddled eggs; poached eggs; scrambled eggs, buttered eggs; dropped eggs, shirred eggs, stuffed eggs, deviled eggs; omelet

26 stuffing, dressing, forcemeat *or* farce

27 bread, the staff of life; loaf of bread; crust, breadcrust, crust of bread; breadstuff; **leaven,** leavening, ferment

28 corn bread; pone, ash pone, corn pone, corn tash, ash cake, hoecake, johnnycake; dodger, corn dodger, corn dab, hush puppy; cracklin' bread <nonformal>; *tortilla* <Sp>

29 biscuit, sinker <nonformal>; hardtack, sea biscuit, ship biscuit, pilot biscuit *or* bread; **cracker,** soda cracker *or* saltine, graham cracker, cream cracker, nacho, potato chip, sultana, water biscuit, butter cracker, oyster cracker, pilot biscuit; wafer; rusk, zwieback, melba toast; pretzel

30 bun, roll, muffin; bagel, bialy *or* bialystoker; brioche, croissant; English muffin; popover; scone; hard roll, kaiser roll, Parker House roll

31 sandwich, *canapé* <Fr>; club sandwich, dagwood; hamburger, burger; submarine *or* sub *or* hero *or* grinder *or* hoagy *or* poorboy

32 noodles, *pasta* <Ital>, paste; **spaghetti,** spaghettini, ziti, fedellini, fettuccine, radiattore, vermicelli, **macaroni,** lasagne; ravioli, *kreplach* <Yiddish>, won ton; **dumpling;** spaetzle, dim sum, gnocchi, linguine; matzo balls, *knaydlach* <Yiddish>

33 cereal, breakfast food, dry cereal, hot cereal; **flour,** meal

34 vegetables, produce, veggies <nonformal>; **greens;** potherbs; **beans,** *frijoles* <Sp>, *haricots* <Fr>; **potato,** spud <nonformal>, tater <nonformal>, Irish potato; **tomato,** love apple; eggplant, *aubergine* <Fr>, mad apple; rhubarb; cabbage, *Kraut* <Ger>

35 salad; greens, *crudités* <Fr>

36 fruit; produce; stone fruit, drupe; citrus fruit; fruit compote, fruit soup, fruit cocktail

37 nut; kernel, meat

38 sweets, sweet stuff, **confectionery; sweet, sweetmeat; confection; candy;** comfit, confiture; **jelly, jam;** preserve, conserve; marmalade; apple butter; prune butter, lekvar; lemon curd; gelatin, Jell-O <trademark>; compote; mousse; blancmange; tutti-frutti; maraschino cherries; honey; icing, frosting, glaze; meringue; whipped cream

39 pastry, *patisserie* <Fr>; French pastry, Danish pastry; **tart;** turnover; timbale; **pie,** *tarte* <Fr>, fruit pie, tart; *quiche* or *quiche*

Lorraine <Fr>; patty, patty cake; patty shell; rosette; dowdy, pandowdy; filo, strudel, baklava; puff pastry; puff, cream puff, croquembouche, profiterole; cannoli, cream horn; éclair, chocolate éclair

40 cake, *gâteau* <Fr>, *torte* <Ger>; *petit-four* <Fr>

41 cookie, biscuit <Brit>

42 doughnut, friedcake, sinker <nonformal>; French doughnut, raised doughnut; glazed doughnut; **cruller,** twister; jelly doughnut, bismarck; fritter; apple fritter

43 pancake, griddlecake, **hot cake,** battercake, flapcake, **flapjack,** flannel cake; buckwheat cake; chapatty <India>; **waffle;** blintz, cheese blintz, *crêpe, crêpe suzette* <both Fr>, Swedish pancake

44 pudding, custard, mousse, flan

45 ice, frozen dessert; **ice cream,** ice milk, French ice cream; **sherbet,** Italian ice; gelato; tortoni; parfait; sundae, ice-cream sundae, banana split; ice-cream soda; frappé; ice-cream cone; frozen pudding; frozen custard, soft ice cream; frozen yogurt

46 dairy products, milk products; **cheese; tofu,** bean curd

47 beverage, drink, thirst quencher, potation, potable, drinkable <nonformal>, **liquor,** liquid; **soft drink,** nonalcoholic beverage; cold drink; carbonated water, soda water, sparkling water, **soda,** pop, soda pop, tonic; milk shake, frosted shake, thick shake, shake *and* frosted <both nonformal>; malted milk, malt <nonformal>; hard drink, alcoholic drink

11 COOKING

NOUNS **1 cooking, cookery, cuisine, culinary art;** food preparation; home economics, domestic science, culinary science; catering; nutrition 7; baking, toasting, roasting, frying, searing, blackening, sautéing, boiling, simmering, stewing, basting, braising, poaching, shirring, barbecuing, steeping, brewing, grilling, broiling, pan-broiling; broil; **dish,** manner of preparation, style of recipe; **condiment,** spice herb; **sauce**

2 cook, chef, kitchener, culinarian, culinary artist; **chief cook, head chef;** fry cook *or* grease-burner <nonformal>, short-order cook; **baker,** pastry cook, pastry chef

3 kitchen, cookroom, cookery, **scullery,** cuisine; kitchenette; **galley,** caboose *or* camboose; cookhouse; **bakery,** bakehouse; **cookware, kitchen ware,** cooker , pots and pans

VERBS **4 cook,** prepare food, prepare, do, cook up, fry up, boil up, rustle up <nonformal>; precook; boil, heat, stew, simmer, parboil, blanch; brew; poach, coddle; bake, fire, ovenbake; **microwave,** micro-cook, nuke <nonformal>; scallop; shirr; roast; toast; fry, deep-fry *or* deep-fat fry, griddle, pan, pan-fry; sauté, stir-fry; frizz, frizzle; sear, blacken, braise, brown; broil, grill, pan-broil; barbecue; fricassee; steam; devil; curry; baste; **do to a turn,** do to perfection

ADJS **5 cooking, culinary,** kitchen

6 cooked, heated, stewed, fried, barbecued, curried, fricasseed, deviled, sautéed, shirred, toasted; roasted, roast; fired, pan-fried, deep-fried *or* deep-fat fried, stir-fried; broiled, grilled, pan-broiled; seared, blackened, braised, browned; boiled, simmered, parboiled; steamed; poached, coddled; baked, fired, oven-baked; scalloped

7 done, well-done, well-cooked; done to a turn *or* to perfection; overcooked, **overdone;** medium, medium-rare; doneness

8 underdone, undercooked, not done, **rare;** sodden, fallen

12 EXCRETION
   <bodily discharge>

NOUNS **1 excretion,** egestion, extrusion, **elimination, discharge;**

emission; eccrisis; **exudation,** transudation; extravasation, effusion, flux, flow; ejaculation, ejection 908; **secretion** 13

2 **defecation,** dejection, **evacuation,** voidance; movement, **bowel movement** or BM, number two <nonformal>, **stool,** shit and crap <both nonformal>; **diarrhea,** loose bowels, flux; trots and runs and shits and GI's and GI shits <all nonformal>; turista and Montezuma's revenge <both nonformal>; lientery; **dysentery,** bloody flux; catharsis, purgation, purge

3 **excrement,** dejection, dejecta, **discharge,** ejection; matter; **waste,** waste matter; **excreta,** egesta, ejecta, ejectamenta; exudation, exudate; transudation, transudate; extravasation, extravasate; effluent

4 **feces,** feculence; defecation, movement, bowel movement or **BM; stool, shit** <nonformal>, **ordure,** night soil, crap and ca-ca and doo-doo <all nonformal>; turd <nonformal>; dingleberry <nonformal>; **manure, dung, droppings;** cow pats, cow flops <nonformal>; cow chips, buffalo chips; guano; coprolite, coprolith; sewage, sewerage

5 **urine,** water, **piss** <nonformal>, number one, pish <Yiddish>, pee and pee-pee and wee-wee and whizz <all nonformal>, piddle, stale; **urination,** micturition, emiction, a piss and a pee and a whizz <all nonformal>; urea

6 **pus; matter,** purulence, ichor, sanies; pussiness; **suppuration, festering,** rankling, mattering, running; leukorrhea

7 **sweat, perspiration,** water; exudation, exudate; diaphoresis, sudor; honest sweat, the sweat of one's brow; beads of sweat, beaded brow; cold sweat; **lather,** swelter; streams of sweat; sudoresis; body odor or **BO,** perspiration odor

8 **hemorrhage,** hemorrhea,

bleeding; nosebleed; ecchymosis, petechia

9 **menstruation,** menstrual discharge or flow or flux, catamenia, catamenial discharge, flowers <old>, **the curse** <nonformal>, the curse of Eve; **menses, monthlies,** courses, period, that time

10 **latrine,** convenience, **toilet,** toilet room, water closet or WC <nonformal>; **john** and johnny and **can** and crapper <all nonformal>; loo <Brit nonformal>; **lavatory,** washroom, public convenience; **bathroom,** basement; **rest room,** comfort station or room; ladies' or women's or girls' or little girls' or powder room <nonformal>; men's or boys' or little boys' room <nonformal>; head; privy, outhouse, backhouse, shithouse <nonformal>, johnny house <nonformal> , closet and necessary <both nonformal>; urinal

11 **toilet,** stool, **water closet; john** and johnny and **can** and crapper and thunderbox <all nonformal>; latrine; commode, potty-chair <nonformal>; **chamber pot,** chamber, pisspot <nonformal>, potty <nonformal>, thunder mug <nonformal>; throne <nonformal>; chemical toilet, chemical closet; urinal; bedpan

VERBS 12 **excrete,** egest, **eliminate, discharge,** emit, give off, pass; ease or relieve oneself, go to the bathroom <nonformal>; **exude,** exudate, transude; weep; effuse, extravasate; **secrete** 13.5

13 **defecate, shit** and crap <both nonformal>, **evacuate,** void, **stool,** dung, have a bowel movement or BM, take a shit or crap <nonformal>, ca-ca or number two <both nonformal>

14 **urinate, pass** or **make water, wet,** stale, **piss** <nonformal>, piddle, pee; pee-pee and wee-wee and whizz and take a whizz and number one <all nonformal>, spend a penny, pump bilge

15 **fester,** suppurate, matter,

rankle, run, weep; ripen, come *or*
draw to a head
16 sweat, perspire, exude; break
out in a sweat, **get all in a lather**
<nonformal>; sweat like a
trooper *or* horse, swelter, wilt
17 bleed, hemorrhage, lose blood,
shed blood, spill blood; bloody;
ecchymose
18 menstruate, come sick, come
around, have one's period
ADJS **19 excretory,** excretive, excre-
tionary; eliminative, egestive; ex-
udative, transudative; **secretory**
13.7
20 excremental, excrementary;
fecal, feculent, shitty *and* crappy
<both nonformal>, scatologic *or*
scatological, stercoral, ster-
corous, stercoraceous, dungy;
urinary, urinative
21 festering, suppurative, rankling,
mattering; pussy, purulent
22 sweaty, perspiry <nonformal>;
sweating, perspiring; wet with
sweat, beaded with sweat, **sticky**
<nonformal>, **clammy;** bathed in
sweat, drenched with sweat,
wilted; in a sweat; sudatory, su-
doric, sudorific, diaphoretic
23 bleeding, bloody, hemorrhag-
ing; ecchymosed
24 menstrual, catamenial

13 SECRETION

NOUNS **1 secretion,** secreta, se-
cernment; **excretion** 12; external
secretion, internal secretion; lactation; weeping, lacrimation
2 digestive secretion *or* juice, salivary secretion, gastric juice,
pancreatic juice, intestinal juice;
bile, gall; endocrine; prostatic
fluid, semen, sperm; thyroxin; au-
tacoid, **hormone;** mucus; tears;
gland
**3 saliva, spittle, sputum, spit,
expectoration;** salivation,
slobber, slabber, slaver, **drivel,**
dribble, **drool;** froth, foam;
mouth-watering
4 endocrinology, eccrinology, hor-
monology
VERBS **5 secrete,** produce, give

out; **excrete** 12.12; water; lactate;
weep, tear
6 salivate, ptyalize; **slobber,** slabber, slaver, **drool, drivel,** dribble;
expectorate, spit, spit up; spew;
hawk, clear the throat
ADJS **7 secretory,** secretive, secre-
tional, secretionary; **excretory**
12.19; lymphatic, serous; seminal, spermatic; watery, watering;
lactational; lacteal, lacteous;
lachrymal, lacrimatory, lachrymose; rheumy; salivary, salivant,
salivous, sialoid, sialagogic
8 glandular, glandulous; **endocrine,** humoral; **hormonal** *or*
hormonic; adrenal, pancreatic,
gonadal; ovarian; luteal; prostatic; splenetic; thymic; thyroidal

14 BODILY DEVELOPMENT

NOUNS **1 bodily** *or* **physical development,** growth, development
860.1, maturation, maturing,
maturescence, coming of age,
growing up, reaching one's full
growth, upgrowth; growing like
a weed <nonformal>; plant
growth, vegetation 310.30, germination, pullulation; sexual
maturity, pubescence, puberty;
nubility, marriageability, mar-
riageableness; adulthood,
manhood, womanhood; re-
production, procreation 78,
burgeoning, sprouting; budding,
gemmation; outgrowth, excrescence; overgrowth 257.5
VERBS **2 grow, develop,** wax, **increase** 251; gather, brew; **grow
up,** mature, maturate, spring up,
ripen, come of age, **shoot up,**
sprout up, upshoot, upspring, upsprout, upspear, overtop, tower;
grow like a weed <nonformal>;
burgeon, **sprout** 310.31, blossom
310.32, reproduce 78.7, procreate
78.8, grow out of, germinate,
pullulate; vegetate 310.31; **flourish, thrive;** mushroom, balloon;
outgrow; overgrow, hypertrophy,
overdevelop, grow uncontrollably
ADJS **3 grown, full-grown, grown-
up,** developed, well-developed,/

fully developed, **mature, adult, full-fledged; growing,** adolescent, maturescent, pubescent; nubile, marriageable; **sprouting,** crescent, budding, flowering 310.35, florescent, **flourishing,** blossoming, blooming, burgeoning, fast-growing, thriving; overgrown, hypertrophied, overdeveloped

15 STRENGTH
<*inherent power*>

NOUNS 1 **strength, might,** mightiness, powerfulness, stamina; **force, potency, power** 18; **energy** 17; **vigor, vitality,** vigorousness, heartiness, lustiness, lustihood; **stoutness, sturdiness,** stalwartness, robustness, hardiness, ruggedness; **guts** *and* gutsiness <both nonformal>, fortitude, intestinal fortitude <nonformal>, **toughness** 1047, **endurance, stamina,** staying *or* sticking power, stick-to-it-iveness <nonformal>; **strength of will,** decisiveness, obstinacy 361

2 **muscularity,** brawniness; beefiness *and* huskiness *and* heftiness *and* hunkiness <all nonformal>, thewiness, sinewiness; **brawn,** beef <nonformal>; **muscle,** brawn, sinew, sinews, thew, thews; musculature, build, physique; tone, elasticity 1046

3 **firmness, soundness,** staunchness, stoutness, **sturdiness, stability,** solidity, **hardness** 1044, temper

4 **impregnability,** impenetrability, **invulnerability,** inexpugnability, inviolability; **unassailability,** unattackableness; resistlessness, **irresistibility; invincibility,** indomitability, insuperability, unconquerableness, unbeatableness

5 **strengthening, invigoration,** fortification; **hardening,** toughening, firming; case hardening, tempering; **restrengthening,** reinforcement; **reinvigoration,** refreshment, revivification

6 **strong man, stalwart, tower of strength,** muscle man, piledriver; bulldozer, hunk <nonformal>; **giant,** Samson, Goliath;

7 <nonformal terms> **hunk, powerhouse, muscle man,** man mountain, big bruiser, strong-arm man, bully, bullyboy, ape, tough, toughie, tough guy, bozo, bimbo, **goon** 671.10, gorilla, meat-eater

8 <comparisons> horse, ox, lion

VERBS 9 **be strong,** overpower, overwhelm; have what it takes, pack a punch

10 **not weaken,** not flag; **bear up, hold up,** keep up, stand up; **hold out,** stay *or* see it out, not give up, **never say die,** not let it get one down

11 <nonformal terms> **tough it out, hang tough, hang in,** stick *or* take it, take it on the chin, sweat it out, stay the distance

12 **exert strength,** put beef *or* one's back into it <nonformal>; use force, get tough <nonformal>, muscle *and* manhandle *and* strong-arm <all nonformal>

13 **strengthen, invigorate, fortify,** beef up <nonformal>, brace, buttress, prop, shore up, support, undergird, brace up; gird, gird up one's loins; steel, harden, case harden, anneal, stiffen, **toughen,** temper, nerve; confirm, sustain; **restrengthen, reinforce; reinvigorate,** refresh, revive, recruit one's strength

14 **proof,** insulate, weatherproof, soundproof

ADJS 15 **strong, forceful,** forcible, **mighty, powerful,** puissant <nonformal>, **potent** 18.12; **stout, sturdy, stalwart, rugged,** hale; hunky *and* husky *and* hefty *and* beefy <all nonformal>, strapping, doughty <nonformal>, **hardy,** hard, hard as nails, cast-iron, iron-hard, steely; **robust,** robustious, gutty *and* gutsy <both nonformal>; strong-willed, obstinate 361.8; **vigorous, hearty,** nervy, **lusty,** bouncing, full- *or* red-blooded; bionic, sturdy as an ox, strong as a lion *or* an ox *or* a horse, strong as brandy, strong as pig-shit <nonformal>, strong as strong; full-strength, double-strength, industrial-strength <nonformal>

16 **able-bodied, well-built,** well-set, well-set-up <nonformal>, well-knit, of good *or* powerful physique, broad-shouldered, barrel-chested, **athletic; muscular,** well-muscled, heavily muscled, thickset, burly, **brawny; thewy,** sinewy, **wiry;** muscle-bound, all muscle

17 **herculean,** gigantic, gigantesque, Brobdingnagian, huge 257.20

18 **firm, sound, stout,** sturdy, tough, hard-boiled <nonformal>, **staunch, stable,** solid; sound as a dollar, solid as a rock, firm as Gibraltar, made of iron; rigid, unbreakable, infrangible

19 **impregnable,** impenetrable, **invulnerable,** inviolable, inexpugnable; **unassailable,** unattackable, insuperable, unsurmountable; resistless, **irresistible; invincible,** indomitable, **unconquerable,** unsubduable, unyielding 361.9, incontestable, unbeatable, more than a match for; overpowering, overwhelming, avalanche

20 **resistant, proof, tight;** impervious; foolproof; shatterproof

21 **unweakened, undiminished,** unallayed, unbated, unabated, unfaded, unwithered, unshaken, unworn, unexhausted; **unweakening, unflagging, unbowed;** in full force *or* swing, **going strong** <nonformal>; in the plenitude of power

22 <of sounds and odors> **intense, penetrating,** piercing; **loud,** deafening, thundering 56.12; **pungent, reeking** 69.10

ADVS 23 **strongly, stoutly, sturdily,** stalwartly, robustly, ruggedly; **mightily, powerfully, forcefully,** forcibly; **vigorously, heartily,** lustily; **soundly, firmly,** staunchly; impregnably, invulnerably, **invincibly, irresistibly,** unyieldingly; resistantly, imperviously; **intensely; loudly,** at the top of one's lungs, clamorously, deafeningly; **pungently**

16 WEAKNESS

NOUNS 1 **weakness,** weakliness, **feebleness,** strengthlessness; **flabbiness, flaccidity,** softness; **impotence** *or* impotency 19; **debility,** debilitation, prostration, invalidism, collapse; **faintness,** faintishness, dizziness, lightheadedness, shakiness, gone *or* blah feeling <nonformal>; **fatigue** 21, exhaustion, weariness, dullness, sluggishness, languor, lassitude, **listlessness,** tiredness, languishment, atony; anemia, bloodlessness, etiolation, asthenia, adynamia, cachexia *or* cachexy

2 **frailty,** slightness, **delicacy, daintiness,** lightness; **flimsiness, unsubstantiality,** wispiness, sleaziness, shoddiness; **fragility,** frangibility *or* frangibleness, brittleness, breakableness, destructibility; disintegration 805; **human frailty,** gutlessness <nonformal>, cowardice 491; moral weakness, irresolution, **indecisiveness,** infirmity of will, velleity, changeableness 853; inherent vice

3 **infirmity, unsoundness,** incapacity, unfirmness, unsturdiness, **instability, unsubstantiality;** decrepitude; **unsteadiness, shakiness,** ricketiness, wobbliness, caducity, senility, invalidism; wishy-washiness, insipidity, vapidity, wateriness

4 **weak point, weakness,** weak place, **weak side,** vulnerable point, chink in one's armor, Achilles' heel *or* heel of Achilles; feet of clay

5 **weakening, enfeeblement, debilitation,** exhaustion, inanition, attrition; languishment; **devitalization,** enervation, evisceration; fatigue; attenuation, extenuation; softening, mitigation, damping, abatement, slackening, relaxing,

relaxation, blunting, deadening, dulling; **dilution,** watering, watering-down, attenuation, thinning, reduction

6 weakling, weak *or* meek soul, weak sister <nonformal>, hot-house plant, softy <nonformal>, softling, **jellyfish,** invertebrate, gutless wonder <nonformal>, **baby,** big baby, crybaby, chicken <nonformal>, Milquetoast, sop, **milksop, namby-pamby, mollycoddle,** mama's boy, mother's boy, mother's darling, teacher's pet; sissy *and* pansy *and* pantywaist <all nonformal>, pushover <nonformal>, lightweight; **wimp,** poor *or* weak *or* dull tool <nonformal>; **nonentity,** hollow man, doormat *and* empty suit *and* nebbish *and* sad sack <all nonformal>

7 <comparisons> a kitten, a reed, thread; a house of cards, a house built on sand; water, gruel, dishwater

VERBS **8** <be weak> **shake,** tremble, quiver, quaver, cringe, cower 491.9, totter, teeter, dodder; halt, limp; be on one's last leg, have one foot in the grave

9 <become weak> **weaken,** grow weak *or* weaker, go soft <nonformal>; **languish, wilt,** faint, **droop,** drop, **sink, decline, flag, pine, fade, tail away** *or* off, fail, fall *or* drop by the wayside; crumble, go to pieces, disintegrate 805.3; go downhill, hit the skids <nonformal>, give way, break, collapse, cave in <nonformal>, surrender, cry uncle <nonformal>; give out, have no staying power, run out of gas <nonformal>, conk *or* peter *or* poop *or* peg *or* fizzle out <nonformal>; come apart, come apart at the seams, come unstuck *or* unglued <both informal>; yield; die on the vine <nonformal>; wear thin *or* away

10 <make weak> **weaken, enfeeble, debilitate,** unstrengthen, unsinew, undermine, soften up <nonformal>, unbrace, unman, unnerve, rattle, shake up <non-

formal>, **devitalize, enervate,** eviscerate; **sap,** sap the strength of, exhaust, take it out of <nonformal>; **shake,** unstring; reduce, lay low; attenuate, extenuate, mitigate, abate; blunt, deaden, dull, damp *or* dampen, take the edge off; draw the teeth, defang; cramp, cripple

11 dilute, cut <nonformal>, **reduce, thin,** thin out, attenuate, rarefy; **water,** water down, adulterate

ADJS **12 weak,** weakly, **feeble,** debilitated, imbecile; **strengthless,** sapless, marrowless, pithless, sinewless, listless, out of gas <nonformal>, nerveless; **impotent, powerless** 19.13; spineless, lily-livered, wimpy *and* wimpish *and* chicken *and* gutless <all nonformal>, cowardly 491.10; unnerved, shookup <nonformal>, unstrung, faint, faintish, lightheaded, dizzy, gone; dull, slack; **soft, flabby,** flaccid, unhardened; **limp,** limber, limp *or* limber as a dishrag, floppy, rubbery; **languorous,** languid, **drooping,** droopy, pooped <nonformal>; asthenic, anemic, bloodless, effete, etiolated; not what one used to be

13 weak as milk and water, weak as a drink of water, weak as a child *or* baby, weak as a chicken, weak as a kitten, weak as a mouse

14 frail, slight, delicate, dainty; puny; light, lightweight; effeminate; namby-pamby, sissified, pansyish; **fragile,** frangible, **breakable,** destructible, shattery, crumbly, brittle, fragmentable, fracturable; **unsubstantial, flimsy,** sleazy, tacky <nonformal>, wispy, cobwebby, gossamery, papery, pasteboardy; gimcrack *and* gimcracky *and* cheapjack *and* ticky-tacky <all nonformal>

15 unsound, infirm, unfirm, **unstable, unsubstantial,** unsturdy, unsolid, decrepit, crumbling, fragmented, fragmentary, disintegrating 805.5; poor, poorish;

rotten, rotten at or rotten to the core

16 unsteady, shaky, rickety, rick-etish, spindly, spidery, teetering, teetery, tottery, tottering, dodder-ing, tumbledown, ramshackle, dilapidated, rocky <nonformal>; groggy, wobbly, staggery

17 wishy-washy, tasteless, bland, **insipid,** vapid, neutral, watery, milky, milk-and-water, mushy; halfhearted, infirm of will or pur-pose, **indecisive,** irresolute, changeable 853.7

18 weakened, enfeebled, dis-abled, incapacitated; **devital-ized,** drained, exhausted, sapped, burned-out, used up, played out, spent, effete, etio-lated; **fatigued, enervated,** eviscerated; **wasted, rundown,** worn, worn-out, worn to a frazzle <nonformal>, worn to a shadow, reduced to a skeleton

19 diluted, cut <nonformal>, **reduced, thinned,** rarefied, attenuated; adulterated; watered, watered-down

20 weakening, debilitating, enfeebling; devitalizing, enervating, sapping, exhausting, fatiguing, grueling, trying, drain-ing, unnerving

21 languishing, drooping, sinking, declining, flagging, pining, fad-ing, failing

ADVS **22 weakly, feebly,** strength-lessly, languorously, listlessly; faintly; delicately, effeminately; daintily; infirmly, unsoundly, unstably, unsubstantially, un-sturdily, flimsily; shakily, un-steadily, teeteringly, totteringly

17 ENERGY

NOUNS **1 energy, vigor, force, power, vitality,** strenuousness, intensity, **dynamism,** demonic energy; **potency** 18; **strength** 15; actual or kinetic energy; dynamic energy; potential energy; **energy source** 1020.1, electrical energy, hydroelectric energy, water power, nuclear energy, solar energy, wind energy

2 vim, verve, fire, adrenalin, **dash, drive; aggressiveness, enter-prise,** initiative, proactiveness, thrust, spunk; **eagerness** 101, zeal, heartiness, keenness, gusto

3 <nonformal terms> **pep,** bang, biff, get-up-and-go, ginger, gism, jazz, sizzle, kick, moxie, oomph, pepper, piss and vinegar, **pizzazz,** poop, punch, push, snap, spiz-zerinctum, starch, steam, zing, zip, zizz

4 animation, vivacity, liveliness, **ardor,** glow, warmth, enthusi-asm, lustiness, robustness, mettle, **zest,** zestfulness, **gusto, élan,** impetus, impetuosity, joie de vivre <Fr>, spiritedness, **brisk-ness,** perkiness, pertness **life, spirit,** life force, vital force or principle, élan vital <Fr>; activity 330

5 <energetic disapproval or criti-cism> **acrimony,** acridity, acerbity, acidity, **bitterness,** tartness, **causticity,** mordancy or mordacity, **virulence; harshness,** fierceness, **rigor,** roughness, **severity, vehemence,** violence 671, stringency, astrin-gency, stridency 58.1, **sharpness, keenness, poignancy,** trench-ancy; edge, point; bite, teeth, grip, sting

6 energizer, stimulus, stimulator, vitalizer, arouser, needle <nonfor-mal>, restorative; **stimulant, tonic** 86.8; **activator,** motivator, motivating force, motive power; **animator,** spark plug and human dynamo and ball of fire <all nonformal>; life, life of the party

7 <units of energy> joule, photon

8 energizing, invigoration, animation, enlivenment, quickening, **vitalization,** revival, revitalization; **exhilaration, stimulation**

9 activation, reactivation; via-bility

VERBS **10 energize,** dynamize; **in-vigorate, animate, enliven, liven, liven up,** vitalize, quicken, goose or jazz up <nonformal>;

exhilarate, stimulate, hearten, galvanize, electrify, fire, build a fire under, inflame, warm, kindle, charge, charge up, psych *or* pump up <nonformal>, rouse, arouse, act like a tonic, be a shot in the arm <nonformal>, **pep** *or* snap *or* jazz *or* zip *or* perk up <nonformal>, put pep *or* zip into it <nonformal>

11 **have energy,** be energetic, be vigorous, **thrive,** burst *or* overflow with energy, flourish, tingle, feel one's oats, be up and doing, be full of beans *or* pep *or* ginger *or* zip <nonformal>, be full of piss and vinegar <nonformal>, champ at the bit <nonformal>

12 **activate,** reactivate, recharge

ADJS 13 **energetic, vigorous, strenuous, forceful, forcible, strong, dynamic,** kinetic, intense, acute, keen, incisive, trenchant, vivid, vibrant; **enterprising, aggressive,** proactive, activist, can-do *and* gung ho *and* take-over *and* take-charge <all nonformal>; **active, lively,** living, **animated, spirited,** go-go <nonformal>, **vivacious,** brisk, bright-eyed and bushy-tailed <nonformal>, lusty, **robust,** hearty, enthusiastic, mettlesome, zesty, zestful, impetuous, spanking, smacking; pumped *and* pumped up *and* jazzed-up *and* charged up *and* switched on <all nonformal>, snappy *and* zingy *and* zippy *and* peppy <all nonformal>, full of pep *or* pizzazz *or* piss and vinegar <all nonformal>

14 **acrimonious, acrid,** acidulous, acid, **bitter,** tart, **caustic,** mordant *or* mordacious, **virulent, violent, vehement,** vitriolic; **harsh,** fierce, **rigorous,** severe, rough, stringent, astringent, strident 58.12, **sharp, keen,** sharpish, incisive, trenchant, **cutting,** biting, stinging, **scathing,** stabbing, **piercing, poignant,** penetrating, edged, double-edged

15 **energizing, vitalizing, enlivening,** quickening; tonic, bracing, rousing; **invigorating,** invigora-

tive; **animating,** animative; **exhilarating,** exhilarative; **stimulating,** stimulative, stimulatory; activating; viable

ADVS 16 **energetically, vigorously, strenuously, forcefully,** forcibly, intensely, like a house afire *and* like gangbusters <both nonformal>, zestfully, lustily, heartily, keenly; **actively,** briskly; **animatedly, spiritedly,** vivaciously

18 POWER, POTENCY
<effective force>

NOUNS 1 **power, potency** *or* potence, prepotency, **force, might,** mightiness, **vigor,** vitality, vim, push, drive, charge; dint, virtue; moxie *and* oomph *and* pizzazz *and* poop *and* punch *and* bang *and* clout *and* steam <all nonformal>; powerfulness, forcefulness; virulence, vehemence; **strength** 15; **energy** 17; **virility** 76.2; cogence *or* cogency, validity, effect, impact, **effectiveness,** effectivity, effectuality, competence *or* competency; productivity, productiveness; power structure; **influence** 893, pull; **authority** 417, weight; **superiority** 249; power pack, amperage, wattage; main force, brute force *or* strength, compulsion, duress; muscle power, sinew, might and main, beef <nonformal>, strong arm; full force, full blast; power struggle; black power; flower power; mana; charisma

2 **ability, capability, capacity,** potentiality, faculty, facility, fitness, qualification, talent, flair, genius, caliber, **competence,** competency, adequacy, sufficiency, **efficiency,** efficacy; **proficiency** 413.1; the stuff *and* the goods *and* what it takes <all nonformal>; susceptibility

3 **omnipotence, almightiness, all-powerfulness;** omnicompetence

4 manpower; horsepower, brake horsepower *or* bhp, electric power, electropower, hydroelectric power; hydraulic power,

water power; steam power; geo-thermal power; solar power; atomic power, nuclear power, thermonuclear power; rocket power, jet power; **propulsion, thrust,** impulse

5 force of inertia; dead force; living force; force of life

6 centrifugal force *or* action, centripetal force *or* action, force of gravity

7 <science of forces> dynamics, statics

8 **empowerment, enablement;** investment, endowment, enfranchisement

9 **work force,** hands, men; **fighting force,** troops, units, firepower; **personnel** 577.11, human resources; **forces**

VERBS 10 **empower, enable;** invest, clothe, invest *or* clothe with power, deputize; enfranchise; endue, endow, **authorize;** arm

11 **be able,** be up to, up to, **lie in one's power; can,** may, can do; make it *or* make the grade <nonformal>; hack it *and* cut it *and* cut the mustard <all nonformal>; charismatize; **wield power,** possess authority 417.13; **take charge** 417.14, get something under one's control *or* under one's thumb, hold all the aces *and* have the say-so <both nonformal>

ADJS 12 **powerful, potent,** prepotent, powerpacked, **mighty,** irresistible, avalanchine, **forceful,** forcible, dynamic; **vigorous,** vital, **energetic,** puissant, ruling, in power; **cogent,** striking, telling, effective, impactful, valid, operative, in force; **strong;** high-powered, high-tension, high-pressure, high-performance, high-potency, bionic; **authoritative;** armipotent, mighty in battle

13 **omnipotent, almighty, all-powerful;** plenipotentiary, absolute, unlimited, **sovereign** 417.17; **supreme** 249.13; omnicompetent

14 **able, capable, equal to,** up to, **competent,** adequate, effective,

effectual, efficient, efficacious; productive; **proficient** 413.22

ADVS 15 **powerfully, potently, forcefully,** forcibly, mightily, with might and main, **vigorously, energetically,** dynamically; **cogently,** strikingly, tellingly, impactfully; **effectively,** effectually; productively; with telling effect, to good account, to good purpose, with a vengeance

16 **ably, capably, competently,** adequately, effectively, effectually, **efficiently, well; to the best of one's ability,** as lies in one's power, so far as one can, as best one can; with all one's might, with everything that is in one

17 **by force,** by main *or* brute force, with the strong arm, with a high hand, high-handedly; **forcibly,** amain, with might and main; by force of arms, at the point of the sword, by storm

19 IMPOTENCE

NOUNS 1 **impotence** *or* impotency, **powerlessness,** forcelessness, feebleness, softness, flabbiness, wimpiness *or* wimpishness <nonformal>, **weakness** 16; power vacuum

2 **inability, incapability, incapacity,** incapacitation, **incompetence** *or* incompetency, inadequacy, insufficiency, ineptitude, **inferiority** 250, inefficiency, unfitness, imbecility; disability, disablement, disqualification; legal incapacity, wardship, minority, infancy

3 **ineffectiveness, ineffectualness,** ineffectuality, inefficaciousness, **inefficacy,** counterproductiveness *or* counterproductivity, invalidity, **futility, uselessness,** bootlessness, failure 410; fatuity, inanity

4 **helplessness, defenselessness,** unprotectedness, vulnerability; **debilitation,** invalidism, effeteness, etiolation, enervation

5 **emasculation,** demasculinization, effeminization, neutering, maiming, castration 255.4

6 impotent, weakling 16.6, invalid, incompetent; flash in the pan, blank cartridge, wimp *and* dud <both nonformal>; eunuch, *castrato* <Ital>, gelding

VERBS **7 be impotent,** lack force; be ineffective, avail nothing, not work *or* do not take <nonformal>; **waste one's effort,** bang one's head against a brick wall, have one's hands tied, spin one's wheels, tilt at windmills, run in circles

8 cannot, not be able, not have it *and* not hack it *and* not cut it *and* not cut the mustard <all nonformal>, not make it *and* not make the grade *and* not make the cut <all nonformal>

9 disable, disenable, unfit, **incapacitate,** drain, de-energize; enfeeble, debilitate, **weaken** 16.9,10; cripple, maim, lame, hamstring, knee-cap, defang, pull the teeth of <nonformal>; wing, clip the wings of; **inactivate,** disarm, unarm, put out of action, put *hors de combat*; **put out of order,** put out of commission <nonformal>, throw out of gear; bugger *and* bugger up *and* queer *and* queer the works *and* gum up *or* screw up <all nonformal>, throw a wrench *or* monkey wrench in the machinery <nonformal>, sabotage, wreck; kibosh *and* put the kibosh on <both nonformal>; spike, spike one's guns, put a spoke in one's wheels

10 <put out of action> paralyze, prostrate, shoot down in flames <nonformal>

11 disqualify; invalidate, knock the bottom out of <nonformal>

12 unman, unnerve, enervate, exhaust, etiolate, **devitalize; emasculate,** cut the balls off <nonformal>, demasculinize, effeminate; desex, desexualize; sterilize; castrate 255.11

ADJS **13 impotent, powerless, forceless, out of gas** <nonformal>; feeble, soft, flabby, **weak** 16.12, weak as a kitten, wimpy *or* wimpish <nonformal>

14 unable, incapable, incompetent, inefficient, ineffective; **unqualified,** inept, unendowed, ungifted, untalented, **unfit,** unfitted; **outmatched,** out of one's depth, in over one's head, outgunned; **inferior** 250.6

15 ineffective, ineffectual, inefficacious, counterproductive, feckless, not up to scratch *or* up to snuff <nonformal>, **inadequate** 250.7; **invalid, inoperative,** of no force; nugatory, nugacious; fatuous, fatuitous; **vain, futile, inutile, useless,** unavailing, bootless, fruitless; all talk and no action, all wind; **empty,** inane; **debilitated,** effete, enervated, etiolated, barren, sterile, washed-out <nonformal>

16 disabled, incapacitated; crippled, hamstrung

17 out of action, out of commission and out of it <both nonformal>

18 helpless, defenseless, unprotected; vulnerable, like a sitting duck <nonformal>, aidless, friendless, unfriended; fatherless, motherless; leaderless, guideless; **untenable,** pregnable, vulnerable

19 unmanned, unnerved, enervated, debilitated, **devitalized;** nerveless, sinewless, marrowless, pithless, lustless; **castrated,** emasculate, emasculated, gelded, eunuchized, unsexed, deballed <nonformal>, demasculinized, effeminized

ADVS **20 beyond one,** beyond one's power *or* capacity *or* ability, beyond one's depth, out of one's league <nonformal>, above one's head, too much for

20 REST, REPOSE

NOUNS **1 rest, repose, ease, relaxation,** slippered *or* unbuttoned ease, decompression <nonformal>; **comfort** 121; restfulness, quiet, tranquility; inactivity 331; sleep 22

2 respite, recess, rest, pause,
halt, stay, lull, **break,** surcease,
suspension, interlude, **intermission,** letup <nonformal>, **time
out** <nonformal>, time to catch
one's breath; **breathing spell,**
breathing time, breathing
place, breathing space, breath;
breather; coffee break, tea break,
cigarette break; cocktail hour,
happy hour <nonformal>; enforced respite, downtime; R and
R *or* rest and recreation

3 vacation; time off; day off, week
off, month off, etc; weekend;
leave, leave of absence, furlough; liberty, shore leave;
sabbatical, sabbatical leave *or*
year; **weekend; busman's holiday**

4 holiday, day off; red-letter day,
gala day, fete day, festival day; national holiday, legal holiday; High
Holiday, High Holy Day; holy
day; feast, feast day, high day,
church feast, fixed feast, movable
feast; half-holiday

5 day of rest; Sabbath, Sunday,
Lord's day

VERBS **6 rest, repose,** take rest,
take one's ease, **take it easy**
<nonformal>, lay down one's
tools, rest from one's labors, rest
on one's oars, take life easy; go to
rest, settle to rest; lie down, have
a lie-down, go to bed, snug down,
curl up, tuck up, bed, bed down,
couch, recline, lounge, drape oneself, sprawl, loll; take off one's
shoes, unbuckle one's belt, get *or*
take a load off one's feet, put one's
feet up

7 relax, unbend, unwind, slack,
slacken, **ease; ease up, let up,**
slack off, **ease off,** let down, **slow
down,** take it slow, let up, take
time to catch one's breath; lay
back *and* kick back *and* decompress <all nonformal>

**8 take a rest, take a break,
break, take time out** *and* grab
some R and R <both nonformal>,
pause, lay off, **knock off** <nonformal>, recess, **take a recess, take
ten** *and* take five <both nonfor-

mal>; stop for breath, catch one's
breath, breathe; stop work, suspend operations, call it a day; go
to bed with the chickens, sleep in;
take a nap

9 vacation, get away from it all,
holiday, take a holiday, make holiday; **take a leave of absence,** take
leave, go on leave, go on furlough,
take one's sabbatical; weekend

ADJS **10 vacational, holiday,** festal;
sabbatical; **comfortable** 121.11;
restful, quiet 173.12

ADVS **11 at rest, at ease,** at one's
ease; abed, in bed

12 on vacation, on leave, on furlough; off duty, on one's own time

21 FATIGUE

NOUNS **1 fatigue, tiredness, weariness,** wearifulness; **burnout,**
end of one's tether, overtiredness,
overstrain; faintness, goneness,
weakness, enfeeblement, lack of
staying power, enervation, debility, debilitation 16.1; jadedness;
lassitude, languor; tension fatigue, stance fatigue, stimulation
fatigue; fatigue disease, fatigue
syndrome; combat fatigue; mental fatigue; strain, mental strain,
heart strain, eyestrain; sleepiness
22.1

2 exhaustion, exhaustedness,
draining; **collapse, prostration,**
breakdown, crack-up <nonformal>, nervous exhaustion *or*
prostration

**3 breathlessness, shortness of
breath,** windedness, shortwindedness; panting, gasping;
dyspnea, labored breathing

VERBS **4 fatigue, tire, weary, exhaust,** wilt, flag, jade, harass;
wear, wear on *or* upon, **wear
down; tire out, wear out, burn
out; use up; do in; wind,** put out
of breath; overtire, overweary,
overfatigue, overstrain; weaken,
enervate, debilitate 16.10; weary
or tire to death; prostrate

**5 burn out, get tired, grow
weary, tire, weary,** fatigue, jade;
flag, droop, faint, sink, feel
dragged out, wilt; **play out,** run

out, run down, burn out; gasp, wheeze, pant, puff, blow, puff and blow, puff like a grampus; collapse, break down, crack up <nonformal>, give out, drop, fall *or* drop by the wayside, drop in one's tracks, succumb

6 <nonformal terms> **beat, poop,** frazzle, fag, tucker; fag out, tucker out, knock out, do in, do up; **poop out,** peter out

ADJS 7 **tired, weary, fatigued,** wearied, weariful, jaded, run-down, good and tired; unrefreshed, unrestored, in need of rest, ready to drop; **faint,** fainting, feeling faint, **weak,** rocky <nonformal>, enfeebled, enervated, debilitated, seedy <nonformal>, weakened 16.13,18; drooping, droopy, wilting, flagging, sagging; languid; worn, worn-down, **worn to a frazzle** *or* shadow, toilworn, weary-worn; wayworn, wayweary; foot-weary, weary-footed, footsore; tired-armed; tiredwinged, weary-winged; wearyladen

8 <nonformal terms> **beat, pooped, bushed,** poohed, paled, frazzled, bagged, fagged, tuckered, plumb tuckered, done, done in, all in, dead, dead beat, dead on one's feet, gone; **pooped out,** knocked out, wiped out, tuckered out, played out, fagged out; run ragged; used up, done up, beat up, washed-up

9 tired-looking, tired-eyed, haggard

10 **burnt-out, exhausted,** drained, **spent,** unable to go on, gone; **tired out, worn-out,** beaten; bone-tired, bone-weary; **dogtired,** dog-weary; **dead-tired, tired to death,** weary unto death, dead-alive *or* dead-and-alive, more dead than alive, ready to drop, on one's last legs; prostrate

11 burnt-out, overtired, overweary

12 **breathless, winded;** wheezing, puffing, panting, **out of breath,** short of breath *or* wind; shortwinded, short-breathed, brokenwinded, touched in the wind, dyspneic

13 fatiguing, wearying, wearing, tiring, straining, stressful, trying, exhausting, draining, grueling

ADVS 14 **out,** to the point of exhaustion

22 SLEEP

NOUNS 1 **sleepiness, drowsiness,** doziness, heaviness, lethargy, oscitation, somnolence *or* somnolency, yawning, stretching, oscitancy, pandiculation; languor 331.6; sand in the eyes, heavy eyelids; REM sleep *or* rapid-eye-movement sleep

2 **sleep, slumber; repose,** the arms of Morpheus; bye-bye *or* beddy-bye <both nonformal>; shut eye < nonformal>; light sleep, fitful sleep, **doze, drowse,** snoozle <nonformal>; beauty sleep <nonformal>; sleepwalking, somnambulism; somniloquy; **land of Nod,** slumberland, sleepland, dreamland; hibernation, winter sleep, aestivation; bedtime, sack time <nonformal>

3 **nap, snooze** <nonformal>, **catnap, wink, forty winks** *and* some Zs <both nonformal>, zizz <Brit nonformal>, wink of sleep, spot of sleep; *siesta* <Sp>, blanket drill *and* sack *or* rack time <all nonformal>

4 sweet sleep, balmy sleep, downy sleep, soft sleep, gentle sleep, smiling sleep, golden slumbers; peaceful sleep, sleep of the just; restful sleep, good night's sleep

5 **deep sleep,** profound sleep, heavy sleep, **sound sleep,** unbroken sleep, wakeless sleep, drugged sleep, dreamless sleep, the sleep of the dead; paradoxical *or* orthodox *or* dreaming *or* REM sleep

6 **stupor,** sopor, **coma, swoon,** lethargy <old>; **trance;** narcosis, narcohypnosis, narcoma, narcotization, narcotic stupor *or* trance; sedation; high <nonformal>; nod <nonformal>; narcolepsy; catalepsy; thanatosis, shock; sleeping sickness, encephalitis lethargica

7 hypnosis, mesmeric or hypnotic sleep, trance

8 **hypnotism, mesmerism;** hypnology; hypnotization, mesmerization; **animal magnetism,** od, odyl, odylic force; hypnotic suggestion, posthypnotic suggestion, autosuggestion

9 **hypnotist, mesmerist,** hypnotizer, mesmerizer; Svengali, Mesmer

10 **sleep-inducer,** sleep-producer, sleep-provoker, sleep-bringer; hypnotic, soporific, somnifacient; poppy, mandrake, mandragora, opium, opiate, morphine, morphia; nightcap; sedative 86.12; anesthetic; lullaby

11 **Morpheus,** Somnus, Hypnos; sandman

12 **sleeper, slumberer;** sleeping beauty; **sleepyhead,** lie-abed, slugabed, sleepwalker, somnambulist; somniloquist

VERBS **13** **sleep, slumber,** rest in the arms of Morpheus; **doze, drowse; nap, catnap,** take a nap, catch a wink, sleep soundly, **sleep like a top** or **log,** sleep like the dead; snore, saw wood <nonformal>; have an early night, go to bed betimes; sleep in; oversleep

14 <nonformal terms> **snooze,** get some shut-eye, get some sack time, flake or sack out, crash, catch forty winks or some Zs; pound the ear

15 **hibernate,** aestivate, lie dormant

16 **go to sleep,** settle to sleep, go off to sleep, **fall asleep,** drop asleep, **drop off,** drift off, drift off to sleep; **doze off, drowse off,** nod off, dope off <nonformal>; close one's eyes

17 **go to bed, retire;** lay me down to sleep; bed, bed down; go night-night and go bye-bye and go beddy-bye <all nonformal>

18 <nonformal terms> **hit the hay, hit the sack,** crash, turn in, crawl in, flop, sack out

19 **put to bed,** bed; nestle, cradle; **tuck in**

20 **put to sleep; lull to sleep,** rock

to sleep; **hypnotize, mesmerize,** magnetize; **entrance,** trance, put in a trance; narcotize, drug, dope <nonformal>; anesthetize, put under; sedate

ADJS **21** **sleepy, drowsy,** dozy, **slumberous,** slumbery, dreamy; **half asleep,** asleep on one's feet; sleepful, sleep-filled; yawny, stretchy <nonformal>, oscitant, yawning, napping, **nodding,** ready for bed; heavy, **heavy-eyed, heavy with sleep,** sleep-swollen, sleep-drowned, sleep-drunk, drugged with sleep; **somnolent,** soporific; **lethargic,** comatose, narcose or narcous, stuporose or **stuporous, in a stupor,** out of it <nonformal>; narcoleptic; cataleptic; narcotized, drugged, doped <nonformal>; sedated; anesthetized; **languid**

22 **asleep, sleeping, slumbering,** in the arms or lap of Morpheus, in the land of Nod; **sound asleep, fast asleep,** dead asleep, deep asleep, in a sound sleep, flaked-out <nonformal>; **unconscious, oblivious, out,** out like a light, out cold; comatose; dormant; dead, **dead to the world;** unwakened, unawakened

23 **sleep-inducing,** sleep-producing, sleep-bringing, sleep-causing, sleep-compelling, sleep-inviting, sleep-provoking, sleep-tempting; **narcotic,** hypnotic, **soporific, somniferous,** somnifacient; sedative 86.45

24 **hypnotic,** hypnoid, hypnoidal, **mesmeric;** odylic; narcohypnotic

23 WAKEFULNESS

NOUNS **1** **wakefulness,** wake; **sleeplessness,** restlessness, tossing and turning; **insomnia,** insomnolence or insomniousness, white night; vigil, all-night vigil, lidless vigil; insomniac; consciousness, sentience; alertness 339.5

2 **awakening, wakening,** rousing, **arousal;** rude awakening, rousting out <nonformal>; reveille

VERBS **3** **keep awake,** keep one's

eyes open; keep alert, be vigilant 339.8; stay awake, **toss and turn, not sleep a wink,** not shut one's eyes, count sheep; have a white night

4 **awake, awaken, wake, wake up, get up,** rouse, come alive <nonformal>; open one's eyes, stir <nonformal>

5 <wake someone up> **awaken, waken, rouse, arouse,** awake, wake, **wake up,** shake up, roust out <nonformal>

6 **get up, get out of bed, arise,** rise, **rise and shine** <nonformal>, greet the day, **turn out** <nonformal>; roll out *and* pile out *and* **show a leg** *and* hit the deck <all nonformal>

ADJS 7 **wakeful, sleepless,** slumberless, **unsleeping,** insomniac, insomnious; restless; watchful, vigilant, lidless

8 **awake,** conscious, **up; wide-awake;** alert 339.14

ADVS 9 **sleeplessly, unsleepingly; wakefully,** with one's eyes open; alertly 339.17

24 SENSATION
<*physical sensibility*>

NOUNS 1 **sensation, sense, feeling;** sense impression, percept, perception, sense perception; experience, sensory experience; **sensuousness,** sensuosity; **consciousness,** awareness, apperception; response, response to stimuli

2 **sensibility,** sensibleness, physical sensibility, sentience *or* sentiency; openness to sensation, readiness of feeling, receptiveness, receptivity; sensation level, threshold of sensation, limen; impressionability, impressibility; affectibility; **susceptibility,** susceptivity, perceptibility

3 **sensitivity, sensitiveness;** perceptivity, perceptiveness; responsiveness; **tact, tactfulness, considerateness,** courtesy, politeness; **compassion, sympathy;** empathy, identification; **concern,** solicitousness, solici-

tude; capability of feeling, passibility; **delicacy, exquisiteness,** tenderness, fineness; **oversensitiveness,** oversensibility, hypersensitivity, **thin skin,** hyperesthesia, hyperpathia, supersensitivity, overtenderness; **irritability,** prickliness, soreness, **touchiness,** tetchiness; ticklishness, nervousness 128; allergy, anaphylaxis; sensitization

4 **sore spot,** sore point, soft spot, raw, exposed nerve, raw nerve, nerve ending, tender spot, the quick, where the shoe pinches, where one lives *and* in the gut <nonformal>

5 senses, five senses, sensorium; touch 74, taste 62, smell 69, sight 27, hearing 48; sixth sense

VERBS 6 **sense, feel,** experience, **perceive,** apprehend, be sensible of, be conscious *or* aware of, apperceive; taste 62.7, smell 69.8, see 27.12, hear 48.11,12, touch 73.6; respond, respond to stimuli; be sensitive to, have a thing about <nonformal>

7 **sensitize,** make sensitive; sensibilize, sensify; **sharpen, whet, quicken,** stimulate, excite, stir, cultivate, refine

8 **touch a sore spot,** touch a soft spot, touch on the raw, touch a raw spot, touch to the quick, hit *or* touch a nerve *or* nerve ending, touch where it hurts, hit one where he lives <nonformal>, strike home

ADJS 9 **sensory,** sensorial; **sensitive,** receptive; **sensuous;** sensorimotor, sensimotor; kinesthetic, somatosensory

10 **neural, nervous,** nerval; neurologic, neurological

11 sensible, sentient, sensile; **susceptible,** susceptive; **receptive,** impressionable, impressible; **perceptive; conscious,** cognizant, **aware,** sensitive to, alive to

12 **sensitive,** responsive, sympathetic, compassionate; empathic, empathetic; passible; delicate, tactful, considerate, courteous, solicitous, tender, refined; **over-**

sensitive, **thin-skinned;** oversensible, hyperesthetic, hyperpathic, hypersensitive, supersensitive, overtender, overrefined; **irritable, touchy,** tetchy <nonformal>, quick on the draw *or* trigger *or* uptake, itchy, ticklish, prickly; goosy <nonformal>, skittish; nervous; allergic, anaphylactic

13 <keenly sensitive> exquisite, poignant, acute, sharp

25 INSENSIBILITY
<physical unfeeling>

NOUNS **1 insensibility,** insensibleness, **insensitivity,** insensitiveness, insentience, impassibility; **unperceptiveness,** imperceptiveness, imperception, imperceptivity, impercipience, blindness, lack of concern, obtuseness; inconsiderateness; unsolicitousness; tactlessness; discourtesy, boorishness; **unfeeling,** unfeelingness, **apathy,** affectlessness, lack of affect; thick skin *or* hide, callousness 94.3; **numbness,** dullness, hypothymia, **deadness;** pins and needles; hypesthesia; anesthesia, analgesia; narcosis, electronarcosis; narcotization

2 unconsciousness, senselessness; nothingness, oblivion, obliviousness, nirvana; nirvana principle; **faint, swoon, blackout,** lipothymia; **coma; stupor;** catalepsy, catatony *or* catatonia, sleep 22

3 anesthetic, analgesic, anodyne; tranquilizer, **sedative,** sleeping pill *or* tablet, knockout drop *and* Mickey Finn <both nonformal>; drug, dope <nonformal>, narcotic, opiate

VERBS **4 deaden, numb,** benumb, blunt, dull, obtund, **desensitize;** paralyze, palsy; **anesthetize, put to sleep,** slip one a Mickey *or* Mickey Finn <nonformal>, chloroform, etherize; narcotize, drug, dope <nonformal>; **stupefy, stun,** bedaze, besot; **knock out,** KO *and* kayo *and* lay out

and knock stiff <all nonformal>

5 faint, swoon, drop, succumb, keel over <nonformal>, fall in a faint, fall senseless, **pass** out <nonformal>, **black out,** go out like a light

ADJS **6 insensible, unfeeling, insensitive,** insentient, insensate, impassible; unsympathetic, uncompassionate; unconcerned, unsolicitous; tactless, boorish, heavy-handed; **unperceptive,** imperceptive, impercipient, blind; thick-skinned, thickwitted, **dull,** obtuse, obdurate; **numb,** numbed, benumbed, dead, **deadened,** asleep, unfelt; **unfeeling, apathetic,** affectless; callous 94.12; anesthetized, narcotized

7 stupefied, stunned, dazed, bedazed

8 unconscious, senseless, oblivious, comatose, asleep, dead, **dead to the world,** cold, out, **out cold;** narcotized, doped *and* stoned *and* spaced out *and* strung out *and* zonked *and* zonked out *and* out of it <all nonformal>

9 deadening, numbing, dulling; **anesthetic,** analgesic, narcotic; stupefying, stunning, numbing, mind-boggling *or* -numbing; anesthetizing, narcotizing

26 PAIN
<physical suffering>

NOUNS **1 pain; suffering, hurt, hurting,** misery <nonformal>, **distress; discomfort,** malaise; aches and pains

2 pang, throe, throes; seizure, spasm, paroxysm; ouch <nonformal>; **twinge; nip, stab,** stitch, **shooting pain,** darting pain, fulgurant pain, lancinating pain; psychalgia

3 smart, smarting, **sting,** stinging, urtication, **tingle,** tingling; **burn,** burning, burning pain, fire

4 soreness, irritation, inflammation, tenderness, sensitiveness; algesia; festering; sore; sore spot 24.4

5 ache, aching, throbbing, throbbing ache *or* pain; **headache,** cephalalgia, misery in the head <nonformal>; splitting headache, **sick headache, migraine,** megrim, hemicrania; **earache,** otalgia; **toothache,** odontalgia; **colic,** collywobbles; **heartburn,** pyrosis; **angina**

6 agony, anguish, torment, torture, the rack, excruciation, crucifixion, martyrdom, martyrization

VERBS **7 pain, hurt, wound, afflict, distress; burn;** sting; nip, bite, tweak, pinch; pierce, prick, stab, cut, lacerate; **irritate, inflame,** harshen, exacerbate, intensify; chafe, gall, fret, rasp, rub, grate; gnaw, grind; gripe; fester; **torture, torment,** rack, **agonize, harrow,** crucify, martyr, martyrize, excruciate, wring, twist, contorse, convulse; kill by inches

8 suffer, feel pain, feel the pangs, anguish 96.19; **hurt, ache;** smart, tingle; throb, pound; shoot; twinge, thrill, twitch; **wince,** blanch, shrink; **agonize,** writhe

ADJS **9 pained,** in pain, **hurt,** hurting, **suffering,** afflicted, wounded, distressed, in distress; **tortured, tormented, racked, agonized, harrowed,** lacerated, crucified, martyred, martyrized, wrung, twisted, convulsed; on the rack, under the harrow

10 painful; hurtful, **hurting,** distressing, afflictive; **acute, sharp,** piercing, stabbing, shooting, stinging, biting, gnawing; **poignant,** pungent, **severe,** cruel, harsh, grave, hard; griping, cramping, spasmic, spasmatic, spasmodic, paroxysmal; **agonizing, excruciating,** exquisite, atrocious, torturous, tormenting, martyrizing, racking **harrowing**

11 sore, raw; smarting, tingling, **burning; irritated, inflamed, tender;** chafed, galled; **festering**

12 aching, achy, **throbbing;** headachy, migrainous, colicky, griping

13 irritating, irritative, irritant; **chafing, galling,** fretting, rasping, boring, grating, grinding, stinging, scratchy

27 VISION

NOUNS **1 vision, sight, eyesight,** seeing; **sightedness;** eye, power of sight, sense of sight, visual sense; **perception,** discernment; perspicacity, perspicuity, visual acuity; **field of vision,** visual field, scope, ken, purview, horizon, sweep, range; line of vision, line of sight, sight-line; peripheral vision, peripheral field; field of view 31.3

2 observation; looking, watching, viewing, seeing, witnessing, espial; **notice,** note, respect, **regard;** watch, lookout; spying, espionage

3 look, sight, the eye and a looksee and a gander <all nonformal>

4 glance, flick of the eye, cast, side-glance; **glimpse; peek, peep;** wink, blink, flicker *or* twinkle of an eye; casual glance, **half an eye**

5 gaze, stare, gape, goggle; sharp *or* piercing *or* penetrating look; **ogle,** glad eye, come-hither look <nonformal>, bedroom eyes <nonformal>; **glare, glower,** glaring *or* glowering look; evil eye, whammy <nonformal>; withering look, hostile look, chilly look, the fisheye <nonformal>

6 scrutiny, overview, **survey,** contemplation; **examination, inspection** 937.3, scrutiny, the once-over <nonformal>, visual examination, ocular inspection, eyeball inspection <nonformal>

7 viewpoint, standpoint, point of view, vantage, vantage point, where one stands; bird's-eye view, worm's-eye view, fly on the wall; **outlook,** angle, angle of vision; mental outlook 977.2

8 observation post *or* point; **observatory; lookout,** outlook, overlook, scenic overlook; **watchtower,** tower; Texas tower;

beacon, lighthouse, pharos; gazebo, belvedere; bridge, conning
tower, crow's nest; peephole,
sighthole, loophole; **ringside,**
ringside seat; **grandstand,**
bleachers; **gallery**; peanut gallery
<nonformal>

9 **eye,** visual organ, organ of vision, oculus, optic, **orb, peeper**
<nonformal>, baby blues
<nonformal>; clear eyes, bright
eyes, starry orbs; saucer eyes,
popeyes *and* goggle eyes *and*
banjo eyes *and* googly eyes <all
nonformal>; naked eye, unassisted eye

10 **sharp eye,** keen eye, gimlet eye,
X-ray eye; **eagle eye,** hawkeye,
peeled eye <nonformal>

11 <comparisons> eagle, hawk, cat,
lynx, ferret, weasel; Argus

VERBS 12 **see, behold, observe,
view, witness, perceive, discern, spy,** espy, **sight,** have in
sight, make out, pick out, descry,
spot <nonformal>, take notice of,
have one's eye on, distinguish,
catch sight of, get a load of
<nonformal>, get an eyeful of
<nonformal>, look on *or* upon,
set *or* lay eyes on, clap eyes on
<nonformal>; **glimpse,** get *or*
catch a glimpse of; see at a glance

13 **look, peer,** have a look, take a
gander *and* take a look <both
nonformal>; **look at,** take a look
at, eye, **eyeball** <nonformal>,
have a look-see <nonformal>,
gaze at *or* upon; **watch, observe,
view, regard;** keep one's eyes
peeled *or* skinned, keep one's eyes
open; keep in sight *or* view; **check
and check out** <both nonfor-
mal>; scope <nonformal>; keep
under observation, spy on, have
an eye out, keep an eye out, keep
an eye on, keep a weather eye on,
tail *and* shadow <both nonfor-
mal>, stake out; **reconnoiter,**
scout, get the lay of the land

14 **scrutinize, survey, eye,** contemplate, look over, give the eye *or*
the once-over <nonformal>;
ogle, ogle at, **leer,** leer at, give
one the glad eye; examine, **inspect** 937.23; **pore,** pore over,
peruse

15 **gaze,** fix one's gaze, fix *or* fasten
or rivet one's eyes upon, keep
one's eyes upon, feast one's eyes
on; **eye, ogle; stare,** stare at,
stare hard, look, goggle, **gape,
gawk** *or* gawp <nonformal>

16 **glare, glower,** look daggers; give
one the evil eye; give one the fish
eye <nonformal>

17 **glance, glimpse,** glint, cast a
glance, glance at *or* upon, take a
squint at <nonformal>

18 **look askance** *or* askant, give a
sidelong look; cock the eye; **look
down one's nose** <nonformal>

19 **look away,** look aside, **avert the
eyes,** look another way; drop
one's eyes *or* gaze

ADJS 20 **visual, ocular,** eye, eyeball
<nonformal>; **sighted; optic, op-
tical;** ophthalmic; retinal; visible
31.6

21 **clear-sighted,** clear-eyed;
twenty-twenty; **farsighted;
sharp-sighted,** keen-sighted,
sharp-eyed, **eagle-eyed,** hawk-
eyed

ADVS 22 **at sight,** as seen, visibly,
at a glance; by sight, by eyeball
<nonformal>, visually; at first
sight, **at the first blush;** out of
the corner of one's eye

28 DEFECTIVE VISION

NOUNS 1 faulty eyesight, bad eyesight, impaired vision, imperfect
vision, blurred vision, reduced
sight, partial sightedness, partial
blindness; legal blindness; **astig-
matism;** nystagmus; **blindness**
30

2 **dim-sightedness,** amblyopia

3 **nearsightedness, myopia,**
shortsightedness

4 **farsightedness,** hyperopia,
presbyopia

5 strabismus; **squint; cross-eye,
cross-eyedness;** walleye

6 <defective eyes> cross-eyes,
cockeyes, squint eyes, lazy eye,
walleyes, bug-eyes

7 **winking, blinking,** nictitation

VERBS **8** see badly *or* poorly, barely
see, see double
9 squint, screw up the eyes
10 wink, blink, nictitate, bat the
eyes <nonformal>
ADJS **11** poor-sighted; visually impaired, sight-impaired; legally
blind; **blind** 30.9; **astigmatic,
astigmatical; nearsighted,
shortsighted, myopic; farsighted,** presbyopic; **squinting,**
strabismal, strabismic; winking,
blinking
12 cross-eyed, cockeyed, goggle-
eyed, bug-eyed *and* popeyed
<both nonformal>, **wall-
eyed**
13 dim-sighted, purblind, half-
blind; bleary-eyed, blear-eyed

29 OPTICAL INSTRUMENTS

NOUNS **1 optical instrument,** optical device, viewer; **microscope;
spectroscope,** spectrometer
2 lens, glass; prism, objective
prism
3 spectacles, specs <nonformal>,
glasses, eyeglasses, pair of
glasses *or* spectacles, cheaters
and peepers <both nonformal>;
reading glasses; bifocals, tri-
focals, pince-nez; lorgnette;
granny glasses; shades <non-
formal>; goggles, blinkers;
contacts, contact lenses, hard
lenses, soft lenses
**4 telescope, spy glass, field
glass; binoculars,** opera glasses
5 sight; sighthole; finder, view-
finder
6 mirror, glass, **looking glass,**
speculum
7 optics; optometry; spectrometry; **photography** 714
8 oculist, ophthalmologist, **optometrist;** optician
ADJS **9 optic, optical,** ophthalmic,
ophthalmological, optometrical;
ocular, binocular, monocular
10 microscopic, telescopic, etc; ster-
eoscopic, three-dimensional, 3-D
11 spectacled, bespectacled;
monocled

30 BLINDNESS

NOUNS **1 blindness, sightless-
ness**; stone-blindness, total blindness; legal blindness; partial
blindness, reduced sight, **blind
side; blind spot;** cataract; glaucoma; trachoma; **blinding,**
making blind, depriving of sight,
putting out the eyes
2 day blindness, hemeralopia;
night blindness, nyctalopia
3 color blindness; Daltonism
4 the blind, the sightless, the unseeing; blind man
5 blindfold; eye patch; blinkers
6 <aids for the blind> sensory aid,
braille, New York point
VERBS **7 blind,** deprive of sight,
strike blind, render *or* make
blind; darken, dim, obscure,
eclipse; **put one's eyes out,**
gouge; throw dust in one's eyes;
dazzle, bedazzle, daze
8 be blind, walk in darkness,
grope in the dark, feel one's way;
go blind, lose one's sight *or* vision;
be blind to, close *or* shut one's
eyes to, wink *or* blink at, look the
other way, blind oneself to, wear
blinkers *or* have blinders on; have
a blind spot *or* side
ADJS **9 blind, sightless, unsighted,**
eyeless, visionless, **unseeing,**
undiscerning, unobserving, unperceiving; in darkness, bereft
of light; **stone-blind,** stark blind,
blind as a bat, blind as an owl;
dim-sighted 28.13; nyctalopic;
color-blind
10 blinded, darkened, obscured;
blindfolded, blindfold, hoodwinked, blinkered; **dazzled,**
bedazzled, dazed; snow-blind,
snow-blinded
11 blinding, obscuring; **dazzling,**
bedazzling

31 VISIBILITY

NOUNS **1 visibility,** visibleness, perceptibility, discernibleness, ob-
servability; **manifestation;** revelation, epiphany
2 distinctness, plainness, manifestness; **clearness, clarity,**

lucidity, limpidity; **definiteness,** definition; resolution; **prominence, conspicuousness,** conspicuity; **exposure,** public exposure, high profile, low profile; high or low visibility

3 field of view, field of vision, range of vision, **sight,** limit of vision, **eyesight,** eyeshot; **vista, view, horizon, prospect, perspective, outlook, viewpoint, observation point** 27.8

VERBS **4 show,** show up, show through, shine through, **surface, appear** 33.8, be seen, be revealed, be evident, be noticeable, meet the gaze, present to the eye, meet or catch or hit or strike the eye; **stand out,** stand forth, loom large, glare, **stare one in the face,** hit one in the eye, **stick out like a sore thumb;** materialize

5 be exposed, be conspicuous, have high visibility, stick out, crop out; live in a glass house; have or keep a high profile

ADJS **6 visible,** visual, **perceptible,** perceivable, **discernible, seeable,** viewable, observable, detectable, noticeable, recognizable; **in sight,** in view, in plain sight, in full view, before one's eyes, under one's eyes, open, naked, exposed, showing, open or exposed to view; **evident,** in evidence, **manifest, apparent**

7 distinct, plain, clear, obvious, evident, patent, unmistakable, much in evidence, for all to see, plain as the nose on one's face, plain as day, clear as day; **definite, defined, well-defined,** in focus; **clear-cut,** clean-cut; crystal-clear, clear as crystal; **conspicuous, prominent,** pronounced, high-profile

ADVS **8 visibly, perceptibly,** perceivably, discernibly, markedly, noticeably; **manifestly, apparently,** evidently; **distinctly, clearly, plainly,** obviously, patently, definitely, unmistakably; conspicuously, undisguisedly, glaringly, starkly

32 INVISIBILITY

NOUNS **1 invisibility,** imperceptibility, indiscernibility; nonappearance; disappearance 34; more than meets the eye; unsubstantiality 763, immateriality 1051, **secrecy** 345, **concealment** 346

2 inconspicuousness, low profile; **indistinctness, unclearness, faintness,** paleness, feebleness, weakness, **dimness, vagueness,** indefiniteness, obscurity, uncertainty; **blurriness, fuzziness, haziness**

VERBS **3** be invisible or unseen, escape notice; disappear 34.2

4 blur, dim, pale, soften, film, mist, fog; defocus, lose resolution or sharpness or distinctness

ADJS **5 invisible; imperceptible,** unperceivable, **indiscernible,** undiscernible, undetectable, **unseeable,** unapparent, insensible; **out of sight; secret** 345.11,15; **unseen,** unobserved, unnoticed, unperceived; behind the scenes; disguised, camouflaged, hidden, **concealed** 346.11,14; unrevealed, in petto <L>; latent

6 inconspicuous, low-profile; **indistinct, unclear, indefinite,** undefined, ill-defined, **faint,** feeble, **dim, shadowy, vague, obscure,** indistinguishable, unrecognizable; half-seen; uncertain, confused, out of focus, **blurred, blurry, fuzzy, hazy,** misty, filmy, foggy

33 APPEARANCE

NOUNS **1 appearance, appearing,** apparition, putting in an appearance; **emergence,** issuance; **arising,** rise, rising, occurrence; **materialization, materializing; manifestation,** incarnation, revelation; epiphany, theophany, avatar; **presentation, disclosure, exposure**

2 appearance, facade, show, outward show, image; glitz and tinsel <both nonformal>, gaudi-

ness, speciousness, meretriciousness, **superficiality**

3 aspect, look, view; feature, lineaments; **seeming, semblance,
image**; effect, impression; **form,
shape,** figure, configuration, gestalt; **manner,** fashion, wise,
guise, style; **respect, regard,** reference, light; **phase; facet, side**

4 **looks, features, lineaments,**
traits, lines; **countenance,** face,
visage, physiognomy; **cut of
one's jib** <nonformal>, cast,
turn; **look, air, mien,** demeanor,
carriage; guise

5 <thing appearing> **apparition,
appearance,** phenomenon; **vision, image, shape, form,** figure,
presence; false image, mirage,
specter, **phantom** 987.1

6 **view, scene, sight;** prospect,
outlook, lookout, vista, **perspective;** scenery; panorama,
sweep; **landscape,** seascape;
bird's-eye view, worm's-eye view

7 **spectacle, sight;** exhibit, **exhibition,** exposition, **show, stage
show** 704.4, **display, presentation,** representation; tableau,
tableau vivant; panorama; *son et
lumière* <Fr>, sound-and-light
show; **pageant,** pageantry; parade, pomp

VERBS 8 **appear; arrive, make
one's appearance,** make *or* put
in an appearance, appear on the
scene, meet *or* catch *or* strike the
eye, **come in sight** *or* **view, show,**
show oneself, show one's face,
show up <nonformal>, **turn up,
materialize,** present oneself,
manifest oneself, become manifest, **reveal oneself,** expose *or*
betray oneself; **come to light,** see
the light, see the light of day;
emerge, issue, issue forth, come
to the fore, come out; **rise, arise,**
rear its head; look forth, peer *or*
peep out; **loom,** heave in sight,
appear on the horizon

9 **burst forth,** break forth, debouch; **pop up, bob up** <non-
formal>, start up, spring up,
burst upon the view

10 appear to be, seem to be, **ap-**

pear, seem, look, feel, sound,
look to be, appear to one's eyes,
have *or* present the appearance
of, give the feeling of, strike one
as; **appear like, seem like, look
like,** have *or* wear the look of,
**sound like; have every appear-
ance of,** have all the earmarks of

ADJS 11 **apparent, seeming, ostensible;** superficial; **visible**
31.6

ADVS 12 **apparently, seemingly,
ostensibly,** to *or* by all appearances, to *or* by all accounts, to the
eye; on the face of it, *prima facie*
<L>; on the surface, outwardly,
superficially; at first sight *or* view,
at first blush

34 DISAPPEARANCE

NOUNS 1 **disappearance,** disappearing, **vanishing; going, passing, departure, loss;** dissipation,
dispersion; dissolution, evanescence, dematerialization 1051.5;
fadeout, blackout; wipe, wipeout,
erasure; eclipse, occultation; vanishing point; elimination 772.2;
extinction 395.6

VERBS 2 **disappear, vanish,** vanish
from sight, do a vanishing act
<nonformal>, depart, fly, **flee**
368.10, **go away,** pass, pass out *or*
away, pass out of sight, exit, pull
up stakes <nonformal>, leave the
scene *or* stage, clear out, pass out
of the picture; **perish, die,** die off;
die out *or* away, dwindle, wane,
fade, **fade out** *or* **away;** sink, sink
away, dissolve, melt, melt away,
dematerialize 1051.6, evaporate,
evanesce, **vanish into thin air,** go
up in smoke; disperse, dispel, dissipate; cease to exist, **cease to be;**
leave no trace; undergo *or* suffer
an eclipse; **hide** 346.8

ADJS 3 **vanishing, disappearing,**
passing, fleeting, fugitive, transient, fading, dissolving, melting,
evaporating, evanescent

4 **gone,** away, gone away, past and
gone, extinct, missing, no more,
lost, lost to sight *or* view, long-
lost, **out of sight; unaccounted
for;** nonexistent

35 COLOR

NOUNS **1 color, hue; tint, tinge, shade, tone,** cast; **coloring, coloration;** color scheme; **complexion,** skin color or coloring or tone; natural color; undercolor; pallor 36.2

2 warmth, warm color; **blush, flush, glow**

3 softness, soft color, pastel, pastel color, pastel shade

4 colorfulness, color, bright color, pure color, **brightness, brilliance, vividness,** intensity, saturation; **richness**

5 garishness, loudness, luridness, glitz <nonformal>, gaudiness 501.3; shocking pink, jaundiced yellow, arsenic green; clashing colors, color clash

6 color quality; brightness, purity, saturation; **hue,** value, lightness; chromaticity; tint, **tone;** chromatic color, achromatic or neutral color; warm color; cool color

7 color system, chromaticity diagram, color triangle, Maxwell triangle

8 <coloring matter> **color, coloring, colorant,** tinction, tincture, **pigment, stain; dye,** dyestuff, color filter; paint, tempera; coat, coating, **coat of paint; undercoat,** undercoating, **primer,** priming, prime coat, **ground, flat coat;** wash, wash coat, flat wash; opaque color, transparent color; medium, vehicle; drier; thinner; turpentine, turps <nonformal>

9 <persons according to hair color> brunet; blond, Goldilocks; bleached blond; ash blond, strawberry blond; towhead; redhead, carrottop <nonformal>

10 <science of colors> chromatology; chromatics, chromatography, chromatoscopy, colorimetry; spectrum analysis, spectroscopy, spectrometry

11 <applying color> **coloring,** coloration; **staining, dyeing; tie-dyeing; tinting,** tinging, tinction; pigmentation; illumination, emblazonry; color printing; lithography

12 painting, coating, covering; **enameling,** glossing, glazing; **varnishing,** japanning, lacquering, shellacking; staining; **calcimining, whitewashing;** gilding; stippling; frescoing; fresco; undercoating, priming

VERBS **13 color,** hue, lay on color; **tinge, tint,** tinct, **tincture,** tone, complexion; pigment; bedizen; **stain, dye,** dip, tie-dye; imbue; dye in the wool; ingrain, grain; shade, shadow; illuminate, emblazon; **paint, coat,** cover, face; dab, **daub,** dedaub, smear, besmear, brush on paint, slap or slop on paint; **enamel,** gloss, glaze; **varnish,** japan, **lacquer, shellac;** white out; **calcimine, whitewash;** wash; **gild;** stipple; fresco; undercoat, prime

14 <be inharmonious> **clash,** conflict, collide, fight

ADJS **15 chromatic; coloring,** colorific, colorative, tinctorial; pigmental, pigmentary; monochrome, monochromatic; dichromatic; many-colored, particolored, rainbow, **variegated** 47.9, polychromatic, kaleidoscopic; prismatic, spectral; cool, cold

16 colored, hued, in color, in Technicolor <trademark>; **tinged, tinted,** tinctured, tinct, toned; **painted, enameled; stained, dyed;** tie-dyed; imbued; complexioned; full-colored; deep, deep-colored

17 deep-dyed, fast-dyed, double-dyed, **dyed-in-the-wool;** ingrained, ingrain; colorfast, fast, indelible

18 colorful; bright, vivid, intense, **rich,** exotic, **brilliant,** burning, **gorgeous, gay**

19 garish, lurid, loud, screaming, shrieking, glaring, flaring, flashy, glitzy <nonformal>, flaunting, crude, blinding, overbright, raw, gaudy 501.20

20 off-color, off-tone; **inharmo-**

nious, discordant, harsh, clashing

21 soft-colored, soft-hued, **soft,** softened, **subdued,** light, creamy, peaches-and-cream, **pastel, pale,** subtle, delicate, quiet, tender, sweet; pearly, nacreous, mother-of-pearl, iridescent, opalescent; somber, simple, sober, sad; flat, eggshell

36 COLORLESSNESS

NOUNS 1 **colorlessness,** lack or absence of color, huelessness, tonelessness; dullness, lackluster 1026.5

2 **paleness, dimness,** weakness, **faintness;** lightness, fairness; **pallor,** pallidity, pallidness; **wanness, sallowness,** pastiness, ashiness, muddiness, dullness; **anemia;** bloodlessness, exsanguination; **ghastliness, haggardness,** lividness, sickly hue, sickliness, cadaverousness

3 **decoloration,** decolorizing, decolorization, discoloration, achromatization, lightening; **fading, paling; dimming, bedimming; whitening,** blanching, etiolation; **bleaching**

4 **bleach,** bleaching agent or substance; decolorizer

VERBS 5 decolor, decolorize, discolor, etiolate; **fade, wash out; dim, dull,** tarnish, tone down; **pale, whiten,** blanch, drain, drain of color; **bleach**

6 **lose color, fade,** fade out; **bleach,** bleach out; **pale, turn pale,** grow pale, **change color,** turn white, **whiten, blanch,** wan

ADJS 7 **colorless, hueless,** toneless, uncolored, achromatic; neutral; dull, flat, mat, dead, dingy, muddy, leaden, lusterless, lackluster 1026.17; **faded, washed-out,** dimmed, discolored, etiolated; **pale, dim,** weak, **faint; pallid, wan, sallow,** fallow; green around the gills; **white,** white as a sheet; **pasty,** waxen; **ashen,** ashy, ashen-hued, gray; **anemic;** bloodless, exsanguinated, exsanguineous; **ghastly,**

livid, lurid, **haggard,** cadaverous, sickly, deadly or deathly pale; pale as death; pale-faced, tallow-faced

8 **bleached,** decolored, decolorized, achromatized, whitened, blanched, lightened, bleached out, bleached white; drained, drained of color

9 **light, fair,** light-colored, light-hued; pastel; whitish 37.8

37 WHITENESS

NOUNS 1 **whiteness;** albescence; **lightness, fairness;** paleness 36.2; chalkiness; pearliness; **creaminess;** milkiness, lactescence; glaucousness; glaucescence; albinism; albino

2 <comparisons> alabaster, bone, chalk, lily, lime, milk, cream, fleece, foam, snow, driven snow, paper

3 **whitening,** blanching; etiolation; **whitewashing; bleaching** 36.3; frosting

4 whitening agent, whiting, **whitewash,** calcimine

VERBS 5 **whiten,** etiolate, **blanch; bleach** 36.5; silver, grizzle, frost; chalk; whitewash

6 **whitewash,** calcimine

ADJS 7 **white,** white as alabaster or chalk or snow, etc 37.2, **snow-white,** snowy, niveous, frosty, frosted; **hoary, grizzled,** grizzly; silver, **silvery,** silvered; platinum; chalky, cretaceous; **milk-white,** milky, lactescent; marble, marmoreal; lily-white, white as a lily; white as a sheet

8 **whitish,** albescent; **light, fair;** pale 36.7; off-white; eggshell; glaucous, glaucescent; pearl, pearly, pearly-white; alabaster, alabastrine; cream, **creamy;** ivory

9 **blond;** flaxen-haired, fair-haired; bleached-blond, peroxide-blond; ash-blond, platinum-blond, strawberry-blond, honey-blond; **towheaded;** golden-haired 43.5

10 **albino,** albinic, albinistic, albinal

38 BLACKNESS

NOUNS **1 blackness,** nigritude, nigrescence; **black, sable, ebony;** melanism

2 **darkness, darkishness; swarthiness; duskiness;** soberness, sobriety, **somberness,** graveness, sadness, funereality; hostility, sullenness, black looks

3 **dinginess, griminess, smokiness,** smudginess, smuttiness, **muddiness,** murkiness

4 <comparisons> ebony, jet, ink, pitch, tar, coal, charcoal, smoke, soot, smut, raven, crow, night, hell, sin

5 **blackening, darkening,** nigrification, melanization, denigration; shading; **smudging,** smutching, **smirching;** smudge, smutch, smirch, smut

6 **blacking,** blackening; charcoal, burnt cork; lampblack, carbon black, soot

VERBS **7 blacken,** black, nigrify, melanize, denigrate; **darken; smudge,** smutch, **smirch,** besmirch, murk, blotch, blot, dinge; smut, soot; **smear** 512.10, 661.9; **blacken one's name** or **reputation,** give one a black eye, tear down

ADJS **8 black,** black as ink or pitch etc 38.4; **ebony; pitch-black, pitch-dark,** black or dark as pitch; black or dark as night; black as midnight; **inky,** inky-black; **jet-black; coal-black,** black as coal, coal-black; black as a crow; **dark** 1026.13-16

9 **dark,** dark-colored, **darkish,** blackish; nigrescent; **swarthy,** swart; **dusky,** dusk; **somber, sober, grave,** funereal; hostile, sullen

10 **dark-skinned,** black-skinned, **dark-complexioned; black, colored;** melanistic, melanous

11 **dingy, grimy, smoky,** sooty, fuliginous, **smudgy,** smutty, blotchy, dirty, **muddy,** murky, smirched, besmirched

12 **livid, black and blue**

13 **black-haired, raven-haired,** raven-tressed

39 GRAYNESS

NOUNS **1 grayness, gray,** grayishness; glaucousness; silveriness; ashiness; mousiness; slatiness; leadenness; lividness, lividity; dullness, drabness, soberness

2 **gray-haired** or **gray-headed person,** graybeard

VERBS **3 gray, grizzle,** silver

ADJS **4 gray, grayish,** griseous; iron-gray, steel-gray; pearl-gray, pearl, pearly; silver-gray, silver, silvery, silvered; **grizzly,** grizzled, grizzle; ash-gray, ashen, ashy, cinereal; dusty, dust-gray; smoky, smoke-gray; charcoal-gray; slaty, slate-colored; leaden, livid, lead-gray; glaucous, glaucescent; mousy, mouse-gray, mouse-colored; taupe; salt-and-pepper; **dull, dingy,** dismal, **somber, sober, sad, dreary;** hoary, frost-gray, rime-gray

5 **gray-haired,** gray-headed, silver-headed; hoary, hoary-haired, hoary-headed; gray-bearded, silver-bearded

40 BROWNNESS

NOUNS **1 brownness, brownishness, brown,** infuscation

VERBS **2 brown,** infuscate; rust; **tan, bronze,** suntan; sunburn, burn; fry, sauté, scorch, braise

ADJS **3 brown, brownish;** fuscous; **brunet;** tawny, fulvous; khaki, khaki-colored; drab, olive-drab; **dun;** beige, ecru; **chocolate;** cocoa, cocoa-brown; coffee, coffee-brown; nut-brown; walnut, walnut-brown; fawn, fawn-colored; grayish-brown; brownish-gray, fuscous, taupe; snuff-colored, snuff-brown; umber; olive-brown; **sepia;** sorrel; brown as a berry

4 **reddish-brown,** rufous-brown; roan; henna; terra-cotta; rufous, foxy; **mahogany,** mahogany-brown; auburn, Titian; **bronze,** bronzed, brazen; copper, coppery, copperish, cupreous, copper-

colored; **chestnut,** chestnut-
brown, castaneous

5 **brunet;** brown-haired; auburn-
haired; xanthous

41 REDNESS

NOUNS 1 **redness, reddishness,**
rufosity, rubricity; **red**; rubicundity, **ruddiness,** floridness,
floridity; erythrism; reddish
brown

2 **pinkness, pinkishness; rosiness; pink,** rose

3 **reddening,** rubefaction, rubi-
fication, rubescence, rufes-
cence; **coloring, blushing,
flushing; blush,** flush, glow;
rubefacient

VERBS 4 <make red> **redden,
rouge,** rubify; inflame; crimson;
vermilion, madder, miniate,
henna, rust, carmine; incarnadine, pinkify

5 **redden,** turn red, **color, mantle,
blush, flush, crimson;** flame,
glow

ADJS 6 **red, reddish; ruddy,** rubicund; rufescent, rufous; fiery,
flaming, flame-red, lurid; inflamed; **scarlet, vermilion,
vermeil; crimson;** maroon;
stammel; cerise; cardinal; cherry,
cherry-red; carmine; **ruby,** ruby-
red; wine, port-wine, wine-red;
carnation, carnation-red; brick-
red, tile-red, lateritious; rust,
rust-red, rusty, ferruginous,
rubiginous; beet-red, red as a
beet; lobster-red, red as a lobster;
copper-red, carnelian; Titian,
Titian-red

7 **sanguine,** sanguineous, **blood-
red,** blood-colored, bloody, gory

8 **pink, pinkish; rose, rosy,** rose-
colored, rose-red, roseate; primrose; flesh-color, flesh-colored,
flesh-pink, incarnadine; coral,
coral-red, coralline; salmon,
salmon-pink

9 **red-complexioned,** ruddy-
complexioned, warm-
complexioned, ruddy-faced,
apple-cheeked, **ruddy,** rubicund,
florid, sanguine; rosy, **rosy-
cheeked;** glowing, blooming;

hectic, flushed, flush; burnt, sun-
burned

10 **redheaded,** red-haired, red-
bearded; carroty, chestnut, auburn, Titian, xanthous

11 reddening, blushing, flushing,
coloring; rubescent, erubescent;
rubificative, rubrific; rubefacient

42 ORANGENESS

NOUNS 1 **orangeness,** oranginess;
orange

ADJS 2 **orange, orangeish,** or-
angey; pumpkin, pumpkin-
colored; tangerine, tangerine-
colored; apricot, peach; carroty,
carrot-colored; orange-red,
orange-yellow

43 YELLOWNESS

NOUNS 1 **yellowness, yellowish-
ness;** goldenness, aureateness;
yellow; gildedness

2 yellow skin, yellow complexion,
sallowness; xanthochroism; **jaundice,** yellow jaundice, xanthism

VERBS 3 **yellow,** turn yellow; **gild;**
aurify; sallow; **jaundice**

ADJS 4 **yellow, yellowish;** lutes-
cent, luteous; xanthous; **gold,
golden,** gilt, gilded, auric, aureate; **canary,** canary-yellow;
citron, citron-yellow, citreous;
lemon, lemon-colored, lemon-
yellow; **sallow,** fallow; cream,
creamy, cream-colored; straw,
straw-colored, tow-colored;
flaxen, flaxen-colored, flax-
colored; buff, buff-colored, buff-
yellow; beige, ecru; saffron,
saffron-colored, saffron-yellow;
primrose

5 **yellow-haired, golden-haired,**
tow-headed, xanthous; blond
37.9

6 yellow-faced, yellow-
complexioned, sallow; **jaundiced,** xanthodermatous

44 GREENNESS

NOUNS 1 **greenness,** viridity;
greenishness, virescence, virides-
cence; verdancy, **verdure,** glaucousness; **green,** chlorosis; chlo-
rophyll

2 verdigris, patina, aerugo; patination

VERBS **3 green;** verdigris, patinate, patinize

ADJS **4 green,** virid; **verdant,** verdurous; vernal, vernant, aestival; **greenish,** viridescent, virescent; **grass-green,** green as grass; **olive,** olive-green, olivaceous; beryl-green, berylline; holly, holly-green; ivy, ivy-green; emerald, emerald-green; chartreuse; glaucous, glaucescent

5 verdigrisy, verdigrised, patinous, patinaed

45 BLUENESS

NOUNS **1 blueness, bluishness;** azureness; **blue, azure;** lividness, lividity; cyanosis

VERBS **2 blue,** azure

ADJS **3 blue, bluish,** cerulescent; cyanic; cerulean; **azure** , azurine, azured, azure-blue; sky-blue; peacock-blue, pavonine, pavonian; beryl-blue, berylline; turquoise, turquoise-blue; sapphire, sapphire-blue; livid; cyanotic

46 PURPLENESS

NOUNS **1 purpleness, purplishness,** purpliness; **purple; violet;** lividness, lividity

VERBS **2 purple,** empurple

ADJS **3 purple,** purpureal, purpurean; **purplish,** purply, purplescent; **violet,** violaceous; plum-colored, plum-purple; amethystine; **lavender,** lavender-blue; lilac; magenta; mauve orchid; livid

47 VARIEGATION

<diversity of colors>

NOUNS **1 variegation, multicolor;** parti-color; riot of color; polychrome, polychromatism

2 iridescence, iridization, **opalescence,** nacreousness, pearliness, **play of colors** or **light;** light show; moiré pattern

3 spottiness, maculation, freckliness, speckliness, mottledness, dappleness, dappledness, stip-

pledness, spottedness, dottedness; **fleck, speck, speckle;** freckle; **spot,** dot, polka dot, macula, macule, blotch, splotch, patch, splash; **mottle, dapple; stipple,** stippling, pointillism, pointillage

4 check, checker, checks, checking, checkerboard; **plaid,** tartan, variegated pattern, harlequin, crazy-work, patchwork; parquet, parquetry, marquetry, mosaic, tesserae, tessellation

5 stripe, striping, candy-stripe, pinstripe; **streak, streaking;** striation, striature, stria

6 <comparisons> spectrum, rainbow, iris, chameleon, leopard, zebra, peacock, butterfly, mother-of-pearl, nacre, tortoise shell, opal, serpentine, marble, mackerel, confetti, crazy quilt, patchwork quilt, moiré, watered silk, Joseph's coat

VERBS **7 variegate,** motley; particolor; **mottle, dapple,** stipple, **fleck,** flake, **speck, speckle,** bespeckle, freckle, **spot,** bespot, dot, sprinkle, spangle, bespangle, pepper, stud, maculate; blotch, splotch; tattoo; **check, checker;** tessellate; **stripe, streak,** striate; marble, marbleize

8 opalesce, opalize, iridesce

ADJS **9 variegated, many-colored, multicolored,** multicolor, **varicolored,** polychromatic; particolored, parti-color; of all the colors of the rainbow; versicolor, versicolored, versicolorous; motley, harlequin; daedal; crazy; kaleidoscopic; prismatic, spectral; shot, shot through

10 iridescent, iridian; **rainbowy,** rainbowlike; **opalescent,** opaline, opaloid; nacreous, nacred, **pearly,** pearlish, mother-of-pearl; tortoise-shell; peacock-like, pavonine, pavonian; moiré, burelé

11 chameleonlike, chameleonic

12 mottled, motley; pied, piebald, pinto; **dappled,** dapple; calico; marbled; pepper-and-salt

13 spotted, dotted, polka-dot,

sprinkled, peppered, studded, pocked, pockmarked; **spotty,** dotty, patchy, pocky; **speckled, specked; stippled,** pointillé, pointillistic; **flecked;** spangled, bespangled; maculate, maculated, macular; freckled, frecked, freckly; blotched, blotchy, splotched, splotchy

14 **checked, checkered, plaid**; tessellated, tessellate, mosaic

15 **striped,** stripy, candy-stripe, pinstripe; **streaked,** streaky; **striated,** striate, strigate or strigose; barred, banded, listed; veined; **brindle,** brindled; marbled, marbleized; watered, tabby

48 HEARING

NOUNS 1 **hearing,** audition; sense of hearing, auditory or aural sense, ear; listening, heeding, attention; auscultation, aural examination; audibility

2 **audition,** hearing, tryout, call <all nonformal>, **audience, interview,** conference; attention, favorable attention, ear; **listening,** listening in; **eavesdropping,** wiretapping, electronic surveillance, bugging <nonformal>

3 good hearing, refined or acute sense of hearing, sensitive ear, nice or quick or sharp or correct ear; **an ear for;** musical ear, ear for music; ear-mindedness; tin ear <nonformal>

4 **earshot, hearing,** range, auditory range, reach, carrying distance, **sound of one's voice**

5 **listener,** hearer, auditor, hearkener; **eavesdropper,** little pitcher with big ears, snoop; fly on the wall

6 **audience, house, congregation;** captive audience, gallery, crowd, house; orchestra, pit; spectator 917

7 **ear** 2.10, auditory apparatus; external ear, **outer ear;** cauliflower ear

8 listening device; **hearing aid;** ear trumpet; amplifier, speaking trumpet, megaphone; stethoscope

9 <science of hearing> otology; otoscopy, auriscopy; otoneurology, otopathy, otography, otoplasty, otolaryngology; otoscope; audiometer

VERBS 10 **listen,** hark, **hearken, heed, hear, attend,** give attention, **give ear,** give or lend an ear, bend an ear; **listen to,** attend to, give a hearing to, give audience to, sit in on; **listen in; eavesdrop,** wiretap, tap, intercept, bug <nonformal>; **keep one's ears open,** be all ears <nonformal>, listen with both ears, strain one's ears; prick up the ears, cock the ears; hang on the lips of, hang on every word; auscultate

11 **hear,** catch, get <nonformal>, take in; **overhear; hear of,** hear tell of <nonformal>; get an earful <nonformal>, get wind of

12 be heard, **fall on the ear, sound** in the ear, catch or reach the ear, come to one's ear, register, make an impression, get across <nonformal>; **have one's ear,** reach, contact, get to; make oneself heard, get through to, gain a hearing, reach the ear of; assault or split or assail the ear

ADJS 13 **auditory,** audio, audile, **hearing, aural,** auricular, otic; audible; acoustic, acoustical, phonic

14 **listening, attentive, all ears** <nonformal>

15 **eared,** auriculate; big-eared, cauliflower-eared, dog-eared, droop-eared, flap-eared, flop-eared, lop-eared, long-eared; **sharp-eared;** tin-eared

49 DEAFNESS

NOUNS 1 **deafness, hardness of hearing,** deaf ears; **stone-deafness; tone deafness;** impaired hearing, hearing or auditory impairment; loss of hearing, **hearing loss; deaf-muteness**

2 **the deaf,** the hard-of-hearing; **deaf-mute,** deaf-and-dumb person; lip reader

3 deaf-and-dumb alphabet, man-

ual alphabet, finger alphabet;
dactylology, sign language; lip
reading

VERBS **4 be deaf;** have no ears, be
earless, lose one's hearing, suffer
hearing loss *or* impairment, go
deaf; shut *or* stop *or* close one's
ears, **turn a deaf ear;** fall on deaf
ears

5 deafen, stun, split the ears *or*
eardrums

ADJS **6 deaf, hard-of-hearing,** dull
or thick of hearing, deaf-eared,
dull-eared; deafened, stunned;
stone-deaf, deaf as a stone, deaf
as a door *or* a doorknob *or* doornail, **deaf as a post; unhearing;**
earless; word-deaf; tone-deaf;
deaf and dumb, deaf-mute

50 SOUND

NOUNS **1 sound,** sonance, acoustic,
acoustical *or* acoustic phenomenon; auditory phenomenon *or*
stimulus, auditory effect; ultrasound; sound wave, sound
propagation; sound intensity,
sound intensity level, amplitude,
loudness 53

2 tone, pitch, frequency, audio
frequency *or* AF; monotone, monotony, tonelessness; overtone,
harmonic; fundamental tone,
fundamental; intonation 524.7

3 timbre, tonality, **tone quality,**
tone color, color, coloring

4 sounding, sonation, sonification

5 acoustics, phonics, radioacoustics; acoustical engineer, acousti-
cian

6 sonics; subsonics; **supersonics,**
ultrasonics; speed of sound 174.2;
sound barrier, transonic barrier,
sonic barrier *or* wall; sonic boom

7 <sound unit> **decibel,** bel, phon

8 loudspeaker, speaker, dynamic
speaker; speaker system; cross-
over network; cone, diaphragm;
acoustical network; horn <non-
formal>; **headphone, ear-
phone,** headset

9 microphone, mike <nonfor-
mal>; concealed microphone,
bug <nonformal>

10 audio amplifier, amplifier,

amp <nonformal>; **pre-
amplifier,** preamp <nonformal>

11 sound reproduction system, audio sound system; **high-fidelity**
system *or* **hi-fi** <nonformal>;
record player, phonograph;
jukebox, nickelodeon; mono-
phonic *or* monaural system,
mono <nonformal>, stereo-
phonic *or* binaural system, stereo
<nonformal>; quadraphonic
sound system; **pickup** *or* cartridge, magnetic pickup *or*
cartridge, ceramic pickup *or*
cartridge, crystal pickup,
photoelectric pickup; stylus,
needle; tone arm; turntable;
public-address system *or*
PA *or* PA system; sound truck;
intercommunication system, **intercom** <nonformal>, squawk
box *and* bitch box <both nonfor-
mal>; **tape recorder,** tape deck,
cassette player, cassette *or* audio-
cassette recorder; compact disk
or CD player; audiophile

12 record, phonograph record,
disc, wax, long-playing record *or*
LP; transcription, digital recording; **recording,** tape recording;
digital disc; tape, tape cassette,
cassette; tape cartridge, cartridge;
compact disk *or* CD; videocassette recorder *or* VCR

13 audio distortion, distortion;
scratching, shredding, hum, rumble, hissing, howling, blurping,
blooping, woomping, fluttering,
flutter, wow, wow-wows, squeals,
whistles, birdies, motorboating;
feedback; static 1033.21

VERBS **14 sound,** make a sound *or*
noise, give forth *or* emit a sound;
noise; speak 524.20; resound;
record, tape, tape-record; pre-
record; play back

ADJS **15 sounding,** sonorous,
soniferous; **sounded;** tonal;
monotone, monotonic, toneless,
droning

16 audible, hearable; **distinct,
clear,** articulate; distinctive; high-
fidelity, hi-fi <nonformal>

17 acoustic, acoustical, phonic,
sonic; subsonic, supersonic, ul-

trasonic, hypersonic; transonic *or* transsonic

ADVS **18 audibly, aloud, out loud;** distinctly, clearly, plainly

51 SILENCE

NOUNS **1 silence,** silentness, **soundlessness,** noiselessness, **stillness, quietness,** quietude, quiescence 173, **quiet, still,** peace, **hush,** mum; lull, rest; deathlike silence, the quiet *or* silence of the grave; hush *or* dead of night, dead; tacitness, taciturnity; inaudibility; tranquillity

2 muteness, mutism, **dumbness,** voicelessness, tonguelessness; speechlessness, wordlessness; inarticulateness; deaf-muteness 49.1; standing mute, refusal to speak, stonewalling <nonformal>, the code of silence *or* omertà <Ital>, keeping one's lip buttoned <nonformal>

3 mute, deaf-mute 49.2

4 silencer, muffler, muffle, **mute,** baffle *or* baffler, quietener, cushion; **damper,** damp; dampener; **soft pedal; gag, muzzle; soundproofing,** acoustic tile, sound-absorbing material

VERBS **5 be silent,** keep silent *or* silence, **keep still *or* quiet; keep one's mouth shut, hold one's tongue,** keep one's tongue between one's teeth, bite one's tongue, seal one's lips, shut *or* close one's mouth, muzzle oneself, **not breathe a word, keep mum, hold one's peace,** not utter a word, not open one's mouth; keep to oneself; not have a word to say, be mute; choke up, have one's words stick in one's throat

6 <nonformal terms> **shut up,** keep one's trap *or* yap shut, button up, button one's lip, save one's breath, dummy up, clam up, not let out a peep, not say 'boo,' play dumb, stonewall

7 fall silent, hush, quiet, quieten, **quiet down,** pipe down <nonformal>

8 silence, put to silence, hush, hush one up, hush-hush, **shush,**

quiet, quieten, **still; soft-pedal,** put on the soft pedal; squash, squelch <nonformal>, stifle, choke, choke off, throttle, put the kibosh on <nonformal>, put the lid on *and* shut down on <both nonformal>, put the damper on <nonformal>, **gag, muzzle,** muffle, cut one short; strike dumb *or* mute, dumbfound; tongue-tie

9 muffle, mute, dull, soften, deaden, cushion, baffle, damp, **dampen,** deafen; subdue, tone down, **soft-pedal**

ADJS **10 silent, still, quiet,** quiescent 173.12, **hushed, soundless,** noiseless; **inaudible,** subaudible, unhearable; quiet as a mouse, mousy; so quiet that one might hear a feather *or* pin drop; silent as the grave *or* tomb, still as death; **unsounded, unvoiced,** unvocalized, unpronounced, unuttered, unarticulated

11 tacit, wordless, unspoken, unuttered, unexpressed, unsaid; **implicit** 519.8

12 mute, mum, dumb, voiceless, tongueless, **speechless,** wordless, breathless, at a loss for words, choked up; inarticulate; **tongue-tied,** dumbstruck, **dumbfounded**

ADVS **13 silently,** in silence, **quietly, soundlessly,** noiselessly; inaudibly

52 FAINTNESS OF SOUND

NOUNS **1 faintness, lowness, softness,** dimness, feebleness, weakness, indistinctness, unclearness, flatness; subaudibility

2 muffled tone, veiled voice; **muteness; dullness, deadness,** flatness

3 thud, dull thud; **thump,** clop, clump, clunk, plunk, plump, bump; pad, pat; **patter,** pitter-patter, pit-a-pat; **tap,** rap, **click;** tinkle, clink

4 murmur, murmuring, **mutter,** muttering; **mumble,** mumbling; small *or* little voice; **undertone,** bated breath; susurration, su-

surus; **whisper,** stage whisper, breathy voice

5 ripple, splash, ripple of laughter, ripple of applause; titter, chuckle

6 rustle, rustling, froufrou

7 hum, humming, thrumming, booming, bombilation, bombination, **droning, buzzing,** whirring, purring

8 sigh, sighing, moaning, sobbing, whining

VERBS **9 steal** *or* **waft on the ear,** float in the air

10 murmur, mutter, mumble; coo; susurrate; **lower one's voice, speak under one's breath; whisper;** aspirate

11 ripple, babble, burble, bubble, gurgle, guggle, **purl, trill; splash,** swish, swash, slosh, wash

12 rustle, crinkle; **swish,** whish

13 hum, thrum, boom, bombilate, bombinate, **drone, buzz,** whiz, whir, burr, purr

14 sigh, moan, sob, whine, sough; **whimper**

15 thud, thump, patter, clop, clump, clunk, plunk; pad, pat; **tap,** rap, **click,** tick; pop; tinkle, clink

ADJS **16 faint, low, soft, gentle, subdued, dim, feeble, weak;** soft-voiced, low-voiced, faint-voiced, weak-voiced; murmured, whispered; half-heard; distant; indistinct, unclear; barely audible, subaudible, near the threshold of hearing

17 muffled, muted, softened, dampened, damped, **smothered,** stifled, bated, deadened, subdued; **dull, dead, flat**

18 murmuring, murmurous, **muttering, mumbling;** susurrant; **whispering; rustling**

19 rippling, babbling, burbling, bubbling, **gurgling, trilling;** lapping, splashing, plashing, sloshing

20 humming, thrumming, **droning,** booming, bombinating, **buzzing,** whirring, purring, burring

ADVS **21 faintly, softly,** gently, sub-

duedly, hushedly, dimly, feebly, weakly, low

22 in an undertone, *sotto voce* <Ital>, **under one's breath,** with bated breath, in a whisper, between the teeth; aside; out of earshot

53 LOUDNESS

NOUNS **1 loudness,** intensity, volume, amplitude, fullness; sonorousness, sonority; crescendo, swell, swelling

2 noisiness, uproariousness, tumultuousness, thunderousness, clamorousness, clangorousness, boisterousness, obstreperousness; vociferousness 59.5

3 noise, blast 56.3, **racket, din, clamor;** outcry, **uproar,** hue and cry; howl; clangor, clatter, clap, jangle, rattle; roar, thunder, thunderclap 56.5; **crash, boom,** sonic boom; **bang,** percussion; brouhaha, **tumult, hubbub;** fracas, **brawl,** commotion; **pandemonium,** bedlam; charivari, shivaree <nonformal>; discord 61

4 <nonformal terms for noisy occasions> row, flap, hullabaloo, brannigan, donnybrook, free-for-all, rumble, rhubarb, dustup, rumpus, ruckus, ruction, Katy-bar-the-door, tzimmes

5 blare, blast, shriek 58.4, peal; **toot,** tootle, **honk,** beep, blat, trumpet; bay, bray; **whistle,** tweedle, squeal; trumpet blast *or* blare, sound *or* flourish of trumpets, Gabriel's trumpet *or* horn, **fanfare,** tarantara; tattoo; taps

6 noisemaker; catcall, cricket, clapper, clack, clacker, cracker; firecracker, cherry bomb; rattle, rattlebox; horn, Klaxon <trademark>; whistle, steam whistle, siren; loud-hailer, bullhorn <nonformal>

VERBS **7 din; boom,** thunder 56.9; **resound,** ring, peal, ring *or* resound in the ears, **blast the ear,** pierce *or* split *or* rend the ears, rend *or* split the eardrums;

deafen, stun; blast 56.8, **bang, crash** 56.6; **rend the air** *or* skies *or* firmament, make the welkin ring; shake *or* rattle the windows; awake the dead; surge, swell, rise, crescendo; **shout** 59.6

8 drown out, outshout, outroar, shout down, overpower, overwhelm; jam

9 be noisy, make a noise *or* **racket,** raise a clamor *or* din *or* hue and cry, noise, racket, **clamor,** roar, clangor; brawl, row, rumpus; **make an uproar,** kick up a dust *or* racket, raise a hullabaloo, raise the roof, raise Cain *or* Ned, raise the devil, raise hell, whoop it up; not be able to hear oneself think

10 blare, blast; shriek 58.8; **toot,** tootle, sound, peal, wind; pipe, trumpet, bugle, clarion; bay, bell, bray; **whistle,** tweedle, squeal; **honk,** honk *or* sound *or* blow the horn, beep; sound taps, sound a tattoo

ADJS **11 loud,** loud-sounding, forte, fortissimo; loudish; **resounding,** ringing, plangent, pealing; full, sonorous; **deafening,** ear-deafening, **ear-splitting,** head-splitting, ear-rending, ear-piercing, piercing; **thunderous,** thundering; **crashing, booming** 56.12; window-rattling, earth-shaking, enough to wake the dead

12 loud-voiced, loudmouthed, full-throated, big-voiced, clarion-voiced, trumpet-voiced, **stentorian**

13 noisy, noiseful, rackety, clattery, clangorous, clanging, **clamorous,** blatant, blaring, brassy, brazen; uproarious, **tumultuous,** turbulent, blustering, brawling, **boisterous,** rip-roaring, rowdy, strepitant, obstreperous, vociferous 59.10

ADVS **14 loudly, aloud,** loud, lustily; **boomingly, thunderously, thunderingly; noisily,** uproariously; ringingly, resoundingly; at the top of one's voice, in full cry

54 RESONANCE

NOUNS **1 resonance, sonorousness,** sonority, plangency, **vibrancy;** mellowness, richness, fullness; **snore,** snoring

2 reverberation, resounding; rumble, rumbling, thunder, thundering, boom, booming, growl, growling, grumble, grumbling, reboation; rebound, resound, **echo,** reecho

3 ringing, tintinnabulation, **pealing, chiming, tinkling,** tingling, **jingling; tolling,** knelling; clangor, clanking, clanging; **ring, peal, chime; toll,** knell; **tinkle,** tingle, **jingle,** dingle; clink, tink, ting, ping, chink; clank, clang; jangle, jingle-jangle; campanology, bell ringing, change ringing; tinnitis, ringing of *or* in the ear

4 bell, tintinnabulum; **gong,** triangle, **chimes,** clapper, tongue; carillon

5 resonator, resounder, reverberator; **sounding board,** sound box; echo chamber

VERBS **6 resonate, vibrate,** pulse, throb; snore

7 reverberate, resound, sound, **rumble,** roll, boom, echo, reecho, rebound, bounce back, be reflected, be sent back, echo back, send back, return

8 ring, tintinnabulate, **peal,** sound; **toll,** knell, sound a knell; **chime;** gong; **tinkle,** tingle, **jingle;** clink, tink, ting, chink; clank, clang, clangor; jangle, jingle-jangle; ring changes; ring in the ear

ADJS **9 resonant, reverberant, vibrant, sonorous,** plangent, rolling; mellow, rich, full; resonating, reverberating, echoing, reechoing, vibrating, pulsing, throbbing

10 deep, deep-toned, deep-pitched, deep-sounding; **hollow, sepulchral; low,** low-pitched, grave, heavy; **bass;** baritone; contralto

11 reverberating, reverberant, reverberatory, reboant, **resounding,** rebounding, reper-

cussive, sounding; **rumbling,**
thundering, booming, growling;
echoing, reechoing, echoic; un-
damped; persistent, lingering
12 **ringing, pealing, tolling,** bell-
ing, sounding, chiming; **tinkling,**
tinkly, tingling, **jingling;** tintin-
nabulous; campanological

55 REPEATED SOUNDS

NOUNS 1 staccato; **drum, thrum,**
beat, pound, roll; drumming,
tom-tom, beating, pounding,
thumping; **throb,** throbbing,
pulsation 915.3; **palpitation,** flutter; sputter, spatter, splutter;
patter, pitter-patter; rat-a-tat;
tattoo, ruff, ruffle, paradiddle;
drumbeat, drum music; drum-
fire, barrage
2 **clicking, ticking, tick, tick-**
tock, ticktack, ticktick
3 **rattle,** rattling; **clatter,** clitter,
clitterclatter, chatter, clack;
racket 53.3
VERBS 4 **drum, thrum, beat,**
pound, thump, thump out, roll;
palpitate, flutter; sputter, splatter, splutter; patter, pitter-patter;
throb, pulsate 915.12; beat or
sound a tattoo, ruffle, beat a ruffle
5 **tick, ticktock,** ticktack, tick
away
6 **rattle,** ruckle; **clatter,** clitter,
chatter, clack; rattle around, clatter about
ADJS 7 staccato; **drumming,**
thrumming, beating, pounding,
thumping; throbbing; palpitant,
fluttering; sputtering, spattering,
spluttering; clicking, ticking
8 **rattly,** rattling, chattering, **clat-**
tery, clattering

56 EXPLOSIVE NOISE

NOUNS 1 **report, crash, crack,**
clap, bang, wham, slam, clash,
burst; **knock, rap, tap,** smack,
whack, whomp, splat, bump,
slap, flap, flop
2 **snap, crack;** click, clack;
crackle, snapping, cracking,
crackling, crepitation, decrepita-
tion, sizzling, spitting; rale

3 **detonation, blast, explosion,**
fulmination, **discharge, burst,**
bang, pop, crack, bark; **shot,**
gunshot; volley, salvo, fusillade
4 **boom,** booming, cannonade,
peal, rumble, grumble, growl,
roll, roar
5 **thunder,** thundering, clap or
peal of thunder; **thunderclap,**
thunderpeal; thunderstorm 316.3
VERBS 6 **crack, clap, crash,**
wham, slam, **bang,** clash; **knock,**
rap, tap, smack, whack, thwack,
whop, whomp, bump, slap, flap
7 **snap, crack;** click, clack;
crackle, crepitate, decrepitate;
spit
8 **blast, detonate, explode, dis-**
charge, burst, go off, **bang, pop,**
crack, fulminate; burst on the ear
9 **boom, thunder, peal, rumble,**
grumble, growl, **roll, roar**
ADJS 10 **snapping, cracking,**
crackling, crackly, crepitant
11 **banging,** crashing, bursting,
exploding, explosive, blasting,
cracking, popping; knocking, rapping, tapping; slapping, flapping
12 **thundering, thunderous,** thun-
dery, fulminating, thunderlike;
booming, pealing, rumbling,
rolling, roaring; cannonading,
volleying

57 SIBILATION

<hissing sounds>

NOUNS 1 sibilation, sibilance; **hiss,**
hissing, white noise; hush, hushing, shush, shushing; fizz, fizzle,
fizzling, effervescing, effervescence; swish, whish, whoosh;
wheeze, *râle* <Fr>, rhonchus;
whistle, whistling; sneeze, sneezing, sternutation; snort, snore,
stertor; **sniff,** sniffle, snuffle; spit,
sputter, splutter; squash, squish,
squelch; lisp
VERBS 2 sibilate; **hiss,** siss; hush,
shush; fizzle, fizz, effervesce;
whiz, buzz, zip; swish, whish;
whistle; wheeze; sneeze; snort;
snore; sniff, sniffle, snuff, snuffle;
spit, sputter, splutter; squash,
squish, squelch; lisp
ADJS 3 **sibilant; hissing,** hushing;

effervescent; **sniffing,** sniffling, snuffling; snoring; wheezing, wheezy

58 STRIDENCY
<harsh and shrill sounds>

NOUNS **1 stridency,** stridulousness, stridulation; **shrillness,** highness, sharpness, acuteness; **screechiness, squeakiness,** creakiness, reediness

2 raucousness, harshness; discord, cacophony 61.1; coarseness, rudeness, gruffness; **raspiness,** scratchiness, **hoarseness,** huskiness; stertorousness; gutturalness, gutturalism

3 rasp, scratch, scrape, grind; crunch, craunch, scrunch; burr, buzz; snore; **jangle, clash, jar;** clank, clang, clangor, twang, twanging; blare, bray; croak, caw, cackle; belch; growl, snarl; grumble

4 screech, shriek, scream, squeal, shrill, keen, squeak, squawk, skirl, screak, creak; **whistle;** pipe; **whine, wail, howl,** ululation, yammer; caterwaul

5 *<insect sounds>* **stridulation;** crick, creak, chirk, chirp, chirping, chirrup

6 *<high voices>* soprano, mezzo-soprano, treble; tenor, alto; male alto, countertenor; falsetto

VERBS **7 stridulate,** crick, creak, chirk, chirp, chirrup

8 screech, shriek, screak, creak, squeak, squawk, **scream, squeal,** shrill, keen; **whistle;** pipe, skirl; **whine,** wail, howl, yammer, ululate; caterwaul

9 *<sound harshly>* **jangle, clash, jar;** blare, blat, bray; croak, caw, cackle; belch; burr, chirr, buzz; snore; growl, snarl; grumble, groan; clank, clang, clangor; twang

10 grate, rasp, scratch, scrape, grind; crunch, scrunch

11 grate on, jar on, grate upon the ear, jar upon the ear, offend the ear, pierce *or* split *or* rend the ears, lacerate the ear, **set the teeth on edge, get on one's**

nerves, jangle *or* wrack the nerves, make one's skin crawl

ADJS **12 strident,** stridulant, stridulous; strident-voiced

13 high, high-pitched, high-toned, high-sounding

14 shrill, thin, sharp, acute, keen, keening, **piercing,** penetrating, ear-piercing; **screechy,** screeching, shrieky, shrieking, **squeaky,** squeaking, screaky, creaky, creaking; whistling, piping, skirling, reedy; whining, wailing, howling, ululating, ululant; vibrato

15 raucous, raucid, **harsh,** harsh-sounding; coarse, rude, rough, gruff, ragged; **hoarse, husky,** cracked, dry; **guttural,** thick, throaty, croaky, croaking; choked; strangled; squawky, **squawking;** brassy, brazen, tinny, metallic; stertorous

16 grating, jarring, grinding; **jangling,** jangly; **rasping,** raspy; scratching, scratchy; scraping

59 CRY, CALL

NOUNS **1 cry, call, shout, yell,** hoot; **whoop; cheer, hurrah; howl,** yowl; bawl, bellow, roar; **scream, shriek,** screech, squeal, squall, caterwaul; yelp, yap, yammer, yawp, bark; war cry, battle cry, war whoop, rallying cry

2 exclamation, ejaculation, outburst, blurt; expletive

3 hunting cry; tallyho

4 outcry, vociferation, clamor, hullabaloo, hubbub, brouhaha, **uproar** 53.3; **hue and cry**

5 vociferousness, clamorousness, blatancy; noisiness 53.2

VERBS **6 cry, call, shout, yell,** hoot; hail, halloo; **whoop; cheer** 116.6; **howl,** yowl, yammer, squawk, yawp; **bawl, bellow,** roar, roar *or* bellow like a bull; cry *or* yell *or* scream bloody murder *or* blue murder; **scream, shriek,** screech, squeal, squall, caterwaul; yelp, yap, bark

7 exclaim, ejaculate, burst out, blurt, blurt out, spout out; stammer out

8 vociferate, cry out, call out, bellow out, yell out, shout out, sing out; sound off <nonformal>, pipe up, **clamor,** make *or* raise a clamor; make an outcry, **raise a hue and cry,** make an uproar

9 cry aloud, raise *or* lift up the voice, give voice *or* tongue; shout *or* cry *or* thunder at the top of one's voice, rend the air

ADJS **10 vociferous,** vociferant, vociferating; **clamorous; blatant;** obstreperous, brawling; **noisy;** crying, shouting, **yelling, bawling,** screaming; yelping, yapping, yappy, yammering; loud-voiced, loudmouthed, stentorian

11 exclamatory, ejaculatory, blurting

60 ANIMAL SOUNDS

NOUNS **1** animal noise; **call, cry;** mating call *or* cry; grunt, howl, bark, howling, caterwaul, ululation, barking; birdcall, note, clang; stridulation 58.5

VERBS **2** cry, call; **howl,** yowl, yawp, ululate; wail, whine, pule; **squeal,** squall, scream, screech, screak, squeak; troat; **roar; bellow,** blare, **bawl; moo,** low; **bleat; bray; whinny, neigh,** nicker; **bay,** bay at the moon, bell; **bark,** give voice *or* tongue; **yelp, yap,** yip; **mew,** mewl, **meow,** miaow, caterwaul

3 grunt, oink; **snort**

4 growl, **snarl,** grumble, gnarl, snap; hiss, spit

5 <birds> **warble, sing,** carol, call; pipe, whistle; **trill,** chirr, roll; **twitter,** tweet, twit, chatter, chitter; **chirp,** chirrup, chirk, **cheep,** peep, pip; **quack,** honk; **croak, caw; squawk,** scold; **crow,** cock-a-doodle-doo; **cackle,** gaggle, gabble, **cluck,** clack; **gobble; hoot; coo; cuckoo;** drum

ADJS **6 howling,** yowling, crying, wailing, whining, puling, bawling, ululant, blatant; lowing

61 DISCORD

<dissonant sounds>

NOUNS **1 discord,** discordance *or* discordancy, **dissonance, cacophony;** stridor; **inharmoniousness,** disharmony; **unmelodiousness,** unmusicality, tunelessness; atonality, atonalism; flatness, sharpness, sourness <nonformal>; dissonant chord; false note, sour note *and* clinker *and* clam <all nonformal>; cipher

2 clash, jangle, jar; noise, confusion *or* conflict *or* jarring of sounds; Babel, witches' *or* devils' chorus; harshness 58.2; clamor 53.3

VERBS **3** sound *or* strike *or* hit a sour note <nonformal>, hit a clinker *or* a clam <nonformal>; not carry a tune; **clash, jar, jangle,** conflict, jostle; grate 58.10,11

ADJS **4 dissonant, discordant, cacophonous,** disconsonant; strident, shrill, harsh, raucous, grating 58.16; **inharmonious,** unharmonious; **unmelodious,** nonmelodious; **unmusical,** untuneful, tuneless; untunable, untuned, atonal; cracked, **out of tune,** out of tone, out of pitch; **off-key, off-tone, off-pitch,** off; flat, sharp, **sour** <nonformal>

5 clashing, jarring, jangling, jangly, confused, conflicting, jostling, ajar; **harsh, grating** 58.16

62 TASTE

<sense of taste>

NOUNS **1** taste; **flavor,** sapor; **smack, tang; savor, relish,** sapidity; palate, tongue, tooth, stomach; taste in the mouth; sweetness, sourness, bitterness, bittersweetness, saltiness; aftertaste; savoriness 63

2 sip, sup, lick, bite

3 tinge, soupçon, hint 248.4

4 sample, specimen, taste, taster; example 785.2

5 taste bud *or* bulb *or* goblet, taste *or* gustatory cell; **tongue; palate**

6 tasting, savoring, gustation

VERBS **7 taste,** taste of, sample; **savor,** savor of; sip, sup <nonformal>, roll on the tongue; lick; smack

ADJS **8 gustatory,** gustative; tastable

9 flavored, flavorous, saporous, saporific; savory, flavorful 63.9; sweet, sour, bitter, bittersweet, salt

10 lingual, glossal; **tonguelike,** linguiform, lingulate

63 SAVORINESS

NOUNS **1 savoriness, palatableness,** palatability, **tastiness,** toothsomeness, goodness, good taste, right taste, **deliciousness,** gustatory delightfulness, scrumptiousness *and* yumminess <both nonformal>, lusciousness, delectability, **flavorfulness,** flavorsomeness, flavorousness, sapidity; full flavor, full-bodied flavor; gourmet quality; succulence, juiciness

2 savor, relish, zest, gusto

3 flavoring, flavor, flavorer; **seasoning, relish, condiment, spice,** condiments

VERBS **4 taste good,** tickle *or* flatter *or* delight the palate, tempt *or* whet the appetite, make one's mouth water, melt in one's mouth

5 savor, relish, like, love, be fond of, be partial to, enjoy, delight in, have a soft spot for, appreciate; smack the lips; taste 62.7

6 savor of, taste of, smack of, have the flavor of, taste like

7 flavor, savor; **season,** salt, pepper, **spice,** sauce

ADJS **8 tasty,** good, fit to eat *and* finger-lickin' good <both nonformal>, good-tasting, **savory, palatable, toothsome,** sapid, **good,** to one's taste, **delicious,** delightful, delectable, exquisite; delicate, dainty; juicy, succulent, **luscious;** for the gods, ambrosial; fit for a king, gourmet; scrumptious *and* yummy <both nonformal>

9 flavorful, flavorsome, flavorous; full-flavored, full-bodied; **rich,** rich-flavored

10 appetizing, mouth-watering, tempting, piquant

64 UNSAVORINESS

NOUNS **1 unsavoriness, unpalatableness,** unpalatability, **distastefulness;** bad taste in the mouth

2 acridness, acridity, tartness, sharpness, acerbity, **sourness** 67; pungency 68; **bitterness,** bitter taste; gall, gall and wormwood, wormwood

3 nastiness, foulness, vileness, loathsomeness, repulsiveness, obnoxiousness, odiousness, offensiveness; **rankness,** rancidity, rancidness, malodorousness, fetor, fetidness; repugnance 99.2; nauseant, emetic

VERBS **4 disgust, repel,** turn one's stomach, nauseate; make one's gorge rise; gross one out <nonformal>

ADJS **5 unsavory, unpalatable, unappetizing,** untasteful, untasty, foul-tasting, **distasteful,** unlikable, uninviting, unpleasant, unpleasing, disagreeable

6 bitter, bitter as gall *or* wormwood; **acrid,** sharp, caustic, tart, astringent; hard, harsh, rough, coarse; acerb, acerbic, sour; pungent

7 nasty, offensive 98.18, fulsome, noisome, noxious, rebarbative, mawkish, cloying, brackish, **foul, vile,** bad; **sickening, nauseating** nauseous; poisonous, rank, rancid, maggoty, stinking, putrid, malodorous, fetid

8 inedible, uneatable, not fit to eat *or* drink, undrinkable, impotable; unfit for human consumption

65 INSIPIDNESS

NOUNS **1 insipidness,** insipidity, **tastelessness, flavorlessness,** blandness, savorlessness, unsavoriness; **weakness, thinness, wishy-washiness; flatness, staleness,** deadness; vapidity, inanity, jejunity, jejuneness

ADJS **2 insipid, tasteless, flavorless,** bland, spiceless, **savorless,** sapless, unsavory, unflavored;

pulpy, pappy, gruelly; **weak, thin, mild, wishy-washy,** milktoast, washy, watery, watered, watered-down, diluted, dilute, milk-and-water; **flat, stale;** vapid, inane, jejune; neither one thing nor the other

66 SWEETNESS

NOUNS **1 sweetness,** sweet, sweetishness, saccharinity; **sugariness,** syrupiness; mawkishness, cloyingness

2 sweetening; sweetener; sugar; sweetening agent, sugar-substitute, artificial sweetener, saccharin, aspartame, cyclamates, sodium cyclamate, calcium cyclamate; molasses, blackstrap; syrup, maple syrup, cane syrup, corn syrup, sorghum; **honey,** comb honey, clover honey; honeydew; **nectar, ambrosia;** sugaring off; saccharification

VERBS **3 sweeten,** dulcify; **sugar,** honey; sugarcoat, glaze, candy; mull; saccharify; sugar off

ADJS **4 sweet,** sweetish, sweetened; sacchariferous; **sugary,** sugared, candied, **honeyed,** syrupy; mellifluous; melliferous, nectarous, ambrosial; sweet as sugar or honey; sugar-coated; bittersweet; sweet and sour, sweet and pungent

5 oversweet, saccharine, rich, **cloying,** mawkish

67 SOURNESS

NOUNS **1 sourness,** sour, **tartness,** tartishness, acerbity; acidity, acidulousness; hyperacidity, subacidity; unsweetness, **dryness; pungency** 68; greenness

2 sour; vinegar, acidulant; **pickle;** lemon, lime, crab apple, green apple, sour cherry, chokecherry; sourgrass; sour balls; sourdough; sour cream, sour milk, yogurt; **acid**

3 souring, acidification, acidulation, acetification; fermentation

VERBS **4 sour, acidify,** acidulate, acetify

ADJS **5 sour,** soured; **tart;** crab, **crabbed;** acerb, acerbic; **vinegarish,** vinegary; pickled; lemony; **pungent** 68.6; **dry,** sec; green, unripe

6 acid, acidulous, acidulent, acidulated; acetic; hyperacid

68 PUNGENCY

NOUNS **1 pungency, piquancy, poignancy; sharpness, keenness,** edge, **causticity,** astringency, mordancy, asperity, trenchancy, **acridity; bitterness** 64.2; acerbity, acidulousness, acidity, **sourness** 67

2 zest, zestfulness, zestiness, **briskness,** liveliness, raciness; **nippiness, tanginess; spiciness,** pepperiness; **tang, spice,** relish; nip, bite; punch, snap, zip, ginger; **kick,** guts <nonformal>

3 strength, strongness; high flavor, highness, rankness, gaminess

4 saltiness, salinity, brininess, brackishness; **salt; brine**

VERBS **5 bite, nip,** cut, penetrate, bite the tongue, sting, make the eyes water

ADJS **6 pungent, piquant, poignant; sharp, keen,** piercing, penetrating, **biting, acrid,** astringent, irritating, harsh, rough, severe, asperous, cutting, trenchant; **caustic,** vitriolic, mordant; **bitter** 64.6; acerbic, **sour**

7 zestful, zesty, **brisk,** lively, racy, **nippy,** snappy, **tangy,** with a kick; spiced, seasoned, high-seasoned; **spicy,** curried, **peppery,** hot, burning, hot as pepper

8 strong, strong-flavored, strong-tasting; **high,** high-flavored; **rank, gamy**

9 salty, salt, salted, saltish, **saline, briny; brackish;** pickled

69 ODOR

NOUNS **1 odor, smell, scent,** aroma, savor; **essence,** redolence, effluvium, emanation, exhalation, whiff, trace; trail, spoor; **fragrance** 70; **stink, stench** 71

2 **odorousness, smelliness,** headiness, pungency 68
3 smelling, olfaction, scenting; sniffing, snuffing, snuffling, whiffing
4 **sense of smell,** scent, olfaction, olfactory sense
5 olfactory organ; **nose; nostrils,** nares
VERBS 6 <have an odor> **smell,** be aromatic, smell of, be redolent of; emit *or* emanate *or* give out a smell, reach one's nostrils; reek, **stink** 71.4
7 odorize; scent, perfume 70.8
8 **smell, scent,** nose; **sniff,** snuff, snuffle, inhale, breathe, breathe in; get a noseful of, smell of, catch a smell of, get *or* take a whiff of, whiff
ADJS 9 **odorous,** odoriferous, odorant, **smelling, smelly, redolent, aromatic;** effluvious; **fragrant** 70.9; **stinking, malodorous** 71.5
10 **strong,** strong-smelling, strong-scented; **pungent,** penetrating, nose-piercing, sharp; reeking; suffocating, stifling
11 **smellable,** sniffable, whiffable
12 **olfactory,** olfactive
13 keen-scented, quick-scented, sharp- *or* keen-nosed, **with a nose for**

70 FRAGRANCE

NOUNS 1 **fragrance, perfume, aroma,** scent, redolence, balminess, **incense, bouquet, odor** 69; spice, spiciness; muskiness; fruitiness
2 perfumery; **perfume, scent, essence,** extract; aromatic, ambrosia; attar, essential *or* volatile oil; aromatic water; balsam, **balm,** aromatic gum; balm of Gilead; myrrh; bay oil; attar of roses; fixative, musk, civet, ambergris
3 **toilet water;** rose water; lavender water; cologne, cologne water, eau de Cologne; bay rum; **lotion,** after-shave lotion
4 **incense;** joss stick; pastille; frankincense , sandalwood
5 **perfumer;** thurifer, censer

bearer; **perfuming,** censing, thurification, odorizing
6 <articles> perfumer, parfumoir <Fr>, fumigator, scenter, odorator, odorizer; atomizer
VERBS 7 **be fragrant,** smell sweet, **smell good,** please the nostrils
8 **perfume, scent,** incense, thurify, odorize, fumigate, embalm
ADJS 9 **fragrant, aromatic,** odoriferous, redolent, **perfumed, scented, sweet, sweet-smelling,** sweet-scented, savory, balmy, ambrosial; **odorous** 69.9; sweet as a rose, fragrant as new-mown hay; musky; spicy

71 STENCH

NOUNS 1 **stench, stink,** funk, malodor, fetidness, fetidity, fetor, offense to the nostrils, bad smell, rotten smell, noxious stench, smell *or* stench of decay, **reek,** reeking, nidor; mephitis, miasma; body odor *or* BO; halitosis, **bad breath,** foul breath
2 **fetidness,** fetidity, malodorousness, **smelliness,** stinkingness, **odorousness,** noisomeness, **rankness, foulness,** putridness, offensiveness; repulsiveness; **mustiness,** funkiness, must, moldiness, mildew, fustiness, frowziness, stuffiness; **rancidness,** rancidity; rottenness 393.7
3 **stinker;** skunk *or* polecat *or* rotten egg; stinkpot, stink bomb; fart
VERBS 4 **stink,** smell, **smell bad,** assail *or* offend the nostrils, smell to heaven *or* high heaven, **reek;** smell up, stink up
ADJS 5 **malodorous, fetid, odorous, stinking, reeking,** nidorous, smelling, bad-smelling, **evil-smelling, smelly,** stenchy; **foul,** vile, putrid, fulsome, noisome, fecal, feculent, excremental, offensive, repulsive, noxious, sulfurous; rotten; **rank,** strong, high, gamy; **rancid, musty,** funky, fusty, frowzy, , stuffy, moldy, mildewed, mil-

dewy; mephitic, miasmic, miasmal

72 ODORLESSNESS

NOUNS **1 odorlessness,** scentlessness; inoffensiveness

2 deodorizing, deodorization, fumigation, ventilation

3 deodorant, deodorizer; antiperspirant; fumigant, fumigator

VERBS **4 deodorize,** fumigate; ventilate, freshen the air

ADJS **5 odorless,** inodorous, nonodorous, **scentless,** unscented; inoffensive

6 deodorant, deodorizing

73 TOUCH

NOUNS **1 touch;** sense of touch, tactile sense; **contact** 223.5; **feel,** feeling; light touch, lambency, whisper, breath, **kiss, caress; brush,** graze, grazing, glance, glancing; stroke, rub; tap, flick

2 touching, feeling, fingering, palpation; **handling,** manipulation; petting, caressing, stroking, rubbing, frottage, frication, friction 1042; fondling; pressure 901.2; feeling up <nonformal>

3 touchableness, **tangibility, palpability,** tactility

4 feeler, tactile organ; **antenna;** tactile hair, vibrissa; cat whisker; barbel, barbule; palp, palpus

5 finger, digit; index finger; ring finger, annulary; middle finger, medius, dactylion; little finger, pinkie <nonformal>, minimus; thumb, pollex

VERBS **6 touch, feel,** palpate; **finger,** pass or run the fingers over; **handle,** palm, paw; **manipulate,** wield, ply; twiddle; poke at, prod; tap, flick

7 touch lightly, touch upon; kiss, **brush,** sweep, graze, brush by, glance, scrape, skim

8 stroke, pet, caress, fondle; **nuzzle,** nose, rub noses; feel up <nonformal>; rub, rub against, massage, knead 1042.6

9 lick, lap, tongue, mouth

ADJS **10 tactile,** tactual

11 touchable, **palpable, tangible,** tactile

12 lightly touching, lambent, playing lightly over, barely touching

74 SENSATIONS OF TOUCH

NOUNS **1 tingle,** tingling, thrill, buzz; **prickle,** prickles, prickling, pins and needles; **sting,** stinging, urtication; paresthesia

2 tickle, tickling, **titillation,** pleasant stimulation, **ticklishness,** tickliness

3 itch, itching, itchiness; pruritus

4 creeps and **cold creeps** and shivers and **cold shivers** <all nonformal>, creeping of the flesh; gooseflesh, goose bumps, goose pimples

VERBS **5 tingle,** thrill; **itch;** scratch; **prickle,** prick, sting

6 tickle, titillate

7 feel creepy, feel funny, creep, crawl; **have the creeps** or **cold creeps** or the heebie-jeebies <nonformal>; have gooseflesh or goose bumps; give one the creeps or the willies <nonformal>

ADJS **8 tingly,** tingling, atingle; **prickly,** prickling

9 ticklish, tickling, tickly, **titillative**

10 itchy, itching; pruriginous

11 creepy, crawly, creepy-crawly

75 SEX

NOUNS **1 sex,** gender; maleness, masculinity 76, femaleness, femininity 77; **genitals, genitalia**

2 sexuality, sexual nature, sexualism, love-life; **love** 104, sexual activity, lovemaking 562, marriage 563; heterosexuality; homosexuality; bisexuality, ambisexuality; **carnality, sensuality** 663; sexiness, voluptuousness, flesh, fleshiness; **libido,** sex drive, sexual instinct or urge; **potency** 76.2; impotence; frigidity, coldness

3 sex appeal, sexual attraction or attractiveness or magnetism, sexiness

4 sex object; piece and meat and piece of meat and ass and piece of ass *and* hot number <all nonformal>; sex queen, sex goddess; stud <nonformal>

5 **sexual desire,** sensuous *or* carnal desire, bodily appetite, **biological urge,** venereal appetite *or* desire, sexual longing, **lust,** desire, lusts *or* desires of the flesh, itch; **erection,** penile erection, hard-on <nonformal>; **passion,** carnal *or* sexual passion, fleshly lust, prurience *or* pruriency, concupiscence, aphrodisia, the hots *and* hot pants *and* hot rocks *and* hot nuts <all nonformal>; lustfulness, goatishness, horniness, libidinousness; lasciviousness 665.5; **eroticism,** erotism; indecency 666; nymphomania, andromania; satyrism, satyriasis, gynecomania; **heat,** rut; estrus, estrum

6 **aphrodisiac, love potion, philter,** love philter; cantharis, Spanish fly

7 **copulation, sex act,** having sex, having intercourse, coupling, mating, coition, **coitus,** pareunia, venery, **sex, intercourse, sexual intercourse,** cohabitation, commerce, sexual commerce, congress, sexual congress, sexual union, sexual relations, relations, marital relations, marriage act, act of love, sleeping together *or* with; screwing *and* balling *and* nookie *and* diddling *and* making it with <all nonformal>; meat *and* ass <both nonformal>, intimacy, connection, carnal knowledge, aphrodisia; foreplay; **oral sex,** oral-genital stimulation, fellatio, fellation, blow job <nonformal>, cunnilingus; **anal sex,** anal intercourse, sodomy, buggery <nonformal>; **orgasm,** climax, sexual climax; unlawful sexual intercourse, adultery, fornication 665.7; coitus interruptus, onanism; group sex; serial sex, gang bang <nonformal>; spouse swapping, wife swapping, husband swapping; casual sex, one-night stand *or* quickie; phone sex; safe sex; sex

shop; **lovemaking** 562; **procreation** 78; germ cell, sperm, ovum 305.12

8 **masturbation,** autoeroticism, self-abuse, onanism, manipulation, playing with oneself, jacking off *and* pulling off *and* hand job <all nonformal>; sexual fantasy; wet dream

9 **sexlessness,** asexuality, neuterness; **impotence** 19; eunuch, *castrato* <Ital>, spado, gelding; steer

10 **sexual preference; sexual orientation; heterosexuality; homosexuality,** homoeroticism, homophilia, the love that dare not speak its name, sexual inversion; autoeroticism; **bisexuality,** bisexualism, ambisexuality, ambisextrousness, amphierotism, swinging both ways <nonformal>; **lesbianism,** sapphism, tribadism *or* tribady; **sexual prejudice,** sexism, genderism, phallicism

11 **perversion,** sexual deviation, sexual deviance, sexual perversion, sexual abnormality; sexual pathology; psychosexual disorder; sexual psychopathy; zoophilia, zooerastia, bestiality; pedophilia, algolagnia, algolagny, **sadomasochism;** active algolagnia, **sadism; masochism;** fetishism; narcissism; pederasty, pedophilia; exhibitionism; necrophilia; coprophilia; scotophilia, voyeurism; transvestitism; **incest,** incestuousness, **sex crime; sexual abuse,** carnal abuse, molestation

12 **intersexuality,** intersexualism, epicenism, epicenity; hermaphroditism, pseudohermaphroditism; androgynism, androgyny, gynandry, gynandrism; transsexuality, transsexualism

13 **heterosexual, straight** <nonformal>

14 **homosexual,** gay person, homosexualist, homophile, invert; catamite; **bisexual; lesbian,** sapphist

15 <nonformal terms for male homosexuals> homo, queer, faggot, fag, fruit, flit, fairy, pansy, nance, auntie, queen, drag queen, closet queen, fruitcake; <nonformal terms for female homosexuals> dyke, bull dyke, butchfemme, boondagger, lez

16 sexual pervert, **pervert, deviant,** deviate, sex *or* sexual pervert, sexual psychopath; sodomist, sodomite, bugger; pederast; paraphiliac; zoophiliac; pedophiliac; sadist; masochist; sadomasochist, algolagniac; fetishist; transvestite *or* TV, cross-dresser; narcissist; exhibitionist; necrophiliac; coprophiliac; scotophiliac, voyeur; erotomaniac, nymphomaniac, satyr; rapist 665.12

17 intersex, epicene; hermaphrodite, pseudohermaphrodite; androgyne, gynandroid; transsexual

18 sexology, sexologist; sexual counselor; sexual surrogate; sexual customs *or* mores *or* practices; sexual morality; sexual freedom, free love; trial marriage

VERBS **19** sex, sexualize; genderize

20 lust, **lust after,** itch for, have a lech and have hot pants for <both nonformal>, **desire; be in heat** *or* **rut,** rut, come in; get physical <nonformal>; get an erection, get a hard-on <nonformal>, tumesce

21 copulate, couple, **mate,** unite in sexual intercourse, **have sexual relations, have sex,** make out <nonformal>, perform the act of love *or* marriage act, come together, cohabit, shack up <nonformal>, sleep with, lie with, go to bed with; fuck *and* screw *and* lay *and* ball *and* frig *and* diddle *and* **make it with** <all nonformal>, go all the way, go to bed with, lie together; cover, mount, serve *or* service <of animals>; commit adultery, fornicate 665.19; **make love**

22 masturbate, play with *or* abuse oneself, jack off *and* whack off <both nonformal>; fellate, suck

and suck off <nonformal>; sodomize, bugger *and* ream <both nonformal>

23 climax, come, achieve satisfaction, achieve *or* reach orgasm; **ejaculate,** get off <nonformal>

ADJS **24 sexual,** gamic, coital, libidinal; **erotic,** sexy, amorous; nuptial; venereal; **carnal, sensual** 663.5, voluptuous, fleshly; **sexy;** erogenous, erogenic, erotogenic; sexed, oversexed, hypersexual, undersexed; procreative 78.15; potent 76.12

25 aphrodisiac, arousing, stimulating, eroticizing, venereal

26 lustful, prurient, hot, steamy, sexy, concupiscent, libidinous, **salacious** 666.9, **passionate,** hot-blooded, itching, **horny** *and* hot to trot *and* sexed-up <all nonformal>, randy, goatish; sex-starved, unsatisfied; lascivious 665.29; **orgasmic,** orgastic, **ejaculatory**

27 in heat, burning, hot; in rut, rutting, rutty, ruttish; in must, must, musty; estrous, estral

28 unsexual, unsexed; **sexless,** asexual, neutral; castrated, emasculated, eunuchized; **cold, frigid; impotent;** frustrated

29 homosexual, homoerotic, gay, queer *and* limp-wristed *and* faggoty <all nonformal>; **bisexual,** bisexed, ambisexual, ambisextrous, amphierotic, AC-DC <nonformal>, autoerotic; lesbian, sapphic, tribadistic; mannish 76.13, butch *and* dykey <both nonformal>; effeminate 77.14; transvestite; **perverted,** deviant

30 hermaphrodite, hermaphroditic, pseudohermaphrodite, pseudohermaphroditic, epicene, monoclinous; androgynous, androgynal, gynandrous, gynandrian

76 MASCULINITY

NOUNS **1 masculinity,** masculineness, maleness; **manliness,** man-

lihood, **manhood,** manfulness,
manlikeness; mannishness; gen-
tlemanliness, gentlemanlike-
ness

**2 male sex, male sexuality, vi-
rility,** virileness, potence *or*
potency, sexual power, manly
vigor, **machismo;** ultra-
masculinity; phallicism; male
superiority

**3 mankind, man, men, man-
hood,** menfolk *or* menfolks
<nonformal>

4 male, male being, masculine;
he, him, his; **man,** male person;
gentleman, gent <nonformal>

5 <nonformal terms> guy, fellow,
feller, lad, chap, guy, cat

6 real man, he-man, *and* two-
fisted man <both nonformal>,
hunk *and* jockstrap *and* jock <all
nonformal>, man with hair on
his chest

7 <forms of address> Mister, Mr,
Messrs +, Master; sir

8 <male animals> cock, rooster,
chanticleer; cockerel; drake; gander; peacock; tom turkey, tom,
turkey-cock, gobbler, turkey gobbler; dog; boar; stag, hart, buck;
stallion, studhorse, stud, top
horse <nonformal>, entire horse,
entire; tomcat, tom; he-goat, billy
goat, billy; ram; wether; bull,
bullock, top cow <nonformal>;
steer

9 <mannish female> **amazon,** virago, androgyne; lesbian, butch
and dyke <both nonformal>;
tomboy, hoyden, romp

VERBS **10** masculinize, virilize

ADJS **11 masculine, male,** bull,
he—; **manly, manlike, mannish,** manful, andric; uneffeminate; **gentlemanly,** gentlemanlike

12 virile, potent, viripotent; ultra-
masculine, **macho, he-mannish**
and hunky <both nonformal>,
two-fisted <nonformal>, broad-
shouldered, hairy-chested

**13 mannish, mannified; un-
womanly, unfeminine,**
uneffeminate, viraginous; **tom-
boyish,** hoyden, rompish

77 FEMININITY

NOUNS **1 femininity,** feminality,
feminacy, femaleness; **womanliness,** womanishness,
womanhood, womanity, mu-
liebrity; girlishness, little-
girlishness; maidenhood,
maidenliness; **ladylikeness,**
gentlewomanliness; **matronli-
ness,** matronage, matronhood,
matronship; the eternal feminine

2 effeminacy, unmanliness, ef-
feminateness, epicenity, epicenism, **womanishness,** mu-
liebrity, **sissiness** <nonformal>,
prissiness <nonformal>; androgyny; feminism

3 womankind, woman, women,
femininity, **womanhood,**
womenfolk *or* womenfolks
<nonformal>, the distaff side;
the female sex; the second sex,
the fair sex, the gentle sex, the
softer sex, **the weaker sex,** the
weaker vessel

4 female, female being; she, her

5 woman, Eve, daughter of Eve,
Adam's rib; **lady,** milady, gentlewoman; feme sole *and* feme
covert <both law>; married
woman, wife; **matron,** dame,
dowager; unmarried woman,
bachelor girl <nonformal>, single
woman, spinster; lass, girl 302.6;
career woman, businesswoman;
superwoman

6 <nonformal terms> **gal, dame,**
hen, biddy, skirt, jane, broad,
doll, babe, chick, wench, tomato,
bitch, minx, momma, mouse, sister, toots

7 fairer sex

8 <forms of address> Ms; Mistress
<old>, Mrs; madam *or* ma'am;
madame, Mme <both Fr>

9 <female animals> hen, biddy;
guinea hen; peahen; bitch, slut,
gyp; sow; ewe, ewe lamb; she-
goat, nanny goat *or* nanny; doe,
hind, roe; jenny; mare, brood
mare; filly; cow, bossy; heifer;
vixen; tigress; lioness; she-bear,
she-lion, etc

10 <effeminate male> **mollycod-**

dle, effeminate; **mother's darling, mother's boy, mama's boy,**
Lord Fauntleroy, sissy, goody-
goody; **pantywaist,** nancy *or*
nance, chicken, lily; cream puff,
weak sister, milksop; old woman

11 feminization, womanization, ef-
femination, effeminization,
sissification <nonformal>

VERBS 12 feminize; womanize, demasculinize, effeminize, effem-
inatize, soften, sissify <non-
formal>; emasculate, castrate,
geld

ADJS 13 **feminine, female;** gynic,
gynecoid; muliebral, distaff,
**womanly, womanish,
womanlike,** petticoat; **ladylike,** gentlewomanlike, gen-
tlewomanly; **matronly,** matron-
like; **girlish,** little-girlish, kittenish; maidenly 301.11

14 **effeminate, womanish,** fem
<nonformal>, old-womanish, **un-
manly,** muliebrous, soft, prissy,
sissified, sissy, **sissyish**

78 REPRODUCTION, PROCREATION

NOUNS 1 **reproduction, making, re-creation,** remaking, refashioning, reshaping, redo-
ing, re-formation, reworking,
rejiggering <nonformal>;
reconstruction, rebuilding, *perestroika* <Russ>; **revision;**
reissue, reprinting; reestablishment, **reorganization,** reinsti-
tution, reconstitution; redevelopment; **rebirth,** renascence, resurrection, revival;
duplication 873, **imitation** 336,
copy 784, **repetition** 848; **restoration** 396, renovation; producing *or* making *or* creating
anew *or* over *or* again *or* once
more; **birth rate,** fertility rate;
baby boom

2 **procreation, reproduction,
generation, begetting,
breeding; propagation,
multiplication,** proliferation;
inbreeding, endogamy; out-
breeding, xenogamy; crossbreeding 796.4

3 **fertilization,** fecundation; **impregnation,** insemination,
begetting, getting with child,
knocking up <nonformal>, mating, servicing; **pollination,**
pollinization; cross-fertilization,
cross-pollination; self-
fertilization, heterogamy,
orthogamy; isogamy, artificial
insemination

4 **conception,** conceiving, inception of pregnancy

5 **pregnancy, gestation, incuba-
tion,** parturiency, gravidness *or*
gravidity, the family way <nonfor-
mal>; brooding, sitting, covering

6 **birth, generation, genesis;
development;** procreation;
abiogenesis, biogenesis,
epigenesis, heterogenesis,
metagenesis, monogenesis,
oögenesis, orthogenesis, par-
thenogenesis, phytogenesis,
sporogenesis, xenogenesis; spontaneous generation

VERBS 7 **reproduce, remake,**
make *or* do over, **re-create,** regenerate, resurrect, revive, reform, refashion, **reshape,** re-
mold, recast, rework, rejigger
<nonformal>, redo, **reconstruct,**
rebuild, redesign, restructure, **revise;** reprint, reissue; reestablish,
reinstitute, reconstitute, refound,
reorganize; redevelop; duplicate 873.3, **copy** 336.5, **repeat**
848.7, **restore** 396.11, renovate

8 **procreate, generate, breed, beget,** get, **engender;** propagate,
multiply; proliferate; mother; father, sire; reproduce after one's
kind; breed true; inbreed; out-
breed; cross-pollinate, crossbreed; copulate

9 **lay** <eggs>, deposit, drop, spawn

10 **fertilize,** fructify, fecundate; **impregnate, inseminate,** knock up
<nonformal>, **get with child** *or*
young; pollinate; cross-fertilize,
cross-pollinate

11 **conceive,** get in the family way
<nonformal>

12 **be pregnant,** be gravid, **be with
child** *or* **young;** be in the family
way *and* have a bun in the oven

and be expecting *and* anticipate a blessed event <all nonformal>, be knocked up <nonformal>; gestate, breed, carry, carry young; **incubate, hatch; brood,** sit, set, cover

13 give birth 1.3

ADJS **14 reproductive, re-creative, reconstructive**; renascent, regenerative, resurgent; **restorative** 396.22; phoenixlike

15 reproductive, procreative, procreant, **propagative,** life-giving; spermatic, spermatozoic, seminal, germinal, fertilizing, fecundative; multiparous

16 genetic, generative; abiogenetic, biogenetic, epigenetic, heterogenetic, homogenetic, isogenetic, monogenetic, oögenetic, orthogenetic, parthenogenetic, phytogenetic, xenogenetic

17 bred, impregnated, inseminated; inbred, endogamic, endogamous; outbred, exogamic, exogamous; crossbred

18 pregnant, *enceinte* <Fr>, knocked-up <nonformal>, **with child** *or* **young, in the family way** <nonformal>, gestating, breeding, parturient; heavy with child *or* young, great *or* big with child *or* young, in a delicate condition, gravid, heavy, great; carrying; **expecting** <nonformal>, anticipating *and* anticipating a blessed event <both nonformal>

79 CLEANNESS

NOUNS **1 cleanness, cleanliness; purity,** pureness; **immaculateness; spotlessness,** stainlessness; freshness; fastidiousness, daintiness; asepsis, sterility; tidiness 806.3

2 cleansing, cleaning, cleaning up; **purge,** cleaning out, purging, purgation, catharsis; **purification,** purifying, lustration; expurgation, bowdlerization

3 sanitation, hygiene; disinfection, decontamination, sterilization, antisepsis; pasteurization; fumigation, delousing

4 refinement, clarification, puri- **fication,** depuration; **straining,** colature; extraction 192.8; **filtering,** filtration; **percolation,** leaching, lixiviation; **sifting,** separation, **screening,** sieving, bolting, winnowing; sublimation; **distillation**

5 washing, ablution; lavation, laving, lavage; **wash, washup;** soaping, lathering; rinse, rinsing; sponge, sponging; shampoo; washout; irrigation, flush, flushing, flushing out; douche, douching; enema; **scrub,** scrubbing, swabbing, mopping, scouring; **cleaning up** *or* **out,** washing up

6 laundering, laundry, tubbing; **wash, washing**

7 bathing, balneation

8 bath, tub <nonformal>; **shower,** shower bath; douche; sponge bath, sponge; hip bath, sitz bath; Turkish bath, Swedish bath, sauna *or* sauna bath, hot tub, whirlpool bath, Jacuzzi <trademark>

9 dip, bath; fixing bath; sheepdip

10 bathing place, bath, baths, public baths, **bathhouse,** sauna; mikvah <Judaism>; watering place, spa; steam room, sweat room, sudatorium, sudarium, caldarium, tepidarium

11 washery, laundry; washhouse; **coin laundry, Laundromat** <trademark>, **launderette,** coin-operated laundry; automatic laundry; hand laundry

12 washbasin, washbowl, basin; **lavatory, washstand; bathtub,** tub, bath; bidet; **shower,** showers, shower room, shower bath, shower stall; **sink,** kitchen sink; dishwasher, automatic dishwasher; washing machine; washer; finger bowl; wash barrel

13 refinery; refiner, purifier, clarifier; **filter; strainer,** colander; **percolator,** lixiviator; **sifter, sieve, screen**; winnow, winnower, winnowing machine

14 cleaner, cleaner-up, cleaner-out; **janitor,** janitress, custodian; cleaning woman *or* lady *or* man

15 washer, launderer; **laundress,** laundrywoman, **washerwoman,** washwoman; **laundryman;** dry cleaner; **dishwasher,** pot-walloper *and* pearl-diver <both nonformal>, scullion, scullery maid

16 sweeper; street sweeper, whitewing; **chimney sweep** *or* sweeper, sweep

17 cleanser, cleaner; cold cream, cleansing cream, **soap, detergent;** shampoo; rinse; **solvent;** water softener; purifier; mouthwash; dentifrice, **toothpaste, tooth powder;** pumice stone, holystone, scouring powder; purge, purgative, cathartic, enema, diuretic, emetic

VERBS **18 clean, cleanse, purge,** deterge, depurate; **purify,** lustrate; sweeten, **freshen;** clean up *or* out, clear out, sweep out, clean up after; houseclean, clean house, spring-clean; spruce, **tidy** 807.12; scavenge; **wipe,** wipe up *or* out, wipe off; dust, dust off; expurgate, bowdlerize

19 wash, bathe, shower, lave; **launder,** tub; wash up *or* out *or* away; **rinse,** rinse out, flush, flush out, irrigate, sluice, sluice out; ritually immerse, baptize; sponge, sponge down *or* off; **scrub,** scrub up *or* out, **swab, mop,** mop up; **scour,** holystone; hose out *or* down; rinse off *or* out; soap, lather; shampoo; syringe, douche; gargle

20 groom, dress, **brush up; preen;** manicure

21 comb, curry, card, rake

22 refine, clarify, clear, purify, rectify, depurate; **strain; extract** 192.10; **filter,** filtrate; **percolate,** leach, lixiviate; **sift,** separate, sieve, **screen,** bolt, winnow; sublimate, sublime; **distill,**

23 sweep, sweep up *or* out, **brush,** brush off, whisk, broom; vacuum <nonformal>

24 sanitize; disinfect, decontaminate, sterilize; boil; pasteurize; fumigate, delouse; chlorinate

ADJS **25 clean, pure; immaculate,** spotless, stainless; **unsoiled, unsullied,** unmuddied, unbesmirched, unblotted, unsmudged, unstained, untarnished, **unspotted,** unblemished; bright, shiny 1024.33; **unpolluted,** untainted, unadulterated, **undefiled;** kosher, ritually pure *or* clean; **sqeaky-clean** *and* clean as a whistle *or* a new penny *or* a hound's tooth <all nonformal>; **sweet, fresh; cleanly,** fastidious, dainty

26 cleaned, cleansed, cleaned up; purged, purified; expurgated, bowdlerized; refined; spruce, spick and span, **tidy** 806.8

27 sanitary, hygienic, prophylactic; sterile, aseptic, antiseptic, **uninfected;** disinfected, decontaminated, sterilized; boiled; pasteurized

28 cleansing, cleaning; detergent, detersive; **purifying,** purificatory; expurgatory; purgative, purging, cathartic, diuretic, emetic

ADVS **29 cleanly,** clean; **purely,** immaculately, spotlessly

80 UNCLEANNESS

NOUNS **1 uncleanness; impurity,** unpureness; **dirtiness,** grubbiness, dinginess, griminess, scruffiness, slovenliness, sluttishness, untidiness 809.6; uncleanliness

2 filthiness, foulness, vileness, feculence, shittiness <nonformal>, ordurousness, nastiness, grossness *and* yuckiness *and* ickiness <all nonformal>; rankness, fetidness 71.2; odiousness, repulsiveness 98.2; hoggishness, piggishness, swinishness, beastliness

3 squalor, squalidness, squalidity, sordidness

4 defilement, befoulment, dirtying, soiling; **pollution, contamination, infection;** abomination; ritual uncleanness *or* impurity *or* contamination

5 soil, smut; **smirch, smudge,**

smutch, smear, **spot,** blot, blotch, **stain** 1003.3

6 dirt, grime; dust; soot, smut; **mud** 1060.8

7 filth, muck, slime, mess, foul matter; ordure, **excrement** 12.3; mucus, snot <nonformal>; scurf, dandruff; putrid matter, pus, corruption, gangrene, decay, carrion, **rot** 393.7; **obscenity,** smut <nonformal> 666.4

8 slime, slop, scum, sludge, slush; glop *and* gunk <both nonformal>, **muck, mire,** ooze

9 offal, offscourings, scurf, scum, riffraff, scum of the earth; **carrion; garbage, swill,** slop, slops; dishwater, bilgewater, bilge; **sewage,** sewerage; **waste, refuse** 391.4

10 dunghill, manure pile; compost heap; refuse heap

11 sty, pigsty, pigpen; **stable,** Augean stables; dump *and* hole *and* shithole <all nonformal>, rathole; tenement; warren, **slum;** the inner city, the ghetto, the slums; hovel

12 <receptacle of filth> **sink;** sump, **cesspool,** cesspit, septic tank; catchbasin; bilge *or* bilges; **sewer,** drain, *cloaca* <L>; purification plant; **dump,** garbage dump, sanitary landfill, landfill; **swamp,** bog, mire, quagmire, marsh

13 pig, swine, hog, slut, sloven, slattern 809.7

VERBS **14 wallow in the mire, live like a pig**

15 dirty, dirty up, grime, **begrime;** muck, muck up <nonformal>; **muddy;** mire, bemire; slime; dust; soot, smoke, besmoke

16 soil; black, **blacken; smirch,** besmirch, sully, smut, **smudge, smear,** besmear, daub; **spot, stain** 1003.6; dirty *or* soil one's hands

17 defile, foul, befoul; sully; foul one's own nest, shit where one eats <nonformal>, mess *and* mess up <both nonformal>; **pollute, corrupt, contaminate, infect; taint,** tarnish

18 spatter, splatter, splash, **be-**

spatter, dabble, bedabble, spot, splotch

19 draggle, bedraggle, **drabble,** bedrabble, drabble in the mud

ADJS **20 unclean, unwashed,** unbathed, unscrubbed, unscoured, unswept, unwiped; **impure,** unpure; **polluted, contaminated, infected, corrupted;** ritually unclean *or* impure *or* contaminated, *tref* <Yiddish>, nonkosher; **uncleanly**

21 soiled, sullied, dirtied, smirched, besmirched, smudged, spotted, **tarnished,** tainted, **stained; defiled,** fouled, **befouled;** draggled, drabbled, bedraggled

22 dirty, grimy, grubby, grungy <nonformal>, smirchy, dingy, messy <nonformal>; scruffy, slovenly, untidy 809.15; miry, **muddy** 1060.14; **dusty;** smutty, smutchy, smudgy; sooty, smoky

23 filthy, foul, vile, mucky, **nasty,** icky *and* yecchy *and* yucky *and* gross *and* grungy *and* scuzzy <all nonformal>; malodorous, mephitic, rank, **fetid** 71.5; **putrid, rotten;** pollutive; nauseating, disgusting; **odious, repulsive** 98.18; **slimy,** scummy <nonformal>; barfy *and* vomity *and* puky <all nonformal>; sloppy, sludgy; gloppy *and* gunky <both nonformal>; wormy, maggoty, flyblown; feculent, ordurous, crappy *and* shitty <both nonformal>, excremental, fecal 12.20

24 hoggish, piggish, swinish, beastly

25 squalid, sordid, wretched, shabby; slumlike, slummy

ADVS **26 uncleanly, impurely,** unpurely; **dirtily,** grimily; **filthily, foully,** nastily, vilely

81 HEALTHFULNESS

NOUNS **1 healthfulness, healthiness, salubrity,** salubriousness, **wholesomeness,** goodness

2 hygiene, hygienics; sanitation 79.3; public health, epidemiology; **preventive medicine,** prophylaxis, mental hygiene

3 hygienist; public health doctor
or physician, epidemiologist; dental hygienist

**VERBS 4 make for health, be good
for,** agree with

**ADJS 5 healthful, healthy, salubrious, salutary, wholesome,
beneficial,** benign, good, **good
for; hygienic, hygienical,** sanitary; constitutional; conditioning; bracing, refreshing, invigorating, tonic

82 UNHEALTHFULNESS

NOUNS 1 unhealthfulness, unhealthiness, insalubrity, insalubriousness, **unwholesomeness;** noxiousness, noisomeness, harmfulness 999.5; health hazard, threat *or* danger *or* menace to health; contamination, pollution, environmental pollution

2 innutritiousness, indigestibility

3 poisonousness, toxicity, venomousness; virulence *or*
virulency, malignancy, noxiousness, destructiveness, deadliness; **infectiousness,** infectivity, contagiousness, communicability; poison, venom 1000.3

VERBS 4 disagree with, not be
good for, sicken

**ADJS 5 unhealthful, unhealthy,
insalubrious, unsalutary, unwholesome,** peccant, bad, **bad
for;** noxious, noisome, injurious, baneful, harmful 999.12; **polluted,** contaminated, tainted, foul, septic; unhygienic, unsanitary, insanitary; pathogenic

6 innutritious, indigestible

7 poisonous, toxic; venomous, envenomed; toxiferous; pollutive; **virulent, noxious, malignant,** malign, destructive, deadly; pestiferous, pestilential; mephitic, miasmal, miasmic; **infectious,** infective, contagious, communicable, catching

83 HEALTH

NOUNS 1 health, well-being; fitness, health and fitness, physical fitness 84; bloom, flush, glow, rosiness; mental health, emotional health; physical condition

2 healthiness, healthfulness, **soundness,** wholesomeness; hea'thy body, healthy constitution; **good health,** good state of health; **robust health,** rugged health, picture of health; **fine fettle,** high feather <nonformal>, **good shape,** good trim, fine shape, top shape <nonformal>, good condition, mint condition; clean bill of health

3 haleness, heartiness, robustness, vigorousness, ruggedness, **vitality,** lustiness, hardiness, strength, vigor; longevity

4 immunity, resistance, nonsusceptibility to disease; **immunization;** antibody, antigen 86.27

5 health *or* **medical care, health
protection,** health *or* medical management, health maintenance, **medical care** 91.1; **wellness,** disease prevention, preventive medicine; health policy, health-care policy; **health
plan, health** *or* **medical insurance,** health-care delivery service *or* plan, health maintenance organization *or* HMO, Medicare, Medicaid; socialized medicine; health club

VERBS 6 enjoy good health, have a clean bill of health, be in the pink; be in the best of health; **feel
good,** feel fine, feel fit, feel like a million dollars *or* like a million <nonformal>, never feel better; feel one's oats, be full of pep; burst with health, bloom, glow, flourish; keep fit, stay in shape; wear well, stay young

7 get well, recover 396.20, mend, be oneself again, feel like a new person, get back on one's feet, get over it; recuperate 396.19

ADJS 8 healthy, healthful, enjoying health, **fine,** in health, in shape, in condition, **fit; in good health,** in the pink of condition, in mint condition, **in good** *or* **fine shape, in fine fettle,** bursting with

health, feeling one's oats; eupeptic

9 <nonformal terms> **in the pink,**
in high feather, chipper, **fit as a
fiddle;** alive and kicking, bright-
eyed and bushy-tailed; full of
beans *or* of piss and vinegar

**10 well, unailing, unsick, un-
sickly;** all right, doing nicely, up
and about, sitting up and taking
nourishment, alive and well

11 sound, whole, wholesome; unimpaired 1001.8; sound of mind
and body, sound as a dollar
<nonformal>

12 hale, hearty, hale and hearty, **robust,** robustious, vital, **vigorous,
strong,** strong as a horse *or* an
ox, bionic <nonformal>, stalwart,
stout, sturdy, **rugged,** rude,
hardy, lusty, bouncing; well-knit;
fit, in condition *or* shape

13 fresh, green, youthful, **blooming;** flush, flushed, **rosy,** rosy-
cheeked, apple-cheeked, ruddy,
pink, pink-cheeked; fresh-faced,
fresh as a daisy *or* rose

14 immune, resistant; health-
conscious; immune response

84 FITNESS, EXERCISE

NOUNS **1 fitness, physical fitness,
physical conditioning, condition, shape,** trim, tone, fettle;
gymnasium, gym <nonformal>,
fitness center, health club,
health spa; **weight, barbell,**
dumbbell, exercise machine,
Nautilus <trademark>, bench,
exercise bike, rowing machine,
stair-climbing machine; whirlpool bath, Jacuzzi <trademark>,
hot tub, spa

2 exercise, motion, movement,
maneuver; **program,** routine,
drill, work-out; **exercise systems; warm-up, stretching,**
warm-down; **calisthenics,**
setting-up exercise *or* set-ups,
daily dozen <nonformal>, constitutional; **gymnastic exercise,
gymnastics; isometrics,** isometric exercise; **violent exercise;
aerobic exercise, aerobics,** aerobic dancing *or* dance;

bodybuilding, weightlifting,
weight training, pumping iron
<nonformal>; **running, jogging,**
roadwork, distance running;
walking, fitness walking, health-
walking; **swimming,** swim-
nastics, water exercise

3 physical fitness test; stress test,
treadmill test

VERBS **4 exercise, work out,** warm
up, lift weights, pump iron <non-
formal>, jog, run, bicycle,
walk

85 DISEASE

NOUNS **1 disease, illness, sickness, malady, ailment, indisposition, disorder,** complaint,
morbidity, **affliction,** affection,
infirmity; disability, defect,
handicap; deformity 265.3; **birth
defect,** congenital defect; abnormality, pathological condition;
signs, symptoms, pathology,
symptomatology, syndrome;
sickishness, malaise; complication; plant disease, blight
1000.2

2 fatal disease, deadly disease,
terminal disease *or* illness; **death**
307, clinical death, loss of vital
signs; apparent death; **brain
death;** sudden death, unexplained death; crib death *or*
sudden infant death syndrome *or*
SIDS

3 unhealthiness, healthlessness;
ill health, poor health, delicate *or*
fragile health; **sickliness,**
peakedness <nonformal>, **feebleness,** fragility, **frailty** 16.2;
infirmity, unsoundness, debility,
debilitation, enervation, exhaustion, decrepitude; wasting, languishing; chronic ill health, invalidity, **invalidism;** morbidity;
hypochondria, hypochondriasis,
valetudinarianism

4 infection, contagion, contamination, taint, virus; **contagiousness, infectiousness, communicability;** carrier, vector; **epidemiology**

5 epidemic, plague, pestilence,
pest, pandemic, scourge; white

plague, tuberculosis; pesthole, plague spot

6 seizure, attack, access, visitation; arrest; blockage, stoppage, occlusion, thrombosis; **stroke,** apoplexy; **spasm, throes, fit, paroxysm, convulsion,** frenzy; **epilepsy;** lockjaw, tetanus

7 fever, feverishness, febrility, febricity, pyrexia; hyperthermia; **heat, fire, fever heat;** flush, hectic flush; delirium 925.8

8 collapse, breakdown, crackup <nonformal>, **prostration,** exhaustion; nervous prostration *or* breakdown *or* exhaustion, neurasthenia

9 <some disease symptoms> anemia; asphyxiation, ataxia; bleeding; colic; dizziness, vertigo; chills; hot flash; dropsy, edema; morning sickness; fainting; fatigue 21; fever; constipation; diarrhea, dysentery; indigestion, upset stomach, dyspepsia; inflammation 85.9; insomnia; itching; backache, lumbago; vomiting, nausea; skin eruption, rash; sore, abscess; hypertension, high blood pressure; low blood pressure; growth; shock; convulsion, seizure, spasm; pain 26; tachycardia; shortness of breath, labored breathing, asthma; nasal discharge, coughing, sneezing; sclerosis

10 inflammation, inflammatory disease; muscle *or* muscular disease *or* disorder, myopathy

11 deficiency diseases, nutritional disease, vitamin-deficiency disease

12 genetic disease, gene-transmitted disease, hereditary *or* congenital disease

13 infectious disease, infection

14 eye disease, ophthalmic disease, disease of the eye *or* of vision; cataract; conjunctivitis *or* pink eye; glaucoma; sty; eye *or* visual defect, defective vision 28

15 ear disease, otic disease; **deafness; earache,** otalgia; tympanitis; otosclerosis; **vertigo,**

dizziness, loss of balance; Ménière's syndrome

16 respiratory disease, upper respiratory disease; lung disease

17 tuberculosis *or* **TB,** white plague, phthisis, consumption

18 venereal disease *or* VD, sexually-transmitted disease *or* STD, social disease, dose <nonformal>; chancre, chancroid; gonorrhea *or* clap *or* the clap *or* claps <nonformal>; syphilis

19 cardiovascular disease; heart disease, heart condition; vascular disease; hypertension *or* high blood pressure; angina *or* angina pectoris; cardiac *or* myocardial infarction; cardiac arrest; congenital heart disease; congestive heart failure; coronary *or* ischemic heart disease; coronary thrombosis; heart attack, coronary, heart failure; tachycardia

20 blood disease, hemic *or* hematic disease, hematopathology

21 endocrine disease, gland *or* glandular disease, endocrinism, endocrinopathy; diabetes; goiter; hyper- *or* hypoglycemia; hyper- *or* hypothyroidism

22 metabolic disease; acidosis, alkalosis, ketosis; gout; galactosemia, lactose intolerance, fructose intolerance

23 liver disease, hepatic disease; jaundice

24 kidney disease, renal disease; nephritis

25 neural *or* **nerve disease,** neuropathy; amyotrophic lateral sclerosis *or* Lou Gehrig's disease; palsy, cerebral palsy; chorea *or* St Vitus's dance; Huntington's chorea; headache, migraine; multiple sclerosis *or* MS; Parkinson's disease *or* Parkinsonism; sciatica; shingles *or* herpes zoster; spina bifida

26 shock, trauma; traumatism

27 paralysis, palsy, impairment of motor function; **stroke,** apoplexy; paresis; motor paralysis, sensory paralysis; hemiplegia, paraplegia, quadriplegia; catalepsy; infantile paralysis, poliomyelitis, polio <nonformal>

28 heatstroke; heat prostration *or* exhaustion; sunstroke, siriasis, insolation

29 gastrointestinal disease; colic; colitis; constipation; diarrhea *or* dysentery *or* looseness of the bowels, the trots *or* the shits <both nonformal>; gastritis; indigestion *or* dyspepsia; ulcer, peptic ulcer

30 nausea, queasiness, squeamishness; motion sickness, travel sickness, **seasickness,** *mal de mer* <Fr>, airsickness, car sickness

31 poisoning, venenation; septic poisoning, blood poisoning, sepsis, septicemia, toxemia; food poisoning, ptomaine poisoning

32 environmental disease, occupational disease, disease of the workplace, environmental *or* occupational hazard

33 allergy; allergic rhinitis, **hay fever; asthma,** bronchial asthma; **hives,** urticaria; eczema; conjunctivitis; allergic gastritis; Chinese restaurant syndrome; allergen

34 skin diseases; acne; dermatitis; eczema; herpes; hives; psoriasis

35 skin eruption, rash, efflorescence, breaking out; diaper rash; prickly heat, heat rash; hives, urticaria

36 sore, lesion; pustule, papule, papula, fester, **pimple,** hickey *and* zit <both nonformal>; pock; ulcer, ulceration; bedsore; blister; **boil,** furuncle; carbuncle; canker; canker sore; sty; abscess; whitlow, felon, paronychia; bubo; chancre; hemorrhoids, piles; bunion; chilblain; polyp; fistula; suppuration, festering

37 trauma, wound, injury, lesion; **cut,** incision, scratch, gash; puncture, stab, stab wound; flesh wound; **laceration,** mutilation; abrasion, gall; frazzle, fray; run, **rip,** rent, slash, **tear; burn,** scald, scorch; flash burn; **break, fracture,** bone-fracture, comminuted

fracture, compound *or* open fracture, greenstick fracture, spiral *or* torsion fracture; rupture; crack, chip, craze, check, crackle; wrench; whiplash injury *or* whiplash; concussion; **bruise, contusion, black-and-blue mark; black eye,** shiner *and* mouse <both nonformal>; **battering;** battered child syndrome

38 growth, neoplasm; **tumor,** intumescence; benign tumor, nonmalignant tumor; malignant tumor, malignant growth, **cancer,** sarcoma, carcinoma; excrescence; cyst, wen; callus, callosity, **corn,** clavus; **wart,** verruca; **mole,** nevus

39 gangrene, necrosis; noma; caries, cariosity, tooth decay; necrotic tissue

40 <animal diseases> anthrax, splenic fever, charbon, milzbrand, malignant pustule; malignant catarrh *or* malignant catarrhal fever; bighead; blackleg, black quarter, quarter evil *or* ill; cattle plague, rinderpest; glanders; foot-and-mouth disease, hoof-and-mouth disease, aphthous fever; distemper

41 germ, pathogen, contagium, bug <nonformal>; **microbe,** microorganism; **virus,** adenovirus, echovirus, reovirus, rhinovirus, enterovirus, picornavirus, retrovirus; rickettsia; bacterium, **bacteria,** coccus, streptococcus, staphylococcus, bacillus, spirochete, aerobe, aerobic bacteria, anaerobe, anaerobic bacteria; protozoon, amoeba, trypanosome; fungus, mold, spore; **carcinogen,** cancer-causing agent

42 sick person, sufferer, victim; valetudinarian, **invalid, shut-in;** incurable, terminal case; **patient, case;** apoplectic, consumptive, dyspeptic, epileptic, rheumatic, arthritic, spastic; **the sick, the infirm**

43 carrier, vector, biological vector, mechanical vector; Typhoid Mary

44 cripple, defective, **handi-**

capped person; amputee; paraplegic, quadriplegic, paralytic; deformity 265.3; the crippled, the handicapped; idiot, imbecile 923.8

VERBS **45 ail, suffer,** labor under, be affected with, complain of; **feel ill,** feel under the weather, feel awful <nonformal>, feel like the walking dead; look green about the gills <nonformal>

46 take sick or **ill, sicken; catch, contract, get,** take, **come down with** <nonformal>, be stricken or seized by, fall a victim to; catch cold; take one's death <nonformal>; **break out,** break out in, break out in a rash, erupt; run a temperature, fever; be struck down, be brought down, be felled; drop in one's tracks, **collapse;** overdose or **OD** <nonformal>; go into shock, be traumatized

47 fail, weaken, sink, decline, run down, lose strength, lose one's grip, dwindle, droop, flag, wilt, wither, wither away, fade, **languish,** waste, waste away, pine, peak

48 go lame, founder

49 afflict, disorder, derange; sicken, indispose; weaken, enfeeble, enervate, reduce, debilitate, devitalize; **invalid,** incapacitate, **disable;** lay up, hospitalize

50 infect, disease, contaminate, taint

51 poison, envenom

ADJS **52 disease-causing, disease-producing, pathogenic;** threatening, life-threatening; unhealthful 82.5

53 unhealthy, in poor health; **infirm, unsound,** invalid, valetudinary, valetudinarian, debilitated, enervated, exhausted, drained; shut-in, housebound, homebound, wheelchair-bound; **sickly,** peaky or peaked <nonformal>; **weakly, feeble, frail** 16.12-21; weakened, with low resistance, **run-down,** reduced in health; **dying** 307.33, **terminal,**

moribund, languishing, failing 16.21

54 unwholesome, unhealthy, unsound, morbid, diseased, pathological

55 ill, ailing, sick, unwell, indisposed, taken ill, on the sick list; **sickish, seedy** and rocky <both nonformal>, **under the weather,** laid low; in a bad way, critically ill, in danger, on the critical list, in intensive care; mortally ill, sick unto death **out of sorts** <nonformal>, below par <nonformal>, off-color, off one's feed <nonformal>; not quite right, not oneself; feeling awful and feeling something terrible <both nonformal>; sick as a dog or a pig <nonformal>, laid low; in

56 nauseated, nauseous, **queasy, squeamish, qualmish,** qualmy; **sick to one's stomach;** pukish and puky and barfy <all nonformal>; seasick, carsick, airsick

57 feverish, fevered, feverous, febrile, pyretic; **flushed,** inflamed, **hot, burning;** hyperthermic; delirious 925.31

58 laid up, invalided, hospitalized; **bedridden, bedfast, sick abed; down,** prostrate, flat on one's back

59 diseased, morbid, pathological, infected, contaminated, tainted, peccant **poisoned,** septic; cankerous, cankered, ulcerous, ulcerated, ulcerative, gangrenous, mortified; **inflamed;** congested; **swollen,** edematous

60 anemic, chlorotic; bilious; dyspeptic, liverish, colicky

61 contagious, infectious, infective, **catching,** taking, spreading, **communicable;** pestiferous, pestilential, **epidemic,** epidemial, pandemic; epizootic, epiphytotic; endemic; sporadic

86 REMEDY

NOUNS **1 remedy, cure, corrective,** alterative, remedial measure; **relief, help, aid, assistance,** succor; balm; restorative, analeptic; specific, specific remedy; **prescription**

2 **nostrum,** patent medicine; snake oil

3 **panacea, cure-all,** catholicon; broad-spectrum drug *or* antibiotic; elixir, elixir of life

4 **medicine, medicament, medication,** medicinal, **drug, physic;** herbs, vegetable remedies; tisane, ptisan; drops; powder; inhalant; **prescription drug,** ethical drug; over-the-counter *or* OTC drug, **nonprescription drug;** proprietary medicine *or* drug, proprietary, patent medicine; proprietary name, generic name; **placebo**

5 **drug, narcotic drug, controlled substance**

6 **dose, draft, potion,** portion, **shot,** injection; booster, booster shot

7 **pill,** bolus, **tablet, capsule,** lozenge, troche

8 **tonic, bracer,** cordial, restorative, **pick-me-up** <nonformal>; **shot in the arm** <nonformal>

9 **stimulant;** Adrenalin <trademark> *or* epinephrine, aloes; amphetamine sulphate, aromatic spirits of ammonia, caffeine, dextroamphetamine sulfate *or* Dexedrine <trademark>, digitalin *or* digitalis, methamphetamine hydrochloride *or* Methedrine <trademark>, smelling salts

10 **palliative, alleviative, lenitive, assuasive;** abirritant

11 **balm, lotion, salve, ointment, unguent,** unction, balsam, oil, emollient, demulcent; **liniment,** embrocation; eyebath, eyewash; ear-drops

12 **sedative, sedative hypnotic, depressant,** barbituric acid, belladonna, chloral hydrate *or* chloral, laudanum, morphine, pentobarbital *or* Nembutal <trademark>, phenobarbital *or* Luminal <trademark>, Quaalude <trademark>, reserpine, scopolamine, secobarbital *or* Seconal <trademark>; **sleeping pill** *or* **tablet** *or* potion; **calmative, tranquilizer,** chlorpromazine, Librium <trademark>, rauwolfia, reserpine, Thorazine <trademark>, Valium <trademark>; abirritant, pacifier; **analgesic,** acetaminophen *or* Tylenol <trademark>, aspirin *or* acetylsalicylic acid, buffered aspirin *or* Bufferin <trademark>, headache *or* aspirin powder, ibuprofen *or* Advil <trademark> *or* Motrin <trademark> *or* Nuprin <trademark>, sodium salicylate; **anodyne,** paregoric <old>; **pain killer** <nonformal>

13 **psychoactive drug, hallucinogen, psychedelic,** psychedelic drug

14 **antipyretic,** febrifuge, fever-reducer

15 **anesthetic;** local *or* topical *or* general anesthetic; differential anesthetic; chloroform, ether, ethyl chloride, gas, laughing gas, nitrous oxide, novocaine *or* Novocain <trademark>, thiopental sodium *or* Pentothal <trademark> *or* truth serum

16 **cough medicine,** cough syrup, cough drops; horehound

17 **laxative, cathartic, physic, purge, purgative,** aperient, carminative, diuretic; stool softener

18 **emetic,** nauseant

19 **enema,** clyster, clysma, lavage

20 **prophylactic, preventive,** preventative, protective

21 **antiseptic, disinfectant,** fumigant, fumigator, **germicide,** bactericide, microbicide; alcohol, carbolic acid, hydrogen peroxide, tincture of iodine

22 **dentifrice, toothpaste,** tooth powder; mouthwash, gargle

23 **contraceptive,** birth control device, prophylactic; condom; **rubber** *and* skin *and* bag <all nonformal>; oral contraceptive, **birth control pill, the pill** <nonformal>, morning-after pill, abortion pill; diaphragm, pessary; spermicide, spermicidal jelly, contraceptive foam; intrauterine device *or* IUD, Dalkon shield <trademark>

24 vermifuge, vermicide, worm
medicine, anthelminthic
25 antacid, gastric antacid, alka-
lizer
26 antidote, counterpoison
27 antitoxin, antitoxic serum;
antivenin; serum, antiserum;
interferon; **antibody;** gamma
globulin; antiantibody; antigen,
Rh antigen, Rh factor; allergen;
immunosuppressive drug
**28 vaccination, inoculation; vac-
cine**
29 antibiotic, bacitracin, ery-
thromycin, neomycin, penicil-
lin, streptomycin, tetracycline
or Terramycin <trademark>; **miracle drug, wonder drug,** magic
bullets; bacteriostat; **sulfa drug**,
sulfa, sulfanilamide, sulfona-
mide, sulfathiazole
30 diaphoretic, sudorific
31 vesicant, vesicatory, epispastic
32 miscellaneous drugs, anabolic
steroid or muscle pill, anti-
histamine, antispasmodic, beta
blocker, counterirritant, decon-
gestant, expectorant, fertility drug
or pill, hormone, vasoconstrictor,
vasodilator
33 dressing, application; plaster,
court plaster, mustard plaster;
poultice; compress; tampon;
bandage, bandaging, binder,
roller or roller bandage; bandage
compress, adhesive compress,
Band-Aid <trademark>; **elastic
bandage,** Ace bandage <trade-
mark>; **tourniquet;** sling; splint,
brace; cast, plaster cast; tape,
adhesive tape; lint, gauze,
sponge
**34 pharmacology, pharmacy,
pharmaceutics;** materia medica
35 pharmacist, druggist, chemist
<Brit>, **apothecary,** dispenser;
pharmacologist
36 drugstore, pharmacy, chemist
and chemist's shop <both Brit>,
apothecary's shop, dispensary
37 pharmacopoeia, dispensatory
VERBS **38** remedy, cure 396.15; prescribe; treat
ADJS **39 remedial, curative, therapeutic, healing,** re-

storative, sanatory; panacean;
medicinal, medicative, iatric
40 palliative, lenitive, alleviative,
assuasive, soothing, balmy, bal-
samic, demulcent, emollient
41 antidotal; antitoxic; antibiotic,
bacteriostatic, antimicrobial;
antiscorbutic; antipyretic,
febrifugal; vermifugal, anthel-
mintic; **antacid**
42 prophylactic, preventive, protective
**43 antiseptic, disinfectant, ger-
micidal,** bactericidal
**44 tonic, stimulating, bracing, in-
vigorating,** reviving, refreshing,
restorative
45 sedative, calmative, calmant,
depressant, **soothing, tranquilizing, quietening; narcotic,**
opiatic; **analgesic,** anodyne, paregoric <old>; anti-inflammatory;
muscle relaxant; hypnotic, soporific, somniferous, somnifacient,
sleep-inducing
46 psychochemical, psychoactive;
antidepressant, mood drug; hallucinogenic, **psychedelic,** mind-
expanding
47 anesthetic, deadening, numbing
48 cathartic, laxative, purgative,
aperient; carminative; diuretic
49 emetic, vomitive

87 SUBSTANCE ABUSE

NOUNS **1 substance abuse, drug
abuse,** glue-sniffing, solvent
abuse; **addiction, addictedness,
drug addiction,** morphine addiction or habit, morphinism, heroin
addiction or habit, cocaine addiction, cocainism, crack habit,
barbiturate addiction, amphetamine addiction; **habit,** drug
habit, drug habituation, drug dependence, physical addiction or
dependence, psychological addiction or dependence, jones and
monkey on one's back and Mighty
Joe Young <all nonformal>; **drug
experience, drug intoxication,**
high and buzz and rush <all non-
formal>; bad trip and bum trip
and bummer <all nonformal>;

alcoholism 88.3, alcohol abuse, drinking habit, chronic alcoholism, dipsomania; **smoking,** smoking habit, nicotine addiction 89.10, chain smoking; **tolerance**; **withdrawal, withdrawal sickness,** withdrawal syndrome, withdrawal symptoms, coming down *and* crash <both nonformal>, abrupt withdrawal *and* cold turkey <both nonformal>; **detoxification** *or* detox <nonformal>, drying out

2 drug, narcotic, dope <nonformal>, controlled substance, abused substance, illegal drug, addictive drug, **hard drug;** soft drug; **opiate; sedative, depressant; hallucinogen,** psychedelic, psychedelic drug, psychoactive drug, mind-altering drug, mind-expanding drug, mind-blowing drug; **stimulant; antidepressant; inhalant**

3 <nonformal terms for amphetamines> bennies, benz, black mollies, brain ticklers, crank, crystal, dexies, diet pills, dolls, ecstasy, footballs, hearts, ice, jelly beans, lid poppers, meth, pep pills, purple hearts, speed, uppers, ups, white crosses

4 <nonformal terms for amyl nitrate> amies, blue angels, blue devils, blue dolls, blue heavens, poppers, snappers; barbiturates, barbs

5 <nonformal terms for chloral hydrate> joy juice, knockout drops, mickey, Mickey Finn, peter

6 <nonformal terms for cocaine> basuco, bernice, big C, blow, C, charlie, coke, crack, crack cocaine, jumps, dust, flake, girl, gold dust, her, jay, joy powder, lady, lady snow, nose candy, snow, star dust, toot, white, white girl, white lady

7 <nonformal terms for hashish> black hash, black Russian, hash

8 <nonformal terms for heroin> big H, boy, brown, caballo, crap, doojee, flea powder, garbage, H, hard stuff, henry, him, his, horse, hombre, jones, junk, mojo,

P-funk, scag, schmeck, smack, white stuff

9 <nonformal terms for LSD> acid, big D, blotter, blue acid, blue cheer, blue heaven, California sunshine, cap, cubes, D, deeda, dots, electric Kool-Aid

10 <nonformal terms for marijuana> Acapulco gold, aunt mary, bomb, boo, bush, doobie, gage, ganja, grass, grefa, hay, hemp, herb, Indian hay, J, jane, kif, mary, maryjane, mary warner, meserole, mighty mezz, moota, muggles, pod, pot, smoke, snop, tea, Texas tea, weed, yerba

11 <nonformal terms for marijuana cigarette> joint, joy stick, kick stick, bone, smoke, puff, reefer, roach, stick, twist, doobie

12 <nonformal terms for mescaline> beans, big chief, buttons, cactus, mesc

13 <nonformal terms for morphine> big M, emm, hocus, M, miss emma

14 <nonformal terms for pentobarbital> nebbies, nemmies

15 <nonformal terms for opium> black pills, brown stuff, hop, O, tar

16 <nonformal terms for peyote> bad seed, big chief, buttons, cactus, P, topi

17 <nonformal terms for phencyclidine> angel dust, animal trank, DOA, dust, elephant, hog, PCP

18 <nonformal terms for psilocybin> magic mushroom, mushroom, shroom

19 dose, hit *and* fix *and* toke *and* rock <all nonformal>; **shot, injection,** bang <nonformal>; **portion, packet,** bag *and* deck <both nonformal>; drug house, shooting gallery *and* needle park <both nonformal>; crack house, opium den, balloon room *and* pot party *and* dope den <all nonformal>

20 addict, drug addict, narcotics addict, user, drug user, drug abuser, junkie *and* head *and* druggy *and* doper *and* toker *and*

fiend *and* freak *and* space cadet
<all nonformal>; cocaine user,
cokie *and* coke head *and* crack-
head *and* sniffer *and* snow drifter
and flaky <all nonformal>; opium
user, opium addict, hophead *and*
hopdog *and* tar distiller <all non-
formal>; heroin user *or* addict,
smackhead *and* smack-sack *and*
schmecker <all nonformal>;
methedrine user *or* methhead
<nonformal>; amphetamine
user, pillhead *and* pill popper *and*
speed freak <all nonformal>;
LSD user, acidhead *and* acid
freak *and* tripper *and* cubehead
<all nonformal>; marijuana
smoker *and* pothead <both non-
formal>; **drug seller** *or* dealer,
pusher, contact, connection; **alcoholic, alcohol abuser** 88;
smoker

VERBS **21 use, be on,** get on; **get a
rush** *or* flush; **sniff,** snort, blow,
toot, one and one <nonformal>;
smoke marijuana, take on a
number *and* blow a stick *and* toke
and blast *and* weed out <all non-
formal>; **smoke opium,** blow a
fill; freebase; **inject,** mainline,
shoot *and* shoot up *and* jab *and*
get down *and* get off <all nonfor-
mal>, pop *and* skin pop <both
nonformal>; **take pills,** pop pills
<nonformal>; **withdraw,** crash
and come down <both nonfor-
mal>, kick *or* go cold turkey *and*
hang tough *and* water out <all
nonformal>, detoxify, dry out,
kick *and* kick the habit <both
nonformal>; **trip,** blow one's
mind *and* wig out <both nonfor-
mal>; **sell drugs,** deal *and* push
<both nonformal>; **buy drugs,**
score *and* make *and* connect <all
nonformal>; **have drugs,** be
heeled *and* carry *and* hold *and*
sizzle <all nonformal>; **drink** *or*
booze 88.24–25; **smoke, smoke
tobacco,** drag, chain-smoke,
smoke like a chimney

ADJS **22 intoxicated,** under the influence, nodding, narcotized,
poppied

23 <nonformal terms> **high,** bent,
blasted, blind, bombed out,
bonged out, buzzed, coked, coked
out, flying, fried, geared, geared
up, geezed, gonged, gorked,
hopped-up, in a zone, junked,
luded out, maxed, noddy, ripped,
smashed, snowed, spaced, space
out, spacey, stoned, strung out,
switched on, tanked, totaled,
tranqued, tripping, trippy, wired,
zoned, zoned out, zonked, zonked
out

24 addicted, hooked *and* zonked
and on the needle <all nonfor-
mal>; dependency-prone;
supplied with drugs, holding
and heeled *and* carrying *and*
anywhere <all nonformal>;
using, on, behind acid <nonfor-
mal>

88 INTOXICATION, ALCOHOLIC DRINK

NOUNS **1 intoxication, inebria-
tion, inebriety,** insobriety,
drunkenness, tipsiness, tip-
sification *and* tiddliness <both
nonformal>; a high; Dutch courage; hangover, morning after
<nonformal>

2 bibulousness, bibulosity, sot-
tishness; serious drinking;
crapulence, crapulousness;
intemperance 669; baccha-
nalianism

3 alcoholism, dipsomania, alcoholic psychosis *or* addiction,
pathological drunkenness, problem drinking, heavy drinking,
habitual drunkenness; delirium
tremens 925.9, 10; gin drinker's
liver, cirrhosis of the liver

**4 drinking, imbibing; social
drinking; tippling,** guzzling,
gargling, bibing; winebibbing,
winebibbery; toping; hard
drinking, serious drinking
<nonformal>; **boozing** *and* swill-
ing <both nonformal>, **hitting
the booze** *or* **bottle** *or* **sauce**
<nonformal>

5 spree, drinking bout, bout, **celebration,** potation, compotation,
symposium, wassail, **carouse,**

carousal; bacchanal, bacchanalia, bacchanalian; **debauch, orgy**

6 <nonformal terms> **binge, drunk,** bust, tear, **bender, toot, bat,** jag, brannigan, guzzle

7 drink, dram, potation, potion, libation, **nip,** draft, drop, spot, finger or two, sip, sup, suck, drench, guzzle, gargle, jigger; peg, swig, swill, pull; **snort,** jolt, **shot,** snifter, wet; quickie; round, round of drinks

8 bracer, refresher, reviver, pickup and **pick-me-up** <both nonformal>, tonic, hair of the dog or hair of the dog that bit one <nonformal>

9 drink, cocktail, highball, long drink, mixed drink; **punch; eye-opener** <nonformal>, **nightcap** <nonformal>; **chaser** <nonformal>; parting cup, stirrup cup, doch-an-dorrach or wee doch-an-dorrach <both Scots>, one for the road; Mickey Finn or Mickey and knockout drops <all nonformal>

10 toast, pledge

11 drinker, imbiber, **social drinker,** tippler, bibber; winebibber; **drunkard, drunk, inebriate, sot,** toper, guzzler, swiller, soaker, barfly, **serious drinker;** swigger; hard drinker, heavy drinker, **alcoholic, dipsomaniac, problem drinker,** chronic alcoholic, chronic drunk, pathological drinker; carouser, reveler, wassailer; bacchanal, bacchanalian

12 <nonformal terms> **drunk, lush, soak,** sponge, **boozer, boozehound,** dipso, ginhound, elbow bender, shikker; **souse, stew,** bum, rummy, rumhound, stewbum; wino

13 spirits, liquor, intoxicating liquor, adult beverage, **hard liquor, whiskey,** firewater, spiritus frumenti, schnapps, **intoxicant, potable,** potation, **beverage, drink, strong drink,** strong liquor, alcoholic drink or beverage, **alcohol,** brew, **grog,** social lubricant, nectar of the gods; **booze** <nonformal>; **rum,** the Demon Rum, John Barleycorn; the bottle, the cup that cheers, little brown jug; punch bowl

14 <nonformal terms> **likker, hooch, juice, sauce,** sheepdip, moonshine, white lightning; **medicine,** snake medicine; **rotgut, poison,** rat poison, formaldehyde, embalming fluid, **panther piss**

15 liqueur, cordial; brandy

16 beer, brew and brewskie and suds <all nonformal>; small beer

17 wine; vintage wine, nonvintage wine; red wine, white wine, rosé wine, pink wine; dry or sweet wine, heavy or light wine, still wine, sparkling wine; extra sec or demi-sec or sec or brut champagne; jug wine

18 bootleg liquor, moonshine <nonformal>; hooch and shine and mountain dew <all nonformal>, white lightning or mule <nonformal>; bathtub gin; home brew

19 liquor dealer, liquor store owner; **vintner,** wine merchant; winegrower, winemaker, oenologist; **bartender,** mixologist, barkeeper, barkeep; barmaid; **brewer,** brewmaster; **distiller; bootlegger, moonshiner** <nonformal>

20 bar, barroom, bistro <Fr>, cocktail lounge; taproom; **tavern, pub,** gin mill <nonformal>, **saloon,** drinking saloon; lounge bar, piano bar, singles bar, gay bar; waterhole or watering hole <nonformal>; wine bar; beer parlor, beer garden, rathskeller; **nightclub, cabaret;** café, wine shop; barrel house and honkytonk and dive <all nonformal>; **speakeasy** and blind tiger and blind pig and after-hours joint <all nonformal>

21 distillery, still, distiller; **brewery; winery,** wine press; bottling works

VERBS **22 intoxicate, inebriate, addle, befuddle,** bemuse, besot, go to one's head, make one see double, make one tiddly

23 <nonformal terms> **plaster,** pickle, swack, crock, stew, souse, stone, pollute, tipsify, booze up, boozify, fuddle, overtake

24 **tipple, drink,** nip; grog, **guzzle,** gargle; **imbibe,** have a drink *or* nip *or* dram *or* guzzle *or* gargle, soak, bib, quaff, sip, sup, lap, lap up, take a drop, slake one's thirst, cheer *or* refresh the inner man, drown one's troubles *or* sorrows, commune with the spirits; **down,** toss off *or* down, toss one's drink, knock back, throw one back, drink off *or* up, drain the cup, drink bottoms-up, drink deep; **drink hard,** drink like a fish, drink seriously, **tope;** take to drink *or* drinking

25 <nonformal terms> **booze,** swig, swill, moisten *or* wet one's whistle; **liquor, liquor up,** lush, souse, tank up, **hit the booze *or* bottle *or* sauce,** exercise *or* bend *or* crook *or* raise the elbow; chug-a-lug

26 **get drunk,** be stricken drunk, get high, take a drop too much; **get plastered *or* pickled,** etc <nonformal>, tie one on *and* get a bun on <both nonformal>

27 **be drunk,** be intoxicated, have a drop too much, have more than one can hold, have a jag on <nonformal>, see double, be feeling no pain; **stagger, reel; pass out** <nonformal>

28 **go on a spree; go on a binge *or* drunk *or* toot *or* bat *or* bender** <nonformal>, **carouse, spree, revel,** wassail, debauch, paint the town red <nonformal>

29 **drink to, toast, pledge,** drink a toast to, drink *or* pledge the health of

30 **distill; brew;** bootleg, moonshine <nonformal>

ADJS 31 **intoxicated, inebriated,** inebriate, **drunk, drunken,** *shikker* <Yiddish>, **tipsy, in one's cups, under the influence,** the worse for liquor; beery; **tiddly, giddy, dizzy,** muddled, addled, flustered, reeling, seeing double; **mellow, merry,** jolly, happy, gay, glorious; **full; besotted,** sotted, sodden, drenched, far-gone; drunk as a lord, drunk as a fiddler *or* piper, drunk as an owl; staggering drunk; crapulent, crapulous; **maudlin**

32 **dead-drunk,** blind drunk, overcome, out *and* out cold *and* passed out <all nonformal>, helpless, under the table

33 <nonformal terms> **fuddled, boozy; swacked, plastered,** stewed, **pickled,** pissed, **soused,** soaked, boiled, fried, canned, tanked, potted, bombed, smashed; **crocked,** sloshed, sozzled, zonked, tight, lushy, squiffy, oiled, lubricated, feeling no pain, polluted, **high,** high as a kite, lit, **lit up,** lit to the gills, full, illuminated, **loaded, stinko,** tanked, stinking drunk, pie-eyed, pissy-eyed, hammered, shitfaced, cockeyed, cockeyed drunk, roaring *or* rip-roaring drunk, skunk-drunk; speaking Inca; half-seas over, three sheets to the wind, **blotto, stiff,** blind, paralyzed, **stoned**

34 **full of Dutch courage, pot-valiant,** pot-valorous

35 **bibulous,** bibacious, drunken, sottish, **liquor-loving,** liquor-drinking, drinking, hard-drinking, swilling <nonformal>, toping, tippling, winebibbing

36 **intoxicating,** intoxicative, **inebriating,** inebriative, inebriant, heady

37 **alcoholic, spirituous, ardent, strong, hard,** with a kick <nonformal>

89 TOBACCO

NOUNS 1 **tobacco; the weed** <nonformal>, filthy weed, sot-weed <old>; carcinogenic substance; smoke, secondhand smoke

2 <tobaccos> flue-cured *or* bright, fire-cured, air-cured; plug tobacco, bird's-eye, canaster, leaf, lugs, seconds, shag

3 smoking tobacco, smokings
<nonformal>, smoke *and* smokes
<both nonformal>

4 cigar; rope *and* stinker <both
nonformal>; **cheroot, stogie,
corona,** belvedere, Havana,
panatella, colorado, trichinopoly;
cigarillo; humidor; cigar cutter

5 cigarette; butt *and* fag *and* coffin nail *and* cancer stick <all
nonformal>; cigarette butt, **butt,**
stub; cigarette case

6 pipe, tobacco pipe; corncob,
corncob pipe, Missouri meerschaum; briar pipe, briar; clay
pipe, clay, churchwarden <Brit>;
meerschaum; water pipe, hoo-
kah, nargileh, kalian, hubble-
bubble; peace pipe, calumet; pipe
rack, pipe cleaner, tobacco pouch

7 chewing tobacco, eating tobacco <nonformal>; navy *or* navy
plug, cavendish, twist, pigtail, cut
plug; **quid, chew,** chaw <nonfor-
mal>; tobacco juice

8 snuff; rappee; pinch of snuff;
snuff bottle, snuffbox

9 nicotine, nicotia <old>

10 smoking, smoking habit, habitual smoking; chain-smoke;
smoke, puff, drag <nonformal>;
chewing; tobacco *or* nicotine
addiction, nicotinism; passive
smoking

11 tobacco user, smoker, cigarette
or pipe *or* cigar smoker, chewer,
snuffer, snuff dipper

12 tobacconist; tobacco store *or*
shop, cigar store

13 smoking room, smoking car,
smoker

VERBS **14** <use tobacco> **smoke;**
inhale, puff, draw, drag <nonfor-
mal>, pull; smoke like a furnace
or chimney; chain-smoke; **chew,**
chaw <nonformal>; **take snuff,**
dip *or* inhale snuff

ADJS **15 tobacco,** tobaccolike; **nic-
otinic;** smoking, chewing; snuffy

90 HEALTH CARE

NOUNS **1 medicine, medical practice, health care,** health-care
industry, health-care delivery;
medical specialty *or* **branch;**

treatment, therapy 91; **health
care, health insurance** 83.5;
care, nursing care, home care,
outpatient care, life care

2 surgery; operation

3 dentistry, dental medicine,
dental care

4 doctor, doc <nonformal>, **physician, medical practitioner,
medical man, medico** <nonfor-
mal>, croaker *and* sawbones
<both nonformal>; **general
practitioner** *or* **GP;** family doctor; country doctor; **intern;
resident,** house physician, resident physician; fellow; medical
attendant, attending physician;
specialist, board-certified physician *or* specialist; **medical
examiner,** coroner; **osteopath,
chiropractor,** podiatrist, oculist,
optometrist

5 surgeon, sawbones <nonfor-
mal>; operative surgeon

6 dentist, tooth doctor; **dental
surgeon,** operative dentist; dental specialist

7 veterinary, veterinarian, vet
<nonformal>, horse doctor, ani-
mal doctor

**8 health-care professional,
health-care provider, physician, nurse, midwife, therapist,**
practitioner

9 healer, nonmedical therapist;
Christian *or* spiritual *or* divine
healer; **Christian Science practitioner,** healer; **faith healer,** witch
doctor <nonformal>

10 nurse; probationer, probationist; caregiver, hospice caregiver;
practical nurse; registered nurse
or RN

11 <hospital staff> paramedic;
medevac; physician's assistant
or PA; orderly, attendant, nurse's
aide; audiologist; anesthetist;
dietitian; radiographer, X-ray
technician; laboratory technician; radiotherapist; physical
therapist, physiotherapist; dietitian; hospital administrator;
ambulance driver

12 Hippocrates, Galen; Aescu-
lapius, Asclepius

13 **practice of medicine,** medical practice; general practice, restricted *or* limited practice; group practice; family practice, community medicine

VERBS 14 **practice medicine,** doctor <nonformal>; treat; intern

ADJS 15 **medical,** iatric, health; surgical; chiropodic, pediatric, orthopedic, obstetric, obstetrical, neurological; dental; orthodontic, periodontic, prosthodontic, exodontic; osteopathic, chiropractic, naturopathic, hydropathic, allopathic, homeopathic; clinical

91 THERAPY, MEDICAL TREATMENT

NOUNS 1 **therapy, therapeutics, treatment, medical care** *or* **treatment,** medication; noninvasive *or* nonsurgical therapy *or* treatment; healing; healing arts; psychotherapy 92; medicines 86

2 **nonmedical therapy; healing;** Christian *or* spiritual *or* divine healing; **faith healing**

3 **hydrotherapy;** hydropathy, water cure; cold-water cure; whirlpool bath

4 **heat therapy,** thermotherapy; heliotherapy, solar therapy

5 **diathermy,** medical diathermy; electrotherapy; **radiothermy;** radiosurgery, electrosurgery, electrosection, electrocautery, electrocoagulation

6 **radiotherapy,** radiation therapy; adjuvant therapy

7 **radiology,** radiography, radioscopy, fluoroscopy, etc 1036.7

8 <radiotherapeutic substances> radium; cobalt; radioisotope, tracer, labeled *or* tagged element, radioelement; radiocarbon, carbon 14, radioiodine; radioactive cocktail

9 <diagnostic pictures and graphs> **X-ray,** radiograph, radiogram; photofluorograph; chest X-ray; pyelogram; orthodiagram; encephalograph, encephalogram; electroencephalograph, electroencephalogram *or* EEG; electrocardiogram *or* ECG *or* EKG; computer-assisted tomography *or* CAT, computerized axial tomography *or* computed tomography *or* computer-assisted tomography *or* computerized tomography *or* CAT; C T scan; magnetic resonance imaging *or* MRI; MR scan; positron emission tomography *or* PET; PET scan; ultrasound, ultrasonography; sonogram

10 case history, medical history, anamnesis; catamnesis, follow-up

11 **diagnostics,** prognostics; symptomatology, semeiology, semeiotics

12 diagnosis; **examination, physical examination;** study, test, work-up <nonformal>; blood test, blood work <nonformal>, urinalysis, uroscopy; biopsy; Pap test *or* smear; electrocardiography, electroencephalography; mammography

13 **prognosis;** prognostic, **symptom, sign**

14 **treatment,** medical treatment *or* attention *or* care; **cure,** curative measures; **medication; regimen,** regime, protocol; first aid; hospitalization

15 **immunization;** immunization therapy, immunotherapy; vaccine therapy, vaccinotherapy; toxin-antitoxin immunization; serum therapy, serotherapy; tuberculin test, scratch test, patch test; **immunology,** immunochemistry; immunity; immunodeficiency

16 **inoculation, vaccination; injection,** hypodermic, hypodermic injection, shot <nonformal>, hypospray *or* jet injection; booster, booster shot <nonformal>; antitoxin, vaccine 86.28

17 <methods of injection> cutaneous, percutaneous, subcutaneous, intradermal, intramuscular, intravenous

18 **transfusion,** blood transfusion; serum; blood bank, blood donor center, bloodmobile; blood donor

19 **surgery,** surgical treatment, **operation,** surgical operation,

surgical intervention, surgical measure, the knife <nonformal>; **instrument**; respirator; unnecessary surgery, tomomania

20 bloodletting, bleeding, venesection, phlebotomy; leeching; cupping

21 **hospital, clinic,** treatment center; hospice, infirmary; nursing home, rest home, sanitarium; sick bay; trauma center

22 pesthouse, lazar house <both old>

23 **health resort, spa, watering place,** baths; mineral spring, warm *or* hot spring; pump room, pump house

VERBS **24 treat, doctor,** minister to, care for; **diagnose;** nurse; **cure, remedy, heal;** dress the wounds, bandage, splint; massage, rub; operate on; physic, purge; **operate,** perform a procedure; transplant

25 medicate, drug, dope <nonformal>, dose; salve, oil, anoint, embrocate

26 irradiate, X-ray

27 bleed, let blood, leech, phlebotomize; cup; **transfuse,** give a transfusion

28 immunize, inoculate, vaccinate, shoot <nonformal>

29 undergo treatment, take the cure, doctor <nonformal>, take medicine; go under the knife <nonformal>

92 PSYCHOLOGY, PSYCHOTHERAPY

NOUNS **1 psychology,** science of human behavior, mental philosophy; psychologism, pop psychology *and* psychobabble <both nonformal>

2 psychological school, school *or* system of psychology, psychological theory

3 psychiatry, psychological medicine; neuropsychiatry; social psychiatry; prophylactic psychiatry

4 psychosomatic medicine, psychological medicine, medico-

psychology; psychosocial medicine

5 psychotherapy, psychotherapeutics, mind cure

6 psychoanalysis, analysis, the couch <nonformal>; psychoanalytic therapy, psychoanalytic method; **depth psychology;** group analysis; dream analysis, interpretation of dreams, dream symbolism; depth interview

7 psychodiagnostics, psychodiagnosis, psychological *or* psychiatric evaluation

8 psychometrics, psychometry, psychological measurement; **intelligence testing;** psychological screening; psychography; lie detector, polygraph, psychogalvanometer

9 psychological test, mental test; standardized test; developmental test, achievement test

10 psychologist; psychotherapist, therapist; clinical psychologist; licensed psychologist, psychological practitioner; **psychiatrist,** alienist, somatist; neuropsychiatrist; **psychoanalyst, analyst; shrink** *and* headshrinker *and* shrinker <all nonformal>; **counselor,** psychological counselor; counseling service

11 personality tendency, humor; somatotype; **introversion,** introvertedness; inner-directedness; **extroversion,** extrovertedness; other-directedness

12 <personality type> **introvert, extrovert,** ambivert; schizoid; choleric, melancholic, sanguine; phlegmatic; endomorph, mesomorph, ectomorph

13 pathological personality, psychopathological personality, sick personality

14 mental disorder, emotional disorder, nervous disorder; reaction; emotional instability; **maladjustment,** social maladjustment; nervous breakdown, crack-up <nonformal>; problems in living; **insanity, mental illness** 925.1; **psychosis** 925.3; **schizo-**

phrenia; **paranoia** 925.4; **manic-depressive psychosis, depression,** melancholia 925.5; premenstrual syndrome *or* PMS; **neurosis, psychoneurosis,** neuroticism, neurotic *or* psychoneurotic disorder; brain disease, nervous disorder

15 **personality disorder, character disorder,** moral insanity, sociopathy, **psychopathy; psychopathic personality;** sexual pathology, sexual psychopathy 75.18

16 **neurotic reaction,** overreaction, disproportionate reaction

17 **psychological stress, stress; frustration;** conflict, ambivalence; **trauma,** psychological *or* emotional trauma, mental *or* emotional shock; rape trauma syndrome

18 **psychosomatic symptom; symptom of emotional disorder,** emotional symptom, psychological symptom; **thought disturbance,** thought disorder *or* disturbances, dissociative disorder, delirium, delusion, disorientation, hallucination; **speech abnormality**

19 **trance,** daze, stupor; catatonic stupor, catalepsy; cataplexy; dream state, reverie, daydreaming 984.2; somnambulism, sleepwalking; hypnotic trance; fugue, fugue state; **amnesia** 989.2

20 **dissociation,** mental *or* emotional dissociation, disconnection; dissociation of personality, personality disorganization *or* disintegration; **schizoid personality;** double *or* dual personality; multiple personality, split personality, alternating personality; schizoidism, **schizophrenia** 925.4; depersonalization; **paranoid personality; paranoia** 925.4

21 **fixation,** libido fixation *or* arrest, **arrested development;** infantile fixation, pregenital fixation, father fixation, mother fixation; **regression**

22 **complex,** inferiority complex, superiority complex, parent complex, Oedipus complex, mother complex, Electra complex, father complex, persecution complex; castration complex

23 **defense mechanism,** defense reaction; biological *or* psychological *or* sociological adjustive reactions; resistance; dissociation; **negativism, alienation; escapism,** escape mechanism, avoidance mechanism; escape, flight, **withdrawal; isolation,** emotional insulation; **fantasy,** escape into fantasy, autistic *or* dereistic thinking, wishful thinking, autism, dereism; wish-fulfillment, wish-fulfillment fantasy; sexual fantasy; **compensation,** overcompensation, decompensation; substitution; **sublimation; projection,** blame-shifting; displacement; **rationalization**

24 **suppression, repression, inhibition,** resistance, restraint, censorship; block, psychological block, blockage, blocking; reaction formation; rigid control; **suppressed desire**

25 **catharsis,** purgation, abreaction, psychocatharsis, **emotional release,** relief of tension; release therapy, acting-out, psychodrama

26 **conditioning,** classical *or* Pavlovian conditioning; psychagogy, reeducation, reorientation; conditioned reflex, conditioned stimulus, conditioned response; reinforcement, positive reinforcement, negative reinforcement; simple reflex, unconditioned reflex, **reflex** 902.1; **behavior** 321

27 **adjustment,** adjustive reaction; **readjustment, rehabilitation;** psychosynthesis, integration of personality; fulfillment, self-fulfillment; self-actualization, peak experience; integrated personality, syntonic personality

28 **psyche, personality, self,** personhood; **mind** 918.1,3,4; preconscious, foreconscious, co-conscious; **subconscious, unconscious,** subconscious *or*

unconscious mind, subliminal, subliminal self; **libido,** psychic *or* libidinal energy, motive force, vital impulse, ego-libido, object libido; **id,** primitive self, pleasure principle, life instinct, death instinct; **ego,** conscious self; **superego,** ethical self, conscience; anima, persona

29 **engram,** memory trace, traumatic trace *or* memory; unconscious memory; archetype, archetypal pattern *or* image *or* symbol; imago, image, father image, etc; race *or* racial memory; cultural memory; **memory** 988

30 **symbol,** universal symbol, father symbol, mother symbol, phallic symbol, fertility symbol, etc; symbolism, symbolization

31 **surrogate,** substitute; father surrogate, father figure, father image; mother surrogate, mother figure

32 **gestalt,** pattern, figure, configuration, sensory pattern; figure-ground

33 **association,** association of ideas, chain of ideas, concatenation, mental linking

34 **cathexis,** cathection, desire concentration

VERBS 35 **psychologize, psychoanalyze;** abreact; fixate, obsess on <nonformal>

ADJS 36 **psychological; psychiatric;** psychometric; **psychopathic,** psychopathological; **psychosomatic; psychotic**

37 **psychotherapeutic;** psychiatric, psychoanalytic, psychoanalytical

38 **neurotic, psychoneurotic,** disturbed, disordered; neurasthenic; hysteric[al], hypochondriac, phobic; stressed

39 **introverted,** introvert, introversive, **subjective, ingoing,** inner-directed

40 **extroverted,** extrovert, extroversive, **out-going,** extrospective; other-directed

41 **subconscious, unconscious;** subliminal, extramarginal; preconscious

93 FEELING

NOUNS 1 **feeling, emotion, affect, sentiment,** affection, affections; emotional charge, cathexis; **feelings, sensitiveness, sensibility,** susceptibility, thin skin; emotional life; **sense,** deep *or* profound sense, gut sense *or* sensation <nonformal>; **sensation** 24; **impression,** undercurrent; hunch, feeling in one's bones, presentiment 933.3; foreboding; **reaction, response,** gut reaction <nonformal>; **instinct** 365.1; emotional coloring *or* shade *or* nuance, **tone,** feeling tone

2 **passion,** passionateness, powerful emotion; **fervor, fervency,** fervidness, impassionedness, **ardor, ardency, warmth, heat, fire,** verve, furor, vehemence; heartiness, gusto, relish, savor; spirit, heart, soul; **liveliness** 330.2; **zeal** 101.2; **excitement** 105; **ecstasy**

3 **heart, soul, spirit, breast, bosom,** inmost heart *or* soul, heart of hearts, secret *or* inner recesses of the heart, secret places, bottom of the heart, being, innermost being, core of one's being; viscera, pit of one's stomach, **gut** *or* guts <nonformal>; bones

4 **sensibility, sensitivity, sensitiveness,** delicacy, fineness of feeling, tenderness, affectivity, susceptibility, impressionability 24.2

5 **sympathy, fellow feeling, sympathetic response,** responsiveness, relating, warmth, **caring,** concern; response, echo, chord, sympathetic chord, vibrations, vibes <nonformal>; **empathy,** identification; involvement, sharing; pathos

6 **tenderness,** tender feeling, softness, gentleness, delicacy; **tenderheartedness,** softheartedness, warmheartedness, tender *or* sensitive *or* warm heart, soft place *or* spot in one's heart; warmth, **fondness, weakness** 100.2

7 bad feeling, hard feelings; disaffinity, personality conflict, bad vibes *or* chemistry <nonformal>, bad blood, **hostility,** animosity 589.4; **hard-heartedness** 94.3

8 sentimentality, sentiment, sentimentalism, oversentimentality, bathos; nostalgia; romanticism; sweetness and light, hearts-and-flowers; bleeding heart; mawkishness, cloyingness, maudlinness, namby-pamby, nambypambyness, namby-pambyism; mushiness *or* sloppiness <both nonformal>; **mush** *and* slush *and* slop *and* goo *and* schmaltz <all nonformal>

9 emotionalism, emotionality, lump in one's throat; emotionalizing; emotiveness, emotivity; visceralness; demonstrativeness, making scenes; **theatrics, theatricality, histrionics, dramatics,** hamminess *and* chewing up the scenery <both nonformal>; **sensationalism, melodrama,** melodramatics, blood and thunder; emotional appeal, human interest, love interest; **overemotionalism,** hyperthymia, excess of feeling

VERBS **10 feel,** entertain *or* harbor *or* cherish *or* nurture a feeling; feel deeply, feel in one's bones, feel in one's gut *or* guts <nonformal>; experience 830.8; have a sensation, get *or* receive an impression, **sense, perceive**

11 respond, react, be moved, be affected *or* touched, be inspired, echo, catch the flame *or* infection, be in tune; **respond to,** warm up to, take to heart, open one's heart to, be turned on to <nonformal>, nourish in one's bosom, feel in one's breast; enter into the spirit of, be imbued with the spirit of; care about, sympathize with, empathize with, identify with, relate to emotionally, dig *and* be turned on by <both nonformal>, be involved, share

12 have deep feelings, be all heart, have a tender heart; have a soft place *or* spot in one's heart;

be a prey to one's feelings; love 104.18–20; hate 103.5

13 emotionalize, emote <nonformal>, give free play to the emotions, make a scene; be theatrical; **sentimentalize,** gush *and* slobber over <both nonformal>

14 affect, touch, move, stir; melt, soften, melt the heart, choke one up, give one a lump in the throat; **penetrate,** pierce, go through one, go deep; touch a chord, **touch a sympathetic chord, touch one's heart,** tug at the heart *or* heartstrings, go to one's heart, get under one's skin; **touch to the quick,** smart, sting

15 impress, affect, strike, hit, smite, rock; **make an impression, get to one** <nonformal>; make a dent in, make an impact upon, sink in <nonformal>, strike home; tell, have a strong effect, traumatize, strike hard, impress forcibly

16 impress upon, bring home to, make it felt; stamp, stamp on, etch, engrave, engrave on

ADJS **17 emotional, affective,** emotive, affectional, **feeling;** soulful, of soul, of heart, of feeling, of sentiment; visceral, gut <nonformal>; demonstrative, overdemonstrative

18 fervent, fervid, passionate, impassioned, intense, **ardent; hearty, cordial,** enthusiastic, exuberant, unrestrained, vigorous; keen, breathless, **excited** 105.18,20,22; **lively** 330.17; zealous; **warm, burning, heated, hot, volcanic,** red-hot, fiery, flaming, glowing, ablaze, afire, on fire, boiling over, steaming, steamy; delirious, fevered, feverish, febrile, flushed; intoxicated, drunk

19 emotionalistic, emotive, overemotional, hysteric, hysterical, melodramatic, theatric, theatrical, histrionic, dramatic, overdramatic, nonrational, unreasoning; overemotional, hyperthymic

20 sensitive, sensible, emotionable,

delicate; responsive, sympathetic, receptive; susceptible, impressionable; **tender, soft, tenderhearted, softhearted,** warmhearted

21 **sentimental,** sentimentalized, soft, **mawkish, maudlin,** cloying; sticky *and* gooey *and* schmaltzy <all nonformal>, oversentimental, oversentimentalized, bathetic; **mushy** *or* sloppy *or* gushing *or* teary <all nonformal>; tearjerking <nonformal>; namby-pamby, romantic; nostalgic

22 **affecting, touching, moving,** emotive, pathetic

23 **affected, moved, touched, impressed;** impressed with *or* by, penetrated with, seized with, imbued with, devoured by, obsessed, obsessed with *or* by; wrought up by; stricken, wracked, racked, torn, agonized, tortured; worked up, all worked up, **excited** 105.18

24 **deep-felt,** from the heart, heartfelt; **deep, profound;** indelible; pervasive, pervading, absorbing; penetrating, penetrant, piercing; **poignant,** keen, sharp, acute

ADVS 25 **feelingly, emotionally,** affectively; affectingly, touchingly, movingly, **with feeling,** poignantly

26 **fervently, fervidly, passionately, impassionedly,** intensely, **ardently,** zealously; keenly, breathlessly, excitedly; warmly, heatedly, glowingly; heartily, cordially; enthusiastically, exuberantly, vigorously; kindly, heart and soul, with all one's heart, from the heart, from the bottom of one's heart

27 **sentimentally,** mawkishly, maudlinly, cloyingly; mushily *and* sloppily *and* gushingly <all nonformal>

94 LACK OF FEELING

NOUNS 1 **unfeeling,** unfeelingness, affectlessness, lack of affect, lack of feeling *or* feeling tone, emotional deadness *or* numbness *or* paralysis, **anesthesia, emotionlessness,** unemotionalism, unexcitability; **dispassion,** dispassionateness, **objectivity;** passionlessness, **spiritlessness, heartlessness; coldness, coolness, frigidity,** chill, chilliness, frostiness, iciness; coldheartedness, cold-bloodedness; **unresponsiveness;** lack of touch *or* contact, autism, self-absorption, withdrawal, catatonia; **impassiveness,** impassibility, impassivity; straight face *and* poker face <both nonformal>, dead pan <nonformal>; **dullness, obtuseness; inexcitability** 106

2 **insensibility,** insensibleness, **unconsciousness,** unawareness, **obliviousness,** oblivion; anesthesia

3 **callousness, insensitivity,** insensitiveness, philistinism; **coarseness, brutalization, hardness, hard-heartedness, hardness of heart,** hard heart, stony-heartedness, heart of stone; **obduracy,** obdurateness, induration, inuredness; imperviousness, **thick skin**

4 **apathy, indifference, unconcern;** aloofness, **detachment,** ataraxia, **dispassion; passiveness,** passivity, supineness, insouciance, nonchalance; inappetence; **listlessness, spiritlessness,** burnout, heartlessness; **lethargy, phlegm,** hebetude, **dullness,** sluggishness, languor, languidness; coma, comatoseness, torpidness, torpor, torpidity, **stupor,** stupefaction; acedia, sloth; **resignation,** stoicism; **numbness;** hopelessness 125

VERBS 5 not be affected by, remain unmoved, not turn a hair, not care less <nonformal>; have a thick skin, have a heart of stone; be cold as ice, be a cold fish; leave one cold *or* unmoved, unimpress, underwhelm <nonformal>

6 **callous, harden,** case harden,

harden one's heart, indurate, inure; brutalize

7 dull, blunt, desensitize, obtund, hebetate

8 numb, benumb, paralyze, **deaden,** anesthetize, freeze, **stun, stupefy,** drug, narcotize, anesthetize

ADJS **9 unfeeling, unemotional,** affectless, emotionally dead *or* numb *or* paralyzed, anesthetized, drugged ; **unpassionate, dispassionate,** unimpassioned, **objective;** passionless, **spiritless, heartless,** soulless; lukewarm; **cold, cool, frigid,** frozen, chill, chilly, arctic, frosty, frosted, icy, **coldhearted, coldblooded; unaffectionate,** unloving; **unresponsive,** unresponding, **unsympathetic;** out of touch *or* contact; in one's shell *or* armor; autistic, self-absorbed, self-centered, egocentric, catatonic; unimpressionable, unimpressible; **impassive;** immovable, untouchable; dull, obtuse, blunt; **inexcitable** 106.10

10 insensible, unconscious, unaware, **oblivious,** blind to, deaf to, dead to, lost to

11 unaffected, unmoved, untouched, dry-eyed, unimpressed, **unstirred,** unruffled, unanimated

12 callous, calloused, insensitive, Philistine; **thick-skinned; hard, hard-hearted, hardened,** case-hardened, coarsened, indurated, stony, stony-hearted, flinthearted, flinty, steely, impervious, inured, steeled against, as hard as nails

13 apathetic, indifferent, unconcerned, uncaring, **disinterested, uninterested; withdrawn, aloof, detached,** Olympian, above it all; **passive,** supine; stoic, stoical; insouciant, nonchalant, blasé, **listless, spiritless,** burned-out, heartless, pluckless, spunkless; **lethargic, phlegmatic,** hebetudinous, **dull,** desensitized, torpid, languid, slack, soporific, comatose, **stupe-**

fied, in a stupor, **numb,** numbed; resigned; hopeless 125.12

ADVS **14 unfeelingly, unemotionally,** emotionlessly; with a straight *or* poker face <nonformal>, deadpan <nonformal>; **dispassionately; spiritlessly, heartlessly,** coldly, coldheartedly, cold-bloodedly, **in cold blood**

15 apathetically, indifferently, unconcernedly, uninterestedly, impassively; **listlessly, spiritlessly,** heartlessly, plucklessly, spunklessly; **lethargically, phlegmatically,** dully, numbly

95 PLEASURE

NOUNS **1 pleasure, enjoyment;** euphoria, well-being, **contentment,** content, **ease, comfort** 121; coziness, warmth; **gratification, satisfaction; self-gratification,** self-indulgence; instant gratification; luxury; **relish, zest, gusto,** *joie de vivre* <Fr>; sweetness of life; kicks <nonformal>, **fun,** entertainment, amusement 743; intellectual pleasure, pleasures of the mind; **strokes** *and* stroking *and* ego massage <all nonformal>; physical pleasure, creature comforts; sexual pleasure, voluptuousness, sensual pleasure, animal pleasure, animal comfort, fleshly *or* carnal delight; forepleasure, titillation, fruition

2 happiness, felicity, gladness, delight, delectation; **joy, joyfulness; cheer,** exhilaration, **exuberance, high spirits, glee,** sunshine; gaiety 109.4, overjoyfulness, overhappiness; intoxication; **rapture,** bewitchment, **enchantment,** unalloyed happiness; elation, exaltation; **ecstasy,** transport; **bliss,** blissfulness; beatitude, beatification, blessedness; paradise, heaven, seventh heaven, cloud nine

3 treat, regalement, regale; **feast, banquet** revelment, regale; round of pleasures, mad round; **festivity,** fete, fiesta, festive occasion, celebration, merrymaking, revel, revelry, jubilation, joyance; carnival, Mardi Gras

4 pleasure-loving, pleasure principle, hedonism; epicureanism

VERBS **5 please, pleasure, give pleasure,** afford one pleasure, be to one's liking, sit well with one, take *or* strike one's fancy, feel good *or* right, strike one right; do one's heart good, warm the cockles of one's heart; **suit**

6 <nonformal terms> **hit the spot,** be just the ticket, be just what the doctor ordered, **make a hit,** go over big, go over with a bang

7 gratify, satisfy, sate, satiate; slake, appease, allay, assuage, quench; regale, feed, feast; do one's heart good, warm the cockles of the heart

8 gladden, make happy; bless, beatify; cheer 109.7

9 delight, delectate, **tickle, titillate, thrill, enrapture, enthrall, enchant,** entrance, fascinate, captivate, bewitch, **charm;** enravish, ravish; transport, carry away

10 <nonformal terms> **give one a bang** *or* kick *or* charge *or* rush, knock out, knock off one's feet *or* dead *or* for a loop, knock one's socks off, thrill to death *or* to pieces, tickle to death, tickle pink, **wow,** slay, send, freak out; **stroke**

11 be pleased, feel happy, feel good, sing, purr, smile, laugh, be wreathed in smiles, beam; **delight,** joy, take great satisfaction; look like the cat that swallowed the canary; walk on air, have stars in one's eyes, be in heaven *or* seventh heaven *or* paradise, be on cloud nine

12 enjoy, pleasure in, be pleased with, receive *or* derive pleasure from, take delight *or* pleasure in, get a kick *or* boot *or* bang *or* charge *or* lift *or* rush out of <nonformal>; **like, love,** adore <nonformal>; **delight in, rejoice in,** indulge in, luxuriate in, revel in, riot in, bask in, wallow in, swim in; feast on, gloat over *or* on; **relish, appreciate,** do justice to, savor, smack the lips; devour, eat up

13 enjoy oneself, have a good time, party, live it up <nonformal>, have the time of one's life

ADJS **14 pleased, delighted; glad,** gladsome; **charmed,** intrigued <nonformal>; **thrilled; tickled,** tickled to death *and* tickled pink <both nonformal>, exhilarated; **gratified, satisfied;** pleased with, taken with, favorably impressed with, sold on <nonformal>; pleased as Punch; euphoric, eupeptic; **content, contented,** easy, **comfortable** 121.11, cozy, in clover

15 happy, glad, joyful, joyous, flushed with joy, radiant, beaming, glowing, starry-eyed, sparkling, laughing, smiling, smirking, purring, singing, dancing, leaping, capering, **cheerful, gay** 109.14; **blissful;** blessed; beatified, beatific; thrice happy; happy as a lark, happy as the day is long, happy as a pig in shit <nonformal>

16 overjoyed, overjoyful, overhappy, brimming *or* bursting with happiness, on top of the world; **rapturous,** raptured, **enraptured, enchanted,** entranced, enravished, ravished, rapt, possessed; sent *and* high *and* freaked-out <all nonformal>, **in raptures,** transported, **carried away,** rapt *or* ravished away, beside oneself, beside oneself with joy; **ecstatic,** in ecstasies; rhapsodic, rhapsodical; **in paradise,** in heaven, in seventh heaven, on cloud nine <nonformal>; **elated,** elate, exalted, jubilant, exultant, flushed

17 pleasure-loving, pleasure-seeking, fun-loving, hedonic, hedonistic; Lucullan; epicurean

ADVS **18 happily, gladly, joyfully, joyously, delightedly,** with pleasure, to one's delight; blissfully, blessedly; **ecstatically,** rhapsod-

ically, **rapturously; elatedly,** jubilantly, exultantly

19 **for fun,** for the hell or heck or
devil of it <nonformal>

96 UNPLEASURE

NOUNS 1 **unpleasure, unpleasantness** 98, **lack of pleasure,**
joylessness, cheerlessness;
nongratification; grimness;
discontent 108; displeasure,
dissatisfaction, **discomfort,**
malaise, **painfulness; disquiet,**
inquietude, **uneasiness,** unease,
discomposure, **anxiety;** angst,
anguish, dread, nausea; the blahs
<nonformal>; **dullness,** flatness,
staleness, tastelessness; ashes in
the mouth; **boredom,** ennui, tedium, tediousness, spleen; emptiness, spiritual void; unhappiness
112.2; dislike 99

2 **annoyance, vexation,** exasperation, **aggravation; nuisance,
pest, bother,** botheration <non-
formal>, public nuisance, **trouble, problem,** pain <nonfor-
mal>, difficulty, hot potato <non-
formal>; **trial; bore,** crashing
bore <nonformal>; **drag** and
downer <both nonformal>;
worry; downside and the bad
news <both nonformal>; **headache** <nonformal>; **pain in the
neck** or **in the ass** <nonformal>;
harassment, molestation, persecution, dogging, hounding,
harrying

3 **irritation, aggravation,** exacerbation, salt in the wound,
twisting the knife in the wound,
embitterment, **provocation;** fret,
gall, chafe; irritant

4 **chagrin, distress; embarrassment, abashment, dis-
comfiture,** egg on one's face
<nonformal>, disconcertment,
discountenance, discomposure,
disturbance, confusion; **humiliation, shame,** mortification, red
face

5 **pain, distress, grief,** stress, suffering, passion; ache, aching;
pang, wrench, throes, cramp,
spasm; wound, injury, hurt; **sore,**
sore spot, tender spot, lesion; cut,
stroke; shock, blow

6 **wretchedness, despair,** bitterness, infelicity, **misery, anguish,
agony, woe,** woefulness, bale,
balefulness; **melancholy,** melancholia, **depression, sadness,**
grief 112.10; **heartache,** aching
heart, heavy heart, bleeding
heart, broken heart; suicidal despair, **despondency,** despond;
desolation, prostration, crushing; extremity, depth of misery;
sloth, acedia

7 **torment, torture,** excruciation,
crucifixion, passion, laceration,
clawing, excoriation; the rack,
the iron maiden, thumbscrews;
**persecution; martyrdom;
purgatory,** living death, hell, hell
on earth; holocaust; nightmare,
horror

8 **affliction,** infliction; **curse,
woe,** distress, grievance, **sorrow,**
tsures <Yiddish>; **trouble,** peck
or pack of troubles; **care,** burden
of care; **burden, oppression,
cross, cross to bear** or **be borne,
load,** encumbrance, weight,
albatross around one's neck,
millstone around one's neck;
thorn, thorn in the side, crown of
thorns; bitter pill, bitter draft;
gall, gall and wormwood; Pandora's box

9 **trial, tribulation,** trials and trib-
ulations; **ordeal,** fiery ordeal

10 **tormentor,** torment; torturer;
nuisance, pest, pesterer, pain
and pain in the neck or ass <non-
formal>, nag, public nuisance;
tease, teaser; annoyer, harasser,
harrier, badgerer, **heckler,** pla-
guer, persecutor, sadist; molester,
bully

11 **sufferer,** victim, prey; **wretch,**
poor devil <nonformal>, object
of compassion; martyr

VERBS 12 give no pleasure or joy or
cheer or comfort, **disquiet,** discompose; discontent; taste like
ashes in the mouth; **bore,** be
tedious

13 **annoy, irk, vex, nettle, provoke, pique,** miff and peeve

<both nonformal>, distemper,
ruffle, disturb, discompose, **roil,**
rile, **aggravate,** make a nuisance
of oneself, **exasperate,** exercise,
try one's patience, try the patience of a saint; **put one's back
up,** make one bristle; **gripe;** give
one a pain <nonformal>; get, get
one down, **get one's goat,** get under one's skin, get in one's hair;
burn up *and* brown off <both
nonformal>; **torment, molest,
bother; harass,** harry, drive up
the wall <nonformal>, **hound,**
dog, nag, **persecute; heckle,**
pick *or* prod at, rub it in *and* rub
one's nose in it <both nonfor-
mal>, badger, hector, bait, worry,
worry at, nip at the heels of,
chivy, hardly give one time to
breathe, make one's life miserable, keep on at; **bug** <nonfor-
mal>, **pester, tease, needle,**
devil, get after *or* get on <non-
formal>, **bedevil, pick on**
<nonformal>, give a bad time
to <nonformal>; **plague,** beset,
beleaguer; catch one off balance, trip one up

14 **irritate, aggravate,** exacerbate,
worsen, rub salt in the wound,
twist the knife in the wound, step
on one's corns; touch a soft spot
or tender spot; touch a raw nerve,
touch where it hurts; provoke,
gall, chafe, fret, grate, rasp; **get
on one's nerves, grate on,** set on
edge; **set one's teeth on edge,**
go against the grain; **rub one** *or*
one's fur the wrong way

15 **chagrin, embarrass, abash,
discomfit, disconcert,** discompose, confuse, throw into confusion *or* a tizzy, **upset,** confound, cast down, mortify, put
out

16 **distress, afflict, trouble,** burden, give one a tough row to hoe,
load with care, **bother, disturb,
perturb, disquiet, discomfort,**
agitate, **upset,** put to it; **worry,**
give one gray hair

17 **pain, grieve,** aggrieve, anguish,
hurt, wound, bruise, **hurt one's
feelings;** pierce, prick, stab, cut,

sting; **cut up** <nonformal>, **cut
to the heart,** wound *or* sting *or*
cut to the quick; be a thorn in
one's side

18 **torture, torment, agonize, harrow,** savage, **rack,** scarify, crucify,
impale, excruciate, lacerate, claw,
rip, bloody, convulse, wring; kill
by inches, make life miserable *or*
not worth living; martyr, martyrize; **tyrannize,** push around
<nonformal>; punish 604.10

19 **suffer, hurt, ache, bleed;** anguish, **suffer anguish;** agonize,
writhe; go hard with, go through
hell; be nailed to the cross

ADJS 20 **pleasureless,** joyless,
cheerless, depressed 112.22,
grim; **sad, unhappy** 112.21; unsatisfied, unfulfilled, ungratified;
bored; anguished, anxious, suffering angst *or* dread, uneasy,
unquiet, prey to malaise; **re-
pelled,** revolted, **disgusted,**
sickened, nauseated, nauseous

21 **annoyed, irritated,** bugged
<nonformal>, galled, chafed;
**bothered, troubled, disturbed,
ruffled, roiled,** riled; **irked,**
vexed, piqued, nettled, provoked, **peeved** *and* miffed <both
nonformal>, **griped, aggravated, exasperated;** burnt-up
and browned-off <both nonfor-
mal>, resentful, angry 152.28

22 **distressed, afflicted, put-upon,**
beset, beleaguered; caught in the
middle *or* in the crossfire; **troubled, bothered, disturbed,**
perturbed, disquieted, discom-
forted, discomposed, agitated;
uncomfortable, uneasy, ill at
ease; **chagrined, embarrassed,**
abashed, discomfited, **disconcerted, upset, confused,** mortified, **put-out,** out of countenance,
cast down, chapfallen

23 **pained, grieved,** aggrieved;
wounded, hurt, injured,
bruised, mauled; **cut,** cut to
the quick; **stung;** anguished,
aching, bleeding

24 **tormented, plagued, harassed,
harried,** dogged **hounded, persecuted,** beset; nipped at,

worried, chivied, **heckled,** badgered, hectored, baited, ragged, **pestered, teased, needled,** deviled, **bedeviled, picked on** <nonformal>, **bugged** <nonformal>

25 **tortured, harrowed,** savaged, **agonized,** convulsed, wrung, racked, crucified, impaled, lacerated, excoriated, clawed, ripped, bloodied; on the rack

26 **wretched, miserable; woeful,** woebegone; crushed, stricken, **cut up** <nonformal>, heartsick; desolate, disconsolate, suicidal

ADVS 27 to one's displeasure, to one's disgust

97 PLEASANTNESS

NOUNS 1 **pleasantness,** pleasingness, **pleasure** 95, pleasurefulness, **pleasurableness,** pleasurability, felicitousness, **enjoyableness; bliss, blissfulness;** sweetness, mellifluousness; mellowness; **agreeableness,** agreeability, rapport, harmoniousness; compatibility; welcomeness; geniality, congeniality, cordiality, affability, amicability, amiability; amenity, graciousness; goodness, goodliness, niceness; **fun** 743.2, 95.1

2 **delightfulness,** exquisiteness, loveliness; **charm,** winsomeness, grace, **attractiveness, appeal,** winningness; sexiness <nonformal>; **glamour;** captivation, enchantment, entrancement, bewitchment, enravishment, **fascination** 377.1; voluptuousness, sensuousness; luxury

3 **delectability,** delectableness, deliciousness, lusciousness; tastiness, flavorsomeness, savoriness; juiciness; succulence

4 **cheerfulness;** brightness, sunniness; sunny side, bright side; fair weather

VERBS 5 make pleasant, brighten, sweeten, gild, gild the lily or pill; sentimentalize, saccharinize

ADJS 6 **pleasant, pleasing, pleasureful, pleasurable;** fair, **enjoyable,** pleasure-giving; felicitous;

likable, desirable, to one's liking, to one's taste, after one's own heart; **agreeable,** harmonious, compatible; **blissful;** sweet, mellifluous, honeyed, dulcet; mellow; **gratifying,** satisfying, rewarding, heartwarming, grateful; **welcome;** genial, congenial, cordial, affable, amiable, amicable, gracious; good, goodly, nice, fine; cheerful 109.11

7 **delightful, exquisite, lovely; thrilling,** titillative; **charming, attractive, endearing, engaging, appealing,** prepossessing, heartwarming, sexy <nonformal>, **enchanting,** bewitching, entrancing, enthralling, intriguing, fascinating; **captivating, irresistible, ravishing; winning,** winsome, taking, fetching; inviting, tempting, tantalizing; voluptuous, sensuous; luxurious, delicious

8 <nonformal terms> **fun, kicky,** chewy, dishy, drooly, sexy, toast, yummy

9 **blissful,** beatific, saintly, divine; sublime; **heavenly,** paradisiacal, empyreal or empyrean, Elysian; out of sight or of this world <nonformal>

10 **delectable, delicious,** luscious; tasty, flavorsome, savory; juicy; succulent

11 **bright, sunny,** fair, mild, balmy; halcyon

ADVS 12 **pleasantly, pleasingly, pleasurably,** fair, **enjoyably; blissfully; gratifyingly,** satisfyingly; agreeably, genially, affably, cordially, amiably, amicably, graciously, kindly; cheerfully 109.17

13 **delightfully, exquisitely; charmingly, engagingly, appealingly, enchantingly,** bewitchingly, entrancingly, intriguingly, fascinatingly; ravishingly; **winningly,** winsomely; invitingly, temptingly, tantalizingly, voluptuously, sensuously; luxuriously

14 **delectably,** deliciously, lusciously, tastily, succulently

98 UNPLEASANTNESS

NOUNS **1 unpleasantness,** displeasure; **disagreeableness,** disagreeability; **abrasiveness,** hostility, unfriendliness; **undesirability,** unappealingness, unattractiveness, unprepossessingness; **distastefulness,** unsavoriness, unpalatability, **undelectability; ugliness** 1014

2 offensiveness, objectionableness; repugnance, contrariety, **odiousness, repulsiveness,** rebarbativeness, grossness *and* yuckiness *and* grunginess *and* scuzziness <all nonformal>; **loathsomeness, hatefulness,** beastliness <nonformal>; **vileness, foulness,** putridness, rottenness, noxiousness; **nastiness,** fulsomeness, noisomeness, **obnoxiousness,** heinousness; **contemptibleness,** contemptibility, despicability, **despicableness,** baseness, ignobility; unspeakableness; coarseness, grossness, crudeness, obscenity

3 dreadfulness, horribleness, horridness, atrociousness, atrocity, hideousness; grimness, direness, banefulness

4 harshness, agony, excruciation, **torture,** torturousness, **torment;** desolation, desolateness; heartbreak, heartsickness

5 distressfulness, distress, grievousness, grief; painfulness, pain 26; **harshness,** bitterness, sharpness; lamentability, deplorability, pitifulness, regrettableness; **woe, sadness, sorrowfulness, mournfulness,** lamentation, woefulness, pathos, poignancy; comfortlessness, discomfort; dreariness, cheerlessness, joylessness, **depression,** bleakness

6 mortification, humiliation, embarrassment, egg on one's face <nonformal>

7 vexatiousness, irksomeness, annoyance, aggravation, exasperation, provocation; **troublesomeness, bothersomeness,** harassment

8 harshness, oppressiveness, burdensomeness, onerousness, weightiness, heaviness

9 intolerability, intolerableness, unbearableness, insufferableness, **unendurability**

VERBS **10 be unpleasant; displease;** be disagreeable *or* undesirable *or* distasteful *or* abrasive

11 offend, give offense, **repel,** put off, turn off <nonformal>, **revolt, disgust,** nauseate, sicken, make one sick, make one sick to *or* in the stomach, make one vomit *or* puke *or* retch, turn the stomach, gross out <nonformal>; stick in one's throat, stick in one's craw; **horrify, appall,** shock; make the flesh creep *or* crawl, make one shudder

12 agonize, excruciate, **torture, torment,** desolate

13 mortify, humiliate, embarrass, disconcert, disturb

14 distress, dismay, grieve, mourn, lament, sorrow; pain, discomfort; get in one's hair, try one's patience, give one a hard time *or* a pain *or* a pain in the neck *or* ass *or* butt <nonformal>

15 vex, irk, annoy, aggravate, exasperate, provoke; **trouble, worry,** give one gray hair, plague, harass, bother, hassle

16 oppress, burden, weigh upon, weight down, wear one down; **tire, exhaust,** weary, wear out, wear upon one; prey on the mind, prey on *or* upon; **haunt,** haunt the memory, obsess

ADJS **17 unpleasant, unpleasing, unenjoyable; displeasing, disagreeable; unlikable,** dislikable; **abrasive,** wounding, hostile, unfriendly; **undesirable,** unattractive, unappealing, unengaging, uninviting, unalluring, unwelcome, thankless; **distasteful, unpalatable,** unsavory, unappetizing, **undelectable; ugly** 1014.6; sour, **bitter**

18 offensive, objectionable,

odious, repulsive, repellent, rebarbative, **repugnant, revolting,** forbidding; **disgusting, sickening, loathsome,** gross *and* yucky *and* grungy *and* scuzzy <all nonformal>, beastly <nonformal>, **vile, foul, nasty, nauseating** 64.7; fulsome, mephitic, miasmic, malodorous, stinking, fetid, noisome, noxious; coarse, gross, crude, obscene; **obnoxious, abhorrent, hateful, abominable,** heinous, **contemptible, despicable,** detestable, execrable, beneath *or* below contempt, **base,** ignoble

19 **horrid, horrible,** horrific, **horrifying,** horrendous, unspeakable, beyond words; **dreadful, atrocious, terrible, rotten,** awful *and* beastly <both nonformal>, **hideous; tragic;** dire, grim, baneful; appalling, shocking, disgusting

20 **distressing,** dismaying; **painful,** sore, **harsh, bitter,** sharp; **grievous,** dolorous; **lamentable, deplorable,** regrettable, pitiable, piteous, rueful, woeful, woebegone, **sad,** sorrowful, wretched, mournful, **depressing,** depressive; **pathetic,** affecting, touching, moving, saddening, poignant; comfortless, discomforting, uncomfortable; **desolate,** dreary, cheerless, joyless, dismal, bleak

21 **mortifying,** humiliating, **embarrassing,** crushing, disconcerting, awkward, disturbing

22 **annoying, irritating,** galling, **provoking, aggravating** <nonformal>, **exasperating; vexatious,** vexing, irking, **irksome,** tiresome, wearisome; **troublesome, bothersome, worrisome,** bothering, troubling, disturbing, plaguing, pestilential, **pesky** *and* pesty *and* pestiferous <all nonformal>; tormenting, harassing, worrying; pestering, teasing; importunate, importune

23 **agonizing, excruciating, harrowing,** racking, rending, **desolating,** consuming; tormenting, torturous; **heartbreaking,** heartrending, **heartsickening**

24 **oppressive, burdensome, crushing,** trying, onerous, heavy, weighty; **harsh,** wearing, wearying, exhausting

25 **insufferable, intolerable, insupportable, unendurable, unbearable,** not to be endured, for the birds <nonformal>, **too much** *or* a bit much <nonformal>, more than flesh and blood can bear, enough to try the patience of Job

ADVS 26 **unpleasantly, distastefully; displeasingly, offensively, objectionably,** odiously, **repulsively,** repellently, rebarbatively, repugnantly, **revoltingly, disgustingly, sickeningly, loathsomely, vilely,** foully, nastily, fulsomely, mephitically, malodorously, fetidly, noisomely, noxiously, obnoxiously, **abhorrently, hatefully, abominably,** contemptibly, **despicably, detestably,** execrably

27 **horridly, horribly, dreadfully, terribly,** hideously; **tragically;** grimly, direly, banefully; appallingly, shockingly

28 **distressingly,** distressfully; **painfully,** sorely, **grievously,** lamentably, deplorably, pitiably, ruefully, woefully, sadly, pathetically; **agonizingly, excruciatingly,** harrowingly

29 **annoyingly, irritatingly, aggravatingly, provokingly, exasperatingly; vexatiously, irksomely; troublesomely, bothersomely,** worrisomely, regrettably

30 **insufferably, intolerably, unbearably, unendurably, insupportably**

99 DISLIKE

NOUNS 1 **dislike, distaste;** disaffection, **disfavor,** disinclination; disaffinity; **displeasure, disapproval,** disapprobation

2 **hostility,** antagonism, **enmity** 589; **hatred, hate** 103; **aversion,**

repugnance, repulsion, **antipathy,** grudge, abomination, **abhorrence, horror; disgust, loathing;** nausea; creeping flesh

VERBS **3 dislike,** mislike, disfavor, not like, have no liking for, be no love lost between, **have no use for** <nonformal>, **not care for,** have no time for, want nothing to do with, not think much of, take a dislike to, not be able to bear *or* endure *or* abide, not give the time of day to <nonformal>, **disapprove of; disrelish,** have no taste for, not be one's cup of tea; be hostile to, have it in for <nonformal>; **hate, abhor, detest, loathe** 103.5

4 feel disgust, be nauseated, **sicken at; gag, retch,** heave, vomit, puke, hurl *and* upchuck *and* barf <all nonformal>

5 shudder at, have one's flesh creep *or* crawl at the thought of; shrink from, **recoil, revolt at; grimace,** make a face, turn up one's nose, look down one's nose, look askance, raise one's eyebrows, take a dim view of

6 repel, disgust 98.11, gross out <nonformal>

ADJS **7 unlikable, distasteful,** dislikable, **uncongenial, displeasing,** unpleasant 98.17; **not to one's taste,** not one's sort, not one's cup of tea, against the grain, uninviting; unlovable; **abhorrent, odious** 98.18; **intolerable** 98.25

8 averse, disaffected, disenchanted, **disinclined, displeased,** put off <nonformal>, not charmed, less than pleased; **disapproving, censorious, judgmental; unfriendly, hostile** 589.10; death on, down on

9 disliked, uncared-for, unvalued, unprized, undervalued; **despised,** lowly, spat-upon, untouchable; **unpopular, out of favor; unappreciated,** misunderstood; unsung, thankless; unlamented, unmourned

10 unloved, unbeloved, un-

cherished, loveless; **lovelorn,** forsaken, **rejected,** jilted, thrown over <nonformal>, spurned, crossed in love

11 unwanted, unwished, undesired; **unwelcome,** unasked, unbidden, uninvited, uncalled-for, unasked-for

100 DESIRE

NOUNS **1 desire, wish,** wanting, **want, need,** desideration; **hope; fancy; will, mind, pleasure,** will and pleasure; heart's desire; **urge,** drive, libido, pleasure principle; concupiscence; wish fulfillment, fantasy; passion, ardor, sexual desire 75.5; **curiosity,** intellectual curiosity, thirst for knowledge, lust for learning; **eagerness** 101

2 liking, love, fondness; infatuation, crush; **affection; relish, taste,** gusto; **passion, weakness** <nonformal>

3 inclination, penchant, partiality, fancy, favor, predilection, preference, propensity, proclivity, **leaning, bent,** tilt, bias, **affinity; sympathy,** fascination

4 wistfulness, nostalgia; wishful thinking; sheep's eyes; daydream, daydreaming

5 yearning, yen <nonformal>; **longing, hankering** <nonformal>, **pining,** aching; **nostalgia, homesickness;** nostomania

6 craving, coveting, lust; hunger, thirst, appetite; aching void; **itch, itching,** prurience *or* pruriency; **sexual desire** 75.5; **mania** 925.12

7 appetite, stomach, relish, taste; **hunger,** hungriness; the munchies <nonformal>; tapeworm <nonformal>; eyes bigger than one's stomach; empty stomach, emptiness <nonformal>; **thirst,** thirstiness, drought <nonformal>, dryness; sweet tooth <nonformal>

8 greed, greediness, graspingness, **avarice, cupidity, avidity, voracity, rapacity, lust,** avariciousness, *avaritia and cupiditas* <both L>; money-grubbing; avidness, esurience, wolfishness; voraciousness, ravenousness, rapaciousness, sordidness, **covetousness,** acquisitiveness; itching palm; grasping; **piggishness, hoggishness,** swinishness; **gluttony** 672, *gula* <L>; inordinate desire, furor, craze, fury *or* frenzy of desire, overgreediness; insatiable desire, insatiability; incontinence, intemperateness 669.1

9 **aspiration,** reaching high, upward looking; high goal *or* aim *or* purpose, dream, ideals; **idealism** 985.7

10 **ambition,** ambitiousness, vaulting ambition; climbing; status-seeking, social climbing, careerism; opportunism; power-hunger; noble *or* lofty ambition

11 <object of desire> **desire,** heart's desire, desideration, *desideratum* <L>; wish; **hope;** catch, quarry, prey, game, plum, prize, trophy; forbidden fruit, temptation; lodestone, magnet; golden vision, mecca, glimmering goal; land of heart's desire 985.11; something to be desired; dearest wish, ambition, the height of one's ambition; a sight for sore eyes, a welcome sight; the light at the end of the tunnel

12 **desirer,** wisher, wanter, hankerer <nonformal>, yearner, coveter; fancier, collector; addict, freak <nonformal>, devotee, votary; **aspirant,** aspirer, solicitant, wannabee *and* hopeful <both nonformal>, candidate; **lover,** swain, suitor

13 **desirability; agreeability,** acceptability, unobjectionableness; **attractiveness,** attraction, magnetism, **appeal,** seductiveness, provocativeness, pleasingness; likability, lovability 104.7

VERBS 14 **desire,** desiderate, be desirous of, **wish,** lust after, bay after, kill for *and* give one's right arm for <both nonformal>, die for <nonformal>, **want,** have a

mind to, choose <nonformal>; **like,** have *or* acquire a taste for, fancy, take to, **take a fancy** *or* a shine to, have a fancy for; have an eye to, have one's eye on; lean toward, tilt toward, have a penchant for, have a weakness *or* soft spot in one's heart for; aim at, set one's cap for, have designs on; wish very much, wish to goodness; **love** 104.18; lust; prefer, favor 371.17

15 **want to, wish to, like to,** love to, dearly love to, choose to; **itch to,** burn to; ache to, long to

16 **wish for, hope for, yearn for,** yen for *and* have a yen for <both nonformal>, **itch for,** lust for, pant for, **long for, pine for,** hone for <nonformal>, ache for, be hurting for <nonformal>, weary for, languish for, **be dying for,** thirst for, sigh for; cry for, clamor for

17 **want with all one's heart, want in the worst way; set one's heart on, have one's heart set on,** give one's kingdom in hell for *or* one's eyeteeth for <nonformal>

18 **crave, covet, hunger after,** thirst after, crave after, **lust after,** have a lech for <nonformal>, pant after, run mad after, **hanker for** *or* **after** <nonformal>; crawl after; aspire after, be consumed with desire; have an itchy *or* itching palm *and* have sticky fingers <all nonformal>

19 **hunger,** hunger for, feel hungry, be peckish <Brit nonformal>; starve <nonformal>, be ravenous, raven; **have a good appetite,** be a good trencherman, have a tapeworm <nonformal>, have a wolf in one's stomach; eye hungrily, lick one's chops <nonformal>; **thirst,** thirst for

20 **aspire, be ambitious;** aspire to, try to reach; aim high, keep one's eyes on the stars, raise one's sights, set one's sights, reach for the sky

ADJS 21 **desirous,** desiring, **wanting, wishing,** needing, hoping; dying to <nonformal>; tempted;

libidinous, libidinal; **eager;** lascivious, **lustful**
22 desirous of *or* **to,** keen on, set on <nonformal>, bent on; fond of, partial to <nonformal>; inclined toward, leaning toward; **itching for** *or* **to,** aching for *or* to, **dying for** *or* **to;** spoiling for <nonformal>
23 wistful, wishful; **longing, yearning,** yearnful, **hankering** <nonformal>, **languishing, pining; nostalgic, homesick**
24 craving, coveting; **hungering,** hungry, thirsting, thirsty; **itching,** prurient; fervid; **devoured by desire,** consumed with desire
25 hungry, hungering; empty <nonformal>, unfilled; ravening, **ravenous,** voracious, **wolfish,** hungry as a bear; **starved, famished,** starving, famishing, perishing with hunger; fasting; half-starved, half-famished
26 thirsty, thirsting; **dry,** parched
27 greedy, avaricious, avid, voracious, rapacious, cupidinous, esurient, **ravening, grasping, grabby** <nonformal>, graspy, acquisitive, mercenary; ravenous, devouring; miserly; money-hungry, money-grubbing, money-mad, venal; **covetous,** coveting; **piggish, hoggish; gluttonous** 672.6; omnivorous, all-devouring; insatiable, insatiate, unsatisfied, unsated, unappeased, unappeasable, limitless, bottomless, unquenchable, quenchless, unslaked
28 aspiring, ambitious; high-flying, social-climbing, careerist, on the make <nonformal>; power-hungry
29 desired, wanted, coveted; **wished-for,** hoped-for, longed-for; in demand, popular
30 desirable, sought-after, **much to be desired; enviable,** worth having; **likable, pleasing,** after one's own heart; **agreeable,** acceptable, unobjectionable; palatable; **attractive,** taking, winning, sexy <nonformal>, **seductive, provocative,** tantalizing, exciting; appetizing, tempting, toothsome, mouth-watering; **lovable,** adorable
ADVS **31 desirously, wistfully,** wishfully, **longingly, yearningly,** languishingly; hungrily, thirstily; aspiringly, ambitiously
32 greedily, avariciously, avidly, ravenously, raveningly, voraciously, rapaciously, **covetously,** graspingly, devouringly; wolfishly, **piggishly, hoggishly,** swinishly

101 EAGERNESS

NOUNS **1 eagerness, enthusiasm, avidity,** avidness, forwardness, **readiness,** promptness, quickness, **alacrity,** cheerful readiness; keen desire, **appetite** 100.7; anxiousness, anxiety; **zest,** zestfulness, gusto, verve, **liveliness,** life, **vitality,** vivacity, élan, spirit, animation; **impatience,** breathless impatience 135.1; keen interest, fascination; **craze** 925.12
2 zeal, ardor, ardency, fervor, fervency, fervidness, spirit, warmth, fire, heat, passion, impassionedness, heartiness, intensity, **abandon,** vehemence; intentness, resolution 359; **devotion,** devoutness, dedication, commitment, committedness; **earnestness, seriousness,** sincerity; loyalty, faithfulness, faith, fidelity 644.7
3 overzealousness, overeagerness, overanxiousness; **overenthusiasm, infatuation; overambitiousness; frenzy, fury; zealotry;** mania, **fanaticism** 925.11
4 enthusiast, zealot, rhapsodist; addict; faddist; pursuer; hobbyist, collector; **fanatic;** visionary 985.13; **devotee,** votary, **fancier,** admirer, **follower; disciple;** amateur, dilettante; collector
5 <nonformal terms> **fan, buff, freak,** hound, fiend, demon, nut, bug, head, junkie, groupie, rooter, booster, sucker for; fan club; eager beaver
VERBS **6 jump at,** catch, grab, grab

at, snatch at, fall all over oneself,
go at hammer and tongs *or* tooth
and nail, go hog wild <nonfor-
mal>; go to great lengths, lean *or*
bend *or* fall over backwards; **desire** 100.14,18

7 **be enthusiastic, rave, enthuse**
< nonformal>; get stars in one's
eyes, **rhapsodize, carry on over**
< nonformal>, make much of,
make a fuss over, make a to-do
over < nonformal>, rave about·
and whoop it up about <both
nonformal>; go nuts *or* gaga *or*
ape over <nonformal>; gush,
gush over; effervesce, bubble over

ADJS 8 **eager, anxious,** agog, all
agog; **avid, keen,** forward,
prompt, quick, ready, ready
and willing, dying to, raring to;
zestful, lively, full of life, vital,
vivacious, vivid, spirited, **animated; impatient** 135.6;
breathless, panting, champing
at the bit; **desirous** 100.21

9 **zealous, ardent, fervent, fervid,** perfervid, **spirited, intense,**
hearty, vehement, abandoned,
passionate, impassioned, **warm,**
heated, hot, hot-blooded, white-
hot, flaming, burning, afire,
aflame, on fire, like a house afire
<nonformal>; **devout, devoted;**
dedicated, committed; **earnest,
sincere, serious,** in earnest;
loyal, faithful 644.20; intent, intent on, resolute 359.11

10 **enthusiastic,** enthused *and* big
<both nonformal>, **gung ho**
<nonformal>, glowing, full of en-
thusiasm

11 <nonformal terms> wild about,
crazy about, mad about, ape
about *or* over, gone on, all in a
dither over, gaga over

12 **overzealous,** ultrazealous,
overeager, over-anxious;
overambitious; overdesirous;
overenthusiastic, infatuated;
feverish, perfervid, at fever *or*
fevered pitch; hectic, frenetic,
frenzied, frantic, **wild,** hysterical, delirious; **insane** 925.26;
fanatical 925.32

ADVS 13 **eagerly, anxiously; impa-**

tiently, breathlessly; **avidly,**
promptly, quickly, keenly, readily;
zestfully, vivaciously, animatedly;
enthusiastically, with enthusiasm; **with alacrity,** with zest,
with gusto, with relish, with open
arms

14 **zealously, ardently, fervently,
fervidly,** perfervidly, heatedly,
heartily, vehemently, **passionately,** impassionedly, intently,
intensely; **devoutly, devotedly;**
earnestly, sincerely, seriously

102 INDIFFERENCE

NOUNS 1 **indifference;** halfheart-
edness, perfunctoriness; **coolness,** coldness, chilliness, chill,
iciness, frostiness; tepidness,
lukewarmness; neutrality; insipidity, vapidity

2 **unconcern, disinterest, detachment; disregard, dis-
passion,** insouciance, **carelessness; heedlessness,** mindlessness, inattention 983;
unmindfulness, incuriosity 981;
insensitivity; recklessness, negligence 340.1; *je-m'en-foutisme* or
je-m'en-fichisme <Fr>; **nonchalance,** ataraxia; indiscrimination,
casualness 944.1; **listlessness,**
lackadaisicalness, lack of feeling
or affect, **apathy** 94.4; sloth,
acedia

3 **undesirousness;** passionlessness; uneagerness, **unam-
bitiousness;** inappetence

VERBS 4 **not care, not mind, not
give** *or* **care a damn,** not give a
hoot *or* shit <nonformal>, care
nothing for *or* about; **shrug off;**
take no interest in, have no desire for, have no taste *or* relish for;
be half-hearted

5 **not matter to,** take it or leave it;
make no difference, make no
never-mind <nonformal>

ADJS 6 **indifferent, halfhearted,**
perfunctory; **cool, cold** 589.9;
tepid, **lukewarm;** neither hot nor
cold, neither one thing nor the
other; **neuter, neutral**

7 **unconcerned, uninterested,
disinterested,** turned-off, **dis-**

passionate, insouciant **careless,**
regardless; easygoing; mindless,
unmindful, heedless, inattentive 983.6; **devil-may-care,** reckless, negligent 340.10; **nonchalant; blasé,** undiscriminating,
casual 944.5; **listless, care-**
lessly, insouciantly, **care-**
sical, sluggish; bovine; numb,
apathetic 94.13

8 **undesirous,** unattracted, de-
sireless; loveless, passionless;
unenthusiastic, uneager; **unambitious**

ADVS 9 **indifferently, with indifference,** with utter indifference;
halfheartedly; perfunctorily; for
all one cares

10 **unconcernedly, uninterestedly, disinterestedly,** dispassionately, insouciantly, **carelessly,** regardlessly; mindlessly;
unmindfully, heedlessly, recklessly, negligently 340.17; **nonchalantly;** listlessly, lackadaisically; numbly, **apathetically**
94.15

103 HATE

NOUNS 1 **hate, hatred; dislike** 99;
**detestation, abhorrence, aver-
sion, antipathy,** repugnance,
loathing, execration, **abomination,** odium; **spite,** spitefulness, **malice, malevolence;** misanthropy; misogamy; anti-
Semitism; race hatred, racism;
bigotry; xenophobia; scorn,
contempt 157

2 **enmity** 589; bitterness, **animosity** 589.4

3 <hated thing> **anathema,
abomination,** detestation, aversion, abhorrence, antipathy,
execration, hate; peeve, pet peeve;
phobia

4 **hater,** man-hater, woman-hater,
misanthropist, misanthrope, misogynist, anti-Semite, racist,
white supremacist, bigot, redneck <nonformal>; xenophobe

VERBS 5 **hate, detest, loathe, abhor,** execrate, **abominate,** take
an aversion to, be death on, not
stand the sight of, not stomach;
scorn, **despise** 157.3

6 **dislike,** have it in for <nonfor-
mal>

ADJS 7 **hating, abhorrent,** loathing, despising, venomous, death
on; averse to 99.8; disgusted
96.20; scornful, **contemptuous**
157.8

8 **hateful, loathsome,** detestable
98.18; **contemptible** 98.18,
661.12

104 LOVE

NOUNS 1 **love, affection, attachment, devotion, fondness,** sentiment, warm feeling, soft spot in
one's heart, weakness <nonfor-
mal>, like, **liking,** fancy, shine
<nonformal>; **partiality, predi-
lection; passion,** tender feeling
or passion, **ardor,** ardency, fervor,
heart, flame; physical love, libido,
sexual love, sex 75; desire, yearning 100.5; lasciviousness 665.5;
charity, brotherly love, agape,
caring; spiritual love, platonic
love; **adoration,** worship, hero
worship; **regard,** admiration;
idolization, idolatry; conjugal
love, uxoriousness; free love;
lovemaking 562

2 **popular regard,** popularity;
faithful love, truelove; married
love

3 **amorousness,** amativeness,
affection, demonstrativeness;
mating instinct, reproductive *or*
procreative drive, libido; carnality, sexiness, hot pants *and*
horniness <both nonformal>;
romantic love, romanticism,
sentimentality, susceptibility;
lovesickness; ecstasy, rapture;
enchantment 95.2

4 **infatuation,** passing fancy;
crush *and* mash *and* case
<all nonformal>; **puppy love**
<nonformal>; love at first sight

5 **parental love, natural affection,** mother love, father love;
filial love; parental instinct

6 **love affair, affair,** affair of the
heart, **amour, romance,** romantic tie *or* bond, liaison,
entanglement, intrigue; **dalliance,** amorous play, the love

game, flirtation, hanky-panky, lollygagging <nonformal>; triangle, eternal triangle; illicit love, forbidden love, adulterous affair, adultery, unfaithfulness, infidelity, cuckoldry

7 loveableness, likeableness, loveliness; cuddliness; amiability, attractiveness 97.2, desirability, agreeability; **charm, appeal,** allurement 377; winsomeness, winning ways

8 Cupid, Amor, Eros, Kama; Venus, Aphrodite

9 <symbols> cupid, cupidon, amor, amourette, amoretto

10 sweetheart, loved one, love, beloved, darling, dear, dear one, dearly beloved, wellbeloved, truelove, beloved object, **object of one's affections,** light of one's eye *or* life, light of love; sex object, prey, quarry, game

11 <nonformal terms> sweetie, honey, honeybunch, honeybunny, honeypie, hon, main squeeze, sweetie-pie

12 lover, admirer, adorer; paramour, **suitor, wooer,** pursuer, follower; **flirt,** coquette; vampire, vamp; conquest, catch; devotee; escort, companion, *and* steady <both nonformal>; significant other

13 beau, inamorato, swain, man, gallant, cavalier; sugar daddy <nonformal>; gigolo; **boyfriend** *and* **fellow** *and* young man *and* flame <all nonformal>; old man <nonformal>; lover-boy <nonformal>; **seducer, lady-killer,** ladies' man, sheik, philanderer; Lothario; Romeo; Casanova, Don Juan

14 ladylove, inamorata, lady, mistress, ladyfriend

15 <nonformal terms> doll, angel, baby, baby-doll, doll-baby, pet, snookums, girl, girlfriend, dream girl; old lady

16 favorite, preference; **darling,** idol, jewel, apple of one's eye, fairhaired boy, man after one's own heart; **pet,** fondling; spoiled child

or darling, lap dog; teacher's pet; matinee idol

17 fiancé, fiancée, bride-to-be, affianced, betrothed, future, intended <nonformal>

18 loving couple, soul mates, lovebirds, turtledoves, bill-and-cooers

VERBS **19 love, be fond of,** be in love with, **care for, like, fancy,** have a fancy for, take an interest in, **dote on** *or* **upon,** burn with love; be partial to, have a soft spot in one's heart for, have a weakness *or* fondness for

20 <nonformal terms> **go for,** have an eye *or* eyes for, only have eyes for, be sweet on, have a crush *or* case on; have it bad, carry a torch *or* the torch for

21 cherish, hold dear, hold in one's heart *or* affections, think much *or* the world of, prize, treasure; **admire, regard,** esteem, revere; **adore, idolize,** worship, think the world of, love to distraction

22 fall in love, lose one's heart, become enamored, be smitten; take to, **take a liking** *or* **fancy to,** take a shine to *and* fall for <both nonformal>, become attached to, bestow one's affections on; fall head and ears *or* head over heels in love, be swept off one's feet; cotton to <nonformal>

23 enamor, endear; win one's heart, win the love *or* affections of, make a hit with <nonformal>; **charm, infatuate,** hold in thrall, **fascinate,** attract, allure, grow on one, strike *or* tickle one's fancy, **captivate,** bewitch, enrapture, carry away, sweep off one's feet, turn one's head; **seduce,** draw on, tempt, tantalize

ADJS **24 beloved, loved, dear, darling, precious;** pet, favorite; **adored, admired,** esteemed, revered; **cherished,** held dear; **well-liked,** popular; **well-beloved,** dearly beloved, dear to one's heart

25 endearing, lovable, likable, adorable, admirable, **lovely,** winning, winsome; **charming;** angelic

26 amorous, amatory, amative,

erotic; **sexual** 75.28,29; **passionate, ardent,** impassioned; desirous 100.21,22; lascivious 665.29

27 **loving, fond, adoring, devoted, affectionate,** demonstrative, **romantic, sentimental, tender**; lovelorn, lovesick, languishing; charitable

28 **enamored, charmed,** becharmed, **fascinated, captivated,** bewitched, enraptured, enchanted; **infatuated; smitten,** lovestruck

29 **in love,** head over heels in love, over head and ears in love

30 **fond of, enamored of,** partial to, **in love with,** attached to, wedded to, devoted to, wrapped up in; **taken with,** smitten with, struck with

31 <nonformal terms> crazy about, mad or nuts or nutty or wild about

ABVS 32 **lovingly, fondly, affectionately, tenderly,** dearly, **adoringly,** devotedly; amorously, ardently, passionately; with love

105 EXCITEMENT

NOUNS 1 **excitement,** emotion, **arousal, stimulation, exhilaration;** manic state or condition

2 **thrill, sensation,** titillation; **tingle,** tingling; **tremor of excitement,** rush <nonformal>; flush, rush of emotion, surge of emotion

3 <nonformal terms> kick, charge, boot, bang, belt, blast

4 **agitation, perturbation,** ferment, **turbulence, turmoil,** tumult, **commotion,** disturbance, ado, brouhaha <Fr>, to-do <nonformal>; pell-mell, **flurry,** ruffle, bustle, stir, swirl, swirling, whirl, vortex, eddy; fermentation, yeastiness, effervescence, ebullience

5 **trepidation; disquiet,** disquietude, inquietude, **unrest, restlessness,** fidgetiness; **fidgets** or **shakes** and shivers and dithers <all nonformal>; **quivering, quavering, quaking, shaking,**

trembling; **quiver,** quaver, shiver, shudder, twitter, **tremor,** tremble, flutter; palpitation, pitter-patter; **throb,** throbbing; panting, heaving

6 **dither, tizzy** <nonformal>, swivet, **twitter, flutter, fluster, fret, fuss,** bother, lather and stew and snit <all nonformal>, flap

7 **fever of excitement, fever pitch,** fever, heat, fever heat, fire; sexual excitement, rut

8 **fury, furor,** fire and fury; **ecstasy,** transport, **rapture,** ravishment; intoxication, abandon; **passion, rage,** raging or tearing passion, towering rage or passion; **frenzy,** orgy, orgasm; madness, craze, **delirium,** hysteria

9 **outburst,** outbreak, **burst, flare-up,** blaze, **explosion,** eruption, irruption, upheaval, convulsion, spasm, seizure, fit, paroxysm

10 **excitability,** perturbability; emotional instability, explosiveness, eruptiveness, inflammability, combustibility, tempestuousness, violence; **irascibility** 110.2; irritability, edginess, touchiness, prickliness, **sensitivity** 24.3; skittishness, **nervousness** 128; **emotionalism** 93.9

11 **excitation, excitement, arousal,** arousing, **stirring,** stirring up, working into a lather <nonformal>, **agitation, perturbation; stimulation, stimulus, exhilaration,** animation; **provocation, irritation,** aggravation, exasperation, exacerbation, **incitement** 375.4

VERBS 12 **excite, impassion, arouse, rouse, stir up,** set astir, stir the feelings, cause a stir or commotion; **work up,** work up into a lather <nonformal>, whip up, **key up,** steam up; **move** 375.12; **foment, incite** 375.17; turn on <nonformal>; **awaken,** awake, wake, waken, wake up; call up, summon up, call forth; **kindle,** light the fuse, **fire, in-**

flame, heat, warm, set fire to, set on fire, fire or warm the blood; fan the fire or flame, feed the fire, add fuel to the fire or flame, pour oil on the fire; raise to a fever heat or pitch, bring to the boiling point; overexcite; annoy, **incense; enrage, infuriate**

13 **stimulate, whet, sharpen,** pique, provoke, pick up, jazz up <nonformal>, animate, **exhilarate,** invigorate, galvanize; infuse life into, give new life to, revive, renew, resuscitate

14 **agitate, perturb, disturb, trouble, disquiet, discompose,** discombobulate <nonformal>, unsettle, **stir, ruffle, shake, shake up, shock, upset,** make waves, jolt, jar, rock, stagger, electrify, bring or pull one up short, give one a turn <nonformal>; fuss <nonformal>, flutter, flurry, rattle, disconcert, **fluster**

15 **thrill, tickle,** thrill to death or to pieces, **give one a kick** or boot or charge or bang or lift <nonformal>; intoxicate, titillate, take one's breath away

16 **be excitable,** excite easily; **get excited, have a fit; explode, flare up,** flash up, flame up, catch fire; **fly into a passion,** have a tantrum, come apart; ride off in all directions at once, run around like a chicken with its head cut off; **rage, rave, rant,** rant and rave, rave on, bellow, **storm,** ramp; be angry, smolder, **seethe** 152.15

17 <nonformal terms> **work oneself up,** work oneself into a sweat, lather, get hot under the collar, race one's motor, get into a dither or tizzy or swivet or pucker or stew; **blow one's top** or stack or cool, **flip,** flip out, flip one's lid or wig, pop one's cork, blow a gasket, fly off the handle, **hit the ceiling,** go ape, go bananas, lose one's cool, go off the deep end

18 <be excited> **thrill, tingle with excitement,** glow; swell with emotion; turn on to and get high on and freak out on <all nonfor-

mal>; heave, pant; **throb,** palpitate; **tremble, shiver, quiver, quaver, quake,** flutter, twitter, **shake,** have the shakes <nonformal>; **fidget,** have the fidgets and have ants in one's pants <both nonformal>; toss and turn; twitch, jerk

19 **change color,** turn color; **pale,** whiten, blanch; darken; turn blue in the face; **flush, blush,** redden, turn or get red

ADJS 20 **excited,** impassioned; **thrilled,** agog, tingling, aquiver, atwitter; **stimulated, exhilarated, high** <nonformal>; manic; **moved, stirred,** stirred up, **aroused, roused,** switched or turned on <nonformal>, inflamed, wrought up, **worked up,** worked up into a lather <nonformal>, whipped up, steamed up; turned-on <nonformal>; carried away; effervescent, yeasty, ebullient

21 **in a dither, in a tizzy** <nonformal>, in a swivet, **in a twitter,** in a pother, in a ferment, in a turmoil, in an uproar, in a stew and in a sweat <both nonformal>, in a lather <nonformal>

22 **heated, passionate, warm, hot,** red-hot, flaming, **burning, fiery, glowing, fervent, fervid; feverish,** febrile, hectic, flushed; sexually excited, in rut 75.20; burning with excitement, het up <nonformal>, hot under the collar <nonformal>; seething, boiling, boiling over, steamy, steaming

23 **agitated, perturbed, disturbed, troubled, disquieted, upset,** antsy <nonformal>, unsettled, **discomposed, flustered,** ruffled, **shaken**

24 **turbulent,** tumultuous, tempestuous, boisterous, clamorous, uproarious

25 **frenzied, frantic; ecstatic,** transported, in a transport or ecstasy; intoxicated; raging, raving, roaring, bellowing, storming, howling, ranting, fulminating, frothing or foaming at the mouth;

wild, hog-wild <nonformal>; **violent,** fierce, ferocious, **furious; mad,** madding, **rabid,** maniacal, demonic, possessed; carried away, **distracted, delirious, beside oneself,** out of one's wits; uncontrollable, berserk, hog-wild <nonformal>; **hysterical**

26 **overwrought, overexcited, overstimulated, hyper** <nonformal>; **overcome,** overwhelmed, overpowered; **upset**

27 **restless,** restive, **uneasy,** unsettled, tense; **fidgety,** antsy <nonformal>, fussy, fluttery

28 **excitable, emotional,** perturbable, flappable <nonformal>; emotionally unstable; explosive, volcanic, eruptive, inflammable; irascible 110.19; irritable, edgy, touchy, prickly, **sensitive** 24.13; **skittish; high-strung,** high-spirited, mettlesome; **nervous**

29 **passionate, fiery, vehement,** hotheaded, **impetuous,** violent, volcanic, furious, fierce, **wild;** tempestuous, stormy

30 **exciting, thrilling, stirring, moving, breathtaking,** eye-popping <nonformal>; agitating, agitative, perturbing, disquieting, unsettling, jarring; heart-stirring, soul-stirring, mind-blowing <nonformal>; impressive, telling; **provocative** 375.27, provoking, tantalizing; **inflammatory** 375.28; **stimulating,** stimulative, stimulatory; exhilarating, heady, intoxicating; **electric,** galvanic, charged; **overwhelming,** overpowering, more than flesh and blood can bear; **suspenseful,** cliff-hanging <nonformal>

31 **penetrating, piercing,** stabbing, cutting, stinging, biting, keen, brisk, sharp, caustic, astringent

32 **sensational, lurid,** yellow, **melodramatic;** spine-chilling, eye-popping <nonformal>; blood-and-thunder

ADVS 33 **excitedly, agitatedly,** perturbedly; with heart going pitapat or pitter-patter <nonformal>, thrilling all over; all agog, all

aquiver or atwitter or atingle; in a sweat or stew or dither or tizzy <all nonformal>

34 **heatedly, passionately,** warmly, hotly, glowingly, fervently, fervidly, **feverishly**

35 **frenziedly, frantically,** furiously, violently, fiercely, distractedly, deliriously, till one is blue in the face <nonformal>

36 **excitingly, thrillingly,** stirringly, movingly; **provocatively,** provokingly; exhilaratingly

106 INEXCITABILITY

NOUNS 1 **inexcitability, imperturbability,** unflappability <nonformal>; steadiness, evenness; **dispassion,** dispassionateness, ataraxia; stoicism; **even temper; patience** 134; **impassiveness,** impassivity, stolidity

2 **composure,** countenance; **calm, calmness, placidity, serenity,** tranquility, peacefulness; peace of mind; easy mind; resignation, acceptance, fatalism, stoic calm; **quiet,** quietness of mind or soul, quietude; decompression, imperturbation, indisturbance, unruffledness; **coolness,** coolheadedness, cool <nonformal>, sangfroid; icy calm

3 **equanimity,** equilibrium, equability, balance; **levelheadedness,** level head, well-balanced mind; **poise,** aplomb, **self-possession, self-control,** self-command, self-restraint, possession, **presence of mind; self-confidence, self-assurance**

4 **sedateness, staidness,** soberness, sobriety, sober-mindedness, **seriousness,** gravity, solemnity; temperance, moderation

5 **nonchalance,** casualness, offhandedness; easygoingness; **indifference**

VERBS 6 **bc cool** or **composed,** not turn a hair, not have a hair out of place, keep one's cool <nonformal>; **tranquilize, calm** 670.7; **set one's mind at ease** or **rest**

7 **compose oneself, control one-**

self, restrain oneself, collect oneself, **get hold of oneself,** get a grip on oneself <nonformal>, master one's feelings, regain one's composure; **calm down, cool off,** cool down, sober down, hold *or* keep one's temper, simmer down *and* cool it <both nonformal>; **relax,** decompress, unwind, take it easy, lay back <nonformal>; **forget it,** get it out of one's mind *or* head

8 <control one's feelings> **suppress, repress,** smother, stifle, choke *or* hold back, fight down *or* back, inhibit

9 **keep cool,** keep one's cool <nonformal>, keep calm, keep one's head, keep one's shirt on and hang loose <both nonformal>

10 **inexcitable, imperturbable,** unflappable <nonformal>, **unirritable; dispassionate; steady;** stoic, stoical; **even-tempered; impassive,** stolid; **patient**

11 **unexcited, unperturbed,** untroubled, unagitated, **unruffled,** unflustered, unimpassioned

12 **calm, placid,** quiet, **tranquil, serene,** peaceful; **cool, coolheaded,** cool as a cucumber <nonformal>

13 **composed, collected, levelheaded; poised,** together <nonformal>, **balanced,** well-balanced; **self-possessed,** self-controlled, self-restrained; confident, assured, **self-confident, self-assured**

14 **sedate, staid,** sober, soberminded, **serious,** grave; temperate, moderate

15 **nonchalant, blasé, indifferent,** unconcerned 102.7; **casual, offhand, relaxed, laid-back** <nonformal>; **easygoing,** devil-may-care, lackadaisical

ADVS 16 inexcitably, **imperturbably, dispassionately;** stoically; **calmly, placidly,** quietly, **tranquilly, serenely; coolly, composedly,** levelheadedly; impassively, stolidly, stodgily

17 **sedately, staidly, soberly, seriously**

18 **nonchalantly, casually, relaxedly,** lackadaisically

107 CONTENTMENT

NOUNS 1 **contentment, content,** contentedness; **satisfaction,** fulfillment; peace of mind, composure 106.2; **comfort 121; quality of life;** well-being, euphoria; **happiness 95.2; acceptance,** resignation, reconciliation; clear *or* clean conscience

2 **complacency; smugness,** self-approval, self-approbation, **self-satisfaction, self-content,** self-contentedness

3 **satisfactoriness, adequacy, sufficiency 990; acceptability,** admissibility, **tolerability,** agreeability, tenability, viability

VERBS 4 **content, satisfy;** gratify; put *or* set at ease, set one's mind at ease *or* rest, achieve inner harmony

5 **be content, rest satisfied, rest easy,** be reconciled to, accept one's lot, rest on one's laurels, let well enough alone, let sleeping dogs lie, take the bitter with the sweet; come to terms with oneself, learn to live in one's own skin; content oneself with, settle for; settle for less, take half a loaf, lower one's sights, cut one's losses; **be pleased 95.11**

6 **be satisfactory, do, suffice 990.4; suit,** suit one down to the ground

ADJS 7 **content, contented, satisfied; pleased 95.12;** happy; **easy, at ease,** easygoing; **composed 106.13; comfortable 121.11;** euphoric, eupeptic; carefree; accepting, resigned, reconciled; uncomplaining

8 **untroubled, unbothered, undisturbed,** unperturbed 106.11, unworried

9 **well-content, well-pleased,** well-contented, **well-satisfied,** highly satisfied

10 **complacent; smug, self-**

complacent, **self-satisfied,** self-content, **self-contented**

11 satisfactory, satisfying; sufficient 990.6, **adequate, enough,** ample, equal to

12 acceptable, admissible, **agreeable,** unobjectionable, unexceptionable, tenable, viable; **passable,** good enough

13 tolerable, bearable, endurable, supportable

ADVS **14 contentedly,** to one's heart's content; **satisfiedly; complacently, smugly**

15 satisfactorily, satisfyingly; **acceptably, agreeably;** sufficiently, adequately, commensurately, amply, enough; **tolerably, passably**

16 to one's satisfaction, to one's delight, to one's great glee; to one's taste, to the king's *or* queen's taste

108 DISCONTENT

NOUNS **1 discontent,** discontentment, discontentedness; **dissatisfaction,** unfulfillment; **resentment, envy** 154; **restlessness, restiveness, uneasiness,** unease; malaise; rebelliousness 327.3; disappointment 132; unhappiness 112.2; **disgruntlement,** sulkiness, petulance, peevishness, querulousness; cold comfort

2 unsatisfactoriness; inadequacy, insufficiency 991; **unacceptability,** inadmissibility, unsuitability; **intolerability** 98.9

3 malcontent; complainer, complainant, **faultfinder, grumbler, murmurer,** mutterer, griper, whiner; reactionary; rebel 327.5

4 <nonformal terms> **grouch, kvetch,** crank, crab, grouser, bellyacher, bitcher, sorehead, picklepuss, sourpuss

VERBS **5 dissatisfy, discontent, disgruntle, displease,** not fill the bill, leave much *or* a lot to be desired, dishearten; **be discontented, complain**

6 <nonformal terms> **beef, bitch, kvetch,** bellyache, crab, gripe,

grouch, grouse, make a stink, squawk

ADJS **7 discontented, dissatisfied, disgruntled,** unaccepting, unaccommodating, **displeased,** let down; **unsatisfied, ungratified,** unfulfilled; resentful, dog-in-the-manger; envious 154.4; restless, restive, uneasy; rebellious 327.11; malcontent, malcontented, **complaining, faultfinding,** grumbling, growling, murmuring, muttering, griping, croaking, **peevish, petulant,** sulky, **querulous,** whiny; unhappy 112.21

8 <nonformal terms> **grouchy, kvetchy,** cranky, beefing, crabby, crabbing, grousing, griping, bellyaching, bitching

9 unsatisfactory; unsatisfying, ungratifying, unfulfilling; **displeasing** 98.17; disappointing, disheartening, not up to expectation; **inadequate, insufficient** 991.9

10 unacceptable, inadmissible, undesirable, **objectionable,** exceptionable, untenable, indefensible; **intolerable** 98.25

ADVS **11 discontentedly, dissatisfiedly**

12 unsatisfactorily; unsatisfyingly, ungratifyingly; inadequately, insufficiently; unacceptably, inadmissibly, objectionably; intolerably 98.30

109 CHEERFULNESS

NOUNS **1 cheerfulness,** cheeriness, **good cheer, cheer;** blitheness; **gladness; happiness** 95.2; **pleasantness,** winsomeness, geniality; brightness, radiance, **sunniness;** sanguineness, sanguinity; **irrepressibility,** irrepressibleness

2 good humor, good spirits; high spirits, exhilaration, rare good humor

3 lightheartedness, levity; **buoyancy,** resiliency, bounce <nonformal>, springiness; **jauntiness,** perkiness, carefreeness; **breeziness,** airiness, pertness, chirpiness, light heart

4 gaiety; liveliness, vivacity, vi-

tality, life **animation, spiritedness, spirit,** esprit, élan, **sprightliness,** high spirits, zestfulness, zest, verve, gusto, **exuberance,** heartiness; **spirits,** animal spirits; piss and vinegar <nonformal>; **friskiness,** skittishness, coltishness; **sportiveness, playfulness, frolicsomeness,** kittenishness

5 merriment, merriness; **hilarity; joy,** joyfulness, joyousness; **glee,** gleefulness, high glee; **jollity, joviality,** jocularity, jocundity; frivolity, **levity; mirth,** mirthfulness, **amusement** 743; **fun; laughter** 116.4

VERBS **6** exude cheerfulness, radiate cheer, not have a care in the world, **beam,** glow, radiate, sparkle, sing, lilt, whistle, **chirp,** chirrup; walk on air, dance, skip, caper, frolic, gambol, romp; **smile, laugh** 116.8

7 cheer, gladden, brighten; encourage, hearten; inspire, inspirit, **raise the spirits,** buoy up, boost, give a lift <nonformal>, put one on top of the world *and* on cloud nine <both nonformal>; **exhilarate,** animate, invigorate, liven, enliven, vitalize; **rejoice,** do the heart good

8 elate, exalt, elevate, lift, uplift, flush

9 cheer up, take heart, drive dull care away; **brighten up,** light up, **perk up;** come out of it, snap out of it <nonformal>, revive

10 be of good cheer, bear up, **keep one's spirits up,** keep one's chin up <nonformal>, keep a stiff upper lip <nonformal>, grin and bear it

ADJS **11 cheerful, cheery,** of good cheer, in good spirits; in high spirits, exalted, elated, exhilarated, high <nonformal>; irrepressible; **blithe; glad, gladsome; happy,** happy as a clam *or* a lark, sitting on top of the world, sitting pretty; **pleasant, genial,** winsome; **bright, sunny, radiant,** sparkling, beaming, glowing, smiling, laughing; sanguine, san-

guineous, euphoric; optimistic, hopeful; **irrepressible**

12 lighthearted, light; **buoyant,** resilient; **jaunty,** perky, **debonair, carefree,** free and easy; **breezy**

13 pert, chirpy, chipper <nonformal>

14 gay, gay as a lark; **spirited,** sprightly, **lively, animated, vivacious,** vital, zestful, **exuberant,** hearty; **frisky,** antic, skittish, coltish; **full of beans** *and* **feeling one's oats** <both nonformal>, full of piss and vinegar <nonformal>; **sportive, playful, frolicsome;** rollicking, rollicky

15 merry, mirthful, hilarious; joyful, joyous, rejoicing; **gleeful,** gleesome; **jolly; jovial,** jocund, jocular; **frivolous**

16 cheering, gladdening; encouraging, heartening, heartwarming; **inspiring,** inspiriting; **exhilarating,** animating, enlivening, invigorating; cheerful, cheery, glad, joyful

ADVS **17 cheerfully,** cheerily, with good cheer; irrepressibly; **lightheartedly,** lightly; jauntily, perkily, airily; **pleasantly,** genially, blithely; **gladly, happily, joyfully;** optimistically, hopefully

18 gaily, exuberantly, heartily, spiritedly, animatedly, vivaciously, zestfully, with gusto

19 merrily, gleefully, hilariously; jovially, jocundly, jocularly; frivolously; **mirthfully,** laughingly

110 ILL HUMOR

NOUNS **1 ill humor, bad temper,** ill *or* evil temper, **ill nature; sourness,** biliousness, liverishness; choler, bile, gall, spleen; **abrasiveness,** causticity, corrosiveness, asperity 144.8; **anger** 152.5; discontent 108

2 irascibility, irritability, excitability, short fuse <nonformal>; **crossness,** disagreeableness, gruffness, shortness, peevishness, querulousness, fretfulness, **crankiness, testiness,** crustiness, huffiness, waspishness; **perversity,** fractiousness

3 <nonformal terms> **crabbiness, grouchiness,** cantankerousness, crustiness, cussedness, huffiness, **meanness, orneriness,** bitchiness, cussedness, feistiness, scrappiness, soreheadedness

4 hot temper, temper, quick *or* short temper, short fuse <nonformal>, feistiness *and* spunkiness <both nonformal>, **hotheadedness,** hot blood

5 touchiness, tetchiness, prickliness, quickness to take offense, **sensitiveness,** hypersensitiveness, hypersensitivity, thin skin

6 petulance *or* petulancy, **peevishness,** pettishness, **querulousness, fretfulness,** resentfulness

7 contentiousness, quarrelsomeness 456.3; **disputatiousness, argumentativeness,** litigiousness; **belligerence**

8 sullenness, sulkiness, surliness, moroseness, glumness; moodiness; dejection, melancholy 112.5

9 scowl, frown, lower, **glower, pout,** grimace; black looks, **long face**

10 sulks, sullens, mopes

11 <ill-humored person> **sorehead, grouch, curmudgeon, grump, crank, crosspatch,** wasp, **bear,** grizzly bear, pit bull; ugly customer <nonformal>; **hothead,** hotspur; fire-eater

12 bitch <nonformal>, **shrew, vixen,** virago, termagant, beldam, cat, tigress, spitfire; **scold,** common scold; battle-ax <nonformal>

VERBS **13** have a temper, have a short fuse <nonformal>, be possessed of the devil; get out on the wrong side of the bed

14 sulk, mope, mope around; grump *and* **grouch** *and* **bitch** <all nonformal>, **fret**

15 look sullen, pull *or* make a long face; **frown, scowl,** knit the brow, lower, **glower, pout,** grimace, make a wry face

16 sour, exacerbate; **embitter,** bitter, envenom

ADJS **17 out of humor,** out of sorts, **in a bad humor; abrasive,** caustic, corrosive, acid; angry; discontented 108.5

18 ill-humored, bad-tempered, ill-tempered, evil-humored, evil-tempered, **ill-natured,** ill-disposed

19 irascible, irritable, excitable, flappable <nonformal>; **cross, cranky, testy;** spiteful, churlish, bearish, snappish, waspish; **gruff,** grumbling; **disagreeable; perverse,** fractious

20 <nonformal terms> **crabby, grouchy,** cantankerous, crusty, grumpy *or* grumpish, cussed, huffy *or* huffish, mean, ornery, bitchy, cussed, feisty, ugly, miffy, salty, scrappy, soreheaded

21 touchy, tetchy, prickly, quick to take offense, **thin-skinned, sensitive,** hypersensitive, high-strung, temperamental, primadonnaish

22 peevish, petulant, pettish, **querulous, fretful,** resentful; shrewish, vixenish; nagging

23 sour, soured, **sour-tempered;** prune-faced <nonformal>; **choleric, dyspeptic, bilious,** liverish, jaundiced; **bitter,** embittered

24 sullen, sulky, surly, morose, dour, **glum,** grim; **moody; mopish,** mopey <nonformal>, moping; **glowering,** lowering, **scowling, frowning;** dejected, melancholy 112.23

25 hot-tempered, hotheaded, passionate, hot, fiery, peppery, feisty, **quick-tempered, short-tempered;** hasty, quick, explosive, volcanic, combustible

26 contentious, quarrelsome 456.17; **disputatious,** controversial, litigious, polemic, polemical; **argumentative;** on the warpath; scrappy <nonformal>; **bellicose, belligerent**

ADVS **27 ill-humoredly, ill-naturedly; irascibly, irritably, crossly, crankily, testily,** huffily, cantankerously <nonformal>, crabbedly, sourly, churlishly, crustily, bearishly, snappily; perversely, fractiously

28 peevishly, petulantly, querulously, fretfully

29 grouchily and **crabbily** and grumpily <all nonformal>, grumblingly

30 sullenly, sulkily, surlily, morosely, grimly; moodily; gloweringly, loweringly, scowlingly

111 SOLEMNITY

NOUNS **1 solemnity, solemness, dignity, sereness, sobriety, gravity,** *gravitas* <L>, weightiness, **somberness, grimness; sedateness, staidness; seriousness, earnestness, thoughtfulness, sober-mindedness;** long face, straight face; **formality** 580

VERBS **2** honor the occasion, keep a straight face, compose one's features, wear an earnest frown; not crack a smile <nonformal>, wipe the smile off one's face

ADJS **3 solemn, dignified, sober, grave,** unsmiling, **somber, grim; sedate, staid;** demure, decorous; **serious, earnest, thoughtful; sober-minded;** straight-faced, stone-faced; sober as a judge; **formal** 580.7

ADVS **4 solemnly, soberly,** gravely, somberly, grimly; **sedately, staidly,** demurely, decorously; **seriously, earnestly,** sobermindedly; with a straight face; formally 580.11

112 SADNESS

NOUNS **1 sadness,** sadheartedness, weight or burden of sorrow; heaviness, **heavyheartedness,** heavy heart, **heaviness of heart;** pathos, bathos

2 unhappiness, infelicity; displeasure 96.1; discontent 108; **uncheerfulness,** cheerlessness; **joylessness,** unjoyfulness; mirthlessness, unmirthfulness, humorlessness, infestivity; **grimness; wretchedness, misery**

3 dejection, depression, oppression, dejectedness, **downheartedness; discouragement, disheartenment,** dispiritedness; malaise 96.1; chilling effect; **low spirits,** drooping spirits, sinking heart; despondence or **despondency,** spiritlessness; **despair** 125.2, pessimism 125.6, death wish, self-destructive urge; weariness of life; sloth, acedia

4 hypochondria, hypochondriasis, morbid anxiety

5 melancholy, melancholia; pensiveness, wistfulness; nostalgia, homesickness

6 blues, doldrums, blahs and mopes and megrims and sulks <all nonformal>

7 gloom, gloominess, murkiness, **dismalness, bleakness, grimness, somberness, gravity, solemnity; dreariness;** wearisomeness

8 glumness, moroseness, sullenness, sulkiness, **moodiness;** mopishness, mopiness <nonformal>

9 heartache, aching heart, bleeding heart, grieving heart; heartsickness, heartsoreness; **heartbreak, broken heart**

10 sorrow, grief, care, woe; heartfelt grief; pining; **anguish, misery, agony;** prostrating grief, prostration; **lamentation** 115

11 sorrowfulness, mournfulness, ruefulness, **woefulness, dolefulness,** dolorousness, **plaintiveness,** lugubriousness; **tearfulness** 115.2

12 disconsolateness, disconsolation, **inconsolability,** inconsolableness; **desolation,** desolateness; forlornness

13 sourpuss and picklepuss and gloomy Gus <all nonformal>; mope, brooder; **melancholic;** depressive

14 killjoy, spoilsport, grinch and crapehanger and drag <all nonformal>; **wet blanket,** party pooper; gloomster *and* doomster <both nonformal>, doomsdayer; skeleton at the feast; pessimist 125.7

VERBS **15** hang one's head, pull *or* make a long face, sing *or* get *or* have the blues <nonformal>; drag one down; carry the weight *or* woe of the world on one's shoulders; hang crape <nonformal>

16 lose heart, despond, give way, give oneself up *or* over to despondency; **despair** 125.10, sink into despair, throw up one's hands in despair, lose the will to live; **droop,** sink, languish; reach *or* plumb the depths, hit rock bottom

17 grieve, sorrow; weep, mourn 115.8,10; be dumb with grief; **pine,** pine away; **brood over, mope, fret; eat one's heart out,** break one's heart over; **agonize,** ache, bleed

18 sadden, darken, cast a pall *or* gloom upon, weigh *or* weigh heavy upon; **deject, depress, oppress, crush,** hit one like a ton of bricks <nonformal>, **cast down,** lower, lower the spirits, get one down <nonformal>, take the wind out of one's sails, **discourage, dishearten,** take the heart out of, **dispirit;** damp *or* dampen the spirits; dash, knock down, beat down; plunge one into despair

19 aggrieve, oppress, **grieve, sorrow,** plunge one into sorrow, embitter; draw tears, bring to tears; **anguish, tear up** *and* **cut up** <both nonformal>, pull at the heartstrings; afflict 96.16, torment 96.18; **break one's heart, make one's heart bleed;** desolate, leave an aching void; prostrate, overwhelm

ADJS **20 sad,** saddened; sadhearted, **sad of heart; heavyhearted;** oppressed, weighed *or* weighted down, bearing the woe of the world, burdened *or* laden with sorrow; sad-eyed

21 unhappy, uncheerful, cheer-

less, **joyless, unjoyful,** unsmiling; mirthless, humorless; **grim; out of humor,** out of sorts, in bad humor *or* spirits; **sorry;** discontented 108.5; **wretched, miserable;** pleasureless 96.20

22 dejected, depressed, downhearted, down, downcast, cast down, bowed down, subdued; **discouraged, disheartened, dispirited; low, feeling low,** low-spirited, **in low spirits; down in the mouth** <nonformal>, **in the doldrums, down in the dumps** *and* **in the dumps** *and* in the doleful dumps <all nonformal>, in the depths; **despondent; despairing** 125.12, weary of life, world-weary; pessimistic 125.16; **woebegone; drooping,** languishing, pining, haggard

23 melancholy, melancholic, **blue** <nonformal>; **pensive, wistful; nostalgic,** homesick

24 gloomy, dismal, murky, bleak, grim, somber, solemn, grave; funereal, crapehanging <nonformal>, saturnine; **dark; dreary;** weary, wearisome

25 glum, morose, sullen, sulky, crestfallen, chapfallen; **moody, brooding,** broody; mopish, mopey <nonformal>, **moping**

26 sorrowful, sorrowing, mournful, rueful, woeful, doleful, plaintive; dolorous, **grievous, lamentable,** lugubrious; **tearful; care-worn; grief-stricken,** aggrieved, plunged in grief, prostrated by grief, **inconsolable**

27 sorrow-stricken, sorrow-torn, sorrow-laden

28 disconsolate, inconsolable, unconsolable, prostrate *or* prostrated, **forlorn; desolate; sick at heart, heartsick,** heartsore

29 overcome, crushed, overwhelmed, inundated, **stricken, cut up** <nonformal>, **desolated,** prostrate *or* prostrated, broken-down, undone; **heart-stricken, brokenhearted,** heartbroken

30 depressing, depressive, depressant, **oppressive; discouraging, disheartening, dispiriting**

ADVS **31 sadly, gloomily, dismally, drearily,** heavily, bleakly, grimly, somberly, solemnly, funereally, gravely; **depressingly**

32 unhappily, uncheerfully, cheerlessly, joylessly

33 dejectedly, downheartedly; discouragedly, disheartenedly, dispiritedly; despondently, despairingly, spiritlessly, heartlessly; **disconsolately,** inconsolably, forlornly

34 pensively, wistfully; nostalgically

35 glumly, grumly, **morosely, sullenly; moodily,** moodishly, broodingly, broodily; mopishly, mopily <nonformal>, mopingly

36 sorrowfully, mournfully, ruefully, woefully, dolefully, dolorously, plaintively, grievously, lugubriously; with a broken voice; **heartbrokenly,** brokenheartedly; **tearfully,** with tears in one's eyes

113 REGRET

NOUNS **1 regret, regrets,** regretfulness; **remorse,** remorsefulness, remorse of conscience; **shame,** shamefulness, shamefacedness; **sorrow, grief, sorriness; contrition,** contriteness, attrition; bitterness; apologies; wistfulness 100.4

2 compunction, qualm, qualms, qualmishness, scruples, scrupulosity, scrupulousness, pang, **pangs of conscience,** throes, sting or pricking or twinge or twitch of conscience, touch of conscience, **voice of conscience,** pricking of heart, better self

3 self-reproach, self-reproachfulness, **self-accusation, self-condemnation,** self-conviction, self-punishment, self-humiliation, self-debasement, **self-hatred; hair shirt; self-analysis, soul-searching**

4 penitence, repentance, change of heart; apology, humble or heartfelt apology, abject apology; guardian angel; reformation

857.2; deathbed repentance; mea culpa; **penance** 658.3; wearing a hairshirt or sackcloth or sackcloth and ashes, mortification of the flesh

5 penitent, confessor; **prodigal son,** prodigal returned

VERBS **6 regret, deplore, repine, be sorry for; rue,** rue the day; **bemoan, bewail;** curse one's folly, **reproach oneself,** kick oneself <nonformal>, bite one's tongue, wear a hair shirt, humiliate or debase oneself, hate oneself for one's actions, hide one's face in shame; examine one's conscience, analyze or search one's motives; cry over spilled milk

7 repent, think better of, change one's mind, have second thoughts; laugh out of the other side of one's mouth; **plead guilty,** humble oneself, **apologize** 658.5, beg pardon or forgiveness, throw oneself on the mercy of the court; **do penance** 658.6; reform

ADJS **8 regretful, remorseful,** full of remorse, **ashamed,** shameful, shamefaced, **sorry, rueful,** repining, unhappy about; **conscience-stricken; self-reproachful,** self-reproaching, self-hating; wistful 100.23

9 penitent, repentant; penitential; contrite, abject, humble, **sheepish, apologetic,** touched, softened, melted

10 regrettable, much to be regretted; **deplorable** 999.9

ADVS **11 regretfully, remorsefully,** ruefully

12 penitently, repentantly; **contritely,** abjectly, **humbly, sheepishly,** apologetically

114 UNREGRETFULNESS

NOUNS **1 unregretfulness, unremorsefulness; remorselessness; shamelessness**

2 impenitence; nonrepentance; uncontriteness, unabjectness; heart of stone, callousness 94.3; **hardness of heart,** hardness, obduracy; **defiance** 454, 327.2; **insolence** 142

VERBS **3 harden one's heart**, steel oneself; **have no regrets**, not cry over spilled milk; have no shame

ADJS **4 unregretful, unremorse-ful, unsorry, unsorrowful**, un-rueful; **remorseless**, regretless; unsorrowing, ungrieving, unre-pining; **shameless**

5 impenitent, unrepentant, un-repenting, unreconstructed; **uncontrite**, unabject; untouched, unsoftened, callous 94.12; hard, hardened, obdurate; **defiant** 453.8/454.7; **insolent** 142.9

6 unregretted, unrepented

ADVS **7 unregretfully, unremorse-fully**, unruefully; **remorselessly**, sorrowlessly, impenitently, shamelessly; **without regret**, without looking back, **with-out remorse**, without compunc-tion, without any qualms *or* scruples

115 LAMENTATION

NOUNS **1 lamentation**, lamenting, **mourning, moaning, grieving, sorrowing, wailing, bewailing, bemoaning**, keening, howling, ululation; **sorrow** 112.10

2 weeping, sobbing, crying, bawling; **blubbering, whimper-ing, sniveling; tears**, flood of tears, fit of crying;; **tearfulness, weepiness** <nonformal>, lach-rymosity; swimming *or* brim-ming *or* overflowing eyes; **tear, teardrop**

3 lament, plaint; **murmur**, mut-ter; **moan, groan; whine, whimper; wail**, wail of woe; **sob, cry**, outcry, scream, **howl**, yowl, bawl, yawp, keen, ululation; jer-emiad, tirade

4 complaint, grievance, peeve, pet peeve, **groan; dissent, pro-test** 333.2; hard luck story <nonformal>; **complaining**, scolding, **faultfinding** 510.4, sniping, **grumbling, murmur-ing**; whining, petulance, queru-lousness

5 <nonformal terms> **beef, kick, gripe**, kvetch, grouse, bellyache, howl, holler, **squawk**, bitch;

beefing, grousing, **kicking, griping**, kvetching, **bellyaching**, squawking, **bitching**, yapping

6 dirge, funeral *or* **death song**, keen, elegy, requiem, monody, threnody, death knell, passing bell, funeral march, muffled drums; eulogy, funeral oration

7 <mourning garments> **mourn-ing, weeds**, widow's weeds, crape, black; sackcloth, sackcloth and ashes;

8 lamenter, griever, mourner 309.7; moaner, weeper; **com-plainer**, faultfinder, malcontent 108.3

9 <nonformal terms> grouch, kvetch, kicker, griper, moaner

VERBS **10 lament, mourn, moan, grieve, sorrow**, keen, weep over, **bewail, bemoan, de-plore, repine, sigh; sing the blues** <nonformal>, **elegize, dirge, knell**

11 wring one's hands, tear one's hair, gnash one's teeth, beat one's breast

12 weep, sob, cry, bawl; blubber, whimper, snivel; shed tears; burst into tears, burst out cry-ing, give way to tears, melt *or* dissolve in tears, break down and cry; cry one's eyes out

13 wail, ululate; moan, groan; howl, yowl; **cry, squall, bawl**, yawp, **yell, scream**, shriek; bay at the moon

14 whine, whimper, yammer <nonformal>, pule

15 complain, groan; grumble, murmur, mutter, growl, clamor, croak, grunt, yelp; **fret**, fuss, make a fuss about, fret and fume; lodge *or* register a complaint; fault, find fault

16 <nonformal terms> beef, bitch, kick, kvetch, bellyache, crab

17 go into mourning; wear mourn-ing

ADJS **18 lamenting, grieving, mourning, moaning, sorrow-ing**; wailing, bewailing, bemoan-ing; **in mourning**, in sackcloth and ashes

19 plaintive, mournful, wailful, ululant; **sorrowful** 112.26; **howling; whining, whiny, whimpering, puling; querulous, fretful,** petulant, peevish; **complaining, faultfinding** 510.24

20 <nonformal terms> **grouchy, kvetchy,** cranky, beefing, crabby, crabbing, grousing, griping, bellyaching, bitching

21 **tearful,** teary, **weepy** <nonformal>; lachrymose; on the edge of tears; **weeping, sobbing, crying;** blubbering, whimpering, sniveling; **in tears,** with tears in one's eyes, with swimming or brimming or overflowing eyes

22 dirgelike, elegiac, elegiacal, threnodic

ADVS 23 **lamentingly, plaintively, mournfully,** wailfully; **sorrowfully** 112.36; complainingly, querulously, fretfully, petulantly, peevishly

116 REJOICING

NOUNS 1 **rejoicing, jubilation,** raucous happiness; **exultation,** elation, triumph; the time of one's life; whoopee and hoopla <both nonformal>, festivity 743.3,4, merriment 109.5; celebration 487

2 **cheer, hurrah, huzzah,** hurray, hooray, yippee, rah; **cry, shout, yell;** hosanna, hallelujah, alleluia, paean; **applause** 509.2

3 **smile,** smiling; gleaming or glowing smile, beam; silly smile or grin; **grin,** grinning; broad grin, ear-to-ear grin, toothful grin; idiotic grin; sardonic grin, **smirk, simper**

4 **laughter, laughing, hilarity** 109.5, risibility; **laugh;** boff and boffola and yuck <all nonformal>; **titter; giggle; chuckle, chortle;** cackle, crow; **snicker,** snigger, snort; guffaw, **horselaugh; hearty laugh, belly laugh** <nonformal>; **shout, shriek,** shout of laughter, burst or outburst of laughter, peal or roar of laughter, gales of laughter; fit of laughter, convulsion

VERBS 5 **rejoice,** jubilate, **exult,**

glory, joy, delight, bless or thank one's stars or lucky stars, congratulate oneself, rub one's hands, clap hands; dance or skip or jump for joy, dance, skip, frisk, rollick, revel, frolic, caper, gambol, romp; sing, carol, chirp, chirrup

6 **cheer,** give three cheers, **cry, shout, yell,** cry for joy, yell oneself hoarse; shout hosanna or hallelujah; **applaud** 509.10

7 **smile,** crack a smile <nonformal>, break into a smile; **beam,** smile brightly; **grin,** grin like a Cheshire cat <nonformal>; **smirk, simper**

8 **laugh,** burst out laughing, burst into laughter; laugh it up <nonformal>; **titter; giggle; chuckle, chortle;** cackle, crow; **snicker,** snigger, snort; ha-ha, hee-haw, hee-hee, ho-ho, tee-hee, yuk-yuk; **guffaw,** belly laugh, horselaugh; **shout, shriek,** give a shout or shriek of laughter; **roar,** roar with laughter; shake with laughter, shake like jelly; be convulsed with laughter, go into convulsions; burst or split with laughter, break up and crack up <both nonformal>, **split one's sides,** laugh fit to burst or bust <nonformal>, **be in stitches** <nonformal>, hold one's sides, roll in the aisles <nonformal>; laugh oneself sick or silly or limp, die or nearly die laughing; laugh up one's sleeve

9 **make laugh, kill** and **slay** <both nonformal>, break or crack one up <nonformal>

ADJS 10 **rejoicing,** delighting, exulting; **jubilant, exultant, elated,** elate, flushed

ADVS 11 **rejoicingly,** delightingly, exultingly; **jubilantly, exultantly, elatedly**

117 DULLNESS
<being uninteresting>

NOUNS 1 **dullness, dryness; stuffiness, stodginess,** woodenness, stiffness; barrenness, sterility, aridity, jejunity; **insipidness,** insipidity, vapidness, vapidity, inanity, hollowness, emptiness, superficiality, **staleness, flatness,** tastelessness; **deadness,** lifelessness, spiritlessness, bloodlessness, paleness, pallor, etiolation, effeteness; **slowness,** pokiness, dragginess <nonformal>, unliveliness; **tediousness** 118.2; **dreariness; heaviness,** leadenness, ponderousness; solemnity 111

2 prosaicness, prosiness; prosaism, prose, plainness; **matter-offactness,** unimaginativeness; **simplicity** 797, **plainness** 499

3 triteness, corniness *and* squareness <both nonformal>, **banality,** unoriginality, sameness, **hackneyedness, commonplaceness,** commonness, platitudinousness; a familiar ring; redundancy, **staleness,** mustiness, fustiness; cliché 973.3

VERBS **4 fall flat; leave one cold** *or* unmoved, go over like a lead balloon <nonformal>, lay an egg *and* bomb <both nonformal>, **wear thin**

5 prose, platitudinize; warm over; banalize

ADJS **6 dull, dry,** dusty, dry as dust; **stuffy, stodgy,** wooden, stiff; arid, barren, blank, sterile, jejune; **insipid,** vapid, inane, hollow, empty, superficial; **flat,** tasteless; characterless, colorless, pointless; **dead,** lifeless, spiritless, bloodless, pale, pallid, etiolated, effete; cold; **slow,** poky, draggy <nonformal>, pedestrian, plodding, unlively; **tedious; dreary,** drearisome, dismal; **heavy,** leaden, ponderous, elephantine; dull as dish water

7 uninteresting, uneventful, **unexciting; uninspiring; unentertaining,** unenjoyable, **unamusing,** unfunny

8 prosaic, prose, prosy, prosing, plain; **matter-of-fact,** unimaginative, unimpassioned

9 trite; banal, unoriginal, platitudinous, **stereotyped,** stock, set, **commonplace, common,** twice-told, **familiar,** bromidic <nonformal>, old hat <nonformal>, back-number, warmedover, **cut-and-dried; hackneyed,** hackney; well-known 927.27; **stale,** musty, fusty; **worn,** timeworn, moth-eaten, threadbare, **worn thin**

ADVS **10 dully, dryly, uninterestingly;** stuffily, stodgily; aridly, barrenly, jejunely, **insipidly, vapidly,** inanely, superficially, tastelessly, **colorlessly,** pointlessly; lifelessly, spiritlessly, bloodlessly, pallidly, effetely; draggily <nonformal>, ploddingly; **tediously;** drearily, dismally; ponderously

11 tritely, cornily <nonformal>, **banally,** commonly, familiarly, hackneyedly, unoriginally, stalely

118 TEDIUM

NOUNS **1 tedium, monotony, humdrum; sameness,** more of the same, the same old thing; broken record, parrot; undeviation, unvariation, invariability; the round, the daily round *or* grind, the rat race <nonformal>, the beaten track *or* path; time on one's hands; time hanging heavily on one's hands; **protraction, prolongation** 826.2

2 tediousness, monotonousness, unrelievedness; humdrumness; dullness 117; **wearisomeness; tiresomeness, irksomeness;** prolixity, **long-windedness** 538.2; redundancy, repetition

3 weariness, tiredness; jadedness, satiation, satiety; **boredom; ennui,** melancholy, worldweariness; **listlessness** 94.4, **dispiritedness** 112.3

4 bore, crashing bore <nonformal>, frightful bore; **pest, nuisance; wet blanket**

5 <nonformal terms> **drag, drip, pill,** deadass, deadfanny; **headache,** pain in the neck *or* ass

VERBS **6 be tedious, drag on,** go on forever; have a certain sameness; **weary, tire, irk,** wear, wear on *or* upon, **make one tired,** fatigue, weary *or* tire to death, jade; give one a swift pain in the ass <nonformal>, **pall, satiate,** glut

7 bore, leave one cold, set *or* send to sleep; **bore stiff** *or* to tears *or* to death *or* to extinction <nonformal>, bore to distraction

8 harp on *or* **upon, dwell on** *or* **upon,** harp upon one *or* the same string, play *or* sing the same old song *or* tune, play the same broken record

ADJS **9 tedious, monotonous, humdrum,** singsong, unvarying, invariable, uneventful, broken-record, parrotlike, harping, everlasting; **dreary,** dry, dusty, **dull** 117.6; protracted, prolonged 826.11; prolix, **long-winded** 538.12

10 wearying, wearing, **tiring; wearisome,** weariful, fatiguing, **tiresome, irksome; boring, boresome,** stupefyingly boring

11 weary, weariful; **tired,** wearied, irked; good and tired, tired to death, weary unto death; sick, **sick of, tired of, sick and tired of;** jaded, satiated, palled, fed up <nonformal>; **blasé;** melancholy, melancholic, life-weary, world-weary, tired of living; **listless** 94.13, **dispirited** 112.22

12 bored, uninterested; bored stiff *or* to death *or* to tears *or* to extinction <nonformal>

ADVS **13 tediously, monotonously,** everlastingly, unvaryingly, endlessly; long-windedly; **boringly; wearisomely, tiresomely, irksomely**

14 on a treadmill, on the beaten track, on the same old round

119 AGGRAVATION

NOUNS **1 aggravation, worsening; exacerbation,** embitterment; deterioration; **intensification, heightening,** sharpening, deepening, **increase,** enhancement, amplification, magnification, augmentation; **exasperation, annoyance, irritation** 96.3; provocation; contentiousness

VERBS **2 aggravate, worsen; exac-**
erbate, embitter; deteriorate; **intensify, heighten,** step up, sharpen, bring to a head, deepen, **increase,** enhance, amplify, enlarge, magnify, build up; augment; rub salt in the wound, add insult to injury, add fuel to the fire *or* flame, heat up *and* hot up <both nonformal>; tighten up, tighten the screws, put the squeeze on <nonformal>; **exasperate,** annoy, irritate 96.14; provoke

3 worsen, take a turn for the worse; go from push to shove, **go from bad to worse; jump out of the frying pan and into the fire,** avoid Scylla and fall into Charybdis

ADJS **4 aggravated, worsened, worse,** exacerbated, embittered, deteriorated; **intensified, heightened,** stepped-up, **increased,** enhanced, amplified, magnified, enlarged, augmented; **exasperated, irritated, annoyed** 96.21; provoked, deliberately provoked

5 aggravating; exasperating; annoying, irritating 98.22; provocative; contentious

ADVS **6** from bad to worse; aggravatingly, exasperatingly; annoyingly 98.29

120 RELIEF

NOUNS **1 relief, easement, easing,** ease; **relaxation,** relaxing, relaxation *or* easing of tension; **reduction,** diminishment, diminution, lessening, abatement, remission; **remedy** 86; **alleviation, mitigation, palliation,** assuagement, defusing, appeasement, mollification; soothing, salving, anodyne; lulling; dulling, deadening, numbing, anesthesia, anesthetizing; sedating, sedation; doping *or* doping up <nonformal>

2 release, deliverance, freeing, removal; suspension, intermission, respite, surcease, reprieve; discharge; catharsis, purging, purgation emotional release

3 lightening, disburdening, unburdening, disembarrassment, a load off one's mind, something out of one's system

4 sense or **feeling of relief,** sigh of relief

VERBS **5 relieve,** give relief; **ease, ease matters; relax,** slacken; **reduce,** diminish, lessen, abate, remit; **alleviate, mitigate, palliate,** cushion, assuage, allay, defuse, appease, mollify, subdue, soothe; salve, pour oil on; slake; lull; **dull, deaden,** dull or deaden the pain, numb, benumb, anesthetize; sedate, dope or dope up <nonformal>

6 release, free, deliver, reprieve, remove, free from; suspend, intermit; **relax,** decompress, ease; act as a cathartic, **purge, purge away, cleanse,** cleanse away

7 lighten, disburden, unburden, ease one's load; **set one's mind at ease** or **rest,** set at ease, **take a load off one's mind,** smooth the ruffled brow of care; relieve oneself, let one's hair down, pour one's heart out, talk it out, let it all hang out and go public <both nonformal>, get it off one's chest

8 be relieved, feel relief, feel better about, get something out of one's system, feel or be oneself again; **breathe easy** or **easier,** breathe more freely; **heave a sigh of relief,** draw a long or deep breath

ADJS **9 relieving, easing, alleviative,** alleviating, **palliative,** lenitive, assuasive, softening, subduing, soothing, demulcent, emollient; **remedial** 86.39; dulling, deadening, numbing, anesthetic, analgesic, anodyne; cathartic, purgative, cleansing; **relaxing**

10 relieved, breathing easy or easier or freely, able to breathe again, out from under and out of the woods <both nonformal>; **relaxed**

121 COMFORT

NOUNS **1 comfort, ease, well-being;** contentment 107; bed of roses; solid comfort

2 comfortableness, easiness; restfulness, peace, peacefulness; softness; **coziness, snugness;** homeyness <nonformal>, homeliness; **commodiousness,** roominess, convenience; luxuriousness 501.5; hospitality 585

3 creature comforts, comforts, conveniences, amenities, good things of life, egg in one's beer <nonformal>, all the comforts of home; all the heart can desire

4 consolation, solace, heart's ease; **encouragement, assurance, reassurance,** support, **comfort,** crumb or shred of comfort; condolence 147, sympathy; **relief** 120

5 comforter, consoler, solacer, encourager

VERBS **6 comfort, console, solace,** give or bring comfort, bear up; sympathize with, extend sympathy; ease, **put** or **set at ease;** bolster, support; relieve 120.5; **assure, reassure; encourage, hearten,** pat on the back; **cheer** 109.7

7 be comforted, take comfort, take heart; take hope, pull oneself together, pluck up one's spirits

8 be at ease, be or feel easy; **make oneself comfortable,** make oneself at home, feel at home, put one's feet up, take a load off <nonformal>; **relax**

9 snug, snug down or up; tuck in

10 snuggle, nestle, cuddle, cuddle up, curl up; nest; bundle; snuggle up to

ADJS **11 comfortable,** comfy <nonformal>; contented 107.7,9,10; **easy,** easeful; **restful,** reposeful, peaceful, **relaxing;** soft, cushioned, cushy <nonformal>; comfortable as an old shoe; **cozy, snug,** snug as a bug in a rug; friendly, warm; **homelike,** downhome <nonformal>, homely, lived-in; **commodious,** roomy; luxurious 501.21

12 at ease, at one's ease, easy, relaxed, laid-back <nonformal>;

at rest, resting easy; **at home,** in one's element

13 comforting, consoling; sympathetic; **assuring, reassuring,** supportive; **encouraging, heartening; cheering** 109.16; relieving 120.9

ADVS **14 comfortably, easily; restfully,** reposefully, peacefully; **cozily, snugly; commodiously,** roomily

15 in comfort, in clover, on or **in velvet** <nonformal>

16 comfortingly, consolingly, assuringly, reassuringly, supportively, hearteningly

122 WONDER

NOUNS **1 wonder,** wonderment, sense of wonder, marveling, marvel, **astonishment, amazement, astoundment;** stupefaction; **surprise; awe,** sense of mystery, admiration; beguilement, fascination 377.1

2 marvel, wonder, prodigy, miracle, phenomenon, phenom <nonformal>; astonishment, amazement, amazing or astonishing thing, quite a thing, really something, **sensation; one for the book** and something to brag about and something to shout about and something to write home about and something else <all nonformal>; **rarity,** nonesuch, nonpareil; **curiosity, sight, spectacle**

3 wonderfulness, wondrousness, **marvelousness, prodigiousness;** fascination, seductiveness, **glamorousness; awesomeness, mysteriousness,** mystery; **transcendence**

4 inexpressibility, ineffability, ineffableness, indescribability, indefinableness, **unutterability, unspeakability**

VERBS **5 wonder, marvel,** be astonished or amazed or astounded, be seized with wonder; **gaze, gape,** look or stand aghast or agog, gawk, **stare,** stare openmouthed, hold one's breath; not know what to make of,

not believe one's eyes or ears or senses

6 astonish, amaze, astound, surprise, startle, stagger, **bewilder, perplex** 970.13, flabbergast <nonformal>, overwhelm, **boggle, boggle the mind; dumbfound, strike dumb, strike dead;** knock one's socks off and bowl down or over <all nonformal>, dazzle, bedazzle, daze; **stun, stupefy,** petrify, paralyze

7 take one's breath away, turn one's head, make one's head swim, make one's hair stand on end, make one sit up and take notice, sweep or carry off one's feet

8 beggar description, stagger belief

ADJS **9 wondering,** marveling, **astonished, amazed, surprised, astounded,** flabbergasted <nonformal>, **bewildered,** puzzled, confounded, **dumbfounded,** dumbstruck, staggered, overwhelmed; **aghast,** agape, agog, all agog, gazing, gaping, wideeyed, openmouthed, **breathless; thunderstruck,** wonderstruck, awestruck; **awed, in awe,** in awe of; spellbound, fascinated, captivated, beguiled, enthralled, enraptured, enchanted, entranced, bewitched, hypnotized, mesmerized, stupefied

10 wonderful, wondrous, marvelous, miraculous, fantastic, fabulous, phenomenal, **prodigious, stupendous,** unheard-of, unprecedented, extraordinary, exceptional, rare, unique, singular, **remarkable,** striking, **sensational; strange,** passing strange; **beguiling, fascinating;** incredible, inconceivable, outlandish, unimaginable, incomprehensible; **bewildering, puzzling,** enigmatic

11 awesome, awful, awe-inspiring; **transcendent,** transcending, surpassing; **mysterious;** weird, eerie, uncanny, bizarre

12 astonishing, amazing, surpris-

ing, startling, **astounding,** confounding, staggering, breathtaking, overwhelming, mindboggling; **spectacular**

13 **indescribable, ineffable,** inexpressible, unutterable, unspeakable, indefinable, undefinable, unmentionable

ADVS 14 **wonderfully,** wondrously, **marvelously, miraculously,** fantastically, fabulously, phenomenally, prodigiously, stupendously, extraordinarily, exceptionally, remarkably, strikingly, **sensationally;** strangely, outlandishly, incredibly, inconceivably, unimaginably, incomprehensibly, **bewilderingly, puzzlingly,** enigmatically; **beguilingly,** fascinatingly

15 **awesomely,** awfully; **mysteriously,** weirdly, eerily, uncannily, bizarrely; **transcendently,** surpassingly, surpassing

16 **astonishingly, amazingly, astoundingly,** staggeringly, confoundingly; **surprisingly,** startlingly, to one's surprise or great surprise

17 **indescribably, ineffably,** inexpressibly, unutterably, **unspeakably**

123 UNASTONISHMENT

NOUNS 1 **unastonishment, unamazement; calm,** calmness, coolness, **cool** <nonformal>, cool or calm or nodding acceptance, composure, composedness, sangfroid, inexcitability 106, expectation 130, refusal to be impressed or awed or amazed; poker face, straight face

VERBS 2 **accept, take for granted** or as a matter of course or in stride or as it comes, treat as routine, not blink an eye, keep one's cool <nonformal>

ADJS 3 **unastonished, unsurprised, unamazed,** unmarveling, unbewildered; undazzled; undazed; **unimpressed,** unmoved; calm, **cool,** cool as a cucumber, composed, inexcitable 106.10

124 HOPE

NOUNS 1 **hope, hopefulness,** hoping, **hopes; aspiration, desire** 100; prospect, **expectation** 130; **trust, confidence, faith,** assured faith, **reliance,** dependence; conviction, assurance, security, wellgrounded hope; assumption, presumption; **promise, prospect,** good prospect, good or hopeful prognosis, best case; great expectations, good prospects, high hopes; hoping against hope

2 **prayerful hope;** doomed hope or hopes

3 **optimism,** optimisticalness, Pollyannaism, cheerful or bright or rosy outlook, rose-colored glasses; **cheerfulness** 109; bright side, silver lining; philosophical optimism, utopianism, perfectionism; millenarianism, millennialism

4 **ray of hope,** gleam or glimmer of hope; faint hope

5 **airy hope,** dream, golden dream, pipe dream <nonformal>, bubble, chimera, fool's paradise

6 **optimist,** hoper, Pollyanna, ray of sunshine <nonformal>, irrepressible optimist, Dr Pangloss; philosophical optimist, utopian, perfectionist; millenarian, millennialist, millennian; aspirer, aspirant

VERBS 7 **hope,** live in hopes, have reason to hope, entertain or harbor the hope, cling to the hope; look for, prognosticate, **expect** 130.5; **trust,** confide, presume, feel confident, rest assured; pin one's hope upon, put one's trust in, hope in, rely on, count on, lean upon, bank on, set great store on; hope for, **aspire to, desire** 100.14; **hope against hope,** hope and pray

8 **be hopeful, get one's hopes up,** keep one's spirits up, never say die, take heart, be of good hope, be of good cheer, keep hoping, keep hope alive, keep the faith <nonformal>; **hope for the best,** knock on wood, cross one's fin-

gers, keep one's fingers crossed, allow oneself to hope; clutch *or* catch at straws

9 **be optimistic, look on the bright side; look through** *or* **wear rose-colored glasses; call the glass half full, think positively** *or* affirmatively, be upbeat <nonformal>, think the best of, **make the best of it,** put a good *or* bold face upon, put the best face upon; see the light at the end of the tunnel

10 **give hope, raise hope,** hold out hope, inspire hope, **raise one's hopes,** raise expectations, **lead one to expect; cheer** 109.7; **assure, reassure,** support; **promise,** hold out promise, augur well, bid fair *or* well

ADJS 11 **hopeful, hoping, in hopes,** full of hope, of good hope, of good cheer; **aspiring** 100.28; **expectant** 130.11; **sanguine,** fond; **confident,** assured

12 **optimistic,** upbeat <nonformal>; **bright, sunny; cheerful** 109.11; **rosy,** rose-colored; pollyannaish, Panglossian; utopian 985.23, perfectionist, millenarian, millennialistic

13 **promising,** of promise, full of promise, bright with promise, best-case; **favorable, auspicious, propitious** 133.18; inspiring, inspiriting, **encouraging,** cheering

ADVS 14 **hopefully; expectantly** 130.15; **optimistically; cheerfully** 109.17; sanguinely

125 HOPELESSNESS

NOUNS 1 **hopelessness, not a prayer** *and* **not a hope in hell** <both nonformal>, not the ghost of a chance; small hope, bleak outlook *or* prospect *or* prognosis, worst case; inexpectation 131; futility 391.2; impossibility 966

2 **despair, desperation,** desperateness; no way <nonformal>, no way out, despondency 112.3; disconsolateness 112.12; forlornness; acedia, sloth; apathy 94.4

3 **irreclaimability, irretrievability,** irredeemability; irrevocability, **irreversibility; irreparability, incurability,** irremediableness, immedicableness; unmitigability

4 **forlorn hope,** vain expectation, doomed *or* foredoomed hope, fond *or* foolish hope

5 **dashed hopes,** blighted hope; disappointment 132

6 **pessimism, cynicism,** nihilism; uncheerfulness 112.2; **gloominess,** gloomy outlook; negativism; defeatism

7 **pessimist, cynic,** nihilist; killjoy 112.14, gloomy Gus *and* calamity howler *and* worrywart <all nonformal>, seek-sorrow, prophet of doom, Cassandra; negativist; defeatist

8 **lost cause, fool's errand, wild-goose chase; hopeless case; goner** *and* gone goose *or* gosling *and* dead duck <all nonformal>; terminal case

VERBS 9 **be hopeless,** have not a hope *or* prayer; **be pessimistic, look on the dark side,** be downbeat <nonformal>, think *or* make the worst of, put the worst face upon, call the glass half empty; not hold one's breath

10 **despair,** despair of, **despond** 112.16, falter, lose hope, **lose heart, abandon hope,** give up hope, **give up,** fall *or* sink into despair, give oneself up *or* yield to despair, throw up one's hands in despair, turn one's face to the wall

11 **shatter one's hopes,** dash *or* crush *or* blight one's hope, burst one's bubble <nonformal>, bring crashing down around one's head, disappoint 132.2, drive to despair *or* desperation

ADJS 12 **hopeless,** affording no hope, worst-case, bleak, grim, dismal, cheerless, comfortless; **desperate, despairing, in despair; despondent** 112.22; **disconsolate** 112.28

13 **futile, vain** 391.13; doomed, foredoomed

14 **impossible,** out of the question,

no-go *and* no-win *and* lose-lose <all nonformal>

15 past hope, beyond recall, past praying for; **irretrievable, irrecoverable, irreclaimable,** irredeemable, unsalvageable; incorrigible; irrevocable, **irreversible; irremediable, irreparable,** inoperable, **incurable,** cureless, remediless, beyond remedy, terminal; unmitigable; **ruined,** undone, kaput <nonformal>; lost, gone, gone to hell *and* gone to hell in a handbasket <both nonformal>

16 pessimistic, pessimist, downbeat <nonformal>, **cynical,** nihilistic; uncheerful 112.21; **gloomy,** dismal, crapehanging, funereal, lugubrious; negative, negativistic; defeatist

ADVS **17 hopelessly, desperately,** forlornly; impossibly

18 irreclaimably, irretrievably, irrecoverably, irredeemably, unsalvageably; irrevocably, **irreversibly; irremediably, incurably, irreparably**

126 ANXIETY
<troubled thought>

NOUNS **1 anxiety, anxiousness; apprehension, apprehensiveness,** misgiving, foreboding, suspense, strain, tension, stress; **dread, fear** 127; **concern,** concernment, **solicitude,** zeal 101.2; **distress,** trouble, vexation; **uneasiness, perturbation, disturbance,** upset, **agitation, disquiet,** disquietude, inquietude; **nervousness** 128; malaise, angst 96.1; pins and needles, tenterhooks; anxiety neurosis

2 worry, worriment <nonformal>; **worries,** troubles, concerns; worrying, fretting

3 worrier, worrywart *and* nervous Nellie <both nonformal>

VERBS **4 concern, trouble, bother, distress, disturb, upset,** frazzle, **disquiet, agitate;** keep one on edge *or* on tenterhooks *or* on pins and needles

5 <make anxious> **worry, upset,**

vex, fret, agitate, get to <nonformal>, **harass,** harry, **torment,** dog, hound, plague, persecute, haunt, beset

6 <feel anxious> **worry,** worry oneself, worry one's head about, worry oneself sick, trouble one's head *or* oneself, lose sleep; have one's heart in one's mouth, have one's heart miss *or* skip a beat, get butterflies in one's stomach; **fret, fuss, chafe,** fret and fume; tense up, bite one's nails, walk the floor, go up the wall <nonformal>, be on tenterhooks *or* pins and needles

ADJS **7 anxious, concerned, apprehensive,** foreboding, misgiving, suspenseful, strained, tense, tensed up <nonformal>, nailbiting; **fearful** 127.32; **solicitous,** zealous 101.9; **troubled, bothered; uneasy, perturbed, disturbed, disquieted, agitated; nervous** 128.11; **on pins and needles,** on tenterhooks; all hot and bothered *and* in a pucker *and* in a stew <all nonformal>; overanxious

8 worried, vexed, fretted; **harassed,** harried, tormented, dogged, hounded, persecuted, haunted, beset, plagued; worried sick, worried to a frazzle, worried stiff <nonformal>

9 careworn, heavy-laden, overburdened

10 troublesome, bothersome, **distressing,** distressful, **disturbing, upsetting, disquieting; worrisome,** worrying; fretting, chafing; **harassing,** tormenting, plaguing; **annoying** 98.22

ADVS **11 anxiously, concernedly, apprehensively,** misgivingly, **uneasily;** worriedly; solicitously

127 FEAR,
FRIGHTENINGNESS

NOUNS **1 fear, fright; scare, alarm, consternation, dismay; dread,** unholy dread, **awe; terror, horror,** mortal *or* abject fear; **phobia, funk** *or* blue funk <both

nonformal>; **panic,** terror; **cow-ardice** 491

2 **frighteningness, frightfulness, awfulness, scariness, fearfulness,** fearsomeness, **dreadfulness, horror, hideousness,** direness, **ghastliness,** grimness, grisliness, **gruesomeness,** ghoulishness; **creepiness, spookiness,** eeriness

3 **fearfulness; timidity, timorousness, hyness;** bashfulness, diffidence, stage fright; skittishness, goosiness <nonformal>

4 **apprehension,** apprehensiveness, **misgiving, qualm,** qualmishness; **anxiety** 126; doubt 954.2; foreboding

5 **trepidation,** trepidity, perturbation, **fear and trembling; quaking, agitation** 105.4; **uneasiness, disquiet,** disquietude, inquietude; palpitation; heebie-jeebies <nonformal>, icy clutch of dread; icy fingers or icy clutch of dread; gooseflesh, goose bumps <nonformal>; sweat, cold sweat; sinking stomach

6 **frightening, intimidation,** bullying, browbeating, cowing, bulldozing <nonformal>, hectoring; **demoralization,** war of nerves

7 **terrorization, terrorizing,** scaremongering, scare tactics; **terrorism,** terror tactics; reign of terror

8 **alarmist,** scaremonger; **terrorist**

9 **frightener, scarer, hair-raiser; bogey,** bogeyman, **bugaboo,** bugbear; hobgoblin; **scarecrow; horror, terror,** holy terror; **ogre, monster,** vampire, werewolf, ghoul; incubus, succubus, nightmare; witch, goblins; **ghost,** specter, phantom; Frankenstein, Dracula

VERBS **10 fear, be afraid; apprehend,** have qualms, misgive, eye askance; **dread,** stand in dread or awe of, be in mortal dread or terror of, stand in awe of; be on pins and needles; have one's heart in one's mouth, have one's heart skip

or miss a beat; **sweat,** break out in a cold sweat, sweat bullets <nonformal>

11 **take fright,** take alarm, push or press or hit the panic button <nonformal>; lose courage 491.8; pale, grow or turn pale, change or turn color; look as if one had seen a ghost; freeze, be paralyzed with fear; shit in one's pants and shit green <both nonformal>

12 **start,** startle, **jump,** jump out of one's skin; **shy,** boggle, jib; **panic,** stampede, skedaddle <nonformal>

13 **flinch, shrink, shy,** shy away from, draw back, recoil, **quail, cringe, wince, blink,** say or cry uncle; put one's tail between one's legs

14 **tremble, shake, quake, shiver, quiver, quaver; tremble** or **quake** or **shake** in one's boots or shoes, shake all over

15 **frighten,** fright, frighten or scare out of one's wits; **scare,** spook <nonformal>, scare one stiff or shitless <nonformal>, scare the life out of, scare the pants off of and scare hell out of and scare the shit out of <all nonformal>; scare one to death, scare the daylights or the living daylights or the wits or the shit out of <nonformal>; give one a fright or scare or turn; **alarm,** disquiet, raise apprehensions; **startle** 131.8; **unnerve, unman,** unstring; give one the creeps or the willies <nonformal>, make one's flesh creep, curl one's hair <nonformal>, make one's hair stand on end, make one's blood run cold, freeze or curdle the blood, make one's teeth chatter, make one tremble, make one shit one's pants or shit green <nonformal>

16 **put in fear,** put the fear of God into, **throw a scare into** <nonformal>; **panic,** stampede

17 **terrify, awe,** strike terror into; **horrify, appall, shock,** make one's flesh creep; **frighten out of one's wits** or senses; strike

dumb, **stun, stupefy, paralyze, petrify,** freeze

18 daunt, deter, stop in one's tracks, set back; **discourage, dishearten;** faze <nonformal>; **awe, overawe**

19 dismay, disconcert, appall, astound, confound, abash, put out, take aback

20 intimidate, cow, browbeat, bulldoze <nonformal>, bludgeon; **bully, hector, harass; bluster,** use terror or terrorist tactics; threaten 514.2; **demoralize**

21 frighten off, scare away, bluff off, put to flight

ADJS **22 afraid, scared,** scared to death <nonformal>, spooked <nonformal>; fear-struck; haunted with fear, phobic

23 fearful, fearing, fearsome, **in fear; cowardly** 491.10; **timorous, timid, shy,** mousy <nonformal>, afraid of one's own shadow; **shrinking,** bashful, diffident; scary; **skittish,** skittery <nonformal>, gun-shy, jumpy, goosy <nonformal>; **tremulous,** trembling, shivery; **nervous**

24 apprehensive, misgiving, antsy <nonformal>, **qualmish,** qualmy; anxious 126.6

25 frightened, frightened to death, in a funk or blue funk <nonformal>; **alarmed,** disquieted; consternated, **dismayed, daunted; startled** 131.13

26 terrified, terror-stricken; awe-stricken, awestruck; **horrified,** horror-stricken, horror-struck; **appalled, astounded, aghast;** frightened out of one's wits or mind, **scared to death, scared stiff** or **shitless; unnerved, unstrung, unmanned, undone, cowed,** awed, **intimidated; stunned, petrified, stupefied,** paralyzed, frozen; white as a sheet, ashen, blanched, pallid

27 panicky, panic-prone, panicked, in a panic, panic-stricken, panic-struck, terror-stricken, out of one's mind with fear

28 frightening, frightful; fearful, fearsome, fear-inspiring, nightmarish; **scary,** scaring, chilling; **alarming, startling,** disquieting, dismaying, disconcerting; **unnerving, daunting,** deterring, **deterrent,** discouraging, disheartening, fazing, stunning, stupefying, mind-boggling

29 terrifying, terrorful; **bloodcurdling, hair-raising** <nonformal>; petrifying, paralyzing, stunning, stupefying; **terrorizing, terror, terroristic**

30 terrible; horrid, horrible, horrifying, horrendous; **dreadful, dread,** dreaded; **awful;** awesome, awe-inspiring; **shocking, appalling,** astounding; **dire,** fell; formidable, redoubtable; **hideous, ghastly,** morbid, grim, grisly, gruesome, ghoulish, macabre

31 creepy, spooky, eerie, weird, uncanny

ADVS **32 fearfully, apprehensively, diffidently,** for fear of; **timorously, timidly, shyly,** shrinkingly; tremulously, tremblingly, quakingly, **with** or **in fear and trembling;** with heart in mouth, with bated breath

33 in fear, in terror, in awe; in mortal fear, in fear of one's life

34 frightfully, fearfully; alarmingly, startlingly, disquietingly, dismayingly, disconcertingly; **shockingly, appallingly,** astoundingly; **terribly; dreadfully, awfully; horridly, horribly,** horrifyingly

128 NERVOUSNESS

NOUNS **1 nervousness, nerves, disquiet, uneasiness, apprehensiveness,** disquietude, qualmishness, malaise, **qualm, qualms, misgiving;** case of nerves, attack of nerves; **agitation, trepidation; fear** 127; panic; **fidgets,** fidgetiness, jitteriness, jumpiness; tic, vellication; stage fright, buck fever <nonformal>; nervous stomach, butterflies in one's stomach <nonformal>

2 <nonformal terms> **jitters,** willies, **heebie-jeebies,** jimjams, **jumps, shakes,** quivers, trembles, butterflies, shivers, creeps, cold sweat

3 **tension,** tenseness, tautness, **strain, stress,** stress and strain, mental strain, nervous tension *or* strain, pressure

4 frayed nerves, frazzled nerves, jangled nerves, shattered nerves, raw nerves *or* nerve endings; neurosis; neurasthenia, nervous prostration, **nervous breakdown**

5 **nervous wreck,** wreck, a bundle of nerves

VERBS 6 **fidget,** have the fidgets; jitter, have the jitters, etc; **tense up; tremble**

7 lose self-control, go into hysterics; **go to pieces,** have a nervous breakdown, fall apart *or* to pieces, come apart, fall *or* come apart at the seams

8 <nonformal terms> **crack, crack up,** go haywire, **blow one's cork** *or* mind *or* stack, **flip,** flip one's lid *or* wig, freak out; come unglued *or* unstuck, go up the wall

9 **get on one's nerves, grate on, jar on,** put on edge, **set one's teeth on edge, go against the grain, send one up the wall** <nonformal>, drive one crazy

10 **unnerve, unman, undo, unstring,** unbrace, reduce to jelly, **demoralize, shake, upset,** psych out <nonformal>, dash, **crush,** overcome, prostrate

ADJS 11 **nervous; high-strung,** overstrung, highly strung, all nerves; **uneasy, apprehensive,** qualmish; nervous as a cat; **excitable; irritable,** edgy, **on edge,** nerves on edge, panicky, **fearful, frightened**

12 **jittery** <nonformal>, **jumpy,** skittish; **shaky,** shivery, quivery, in a quiver; tremulous, tremulant, trembly; jumpy as a cat on a hot tin roof; **fidgety; fluttery, all of a flutter** *or* twitter; **agitated;** shaking, trembling, quivering,

shivering; shook up *and* all shook up <both nonformal>

13 **tense,** tensed-up, uptight <nonformal>, **strained,** stretched tight, taut, unrelaxed, **under a strain**

14 **unnerved, unmanned, unstrung, undone,** reduced to jelly, unglued <nonformal>, **demoralized, shaken, upset,** dashed, stricken, **crushed; shot;** prostrate, prostrated

15 **unnerving, nerve-racking,** nerve-rending, nerve-jangling; jarring

ADVS 16 **nervously, shakily,** tremulously, tremblingly

129 UNNERVOUSNESS

NOUNS 1 **unnervousness, nervelessness; sangfroid, calmness, inexcitability** 106; **steadiness,** steady nerves; no nerves, iron nerves, nerves of steel, icy nerves

ADJS 2 **unnervous, nerveless,** without a nerve in one's body; iron-nerved, steel-nerved; coolheaded, **calm, inexcitable** 106.10; calm, cool, and collected; cool as a cucumber <nonformal>; **steady,** steady as a rock; without a tremor; unflinching, unfaltering, unwavering, unshrinking, unblinking; **relaxed**

130 EXPECTATION

NOUNS 1 **expectation, expectancy,** state of expectancy; **predictability,** predictableness; **anticipation, prospect; contemplation; probability** 967; **confidence, reliance** 952.1; **certainty** 969

2 optimism, eager expectation, **hope** 124; the light at the end of the tunnel

3 **suspense,** state of suspense, cliff-hanging *and* nail-biting <both nonformal>; **waiting,** hushed expectancy; uncertainty 970; **anxiety, dread, pessimism,** apprehension 126.1

4 **expectations,** prospects, outlook, hopes, apparent destiny *or*

fate, future prospects; likeli-
hoods, probabilities
VERBS **5 expect,** be expectant, **anticipate, have in prospect,** face,
think, **contemplate,** have in
mind, envision, envisage; **hope**
124.7; presume 950.10; dread;
take for granted; foresee 960.5
6 look forward to, reckon *or* calculate *or* count on, predict, foresee; look to, **look for, watch for,**
look out for, watch out for, be on
the watch *or* lookout for, keep a
good *or* sharp lookout for
7 be expected, be in store
8 await, wait, wait for, wait on *or*
upon; have *or* keep an eye out for,
lie in wait for; wait around *or*
about, watch, watch and wait;
bide one's time, bide, abide,
mark time; cool one's heels
<nonformal>; be on tenterhooks,
be on pins and needles, hold one's
breath, sweat out *or* sweat it out
<all non-
formal>; **wait up for,** stay up for
9 expect to, plan on 380.4,6,7
10 be as expected, turn out that
way, come as no surprise; **be just
like one; expect it of,** think that
way about, **not put it past** <non-
formal>; **impend,** be imminent
839.2; lead one to expect 133.13
ADJS **11 expectant,** expecting, in
anticipation; **anticipative,** anticipating, anticipatory; **holding
one's breath; waiting,** awaiting,
waiting for; forewarned, fore-
armed, forestalling, ready, prepared; **looking forward to,** looking for, watching for, on the watch
or lookout for; **eager;** sanguine,
optimistic, hopeful 124.11; certain 969.13
12 in suspense, on tenterhooks,
on pins and needles, **on edge,
with bated breath,** tense, keyed-
up, biting one's nails; anxious,
apprehensive; suspenseful,
cliff-hanging <nonformal>
**13 expected, anticipated,
awaited, predicted, foreseen;**
presumed 950.14; probable
967.6; **looked-for,** hoped-for;
due, promised; long-expected,

long-awaited, overdue; **in prospect, prospective; in view,** on
the horizon
14 to be expected, as expected, up
to *or* according to expectation,
just as one thought, just as predicted, **as one may have suspected,** as one might think *or*
suppose; **expected of, taken
for granted;** in character
ADVS **15 expectantly,** expectingly;
anticipatively, **anticipatingly;**
hopefully 124.14; **with bated
breath,** in hushed expectancy

131 INEXPECTATION

NOUNS **1 inexpectation, unan-
ticipation; unexpectedness;**
unforeseeableness, unpredictableness, unpredictability; unreadiness, unpreparedness;
the unforeseen, the last thing
one expects; **improbability**
968
2 surprise; astonishment 122.1,
2; shocker, **blow, eye-opener,**
revelation; **bolt out of** *or* **from
the blue,** thunderbolt; **bombshell,** bomb; blockbuster; sudden
turn *or* development, switch; surprise ending, kicker *or* joker *or*
catch <all nonformal>
3 start, shock, jar, jolt, turn
VERBS **4 not expect,** hardly expect,
not anticipate, not look for, not
bargain for, **not foresee,** not
think of, have no thought of,
think unlikely
**5 be startled, be taken by sur-
prise,** be taken aback, be given a
start; **start,** startle, **jump,** jump
out of one's skin; **shy,** flinch
**6 be unexpected, come un-
awares,** come as a surprise *or*
shock, come out of left field
<nonformal>, come out of no-
where, turn up, drop from the
clouds, appear like a bolt out of
the blue, come *or* burst like a
thunderclap *or* thunderbolt, burst
upon one, fall *or* pounce upon,
steal *or* creep up on
7 surprise, take by surprise, do
the unexpected, spring a surprise

<nonformal>, **open one's eyes; catch** or **take unawares,** take aback, pull up short, raise some eyebrows, **catch off-guard** 940.7, cross one up <nonformal>; throw a curve <nonformal>, come from an unexpected quarter, come upon without warning, spring or pounce upon; drop a bombshell; **blindside** <nonformal>, ambush, bushwhack; drop in on <nonformal>; give a surprise party; **astonish** 122.6

8 **startle, shock, electrify, jar, jolt, shake,** stun, **stagger, give one a turn** <nonformal>, give the shock of one's life, make one jump out of his skin, take aback, take one's breath away, bowl over <nonformal>; **frighten**

ADJS 9 **inexpectant,** nonexpectant; **unanticipative,** unanticipating; **unsuspecting, unaware; uninformed, unwarned,;** unready, unprepared; off one's guard 983.8

10 **unexpected, unanticipated, unlooked for,** unhoped for, unprepared for, **unforeseen;** unforeseeable, unpredictable, off-the-wall <nonformal>; **improbable** 968.3; contrary to expectation, more than expected, more than one bargained for; out of the blue, out of left field and from out in left field <both nonformal>; without warning, unheralded, unannounced; sudden 829.5; out-of-the-way, **extraordinary**

11 **surprising, astonishing** 122.12; eye-opening, eye-popping <nonformal>; **startling, shocking,** electrifying, staggering, stunning, jarring, jolting

12 **surprised,** openmouthed; **astonished** 122.9; **taken by surprise,** taken unawares

13 **startled, shocked, electrified,** jarred, jolted, shaken, shook <nonformal>, staggered, **given a turn** or **jar** or **jolt,** taken aback, bowled over <nonformal>, able to be knocked down with a feather

ADVS 14 **unexpectedly,** unan-

ticipatedly, improbably, implausibly, unpredictably, **unforeseeably, by surprise, unawares,** contrary to all expectation, when least expected, without notice or warning, in an unguarded moment; **out of a clear sky, out of the blue, like a bolt from the blue;** suddenly 829.9

15 **surprisingly, startlingly, to one's surprise; shockingly, staggeringly, astonishingly** 122.16

132 DISAPPOINTMENT

NOUNS 1 **disappointment,** bitter or cruel disappointment; **dashed hope, blighted hope,** hope deferred, forlorn hope; blow, buffet; **frustration,** discomfiture, bafflement, defeat, balk, foiling; **comedown,** setback, **letdown** <nonformal>; failure, fizzle <nonformal>, fiasco; **disillusionment** 976; tantalization, mirage

VERBS 2 **disappoint,** defeat expectation or hope; **dash,** dash or blight or blast or crush one's hope; **balk,** bilk, **thwart, frustrate, baffle, defeat,** foil, cross; put one's nose out of joint; **let down,** cast down; **disillusion** 976.2; tantalize, tease; dissatisfy

3 **be disappointing, let one down** <nonformal>, **not come up to expectation,** turn sour, disappoint one's expectations, fall short; peter out or fizzle or fizzle out <all nonformal>, not make it and not hack it <both nonformal>

4 **be disappointed,** run into a stone wall, be let down; look blue, laugh on the wrong side of one's mouth <nonformal>; be crestfallen or chapfallen

ADJS 5 **disappointed,** bitterly or sorely disappointed; **let down,** betrayed; **dashed,** blighted, blasted, crushed; **balked,** bilked, **thwarted, frustrated,** baffled, crossed, defeated, foiled; caught in one's own trap; disillusioned 976.5; crestfallen, chapfallen, out of countenance; soured; dissatisfied; regretful 113.8

6 disappointing, not up to expectation, falling short, out of the running, not up to one's hopes; tantalizing, teasing; **unsatisfactory**

133 PREMONITION

NOUNS **1 premonition, presentiment,** presagement; **hunch** 933.3, **feeling in one's bones;** prediction 961

2 **foreboding; apprehension, misgiving; wind of change**

3 **omen, portent; augury,** auspice, soothsay, prognostic, prognostication; **premonitory sign** or **symptom,** premonitory chill, **foretoken,** foretokening, foreshowing, prefiguration, presignification, **preindication,** indicant, indication, **sign, token,** type, **promise,** sign of the times; **foreshadowing, adumbration,** foreshadow, shadow

4 **warning, forewarning**

5 **harbinger, forerunner, precursor, herald,** announcer; presager, premonitor, foreshadower

6 <omens> bird of ill omen, owl, raven, stormy petrel; gathering clouds, clouds on the horizon, dark or black clouds, angry clouds, storm clouds; black cat; broken mirror; rainbow; ring around the moon; shooting star; woolly bear, groundhog

7 **ominousness, portentousness, portent,** significance, **meaning** 518, meaningfulness; fatefulness

8 **inauspiciousness, unpropitiousness, unfavorableness, unfortunateness, unluckiness,** ill-fatedness

9 **auspiciousness, propitiousness, favorableness; luckiness, fortunateness,** prosperousness, beneficence, benignancy, benevolence; good omen, good auspices

VERBS **10 foreshow, presage;** omen, be the omen of; **foreshadow, adumbrate; predict** 961.9; have an intimation, have a hunch <nonformal>, feel or know in one's bones

11 **forebode, bode,** portend; **threaten, menace, lower,** spell trouble; **warn, forewarn,** raise a warning flag, give pause; have a premonition or presentiment

12 **augur,** hint; **foretoken, preindicate,** presignify, **prefigure,** betoken, token, typify, **signify, mean** 518.8, spell, **indicate,** point to, **be a sign of,** show signs of

13 **promise, suggest, hint, imply,** give prospect of, make likely, give ground for expecting, **lead one to expect,** hold out hope, show promise, **bid fair, stand fair to**

14 **herald, harbinger, forerun; speak of, announce, proclaim; give notice, notify, talk about**

ADJS **15** augured, **foreshadowed, adumbrated, foreshown;** indicated, signified; **preindicated,** prognosticated, **foretokened,** prefigured; **presaged; promised; threatened;** predicted 961.14

16 **premonitory, forewarning,** monitory, presaging, **foretokening, preindicative,** indicative, prognostic, prefigurative; **significant, meaningful** 518.10, speaking; **foreshowing, foreshadowing;** pregnant or heavy with meaning; forerunning, precursory, precursive; intuitive 933.5; predictive 961.11

17 **ominous, portentous,** portending; **foreboding,** boding, **bodeful; inauspicious, ill-omened,** of ill or fatal omen, of evil portent, looming, looming over; fateful; apocalyptic; **unpropitious, unpromising, unfavorable, unfortunate, unlucky; sinister,** dark, black, gloomy, somber; **threatening, menacing, lowering;** bad, evil, ill, untoward; dire, baleful, baneful; **ill-fated,** ill-starred, star-crossed

18 **auspicious,** of good omen, of happy portent; **propitious, favorable,** favoring, fair, good; **promising,** of promise, full of promise; **fortunate, lucky,** prosperous; benign, benignant

ADVS **19 ominously, portentously, bodefully, forebodingly;** significantly, meaningly, meaningfully, sinisterly; **threateningly, menacingly,** loweringly
20 inauspiciously, unpropitiously, unpromisingly, unfavorably, unfortunately, unluckily
21 auspiciously, propitiously, promisingly, favorably; fortunately, luckily, happily; brightly

134 PATIENCE

NOUNS **1 patience; tolerance,** toleration, **acceptance; indulgence,** lenience, leniency 427; **forbearance,** forbearing; **sufferance, endurance; longsuffering,** long-sufferance; **stoicism,** fortitude, self-control; patience of Job; waiting game, waiting it out; **perseverance** 360
2 resignation, meekness, humility, humbleness; obedience; amenability; submission, **submissiveness** 433.3; acquiescence, compliance; **fatalism; quietude,** passivity, **passiveness** 329.1; passive resistance, nonviolent resistance, nonresistance; Quakerism
3 stoic, Spartan, man of iron; Job
VERBS **4 be patient,** forbear, bear with composure, **wait,** wait it out, play a waiting game, wait around, wait one's turn, watch for one's moment, keep one's shirt or pants on <nonformal>, not hold one's breath <nonformal>; contain oneself
5 endure, bear, stand, support, sustain, **suffer, tolerate, abide,** bide, live with; persevere; **bear up under, bear the brunt, bear with, put up with, stand for,** tolerate, carry one's cross, take what comes, take the bitter with the sweet, abide with, brook, brave, brave out, hang in there, keep it up
6 <nonformal terms> **take it,** take it on the chin, take it like a man, stand the gaff; bite the bullet;

hang in, hang in there, hang tough, tough or stick it out
7 accept, condone, countenance; overlook, not make an issue of, let go by, let pass; **reconcile oneself to,** resign oneself to, yield or submit to; obey; accustom or accommodate or adjust oneself to; accept one's fate, take things as they come, roll with the punches <nonformal>; **make the best of it,** make the best of a bad bargain, make a virtue of necessity; **grin and bear it,** shrug it off; take in good part, take in stride
8 take, pocket, swallow, down, stomach, eat, digest, disregard, turn a blind eye, ignore; swallow an insult, turn the other cheek, take it lying down
ADJS **9 patient,** patient as Job, Joblike; **tolerant,** tolerating, accepting; understanding, **indulgent,** lenient; **forbearing;** philosophical; **long-suffering; enduring,** endurant; stoic, stoical, Spartan; disciplined, self-controlled; **persevering**
10 resigned, reconciled; **meek,** humble; obedient, amenable, **submissive** 433.12; acquiescent, compliant; accommodating, adjusting, adapting, adaptive; unresisting, **passive** 329.6; **uncomplaining**
ADVS **11 patiently,** enduringly, stoically; **tolerantly, indulgently,** philosophically, more in sorrow than in anger; perseveringly
12 resignedly, meekly, submissively, passively, acquiescently, compliantly, uncomplainingly

135 IMPATIENCE

NOUNS **1 impatience,** impatientness; **anxiety, eagerness** 101; **restlessness,** restiveness, ants in one's pants <nonformal>; **disquiet,** disquietude, unquietness, uneasiness; sweat and lather and stew <all nonformal>; **fretfulness,** fretting, chafing; **impetuousness** 365.2; **haste** 401; excitement 105

2 **intolerance,** intoleration, unfor-
bearance, nonendurance

3 **the last straw,** the straw that
breaks the camel's back, the limit
of one's patience, all one can bear

VERBS 4 **be impatient; hasten**
401.4, 5; **itch to, burn to; champ
at the bit, pull at the leash;
chafe, fret, fuss,** squirm; **stew,**
sweat, get into a dither, get into
a stew <nonformal>, work oneself into a lather *or* sweat <non-
formal>, get excited; wait impatiently, sweat it out <nonfor-
mal>, pace the floor; beat the
gun, jump the gun <nonformal>,
go off half-cocked, shoot from the
hip

5 **have no patience with; lose patience,** run out of patience, have
had it <nonformal>, blow the
whistle <nonformal>

ADJS 6 **impatient; breathless;
champing at the bit, rarin' to go**
<nonformal>; **dying, anxious,
eager;** hopped-up *and* in a lather
and in a sweat *or* stew <all non-
formal>, excited 105.18; edgy, **on
edge; restless,** restive, unquiet,
uneasy; **fretful,** fretting, chafing,
squirming, squirmy, about to pee
or piss one's pants <nonformal>;
impetuous 365.9; **hasty** 401.9

7 **intolerant, unforbearing, un-
indulgent**

ADVS 8 **impatiently,** breathlessly;
anxiously; fretfully; restlessly,
restively, uneasily; intolerantly

136 PRIDE

NOUNS 1 **pride,** proudness,
pridefulness; **self-esteem, self-
respect,** self-confidence, self-
consequence, face; obstinate
or stiff-necked pride, stiff-
neckedness; **vanity, conceit**
140.4; haughtiness, **arrogance**
141; boastfulness 502.1; purse-
pride

2 **proud bearing,** pride of bearing, military *or* erect bearing,
dignity, stateliness, courtliness,
grandeur, **loftiness;** pride of
place; **nobility, majesty,** regality;
worthiness, augustness, ven-

erability; **sedateness, solemnity**
111, gravity, sobriety

3 proudling; stiff neck; egoist
140.5; boaster 502.5; the
proud

VERBS 4 **be proud,** hold up one's
head, hold one's head high, hold
oneself erect; look one in the face
or eye; stand on one's own two
feet

5 **take pride, pride oneself,
congratulate oneself,** hug oneself; **be proud of,** glory in, exult
in, **burst with pride**

6 **make proud,** do one's heart
good, do one proud <nonfor-
mal>, **gratify, elate,** flush

7 save face, save one's face, guard
or preserve one's honor, be jealous of one's good name

ADJS 8 **proud, prideful,** proudful
<nonformal>; **self-esteeming,
self-respecting;** self-confident,
self-reliant, **independent, self-
sufficient;** proudhearted; proud-
looking; proud as Punch, proud
as a peacock; erect, **stiff-necked;**
purse-proud

9 **vain, conceited** 140.11;
haughty, **arrogant** 141.9; boastful
502.10

10 **puffed up,** swollen, bloated,
puffed-up with pride; flushed
with pride

11 **lofty, elevated,** triumphal, high,
high-flown, highfalutin *and* highfaluting <both nonformal>, high-
toned <nonformal>; high-
minded

12 **dignified, stately, imposing,
grand, courtly,** aristocratic;
noble, majestic, regal, royal;
worthy, **august, venerable;** statuesque; **sedate, solemn** 111.3,
sober, grave

ADVS 13 **proudly,** pridefully, **with
pride;** self-respectingly, self-
confidently, self-reliantly, independently; erectly, with head held
high, with nose in air; stiffneckedly

14 **dignifiedly, with dignity;** nobly,
stately, imposingly, loftily,
grandly, magisterially; majestically, regally, royally; worthily,

augustly, venerably; sedately, solemnly, soberly, gravely

137 HUMILITY

NOUNS **1 humility, humbleness, meekness; lowliness,** ingloriousness, undistinguishedness; unimportance 997; innocuousness 998.9; submissiveness 433.3; **modesty,** unpretentiousness 139.1; plainness, simpleness

2 humiliation, egg on one's face <nonformal>, chagrin, **embarrassment** 96.4, egg on one's face <nonformal>; **abasement,** debasement, letdown, setdown; **comedown,** deflation, wounded or humbled pride; self-diminishment, **self-abasement, self-abnegation** 652.1; **shame, disgrace;** shamefacedness

3 condescension, condescendence, deigning, lowering oneself, stooping from one's high place

VERBS **4 humiliate, humble; embarrass** 96.15; put out; **shame, disgrace,** put to shame; **deflate,** prick one's balloon

5 abase, debase, crush, abash, **degrade, reduce,** diminish, **demean,** lower, **bring low,** bring down, trip up, take down, set down, put in one's place, put down, dump *and* dump on <both nonformal>, knock one off his perch; take down a peg *or* notch or two <nonformal>, make a fool *or* an ass *or* a monkey of one

6 <nonformal terms> beat *or* knock *or* **cut one down to size,** take the starch out of, take the wind out of one's sails; put one's nose out of joint

7 humble oneself, demean oneself, abase oneself, climb down *and* get down from one's high horse <both nonformal>; put one's pride in one's pocket; **eat humble pie,** eat crow *or* dirt, eat one's words, swallow one's pride, lick the dust, take *or* eat shit <nonformal>; come on bended

knee, come hat in hand; go down on one's knees; pull in one's horns; come down a peg *or* a peg or two; **deprecate** *or* **deprecate oneself,** diminish oneself; kiss one's ass <nonformal> 138.7

8 condescend, deign, vouchsafe; stoop, descend; lower *or* demean oneself, set one's dignity aside *or* to one side; **patronize;** be so good as to, so forget oneself, dirty *or* soil one's hands; talk down to

9 be humiliated; be crushed, feel small, feel cheap, look foolish *or* silly, be ready to sink through the floor; **take shame, be ashamed, feel ashamed of oneself;** bite one's tongue; hang one's head, hide one's face, not dare to show one's face, not have a word to say for oneself

ADJS **10 humble, lowly,** low, **poor, mean,** small, inglorious, undistinguished; unimportant 997.16; innocuous; biddable, teachable 570.18; **modest, unpretentious** 139.9; **plain, simple,** homely

11 humble-hearted, humble-spirited; **meek,** meek-hearted, lamblike; **abject,** submissive 433.12

12 self-abasing, self-abnegating, self-deprecating, self-depreciating 139.10, self-doubting

13 humbled, reduced, diminished, lowered, brought down *or* low; on one's knees

14 humiliated, humbled, **embarrassed, chagrined, abashed, crushed;** blushing, red-faced, **ashamed,** shamefaced; crestfallen, chapfallen, hangdog

15 humiliating, humbling, chastening, mortifying, **embarrassing,** crushing

ADVS **16 humbly, meekly;** modestly 139.14; with due deference, with bated breath; submissively 433.17; **abjectly,** on bended knee, **on one's knees,** with one's tail between one's legs, hat-in-hand

138 SERVILITY

NOUNS **1 servility, slavishness,** subservience *or* subserviency, menialness, abjectness, **baseness,** meanness; **submissiveness** 433.3; slavery, peonage

2 obsequiousness, sycophancy, toadyism; sponging; **ingratiation,** insinuation; **truckling, fawning, toadying,** groveling, cringing, **bootlicking** <nonformal>, back scratching; **apple-polishing** *and* **handshaking** <both nonformal>; ass-licking *and* ass-kissing *and* brown-nosing *and* sucking up <all nonformal>; obeisance, prostration

3 sycophant, flatterer, toady, lickspittle, **truckler, fawner** kowtower, groveler, cringer; flunky; **puppet,** minion, lap dog, **tool,** cat's-paw, dupe, slave, peon; mealymouth

4 <nonformal terms> **apple-polisher, ass-kisser, brown-nose,** brown-noser, ass-licker, suck-ass; **backslapper,** back-scratcher; **bootlicker,** bootlick; **handshaker; yes-man, stooge**

5 parasite, barnacle, leech; **sponger,** sponge <nonformal>, freeloader <nonformal>; deadbeat <nonformal>

6 hanger-on, adherent, appendage, **dependent, satellite, follower,** cohort, retainer, servant, man, **henchman**

VERBS **7 fawn, truckle; flatter; toady; bootlick** <nonformal>, lickspittle, lick one's shoes, lick the feet of; **grovel,** crawl, creep, cower, cringe, crouch, stoop, kneel, bend the knee, prostrate oneself, throw oneself at the feet of, fall at one's feet, kiss *or* lick *or* suck one's ass *and* brown-nose <all nonformal>, kiss one's feet, make a doormat of oneself; **kowtow, bow and scrape**

8 toady to, truckle to, pander to, cater to; wait on *or* **upon,** wait on hand and foot, dance attendance, do *or* jump at the bidding of

9 curry favor, court, pay court to, run after <nonformal>, dance attendance on; **shine up to,** make up to <nonformal>; **suck up to** *and* **play up to** *and* act up to <all nonformal>; be a yes-man <nonformal>; fall over *or* all over <nonformal>; **polish the apple** <nonformal>

10 ingratiate oneself, insinuate oneself, worm oneself in, creep into the good graces of, get in with *or* next to <nonformal>, **get on the good** *or* **right side of,** rub the right way <nonformal>

11 attach oneself to, hang on the skirts of, become an appendage of, **follow; follow the crowd, get on the bandwagon**

12 sponge *and* **sponge on** *and* **sponge off of** <all nonformal>; feed on, fatten on, batten on, live off of, use as a meal ticket

ADJS **13 servile, slavish,** subservient, **menial, base,** mean; **submissive** 433.12

14 obsequious, flattering, sycophantic, fawning, flattering, truckling, ingratiating, toadying, bootlicking *and* back scratching *and* backslapping *and* ass-licking *and* brown-nosing <all nonformal>; **groveling,** sniveling, cringing, cowering, crawling; **parasitic,** leechlike, sponging <nonformal>; **abject,** beggarly, hangdog; obeisant, prostrate, on one's knees, on bended knee

ADVS **15 servilely, slavishly,** subserviently, menially; **submissively** 433.17

16 obsequiously, sycophantically, ingratiatingly, fawningly, trucklingly; hat-in-hand, cap-in-hand; **abjectly,** on one's knees; parasitically

139 MODESTY

NOUNS **1 modesty, meekness;** humility 137; **unpretentiousness,** unpresumptuousness, **unostentatiousness,** unobtrusiveness

2 self-effacement, self-depreciation, self-deprecation, self-

detraction, **diffidence;** hiding
one's light under a bushel; low
self-esteem, lack of self-confidence

3 **reserve, restraint, constraint,**
retiring disposition; low visibility,
low profile

4 **shyness, timidity,** timidness,
timorousness, **bashfulness,**
shamefacedness; **coyness, demureness,** mousiness; self-
consciousness; stagefright

5 **blushing, flushing,** coloring;
blush, flush, suffusion

6 shrinking violet, mouse

VERBS 7 **efface oneself; have low
self-esteem;** retire into one's
shell, **keep in the background,**
not thrust oneself forward, **keep
a low profile,** remain in the
shade, take a back seat *and* play
second fiddle <both nonformal>,
hide one's face, hide one's light
under a bushel, avoid the limelight

8 **blush, flush, color,** change
color, color up, redden, get red
in the face; squirm with embarrassment

ADJS 9 **modest, meek;** humble; **unpretentious,** unpretending, **unassuming,** unpresuming, unpre-
sumptuous, **unostentatious,** unobtrusive, unimposing, unboast-
ful; unambitious, unaspiring

10 **self-effacing, self-deprecia-
tive, self-depreciating,** self-
deprecating; **diffident,** deprecatory, deprecative, self-doubting,
unself-confident, unsure of oneself; low in self-esteem

11 **reserved, restrained, constrained;** quiet; low-keyed,
keeping low visibility *or* a low
profile; **backward, retiring,
shrinking**

12 **shy, timid,** timorous, **bashful,**
shamefaced; **coy, demure,** skittish, mousy; stammering, inarticulate

13 **blushing; flushed,** red, ruddy,
red-faced, red in the face; **sheepish; embarrassed**

ADVS 14 **modestly, meekly;** humbly; **unpretentiously,** unpretend-

ingly, **unassumingly, unosten-
tatiously,** unobtrusively

15 **shyly, timidly,** timorously, **bash-
fully, coyly, demurely,** diffidently; **shamefacedly, sheepishly,** blushingly

140 VANITY

NOUNS 1 **vanity, vainness;** overweening pride; **self-importance,**
consequentiality, **self-esteem,**
self-respect, self-assumption;
self-admiration, self-delight,
self-worship, **self-love,** self-
infatuation, narcissism; autoeroticism, masturbation; **self-
satisfaction, self-content,** ego
trip <nonformal>, self-approbation, self-congratulation, self-
complacency, **smugness,** complacency; vainglory, vaingloriousness

2 **pride** 136; arrogance 141;
boastfulness 502.1

3 **egotism, egoism, ego** <nonfor-
mal>, self-interest; **egocentricity,**
egocentrism, self-centeredness;
selfishness 651

4 **conceit, conceitedness, self-
conceit, self-conceitedness, immodesty,** side, **self-assertiveness;**
chestiness <nonformal>, swelled
head, big head, large hat size;
cockiness <nonformal>, pertness, perkiness; obtrusiveness,
bumptiousness

5 **egotist, egoist, egocentric,** individualist; narcissist, narcist,
Narcissus; **swellhead** <nonfor-
mal>, **braggart** 502.5, know-it-all
or know-all, smart-ass *and* wise-
ass <both nonformal>, smart aleck, no modest violet

VERBS 6 **be stuck on oneself**
<nonformal>, be impressed *or*
overly impressed with oneself;
ego-trip *and* be *or* go on an ego
trip <all nonformal>; think well
of oneself, think one is it *or* one's
shit doesn't stink <nonformal>,
get too big for one's breeches,
have a swelled head, know it all,
have no false modesty, have no
self-doubt, love the sound of one's
own voice; fish for compliments;

toot one's own horn, **boast**
502.6,7; be vain as a peacock

7 puff up, inflate, swell; go to
one's head, turn one's head

ADJS **8 vain, vainglorious,** over-
proud, overweening; **self-
important, self-esteeming,** having high self-esteem *or* self-valua-
tion, self-respecting, self-assum-
ing, consequential; **self-admiring,** self-delighting, self-worship-
ing, self-loving, narcissistic; **self-
satisfied, self-content,** self-contented, self-approving, self-con-
gratulating, self-congratulatory,
self-complacent, **smug,** complacent

9 proud 136.8; arrogant 141.9;
boastful 502.10

10 egotistic, egotistical, egoistic,
egoistical, self-interested; **egocentric,** self-centered, self-
obsessed, narcissistic; selfish
651.5

**11 conceited, self-conceited, im-
modest,** self-opinionated; **stuck-
up** <nonformal>, **puffed up,**
chesty <nonformal>; swollen-
headed, **big-headed** *and* too big
for one's shoes *or* britches *and*
cocky <all nonformal>; pert,
perk, perky; peacockish, peacocky; know-all *or* know-it-all,
smart-ass *and* wise-ass <both
nonformal>, smarty, smart-
alecky; aggressively self-confident, obtrusive, bumptious

12 stuck on oneself <nonformal>,
full of oneself, all wrapped up in
oneself

ADVS **13 vainly,** self-importantly;
egotistically, egoistically; **con-
ceitedly,** immodestly; cockily
<nonformal>, pertly, perkily

141 ARROGANCE

NOUNS **1 arrogance; overbearingness, overbearing pride, overweening pride,** domineering;
pride, proudness; sin of pride;
haughtiness, hauteur; loftiness;
stuckupness *and* uppishness *and*
uppityness <all nonformal>,
hoity-toity; high horse <nonfor-

mal>; **condescension,** patronizing, patronizing attitude

2 presumptuousness, presumption, overweening, overweeningness; hubris; **insolence**
142

**3 lordliness, imperiousness,
high-and-mightiness; elit-
ism**

4 aloofness, standoffishness,
coolness, distantness, remoteness

5 disdainfulness, disdain, aristocratic disdain, **contemptuousness, superciliousness,** con-
tumeliousness, cavalierness

6 snobbery, snobbishness, snob-
biness, snobbism; **priggishness,
priggery; snootiness** *and* snottiness *and* sniffiness *and* high-
hattedness <all nonformal>

7 snob, prig; elitist; highbrow
and egghead <both nonformal>,
Brahmin, mandarin; name-
dropper

VERBS **8 give oneself airs** 501.14;
**hold one's nose in the air, look
down one's nose; mount** *or* get
on one's high horse *and* ride the
high horse <all nonformal>; **condescend, patronize, deign,**
stoop, descend, lower *or* demean
oneself, so forget oneself, dirty *or*
soil one's hands; talk down to

ADJS **9 arrogant, overbearing, superior,** domineering, **proud,
haughty; lofty; high-flown,
high-falutin** *and* high-faluting
<both nonformal>; **stuck-up** *and*
uppish *and* uppity *and* **upstage**
<all nonformal>; **hoity-toity,** big,
big as you please; on one's high
horse; **condescending, patronizing**

10 presumptuous, presuming, assuming, overweening, would-be,
self-elect, self-elected, self-
appointed, self-proclaimed; **insolent**

11 lordly, imperious, aristocratic;
hubristic; masterful, magisterial,
high-and-mighty; elitist; dictatorial 417.16

12 aloof, standoffish, standoff, offish <nonformal>, chilly, cool,

distant, remote, above all that; Olympian

13 disdainful, dismissive, **contemptuous, supercilious,** contumelious, cavalier

14 snobbish, snobby, **priggish,** snippy <nonformal>; **snooty** and **snotty** and sniffy <all nonformal>; **high-hat** and high-hatted and high-hatty <all nonformal>

ADVS **15 arrogantly, haughtily, proudly,** aloofly; **condescendingly, patronizingly;** loftily; **imperiously, magisterially; disdainfully, contemptuously,** superciliously, contumeliously; with nose in air, with head held high

16 presumptuously, overweeningly, aristocratically; hubristically; **insolently**

17 snobbishly, snobbily, **priggishly;** snootily and snottily <both nonformal>

142 INSOLENCE

NOUNS **1 insolence; presumption,** presumptuousness; **audacity, effrontery,** boldness, assurance, bumptiousness; hubris; overweening, overweeningness; **contempt** 157, **contemptuousness,** contumely; **disdain** 141.5; **arrogance** 141, uppishness and uppityness <both nonformal>; obtrusiveness, pushiness <nonformal>

2 impudence, impertinence, flippancy, pertness, **sauciness,** sassiness <nonformal>, **cockiness,** and cheekiness <both nonformal>, freshness <nonformal>, **brazenness,** brazenfacedness, brassiness <nonformal>, **rudeness** 505.1, **brashness,** disrespect, disrespectfulness, derision, ridicule 508

3 <nonformal terms> **cheek,** face, brass, **nerve, gall, chutzpah,** crust

4 sauce and sass and lip <nonformal>, **back talk**

5 <impudent person> minx, hussy; whippersnapper, puppy,

pup, upstart; boldface, brazenface; swaggerer 503.2

6 <nonformal terms> smart aleck, wise-ass

VERBS **7 have the audacity, have the cheek; have the gall** or a nerve or one's nerve <nonformal>; **get fresh** <nonformal>, get smart <nonformal>, forget one's place, **dare, presume,** take liberties, make bold or free; hold in contempt 157.3, ridicule, taunt, deride 508.8

8 sauce and sass <both nonformal>, **talk back,** answer back, give one the lip <nonformal>, provoke

ADJS **9 insolent,** insulting; **presumptuous,** presuming, overpresumptuous, overweening; **audacious, bold,** assured, hardy, bumptious; **contemptuous** 157.8, contumelious; **disdainful** 141.13, **arrogant** 141.9, uppish and uppity <both nonformal>; hubristic; forward, pushy <nonformal>, obtrusive, pushy <nonformal>, familiar, cool, cold

10 impudent, impertinent, pert, flip <nonformal>, flippant, **cocky** and cheeky and **fresh** and facy and crusty and nervy <all nonformal>; uncalled-for, gratuitous, biggety <nonformal>; **rude** 505.4,6, disrespectful, derisive 508.12, brash, bluff; **saucy,** sassy <nonformal>; smart or smart-alecky <nonformal>, smart-ass or wise-ass <nonformal>

11 brazen, brazenfaced, barefaced, brassy, **bold,** bold as brass <nonformal>, unblushing, unabashed, **shameless; swaggering** 503.4

ADVS **12 insolently, audaciously,** bumptiously, contumeliously; **arrogantly** 141.15; **presumptuously,** obtrusively, pushily <nonformal>; **disdainfully** 141.15

13 impudently, impertinently, pertly, flippantly, **cockily** and cheekily <both nonformal>, saucily; **rudely** 505.8, brashly, disrespectfully, contemptuously 157.9, derisively 508.15

14 brazenly, brazenfacedly, **boldly,** boldfacedly, **shamelessly,** unblushingly

143 KINDNESS, BENEVOLENCE

NOUNS **1 kindness, kindliness,** kindly disposition; **benignity; goodness, decency,** niceness; **graciousness; kindheartedness,** goodheartedness, warmheartedness, softheartedness, tenderheartedness, warmth, **loving kindness; soul of kindness,** heart of gold; **brotherhood, sympathy,** fraternal feeling, feeling of kinship; **pity** 145, **mercy, compassion; humaneness,** humanity; charitableness

2 good nature, good humor, good disposition, good temper, good-naturedness, goodhumoredness, bonhomie; **amiability,** affability, geniality, cordiality; **gentleness,** mildness, lenity

3 considerateness, consideration, thoughtfulness, mindfulness, heedfulness, regardfulness, attentiveness, **solicitousness,** solicitude, thought, regard, concern, delicacy, **sensitivity,** tact, tactfulness; indulgence, toleration, leniency 427; **helpfulness,** agreeableness

4 benevolence, beneficence, charity, charitableness, **philanthropy; altruism,** philanthropism, **humanitarianism,** do-goodism; **goodwill,** grace, brotherly love, charity, Christian charity or love, love of mankind, good will to or toward man, love; brotherhood of man; **bigheartedness; generosity** 485; giving 478

5 welfare; welfare work, social service, social welfare, social work; child welfa e, etc; public welfare; welfare state, welfare statism

6 benevolences, philanthropies, charities; works, **good works,** public service

7 act of kindness, kindness, favor, mercy, **benefit,** benefaction, benevolence, benignity, blessing, **service, good turn, good** or **kind deed,** *mitzvah* <Heb>, office, good offices, obligation, grace, act of grace, courtesy, labor of love

8 philanthropist, altruist, humanitarian, man of good will, **do-gooder,** power for good; welfare worker, social worker, caseworker; almsgiver; Robin Hood, Lady Bountiful

VERBS **9 be kind,** be good or nice, show kindness; treat well, do right by; favor, oblige, accommodate

10 be considerate, consider, respect, regard, think of, **be thoughtful of,** have consideration or regard for; be at one's service, fuss over one, spoil one <nonformal>

11 be benevolent, bear good will, wish well, have one's heart in the right place; follow the golden rule; make love not war

12 do a favor, do good, do a good turn or deed, do a *mitzvah* <Heb>, use one's good offices; benefit, help 449.11

ADJS **13 kind, kindly,** kindlydisposed; **benign; good as gold, good, nice, decent; gracious; kindhearted, warm, warmhearted,** softhearted, tenderhearted, tender, loving, affectionate; **sympathetic,** sympathizing, **compassionate** 145.7, merciful; brotherly, fraternal; humane, human; charitable

14 good-natured, good-humored, good-tempered, sweet, sweet-tempered; amiable, affable, genial, cordial; gentle, mild, mildmannered; easy, easy to get along with, able to take a joke, **agreeable**

15 benevolent, charitable, beneficent, philanthropic, altruistic, humanitarian; **bighearted; generous** 485.4; eleemosynary

16 considerate, thoughtful, mindful, heedful, regardful, solicitous, attentive, delicate, tactful, mindful of others; complaisant, **accommodating**, accommodative, at one's service, **helpful**, agreeable, **obliging**, indulgent, tolerant, lenient 427.7

17 well-meaning, well-meant, well-disposed, **well-intentioned**

ADVS **18 kindly**, benignly; **kindheartedly, warmly**, warmheartedly, softheartedly, tenderheartedly; humanely, humanly

19 good-naturedly, good-humoredly; sweetly; amiably, affably, genially, cordially; graciously

20 benevolently, beneficently, charitably, philanthropically, altruistically, bigheartedly

21 considerately, thoughtfully, mindfully, heedfully, regardfully, tactfully, **sensitively**, solicitously, attentively

144 UNKINDNESS, MALEVOLENCE

NOUNS **1 unkindness, unkindliness; unamiability**, uncordiality, ungraciousness, inhospitality; uncompassionateness; disagreeableness

2 unbenevolentness, uncharitableness, ungenerousness

3 inconsiderateness, inconsideration, unthoughtfulness, unmindfulness, unheedfulness, **thoughtlessness**, heedlessness, forgetfulness; **unhelpfulness**

4 malevolence, ill will, bad will, bad blood, bad temper, ill nature, evil disposition; evil eye, whammy <nonformal>

5 malice, maliciousness, maleficence; malignance *or* **malignancy**, malignity; **meanness** *and* orneriness *and* cussedness *and* bitchiness <all nonformal>, hatefulness, nastiness, invidiousness; **wickedness**, iniquitousness 654.4; deviltry, devilment; malice aforethought, evil intent; **harmfulness, noxiousness** 999.5

6 spite, despite; **spitefulness**, cat-

tiness; gloating pleasure, unwholesome *or* unholy joy

7 rancor, virulence, venom, vitriol, gall

8 causticity, causticness, corros'veness, mordancy; **acrimony, asperity**, acidity, acidulousness, acerbity, **bitterness**, tartness; sharpness, keenness, incisiveness, trenchancy

9 harshness, roughness, ungentleness; **severity**, austerity, hardness, sternness, grimness, inclemency; stringency

10 heartlessness, unfeeling, unresponsiveness, insensitivity, coldness, **cold-heartedness**, cold-bloodedness; **hardheartedness**, hardness, heart of stone; **callousness; obduracy; pitilessness, unmercifulness** 146.1

11 cruelty, cruelness, sadism, wanton cruelty; **ruthlessness** 146.1; **inhumanity**, atrociousness; **brutality**, mindless *or* senseless brutality, brutalness, **brutishness, bestiality, animality**, beastliness; **barbarity**, barbarousness, vandalism; **savagery, viciousness, violence**, fiendishness; **child abuse** 389.2; truculence, fierceness, **ferocity**; piling on <nonformal>; bloodthirstiness, bloodlust, bloodiness, bloody-mindedness, sanguineousness; cannibalism

12 act of cruelty, atrocity, cruelty, brutality, bestiality, barbarity, inhumanity

13 bad deed, disservice, ill turn, bad turn

14 beast, animal, brute, monster, devil, devil incarnate; **sadist**, torturer, tormenter

VERBS **15 bear malice** *or* ill will; **harshen, dehumanize**, brutalize, bestialize; torture, torment; **have a cruel streak**, go for the jugular, have the killer instinct

ADJS **16 unkind, unkindly**, ill; **unamiable**, disagreeable, **uncordial, ungracious**, inhospitable, unaffectionate, unloving;

unsympathetic, unsympathizing, uncompassionate

17 unbenevolent, uncharitable, unphilanthropic, unaltruistic, ungenerous

18 inconsiderate, unthoughtful, unmindful, unheedful, disregardful, thoughtless, heedless, mindless, unthinking, forgetful; tactless, insensitive; unhelpful, unaccommodating, unobliging, disobliging, uncooperative

19 malevolent, ill-disposed, ill-natured, ill-intentioned

20 malicious, maleficent, malefic; malignant, malign; mean and ornery and cussed and bitchy <all nonformal>, hateful, nasty, baleful, invidious; wicked, iniquitous 654.16; harmful, noxious 999.12

21 spiteful; catty, cattish, bitchy <nonformal>; snide

22 rancorous, virulent, vitriolic; venomous

23 caustic, mordant, mordacious, corrosive, corroding; acrimonious, acrid, acid, acidic, acidulous, acerb, acerbic, bitter, tart; sharp, keen, incisive, trenchant, cutting, penetrating, piercing, biting, stinging, stabbing, scathing, scorching, withering, scurrilous, abusive, foulmouthed

24 harsh, rough, rugged; severe, austere, stringent, hard, stern, dour, grim, unsparing

25 heartless, unfeeling, unnatural, unresponsive, insensitive, cold, coldhearted, cold-blooded; hard, hardened, hard-hearted; callous, calloused; obdurate; unmerciful 146.3

26 cruel, cruel-hearted, sadistic; ruthless 146.3; brutal, brutish, brute, bestial, beastly, animal; mindless, soulless, insensate, senseless, subhuman, dehumanized, brutalized; slavering; barbarous, barbaric, uncivilized, unchristian; savage, ferocious, feral, vicious, fierce, atrocious, truculent, fell; inhuman, inhumane, unhuman; fiendish,

fiendlike; demoniacal, diabolic, diabolical, devilish, satanic, hellish, infernal; bloodthirsty, bloody-minded, bloody, sanguinary; cannibalistic, anthropophagous; murderous

ADVS 27 unkindly, ill; unbenignly; unamiably, disagreeably, uncordially, ungraciously, inhospitably, ungenially, unaffectionately, unlovingly; unsympathetically, uncompassionately

28 unbenevolently, uncharitably, unphilanthropically, unaltruistically, ungenerously

29 inconsiderately, unthoughtfully, thoughtlessly, heedlessly, unthinkingly; unhelpfully, uncooperatively

30 malevolently, maliciously, malignantly; meanly and cussedly and bitchily and cattily <all nonformal>, hatefully, nastily, invidiously, balefully; wickedly, iniquitously 654.19; harmfully, noxiously 999.15, spitefully; with bad intent, with malice aforethought

31 rancorously, virulently, vitriolically; venomously

32 caustically, mordantly, mordaciously, corrosively, corrodingly; acrimoniously, acridly, acidly, acerbically, bitterly, tartly; sharply, keenly, incisively, trenchantly, cuttingly, penetratingly, piercingly, bitingly, stingingly, stabbingly, scathingly, scorchingly, witheringly, scurrilously, abusively

33 harshly, roughly; severely, austerely, stringently, sternly, grimly, inclemently, unsparingly

34 heartlessly, soullessly, unfeelingly, callously, coldheartedly; cold-bloodedly, in cold blood

35 cruelly, brutally, brutishly, bestially, subhumanly, slaveringly; barbarously, savagely, ferociously, ferally, viciously, fiercely, atrociously, truculently; ruthlessly 146.4; inhumanely, inhumanly, unhumanly; fiendishly, diabolically, devilishly

145 PITY

NOUNS 1 **pity, sympathy,** feeling, **commiseration,** condolence, condolences; **compassion, mercy,** ruth, rue, humanity; **sensitivity; clemency,** quarter, reprieve, mitigation, relief 120, favor, grace; **leniency,** lenity, gentleness; forbearance; **kindness, benevolence** 143; pardon, **forgiveness** 601.1; self-pity; **pathos**

2 **compassionateness, mercifulness,** ruthfulness, ruefulness, softheartedness, tenderness, gentleness

VERBS 3 **pity, be** or **feel sorry for,** feel sorrow for; **commiserate; open one's heart; sympathize, sympathize with,** feel for, weep for, lament for, bleed, bleed for

4 **have pity, have mercy upon, take pity on** or **upon;** melt, thaw; relent, forbear, relax, give quarter, spare, go easy on and let up or ease up on <all nonformal>; **reprieve, pardon,** remit, **forgive** 601.4; put out of one's misery

5 <excite pity> **move, touch,** affect, reach, **soften,** melt, melt the heart, appeal to one's better feelings; sadden, grieve 112.17

6 **beg for mercy,** ask for pity, cry for quarter; fall on one's knees, throw oneself at the feet of

ADJS 7 **pitying, sympathetic,** sympathizing, commiserative, condolent, understanding; **compassionate, merciful,** ruthful, rueful, **clement,** gentle, soft, melting, bleeding, tender, **tenderhearted,** softhearted, warmhearted; **humane,** human; lenient, forbearant 427.7

8 **pitiful, pitiable, pathetic, piteous, touching, moving, affecting,** heartrending, grievous, doleful 112.26

9 self-pitying, self-pitiful, sorry for oneself

ADVS 10 **pitifully,** sympathetically; **compassionately, mercifully,** ruthfully, ruefully, clemently

146 PITILESSNESS

NOUNS 1 **pitilessness, unmercifulness, uncompassionateness, ruthlessness,** inclemency, relentlessness, inexorableness, unyieldingness 361.2, unforgivingness; **heartlessness,** heart of stone, hardness, steeliness, flintiness, harshness, **cruelty** 144.11; remorselessness, unremorsefulness; short shrift, tender mercies

VERBS 2 **show no mercy,** give no quarter, turn a deaf ear, claim one's pound of flesh, harden or steel one's heart

ADJS 3 **pitiless,** unpitying, unpitiful; **unsympathetic,** unsympathizing; **uncompassionate; merciless, unmerciful,** without mercy, **ruthless,** dog-eat-dog; unfeeling, relentless, inexorable, unyielding 361.9, unforgiving; **heartless,** hard, hard as nails, steely, flinty, harsh, savage, **cruel;** remorseless, unremorseful

ADVS 4 **pitilessly,** unsympathetically; mercilessly, **unmercifully, ruthlessly,** uncompassionately, relentlessly, inexorably, unyieldingly, unforgivingly; heartlessly, harshly, savagely, cruelly; remorselessly, unremorsefully

147 CONDOLENCE

NOUNS 1 **condolence, condolences, consolation,** comfort, balm, **sympathy,** sharing of grief or sorrow

VERBS 2 **condole with, commiserate, sympathize with,** feel with, empathize with, express sympathy for, send one's condolences; pity 145.3; **console,** comfort, speak soothing words; sorrow with, share or help bear one's grief, grieve or weep with, grieve or weep for, share one's sorrow

ADJS 3 condoling, comforting, commiserating, **sympathetic,** empathic, empathetic; pitying 145.7

148 FORGIVENESS

NOUNS **1 forgiveness,** forgiving-
ness; **condoning,** overlooking,
disregard; **patience** 134; **indulgence, forbearance,** long-
suffering; **kindness, benevolence** 143; **magnanimity** 652.2;
brooking, **tolerance** 978.4

  2 pardon, excuse, sparing, **amnesty,** indemnity, exemption,
immunity, reprieve, grace; **absolution,** shrift, remission; redemption; **exoneration, exculpation** 601.1

VERBS **3 forgive, pardon, excuse,**
give *or* grant forgiveness, spare;
grant amnesty to, grant immunity
or exemption; hear confession,
absolve, remit, give absolution,
shrive, grant remission; **exonerate, exculpate** 601.4; wipe the
slate clean

  4 condone 134.7, **overlook, disregard, ignore,** accept, give one
another chance, let one off this
time *and* let one off easy <both
nonformal>, close *or* shut one's
eyes to, **blink** *or* **wink at,** connive
at; allow for, make allowances
for; bear with, endure, regard
with indulgence; turn the other
cheek, bury *or* hide one's head in
the sand

  5 forget, forgive and forget, dismiss from one's thoughts, not
give it another *or* a second
thought, let it go <nonformal>,
let it pass, **let bygones be bygones;** write off; bury the
hatchet

ADJS **6 forgiving,** sparing, conciliatory; **kind, benevolent** 143.15;
magnanimous, generous 652.6;
patient 134.9; **forbearing,** long-
suffering; unresentful, unre-
vengeful; **tolerant** 978.11, more
in sorrow than in anger

  7 forgiven, pardoned, excused,
spared, reprieved, remitted; overlooked, disregarded, forgotten,
not held against one, wiped away,
removed from the record, blotted,
canceled, **condoned,** indulged;
absolved, shriven; redeemed; ex-

onerated, exculpated, acquitted;
unavenged

149 CONGRATULATION

NOUNS **1 congratulation, congratulations,** congrats <nonfor-
mal>, **felicitation,** blessing,
compliment, pat on the back;
good wishes, best wishes; **applause** 509.2, **praise** 509.5,
flattery 511

VERBS **2 congratulate, felicitate,**
bless, **compliment,** tender *or*
offer one's congratulations *or*
felicitations *or* compliments;
shake one's hand, pat one on the
back; **rejoice with one,** wish one
joy; **applaud** 509.10, **praise**
509.12, flatter 511.5

ADJS **3 congratulatory,** congrat-
ulant; **complimentary** 509.16,
flattering 511.8

150 GRATITUDE

NOUNS **1 gratitude, gratefulness,
thankfulness, appreciation,
appreciativeness**

  2 thanks, thanksgiving, praise,
laud, hymn, paean, benediction;
grace, prayer of thanks; **thank-
you; acknowledgment,** cognizance, recognition

VERBS **3 be grateful, be obliged,**
feel *or* be under an obligation, be
obligated *or* indebted, be in the
debt of, give credit *or* due credit;
be thankful, thank one's lucky
stars, thank *or* bless one's stars;
appreciate, be appreciative of;
never forget; overflow with gratitude; not look a gift horse in the
mouth

  4 thank, extend gratitude *or*
thanks, bless; give one's thanks,
**express one's appreciation; of-
fer** *or* **give thanks,** tender *or*
render thanks; acknowledge,
make acknowledgments of,
credit, recognize, give credit *or*
recognition; fall all over one with
gratitude; fall on one's knees

ADJS **5 grateful, thankful; appreciative,** appreciatory, sensible;
obliged, much obliged, beholden, indebted to, cognizant of

151 INGRATITUDE

NOUNS 1 **ingratitude, ungrate-
fulness, unthankfulness,**
thanklessness, **unappreciative-
ness;** nonrecognition, denial of
due or proper credit; halfhearted
thanks

  2 **ingrate,** ungrateful wretch

VERBS 3 **be ungrateful,** feel no
obligation, owe one no thanks;
look a gift horse in the mouth;
bite the hand that feeds one

ADJS 4 **ungrateful, unthankful,**
unthanking, thankless, unap-
preciative, unmindful

  5 **unthanked,** unacknowledged,
unrecognized, uncredited, denied
due or proper credit, unrequited,
unrewarded, forgotten, neglected, unduly or unfairly
neglected, ignored

152 RESENTMENT, ANGER

NOUNS 1 **resentment,** resentfulness; **displeasure,** disapproval,
disapprobation, dissatisfaction,
discontent; vexation, irritation,
annoyance, exasperation

  2 **offense, umbrage, pique;**
glower, scowl, dirty look <non-
formal>, glare, frown

  3 **bitterness, bitter resentment,**
bitterness of spirit; **rancor,** virulence, **acrimony,** acerbity,
asperity; **choler,** gall, bile, spleen,
acid, acidity, acidulousness; hard
feelings, **animosity** 589.4; rankling, slow burn <nonformal>

  4 **indignation,** righteous indignation

  5 **anger, wrath, ire,** mad <non-
formal>; angriness, irateness,
wrathfulness; grapes of wrath;
heat, more heat than light
<nonformal>

  6 **temper,** dander and Irish <both
nonformal>; bad temper 110.1

  7 **dudgeon,** high dudgeon; **huff,**
pique, pet, tiff, miff and stew
<both nonformal>, fret, **fume,**
ferment

  8 **fit,** fit of anger, fit of temper,
rage, **tantrum,** temper tantrum;
conniption or conniption fit and

snit <all nonformal>, paroxysm,
convulsion

  9 **outburst, explosion,** eruption,
blowup and **flare-up** <both non-
formal>; **storm, scene**

  10 **rage, passion; fury,** furor; towering rage or passion, blind or
burning rage, furious rage; vehemence, violence

  11 **provocation, affront, offense;**
casus belli <L>, sore point, sore
spot, tender spot, raw nerve, the
quick, where one lives; slap in the
face

VERBS 12 **resent,** be resentful, feel
or harbor or nurse resentment,
feel hurt, smart, feel sore and
have one's nose out of joint <both
nonformal>; bear or hold or have
a grudge

  13 **take amiss,** take ill, **take in bad
part,** take to heart, not take it as a
joke, **mind; take offense, take
umbrage,** get miffed or huffy
<nonformal>; be cut or cut to the
quick

  14 <show resentment> redden,
color, flush, mantle; **growl, snarl,**
gnarl, **snap,** show one's teeth,
spit; gnash or grind one's teeth;
glower, lower, scowl, **glare,
frown,** give a dirty look <nonfor-
mal>, look daggers; **stew,** stew in
one's own juice

  15 <be angry> **burn, seethe, simmer,** sizzle, smoke, smolder,
steam; be pissed or pissed off or
browned off <all nonformal>, be
livid, be beside oneself, **fume,**
stew <nonformal>, boil, fret,
chafe; foam at the mouth;
breathe fire and fury; **rage,
storm, rave,** rant, bluster; take
on and go on and carry on <all
nonformal>, rant and rave, kick
up a row or dust or a shindy
<nonformal>; raise Cain or raise
hell or raise the devil or raise the
roof <all nonformal>, tear up the
earth; throw a fit, have a conniption or conniption fit or duck fit or
cat fit <nonformal>, go into a tantrum; stamp one's foot

  16 **vent one's anger,** vent one's rancor or choler or spleen, pour out

the vials of one's wrath; **snap at, bite** or **snap one's nose off, bite** or **take one's head off, jump down one's throat;** expend one's anger on, take it out on <nonformal>

17 <become angry> **anger, lose one's temper,** become irate, forget oneself, let one's angry passions rise; **get one's gorge up,** get one's blood up, **bridle,** bridle up, **bristle,** bristle up, raise one's hackles, get one's back up; reach boiling point, boil over, climb the wall, go through the roof

18 <nonformal terms> **get mad** or **sore,** get one's Irish or dander or hackles up, get one's monkey up <Brit>; **see red, get hot under the collar,** flip out, work oneself into a lather or sweat or stew, get oneself in a tizzy, do a slow burn

19 **flare up, blaze up,** fire up, flame up, spunk up, ignite, kindle, take fire

20 **fly into a rage** or **passion** or **temper,** fly out, fly off at a tangent; **fly off the handle** and **hit the ceiling** and go into a tailspin and have a hemorrhage <all nonformal>; **explode, blow up** <nonformal>, blow one's top or stack <nonformal>, blow a fuse or gasket <nonformal>, flip one's lid or wig <nonformal>, wig out <nonformal>; kick or piss up a fuss or a row or a storm <all nonformal>

21 **offend, give offense, give umbrage,** affront, outrage; grieve, aggrieve; wound, hurt, cut, cut to the quick, hit one where one lives <nonformal>, **sting,** hurt one's feelings; step or tread on one's toes

22 **anger, make angry, make mad,** raise one's gorge or choler; make one's blood boil

23 <nonformal terms> **piss** or tee off, tick off, piss, **get one's goat, get one's Irish** or back or dander or hackles up, **make sore,** get one's mad up, make one hot under the collar, put one's nose out

of joint, burn one up, burn one's ass or butt, steam

24 **provoke, incense,** arouse, inflame, embitter; **vex, irritate, annoy, aggravate** <nonformal>, **exasperate, nettle,** fret, chafe; **pique, peeve** and miff <both nonformal>, huff; **ruffle, roil, rile** <nonformal>, ruffle one's feathers, **rankle;** bristle, put or get one's back up, set up, put one's hair or fur or bristles up; stick in one's craw <nonformal>; **stir up, work up,** stir one's bile, stir the blood; wave the bloody shirt

25 **enrage, infuriate, madden,** drive one mad, frenzy, lash into fury, work up into a passion, **make one's blood boil**

ADJS 26 **resentful,** resenting; **bitter,** embittered, rancorous, virulent, **acrimonious,** acerb, acerbic, acerbate; caustic; **choleric,** splenetic, acid, acidic, acidulous, acidulent; **sore** <nonformal>, rankled, burning and stewing <both nonformal>

27 **provoked, vexed, piqued; peeved** and miffed and huffy <all nonformal>, **nettled, irritated, annoyed,** aggravated <nonformal>, exasperated, put-out

28 **angry,** angered, **incensed, indignant, irate,** ireful; **livid,** livid with rage, beside oneself, **wroth, wrathful,** wrathy, **cross,** wrought-up, worked up, riled up <nonformal>

29 **burning, seething,** simmering, smoldering, sizzling, boiling, **steaming;** flushed with anger

30 <nonformal terms> **mad, sore,** mad as a hornet or as a wet hen or as hell, sore as a boil, pissed; **pissed-off** or PO'd; teed off or TO'd; ticked off, browned-off, waxy and stroppy <both Brit>, **hot,** het up, **hot under the collar,** burned up, hot and bothered, boiling, boiling or hopping or fighting or roaring mad, fit to be tied, good and mad, steamed, hacked, bent out of shape, in a lather or lava or pucker, red-assed

31 **in a temper, in a huff, in a pet,**

in a snit *or* a stew <both nonformal>; in a wax <Brit nonformal>, **in high dudgeon**

32 infuriated, infuriate, in a rage *or* passion *or* fury; **furious,** fierce, wild, savage; raving mad <nonformal>, **rabid,** foaming *or* frothing at the mouth; **fuming,** in a fume; **enraged, raging, raving, ranting, storming**

ADVS **33 angrily, indignantly, irately,** wrathfully, infuriatedly, infuriately, furiously, heatedly; **in anger,** in hot blood, in the heat of passion

153 JEALOUSY

NOUNS **1 jealousy,** *jalousie* <Fr>, jealousness, heartburning, heartburn, **jaundice,** jaundiced eye, green in the eye <nonformal>; Othello's flaw; **envy 154**

2 suspiciousness, suspicion, doubt, misdoubt, mistrust, distrust, distrustfulness

VERBS **3 suffer pangs of jealousy, have green in the eye** <nonformal>, be possessive *or* overpossessive, view with a jaundiced eye; **suspect,** distrust, mistrust, doubt, misdoubt

4 make one jealous, put someone's nose out of joint

ADJS **5 jealous, jaundiced,** jaundice-eyed, yellow-eyed, green-eyed, yellow, green, green with jealousy; horn-mad; invidious, **envious** 154.4; **suspicious,** distrustful

154 ENVY

NOUNS **1 envy,** enviousness, **covetousness;** invidia, deadly sin of envy, **invidiousness;** grudging, grudgingness; resentment, resentfulness; **jealousy** 153; rivalry

2 meanness, meanspiritedness, ungenerousness

VERBS **3 envy,** be envious *or* covetous of, covet, cast envious eyes; resent; **grudge, begrudge**

ADJS **4 envious,** envying, **invidious,** green with envy; **jealous** 153.4; **covetous,** desirous of;

resentful; **grudging, begrudging;** mean, mean-spirited, ungenerous

155 RESPECT

NOUNS **1 respect, regard,** consideration, appreciation, favor; approbation, approval; **esteem,** estimation, prestige; **reverence, veneration,** awe; **deference; honor, homage,** duty; great respect, high regard, **admiration;** adoration, exaggerated respect, worship, hero worship, **idolization;** idolatry, deification, apotheosis; courtesy 504

2 obeisance, reverence, homage; **bow, nod, bob,** bend, inclination, inclination of the head, **curtsy, salaam, kowtow,** scrape, bowing and scraping; **genuflection,** kneeling, bending the knee; prostration; dipping the colors, standing at attention; **submissiveness, submission 433; obsequiousness, servility 138**

3 respects, regards; duties; attentions

VERBS **4 respect,** accord respect to, **regard, esteem,** hold in esteem, favor, **admire,** think much of, think well of, think highly of, have *or* hold a high opinion of; **appreciate, value,** prize; **revere, reverence,** hold in reverence, **venerate, honor, look up to, defer to, bow to,** exalt, put on a pedestal, **worship,** hero-worship, deify, apotheosize, **idolize, adore,** worship the ground one walks on, stand in awe of

5 do *or* **pay homage to,** show respect for, pay respect to, pay tribute to, **do** *or* **render honor to; doff one's cap to, take off one's hat to;** salute, present arms, dip the colors, stand at *or* to attention; roll out the red carpet

6 bow, make obeisance, salaam, kowtow, bow down, **nod,** incline *or* bend *or* bow the head, **curtsy,** bend, scrape, **bow and scrape; genuflect, kneel,** bend the knee, get down on one's knees, fall down before, fall at the feet of, prostrate oneself, kiss the hem of one's garment

7 command respect, inspire respect, stand high, have prestige, rank high, be widely reputed, be up there *or* way up there <nonformal>; awe 122.6

ADJS **8 respectful, regardful,** attentive; **deferential,** conscious of one's place, dutiful, honorific, ceremonious, cap in hand; **courteous** 504.14

9 reverent, reverential; **adoring, worshiping,** worshipful, **idolizing,** idolatrous, deifying, apotheosizing; **venerative,** venerational; awestruck, awestricken, in awe

10 obeisant, prostrate, on one's knees, on bended knee; **submissive** 433.12; **obsequious**

11 respected, esteemed, revered, adored, worshiped, **venerated, honored,** admired, much-admired, appreciated, valued, prized, well-considered, held in respect *or* regard *or* favor *or* consideration, prestigious

12 venerable, reverend, estimable, honorable, worshipful, august, awe-inspiring, awesome, awful, dreadful; time-honored

ADVS **13 respectfully,** deferentially, reverentially; dutifully

ADVS, PREPS **14 in deference to,** with due respect, with all respect, **with all due respect to** *or* **for; out of respect** *or* consideration for, out of courtesy to

156 DISRESPECT

NOUNS **1 disrespect, disrespectfulness,** lack of respect, low esteem, **disesteem,** dishonor, **irreverence; ridicule** 508; **disparagement** 512; **discourtesy** 505; **impudence,** insolence 142

2 indignity, affront, offense, injury, humiliation; scurrility, contempt 157, contumely, flout, flouting, mockery, jeering, jeer, mock, scoff, gibe, taunt, brickbat <nonformal>; **insult, aspersion,** slap *or* kick in the face, back-handed compliment, damning with faint praise; cut; **outrage, atrocity,** enormity

3 <nonformal terms> put-down, dump, bringdown, dis

VERBS **4 disrespect, disesteem,** hold a low opinion of, hold in low esteem, not care much for, pay a lefthanded *or* backhanded compliment, damn with faint praise; **show disrespect for, be disrespectful,** be overfamiliar with; trifle with, make bold *or* free with, take liberties with, play fast and loose with; **ridicule** 508.8; **disparage** 512.8

5 offend, affront, give offense to, disoblige, outrage; dishonor, humiliate, treat with indignity; flout, mock, jeer at, scoff at, gibe at, taunt; **insult,** call names, slap in the face; **add insult to injury**

6 <nonformal terms> **bad-mouth, put down, trash,** rubbish, dump on, ride, roast, slam, hurl a brickbat

ADJS **7 disrespectful, irreverent; discourteous** 505.4; **insolent, impudent; derisive** 508.12; **disparaging** 512.13

8 insulting, insolent, abusive, offensive, humiliating, degrading, contemptuous 157.8, contumelious, calumnious; scurrilous; backhand, backhanded, lefthanded; outrageous, atrocious, unspeakable

9 unrespected, unregarded, unrevered, unvenerated, unhonored, unenvied

157 CONTEMPT

NOUNS **1 contempt, disdain, scorn,** contemptuousness, disdainfulness, superciliousness, snootiness, snottiness, scornfulness, contumely; snobbishness, clannishness, cliquishness, exclusiveness, exclusivity, hauteur, airs, arrogance 141; **ridicule** 508; **insult** 156.2; **disparagement** 512

2 snub, rebuff, repulse; **slight,** humiliation, spurning, spurn, disregard; cut, **the cold shoulder** <nonformal>; sneer, snort, sniff;

dismissal 907.2, kiss-off <nonformal>; **rejection** 372

VERBS **3 disdain, scorn, despise,** hold in contempt, rate *or* rank low, be contemptuous of, feel contempt for, **hold in contempt,** hold cheap, look down upon, think little *or* nothing of, hold beneath one *or* beneath contempt, view with a scornful eye, give one the fish-eye *or* the beady eye; **put down** *or* dump on <both nonformal>; deride, **ridicule** 508.8; **insult; disparage** 512.8; thumb one's nose at, sniff at, sneeze at, snap one's fingers at, sneer at, snort at, curl one's lip at, shrug one's shoulders at; care nothing for, couldn't care less about, think nothing of

4 spurn, turn up one's nose at, not want any part of; spit upon

5 snub, rebuff, cut *or* cut dead <nonformal>, drop, repulse; **high-hat** *and* upstage <both nonformal>; **look down one's nose at;** turn a cold shoulder upon *or* **give the cold shoulder** <nonformal>, give the kiss-off <nonformal>; turn one's back upon, turn away from, turn on one's heel, set one's face against, slam the door in one's face, show one his place, put one in his place

6 slight, ignore, pooh-pooh <nonformal>, make little of, dismiss, pretend not to see, disregard, overlook, neglect, pass by, pass up <nonformal>, leave out in the cold <nonformal>, take no note *or* notice of, pay no attention *or* regard to, refuse to acknowledge *or* recognize

7 avoid 368.6, avoid like the plague, go out of one's way to avoid, shun, dodge, steer clear of *and* have no truck with <both nonformal>; **keep one's distance,** keep at a respectful distance, **keep** *or* **stand** *or* **hold aloof;** keep at a distance, hold at arm's length; **be stuck-up** <nonformal>, act holier than thou

ADJS **8 contemptuous, disdainful,** supercilious, snooty, snotty, sniffy, **scornful,** sneering, withering, contumelious; snobbish, snobby; clannish, cliquish, exclusive; stuck-up <nonformal>, **conceited** 140.11; haughty, **arrogant** 141.9

ADVS **9 contemptuously, scornfully, disdainfully;** in *or* with contempt, in disdain, in scorn; sneeringly

158 SPACE
<indefinite space>

NOUNS **1 space, extent,** space continuum, continuum; **expanse,** expansion; spread, breadth; depth, deeps; height, vertical space, air space; **measure,** volume; **dimension,** proportion; **area, expanse,** tract, surface; **field,** arena, sphere; acreage; **void,** empty space, emptiness, nothingness; infinite space, outer space, deep space, interstellar *or* intergalactic space

2 range, scope, compass, reach, stretch, expanse, radius, sweep; **gamut, scale,** register; **spectrum**

3 room, latitude, way; room to spare, room to swing a cat <nonformal>, **elbowroom, margin, leeway;** breathing space; headroom, clearance

4 open space, clear space; **clearing,** clearance, glade; wide-open spaces, **terrain,** prairie, steppe, plain 236; wilderness, back country, boonies *and* boondocks <both nonformal>; desert; distant prospect *or* perspective, empty view, far horizon; **territory;** living space

5 spaciousness, roominess, size commodiousness, capacity, amplitude, extensiveness, extent, expanse

6 fourth dimension, space-time, space-time continuum; **relativity,** theory of relativity, Einstein's theory, principle of relativity, general theory of relativity, special *or* restricted theory of relativity, continuum theory; time warp

7 inner space, psychological

space, the realm of the mind; personal space, private space

VERBS **8 extend, reach, stretch,** sweep, spread, run, **go** or **go out,** cover, carry, **range,** lie; **reach** or stretch or thrust out; span, straddle, take in, hold, encompass, surround

ADJS **9 spatial,** space; **dimensional,** proportional; twodimensional, flat, surface or superficial, three-dimensional or 3-D, spherical, cubic, volumetric; galactic, intergalactic, interstellar

10 spacious, sizeable, roomy, commodious, capacious, ample; **extensive,** expansive, extended, wide-ranging; farreaching, extending, spreading, **vast, wide,** voluminous; widespread 863.13; **infinite** 822.3

ADVS **11 extensively, widely,** broadly, vastly; **far and wide,** far and near; **right and left,** on all sides, on every side; infinitely

12 everywhere, here, there, and everywhere; in all places, in every quarter, in all quarters; **all over,** all round, all over hell and all over the map and all over the place and all over town <all nonformal>, all over the world, the world over, on the face of the earth, under the sun, throughout the length and breadth of the land; from end to end, from pole to pole; **high and low,** upstairs and downstairs, in every nook and cranny; **universally**

13 from everywhere, from all points of the compass, from every quarter or all quarters; everywhere, to the four winds, to hell and back <nonformal>

159 LOCATION

NOUNS **1 location, situation, place, position,** spot, stead; **whereabouts; area, district, region** 231; **locality, locale,** locus; **abode** 228; **site,** situs; **spot, point,** pinpoint; *locus classicus* <L>; bearings, latitude and longitude

2 station, status, **stand, standing,** standpoint; **viewpoint,** point of reference, reference-point, angle, perspective, distance; **seat, post,** base, footing, ground, venue

3 navigation, guidance; dead reckoning; celestial guidance, celestial navigation; loran; radar navigation; radio navigation; **position, orientation,** lay, lie, set, **attitude,** aspect, exposure, frontage, **bearing** or **bearings,** radio bearing, azimuth; **fix**

4 place, stead, lieu

5 map, chart; hachure, contour line; **scale,** graphic scale; **legend;** grid line, meridian, parallel, latitude, longitude; inset; index; **projection,** map projection, conic projection, Mercator projection; **cartography, mapmaking; cartographer, mapmaker, mapper**

6 <act of placing> **placement, positioning, emplacement, situation, location, siting, locating, placing,** putting; **allocation, disposition,** assignment, **deployment, stationing,** spotting; **deposit,** disposal, dumping; **stowage,** storage

7 establishment, foundation, settlement, settling, colonization, population, peopling, plantation; anchorage, mooring; **installation,** investiture, placing in office, initiation

8 topography, geography; cartography; surveying, navigation; orbiting geophysical observatory or OGO

VERBS **9 have place,** be there; have its place or slot, **belong, go, fit,** fit in

10 be located or **situated, lie, be found,** stand, rest, repose; lie in, have its seat in

11 locate, situate, site, place, position; emplace, spot <nonformal>, **install,** put in place; **allocate, dispose, deploy,** assign; **localize,** narrow or pin down; **map, chart,** put on the map or chart; put one's finger on, **fix,** assign or consign or relegate to a place; **pinpoint,** zero in on, home in on; find *or* fix *or* calculate one's position, triangulate, **get a fix on** *or* navigational fix, navigate

12 **place, put, set, lay,** pose, site, seat, **station, post; park,** plump down <nonformal>; **dump**

13 <put violently> **clap,** slap, **thrust, fling, hurl,** throw, cast, chuck, toss; **plump**

14 **deposit,** repose, rest, **lay,** lodge; **put down,** set down, lay down

15 **load, lade,** freight, burden; fill 793.7; **stow,** store, warehouse; **pack,** pack away; pile, dump, heap, heap up, stack, mass; bag, sack, pocket

16 **establish, fix, plant, site,** pitch, seat, **set; found, base,** lay the foundation; **build,** put up, set up; build in; **install, invest,** vest, place in office

17 **settle, settle down,** sit down, locate, park <nonformal>, ensconce, ensconce oneself; make one's home, **reside, inhabit** 225.7; **move,** locate, relocate, establish residence, make one's home, **take up residence,** put up *or* live *or* stay at, hang up one's hat <nonformal>; take root, put down roots, plant oneself, get a footing, take one's stand *or* position; **anchor,** drop anchor, moor; **squat;** camp, bivouac, perch, roost, nest, burrow; domesticate, **set up housekeeping,** keep house; **colonize,** populate, people; **set up in business,** go in business for oneself, set up shop, hang up one's shingle <nonformal>

ADJS 18 **located, placed, sited, situated, positioned,** installed, emplaced, spotted <nonformal>, **set,** seated; **stationed, posted,** deployed, assigned, positioned; **established,** fixed, in place, **settled,** planted, ensconced

19 locational, positional, situational; **cartographic;** topographic, geographic, geodetic; navigational; **regional** 231.8

ADVS 20 **in place,** in position, in situ, in loco

21 **where,** whereabouts, in what place, in which place; **whither,** to what *or* which place

22 **wherever, wheresoever,** whithersoever, wherever it may be; **anywhere,** anyplace <nonformal>

23 **here,** in this place, on the spot; **hereabouts,** hereabout, in this vicinity, near here; **aboard,** on board, with *or* among us; **hither,** hereto, hereunto, to this place

24 **there,** thereat, in that place, in those parts; thereabout, **thereabouts,** in that vicinity *or* neighborhood; **thither,** to that place

25 **here and there, in places,** in various places, in spots, *passim* <L>

26 **somewhere, someplace,** someplace or other

160 DISPLACEMENT

NOUNS 1 **dislocation, displacement;** unhinging, luxation; **shift, removal,** forcible removal; eviction; **uprooting,** deracination; rootlessness; **disarrangement** 810; incoherence 803.1; discontinuity 812

2 **dislodgment;** unplacement, **unseating,** upset, unsaddling, unhorsing; **deposal** 447

3 **misplacement, mislaying,** misputting

4 displaced person *or* DP, stateless person, homeless person, man without a country, exile, drifter, vagabond, deportee; displaced population

VERBS 5 **dislocate, displace, disjoint,** disarticulate, unjoint, luxate, unhinge, **put** *or* **throw out of joint, disarrange** 810.2

6 **dislodge,** unplace; evict; **uproot,** root out, deracinate; depose 447.4, **unseat,** unsaddle; **unhorse,** dismount

7 **misplace, mislay,** misput

ADJS 8 dislocatory, dislocating, heterotopic

9 **dislocated, displaced; disjointed,** unhinged, out, **out of joint; disarranged** 809.13

10 unplaced, unestablished, unsettled; **uprooted,** deracinated; unhoused, evicted, made homeless, stateless, exiled, outcast

11 misplaced, mislaid, misput; **out of place,** out of one's element, like a fish out of water, in the wrong place

12 eccentric, off-center, off-balance, unbalanced

161 DIRECTION

<compass direction or course>

NOUNS **1 direction,** directionality; **line,** point, quarter, **aim, way,** track, range, **bearing,** azimuth, compass reading, **heading, course;** tendency, trend, inclination, bent, tenor, drift; **orientation,** lay, lie, steering, helmsmanship, piloting; navigation 182.1,2

2 *<nautical & aviation terms>* vector, tack; compass direction, azimuth, compass bearing *or* heading, magnetic bearing *or* heading, relative bearing *or* heading, true bearing *or* heading *or* course; lee side, weather side 218.3

3 points of the compass, cardinal points

4 orientation, bearings; adaptation, adjustment, accommodation, alignment, collimation; disorientation; deviation

VERBS **5 direct, point, aim, turn, bend, train,** fix, set, determine; point to *or* at, hold on, fix on, sight on; take aim, aim at; give a push in the right direction

6 direct to, give directions to, lead *or* conduct to, point out to, show, **show** *or* **point the way,** steer, put on the track, put on the right track, set straight, set *or* put right

7 *<have or take a direction>* **bear, head, turn, point, aim,** take *or* hold a heading, lead, go, steer, direct oneself, align oneself; **incline, tend, trend,** set, dispose, verge, tend to go

8 go west, go east, go north, go south

9 head for, bear for, **go for, make for,** hit *or* hit out for <nonformal>, **steer for, set out** *or* **off for,** strike out for, lay for, set in towards; set *or* direct *or* shape one's course for, set one's compass for, sail for 182.35; **break for,** make a break for <nonformal>, run *or* dash for, make a run *or* dash for

10 go directly, go straight, follow one's nose, **head straight for,** vector for, go straight to the point, steer a straight course, follow a course, keep *or* hold one's course; **make a beeline,** go as the crow flies; stay on the beam

11 orient, orientate, orient *or* orientate oneself, **take** *or* **get one's bearings,** get the lay *or* lie of the land, see which way the wind blows; adapt, adjust, accommodate

ADJS **12 directional,** azimuthal; **direct, straight,** straight-ahead, straightforward, straightaway, straightway; **undeviating,** unswerving; uninterrupted, unbroken; one-way, unidirectional

13 directable, trainable; **steerable, leadable; directed,** guided, aimed; on the mark, on the nose *or* money <nonformal>; **directional**

14 northern, north, arctic; southern, south, southbound, antarctic; eastern, east, oriental; western, west, occidental

ADVS **15 north,** northerly, northward, northwards, northwardly; north about

16 south, southerly, southward, southwards, southwardly; south about

17 east, easterly, eastward, eastwards, eastwardly, where the sun rises; eastabout

18 west, westerly, westward, westwards, westwardly, where the sun sets; westabout

19 northeast, northeasterly, northeastward, northeastwards, northeastwardly

20 northwest, northwesterly,

northwestward, northwest-
wards, northwestwardly
21 southeast, southeasterly,
southeastward, southeast-
wards, southeastwardly
22 southwest, southwesterly,
southwestward, southwest-
wards, southwestwardly
23 directly, direct, straight,
straightforward, undeviatingly,
unswervingly, unveeringly;
straight ahead, dead ahead; due,
dead, due north, etc; right, forthright; in line with, in a line for, in
a beeline, as the crow flies;
straight as an arrow
24 clockwise, rightward 219.7;
counterclockwise, anticlockwise, leftward 220.6; homeward;
landward; seaward; earthward;
heavenward; leeward, windward
218.9
25 in every direction, in all directions, every which way <non-
formal>, everyway, every-
where, at every turn, in all directions at once, all over the place
or the map <nonformal>; around,
all round, round about; forty
ways or six ways from Sunday
<nonformal>; from every quar-
ter; from or to the four corners
of the earth, from or to the four
winds

162 PROGRESSION
<motion forwards>

NOUNS 1 progression, progress,
going, going forward; ongoing,
rolling on; advance, advancing,
advancement, promotion, furtherance, furthering; forward
motion, forwarding; headway,
way; leap, jump, forward leap
or jump, quantum jump or leap,
spring; progressiveness, prog-
ressivity; passage, course,
march, career; midpassage, midcourse, midcareer; travel 177;
improvement 392
VERBS 2 progress, advance, proceed, go, go or move forward,
step forward, go on, go ahead,
go along, push ahead, pass on or
along; move, travel; make prog-

ress, come on, get along, come
along <nonformal>, get ahead;
further oneself; make headway,
roll; make strides or rapid
strides, cover ground, make good
time, leap or jump or spring forward, catapult oneself forward;
make up for lost time, gain
ground
3 march on, run on, rub on, jog
on, roll on, flow on; drift along,
go with the stream
4 make or wend one's way, work
or weave one's way, inch forward,
feel one's way, muddle through;
go slow 175.6; push or force one's
way, fight one's way, go or swim
against the current, swim upstream; come a long way, move
up in the world; forge ahead,
drive on or ahead, push or press
on or onward, push or press forward, push, crowd
5 advance, further, promote,
forward, hasten, contribute to,
foster, aid, facilitate, expedite,
abet
ADJS 6 progressive, progressing,
advancing, proceeding, ongoing, forward-looking; moving
ADVS 7 in progress, in midcourse,
in midcareer, in full career; going
on; by leaps and bounds
8 forward, forwards, onward,
onwards, forth, on, along,
ahead; on the road or high road
to, en route to

163 REGRESSION
<motion backwards>

NOUNS 1 regression; recession
168; retrogression, retrocession,
reaction, return, reentry; setback, throwback, rollback;
backsliding, lapse, relapse, recidivism, recidivation
2 retreat, withdrawal, strategic
withdrawal, exfiltration; retirement, fallback, pullout,
pullback; rout; disengagement;
backing down or off or out <all
nonformal>; reneging, copping
or weaseling out <nonformal>

3 reverse, reversal, reversion; **backing,** backup; **about-face,** *volte-face* <Fr>, about-turn, right-about, right-about-face, turn to the right-about, U-turn, turn-around

4 countermotion; countermarch

VERBS **5 regress,** go backwards, **recede,** return, revert; **retrogress,** retrograde, retroflex, retrocede; pull back, jerk back, reach back; fall *or* get *or* go behind, fall astern, lose ground, slip back; **backslide,** lapse, relapse, recidivate

6 retreat, sound *or* beat a retreat, beat a hasty retreat, **withdraw, retire,** pull out *or* back, exfiltrate, disengage; **fall back,** move back, go back, stand back; run back; **draw back,** draw off; **back out** *or* **out of** *and* back off *and* back down <all nonformal>; defer, give ground, take a back seat, play second fiddle

7 reverse, go into reverse; **back, back up,** backpedal, back off *or* away; **backwater; backtrack; countermarch; reverse one's field;** have second thoughts, think better of it, cut one's losses

8 turn back; double back, retrace one's steps; turn one's back upon; **return,** go *or* come back

9 turn round *or* **around** *or* **about,** turn, make a U-turn, turn on a dime, turn tail, **come** *or* **go about,** put about; veer, veer around; **swivel,** pivot, pivot about, swing, round, swing round; wheel, wheel about, whirl, spin

10 about-face, *volte-face* <Fr>, right-about-face, **do an about-face** *or* **a right-about-face** *or* **an about-turn,** perform a *volte-face,* **face about**

ADJS **11 regressive; retrogressive,** retrocessive, retrograde; retroactive; reactionary

12 backward, reversed, reflex, **turned around,** back, **backward;** wrong-way around, assbackwards *and* bassackwards <both nonformal>

ADVS **13 backwards,** backward, **hindwards,** hindward, **rearwards,** rearward, astern; **back,** away, fro; **in reverse,** assbackwards <nonformal>; against the grain; counterclockwise

164 DEVIATION
<indirect course>

NOUNS **1 deviation,** deviance *or* deviancy, deviousness, **departure, digression,** diversion, **divergence,** divarication, branching off, divagation, declination, aberration, aberrancy, **variation,** indirection; detour, excursion; obliquity, bias, skew, slant; **circuitousness** 913; **wandering,** rambling, **straying, drift, drifting; turning, shifting, swerving, swinging; turn, corner, bend, curve,** dogleg, crook, hairpin, zigzag, twist, warp, swerve, **veer,** sheer, sweep; shift, double; tack, yaw

2 deflection, bending, flection; torsion, distortion, contortion, twisting, warping, skewness; **refraction, diffraction, scatter,** diffusion, dispersion

VERBS **3 deviate, depart from,** vary, **diverge,** branch off, angle, angle off; **digress,** divagate, turn aside, go out of the way, detour, take a side road; **swerve, veer,** sheer, curve, **shift, turn,** trend, bend, heel, bear off; turn right, turn left, hang a right *or* left <nonformal>; alter one's course, make a course correction; tack 182.30

4 stray, go astray, lose one's way, err; take a wrong turn; drift, go adrift; **wander,** wander off, ramble, rove, straggle; meander, wind, twist, snake, twist and turn

5 deflect, deviate **divert,** diverge, **bend,** curve, pull, zigzag; **warp,** bias, twist, distort, contort, torture, skew; refract, diffract, **scatter, diffuse, disperse**

6 avoid, evade, dodge, duck <nonformal>, turn aside *or* to the side, draw aside, **turn away,** jib, shy, shy off; **sidetrack,** shove aside, shunt, switch; **avert; head off,** turn back 907.3; **step aside,** sidestep, sidle; **steer clear of,** make way for, get out of the way of; go off, bear off, sheer off, veer off, ease off, edge off; fly off, go or fly off at a tangent; glance off

ADJS **7 deviative, deviant,** departing, aberrant, shifting, turning, swerving, veering; **digressive,** discursive, excursive, **circuitous; devious,** indirect, out-of-the-way; errant, erratic, **wandering,** rambling, roving, winding, twisting, meandering, serpentine, labyrinthine, vagrant, stray, desultory

8 deflective, inflective, diffractive, refractive; refrangible; deflected, refracted, diffracted, scattered; diffuse, diffused, dispersed; distorted, skewed, skew

9 avertive, evasive, dodging, dodgy,

165 LEADING
<going ahead>

NOUNS **1 leading, heading; preceding,** precedence 813; priority 833.1; front, point, leading edge, cutting edge, forefront, vanguard, van 216.2; herald, precursor 815

VERBS **2 lead, head,** spearhead, stand at the head, stand first, be way ahead <nonformal>, head the line; take the lead, go in the lead, **lead the way,** break the trail, lead the pack; be the point or point man; **light the way,** show the way, guide; get ahead or in front of, come to the fore, lap, outstrip, pace, set the pace; not look back; get a head start, steal a march upon; **precede** 813.2, **go before** 815.3

ADJS **3 leading, heading,** precessional, precedent, precursory, foregoing; **first, foremost,** headmost; **preceding,** antecedent 813.4; **prior** 833.4; **chief** 249.14

ADVS **4 before** 813.6, in front, out in front, outfront, foremost, headmost, in the the van, in the forefront, in advance 216.12

166 FOLLOWING
<going behind>

NOUNS **1 following, trailing,** tailing <nonformal>, shadowing; **hounding, dogging,** chasing, **pursuit,** pursuance; sequence 814; sequel 816; series 811.2

2 follower, successor; shadow and tail <both nonformal>; **pursuer; attendant** 768.4, **satellite, hanger-on,** dangler, adherent, appendage, dependent, parasite, stooge <nonformal>, flunky; **henchman,** ward heeler, partisan, supporter; camp follower, groupy <nonformal>; fan and buff <both nonformal>; **public; entourage, following** 768.6; disciple 572.2

VERBS **3 follow,** go after or behind, come after or behind; **pursue, shadow** and **tail** <both nonformal>, **trail,** trail after, follow in the trail of, **heel,** follow or tread or step on the heels of, follow in the steps or footsteps or footprints of, breathe down the neck of, follow in the wake of, hang on the skirts of, tailgate <nonformal>, bring up the rear, eat the dust of, swallow one's dust; **tag after** and **tag along** <both nonformal>; string along <nonformal>; **dog, hound,** chase, take out or take off after, **pursue**

4 lag, lag behind, straggle, drag, trail, **trail behind,** hang back or behind, loiter, linger, **loiter** or **linger behind,** dawdle, get behind, fall behind, let grass grow under one's feet

ADJS **5 following,** trailing; succeeding 814.4; back-to-back <nonformal>, consecutive 811.9

ADVS **6 behind, after,** in the rear, in the wake of

167 APPROACH
<motion towards>

NOUNS **1 approach,** approaching, coming or going toward, coming or going near, proximation, **access,** accession, nearing; advance, oncoming; **advent,**

coming, forthcoming; flowing toward; nearness 223; imminence
839; approximation 223.1
2 **approachability, accessibility,
access,** attainability, openness
VERBS 3 **approach, near, draw
near** *or* nigh, go *or* come near, go
or come toward, come to close
quarters; **close,** close in, close in
on, close with; zoom in on; **ac-
cost,** encounter, confront;
proximate; **advance,** come,
come forward, come on, come
up, bear up, step up; ease *or* edge
or sidle up to; bear down on *or*
upon, be on a collision course
with
ADJS 4 **approaching, nearing,**
advancing; attracted to, drawn to;
**coming, oncoming, forthcom-
ing,** upcoming; approximate;
near 223.14; imminent 839.3
5 **approachable, accessible,** attainable, open, easy to find, meet,
etc

168 RECESSION
<*motion from*>

NOUNS 1 **recession,** recedence; **retreat, retirement, withdrawing,
withdrawal;** retraction; fleetingness, fugitiveness, evanescence
VERBS 2 **recede,** retrocede; **retreat, retire, withdraw;** move off
or away, stand off *or* away, stand
out from the shore; go, **go away;
die away,** fade away, drift away;
erode, wash away; **diminish,** decline, sink, shrink, dwindle, **fade,
ebb,** wane; shy away, tail off; fade
into the distance
3 **retract,** withdraw, **draw** *or* **pull
back,** draw *or* pull in; draw in
one's claws; take a back seat, play
second fiddle; **shrink,** wince,
cringe, flinch, shy
ADJS 4 **recessive,** recessionary; ret-
rocedent
5 **receding, retreating,** retiring,
withdrawing; **diminishing, declining,** shrinking, eroding,
dwindling, **ebbing,** waning;
fading; fleeting, fugitive
6 **retractile,** retractable

169 CONVERGENCE
<*coming together*>

NOUNS 1 **convergence,** confluence, concourse; **meeting,**
congress, concurrence; **concentration,** focus 208.4; point
of convergence, vanishing
point; union, merger; crossing
point, crossroads, crossing 170;
collision course, narrowing gap;
funnel, bottleneck; hub, spokes
VERBS 2 **converge, come together,** approach 167.3, run together, **meet,** unite, connect,
merge; **cross, intersect** 170.6;
fall in with, link up with; be on a
collision course; go toward, narrow the gap, close with, close up,
close in; funnel; taper; center on
or around, **concentrate,** come to
a point; **come to a focus** 208.10
ADJS 3 **converging,** convergent;
meeting, uniting, merging; concurrent, confluent; **crossing, intersecting** 170.8; **focal,** focusing,
focused; centripetal; asymptotic;
tangent, tangential

170 CROSSING

NOUNS 1 **crossing, intercrossing,**
intersecting, **intersection;** cross
section, transection; cruciation;
transit, transiting
2 **crossing,** crossway, **crosswalk,
crossroad; intersection;** cross-
over, overpass,; traffic circle,
rotary; interchange, cloverleaf
3 **network, webwork, weaving**
740, **meshwork,** interlacement,
intertwinement, texture, reticulation; crossing-out, cancellation;
net, netting; **mesh; web,** web-
bing; weave, weft; lace, lacework;
screen, screening; sieve, riddle,
raddle; wicker, wickerwork;
basketwork, basketry; lattice,
latticework; hachure *or* hatchure,
hatching, cross-hatching; trellis,
trelliswork; grate, grating; grille,
grillwork; **grid,** gridiron; tracery,
fretwork, filigree; reticle, reticule;
wattle
4 **cross,** crux, cruciform; **crucifix,**

rood; **swastika; crossbones; dagger**

5 **crosspiece**, traverse, transverse, transept; diagonal; **crossbar,** crossarm

VERBS 6 **cross, crisscross; intersect**, intercross; **cut across,** crosscut; **traverse**, transverse; crossbar

7 net, web, mesh; lattice, trellis; grate, grid

ADJS 8 **cross, crossing, crossed; crisscross, crisscrossed; intersecting, intersected; crosscut, cut across**

9 **transverse**, traverse; **across,** cross, crossway, **crosswise** or crossways, athwart; oblique 204.13

10 **cruciform, crosslike,** crossshaped, crossed; cruciferous

11 **netlike,** retiform, plexiform; **reticulated,** reticular, reticulate; **netted; meshed,** meshy; laced, lacy, lacelike; filigreed; latticed, latticelike

12 **webbed,** weblike, woven, interwoven, interlaced, intertwined

ADVS 13 **crosswise** or crossways or crossway; **cross, crisscross, across, athwart; traverse,** traversely; **transverse,** transversely; obliquely 204.21; **sideways** or sidewise; contrariwise; crossgrained, across the grain, against the grain

171 DIVERGENCE
<recession from one another>

NOUNS 1 **divergence** or divergency; aberration, deviation 164; **separation,** division, decentralization; **radial, radiating; spread,** spreading out, splaying, fanning out, deployment

2 **radiation,** ray, sunray, radius, spoke; radiance, diffusion, scattering, dispersion, emanation; halo, aureole, glory, corona

3 **forking,** bifurcation, trifurcation, divarication; **branching,** branching off or out, **ramification**

4 **fork, prong,** trident; **branch,** ramification, stem, offshoot;

crotch, crutch; **fan, delta; groin;** wishbone

VERBS 5 **diverge,** divaricate; aberrate; **separate,** divide; **spread out,** splay, fan out, deploy; go off or away, **fly** or **go off at a tangent**

6 **radiate,** ray, diffuse, emanate, spread, disperse, scatter

7 **fork,** bifurcate, trifurcate, divaricate; **branch,** stem, ramify

ADJS 8 **diverging,** divergent; divaricate, divaricating; fanlike, fanshaped; deltoid, deltoidal, deltashaped; splayed; centrifugal

9 **radiating,** radial, radiated; rayed, spoked; radiative

10 **forked, forking,** bifurcated, forklike, trifurcated, tridentlike, pronged; **crotched; branched, branching;** tree-shaped, dendriform, dendritic; branchlike, ramous

172 MOTION
<motion in general>

NOUNS 1 **motion; movement, momentum; stir,** unrest, restlessness; **going,** running, stirring; **operation,** operating, **working,** ticking; **activity** 330; kinesis, kinetics, kinematics; dynamics; **actuation,** motivation; mobilization

2 **course, career,** midcareer, **passage, progress,** trend, **advance,** forward motion; **travel** 177; **flow,** flux, flight, **trajectory; stream, current,** run, rush, onrush, ongoing; backward motion, **regression,** retrogression, going or moving backwards; backflowing, ebbing, subsiding, withdrawing; downward motion, **descent,** descending, sinking, plunging; upward motion, mounting, climbing, rising, **ascent,** ascending, **soaring;** radial motion, angular motion, axial motion; random motion, Brownian movement; perpetual motion

3 **mobility, motivity,** motility, movableness; **locomotion;** motive power

4 **velocity** 174.1,2, rate, gait, pace,

tread, step, stride, clip *and* lick
<both nonformal>

VERBS **5 move, budge, stir**; go,
run, flow, stream; **progress**, advance; wend, wend one's way;
back, back up, regress, retrogress; ebb, subside, wane; **descend**, sink, plunge; **ascend**,
mount, rise, climb, soar; circle,
rotate, gyrate, spin, whirl; travel;
shift, change, shift *or* change
place; **speed** 174.8; **hurry** 401.5,
do on the fly *or* run

6 set in motion, move, actuate,
motivate, push, shove, nudge,
drive, impel, propel; mobilize

ADJS **7 moving, stirring, in motion**; transitional; **mobile**, motile; motivational, impelling,
propelling, propellant, driving;
traveling; **active** 330.17

8 flowing, fluent, passing, streaming, flying, **running, going, progressive**; **drifting**; **regressive**,
retrogressive, back, **backward**;
descending, sinking, plunging,
downward, down-trending; ascending, mounting, rising, soaring, **upward**, up-trending; **rotary**, rotatory, rotational; axial,
gyrational, gyratory

ADVS **9 under way**, under sail, on
one's way, on the go *or* move *or* fly
or run *or* march, **in motion**, astir

173 QUIESCENCE

<*being at rest; absence of
motion*>

NOUNS **1 quiescence, stillness**, silence 51, quietness, **quiet; calmness**, restfulness, **peacefulness**,
imperturbability, passiveness,
passivity, **placidity, tranquillity,
serenity, peace, composure**;
contemplation, satori, nirvana,
samadhi, ataraxia; **rest, repose;
sleep, slumber** 22.2

**2 motionlessness, immobility;
inactivity, inaction**; fixity, fixation 854.2

**3 standstill, stand; stop, halt,
cessation** 856; dead stop; deadlock, dead set; running *or* dying
down, subsidence, waning,
ebbing, wane, ebb

**4 inertness, dormancy; inertia;
passiveness, passivity; suspense, abeyance, latency; torpor, apathy, indifference, indolence, lotus-eating, languor;
stagnation**, stagnancy, **vegetation**; deathliness, deadliness;
catalepsy

5 calm, lull, calm before the
storm; dead calm, deathlike calm;
doldrums, horse latitudes

6 stuffiness, airlessness, closeness, oppressiveness

VERBS **7 be still, keep quiet**, lie
still; **stop moving**, cease motion,
freeze *or* seize up, come to a
standstill; **rest, repose; remain,
stay**, tarry; remain motionless,
freeze <nonformal>; **stand still**,
be at a standstill; stand fast, stand
firm, stay put <nonformal>; **not
stir**, not move a muscle; hold
one's breath; bide one's time,
mark time, tread water, coast;
rest on one's oars, put one's
feet up

8 quiet, lull, soothe, calm, calm
down, tranquilize 670.7, pacify,
pour oil on troubled waters; **stop**
856.7, halt, bring to a standstill;
cease 856.6, wane, subside, ebb,
run *or* die down, die off, dwindle

**9 stagnate, vegetate; sleep,
slumber; smolder, hang fire;
idle**

10 sit, sit down, be seated, remain
seated; perch, roost

11 becalm, take the wind out of
one's sails

ADJS **12 quiescent, quiet, still**,
hushed; quiet as a mouse;
waning, subsiding, ebbing,
dwindling; **at rest**, resting, reposing; restful, reposeful, relaxed; cloistered, sequestered,
sequestrated, isolated, secluded,
sheltered; **calm, tranquil, peaceful**, peaceable, pacific, halcyon;
placid, smooth; unruffled, untroubled, cool, undisturbed,
unperturbed, unagitated, laidback <nonformal>; stolid, stoic,
stoical, impassive; still as death

13 motionless, unmoving, unmoved, **immobile; still, fixed,**

stationary, static, at a standstill; **stock-still,** dead-still; still as a mouse; riding at anchor; **idle,** unemployed; out of commission, down

14 **inert, inactive, static,** dormant, passive, sedentary; **latent,** suspended, abeyant, in suspense or abeyance; sleeping, slumbering; **stagnant,** standing, foul; **torpid, languorous, languid,** apathetic, phlegmatic, **sluggish,** logy, dopey <nonformal>, groggy, heavy, leaden, **dull,** flat, slack, tame, **dead,** lifeless; catatonic, cataleptic

15 **untraveled, stay-at-home,** stick-in-the-mud <nonformal>

16 **stuffy, airless,** breathless, breezeless, windless; **close, oppressive, stifling, suffocating,** stirless, unstirring, not a breath of air, not a leaf stirring; unventilated

17 **becalmed,** in a dead calm

ADVS 18 quiescently, **quietly,** stilly, still; **calmly, tranquilly, peacefully; placidly,** unperturbedly, **coolly**

19 **motionlessly,** fixedly

20 **inertly, inactively,** statically, dormantly, passively; stagnantly; **torpidly, languorously, languidly; like a bump on a log; sluggishly,** heavily, dully, coldly, lifelessly, apathetically, phlegmatically; stoically, stolidly, impassively

174 SWIFTNESS

NOUNS 1 **velocity, speed; rapidity,** celerity, **swiftness,** fastness, **quickness, speediness;** haste 401.1, hurry, flurry, rush; **dispatch, expedition, promptness;** lightning speed; smart or rattling or spanking or lively or snappy pace

2 **speed of sound, sonic speed,** Mach, Mach number, Mach one, Mach two, etc; subsonic speed; supersonic or ultrasonic or hypersonic or transsonic speed; transsonic barrier, sound barrier

3 **run, sprint; dash, rush,** plunge, headlong rush or plunge, **race, scurry, scamper,** scud, **spurt, burst of speed;** canter, **gallop,** lope; **trot,** dogtrot; **full speed,** open throttle; **fast-forward**

4 **acceleration, quickening; pickup,** getaway; step-up, speedup; thrust, drive, impetus

5 **speeder, sprinter; speed demon** or maniac or merchant <nonformal>; **racer, runner**

6 <comparisons> lightning, greased lightning <nonformal>, thunderbolt, flash, streak of lightning, streak, blue streak <nonformal>, bat out of hell <nonformal>, wind, shot, bullet

7 **speedometer,** accelerometer; cyclometer; tachometer; Mach meter; windsock; wind gauge, anemometer

VERBS 8 **speed, go fast,** skim, **fly,** flit, outstrip the wind; **zoom;** break the sound barrier; go like the wind, go like a shot or flash, go like lightning or a streak of lightning, go like greased lightning; **rush, tear,** dash, dart, shoot, hurtle, bolt, fling, **scamper, scurry,** scour, scud, scuttle, scramble, **race,** careen; **hasten,** make haste, **hurry** 401.4, hie, post; **run, sprint, trip,** spring, **bound,** leap; gallop, lope, canter; trot; **make time,** make good time, **cover ground,** get over the ground, **make strides** or **rapid strides**

9 <nonformal terms> barrel, clip, spank or cut along, tear or tear along, bowl along, thunder along, storm along, breeze or breeze along, tear up the track or road

10 **accelerate, speed up, step up** <nonformal>, **hurry up, quicken; hasten** 401.4; put on steam, pour on the coal, put on more speed, open the throttle; pick up speed, gain ground

11 <naut terms> put on sail, crack or pack on sail, crowd sail, press her

12 **spurt,** make a spurt or dash, **dash** or dart or shoot ahead, rush

ahead, put on *or* make a burst of
speed; make one's move

13 overtake, outstrip, overhaul,
catch up, **catch up with,** come
up with *or* to, gain on *or* upon,
pass, lap; outpace, outrun, out-
sail; leave behind, leave standing
or looking *or* flatfooted

14 keep up with, keep pace with,
run neck and neck

ADJS **15 fast, swift, speedy, rapid;
quick,** double-quick, express,
fleet, hasty, expeditious, hustling, rushing, dashing, galloping,
running, **agile, nimble,** lively,
nimble-footed; winged; mercurial; quick as lightning; **breakneck,** reckless, headlong, precipitate; quick as a wink, quick on
the trigger <nonformal>, hair-
trigger <nonformal>; **prompt**
844.9

16 supersonic, transsonic, ultrasonic, hypersonic, faster than
sound; **high-speed,** high-velocity

ADVS **17 swiftly, rapidly, quickly,**
snappily <nonformal>, **speedily, fast, quick,** apace; at a great
rate, at a good clip <nonformal>,
in seven-league boots, **by leaps
and bounds,** trippingly; **lickety-
split** <nonformal>; hell-bent *and*
hell-bent for election *and* hell-
bent for leather <all nonformal>;
posthaste, hastily, expeditiously,
promptly; double-quick, in double time, on the double <nonfor-
mal>; in high gear, in high

18 <nonformal terms> **like a shot,**
as if shot out of a cannon, **like a
flash,** like a streak, like a blue
streak, like greased lightning,
**like a bat out of hell, like a
scared rabbit,** like a house afire,
like sixty, like mad *and* **crazy** *and*
fury, like sin, to beat the band

19 in short order, in no time, instantaneously, immediately if not
sooner, in less than no time, in
nothing flat <nonformal>; in a
jiffy <nonformal>, before you
can say Jack Robinson, **in a
flash, in a twinkling, pronto**
<**nonformal>, PDQ** *or* pretty
damn quick <nonformal>

20 at full speed, with all speed, at
full throttle, **for all one is worth**
<nonformal>, hit the ground run-
ning <nonformal>, as fast as
one's legs will carry one; **at full
blast; under full steam; all out**
<nonformal>, **wide open;** full
speed ahead

175 SLOWNESS

NOUNS **1 slowness, leisureliness,**
pokiness, slackness, creeping;
sluggishness, sloth, laziness,
idleness, indolence, languor, inertia, inertness; deliberateness,
deliberation, circumspection,
foot-dragging <nonformal>

2 slow motion, leisurely gait,
snail's pace; **creep, crawl; walk,**
trudge, waddle, saunter, stroll;
slouch, shuffle, plod, shamble;
limp, hobble; jog; mincing steps;
slow march, funeral march

**3 dawdling, lingering, loitering,
tarrying, dallying,** dillydallying,
shillyshallying, dilatoriness, delaying tactic, delayed action,
procrastination 845.5, lag, **lagging,** goofing off <nonformal>

**4 slowing, retardation, slack-
ening,** flagging, slowing down;
**slowdown, letup, letdown,
slack-up, slack-off,** ease-up;
deceleration, negative acceleration; **delay** 845.2, **detention,
setback, holdup** <nonformal>,
check, arrest, obstruction; lag,
drag

5 slowpoke <nonformal>, plodder, slow goer, **lingerer, loiterer,
dawdler,** dawdle, **laggard,** procrastinator, foot-dragger, stick-in-
the-mud <nonformal>, drone,
slug, sluggard, lie-abed, sleepyhead, goof-off <nonformal>,
goldbrick <nonformal>; tortoise,
snail

VERBS **6 go slow** *or* **slowly,** go at a
snail's pace, take it slow, get no
place fast <nonformal>; **drag;
creep, crawl;** laze, idle; get nowhere fast; inch, inch along;
worm, worm along; poke, **poke
along;** shuffle *or* stagger *or* totter
or toddle along; drag along, drag

one's feet, walk, traipse *and* **mo-sey** <both nonformal>; **saunter, stroll, amble,** waddle, toddle <nonformal>; dogtrot; limp, hobble

7 **plod,** plug <nonformal>, peg, shamble, **trudge,** tramp, lumber; plod along, plug along <nonformal>, schlep <nonformal>

8 **dawdle, linger, loiter, tarry, delay, dally, dillydally,** shilly-shally, waste time, **take one's time,** take one's own sweet time; goof off <nonformal>; lag, drag, trail; flag, falter, halt

9 **slow, slow down** *or* **up, let down** *or* **up, ease off** *or* **up, slack off, slacken,** relax, moderate, taper off; **decelerate, retard, delay** 845.8, **detain,** impede, obstruct, arrest, stay, **check,** curb, **hold up, hold back,** keep back, hold in check; rein in; throttle down, take one's foot off the gas; idle; brake, **put on the brakes;** backpedal; lose ground; clip the wings

ADJS 10 **slow, leisurely,** slack, moderate, gentle, **easy,** deliberate, unhurried, relaxed, gradual, circumspect, tentative, cautious, reluctant, foot-dragging <nonformal>; **creeping, crawling; poking,** poky; tottering, staggering, toddling, trudging, **lumbering,** ambling, waddling, shuffling, **sauntering,** strolling; **sluggish,** languid, languorous, lazy, slothful, indolent, idle; **slow-going, slow-moving; slow-footed; snail-paced** ; limping, hobbling, hobbled; halting; faltering, flagging; slow as molasses *or* molasses in January, slow as death

11 **dawdling, lingering, loitering, tarrying, dallying, dillydallying,** shilly-shallying, dilatory, delaying 845.17, **lagging,** dragging

12 **retarded,** slackened; **delayed, detained,** checked, **arrested,** impeded, set back; late, **tardy** 845.16

ADVS 13 **slowly,** slow, **leisurely,** unhurriedly, moderately, gently;

creepingly; pokingly, pokily; **sluggishly,** languidly, languorously, lazily, indolently, idly, deliberately, circumspectly, tentatively, cautiously, reluctantly; **lingeringly,** loiteringly; haltingly, falteringly; in **slow motion,** at a funeral pace, with halting steps; at a snail's pace; with agonizing slowness; in low gear

14 **gradually,** little by little 245.6

176 TRANSFERAL, TRANSPORTATION

1 **transferal, transfer; transmission,** transference, transmittal, transmittance; transposition, transposal, transplacement; metathesis; translocation, **transplantation,** translation; migration, transmigration; **import, importation; export, exportation;** deportation, extradition, expulsion, **transit,** transition, **passage; communication,** dissemination, diffusion, contagion; metastasis; transmigration of souls, metempsychosis; passing over; osmosis; transfusion

2 transferability, conveyability; transmissibility; **portability,** transportability; communicability

3 **transportation, conveyance, transport, carrying,** bearing, packing, toting *and* lugging <both nonformal>; **carriage,** carry, **hauling,** portage; **cartage,** drayage; freight, railway express; **airfreight, air express,** airlift; **shipment, shipping,** transshipment; containerization, cargo-handling; delivery 478.1

4 **moving, removal, movement,** relocation, shift; **displacement**

5 people mover, moving sidewalk; conveyor belt; elevator, escalator 911.4

6 **freight; shipment, consignment; cargo,** payload, lading, load, pack; **baggage, luggage**

7 **carrier, conveyer;** hauler, carter, shipper, trucker, common carrier, truck driver; freighter; steve-

dore, cargo handler; **bearer, porter,** redcap, skycap; coolie; litter-bearer, stretcher-bearer; caddie; water boy; letter carrier 353.5; cupbearer

8 **beast of burden; pack** or **draft animal; horse** 311.10-15, ass, mule; ox; camel, ship of the desert, dromedary, llama; reindeer; elephant; sledge dog, husky, malamute, Siberian husky

9 <geological terms> **deposit,** sediment; drift, silt, loess, moraine, scree, sinter; alluvium, alluvion, diluvium; detritus, debris

VERBS 10 **transfer, transmit, transpose,** translocate, metathesize, switch; **transplant,** translate; **pass,** pass over, **hand over,** turn over, consign, assign; **deliver** 478.13; pass the buck <nonformal>, hand forward, hand on, relay; **import, export;** deport, extradite, expel; communicate, diffuse, disseminate, spread, impart; transfuse, perfuse

11 **remove, move, relocate, shift,** send, shunt; displace, dislodge; **take away,** cart off or away, carry off or away; manhandle; set or lay or put aside, put or set to one side

12 **transport, convey,** freight, conduct, **take; carry, bear,** pack, tote and lug <both nonformal>, manhandle; lift, waft, whisk

13 **haul, cart,** truck, bus; **ship,** barge, lighter, ferry

14 <convey through a channel> **channel; pipe,** tube, pipeline, flume, **siphon, funnel,** tap

15 **send,** send off or away, send forth; **dispatch,** transmit, remit, consign, forward; expedite; **ship,** freight, airfreight, embark, containerize; **transship; express,** air-express; express-mail; **post, mail,** airmail; export

16 **fetch, bring, go get,** go and get, **go after, go for,** call for, pick up; **get,** obtain, procure, secure; **bring back, retrieve;** chase after

17 **ladle, dip, scoop; bail,** bucket; **dish,** dish out or up; cup; **shovel,** spade, fork; spoon; **pour,** decant

ADJS 18 **transferable, conveyable;**

transmittable, consignable, deliverable; **movable,** removable; **portable; transportable;** transposable, interchangeable; **communicable,** contagious; metastatic; assignable 629.5

ADVS 19 by transfer, from hand to hand, from door to door; by freight, by express, by rail, by trolley, by bus, by steamer, by airplane, by mail, by messenger, by hand

20 **on the way,** along the way, on the road, **en route, in transit,** on the wing; in passing

177 TRAVEL

NOUNS 1 **travel,** traveling, going, journeying, touring, moving, **movement, motion, locomotion, transit, progress, passage,** course, crossing, commutation, straphanging; world travel, globetrotting <nonformal>; junketing; **tourism**

2 **travels,** journeys, peregrinations, migrations, transmigrations; odyssey

3 **wandering, roving, roaming, rambling, gadding,** traipsing <nonformal>, wayfaring, drifting, gallivanting, peregrination, divagation; roam, rove, ramble; **itinerancy,** itinerary; **nomadism;** vagabondage; **vagrancy,** hoboism; bumming <nonformal>; the open road; **wanderlust**

4 **migration, transmigration,** passage, trek; run <of fish>, flight <of birds and insects>; swarm, swarming <of bees>; **immigration; emigration,** expatriation

5 **journey, trip,** peregrination, **trek;** progress, course, run; **tour,** grand tour; **conducted tour,** package tour; **excursion, jaunt, junket, outing,** pleasure trip; sight-seeing trip; day-trip; **cruise; expedition,** campaign; safari; **pilgrimage,** hajj; **voyage** 182.6

6 **riding, driving; motoring; busing; motorcycling, bicycling, cycling,** biking <nonformal>; **horseback riding,** equitation; horsemanship, manège

7 ride, drive; joyride <nonformal>; airing

8 walking, perambulation, pedestrianism, shank's mare <nonformal>, going on foot *or* afoot, footing it *or* hoofing it; strolling, sauntering, ambling; **tramping, marching, hiking,** backpacking, trudging; lumbering, waddling; toddling, staggering, tottering; **hitchhiking** *and* hitching <both nonformal>, thumbing *and* thumbing a ride <both nonformal>; jaywalking

9 nightwalking, noctambulation, noctambulism; **sleepwalking,** somnambulation, somnambulism

10 walk, ramble, amble, **hike, tramp,** traipse <nonformal>; slog, trudge; **stroll,** saunter; **promenade;** jaunt, airing; **constitutional** <nonformal>, stretch; turn; excursion; **march; parade**

11 step, pace, stride; footstep, footfall, tread; hop, jump; skip

12 gait, pace, walk, step, stride, tread; saunter, stroll; shuffle, shamble, hobble, limp, waddle; totter, stagger, lurch; mince, mincing steps, scuttle, prance, flounce, stalk, strut, swagger; slink, slither, sidle; jog; amble; trot, gallop 174.3; lock step; velocity 174.1, 2; slowness 175

13 march; quick march, quickstep, quick time; lockstep; double time; slow time; goose step

14 leg, limb, shank; hind leg, foreleg; shin, cnemis; ankle, tarsus; calf; knee; thigh; ham, drumstick

15 <nonformal terms> gams, stems, trotters, underpinnings, wheels, shanks, pins, stumps

16 gliding, sliding, slipping, slithering, coasting, sweeping, flowing, sailing; **skating, skiing, tobogganing, sledding;** glide, slide, slither, sweep, skim, flow

17 creeping, crawling, going on all fours; sneaking, stealing, slinking, sidling, pussyfooting <nonformal>, padding, prowling;

tiptoeing, tiptoe; creep, crawl, scramble, scrabble

VERBS **18 travel, go, move, pass,** fare, fare forth, hie, sashay <nonformal>; **progress** 162.2; move on *or* along, go along; wend, **wend one's way;** course, run, flow, stream; roll, roll on; commute

19 <go at a given speed> go, go at, reach, make, do, hit <nonformal>, clip off <nonformal>

20 traverse, cross, travel over *or* through, pass through, **go** *or* **pass over, cover,** measure, transit, track, range, course, perambulate, peregrinate; patrol, reconnoiter, scout; sweep, go *or* make one's rounds, scour, scour the country; ply, voyage 182.13

21 journey, travel, make *or* take *or* go *or* go on a journey, **take** *or* **make a trip, gad around** *or* about, get around *or* about, navigate, trek, jaunt, peregrinate; junket, go on a junket; **tour;** hit the trail <nonformal>; **cruise, go on a cruise,** voyage 182.13; go abroad, globe-trot <nonformal>; travel light, live out of a suitcase; go on *or* make a pilgrimage; campaign, go on an expedition, go on safari

22 migrate, transmigrate, trek; flit, take wing; run <of fish>, swarm <of bees>; **emigrate,** expatriate; **immigrate**

23 wander, roam, rove, range, **gad,** gad around *or* about, follow the seasons, traipse <nonformal>, gallivant, knock around *or* about *and* bat around <all nonformal>, prowl, **drift, stray,** float around, straggle, **meander, ramble,** stroll, saunter, jaunt, peregrinate, divagate; **tramp,** vagabond, take to the road, beat one's way; **hit the road** <nonformal>, walk the tracks <nonformal>, pound the pavement

24 go for an outing *or* **airing,** take the air, get some air; go for a walk

25 go to, repair to, resort to, hie to, hie oneself to, make one's way to, set foot in, **visit,** drop in *or*

around *or* by, make the scene <nonformal>

26 creep, crawl, scramble, scrabble, grovel, **go on hands and knees,** go on all fours; worm, worm one's way, snake; inch, inch along; **sneak, steal;** slink, sidle, pad, prowl; **tiptoe,** go on tiptoe

27 walk, ambulate, traipse <nonformal>; **step, tread, pace, stride,** pad; leg it; hoof it, ride shank's mare <nonformal>; shuffle on *or* along; perambulate; jaywalk; power walk

28 <ways of walking> **stroll,** saunter; shuffle, scuff, scuffle, straggle, shamble, slouch; stride, straddle; **trudge, plod,** peg, traipse <nonformal>, clump, stump, slog, footslog, drag, **lumber ;** stamp, stomp <nonformal>; swing, roll, lunge; hobble, halt, limp, hitch, lurch; totter, stagger; toddle, paddle; waddle, wobble, wiggle; slither, sidle; stalk; **strut, swagger;** mince, sashay <nonformal>, prance, flounce, trip, skip; hop, jump; jog; **amble,** pace

29 go for a walk, perambulate, take a walk, take one's constitutional <nonformal>; **promenade,** parade

30 march, mush, footslog, **tramp, hike,** backpack; file, defile; **parade;** goose-step

31 hitchhike *or* **hitch** <nonformal>, **thumb** *or* **thumb one's way** <nonformal>, **catch a ride;** hitch *or* bum *or* thumb a ride <nonformal>

32 nightwalk, noctambulate; **sleepwalk,** somnambulate, walk in one's sleep

33 ride, go for a ride *or* **drive;** go for a spin <nonformal>; **drive, chauffeur; motor,** taxi; bus; bike *and* cycle *and* wheel *and* pedal <all nonformal>; **motorcycle, bicycle;** joyride *or* take a joyride <nonformal>; catch *or* make a train <nonformal>

34 go on horseback, ride; ride bareback; mount, take horse; hack; trot, amble, pace, canter, gallop, lope; prance, frisk

35 glide, coast, skim, sweep, flow; **sail, fly; slide,** slip, skid, slither; skate; ski; toboggan, sled, sleigh

ADJS **36 traveling, going, moving,** trekking; **progressing; itinerant,** itinerary; **journeying, wayfaring,** strolling; **peripatetic;** ambulant, ambulatory; perambulating; peregrine; locomotive; **walking, pedestrian, touring,** on tour, globe-trotting <nonformal>; touristic; expeditionary

37 wandering, roving, roaming, ranging, **rambling, meandering,** strolling, **straying,** straggling, shifting, divagatory; **gadding,** traipsing <nonformal>, gallivanting; **nomad,** nomadic, floating, drifting; **transient,** transitory, fugitive; **vagrant,** vagabond; **footloose,** footloose and fancy-free; **migratory**

38 nightwalking, noctambulant; **sleepwalking,** somnambulant

39 creeping, crawling, on hands and knees, on all fours; on tiptoe, tiptoeing

40 traveled, well-traveled, cosmopolitan

41 wayworn, leg-weary, **travelworn,** travel-weary

ADVS **42 on the move** *or* **go,** en route, in transit, on the wing; on the run, on the jump <nonformal>, on the road

43 on foot, afoot, by foot; on *or* by shank's mare <nonformal>

44 on horseback, horseback, by horse, mounted

178 TRAVELER

NOUNS **1 traveler, goer,** viator; **wayfarer, journeyer,** trekker; **tourist; cicerone, travel guide; visitor,** visiting fireman <nonformal>; **excursionist, sightseer,** rubberneck *or* rubbernecker <nonformal>; **voyager,** sailor, mariner 183; **globe-trotter** <nonformal>, world-traveler, cosmopolite; jet set, jet-setter; **pilgrim,** hajji; **passenger,** fare; **commuter,** straphanger <nonformal>; transient; passerby;

explorer, forty-niner, pioneer, pathfinder, trailblazer, trail-breaker

2 **wanderer, rover, roamer,** rambler, stroller, straggler, mover; **gad, gadabout** <nonformal>, runabout; **itinerant,** peripatetic, rolling stone, peregrine, visitant; **drifter** *and* **floater** <both nonformal>; wandering scholar; strolling player, wandering minstrel, troubadour

3 **vagabond, vagrant; bum** <nonformal>, loafer, wastrel; **tramp,** knight of the road, easy rider, **hobo** <nonformal>, bindlestiff <nonformal>; beggar 440.8; **waif,** dogie, stray; ragamuffin, tatterdemalion; **gamin,** gamine, urchin, street urchin, guttersnipe <nonformal>; beachcomber, loafer, idler; ski bum, beach bum, surf bum, tennis bum

4 **nomad,** Bedouin; gypsy, Bohemian

5 **migrant,** trekker; **immigrant; migrant** *or* migratory worker, wetback <nonformal>; **emigrant,** émigré <Fr>; expatriate; **evacuee; displaced person, stateless person,** exile

6 **pedestrian, walker; foot traveler,** hoofer <nonformal>, peripatetic; **hiker,** backpacker; marcher, footslogger, foot soldier, infantryman; **hitchhiker** <nonformal>; jaywalker; power walker

7 **nightwalker,** noctambulist, **sleepwalker,** somnambulist

8 **rider, equestrian, horseman,** horserider, horseback rider; horse soldier, cavalryman, mounted policeman; horsewoman, equestrienne; cowboy, cowgirl, puncher *or* cowpuncher *or* cowpoke <all nonformal>; broncobuster <nonformal>, buckaroo; **jockey;** steeplechaser

9 **driver,** Jehu, skinner <nonformal>; **coachman,** coachy <nonformal>, gharry-wallah <India>; stage coachman; charioteer; **cabdriver,** cabby <nonformal>, hack *or* hacky <nonformal>; drayman,

truckman; **carter; teamster;** mule skinner <nonformal>; mahout; cameleer

10 **driver, motorist; chauffeur; taxidriver,** cabdriver, cabby <nonformal>, **hack** *or* hacky <nonformal>; **truck driver, teamster,** truckman, **trucker; bus driver,** busman; road hog <nonformal>, Sunday driver, joyrider <nonformal>; hit-and-run driver; backseat driver

11 cyclist; **bicyclist,** bicycler; **motorcyclist,** biker <nonformal>

12 **engineer; Casey Jones; motorman**

13 **trainman,** railroad man, **railroader;** conductor; brakeman; fireman, stoker; switchman; yardman; yardmaster; trainmaster; dispatcher; stationmaster; lineman; baggage man; porter, redcap

179 VEHICLE
<means of conveyance>

NOUNS 1 **vehicle, conveyance,** carrier, means of transport, carriage; watercraft 180.1, aircraft 181

2 **wagon; haywagon; dray, van; covered wagon, prairie schooner, Conestoga wagon**

3 **cart; oxcart, horsecart, ponycart, dogcart; handcart;** jinrikisha, ricksha

4 **carriage,** gharry <India>; **chaise,** shay <nonformal>

5 **rig, equipage,** coach-and-four; team, pair, span; tandem

6 **baby carriage,** baby buggy <nonformal>, perambulator; gocart; **stroller,** walker

7 **wheel chair,** push chair

8 **cycle,** wheel <nonformal>; **bicycle,** bike <nonformal>, velocipede; **tricycle,** three-wheeler; **motorcycle,** motocycle

9 **automobile, car, auto,** motorcar, **machine,** motor, motor vehicle

10 <nonformal terms> **jalopy,** bus, buggy, wheels, tub, heap, crate, wreck, clunker, junker

11 **police car, patrol car; prowl car,** squad car; **police van,** patrol wagon; wagon *and* paddy wagon *and* Black Maria <all nonformal>

12 **truck; trailer truck,** tractor trailer, rig *and* semi <both nonformal>; eighteen-wheeler <nonformal>

13 <public vehicles> **commercial vehicle; bus,** omnibus, motor coach; schoolbus; **cab, taxicab, taxi,** hack <nonformal>, gypsy cab <nonformal>; rental car; limousine, limo *and* stretch limo <both nonformal>

14 **train,** railroad train; choo-choo *and* choo-choo train <both nonformal>; passenger train,; bullet train; local, milk train; shuttle; express train, express; flier, cannonball express <nonformal>; freight train, freighter; electric train; cable railroad; funicular; cog railroad *or* railway; subway, tube; elevated, el <nonformal>; monorail; streamliner; rolling stock

15 **railway car,** car; baggage car, boxcar, caboose, coach; diner, dining car; freight car; parlor car; Pullman *or* Pullman car; refrigerator car *or* reefer <nonformal>; roomette, sleeper *or* sleeping car; smoker *or* smoking car *or* compartment

16 **handcar; push car, trolley**

17 **streetcar, trolley** *or* trolley car; electric car, electric <nonformal>; trolley bus; horsecar; cable car

18 **tractor,** traction engine; Caterpillar tractor <trademark>, Caterpillar <trademark>; bulldozer, dozer <nonformal>

19 **trailer; house trailer, mobile home; recreation vehicle** *or* RV; truck trailer, **semitrailer; camp** trailer; **camper**

20 **sled, sleigh; snowmobile,** skimobile; runner, blade; toboggan

21 **skates,** ice skates, hockey skates, figure skates; roller skates, skateboard; **skis, snowshoes**

22 **Hovercraft** <trademark>, aircushion vehicle *or* ACV, ground-effect machine *or* GEM, captured-air vehicle *or* CAV, captured-air bubble *or* CAB, surface-effect ship

ADJS 23 **vehicular; automotive,** locomotive

180 SHIP, BOAT

NOUNS 1 **ship,** argosy, cargo ship, container ship, cruise ship, dredge, freighter, liner, merchant ship *or* merchantman, paddle boat *or* steamer, refrigeration ship, supertanker, tanker, trawler, whaler; **boat,** ark, canoe, gondola, kayak, lifeboat, motorboat, shell, skiff, whaleboat; vessel, craft, bark, argosy, hull, hulk, keel, watercraft; tub *and* bucket *and* rustbucket <all nonformal>; packet; leviathan

2 **steamer, steamboat, steamship;** motor ship

3 **sailboat, sailing vessel,** sailing boat, wind boat, tall ship, sail, **windjammer** <nonformal>; **yacht,** pleasure boat

4 **motorboat, powerboat,** speedboat, stinkpot <nonformal>; **launch,** motor launch; **cruiser,** power cruiser, cabin cruiser

5 **liner, ocean liner,** ocean greyhound <nonformal>, passenger steamer, floating hotel *or* palace, luxury liner; **cruise ship**

6 **warship,** war vessel, naval vessel; warship; **man-of-war,** man-o'-war; ship of the line; aircraft carrier *or* flattop <nonformal>, battle cruiser, battleship, coast guard cutter, cruiser, destroyer, destroyer escort, guided missile cruiser, heavy cruiser, hospital ship, mine layer, mine sweeper

7 **battleship,** battlewagon <nonformal>, capital ship; **cruiser,** battle-cruiser; **destroyer,** can *or* tin can <nonformal>

8 **carrier, aircraft carrier, flattop** <nonformal>

9 **submarine, sub,** submersible; **U-boat,** pigboat <nonformal>; nuclear *or* nuclear-powered submarine; Polaris submarine; Trident submarine

10 **ships, shipping,** merchant marine, merchant navy *or* fleet, tonnage; **fleet,** flotilla, argosy; fishing fleet, whaling fleet, etc; **navy** 461.26

11 **float, raft;** balsa, balsa raft, Kon Tiki; life raft; boom; pontoon; buoy, life buoy; **life preserver** 397.5; surfboard

12 **rigging,** rig, **tackle,** tackling, **gear; ropework,** roping; boatswain's stores; ship chandlery

13 **spar,** timber; **mast,** pole, stick <nonformal>

14 **sail, canvas,** muslin; **full** *or* **plain sail;** square sail; fore-and-aft sail

15 **oar; paddle,** scull, sweep, pole; steering oar

16 **anchor,** mooring, hook *and* mudhook <nonformal>; **anchorage,** moorings; **berth,** slip

ADJS 17 **rigged,** decked, trimmed; square-rigged, fore-and-aft rigged, gaff-rigged, lateen-rigged

18 **seaworthy, snug, bold; watertight,** waterproof; stiff, tender; weatherly; yare

19 **trim,** in trim; on an even keel

20 **shipshape,** trim, trig, neat, tight, taut, bungup and bilge-free

181 AIRCRAFT

NOUNS 1 **aircraft, airplane, plane, ship,** fixed-wing aircraft; heavier-than-air craft; **shuttle, space shuttle,** lifting body; **airplane part; flight instrument,** aircraft instrument; **aircraft engine; piston engine,** radial engine, rotary engine; **jet engine,** fan-jet engine, rocket motor, turbofan, turbojet, turboprop, pulse jet, ramjet, reaction engine

2 **propeller plane; tractor, tractor plane; pusher, pusher plane; piston plane; turbo-propeller plane, turbo-prop, prop-jet**

3 **jet plane, jet; turbojet,** ramjet, pulse jet, blowtorch <nonformal>; business jet; jumbo jet; subsonic jet; supersonic transport *or* SST, Concorde

4 **rocket plane; rocket ship, spaceship** 1073.2

5 **rotor plane,** rotary-wing aircraft; gyroplane, gyro, **autogiro,** windmill <nonformal>; **helicopter,** copter *and* whirlybird *and* chopper *and* eggbeater <all nonformal>

6 **ornithopter,** orthopter, mechanical bird

7 **flying platform,** flying bedspring; **Hovercraft** <trademark>, ground-effect machine, aircushion vehicle, cushioncraft; flying motorcycle, flying bathtub

8 **seaplane, hydroplane, floatplane; flying boat,** clipper; **amphibian**

9 **military aircraft, warplane; carrier fighter, carrier-based plane, dive bomber, fighter, helicopter gunship, jet bomber, jet fighter, jet tanker, night fighter, photo-reconnaissance plane, Stealth Bomber, Stealth Fighter, tactical support bomber, torpedo bomber, troop carrier** *or* **transport;** kamikaze; air fleet, air armada; air force 461.29

10 **trainer;** Link trainer; **flight simulator**

11 **aerostat,** lighter-than-air craft; **airship, ship, blimp** <nonformal>; rigid airship, semirigid airship; **dirigible,** zeppelin, Graf Zeppelin

12 **glider; sailplane; rocket glider**

13 **parachute, chute** <nonformal>; pilot chute, drogue chute; rip cord, safety loop, shroud lines, harness, pack, vent; parachute jump; sky dive; braking parachute; parawing *or* paraglider *or* parafoil

14 **kite,** box kite, cellular kite, tetrahedral kite

182 WATER TRAVEL

NOUNS 1 water travel, ocean travel, **seafaring, sailing,** steaming, voyaging, **cruising,** coasting; **boating, yachting,** motorboating, canoeing, rowing, sculling

2 **navigation,** navigating, circum-navigation

3 **seamanship,** shipmanship; sea legs

4 **pilotship, helmsmanship;** steerage

5 embarkation 188.3; disembarkation 186.2

6 **voyage,** ocean trip, **cruise,** sail; course, **run, passage; crossing;** shakedown cruise; leg

7 **wake,** track; wash, backwash

8 <submarines> **surfacing,** breaking water; **submergence, dive;** stationary dive, running dive, crash dive

9 **way, progress; headway,** sternway, leeway

10 **seaway, waterway,** fairway, road, channel, ocean or sea lane; approaches

11 aquatics, **swimming, bathing,** natation, **swim, bathe;** crawl, freestyle, trudgen, Australian crawl, breaststroke, butterfly, sidestroke, dog paddle, backstroke; waterskiing, aquaplaning, surfboarding; surfing; windsurfing

12 **swimmer, bather,** natator, merman; bathing girl, mermaid; bathing beauty; frogman; diver 367.4

VERBS 13 **navigate, sail, cruise,** steam, run, **seafare, voyage,** ply, go by ship, go on or take a voyage; go to sea, sail the sea, sail the ocean blue; **boat, yacht,** motorboat, canoe, row, scull; surf, windsurf; steamboat; cross, traverse, make a passage or run; sail round, circumnavigate; coast

14 **pilot,** helm, coxswain, **steer,** guide, be at the helm or tiller, direct, manage, handle, run, operate; **navigate,** chart a course

15 **anchor, cast anchor,** drop the hook; **dock, tie up; moor; lash, lash and tie; foul the anchor; disembark 186.8**

16 **ride at anchor,** ride, lie, rest; ride easy; lie athwart; set an anchor watch

17 **lay** or **lie to,** lay or lie by; lie near or close to the wind, head to wind

or windward; lie off, lie off the land; lay or lie up

18 **weigh anchor,** up-anchor, bring the anchor home, loose for sea; **unmoor,** drop the mooring, cast off or loose or away

19 **get under way,** put or have way upon, **put** or **push** or **shove off; put to sea,** put out to sea, go to sea, head for blue water; **sail,** sail away; embark

20 **set sail,** hoist sail, spread sail, **make sail,** trim sail; square the yards; **crowd** or **clap** or **crack** or **pack on sail,** put on [more] sail; clap on, crack on, pack on; give her beans <nonformal>

21 **make way,** gather way, **make headway,** make sternway; **go full speed ahead,** go full speed astern

22 **run, run** or **sail before the wind,** run or sail with the wind, run or sail down the wind, sail off the wind, sail free, sail with the wind aft; run or sail with the wind quartering

23 **bring off the wind, pay off,** bear off or away, bear or head to leeward, pay off the head

24 **sail against the wind,** sail on or by the wind, sail to windward; **bring in** or **into the wind;** put the helm up; haul, haul off, haul up; **haul to, bring to, heave to;** sail in or into the wind's eye or the teeth of the wind; sail to the windward of, weather

25 **sail near the wind,** sail close to the wind, lie near or close to the wind, **sail close-hauled,** close-haul; work or go or beat or eat to windward, **beat, ply; luff,** sail closer to the wind; sail too close to the wind

26 **gain to windward of,** eat the wind out of, have the wind of, be to windward of

27 **chart** or **lay out a course;** shape a course, lay a course

28 take or follow a course, **keep** or **hold the course** or **a course,** maintain or keep the heading, keep her steady

29 **drift off course, yaw,** bear off, drift, sag; sag or bear or ride or

drive to leeward, drive, fetch away; drift with the current

30 **change course,** change the heading, bear off *or* away; sheer, swerve; **tack,** cast, break, yaw, slew, shift, turn; **cant,** cant round *or* across; **beat, ply; veer, wear, wear ship; put about,** come *or* go *or* bring *or* fetch about, cast *or* throw about; bring *or* swing *or* heave *or* haul round; **about ship,** turn *or* put back, turn on her heel; swing the stern

31 put the rudder hard left *or* right, put the rudder *or* helm hard over, give her more *or* less rudder

32 **veer** *or* **wear short, broach to,** lie beam on to the seas

33 <come to a stop> **fetch up, heave to,** haul up

34 **backwater,** back, reverse, go astern; **go full speed astern;** make sternway

35 **sail for, put away for, make for** *or* toward, make at, **run for,** stand for, head *or* steer toward, lay for, **lay a** *or* **one's course for,** bear up for; bear up to, **bear down on** *or* **upon,** run *or* bear in with, **close with; put in** *or* into, put into port, approach anchorage

36 **sail away from,** head *or* steer away from, run from, **stand from,** lay away *or* off from; **stand off,** bear off, put off, shove off, haul off; stand off and on

37 **clear the land,** bear off the land, lay *or* settle the land, make *or* get sea room

38 **make land; close with the land; smell land; make a land-fall**

39 **coast,** sail coast-wise, range the coast, skirt the shore, lie along the shore, **hug the shore** *or* **land**

40 **weather the storm,** weather, **ride out,** ride *or* ride out a storm; make heavy *or* bad weather

41 **sail into,** run down, run in *or* into, **ram; come** *or* **run foul** *or* **afoul of,** collide; **nose** *or* head into, run prow *or* end *or* head on; run broadside on

42 **shipwreck,** wreck, pile up <nonformal>, cast away; **go** *or* **run**

aground, ground, beach, run on the rocks; ground hard and fast

43 **careen, list, heel,** tip, cant, heave *or* lay down, lie along; be on beam ends

44 **capsize, upset, overturn,** turn over, turn turtle, keel, keel over *or* up; **sink, founder,** go down, go to the bottom, go to Davy Jones's locker; scuttle

45 **go overboard,** go by the board, go over the side

46 **maneuver; heave in together,** maintain position, **keep station,** steam in line; convoy

47 <submarines> **surface,** break water; **submerge, dive,** crash-dive; rig for diving; flood the tanks

48 <activities aboard ship> lay, heave, haul

49 **trim ship,** trim, trim up; trim by the head *or* stern, **put on an even keel; ballast,** shift ballast, wing out ballast; break out ballast, break bulk, shoot ballast; **clear the decks,** clear for action

50 **reduce sail,** shorten *or* take in sail, **reef,** reef one's sails; lower sail, dowse sail; snug down; **furl**

51 **take bearings,** cast a traverse; correct distance and maintain the bearings; **take a sight,** shoot the sun; **box the compass; take soundings** 275.9

52 **signal,** hail and speak; dress ship; unfurl *or* hoist a banner, unfurl an ensign, **break out a flag;** show one's colors, **exchange colors;** dip the ensign

53 **row, paddle, pull, scull, punt;** give way, row away; feather, feather an oar; sky an oar <nonformal>; ship oars

54 **float,** ride, drift; **sail, scud, run,** shoot; skim, foot; ride the sea, plow the deep

55 **pitch, toss, tumble, plunge,** pound, rear, rock, roll, reel, swing, sway, lurch, yaw, heave, flounder, welter, wallow; make heavy weather

56 **swim, bathe; tread water; float,** do the deadman's float; **wade; skinny-dip;** dive 367.6

ADJS 57 **nautical, marine, mar-**

itime, naval, navigational; seafaring, seagoing, oceangoing,
seaborne, water-borne; seamanly,
salty <nonformal>

58 aquatic, water-dwelling, water-
living; **swimming,** balneal, na-
tant, natatorial; tidal, estuarine,
littoral; riverine; deep-sea 275.14

59 navigable, boatable

60 floating, afloat, awash; water-
borne

61 adrift, afloat, unmoored, untied, loose, unanchored, aweigh;
cast-off, started

ADVS **62 on board,** on shipboard,
on board ship, **aboard,** all
aboard, afloat; **on deck,** topside; aloft; in sail; before the
mast

63 under way, making way, with
steerageway, with way on; **at sea,**
on the high seas, in blue water;
under sail or **canvas,** with sails
spread; under steam or power; on
or off the heading or course;
homeward bound

64 before the wind, with the wind,
down the wind, running free; off
the wind, with the wind aft, with
the wind abaft the beam, under
the wind, under the lee

65 against the wind, on the wind,
in or into the wind, up the wind,
by the wind; in the teeth of the
wind

66 near the wind, close to the
wind, **close-hauled**

**67 coastward, landward; coast-
wise,** coastways

68 leeward, to leeward, downwind;
windward, to windward, weatherward

69 aft, abaft, baft, **astern;** fore and
aft

70 alongside, board and board,
yardarm to yardarm

71 at anchor, riding at anchor;
lying to, hove to

72 afoul, foul, in collision; head
and head, head or end or prow
on; broadside on

73 aground, on the rocks; hard and
fast

74 overboard, over the side, by the
board; aft the fantail

183 MARINER

NOUNS 1 **mariner, seaman, sailor,
navigator, seafarer,** seafaring
man, sea dog <nonformal>; jack-
tar, **tar, salt** <nonformal>, wind-
sailor, windjammer; saltwater or
bluewater or deepwater sailor;
fresh-water sailor; fair-weather
sailor; whaler, fisherman, lobster-
man; viking, sea rover, buccaneer,
privateer, pirate; **yachtsman,
yachtswoman**

2 <novice> **lubber, landlubber;**
polliwog

3 <veteran> **old salt** and old sea
dog and shell-back and barnacle-
back <all nonformal>; **master
mariner**

4 **navy man, bluejacket; gob** and
swabbie and swabber <all nonfor-
mal>; **marine, leatherneck** and
gyrene and devil dog <all nonfor-
mal>; **boot** <nonformal>; **midshipman,** middy <nonformal>;
cadet, naval cadet

5 **boatman,** boatsman, **boater;
oarsman,** oar, rower, sculler; **fer-
ryman; bargeman,** bargemaster;
gondolier

6 hand, **deckhand,** roustabout
<nonformal>; stoker, fireman;
black gang; wiper, oiler, boiler-
man; cabin boy; yeoman; purser;
ship's carpenter; ship's cooper;
steward, stewardess; navigator;
radio operator; complement;
watch

7 <ship's officers> **captain,** ship-
master, **master, skipper** <non-
formal>, **commander; mate;
boatswain,** bos'n; quartermaster

8 **steersman, helmsman; quartermaster;** coxswain, cox
<nonformal>; **pilot**

9 **longshoreman,** dockhand,
dockworker, dock-walloper
<nonformal>; **stevedore; roust-
about** <nonformal>

184 AVIATION

NOUNS 1 **aviation, aeronautics;
flying, flight; gliding,** sail-
planing, soaring; ballooning;

barnstorming <nonformal>; **air traffic,** airline traffic; commercial aviation, general aviation, private aviation, private flying; astronautics 1073.1; air show, flying circus

2 air sciences, aeronautical sciences

3 **airmanship; flight plan;** briefing, brief, rundown <nonformal>; debriefing; flight *or* pilot training

4 air-mindedness, aerophilia; air legs

5 airsickness; aerophobia, aeropathy

6 **navigation; celestial navigation;** radio navigation, radar, tacan, loran, shoran

7 <aeronautical organizations> Civil Aeronautics Administration *or* CAA; Federal Aviation Agency *or* FAA

8 **takeoff; taxiing, takeoff run; daisy-clipping** *and* grass-cutting <both nonformal>; ground loop; jet-assisted takeoff *or* JATO

9 **flight, trip, run; hop** *and* **jump** <both nonformal>; powered flight; solo flight, **solo;** test flight, **test hop** <nonformal>; **airlift;** airdrop

10 **air travel,** air transport; **airfreight, air cargo; airline travel, airline,** feeder airline, commuter airline, scheduled airline, charter airline, nonscheduled airline; **shuttle,** air shuttle, shuttle service, shuttle trip; air taxi

11 <Air Force> **mission; training mission; gunnery mission; dry run** <nonformal>; reconnaissance mission, search mission; **milk run** <nonformal>; combat flight; **sortie,** scramble <nonformal>; **air raid;** shuttle raid; bombing mission; bombing, strafing 459.7; **air support** <for ground troops>, **air cover,** air umbrella

12 flight formation, formation flying, formation; close formation, loose formation, wing formation

13 <maneuvers> acrobatic *or* tactical maneuvers, acrobatics, **aerobatics;** stunting *and* **stunt flying** <both nonformal>, rolling, crabbing, banking, porpoising, fishtailing, diving; **dive, nose dive, power dive; glide**

14 **roll, barrel roll,** aileron roll, **snap roll**

15 **spin,** autorotation, **tailspin,** flat spin, inverted spin, normal spin, power spin; whipstall

16 **loop,** spiral loop, ground loop, normal loop, outside loop, inverted normal *or* outside loop, dead-stick loop, wingover, looping the loop

17 **buzzing, hedgehopping** <nonformal>

18 **landing,** coming in <nonformal>, touching down, touchdown; arrival

19 flying and landing guides marker, pylon; beacon; radio beacon, radio range station, radio marker; fan marker; radar beacon, racon; beam, radio beam; beacon lights; runway lights, high-intensity runway approach lights, sequence flashers, flare path; wind indicator, wind cone *or* sock, air sleeve

20 **crash, crack-up; crash landing; collision, mid-air collision; near-miss, near collision**

21 **blackout;** grayout; anoxia; useful consciousness; pressure suit, antiblackout suit

22 **airport, airfield, airdrome,** air harbor <Can>, aviation field, **landing field; air terminal, jetport; air base,** air station, naval air station; **heliport; control tower**

23 **runway, taxiway,** strip, landing strip, **airstrip, flight strip,** takeoff strip; apron; **flight deck,** landing deck; helipad

24 **hangar,** housing, dock, airdock, shed, airship shed; mooring mast

25 <propulsion> rocket propulsion, rocket power; **jet propulsion,** jet power; turbojet propulsion, pulse-jet propulsion, ram-jet propulsion; constant *or* ram pressure, air ram; reaction propulsion, reaction; aircraft engine, power plant

26 lift, lift ratio, lift force *or* component; dynamic lift, gross lift, useful lift

27 drag, resistance; drag ratio, drag force *or* component, induced drag, wing drag, parasite *or* parasitic *or* structural drag, profile drag, head resistance, drag direction, cross-wind force

28 drift, drift angle; lateral drift, leeway

29 flow, air flow, laminar flow; **turbulence,** turbulent flow, eddies

30 wash, wake, stream; downwash; backwash, **slipstream,** propwash; **exhaust,** jet exhaust; **vapor trail,** condensation trail, contrail, vortex

31 <speed> **air speed,** true air speed, operating *or* flying speed, cruising speed, knots, minimum flying speed; **speed of sound** 174.2; Mach cone; **sound barrier,** sonic barrier *or* wall; sonic boom, shock wave, Mach wave

32 <air, atmosphere> **airspace,** navigable airspace; **aerospace; weather, weather conditions; ceiling; ceiling and visibility unlimited;** cloud layer *or* cover, ceiling zero; visibility, visibility zero; **overcast; fog, soup** <nonformal>; **high-pressure area, low-pressure area,** trough; **front; air pocket** *or* **hole,** air bump, pocket, hole, bump; **turbulence;** clear-air turbulence *or* CAT; roughness; head wind; tail wind, favorable *or* favoring wind; cross wind; jetstream

33 airway, air lane, air line, air route, skyway, corridor, flight path, lane, path

34 course, heading, vector; compass heading *or* course, compass direction, magnetic heading, true heading *or* course

35 <altitude> altitude of flight, absolute altitude, critical altitude

VERBS **36 fly,** be airborne, take wing, take to the air; **jet;** travel by air, go *or* travel by airline, ride the skies; hop <nonformal>; **soar,** drift, hover; **cruise; glide; hydroplane, seaplane; balloon;**

ferry; airlift; break the sound barrier

37 pilot, control, be at the controls, **fly,** fly left seat; **copilot,** fly right seat; solo; **barnstorm** <nonformal>; fly blind, fly by the seat of one's pants <nonformal>; follow the beam, ride the beam, fly on instruments; fly in formation, take position; peel off

38 take off, hop *or* jump off <nonformal>, become airborne, get off *or* leave the ground, take to the air, clear; power off; **taxi**

39 ascend, climb, gain altitude, mount; **zoom**

40 <maneuver> **stunt** <nonformal>, perform aerobatics; crab, fishtail; **spin,** go into a tailspin; **loop,** loop the loop; **roll,** wingover, spiral, undulate, porpoise, feather, yaw, sideslip, skid, bank, dip, nose down, nose up, pull up, push down, pull out, plow, mush through

41 dive, nose-dive, power-dive, go for the deck; lose altitude, settle, dump altitude <nonformal>

42 buzz, hedgehop <nonformal>

43 land, set her down <nonformal>, **alight, light,** touch down; **descend,** come down, dump altitude <nonformal>, fly down; come in, come in for a landing; **level off,** flatten out; upwind, downwind; overshoot, undershoot; make a dead-stick landing; pancake, thump in <nonformal>; fishtail down; **crashland;** ditch <nonformal>; nose up, nose over

44 crash, crack up, spin in, fail to pull out

45 stall, lose power, conk out <nonformal>; flame out

46 black out, gray out

47 parachute, bail out, jump, make a parachute jump, hit the silk, sky-dive

48 brief, give a briefing; debrief

ADJS **49 aviation, aeronautic, aeronautical,** aerial; **aerospace,** aerodynamic, avionic; aerobatic; airworthy, air-minded; airsick

50 flying, airborne, winging, soaring; volant, volitant, volitational, hovering, fluttering; gliding; jet-propelled, rocket-propelled

ADVS **51 in flight, on the wing,** while airborne

185 AVIATOR

NOUNS 1 **aviator, airman, flier, pi-lot,** licensed pilot, private pilot, airline pilot, commercial pilot, flyboy *and* airplane driver *and* birdman <all nonformal>; captain, chief pilot; copilot, second officer; flight engineer, third officer; jet pilot; test pilot; bush pilot; astronaut 1073.8; cropduster; barnstormer <nonformal>

2 **aviatrix, airwoman; stunt-woman**

3 **military pilot; fighter pilot; bomber pilot; observer; avia-tion cadet; flyboy** <nonformal>; **ace**

4 **crew, aircrew,** flight crew; **navi-gator; bombardier;** gunner; crew chief; **flight attendant, steward, stewardess**

5 **ground crew,** plane handlers; crew chief

6 aircraftsman, aeromechanic, air-craft mechanic

7 **balloonist,** ballooner, aeronaut

8 **parachutist,** chutist *or* chuter <nonformal>, parachute jumper; sky diver; smoke jumper; **para-trooper;** paramedic; jumpmaster

186 ARRIVAL

NOUNS 1 **arrival, coming, advent,** approach, appearance, **reaching; attainment, accomplishment, achievement**

2 **landing,** landfall; docking, mooring, dropping anchor; **dis-embarkation,** disembarkment, debarkation, coming *or* going ashore; **deplaning**

3 **return, homecoming; reen-trance, reentry**

4 **welcome,** greetings 585.3

5 **destination, goal; port, haven, harbor, anchorage, journey's end;** end of the line, terminus, **terminal,** terminal point; stop,

stopping place, last stop; **airport, air terminal** 184.22

VERBS 6 **arrive,** arrive at, arrive in, come, **come** *or* **get to,** approach, access, **reach, hit** <nonformal>; find, **gain,** attain, attain to, ac-complish, achieve, make, **make it** <nonformal>, fetch up at, reach one's destination, come to one's journey's end, end up; **come to rest,** settle, settle in; **make** *or* **put in an appearance, show up** <nonformal>, turn up, **surface,** pop *or* bob up *and* make the scene <all nonformal>; **get in, come in,** blow in <nonformal>, pull in, roll in; **check in;** clock *or* punch *or* ring in <all nonformal>, sign in; hit town <nonformal>

7 **arrive at,** come at, **reach,** arrive upon, **come upon, hit upon,** strike upon, fall upon, light upon, pitch upon, stumble on *or* upon

8 **land,** come to land, make a land-fall, set foot on dry land; reach *or* make land, make port; put in *or* into, put into port; dock, moor, tie up, anchor, drop anchor; go ashore, **disembark,** debark; **de-train, deplane, disemplane;** alight

ADJS 9 **arriving,** approaching, en-tering, **coming,** incoming; in-bound, inwardbound; homeward, homeward-bound

ADVS 10 **arriving,** on arrival *or* ar-riving

187 RECEPTION

NOUNS 1 **reception, taking in,** re-ceipt, receiving; **welcome,** wel-coming, open *or* welcoming arms; refuge 1008

2 **admission,** admittance, accep-tance; intromission 191.1; **instal-lation,** installment, instatement, inauguration, initiation; baptism, investiture, ordination; enlist-ment, enrollment, induction

3 **entree, entrée,** in <nonformal>, entry, **entrance** 189, **access,** opening, **open door,** open arms; a foot in the door, opening wedge

4 **ingestion; eating** 8; **drinking**

8.3, imbibing ; **swallowing,** gulping; swallow, gulp, slurp

5 <drawing in> **suction,** suck, sucking; **inhalation,** inspiration, aspiration; snuff, snuffle, sniff, sniffle

6 sorption, **absorption,** adsorption, engrossment, digestion; **assimilation,** infiltration; **sponging, blotting; seepage,** percolation; **osmosis; absorbency; absorbent,** adsorbent, **sponge, blotter**

7 <bringing in> **introduction; importing,** import, **importation**

8 readmission; reabsorption, resorbence

9 **receptivity, receptiveness,** welcoming, welcome, invitingness, openness, hospitality, cordiality; admissibility

VERBS 10 **receive, take in; admit, let in,** intromit, give entrance or admittance to; **welcome,** bid welcome, give a royal welcome, roll out the red carpet; open the door to, give refuge or shelter or sanctuary to, throw open to

11 **ingest, eat** 8.18, put away; imbibe, **drink; swallow, devour; engulf,** engorge; **gulp,** gulp down, swill, swill down, wolf down, gobble

12 **draw in, suck,** suckle, suck in or up, aspirate; **inhale,** inspire, breathe in; snuff, snuffle, sniff, sniffle, snuff in or up, slurp

13 **absorb,** adsorb, **assimilate,** engross, digest, **drink,** imbibe, take up or in, drink up or in, slurp up, swill up; **blot up, soak up,** sponge; infiltrate; **soak in, seep in**

14 **bring in, introduce, import**

15 readmit; reabsorb, resorb

ADJS 16 **receptive,** recipient; welcoming, open, hospitable, cordial, inviting; **admissive; receivable, receptible, admissible; intromissive; ingestive, imbibitory**

17 sorbent, **absorbent,** adsorbent, **assimilative,** digestive; bibulous, imbibitory, thirsty, soaking, blotting; spongy; osmotic; resorbent

18 **introductory,** introductive; **initiatory,** baptismal

188 DEPARTURE

NOUNS 1 **departure, leaving, going,** passing, **parting; exit; egress** 190.2; **withdrawal,** removal, retreat 163.2, retirement; evacuation, abandonment, desertion; escape, flight, getaway <nonformal>; exodus, hegira; migration; defection

2 **start,** starting, start-off, setout, takeoff and getaway <both nonformal>; the starting gun or pistol

3 **embarkation,** embarkment, boarding; entrainment; **takeoff**

4 **leave-taking, leave, parting, departure; send-off,** Godspeed; **adieu, farewell,** aloha, **good-bye;** valedictory address, valedictory, valediction; parting or Parthian shot; swan song; viaticum; stirrup cup, one for the road

5 **point of departure, starting place** or **point,** takeoff, **start,** base, baseline, basis; starting line or post or gate, starting blocks

VERBS 6 **depart,** make off, begone, be off, take oneself off or away, take one's departure, take leave or take one's leave, **leave, go, go away, go off, get off** or **away,** get under way, be getting along, go on, get on; move off or away, move out, march off or away; **pull out;** decamp; exit; take or break or tear oneself away, take wing or flight

7 <nonformal terms> **beat it, split,** scram, toddle, stagger along, mosey or sashay along, buzz off, buzz along, bug out, get rolling, hightail it, pull up stakes, check out, clear out, cut out, haul ass, hit the road or trail, get lost, flake off, get going, shove off, push along, push off, get out, get or git, clear out, get the hell out, make oneself scarce, vamoose, take off, skip, skip out, lam, take it on the lam, powder, take a powder, take a runout powder, skedaddle

8 **set out, set forth,** put forth, go

forth, **sally forth,** sally, issue, issue forth, launch forth, set forward, **set out** or **off,** be off, be on one's way, **start, start out** or **off, strike out,** get off, get away, get off the dime <nonformal>

9 quit, vacate, evacuate, abandon, desert, turn one's back on, walk away from, leave to one's fate, leave flat or high and dry; leave or desert a sinking ship; **withdraw,** retreat, **beat a retreat,** retire, remove; walk away, abscond, disappear, vanish; **bow out** <nonformal>, make one's exit; jump ship

10 hasten off, hurry away; scamper off, dash off, whiz off, tear off or out, **light out** <nonformal>

11 fling out or **off,** flounce out or off

12 run off or **away,** run along, flee, take to one's heels, cut and run and hightail and make tracks <all nonformal>; run for one's life; beat a retreat or a hasty retreat

13 check out; clock and ring and punch out <all nonformal>, sign out

14 decamp, break camp, strike camp, **pull up stakes**

15 embark, go aboard, board, go on board; **entrain,** enplane; weigh anchor, up-anchor, put to sea 182.19

16 say or bid good-bye or farewell, take leave, make one's adieus; bid Godspeed, give one a send-off or a big send-off, see off; have one for the road

17 leave home; leave the country, emigrate, expatriate, defect; vote with one's feet; burn one's bridges

ADJS **18 departing, leaving; parting,** last, final, farewell; valedictory; outward-bound

19 departed, left, gone, gone off or away

ADVS **20 hence,** thence, whence; off, **away,** forth, out; therefrom, thereof

189 ENTRANCE

NOUNS **1 entrance, entry,** access, entree, entrée; **ingress; admission, reception** 187; **ingoing, incoming; importation,** import, importing; **input, intake; penetration,** injection; infiltration, percolation, seepage, leakage; insinuation; intrusion 214; introduction, **insertion** 191

2 influx, inflow, incursion, inrush

3 immigration, foreign influx; border-crossing

4 incomer, entrant, comer, arrival; **visitor,** visitant; **immigrant;** newcomer 773.4; settler 227.9; **trespasser, intruder** 214.3

5 entrance, entry, gate, door, portal, **entranceway,** entryway; **inlet,** ingress, intake, adit, approach, **access,** means of access, in <nonformal>, way in; a foot in the door, an opening wedge; **opening** 292; **passageway,** corridor, companionway, hall, hallway, passage, way; jetway; gangway, gangplank; **vestibule** 197.19; air lock

6 porch; portal, threshold, doorjamb, gatepost, doorpost, lintel; **door, doorway; gate, gateway; hatch,** hatchway

VERBS **7 enter, go in** or **into,** access, cross the threshold, **come in,** find one's way into, put in or into; be admitted, gain admission or admittance, have an entree, have an in <nonformal>; **set foot in,** step in, walk in; **get in, drop in,** look in, visit, drop by or in, pop in <nonformal>; **breeze in,** come breezing in; break or burst in; **barge in** or come barging in and wade in <all nonformal>; thrust in, push or press in, crowd in, jam in, wedge in, pack in, squeeze in; slip or creep in, wriggle or worm oneself into, get one's foot in the door, edge in, work in, insinuate oneself, weigh in <nonformal>; intrude 214.5; take in, admit 187.10; insert 191.3

8 penetrate, interpenetrate, **pierce,** pass or go through, get through, get into, make way into,

make an entrance, gain entree;
crash <nonformal>

9 flow in, inpour, **pour in**

10 filter in, infiltrate, seep in, percolate into, leak in, soak in,
perfuse

11 immigrate; cross the border

ADJS **12 entering, incoming, ingoing,** in, inward; **inbound,**
inward-bound; inflowing, influent, inrushing; invasive, intrusive; ingrowing

ADVS **13 in,** inward, inwards, inwardly; thereinto

190 EMERGENCE

NOUNS **1 emergence,** coming
forth, coming into view, rising to
the surface, surfacing; **issuing,**
issuance; extrusion; **emission,**
emitting, giving forth, giving out;
emanation; **vent,** venting, discharge

2 egress, egression; **exit,** exodus;
outgoing, outgo; **departure** 188;
extraction 192

3 outburst 671.6, ejection 908

4 outflow, outflowing; discharge;
outpouring, outpour; effluence,
effusion, exhalation; **exhaust;
runoff, flowoff;** drainage, drain;
gush 238.4

5 leakage, leaking, weeping
<nonformal>; **leak; dripping,**
drippings, **drip,** dribble, drop,
trickle; distillation

6 exuding, exudation, transudation; **filtration,** exfiltration;
filtering; straining; **percolation,**
percolating; leaching; effusion;
seepage, seep; **oozing,** ooze;
weeping, weep; **excretion** 12

7 emigration; exile, expatriation, defection, deportation

8 export, exporting, exportation

9 outlet, egress, **exit,** outgo, outcome, out <nonformal>, way out;
loophole, escape; **opening** 292;
estuary; chute, flume, sluice,
weir, floodgate; **vent,** ventage,
venthole, port; safety valve; avenue, channel; spout, tap; **exhaust;** outgate, sally port; vomitory; pore; blowhole, spiracle

10 goer, outgoer, leaver, departer;

emigrant, émigré; defector, refugee

VERBS **11 emerge, come out, issue,** issue forth, come into view,
extrude, **come forth; surface,**
rise to the surface; sally forth,
come to the fore; emanate, effuse,
arise, come; bail out; **burst forth,
break forth, erupt;** break cover,
come out in the open; protrude

12 exit, make an exit, **make one's
exit;** egress, **go out,** get out, walk
out, march out, run out, pass out,
bow out *and* include oneself out
<both nonformal>; leave cold
<nonformal>; **depart** 188.6

13 run out, empty, find vent; **exhaust, drain,** drain out; **flow out,**
outflow, outpour, **pour out,** sluice
out, well out, gush *or* spout out,
spew, flow, pour, well, surge,
gush, jet, spout, spurt, vomit
forth, blow out, spew out

14 leak, leak out, drip, dribble,
drop, trickle

15 exude, transude, reek; **emit,
discharge; filter,** filtrate, exfiltrate; strain; **percolate;** leach;
effuse; **seep, ooze;** bleed; weep

16 emigrate; exile, expatriate, defect; deport

17 export, send abroad

ADJS **18 emerging,** emergent; **issuing,** arising, surfacing, coming,
forthcoming; emanating, transient

19 outgoing, outbound, outwardbound; **outflowing,** outpouring,
effusive, effluent

**20 exuding; porous, permeable, pervious, oozy, runny, weepy, leaky

ADVS **21 forth; out,** outward, outwards, outwardly

191 INSERTION
<putting in>

NOUNS **1 insertion, introduction,**
insinuation, injection, infusion,
inoculation, intromission; **entrance** 189; **penetration** 292.3;
interjection, interpolation 213.2;
infixing, implantation, embedment, impactment, impaction

2 insert, insertion; **inset, inlay;**
gore, gusset; **graft,** scion *or* cion

VERBS **3 insert, introduce,** insinuate, inject, infuse, inoculate, intromit; **enter** 189.7; **penetrate;
put in, stick in,** set in, throw in,
pop in, tuck in, whip in; interject

4 install, instate, inaugurate, initiate, invest, ordain; enlist, enroll,
induct, sign up, sign on

5 inset, inlay; embed or bed, bed
in

6 graft, engraft, **implant; bud**

**7 thrust in, drive in, run in,
plunge in,** force in, push in, **ram
in,** press in, stuff in, crowd in,
squeeze in, cram in, jam in, tamp
in, pound in, pack in, poke in,
knock in, wedge in

8 implant, transplant; infix 854.9;
fit in, **inlay**

192 EXTRACTION
<taking or drawing out>

NOUNS **1 extraction, withdrawal,**
removal; **drawing, pulling,**
drawing out; ripping or tearing or
wresting out; eradication, **uprooting,** deracination; squeezing
out, pressing out, expressing, expression; extirpation, excision;
extrication, disentanglement, un-
ravelment; excavation, mining,
quarrying, drilling; dredging

**2 disinterment, exhumation, un-
earthing,** uncovering, digging
out

3 drawing, drafting, sucking, **suction,** aspiration, pipetting;
pumping, siphoning, tapping;
broaching; milking; bloodletting,
bleeding, phlebotomy

4 evisceration, gutting, **disembowelment**

5 elicitation, eduction, drawing
out or forth, bringing out or forth;
evocation; arousal

6 extortion, exaction, claim, demand; **wresting, wrenching,
wringing, rending,** tearing, ripping; wrest, wrench, wring

7 <obtaining an extract> **squeezing, pressing,** expression; **distillation;** decoction; **rendering,**
rendition; **steeping,** soaking, infusion; concentration

8 extract, extraction; **essence,**

quintessence, spirit, elixir; decoction; **distillate,** distillation;
concentrate, concentration; infusion

9 extractor, separator; siphon; as-
pirator, pipette; pump, vacuum
pump; press, wringer

VERBS **10 extract, take out,** get
out, **withdraw, remove;** pull;
draw; **pull out, draw out,** tear
out, rip out, wrest out, pluck out,
pick out, weed out, rake out; **pry
out; pull up,** pluck up; **root out** or
out, uproot, eradicate, deracinate, pull or pluck out by the
roots; cut out, excise; gouge out;
extricate, disentangle, unravel;
dig up or **out,** grub up or out, excavate, **unearth,** mine, quarry;
dredge, dredge up or out

11 disinter, exhume, disentomb,
dig up, uncover

12 draw off, draft off, draft, draw,
draw from; **suck,** suck out or up,
siphon off; pipette; pump, pump
out; tap, broach; bleed; let blood,
phlebotomize; milk; **drain,** decant; exhaust, empty

13 eviscerate, disembowel, gut

14 elicit, educe, deduce, induce, derive, obtain, procure, secure; **get
from,** get out of; **evoke, call up,**
summon up, call or summon
forth; rouse, arouse, stimulate;
draw out or **forth,** bring forth,
pry out, drag out, worm out,
bring to light; wangle, wangle out
of, worm out of

15 extort, exact, squeeze, claim,
demand; **wrest, wring from,
wrench from, rend from,** wrest
or tear from

16 <obtain an extract> **squeeze** or
press out, express, wring, wring
out; **distill,** distill out; **filter,** filter
out; decoct; **render,** melt down;
refine; **steep,** soak, infuse; **concentrate**

ADJS **17 extractive,** eductive; eradicative, uprooting; **evocative,**
arousing; **exacting,** exactive;
extortionate, extortionary, ex-
tortive

18 essential, quintessential, pure
797.6

193 ASCENT
<motion upwards>

NOUNS **1 ascent,** ascension, levitation, **rise, rising,** uprising, **up-rise,** uprisal; **upgoing,** upgo, uphill; upcoming; **taking off,** leaving the ground, takeoff; **soaring,** zooming, gaining altitude; spiraling up; shooting or rocketing up; **jump,** vault, spring, **leap** 366; mount, **mounting; climb, climbing,** clamber, escalade; surge, upsurge, upshoot, uprush; **gush, jet,** spurt, spout, fountain; updraft; upgrowth; upgrade 204.6; **uplift,** elevation 911; **up-tick** <nonformal>, **increase** 251

2 upturn, uptrend, upsweep, upcurve

3 stairs, stairway, staircase, flight of stairs, pair of stairs; **steps,** treads and risers; stepping-stones; stile; back stairs; fire escape; landing; ramp, incline

4 ladder; stepladder, folding ladder, rope ladder, fire ladder; hook ladder, extension ladder;

5 step, stair, footstep, rest, footrest, stepping-stone; **rung, round,** spoke, stave, scale; doorstep; tread; riser

6 climber, ascender, upclimber; mountain climber, **mountaineer,** alpinist, rock climber

7 <comparisons> rocket, skyrocket; lark, eagle

VERBS **8 ascend, rise, mount,** arise, up, uprise, levitate, **go up,** rise up, come up; go onwards and upwards; upsurge, **surge,** upstream, upheave; swarm up; spiral, spire, curl upwards; stand up, **rear,** rear up, **tower,** loom

9 shoot up, spring up, jump up, **leap up,** vault up, start up, fly up, pop up, bob up; float up, surface; **gush, jet,** spurt, fountain; upspring, rocket, **skyrocket**

10 take off, leave the ground, gain altitude; become airborne; **soar,** zoom, fly, plane, fly aloft; aspire; spire, spiral upward; **hover,** hang, poise, float

11 climb, climb up, **mount,** clamber, **clamber up,** scramble or scrabble up, claw one's way up, shinny or shin up <nonformal>, work or inch one's way up; **scale,** scale the heights; climb over, surmount

12 mount, get on, climb on, back; **bestride,** bestraddle; **board,** go aboard, go on board; **get in,** jump in, hop in, pile in <nonformal>

13 upturn, turn up; trend upwards, slope up; upsweep, upcurve

ADJS **14 ascending,** in the ascendant, **mounting, rising,** uprising; ascendant; **leaping,** springing; spiraling, skyrocketing; **upward; uphill,** upgrade, upsloping; rearing, rampant; climbing

15 upturned, upcast, uplifted, **turned-up,** retroussé

ADVS **16 up, upward, upwards; skyward,** heavenward; upstream; uphill; upstairs; uptown

194 DESCENT
<motion downward>

NOUNS **1 descent, descending, comedown,** down; **dropping, falling,** plummeting, **drop, fall, freefall, downfall,** debacle, **collapse,** crash; **swoop,** stoop, **pounce,** downrush, cascade, waterfall, cataract, **downpour; downturn, downcurve, downbend, downward trend, downtrend;** declination, inclination; downgrade 204.5; **down tick; decrease** 252

2 sinkage, lowering, **decline, slump,** subsidence, submergence, lapse; cadence; **droop, sag**

3 tumble, fall, cropper and **spill** <both nonformal>, **flop** <nonformal>; **header** <nonformal>; sprawl; **pratfall** <nonformal>; **stumble,** trip; **dive, plunge** 367

4 slide; slip, slippage; **glide,** coast; slither; **skid,** sideslip; **landslide,** mudslide, landslip, subsidence; **snowslide; avalanche**

VERBS **5 descend, go** or **come**

down, down, dip down, lose altitude; gravitate; **fall, drop,** precipitate, rain, fall or drop down; **collapse,** crash; **swoop,** stoop, pounce; **pitch, plunge** 367.6, **plummet;** cascade, cataract; parachute; come down a peg <nonformal>; **fall off,** drop off; trend downward, go downhill

6 **sink, go down,** submerge; **set, settle,** settle down; **decline,** lower, **subside,** give way, lapse, cave, cave in; **droop,** slouch, **sag; slump,** slump down; plump, plop or plop down, plunk or plunk down <nonformal>; founder 367.8

7 **get down, alight,** touch down, **light; land,** settle, perch, come to rest; **dismount, get off**

8 **tumble, fall, fall down,** come a cropper <nonformal>, take a fall or tumble, precipitate oneself; fall over, tumble over, trip over; **sprawl,** sprawl out, take a pratfall <nonformal>, spread-eagle <nonformal>; fall headlong, **take a header** <nonformal>; fall prostrate, fall flat, fall on one's face; **fall over,** topple down or over; capsize, turn turtle; **topple,** lurch, pitch, **stumble,** stagger, totter, careen, list, tilt, trip, flounder

9 **slide, slip,** slip or slide down; **glide,** skim, coast; **slither; skid,** sideslip

10 **light upon,** alight upon, settle on; **descend upon, come down on, fall on,** drop on, hit upon

ADJS 11 **descending,** descendant; **down,** downward, declivitous; deciduous; **downgoing,** downcoming; **dropping, falling, plunging, plummeting; sinking,** foundering, submerging, setting; declining, **subsiding;** collapsing, tumbledown, tottering, drooping, sagging; on the downgrade, downhill 204.16

12 **downcast, downturned;** hanging, down-hanging

ADVS 13 **down, downward, downwards,** from the top down; below; downright; downhill, downgrade; downstream; downstairs; downtown

195 CONTAINER

NOUNS 1 **container, receptacle;** receiver 479.3, holder, vessel, utensil; basin, pot, pan, cup, glass, ladle, bottle; cask; box, case; basket; luggage, baggage; cabinet, cupboard

2 **bag, sack,** sac, poke <nonformal>; **pocket; balloon, bladder**

196 CONTENTS

NOUNS 1 **contents, content; insides** 207.4, innards <nonformal>, guts; **components, constituents, ingredients,** elements **items, parts, divisions,** subdivisions; **inventory,** index, census, list 870; part 792; whole 791; composition 795

2 **load, lading, cargo, freight,** charge, burden; payload

3 **lining,** liner; **interlining;** inside layer, **inlay; filling,** filler; **packing,** padding, wadding, **stuffing;** facing

4 <contents of a container> cup, cupful, etc

5 <essential content> **substance, sum and substance, stuff, material, matter,** medium, building blocks, fabric; **gist, heart, soul, meat, nub;** the nitty-gritty and the bottom line and the name of the game <all nonformal>, **core,** kernel, marrow, pith, sap, spirit, **essence,** quintessence, elixir, distillate, distillation, distilled essence; sine qua non, irreducible or indispensable content

6 **enclosure,** the enclosed

VERBS 7 **fill, pack** 793.7, **load; line,** interline, interlineate; inlay; face; **pad,** wad, **stuff**

197 ROOM
<compartment>

NOUNS 1 **room, chamber,** four walls

2 **compartment,** chamber, space, enclosed space; **cavity,** hollow, hole, concavity; **cell; booth, stall,**

crib, manger; box, pew; crypt, vault

3 **nook, corner, cranny, niche, recess,** cove, bay, oriel, alcove; cubicle, roomlet, carrel, hole-in-the-wall <nonformal>, **cubbyhole,** snuggery

4 **hall;** assembly hall, exhibition hall, convention hall; gallery; meetinghouse, meeting room; **auditorium; concert hall; theater,** music hall; lecture hall, lyceum, amphitheater; operating theater; dance hall; ballroom; **chapel** 703.3

5 **parlor, living room, sitting room, drawing room, front room, salon; sun parlor** or sunroom, sun lounge, sunporch, solarium

6 **library,** stacks; **study,** studio, workroom; **office,** workplace; loft

7 **bedroom, boudoir,** chamber, **bedchamber,** cubicle; nursery; dormitory

8 <private chamber> **sanctum,** sanctum sanctorum, holy of holies; **den,** retreat

9 <ships> cabin, stateroom; saloon; house

10 <trains> drawing room, stateroom, parlor car, Pullman car

11 **dining room,** dinette, dining hall, refectory, mess or mess hall, commons; dining car or diner; **restaurant, cafeteria**

12 **playroom,** recreation room, rec room <nonformal>, game room, **rumpus room** <nonformal>

13 **utility room,** laundry room, sewing room

14 **kitchen** 11.3, **storeroom** 386.6, smoking room 89.13

15 **closet,** clothes closet, wardrobe, cloakroom; checkroom; linen closet; dressing room pantry

16 **attic, garret, loft;** hayloft; storeroom

17 **cellar, basement;** subbasement; wine cellar, potato cellar, storm cellar, cyclone cellar

18 **corridor, hall,** hallway; passage, **passageway; gallery; arcade,** colonnade, pergola, cloister; breezeway

19 **vestibule, portico,** entry, entryway, **entrance hall,** entranceway, **threshold; lobby, foyer**

20 **anteroom,** antechamber; **waiting room; reception room;** throne room; lounge, greenroom, wardroom

21 **porch,** stoop, **veranda,** piazza <nonformal>, patio, lanai, gallery; sleeping porch

22 **balcony,** gallery, terrace

23 **floor, story,** level, flat; first floor or story, ground or street floor; mezzanine

24 **showroom,** display room, exhibition room, gallery

25 **hospital room; ward,** maternity ward; examination room, consulting room; **operating room** or OR, operating theater; surgery; labor room, delivery room; recovery room; emergency room; intensive care unit or ICU; pharmacy, dispensary; clinic, nursery; laboratory or blood bank

26 **bathroom, lavatory, washroom** 79.10, **water closet** or **WC,** closet, **rest room, toilet** 12.10

27 <for vehicles> **garage,** carport; carriage house; roundhouse; hangar; boathouse

198 TOP

NOUNS 1 **top,** top side, upper side; surface 206.2; **topside** or **topsides;** upper story, top floor; clerestory; **roof; rooftop**

2 **summit,** top; **tip-top, peak** 3.6, pinnacle; **crest, brow;** ridge, edge; **crown,** cap, **tip,** point, spire, pitch; highest pitch, **apex,** vertex, **acme, zenith, climax,** apogee, pole; **culmination; extremity, maximum, limit,** upper extremity, top of the world; **sky,** heaven or heavens, seventh heaven, cloud nine <nonformal>; meridian, noon, high noon

3 **topping,** icing, frosting

4 <top part> **head,** heading, **headpiece,** cap, **crown, crest;** topknot

5 **architectural topping, capital, head, crown, cap;** cornice

6 head, headpiece, **pate,** poll
<nonformal>, crown, **noodle**
and noggin *and* **bean** *and* dome
<all nonformal>; brow, ridge
7 skull, cranium, pericranium,
epicranium; brain box *or* case
8 phrenology, craniology
VERBS **9 top,** top off, **crown, cap,**
crest, **head,** tip, peak, surmount;
over-arch; **culminate,** consummate, climax; ice, frost [a cake];
fill, top up
ADJS **10 top,** topmost, **uppermost,
highest;** tip-top, **maximum,**
maximal, ultimate; vertical, ze-
nithal, climactic, **consummate;
meridian; head,** headmost, capital, chief, paramount, supreme,
preeminent; **top-level,** highest
level, top-echelon, top-flight, top-
ranking, top-drawer <nonfor-
mal>
11 topping, crowning, capping,
heading, surmounting, overarching; **culminating,** consummat-
ing, climaxing
12 topped, headed, **crowned,
capped,** crested, plumed,
tipped, peaked
13 topless, headless, crownless
14 cranial; cephalic, encephalic
ADVS **15 atop, on top,** at *or* on the
top, topside <nonformal>; on top
of the heap; on the crest *or* crest
of the wave; at the head, at the
peak *or* pinnacle *or* summit

199 BOTTOM

NOUNS **1 bottom, underside,**
nether side, **underneath,** fundament; belly, underbelly; buttocks
217.4, breech; **rock bottom, bedrock,** bed, hardpan; **grass roots;**
substratum, underlayer; **nadir,**
the pits <nonformal>
2 base, basement, **foot,** footing,
sole, toe; **foundation** 900.6; base-
board; wainscot, dado; skeleton,
bare bones, chassis; keel
3 ground covering, ground, earth,
terra firma <L>; **floor,** flooring,
parquet; **deck; pavement,** paving, surfacing, asphalt, blacktop,
macadam, concrete; **cover,** car-

pet, floor covering; artificial turf,
Astroturf <trademark>
4 bed, bottom, floor, ground, **basin, channel; seabed, ocean
bottom** 275.4
5 foot, extremity, trotter, pedal extremity, dog, tootsy
<nonformal>; **hoof; paw,** pad;
forefoot, forepaw; **toe,** digit;
heel; sole; instep, arch; fetlock
VERBS **6 base on, found on,
ground on, build on,** bottom on,
bed on, set on; root in; **underlie,**
undergird; bottom, bottom out;
hit bottom
ADJS **7 bottom, undermost,**
nethermost, deepest, **lowest;
rock-bottom,** bedrock; ground
8 basic; basal, basilar; **underlying, fundamental,** essential, elemental, primary, primal, primitive, rudimentary, original, grass-
roots; radical; nadiral
9 pedal; plantar; footed, hoofed,
ungulate

200 VERTICALNESS

NOUNS **1 verticalness,** verticality;
erectness, uprightness; steepness, sheerness, precipitousness;
perpendicularity, plumbness;
right-angularity, squareness, orthogonality
**2 vertical, upright, perpendicu-
lar,** plumb, normal; right angle,
orthodiagonal
3 precipice, cliff, sheer *or* yawning cliff *or* precipice *or* drop,
steep, bluff, wall, face, scar; crag;
scarp, **escarpment; palisade,**
palisades
4 erection, erecting, **elevation;
rearing,** raising; **uprearing,** upraising, lofting, uplifting; standing on end *or* upright *or* on its feet
or on its legs
5 rising, uprising, ascension, ascending, ascent; vertical height *or*
dimension; **gradient,** rise, uprise
6 <instruments> square, T square,
try square, set square, carpenter's
square; plumb, plumb line, plumb
rule, plummet, bob, plumb bob,
lead
VERBS **7 stand, stand erect, stand**

up, stand upright, stand up
straight, be erect, be on one's
feet; hold oneself straight or stiff,
stand ramrod-straight; stand at
attention, brace <both military>

8 rise, arise, ascend, mount, uprise, **rise up, get up,** get to one's
feet; **stand up, stand on end;
stick up; bristle; rear,** rear up,
rise on the hind legs; upheave; sit
up, sit bolt upright; spring to
one's feet

9 erect, elevate, rear, raise, pitch,
set up, raise or lift or cast up;
raise or heave or rear aloft; upraise, uplift; upright; **upend,**
stand upright or on end; set on
its feet or legs or base or bottom

10 plumb, plumb-line, **square,**
square up

ADJS **11 vertical, upright,** bolt upright, ramrod straight, **erect,** upstanding, stand-up; rearing,
rampant; **upended,** upraised

**12 perpendicular, plumb, up-and-
down;** sheer, steep, precipitous,
plunging; **right-angled,** right-
angle, right-angular, orthogonal

ADVS **13 vertically, erectly,** uprightly, **upright,** up, stark or bolt
upright; **on end,** up on end, endwise, endways; on one's feet or
legs, on one's hind legs <nonfor-
mal>; at attention, braced

14 perpendicularly, sheer, sheerly;
straight up and down; plumb;
at right angles, square

201 HORIZONTALNESS

NOUNS **1 horizontalness,** horizon-
tality; **levelness, flatness,** evenness, smoothness; unbrokenness

2 recumbency, recumbence;
prostration, proneness; supineness, reclining; lying, lounging,
repose 20; sprawl, loll

3 horizontal, plane, level, flat,
dead level or flat; **horizontal** or
level plane; horizontal projection;
horizontal surface, fascia; water
level, sea level; ground, earth,
steppe, **plain, flatland,** prairie,
savanna, sea of grass, bowling
green, table, billiard table; floor,
platform, ledge, terrace

4 horizon, skyline; sea line; apparent or local or visible horizon,
sensible horizon, celestial or rational or geometrical or true
horizon, artificial or false horizon; azimuth

VERBS **5 lie, lie down,** lay <nonfor-
mal>, **recline, repose,** lounge,
sprawl, loll, splay, lie limply; **lie
flat** or prostrate or prone or supine, lie on one's face or back, hug
the ground or deck; **grovel,
crawl,** kowtow

6 level, flatten, even, equalize,
align, smooth or smoothen, level
out, smooth out, flush; grade,
roll, steamroller or steamroll; **lay,**
lay down or out; **raze,** rase, lay
level; lay low or flat; **fell** 912.5

ADJS **7 horizontal, level, flat,** flattened; **even,** smooth, smoothed
out; **flush; plane,** plain; rolled,
trodden, squashed; flat as a pancake, flat as a board

8 recumbent, accumbent, pro-
cumbent, decumbent; **prostrate,
prone,** flat; **supine; lying, reclining, reposing,** flat on one's back;
sprawling, lolling, lounging;
sprawled, spread, splay, splayed,
draped; groveling, crawling, flat
on one's belly

ADVS **9 horizontally, flat,** flatly;
evenly, flush; **level, on a level;**
lengthwise, lengthways, at full
length, on one's back or belly

202 PENDENCY

NOUNS **1 pendency,** pendulous-
ness or pendulosity; **hanging,
suspension,** dangling, suspense,
dependence or dependency

2 hang, droop, dangle, swing, fall;
sag, swag, bag

**3 overhang, overhanging, pro-
jection,** jutting; cantilever

4 pendant, hanger; **hanging,**
drape; **lobe,** ear lobe, wattle;
uvula

5 suspender, hanger, supporter;
suspenders, pair of suspenders,
galluses <nonformal>

VERBS **6 hang,** hang down, fall; **depend; dangle,** swing, flap, flop
<nonformal>; flow, drape, cas-

cade; **droop; nod, weep; sag,**
bag; trail, drag, draggle
7 **overhang,** hang over, hang out,
impend, project, project over,
beetle, **jut,** beetle *or* jut *or* thrust
over
8 **suspend, hang, hang up,** put
up, fasten up; sling
ADJS 9 **pendent,** pendulous, pen-
dulant; **suspended,** hung; **hang-**
ing, pending, depending, dependent; **falling; dangling,** swinging; weeping; flowing, cascad-
ing
10 **drooping, droopy,** limp, loose,
nodding, floppy <nonformal>;
sagging, saggy; **bagging,** baggy,
ballooning; lop-eared
11 **overhanging,** overhung, lowering, **impending, pending;**
incumbent, superincumbent;
projecting, jutting; beetling,
beetle; beetle-browed
12 lobular, lobar, lobed, lobate, lo-
bated

203 PARALLELISM
<physically parallel direction or
state>

NOUNS 1 **parallelism,** noncon-
vergence, nondivergence, concurrence, equidistance; collimation;
alignment; **analogy** 942.1
2 **parallel; parallelogram, paral-**
lelepiped
3 <instruments> parallel rule or
rules or ruler
VERBS 4 **parallel,** be parallel, coex-
tend; run parallel, go alongside,
go beside, run abreast; match,
equal
5 **parallelize,** equidistance; line
up, align, realign; collimate;
match; correspond, follow,
equate
ADJS 6 **parallel,** paralleling; coex-
tending, coextensive, noncon-
vergent, nondivergent, **equi-**
distant, collateral, concurrent;
lined up, aligned; equal, even;
analogous 942.8
ADVS 7 **in parallel; side-by-side,**
alongside, abreast; equidistantly,
nonconvergently, nondivergently;
collaterally, coextensively

204 OBLIQUITY

NOUNS 1 **obliquity,** obliqueness;
deviation 164, deviance, divergence, digression, divagation,
vagary, excursion, skewness, aberration, squint, declination;
deflection; nonconformity 867;
indirection, indirectness, deviousness, circuitousness 913
2 **inclination, leaning,** lean, angularity; **slant, slope; tilt, tip,**
pitch, **list, cant,** sway
3 **bias, bend,** bent, **crook, warp,**
twist, turn, skew, veer, sheer,
swerve, lurch
4 **incline,** inclination, **slope,**
grade, gradient, pitch, **ramp,**
gentle *or* easy slope; rapid *or*
steep slope, stiff climb, scarp,
chute; inclined plane <phys>;
bevel, bezel; hillside, side
5 **declivity, descent,** dip, drop,
fall, falling-off *or* -away, **decline;**
hang, hanging; **downgrade,**
downhill
6 **acclivity, ascent,** climb, **rise,**
rising, uprise, uprising; **upgrade,**
uphill, uplift, steepness, precipitousness, abruptness, verticalness 200
7 **diagonal,** oblique, transverse,
bias, slash, **slant,** virgule, solidus;
oblique angle *or* figure, rhomboid
8 **zigzag,** zig, zag; **crookedness;**
switchback, hairpin, dogleg
VERBS 9 **oblique, deviate, di-**
verge, deflect, divagate, **bear off;**
angle, **angle off, swerve,** shoot
off at an angle, **veer,** sheer, sway,
slue, **skew, twist, turn,** bend,
bias; crook
10 **incline, lean; slope, slant,**
pitch, grade, bank, shelve; **tilt,**
tip, list, cant, careen, keel, sidle,
sway; **ascend, rise,** climb, go **up-**
hill; descend, decline, dip, drop,
fall, fall off *or* away, go **downhill;**
retreat
11 cut, cut across, cut crosswise *or*
transversely *or* diagonally, catercorner, slash, slash across
12 **zigzag,** zig, zag, **stagger,** wind in
and out
ADJS 13 **oblique; devious,** deviant,

divergent, digressive, divagational, deflectional; **indirect,** sidelong; left-handed, sinister, sinistral; backhand, backhanded; circuitous 913.7

14 askew, skew, skewed; **awry; askance,** squinting, **cockeyed** <nonformal>; **crooked** 265.10

15 inclining, inclined; **leaning,** recumbent; **sloping,** sloped; pitched; **slanting,** slanted, slant, aslant, slantways, slantwise; bias, biased; **tilting,** tilted, tipped, **tipping,** tipsy, listing, **canting,** careening; sidelong; out of the perpendicular or square or plumb, bevel, beveled

16 <sloping downward> **downhill, downgrade; descending,** falling, dropping, dipping; **declining;** declivitous

17 <sloping upward> **uphill, upgrade; rising, ascending,** climbing; acclivitous

18 steep, precipitous, bluff, plunging, abrupt, bold, **sheer,** sharp, rapid; **headlong,** breakneck; vertical 200.11

19 transverse, crosswise or crossways, thwart, athwart, across 170.9; **diagonal; catercorner** or **catercornered** or cattycorner or cattycornered; slant, bias, biased

20 crooked, zigzag, zigzagged, zigzaggy, dogleg or doglegged; flexuous, twisty, hairpin, curvy; staggered

ADVS **21 obliquely, deviously, indirectly,** circuitously 913.9; divergently, digressively, excursively, divagationally; **sideways** or sidewise, sidelong, on or to one side; at an angle

22 askew, awry; askance, asquint

23 slantingly, slopingly, aslant, slantwise, slantways, on or at a slant; off plumb or the vertical; **downhill, downgrade; uphill, upgrade**

24 transversely, crosswise or crossways, athwart, across 170.13

25 diagonally; on the bias, bias; **cornerwise,** cornerways; **catercorner** or cattycorner

205 INVERSION

NOUNS **1 inversion,** turning over or around or upside down; turning inside out, invagination; introversion, turning inward; **reversing, reversal** 858.1, turning front to back or side to side; **reversion,** turning back or backwards, retroversion, revulsion; devolution, atavism; recidivism; **transposition,** transposal; topsy-turviness; the world turned upside-down, the tail wagging the dog; pronation, supination

2 overturn, upset, overset, **overthrow,** upturn, **turnover,** spill <nonformal>; subversion; **revolution** 859; **capsizing,** turning turtle; **somersault; turning head over heels**

3 <grammatical and rhetorical terms> metastasis, metathesis; anastrophe, chiasmus, hypallage, hyperbaton, hysteron proteron, palindrome, parenthesis, synchysis, tmesis

4 inverse, reverse, converse, opposite 215.5, other side of the coin, the flip side <nonformal>

VERBS **5 invert,** inverse, turn over or around or upside down; introvert, turn in or inward; **turn down; turn inside out,** invaginate; **revert,** recidivate, relapse, lapse, back-slide; **reverse** 858.4, **transpose,** convert; put the cart before the horse; turn the tables; rotate, revolve, pronate, supinate

6 overturn, turn over, turn upside down, turn bottom side up, upturn, **upset, overthrow,** subvert; go or turn ass over elbows or ass over tincups <all nonformal>, go or turn head over heels; **turn turtle, turn topsy-turvy,** topsyturvy; **tip over,** keel over, topple over; **capsize;** set on its ears

ADJS **7 inverted,** back-to-front, **backwards, reversed, transposed, back side forward, tail first; inside out,** outside in, invaginated, wrong side out; reverted, lapsed, recidivist or recidivistic; atavistic; **upside-**

down, topsy-turvy, ass over elbows *and* ass over tincups *and* arsy-varsy <all nonformal>; **capsized,** head-over-heels; palindromic; introverted

ADVS **8 inversely, conversely,** contrarily, contrariwise, **vice versa,** the other way around, **backwards,** turned around; **upside down,** over, **topsy-turvy; bottom up,** bottom side up; head over heels

206 EXTERIORITY

NOUNS **1 exteriority,** externality, **outwardness; appearance, outward appearance,** mien, **front,** manner; window-dressing, cosmetics; openness; extrinsicality 767; **superficiality, shallowness** 276

2 exterior, external, **outside; surface,** covering 295, skin 2.4, outer skin *or* layer, epidermis, integument, envelope, crust, cortex, rind, shell 295.16; cladding, plating; top; **periphery, fringe,** circumference, outline, border; **face,** outer face *or* side, facade, **front;** facet; back

3 outdoors, outside, **the out-of-doors,** the great out-of-doors, the open, **the open air**

4 externalization, bringing into the open, show, showing, display, displaying; **objectification,** actualization, realization

VERBS **5 externalize,** bring into the open, bring out, show, display, exhibit; **objectify,** actualize, project, realize

6 scratch the surface; give a lick and a promise, give a once-over-lightly, whitewash, give a nod

ADJS **7 exterior, external;** extrinsic 767; **outer, outside, out, outward,** outward-facing; **outermost; surface, superficial** 276.5; **cosmetic; peripheral, fringe,** roundabout; apparent, seeming; open 348.10, public 352.17

8 outdoor, out-of-door, out-of-doors, **outside, without-doors; open-air,** alfresco; out and about

9 extraterritorial; extraterrestrial, extramundane; extragalactic; foreign, outlandish, **alien**

ADVS **10 externally, outwardly,** on the outside; **without, outside, outwards, out;** apparently, to all appearances; openly, to judge by appearances; superficially, on the surface

11 outdoors, out of doors, outside, abroad; in the open, **in the open air,** alfresco

207 INTERIORITY

NOUNS **1** interiority, **inwardness, innerness; introversion, internalization; intrinsicality** 766; depth 275

2 interior, inside, inner, inward, internal; inner recess, recesses, **innermost** *or* **deepest recesses,** penetralia, intimate places, secret place *or* places; bosom, secret heart, heart, heart of hearts, soul, vitals, vital center; inner self, inner life, inner landscape, inner nature; core, center 208.2

3 inland, inlands, **interior,** upcountry; **midland,** midlands; heartland; hinterland 233.2; Middle America

4 insides, innards <nonformal>, inwards, internals; inner mechanism, what makes it tick *and* works <both nonformal>; **guts** <nonformal>, **vitals, viscera,** giblets; entrails, bowels, guts

VERBS **5** internalize, keep within; enclose, embed, surround, contain, comprise, include, enfold, take to heart, assimilate

ADJS **6 interior, internal, inner, inside, inward;** intestine; **innermost,** inmost, **intimate,** private; visceral, gut <nonformal>; **intrinsic** 766.7; deep 275.10; central 208.11; indoor; live-in

7 inland, interior, up-country, up-river; hinterland; **midland,** mediterranean; Middle American

8 intramarginal, intramural, intramundane, intramontane, intraterritorial, intracoastal

ADVS **9 internally, inwardly, inti-**

mately, deeply, profoundly; **intrinsically** 766; centrally
10 **in, inside, within;** herein,
therein, wherein
11 **inward, inwards, inwardly; inland, inshore**
12 **indoors,** indoor, withindoors

208 CENTRALITY

NOUNS 1 **centrality,** centralness,
middleness; equidistance; con-
centricity; centripetalism
2 **center,** centrum; **middle** 818,
**heart, core, nucleus; core of
one's being, where one lives;
kernel; pith,** marrow; **nub, hub,**
nave, axis, pivot; **navel,** umbil-
icus, omphalos, belly button
<nonformal>; bull's-eye; dead
center; storm center, eye of the
storm
3 <biological terms> central body,
centriole
4 **focus,** focal point, prime focus,
point of convergence; **center of
interest** or attention, focus of attention; center of consciousness;
**center of attraction, center-
piece,** mecca, cynosure, cynosure
of all eyes; polestar, lodestar;
magnet
5 **nerve center,** center of activity,
vital center; control center, guidance center
6 **headquarters** or **HQ,** main office, central administration, seat,
base, **base of operations,** center
of authority; general headquarters or **GHQ**
7 **metropolis, capital;** urban center, cultural center
8 **centralization,** centering; **focal-
ization,** focus, focusing; convergence 169; **concentration**
VERBS 9 **centralize, center,** middle; center on or in
10 **focus,** bring to or into focus;
bring or come to a head, get to the
heart of the matter, home in on;
zero in on; draw a bead on and
get a handle on <nonformal>;
concentrate, get it together
<nonformal>; **channel,** direct,
channelize; converge 169.2
ADJS 11 **central, middle** 818; mid-

dlemost, **midmost; equidistant;**
centralized, concentrated; umbil-
ical, omphalic; axial, **pivotal,** key;
geocentric
12 **nuclear,** nucleate
13 **focal; converging;** centripetal
14 **concentric; coaxial**
ADVS 15 **centrally,** in the middle of,
at the heart of

209 ENVIRONMENT

NOUNS 1 **environment, surroundings, environs,** surround, ambience, entourage, circle, **circumstances; precincts,** ambit, purlieus, **milieu; neighborhood,
vicinity; suburbs;** outskirts,
outposts, borders, boundaries,
limits, periphery, perimeter, compass, circuit; **context, situation;**
habitat 228; gestalt
2 **setting, background,** backdrop,
ground, surround, field, scene,
arena, theater, locale; back, rear,
hinterland, distance; stage, stage
setting, stage set
3 <surrounding influence or con-
dition> **milieu, ambience, atmosphere, climate, air,** aura,
spirit, feeling, feel, quality, color,
local color, sense, sense of place,
note, tone, overtone, undertone
4 <natural or suitable environ-
ment> **element,** medium; **the
environment**
5 **surrounding, encompassment,**
environment; containment, **enclosure** 212; **encirclement,** circling, girdling, girding; **envelopment,** encompassing, compass-
ing; inclusion 771, involvement
897
VERBS 6 **surround, environ,** compass, **encompass,** enclose, close;
go round or around; **envelop,** enfold, lap, wrap, embrace, involve,
invest
7 **encircle, circle,** belt, belt in;
zone; **girdle,** gird; ring, band;
loop; wreathe or twine around
ADJS 8 **environing, surrounding,**
encompassing, enclosing; **enveloping,** wrapping, embracing;
encircling, circling; bordering,
peripheral; circumferential, cir-

cumambient, ambient; **round-about,** neighboring
9 **environmental; ecological**
10 **surrounded,** compassed, **encompassed,** enclosed; **enveloped,** wrapped, enfolded, lapped, wreathed
11 **encircled, circled,** ringed, belted, girdled, girt
ADVS 12 **around,** round, **about,** round about, in the neighborhood *or* vicinity; close, close about
13 **all round, all about,** on every side, on all sides, on all hands, right and left

210 CIRCUMSCRIPTION

NOUNS 1 **circumscription, limiting,** circumscribing, **bounding, demarcation,** delimitation, definition, determination, specification; limit-setting, boundary-marking
2 **limitation, limiting, restriction,** restricting, confinement 212.1, prescription, proscription, restraint, discipline, moderation, continence; qualification, **hedging;** bounds 211, boundary, limit 211.3; time-limit, time constraint
3 **patent, copyright; trademark, logo** *or* logotype, registered trademark, trade name, service mark
VERBS 4 **circumscribe, bound; mark off** *or* mark out, stake out, lay off, rope off; **demarcate,** delimit, draw *or* mark *or* set *or* lay out boundaries, hedge in, set the limit; **define,** determine, fix, specify; surround 209.6; enclose 212.5
5 **limit, restrict, restrain, bound, confine,** ground <nonformal>; straiten, narrow, tighten; specialize; stint, scant; **condition,** qualify, hedge, hedge about; draw the line; discipline, moderate, contain; restrain oneself, pull one's punches <nonformal>; **patent, copyright,** register
ADJS 6 **circumscribed; ringed** *or* circled *or* hedged about; **demarcated, delimited, defined,** definite, determined, determinate, specific, stated, set, fixed; surrounded 209.10, encircled 209.11
7 **limited, restricted,** bound, **bounded, finite; confined** 212.10, prescribed, proscribed, cramped, strait, straitened, narrow; conditioned, qualified, hedged; disciplined, moderated; **deprived,** in straitened circumstances, pinched, on short rations, strapped; patented, registered, protected, copyrighted
8 **restricted,** out of bounds, off-limits
9 **limiting, restricting,** defining, determining, confining; restrictive, definitive, exclusive
10 **terminal,** limital; limitable, terminable

211 BOUNDS

NOUNS 1 **bounds, limits,** boundaries, limitations, **confines, pale,** edges, outlines, outer markings, outskirts, **fringes,** metes and bounds; periphery, **perimeter; compass, circumference,** circumscription 210
2 **outline, contour,** delineation, shapes, figure, figuration, **configuration,** gestalt; **features; profile, silhouette;** relief; skeleton, framework, armature
3 **boundary, bound, limit,** limitation, extremity 793.5; **barrier,** block; delimitation, hedge, break point, cutoff, cutoff point, terminus; finish, **end** 819, tail end; **start,** starting line *or* point, mark; **limiting factor,** determinant, boundary condition; bracket, brackets, **bookends** <nonformal>; threshold; upper limit, ceiling, apogee, high-water mark; lower limit, floor, low-water mark, nadir; **confine,** compass, circumscription; **boundary line, border line,** frontier, interface, break, boundary, line of demarcation
4 **border, edge,** limb, **verge, brink,** brow, **brim, rim, margin, fringe, hem,** list, selvage *or* selvedge, side; **forefront, cutting**

edge, front line, vanguard 216.2; sideline; shore, bank, coast; **lip; flange; ledge; frame,** mat

5 **frontier, border, borderland,** border ground; outskirts, outpost; frontier post; iron curtain, bamboo curtain

6 **curb,** curbing; border stone, curbstone, edgestone

7 **edging, bordering, trimming,** binding, skirting; fringe; **hem,** selvage; welt; frill; beading, flounce, furbelow, ruffle, valance

VERBS 8 **bound,** circumscribe 210.4, surround 209.6, limit 210.5, enclose 212.5, divide, separate

9 **outline,** contour; **delineate;** silhouette, profile

10 **border, edge, bound, rim, skirt, hem, hem in, ringe,** verge, line, side; **adjoin** 223.9; **frame,** enframe, set off; trim, bind

ADJS 11 **bordering, fringing,** rimming, skirting; **bounding,** boundary, **limiting,** limit, determining or determinant or determinative; threshold; extreme, terminal; **marginal, borderline,** frontier; coastal, littoral

12 **bordered,** edged; **fringed,** trimmed, skirted

13 lipped, labial, labiate

14 outlining, delineatory; peripheral, circumferential; outlined, **in outline**

ADVS 15 **on the verge, on the brink,** on the borderline, on the point, on the edge, on the ragged edge, at the threshold, at the limit or bound; **peripherally,** marginally, at the periphery

16 **thus far,** so far, thus far and no farther

212 ENCLOSURE

NOUNS 1 **enclosure; confinement,** containment, circumscription 210, immurement, walling- or hedging- or hemming- or boxing- or fencing- or walling-in; **imprisonment,** incarceration, jailing; **siege,** beleaguerment, blockade, blockading, cordoning, quaran-

tine; inclusion 771; **envelopment** 209.5

2 **packaging, packing,** package; encasement; canning; bottling; **wrapping,** bundling; shrink-wrapping

3 <enclosed place> **enclosure,** close, **confine,** precinct, enclave, pale, paling; **cloister; pen, coop,** fold; **yard,** park, court, courtyard; square, quadrangle, quad <nonformal>; **field, arena,** theater, ground; **container** 195

4 **fence, wall,** boundary 211.3, **barrier;** stone wall; paling, palisade; rail, railing; arcade

VERBS 5 **enclose,** close in, bound, include, **contain;** compass, encompass; **surround,** encircle 209.7; **shut** or **pen in,** coop in; **fence in,** wall in, wall up, rail in, rail off, screen off, curtain off; **hem** or **hedge in,** box in; shut or coop up; pen, coop, corral, cage, impound; **imprison,** incarcerate, jail, lock up; **besiege,** beset, beleaguer, cordon, cordon off, quarantine, blockade; house in; stable, kennel; **wrap** 295.20

6 **confine, immure;** cramp, straiten, encase; cloister, closet, crib; entomb; bottle up or in, box up or in

7 **fence, wall,** fence in; hem, hem in, hedge, hedge in; palisade

8 parenthesize, bracket, precede and follow

9 **package, pack, parcel;** box, box up, case, encase, crate, carton; can; bottle, jar, pot; barrel, cask, tank; sack, bag; capsule, encyst; **wrap,** bundle; shrink-wrap

ADJS 10 **enclosed,** closed-in; **confined,** bound, immured, cloistered; **imprisoned,** incarcerated, jailed; caged, restrained, corralled; besieged, beleaguered, beset, cordoned, cordoned off, quarantined, blockaded; **shut-in,** pent-up, penned, cooped, walled- or hedged- or hemmed- or boxed- or fenced-in, walled, barred; hemmed, hedged

11 enclosing, confining, **cloistered,**

cloisterlike, surrounding 209.8;
limiting 210.9
12 packed, packaged, boxed,
crated, canned, cased, encased;
bottled; capsuled, encapsuled;
wrapped, enwrapped, bundled;
shrink-wrapped; prepacked;
vacuum-packed

213 INTERPOSITION

<a putting or lying between>

NOUNS **1 interposition, interposing; intervention,** intervenience,
sandwiching; interleaving, interfoliation, tipping-in; **intrusion**
214

2 interjection, interpolation,
introduction, **injection,** insinuation; interlineation; **insertion** 191; interlocution, remark, parenthetical or side or
casual remark, obiter dictum
<L>, aside, parenthesis; episode; infix, insert

3 interspersion, interfusion, interpenetration

4 intermediary, medium; link,
connecting link, tie, connection,
go-between, liaison; middleman;
mediator 466.3

5 partition, dividing wall, division, separation; **wall, barrier;**
panel; bulkhead; diaphragm,
midriff, midsection; septum;
border 211.4, **dividing line,**
property line, party wall; **buffer,
bumper,** mat, fender, cushion,
pad; buffer state

VERBS **6 interpose, interject, interpolate; mediate, go between;
intervene;** sandwich; **insert in,**
stick in, introduce in, insinuate
in, sandwich in, slip in, inject in,
implant in; leaf in, interleaf; **foist
in,** work in, drag in, lug in, worm
in, squeeze in, smuggle in, throw
in, run in, thrust in, edge in; **intrude** 214.5

7 intersperse, interfuse, interlard

8 partition, set apart, separate, divide; **wall off,** fence off, screen
off, curtain off

ADJS **9** interjectional; parenthetical,
episodic

10 intervening, interjacent; intermediate, intermediary, medial,
mean, medium, median, **middle**
11 partitioned, walled; mural

214 INTRUSION

NOUNS **1 intrusion,** obtrusion, **interloping;** interposition 213, imposition, insinuation, **interference,** intervention, interruption,
injection, interjection 213.2; **encroachment,** trespass, trespassing; impingement, **infringement,**
invasion, incursion, inroad, influx, irruption, infiltration; entrance 189

2 meddling; butting-in and kibitzing and sticking one's nose in
<all nonformal>; **meddlesomeness, intrusiveness, forwardness,** obtrusiveness; **officiousness,** impertinence, presumption, presumptuousness; inquisitiveness 980.1

3 intruder, interloper, trespasser; crasher and gate-crasher
<both nonformal>, unwelcome
or uninvited guest; invader, encroacher

4 meddler; busybody, pry, snoop
or snooper, **kibitzer** and backseat
driver <both nonformal>

VERBS **5 intrude,** obtrude, **interlope;** come between, **interpose**
213.6, insert oneself, **intervene,
interfere,** insinuate, impose; **encroach, infringe,** impinge, **trespass,** trespass on or upon, invade, infiltrate; **break in upon,**
break in, burst in, charge in,
crash in, smash in, storm in;
barge in <nonformal>, irrupt,
cut in, thrust in 191.7, push in,
press in, rush in, throng in, crowd
in, squeeze in, elbow in, muscle
in <nonformal>; **butt in** and
horn in and muscle in <all nonformal>; appoint oneself; crash
and crash the gate <both nonformal>; **get in,** get in on, creep in,
steal in, sneak in, slink in, slip in;
worm or work in, edge in, put in
one's oar; **foist oneself upon,**
thrust oneself upon; put one's two
cents in <nonformal>

6 interrupt, put in, cut in, break in; jump in, chime in *and* chip in *and* put in one's two-cents worth <all nonformal>

7 meddle, intermeddle, not mind one's business; **meddle with, tamper with,** inject oneself into, monkey with, fool with *or* around with <nonformal>, mess in *or* around with <nonformal>; **pry,** snoop, nose, **stick** *or* poke one's nose in; have a finger in, have a finger in the pie; kibitz <nonformal>

ADJS **8 intrusive,** obtrusive, **interfering,** invasive

9 meddlesome, meddling; **officious,** self-appointed, impertinent, presumptuous; **busybody;** pushy, forward; **prying,** nosy *or* nosey *and* snoopy <both nonformal>; inquisitive 980.5

215 CONTRAPOSITION
<a placing over against>

NOUNS **1** contraposition, anteposition; **opposition,** opposing; **antithesis,** contrast; **confrontation;** polarity, **polarization; contrariety** 778; contention 457; hostility 451.2

2 opposites, antipodes, polar opposites; **poles,** opposite poles; antipodal points; night and day, black and white

3 opposite side, other side, the other side of the coin, other face; **reverse, inverse, obverse, converse;** heads, tails <of a coin>; flip side *and* B-side <both nonformal>

VERBS **4** contrapose, **oppose,** contrast, match, **set over against,** put in opposition, set *or* pit against one another; **confront,** face, front, stand *or* lie opposite; be at loggerheads, be eyeball to eyeball, bump heads, meet head-on; counteract 451.3; contend; subtend; **polarize**

ADJS **5** contrapositive, **opposite,** opposing, **facing,** confronting, confrontational, eyeball-to-eyeball; **opposed,** adversarial, at loggerheads, at daggers drawn, antithetical; **reverse, inverse, obverse, converse;** antipodal; polar

ADVS **6 opposite, poles apart,** at opposite extremes; contrary, contrariwise, counter; just opposite, **face-to-face,** vis-à-vis, nose to nose, one on one, eyeball-to-eyeball, back to back

216 FRONT

NOUNS **1 front, fore,** forehand; **priority; frontier** 211.5; **foreground;** proscenium; frontage; frontispiece; **preface,** front matter, foreword; prefix; front view, front elevation; **head,** heading; **face,** facade; fascia; **false front,** window dressing, display; front man; bold *or* brave front; facet; obverse <of a coin or medal>, head <of a coin>

2 vanguard, van, point, point man; **spearhead,** advance guard, **forefront, cutting edge,** avantgarde; scout; **pioneer; precursor** 815; **front-runner,** leader; **front,** battlefront, line, line of departure; **outpost; bridgehead,** beachhead, airhead, railhead

3 prow, bow, stem, rostrum, figurehead, nose, beak; bowsprit; forecastle

4 face, visage; physiognomy; **countenance,** features, lineaments; mug *and* mush *and* pan *and* kisser *and* map *and* puss <all nonformal>

5 forehead, brow, lofty brow

6 chin, point of the chin, button <nonformal>

VERBS **7** be *or* stand in front, **lead, head,** head up; **get ahead of,** steal a march on, take the lead, forge ahead; be the front-runner, lead the pack *or* field, be first; **pioneer;** front, front for, represent, speak for

8 confront, front, face, meet, encounter, breast, stem, brave, meet squarely, come to grips with, head *or* wade into, meet face to face *or* eyeball to eyeball

or one-on-one, come face to face
with, look in the face *or* eye, stand
up to, stand fast, hold one's
ground, hang tough *and* tough it
out *and* gut it out <all nonfor-
mal>; call someone's bluff, call *or*
bring someone to account; **confront with, face with,** bring face
to face with, tell one to one's face,
cast *or* throw in one's teeth, **put
or bring before,** set *or* place before, lay before, put *or* lay it on
the line; bring up, bring forward;
put it to, put it up to; **challenge,**
dare, defy, fly in the teeth of,
throw down the gauntlet, start
something, do something about it

9 **front on, face upon, give upon,**
look toward, look out upon, look
over, **overlook**

ADJS 10 **front, frontal, anterior;
full-face, full-frontal; fore, forward,** forehand, foremost;
headmost; first, earliest, **pioneering, trail-blazing, advanced;
leading,** up-front <nonformal>,
first, chief, head, prime, primary;
confronting, confrontational,
head-on, one-on-one *and* eyeball-
to-eyeball <both nonformal>;
ahead, in front, one-up, one
jump *or* move ahead

11 **fronting, facing,** looking on *or*
out on, opposite

ADVS 12 **before, ahead,** out *or* up
ahead, **in front,** in the front, in
the lead, in the van, **in the forefront,** in the foreground; **to the
fore,** to the front; foremost, first;
before one's eyes, under one's
nose

13 **frontward,** frontwards, **forward, headward,** headwards,
onward; facing 215.7

217 REAR

NOUNS 1 **rear, rear end, hind end,**
rearward, **posterior, behind,**
breech, stern, tail, tail end; **back,**
back side, reverse <of a coin or
medal>, **tail** <of a coin>; back
door; back seat, rumble seat

2 rear guard, rear, rear area

3 **back;** lumbar region; hindquar-
ter; loin

4 **buttocks, rump,** bottom, posterior, derrière; haunches; nates

5 <nonformal terms> **ass,** behind,
backside, **butt, can,** stern, tail,
fanny, prat, keister, rear, rear end,
tuchis *or* tushy *or* tush

6 **tail,** caudal appendage; tailpiece; rattail, rat's-tail; dock, stub;
caudal fin; **queue, pigtail**

7 **stern,** heel; poop, fantail; stern-
post

VERBS 8 <be behind> **bring up the
rear,** come last, **follow,** come after; trail, trail behind, lag behind,
draggle, **straggle;** fall behind, fall
back, fall astern; **back up, back,**
go back, go backwards, regress
163.5, retrogress, get behind; revert 858.4

ADJS 9 **rear,** rearward, **back,** backward, retrograde, **posterior,** tail;
after *or* aft; **hind, hinder; hind-
most, aftermost,** rearmost

10 <anatomy> dorsal, tergal, lumbar, gluteal, sciatic, occipital

11 **tail,** caudal, caudate, caudated,
tailed

12 backswept, swept-back

ADVS 13 **behind, in the rear, in
back of;** in the background; behind the scenes; behind one's
back

14 **after;** aft, abaft, baft, astern;
aback

15 **rearward,** rearwards, **hindward,** hindwards, **backward,**
backwards, tailward, tailwards

218 SIDE

NOUNS 1 **side, flank, hand;** lat-
erality, handedness; unilaterality,
bilaterality, multilaterality; border 211.4; parallelism 203; bank,
shore, coast; quarter; hip, haunch;
cheek, jowl, chop; temple; **profile**

2 **lee side, lee,** leeward

3 **windward side, windward,**
windwards, weather side,
weather

VERBS 4 **side, flank;** edge, skirt,
border 211.10

5 **go sideways, sidle, edge, veer,
angle, slant, skew,** sidestep; go
crabwise; **sideslip, skid**

ADJS **6 side, lateral;** flanking, skirting; **beside,** to the side, off to one side; **alongside, parallel** 203.6; **sidelong, sidewise,** sideway, **sideways,** sideward, **sidewards,** glancing; leeward, lee; windward, weather

7 sided, flanked, handed; lateral; **one-sided,** unilateral, **two-sided, bilateral; dihedral, bifacial; three-sided, trilateral,** trihedral; **four-sided, quadrilateral; many-sided, multilateral,** multifaceted, polyhedral

ADVS **8 laterally; sideways,** sideway, **sidewise, sidewards,** sideward, sidelong, crabwise; side-to-side; **edgeways,** edgeway, **edgewise; askance,** glancingly; broadside, **broadside on; on its side; on the other hand**

9 leeward, to leeward, downwind; **windward,** to windward, weatherward, upwind

10 aside, on one side, **to one side,** to the side, sidelong, on the side, on the one hand, on the other hand; **alongside,** in parallel 203.7, side-by-side; nearby, in juxtaposition 223.21

219 RIGHT SIDE

NOUNS **1 right side, right,** starboard; recto <of a book>; right field; right wing; right-winger, conservative, reactionary

2 rightness, dextrality; dexterity, **right-handedness**

3 right-hander; righty <nonformal>

ADJS **4 right, right-hand; off, starboard;** rightmost; **clockwise; right-wing,** right-of-center, conservative, reactionary

5 right-handed, dexterous

6 ambidextrous, ambidextral; dextrosinistral, sinistrodextral

ADVS **7 rightward,** rightwards, **right, to the right,** dextrally; on the right; starboard

220 LEFT SIDE

NOUNS **1 left side, left, left hand,** left-hand side, wrong side <nonformal>, near side <of a

horse or vehicle>, portside, port, larboard; verso <of a book>; left field; left wing, left-winger, radical, liberal, progressive

2 leftness, sinistrality, **left-handedness;** sinistration

3 left-hander, southpaw and lefty and portsider <all nonformal>

ADJS **4 left, left-hand,** sinister, sinistral; near, nigh; **larboard, port;** left-wing, left-of-center, radical, liberal, progressive

5 left-handed, sinistral, lefty and southpaw <both nonformal>

ADVS **6 leftward,** leftwards, **left, to the left,** sinistrally, sinister; on the left; larboard, port

221 PRESENCE

NOUNS **1 presence,** physical or actual presence, spiritual presence; **immanence, inherence; immediacy;** availability, accessibility; nearness 223; **occurrence** 830.2, existence 760

2 omnipresence, ubiquity; continuum; infinity

3 permeation, pervasion, penetration; **suffusion,** transfusion, perfusion, diffusion; absorption; **overrunning,** overspreading, ripple effect, overwhelming

4 attendance, frequenting; number present; turnout and box office and draw <all nonformal>

5 attender, visitor; patron; fan and buff <both nonformal>, aficionado, supporter; **frequenter,** habitué, haunter; spectator 917; theatergoer; audience 48.6

VERBS **6 be present,** be located or situated 159.10; **occur** 830.5, exist 760.8; lie, stand, remain; fall in the way of; dwell in, inhere

7 pervade, permeate, penetrate; **suffuse,** inform, transfuse, diffuse, leaven, imbue; **fill,** leave no void, occupy; **overrun,** overspread, meet one at every turn, overwhelm; creep or crawl or swarm with, be lousy with <nonformal>, teem with

8 attend, be at, be present at, **go or come to; appear** 33.8, turn up, set foot in, show up <nonformal>, show one's face, make or put in an appearance, make a personal appearance, **visit**, **take in** and do and catch <all nonformal>; sit in or at; be on hand; watch, see; witness, look on

9 **revisit**, return to, go back to, come again

10 **frequent, haunt**, resort to, hang and hang around and hang about and hang out <all nonformal>

11 **present oneself, report**; report for duty

ADJS 12 **present**, attendant; **on hand**, on deck <nonformal>, on board; **immediate**, inherent, **available, accessible, at hand**, in view, within reach, in place

13 **omnipresent, all-present**, ubiquitous, everywhere; continuous, uninterrupted, infinite

14 **pervasive**, pervading, suffusive, suffusing

15 **permeated**, saturated, shot through, filled with, suffused; honeycombed; crawling, creeping, swarming, teeming, lousy with <nonformal>

ADVS 16 **here, there**

17 **in person**, personally, bodily, **in the flesh** <nonformal>, in one's own person

222 ABSENCE

NOUNS 1 **absence**, nonpresence; **nonexistence** 761; want, **lack**, deprivation; nonoccurrence; **subtraction** 255

2 **vacancy**, vacuity, voidness, **emptiness**, blankness, hollowness, inanition; **bareness**, barrenness, desolateness, bleakness; **nonoccupancy**, vacancy, nonresidence; opening, open place or post, vacant post

3 **void, vacuum**, blank, emptiness, empty space, inanity; **nothingness;** clean slate; **nothing** 761.2

4 **absence**, nonattendance, **absenting, leaving**, taking leave, **departure** 188; running away, fleeing, decamping, bolting,

skedaddling; **disappearance** 34, escape 369; **absentation**, default, unauthorized or unexcused absence; **truancy, hooky** <nonformal>, French leave, cut <nonformal>; **absence without leave** or AWOL; **absenteeism**, truantism; **leave, leave of absence**, furlough; **vacation**, holiday, day off; authorized or excused absence, sick leave; sabbatical leave

5 **absentee, truant**, no-show

6 **nobody, no one**, no man, not one, not a single one or person, **not a soul** or **blessed soul** or **living soul**, nary one <nonformal>, nobody on earth or under the sun; nonperson, unperson

VERBS 7 **be absent, stay away**, keep away, keep out of the way, not show up <nonformal>, turn up missing <nonformal>, stay away in droves <nonformal>, fail to appear, default, sit out

8 **absent oneself**, take leave or leave of absence, go on leave or furlough; **vacation**, go on vacation, take time off, take off from work; slip off or away, duck or sneak out <nonformal>, slip out, make oneself scarce <nonformal>, leave the scene, bow out, exit, **depart** 188.6, **disappear** 34.2, escape 369.6

9 **play truant, go AWOL**, take French leave; play hooky, cut classes; jump ship

10 <nonformal terms> **split**, bugger off, fuck off, f off, make tracks, pull up stakes, push off, skedaddle, **haul ass, beat it, blow**, bug out, cut, **cut out**, cut and run, make tracks, scram, shove off

ADJS 11 **absent**, not present, **away, gone**, departed, disappeared, vanished, absconded; **missing**, among the missing, wanting, **lacking**, nowhere to be found, omitted, taken away, subtracted, deleted; no longer present or with us or among us; long-lost; **nonexistent**

12 **nonresident**, away from home,

on leave *or* vacation, on sabbatical leave; on tour, on the road; abroad, overseas

13 truant, absent without leave *or* **AWOL**

14 vacant, empty, hollow, inane, **bare, vacuous, void,** without content, null, null and void; **blank,** clear, white, bleached; featureless, unrelieved, characterless, bland, insipid; **barren** 890.4

15 available, open, free, **unoccupied, uninhabited,** unpopulated, unpeopled, unmanned, unstaffed; **deserted,** abandoned, forsaken, godforsaken <nonformal>

ADVS **16 absently; vacantly, emptily,** hollowly, vacuously, blankly

17 nowhere, neither here nor there

18 away 188.21, **elsewhere,** somewhere else, not here

223 NEARNESS

NOUNS **1 nearness, closeness, proximity,** propinquity, intimacy, immediacy; approximation, approach, convergence; **vicinity, neighborhood,** environs, surroundings, setting, confines, precinct; **foreground**

2 short distance, short way, step, short step, span, brief span, short piece <nonformal>; short range; close quarters *or* range; **stone's throw,** spitting distance <nonformal>; earshot, bit <nonformal>, **hair, hairbreadth** *or* **hairsbreadth,** finger's breadth *or* width, an inch

3 juxtaposition, apposition, adjacency; **contiguity,** contiguousness; butting, abutment; junction 799.1, connection, union; **conjunction;** syzygy; perigee, perihelion

4 meeting, joining, joining up, **encounter;** confrontation; near-miss, collision course, near thing, narrow squeak *or* brush

5 contact, touch, touching, tangency; gentle *or* tentative contact, caress, brush, glance, nudge, kiss, rub, graze; impingement, impingence; osculation

6 neighbor, immediate neighbor; abutter, adjoiner; bystander, onlooker; tangent

VERBS **7 near, come near,** nigh, draw near *or* nigh, **approach** 167.3, come within shouting distance; **converge; come within an inch**

8 be near *or* **around,** be in the vicinity *or* neighborhood, **approximate, approach,** get warm <nonformal>, come near, have something at hand *or* at one's fingertips

9 adjoin, join, conjoin, **connect,** butt, **abut,** abut on, be contiguous, be in contact; **neighbor,** border, **border on** *or* **upon,** verge on *or* upon

10 contact, come in contact, touch, feel, impinge, bump up against, hit; osculate; **graze,** caress, kiss, nudge, rub, brush, glance, scrape, sideswipe, skim, skirt, shave; grope *and* feel up *and* cop a feel <all nonformal>; have a near miss

11 meet, encounter; come across, run across, meet up, cross the path of; **come upon,** run upon, fall upon; **meet with,** meet up with <nonformal>, come face to face with, **confront,** meet head-on *or* eyeball to eyeball; **run into, bump into** *and* run smack into <both nonformal>, join up with, run *and* fall foul of; be on a collision course

12 stay near, keep close to; go with, march with, follow close upon, breathe down one's neck, stay on one's tail, tailgate <nonformal>; hang about *or* around, hover over; **cling to,** clasp, hug, huddle; hug the shore *or* land

13 juxtapose, join 799, **adjoin, abut,** butt against, neighbor; bring near, put with, set side by side

ADJS **14 near, close, nigh,** close-in, nearish, intimate, cheek-by-jowl, side-by-side, hand-in-hand, armin-arm; **approaching**, nearing, proximate, proximal; **short-range;** near the mark

15 **nearby, handy, convenient,** neighboring, ready at hand, easily reached *or* attained

16 **adjacent, next,** immediate, contiguous, **adjoining, abutting; neighboring,** neighbor; **juxtaposed; bordering,** connecting; **face-to-face** 215.6; end-to-end; **joined**

17 **in contact,** contacting, **touching, meeting,** contingent; impinging; tangent, tangential; osculatory; grazing, kissing, glancing, brushing, rubbing, nudging

18 **nearer,** nigher, **closer**

19 **nearest, closest,** next, immediate

ADVS 20 **near, nigh, close;** hard, at close quarters; **nearby, close by,** hard by, in the vicinity *or* **neighborhood of,** at hand, at close range, **near** *or* **close at hand;** **about, around** <nonformal>, along toward <nonformal>; at no great distance; **within reach** *or* **range,** within call *or* hearing, within earshot, within a whoop *or* two whoops and a holler <nonformal>, a stone's throw away, in spitting distance <nonformal>, at one's elbow, at one's fingertips, under one's nose, at one's side, within one's grasp; just around the corner, just across the street, next-door

21 **in juxtaposition, in conjunction,** in apposition; beside 218.11

22 **nearly, near,** pretty near <nonformal>, close, **closely; almost,** as near as makes no difference; **well-nigh, just about;** nigh

23 **approximately,** practically <nonformal>, for practical purposes, give or take a little, **more or less;** roughly, roundly, in round numbers; **generally,** generally speaking, roughly speaking, say; in the ballpark <nonformal>

224 INTERVAL
<space between>

NOUNS 1 **interval, gap, space** 158, intervening *or* intermediate space, **interspace,** distance *or* space between, interstice; **clearance,** margin, leeway, **room** 158.3; discontinuity 812, jump, leap, interruption; hiatus, caesura, lacuna; time interval, interim 825

2 **crack, cleft,** cranny, chink, check, craze, chap, **crevice,** fissure, incision, notch, score, cut, gash, slit, split, **rift,** rent; **opening,** excavation, cavity, hole; **gap,** gape, **abyss, gulf, chasm,** void 222.3; **breach, break,** fracture, rupture; fault, flaw; slot, groove, furrow, moat, ditch, trench, dike; joint, seam; **valley**

VERBS 3 **interspace, space,** make a space, set at intervals, dot, scatter 770.4, **space out, separate,** split off, part, dispart, set *or* keep apart

4 **cleave, crack,** check, incise, craze, **cut, cut apart,** gash, slit, **split,** rive, rent, rip open; **open; gap,** breach, break, fracture, rupture; slot, groove, furrow, ditch, trench

ADJS 5 interspatial, interstitial

6 **interspaced, spaced, spaced out,** set at intervals, dotted, scattered 770.9, **separated, parted,** split-off

7 **cleft, cut,** cloven, **cracked,** sundered, rift, rent, chinky, chapped, crazed; **slit, split;** ;aping, gappy; hiatal, caesural, lacunar; fissured

225 HABITATION
<an inhabiting>

NOUNS 1 **habitation,** inhabiting, habitancy, inhabitancy, **tenancy, occupancy,** occupation, **residence** *or* **residency,** residing, abiding, **living,** nesting, **dwelling,** lodging, staying, stopping, sojourning, staying over; squatting; cohabitation, living together, sharing quarters; living in sin; **abode, habitat** 228

2 **peopling, population,** inhabiting; **colonization, settlement,** plantation

3 **housing; lodging, quartering,** billeting, hospitality; living quarters; **housing development,** subdivision, tract

4 **camping, encampment,** bivouacking; camp 228.29

5 **sojourn,** sojourning, temporary stay; **stay,** stop; **stopover,** stopoff, stayover, layover

6 **habitability,** inhabitability, **livability**

VERBS 7 **inhabit, occupy,** tenant, take up one's abode, make one's home; rent, lease; **reside, live, live in, dwell, lodge, stay,** remain, abide, hang *or* hang out <nonformal>, domicile; **room,** bunk, crash <nonformal>, berth; perch *and* roost *and* squat <all nonformal>; nest; room together; cohabit, live together; live in sin

8 **sojourn,** stop, stay, **stop over,** stay over, lay over

9 **people, populate, inhabit; colonize, settle**

10 **house,** domicile; have as a guest *or* lodger, shelter, harbor; **lodge, quarter, put up,** billet, room, bed, berth, bunk; stable

11 **camp, encamp,** tent; pitch, **pitch camp,** pitch one's tent, drive stakes <nonformal>; bivouac; go camping, camp out, sleep out, rough it

ADJS 12 **inhabited, occupied,** tenanted; **peopled,** populated, colonized, settled; populous

13 **resident, in residence; residing, living, dwelling,** lodging, **staying,** remaining, abiding, living in; cohabiting, live-in

14 **housed,** domiciled, **lodged,** quartered, billeted; stabled

15 **habitable,** inhabitable, tenantable, **livable, fit to live in, fit for occupation;** homelike 228.33

ADVS 16 **at home,** in the bosom of one's family; in one's element; back home *and* down home <both nonformal>

226 NATIVENESS

NOUNS 1 **nativeness,** nativity, indigenousness, aboriginality, autochthonousness, **nationality;** nativism

2 **citizenship,** citizenhood, subjecthood

3 **naturalization,** nationalization, adoption, admission, affiliation, **assimilation;** indigenization; acculturation, enculturation

VERBS 4 **naturalize,** grant *or* confer citizenship, adopt, admit, affiliate, **assimilate;** acculturate; indigenize, go native <nonformal>

ADJS 5 **native,** natal, **indigenous,** endemic, autochthonous; mother, maternal, original, aboriginal, primitive; native-born, home-grown, homebred

6 **naturalized,** adopted, **assimilated;** indoctrinated; acculturated; indigenized

227 INHABITANT, NATIVE

NOUNS 1 **population, inhabitants,** dwellers, **populace, people,** citizenry, body, whole body, warm bodies <nonformal>; **public,** general public; community, society, **nation,** commonwealth, constituency, body politic, electorate; **census,** head count; population statistics, demography, demographics

2 **inhabitant,** inhabiter, habitant; **occupant,** occupier, **dweller, tenant, denizen,** inmate; **resident; inpatient;** live-in maid; writer- *or* poet- *or* artist- *or* composer-in-residence; incumbent, *locum tenens* <L>; sojourner

3 **native,** autochthon, earliest inhabitant; primitive; **aborigine,** aboriginal; local *and* local yokel <both nonformal>

4 **citizen, national,** subject; **naturalized citizen,** citizen by adoption, immigrant; hyphenated American; **cosmopolitan,** cosmopolite, citizen of the world

5 **fellow citizen,** fellow country-

man, **compatriot, countryman,**
countrywoman; home boy *and*
home girl *and* hometowner <all
nonformal>

**6 townsman, townswoman, vil-
lager,** city dweller, city person;
city slicker <nonformal>; urban-
ite; suburbanite; exurbanite;
townspeople, townfolks, town-
folk

7 householder, homeowner; cot-
tager, crofter; head of household

8 lodger, roomer, paying guest;
boarder, transient, transient
guest *or* boarder; **renter, tenant,**
lessee

9 settler, *habitant* <Canadian &
Louisiana Fr>; **colonist,** colo-
nizer, colonial, immigrant;
homesteader; squatter, nester;
pioneer

10 wilderness settler; **frontiersman,** mountain man; **back-
woodsman,** woodsman; **mountaineer, hillbilly** *and* ridge runner <both nonformal>; **cracker**
and redneck <both nonformal>,
desert rat <nonformal>, clam
digger <nonformal>

11 <regional inhabitants> East-
erner; Midwesterner; Westerner;
Southerner; Northener, Yankee;
New Englander

228 ABODE, HABITAT
<place of habitation or resort>

NOUNS **1 abode, habitation,
place, dwelling,** dwelling place,
place to live, roof, roof over one's
head, **residence,** place of residence, **domicile; lodging,**
lodging place; seat, nest, living
space, place to rest one's head,
crash pad <nonformal>; native
heath, turf, home turf; **address,**
permanent residence; **housing;
affordable housing,** low-cost
housing, low-and-middle-income
housing, public housing

2 home, home sweet home; **fireside, hearth,** hearth and home,
hearthstone, fireplace, *foyer*
<Fr>, chimney corner, ingle, in-
gleside *or* inglenook; **household,**

ménage; **homestead,** roof; family
homestead, ancestral halls

3 domesticity; housewifery,
housekeeping, homemaking;
householding

**4 quarters, living quarters; lodg-
ings,** lodging; **pad** *and* **crib** <both
nonformal>, room; **rooms,** berth,
roost, accommodations; **housing**
225.3, shelter

5 house, dwelling, dwelling
house; house and grounds, home-
site; **building, structure, edifice,**
fabric, **hall** 197.4; roof; lodge;
town house; country house;
ranch house, farmhouse, farm;
lake dwelling 241.3; houseboat;
cave *or* cliff dwelling; penthouse;
split-level; parsonage 703.7, **rectory,** vicarage, deanery, manse

6 farmstead; ranch, grange

**7 estate; mansion; villa, châ-
teau, castle,** tower; **palace,**
court

8 cottage, bungalow, box; **cabin,**
log cabin; **second home, vacation home;** chalet, lodge, snuggery; home away from home,
pied-à-terre <Fr>

9 hut, hutch, **shack, shanty,** crib,
hole-in-the-wall <nonformal>,
shed; lean-to; booth, stall; toll-
house, sentry box, gatehouse;
outhouse, outbuilding; privy; **pa-
vilion,** kiosk

10 <Native American houses> wigwam, tepee, hogan, wickiup,
jacal, longhouse; tupik, igloo
<both Eskimo>

11 hovel, dump <nonformal>,
rathole, hole, sty, pigsty, pigpen,
tumbledown shack

12 summerhouse, arbor, bower,
gazebo, pergola, kiosk, alcove,
retreat; **conservatory, greenhouse,** lathhouse

13 apartment, flat, tenement,
rooms; studio apartment *or* flat;
granny flat, flatlet; **suite;
walkup, cold-water flat; penthouse;** garden apartment; duplex
apartment; railroad flat

**14 apartment house, flats, tene-
ment;** duplex; apartment complex; cooperative apartment

house *or* co-op <nonformal>, condominium *or* condo <nonformal>; high-rise apartment building *or* high rise

15 **inn, hotel,** hostel, **tavern; roadhouse,** guest house, bed and breakfast; youth hostel, hospice; **lodging house,** rooming house; **boardinghouse; dormitory,** dorm <nonformal>, fraternity *or* sorority house; bunkhouse; **flophouse** *and* fleabag <both nonformal>

16 **motel,** motor court, motor hotel, auto court

17 **trailer,** house *or* camp trailer, **mobile home,** camper; trailer court *or* camp *or* park, campground

18 **habitat,** home, **range,** stamping grounds, locality

19 **zoo, menagerie,** zoological garden *or* park

20 **barn, stable,** stall; **cowbarn,** cowhouse, cowshed

21 **kennel, doghouse;** pound, dog pound

22 **coop, chicken house** *or* **coop,** henhouse; brooder

23 **birdhouse, aviary,** bird cage; dovecote, pigeon house *or* loft; roost, perch; rookery; eyrie

24 **vivarium, terrarium, aquarium;** fishpond

25 **nest; beehive, apiary,** hive, hornet's nest, wasp's nest

26 **lair, den,** cave, **hole,** covert; **burrow,** tunnel, earth, run

27 **resort, haunt,** purlieu, **hangout** <nonformal>, **stamping ground** <nonformal>; gathering place, rallying point, meeting place, clubhouse, club; casino, gambling house; health resort; **spa,** baths, springs, watering place

28 <disapproved place> **dive** <nonformal>, **den, lair,** den of thieves; hole *and* dump *and* **joint** <all nonformal>; gyp *or* clip joint <nonformal>; **whorehouse,** cathouse <nonformal>, sporting house, brothel, bordello

29 **camp, encampment; bivouac; barracks,** cantonment; hobo jungle *or* camp; detention camp, concentration camp; campground *or* campsite

30 <deities of the household> lares and penates, Vesta, Hestia

VERBS 31 **keep house,** practice domesticity, maintain *or* run a household

ADJS 32 **residential,** residentiary; domestic, domiciliary; **home, household**

33 **homelike, homey** <nonformal>, homely; comfortable, friendly, cheerful, peaceful, cozy, snug, intimate; simple, plain, unpretending

34 **domesticated, tame,** tamed, broken; housebroken

229 FURNITURE

NOUNS 1 **furniture,** furnishings, home furnishings, house furnishings, household effects, household goods; **cabinetmaking,** cabinetwork, cabinetry; **furniture design, furniture style; period furniture; piece of furniture,** chair, sofa, bed, table, desk, cabinet, mirror, clock, screen; **suite, set of furniture,** ensemble, decor

230 TOWN, CITY

NOUNS 1 **town,** township; **city, metropolis,** metropolitan area, megalopolis, conurbation, urban complex, urban sprawl, urban corridor, strip city, **municipality,** city *or* municipal government; **borough, burg** <nonformal>; **suburb,** suburbia, burbs <nonformal>, outskirts; exurb, exurbia; boom town, ghost town

2 **village, hamlet;** country town, crossroads, wide place in the road

3 <nonformal terms> **one-horse town,** jerkwater town, **tank town** *or* station, **whistle-stop; hick town,** rube town, podunk; hoosier town; wide place in the road

4 **capital,** capital city, **seat,** seat of government; **county seat**

5 town hall, city hall, municipal building; courthouse; county building, county courthouse; community center

6 <city districts> East Side *or* End, West Side *or* End; **downtown,** uptown, midtown; city center, urban center, central *or* center city, inner city, suburbs, suburbia, burbs <nonformal>, outskirts, greenbelt, residential district, business district *or* section, shopping center; **asphalt** *or* **concrete jungle; slum** *or* **slums,** the other side *or* the wrong side of the tracks, tenement district, shantytown, hell's kitchen *or* half-acre; tenderloin, red-light district, **skid row** <nonformal>; **ghetto, inner city,** urban ghetto, barrio

7 block, city block, square

8 square, plaza, marketplace, market, forum, agora

9 circle; crescent

10 city planning, urban planning; urban studies

ADJS **11 urban, metropolitan, municipal, civic; citywide; city, town, village; citified; suburban; interurban; downtown, uptown, midtown; inner-city,** ghetto; small-town; boom-town

231 REGION

NOUNS **1 region, area, zone,** belt, **territory,** terrain; **place** 159.1; **space** 158; **country 232, land 234,** ground, soil; territoriality; continental shelf; air space; heartland; hinterland; **district, quarter, section;** vicinity, neck of the woods <nonformal>, purlieus; premises, confines, precincts, environs, milieu

2 sphere, hemisphere, orb, **orbit,** ambit, circle; **circuit, beat, round,** walk; **realm, domain,** dominion, jurisdiction, bailiwick; **province,** precinct, department

3 zone; longitude; meridian, prime meridian; latitude, parallel; equator; tropic, tropics, subtropics; Temperate Zones; Frigid Zones, Arctic Zone, Antarctic Zone; horse latitudes, roaring forties

4 plot, parcel of land, **patch, tract, field;** lot; air space; block, square; section <square mile>, forty <sixteenth of a section>; close, quadrangle, quad, enclave, pale

5 <territorial divisions> **state, territory, province,** region, duchy, electorate, government, principality; **county,** shire, canton; **borough, ward,** riding; **township,** commune; metropolis, metropolitan area, **city, town 230; village,** hamlet; **district,** precinct; magistracy, bailiwick

6 <regions of the world> continent, landmass; Old World, the old country; New World, America; Northern Hemisphere, North America; Central America; Southern Hemisphere, South America; Latin America; Western Hemisphere, Occident, West; Eastern Hemisphere, Orient, Levant, East, eastland; Far East, Mideast *or* Middle East, Near East; Asia, Europe, Eurasia, Asia Major, Asia Minor, Africa; Antipodes, down under, Australasia, Oceania

7 <some regions of the US> the West, the wild West, the West Coast, the left Coast <nonformal>; the Northwest, the Pacific Northwest; the Rockies; the Southwest, the Middle West, Middle America; the Great Plains, the heartlands; the Rust Belt; the East, the East Coast, the Middle Atlantic; the Northeast, the Southeast; the North, the Snow Belt, the Frost Belt; Appalachia; the South, Dixie, Dixieland; the Deep South, the Old South; the Delta, the bayous; the Bible Belt; the Sunbelt; the Gulf Coast; New England, Down East

ADJS **8 regional, territorial, geographical,** sectional, zonal, topographic *or* topographical

9 local, localized, geographically limited, topical, vernacular, parochial, provincial, insular, limited, confined

232 COUNTRY

NOUNS **1 country,** land; **nation,**
nationality, **state,** nation-state,
sovereign nation *or* state, polity,
body politic; power, super-
power, world power; **republic,**
commonwealth, commonweal;
kingdom, sultanate; **empire;**
realm, dominion, domain; **prin-**
cipality, principate; duchy,
dukedom; grand duchy, arch-
duchy, archdukedom, earldom,
county, palatinate, seneschalty;
city-state, free city; **province,**
territory, possession; colony, settlement; protectorate, mandate,
mandated territory; **ally,** cobel-
ligerent, treaty partner; satellite,
puppet regime *or* government;
free nation, captive nation; nonaligned *or* unaligned *or* neutralist
nation; developed nation, industrial *or* industrialized nation; underdeveloped nation, third-world
nation

2 fatherland, motherland,
mother country, **native land,** native soil, the old country, country
of origin, **birthplace,** cradle;
home, homeland, homeground,
God's country; the home front

3 United States, United States of
America, US, USA; America, the
States, Land of Liberty, the melt-
ing pot; stateside

4 Britain, Great Britain, United
Kingdom, the UK, Britannia

5 <national personifications> Uncle Sam *or* Brother Jonathan
<US>; John Bull <England>

6 nationhood, peoplehood, **na-**
tionality; statehood, nation-
statehood, sovereignty, independence, self-government, self-
determination; internationalism;
nationalism

233 THE COUNTRY

NOUNS **1 the country,** agricultural
region, farm country, farmland,
arable land, grazing region *or*
country, rural district, province
or **provinces,** countryside, woodland 310.11, grassland 310.8, the
soil, grass roots; **the sticks** *and*
the tall corn *and* yokeldom *and*
hickdom <all nonformal>; cotton
belt, tobacco belt, black belt,
farm belt, corn belt, fruit belt,
wheat belt, citrus belt; dust bowl;
highlands, moors, uplands, foot-
hills; lowlands, veld *or* veldt,
savanna *or* savannah, plains,
prairies, steppes, wide-open
spaces

2 hinterland, back country, outback <Australia>, up-country,
boonies *and* boondocks <both
nonformal>; **the bush,** bush
country, **woods,** woodlands,
backwoods, forests, timbers,
brush; wilderness, wilds, uninhabited region, virgin land *or*
territory; **wasteland** 890.2; **fron-**
tier, borderland, outpost; cow
country

3 rusticity, ruralism, agrarianism, bucolicism, **provin-**
cialism, provinciality, simplicity, pastoral simplicity, unspoiledness; yokelism, hickishness,
backwoodsiness; **boorishness,**
churlishness, unrefinement, uncultivation

4 ruralization, rustication, pas-
toralization

VERBS **5 ruralize, countrify, rusti-**
cate; farm 1067.16

ADJS **6 rustic, rural, country, pro-**
vincial, farm, pastoral, bucolic,
Arcadian, **agrarian; agricultural**
1067.20; lowland, highland, prairie, plains

7 countrified, inurbane; country-
bred, up-country; hobnailed,
clodhopping; **boorish,** clownish,
loutish, cloddish, churlish; **un-**
couth, unpolished, uncultivated,
uncultured, unrefined

8 <nonformal terms> **hick,** hick-
ified, from the sticks, rube, hay-
seed, yokel, yokelish, down-
home, shit-kicking, hillbilly,
redneck

9 hinterland, back, **back-**
country, up-country, outback
<Australia>, wild, wilderness, vir-
gin; cow-country; **waste** 890.4;

backwood *or* **backwoods,** back-
woodsy; woodland, sylvan

234 LAND

NOUNS **1 land, ground,** landmass,
earth, **sod,** clod, **soil, dirt,** dust,
clay; **terra firma;** terrain; **dry
land;** arable land; grassland
310.8, woodland 310.11; earth's
crust, lithosphere; topsoil, sub-
soil; **real estate,** real property,
landholdings, acres, territory; region 231

2 shore, coast; strand, beach,
beachfront, lido, sands, berm;
waterfront; shoreline, coastline;
bank, embankment; **seashore,
coast, seacoast, seaside, sea-
board,** oceanfront, oceanside,
seafront, seaside, shorefront,
tidewater, tideland, coastland, littoral; wetland, wetlands; **bay,**
bayfront; drowned *or* submerged
coast

3 landsman, landman, **landlubber**

ADJS **4 terrestrial, earth, earthly,**
tellurian; earthbound; sublunar,
subastral; geophilous; terraque-
ous

5 earthy, earthen, soily, loamy,
gumbo; clayey; adobe

6 alluvial, estuarine, fluviomarine

**7 coastal, littoral, seaside,
shore,** shoreside; shoreward; ri-
parian *or* riparious; riverine;
riverside; lakefront, lakeshore;
oceanfront, oceanside; seaside,
seafront, shorefront, shoreline;
beachfront, beachside; bayside;
tideland, tidal, wetland

ADVS **8 on land,** on dry land, on
terra firma; onshore, ashore;
shoreward; overland

9 on earth, on the face of the earth
or globe, in the world, in the
whole wide world; **under the
sun,** under the stars, beneath the
sky, below, **here below**

235 BODY OF LAND

NOUNS **1 continent, mainland,**
landform, continental landform,
landmass; subcontinent; penin-
sula; **plate,** crustal plate, crustal

segment; continental divide, continental drift

2 island, isle; islet; continental island; oceanic island; **key,** cay;
sandbank, sandbar, bar; **reef,**
coral reef, coral head; coral island, atoll; archipelago, island
group *or* chain; insularity

3 continental, mainland

4 islander, island-dweller, insular

VERBS **5** insulate, isolate; island-
hop

ADJS **6 continental,** mainland

7 insular, insulated, isolated; island, islandlike; island-dotted;
seagirt; archipelagic *or* archi-
pelagian

236 PLAIN

<open country>

NOUNS **1 plain, plains,** flatland,
flats, flat, level; open country,
wide-open spaces; prairie,
grassland 310.8, sea of grass,
steppe, pampas, savanna, tun-
dra; **veld; moor,** moorland,
down, **downs, heath;** lowland,
lowlands, bottomland; basin;
sand plain, sand flat; tidal flat,
salt marsh; salt pan; salt flat, alkali flat; **desert** 890.2; **plateau,**
upland, tableland, table, **mesa;**
peneplain; coastal plain, tidal
plain, alluvial plain, delta, delta
plain; mare, lunar mare

ADJS **2 plain, flat,** open; campestral
or campestrian

237 HIGHLANDS

NOUNS **1 highlands, uplands,**
highland, upland, high country,
elevated land, dome, **plateau, tableland,** upland area, piedmont,
moor, moorland, **hills, heights,**
hill *or* hilly country, downs, foot-
hills, rolling country, **mountains,**
high terrain, peaks, range

2 slope, declivity, steep, incline,
rise, talus, mountainside, hillside,
bank, gentle *or* easy slope, steep
or rapid slope, fall line, bluff, cliff,
precipice, steep, wall, palisade,
escarpment, scarp, fault scarp,
rim, face; upper slopes, upper
reaches, timberline *or* tree line

3 **plateau, tableland,** high plateau, table, mesa, table mountain, butte, moor

4 **hill; hillock, knob,** butte, **knoll,** hummock, eminence, rise, mound, swell, barrow, tumulus; **dune,** sand dune; moraine, drumlin; anthill, molehill; **dune,** sand dune, sandhill

5 **ridge,** ridgeline, chine, spine, esker, cuesta, moraine, terminal moraine; **saddle, hogback,** hog's-back, saddleback, horseback; **pass,** gap, notch, wind gap, water gap

6 **mountain,** mount, alp, hump, tor, height, dizzying height, dome; **peak, pinnacle, summit** 198.2, mountaintop, point, topmost point *or* pinnacle, **crest,** tor; crag, spur, cloud-capped *or* cloud-topped *or* snow-clad peak, the roof of the world; needle, horn; **volcano;** submarine mountain; **mountain range,** range; **mountain system, chain,** mountain chain, cordillera, sierra; hill heaped upon hill; mountain-building, orogeny, folding, faulting, block-faulting, volcanism

7 **valley,** vale, glen, dale, dell, hollow, holler <nonformal>, flume; **ravine, gorge, canyon,** box canyon, coulee, gully, gulch, dingle, rift, rift valley, gully, draw, wadi, basin, cirque, corrie; **crevasse; chimney, defile,** pass, passage; **crater,** volcanic crater, caldera, meteorite *or* meteoritic crater

ADJS 8 **hilly, rolling,** undulating; **mountainous,** montane, alpine

238 STREAM
<*running water*>

NOUNS 1 **stream, waterway, watercourse** 239.2, **channel** 239; lazy stream, racing stream, braided stream; spill stream; adolescent stream; **river;** navigable river, underground *or* subterranean river; dry stream, stream bed, winterbourne, wadi; **brook,** branch; kill, bourn, **creek,** crick <nonformal>; **rivulet,** rill, **streamlet,** brooklet, runlet, runnel, rundle <nonformal>; **freshet;** millstream, race; midstream, midchannel; fluviation

2 **headwaters, headstream,** headwater, head, riverhead; **source,** fountainhead 885.6

3 **tributary,** feeder, **branch, fork,** prong <nonformal>, confluent, confluent stream, affluent; effluent, anabranch; bayou

4 **flow,** flowing, **flux,** fluid motion *or* movement; hydrodynamics; **stream, current,** set, trend, tide, water flow; drift, driftage; **course,** onward course, **surge, gush, rush,** onrush, spate, run; race; millrace, mill run; undercurrent, undertow; crosscurrent, crossflow; affluence, confluence, concourse; **downflow; downpour;** inflow 189.2; outflow 190.4

5 **torrent, river, flood,** flash flood, wall of water, **deluge;** spate, **pour,** freshet

6 **overflow,** spillage, spill, spillover, overflowing, overrunning, alluvium, **inundation, flood, deluge,** engulfment, submersion 367.2, cataclysm; the Flood, the Deluge; washout

7 **trickle,** tricklet, **dribble, drip,** dripping, drop; percolation; leaching; distillation, condensation, sweating; seeping, seepage

8 **lap, swash, wash, slosh, plash, splash;** lapping, washing, etc

9 **jet, spout, spurt,** squirt, spit, spew, spray, spritz <nonformal>; rush, **gush,** flush; **fountain,** fount, font; geyser; spouter <nonformal>

10 **rapids, rapid,** white water, wild water; ripple, **riffle,** riff <nonformal>; chute, shoot, sault

11 **waterfall, cataract,** fall, **falls, Niagara, cascade,** sault; watershoot

12 **eddy,** back stream, gurge, **swirl,** twirl, whirl; **whirlpool,** vortex, gulf, **maelstrom;** Maelstrom, Charybdis; countercurrent, counterflow, counterflux, backflow, reflux, refluence, regurgitation, backwash, backwater, snye <Can>

13 tide, tidal current *or* stream, tidal flow *or* flood, **tide race; tidewater;** tideway, tide gate; **riptide,** rip, tiderip, overfalls; **spring tide; high tide,** high water; **low tide,** low water; **neap tide,** neap; lunar tide, solar tide; **flood tide, ebb tide;** rise of the tide, flux, flow, flood; ebb, reflux, refluence; ebb and flow, flux and reflux; tidal amplitude, tidal range; tide chart *or* table, tidal current chart

14 wave, billow, surge, **swell,** heave, undulation, lift, rise; trough, peak; **sea,** ocean swell, ground swell; **roller,** roll; **comber,** comb; **surf, breakers;** wavelet, **ripple,** riffle; **tidal wave,** tsunami; **whitecap,** white horse; rough *or* heavy sea, rough water, choppy *or* chopping sea; standing wave

15 water gauge, fluviometer; marigraph; Nilometer

VERBS **16 flow,** stream, issue, pour, **surge, run,** course, **rush, gush, flush, flood;** empty into, flow into, join, join with; flow in 189.9; flow out 190.13; flow back, surge back, ebb

17 overflow, flow over, wash over, **run over, well over, brim over,** lap, lap at, lap over, pour out *or* over, **spill, slop, slosh,** spill out *or* over; **cataract, cascade; inundate,** engulf, swamp, sweep, **flood,** deluge

18 trickle, dribble, drip, drop; **filter,** percolate, leach; distill, condense, sweat; seep, weep; **gurgle** 52.11

19 lap, plash, splash, wash, swash, slosh

20 jet, spout, spurt, squirt, spit, spew, spray, play, **gush,** well, surge; vomit out *or* forth

21 eddy, gurge, **swirl,** whirl, purl, reel, spin

22 billow, surge, swell, heave, lift, rise, send, toss, **roll,** wave, **undulate; peak,** draw to a peak, be poised; comb, **break,** dash, crash, smash; rise and fall, ebb and flow

ADJS **23 streamy,** rivery, brooky,

creeky; streamlike, riverine; fluvial, fluviatile *or* fluviatic

24 flowing, streaming, running, pouring, coursing, racing, gushing, rushing, onrushing, surging, surgy, torrential, rough, whitewater; **fluent,** profluent, affluent, defluent, decurrent, confluent, diffluent; tidal; gulfy, vortical; meandering, mazy, sluggish, serpentine

25 flooded, deluged, inundated, engulfed, swamped, swept, drowned, awash; washed, waterwashed; in flood, at flood, in spate

239 CHANNEL

NOUNS **1 channel, conduit, duct,** canal, course; **way, passage, passageway;** trough; tunnel; ditch, trench 290.2; adit; ingress, entrance 189; egress, exit; **stream** 238

2 watercourse, waterway, aqueduct, water channel, water gate, culvert, **canal;** streamway, riverway; **bed,** stream bed, river bed, creek bed, runnel; water gap; dry bed, wadi, winterbourne, **gully,** gulch; race, headrace, tailrace; flume; sluice; spillway; spillbox; irrigation ditch, water furrow; waterworks

3 gutter, trough; flume, chute, shoot; penstock; guide

4 <metal founding> gate, ingate, runner, sprue, tedge

5 drain, sluice, scupper; **sink,** sump; **gutter; sewer,** cloaca, headchute

6 tube; pipe; tubing, piping; nipple, pipette, tubulet, tubule; reed, stem, straw; **hose,** garden hose, fire hose; pipeline; catheter; **siphon;** tap; funnel; snorkel; siamese connection *or* joint

7 main, water main, gas main, fire main

8 spout, beak, waterspout, downspout; gargoyle

9 nozzle, bib nozzle, pressure nozzle, spray nozzle, nose, snout; rose, rosehead

10 valve, gate; **faucet, spigot, tap;** cock, **petcock,** draw cock, stop-

cock, sea cock, drain cock, ball
cock

11 **floodgate,** gate, **head gate,** penstock, water gate, **sluice,** sluice
gate; tide gate, aboiteau <Can>;
weir; **lock,** lock gate, dock gate;
air lock

12 **hydrant,** fire hydrant, **plug,** water plug, fireplug

13 air passage, air duct, airway, air
shaft, shaft, **air hole,** air tube;
speaking tube *or* pipe; **blowhole,**
breathing hole, spiracle; nostril;
vent, venthole, ventage; **ventilator,** ventilating shaft; transom,
louver

14 **chimney, flue,** flue pipe, funnel,
stovepipe, stack, smokestack,
smoke pipe, smokeshaft; fuma-
role

VERBS 15 **channel,** channelize,
canalize, **conduct, convey,** put
through; pipe, funnel, siphon;
trench 290.3; direct 573.8

ADJS 16 **tubular,** tubate, tubiform,
tubelike, pipelike; cylindrical;
tubed, piped; cannular; tubal

17 **valvular,** valval, valvelike; valved

240 SEA, OCEAN

NOUNS 1 **ocean, sea, main** *or*
ocean main, the bounding main,
tide, salt sea, salt water, deep water, open sea, **the brine,** the briny
<nonformal>, the briny deep, **the
deep,** the deep sea, the deep blue
sea, drink *and* big drink <both
nonformal>, **high sea, high seas;**
the seven seas; **ocean depths,**
ocean deeps and trenches
275.4, 17

2 <methods> celestial navigation,
radar

3 **ocean**; **sea,** tributary sea, gulf,
bay

4 spirit of the sea, **Davy Jones;** sea
god, **Neptune; mermaid,** siren;
merman, seaman

5 <ocean zones> pelagic zone,
benthic zone, estuarine area,
sublittoral, littoral, intertidal
zone, splash zone, supralittoral

6 oceanography, thalassography,
hydrography, bathymetry; marine biology; aquaculture

7 oceanographer, thalassographer,
hydrographer

ADJS 8 **oceanic, marine, mar-
itime,** pelagic, thalassic; nautical
182.57; oceanographic, ocean-
ographic, hydrographic, hydro-
graphical, bathymetric, bathy-
metrical, bathyorographical,
thalassographic, thalassograph-
ical; terriginous; deep-sea 275.14

ADVS 9 **at sea,** on the high seas;
afloat 182.62; by water, by sea

10 **oversea, overseas,** beyond seas,
over the water, transmarine,
across the sea

11 **oceanward,** oceanwards, **seaward,** seawards; offshore, in blue
water

241 LAKE, POOL

NOUNS 1 **lake,** loch <Scots>, mere,
freshwater lake; oxbow lake,
bayou lake, glacial lake; volcanic
lake; tarn; inland sea; **pool,
pond,** dew pond; standing water,
still water, stagnant water, dead
water; **water** *or* watering hole;
oasis; farm pond; fishpond; mill-
pond; salt pond, tidal pond *or*
pool; **puddle,** sump <nonfor-
mal>; **lagoon; reservoir;** dam;
well, cistern, tank, artesian well,
spring

2 **lake dweller,** lacustrine, lacustrine dweller *or* inhabitant,
pile dweller *or* builder; laker

3 **lake dwelling,** lacustrine dwelling, **pile house** *or* **dwelling,**
palafitte

4 limnology, limnologist; limnime-
ter, limnograph

ADJS 5 **lakish,** lakelike; lacustrine,
lacustral, lacustrian; pondlike;
limnologic, limnological

242 INLET, GULF

NOUNS 1 **inlet, cove,** arm of the
sea, arm, canal, reach, loch
<Scots>, **bay, fjord,** bight; cove;
gulf; estuary, firth *or* frith,
bayou, mouth; **harbor,** natural
harbor; road *or* roads, roadstead; **strait** *or* straits, **narrow**
or **narrows,** belt, narrow seas;
sound

ADJS **2** gulflike; gulfed, bayed, em-
bayed; estuarine, tidewater;
drowned

243 MARSH

NOUNS **1 marsh,** marshland,
swamp, swampland, fen,
morass, bog, mire, quagmire;
sump <nonformal>, wash; glade,
everglade; slough, swale, wallow,
hog wallow, buffalo wallow; bottom, **bottoms,** bottomland, slob
land, meadow; **moor,** moorland,
peat bog; salt marsh; quicksand;
taiga; mud flat, **mud** 1060.8, 9
VERBS **2 mire,** bemire, sink in,
bog, mire *or* bog down, stick in
the mud; stodge
ADJS **3 marshy, swampy,** swamp-
ish, **moory,** moorish, fenny,
paludal; **boggy, miry,** quaggy,
quagmiry; **muddy** 1060.14; ul-
iginous

244 QUANTITY

NOUNS **1 quantity,** quantum,
amount, **whole** 791; mass, **bulk,**
substance, matter, magnitude,
amplitude, **extent, sum; measure,** measurement; strength,
force, numbers
  2 amount, quantity, **sum, number,** count, group, total, reckoning, **measure,** parcel, passel <nonformal>, **part** 792,
portion, clutch, ration, share, issue, allotment, lot, deal; **batch,**
bunch, heap <nonformal>, pack,
mess <nonformal>, gob *and*
chunk *and* hunk <all nonfor-
mal>, dose
  3 some, somewhat, something
VERBS **4 quantify,** quantize, **count,
number off, enumerate, num-
ber** 1016.10, rate, fix; parcel,
apportion, mete out, issue, allot,
divide 801.18; **increase** 251.4, 6,
decrease 252.6, reduce 252.7;
measure 300.11
ADJS **5 quantitative,** quantified,
quantized, measured; **some,** certain, one; a, an; **any**
ADVS **6 approximately,** nearly,
some, about, circa; more or less,
by and large, upwards of

245 DEGREE

NOUNS **1 degree, grade, step,**
leap; round, rung, tread, stair;
point, mark, peg, tick; **notch,**
cut; **plane,** level, plateau; **period,**
space, interval; **extent, measure,**
amount, ratio, proportion, stint,
standard, height, pitch, reach, remove, compass, range, scale,
scope, caliber; **shade,** shadow,
nuance
  2 rank, standing, level, footing,
status, station; **position,** place,
sphere, orbit, echelon; **order,** estate, precedence, condition; rate,
rating; **class,** caste; **hierarchy,**
power structure
  3 gradation, graduation, grading, tapering, shading
VERBS **4 graduate, grade,** calibrate; phase in, phase out, taper
off, shade off; **increase** 251, **decrease** 252.6, 7
ADJS **5 gradual,** gradational, calibrated, graduated, phased,
staged, tapered; regular, progressive; hierarchic, hierarchical
ADVS **6 by degrees; gradually;
step by step, bit by bit, little by
little,** inch by inch, step by step,
drop by drop; a little, fractionally;
a little at a time, by slow degrees,
by inches, a little at a time; slowly
175.13
  7 to a degree, to some extent, in a
way, in some measure; some-
what, kind of <nonformal>, sort
of <nonformal>, rather, quite,
fairly; a little, a bit; slightly,
scarcely, to a small degree
248.9, 10; very, extremely, to a
great degree 247.19-22

246 MEAN

NOUNS **1 mean, median, middle**
818; **golden mean; medium,**
happy medium; middle of the
road, middle course; middle state
or ground *or* position *or* echelon
or level *or* point, midpoint; **average,** balance, par, normal, norm,
rule, run, generality; **mediocrity,**
adequacy; averaging; **center**
208.2

VERBS **2 average,** average out, **split the difference,** strike a balance; strike a happy medium; keep to the middle, avoid extremes; **do,** just do, pass, barely pass

ADJS **3 medium,** mean, **intermediate,** intermediary, median, medial; **average,** normal, standard, par for the course; middle-of-the-road, moderate; **middling, ordinary,** usual, routine, common, mediocre, passing, banal, so-so; **central** 208.11

ADVS **4 mediumly,** medianly; medially, midway 818.5, intermediately, in the mean; **centrally** 208.15

5 on the average, in the long run, over the long haul; taking one thing with another, taking all things together, **all in all, on the whole,** all things considered, on balance; **generally** 863.17

247 GREATNESS

NOUNS **1 greatness, magnitude; amplitude,** fullness, plenitude, great scope *or* compass *or* reach; **grandeur,** grandness; **immensity,** enormousness, **vastness,** vastitude, expanse, boundlessness, infinity 822; prodigiousness, humongousness <nonformal>; **might,** mightiness, strength, power, intensity; **largeness** 257.6, **hugeness,** gigantism, bulk; **superiority** 249

2 glory, eminence, preeminence, majesty, loftiness, prominence, distinction, outstandingness, consequence, notability; **magnanimity,** nobility, sublimity; **fame,** renown, celebrity; heroism

3 quantity 244, **numerousness** 883; **quantities, much, abundance,** copiousness, superabundance, superfluity, profusion, plenty, plenitude; **volume, mass,** mountain, load; peck, bushel; bag, barrel, ton; flood, spate; **multitude** 883.3, countlessness 822.1

4 lot, lots, deal, no end of, **good** *or* **great deal, considerable,** sight,

heap, pile, stack, loads, **raft, slew,** spate, wad, **batch,** mess, mint, peck, pack, pot, **tidy sum,** quite a little; **oodles, gobs, scads**

VERBS **5 loom, bulk,** loom large, bulk large, stand out; **tower,** rear, soar; **tower above,** rise above; **exceed, transcend,** outstrip

ADJS **6 great, grand, considerable,** consequential; **mighty,** powerful, strong, irresistible, intense; main, maximum, **total, full,** plenary, comprehensive, exhaustive; grave, **serious,** heavy, deep

7 large 257.16, **immense, enormous, huge** 257.20; **gigantic,** mountainous, titanic, colossal, mammoth, Gargantuan, gigantesque, monster, monstrous, outsize, sizable, larger-than-life, overgrown, king-size, monumental; **massive,** weighty, bulky, voluminous, **vast,** boundless, **infinite** 822.3, immeasurable, cosmic, astronomical, galactic; **spacious,** extensive; **tremendous,** stupendous, awesome, prodigious

8 much, many, beaucoup <nonformal>, ample, **abundant,** copious, generous, overflowing, superabundant, multitudinous, plentiful, **numerous** 883.6, countless 822.3

9 eminent, prominent, outstanding, standout, high, elevated, towering, soaring, exalted, **lofty,** sublime; august, majestic, noble, distinguished; **magnificent,** magnanimous, heroic, godlike, superb; famous, renowned, lauded, glorious

10 remarkable, outstanding, extraordinary, **superior** 249.12, **marked,** signal, conspicuous, **striking; notable,** much in evidence, noticeable, noteworthy; **marvelous,** wonderful, formidable, exceptional, uncommon, astonishing, humongous <nonformal>, fabulous, fantastic, incredible, egregious

11 <nonformal terms> **terrific,** terrible, horrible, **dreadful, awful,**

fearful, frightful, deadly; **whacking, thumping, rousing,** howling

12 **downright, outright, out-and-out; absolute, utter, perfect, consummate,** superlative, surpassing, positive, definitive, classical, **pronounced,** decided, regular <nonformal>, precious, profound, stark; **thorough,** thoroughgoing, **complete,** total; **unmitigated,** unqualified, unrelieved, unspoiled, undeniable, unquestionable, unequivocal; **flagrant,** arrant, shocking, shattering, egregious, intolerable, unbearable, unconscionable, glaring, **rank,** crass, gross

13 **extreme, radical,** out of this world, way or far out <nonformal>, too much <nonformal>; **greatest,** furthest, **most, utmost; ultra;** at the height or peak or limit or summit or zenith

14 **undiminished,** unabated, unrestricted, unmitigated

ADVS 15 **greatly, largely,** to a large or great extent, in great measure, on a large scale; **much,** pretty much, very much, so, ever so much, ever so, never so; **considerably,** considerable <nonformal>; abundantly, plenty <nonformal>, no end of, not a little, galore <nonformal>, **a lot,** a deal <nonformal>, **a great deal; highly,** to the skies; like all creation <nonformal>, like all get-out <nonformal>, in spades and with bells on and with bells on one's toes <all nonformal>; **undiminishedly,** unabatedly, unrestrictedly, unmitigatedly

16 **vastly, immensely, enormously, hugely, tremendously,** gigantically, colossally, titanically, prodigiously, stupendously, humongously <nonformal>

17 **by far, far and away,** far, far and wide, by a long shot, by all odds

18 **very, exceedingly,** awfully and terribly and terrifically <all nonformal>, **quite,** just, so, **really, pretty,** only too, mightily, **mighty** and almighty and powerfully and powerful <all nonformal>

19 <in a positive degree> **positively, decidedly, clearly,** manifestly, unambiguously, patently, **obviously,** visibly, unmistakably, unquestionably, observably, **noticeably,** demonstrably, sensibly, quite; **certainly,** actually, **really, truly,** verily, **undeniably,** indubitably, without doubt, assuredly, **indeed,** for a certainty, for real <nonformal>, seriously, in all conscience

20 <in a marked degree> **intensely, acutely,** exquisitely, **exceptionally,** surpassingly, superlatively, eminently, preeminently; **remarkably, markedly, notably, strikingly,** signally, emphatically, pointedly, prominently, conspicuously, pronouncedly, impressively, famously, glaringly; **particularly, singularly,** peculiarly; uncommonly, extraordinarily, **unusually; wonderfully,** wondrous, amazingly, magically, surprisingly, astonishingly, marvelously, exuberantly, incredibly, awesomely; **abundantly,** richly, profusely, amply, **generously,** copiously; **magnificently,** splendidly, nobly, worthily, magnanimously

21 <in a distressing degree> **distressingly, sadly, sorely, bitterly,** piteously, grievously, miserably, **cruelly,** woefully, lamentably, shockingly; **terribly, awfully, dreadfully, frightfully, horribly,** abominably, **painfully,** excruciatingly, torturously, **agonizingly,** deathly, deadly, something awful or fierce or terrible <all nonformal>, within an inch of one's life; shatteringly, staggeringly; **excessively,** exorbitantly, extravagantly, **inordinately,** preposterously; **unduly, improperly,** intolerably, unbearably; **inexcusably,** unpardonably, unconscionably; **flagrantly,** blatantly, egregiously; **unashamedly,** unabashedly, baldly, nakedly, brashly, openly; **cursedly,** confoundedly, **damnably,** infernally, hellishly

22 <in an extreme degree> **extremely, utterly, totally** in the extreme, **most; immeasurably,** incalculably, indefinitely, **infinitely;** beyond compare *or* comparison, **beyond measure,** beyond all bounds, all out <nonformal>; **perfectly, absolutely,** essentially, fundamentally, radically; **purely, totally,** completely; unconditionally, with no strings attached, unequivocally, downright, dead; with a vengeance

23 <in a violent degree> **violently,** furiously, hotly, fiercely, severely, **desperately,** madly, **like mad** <nonformal>; **wildly,** demonically, like one possessed, **frantically,** frenetically, fanatically, uncontrollably

248 INSIGNIFICANCE

NOUNS **1 insignificance,** unimportance 997, inconsequentiality, lowness, pettiness, meanness, triviality, nugacity; **smallness,** tininess, diminutiveness, minuteness, exiguousness; **slightness,** moderateness, scantiness, puniness, picayunishness, meanness, meagerness; daintiness, delicacy; **littleness** 258; **fewness** 884; insufficiency 991

2 modicum, minim; **minimum; little, bit,** little *or* wee *or* tiny bit <nonformal>, bite, **particle,** fragment, spot, **speck,** flyspeck, fleck, point, dot, jot, tittle, **iota,** ounce, **dab** <nonformal>, mote, **mite** <nonformal> 258.7; whit, ace, **hair,** scruple, pittance, dole, trifling amount, **smidgen** *and* skosh *and* smitch <all nonformal>, pinch, dribble, driblet, dram, drop, drop in a bucket *or* in the ocean, tip of the iceberg; grain, granule, pebble; molecule, **atom;** thimbleful, spoonful, handful, nutshell; trivia, minutiae; dwarf

3 scrap, tatter, smithereen <nonformal>, patch, **stitch, shred;** snip, **snippet,** chip, nip; splinter, sliver, shiver; **morsel, crumb**

4 hint, *soupçon* <Fr>, **suspicion, suggestion,** intimation; tip of the iceberg; **trace, touch, dash,** cast, **smattering,** sprinkling; tinge, tincture; **taste, lick, smack,** sip, sup, **smell;** look, **thought,** idea; **shade,** shadow; gleam, spark, scintilla

5 hardly anything, mere nothing, next to nothing, less than nothing, **trifle,** bagatelle, **a drop in the bucket** *or* **in the ocean**

ADJS **6 insignificant, small, inconsiderable, inconsequential, negligible,** no great shakes, one-horse *and* pint-size *and* vest-pocket <all nonformal>; unimportant, no skin off one's nose *or* ass, **trivial,** trifling, nugatory, petty, mean, niggling, picayune *or* picayunish, nickel-and-dime *and* penny-ante *and* Mickey-Mouse *and* chickenshit <all nonformal>; shallow, depthless, cursory, superficial, skin-deep; **little** 258.10, **tiny** 258.11, **miniature** 258.12, **meager** 991.10, **few** 884.4; **short** 268.8; **low** 274.7

7 dainty, delicate, gossamer, diaphanous; subtle, tenuous, thin 270.16, rarefied 299.4

8 mere, sheer, stark, bare, bare-bones, plain, simple, unadorned, unenhanced

ADVS **9** <in a small degree> **scarcely, hardly, barely,** only just, by a hair, by an ace *or* a jot *or* a whit *or* an iota, **slightly,** lightly, exiguously, fractionally, scantily, inconsequentially, **insignificantly, negligibly,** imperfectly, minimally, inappreciably, **little; minutely,** meagerly, triflingly, faintly, weakly, feebly; **a little, a bit,** just a bit, to a small extent, on a small scale; ever so little

10 <in a certain or limited degree> **to a degree, to a certain extent, to some degree,** in some measure, to such an extent; **moderately,** mildly, **somewhat,** detectably, modestly, appreciably, visibly, **fairly,** tolerably, **partially,** partly, part, in part, incompletely; **comparatively, relatively;**

merely, simply, purely, only; **at least,** at the least, leastwise, at worst, at any rate; **at most,** at the most, at best, at the outside <nonformal>; in a manner of speaking, **in a way,** after a fashion; so far, thus far

11 <in no degree> **noway,** noways, **nowise,** in no wise, in no case, in no respect, **by no means,** by no manner of means, **on no account,** not on any account, not for anything in the world, **under no circumstances,** at no hand, nohow <nonformal>, **not in the least,** not much, **not at all,** never, not by a damn sight <nonformal>, not by a long shot <nonformal>; not nearly, **nowhere near; not a bit,** not a bit of it, not a whit, not a speck, not a jot, not an iota

249 SUPERIORITY

NOUNS **1 superiority, preeminence, greatness** 247, **lead,** transcendence *or* transcendency, ascendancy *or* ascendance, prestige, favor, preponderance; predominance, hegemony; precedence 813, **priority,** prerogative, privilege; **excellence** 998.1, virtuosity, inimitability, incomparability; **seniority,** precedence; **success** 409, accomplishment 407, **skill** 413

2 advantage, vantage, odds, leg up *and* inside track *and* pole position <all nonformal>; **upper hand,** whip hand; start, head *or* flying *or* running start; **edge,** bulge *and* jump *and* drop <all nonformal>; **card up one's sleeve** <nonformal>, ace in the hole <nonformal>; vantage point

3 supremacy, primacy, first place, height, acme, zenith, be-all and end-all, summit, top spot <nonformal>; **sovereignty, rule, hegemony,** control 417.5; **dominion** 417.6; **command,** sway; **mastery; leadership,** presidency; **authority** 417, management, jurisdiction, power, say *and* last word <both nonformal>; influence 893; effectiveness; **maximum,** highest; most; **championship,** crown, laurels, first prize, blue ribbon, record

4 superior, chief, head, boss 575.1, honcho <nonformal>, commander, **ruler, leader, master** 575; higher-up <nonformal>, senior, principal, big shot <nonformal>; superman, **genius** 413.12; prodigy, nonpareil, paragon, virtuoso, ace, **star, superstar,** champion, winner, top dog *and* top banana <both nonformal>, laureate, Cadillac *and* Rolls-Royce <both trademark>, standout, the greatest *and* world-beater *and* a tough act to follow <all nonformal>

5 the best 998.8, the top of the line <nonformal>; the best people, nobility 608; **aristocracy, elite,** cream, upper crust, upper class, one's betters; **the brass** <nonformal>, higher-ups, movers and shakers, lords of creation, ruling circles, **establishment,** power elite, power structure, **ruling class,** bigwigs <nonformal>

VERBS **6 excel, surpass, exceed, transcend,** have the ascendancy, have the edge, have it all over <nonformal>, overcome, best, **better,** improve on, perfect, go one better <nonformal>; **cap,** trump; top, tower above *or* over; **predominate,** prevail, preponderate; **outweigh,** overbear

7 best, beat, beat out, defeat 412.6; beat all hollow <nonformal>, trounce, clobber *and* take to the cleaners *and* skin alive <all nonformal>, worst, whip *and* lick *and* have it all over *and* cut down to size <all nonformal>; take the cake <nonformal>, bring home the bacon <nonformal>; **triumph; win** 411.4

8 overshadow, eclipse, throw into the shade, top, extinguish; put to shame, show up <nonformal>, put one's nose out of joint, put down <nonformal>

9 outdo, outrival, edge out, **outclass, outshine,** overmatch, outgun <nonformal>; **outstrip, outreach, outpoint, outperform;** outmaneuver, outwit; outrun, outpace, run rings or circles around <nonformal>; override; outleap

10 **outdistance, distance; pass, surpass; get ahead,** pull ahead, shoot ahead; **leave behind,** leave at the post, leave in the dust; **come to the front,** have a healthy lead <nonformal>; steal a march

11 **rule, command, lead,** possess authority 417.13, have the say or the last word, have the whip hand and hold all the aces <both nonformal>; **take precedence, precede** 813.2; **come** or **rank first, outrank,** rank; **come to the fore,** come to the front, **lead** 165.2; **star**

ADJS 12 **superior, greater,** better, finer; **higher,** upper; ascendant, in the ascendant, in ascendancy, coming <nonformal>; **eminent,** outstanding, rare, distinguished, marked, of choice, chosen; **surpassing, exceeding, excellent** 998.12, **excelling, rivaling, eclipsing,** capping, topping, **transcending,** transcendent; **ahead,** a cut or stroke above, one up on <nonformal>; more than a match for

13 **superlative, supreme, greatest, best, highest,** maximum, most, utmost, outstanding; top, topmost, **uppermost,** tip-top, top-level, top-echelon, top-notch and top-of-the-line <both nonformal>, **first-rate,** first-class, of the first water, top of the line, far and away the best, the best by a long shot, head and shoulders above, A1, A number 1

14 **chief, main, principal,** paramount, **foremost, leading, dominant,** crowning, capital, **cardinal;** great, banner, master; central, focal, prime, **primary,** primal, first; **preeminent; predominant,** preponderant, prevailing, hegemonic; ruling; **sovereign** 417.17; topflight,

highest-ranking, ranking; **star,** superstar, stellar, world-class

15 **peerless, matchless, champion; unmatched,** unmatchable, unrivaled, unparalleled, immortal, **unequaled,** never-to-be-equaled, unexampled, unapproached, unapproachable, **unsurpassed, unexcelled;** unsurpassable; inimitable, **incomparable,** beyond compare or comparison, **unique;** without equal or parallel; in a class by itself, *sui generis* <L>; second to none; **unbeatable,** invincible

ADVS 16 **superlatively, exceedingly, surpassingly;** eminently, egregiously, prominently; supremely, preeminently, **the most,** transcendently; inimitably, incomparably; to or in the highest degree, far and away

17 **chiefly, mainly, in the main; predominantly; mostly, for the most part; principally, especially, particularly,** peculiarly; **primarily, in the first place,** first of all, **above all; indeed,** even, yea, still more, more than ever, all the more; ever so, never so

18 **peerlessly, matchlessly,** unmatchably; unsurpassedly, unsurpassably; inimitably, **incomparably; uniquely,** second to none; **unbeatably,** invincibly

19 **advantageously,** favorably; melioratively, amelioratively, improvingly

250 INFERIORITY

NOUNS 1 **inferiority, subordinacy,** subordination; **juniority,** minority; **subservience, subjection,** servility, lowliness, humbleness, humility; back seat and second fiddle <both nonformal>, second or third string <nonformal>

2 **inferior, underling, subordinate,** subaltern, **junior;** secondary, second fiddle and second stringer and third stringer and benchwarmer and low man on the totem pole <all nonformal>, loser and nonstarter <both nonformal>; lightweight, fol-

lower, pawn, cog, flunky, yes-
man, creature; infrastructure *or*
commonality, *hoi polloi* <Gk>,
masses

3 inadequacy, mediocrity 1004,
deficiency, imperfection, insufficiency 991; **incompetence,** *or*
incompetency, maladroitness,
unskillfulness 414; **failure** 410;
smallness 248.1; littleness 258;
meanness, lowness, baseness,
pettiness, triviality, shabbiness,
vulgarity 497

VERBS **4 be inferior, not come up
to, not measure up, fall short,
fail** 410.8, not hack it *and* not cut
the mustard *and* not make the cut
<all nonformal>; want, leave
much to be desired, be found
wanting; **not compare,** have
nothing on <nonformal>, **not
hold a candle to** <nonformal>,
not approach, not come near;
serve, follow, play second fiddle
and take a back seat *and* sit on the
bench <all nonformal>

5 bow to, hand it to <nonfor-
mal>; retire into the shade; give
in <nonformal>, lose face

ADJS **6 inferior, subordinate,**
subaltern, **secondary; junior,
minor;** second *or* third string *and*
one-horse *and* penny-ante *and*
dinky <all nonformal>, second *or*
third rank, low in the pecking order; **subservient,** subject, servile,
low, **lowly,** humble, modest;
lesser, less, lower; **common,** vulgar, **ordinary;** underprivileged,
disadvantaged; **beneath one's
dignity** *or* station, demeaning

7 inadequate, mediocre, deficient, imperfect, **insufficient;
incompetent,** unskillful, maladroit; small, little, mean, base,
petty, trivial, shabby; **not to be
compared, not comparable, not
a patch on** <nonformal>; **out-
classed,** not in the same league
with <nonformal>, out of it *and*
out of the picture *and* **out of the
running** <all nonformal>

8 least, smallest, littlest, slightest,
lowest, shortest; minimum, minimal; few 884.4

ADVS **9 poorly, incompetently, inadequately,** badly, maladroitly;
least of all, at the bottom of the
heap *and* in the gutter <both non-
formal>; at a disadvantage

251 INCREASE

NOUNS **1 increase, gain,** augmentation, **enlargement, amplification, growth,** development,
widening, spread, elevation, **extension,** aggrandizement, access,
increment, accretion; **addition**
253; **expansion** 259; **inflation,**
swelling, ballooning, edema, fattening, tumescence, bloating;
proliferation, productiveness
889; accrual, accumulation; **advance,** appreciation, ascent,
mounting, crescendo, waxing,
snowballing, **rise** *or* raise, fattening *and* boost *and* hike <all
nonformal>, buildup; **upturn,**
uptick <nonformal>, upsurge,
upswing; **leap,** jump; **flood,**
surge, gush

**2 intensification, heightening,
deepening,** tightening, turn of
the screw; **strengthening,**
beefing-up <nonformal>, enhancement, **magnification,**
blowup, exaggeration; aggravation, exacerbation, heating-up;
concentration, condensation,
consolidation; **reinforcement,**
redoubling; **acceleration,**
speedup; **boom, explosion,** baby
boom, population explosion, information explosion

3 gains, winnings, cut *and* take
<both nonformal>, **profits** 472.3

VERBS **4 increase, enlarge,** aggrandize, **amplify, augment, extend,** maximize, **add to; expand**
259.4, **inflate;** lengthen, broaden,
fatten, fill out, thicken; **raise,** exalt, boost <nonformal>, hike *and*
hike up *and* jack up <all nonfor-
mal>, mark up, put up, **up**
<nonformal>; **build, build up;**
pyramid, parlay

5 intensify, heighten, deepen,
enhance, **strengthen,** beef up
<nonformal>, aggravate, exacer-
bate; **exaggerate,** blow up *and*

puff up <both nonformal>, **magnify;** whet, sharpen; **reinforce;** **concentrate,** condense, consolidate; **complicate,** ramify; give a boost to, **step up** <nonformal>, accelerate; key up, hop up *and* soup up *and* jazz up <all nonformal>; add fuel to the flame *or* the fire

6 **grow, increase, advance,** appreciate; **spread, widen,** broaden; **gain,** get ahead; wax, swell, balloon, bloat, mount, **rise,** go up, snowball; **intensify, develop,** gain strength, strengthen; accrue, accumulate; **multiply, proliferate,** breed, teem; run *or* shoot up, **boom, explode**

ADJS 7 **increased, heightened,** raised, elevated, stepped-up <nonformal>; **intensified,** deepened, reinforced, strengthened, fortified, beefed-up <nonformal>, tightened, stiffened; **enlarged, extended,** augmented, aggrandized, amplified, **enhanced,** boosted, hiked <nonformal>; broadened, widened, spread; **magnified, inflated, expanded,** swollen, bloated; **multiplied,** proliferated; **accelerated,** hopped-up *and* jazzed-up <both nonformal>

8 **increasing, rising,** fast-rising, skyrocketing, meteoric; on the upswing, on the increase, on the rise; **growing,** fast-growing, flourishing, burgeoning, blossoming, waxing, swelling, lengthening, **multiplying,** proliferating; spreading, spreading like a cancer *or* like wildfire, expanding; tightening, intensifying; incremental; **on the increase,** snowballing, mushrooming

ADVS 9 **increasingly,** more, **more and more,** on and on, greater and greater, ever more

252 DECREASE

NOUNS 1 **decrease,** decrement, diminution, **reduction, lessening, lowering,** waning, shrinking *or* shrinkage, withering, withering away, scaledown, downsizing,

build-down; miniaturization; depression, damping, dampening; **letup** <nonformal>, abatement, easing, easing off; de-escalation; **alleviation,** relaxation, mitigation; attenuation, extenuation; weakening, sagging, dying, dying off *or* away, trailing off, tailing off, tapering off, fade-out, languishment; depreciation, **deflation; deduction** 255.1; subtraction, **abridgment** 268.3; **contraction** 260

2 **decline,** declension, **subsidence,** slump <nonformal>, lapse, **drop,** downtick <nonformal>; **collapse,** crash; dwindling, wane, ebb; downturn, downtrend, retreat; **fall, plunge,** dive; catabasis, deceleration, slowdown

3 **decrement, waste, loss,** dissipation, wear and tear, erosion, ablation, wearing away, depletion, corrosion, attrition, consumption, shrinkage, exhaustion; deliquescence, dissolution

4 **curtailment, retrenchment,** cut, cutback, drawdown, rollback, scaleback, pullback

5 **minimization,** making light of, devaluing, undervaluing, **belittling,** detraction; qualification 958

VERBS 6 **decrease, diminish, lessen; let up,** abate; **decline, subside,** shrink, wane, wither, ebb, dwindle, languish, sink, sag, die down *or* away, wind down, taper off *and* trail off *or* away *and* tail off *or* away <all nonformal>; **drop,** drop off, dive, take a nose dive, plummet, plunge, fall, fall off, fall away, run low; **waste,** wear, waste *or* wear away, crumble, erode, ablate, corrode, consume, be eaten away; melt away, deliquesce

7 **reduce, decrease, diminish, lessen; lower, depress,** de-escalate, damp, dampen, **step down** *and* phase down *or* out *and* scale back *or* down *and* roll back <all nonformal>; **downgrade;** depreciate, **deflate; curtail,** re-

trench; **cut,** cut down *or* back, chip away at, whittle away *or* down, pare, roll back <nonformal>; deduct 255.9; **shorten** 268.6, abridge; **compress** 260.7, shrink, downsize; **simplify** 797.4

8 **abate,** ease; **weaken,** dilute, water down, attenuate, extenuate; alleviate, mitigate, slacken

9 **minimize, belittle,** detract from; dwarf; play down, underplay, downplay, de-emphasize

ADJS 10 **reduced, decreased, diminished, lowered,** dropped; **abated; deflated,** contracted, shrunk, shrunken; **simplified** 797.9; back-to-basics, no-frills; dissipated, **eroded,** consumed, ablated, **worn;** curtailed, shorn, retrenched, cutback; weakened, attenuated, watered-down; minimized, belittled; **lower,** less, lesser, smaller, shorter; off-peak

11 **decreasing, diminishing, lessening, subsiding, declining,** languishing, dwindling, waning, on the wane, wasting; decrescent, reductive, deliquescent, **contractive**

ADVS 12 **decreasingly, diminishingly, less and less,** ever less; at a declining rate

253 ADDITION

NOUNS 1 **addition,** accession, annexation, affixation, agglutination, attachment, junction, **joining** 799, uniting; **increase** 251; **augmentation,** reinforcement; superposition; juxtaposition 223.3; adjunct 254, add-on

2 <math terms> plus sign, plus; addend; sum, summation, total; subtotal

3 **adding,** totalizing *or* totalization, computation; **adding machine,** calculator

VERBS 4 **add,** put with, **join** *or* **unite with, bring together, affix, attach,** annex, adjoin, append, conjoin, subjoin, tag on, **tack on** <nonformal>, glue on, paste on; burden, encumber, saddle with; **complicate,** ornament, decorate

5 **add to, augment, supplement; increase** 251.4; **reinforce,** strengthen, fortify, beef up <nonformal>; recruit, swell the ranks of

6 **compute,** add up; sum, total up, tot *and* tot up *and* tote *and* tote up <all nonformal>, tally

7 **be added,** advene, supervene

ADJS 8 **additive,** additional; **cumulative,** accumulative

9 **added,** affixed, add-on, **attached,** annexed, appended; adjoined, adjunct, conjoined, subjoined

10 **additional, supplementary, supplemental; extra,** plus, further, farther, fresh, **more,** new, **other,** another, ulterior; **auxiliary,** ancillary, supernumerary, contributory, **accessory,** collateral; **surplus,** spare

ADVS 11 **additionally, in addition, also,** and then some, even more, more so, and also, and all <nonformal>, and so, **as well, too,** else, beside, **besides, to boot, not to mention, let alone, into the bargain;** on top of, over, above; **beyond, plus; extra,** on the side <nonformal>; **more, moreover,** thereto, farther, further, **furthermore,** at the same time, then, again, yet; similarly, likewise, by the same token, by the same sign; item; therewith; all included, altogether; among other things, *inter alia* <L>

254 ADJUNCT
   <thing added>

NOUNS 1 **adjunct, addition,** increase, **increment,** augmentation, addendum, addenda <pl>, accession, fixture; **annex,** annexation; **appendage,** pendant, coda; undergirding, reinforcement; appurtenance, appurtenant; **accessory,** attachment; **supplement,** complement, continuation, extrapolation, extension; offshoot, side issue, corollary, sidebar <nonformal>, side effect, spin-off <nonformal>,

concomitant, **accompaniment**
768, **additive**

2 <written text> **postscript, appendix;** rider, codicil; **epilogue,**
envoi, coda, tail; note, marginalia, commentary; **interpolation,**
interlineation

3 <building> wing, **addition, annex,** extension

4 **extra, bonus, premium,** something extra, extra added attraction, lagniappe, something into
the bargain, something for good
measure, baker's dozen; **padding,** stuffing, filling; trimming,
frill, flourish, filigree, decoration,
ornament; bells and whistles
<nonformal>; fillip, wrinkle,
twist

255 SUBTRACTION

NOUNS **1 subtraction, deduction,
removal,** taking away; erosion,
abrasion, wearing, wearing away

2 **reduction, diminution,** decrease 252, build-down, phase-
down, drawdown, decrement, impairment, **cut** or **cutting,** curtailment, shortening, truncation;
shrinkage, depletion, **attrition,**
remission; **depreciation,** detraction, disparagement, derogation;
retraction, retrenchment; **extraction**

3 **excision,** abscission, rescission,
extirpation; **elimination,** exclusion, extinction, eradication,
destruction 395, annihilation;
cancellation, write-off, erasure;
amputation, mutilation

4 **castration,** gelding, emasculation, **deballing** <nonformal>,
altering and fixing <both nonformal>, spaying

5 <written text> **deletion,** erasure, cancellation, omission;
expurgation, bowdlerization,
censoring or censorship; abridgment, abbreviation

6 <math terms> subtrahend, minuend; negative; minus sign,
minus

7 <thing subtracted> deduction,
decrement, minus

8 <result> difference, remainder

256, epact <astronomy>, discrepancy, net, balance, surplus 992.5,
deficit, credit

VERBS **9 subtract, deduct, remove,** withdraw, abstract; **reduce,** shorten, curtail, retrench,
lessen, **diminish, decrease,**
phase down, impair, abate; **depreciate,** disparage, detract,
derogate; **erode,** abrade; **extract,**
leach, drain, wash away; thin,
thin out, weed; **refine,** purify

10 **excise,** cut out, cut, extirpate;
cancel, write off; **eradicate,** root
out, wipe or stamp out, **eliminate,** kill, kill off, liquidate,
annihilate, destroy 395.10, extinguish; **exclude,** except, cancel,
cancel out, bleep out <nonformal>, rule out, bar, ban; **cut off**
or **away,** shear or take or strike or
knock or lop off, truncate; **amputate,** mutilate, abscind; **prune,**
pare, peel, clip, crop, bob, dock,
lop, nip, shear, shave, strip, strip
off or away

11 **castrate,** geld, emasculate, eunuchize, neuter, spay, fix or alter
<both nonformal>, unsex, deball
<nonformal>

12 <written text> delete, erase, expunge, cancel, omit; edit, edit
out, blue-pencil; strike, strike out
or off, rub or blot out, cross out
or off, kill, cut

ADJS **13 subtractive, reductive,**
deductive; erosive

256 REMAINDER

NOUNS **1 remainder, remains,
remnant, residue,** residuum,
rest, balance; holdover; **leavings, leftovers; refuse,** odds and
ends, scraps, **rubbish, waste;**
parings, sweepings, filings, shavings, sawdust; chaff, straw,
stubble, husks; **debris,** detritus,
ruins; stump, butt or butt end,
roach <nonformal>, rump; survival, vestige, trace, hint, shadow;
fossil, relics

2 **dregs, grounds, lees,** dross,
slag, scoria, feces; **sediment, settlings, deposits,** deposition; silt,
loess, moraine; scum, froth; ash,

ember, cinder, sinter, clinker;
soot, smut
3 **survivor,** heir, successor;
widow, widower, relict, **orphan**
4 **excess** 992, **surplus,** surplusage,
overage; superfluity, redundancy
VERBS 5 **remain, be left** *or* **left
over, survive,** subsist, rest
6 **leave,** leave over, leave behind
ADJS 7 **remaining, surviving, extant,** vestigial, over, left, **leftover,
still around, remnant,** rema-
nent, odd; **spare,** to spare;
unused, unconsumed; **surplus,**
superfluous; **outstanding,** un-
met, unresolved; net
8 **residual,** residuary; sedimental,
sedimentary

257 SIZE, LARGENESS

NOUNS 1 **size, largeness, bigness,
greatness** 247, vastness, **magnitude,** order of magnitude,
amplitude; mass, bulk, **volume,**
body; **dimensions, proportions,**
dimension, caliber, scantling,
proportion; **measure,** measurement 300, gauge, **scale; extent,**
extension, expansion, expanse,
scope, reach, range, ballpark
<nonformal>, spread ambit,
girth, diameter, radius, boundary,
border, periphery
2 **capacity, volume, content,** accommodation, room, space,
measure, limit, burden; poundage, tonnage, cordage; stowage;
quantity 244
3 **full size,** full growth; life size
4 **large size,** economy size, family
size
5 **oversize,** outsize; **overgrowth,**
overdevelopment, sprawl; **overweight;** bloat, bloatedness,
obesity; gigantism, giantism,
titanism; hypertrophy
6 <large size> **sizableness, largeness, bigness,** grandiosity;
voluminousness, capaciousness,
copiousness, ampleness; profundity; extensiveness, expansive-
ness, comprehensiveness; spaciousness 158.5
7 <very large size> **hugeness,
vastness;** humongousness

<nonformal>; **enormousness,
immenseness, immensity, prodigiousness,** stupendousness;
gigantism, giantism; monumen-
talism; **monstrousness, monstrosity**
8 **corpulence, obesity, stoutness,
fatness,** adiposity, fleshiness,
beefiness, meatiness, heftiness,
grossness; **plumpness,** rotundity,
tubbiness <nonformal>; pudginess; chubbiness, chunkiness
<nonformal>; stockiness, portli-
ness; blowziness; steatopygia
9 **bulkiness, bulk, massiveness,**
lumpishness; **ponderousness,**
cumbersomeness; clumsiness,
awkwardness, unwieldiness
10 **lump,** clump, **hunk** *and* **chunk**
<both nonformal>; **mass,** piece,
gob *and* glob <both nonformal>;
batch, **wad,** block, loaf; pat <of
butter>; clod; nugget; **quantity**
244
11 <something large> **whopper**
and thumper *and* whale *and*
jumbo <all nonformal>; hulk
12 <corpulent person> **heavyweight, pig,** porker, man
mountain <nonformal>; **fat person, fatty** *and* **fatso** <both
nonformal>, roly-poly, **tub, tub
of lard,** whale, blimp <nonfor-
mal>, **potbelly**
13 **giant, amazon, colossus, titan**
14 **behemoth, leviathan, monster;** mammoth, mastodon; elephant, jumbo <nonformal> **dinosaur**
VERBS 15 **size, adjust, grade,**
group, range, rank, graduate,
sort, match; gauge, **measure**
300.11, proportion; **bulk** 247.5;
enlarge 259.4, 5; fatten
ADJS 16 **large, sizable, big, great**
247.6, **grand, considerable,
goodly,** healthy, **substantial,**
bumper; as big as all outdoors;
numerous 883.6; large-scale,
larger than life; man-sized
<nonformal>
17 **voluminous, capacious, generous, ample,** copious, broad,
wide, extensive, expansive; **spacious**

**18 corpulent, stout, fat, over-
weight, obese,** adipose, gross,
fleshy, beefy, meaty, hefty;
paunchy, bloated, puffy, blowzy,
distended, swollen; abdominous,
potbellied, **plump, buxom,** *zaf-
tig* <Yiddish>, rotund, **tubby**
<nonformal>, roly-poly; **pudgy;**
thickbodied, **heavyset, thickset,
chubby,** chunky <nonformal>,
stocky, squat, squatty, dumpy,
square; pyknic, endomorphic;
stalwart, brawny, burly; strapping <nonformal>; **portly,**
imposing; well-fed, corn-fed;
moonfaced; steatopygic, fat-assed
and lard-assed <both nonfor-
mal>, broad in the beam <non-
formal>; bosomy, full-bosomed,
chesty, busty <nonformal>, top-
heavy

19 bulky, hulky, hulking, lumpish,
lumpy, lumbering; **massive,**
massy; elephantine; **ponderous,**
cumbersome; **clumsy,** awkward,
unwieldy

**20 huge, immense, vast, enor-
mous,** astronomical, humongous
and jumbo <both nonformal>,
tremendous, prodigious, stupendous; larger than life, mighty,
titanic, colossal, monumental,
heroic, epic, epical, towering,
mountainous; profound, abysmal, deep as the ocean; **monster,**
monstrous; **mammoth,** masto-
donic; **gigantic, giant;** Brobdingnagian, Gargantuan; elephantine;
jumbo <nonformal>; **infinite**
822.3

21 <nonformal terms> **whopping,
walloping, whaling, whacking,**
spanking, slapping, thumping

22 full-sized, full-scale; **full-
grown, full-fledged,** full-blown;
full-formed, **life-sized,** larger
than life

23 oversize, oversized; **outsize,**
outsized, **overlarge; overgrown,**
overdeveloped; **overweight;** over-
fleshed, obese

24 this big, so big, yay big <nonfor-
mal>

ADVS **25** largely, on a large scale, in
a big way

258 LITTLENESS

NOUNS **1 littleness, smallness, diminutiveness,** slightness, exiguity; puniness, dinkiness <non-
formal>; **minuteness;** undersize;
petiteness; dwarfishness, runti-
ness, shrimpiness; **shortness**
268; **scantiness** 884.1

2 infinitesimalness; inapprecia-
bility, evanescence; intangibility,
impalpability, tenuousness, imponderability

3 <small space> **tight spot** *and*
corner *and* squeeze *and* **pinch**
<all nonformal>, not enough
room to swing a cat <nonfor-
mal>; cubbyhole; dollhouse,
playhouse, doghouse

4 <small person or creature>
runt, shrimp <nonformal>,
wisp, chit, slip, snip, snippet,
peanut *and* **peewee** <both non-
formal>, pipsqueak, small fry
<nonformal>; lightweight, feath-
erweight; mouse, titmouse,
tomtit <nonformal>

5 <creature small by species or
birth> **dwarf, midget,** midge,
pygmy, manikin, homunculus,
hop-o'-my-thumb; elf, gnome,
brownie; Lilliputian, Tom
Thumb, Thumbelina

6 miniature; scaled-down *or* miniaturized version; microcosm;
baby; doll, puppet

7 <minute thing> minutia, **minutiae** <pl>, **drop,** droplet, **mite**
<nonformal>, **point,** vanish-
ing point, pinpoint, pinhead,
dot; mote, fleck, **speck,** flyspeck, jot, tittle, iota, **trace,**
trace amount, suspicion,
soupçon <Fr>; **particle,** crumb,
scrap, bite, snip, snippet; grain,
grain of sand; midge, gnat; microbe, **microorganism,** amoeba,
bacillus, bacteria, diatom, germ,
microbe, paramecium, protozoon, virus

8 atom, monad; **molecule,** ion;
electron, proton, meson, neu-
trino, quark, parton, subatomic
or nuclear particle

9 make small, contract 260.7;

shorten 268.6; **miniaturize,**
scale down; **reduce** 252.7

ADJS **10 little, small** 248.6, small-
ish; **slight,** exiguous; **puny, trifling,** piffling *and* piddling *and*
piddly <all nonformal>, **dinky**
<nonformal>; cramped, limited;
one-horse, two-by-four <nonfor-
mal>; pintsized <nonformal>,
half-pint; knee-high to a grasshopper; petite; short 268.8

11 tiny; teeny *and* teeny-weeny *and*
eentsy-weentsy <all nonformal>,
wee *and* peewee <both nonfor-
mal>, bitty *and* little-bitty *and*
itsy-bitsy <all nonformal>; **minute**

**12 miniature, diminutive, mi-
nuscule,** miniaturized, submin-
iature, **small-scale,** minimal;
pony, bantam; **baby,** baby-sized;
pocketsized, **vest-pocket; toy;**
compact

13 dwarf, dwarfish, **pygmy,
midget,** elfin; Lilliputian, Tom
Thumb; **undersized,** squat,
dumpy; **stunted,** runty, pint-size
or -sized *and* sawed-off <all non-
formal>; wizened, shriveled;
meager, scrubby, scraggy

14 infinitesimal, microscopic, ul-
tramicroscopic; evanescent, thin,
tenuous; inappreciable; impalpable, intangible; imperceptible;
indiscernible, invisible; subatomic; molecular; embryonic,
germinal

15 microbic, microbial, **micro-
organic;** bacterial; microzoic;
protozoan, microzoan, amoebic
or amoeboid

ADVS **16 small,** little, **slightly**
248.9, fractionally; **on a small
scale,** in a small compass, in a
small way, on a minuscule scale;
in miniature; in a nutshell

259 EXPANSION, GROWTH
<increase in size>

NOUNS **1 expansion, extension,
enlargement, increase** 251,
raising, hiking, magnification,
aggrandizement, amplification,
broadening, widening; **spread,**
spreading, creeping, fanning out,

dispersion; **flare,** splay; deployment; augmentation, **addition**
253; adjunct 254

2 distension, stretching; **inflation,** blowing up; **dilation,**
dilatation, dilating; **swelling,**
swell 283.4; puffiness, **bloating,
flatulence** *or* flatulency, flatus;
turgidity, turgidness; tumidity,
tumefaction; tumescence,
intumescence; **swollenness,**
bloatedness; edema

3 growth, development 860.1;
bodily development 14, **maturation,** maturing, coming of age;
vegetation 310.30; reproduction,
procreation 78, germination; burgeoning, sprouting; budding,
gemmation; outgrowth, excrescence

VERBS **4** <make larger> **enlarge,
expand, extend, widen,
broaden,** build up, aggrandize,
amplify, magnify, increase
251.4, augment, add to 253.5,
raise, scale up, hike *or* hike up;
develop, bulk *or* bulk up; **stretch,
distend, dilate, swell, inflate,
blow up,** puff up, bloat; pump up

5 <become larger> **enlarge,
expand, extend, increase,
develop, widen, broaden,** bulk;
**stretch, distend, dilate, swell,
swell up, swell out, puff up,
puff out, pump up,** bloat, tu-
mefy, balloon, fill out; snowball

6 spread, spread out; **expand,
extend,** widen; open, **open up,**
unfold; **flare,** flare out, broaden
out, splay; sprawl; branch,
branch out, ramify; fan, fan out,
disperse, deploy; spread like wildfire; overrun, overgrow

7 grow, develop, wax, **increase**
251; gather, brew; **grow up,** mature, spring up, ripen, come of
age; **shoot up,** sprout up, tower;
burgeon, **sprout** 310.31, blossom
310.32, reproduce 78.7, procreate
78.8, germinate; vegetate 310.31;
flourish, thrive, grow like a
weed; mushroom; hypertrophy,
grow uncontrollably

8 fatten, fat, plump; **gain weight,**

take *or* put on weight, become overweight

ADJS **9 expansive, extensive;** expansible, inflatable; distensive; inflationary

10 expanded, extended, enlarged, increased 251.7, raised, hiked, **amplified,** widened, broadened, built-up, beefed-up <nonformal>

11 spread, spreading; sprawling, sprawly; **outspread, outstretched,** spreadout; open, gaping, patulous; widespread, wide-open; flared, splayed; flaring, flared, flared-out, splaying; splay; fanned, fanning

12 grown, full-grown, grown-up, mature, developed, well-developed, fully developed, full-fledged; growing, sprouting, budding, flowering 310.35, florescent, **flourishing,** blossoming, blooming, burgeoning, thriving; overgrown, hypertrophied, overdeveloped

13 distended, dilated, inflated, blown up, puffed up, swollen, swelled, **bloated,** turgid, tumid, plethoric; **puffy;** flatulent, gassy, windy, ventose; tumefacient; edematous; fat; puffed out, bouffant

260 CONTRACTION
<decrease in size>

NOUNS **1 contraction;** systole; **compression,** pressurizing, pressurization; **compacting,** compaction; **condensation, concentration,** consolidation, solidification; **circumscription, narrowing;** reduction, **decrease** 252; abbreviation, curtailment, shortening 268.3; **constriction,** stricture, strangulation, **choking,** choking off; bottleneck, hourglass, hourglass figure, wasp waist; neck, cervix, isthmus, narrow place; astringency, constringency; puckering, pursing; knitting, wrinkling

2 squeezing, compression, clamping *or* clamping down, tightening; **pressure,** press, crush; **pinch, squeeze, tweak, nip**

3 shrinking, shrinkage, atrophy; **shriveling, withering;** searing, parching, drying *or* drying up; attenuation, thinning; wasting, consumption, emaciation; skin and bones

4 collapse, prostration, cave-in; implosion; **deflation**

5 contractibility, compactability, **compressibility,** condensability, reducibility

6 contractor, constrictor, clamp, compressor, vise, pincer, squeezer; thumbscrew; **astringent,** styptic

VERBS **7 contract, compress,** cramp, compact, condense, concentrate, consolidate, solidify; **reduce, decrease** 252; abbreviate, curtail, **shorten** 268.6; **constrict,** circumscribe, **narrow,** draw, draw in; strangle, strangulate, choke, choke off; **pucker,** pucker up, **purse; knit, wrinkle**

8 squeeze, compress, clamp, tighten; roll *or* wad up, roll up into a ball; **press,** pressurize, crush; **pinch, tweak, nip**

9 shrink, shrivel, wither, sear, parch, dry up; **wizen,** weazen; consume, waste, waste away, attenuate, thin, emaciate

10 collapse, cave, cave in; fold, fold up; implode; **deflate,** take the wind out of; puncture

ADJS **11 contractive,** contractible, contractile, compactable; **astringent,** styptic; **compressible,** condensable, reducible; **collapsible;** deflationary

12 contracted, compressed, cramped, compact *or* compacted, concentrated, condensed, consolidated, solidified; **constricted,** strangled, choked, choked off, **squeezed,** clamped, nipped, pinched, wasp-waisted; puckered, pursed; knitted, wrinkled

13 shrunk, shrunken; shriveled, shriveled up; **withered,** sear, parched, dried-up; **wasted,** wasted away, consumed, emaciated, emacerated, thin, attenuated; **wizened,** wizen, weazened

14 deflated, punctured, flat, holed

261 DISTANCE, REMOTENESS

NOUNS **1 distance, remoteness,** farness, far-offness; **separation,** divergence, clearance, margin, leeway; **extent, length,** space 158, **reach,** stretch, range, compass, span, stride, haul, a way; perspective; **infinity** 822; **mileage**

2 long way, great distance, far cry, far piece <nonformal>; giant step; long run *or* haul, long road; long range

3 the distance, **remote distance, offing; horizon,** the far horizon, where the earth meets the sky

4 <remote region> jumping-off place *and* godforsaken place *and* God knows where *and* the middle of nowhere <all nonformal>, Thule *or* Ultima Thule, Timbuktu, Siberia, pole, antipodes, end of the earth, North Pole, South Pole, Tierra del Fuego, remotest corner of the world; outpost, outskirts; the sticks *and* the boondocks *and* the boonies <all nonformal>; **nowhere;** frontier, outback <Australia>

VERBS **5 reach out, stretch out,** extend, go *or* go out; outstretch, outlie, outdistance

6 extend to, stretch to, **reach to,** lead to, get to, run to

7 keep one's distance, distance oneself, remain at a distance, keep at a respectful distance, separate oneself, **keep away,** stand off *or* away; keep *or* stand clear of, **steer clear of** <nonformal>, give a wide berth to, keep out of the way of, keep at arm's length, not touch with a ten-foot pole <nonformal>, keep *or* stay *or* stand aloof

ADJS **8 distant, remote, removed, far, far-off,** away, **faraway,** way-off, at a distance, exotic, separated, apart, asunder

9 out-of-the-way, godforsaken, upcountry; **out of reach, inaccessible,** unapproachable, untouchable, antipodean

10 thither, ulterior; **yonder,** yon; **farther, further**

11 transoceanic, transmarine, ultramarine, overseas; transatlantic, transpacific; tramontane, transmontane, ultramontane, transalpine

12 farthest, furthest, farthest off, ultimate, extreme, remotest

ADVS **13 yonder,** yon; **in the distance; in the offing,** on the horizon

14 at a distance, away, off, aloof, at arm's length

15 far, far off, far away, **afar,** afar off, a long way off, a good ways off <nonformal>, as far as the eye can see, out of sight; clear to hell and gone <nonformal>

16 far and wide, far and near, widely, broadly, abroad

17 apart, away, aside, wide apart

18 out of reach, beyond reach, **out of range,** beyond the bounds, out-of-the-way; out of sight; out of earshot

19 wide, clear; wide of the mark, abroad, all abroad, astray, afield, far afield

262 FORM

NOUNS **1 form, shape, figure; configuration;** formation, **conformation; structure** 266; **build,** make, frame; **arrangement** 807; makeup, format, layout; **composition** 795; mold, impression, pattern, matrix, model, mode, modality; archetype, prototype 785.1; style, fashion; genre

2 contour; broad lines, silhouette, profile, **outline** 211.2; organization 806.1

3 appearance 33, lineaments, features, physiognomy

4 <human form> **figure, form,** shape, frame, anatomy, **physique,** build, body-build, person

5 forming, shaping, molding, modeling, fashioning; **formation,** conformation, configuration; sculpture; creation

6 <grammatical terms> form, morph, allomorph, morpheme; morphology, morphemics

VERBS **7 form,** formalize, **shape, fashion,** tailor, frame, figure, work, knead; set, fix; **forge,** drop-forge; **mold,** sculpt or sculpture; cast, found; stamp, mint; carve, whittle, cut, chisel; roughhew, roughcast, rough out, block out, lay out, sketch out; hammer or knock out; create; organize 806.4

8 <be formed> **form,** take form, shape, **shape up, take shape;** materialize

ADJS **9 formative,** plastic; **formed, shaped,** patterned, fashioned, tailored, framed; **forged,** molded, modeled, sculpted; cast, founded; stamped, minted; carved, cut, whittled, chiseled, hewn; hammered-out, knocked-out, cobbled-up; **made, produced**

10 <biological terms> plasmatic, plasmic, protoplasmic, plastic, metabolic

11 <grammatical terms> morphologic, morphological, morphemic

263 FORMLESSNESS

NOUNS **1 formlessness, shapelessness;** amorphousness; **chaos** 809.2, confusion, messiness, mess, muddle 809.2, untidiness; **disorder** 809; anarchy 418.2; **indeterminateness, indefiniteness,** indecisiveness, vagueness, haziness, fuzziness, blurriness, obscurity; lumpishness

2 unlicked cub, diamond in the rough, raw material

VERBS **3 deform, distort** 265.5; misshape; disorder, jumble, mess up, muddle, confuse; obfuscate, obscure, fog up, blur

ADJS **4 formless, shapeless,** featureless, characterless, nondescript, inchoate, lumpish, baggy <nonformal>; amorphous, **chaotic, orderless,** disorderly 809.13, unordered, unorganized, confused, anarchic 418.6; **indeterminate, indefinite,** undefined, indecisive, vague, misty, hazy, fuzzy, blurred or blurry, unclear, obscure; obfuscatory

5 unformed, unshaped, unfashioned, unlicked; unstructured

264 SYMMETRY

NOUNS **1 symmetry, proportion,** proportionality, **balance** 789.1, equilibrium; **regularity,** uniformity 780, evenness; equality 789; finish; harmony, congruity, consistency, conformity 866, **correspondence,** keeping; parallelism 203, polarity; shapeliness

2 harmonization; evening, equalization; coordination, integration; **compensation,** playing off, playing off against

VERBS **3** regularize, **balance,** balance off, compensate; harmonize; **proportion,** proportionate; even, even up, equalize; coordinate, integrate; play off, play off against

ADJS **4 symmetric, symmetrical, balanced,** balanced off, proportioned, harmonious; **regular,** uniform 780.5, even, equal 789.7, fifty-fifty <nonformal>, square, squared-off; coordinate, equilateral; **well-balanced,** well-set-up <nonformal>; finished

5 shapely, well-shaped, well-proportioned, well-formed; comely; trim, neat, spruce, clean, clean-cut

265 DISTORTION

NOUNS **1 distortion,** torsion, twist, twistedness, **contortion, crookedness; asymmetry,** disproportion, lopsidedness, imbalance, irregularity, **deviation; twist,** quirk, turn, screw, wring, wrench, wrest; **warp,** buckle; knot, gnarl

2 perversion, corruption, misdirection, misrepresentation 350, misinterpretation, misconstruction; **falsification** 354.9; **twisting,** false coloring, bending the truth, **spin,** spin control, slanting, straining, torturing; misuse 389

3 deformity, deformation, **malformation,** monstrosity 869.6, teratology, freakishness, misproportion, **misshapenness,** misshape; **disfigurement, defacement;** humpback, hunchback, kyphosis; swayback, lordosis; clubfoot, talipes, flatfoot, splayfoot; knock-knee; bowlegs; harelip; cleft palate

4 grimace, wry face, snarl; moue, pout

VERBS **5 distort, contort,** turn awry; **twist,** turn, screw, wring, wrench, wrest; writhe; **warp,** buckle, crumple; knot, gnarl; **crook,** bend, spring

6 pervert, falsify, twist, garble, put a false construction upon, give a spin, give a false coloring, color, varnish, slant, strain, torture; put words in someone's mouth; **bias;** misrepresent 350.3, misconstrue, misinterpret; misuse 389.4; send *or* deliver the wrong signal *or* message

7 deform, misshape, twist, torture, disproportion; **disfigure, deface;** mutilate; blemish, mar

8 grimace, make a face, make a wry face *or* mouth, pull a face, **screw up one's face;** pout

ADJS **9** distortive, contortive, contortional, torsional

10 distorted, contorted, warped, twisted, crooked; tortuous, labyrinthine, buckled, sprung, bent, bowed; cockeyed <nonformal>, crazy; crunched, crumpled; unsymmetrical, asymmetrical, nonsymmetrical; lopsided; askew 204.14, off-center

11 falsified, perverted, twisted, garbled, slanted, doctored, biased, crooked; strained, tortured; misrepresented, misquoted

12 deformed, malformed, misshapen, misbegotten, misproportioned, ill-proportioned, illmade, ill-shaped, **out of shape;** bloated; **disfigured,** defaced, blemished, marred; mutilated; grotesque, **monstrous** 869.13; sway-backed, round-shouldered; bowlegged, bandy-legged, bandy; knock-kneed; rickety; clubfooted, talipedic; flatfooted, splayfooted, pigeon-toed

13 humpbacked, hunchbacked, humped, gibbous, kyphotic

266 STRUCTURE

NOUNS **1 structure, construction,** architecture, tectonics, architectonics, **frame, make, build,** fabric, tissue, warp and woof *or* weft, web, weave, texture, contexture, mold, **shape, pattern, plan,** fashion, arrangement, **organization** 806.1; **constitution, composition; makeup,** getup <nonformal>, setup; **formation,** conformation, **format; arrangement** 807, configuration; **composition** 795; anatomy, physique; form 262; **morphology**

2 structure, building, edifice, construction, erection, establishment, fabric; house; tower, pile, pyramid, skyscraper, ziggurat; prefab; superstructure

3 understructure, crypt; **substructure;** infrastructure

4 frame, framing; **framework, skeleton,** fabric, chassis, shell, armature; sash, casement *or* case, casing

VERBS **5 construct, build; structure; organize** 806.4; **form** 262.7

ADJS **6 structural,** morphological, tectonic, textural; **anatomic,** anatomical, **organic,** organismic; **structured, patterned,** shaped, formed; **architectural,** architectonic; superstructural, substructural

267 LENGTH

NOUNS **1 length,** lengthiness; wheelbase; **extent,** extension, **measure, span, reach, stretch; distance** 261; infinity 822; perpetuity 828; linear measures; longitude

2 a length, **piece, portion,** part; coil, **strip,** bolt, roll; run

3 line, strip, bar; stripe 517.6; string

4 lengthening, prolongation, elongation, protraction; prolixity; **extension,** stretching *or* spinning *or* stringing out

VERBS **5 be long, be lengthy, extend,** be prolonged, **stretch; stretch out,** extend out, reach out; stretch oneself, crane, crane one's neck, rubberneck; outstretch, outreach; sprawl, straggle

6 **lengthen, prolong, elongate, extend, protract,** continue; make prolix; let out, **draw** or drag or stretch or string or spin out; **stretch,** draw, pull

ADJS 7 **long, lengthy;** tall; **extensive, far-reaching,** far-flung; sesquipedalian; **time-consuming,** interminable, without end

8 **lengthened, prolonged, elongated, extended, protracted;** prolix; **long-winded; drawn-out,** dragged out, long-drawn-out, stretched or spun or strung out; **stretched,** drawn, pulled

9 **oblong, elongated;** rectangular; elliptical

ADVS 10 lengthily, extensively, at length, ad nauseam

11 **lengthwise** or lengthways, longways, longitudinally, along, in length, at length; **endwise**

268 SHORTNESS

NOUNS 1 **shortness, briefness, brevity; succinctness,** curtness, terseness, compactness; **conciseness** 537; transience 827, instantaneousness 829

2 **stubbiness,** stumpiness <nonformal>, **stockiness, fatness** 257.8, chubbiness, chunkiness <nonformal>, squatness, dumpiness; pudginess; snubbiness

3 **shortening, abbreviation; reduction; abridgment, condensation,** compression, epitome, summary, summation, précis, abstract, recapitulation, recap <nonformal>, wrapup, synopsis, encapsulation; **curtailment,** truncation, retrenchment; elision, ellipsis, syncope, apocope; foreshortening

4 shortener, cutter, abridger; abstracter, epitomizer

5 **shortcut,** cut, cutoff; shortest way; **beeline**

VERBS 6 **shorten, abbreviate, cut; reduce** 260.7; **abridge, con-**

dense, compress, contract, **boil down,** abstract, sum up, summarize, recapitulate, recap <nonformal>, synopsize, epitomize, encapsulate, capsulize; **curtail,** truncate, retrench; bowdlerize; elide, **cut short,** cut down; **dock,** bob, shear, shave, trim, clip, snub, nip; mow, reap, **crop; prune,** poll; stunt, check the growth of; foreshorten

7 **take a short cut; cut across,** cut through; **cut a corner,** cut corners; **make a beeline,** go as the crow flies

ADJS 8 **short, brief, abbreviated; concise** 537.6; **curt,** curtate, decurtate; **succinct, summary,** synoptic, synoptical, compact; **little** 258.10; **low** 274.7; transient 827.7

9 **shortened, abbreviated; abridged,** compressed, condensed, epitomized, digested, abstracted, capsulized, encapsulated; bowdlerized; nutshell, vestpocket; **curtailed,** cut short, **docked,** bobbed, sheared, shaved, trimmed, clipped, snub, snubbed, nipped; mowed, mown, reaped, **cropped; pruned,** polled; elided, elliptic, elliptical

10 **stubby,** stubbed, stumpy <nonformal>, **thickset, stocky, chunky** <nonformal>, **fat** 257.18, **chubby,** tubby <nonformal>, dumpy; **squat; pudgy;** snub-nosed; turned-up, retroussé <Fr>

11 short-legged; short-winged

ADVS 12 **shortly, briefly,** summarily, economically, sparely, curtly, succinctly, in a nutshell, in few words; for short; **concisely** 537.7, synoptically

13 **short, abruptly,** suddenly 829.9, all of a sudden

269 BREADTH, THICKNESS

NOUNS 1 **breadth, width,** amplitude, latitude, distance across, extent, **span, expanse, spread;** beam

2 **thickness,** the third dimension, distance through; **mass, bulk,**

body; corpulence, fatness 257.8;
coarseness, grossness 294.2

3 **diameter, bore, caliber; radius**

VERBS 4 **broaden, widen,** deepen;
expand, extend, extend to the
side *or* sides; **spread** 259.6,
spread out

5 **thicken,** grow thick, thick; fatten 259.8

ADJS 6 **broad, wide,** deep; wide-
scale, wide-ranging, exhaustive,
comprehensive, in-depth, extensive; spread-out; **expansive;**
spacious, **roomy;** ample, full;
widespread 863.13

7 broad of beam, broad-beamed

8 **thick,** three-dimensional; **thickset, heavyset,** thick-bodied;
massive, bulky 257.19, corpulent
257.18; coarse, heavy, gross,
crass, fat; full-bodied, viscous;
dense 1043.12; thicknecked

ADVS 9 breadthwise, in breadth;
broadside, broad side foremost;
sideways; through, in depth

270 NARROWNESS, THINNESS

NOUNS 1 **narrowness, slenderness; closeness,** nearness; **strait-
ness,** restriction, limitation,
strictness, confinement; crowdedness, incapaciousness, incom-
modiousness; **tightness,** tight
squeeze; hair, hairbreadth; narrow gauge

2 **narrowing, tapering,** taper;
contraction 260; stricture, constriction, strangulation

3 <narrow place> narrow, **narrows, strait; bottleneck,**
chokepoint; isthmus; channel
239, canal; pass, defile; neck,
throat, craw

4 **thinness, slenderness, slim-
ness, frailty,** slightness, lightness, airiness, delicacy, flimsiness, wispiness, insubstantiality,
mistiness, vagueness; light *or* airy
texture; **fineness** 294.3; **tenuity,
rarity,** exiguity; **attenuation;**
dilution, wateriness 1059.1,
weakness

5 **leanness, skinniness,** fleshless-
ness, slightness, frailness, spare-

ness, meagerness, **scrawniness,
gauntness, lankiness,** gawkiness, **boniness,** skin and bones;
haggardness, peakedness <non-
formal>, puniness; undernourishment, underweight; hatchet
face, lantern jaws

6 **emaciation,** attenuation, atrophy

7 <comparisons> paper, wafer,
lath, slat, rail

8 <thin person> **slim, lanky;**
shadow, **skeleton,** stick, walking
skeleton, corpse, bag of bones;
rattlebones *or* **spindleshanks** *or*
spindlelegs <all nonformal>,
beanpole, beanstalk, broomstick

9 **reducing, slenderizing, slimming down;** weight-watching,
calorie-counting

10 **thinner,** solvent 1062.4

VERBS 11 **narrow,** constrict, diminish; restrict, limit, straiten,
confine; **taper; contract** 260.7

12 **thin,** thin down, thin out; **rarefy,
attenuate;** dilute, water, water
down, weaken; undernourish;
emaciate

13 **slenderize, reduce,** watch one's
weight, weight-watch, count calories, diet; slim, **slim down,** thin
down

ADJS 14 **narrow, slender; close,**
near; **tight, strait;** close-fitting;
restricted, limited, circumscribed, **confined,** constricted;
cramped; incommodious,
crowded; **meager,** scant, scanty

15 **tapered,** taper, tapering, cone-
or wedge-shaped

16 **thin, slender, slim,** gracile;
thin-bodied, narrow- *or* wasp-
waisted; **svelte,** slinky, sylphlike,
willowy; girlish, boyish; **slight;
frail,** delicate, light, airy, wispy,
lacy, gauzy, papery, gossamer, diaphanous, insubstantial, ethereal, misty, vague, flimsy, wafer-
thin, **fine; finespun,** fine-drawn;
threadlike, slender as a thread;
tenuous, subtle, rare, **rarefied;**
attenuated, **watery, weak,** diluted, watered-down

17 **lean, skinny** <nonformal>,
fleshless, **spare,** meager,

scrawny, scraggy, **gaunt, lank, lanky; gangling** *and* gangly <both nonformal>; gawky, **spindling,** spindly; **bony, rawboned,** bare-boned, rattleboned <nonformal>, skeletal, **mere skin and bones, nothing but skin and bones; underweight,** undersized, undernourished, spidery, thin *or* skinny as a rail

18 lean-limbed, thin-legged, lath- or stick-legged <nonformal>

19 **hatchet-faced;** lean- *or* thin-cheeked; lean- *or* lantern-jawed

20 **haggard, poor,** puny, **peaked** <nonformal>, **pinched;** shriveled, withered; **wizened;** **emaciated, wasted,** attenuated, corpselike, skeletal, hollow-eyed, wraithlike, cadaverous; **starved;** **undernourished,** underfed, jejune; worn to a shadow

21 **slenderizing,** reducing, slimming

ADVS 22 **narrowly,** closely, nearly, **barely,** hardly, only just, **by the skin of one's teeth**

23 thinly, thin; meagerly, sparsely, sparingly, scantily

271 FILAMENT

NOUNS 1 **filament; fiber; thread; strand,** suture; **hair** 3; fibril, fibrilla; **tendril,** cirrus; flagellum; **web,** cobweb, gossamer, spider *or* spider's web

2 **cord, line, rope, wire, cable; yarn,** skein, hank; **string, twine;** braid; **ligament,** ligature, ligation; **tendon**

3 **cordage,** cording, **ropework,** roping; tackle, tack, gear, rigging

4 **strip, strap,** strop; **lace,** thong; **band,** bandage, fillet; **belt,** girdle; **ribbon; tape,** tapeline, tape measure; slat, lath, batten, spline

5 **spinner,** spinster; silkworm, spider; spinning wheel, spinning jenny, jenny, mule; spinneret; rope walk

VERBS 6 <make threads> **spin; braid,** twist

ADJS 7 **threadlike,** thready; **stringy,** ropy, wiry; **hairlike** 3.23, hairy 3.24; filamentary, filamen-

tous; fibrous, fibered, fibroid; ligamental; capillary, capilliform; cirrose, cirrous; ligulate, ligular; gossamer, flossy, silky

272 HEIGHT

NOUNS 1 **height,** vertical *or* perpendicular distance; **highness, tallness; altitude, elevation,** ceiling; **loftiness,** sublimity, exaltation; hauteur, toploftiness 141.1; eminence, prominence; **stature**

2 **height, elevation,** eminence, **rise,** raise, **uprise,** lift, rising ground, vantage point *or* ground; **heights,** Olympian heights, dizzy *or* dizzying heights; upmost *or* uppermost *or* utmost *or* extreme height; **zenith, apex, acme**

3 **highlands** 237.1, uplands, moorland, moors, rolling country

4 **plateau,** tableland, mesa, table mountain; **hill; ridge; mountain; peak; mountain range**

5 **watershed, divide;** Great Divide, Continental Divide

6 **tower; turret;** campanile, bell tower, belfry; **spire,** church spire; **lighthouse;** cupola, lantern; dome; martello tower; barbican; **derrick,** pole; **mast,** antenna tower; water tower, standpipe; **pinnacle; steeple;** minaret; stupa, pagoda; pyramid; pylon; **shaft,** pillar, column; pilaster; obelisk; monument; colossus; skyscraper

7 <tall person> **longlegs** *and* highpockets *and* long drink of water <all nonformal>; beanpole 270.8; **giant** 257.13

8 **high tide,** high water, flood tide, spring tide, flood

9 <measurement of height> altimetry, hypsometry, hypsography; altimeter, hypsometer

VERBS 10 **tower, soar,** spire; **rise, uprise, mount, rear;** stand on tiptoe

11 **rise above, tower above** *or* **over,** clear, **top, surmount; overlook,** look down upon *or* over; **command,** dominate, overarch, overshadow, command a view of; bestride, bestraddle

12 <become higher> **grow,** grow
up, upgrow; uprise, **rise** *or* **shoot
up,** mount
13 **heighten, elevate** 911.5
ADJS **14 high,** high-reaching, **lofty,
elevated,** altitudinous, uplifted,
eminent, exalted, prominent,
superlative, sublime; **towering, soaring,** spiring, aspiring,
mounting, ascending; towered,
turreted, steepled; **topping;** overarching, **overlooking, dominat-
ing;** airy, aerial, ethereal; Olympian; monumental, colossal; topless; high-rise, multistory;
haughty 141.9, 157.8
15 skyscraping, **sky-high;** cloud-
touching *or* -topped *or* -capped;
mid-air
16 **giant** 257.20, gigantic, colossal,
statuesque; **tall, lengthy,** long
267.8; **rangy, lanky,** lank; **gangling** *and* gangly <both nonfor-
mal>; **long-legged,** leggy
17 **highland,** upland; mountain-
dwelling
18 **hilly,** knobby, rolling; **mountainous,** mountained, **alpine;**
subalpine
19 **higher,** superior, greater; **over,
above;** upper, upmost *or* uppermost; highest 198.10
20 altimetric, altimetrical
ADVS **21 on high,** high up, high;
aloft, aloof; **up,** upward, upwards, to the zenith; **above, over,**
o'er, **overhead;** skyward, airward,
in the air, in the clouds; on the
peak *or* summit *or* crest *or* pinnacle; tiptoe, on tiptoe; on stilts; on
the shoulders of

273 SHAFT

NOUNS 1 **shaft, pole, bar, rod,
stick; stalk, stem;** tongue, wagon
tongue; flagstaff; totem pole;
Maypole; tent pole
2 **staff,** stave; **cane, stick, walking stick,** shillelagh; Malacca
cane; baton; swagger stick; pilgrim's staff; crosier, cross-staff,
cross; alpenstock; quarterstaff;
crutch
3 **beam, timber,** pole, spar
4 **post, standard, upright;** ban-

ister, baluster; **balustrade,** balus-
trading; gatepost; doorpost,
jamb, doorjamb; signpost, milepost; stile, mullion; stanchion;
hitching post
5 **pillar, column,** post, pier, pilaster; caryatid; atlas, atlantes <pl>;
telamon, telamones; **colonnade,
arcade,** pilastrade, portico, peri-
style
6 **leg,** shank; **stake,** peg; **pile, stud;**
picket, pale, palisade

274 LOWNESS

NOUNS 1 **lowness, shortness,**
squatness, stumpiness; **prostration,** supineness, proneness,
recumbency, **lying, lying down,
reclining;** depression, debasement
2 **low tide,** ebb tide, neap tide,
neap
3 lowland, **lowlands,** bottomland,
swale
4 **base, bottom** 199, nadir; the
lowest of the low; lower strata,
bedrock
VERBS **5 lie low, squat, crouch,**
lay low <nonformal>; crawl,
grovel, lie prone *or* supine *or*
prostrate, hug the earth; underlie
6 lower, debase, depress 912.4
ADJS **7 low, unelevated, flat, low-
lying; short, squat,** squatty,
stumpy, runty 258.13; **lowered,**
debased, depressed 912.12; de-
moted; **reduced** 252.10; prone,
supine, prostrate *or* prostrated,
stooped, recumbent; laid low,
knocked flat, decked <nonfor-
mal>; **low-built,** low-statured;
low-level, low-leveled; neap;
knee-high, knee-high to a grasshopper <nonformal>
8 **lower,** inferior, **under, nether;**
down; less advanced; earlier; lowest 199.7
ADVS 9 **low,** near the ground; at a
low ebb
10 **below,** down below, **under;**
hereunder; thereunder; below-
stairs, downstairs, below deck;
underfoot; below par, below the
mark

275 DEPTH

NOUNS **1 depth, deepness,** profoundness, profundity; deep-seatedness, deep-rootedness; bottomlessness, fathomlessness

2 pit, deep, depth, hole, hollow, **cavity,** shaft, well, **gulf, chasm, abyss,** yawning abyss; crevasse

3 depths, deeps, bowels, bowels of the earth; bottomless pit; hell, nether world, underworld; dark *or* yawning *or* gaping depths, un-fathomed deeps; deep space

4 ocean depths, the deep sea, the deep, trench, deep-sea trench, **the deeps, the depths,** bottomless depths, inner space, abyss; bottom waters; abyssal zone, bathyal zone, pelagic zone; **seabed, bottom of the sea,** ocean bottom *or* floor *or* bed, ground, benthos; Davy Jones's locker <nonformal>

5 sounding *or* **soundings,** fathoming, depth sounding; **echo sounding,** echolocation; **depth indicator**

6 draft, submergence, submersion, **displacement**

7 deepening, lowering, depression; excavation, digging, mining, tunneling; drilling, probing

VERBS **8 deepen, lower, depress, sink;** countersink, **dig,** excavate, tunnel, mine, **drill; dive** 367.6

9 sound, take soundings, make a sounding, **fathom, plumb,** plumb-line, plumb the depths

ADJS **10 deep, profound,** deep-down; **deep-going; deep-set,** deep-laid; deep-sunk; **deep-seated, deep-rooted;** deep-cut; knee-deep, ankle-deep

11 abysmal, abyssal, yawning, cavernous, gaping, plunging; **bottomless,** unsounded, plumbless, **fathomless,** unfathomed, unfathomable; deep as the sea

12 underground, subterranean, buried

13 underwater; submarine, undersea; submerged, immersed, buried, engulfed, inundated, flooded, drowned, sunken

14 deep-sea, deep-water; ocean-ographic, bathyal; benthic, benthal, benthonic; abyssal

15 deepest, profoundest; bedrock, rock-bottom

ADVS **16 deep; beyond one's depth,** out of one's depth; over one's head; at bottom, at the core

276 SHALLOWNESS

NOUNS **1 shallowness, depthlessness; superficiality,** triviality, **cursoriness,** slightness; insufficiency 991; a lick and a promise *and* once-over-lightly <both non-formal>; **surface,** skin, rind, epidermis; veneer, gloss; pinprick

2 shoal, shallow, shallows, flat, shelf; **bank, bar,** sandbank, sandbar; **reef,** coral reef; ford; wetlands

VERBS **3 shoal,** shallow; fill in *or* up, silt up

4 scratch the surface, touch upon, hardly touch, skim over, skim *or* graze the surfaceonce over lightly <nonformal>, apply a Band-Aid <trademark> <nonformal>

ADJS **5 shallow,** shoal, **depthless; surface,** on *or* near the surface; **superficial, cursory,** slight, light, cosmetic, thin, jejune, trivial; **skin-deep,** epidermal; ankle-deep, knee-deep

6 shoaly, shelfy; reefy; unnavigable

277 STRAIGHTNESS

NOUNS **1 straightness,** directness, unswervingness, **linearity,** rectilinearity; verticalness 200; flatness

2 straight line, direct line; straight stretch, straightaway; **beeline; shortcut** 268.5; great-circle course; edge, side, diagonal, chord, tangent, perpendicular, segment, diameter, axis, radius, vector <all mathematics>

3 straightedge, rule, ruler; square, T square, triangle

VERBS **4** have no turning; go straight, make a beeline

5 straighten, set *or* **put straight,** rectify, make right *or* good, square away; **unbend,** unkink, uncurl, unsnarl, disentangle 797.5; straighten up, square up; straighten out, extend; flatten, smooth 201.6

ADJS **6 straight;** dead straight, straight as an edge *or* a ruler, even, right, true, straight as an arrow; **rectilinear; linear; direct, undeviating, unswerving,** unbending, undeflected; **unbent, unbowed,** unturned, uncurved; **uninterrupted, unbroken;** upright, vertical 200.11; flat, level, smooth, horizontal 201.7

ADVS **7 straight,** straightly, unswervingly, undeviatingly, **directly;** straight to the mark; in the groove *and* on the beam *and* on the money <all nonformal>

278 ANGULARITY

NOUNS **1 angularity,** crookedness; squareness, orthogonality, rectangularity; flexure

2 angle, point, bight; vertex, apex 198.2; **corner,** quoin, nook; **crook, hook,** crotchet; **bend,** curve, swerve, veer, inflection, deflection; cant; furcation, bifurcation, fork 171.4; zigzag, zig, zag; elbow, knee, dogleg <nonformal>

3 <angular measurement> goniometry; trigonometry

4 <instruments> goniometer; radiogoniometer; pantometer; clinometer; graphometer; astrolabe; protractor

VERBS **5 angle, crook, hook, bend,** elbow; angle off *or* away, curve, swerve, veer, veer off, go off on a tangent; furcate, bifurcate, branch, fork 171.7; zigzag, zig, zag

ADJS **6 angular;** cornered, **crooked, hooked, bent,** flexed; akimbo; doglegged <nonformal>; crotched; furcate, forked 171.10; sharp-cornered, **sharp, pointed;** zigzag, jagged, serrate, sawtooth

7 right-angled, rectangular, right-angle; **orthogonal,** orthodiagonal; **perpendicular,** normal

8 triangular, trilateral, deltoid;

wedgeshaped, cuneiform, cuneate

9 quadrangular, quadrilateral; rectangular, square; foursquare, orthogonal; tetragonal, tetrahedral; **oblong;** trapezoid *or* trapezoidal, rhombic, rhomboid; **cubic,** cube-shaped, cubed, diced

10 pentagonal, hexagonal, heptagonal, octagonal, decagonal, dodecagonal, etc; pentahedral, hexahedral, octahedral, dodecahedral, icosahedral, etc

11 multilateral, multiangular, polygonal; polyhedral, pyramidal; prismatic, prismoid

279 CURVATURE

NOUNS **1 curvature,** curving; incurvature; excurvature; decurvature; recurvature; **arching, vaulting,** arcuation; aquilinity; crookedness, hookedness; sinuosity, sinuousness, tortuosity, tortuousness; circularity 280; convolution 281; rotundity 282; convexity 283; concavity 284; curvaceousness

2 curve, sinus; **bow, arc; crook, hook;** parabola, hyperbola; ellipse; catenary, festoon, swag; tracery; circle 280.2; curl 281.2

3 bend, bending; **bow,** bowing, oxbow; Cupid's bow; **turn,** turning, sweep, meander, hairpin turn *or* bend; **flexure,** flex, **flection,** inflection, deflection; reflection

4 arch, span, vault, vaulting, camber; ogive; apse; **dome,** cupola, geodesic dome, igloo; cove; **arcade, archway,** arcature; keystone

5 crescent, semicircle, scythe, sickle, meniscus; horseshoe

VERBS **6 curve, turn,** arc, sweep; **crook, hook,** loop; incurve; recurve, decurve, retroflex; sag, swag <nonformal>; **bend,** flex; deflect, inflect; reflect, reflex; **bow, arch,** vault; dome; **hump;** wind, curl 281.5; round 282.6

ADJS **7 curved,** curve, curvate, **curving,** curvy, curvaceous <nonformal>; curvilinear; wavy, undulant, billowy, billowing; sinuous, tortuous, serpentine, mazy, labyrinthine, meandering; **bent**, flexed; incurved, incurvated; recurved, recurvated

8 hooked, crooked, aquiline; **hook-shaped**, uncinate, unciform; claw-like, unguiform; **hook-nosed**, aquiline-nosed, Roman-nosed, crooknosed; **beaked**, billed; **beak-shaped**, beak-like; bill-shaped, bill-like; rostrate

9 turned-up, upcurving, *retroussé* <Fr>

10 bowed, bandy; bow-shaped, ox-bow; **convex, concave** 284.16; arcuate, arclike; **arched**, vaulted; **humped**, hunched, humpy; gibbous; humpbacked 265.13

11 crescent-shaped, crescentlike, crescent; meniscoid[al]; sigmoid; **semicircular**, semilunar; horn-shaped, horned, corniform; sickle-shaped, falciform; moon-shaped, lunar, lunate

12 lens-shaped, lenticular, lentiform

13 parabolic, paraboloid; saucer-shaped; elliptic, elliptical; bell-shaped, campanular, campaniform

14 pear-shaped, pearlike, pyriform

15 heart-shaped; cordate, cardioid, cordiform

16 kidney-shaped, reniform

17 turnip-shaped, napiform

18 shell-shaped; conchate, conchiform

19 shield-shaped; scutiform

20 helmet-shaped, helmetlike, galeiform, cassideous

280 CIRCULARITY

NOUNS **1 circularity, roundness**, ring-shape, ringliness, annularity; annulation

2 circle, circus, rondure, **ring**, annulus; **circumference**, radius; **round**, roundel, rondelle; **cycle, circuit**; orbit 1070.16; vicious circle; fairy ring; circular reasoning; **wheel** 914.4; **disk**, discus, saucer; **loop**; noose, lasso; crown, diadem, coronet, corona; garland;

wreath; halo, aureole; annular muscle, sphincter

3 <thing encircling> **band, belt, cincture, girdle, girth**, zone, fascia, fillet; collar, collarband, neckband; necktie; necklace, bracelet, armlet, wristband, anklet; ring, earring, nose ring, finger ring; hoop; quoit; zodiac, ecliptic, equator, great circle

4 rim; tire

5 circlet, **ringlet**, annulet, **eyelet**, grommet

6 oval, ovule, ovoid; ellipse

7 cycloid; epicycloid, epicycle; cardioid

8 semicircle, half circle; crescent 279.5; quadrant, sextant, sector

9 <music and poetry> **round**, canon; rondo, rondino, rondeau, rondelet

VERBS **10 circle, round**; orbit; **encircle** 209.7, surround, encompass, girdle

ADJS **11 circular, round**, annular, annulate ring-shaped; disklike, discoid; cyclic, cyclical, cycloid, cycloidal; epicyclic; planetary; crownlike

12 oval, ovate, ovoid, oviform, egg-shaped, obovate

281 CONVOLUTION

<complex curvature>

NOUNS **1 convolution**, involution, **winding, twisting, turning; meander, meandering**; crinkle, crinkling; circuitousness, circumlocution, ambagiousness; Byzantinism; tortuousness, tortuosity; torsion, intorsion; sinuousness, **sinuosity**, slinkiness; snakiness; flexuosity; undulation, wave, waving; **complexity** 798

2 coil, whorl, roll, **curl**, curlicue, ringlet, pigtail, **spiral**, helix, volute, volution, involute, evolute, scroll; **kink, twist, twirl**; corkscrew; tendril; whirl, swirl, vortex

3 curler, curling iron; curlpaper, papillote

VERBS **4** convolve, **wind, twine**, twirl, **twist, turn, twist and turn, meander**; serpentine, snake,

slink, worm; corkscrew; whirl,
swirl; whorl; wring; contort
5 curl, coil; crisp, kink, crimp
ADJS **6 convolutional, winding,
twisting,** twisty, turning; **meandering,** labyrinthine; **serpentine,** snaky, anfractuous; roundabout, circuitous, ambagious, circumlocutory; labyrinthine; Byzantine; **sinuous; tortuous,** torsional; involute, involuted; sig-
moidal; wreathlike; whorled
**7 coiled, snakelike, snaky, ser-
pentine;** anguiform; eelshaped,
anguilliform; wormlike, vermiform, lumbricoid
8 spiral, spiroid, volute, voluted;
helical, helicoidal; anfractuous;
whorled, scrolled; cochlear, co-
chleate
9 curly, curled; kinky, kinked;
frizzly, frizzy, frizzled, frizzed;
crisp
10 wavy, undulant, undulatory, undulating; **billowy,** billowing,
rolling
ADVS **11 windingly, twistingly,** sin-
uously, tortuously, meanderingly;
in and out, round and round

282 SPHERICITY, ROTUNDITY

NOUNS **1 sphericity, rotundity,
roundness,** orbicularity, **spher-
icalness,** sphericality, globularity,
globularness; spheroidicity; belly;
cylindricality; convexity 283
2 sphere; ball, orb, orbit, **globe,**
rondure; spheroid, globoid, ellipsoid; spherule, globule; **pellet;**
boll; **bulb; gob,** glob <nonfor-
mal>, blob, gobbet; pill, bolus;
balloon, bladder, bubble
3 drop, droplet; raindrop, teardrop; bead, pearl
4 cylinder, pillar, column; barrel,
drum, cask; pipe, tube; roll, rou-
leau, roller; bole, trunk
5 cone, conelet; funnel; ice-cream
cone; pine cone
VERBS **6 round; round out, fill
out;** cone
7 ball, snowball; sphere, spherify,
globe, conglobulate; roll; bead;
balloon, mushroom

ADJS **8 rotund, round,** rounded,
rounded out; bellied, bellylike;
convex, bulging
9 spherical, spherelike, sphere-
shaped; **globular, global,** globed,
globose, globe-shaped; orbicular,
orbiculate, orblike; spheroid,
spheroidal, ellipsoid; hemi-
spheric, hemispherical; **bulbous,**
bulging; ovoid
10 beady, beaded, bead-shaped
11 cylindrical, cylindroidal; **col-
umnar,** columned; **tubular,** tube-
shaped; barrel-shaped, drum-
shaped
12 conical, conic, cone-shaped;
funnel-shaped, funnellike, fun-
nelled, infundibular

283 CONVEXITY, PROTUBERANCE

NOUNS **1 convexity,** convexness;
excurvature, excurvation; camber; gibbosity; tuberosity;
bulging, bellying
2 protuberance or protuberancy,
**projection, protrusion, extru-
sion;** prominence, eminence,
salience, boldness, **bulging,** bellying; gibbosity; excrescence;
tuberosity, puffiness; salient; relief, high relief, low relief, bas-
relief, embossment
3 bulge, bow, convex; **bump;**
cahot <Can>; hill, mountain;
hump, hunch; **lump,** clump,
bunch, blob; nubbin, nub; **mole,**
nevus; **wart,** verruca; **knob,** boss,
bulla, button, bulb; stud, peg,
dowel; flange, lip; tab, ear, flap,
loop, ring, handle; **knot,** knurl,
burl, gall; **ridge,** rib, chine, spine,
shoulder; welt, wale; blister,
vesicle <anat>; bubble; bubo;
tubercle or tubercule
4 swelling, swollenness, edema;
rising, lump, bump, pimple;
pock, furuncle, boil, carbuncle;
corn; pustule; dilation, dilatation;
turgidity, turgescence, tumescence, intumescence; tumor,
tumefaction; wen, cyst, sebaceous cyst; bunion
5 node, nodule, nodulus, nodula-
tion, nodosity

6 breast, bosom, bust, chest,
crop, brisket; thorax; **breasts,**
dugs, teats; **nipple,** papilla, mam-
milla; mammary gland; udder,
bag

7 <nonformal terms> **tits,** titties,
boobs, boobies, jugs, headlights,
knockers, knobs, bazooms

8 nose, olfactory organ; **snout,
snoot** <nonformal>; **muzzle;
proboscis, trunk; beak,** rostrum; **bill** and pecker <both
nonformal>; smeller and schnoz-
zle and schnoz and schnozzola
<all nonformal>; muffle; nostrils,
nares

9 <point of land> **point,** hook,
spur, **cape,** tongue, bill; **promon-
tory,** foreland, **headland; pen-
insula; delta; spit,** sandspit;
reef, coral reef; breakwater 900.4

**VERBS 10 protrude, protuberate,
project, extrude; stick out,** jut
out, shoot out; **stick up,** bristle
up, shoot up

11 bulge, belly, bag, balloon,
pouch; pout; **goggle,** bug <non-
formal>, pop; **swell, swell up,
dilate, distend,** billow; swell out,
belly out

12 emboss, boss, chase, raise;
ridge

ADJS 13 convex; excurvate; **bowed,**
arched 279.10; gibbous, gibbose;
humped 279.10; rotund 282.8

**14 protruding, protrusive; pro-
tuberant,** protuberating; **projecting, extruding;** jutting;
prominent, eminent, salient,
bold; prognathous; excrescent;
protrusile

15 bulging, swelling, distended,
bloated, potbellied, bellying,
pouching; bagging, baggy;
rounded, hummocky; billowing,
billowy, bosomy, ballooning;
bumpy; bulbous, warty, ver-
rucose

16 bulged, bulgy, bugged-out
<nonformal>; swollen 259.13,
turgid, tumid, turgescent, tumescent, tumorous; bellied, ventri-
cose; pouched; goggled, goggle;
exophthalmic, bug-eyed <nonfor-
mal>, popeyed <nonformal>

17 studded, knobbed, knobby,
knoblike, nubby; **knotty, knotted; gnarled,** knurled, burled,
gnarly; noduled, nodular; bu-
bonic; tuberculous, tubercular;
tuberous

18 in relief, in bold or high relief,
raised; chased, bossed, embossed

19 pectoral, chest, thoracic;
pigeon-breasted; mammary,
mammillary, mammiform; mammalian; papillary, papillose;
breasted, bosomed; teated, nip-
pled; busty, bosomy, chesty

20 peninsular; deltaic, deltal

284 CONCAVITY

NOUNS 1 concavity, hollowness;
incurvature, incurvation; depression, impression

2 cavity, concavity, concave; **hollow,** hollow shell, shell; **hole, pit,
depression, dip,** sink; scoop,
pocket; **basin,** trough, **bowl,** cup,
container 195; **crater;** lacuna;
crypt; armpit; socket

3 pothole, sinkhole, chuckhole,
mudhole, rut 290.1

4 pit, well, shaft, sump; **chasm,
gulf, abyss; excavation,** dig, diggings, workings; mine, quarry

5 cave, cavern, hole, grotto; lair
228.26; **tunnel, burrow,** warren;
subway; bunker, foxhole, dugout

6 indentation, indent, dent;
gouge, **furrow** 290; **dimple;
pit,** pock, pockmark; impression,
impress; imprint, print; **notch**
289

7 recess, niche, nook, inglenook,
corner; cove, alcove

8 <hollow in the side of a moun-
tain> combe, cirque

9 valley, vale, dale, dell; **glen,** bottom, bottoms, intervale, wadi,
grove; trench, trough, lunar rill;
gap, pass, ravine

10 excavator, digger; sapper;
miner; tunneler, sandhog and
groundhog <both nonformal>;
driller; dredge, dredger

11 excavation; mining; indentation, **engraving**

VERBS 12 <be concave> **sink, dish,**
cup, bowl, hollow; retreat, retire

13 hollow, hollow out, concave,
dish, cup, bowl; cave, cave in
14 indent, dent, dint, **depress,**
press in, stamp, tamp, punch,
impress, imprint; **pit;** pock,
pockmark; dimple; **recess,** set
back; set in; **notch** 289.4; engrave
15 excavate, dig, dig out, **scoop,**
scoop out, **gouge,** gouge out,
grub, shovel, spade, scrape,
scratch, scrabble; dredge; **trench,**
trough, furrow, groove; **tunnel,
burrow; mine,** sap; quarry; drill,
bore
ADJS **16 concave, incurved,** incur-
vate; **sunk,** sunken; retreating, re-
cessed, retiring; **hollow,** empty;
dish-shaped, bowl-shaped; crater-
shaped, saucer-shaped; **cupped,**
scyphate; funnel-shaped, infundibular; boat-shaped, navicular,
scaphoid; **cavernous**
17 indented, dented, depressed;
dimpled; pitted; cratered;
pocked, pockmarked; honeycombed; **notched** 289.5;
engraved

285 SHARPNESS

NOUNS **1 sharpness, keenness,
edge;** acuteness; **pointedness,**
acumination; thorniness, prickliness, spinosity; acridity 68.1
2 <sharp edge> **edge, cutting
edge, honed edge, knife-edge,
razor-edge;** featheredge
3 point, tip, cusp; acumination;
nib; needle; **drill,** borer, auger,
bit; **prick, prickle;** sting, acus;
tooth 2.8
4 <pointed projection> **projection,** spur, jag, **snag,** snaggle;
horn, antler; crag, peak; spire,
steeple; **cog, sprocket,** ratchet;
sawtooth
5 thorn, bramble, brier, nettle,
burr, prickle; **spike,** spicule;
spine; bristle; quill; **needle; this-
tle**
VERBS **6** come to a point, acuminate; prick, sting, stick, bite; be
keen, have an edge, cut; bristle
with
7 sharpen, edge, acuminate,
spiculate, taper; **whet, hone,** oil-
stone, file, grind; strop, strap; set,
reset; **point**
ADJS **8 sharp, keen, edged, acute,**
fine, **cutting,** knifelike; razor-
edged, knife-edged; featheredged;
acrid 68.6; sharp as a razor *or*
needle *or* tack; sharpened, set
9 pointed, acuminate, aculeate,
aculeated, acute; tapered, tapering; cusped, cuspate, cuspidate;
sharp-pointed; needlelike,
needle-sharp; toothed; **spiked,**
spiculate; **barbed, tined,
pronged; horned,** horny, cornu-
ted, cornified, ceratoid; **spined,
spiny,** spinous, acanthous
10 prickly, echinate, aculeolate;
pricking, stinging; **thorny,** bram-
bly, briery, thistly; bristly
11 arrowlike, arrowheaded; sagit-
tal, sagittate
12 spearlike; lancelike, lanceolate,
lanceolar; **spindle-shaped**
13 swordlike, gladiate, ensate, en-
siform
14 toothlike, dentiform, dentoid,
odontoid; **toothed, fanged,
tusked;** snaggle-toothed
15 star-shaped, starlike, star-
pointed

286 BLUNTNESS

NOUNS **1 bluntness, dullness,**
obtuseness; bluffness; abruptness; toothlessness, lack of incisiveness
VERBS **2 blunt, dull,** obtund, **take
the edge off;** weaken, repress;
draw the teeth *or* fangs
ADJS **3 blunt, dull,** obtuse; **un-
sharp,** unsharpened; **unedged,**
edgeless; rounded, faired,
smoothed, streamlined; **un-
pointed,** pointless; blunted,
dulled; blunt-edged, dull-edged;
bluff, abrupt
4 toothless, teethless, edentate,
edental, biteless

287 SMOOTHNESS

NOUNS **1 smoothness, flatness,
levelness,** evenness, uniformity,
regularity; **sleekness,** glossiness;
slickness, slipperiness, lubricity,
oiliness, greasiness; silkiness, vel-

vetiness; glabrousness; suavity
504.5

2 polish, gloss, glaze, burnish,
shine, luster; patina

3 <smooth surface> **plane, level,
flat;** glass, ice; marble, alabaster,
ivory; silk, satin, velvet, a baby's
ass <nonformal>

4 smoother; roller; sleeker,
slicker; **polish,** burnish; **abrasive,** abrader; lubricant

VERBS **5 smooth, flatten, plane,
level,** even; **dress;** smooth down
or out, lay; plaster; roll; harrow,
drag; grade; mow, shave; lubricate, oil, grease

6 press, hot-press, **iron, mangle,**
calender; roll

7 polish, shine, burnish, furbish,
slick down, gloss, glaze; **rub,**
scour, **buff;** wax, varnish; finish

8 grind, file, sand, scrape, sandpaper, emery, pumice; abrade;
sandblast

ADJS **9 smooth;** smooth-textured or
-surfaced, **even, level, plane,
flat,** uniform, **unbroken;** unruffled, unwrinkled; glabrous;
downy; silky, satiny, velvety,
smooth as silk or satin or velvet,
smooth as a baby's ass <nonformal>; lissotrichous; smooth-
shaven 6.17; suave 504.18

10 sleek, slick, glossy, shiny,
gleaming; silky, silken, satiny,
velvety; **polished,** burnished;
buffed, rubbed, finished; varnished, lacquered, shellacked,
glazed; **glassy,** smooth as glass

11 slippery, slick, slithery <nonformal>, slippery as an eel;
lubricious, oily, oleaginous,
greasy; lubricated, oiled, greased

ADVS **12 smoothly, evenly,** uniformly; **like clockwork**

288 ROUGHNESS

NOUNS **1 roughness, unsmoothness, unevenness,** irregularity,
nonuniformity 781; **bumpiness;
abrasiveness, abrasion,** harshness, asperity; **ruggedness,** jaggedness, cragginess; bumpiness;
turbulence; choppiness; hispidity,
bristliness, thorniness; nubbiness

2 <rough surface> **rough,** broken
ground; broken water, chop; **corrugation,** washboard; gooseflesh,
goose bumps, goose pimples;
sandpaper

3 bristle, barb, barbel, striga, seta;
stubble; whisker

VERBS **4 roughen,** rough up;
coarsen; granulate; gnarl; pimple

5 ruffle, wrinkle, corrugate, crinkle, **rumple; bristle; rub the
wrong way, go against the grain**

ADJS **6 rough, unsmooth; uneven,
broken,** irregular, textured;
bumpy, rutted, pitted, potholed;
pimply; **corrugated; choppy;**
ruffled, unkempt; **shaggy;
coarse,** rank, unrefined; unpolished; grainy, granulated;
rough-hewn, rough-cast; homespun

7 rugged, ragged, harsh; rugose,
wrinkled, crinkled, crumpled,
corrugated; **scratchy, abrasive;
jagged; snaggy,** snagged, snaggled; **scraggy,** scraggly; sawtooth,
sawtoothed, serrate, serrated;
craggy, cragged, **rocky,** gravelly,
stony; rockbound, ironbound

8 gnarled; knurled; knotted,
knotty, nodular, studded, lumpy

9 bristly, bristling, hispid, hirsute, whiskery; whiskered, setose;
strigose, strigate, studded; **stubbled,** stubbly; hairy 3.24

10 bristlelike, setiform, aristate, setarious

ADVS **11 roughly,** in the rough; **unsmoothly,** brokenly, **unevenly,** irregularly, choppily, jaggedly;
abrasively

12 cross-grained, **against the
grain,** the wrong way

289 NOTCH

NOUNS **1 notch, nick, cut,** cleft, **incision, gash,** blaze, **score,** kerf,
jag; joggle; **indentation** 284.6

2 notching, serration, saw tooth;
denticulation, dogtooth; crenelation, crenulation; **scallop;** rickrack; deckle edge; cockscomb

3 battlement, crenel, castellation,
machicolation

VERBS **4 notch, nick, cut, incise,**

gash, slash, chop, crimp, **score,**
blaze, scarify; **indent** 284.14;
scallop, crennellate, crenulate,
machicolate; serrate

ADJS **5 notched, nicked,** incised,
gashed, scored, blazed; **indented**
284.17; serrated, **saw-toothed;**
crenated, crenulate; scalloped;
toothed, tooth-shaped; lacerate,
lacerated; **jagged**

290 FURROW

NOUNS **1 furrow, groove,** scratch,
crack, cranny, chase, chink,
score, **cut,** gash, striation, streak;
rut, well-worn groove; wrinkle
291.3; **corrugation;** rifling;
chamfer, bezel, rabbet, dado

  2 trench, trough, channel, ditch,
fosse, **canal,** cut, gutter; moat;
aqueduct 239.2; pleat, crimp

VERBS **3 furrow, groove,** score,
scratch, incise, cut, carve, chisel,
gash, striate, streak, gouge, slit,
crack; plow; rifle; **channel,**
trough, flute, chamfer, rabbet,
dado; **trench,** canalize, **ditch,**
gully, **rut; corrugate;** wrinkle
291.6; pleat, crimp

ADJS **4 furrowed, grooved,**
scratched, scored, incised, cut,
gashed, gouged, slit, striated;
channeled, troughed, trenched,
ditched; fluted, chamfered, rab-
beted, dadoed; rifled; canalicu-
lated; **corrugated;** corduroy, cor-
duroyed, **rutted,** rutty; wrinkled
291.8, pleated, crimped; ribbed,
costate   \

291 FOLD

NOUNS **1 fold, double,** fold on itself, doubling; ply; plicature; flexure; **crease,** creasing; crimp;
tuck, gather; ruffle, frill; flounce;
dog-ear

  2 pleat, pleating, plait

  3 wrinkle, corrugation, ridge,
furrow 290, **crease, crimp,**
pucker; crinkle, ripple, wimple;
crumple, rumple; crow's-feet

  4 folding, creasing, infolding;
plication, plicature; origami

VERBS **5 fold,** fold on itself, fold
up; **double,** ply, plicate; fold over,

double over, turn under; **crease,**
crimp; pleat, plait; **tuck, gather;**
ruffle, ruff, frill; flounce; flute;
dog-ear; **fold in,** wrap, lap; inter-
fold

  6 wrinkle, corrugate, shirr, ridge,
furrow, crease, crimp, **pucker,**
purse; knit; crumple, rumple;
crinkle, ripple, wimple

ADJS **7 folded, doubled;** plicate,
plicated; **pleated,** plaited;
creased, crimped; tucked, gathered; flounced, ruffled; fluted;
dog-eared; foldable, flexural, flexible, pliable, pliant, willowy

  8 wrinkled, wrinkly; corrugated;
creased, furrowed 290.4, ridged;
puckered; pursed; knitted, knotted; rugged, rugose; **crinkled,**
crinkly, rippled; crimped; **crum-**
pled, rumpled

292 OPENING

NOUNS **1 opening, aperture, hole,**
hollow, **cavity** 284.2, **orifice; slot,**
split, crack, check, leak; opening
up, unstopping, throwing open,
broaching, cutting through; passageway; inlet 189.5; outlet 190.9;
gap, yawn, hiatus, lacuna, interval; **chasm, gulf;** cleft 224.2;
fontanel; foramen, fenestra; pore,
porosity; fistula; **disclosure** 351

  2 gaping, yawning, oscitancy, de-
hiscence; **gape, yawn**

  3 hole, perforation, penetration,
piercing, puncture, boring,
puncturing, punching, pricking,
lancing; acupuncture; trephining;
impalement, skewering, fixing;
borehole, drill hole

  4 mouth; maw, oral cavity; **muz-**
zle, jaw, lips, embouchure; kisser
or mush or trap or yap <all non-
formal>; **jaws,** mandibles, chops,
jowls

  5 anus; asshole and bumhole and
bunghole <all nonformal>; bung

  6 door, doorway 189.6; **entrance,**
entry 189.5

  7 window, casement; **window-**
pane, light

  8 porousness, porosity; screen,
sieve, strainer, colander, net;
honeycomb

9 permeability, perviousness

10 opener; can opener; corkscrew, bottle opener; latchstring; **key;** latchkey; passkey; open sesame

VERBS **11 open, open up;** lay open, throw open; **tap, broach;** cut open, cleave, split, slit, crack, incise; tear open, rent, tear, rip, rip open, part, separate, divide; spread, spread out, splay

12 unclose, unshut; **unfold,** unwrap, unroll; **unstop, unclog, unblock,** clear, unfoul, free; **unplug;** crack; **unlock,** unlatch, undo; **uncover,** unsheathe, unveil, undrape; **disclose** 351.4, expose, reveal, bare, manifest

13 make an opening, find an opening, make place *or* space, **make way, make room**

14 breach, rupture; **break open,** force *or* pry open, crack *or* split open, rip *or* tear open; break in, burst in, bust in <nonformal>, stave in

15 perforate, pierce, penetrate, puncture, punch, hole, prick; **tap, broach; stab, stick,** pink, run through; **transfix,** fix, **impale,** spit, skewer; gore, spear, lance, spike, needle; **bore, drill,** auger; **ream,** ream out, countersink, gouge, gouge out; trephine; punch full of holes, **riddle, honeycomb**

16 gape, yawn, oscitate, dehisce, hang open

ADJS **17 open, unclosed,** uncovered; **unobstructed, unstopped, unclogged;** wide-open, unrestricted; **disclosed** 348.10; bare, exposed, naked, bald

18 gaping, yawning, oscitant, slack-jawed, openmouthed; dehiscent; ajar, cracked

19 apertured, slotted; pierced, **perforated;** honeycombed, riddled, shot through, peppered; windowed, fenestrated

20 porous; sievelike, cribriform; spongelike; percolating, leachy

21 permeable, pervious, penetrable, accessible

22 mouthlike, oral; mandibular, maxillary

293 CLOSURE

NOUNS **1 closure, closing, shutting,** occlusion; **shutdown; exclusion** 772, **ruling out;** blockade, embargo

2 imperviousness, impermeability, impenetrability, impassability; imperforation

3 obstruction, clog, block, blockade, sealing off, **blockage,** strangulation, choking, choking off, **stoppage, bar, barrier, obstacle,** impediment; **bottleneck,** chokepoint; **congestion,** jam, traffic jam, gridlock; constipation, costiveness; infarct, infarction; embolism, embolus; bottleneck; **blind alley,** blank wall, **dead end,** cul-de-sac, dead-end street, impasse; cecum

4 stopper, stopple, stopgap; **plug, cork,** bung, tap, faucet, spigot, valve, check valve, cock, sea cock, peg, pin; lid 295.5

5 stopping, **wadding, stuffing,** padding, **packing,** pack, tampon; gland; **gasket**

VERBS **6 close, shut,** occlude; contract, constrict, strangle, strangulate, choke, choke off, squeeze; **exclude** 772.4, shut out, squeeze out; **rule out** 444.3; **fasten,** secure; **lock,** lock up, lock out, key, padlock, latch, bolt, bar, barricade; **seal,** seal up, seal in, seal off; button, button up; zipper, zip up; batten down; put *or* slap the lid on, **cover; shut the door,** slam

7 stop, stop up; obstruct, bar, stay; **block,** block up; **clog,** clog up, foul; **choke,** choke up *or* off; **fill,** fill up; **stuff,** pack, jam; **congest,** stuff up; **plug,** plug up; stopper, stopple, **cork,** bung; cover; **dam,** dam up; stanch; chink; caulk; blockade, embargo; constipate, bind

8 close shop, **close up** *or* **down,** shut up, **shut up shop, shut down,** go out of business, fold *or* fold up <nonformal> shutter; cease 856.6

ADJS **9 closed, shut, unopen,** unopened; unvented, unventilated;

excluded 772.7, shut-out; **ruled out, barred** 444.7; contracted, constricted, choked, choked off, strangulated; blind, dead; dead-end, blind-alley; **exclusive,** exclusionary, closed-door, private, closed to the public

10 **unpierced, unperforated,** imperforate; intact; **untrodden,** pathless, trackless

11 **stopped, stopped up; obstructed,** infarcted, **blocked; plugged,** plugged up; **clogged,** clogged up; fouled; **choked,** choked up, strangulated; **full, stuffed,** packed, jammed, bumper-to-bumper <nonformal>, jam-packed; **congested;** constipated, costive, bound

12 **close, tight, compact,** fast, shut fast, **snug; sealed;** hermetic, hermetically sealed; airtight, dustproof, gasproof, lightproof, oilproof, rainproof, smokeproof, stormproof, waterproof, windproof; water-repellant *or* -resistant

13 **impervious, impenetrable, impermeable; impassable,** unpassable; **punctureproof,** holeproof

294 TEXTURE
<surface quality>

NOUNS 1 texture; **surface; finish,** feel; **grain,** granular texture; **weave,** woof 740.3, wale; **nap,** pile, shag, protuberance 283; **pit,** pock, indentation 284.6

2 **roughness** 288; irregularity; **coarseness, grossness, unrefinement; graininess,** granularity, grittiness

3 **smoothness** 287, **fineness, refinement,** fine-grainedness; **delicacy, daintiness;** filminess; down, **downiness,** fluff, fluffiness, velvet, fuzz, fuzziness, pubescence; satin; silk; softness 1045

VERBS 4 coarsen; granulate; **roughen** 288.4; smooth 287.5

ADJS 5 textural, textured

6 **rough** 288.6, **coarse, gross, unrefined, coarse-grained;**

grained, **grainy,** granular, granulated, gritty, gravelly

7 **nappy, shaggy,** hairy, hirsute; bumpy, lumpy; studded, knobbed; pocked, pitted 284.17

8 **smooth** 287.9; **fine, refined,** attenuated, **fine-grained; delicate, dainty; finespun;** gauzy, filmy, gossamer, **downy,** fluffy, velvety, fuzzy, pubescent; satiny, silky

295 COVERING

NOUNS 1 <act of covering> **covering;** coating, cloaking; **screening,** shielding, hiding, **veiling,** clouding, obscuring, fuzzing, masking, shrouding, blanketing; blotting out, eclipsing, occultation; **wrapping,** sheathing, envelopment; **overlaying,** overspreading, superimposition, superposition; upholstering, upholstery; incrustation

2 **cover, covering,** coverage, housing, hood, cowl, cowling, **shelter; screen,** shroud, shield, veil, pall, mantle, curtain, hanging, drape, drapery; **coat,** cloak, mask, guise; vestment 5.1

3 **skin,** dermis; **cuticle; rind; flesh;** the buff; integument, tegument 206.2, **pelt, jacket, fleece, fur, hair; peel, peeling, rind; skin; bark;** cork

4 **overlayer,** overlay; appliqué, **lap, overlap,** overlapping, imbrication; **flap,** fly

5 **cover, lid, top, cap;** operculum; stopper 293.4

6 **roof,** roofing, roofpole, ridgepole; shingles, slates, tiles; eaves; **ceiling;** skylight, cupola

7 **umbrella,** bumbershoot <nonformal>; **sunshade, parasol**

8 **tent,** canvas; top, big top; tentage

9 **rug, carpet,** floor cover *or* covering; carpeting; **mat; flooring,** floorboards, duckboards; **tiling; pavement**

10 **blanket, coverlet,** cover, covers, **spread,** robe, **afghan; bedspread; bedcover;** counterpane; **comforter, duvet, quilt,** feather bed, eiderdown; patchwork quilt;

bedding, bedclothes; linen, bed linen; sheet, sheeting; pillow-case, pillow slip; duvet cover

11 horsecloth, horse blanket; saddle blanket, saddlecloth

12 blanket, coating, coat; veneer, facing; film, scum, skin, scale; varnish, enamel, lacquer, paint 35.8

13 plating, plate, cladding

14 crust, incrustation, shell; stalactite, stalagmite; scale, scab

15 shell, seashell, conch; armor, mail, shield; carapace, plate, chitin; protective covering, cortex, thick skin or hide, elephant skin

16 hull, shell, pod, capsule, case, husk, shuck; bark, jacket; chaff, bran

17 case, casing, encasement; sheath, sheathing

18 wrapper, wrapping, wrap; binder, binding; bandage, bandaging; envelope, envelopment; jacket, jacketing

VERBS 19 cover, cover up; apply to, put on; superimpose, superpose; lay over, overlay; spread over, overspread; clothe, cloak, mantle, muffle, blanket, canopy, cowl, hood, veil, curtain, screen, shield, screen off, mask, cloud, obscure, fog, fuzz; block, eclipse, occult; film, film over

20 wrap, enwrap, wrap about or around; envelop, sheathe; surround, encompass, lap, smother, enfold, embrace, invest; shroud, enshroud; swathe, swaddle; box, case, encase, crate, pack; containerize; package, encapsulate

21 top, cap, tip, crown; put the lid on, cork, plug; roof, roof in or over; dome

22 floor; carpet; pave, causeway, cobblestone, flag, pebble; cement, concrete; pave, surface, pave over; blacktop, tar, asphalt, macadamize

23 face, veneer, revet; sheathe; shingle, shake; tile, stone, brick, slate; thatch; glass, glaze; paper, wallpaper; wall in or up

24 coat, spread on, spread with;

smear, smear on, slap on, dab, daub, plaster; lay on, lay it on thick, slather; undercoat, prime

25 plaster, stucco, cement, concrete, mastic, grout, mortar; face, line

26 plate, chromium plate, copper-plate

27 crust, incrust, encrust; scab, scab over

28 upholster, overstuff

29 re-cover, reupholster, recap

30 overlie, lie over; overlap, lap, lap over, imbricate, shingle; extend over, span, bridge, overarch, overhang

ADJS 31 covered, covert, under cover; cloaked, mantled, blanketed, muffled, hooded, shrouded, veiled, clouded, obscured, fogged; eclipsed, occulted, curtained; screened; shielded, masked; housed; wrapped, jacketed, enveloped, sheathed, swathed; boxed, cased, encased, encapsulated; packaged; coated, filmed, filmed-over; armored; floored; paved, surfaced; plastered, stuccoed

32 cutaneous; epidermal; cortical; epicarpal; testaceous; integumentary, tegumentary, vaginal

33 plated; electroplated, galvanized, anodized

34 upholstered, overstuffed

35 covering, coating; cloaking, blanketing, shrouding, obscuring, veiling, screening, shielding, sheltering; wrapping, enveloping, sheathing

36 overlying, incumbent, superimposed; overlapping, lapping, imbricate, imbricated; spanning, bridging; overarched, overarching

296 LAYER

NOUNS 1 layer, thickness; level, tier, stage, story, floor, gallery; stratum, belt, band, bed, course; zone; shelf; overlayer, superstratum, overstory; underlayer, substratum, understory; floor, bedding

2 lamina, lamella; **sheet,** leaf, foil;
wafer, disk; **plate,** plating, cladding; covering 295, **coat,** coating,
veneer, film, patina, scum, membrane, peel, skin, rind, hide; **slice,**
cut, rasher; **slab,** plank, slat;
panel; **fold,** lap, flap, **ply,** plait

3 **flake,** flock, floccule, flocculus;
scale, scurf, dandruff; chip;
shaving, paring

4 **stratification, lamination,**
lamellation; foliation; flakiness,
scaliness

VERBS 5 **layer,** lay down, lay up,
stratify, laminate; flake, scale;
delaminate, exfoliate

ADJS 6 **layered; laminated,** laminate, laminous; lamellated;
plated, coated; veneered, faced;
stratified; foliated, leaflike

7 **flaky,** flocculent; **scaly,** scurfy,
squamous, lentiginous; scabby,
scabious, scabrous

297 WEIGHT

NOUNS 1 **weight, heaviness,**
weightiness, ponderousness,
ponderosity, leadenness, heftiness *and* heft <both nonformal>;
body weight, avoirdupois <non-
formal>, fatness 257.8, beef *and*
beefiness <both nonformal>;
poundage, tonnage; **net weight;**
short-weight; underweight; overweight; **solemnity, gravity** 111.1,
580.1

2 onerousness, **burdensomeness,**
oppressiveness, deadweight,
overburden, cumbersomeness,
cumbrousness; massiveness,
massiness <old>; bulkiness
257.9, lumpishness, unwieldiness

3 <sports> bantamweight, featherweight, flyweight, heavyweight,
light heavyweight, lightweight,
middleweight, cruiser weight,
welterweight

4 **counterbalance** 899.4; **ballast,**
ballasting

5 <physics terms> **gravity, grav-**
itation, G, supergravity; specific
gravity; gravitational field; **mass;**
atomic weight, molecular weight,
molar weight

6 **weight,** paperweight; sinker;

lead, plumb, plummet, bob; sandbag

7 **burden,** pressure, **oppression,**
deadweight; burdening, taxing;
overburden, overtaxing, weighing
or weighting down; charge, **load,**
loading, lading, freight, cargo;
cumbrance, **encumbrance;** incubus; incumbency; handicap,
drag, millstone; surcharge, overload

8 <systems of weight> avoirdupois weight, troy weight,
apothecaries' weight; atomic
weight, molecular weight;
pound, ounce, gram etc, **unit**
of weight

9 **weighing,** hefting <nonformal>,
balancing; weigh-in, weigh-out;
scale

VERBS 10 **weigh,** weight; **heft**
<nonformal>, **balance,** weigh in
the balance, strike a balance, put
on the scales; **counterbalance;**
weigh in, weigh out; weigh
heavy, lie heavy, carry weight;
tip the scales, tilt the scales

11 **weigh on** *or* **upon,** rest on *or*
upon, lie on, press down, press to
the ground

12 **weight, weigh** *or* **weight down;**
hang like a millstone; **ballast;**
lead, sandbag

13 **burden, load,** load down *or* up,
lade, **encumber, charge, freight,**
tax, handicap, hamper, saddle;
oppress, weigh one down,
weigh on *or* **upon, weigh heavy**
on, lie hard *or* heavy upon, press
hard upon, be an incubus to;
overburden, overweight, overtax, **overload** 992.15

14 **outweigh,** overweigh, overweight, **outbalance**

15 **gravitate, descend** 194.5, drop,
plunge 367.6, precipitate, sink,
settle, subside; **incline,** point,
head, lead, lean

ADJS 16 **heavy, ponderous, mas-**
sive, weighty, hefty <nonformal>,
fat 257.18; **leaden,** heavy as lead;
deadweight; heavyweight; overweight; **solemn, grave** 111.3,
580.8

17 **onerous, oppressive, burden-**

some, incumbent *or* superincumbent, **cumbersome;** massive; lumpish, **unwieldy**

18 **weighted, weighed** *or* **weighted down; burdened, oppressed, laden, encumbered,** charged, loaded, fraught, freighted, taxed, saddled, hampered; **overburdened,** overloadedovertaxed; borne-down, sinking, foundering

19 **weighable; appreciable,** palpable, sensible

20 **gravitational,** mass

ADVS 21 **heavily,** heavy, weightily, leadenly; burdensomely, onerously, oppressively; **ponderously,** cumbersomely

298 LIGHTNESS

NOUNS 1 **lightness, levity,** lack of weight; **weightlessness; buoyancy;** levitation, ascent 193; **volatility; airiness,** ethereality; foaminess, frothiness, yeastiness; downiness, fluffiness; softness, gentleness, delicacy, daintiness, tenderness

2 <comparisons> air, ether, feather, down, fluff, fuzz, sponge, gossamer, cobweb, bubble

3 **lightening,** easing, **easement, alleviation, relief;** unburdening, **unloading,** unlading, unsaddling, untaxing, unfreighting; unballasting

4 **leavening, fermentation; leaven, ferment**

5 <indeterminacy of weight> **imponderableness** *or* imponderability, unweighability

VERBS 6 **lighten,** make light, reduce weight; unballast; **ease, alleviate, relieve; disburden, disencumber,** unburden, unload; **be light,** weigh lightly, have little weight

7 **leaven,** raise, **ferment**

8 **buoy,** buoy up; float, float high, ride high, waft; **sustain, hold up,** bear up, uphold, upbear, uplift

9 **levitate, rise,** ascend 193.8; hover, **float**

ADJS 10 **light; weightless; airy,**

ethereal; volatile; frothy, foamy, spumy, bubbly, yeasty; downy, feathery, fluffy; light as air *or* a feather *or* gossamer, etc 298.2

11 **lightened, eased, unburdened,** disencumbered, unencumbered, relieved, alleviated, out from under, breathing easier; mitigated

12 **light, gentle, soft, delicate,** dainty, tender, **easy**

13 **lightweight,** bantamweight, featherweight; underweight

14 **buoyant,** floatable; floating, supernatant

15 levitative, levitational

16 **lightening, easing,** alleviating, alleviative, relieving, unburdening, disencumbering

17 **leavening,** raising, **fermenting,** working; yeasty

18 **imponderable,** unweighable

299 RARITY

<*lack of density*>

NOUNS 1 **rarity,** rareness; **thinness, tenuousness,** tenuity; **subtlety; fineness,** slightness, flimsiness, **unsubstantiality** *or* **insubstantiality** 763; **ethereality,** airiness, immateriality, incorporeality; **diffuseness,** dispersedness, scatter, scatteredness

2 **rarefaction,** attenuation, subtilization, etherealization; **diffusion,** dispersion, scattering; **thinning,** thinning-out, dilution, adulteration, watering, watering-down; decompression

VERBS 3 **rarefy, attenuate,** thin, thin out; dilute, adulterate, water, water down, cut; **etherealize; diffuse,** disperse, scatter; expand 259.4; decompress

ADJS 4 **rare,** rarefied; **subtle; thin,** thinned, dilute, attenuated; thinned-out, diluted, adulterated, watered, watered-down, cut; **tenuous, fine,** flimsy, slight, **unsubstantial** *or* **insubstantial** 763; **airy, ethereal,** vaporous, gaseous, windy; **diffused,** diffuse, dispersed, scattered; uncompressed, decompressed

5 rarefactive, rarefactional

300 MEASUREMENT

NOUNS **1 measurement, measure;** mensuration, measuring, **gauging; estimation,** estimate, approximation, ballpark figure <nonformal>; **quantification,** quantization; **appraisal, stocktaking, assay,** assaying; **assessment,** determination, rating, evaluation; sizing up <nonformal>; **survey,** surveying; triangulation; **instrumentation;** telemetry, telemetering; metric system; metrication; English system of measurement; calibration, correction, computation, calculation

2 measure, measuring instrument, **meter, instrument, gauge,** barometer, **rule, yardstick, standard,** norm, canon, **criterion,** test, touchstone, check; **pattern,** model, type; **scale,** graduated *or* calibrated scale; value, degree, quantity; parameter

3 extent, quantity 244, degree 245, size 257, distance 261, length 267, breadth 269; **weight** 297

4 <measures> US liquid measure, British imperial liquid measure, US dry measure, British imperial dry measure, apothecaries' measure

5 coordinates, Cartesian coordinates, rectangular coordinates, polar coordinates; latitude, longitude; altitude, azimuth

6 waterline; floodmark, **highwater mark;** load waterline, Plimsoll mark *or* line

7 measurability, mensurability, quantifiability

8 science of measurement, **mensuration,** metrology

9 measurer, meter, gauger; **geodesist,** geodetic engineer; **surveyor,** land surveyor; topographer, cartographer, oceanographer; **appraiser, assessor;** assayer; evaluator; estimator

VERBS **10 measure, gauge, quantify,** quantize, take the measure of, mensurate, triangulate, apply the yardstick to; **estimate; as-**sess, **rate, appraise, value,** evaluate, appreciate, prize; **assay;** size *or* size up <nonformal>; **weigh,** weigh up 297.10; survey; plumb, probe, sound, fathom; span, pace, step; calibrate, graduate; divide; caliper; meter; compute, calculate

11 measure off, mark off, lay off, set off, rule off; **step off,** pace off *or* out; **measure out,** mark out, lay out; put at

ADJS **12 measuring, metric, metrical,** mensural, mensurational; **quantitative,** numerative; approximative, estimative

13 measured, gauged, metered, **quantified;** quantitated, quantized; **appraised, assessed, valuated,** valued, rated, ranked; **assayed; surveyed,** plotted, mapped, triangulated

14 measurable, mensurable, **quantifiable,** numerable, fathomable, **determinable,** computable, calculable; quantifiable, quantizable; estimable; assessable, appraisable, ratable; appreciable, perceptible, noticeable

ADVS **15 measurably, appreciably, perceptibly, noticeably**

301 YOUTH

NOUNS **1 youth, youthfulness, juvenility,** juvenescence, tenderness, tender age, early years, school age, prime of life, flower of life, salad days, springtime of life, bloom, florescence, budtime, golden season of life, heyday of youth *or* of the blood, young blood

2 childhood; boyhood; girlhood, maidenhood *or* maidenhead; subteens, pre-teens

3 immaturity, undevelopment, inexperience, **callowness, unripeness,** greenness, rawness, sappiness, freshness, juiciness, dewiness; **minority,** juniority, infancy, nonage

4 childishness, childlikeness, **puerility; boyishness; girlishness,** maidenliness

5 infancy, babyhood, the cradle, the crib, the nursery

6 adolescence, maturation, pubescence, **puberty;** nubility

7 teens, teen years or age, **awkward age**

VERBS **8** make young, **rejuvenate,** reinvigorate; turn back the clock

ADJS **9 young,** youngish, **juvenile,** juvenescent, **youthful,** youthlike, in the flower or bloom of youth, blooming, florescent, flowering, dewy, fresh-faced; young-looking, well-preserved

10 immature, unadult; **inexperienced,** unseasoned, unfledged, new-fledged, **callow, unripe,** ripening, unmellowed, **raw, green,** vernal, dewy, juicy, sappy, budding, tender, virginal, intact, innocent, naive, ingenuous, **undeveloped,** growing, unformed, unlicked, wet or not dry behind the ears; **minor,** underage

11 childish, childlike, kiddish <nonformal>, **puerile; boyish,** boylike, beardless; **girlish,** girl-like, maiden, maidenly; puppyish, puppylike, puplike, calflike, coltish, coltlike

12 infant, infantile, infantine, **babyish,** baby; doll-like; kittenish, kittenlike; **newborn,** neonatal; in the cradle or crib or nursery, in swaddling clothes, in diapers, in arms, at the breast, tied to mother's apron strings

13 adolescent, pubescent, nubile, marriageable

14 teen-age, teen-aged, teenish, **in one's teens;** sweet sixteen <nonformal>

15 junior, Jr; **younger**

302 YOUNGSTER

NOUNS **1 youngster,** young person, **youth, juvenile,** young'un <nonformal>; **stripling,** slip, sprig, sapling; fledgling; hopeful, young hopeful; **minor,** infant; **adolescent,** pubescent; **teenager,** teenybopper <nonformal>; junior, younger, youngest, baby

2 young people, youth, young, **younger generation,** new generation, young blood, young fry <nonformal>; **children,** tots; small fry and **kids** and **little kids** and little guys <all nonformal>; boyhood, girlhood; babyhood

3 child; nipper, **kid** and kiddy and kiddo <all nonformal>, **little one,** little fellow or guy, little bugger <nonformal>, shaver and little shaver <both nonformal>, little squirt <nonformal>, **tot, little tot,** tad or little tad, tyke, mite, chit <nonformal>, innocent, little innocent, moppet; darling, cherub, lamb, lambkin, kitten, **offspring** 561.3

4 brat, urchin; minx, imp, puck, elf, gamin, little monkey, **whippersnapper,** holy terror; spoiled brat; snotnose kid <nonformal>; juvenile delinquent, JD <nonformal>, punk and punk kid <both nonformal>

5 boy, lad, laddie, **youth,** young man, schoolboy, schoolkid <nonformal>, fledgling; fellow 76.5; pup, puppy, whelp, cub, colt; master; sonny, sonny boy; bud and buddy <both nonformal>; bub and bubba <both nonformal>; buck, young buck

6 girl, girlie <nonformal>, **maid, maiden, lass,** girlchild, **lassie,** young lady, damsel in distress, **damsel,** demoiselle, miss, missy, little missy, slip, wench <dial or nonformal>, colleen <Irish>

7 <nonformal terms> **gal,** dame, **chick,** tomato, **babe** or baby, **broad,** frail, **doll,** skirt, jill, chit, cutie, filly, heifer; teenybopper <nonformal>

8 schoolgirl, schoolmaid, school-miss, junior miss, subteen; subdebutante, subdeb <nonformal>; bobbysoxer <nonformal>, **tomboy,** hoyden; nymphet; virgin

9 infant, baby, babe, babe in arms, little darling or angel or doll or cherub, bouncing baby, puling infant, mewling infant, babykins <nonformal>, baby bunting; papoose; **toddler; suckling,** nursling, fosterling, weanling; neonate; yearling, yearold;

premature baby, preemie <nonformal>, incubator baby; preschooler

10 <animals> **fledgling,** birdling, nestling; **chick,** chicky, chickling; **pullet,** fryer; **duckling;** gosling; **kitten,** kit, catling; **pup,** puppy, whelp; **cub; calf,** dogie, weaner; **colt,** foal; piglet, pigling, shoat; **lamb,** lambkin; kid, yeanling; fawn; **tadpole,** polliwog; litter, nest

11 <plants> **sprout, seedling,** set; sucker, shoot, slip; **twig,** sprig, scion, sapling

12 <insects> **larva, chrysalis,** aurelia, **cocoon,** pupa; nymph, nympha; wriggler, wiggler; caterpillar, maggot, grub

303 AGE

<time of life>

NOUNS 1 **age,** years; time of life; lifespan, life expectancy

2 **maturity, adulthood, majority,** full growth, mature age, legal age, voting age, driving age, drinking age; age of consent; ripe age, riper years, full age or growth or bloom, **prime, prime of life,** age of responsibility, age or years of discretion; **manhood,** virility, masculinity, maleness, manliness; **womanhood,** womanness, femininity, femaleness, womanliness

3 **seniority, eldership,** deanship, primogeniture

4 **middle age,** the middle years, the wrong side of forty, the dangerous age

5 **old age, oldness, elderliness,** senectitude, advanced age or years; superannuation, age of retirement; **ripe old age,** the golden years, senior citizenship, hoary age, gray or white hairs; **decline of life,** declining years, youth deficiency, the vale of years; sunset or twilight or evening or autumn or winter of one's days; **decrepitude,** infirm old age, infirmity, debility, feebleness; **dotage,** second childhood; senility 921.10, anility; **longevity,** long life, length of years

6 **maturation, development,** growth, ripening, blooming, blossoming, flourishing; **mellowing,** seasoning, tempering; **aging,** senescence

7 **change of life, menopause,** climacteric

8 **geriatrics,** gerontology

VERBS 9 **mature, grow up,** grow, **develop, ripen,** flower, flourish, bloom, blossom; fledge, leave the nest, put up one's hair, put on long pants; **come of age,** come to maturity, attain majority, **reach one's majority,** reach the age of consent, reach manhood or womanhood, put on long trousers or pants, be in the prime of life, cut one's wisdom teeth or eyeteeth <nonformal>, have sown one's wild oats, settle down; **mellow,** season, temper

10 **age, grow old,** get on or along, **get on** or **along in years,** be over the hill <nonformal>, turn gray or white; **decline,** wane, fade, fail, sink, waste away; **dodder,** totter, shake; wither, wrinkle, shrivel, wizen; **live to a ripe old age,** cheat the undertaker <nonformal>; be in one's dotage or second childhood

11 **have had one's day, have seen better days; show one's age,** have one foot in the grave

ADJS 12 **adult, mature, of age,** out of one's teens, big, grown, **grown-up;** old enough to know better; **marriageable,** of marriageable age, nubile

13 **mature, ripe,** ripened, of full or ripe age, **developed,** fully developed, well-developed, **full-grown,** full-fledged, fully fledged, full-blown, in full bloom, in one's prime; **mellow** or mellowed, seasoned, tempered, aged

14 **middle-aged,** mid-life, fortyish, matronly

15 **past one's prime,** senescent, on the shady side <nonformal>, of a certain age, over the hill <nonformal>

16 **aged, elderly, old,** grown old in years, along or up or advanced or

on in years, advanced in life, **at an advanced age, ancient,** geriatric, geronti℮; **venerable,** old as Methuselah *or* as the hills; patriarchal; hoary, hoar, **gray,** white, gray- *or* white-haired, gray- *or* white-bearded, gray with age; wrinkled; wrinkly

17 **aging,** growing old, senescent, **getting on** *or* **along,** getting on *or* along *or* up in years, not as young as one used to be, long in the tooth; **declining,** sinking, waning, fading

18 **decrepit, infirm,** weak, debilitated, feeble, geriatric, timeworn, the worse for wear, fossilized, wracked *or* ravaged with age, run to seed; **doddering,** doddery, doddered, tottering, tottery, rickety, shaky, palsied; on one's last legs, with one foot in the grave; **wizened,** crabbed, **withered,** shriveled; **senile** 921.23, anile

304 ADULT OR OLD PERSON

NOUNS 1 **adult, grownup,** mature man *or* woman, grown man *or* woman; **man, woman;** no chicken *and* no spring chicken <both nonformal>

2 **old man, elder, oldster** <nonformal>; golden-ager, senior citizen, geriatric; old party, **old gentleman,** old gent <nonformal>, old codger <nonformal>, geezer *and* old geezer <both nonformal>; gramps <nonformal>, gaffer, old duffer <nonformal>, old dog *and* old-timer <both nonformal>, dotard, veteran; **patriarch,** graybeard; grandfather; Father Time, Methuselah; sexagenarian, septuagenarian, octogenarian, nonagenarian, centenarian

3 **old woman, old lady,** dowager, granny; old hen *and* bag *and* girl <all nonformal>; old bag *and* old bat *and* old battleax <all nonformal>; **crone,** hag, witch, frump <nonformal>, old wife; grandmother

4 <elderly couples> Darby and Joan, Baucis and Philemon

5 **senior,** Sr, **elder,** older; dean; father, sire; first-born, **eldest,** oldest

VERBS 6 **mature** 303.9; grow old 303.10

ADJS 7 **mature** 303.12; middle-aged 303.14; aged 303.16, older 841.19

305 ORGANIC MATTER

NOUNS 1 **organic matter,** animate *or* living matter, all that lives, living nature, organic nature; **biology** 1066; **flesh, tissue,** fiber, brawn; **flora and fauna,** plant and animal life, animal and vegetable kingdom, biosphere, biota, ecosphere

2 **organism,** organization, lifeform, **living being** *or* **thing,** being, creature, **individual,** genetic individual, physiological individual, morphological individual; virus; aerobic organism, anaerobic organism; heterotrophic organism, autotrophic organism; microbe, microorganism

3 biological classification, taxonomy, kingdom, phylum, etc

4 **cell,** cellule; procaryotic cell, eucaryotic cell; plant cell, animal cell; germ cell, somatic cell; **protoplasm;** germ plasm; cytoplasm; ectoplasm, endoplasm; cellular tissue

5 organelle; plastid; chromoplast, plastosome, chloroplast

6 metaplasm; cell wall, cell plate; structural polysaccharide

7 **nucleus,** cell nucleus; macronucleus, meganucleus; micronucleus

8 chromosome; allosome; heterochromosome, sex chromosome, idiochromosome; X chromosome, accessory chromosome, monosome; Y chromosome

9 **genetic material, gene;** allele; structural gene, regulator gene, operator gene; altered gene; deoxyribonucleic acid *or* **DNA;** DNA double helix; ribonucleic acid *or* **RNA;** messenger RNA, mRNA; transfer RNA, tRNA; ribosomal RNA; genotype, biotype; **hereditary character,** heredity 560.6;

genetic counseling; genetic screening; **recombinant DNA technology,** gene mapping, gene splicing; gene transplantation, gene transfer; **genetic engineering;** designer gene

10 **gamete, germ cell,** reproductive cell; gametophyte; germ plasm, idioplasm

11 **sperm, spermatozoa, seed, semen,** jism *or* gism *and* come *or* cum *and* scum *and* spunk <all nonformal>; seminal *or* spermatic fluid, milt; **sperm cell,** male gamete; pollen; androcyte, spermatid, spermatocyte

12 **ovum, egg, egg cell,** female gamete, oösphere; oöcyte; oögonium; ovicell, oöecium; ovule; donor egg

13 **spore;** microspore; macrospore, megaspore; zygospore; sporangium; sporophyte; sporophore

14 **embryo,** zygote, oösperm, oöspore, blastula; **fetus,** germ, rudiment; **larva,** nymph

15 **egg;** ovule; **roe,** fish eggs, caviar, spawn; **yolk,** yellow, vitellus; white, **egg white,** albumen; eggshell

16 **cell division; mitosis; meiosis**

ADJS 17 **organic,** organismic; organized; **animate, living,** vital; **biological,** biotic; physiological

18 **protoplasmic,** plasmic, plasmatic; **genetic,** genic, hereditary

19 **cellular;** unicellular, multicellular; corpuscular

20 gametic, gamic, sexual; **spermatic,** spermic, **seminal,** spermatozoan, spermatozoic; sporous, sporoid; sporogenous

21 **nuclear;** nucleate; nucleolar, nucleolated; **chromosomal;** chromatinic; haploid, diploid, polyploid

22 **embryonic, germinal,** germinative; larval; fetal; germiparous

23 **egglike,** ovicular, eggy; albuminous, albuminoid; yolked, yolky; oviparous

306 LIFE

NOUNS 1 **life, living, vitality,** being alive, having life, animation, animate existence; breath; liveliness, animal spirits, vivacity, spriteliness; long life, longevity; life expectancy, life-span; viability; lifetime 826.5; immortality 828.3; birth 1; existence 760

2 indwelling spirit; impulse of life

3 **life force, soul,** spirit, force of life, living force, **vital force** *or* energy, animating force *or* power *or* principle, élan vital, vital principle, **vital spark** *or* **flame,** spark of life, divine spark, life principle, vital spirit, vital fluid, anima; **breath, breath of life,** divine breath, life essence, essence of life; blood, **lifeblood,** heartblood, heart's blood; **heart,** heartbeat, beating heart; seat of life; growth force; **life process;** biorhythm, biological clock, life cycle

4 **the living,** the living and breathing; the quick and the dead

5 vivification, vitalization, animation, quickening

6 biosphere, ecosphere; biotype, biocycle

VERBS 7 **live,** be alive *or* animate *or* vital, have life, exist 760.8, breathe, respire, live and breathe, draw breath, draw the breath of life, walk the earth, subsist

8 **come to life,** come into existence *or* being, come into the world, see the light, be incarnated, **be born** *or* begotten *or* conceived; quicken; **revive, come to,** come alive, show signs of life; **awake, awaken;** rise again, live again, rise from the grave, resurge, resuscitate, reanimate, return to life

9 **vivify, vitalize, energize, animate, quicken,** inspirit, imbue *or* endow with life, give life to, put life *or* new life into, breathe life into, bring to life, bring *or* call into existence *or* being; conceive; give birth

10 **keep alive,** keep body and soul together, endure, survive, persist, last, last out, hang on, hang in <nonformal>, be spared, have nine lives; support life; cheat death

ADJS 11 **living, alive,** having life,
live, very much alive, alive and
well, alive and kicking <nonfor-
mal>, conscious, breathing,
animate, animated, **vital,** imbued or endowed with life,
vivified, enlivened, inspirited; in
the flesh, among the living, in the
land of the living, on this side of
the grave, above-ground; existent
760.13; long-lived; capable of survival, viable

12 **life-giving,** animating, quickening, vivifying

307 DEATH

NOUNS 1 **death, dying,** somatic
death, clinical death, biological
death, abiosis, **decease, demise;**
brain death; perishing, release,
passing away, passing, passing
over, leaving life, departure, parting, going, exit, ending, **end** 819,
end of life, cessation of life, end
of the road or line <nonformal>;
loss of life, expiration, **dissolution, extinction,** annihilation,
extinguishment, quietus; doom,
final summons, sentence of
death, death knell, knell; **sleep,
rest,** eternal rest or sleep, last
sleep, last rest; **grave** 309.16; reward, debt of nature, last debt;
last roundup, curtains <nonfor-
mal>; jaws of death, hand or
finger of death, shadow or shades
of death; rigor mortis; near-death
experience or NDE

2 making an end, going off or
away

3 <personifications and symbols>
Death, Grim Reaper, Reaper;
pale horse, pale rider; angel of
death, death's bright angel; scythe
or sickle of Death; **skull,** death's-
head, grinning skull, crossbones,
skull and crossbones; *memento
mori* <L>; white cross

4 river of death, Styx, Stygian
shore, Acheron; Jordan; Heaven
681; Hell 682

5 early death, early grave, **untimely end,** premature death;
sudden death; deathblow

6 **violent death,** killing 308; suf-

focation, smothering, smotheration <nonformal>;
asphyxiation; choking, choke,
strangulation, strangling; drowning, watery grave; starvation

7 **natural death;** easy or quiet or
peaceful death or end, eutha-
nasia, blessed or welcome release

8 dying day, deathday; final or fatal
hour, dying hour, running-out of
the sands

9 moribundity, extremity, last or final extremity; **deathbed;** deathwatch; death struggle, agony, last
agony, death agony, death throes;
last breath or gasp, dying breath;
death rattle

10 **swan song,** death song

11 **bereavement** 473.1

12 **deathliness,** deadliness; **weirdness, eeriness, uncanniness,**
unearthliness; ghostliness; **ghastliness, grisliness, gruesomeness,** macabreness; paleness,
haggardness, wanness, pallor; cadaverousness; mask of death

13 **death rate,** death toll; **mortality;** transience 827; mutability
853.1

14 **obituary,** obit <nonformal>,
necrology; casualty list; martyrology; death toll, body count

15 terminal case; **dying**

16 **corpse,** dead body, dead man or
woman, dead person, **cadaver,
carcass, body;** *corpus delicti*
<L>; **stiff** <nonformal>; **the
dead,** the defunct, **the deceased,**
the departed, the loved one; **dece-
dent,** late lamented; **remains,**
mortal or organic remains, bones,
skeleton, relics, reliquiae; dust,
ashes, earth, clay; **carrion,** food
for worms; **mummy,** mummification; embalmed corpse

17 **dead,** the majority, the great
majority; one's fathers, one's
ancestors

18 **autopsy, postmortem, inquest,**
postmortem examination, ne-
cropsy, medical examiner,
coroner

VERBS 19 **die, decease, succumb,
expire, perish,** be taken by
death, up and die <nonformal>,

cease to be or live, part, depart, quit this world, make one's exit, go, go the way of all flesh, go out, pass, pass on or over, **pass away, meet one's death** or **end** or **fate,** end one's life or days, depart this life, put off mortality, **lose one's life,** fall, be lost, relinquish or surrender one's life, resign one's life, **give up the ghost,** take one's last breath, breathe one's last, fall asleep, close one's eyes, take one's last sleep, pay the debt of or to nature, return to dust or the earth

20 <nonformal terms> **croak,** go west, kick the bucket, pop off, conk out, go home feet first, kick off, shove off, bow out, pass out, push up daisies, belly up, go belly up, bite the dust, take the last count; check out, check in, cash in, hand or cash in one's checks or chips; turn up one's toes; buy the farm or the ranch

21 **meet one's Maker,** go to glory, go to kingdom come <nonformal>, go to the happy hunting grounds, go to one's rest or reward, go home, go home feet first <nonformal>, **be gathered to one's fathers,** join one's ancestors, join the angels, go to Abraham's bosom, pass over Jordan, cross the Stygian ferry; awake to life immortal

22 **drop dead, fall dead,** fall down dead; come to an untimely end; predecease

23 die in harness, die with one's boots on, die fighting, die like a man

24 die a natural death; die a violent death, be killed; **starve,** famish; smother, **suffocate;** asphyxiate; choke, strangle; **drown,** go to a watery grave, go to Davy Jones's locker <nonformal>; catch one's death of cold

25 **lay down** or **give one's life for one's country, die for one's country,** make the supreme sacrifice

26 die out, become extinct

27 be dead, be no more, sleep with the Lord, sleep with one's ancestors; lie in the grave, lie in Abraham's bosom <nonformal>

28 **bereave;** leave, leave behind; orphan, widow

ADJS 29 **deathly, deathlike,** deadly; **weird, eerie, uncanny,** unearthly; ghostly, ghostlike; **ghastly, grisly, gruesome, macabre;** pale, deathly pale, livid, haggard; **cadaverous,** corpselike

30 **dead, lifeless,** breathless, without life, without vital functions; **deceased, demised, defunct,** croaked <nonformal>, departed, departed this life, **gone, passed on,** gone the way of all flesh, gone west <nonformal>, dead and gone, done for <nonformal>, dead and done for <nonformal>, released, fallen, bereft of life; **at rest,** out of one's misery; **asleep,** sleeping, reposing; **called home,** gone to a better world, gone to glory, gone to kingdom come <nonformal>, with the saints, sainted, numbered with the dead; in the grave, six feet under and pushing up daisies <both nonformal>; food for worms; stillborn; late, late lamented

31 **stone-dead;** dead as a doornail <nonformal>; cold, stone-cold, stiff <nonformal>

32 **drowned,** in a watery grave, in Davy Jones's locker

33 **dying, terminal,** expiring, going, slipping away, sinking, sinking fast, given up for dead, not long for this world, hopeless, **moribund,** near death, near one's end, at the end of one's rope <nonformal>, done for <nonformal>, at the point of death, **at death's door,** in extremis <L>, in the jaws of death, facing death; **on one's last legs** <nonformal>, with one foot in the grave, tottering on the brink of the grave; on one's deathbed; at the last gasp; nonviable, incapable of life

34 **mortal, perishable,** subject to death, ephemeral, transient 827.7, mutable 853.6

35 **bereaved,** bereft, deprived; widowed; orphan, **orphaned,**
parentless, fatherless, motherless
36 **postmortem,** post-obit, post-
obituary, **posthumous**
ADVS 37 **deathly, deadly;** to the
death

308 KILLING

NOUNS 1 **killing, slaying, slaughter, dispatch, extermination,
destruction,** taking of life, death-
dealing; **bloodshed,** bloodletting,
blood, gore; mercy killing, eutha-
nasia; ritual murder *or* killing,
immolation, sacrifice; *auto-da-fé*
<Sp, literally, act of faith>, mar-
tyrdom, martyrization; lynching;
defenestration; braining; shooting; poisoning; execution 604.7;
mass killing, biocide, ecocide,
genocide; Holocaust; mass murder

2 **homicide, manslaughter; negligent homicide; murder,**
bloody murder <nonformal>; serial killing; hit *and* bump-off *and*
bumping-off <all nonformal>,
gangland-style execution; kiss of
death; foul play; **assassination;**
removal, elimination; liquidation,
purge, purging; justifiable homicide

3 **butchery,** butchering, **slaughter,** shambles, slaughtering,
hecatomb, holocaust

4 **carnage, massacre, bloodbath,
decimation; mass murder, mass
destruction,** mass extermination, wholesale murder, pogrom,
ethnic cleansing, genocide, **the
Holocaust,** the final solution

5 **suicide,** autocide, self-
destruction, death by one's own
hand, self-immolation, self-
sacrifice; **disembowelment,** ritual suicide, *hara-kiri, seppuku*
<both Jap>, suttee, sutteeism;
mass suicide

6 **suffocation,** smothering,
smotheration <nonformal>, **asphyxiation,** asphyxia; **strangulation,** strangling, throttling, stifling, garrote, garroting; **choking,**
choke; **drowning**

7 **fatality,** fatal accident, violent
death, **casualty,** disaster, calamity; **DOA** *or* dead-on-arrival

8 **deadliness, lethality,** mortality,
fatality; **virulence, pernicious-
ness,** banefulness

9 **deathblow,** death stroke, final
stroke, fatal *or* mortal *or* lethal
blow, *coup de grâce* <Fr>

10 **killer, slayer, slaughterer,
butcher; homicide, murderer,**
man-killer, bloodletter, Cain; **as-
sassin; cutthroat,** thug, desperado, bravo, gorilla <nonformal>,
gunman; professional killer, hired
killer, hit man *or* gun *or* trigger
man *or* torpedo *or* gunsel <all
nonformal>; **hatchet man;** poi-
soner; strangler, garroter; cannibal, maneater, anthropophagus;
headhunter; mercy killer; thrill
killer, homicidal maniac; serial
killer; executioner 604.8; exterminator, eradicator; death
squad; poison, pesticide
1000.3

11 <place of slaughter> field of
blood *or* bloodshed; **slaughter-
house,** abattoir; stockyard; gas
chamber, concentration camp,
death camp, killing fields; Ausch-
witz, Belsen, etc

VERBS 12 **kill, slay, put to death,**
deprive of life, **take life,** take the
life of, **do away with, put out of
the way,** put to sleep, end, **put an
end to,** end the life of, **dispatch,**
do for, finish, finish off, kill off,
**dispose of, exterminate, de-
stroy,** annihilate; **liquidate,**
purge; carry off *or* away, remove
from life; put down, put away, put
one out of one's misery; send to
kingdom come <nonformal>,
send to one's last account; **martyr,** martyrize; immolate, sacrifice; lynch; cut off, cut down, nip
in the bud; poison; chloroform;
starve; **execute**

13 <nonformal terms> **waste, zap,**
nuke, rub out, croak, snuff, bump
off, knock off, bushwhack, lay
out, polish off, blow away, erase,
wipe out, blast, do in, off, hit, ice,
gun down, pick off, take care of,

take out, take for a ride, give the business *or* works, get

14 shed blood, spill blood, let blood, bloody one's hands with, have blood on one's hands

15 murder, commit murder; **assassinate;** remove, **purge, liquidate,** eliminate, get rid of

16 slaughter, butcher, massacre, decimate, commit carnage, depopulate; commit mass murder *or* destruction, murder wholesale, commit genocide

17 strike dead, fell, bring down, lay low; drop, drop *or* stop in one's tracks; **shoot,** shoot down, pistol, shotgun, machinegun, gun down, riddle, shoot to death; cut down, cut to pieces *or* ribbons, **put to the sword,** stab to death, cut *or* slash the throat; **deal a deathblow,** give the *coup de grâce* <Fr>, silence; **brain,** blow *or* knock *or* dash one's brains out, poleax; **stone,** stone to death; defenestrate; blow up, blow to bits *or* pieces *or* kingdom come, frag; disintegrate, vaporize; burn to death, incinerate, burn at the stake

18 strangle, garrote, **throttle, choke; suffocate, stifle, smother, asphyxiate,** stop the breath; **drown**

19 condemn to death, sign one's death warrant, finger <nonformal>; give the kiss of death to

20 be killed, get killed, die a violent death, **come to a violent end,** meet with foul play

21 commit suicide, take one's own life, kill oneself, die by one's own hand, do away with oneself, put an end to oneself; blow one's brains out, take an overdose <of a drug>, overdose *or* OD <nonformal>; commit hara-kiri *or* seppuku; sign one's own death warrant, doom oneself

ADJS **22 deadly, deathly, killing, destructive,** death-dealing, death-bringing; savage, brutal; internecine; **fatal, mortal, lethal, malignant,** malign,

virulent, pernicious, baneful; **life-threatening, terminal**

23 murderous, slaughterous; cutthroat; **homicidal,** man-killing, death-dealing; biocidal, genocidal; suicidal, self-destructive; **bloodthirsty,** bloody-minded; **bloody, gory,** sanguinary

309 INTERMENT

NOUNS **1 interment, burial,** burying, inhumation, sepulture, **entombment;** inurnment, urn burial; reburial; disposal of the dead; burial *or* funeral customs

2 cremation, incineration, burning

3 embalmment, embalming; mummification

4 last offices, last honors, **last rites,** funeral rites, funeral service, burial service, exequies, **obsequies;** Office of the Dead, requiem, requiem mass; **extreme unction;** funeral oration *or* sermon, eulogy; **wake,** deathwatch

5 funeral, burial, burying; funeral procession, cortege; dead march, muffled drum, taps; dirge; burial at sea

6 knell, passing bell, tolling, tolling of the knell

7 mourner, griever, lamenter, keener; professional mourner; **pallbearer,** bearer

8 undertaker, mortician, funeral director; embalmer; gravedigger; sexton

9 mortuary, morgue, charnel house; ossuary *or* ossuarium; **funeral home *or* parlor; crematorium,** crematory, cinerarium; pyre, funeral pile

10 hearse, funeral car *or* coach; catafalque

11 coffin, casket; wooden kimono *or* overcoat <nonformal>; **sarcophagus;** mummy case

12 urn, cinerary urn, funerary *or* funeral urn *or* vessel, bone pot, ossuary *or* ossuarium

13 bier, litter

14 graveclothes, shroud, winding sheet, cerecloth, cerements; pall

15 graveyard, cemetery, burial

ground or place, burying place *or ground,* necropolis, **memorial park,** city of the dead; **churchyard,** God's acre; **potter's field;** Golgotha, Calvary

16 **tomb, sepulcher; grave,** gravesite, burial, pit, deep six <nonformal>; resting place; last home, house of death; **crypt, vault,** burial chamber; ossuary *or* ossuarium; charnel house, bone house; **mausoleum; catacombs; shrine,** reliquary, monstrance; cenotaph; pyramid, mummy chamber; burial mound, tumulus, barrow, cromlech, dolmen

17 **monument,** gravestone 549.12

18 **epitaph,** inscription, tombstone marking

VERBS 19 **inter,** inhume, **bury,** sepulture, **lay to rest, consign to the grave,** lay in the grave *or* earth, lay under the sod, put six feet under <nonformal>; tomb, **entomb,** ensepulcher, hearse; enshrine; inurn; hold *or* conduct a funeral

20 **cremate, incinerate, burn,** reduce to ashes

21 **lay out; embalm;** mummify; lie in state

ADJS 22 **funereal,** funeral, funerary, funebrous; mortuary, exequial, obsequial; graveside; sepulchral, tomblike; cinerary; necrological, obituary, epitaphic; **dismal** 112.24; **mournful** 112.26; dirgelike

ADVS 23 beneath the sod, underground, six feet under <nonformal>; at rest, resting in peace

310 PLANTS

NOUNS 1 **plants, vegetation; flora, plant life,** vegetable life; **vegetable kingdom,** plant kingdom; herbage, verdure, greenery; botany 1,5,6,7

2 **growth,** stand, crop; plantation, planting; **clump,** tuft, tussock, hassock

3 **plant; vegetable; weed;** seedling; cutting; gymnosperm; angiosperm; monocotyledon *or* monocot *or* monocotyl;

dicotyledon *or* dicot *or* dicotyl; thallophyte, fungus; gametophyte, sporophyte; ephemeral, annual, biennial, triennial, perennial; evergreen, deciduous plant; hydrophyte

4 <varieties> **legume,** vetch, bean, pea, lentil; **herb;** succulent; **vine,** creeper, ivy, climber, liana; **fern,** bracken; **moss; wort,** liverwort; **algae; seaweed,** kelp, sea moss, sargasso *or* sargassum, sea wrack; **fungus,** mold, rust, puffball, mushroom; lichen; parasite, saprophyte, autophyte

5 grass, gramineous or graminaceous plant, pasture or forage grass, lawn grass, ornamental grass

6 **turf, sod, sward,** greensward; divot

7 **green, lawn;** artificial turf, Astroturf <trademark>; grounds; **common, park, village green;** golf course *or* links, fairway; bowling green, putting green; grass court

8 **grassland,** grass; parkland; **meadow,** meadow land, swale, lea; bottomland; **pasture,** pastureland, pasturage; **range,** grazing land; **prairie, savanna, steppe,** steppeland, **pampas,** pampa, campo, llano, **veld**

9 **shrubbery; shrub, bush;** scrub, bramble, brier, brier bush; topiary

10 **tree,** timber; shade tree, fruit tree, timber tree; softwood tree, hardwood tree; sapling, seedling; conifer, evergreen; pollard, pollarded tree

11 **woodland, wood, woods, timberland; timber,** stand of timber, **forest,** forest land, forest cover, forest preserve, state *or* national forest; forestry, dendrology, silviculture; afforestation, reforestation; **bush,** scrub; scrubland; pine barrens, palmetto barrens; **park,** parkland; arboretum

12 **grove, woodlet; orchard;** wood lot; coppice, copse

13 **thicket,** thicket, **copse, coppice,** copsewood; boscage; co-

vert; **brake,** canebrake; chaparral

14 brush, scrub, bush, **brushwood,** shrubwood, scrubwood

15 undergrowth, underwood, underbrush, copsewood, undershrubs, boscage; ground cover

16 foliage, leafage, leafiness, umbrage, foliation

17 leaf, frond; leaflet; **blade,** spear, spire, pile, flag; **needle,** pine needle; floral leaf, **petal,** sepal; bract, bractlet, bracteole, spathe, involucre, involucrum; cotyledon, seed leaf; stipule, stipula

18 branch, fork, **limb, bough;** deadwood; **twig, sprig,** switch; spray; **shoot,** offshoot, spear, frond; scion; **sprout,** sprit, slip, burgeon, thallus; sucker; **runner,** stolon, flagellum; **tendril;** ramification

19 stem, stalk, stock, axis; **trunk,** bole; spear, spire; straw; reed; cane; culm; pedicel, peduncle; leafstalk, petiole

20 root, radix, radicle; rootlet; **taproot,** tap; **rhizome,** rootstock; **tuber,** tubercle; **bulb,** bulbil, corm

21 bud, burgeon; gemmule, gemmula; leaf bud, flower bud

22 flower, posy, blossom, bloom; floweret, floret; **wildflower; gardening,** horticulture, floriculture

23 bouquet, nosegay, posy, flower arrangement; **boutonniere; corsage; spray; wreath;** festoon; **garland,** lei

24 flowering, florescence, efflorescence, **blossoming, blooming;** inflorescence; **blossom, bloom;** unfolding, unfoldment; anthesis

25 <types of inflorescence> raceme, corymb, umbel, panicle, spadix; head, capitulum; spike, spikelet; catkin; cone, pine cone

26 <flower parts> petal, perianth; calyx, epicalyx; corolla, corolla tube, corona; anther, stamen; pistil, gynoecium; style; stigma, carpel; receptacle, torus

27 ear, spike; auricle; ear of corn; **cob,** corncob

28 seed vessel, seedcase, seedbox, pericarp; hull, husk; **capsule, pod,** cod <nonformal>, seed pod; legume, legumen, boll, burr; follicle

29 seed; stone, pit, nut; pip; fruit; **grain, kernel, berry;** flaxseed, linseed; hayseed; bird seed

30 vegetation, growth; germination, pullulation; burgeoning, sprouting; budding, luxuriation

VERBS **31 vegetate, grow;** germinate, pullulate; root, take root; shoot up, upsprout; **burgeon,** put forth, burst forth; **sprout,** shoot; **bud,** gemmate, put forth *or* put out buds; **leaf,** leave, leaf out, put forth leaves; flourish, luxuriate, riot, grow rank *or* lush; overrun

32 flower, be in flower, **blossom, bloom,** be in bloom, effloresce, floreate, burst into bloom

ADJS **33 vegetable,** vegetal, vegetative; **plantlike; herbaceous,** herbal; leguminous; cereal, farinaceous; weedy; fruity, fruitlike; tuberous, bulbous; rootlike, rhizoid, radicular; botanical

34 algal, fucoid; phytoplanktonic, diatomaceous; fungous, fungoid; fungiform

35 floral; flowery; flowered, floreate; **flowering, blossoming, blooming,** florescent, inflorescent, efflorescent, in flower, in bloom, in blossom; **garden,** horticultural, floricultural

36 arboreal, arboreous; **treelike,** arboriform, dendroid, dendriform, dendritic; deciduous, nondeciduous; evergreen; softwood, hardwood; piny; coniferous; citrous; **bosky,** bushy, shrubby, scrubby; bushlike, shrublike, scrublike

37 sylvan, woodland, forest; dendrological, silvicultural; **wooded,** timbered, forested, arboreous; **woody,** bosky, bushy, shrubby, scrubby; braky

38 leafy, bowery; foliated, foliate, foliaged, leaved; **branched,** branchy, branching, ramified, ramate, ramose; twiggy

39 verdant, verdurous, verdured; **mossy,** moss-covered, moss-grown; **grassy,** grasslike, gramineous, graminaceous; turfy, turflike, tufted; meadowy

40 luxuriant, flourishing, **rank, lush,** riotous, exuberant; dense, impenetrable, thick, heavy, gross; overgrown, overrun; **weedy,** unweeded, weed-choked; gone to seed

41 perennial, ephemeral; hardy; **deciduous,** evergreen

311 ANIMALS, INSECTS

NOUNS **1 animal life, animal kingdom, fauna;** animal behavior, biology; the beasts of the field, the fowl of the air, and the fish of the sea; domestic animals, livestock, stock <nonformal>; cattle; wild animals *or* beasts, wildlife, denizens of the forest *or* jungle, furry creatures; predators, beasts of prey; game, big game, small game

2 animal, creature, critter <nonformal>, living being *or* thing, creeping thing, **brute, beast,** varmint <nonformal>, dumb animal

3 <varieties> **vertebrate; invertebrate; biped, quadruped; mammal, primate; marsupial;** canine; **feline; rodent; ungulate; ruminant;** insectivore, herbivore, carnivore, omnivore; cannibal; scavenger; reptile; amphibian; aquatic; vermin, varmint <nonformal>

4 pachyderm; elephant, Jumbo; mammoth, woolly mammoth; mastodon; **rhinoceros,** rhino; **hippopotamus,** hippo

5 <hoofed animals> **deer, buck, doe, fawn; stag,** hart, hind; roe deer, roe, roebuck; **elk,** wapiti; **moose; reindeer,** caribou; **antelope;** gazelle, wildebeest *or* gnu, hartebeest, springbok, reebok, dik-dik, eland *or* Cape elk, koodoo; **camel,** dromedary, ship of the desert; **giraffe,** okapi

6 cattle, kine <old pl>; beef cattle; dairy cattle *or* cows; bovine animal, **bovine,** critter <nonformal>; **cow,** moo-cow *and* bossy <both nonformal>; milk *or* milch cow, milker, milcher, dairy cow; **bull,** bullock, top cow <nonformal>; **steer, ox,** oxen <pl>; **calf, heifer,** yearling, **dogie,** leppy <both W US>; maverick <W US>; hornless cow; zebu, Brahman; yak; musk-ox; **buffalo,** water buffalo, carabao; bison, aurochs, wisent

7 sheep; lamb, lambkin, yeanling; **ewe; ram,** wether; bellwether; mutton

8 goat; he-goat, buck, **billy goat** *and* billy <both nonformal>; she-goat, doe, **nanny goat** *and* nanny <both nonformal>; **kid;** mountain goat

9 swine, pig, hog, porker, **shoat,** piglet; suckling pig; gilt; **boar, sow;** barrow; wild boar, tusker, razorback; warthog

10 horse; horseflesh, hoss <nonformal>, critter <nonformal>; **equine,** mount, **nag** <nonformal>; **steed,** prancer, dobbin; charger, courser, war-horse; **colt,** foal, filly; **mare,** brood mare; **stallion, studhorse, stud,** top horse <nonformal>; gelding, purebred horse, blood horse; wild horse, **pony,** Shetland pony, Shetland, shelty; **bronco,** Indian pony, cayuse, mustang; bucking bronco; cowcutting horse, stock horse, roping horse, cow pony

11 <colored horses> appaloosa, bay, bayard, chestnut, gray, dapple-gray, grizzle, roan, sorrel, dun, buckskin <W US>, pinto, paint, piebald, skewbald, calico pony, painted pony

12 <inferior horse> **nag, plug,** hack, jade, crowbait <nonformal>, scalawag; balky horse, balker, jughead; rackabones, scrag, stack of bones

13 hunter; stalking-horse; **saddle horse,** saddler, **riding horse,** rider, palfrey, **mount;** remount; polo pony; **driving horse,** carriage horse, coach horse; hack, hackney; **draft horse,** dray horse, cart horse, **workhorse,** plow horse; wheelhorse, wheeler, lead, leader; pack horse, sumpter, sumpter horse

14 race horse; show-horse, gaited horse, galloper, trotter, pacer, sidewheeler <nonformal>; stepper, high-stepper, cob, prancer; ambler; racker

15 <race horses> Affirmed, Alydar, Assault, Citation, Dr Fager, Forego, John Henry, Kelso, Man O'War, Nashua, Native Dancer, Northern Dancer, Personal Ensign, Ruffian, Seabiscuit, Seattle Slew, Secretariat, Spectacular Bid, Swaps, Whirlaway

16 ass, donkey, burro, Rocky Mountain canary <W US>; **jackass;** jenny, jenny ass, jennet; **mule,** sumpter mule, sumpter; hinny, jennet

17 dog, canine, pooch and bowwow <both nonformal>; **pup, puppy, whelp;** bitch; toy dog, lap dog; working dog; ratter; watchdog; sheep dog, shepherd dog; Seeing Eye dog, guide dog; sled dog; show dog; kennel, pack of dogs

18 sporting dog, **hunting dog,** hunter, field dog, bird dog, gundog, water dog

19 cur, mongrel, mutt <nonformal>

20 fox, reynard; **wolf,** timber wolf, lobo <W US>, **coyote,** brush wolf, prairie wolf; dingo, jackal, **hyena**

21 cat, feline, pussy and **puss** and pussycat <all nonformal>, tabby, grimalkin; house cat; **kitten, kitty** and kitty-cat <both nonformal>; **tomcat,** tom; mouser; ratter; Cheshire cat; blue cat, Maltese cat; tiger cat, tabby cat; tortoise-shell cat, calico cat; alley cat

22 <wild cats> **big cat, jungle cat; lion,** Leo <nonformal>, simba <Swah>; **tiger; leopard,** panther, jaguar, cheetah; cougar, painter <S US>, puma, mountain lion, catamount or cat-a-mountain; lynx, ocelot; wildcat, bobcat

23 <wild animals> **bear,** bar <nonformal>; guinea pig; hedge-hog, **porcupine**; woodchuck, **groundhog, whistle-pig** <nonformal>; prairie dog; **raccoon,** coon; **opossum,** possum; **weasel; wolverine**; ferret; **skunk,** polecat <nonformal>; **primate, simian; ape; monkey,** chimpanzee, chimp

24 hare, leveret, jackrabbit; **rabbit, bunny** and bunny rabbit <both nonformal>; cottontail; leporide; buck, doe

25 reptile, reptilian; **lizard;** saurian, dinosaur; crocodile, crocodilian, alligator, gator <nonformal>; tortoise, turtle, terrapin

26 serpent, snake, ophidian; **viper,** pit viper; sea snake

27 amphibian, batrachian, croaker; **frog,** tree toad or frog, bullfrog; **toad;** newt, salamander; **tadpole, polliwog**

28 bird, fowl; birdlife, avifauna, feathered friends; baby bird, chick, nestling, fledgling; wildfowl, game bird; waterfowl, water bird, wading bird, diving bird; sea bird; shore bird; migratory bird, migrant, bird of passage; **songbird,** warbler, passerine bird, perching bird; cage bird; **raptor,** bird of prey; **eagle,** eaglet; **hawk, falcon; owl;** peafowl, peahen, **peacock; swan,** cygnet; **pigeon, dove,** squab; stormy or storm petrel

29 poultry, fowl, domestic fowl, barnyard fowl; **chicken,** chick; **cock, rooster,** chanticleer; **hen,** biddy <nonformal>; cockerel, pullet; setting hen, brooder, broody hen; capon; broiler, fryer, spring chicken, roaster, stewing chicken; Bantam, banty <nonformal>; game fowl; guinea fowl, guinea cock, guinea hen; **goose,** gander, gosling; **duck,** drake, duckling; **turkey,** gobbler, turkey gobbler; tom, tom turkey; poult

30 marine animal, denizen of the deep; **whale,** cetacean; **porpoise, dolphin; sea serpent,** sea snake, Loch Ness monster, sea monster, Leviathan <Bible>; **fish,** game fish, tropical fish; **shark,** man-eating shark, man-eater; **salmon,** kipper; **minnow,** fry, fingerling; **sponge; plankton,** zooplankton, nekton, benthon, benthos, zoobenthos; **crustacean,** lobster, **crab,** Dungeness crab, king crab, spider crab, land crab, stone crab, soft-shell crab; crayfish *or* crawfish; **mollusc,** whelk, snail, cockle, mussel, **clam, oyster,** quahog, steamer

31 **insect, bug; beetle;** arthropod; hexapod, myriapod; centipede, chilopod; millipede, diplopod; **mite; arachnid, spider,** tarantula, black widow spider, daddy longlegs *or* harvestman; **scorpion; tick;** larva, maggot, nymph, **caterpillar; insect; fly**

32 **ant,** pismire, pissant *and* antymire <both nonformal>; carpenter ant, army ant; slave ant, slave-making ant; **termite,** white ant; queen, worker, soldier

33 **bee,** honeybee, bumblebee; queen bee, worker, drone; **wasp; hornet,** yellow jacket

34 **locust; grasshopper; cricket;** cicada, seventeen-year locust

35 **vermin;** parasite; **louse,** head louse, body louse, cootie <nonformal>; crab; weevil; nit; **flea,** sand flea, chigoe, chigger, red bug, mite, harvest mite; **roach, cockroach**

36 bloodsucker, parasite; **leech; tick,** wood tick, deer tick; **mosquito,** culex; bedbug

37 **worm;** earthworm, angleworm, fishworm, night crawler; measuring worm, inchworm; tapeworm, helminth

ADJS 38 **animal,** animal-like, zoic, zooidal; zoologic, zoological; **brutish, brutal,** brute, brutelike; **bestial, beastly,** beastlike; **wild,** feral; subhuman, soulless; dumb; instinctual *or* instinctive, mindless, nonrational; half-animal, half-human, anthropomorphic

39 **vertebrate,** chordate, mammalian; viviparous; marsupial, cetacean

40 **canine,** doggish, doglike; vulpine, foxy, foxlike; lupine, wolfish, wolflike

41 **feline,** cattish, catty, catlike; kittenish; leonine, lionlike; tigerlike

42 ursine, bearish, bearlike

43 **rodent;** verminous; mousy, mouselike; ratty, ratlike

44 **ungulate,** hoofed, hooved; **equine,** horselike; **equestrian;** mulish; bovid, ruminant; **bovine,** cowlike, cowish; bull-like, bullish, taurine; cervine, deerlike; caprine, caprid, hircine, goatish, goatlike; ovine, sheepish, sheeplike; porcine, swinish, piggish, hoggish

45 elephantlike, elephantine, pachydermous

46 **reptile,** reptilian, **reptilelike;** reptiliform; reptant, creeping, crawling, slithering; **lizardlike,** saurian; crocodilian; **serpentine,** serpentile, **serpentlike;** snakish, **snaky, snakelike;** ophidian; viperish, viperous, viperine, viperlike; amphibian, batrachian

47 **birdlike;** avian; gallinaceous, rasorial; oscine, passerine, perching; psittacine; aquiline, hawklike; anserine, anserous; nesting, nest-building; nidicolous, altricial

48 **fishlike,** fishy; piscine, pisciform; piscatorial, piscatory; eellike; selachian, sharklike, sharkish

49 **invertebrate,** invertebral; protozoan, protozoic; crustaceous, crustacean; molluscan, molluscoid

50 **insectile, insectlike,** buggy; verminous; lepidopterous, lepidopteran; weevily

51 **wormlike,** vermicular, vermiform; wormy

52 planktonic, nektonic, benthonic, zooplanktonic, zoobenthoic

312 HUMANKIND

NOUNS 1 **humankind, mankind, man, human race,** race of man, human family, the family of man, **humanity,** human beings, mortals, mortality, flesh, mortal flesh, clay; **Homo sapiens,** hominids;

race, strain, stock; **culture** 373.3; ethnic group; ethnicity; **society, ethnic group;** community, **the people, the populace; nationality**

2 <races of humankind> Caucasoid *or* Caucasian *or* white race; Nordic subrace, Alpine subrace, Mediterranean subrace; Archaic Caucasoid *or* archaic white *or* Australoid race; Polynesian race; Negroid *or* black race

3 Caucasian, white man *or* woman, white person, the Man *and* whitey *and* honky <all nonformal>; Australian aborigine, blackfellow <Australia>; Negro, black man *or* woman, black, colored person, person of color; African-American; Indian, American Indian, Amerind, red man *or* woman; injun *and* redskin <both nonformal>; Mongolian, yellow man *or* woman, Oriental

4 **the people** 606, the populace, the population, the public

5 **person, human, human being, man, woman, child,** member of the human race *or* family; ethnic; **mortal,** life, **soul,** living soul; **being,** creature, clay, ordinary clay; **individual;** personage, **personality, personhood,** individuality; **body;** earthling, groundling, tellurian; **ordinary person;** head, hand, nose; fellow <nonformal> 76.5; gal <nonformal> 77.6

6 **human nature, humanity;** frail *or* fallen humanity, Adam, the generation of Adam, Adam's seed

7 **God's image, lord of creation;** homo faber, symbol-using animal

8 **humanness, humanity,** mortality; **human nature; frailty,** human frailty, weakness, **human weakness,** weakness of the flesh, the weaknesses human flesh is heir to; human equation

9 humanization, humanizing; **anthropomorphism,** pathetic fallacy, anthropomorphology

10 **anthropology,** science of man; anthropogeny, anthropography, anthropogeography, human geography, demography, human ecology, anthropometry, ethnology, ethnography; behavioral science, sociology, social anthropology, social psychology, psychology 92; anatomy; **anthropologist,** ethnologist, ethnographer; sociologist; demographics, population study, population statistics; demographer

11 **humanism;** naturalistic humanism, scientific humanism, secular humanism; religious humanism; Christian humanism, integral humanism; new humanism; anthroposophy

VERBS 12 **humanize,** anthropomorphize, make human, civilize

ADJS 13 **human;** hominal; **frail, weak,** fleshly, finite, **mortal; only human;** earthborn, of the earth, earthy, tellurian; humanistic; man-centered, homocentric, anthropocentric; anthropological, ethnographic, ethnological; demographic

14 **manlike, anthropoid,** humanoid, hominid; anthropomorphic, therioanthropic

15 **personal, individual,** private, peculiar, idiosyncratic; person-to-person, one-to-one, one-on-one

16 **public, general, common; communal, societal, social;** civic, civil; **national,** state; international, cosmopolitan, supernational, supranational

ADVS 17 **humanly,** mortally, after the manner of men

313 SEASON
<time of year>

NOUNS 1 **season,** time of year, season of the year, **period,** annual period; dry *or* rainy *or* cold season, monsoon; theatrical *or* opera *or* concert season; **social season,** the season; dead *or* off-season; baseball season, football season, basketball season, etc; seasonality, periodicity 849.2; **seasonableness** 842.1

2 **spring,** springtide, **springtime,** seedtime *or* budtime, Maytime, Eastertide; prime

3 **summer,** summertide, **summer-**

time, good old summertime;
growing season; midsummer;
dog days; the silly season

4 autumn, fall, fall of the year, fall
of the leaf, harvest, harvest time

5 Indian summer, St Martin's
summer, St Luke's summer

6 winter, wintertide, **wintertime;**
midwinter; Christmastime or
Christmastide, Yule or Yuletide

7 equinox, vernal equinox, autumnal equinox; **solstice,**
summer solstice, winter solstice

VERBS **8** summer, winter, overwin-
ter, spend or pass the spring, summer, etc

ADJS **9 seasonal,** in or out of season, in season and out of season,
off-season; early-season, mid-
season, late-season; **spring,**
springlike, vernal; **summer,** summery, summerlike, aestival;
autumn, autumnal;
winter, wintry, hibernal, hiemal,
boreal, arctic 1022.14, winterlike,
snowy, icy; midwinter; equinoctial, solstitial

314 MORNING, NOON

NOUNS **1 morning,** morn, morn-
ingtide, morning time, matins,
waking time, reveille, get-up time
<nonformal>, **forenoon;** ante
meridiem <L> or AM

2 Morning, Aurora, Eos

3 dawn, the dawn of day, dawning, **daybreak, sunrise, sunup**
<nonformal>, cockcrowing, light
1024, first light, daylight, aurora;
break of day, peep of day, **crack
of dawn,** prime, first blush or
flush of the morning, brightening
or first brightening; chanticleer

4 foredawn, twilight, half-light,
glow, dawnlight, first light, crepuscule, aurora; **the small
hours;** alpenglow

5 noon, noonday, noontide, noon-
time, **high noon, midday,**
meridian, meridian <L>, twelve
o'clock, 1200 hours, eight bells

ADJS **6 morning,** matin, matinal,
matutinal, **antemeridian;** au-
roral, dawn, dawning

7 noon, noonday, noonish, **mid-**

day, meridian, twelve-o'clock;
noonlit

ADVS **8 in the morning,** before
noon, mornings <nonformal>; at
sunrise, at dawn, at dawn of day,
at cockcrow, at first light, **at the
crack or break of dawn;** with the
sun, with the lark

9 at noon, at midday, at twelve-
o'clock sharp

315 EVENING, NIGHT

NOUNS **1 afternoon,** post meridiem
<L> or **PM;** this afternoon, this
PM <nonformal>

2 evening, eve, even, evensong
time or hour, **eventide,** vesper;
close of day, gray of the evening,
grayness 39, evening's close,
when day is done; **nightfall, sunset, sundown,** setting sun, going
down of the sun; shank of the afternoon or evening <nonformal>,
the cool of the evening

3 dusk, twilight, crepuscule, crepuscular light, gloam, **gloaming,**
glooming; duskiness, duskish-
ness, brown of dusk, brownness
40, candlelight, candlelighting,
owllight or owl's light

4 night, nighttime, lights-out,
taps, bedtime, sleepy time
<nonformal>, **darkness** 1026,
blackness 38

5 eleventh hour, curfew

6 midnight, dead of night, hush
of night, the witching hour

ADJS **7 afternoon,** postmeridian

8 evening, evensong, vesper, ves-
pertine; **twilight,** crepuscular;
dusk, dusky, duskish

9 nocturnal, night, **nightly,** nighttime; nightlong, all-night; midnight

10 benighted, night-overtaken

ADVS **11 nightly,** nights <nonfor-
mal>, at or by night; **overnight,**
through the night, all through the
night, nightlong, the whole night,
all night

316 RAIN

NOUNS **1 rain, rainfall,** fall, **precipitation,** moisture, wet, rain-
water; **shower, sprinkle,** flurry,

pitter-patter, splatter; streams of rain, sheet of rain; **drizzle**; **mist, misty rain**, Scotch mist; evening mist; raindrop

2 **rainstorm**; **cloudburst**, rainburst, burst of rain, torrent of rain, torrential rain or downpour; waterspout, spout, rainspout, **downpour**, pour, pouring or pelting or teeming rain, **deluge, flood**, heavy rain, driving rain, drenching or soaking rain, drencher, soaker, lovely weather for ducks

3 **thunderstorm**, thundersquall, thundershower

4 **wet weather, raininess**, rainy weather, stormy or dirty weather, cat-and-dog weather <nonformal>, spell of rain, wet; rainy day; **rains**, rainy or wet season, spring rains, **monsoon**

5 **rainmaking**, seeding, cloud seeding, nucleation, artificial nucleation; **rainmaker**, rain doctor, cloud seeder; dry ice, silver iodide

6 Jupiter Pluvius, Zeus; Thor

7 **rain gauge**, pluviometer, pluvioscope, pluviograph; ombrometer, ombrograph; udometer, udomograph; hyetometer, hyetometrograph, hyetograph

8 <science of precipitation> hydrometeorology, hyetology, hyetography; pluviography, pluviometry, ombrology

VERBS 9 **rain, precipitate,** rain down, fall; weep; **shower,** shower down; **sprinkle,** spit and spritz <both nonformal>, spatter, patter, pitter-patter; **drizzle**; **pour,** stream, stream down, pour with rain, **pelt,** pelt down, drum, come down in torrents or sheets or buckets or curtains, **rain cats and dogs** <nonformal>, rain tadpoles or bullfrogs or pitchforks <nonformal>

ADJS 10 **rainy, showery**; pluvious or pluviose or pluvial; **drizzly,** drizzling, drippy; **misty**, torrential, pouring, streaming, pelting, drumming, driving, blinding

11 pluviometric or pluvioscopic or pluviographic, ombrometric or

ombrographic, udometric or udographic, hyetometric, hyetographic, hyetometrographic; hydrometeorological, hyetological

317 AIR, WEATHER

NOUNS 1 **air**; ether; ozone <nonformal>; thin air

2 **atmosphere**; aerosphere, gaseous envelope or environment or medium or blanket; biosphere, ecosphere, noösphere; air mass; atmospheric component, atmospheric gas; atmospheric layer or stratum or belt

3 **weather, climate,** clime; **the elements,** forces of nature; microclimate, macroclimate; fair weather, calm weather, halcyon days, good weather; stormy weather 671.4; rainy weather 316.4; windiness 318.15; heat wave, hot weather 1018.7; cold wave, cold weather 1022.3

4 **weather map**; isobar, isobaric line; isotherm, isothermal line; isometric, isometric line; high, high-pressure area; low, low-pressure area; front, wind-shift line, squall line; cold front, polar front, cold sector; warm front; occluded front, stationary front; air mass; cyclone, anticyclone

5 **meteorology,** weather science, aerology, aerography, air-mass analysis, weatherology, climatology, climatography, microclimatology, forecasting, long-range forecasting; barometry; anemology 318.16; nephology 319.4

6 **meteorologist,** weather scientist, aerologist, aerographer, weatherologist; climatologist, microclimatologist; **weatherman, weather forecaster,** weather prophet; **weather report,** weather forecast; weather bureau; weather ship; weather station; weather-reporting network

7 **weather instrument,** meteorological or aerological instrument; **barometer,** aneroid barometer, glass, weatherglass;

barograph, barometrograph, recording barometer; aneroidograph; vacuometer; hygrometer; weather balloon, radiosonde; weather satellite; hurricane-hunter aircraft; weather vane 318.17

8 ventilation, cross-ventilation, **airing; aeration; air conditioning,** air cooling; oxygenation, oxygenization

9 ventilator; aerator; air conditioner, air filter, air cooler, ventilating or cooling system; blower; heat pump; air passage; fan

VERBS **10 air,** air out, **ventilate,** cross-ventilate, refresh, freshen; **air-condition,** air-cool; **fan; aerate,** airify; oxygenate, oxygenize

ADJS **11 airy, aerial,** aeriform, air-like, **pneumatic,** ethereal; exposed, roomy, light; breezy; open-air, alfresco; **atmospheric,** tropospheric, stratospheric

12 climatal, climatic, climatical, climatographical, **elemental;** meteorological, aerologic, aerological, aerographic, aerographical, climatologic, climatological; macroclimatic, microclimatic, microclimatologic; barometric, barometrical, baric, barographic; isobaric, isometric; high-pressure, low-pressure; cyclonic, anti-cyclonic

318 WIND
<air flow>

NOUNS **1 wind,** current, **air current, draft,** stream, stream of air, flow of air; updraft, uprush; downdraft, downrush; inflow, inrush; crosscurrent, undercurrent; gravity wind, katabatic wind; head wind, tail wind, following wind; wind aloft; jet stream, upper-atmosphere or upper-atmospheric wind

2 current of air, movement of air

3 <wind gods; the wind personified> Aeolus, Vayu; Boreas; Eurus; Zephyr or Zephyrus, Favonius; Notus; Caurus; After

4 puff, puff of air or wind, breath, breath of air, flatus, waft, whiff, stir of air

5 breeze, light or gentle wind or breeze, **zephyr,** gale, air, light air, moderate breeze; fresh or stiff breeze; cool or cooling breeze; sea breeze, onshore breeze, ocean breeze, cat's-paw

6 gust, wind gust, **blast,** blow, flaw, **flurry**

7 hot wind; snow eater, thawer; chinook, **chinook wind;** simoom; sirocco; Santa Ana; volcanic wind

8 wintry wind, winter wind, raw wind, chilling or freezing wind, bone-chilling wind, sharp or piercing wind, cold or icy wind, biting wind, nippy wind, icy blasts; Arctic or boreal or hyperboreal or hyperborean blast; wind chill or wind chill factor

9 north wind, norther, mistral, tramontane; northeaster, **nor'easter;** northwester, **nor'wester;** southeaster, **sou'easter;** southwester, **sou'wester; east wind,** easter, easterly, levanter; **west wind,** wester, westerly; **south wind,** souther

10 prevailing wind; polar easterlies; prevailing westerlies, antitrades; trade wind, trades; doldrums; horse latitudes; roaring forties

11 <naut terms> **head wind, beam wind, tail wind,** following wind, fair or favorable wind, apparent or relative wind, backing wind, veering wind, slant of wind; onshore wind, offshore wind

12 windstorm, big or great or fresh or strong or stiff or high or howling or spanking wind, ill or dirty or ugly wind; storm, storm wind, stormy winds, **tempest,** tempestuous wind; williwaw; **blow,** violent or heavy blow; **squall,** thick squall, black squall, white squall; squall line, wind-shift line, line squall; line storm; equinoctial; **gale,** half a gale, whole gale; tropical cyclone, **hurricane,** typhoon, tropical storm, **blizzard**

1022.8; **thundersquall,** thunder-
gust; wind shear
13 **dust storm, sandstorm,** devil,
sirocco, simoom
14 **whirlwind,** whirlblast, tour-
billion, wind eddy; **cyclone,
tornado, twister,** rotary storm,
typhoon; sandspout, sand column, dust devil; waterspout,
rainspout
15 **windiness,** gustiness; airiness,
breeziness; draftiness
16 **anemology,** anemometry; **wind
direction; wind force, Beaufort
scale,** half-Beaufort scale, International scale; wind rose, barometric wind rose, humidity wind
rose, hyetal *or* rain wind rose,
temperature wind rose, dynamic
wind rose; wind arrow, wind
marker
17 **weather vane, weathercock,**
vane, cock, wind vane, wind indicator, wind cone *or* sleeve *or* sock,
anemoscope; anemometer, wind-
speed indicator, anemograph, an-
emometrograph
18 **blower,** bellows; blowpipe,
blowtube, blowgun
19 **fan;** punkah, electric fan, blower,
window fan, attic fan, exhaust
fan; ventilator; windsail, wind-
scoop, windcatcher
VERBS 20 **blow, waft; puff,** huff,
whiff; whiffle; **breeze;** freshen;
gather, brew, set in, blow up,
pipe up, come up, **blow up a
storm;** bluster, squall; **storm,**
rage, blast, blow a hurricane;
blow over
21 **sigh,** sough, whisper, mutter,
murmur, **sob, moan,** groan,
growl, snarl, **wail, howl,** scream,
screech, shriek, **roar,** whistle,
pipe, sing, sing in the shrouds
ADJS 22 **windy, blowy; breezy,
drafty,** airy, airish; brisk, fresh;
gusty, blasty, puffy; **squally;** blustery, blustering, blusterous;
aeolian, favonian
23 **stormy, tempestuous,** raging,
storming, angry; turbulent; dirty,
foul; cyclonic, tornadic, ty-
phoonish; rainy 316.10; cloudy
319.7

24 **windblown,** blown; **windswept,**
bleak, raw
25 **anemological,** anemographic,
anemometric

319 CLOUD

NOUNS 1 **cloud,** high fog; fleecy
cloud, cottony cloud, billowy
cloud; **cloud bank,** cloud mass,
cloud cover, cloud drift; cloud
band
2 **fog,** pea soup *and* peasouper *and*
pea-soup fog <all nonformal>;
London fog; fog-bank; **smog,**
smaze; frost smoke; mist, drizzling mist; haze, gauze, film;
vapor 1065
3 **cloudiness, haziness, mistiness, fogginess,** nebulosity,
nubilation, nimbosity, **overcast,**
heavy sky, dirty sky, lowering *or*
louring sky
4 nephology, nephelognosy; neph-
ologist
5 nephelometer, nepheloscope
VERBS 6 **cloud,** becloud, cloud
over, cloud up, **overcast,** overshadow, shadow, shade, **darken**
1026.9, darken over, nubilate, ob-
nubilate, obscure; **smoke,** over-
smoke; **fog,** befog; fog in; smog;
mist, mist over, mist up; **haze**
ADJS 7 **cloudy,** nebulous, nubilous;
clouded, overclouded, **overcast;**
dirty, heavy, lowering *or* louring;
dark 1026.13; **gloomy** 1026.14;
cloud-flecked; cirrous; cumulous,
cumuliform, stratous, stratiform;
thunderheaded, stormy, squally
8 **cloud-covered,** cloud-laden,
cloud-curtained, cloud-decked,
cloud-hidden, cloud-girt, cloud-
flecked, **cloud-capped,** cloud-
topped
9 **foggy,** soupy *or* pea-soupy
<nonformal>, nubilous; fog-
bound, fogged-in; smoggy; hazy,
misty; so thick you can cut it with
a knife
10 nephological

320 BUBBLE

NOUNS 1 **bubble, globule;** vesicle,
bulla, **blister,** blood blister, fever
blister; air bubble, soap bubble

2 **foam, froth; spume,** sea foam, scud; **spray, surf,** breakers, white water, spoondrift *or* **spindrift;** **suds, lather,** soap-suds; beer-suds, head; **scum;** head, collar; puff, mousse, soufflé, meringue

3 **bubbling,** bubbliness, **effervescence, sparkle,** spumescence, frothiness, frothing, foaming; **fizz,** fizzle, carbonation; ebullience *or* ebulliency; **ebullition,** boiling; **fermentation,** ferment

VERBS 4 **bubble,** bubble up, burble; **effervesce, fizz, fizzle;** hiss, **sparkle; ferment,** work; **foam, froth,** froth up; have a head, foam over; **boil,** seethe, simmer; gurgle; bubble over, **boil over**

5 **foam, froth,** spume, cream; **lather,** suds, sud; scum; **aerate,** whip, beat, whisk

ADJS 6 **bubbly, bubbling; effervescent,** spumescent, **fizzy, sparkling;** carbonated; ebullient; puffed, soufflé *or* souffléed, beaten, whipped, chiffon; **blistered,** blistery, vesicated; blistering, vesicant

7 **foamy,** foam-flecked, **frothy,** spumy, spumose; yeasty; **sudsy, lathery,** soapy, soapsudsy; heady, with a head *or* collar on

321 BEHAVIOR

NOUNS 1 **behavior, conduct, deportment, comportment, manner, manners, demeanor, mien, carriage, bearing,** poise, posture, guise, **air,** presence; tone, style, lifestyle; way of life, modus vivendi; **way, way of acting, ways; trait behavior,** behavior trait; methods, **method, methodology; practice,** praxis; procedure; **actions,** acts, goings-on, doings, what one is up to, movements, moves, tactics; action, doing 328.1; activity 330; objective *or* observable behavior; motions, gestures; pose, affectation 500; pattern, behavior pattern; culture pattern, behavioral norm, folkway, **custom** 373; behavioral science, social science

2 **good behavior,** sanctioned be-

havior; good citizenship; good manners, correct deportment, **etiquette** 580.3; **courtesy** 504; social behavior, sociability 582; **misbehavior** 322; **discourtesy** 505

3 **behaviorism,** behavioral science, behavioristic psychology, Watsonian psychology, Skinnerian psychology; behavior modification, ethology, animal behavior, human behavior, social behavior

VERBS 4 **behave, act, do,** go on; **behave oneself, conduct oneself,** manage oneself, **handle oneself, comport oneself, deport oneself,** demean oneself, **bear oneself, carry oneself;** acquit oneself; move, swing into action; **misbehave** 322.4

5 **behave oneself, behave,** act well, clean up one's act <nonformal>, act one's age, **be good, do right,** do what is right, do the right *or* proper thing, keep out of mischief, play the game *and* mind one's P's and Q's <both nonformal>, be on one's good *or* best behavior, play one's cards right

6 **treat, use, do by,** deal by, **act *or* behave toward,** conduct oneself toward, act with regard to; **deal with,** cope with, **handle;** respond to

ADJS 7 **behavioral;** behaviorist, behavioristic; ethological; **behaved, mannered,** demeanored

322 MISBEHAVIOR

NOUNS 1 **misbehavior, misconduct;** unsanctioned behavior; **naughtiness,** badness; impropriety; venial sin; **disorderly conduct,** disorder, disorderliness, disruptiveness, disruption, **rowdiness,** rowdyism, riotousness, ruffianism, hooliganism, hoodlumism, vandalism, trashing; roughhouse, horseplay; discourtesy 505; vice 654; misfeasance, malfeasance, misdoing, delinquency, **wrongdoing** 655

2 **mischief, mischievousness; devilment, deviltry;** roguish-

ness, roguery, scampishness; **waggery,** waggishness; **impishness,** devilishness, puckishness, elfishness; **prankishness;** sportiveness, playfulness; high spirits, youthful spirits; foolishness 922

3 mischief-maker, mischief, **rogue, devil,** knave, **rascal,** rapscallion, scapegrace, **scamp; wag** 489.12; buffoon 707.10; joker, jokester, practical joker, prankster, life of the party, **cutup** <nonformal>; **rowdy,** ruffian, hoodlum, hood <nonformal>; hooligan; **imp, elf, puck,** pixie, **minx,** bad boy, little devil, little rascal, little monkey, *enfant terrible* <Fr>

VERBS **4 misbehave, misbehave oneself, misconduct oneself,** behave ill; get into mischief; **act up** *and* make waves *and* **carry on** *and* carry on something scandalous <all nonformal>, sow one's wild oats; **cut up** <nonformal>, horse around <nonformal>, roughhouse *and* cut up rough <both nonformal>

ADJS **5 misbehaving, unbehaving; naughty, bad;** out-of-order *and* off-base *and* out-of-line <all nonformal>; **disorderly,** disruptive, **rowdy,** rowdyish, **ruffianly**

6 mischievous, mischief-loving, full of mischief, full of the devil; **roguish,** scapegrace, arch, knavish; **devilish; impish, puckish, elfish,** elvish; **waggish, prankish,** pranky, pranksome; **playful,** sportive, high-spirited; foolish 922.8, 9

ADVS **7 mischievously, roguishly,** knavishly; impishly, puckishly, elfishly; waggishly; prankishly, playfully, sportively

323 WILL

NOUNS **1 will, volition; choice,** determination, **decision** 371.1; **wish, mind, fancy,** discretion, pleasure, **inclination, disposition,** liking, **desire** 100; half a mind, idle wish, velleity; **appetite, passion, lust, sexual desire** 75.5; animus, **objective, inten-**

tion 380; **command** 420; **free choice,** one's own will *or* discretion *or* initiative, **free will** 430.6; will power, **resolution** 359

VERBS **2 will, wish,** see *or* think fit, think proper, **choose to, have a mind to;** have half a mind *or* notion to; **choose,** determine, **decide** 371.14, 16; **resolve** 359.7; command, decree; **desire** 100.14, 18

3 have one's will, **have** *or* **get one's way, get one's wish, have one's druthers** <nonformal>, **write one's own ticket,** have it all one's way, do *or* go as one pleases, please oneself; take the bit in one's teeth, take charge of one's destiny; stand on one's rights; take the law into one's own hands; have the last word, impose one's will

ADJS **4 volitional, volitive; willing, voluntary**

ADVS **5 at will,** at choice, at pleasure, **at one's pleasure,** at one's own sweet will, **at one's discretion;** ad lib; as one wishes, as it pleases *or* suits oneself, **in one's own way,** in one's own sweet way *or* time <nonformal>, **as one thinks best;** of one's own free will, of one's own accord, on one's own; without coercion, unforced

324 WILLINGNESS

NOUNS **1 willingness, gameness** <nonformal>, readiness; **unreluctance;** agreeableness, **agreeability; acquiescence, consent** 441; **compliance,** cooperativeness; receptivity, receptiveness, responsiveness; amenability, tractability, docility, pliancy, pliability, malleability; **eagerness,** keenness, promptness, forwardness, alacrity, zeal, zealousness, ardor, enthusiasm; goodwill, cheerful consent; **willing heart** *or* **mind** *or* **humor, favorable disposition,** receptive mood, willing ear

2 voluntariness, volunteering; **gratuitousness; spontaneity,** spontaneousness, unforcedness;

self-determination, autonomy, independence, free will 430.5-7; **volunteerism,** voluntarism; volunteer

VERBS **3 be willing, be game** <nonformal>, be ready; take the trouble, find it in one's heart, have a willing heart; **incline, lean;** look kindly upon; be open to, bring oneself, **agree,** be agreeable to; **acquiesce, consent** 441.2; not hesitate to, not care *or* mind if one does <nonformal>; **play** *or* **go along** <nonformal>, do one's part *or* bit; be eager, be keen, be dying to, fall all over oneself, be spoiling for, be champing at the bit; be Johnny on the spot, step into the breach; **enter with a will,** lean *or* bend over backward, go the extra mile, plunge into; **cooperate,** collaborate 450.3; lend *or* give *or* turn a willing ear

4 volunteer, do voluntarily, **do of one's own accord,** do of one's own volition, **do of one's own free will** *or* **choice;** do independently

ADJS **5 willing, willinghearted, ready, game** <nonformal>; **disposed, inclined, minded, willed; well-disposed,** well-inclined, favorably inclined *or* disposed; predisposed; **favorable, agreeable, cooperative; compliant, acquiescent** 332.13, **consenting** 441.4; **eager;** keen, prompt, quick, ready and willing, zealous, ardent, enthusiastic; in the mood *or* vein *or* humor, in a good mood; receptive, responsive; amenable, tractable, docile; pliant

6 ungrudging, unreluctant, nothing loath, unaverse, unshrinking

7 voluntary, volunteer; gratuitous; spontaneous, free, freewill; offered, proffered; **discretionary,** discretional, **optional,** elective; arbitrary; **self-determined,** self-determining, autonomous, independent; **unsought, unasked,** unrequested, **unsolicited, uninvited,** unbidden, uncalled-for; **unforced,** unpressured, uncompelled; unprompted, uninfluenced

ADVS **8 willingly, with a will,** with good will, with right good will; **eagerly,** with zest, with relish, with open arms, without question, zealously, ardently, enthusiastically; **readily,** promptly, at the drop of a hat <nonformal>

9 agreeably, favorably, compliantly; lief, lieve <nonformal>, as lief, as lief as not; **ungrudgingly, unreluctantly, nothing loath,** without hesitation, unstintingly, unreservedly

10 voluntarily, freely, gratuitously, spontaneously; optionally, electively, by choice; **of one's own accord,** of one's own free will, of one's own volition, without reservation, of one's own choice, at one's own discretion; without coercion *or* pressure *or* compulsion *or* intimidation; independently

325 UNWILLINGNESS

NOUNS **1 refusal** 442, **unwillingness, disinclination, indisposition, reluctance,** grudging consent; unenthusiasm, lack of enthusiasm *or* zeal *or* eagerness, slowness, backwardness, dragging of the feet *and* foot-dragging <both nonformal>; sullenness, sulkiness; cursoriness, perfunctoriness; recalcitrance *or* recalcitrancy, disobedience, refractoriness, fractiousness, intractableness, indocility; averseness, aversion, repugnance, antipathy, distaste, disrelish; **obstinacy, stubbornness** 361.1; opposition 451; **resistance** 453; **disagreement,** dissent 456.3

2 demur, demurral, **scruple, qualm,** qualm of conscience, reservation, compunction; **hesitation,** hesitancy *or* hesitance, pause, boggle, **falter;** qualmishness, scrupulousness, scrupulosity; **stickling,** boggling; **fal-**

tering; shrinking; shyness, **diffidence,** modesty, bashfulness;
recoil; **protest, objection** 333.2

VERBS **3 refuse** 442.3, **be unwilling, would** or **had rather not,
not care to,** not feel like <nonfor-
mal>, not find it in one's heart to,
not have the heart or stomach to;
mind, object to, draw the line at,
be dead set against, **balk at;**
grudge, begrudge

4 demur, scruple, have qualms or
scruples; **stickle, stick at,** boggle, strain; falter, waver; **hesitate,**
pause, be half-hearted, **hang
back,** hold off; **fight shy of,** shy
at, shy, shrink, recoil, flinch,
wince, quail, pull back; make
bones about

ADJS **5 unwilling, disinclined, indisposed,** not in the mood,
averse; **unconsenting** 442.6;
dead set against, opposed 451.8;
resistant 453.5; **disagreeing,** differing, at odds 456.16; disobedient, recalcitrant, refractory,
fractious, sullen, sulky, indocile,
mutinous; cursory, perfunctory;
involuntary, forced

6 reluctant, grudging, loath;
backward, laggard, dilatory, slow,
slow to; unenthusiastic, indifferent, apathetic, perfunctory;
balky, balking, restive

7 demurring, qualmish, boggling, stickling, hedging,
squeamish, **scrupulous; diffident,** shy, modest, bashful;
hesitant, hesitating, faltering;
shrinking

ADVS **8 unwillingly, involuntarily,
against one's will;** under compulsion or coercion or pressure;
in spite of oneself

9 reluctantly, grudgingly, sullenly, sulkily; unenthusiastically,
perfunctorily; with dragging feet,
under protest; with a heavy
heart, with no heart or stomach;
over one's dead body, not on one's
life

326 OBEDIENCE

NOUNS **1 obedience** or **obediency,**
compliance; acquiescence, con-

sent 441; **deference** 155.1, self-
abnegation, submission, submissiveness 433.3; servility 138;
eagerness or readiness or willingness to serve, **dutifulness,**
duteousness; **service,** homage,
fealty, **allegiance, loyalty,** faithfulness, faith; doglike devotion or
obedience; **conformity** 866, lockstep

VERBS **2 obey, mind, heed, keep,
observe,** listen or hearken to;
comply, conform 866.3, walk in
lockstep; stay in line and not get
out of line and not get off base
<all nonformal>, **toe the line** or
mark, fall in line, fall in line, obey the
rules, follow the book, **do what
one is told;** do as one says, do the
will of, defer to 155.4, do one's
bidding, come at one's call, lie
down and roll over for <nonfor-
mal>; take orders, follow the lead
of; **submit** 433.6,9

ADJS **3 obedient, compliant,** complying; **acquiescent,** consenting
441.4, **submissive** 433.12, deferential 155.8, self-abnegating;
willing, **dutiful,** duteous; loyal,
faithful, devoted; uncritical, doglike; conforming, in conformity;
law-abiding

4 at one's command, at one's
whim or pleasure, at one's disposal, at one's call, **at one's beck
and call**

**5 henpecked, tied to one's apron
strings,** on a string, on a leash;
wimpish <nonformal>; milk-
toast or milquetoast, Caspar
Milquetoast

ADVS **6 obediently, compliantly;
acquiescently, submissively**
433.17; willingly, **dutifully,** duteously; loyally, faithfully, devotedly; in obedience to, in compliance or conformity with

7 at your service or **command, as
you please, as you will**

327 DISOBEDIENCE

NOUNS **1 disobedience, noncompliance; undutifulness,** undu-
teousness; willful disobedience;
insubordination, indiscipline;

unsubmissiveness, **intractability,** indocility 361.4; **nonconformity** 867; **disrespect** 156; **lawlessness,** waywardness, frowardness, naughtiness; violation, transgression, infraction, infringement, lawbreaking; civil disobedience, passive resistance; uncooperativeness, noncooperation; **dereliction,** default, delinquency, nonfeasance

2 **defiance, refractoriness, recalcitrance** or recalcitrancy, defiance of authority, **contumaciousness, obstreperousness, unruliness,** restiveness, fractiousness, orneriness and feistiness <both nonformal>; wildness 430.3; **obstinacy, stubbornness** 361.1

3 **rebelliousness, mutinousness;** insurrectionism; **sedition,** seditiousness; subversiveness; extremism 611.4

4 **revolt, rebellion, revolution, mutiny, insurrection, insurgence** or insurgency, **uprising,** rising, outbreak, general uprising, **riot,** civil disorder; putsch, coup d'état; **strike, general strike;** intifada

5 **rebel; insurgent,** insurrectionary, **insurrectionist;** malcontent; **insubordinate; mutineer,** rioter, brawler; maverick <nonformal>, troublemaker, refusenik <nonformal>; nonconformist 867.3; agitator 375.11; extremist 611.12; revolutionary, revolutionist 859.3; traitor, subversive 357.11; freedom fighter

VERBS 6 **disobey,** not mind, not heed, not keep or observe, not listen, pay no attention to, **ignore, disregard, defy,** fly in the face of, snap one's fingers at, scoff at, flout, go counter to; be a law unto oneself, step out of line, get off-base <nonformal>, refuse to cooperate; not conform 867.4, hear a different drummer; **violate,** transgress 435.4; break the law 674.5

7 **revolt, rebel,** kick over the traces; **rise up,** rise, arise, rise up in arms, mount the barricades; mount or make a coup d'état; **mutiny; riot,** run riot; revolutionize, subvert, overthrow 859.4; call a general strike, strike 727.8; secede, break away

ADJS 8 **disobedient, transgressive,** uncomplying, lawless, wayward, froward, naughty; nonconforming 867.5; **undutiful;** self-willed, willful, obstinate 361.8; **defiant** 454.7; **undisciplined,** ill-disciplined

9 **insubordinate, unsubmissive,** indocile, **uncompliant, uncooperative,** noncooperative, noncooperating, **intractable** 361.12

10 **defiant, refractory, recalcitrant, contumacious, obstreperous, unruly,** restive; fractious, ornery and feisty <both nonformal>; wild, untamed 430.29

11 **rebellious,** rebel, breakaway; **mutinous,** mutineering; **insurgent, insurrectionary,** riotous, turbulent; **seditious,** seditionary; revolutionary; traitorous, treasonable, subversive; extreme

ADVS 12 **disobediently,** uncompliantly, contrary to order and discipline; **insubordinately, unsubmissively,** indocilely, **uncooperatively;** unresignedly; floutingly, **defiantly;** intractably 361.17; obstreperously, contumaciously, restively; **rebelliously,** mutinously; riotously

328 ACTION
<voluntary action>

NOUNS 1 **action, activity** 330, act, willed action or activity; **acting, doing,** activism, direct action, not words but action; **practice,** actual practice, praxis; **exercise,** drill; **operation,** working, function, functioning; play; **operations,** affairs, workings; **business,** employment, work, occupation; **behavior** 321

2 **performance, execution,** carrying out, enactment; **transaction; discharge, dispatch;** conduct,

handling, management, administration; **achievement, accomplishment, implementation; commission, perpetration;** completion 407.2

3 **act, action, deed, doing,** thing, thing done; **turn; feat, stunt** *and* **trick** <both nonformal>; **master stroke,** *tour de force* <Fr>, **exploit,** adventure, **enterprise, initiative,** achievement, accomplishment, **performance,** production, track record <nonformal>; effort, endeavor, job, undertaking; **transaction;** dealing, deal <nonformal>; **operation, proceeding, step, measure, maneuver, move, movement;** coup, stroke; blow, go <nonformal>; *fait accompli* <Fr>, done deal <nonformal>; overt act <law>; **doings, dealings; works;** work, handiwork, hand

VERBS 4 **act, serve, function; operate, work, move,** practice, do one's thing <nonformal>; **move,** proceed; make, play, **behave** 321.4

5 **take action, take steps** *or* **measures; proceed,** proceed with, go ahead with, go with, go through with; do something, go *or* swing into action, **do something about, act on** *or* **upon,** take it on, run with it <nonformal>, get off the dime *or* one's ass *or* one's dead ass <nonformal>, get with it <nonformal>; fish or cut bait, shit or get off the pot *and* put up or shut up *and* put one's money where one's mouth is <all nonformal>; **go,** take a whack *or* a cut <nonformal>, lift a finger, **take a hand;** play a role *or* part in; strike a blow; **maneuver,** make moves <nonformal>

6 **do, effect,** effectuate, **make; bring about,** bring to pass, **bring off, produce, deliver** <nonformal>, **do the trick,** put across *or* through; swing *or* swing it *and* hack it *and* cut it *and* cut the mustard <all nonformal>; **do one's part,** carry one's weight, carry the ball <nonformal>, hold up

one's end *or* one's end of the bargain; tear off <nonformal>, **achieve, accomplish,** realize 407.4; **render, pay; inflict, wreak,** do to; **commit, perpetrate;** pull off <nonformal>; go and do <nonformal>

7 **carry out,** carry through, go through, fulfill, work out; **bring off,** carry off; **put through,** get through; **implement; put into effect,** put in *or* into practice, **translate into action;** suit the action to the word; rise to the occasion

8 **practice, put into practice,** exercise, employ, use; carry on, **conduct, prosecute, wage; follow, pursue; engage in,** work at, devote oneself to, **do,** turn to, apply oneself to; play at; **take up,** take to, **undertake, tackle,** take on, address oneself to, have a go at, turn one's hand to, **go in** *or* **out for** <nonformal>, make it one's business, set up shop; specialize in 865.4

9 **perform, execute, enact;** transact; **discharge, dispatch;** conduct, **manage, handle;** dispose of, take care of, **deal with,** cope with; **make, accomplish,** complete 407.6

ADJS 10 **acting,** performing, practicing, serving, functioning, functional, operating, operative, operational, working; in action 888.11; behavioral 321.7

329 INACTION
<voluntary inaction>

NOUNS 1 **inaction,** passiveness, **passivity;** passive resistance; nonresistance, nonviolence; pacifism; neutrality, **nonparticipation, noninvolvement;** do-nothingism, do-nothingness, **laissez-faireism;** *laissez-faire* <Fr>; watching and waiting, watchful waiting, waiting game, a wait-and-see attitude; **inertia,** inertness, **immobility,** dormancy, stagnation, stagnancy, vegetation, stasis, paralysis; **procrastination; idleness,** indolence, torpor, torpidness, torpidity, sloth; **immobility** 852.1; equilibrium, dead center; **inactivity** 331; **quietude, serenity, quiescence** 173; **quietism,** contemplation, meditation; contemplative life

VERBS **2 do nothing,** not stir, not budge, **not lift a finger** or **hand, sit back, sit on one's hands** <nonformal>, sit on one's ass or dead ass or butt or duff <nonformal>, sit on the sidelines, sit it out, take a raincheck <nonformal>, twiddle one's thumbs; **cool one's heels** <nonformal>; **bide one's time, delay,** watch and wait, wait and see, play a waiting game, lie low; hang fire, not go off half-cocked; lie or sit back, lie or rest upon one's oars, rest, be still 173.7; drift, coast; **stagnate,** vegetate, lie dormant, hibernate; lay down on the job <nonformal>, idle 331.11

3 refrain, abstain, hold, **spare, forbear, forgo,** keep from; hold or stay one's hand, sit by or idly by, sit on one's hands

4 let alone, leave alone, **leave** or **let well enough alone;** look the other way, not make waves, not look for trouble, not rock the boat; **let be,** leave be <nonformal>, let things take their course, let it have its way; leave things as they are; *laissez faire* <Fr>, live and let live; **take no part in,** not get involved in, **have nothing to do with,** have no hand in, stand or hold or remain aloof

5 let go, let pass, **let slip, let slide** and let ride <both nonformal>; procrastinate

ADJS **6 passive; neutral,** neuter; standpat <nonformal>, **donothing;** *laissez-faire* <Fr>; **inert,** like a bump on a log <nonformal>, immobile, dormant, stagnant, stagnating, vegetative, vegetable, static, stationary, motionless, immobile, unmoving, paralyzed, paralytic; procrastinating; **inactive, idle** 331.16; quiescent 173.12; quietist, contemplative, meditative

330 ACTIVITY

NOUNS **1 activity, action,** activeness; **movement,** motion, **stir; proceedings, doings, goings-on; activism; militancy;** business 724

2 liveliness, animation, vivacity, sprightliness, spiritedness, bubbliness, ebullience, effervescence, **briskness, breeziness, peppiness** <nonformal>; **life, spirit, verve,** energy, adrenalin; pep and and pizzazz and piss and vinegar <all nonformal>, **vim** 17.2

3 quickness, swiftness, speediness, alacrity, celerity, readiness, smartness, sharpness, briskness; **promptness;** dispatch, expeditiousness, expedition; **agility, nimbleness, spryness,** springiness

4 bustle, fuss, flurry, flutter, fluster, scramble, ferment, stew, sweat, whirl, swirl, vortex, maelstrom, **stir,** hubbub, hullabaloo, ado, to-do <nonformal>, bother, botheration <nonformal>; fussiness, flutteriness; tumult, commotion, **agitation; restlessness,** unquiet, fidgetiness; **spurt, burst,** fit, spasm

5 busyness, press of business; plenty to do, many irons in the fire, much on one's plate; the rat race <nonformal>

6 industry, industriousness, assiduousness, **assiduity, diligence, application,** concentration, laboriousness, **sedulousness,** unsparingness, relentlessness, zealousness, ardor, fervor, vehemence; **energy,** strenuousness, tirelessness, indefatigability

7 enterprise, dynamism, **initiative,** aggression, **aggressiveness,** killer instinct, force, forcefulness, **pushiness, push, drive, hustle, go,** getup, **get-up-and-go** <nonformal>, go-ahead, go-getting, go-to-itiveness <nonformal>; **adventurousness,** venturesomeness; spirit, gumption *and* spunk <both nonformal>; **ambitiousness** 100.10

8 **man** *or* **woman of action, doer,** man of deeds; **hustler** *and* self-starter <both nonformal>; go-getter *and* ball of fire *and* live wire *and* powerhouse *and* human dynamo *and* spitfire <all nonformal>; **workaholic,** overachiever; beaver, busy bee, **eager beaver** <nonformal>; operator *and* big-time operator *and* wheeler-dealer <all nonformal>; winner <nonformal>; **activist, militant;** enthusiast 101.4; new broom, take-charge guy <nonformal>

9 **overactivity,** hyperactivity; frenziedness; overexertion, overextension; officiousness 214.2

VERBS 10 **be busy, have one's hands full,** have many irons in the fire, have a lot on one's plate; not have a moment to spare, not have a moment to call one's own, not be able to call one's time one's own; do it on the run; have other things to do, have other fish to fry; **work, labor, drudge** 725.14; **busy oneself** 724.10,11

11 **stir,** stir about, **bestir oneself,** get down to business, sink one's teeth into it, take hold, be up and doing

12 **bustle, fuss,** make a fuss, stir, stir about, rush around *or* about, tear around, hurry about, dart to and fro, run around like a chicken with its head cut off

13 **hustle** <nonformal>, **drive,** drive oneself, **push, scramble,** go all out <nonformal>, **make things hum,** step lively <nonformal>, make the sparks fly <nonformal>; press on, drive on; go ahead, forge ahead, go full steam ahead

14 <nonformal terms> **hump,** break one's neck, bear down on it, put one's back into it, get off the dime, get off one's ass *or* duff *or* dead ass, **hit the ball,** pour it on, shake a leg, get the lead out

15 **keep going, keep on,** keep on the go, **carry on,** peg *or* plug

away <nonformal>, **keep at it,** keep moving, **keep the pot boiling,** keep the ball rolling; keep busy, **keep one's nose to the grindstone**

16 make the most of one's time, make hay while the sun shines, not let the grass grow under one's feet

ADJS 17 **active, lively, animated, spirited,** bubbly, ebullient, effervescent, **vivacious, sprightly,** chipper *and* perky <both nonformal>, pert; **spry, breezy, brisk, energetic,** eager, keen, can-do <nonformal>; alive, live, full of life, full of pep *or* go *and* pizzazz; **peppy** *and* snappy *and* zingy <all nonformal>; frisky, bouncing, bouncy; mercurial, quicksilver; **activist, militant**

18 **quick, swift, speedy, expeditious, snappy** <nonformal>, **prompt,** ready, smart, sharp, quick on the draw *or* trigger *or* upswing <nonformal>; **agile, nimble, spry**

19 **astir, stirring,** afoot, **on foot;** in full swing

20 **bustling,** fussing, fussy; **fidgety,** restless, fretful, jumpy, unquiet, unsettled 105.23; **agitated, turbulent**

21 **busy; occupied, engaged, employed, working; at work,** on duty, on the job, in harness; hard at work, **hard at it; on the move, on the go,** on the run, **on the hop** *or* **jump** <nonformal>; busy as a bee *or* beaver, busier than a one-armed paper hanger <nonformal>; up to one's ears *or* elbows *or* asshole *or* neck *or* eyeballs in <nonformal>

22 **industrious, assiduous, diligent, sedulous, hardworking;** unremitting, unsparing, relentless, zealous, ardent, fervent; **energetic,** strenuous; sleepless, unsleeping; tireless, unwearied, unflagging, indefatigable

23 **enterprising, aggressive, dynamic,** activist, driving, forceful, **pushing, pushy, up-and-coming, go-ahead** *and* **hustling**

<both nonformal>; adventurous, venturous, venturesome; **ambitious** 100.28

24 overactive, hyperactive, hyper <nonformal>; hectic, frenzied, frantic, frenetic; hyperkinetic; intrusive, officious 214.9

ADVS **25 actively, busily; lively, briskly, breezily, energetically, animatedly, vivaciously, spiritedly**, with gusto; full tilt, in full swing, all out <nonformal>; like a house afire

26 quickly, swiftly, expeditiously, with dispatch, readily, **promptly; agilely, nimbly, spryly**

27 industriously, assiduously, diligently, sedulously, laboriously; unsparingly, relentlessly, zealously, ardently, fervently, vehemently; **energetically,** strenuously, tirelessly, indefatigably

331 INACTIVITY

NOUNS **1 inactivity, inaction** 329, inactiveness; lull, suspension; suspended animation; dormancy, hibernation; immobility, motionlessness, quiescence 173; **inertia** 329.1; underactivity

2 idleness, unemployment, nothing to do, otiosity; **leisure,** leisureliness; idle hands, idle hours, time on one's hands; **relaxation,** letting down, unwinding, putting one's feet up

3 unemployment, lack of work, joblessness; layoff, furlough

4 idling, loafing, lazing, goofing off <nonformal>, goldbricking <nonformal>; trifling; dallying, dillydallying; dawdling; loitering, tarrying, lingering; lounging, **lolling**

5 indolence, laziness, sloth, slothfulness, bone-laziness; laggardness, slowness, dilatoriness, remissness; inexertion, inertia; **shiftlessness;** hoboism, vagrancy; spring fever

6 languor, languidness, languorousness, lackadaisicalness, lotus-eating; **listlessness,** lifelessness, inanimation, enervation, slowness, **dullness, slug-**gishness, heaviness, dopiness <nonformal>, hebetude, supineness, **lassitude, lethargy,** loginess; nodding; phlegm, **apathy, indifference, passivity;** torpidness, **torpor,** torpidity; stupor, stuporousness, stupefaction; **sloth,** slothfulness, acedia; **sleepiness, somnolence, oscitancy, yawning, drowsiness** 22.1; **weariness, fatigue** 21; jadedness, satedness 993.2; world-weariness, ennui, boredom 118.3

7 lazybones, indolent, lie-abed, slugabed

8 idler, loafer, lounger, loller, couch potato <nonformal>, lotus-eater, **do-nothing,** dolittle, goof-off *and* fuck-off *and* goldbrick *and* goldbricker <all nonformal>, clock watcher; **sluggard,** slug, slouch, sloucher, lubber, stick-in-the-mud <nonformal>; **time waster,** time killer; **dallier, dillydallier,** mope, moper, doodler, **dawdler,** dawdle, laggard, **loiterer,** lingerer; trifler; **putterer**

9 bum, stiff <nonformal>, derelict, skid-row bum, Bowery bum; beachcomber; **good-for-nothing, ne'er-do-well,** wastrel; drifter, vagrant, hobo, tramp 178.3; beggar 440.8

10 homeless person; street person; shopping-bag lady

11 nonworker, drone; cadger, bummer *and* moocher <both nonformal>, **sponger,** freeloader, lounge lizard <nonformal>, social parasite, parasite; beggar, mendicant, panhandler <nonformal>; **the unemployed;** the unemployable; discouraged workers; leisure class, couponclippers, idle rich

VERBS **12 idle,** do nothing, **laze,** lazy <nonformal>, take one's ease *or* leisure, take one's time, **loaf, lounge; lie around,** lounge around, loll around, moon, moon around, sit around, sit on one's ass *or* butt *or* duff <nonformal>, stand *or* hang around, **loiter about** *or* **around,** slouch around,

bum around *and* mooch around <both nonformal>; **shirk, goof off** *and* fuck off *and* **lie down on the job** <all nonformal>; let the grass grow under one's feet; twiddle one's thumbs

13 **waste time,** consume time, **kill time,** idle *or* trifle *or* fritter *or* fool away time, **while away the time,** pass the time, lose time, waste the precious hours; **trifle,** dabble, fribble, putter, potter, piddle

14 **dally, dillydally,** piddle, diddle, doodle, **dawdle, loiter,** lollygag <nonformal>, linger, lag, poke, take one's time

15 **take it easy,** take things as they come, **drift,** drift with the current, go with the flow, coast, lead an easy life, **live a life of ease,** rest on one's oars; rest on one's laurels

16 **lie idle, lie fallow;** aestivate, hibernate, lie dormant; lay off, charge *or* recharge one's batteries <nonformal>; lie up, lie on the shelf; ride at anchor, lay *or* lie by, lay *or* lie to; have nothing to do, have nothing on <nonformal>

ADJS 17 **inactive,** unactive; stationary, static, at a standstill; sedentary; **quiescent,** motionless 173.13

18 **idle,** fallow, otiose; **unemployed, unoccupied,** disengaged, **jobless, out of work,** out of a job, out of harness; free, available, at liberty, at leisure; at loose ends; unemployable; leisure, leisured; off duty, off work, off

19 **indolent, lazy, slothful; do-nothing, laggard,** slow, **dilatory,** procrastinative, remiss, slack, lax; easy; **shiftless; unenterprising;** good-for-nothing, ne'er-do-well; parasitic, cadging, sponging, scrounging

20 **languid, languorous, listless,** lifeless, inanimate, enervated, debilitated, **pepless** <nonformal>, lackadaisical, slow, wan, **lethargic,** logy, hebetudinous, supine, apathetic, **sluggish,** dopey <nonformal>, drugged,

nodding, droopy, **dull,** heavy, leaden, lumpish, **torpid,** stultified, stuporous, **inert,** stagnant, stagnating, vegetative, vegetable, dormant; phlegmatic, numb, benumbed; moribund, dead; sleepy, somnolent 22.21; **pooped** <nonformal>, weary; jaded, sated 993.6; **blasé,** world-weary, bored

332 ASSENT

NOUNS 1 **assent, acquiescence, concurrence, concurring, concurrency, compliance, agreement, acceptance;** welcome; agreement in principle, general agreement; support; **consent** 441

2 **affirmative; yes,** yea, aye, amen; nod, nod of assent; thumbs-up; **affirmativeness,** yea-saying; **metooism;** toadying, subservience, ass-licking <nonformal>

3 **acknowledgment, recognition, acceptance;** appreciation; **admission,** confession, concession, allowance; avowal, profession, declaration

4 **ratification, endorsement, acceptance, approval, approbation** 509.1, subscription, imprimatur, **sanction, permission, the OK** *and* the okay *and* **the green light** *and* **the go-ahead** *and* the nod <all nonformal>, **certification, confirmation, validation, authentication,** authorization, warrant; **affirmation;** rubber stamp, **stamp of approval;** seal, signet, sigil; **subscription, signature,** John Hancock <nonformal>; countersignature; visa; notarization

5 **unanimity,** universal *or* unambiguous assent; **like-mindedness, meeting of minds,** one *or* same mind; total agreement; **understanding,** mutual understanding; **concurrence, consent,** general consent, **accord, concord, agreement; consensus;** universal agreement *or* accord, shared sense, sense of the meeting; **acclamation;** uni-

son, harmony, **chorus, concert,**
one or single voice

6 assenter, consenter, accepter;
yea-sayer; **yes-man,** toady, ass-
licker and ass-kisser and brown-
nose and boot-licker <all nonfor-
mal>

7 endorser, subscriber, ratifier,
approver, upholder, certifier, con-
firmer; **signer,** signatory, the
undersigned; cosigner, cosig-
natory, party; underwriter, guarantor, insurer; notary, notary
public

VERBS **8 assent,** give or yield assent, **acquiesce, consent** 441.2,
comply, accede, agree, agree to
or with, have no problem with;
find it in one's heart; take kindly
to and hold with <both nonfor-
mal>; **accept,** receive, buy
<nonformal>, take one up on
<nonformal>; **subscribe to,** ac-
quiesce in, abide by; yes, **say 'yes'
to; nod,** nod assent, give one's
voice for; welcome, hail, cheer,
acclaim, applaud, accept in toto

9 concur, accord, coincide,
**agree, agree with; see eye to
eye, be at one with,** be of one
mind with, go with, **go along
with,** fall in with, close with,
meet, conform to, side with, identify oneself with; cast in one's lot,
fall in or into line, lend oneself to,
play or go along, take kindly to;
echo, say 'amen' to; join in the
chorus, go along with the crowd
<nonformal>, run with the pack;
get on the bandwagon <nonfor-
mal>

**10 come to an agreement, agree,
concur on, settle on,** agree with,
agree on or **upon, arrive at an
agreement, come to an understanding, come to terms, reach
an understanding** or **agreement**
or **accord,** strike a bargain, covenant, get together <nonformal>;
shake hands on, shake on it
<nonformal>; come around to

**11 acknowledge, admit, own,
confess, allow,** avow, **grant,** warrant, **concede; accept, recognize;** agree in principle, express

general agreement, go along with,
agree provisionally or for the sake
of argument; assent grudgingly or
under protest

12 ratify, endorse, sign off on, second, support, **certify, confirm,
validate, authenticate, accept,**
give the nod or the green light or
the go-ahead or the OK <all non-
formal>, give a nod of assent, give
one's imprimatur, permit, give
permission, **approve** 509.9; sanction, **authorize,** warrant; **pass,**
pass on or upon, give thumbs up
<nonformal>; amen, say amen
to; underwrite, subscribe to; **sign,**
sign on the dotted line, put one's
John Hancock on <nonformal>,
initial, put one's mark or X or
cross on; autograph; cosign,
countersign; seal, sign and seal,
set one's seal, **set one's hand and
seal;** affirm, swear and affirm,
take one's oath, swear to; rubber
stamp <nonformal>; notarize

ADJS **13 assenting, agreeing,** ac-
quiescing, **acquiescent, compliant,** consenting, consentient,
consensual, submissive, conced-
ing, **agreed, content**

14 accepted, approved, received;
acknowledged, admitted, allowed, granted, conceded, recognized, professed, confessed,
avowed, warranted; self-
confessed; **ratified, endorsed,
certified,** confirmed, validated,
authenticated; confirmatory, val-
idating, warranting; **signed,**
sealed, signed and sealed, coun-
tersigned, underwritten;
stamped; sworn to, notarized, affirmed

15 unanimous, solid, consen-
taneous, **with one consent** or
voice; uncontradicted, unchallenged, uncontroverted,
uncontested, unopposed; **concurrent, of one accord; agreeing,
in agreement, like-minded, of
one mind,** of the same mind; of a
piece, **at one,** at one with

ADVS **16 affirmatively,** assentingly,
in the affirmative

17 unanimously, concurrently,

consentaneously, **by common** or **general consent, with one accord,** with one voice, without contradiction, without a dissenting voice, in chorus, in concert, in unison, in one voice, univocally, unambiguously, to a man, **together,** all together, **as one,** as one man, one and all; by acclamation

333 DISSENT

NOUNS **1 dissent, dissidence,** dissentience; nonconcurrence, nonagreement; minority opinion or report or position; **disagreement, difference, variance,** diversity, disparity; **dissatisfaction, disapproval,** disapprobation; repudiation, **rejection; refusal, opposition** 451; dissension, disaccord 456; **alienation,** withdrawal, secession; **nonconformity** 867; apostasy 363.2; counterculture, underground

2 objection, protest; kick and **beef** and **bitch** and squawk and howl <all nonformal>, protestation; **remonstrance, remonstration,** expostulation; **challenge; demur,** demurrer; **reservation, scruple,** compunction, qualm, twinge of conscience; **complaint, grievance; exception;** peaceful or nonviolent protest; **demonstration,** counterdemonstration, **rally,** march, boycott, strike, picketing; **rebellion** 327.4

3 dissenter, dissident, dissentient; **objector,** demurrer; minority or opposition voice; **protester,** protestant; **separatist,** schismatic; nonconformist 867.3; apostate 363.5

VERBS **4 dissent,** say nay, **disagree, differ,** not agree, disagree with, agree to disagree or differ; be at variance; **take exception,** withhold assent, **take issue, beg to differ,** raise an objection; be in opposition to, oppose; march to or hear a different drummer, swim against the tide or against the current or upstream; **split off, withdraw,** secede

5 object, protest, kick and **beef** <both nonformal>, put up a struggle or fight; **bitch** and **beef** and **squawk** and put up a squawk and raise a howl <all nonformal>; cry out against, make or create or raise a stink about <all nonformal>; yell bloody murder <nonformal>; **remonstrate,** expostulate; raise one's voice against, enter a protest; **complain,** state a grievance, air one's grievances; **dispute, challenge,** call in question; **demur, scruple; demonstrate, demonstrate against,** rally, boycott, strike, picket; **rebel** 327.7

ADJS **6 dissenting, dissident,** dissentient; **disagreeing, differing; opposing** 45¹.8, in opposition; alienated; counterculture, antiestablishment, underground; at variance with, at odds with; schismatic, sectarian; nonconforming 867.5; rebellious 327.11; resistant 453.5

7 protesting, protestant; **objecting,** remonstrant; under protest

334 AFFIRMATION

NOUNS **1 affirmation, assertion, asseveration, declaration,** allegation; **avowal; position, stand,** stance; profession, **statement, word,** say, saying, say-so <nonformal>; manifesto, position paper; statement of principles, **creed** 952.3; **pronouncement, proclamation,** announcement, annunciation, enunciation; proposition, conclusion; predication, predicate; protest, protestation; utterance, dictum

2 affirmativeness; assertiveness, absoluteness, speaking out, table-thumping <nonformal>

3 deposition, sworn statement, affidavit, sworn testimony, affirmation; **vouching, swearing; attestation;** certification; **testimony**

4 oath, vow, word, assurance, guarantee, warrant, solemn oath or affirmation or word or declaration; **pledge** 436.1

VERBS **5 affirm, assert,** asseverate,
aver, protest, avow, **declare,** say,
say loud and clear, sound off
<nonformal>, have one's say,
speak, speak one's piece *or* one's
mind, speak up *or* out, **state,** set
down, express, put, put it, put in
one's two-cents worth <nonfor-
mal>; **allege,** profess; predicate;
issue a manifesto *or* position paper, manifesto; announce, **pronounce,** annunciate, enunciate,
proclaim; maintain, have, **contend,** argue, **insist, hold,** submit,
maintain with one's last breath

6 depose, depone; **testify,** take the
stand, witness; **warrant, attest,**
certify; **guarantee, assure;
vouch, vouch for, swear, swear
to,** swear the truth, **assert under
oath; vow;** swear to God, swear
on the Bible, hope to die, cross
one's heart *or* cross one's heart
and hope to die; swear till one is
blue in the face <nonformal>

7 administer an oath, **place** *or* **put
under oath,** put to one's oath;
swear, swear in

ADJS **8 affirmative,** affirming, af-
firmatory, certifying; **assertive,**
assertative; **declarative,** declar-
atory; **predicative; positive,** absolute, emphatic, decided, table-
thumping <nonformal>, unambiguously, unmistakably, loud
and clear

9 affirmed, asserted, asseverated,
avowed, averred, **declared; alleged,** professed; **stated,** pronounced, announced, enunci-
ated; predicated; **deposed,** warranted, **attested, certified,**
vouched, **vouched for,** vowed,
pledged, **sworn, sworn to**

ADVS **10 affirmatively,** assertively,
declaratively, predicatively; **positively,** absolutely, decidedly,
loudly, loud and clear, at the top
of one's voice *or* one's lungs; without fear of contradiction; under
oath, on one's honor *or* one's word

335 NEGATION, DENIAL

NOUNS **1 negation,** negating, abnegation; negativeness, nega-

tivity, **negativism,** naysaying; **obtuseness,** perversity, orneriness
<nonformal>; **negative, no,** nay,
nix <nonformal>

**2 denial, disavowal, disaffirma-
tion, disownment,** disallowance;
disclaimer; **renunciation, retraction, repudiation,** recantation; revocation, nullification, annulment, abrogation; abjuration,
forswearing; **contradiction,** flat
or absolute contradiction, contravention, countering, crossing,
gainsaying, impugnment; **refutation, disproof** 957; **apostasy,
defection** 363.2; **about-face, reversal** 363.1

VERBS **3 negate,** abnegate, negative; shake the head

4 deny, not admit, not accept, refuse to admit *or* accept; **disclaim,
disown, disaffirm, disavow,
disallow,** abjure, forswear, **renounce, retract,** take back, recant; revoke, nullify, **repudiate;
contradict,** fly in the face of,
cross, contravene, controvert, impugn, **dispute,** gainsay, **oppose,
counter,** go counter to, contest,
take issue with, run counter to;
belie, give the lie to; **refute** 957.5,
disprove 957.4; **reverse oneself**
363.6; **defect, apostatize** 363.7

ADJS **5 negative,** abnegative; **denying, disclaiming,** disowning, dis-
affirming, disavowing, recanting;
contradictory, contradicting, **opposing, contrary,** nay-saying,
repugnant; **obtuse,** perverse, ornery <nonformal>

ADVS **6 negatively, in the negative;**
in contradiction

336 IMITATION

NOUNS **1 imitation, copying,**
counterfeiting, repetition; emulation, the sincerest form of flattery,
following, mirroring; **simulation**
354.3, modeling; fakery, forgery,
plagiarism, plagiarizing; **imposture, impersonation, takeoff**
and hit-off <both nonformal>,
impression, burlesque, pastiche;
mimesis; parody, onomatopoeia

2 mimicry, mockery, apery, parrotry, mimetism; protective coloration *or* mimicry, playing possum

3 reproduction, duplication, imitation 784.1, **copy** 784.1, dummy, mock-up, **replica,** facsimile, representation, paraphrase, approximation, model, version, knockoff <nonformal>; computer model *or* simulation; parody, burlesque, pastiche, travesty 508.6

4 imitator, simulator, **impersonator, impostor** 357.6, **mimic,** mimicker, mime, **mocker; parrot, ape,** monkey; **echo,** echoist; **copier,** copyist, **copycat** <nonformal>; **faker, impostor,** counterfeiter, forger, plagiarist; dissimulator, dissembler, deceiver, hypocrite, phony <nonformal>, poseur; conformist, sheep

VERBS **5 imitate, copy, repeat,** ditto <nonformal>; act *or* go *or* make like <nonformal>; **mirror, reflect; echo,** reecho, chorus; **borrow,** steal one's stuff <nonformal>, take a leaf out of one's book; assume, **affect; simulate;** counterfeit, fake <nonformal>, hoke *and* hoke up <both nonformal>, forge, plagiarize, crib, lift <nonformal>; **parody,** pastiche; **paraphrase,** approximate

6 mimic, impersonate, mime, **ape, parrot,** copycat <nonformal>; take off, hit off, hit off on, take off on

7 emulate, follow, follow in the steps *or* footsteps of, walk in the shoes of, put oneself in another's shoes, follow in the wake of, jump on the bandwagon; **copy after,** model after, model on, pattern after, pattern on, shape after, take after, take a leaf out of one's book, take as a model

ADJS **8 imitation, mock, sham,** copied, fake *and* phony <both nonformal>, counterfeit, forged, plagiarized, unoriginal, ungenuine; **pseudo,** ersatz, hokey *and* hoked-up <both nonformal>

9 imitative; mimic, mimetic, **apish,** parrotlike; **emulative;**

echoic, onomatopoetic, onomatopoeic

10 imitable, copiable, duplicable, replicable

ADVS **11** imitatively, apishly; onomatopoetically; synthetically

337 NONIMITATION

NOUNS **1 nonimitation, originality, novelty,** innovation, freshness, uniqueness; **authenticity;** inventiveness, creativity, creativeness 985.3

2 original, model 785, archetype, prototype 785.1, **pattern, mold; innovation,** new departure

3 autograph, holograph, first edition

VERBS **4 originate, invent; innovate; create;** revolutionize

ADJS **5 original, novel, unprecedented; unique,** *sui generis* <L>; new, fresh 840.7; **firsthand; authentic, imaginative, creative** 985.18; **avant-garde,** revolutionary; **pioneer,** trail-blazing

6 unimitated, uncopied, **unduplicated,** unprecedented, unexampled; **archetypal,** archetypical, prototypal 785.9; **prime,** primary, primal, primitive, pristine

338 COMPENSATION

NOUNS **1 compensation, recompense,** repayment, payback, indemnification, measure for measure, rectification, restitution, **reparation; amends,** expiation, atonement; **redress,** satisfaction; commutation, substitution; **offsetting,** balancing, **counterbalancing,** counteraction; **retaliation** 506, revenge

2 offset; counterbalance, counterpoise, equipoise, counterweight; **balance,** ballast; **tradeoff,** equivalent, consideration, *quid pro quo* <L, something for something>, tit for tat, give-and-take 862.1

3 counterclaim, counterdemand

VERBS **4 compensate,** make compensation, make good, set right, pay back, rectify, **make up for; make amends,** expiate, do penance, atone; **recompense,** repay, indemnify, cover; **trade off;** **retaliate** 506

5 **offset** 778.4, set off, **counteract,** countervail, **counterbalance,** counterweigh, counterpoise, **balance,** play off against, set against, set over against, equiponderate; **square,** square up

ADJS 6 **compensating, compensatory;** rectifying; **offsetting,** counteracting or counteractive, countervailing, balancing, **counterbalancing,** zero-sum; **expiatory,** penitential; **retaliatory** 506

ADVS 7 **in compensation,** in return, back; in consideration, for a consideration

339 CAREFULNESS
<close or watchful attention>

NOUNS 1 **carefulness, care, heed, concern, regard; attention** 982; **heedfulness,** mindfulness, **thoughtfulness; consideration,** solicitude, caring, loving care, tender loving care, TLC <nonformal>; circumspectness, circumspection; forethought, anticipation, preparedness; **caution** 494

2 **painstakingness,** painstaking, **pains; diligence,** assiduousness, assiduity, sedulousness, industriousness, industry; **thoroughness**

3 **meticulousness,** exactingness, **scrupulousness,** scrupulosity, **conscientiousness,** punctiliousness, fine-tuning; **particularness,** particularity; **fussiness, criticalness,** criticality; **finicalness,** finickiness; **exactness, exactitude, accuracy, preciseness, precision,** punctuality, correctness, prissiness; **strictness, rigor,** rigorousness, spit and polish; nicety, subtlety, refinement, exquisiteness

4 **vigilance, wariness,** prudence, **watchfulness, surveillance; watch, vigil, lookout;** invigilation, proctoring, monitoring; watch and ward; custody, custodianship, guardianship, stewardship; **guard,** guardedness; **sharp eye, weather eye,** peeled eye, watchful eye, eagle eye

5 **alertness, attentiveness; attention** 982; **wakefulness,** sleeplessness; **readiness,** promptness, punctuality; **quickness,** agility, nimbleness; **smartness,** brightness, keenness, sharpness, acuteness, acuity

VERBS 6 **care, mind, heed,** think, consider, regard, pay heed to, take heed of; **take an interest,** be concerned; **pay attention** 982.8

7 **be careful, take care** or good care, take heed, exercise care; **be cautious** 494.5; **take pains,** take trouble, **be painstaking,** go to great pains, go to great lengths, go out of one's way, go the extra mile <nonformal>, bend over backwards <nonformal>, use every trick in the book; mind what one is doing or about, mind one's business, **mind one's P's and Q's** <nonformal>; **watch one's step** <nonformal>, tread on eggs, feel one's way; **handle with gloves** or **kid gloves**

8 **be vigilant,** be watchful, **be on the watch** or **lookout,** keep a sharp lookout, keep in sight or view; **keep watch,** keep vigil; **watch, look sharp,** look about one, **be on one's guard,** keep an eye out, sleep with one eye open, have all one's wits about one, keep one's eye on the ball <nonformal>, keep one's eyes open, keep a weather eye open *and* **keep one's eyes peeled** <both nonformal>, keep the ear to the ground; **be on the alert; look out, watch out;** look lively or alive; stop, look, and listen

9 **look after,** nurture, foster, **take care of** 1007.19

ADJS 10 **careful, heedful, regardful, mindful, thoughtful, considerate, caring,** solicitous, loving, tender; circumspect; **attentive** 982.15; **cautious** 494.8

11 **painstaking, diligent, assiduous,** sedulous, **thorough, thoroughgoing,** industrious

12 meticulous, exacting, scrupulous, conscientious, religious, punctilious, punctual, particular, fussy, critical, attentive, scrutinizing; thorough,
thoroughgoing; finicky; exact,
precise, accurate, correct;
close, narrow; strict, rigorous,
spit-and-polish, exigent, demanding; nice, delicate, subtle, fine,
refined, minute, detailed, exquisite

13 vigilant, wary, prudent, watchful, sleepless, observant; on the
watch, on the lookout; on
guard, on one's guard, guarded;
with open eyes, with one's eyes
peeled or with a weather eye
open <both nonformal>; sharp-
eyed, eagle-eyed, hawk-eyed;
all eyes, all ears, all eyes and
ears

14 alert, on the alert, on one's
toes, on top and on the job and
on the ball <all nonformal>, attentive; awake, wakeful, wide-
awake, unwinking, unnodding,
alive, ready, prompt, quick, agile,
nimble, quick on the trigger or
draw or uptake <all nonfor-
mal>; smart, bright, keen,
sharp

ADVS **15** carefully, heedfully, regardfully, mindfully, thoughtfully, considerately, solicitously,
tenderly, lovingly; circumspectly;
cautiously 494.12; with care,
with great care; painstakingly,
diligently, assiduously, industriously, sedulously, thoroughly,
thoroughgoingly, to a t or a turn
and to a fare-thee-well <all non-
formal>

16 meticulously, exactingly, scrupulously, conscientiously,
religiously, punctiliously, punctually, fussily; strictly, rigorously;
exactly, accurately, precisely,
with exactitude, with precision;
nicely, with great nicety, refinedly,
minutely, in detail, exquisitely

17 vigilantly, warily, prudently,
watchfully, observantly; alertly,
attentively; sleeplessly, unwink-
ingly, unblinkingly, unnoddingly

340 NEGLECT

NOUNS **1** neglect, neglectfulness,
negligence, inadvertence or inadvertency, dereliction, criminal
negligence; remissness, laxity,
laxness, slackness, looseness; permissiveness; noninterference,
laissez-faire <Fr>; disregard,
slighting; inattention 983; oversight, overlooking; omission,
nonperformance, lapse, failure,
default; poor stewardship or
guardianship or custody; procrastination 845.5

2 carelessness, heedlessness,
unheedfulness; unperceptiveness, impercipience, blindness;
uncaring, unsolicitude, unsolicitousness, thoughtlessness,
tactlessness, inconsiderateness,
inconsideration; unmindfulness, oblivion, forgetfulness;
unpreparedness, unreadiness,
lack of foresight or forethought;
recklessness 493.2; indifference 102; laziness 331.5;
perfunctoriness; cursoriness,
hastiness, offhandedness, casualness; nonconcern, insouciance;
abandon

3 slipshodness, slovenliness,
sluttishness, untidiness, sloppiness and messiness <both
nonformal>; haphazardry;
slapdash, a lick and a promise
<nonformal>, loose ends; botch,
slovenly performance; bungling
414.4

4 unmeticulousness, unscrupulousness, unrigorousness,
unconscientiousness, un-
punctuality, uncriticalness;
inexactness, inexactitude, inaccuracy, imprecision, unpreciseness

5 neglecter, ignorer, disregarder;
procrastinator; slacker, shirker,
malingerer, dodger, goof-off and
goldbrick <both nonformal>,
idler; skimper <nonformal>; trifler; sloven, slut; bungler 414.8

VERBS **6** neglect, overlook, disregard, not heed, not attend to,
take for granted, ignore; not care

for, not take care of; **pass over,** gloss over; **let slip, let slide** <nonformal>, **let go,** let ride <nonformal>, let take its course; let the grass grow under one's feet; not think *or* consider, not give a thought to, take no thought *or* account of, blind oneself to, turn a blind eye to; lose sight of, lose track of; **be neglectful** *or* **negligent,** fail in one's duty, **fail,** lapse, **default,** let go by default; not get involved; nod, nod *or* sleep through, be caught napping, be asleep at the switch <nonformal>

7 **leave undone,** leave, **let go,** leave half-done, **skip,** jump, **miss, omit,** let be *or* alone, pass over, pass up <nonformal>, abandon; leave loose ends; **slack, shirk,** malinger, goof off *and* goldbrick <both nonformal>; trifle; **procrastinate** 845.11

8 **slight;** turn one's back on, turn a cold shoulder to, get *or* give the cold shoulder *and* get *or* give the cold-shoulder <all nonformal>, leave out in the cold; not lift a finger, leave undone; scamp, skimp <nonformal>; slur, **slur over,** pass over, **skip over,** dodge, fudge, blink; skim, **skim over,** skim the surface, **touch upon,** touch upon lightly *or* in passing, go once over lightly, **hit the high spots** *and* **give a lick and a promise** <both nonformal>; **cut corners,** cut a corner

9 **do carelessly,** do by halves, do in a half-assed way <nonformal>, do in a slipshod fashion, do in any old way <nonformal>; botch, **bungle** 414.11; **trifle with,** play fast and loose with, mess around *or* about with *and* muck around *or* about with *and* piss around *or* about with <all nonformal>; **do offhand,** dash off, knock off *and* throw off <both nonformal>, **toss off** *or* **out** <nonformal>; **roughhew,** roughcast, rough out; **knock out** <nonformal>, bat out <nonformal>; toss *or* **throw together,** knock together, throw *or*

slap together, patch together, patch, patch up, fudge up; jury-rig

ADJS 10 **negligent, neglectful,** derelict, culpably negligent; inadvertent, uncircumspect; **inattentive** 983.6; unwary, unwatchful, asleep at the switch, off-guard, unguarded; **remiss,** slack, lax, relaxed, laid-back <nonformal>, loose, unrigorous, permissive, overly permissive; noninterfering; slighting; slurring, scamping, skimping <nonformal>; procrastinating 845.17

11 **careless, heedless, unheeding, unheedful, disregardful, unsolicitous, uncaring;** tactless, **thoughtless, unthinking, inconsiderate,** untactful, undiplomatic, **unmindful,** forgetful, oblivious; **unprepared,** unready; **reckless** 493.8; **indifferent** 102.6; lazy; perfunctory, cursory, casual, offhand; easygoing, airy, flippant, insouciant, free and easy

12 **slipshod, slovenly,** sloppy *and* **messy** *and* half-assed <all nonformal>, sluttish, untidy; **clumsy, bungling** 414.20; **haphazard, promiscuous, hit-or-miss,** hit-and-miss; half-assed <nonformal>, botched

13 **unmeticulous, unexacting, unpainstaking, unscrupulous,** unrigorous **unconscientious,** unpunctilious, unpunctual, **unparticular, unfussy, uncritical;** inexact, inaccurate, unprecise

14 **neglected,** unattended to, untended, unwatched, unchaperoned, uncared-for; **disregarded,** unconsidered, **overlooked, missed,** omitted, passed by, passed over, passed up <nonformal>, gathering dust, **ignored, slighted;** unasked, unsolicited; half-done, undone, left undone; deserted, abandoned; in the cold *and* out in the cold <both nonformal>; on the shelf, shelved, pigeonholed, on hold *and* on the back burner <both nonformal>, **put** *or* **laid aside,** sidetracked

and sidelined <both nonformal>, shunted

15 unheeded, unobserved, unnoticed, unnoted, unperceived, unseen, undiscerned, unmarked, unremarked, unregarded, unmissed

16 unexamined, unstudied, unconsidered, unsearched, unscanned, unweighed, unsifted, unexplored, uninvestigated

ADVS **17 negligently, neglectfully,** inadvertently; **remissly,** laxly, slackly, loosely; **unrigorously,** permissively; **slightingly,** lightly, slurringly; scampingly, skimpingly <nonformal>

18 carelessly, heedlessly, unheedingly, unheedfully, regardlessly, **thoughtlessly, unthinkingly, unsolicitously,** tactlessly, **inconsiderately,** unmindfully, forgetfully; **inattentively, unwarily,** unvigilantly, unguardedly, unwatchfully; **recklessly** 493.11; perfunctorily; once over lightly, cursorily; casually, offhand, offhandedly, airily; clumsily, bunglingly 414.24; **sloppily** *and* **messily** <both nonformal>, sluttishly, shoddily, shabbily; haphazardly, promiscuously, hit or miss *and* hit and miss *and* helter-skelter *and* slapdash *and* anyhow *and* any old way *and* any which way <all nonformal>

19 unmeticulously, unscrupulously, unconscientiously, unfussily, **uncritically;** inexactly, inaccurately, unprecisely, imprecisely, unrigorously, unpunctually

341 INTERPRETATION

NOUNS **1 interpretation, construction, reading,** way of seeing *or* understanding *or* putting; constructionism, strict constructionism; **diagnosis; definition;** description; **meaning** 518; over-interpretation, laboring

2 rendering, rendition; text; version; reading, lection, variant, variant reading; **edition;** variorum edition *or* variorum; conflation

3 translation, transcription, transliteration; **paraphrase,** loose *or* free translation; amplification, restatement, rewording; word-for-word translation; **pony** *and* trot *and* crib <all nonformal>; interlinear, interlinear translation, bilingual text *or* edition; **gloss, glossary;** key

4 explanation, explication, **elucidation,** illumination, enlightenment, light, **clarification,** simplification; take <nonformal>; **exposition,** expounding, exegesis; **illustration, demonstration,** exemplification; **reason,** rationale; demythologization; decipherment, decoding, cracking, unlocking, **solution** 939; editing, emendation

5 <explanatory remark> **comment, word of explanation; annotation,** notation, **note,** footnote, gloss, scholium; exegesis; commentary

6 interpretability, construability; **definability, describability; explicability,** accountableness

7 interpreter, exegete, hermeneut; constructionist, strict constructionist; **commentator,** annotator, scholiast; critic, **editor,** emender, emendator; cryptographer, cryptologist, decoder, decipherer, cryptanalyst; **explainer,** lexicographer, definer, **explicator,** exponent, expositor, expounder, clarifier; demonstrator, demythologizer; go-between 576.4; **translator;** guide, dragoman

8 <science of interpretation> exegetics, hermeneutics; tropology; criticism, literary criticism, textual criticism; paleography, epigraphy; cryptology, cryptography, cryptanalysis; lexicography; semeiology, semeiotics; pathognomy; physiognomy

VERBS **9 interpret, diagnose; construe, take;** understand, **understand by, take to mean,** take it that; **read; read into,** read between the lines; read in view of, take an approach to, **define, describe**

10 **explain, explicate, expound,** make of, exposit; **give the meaning,** tell the meaning of; **spell out,** unfold; **account for,** give reason for; **clarify, elucidate,** clear up, clear the air, **cover** *and* cover the waterfront *or* the territory <all nonformal>, **make clear,** make plain; **simplify,** popularize; **illuminate,** enlighten, **shed** *or* **throw light upon;** rationalize, demythologize; tell *or* show how, show the way; **demonstrate, show, illustrate,** exemplify; get to the bottom of *or* to the heart of, make sense of, make head or tails of; decipher, crack, unlock, find the key to, unravel, read between the lines, read into, **solve** 939.2; explain away; overinterpret

11 **comment upon,** remark upon; **annotate,** gloss; **edit,** make an edition

12 **translate, render,** transcribe, transliterate, put *or* turn into; construe

13 **paraphrase, rephrase, reword, restate,** rehash

ADJS 14 **interpretative,** interpretive, interpretational, exegetic, hermeneutic; constructive, constructional; **diagnostic;** semeiological; **descriptive**

15 **explanatory,** explaining, exegetic, **explicative,** explicatory; **expository; clarifying, elucidative; illuminating,** illuminative, enlightening; **demonstrative, illustrative;** annotate, critical, editorial; rationalizing, demythologizing

16 **translational,** translative; paraphrastic

17 **interpretable, construable; definable,** describable; translatable, renderable; explainable, explicable, accountable

ADVS 18 **by interpretation,** as here interpreted, as here defined, according to this reading; **in explanation, to explain; that is,** that is to say, as it were, *id est*

<L>, i.e.; **to wit, namely,** *videlicet* <L>, viz, *scilicet* <L>, sc; **in other words**

342 MISINTERPRETATION

NOUNS 1 **misinterpretation, misunderstanding, misapprehension, misreading, misconstruction,** mistaking, **misconception; misrendering,** mistranslation; misapplication; gloss; **perversion, distortion,** wrenching, twisting, contorting, torturing, squeezing, garbling; reversal; misuse of words, catachresis; misquotation; misjudgment 947; **error** 974

VERBS 2 **misinterpret, misunderstand,** misconceive, **mistake, misapprehend; misread, misconstrue,** put a false construction on, miss the point, **take wrong, get wrong,** take the wrong way; **get backwards,** reverse, put the cart before the horse; misapply; **misrender,** mistranslate; quote out of context; misquote, give a false impression *or* idea, gloss; **garble, pervert, distort,** wrench, contort, torture, squeeze, twist the words *or* meaning, **misjudge** 947.2; bark up the wrong tree

ADJS 3 **misinterpreted, misunderstood, mistaken, misapprehended, misread,** misconceived, **misconstrued; garbled, perverted, distorted,** catachrestic; backwards, reversed, assbackwards <nonformal>

4 **misinterpretable, misunderstandable,** mistakable

343 COMMUNICATION

NOUNS 1 **communication,** communion, congress, **commerce, intercourse;** speaking, **speech** 524, utterance, talking, converse, **conversation** 541; **contact, touch, connection; interpersonal communication, intercommunication, interplay,** interaction; **exchange,** interchange; answer, response, reply; **dealings,** dealing, **traffic, truck**

<nonformal>; information 551; message 552.4; ESP, telepathy 689.9; correspondence 553; social intercourse 582.4

2 **informing, telling,** imparting, **conveyance, telling, transmission,** transmittal, transfer, transference, sharing, giving, sending, signaling; notification, alerting, **announcement** 352.2, publication 352, **disclosure** 351

3 **communicativeness, talkativeness** 540, **sociability** 582; **unreserve,** unreservedness, **unreticence,** unrestraint, **unconstraint; unsecretiveness;** candor, **frankness** 644.4; **openness,** plainness, freeness, outspokenness, plainspokenness; **accessibility,** approachability; **extroversion,** outgoingness; **uncommunicativeness** 344, reserve, taciturnity

4 **communicability, impartability, conveyability, transmittability,** transmissibility, transferability

5 **communications,** media, communications medium or media, communications network; telecommunication 347.1

VERBS 6 **communicate, be in touch** or **contact,** have intercourse; **intercommunicate,** interchange, commune with; **deal with, traffic with, have dealings with, have truck with** <nonformal>; **speak, talk, converse** 541.9, pass the time of day

7 **communicate, impart, tell, convey, transmit,** transfer, send, send word, deliver or send a signal or message, **disseminate,** broadcast, pass, **pass on** or **along, hand on;** report, render, **make known,** get across or over; give or send or leave word; **signal;** share, share with; **leak,** let slip out, **give** 478.12; tell 551.8

8 **communicate with, get in touch** or **contact with, contact** <nonformal>, **make contact with,** raise, reach, get to, get through to, get hold of; **make advances,** make overtures, **approach,** make up to <nonformal>; relate to; keep in touch or contact with, maintain connection; **answer,** respond or reply to, get back to; **question,** interrogate; **correspond,** drop a line

ADJS 9 **communicational, communicating;** speech, **verbal,** linguistic, oral; **conversational** 541.13; **intercommunicational,** intercommunicative, interactive, interacting, responsive, answering; questioning, interrogatory; telepathic

10 **communicative, talkative** 540.9, gossipy, newsy; **sociable; unreserved, unreticent,** unshrinking, **unrestrained, unconstrained,** unhampered, unrestricted; demonstrative, expansive, effusive; **unrepressed, unsuppressed; unsecretive;** candid, **frank** 644.17; self-revealing; **open,** free, outspoken, free-speaking, free-spoken; **accessible, approachable,** easy to speak to; **extroverted,** outgoing; **uncommunicative** 344.8

11 **communicable, impartable, conveyable, transmittable,** transmissible, transferable

12 communicatively; verbally, talkatively, by word of mouth, orally, viva voce

344
UNCOMMUNICATIVENESS

NOUNS 1 **uncommunicativeness,** closeness; **unsociability** 583; nondisclosure, **secretiveness** 345.1; lack of meaning, meaninglessness 520

2 **taciturnity, untalkativeness;** silence 51; **speechlessness,** wordlessness, dumbness, **muteness** 51.2; quietness, quietude; curtness, shortness, terseness; brusqueness, briefness, brevity, conciseness, economy or sparingness of words

3 **reticence** or reticency; **reserve,** reservedness, restraint, low key, **constraint;** guardedness, discreetness, discretion; suppression, repression; backwardness,

retirement, low profile; **aloofness, standoffishness,** distance,
remoteness, **detachment,** withdrawal, reclusiveness, solitariness; impersonality; **coolness,** coldness, frigidity, iciness,
frostiness, chilliness; **inaccessibility, unapproachability;
undemonstrativeness,** unexpan-
siveness, unaffability, uncongeniality; **introversion;** modesty,
bashfulness 139.4; blankness, impassiveness, impassivity; straight
or poker face, mask

4 **prevarication, equivocation,**
tergiversation, **evasion,** shuffle,
fencing, dodging, waffling and
tap-dancing <both nonformal>;
weasel words

5 **man of few words,** clam
<nonformal>, strong silent type;
Spartan; evader, weasel

VERBS 6 **keep to oneself,** keep
one's own counsel; not open one's
mouth, not say a word, not
breathe a word, stand mute, **hold
one's tongue** 51.5, clam up
<nonformal>; bite one's tongue;
have little to say, waste no words,
save one's breath; **keep one's distance,** keep at a distance, **stand
aloof,** hold oneself aloof; keep secret 345.7

7 **prevaricate, equivocate,** waffle
<nonformal>, tergiversate,
evade, dodge, sidestep, say in a
roundabout way, duck, weasel
and weasel out <both nonfor-
mal>; **hem and haw; mince
words**

ADJS 8 **uncommunicative,** indisposed or disinclined to communicate; **unsociable** 583.5; **secretive**
345.15; meaningless 520.6

9 **taciturn, untalkative,** unlo-
quacious, indisposed to talk;
silent, speechless, wordless,
mum; mute 51.12, dumb, quiet;
close, **closemouthed, tight-
lipped;** close-lipped, tongue-tied;
laconic, curt, brief, terse,
brusque, short, concise, **sparing
of words,** economical of words,
of few words

10 **reticent, reserved,** restrained,

nonassertive, low-key, low-keyed,
constrained; **suppressed,** repressed; subdued; guarded,
discreet; backward, **retiring,**
shrinking; **aloof, standoffish,**
standoff, **distant,** remote, removed, **detached,** withdrawn;
impersonal; **cool,** cold, frigid, icy,
frosty, chilled, chilly; **inaccessible, unapproachable,** forbidding; **undemonstrative,** unex-
pansive, uncongenial; **introverted;** modest, bashful 139.12;
expressionless, blank, impassive

11 **prevaricating, equivocal,** ter-
giversating, waffling <nonfor-
mal>, **evasive**

345 SECRECY

NOUNS 1 **secrecy,** secretness; the
dark; hiddenness, **concealment**
346; **secretiveness,** closeness;
discreetness, discretion, **uncommunicativeness** 344;
evasiveness, evasion, subterfuge

2 **privacy,** retirement, isolation,
sequestration, seclusion; incognito, anonymity; **confiden-
tialness,** confidentiality

3 **veil of secrecy, veil,** curtain,
pall, wraps; iron curtain, bamboo
curtain; wall of secrecy; **suppression,** repression, stifling, smothering; **censorship,** blackout
<nonformal>, **hush-up, cover-
up; seal of secrecy;** security

4 **stealth,** stealthiness, **furtiveness, clandestineness,
surreptitiousness, covertness,**
shiftiness, sneakiness, slinkiness,
underhand dealing, undercover
activity, **covert activity or operation;** prowl, prowling; stalking

5 **secret, confidence;** private or
personal matter; trade secret;
confidential or **privileged information or communication;**
more than meets the eye; deep,
dark secret; solemn secret; hush-
hush matter, classified information, eyes-only or top-secret
information, restricted information; inside information;
mystery, enigma 522.8; the arcane, arcanum; esoterica, cabala,

the occult, hermetism; deep secret, mystery of mysteries; skeleton in the closet

6 cryptography, cryptoanalysis; **code, cipher;** code book, code word, code name; **secret writing,** cryptogram, cryptograph; invisible ink; cryptographer

VERBS **7 keep secret, keep mum, veil,** keep dark; keep it a deep, dark secret; secrete, **conceal;** keep to oneself 344.6, keep close, keep back, keep from, **withhold,** hold out on <nonformal>; not let it go further, keep within these walls, keep between us; **not tell,** hold one's tongue 51.5, never let on <nonformal>, make no sign, not breathe *or* whisper a word, clam up <nonformal>, be the soul of discretion; **not give away** <nonformal>, **keep it under one's hat** <nonformal>, keep under wraps <nonformal>, keep buttoned up <nonformal>, keep one's own counsel; play one's cards close to the chest *or* to one's vest; not let the right hand know what the left is doing; keep in the dark; **have secret** *or* **confidential information,** be in on the secret *and* know where the bodies are buried <both nonformal>

8 cover up, muffle up; **hush up, hush,** hush-hush; **suppress,** repress, **stifle,** muffle, **smother,** squash, quash, squelch, kill, sit on, put the lid on <nonformal>; **censor,** black out <nonformal>

9 tell confidentially, tell for one's ears only, **whisper, breathe, whisper in the ear;** talk to in private, speak in privacy; say under one's breath

10 code, encode, encipher, cipher

ADJS **11 secret,** close, closed, closet; cryptic, dark; unuttered, unrevealed, undivulged, undisclosed, unspoken, untold; **hush-hush, top secret,** eyes-only, classified, restricted, under wraps <nonformal>; **censored,** suppressed, stifled, smothered, hushed-up; **unrevealable, undivulgable, undisclosable,**

unbreathable, unutterable; latent, ulterior, concealed, hidden 346.11; arcane, esoteric, occult, cabalistic, hermetic; enigmatic, mysterious 522.18

12 covert, clandestine, quiet, unobtrusive, **surreptitious, undercover,** underground, under-the-table, **cloak-and-dagger,** underhand, **underhanded; furtive, stealthy, sly, shifty, sneaky,** skulking, slinking, slinky

13 private, privy, closed-door; intimate, inmost, innermost, interior, inward, **personal; priviliged,** protected; **secluded, sequestered,** isolated, withdrawn, retired; incognito, anonymous

14 confidential, auricular, **inside** <nonformal>, esoteric; close to one's chest *or* vest <nonformal>, under one's hat <nonformal>; **off the record,** not for the record, within these four walls, eyes-only, between us; not to be quoted, not for publication; not for attribution; unquotable, sealed; sensitive, privileged

15 secretive, close-lipped, secret, close, dark; discreet; evasive, shifty; **uncommunicative, close-mouthed**

16 coded, encoded; ciphered, enciphered; cryptographic

ADVS **17 secretly, in secret,** up one's sleeve; in the closet; nobody the wiser; **covertly, undercover,** under the cloak of; **behind the scenes,** in the dark, behind the veil of secrecy; *sub rosa* <L>; underground; with bated breath

18 surreptitiously, clandestinely, secretively, furtively, stealthily, slyly, shiftily, sneakily, skulkingly, slinkily; by stealth, **on the sly** *and* **on the quiet** *and* on the qt <all nonformal>, behind one's back, by a side door, **like a thief in the night,** underhand, underhandedly

19 privately, in private, in privacy; **behind closed doors,** *in camera* <L>, in chambers

20 confidentially, in confidence,

in strict confidence, **off the record; between ourselves,** strictly between us, *entre nous* <Fr>, for your ears or eyes only, between you and me, between you and me and the lamppost <nonformal>

346 CONCEALMENT

NOUNS **1 concealment, hiding, secretion;** burial, burying, interment; **cover, covering,** covering up, masking, screening 295.1; obscuration; darkening, obscurement, clouding 1026.6; hiddenness, concealedness, **covertness**; **secrecy** 345; uncommunicativeness 344; invisibility 32; **subterfuge, deception** 356

2 veil, curtain, **cover, screen** 295.2; fig leaf; **wraps** <nonformal>; **cover, disguise**

3 ambush, ambuscade; surveillance, shadowing 937.9; blind; booby trap, trap

4 hiding place, hideaway, hideout, concealment, **cover**; safe house; drop; **recess, corner,** nook, cranny, niche; **hole,** foxhole, dugout, lair, den; **asylum, sanctuary, retreat, refuge** 1008; **cache,** stash <nonformal>; cubbyhole, pigeonhole

5 secret passage; back way, back door, side door; escape route, escape hatch, escapeway; **underground,** underground route, underground railroad

VERBS **6 conceal, hide,** ensconce; **cover, cover up,** blind, **screen, cloak, veil,** screen off, curtain, blanket, shroud, envelop; **disguise, camouflage, mask,** dissemble; whitewash <nonformal>; **paper over,** gloss over, varnish, slur over; **obscure,** obfuscate, cloud, shade, throw into the shade; **eclipse,** occult; put out of sight, sweep under the rug, keep under cover; cover up one's tracks, hide one's trail

7 secrete, hide away, keep hidden, put away, store away, stow away, file and forget, bottle up, lock up, seal up, put out of sight;

keep secret 345.7; **cache,** stash <nonformal>, deposit, plant <nonformal>; **bury**

8 <hide oneself> **hide, conceal oneself, take cover, hide out** <nonformal>, hide away, **go into hiding; lie hidden,** lie or lay low <nonformal>, **hole up** <nonformal>, **go underground;** play hide and seek; keep out of sight, drop from sight, disappear 34.2, crawl or retreat into one's shell, keep in the background, keep a low profile; **disguise oneself,** masquerade, take an assumed name, assume a cover, change one's identity, go under an alias, be incognito, go or sail under false colors

9 lurk; lie in wait; sneak, skulk, slink, prowl, steal, creep, pussyfoot <nonformal>, tiptoe; **stalk,** shadow 937.34

10 ambush, ambuscade, **waylay; lie in ambush, lie in wait for,** lay for <nonformal>; stalk

ADJS **11 concealed, hidden, hid,** occult, blind; **covered** 295.31; **covert, under cover,** under wraps <nonformal>; **obscured,** obfuscated, clouded, clouded over, in a cloud or fog or mist or haze; eclipsed, in eclipse; in the wings; buried; underground; close, secluded, sequestered; under house arrest, incommunicado; **obscure,** abstruse, mysterious 522.18; **secret** 345.11; unknown 929.17, latent 519.5

12 unrevealed, undisclosed, undivulged, **unexposed; invisible, unseen,** unperceived, undetected; undiscovered, unexplored, untracked; unaccounted for, unexplained, unsolved

13 disguised, camouflaged, in disguise; incognito

14 in hiding, under cover; in ambush; lying in wait; in the wings; lurking, skulking, prowling, sneaking, stealing; stealthy, furtive, surreptitious 345.12

15 concealing, hiding, obscuring, obfuscatory; covering; unrevealing, nonrevealing, undisclosing

347 COMMUNICATIONS

NOUNS **1 communications,** signaling, telecommunication; electronic communication; satellite communication; media, communications medium *or* media; information theory 551.7; information explosion

 2 telegraph, ticker; **telegraphy; teleprinter,** Telex <trademark>, teletypewriter; telex; wire service; code 345.6; **key,** transmitter; sender; receiver

 3 radio 1033, **radiotelephony, radiotelegraphy,** wireless telegraphy; radiophotography; **television** 1034; electronics 1032

 4 telephone, phone *and* horn <both nonformal>; telephony; receiver; transmitter; cellular telephone *or* phone <nonformal>; caller ID service

 5 radiophone, radiotelephone, wireless telephone, wireless; headset, headphone 50.8

 6 intercom <nonformal>, intercommunication system

 7 telephone exchange, central office, **central;** step-by-step switching, crossbar switching, electronic switching

 8 switchboard; PBX *or* private branch

 9 telephone operator, operator, switchboard operator, **central;** long distance; PBX operator

 10 telephone man; lineman

 11 telephoner, caller, **party,** calling party

 12 telephone number, **phone number** <nonformal>, unlisted number; telephone exchange, exchange; telephone area, area code

 13 telephone call, **phone call** <nonformal>, **call, ring** *and* buzz <both nonformal>; video teleconference, teleconference; hot line; voicemail, phonemail; telemarketing

 14 telegram, telegraph, wire <nonformal>, telex; **cablegram, cable; radiogram**

 15 Telephoto <trademark>, Wire-photo <trademark>, Telecopier <trademark>, facsimile, fax <nonformal>

 16 telegrapher, telegraphist, telegraph operator

 17 line, wire line, telegraph line, telephone line; private line, direct line; party line; hot line; trunk, trunk line; WATS *or* wide area telecommunications service, WATS line

VERBS **18 telephone, phone** <nonformal>, **call,** call on the phone <nonformal>, put in *or* make a call, **call up, ring,** give a ring *or* buzz <nonformal>, buzz <nonformal>; listen in; hold the phone *or* wire; hang up

 19 telegraph, telegram, flash, **wire** *and* send a wire <both nonformal>, telex; **cable;** Teletype; radio

ADJS **20 communicational, communications,** communication, signal; **telephonic; telegraphic; Teletype;** Wirephoto, facsimile; **radio**

348 MANIFESTATION

NOUNS **1 manifestation, appearance; expression; indication, evidence,** proof 956; embodiment, incarnation, materialization; epiphany, avatar; **revelation, disclosure** 351; dissemination, **publication** 352

 2 display, demonstration, show, showing; presentation, presentment, **exhibition, exhibit, exposition,** retrospective; production, performance, representation, enactment, projection; opening, unfolding; **showcase,** showcasing, unveiling, exposure

 3 manifestness, obviousness, plainness, clearness, crystal-clearness, perspicuity, distinctness, patency, patentness, palpability, tangibility; **self-evidence; openness,** overtness; visibility 31; unmistakableness, unquestionability 969.3

 4 conspicuousness, prominence, salience *or* saliency, bold *or* high *or* strong relief, boldness,

noticeability, pronouncedness, strikingness; highlighting, spotlighting, featuring; obtrusiveness; **flagrance** or flagrancy, arrantness, blatancy, notoriousness, notoriety; ostentation 501

VERBS 5 **manifest, show, exhibit, demonstrate, display,** breathe, unfold, develop; **present, evince, evidence; in.licate,** token, betoken, mean 518.8; **express,** set forth; show off, showcase; **make plain, make clear;** produce, bring out, roll out, trot out <nonformal>, bring forth, bring to notice, expose to view, bring into view; **reveal, divulge, disclose** 351.4; **illuminate, highlight, spotlight, feature,** bring to the fore, place in the foreground; **flaunt,** dangle, wave, **flourish,** brandish, parade; affect, make a show or a great show of; perform, enact, dramatize; **embody,** incarnate, **materialize**

6 <manifest oneself> **come out, come into the open,** come out of the closet <nonformal>, come forth, **surface; show one's colors** or true colors, wear one's heart upon one's sleeve; **speak up, speak out, assert oneself,** let one's voice be heard, speak one's piece or one's mind, **stand up and be counted,** take a stand; open up, have no secrets; **appear, materialize**

7 **be manifest,** be there for all to see, make an appearance, **surface,** be seen with half an eye; need no explanation, **speak for itself,** tell its own story or tale; **go without saying; leap to the eye, stare one in the face,** hit one in the eye, strike the eye, glare, shout; come across, project; stand out, stick out, stick out a mile, stick out like a sore thumb, hang out <nonformal>

ADJS 8 **manifest, apparent, evident, self-evident,** axiomatic, indisputable, **obvious, plain, clear,** perspicuous, distinct, palpable, patent, tangible; **visible, perceptible, perceivable, discernible,**

observable, **noticeable, much in evidence; to be seen,** easy to be seen; plain as day, plain as the nose on one's face, big as life, big as life and twice as ugly; **crystal-clear,** clear as crystal; **express, explicit, unmistakable,** open-and-shut <nonformal>; self-explanatory; **indubitable** 969.15

9 **manifesting, manifestative,** showing, displaying, showcasing, demonstrating, **demonstrative,** expository, **expressive; indicative,** indicatory; appearing, incarnating, materializing; epiphanic; **revelational,** revelatory, **disclosive** 351.10

10 **open,** overt, open to all, out of the closet <nonformal>; **revealed, disclosed, exposed;** bare, bald, naked

11 **unhidden, unconcealed; unobscure,** unobscured, undarkened, unclouded; **undisguised,** uncamouflaged

12 **conspicuous, noticeable,** ostensible, **prominent, bold, pronounced, salient,** in bold or high or strong relief, **striking, outstanding** ; highlighted, spotlighted, featured; obtrusive; **flagrant,** arrant, blatant, notorious; **glaring,** staring, stark-staring

13 **manifested,** demonstrated, exhibited, shown, displayed, showcased; demonstrable

ADVS 14 **manifestly, apparently, evidently, obviously, patently, plainly, clearly,** distinctly, **unmistakably,** expressly, explicitly, palpably, tangibly; **visibly, perceptibly,** discernibly, **noticeably**

15 **openly, overtly, before one's eyes** or very eyes, under one's nose <nonformal>; to one's face, face-to-face; **publicly,** in public; **in the open,** out in the open, **in plain sight,** in broad daylight, for all to see, in public view, in plain view; aboveboard, on the table

16 **conspicuously, prominently, noticeably,** ostensibly, **notably, markedly, pronouncedly, saliently, strikingly, boldly,**

outstandingly; obtrusively; arrantly, flagrantly, blatantly, notoriously; glaringly, staringly

349 REPRESENTATION, DESCRIPTION

NOUNS **1 representation, delineation,** drawing, **portrayal, portraiture, depiction,** rendering, rendition, characterization, imaging; **illustration,** exemplification, demonstration; projection, **realization;** imagery, iconography; **art** 712; **drama** 704.1, 4–6; plan, diagram, schema, schematization, **blueprint, chart, map; notation,** tablature; choreography; **writing,** script, text; **writing system; alphabet,** syllabary; letter, ideogram, pictogram, logogram, logograph, hieroglyphic; printing 548; **symbol**

2 description, portrayal, portraiture, **depiction,** rendering, rendition, **delineation, representation** 349; imagery; **word painting** or **picture, picture, portrait, image,** photograph; evocation, impression; **sketch,** vignette, cameo; **characterization,** character sketch; profile; slice of life, graphic account; specification, particularization, details, itemization, catalog, cataloging; **narration**

3 account, recounting, statement, report, word; play-by-play description, blow-by-blow account or description; case study

4 impersonation; mimicry, mimicking, mime, miming, pantomime, pantomiming, aping, dumb show; mimesis, **imitation** 336; personification, embodiment, incarnation; **characterization,** portrayal; **acting,** playing, dramatization, enacting, enactment, performing, performance; **posing,** masquerade

5 image, likeness; resemblance, semblance, similitude, simulacrum; **effigy,** icon, idol; **copy** 784; **picture; portrait,** likeness;

photograph 714.3, 6; **perfect** or **exact likeness, duplicate, double;** match, fellow, mate, companion, **twin;** living image, dead ringer <nonformal>, spitting image or spit and image <nonformal>; miniature, model; **reflection,** shadow, mirroring; trace, tracing; rubbing

6 figure, figurine; doll; puppet, marionette; mannequin or manikin, model, dummy, lay figure; wax figure, waxwork; scarecrow, gingerbread woman or man; **sculpture, bust, statue, statuette,** statuary; portrait bust or statue; death mask, life mask; carving, wood carving; figurehead

7 representative, representation, **type, specimen,** typification, embodiment; **cross section;** exponent; **example** 785.2, exemplar; exemplification, representativeness

VERBS **8 represent, delineate, depict,** render, characterize, hit off, **portray, picture,** draw, paint 712.20; **register,** convey an impression of; **notate, write,** print, map, chart, diagram, schematize; trace, trace out, trace over; rub, take a rubbing; **symbolize** 517.18

9 describe, portray, picture, render, **depict, represent, delineate, paint,** draw; evoke, bring to life, make one see; outline; sketch; **characterize,** character; **express,** set forth, give words to; **write** 547.21

10 go for or **as, pass for** or **as, count for** or **as,** answer for or as, stand in the place of, be taken as, be regarded as, be the equivalent of; **serve as**

11 image, mirror, hold the mirror up to nature, reflect, figure; **embody,** incarnate, **personify, impersonate; illustrate,** demonstrate, exemplify; project, realize; shadow; **prefigure, pretypify,** foreshadow, adumbrate

12 impersonate; mimic, mime, pantomime, take off, do or give an impression of, mock; ape,

copy; **pose as, masquerade as,**
affect the manner of, pass for,
pretend to be, represent oneself
to be; **act,** enact, perform, do;
play, act as, act *or* play a part, act
the part of, act out

ADJS **13 representational, representative, depictive, delineatory; illustrative,** illustrational;
pictorial, graphic, vivid; ideographic, pictographic, figurative;
representing, portraying, illus-
trating; **typifying, symbolizing,**
personifying, incarnating, embodying; imitative, mimetic,
apish, mimish; echoic, onomatopoeic

14 descriptive, depictive, expositive, **representative, deline-
ative; expressive, vivid,
graphic;** realistic, naturalistic,
true to life, lifelike, faithful

15 typical; exemplary, sample;
characteristic, distinctive, distinguishing, quintessential;
**realistic, naturalistic; natural,
normal,** usual, regular, par for
the course <nonformal>; **true to
type, true to form**

ADVS **16 descriptively; expressively, vividly, graphically;** faithfully, realistically, naturalistically

350 MISREPRESENTATION

NOUNS **1 misrepresentation, perversion, distortion,** deformation, garbling, twisting, slanting;
inaccuracy; **coloring, false coloring; falsification** 354.9, **spin,**
spin control, disinformation; injustice; misstatement, misquotation; abstractionism, expression-
ism; overstatement, exaggeration,
hyperbole, overdrawing; understatement, litotes

2 bad likeness, **daub,** botch; scribble, hen tracks *or* scratches
<nonformal>; distortion, astig-
matism; **travesty,** parody, **caricature, burlesque**

VERBS **3 misrepresent, belie,** pass
or pawn *or* foist *or* fob off as, send
or deliver the wrong signal *or*
message; put in a false light, **pervert, distort, garble, twist,**

warp, wrench, slant, put a spin
on, twist the meaning of; **color,
give a false coloring,** put a false
construction upon, falsify 354.18;
misteach 569.3; **disguise,** camouflage; misstate, misreport, misquote, put words into one's
mouth, quote out of context; overstate, exaggerate, blow out of all
proportion; understate; **travesty,**
parody, **caricature, burlesque**

4 misdraw, mispaint; daub,
botch, butcher, scribble

351 DISCLOSURE

NOUNS **1 disclosure,** disclosing;
revelation, revealing, making
public, publicizing, broadcasting;
apocalypse; discovery, discover-
ing; manifestation 348; unfolding, **uncovering,** unwrapping,
taking the wraps off, **unveiling,
unmasking; exposure, exposé;
baring,** stripping *or* laying bare;
showing up

2 divulgence, divulging, divulga-
tion, letting out; **betrayal,**
unwitting disclosure, indiscretion; leak; **giveaway** *and* dead
giveaway <both nonformal>; telltale, telltale sign, obvious clue;
blabbing *and* blabbering <both
nonformal>; **tattling**

3 confession, confessing, shrift,
acknowledgment, admission,
concession, avowal, owning up
and coming clean <both nonfor-
mal>, unbosoming, unburdening
oneself, getting a load off one's
mind <nonformal>, making a
clean breast

VERBS **4 disclose, reveal, let out,
show, leak,** let slip out, let the cat
out of the bag *and* spill the beans
<both nonformal>; manifest
348.5; **open,** open up, lay open,
get out in the open, bring out of
the closet; **expose, show up;
bare,** strip *or* lay bare, blow the
lid off *and* blow wide open *and*
rip open *and* crack wide open <all
nonformal>; take the lid off,
bring to light, bring into the
open, hold up to view; hold up the
mirror to; **unmask, uncover,** un-

veil, take the lid off <nonformal>, ventilate, take the wraps off, lift *or* draw the veil, raise the curtain, let daylight in, unwrap; put one wise *and* clue one in *and* bring one up to speed <all nonformal>, open one's eyes

5 **divulge**; **reveal, make known, tell**, breathe, utter, vent, ventilate, air; give vent to, **give out**, let get around, come out with; break it to, **break the news;** let in on, **confide,** confide to, let one's hair down <nonformal>, unbosom oneself, let into the secret; **publish** 352.10

6 **betray,** inform, **inform on** 551.12; rat *and* stool *and* sing *and* squeal <all nonformal>, turn state's evidence; leak <nonformal>, spill <nonformal>, **spill the beans** <nonformal>; **let the cat out of the bag** <nonformal>, be unguarded *or* indiscreet, kiss and tell, **give away** *and* give the show away *and* give the game away <all nonformal>, betray a confidence; have a big mouth <nonformal>, **blab** *or* blabber <nonformal>; babble, **tattle, tell** *or* tattle on, tell tales, **tell tales out of school;** talk out of turn, let slip, let fall *or* drop; **blurt, blurt out**

7 **confess,** break down and confess, **admit, acknowledge,** tell all, **own, own up** <nonformal>, let on, incriminate oneself, come clean <nonformal>; spill *and* spill it *and* spill one's guts <all nonformal>; **tell the truth,** tell all, let it all hang out <nonformal>; **plead guilty,** cop a plea <nonformal>; **unbosom oneself, make a clean breast, get it off one's chest** <nonformal>, **get it out of one's system** <nonformal>, unburden one's mind *or* conscience *or* heart, **get a load off one's mind** <nonformal>, fess up <nonformal>; throw oneself on the mercy of the court; **reveal oneself,** show one's colors *or* true colors, come out of the closet <nonformal>, show one's hand *or* cards,

put *or* lay one's cards on the table

8 **be revealed, become known, surface, come to light,** appear, manifest itself, transpire, **leak out, get out, come out,** out, come home to roost, show its face; show its colors, stand revealed; blow one's cover <nonformal>

ADJS 9 **revealed, disclosed** 348.10

10 **disclosive, revealing,** revelatory; **disclosing,** showing, exposing, betraying; kiss-and-tell; **talkative** 343.10, 540.9; admitted, self-confessed

11 confessional, admissive

352 PUBLICATION

NOUNS 1 **publication, publishing, promulgation, propagation, dissemination, diffusion, broadcast, broadcasting, spread, spreading, circulation,** ventilation, airing, noising, bandying, bruiting about; **display;** issue, issuance; telecasting; printing 548

2 **announcement**; **proclamation,** pronouncement, pronunciamento; **report,** communiqué, **declaration, statement;** public declaration *or* statement, program, **notice, notification,** public notice; circular, encyclical; manifesto, position paper; broadside; rationale; white paper, white book; ukase, edict 420.4

3 **press release,** release, handout, bulletin, notice

4 **publicity, notoriety, fame,** notice, public notice, **celebrity;** limelight *and* spotlight <both nonformal>, daylight, bright light, glare, public eye *or* consciousness, **exposure, currency,** common *or* public knowledge; **ballyhoo** *and* hoopla <both nonformal>; hue and cry; **public relations** *or* PR, flackery <nonformal>; **publicity story,** press notice; **writeup, puff** <nonformal>, **plug** <nonformal>, **blurb** <nonformal>

5 **promotion, buildup** *and* promo

<both nonformal>, flack <nonformal>, publicizing, promoting, advocating, advocacy, tub-thumping, press-agentry; **advertising,** salesmanship 734.2, Madison Avenue, hucksterism <nonformal>; advocacy, advocacy group

6 **advertisement, ad** <nonformal>, notice; **commercial,** message; testimonial

7 **poster, bill, placard, sign,** show card, banner; **signboard, billboard,** highway sign; sandwich board; marquee

8 **advertising matter,** promotional material, public relations handout *or* release, **literature** <nonformal>; **leaflet,** leaf, **folder, handbill, bill, flier, throwaway, handout, circular**

9 **publicist,** publicizer, public relations officer, PR man, pitchman <nonformal>, **publicity man** *or* agent, **press agent; advertiser; adman** *and* huckster *and* pitchman <all nonformal>; ad writer <nonformal>, copywriter; **promoter, booster** <nonformal>, plugger <nonformal>; **barker,** spieler <nonformal>, skywriter; sandwich man

VERBS 10 **publish, promulgate, propagate, circulate,** circularize, **diffuse, disseminate,** distribute, **broadcast,** televise, telecast, air, **spread,** spread around *or* about, spread far and wide, **pass the word around,** bruit about, **advertise,** repeat, retail, **bandy about, noise about, spread a report; rumor,** launch a rumor, whisper, buzz, **rumor about**

11 **make public,** go public with <nonformal>; bring *or* lay *or* drag before the public, **display,** take one's case to the public, **give** *or* **put out, make known; divulge** 351.5; **ventilate,** air, bring into the open, get out in the open, open up, broach

12 **announce,** annunciate, enunciate; **declare, state,** affirm,

pronounce, give notice; **say,** make a statement, send a message *or* signal; **report,** issue a statement, hold a press conference

13 **proclaim, promulgate,** give voice to; **herald;** blare forth *or* abroad, thunder, declaim, shout, trumpet, trumpet *or* thunder forth; shout from the housetops

14 **issue, bring out, put out, get out, launch** get off, emit, put *or* give *or* send forth, offer to the public

15 **publicize,** give publicity; go public with <nonformal>; bring *or* drag into the limelight, throw the spotlight on <nonformal>; **advertise, promote,** build up, puff <nonformal>, **boost** <nonformal>, **plug** <nonformal>, **ballyhoo** <nonformal>; put on the map, make a household word of, establish; make a pitch for *and* beat the drum for *and* thump the tub for <all nonformal>; **write up;** circularize; **post bills,** placard; skywrite

16 <be published> **come out, appear,** break, hit the streets <nonformal>, **issue,** see the light of day, become public; **circulate, spread,** spread about, have currency, **get around** *or* about, get abroad, get exposure, **go the rounds,** pass from mouth to mouth, be on everyone's lips; spread like wildfire

ADJS 17 **published, public,** made public, **circulated,** in circulation, promulgated, propagated, **disseminated,** issued, spread, diffused, distributed; in print; **broadcast,** telecast, televised; **announced,** proclaimed, declared, **stated,** affirmed; **reported,** brought to notice; common knowledge, common property, current; **open,** accessible, open to the public

18 promulgatory, propagatory, proclamatory

ADVS 19 **publicly, in public; openly** 348.15; in the public eye, in the limelight *or* spotlight <nonformal>, reportedly

353 MESSENGER

NOUNS **1 messenger,** message-
bearer, **dispatch-bearer, courier,**
diplomatic courier, carrier, **runner,** dispatch-rider, pony-express
rider, postrider; bicycle *or* motorcycle messenger; **go-between**
576.4; **emissary** 576.6

2 **herald, harbinger,** forerunner;
evangelist, bearer of glad tidings

3 **announcer,** annunciator, enun-
ciator; **proclaimer; crier, town
crier**

4 errand boy, office boy, messen-
ger-boy, copyboy; bellhop <non-
formal>, bellboy, bellman

5 **postman, mailman,** mail carrier, letter carrier; postmaster,
postmistress; postal clerk

6 <mail carriers> carrier pigeon,
carrier, homing pigeon, homer
<nonformal>

354 FALSENESS

NOUNS **1 falseness, falsehood,** falsity, inveracity, untruth, **truthlessness, untrueness; fallaciousness,** fallacy, **erroneousness** 974.1

2 **spuriousness, phoniness**
<nonformal>, **unauthenticity,**
artificiality, factitiousness

3 **sham, fakery,** faking, falsity,
feigning, pretending; feint, pretext, **pretense, pretension, false
pretense;** humbug, humbuggery;
bluff, bluffing, four-flushing
<nonformal>; speciousness, mer-
etriciousness; cheating, fraud;
imposture; deception, delusion
356.1; representation, **simulation;** dissembling, **dissem-
blance, dissimulation;** seeming,
semblance, appearance, face, ostentation, **show, false show,**
outward show; window dressing,
front, **false front, façade,** gloss,
varnish; gilt; color, coloring; masquerade, facade, disguise;
posture, pose, posing, attitudinizing; mannerism, affectation 500

4 **falseheartedness, falseness,
duplicity, two-facedness,
double-dealing,** ambidexterity;

double standard; **dishonesty,** improbity, lack of integrity, Machiavellianism, bad faith; **cunning,**
artifice, wile 415.1, 3; **deceitfulness** 356.3; faithlessness,
treachery 645.6

5 **insincerity, uncandidness, unfrankness,** disingenuousness;
mockery, hollow mockery;
crossed fingers, tongue in cheek,
unseriousness; sophistry, casuistry 935.1

6 **hypocrisy,** hypocriticalness;
pharisaism, **sanctimony** 693,
sanctimoniousness, religiosity,
false piety, ostentatious devotion,
pietism, Bible-thumping
<nonformal>; **mealymouthed-
ness, unctuousness,** oiliness;
cant, mouthing; lip service; to-
kenism; token gesture, empty
gesture; smooth tongue, smooth
talk, sweet talk *and* soft soap
<both nonformal>; crocodile
tears

7 **quackery, chicanery,** quack-
ishness, **mountebankery,
charlatanry,** charlatanism; **imposture; humbug,** humbuggery

8 **untruthfulness, dishonesty,**
falsehood, **unveracity,** un-
veraciousness, truthlessness,
mendaciousness, mendacity;
credibility gap; **lying, fibbing;**
pathological lying

9 **deliberate falsehood, disinformation, falsification,** disinform-
ing, falsifying; confabulation;
**perversion, distortion, bend-
ing; misrepresentation,** misconstruction, misstatement, coloring, false coloring, slanting, imparting a spin <nonformal>; tam-
pering, cooking *and* fiddling
<both nonformal>; stretching,
exaggeration 355; **prevarication,** equivocation 344.4; **perjury**

10 **fabrication, invention, concoction, disinformation;** canard;
forgery; fiction, figment, **myth,**
fable, romance

11 **lie, falsehood,** falsity, **untruth,**
mendacity, **prevarication, fib,**
flimflam *or* flam, a crock *and* a
crock of shit <both nonformal>;

fiction, pious fiction; story <nonformal>, trumped-up story, farrago; yarn <nonformal>, tale, fairy tale <nonformal>; tall tale *and* tall story <both nonformal>, cock-and-bull story, fish story <nonformal>; exaggeration 355; half-truth, stretching of the truth, white lie, little white lie; a pack of lies

12 monstrous lie, consummate lie, out-and-out lie, whopper <nonformal>, gross *or* flagrant *or* shameless falsehood, barefaced lie, dirty lie <nonformal>; slander, libel 512.3; the big lie

13 fake, put-up job <nonformal>, phony <nonformal>, rip-off <nonformal>, sham, mock, imitation, dummy; shoddy, junk; counterfeit, forgery; put-up job *and* frame-up <both nonformal>, put-on <nonformal>; hoax, cheat, fraud, swindle 356.8; whitewash job <nonformal>; impostor 357.6

14 humbug, humbuggery; bunk <nonformal>, bunkum; hooey *and* hoke *and* hokum <all nonformal>, bosh <nonformal>, bull *and* bullshit *and* crap <all nonformal>, baloney <nonformal>, flimflam, flam, smoke and mirrors <nonformal>, claptrap, moonshine, eyewash, hogwash

VERBS 15 ring false, not ring true

16 falsify, belie, misrepresent; misstate, misquote; overstate, understate; pervert, distort, strain, warp, slant, twist, impart spin <nonformal>; put a false appearance upon, color, gild, gloss, gloss over, whitewash, varnish, paper over <nonformal>; fudge <nonformal>, dress up, titivate, embellish, embroider; make smell like roses; disguise, camouflage, mask

17 tamper with, manipulate, fake, juggle, doctor *and* cook <both nonformal>, rig, cook *or* juggle the books *or* the accounts <nonformal>; adulterate; retouch; load; salt, plant <nonformal>

18 fabricate, invent, manufacture, trump up, make up, hatch, concoct, cook up *and* make out of whole cloth <both nonformal>, fudge <nonformal>, fake, hoke up <nonformal>; counterfeit, forge

19 lie, tell a lie, falsify, speak with forked tongue <nonformal>, trifle with the truth, deviate from the truth, fib, story <nonformal>; stretch the truth, strain *or* bend the truth; exaggerate 355.3; lie flatly, lie through one's teeth, prevaricate, equivocate 344.7; deceive, mislead

20 swear falsely, perjure oneself, bear false witness

21 sham, fake <nonformal>, feign, counterfeit, simulate; pretend, make believe, make a show of, make as if *or* as though; go through the motions <nonformal>; let on like <nonformal>; affect, profess, assume, put on; dissimulate, dissemble, cover up; act, play, play-act, put on an act <nonformal>, act *or* play a part; put up a front <nonformal>, put on a front *or* false front <nonformal>; four-flush <nonformal>, bluff, pull *or* put up a bluff <nonformal>; play possum <nonformal>, roll over and play dead

22 pose as, masquerade as, impersonate, pass for, assume the identity of, set up for, act the part of, represent oneself to be, claim *or* pretend to be, make false pretenses, go under false pretenses, sail under false colors

23 be hypocritical, act *or* play the hypocrite; cant, be holier than thou, reek of piety; shed crocodile tears, snivel, mouth; render *or* give lip service; sweet-talk, softsoap, blandish 511.5

24 play a double game *or* role, play both ends against the middle, work both sides of the street, have it both ways at once, have one's cake and eat it too; two-time <nonformal>

ADJS 25 false, untrue, truthless,

not true, contrary to fact, **fallacious, erroneous** 974.16; unfounded 935.13

26 spurious, ungenuine, unauthentic, supposititious, bastard, **pseudo,** apocryphal, **fake** <nonformal>, **phony** <nonformal>, **sham, mock, counterfeit, bogus,** queer <nonformal>, **make-believe,** so-called, **imitation** 336.8; not what it's cracked up to be <nonformal>; **falsified;** dressed up, titivated, embellished, embroidered; garbled; twisted, distorted, warped, perverted, slanted; **simulated, faked, feigned,** colored, fictitious, fictive, **counterfeited, pretended, affected, assumed, put-on; artificial, synthetic,** ersatz; unreal; factitious, unnatural, man-made; illegitimate; self-styled; tinsel, shoddy, junky

27 specious, meretricious, gilded, tinsel, **seeming,** apparent, colored, colorable, plausible, **ostensible**

28 quack, quackish; charlatan, charlatanish

29 fabricated, invented, manufactured, **concocted, hatched, trumped-up, made-up,** put-up, cooked-up <nonformal>; **forged;** fictitious, **mythical,** fabulous; fantastic

30 tampered with, **manipulated, cooked** and **doctored** <both nonformal>, juggled, **rigged;** packed

31 falsehearted, false; double, duplicitous, **double-dealing, two-faced;** Machiavellian, dishonest; **crooked, deceitful;** creative, artful, cunning, crafty 415.12; faithless, perfidious, treacherous 645.21

32 insincere, uncandid, unfrank, mealymouthed, unctuous, oily, disingenuous; dishonest; **empty, hollow;** tongue in cheek; sophistic or sophistical, casuistic 935.10

33 hypocritic or hypocritical, canting, pharisaical, **sanctimonious,** holier-than-thou, simon-pure

34 untruthful, dishonest, unveracious, truthless, **lying, mendacious;** prevaricating, equivocal 344.11

ADVS **35 falsely, untruly;** erroneously 974.20; **untruthfully,** unveraciously; **spuriously,** ungenuinely; artificially, synthetically; unnaturally, factitiously; speciously, seemingly, apparently, plausibly, ostensibly; nominally, in name only

36 insincerely, uncandidly; emptily, hollowly; unseriously; **hypocritically,** unctuously

355 EXAGGERATION

NOUNS **1 exaggeration,** exaggerating; **overstatement,** big talk <nonformal>, **hyperbole; superlative; extravagance,** profuseness, **prodigality** 486; **magnification, enlargement,** dilation, **inflation,** expansion, blowing up, puffing up, aggrandizement; **stretching, heightening,** enhancement; **extreme,** inordinacy, **overkill, excess** 992; burlesque, travesty, caricature; puffery and ballyhoo <both nonformal>, touting, huckstering; grandiloquence 545

2 overreaction, much ado about nothing, storm or tempest in a teapot, making a mountain out of a molehill

VERBS **3 exaggerate,** hyperbolize; **overstate,** overreach, **overdraw;** overstress; **overdo, carry too far, go to extremes;** push to the extreme, indulge in overkill, overestimate 948.2; overpraise, oversell, tout, puff and ballyhoo <both nonformal>; **stretch,** stretch the truth, stretch the point; **magnify, inflate;** aggrandize, build up; pile or lay it on and pour or spread or lay it on thick and lay it on with a trowel <all nonformal>; talk big <nonformal>, make much of; **overreact,** make a Federal case out of it <nonformal>, make a mountain out of a molehill; caricature, travesty, burlesque

ADJS **4 exaggerated,** hyperbolical,

magnified, inflated, aggrandized; stretched, disproportionate, blown up out of all proportion; overpraised, oversold, touted, puffed *and* ballyhooed <both nonformal>; overemphatic, overstressed; overstated, overdrawn; overdone, overwrought; overestimated 948.3; extreme, pushed to the extreme, inordinate, excessive 992.16; superlative, extravagant, profuse, prodigal 486.8; grandiloquent 545.8

5 exaggerating, exaggerative, hyperbolical

356 DECEPTION

NOUNS 1 deception, calculated deception, deceptiveness, subterfuge, trickiness; falseness 354; fallaciousness, fallacy; self-deception, wishful thinking; vision, hallucination, mirage, will-o'-the-wisp, delusion, illusion 975; deceiving, victimization, dupery; bamboozlement <nonformal>, hoodwinking; swindling, defrauding, conning, flimflam <nonformal>; fooling, tricking, kidding *and* putting on <both nonformal>; spoofing *and* spoofery <both nonformal>; bluffing; circumvention, overreaching, outwitting; ensnarement, entrapment

2 misleading, misguidance, misdirection; bum steer <nonformal>; misinformation 569.1

3 deceit, deceitfulness, guile, falseness, underhandedness; shiftiness, furtiveness, surreptitiousness; hypocrisy 354.6; falseheartedness, duplicity 354.4; treacherousness 645.6; artfulness, craft, cunning 415; sneakiness 345.4

4 chicanery, skulduggery <nonformal>, trickery, pettifogging, pettifoggery, artifice, sleight, machination; sharp practice, underhand dealing, foul play; connivance, collusion, conspiracy

5 juggling, jugglery, trickery, dirty pool <nonformal>, prestidigitation, conjuration, legerdemain, sleight of hand, smoke and mirrors <nonformal>; mumbo jumbo, hocus-pocus, hanky-panky *and* monkey business *and* hokey-pokey <all nonformal>

6 trick, artifice, device, ploy, gambit, stratagem, scheme, design, subterfuge, blind, ruse, wile, dodge, artful dodge, sleight, pass, feint, fetch, chicanery; bluff; gimmick, joker, catch; curve, curve-ball; dirty trick, dirty deal, fast deal; sleight of hand, sleight-of-hand trick; bag of tricks, tricks of the trade

7 hoax, deception, spoof <nonformal>, humbug, flam, fake, rip-off <nonformal>, sham

8 fraud, fraudulence, dishonesty; imposture; imposition, cheat, cheating, swindle, dodge; insider-trading, short weight, chiseling; gyp joint <nonformal>; racket <nonformal>; graft <nonformal>, grift <nonformal>; bunco; cardsharping

9 <nonformal terms> gyp, diddling, scam, flimflam, flam, scam, snow job, song and dance, number, bill of goods, double cross, fiddle, hosing, the old army game, reaming, suckering, sting

10 confidence game, con game <nonformal>, skin game <nonformal>, bunco game; shell game; bucket shop, boiler room <nonformal>; goldbrick; bait-and- switch, the wire, the pay-off

11 cover, disguise, camouflage, protective coloration; false colors, false front 354.3; incognito; smoke screen; masquerade; mask, visor, false face, domino, domino mask

12 trap, gin; pitfall; deathtrap, firetrap; booby trap, mine; decoy 357.5

13 snare; noose, lasso, lariat; net, trawl, dragnet, seine; cobweb; meshes, toils; fishhook, hook;

bait; **lure,** fly, jig, squid, plug, wobbler, spinner

VERBS **14 deceive, beguile, trick, hoax, dupe, gull,** pigeon, play one for a sucker, **bamboozle** *and* snow *and* **hornswoggle** *and* diddle *and* scam <all nonformal>, **humbug, take in,** put on <nonformal>, string along, **put something over** *or* **across,** slip one over on <nonformal>, pull a fast one on; **delude,** mock; **betray,** let down, leave in the lurch, leave holding the bag, **doublecross** <nonformal>, cheat on; two-time <nonformal>; **bluff;** cajole, **circumvent,** get around; **overreach,** outreach, outwit, outmaneuver, outsmart

15 fool, make a fool of, **pull one's leg,** make an ass of; **trick; spoof** *and* **kid** *and* put one on <all nonformal>; **play a trick on,** send on a fool's errand; fake one out <nonformal>; sell one a bill of goods, give one a snow job

16 mislead, misguide, misdirect, lead astray, lead up the garden path, **give a bum steer** <nonformal>; feed one a line <nonformal>; throw off the track *or* trail; throw one a curve *or* curve ball <nonformal>; misinform 569.3

17 hoodwink, blindfold, blind, throw dust in one's eyes, **pull the wool over one's eyes**

18 cheat, victimize, gull, fudge, **swindle, defraud,** practice fraud upon, **con,** finagle, **fleece,** mulct, **bilk, cheat out of, do out of,** obtain under false pretenses; live by one's wits; bunco, play a bunco game; sell gold bricks <nonformal>; shortchange, shortweight, skim off the top; stack the cards *or* deck, deal off the bottom of the deck, play with marked cards; load the dice; throw a fight *or* game <nonformal>, take a dive <nonformal>

19 <nonformal terms> **gyp, clip, scam,** rope in, hose, shave, beat, rook, flam, flimflam, do a number on, hustle, fuck, screw, have, pull something, pull a trick *or* stunt, give the business, stick, sting, burn, gouge, chisel, play *or* take for a sucker, make a patsy of, do, run a game on, slicker, take for a ride

20 trap, catch, catch out; **ensnare, snare,** hook, **hook in,** noose; inveigle; net, mesh, enmesh, ensnarl, wind, tangle, entangle; trip, trip up; **set** *or* **lay a trap for,** bait the hook; **lure, decoy** 377.3

ADJS **21 deceptive, deceiving, misleading,** beguiling, **false, fallacious,** delusive, delusory; hallucinatory, illusive, **illusory;** tricky, trickish, catchy; **fishy** <nonformal>, questionable, dubious

22 deceitful, false; fraudulent, sharp, guileful, insidious, slippery, slippery as an eel, **shifty, tricky,** cute, finagling, chiseling <nonformal>; **underhanded, furtive, surreptitious;** collusive, **two-faced; treacherous** 645.21; sneaky 345.12; **cunning,** artful, **wily, crafty** 415.12; calculating, scheming

ADVS **23 deceptively,** beguilingly, **falsely,** fallaciously, delusively, **trickily, misleadingly,** with intent to deceive; under false colors, under cover of

24 deceitfully, fraudulently, guilefully, shiftily, trickily; underhandedly, furtively, surreptitiously, like a thief in the night; **treacherously** 645.25

357 DECEIVER

NOUNS **1 deceiver, deluder,** duper, **beguiler, bamboozler** <nonformal>; **dissembler,** dissimulator; confidence man; **double-dealer,** Machiavelli; **counterfeiter, forger, faker;** plagiarist; **enchanter,** charmer, mesmerizer; **seducer,** Don Juan, Casanova; tease, teaser; jilter; gay deceiver; **fooler, joker,** jokester, **hoaxer,** practical joker; spoofer *and* **kidder** *and* ragger *and* leg-puller <all nonformal>

2 trickster; juggler, magician, il-

lusionist, conjurer, **prestidigitator**

3 **cheat, cheater;** two-timer
<nonformal>; **swindler, de-
frauder; sharper, sharp,**
pitchman; **confidence man;
cardsharp**;shortchanger; **shyster** and pettifogger <both
nonformal>; carpetbagger

4 <nonformal terms> **gyp,** gyp
artist, flimflammer, flimflam
man, chiseler, bilker, fleecer, did-
dler, crook, sharpie, shark,
slicker, con man, con artist,
bunco, bunco artist, scammer,
clip artist, smoothie, hustler

5 **shill,** decoy, **come-on man**
<nonformal>, plant, stool pigeon

6 **impostor, ringer; impersonator; pretender;** sham,
shammer, **humbug, fraud**
<nonformal>, **fake** and **faker**
and **phony** <all nonformal>,
fourflusher <nonformal>,
bluffer; **charlatan, mountebank;
wolf in sheep's clothing;** poser,
poseur; malingerer

7 **masquerader, impersonator;**
mummer; incognito, incognita

8 **hypocrite, phony** <nonformal>,
sanctimonious fraud, pharisee,
whited sepulcher, **canter,**
snuffler, mealy-mouth; false
friend, fair-weather friend

9 **liar, fibber,** fabricator, fabulist;
falsifier; **prevaricator,** equivo-
cator, waffler <nonformal>;
storyteller; yarner and yarn spinner and spinner of yarns <all
nonformal>; consummate liar;
dirty liar; pathological liar, confirmed or habitual liar; **perjurer,**
false witness

10 **traitor, betrayer, quisling, rat**
<nonformal>, serpent, snake,
**snake in the grass, double-
crosser** <nonformal>, double-
dealer; double agent; trimmer;
turncoat 363.5; informer 551.6;
archtraitor; Judas, Judas Iscariot,
Quisling, Brutus; **schemer, plotter,** intriguer, **conspirator,**
conniver

11 **subversive; saboteur, fifth
columnist; collaborationist,**
collaborator, fraternizer; fifth column, underground; Trojan horse

358 DUPE

NOUNS 1 **dupe, gull; victim;** trusting or simple soul, innocent, *naïf*
<Fr>; babe in the woods; green-
horn; **fool** 923; stooge, **cat's-paw**

2 <nonformal terms> **sucker,
patsy,** pigeon, chicken, fall guy,
doormat, fish, easy mark, sitting
duck, pushover, cinch, mark, easy
pickings, chump, boob, schlemiel, sap, easy touch, soft touch

359 RESOLUTION

NOUNS 1 **resolution,** resolve, **determination, decision,** fixed or
firm resolve, **will,** purpose; **resoluteness, determinedness,**
decisiveness, **purposefulness;**
definiteness; **earnestness, seriousness,** sincerity, devotion,
dedication, commitment; single-
mindedness, relentlessness, persistence, tenacity, perseverance
360

2 **firmness,** firmness of mind or
spirit, **staunchness,** steadiness,
constancy, steadfastness; **stability** 854; concentration; flintiness,
steeliness; inflexibility, rigidity;
loyalty 644.7

3 **pluck, spunk** <nonformal>,
mettle, backbone <nonformal>,
grit, true grit, spirit, **stamina,
guts** and moxie <both nonfor-
mal>, **toughness** <nonformal>;
pluckiness, spunkiness <nonfor-
mal>, **gameness,** feistiness
<nonformal>; courage 492

4 **will power, will, strong-
mindedness,** strength or fixity of
purpose, strength, fortitude,
moral fiber; iron will, will of
iron or steel; a will or mind of
one's own, law unto oneself; the
courage of one's convictions

5 **self-control, self-command,
self-possession,** self-mastery,
self-restraint, self-discipline,
self-denial; control, restraint,
discipline; composure, possession, aplomb; **independence**
430.5

6 self-assertion, self-assertiveness, forwardness, **nerve** and pushiness <both nonformal>, importunateness; self-expression, self-expressiveness

VERBS **7 resolve, determine, decide, will, purpose, make up one's mind,** make a resolution, make a point of; **settle,** settle on, fix, seal; conclude, come to a determination or conclusion or decision, determine once for all

8 be determined, be resolved; **have a mind** or **will of one's own,** know one's own mind; **be in earnest, mean business** <nonformal>, mean what one says; be out for blood <nonformal>; **set one's mind** or **heart upon;** put one's heart into, dedicate oneself to, give oneself up to; buckle down; steel oneself, brace oneself, grit one's teeth; put one's shoulder to the wheel; take the bull by the horns, take the plunge, cross the Rubicon; burn one's bridges, go for broke and shoot the works <both nonformal>; never say die, die with one's boots on

9 remain firm, stand fast or **firm, hold out,** hold fast, get tough <nonformal>, **take one's stand,** set one's back against the wall, **stand** or **hold one's ground,** keep one's footing, hang in and hang in there and hang tough <all nonformal>, dig in, dig one's heels in; **stick to one's guns,** stick with it, stick fast, adhere to one's principles; take what comes, stand the gaff; **put one's foot down** <nonformal>, stand no nonsense

10 not hesitate, think nothing of, **make no bones about** <nonformal>, **stick at nothing,** stop at nothing; not look back; go the whole nine yards <nonformal>

ADJS **11 resolute, resolved, determined,** bound and bound and determined <both nonformal>, **decided,** decisive, **purposeful;** definite; **earnest, serious,** sincere; devoted, dedicated, committed, wholehearted; single-minded, relentless, persistent, tenacious, persevering; **obstinate** 361.8

12 firm, staunch, standup <nonformal>, fixed, settled, steady, steadfast, constant, flinty, steely; unshaken, unflappable <nonformal>; **unswerving;** immovable, unbending, inflexible, **unyielding** 361.9; true, loyal 644.20

13 unhesitating, unfaltering, unflinching, unshrinking

14 plucky, spunky and feisty and gutsy <all nonformal>, gritty, **mettlesome,** dauntless, **game,** game to the last or end; **courageous** 492.17

15 strong-willed, strong-minded; self-controlled, controlled, self-disciplined; **self-possessed; self-assertive,** forward, pushy <nonformal>, importunate; **independent**

16 determined upon, resolved upon, intent upon, settled upon, **set on,** dead set on <nonformal>, **bent on,** hell-bent on <nonformal>

ADVS **17 resolutely, determinedly, decidedly,** decisively, **purposefully, with a will;** firmly, steadfastly, steadily, fixedly, staunchly; **seriously, earnestly,** in earnest, sincerely; devotedly, with total dedication; hammer and tongs, tooth and nail; heart and soul, with all one's heart or might, wholeheartedly; **unswervingly;** singlemindedly, relentlessly, persistently, tenaciously, like a bulldog, like a leech, perseveringly; **obstinately, unyieldingly, inflexibly** 361.15

18 pluckily, spunkily and feistily and gutsily <all nonformal>, **gamely,** dauntlessly; on one's mettle; **courageously, heroically** 492.23

19 unhesitatingly, unhesitantly, **unfalteringly,** unflinchingly, unshrinkingly

360 PERSEVERANCE

NOUNS **1 perseverance, persistence** or persistency, singleness of purpose; **resolution** 359; **steadfastness, steadiness; constancy, permanence** 852.1; loyalty, fidelity 644.7; **single-mindedness,** undivided or unswerving attention, engrossment, preoccupation 982.3; **endurance, stick-to-itiveness** <nonformal>, staying power, **pertinacity, tenacity, doggedness,** relentlessness, dogged perseverance, bulldog tenacity; plodding, plugging, slogging; **obstinacy, stubbornness** 361.1; **diligence,** application, sedulousness, industry, assiduousness; **tirelessness, indefatigability, stamina; patience,** patience of Job 134.1

VERBS **2 persevere, persist, carry on,** go on, **keep on,** keep up, keep at, **keep at it,** keep going, keep driving, keep trying, try and try again, **keep the ball rolling**; not take 'no' for an answer; not accept compromise or defeat; **endure,** last, **continue** 826.6

3 keep doggedly at, **plod,** drudge, slog or slog away, put one foot in front of the other, peg away; **plug,** plug away; pound or hammer away; **keep one's nose to the grindstone**

4 stay with it, hold on, hold fast, **hang on,** hang on like a bulldog, **stick to one's guns**; not give up, **never say die,** not give up the ship; come up fighting, come up for more; **stay it out, stick out, hold out;** hold up, last out, **bear up,** stand up; **live with it,** live through it; stay the distance or the course; sit tight, be unmoved; brazen it out

5 prosecute to a conclusion, **go through with it, carry through, follow through, see it through,** see it out, follow out or up; go to the bitter end, go the distance, go all the way, go to any length; **leave no stone unturned,** overlook nothing; move heaven and earth, go through fire and water

6 die trying, die in harness, **die with one's boots on,** die in the attempt, die hard, **go down with flying colors**

7 <nonformal terms> **stick,** stick to it, stick with it, stick it out, hang on for dear life, hang in there, hang tough, tough it out; **go the limit,** go the whole nine yards, go all out, shoot the works, go for broke, go through hell and high water

ADJS **8 persevering, persistent,** persisting, insistent; **enduring,** permanent, **constant, lasting;** continuing 852.7; **stable, steady, steadfast** 854.12; immutable, inalterable; **resolute** 359.11; **diligent, assiduous, sedulous,** industrious; dogged, plodding, slogging, plugging; **pertinacious, tenacious, stick-to-itive** <nonformal>; loyal, faithful 644.20; **unswerving,** unremitting, unabating, uninterrupted; single-minded; rapt, preoccupied 982.17; **unfaltering, unwavering,** unflinching; relentless, **unrelenting; obstinate, stubborn** 361.8; **unrelaxing,** unfailing, **untiring,** unflagging, **tireless, indefatigable,** sleepless; undiscouraged, undaunted, indomitable, unconquerable, invincible, game to the last or to the end; **patient,** patient as Job 134.9

ADVS **9 perseveringly, persistently,** persistingly; resolutely 359.17; loyally, faithfully, devotedly 644.25; **diligently,** industriously, assiduously, sedulously; **doggedly,** sloggingly, ploddingly; pertinaciously, tenaciously; unremittingly, uninterruptedly; unswervingly, unwaveringly, unfalteringly, unflinchingly; relentlessly, unrelentingly; **indefatigably, tirelessly,** untiringly, unflaggingly; **patiently**

10 through thick and thin, through fire and water, come hell or high water, rain or shine, fair or foul, in sickness and in health; **come what may** 359.20, **all the way, down to the wire,** to the bitter end

361 OBSTINACY

NOUNS **1 obstinacy,** obstinateness, pertinacity, **stubbornness, willfulness,** hardheadedness, **headstrongness;** mind *or* will of one's own; **perseverance** 360, **doggedness, determination,** tenacity; **bullheadedness, pigheadedness, mulishness; obduracy;** balkiness; uncooperativeness; overzealousness, fanaticism 925.11; intolerance, bigotry 979.1

2 unyieldingness, unbendingness, **inflexibility, obduracy,** toughness, **firmness,** stiffness, **rigidity,** stuffiness; **hard line,** hard-nosedness <nonformal>; unalterability, unchangeability, immutability, immovability; irreconcilability, **intransigence** *or* intransigency; **implacability,** inexorability, **relentlessness,** unrelentingness; sternness, grimness, dourness, flintiness, **steeliness**

3 perversity, perverseness, **contrariness, wrongheadedness, waywardness,** cantankerousness, feistiness *and* orneriness *and* cussedness <all nonformal>; sullenness, sulkiness, dourness, stuffiness; irascibility 110.2

4 ungovernability, unmanageability, uncontrollability; indomitability, **intractability,** refractoriness; incorrigibility; **unsubmissiveness, indocility;** irrepressibility; recidivism; **recalcitrance** *or* recalcitrancy, contumacy, contumaciousness; **unruliness,** obstreperousness, restiveness, fractiousness, wildness; defiance 454; resistance 453

5 unpersuadableness, deafness, blindness; closed-mindedness; dogmatism 969.6

6 <obstinate person> **mule** *and* donkey <both nonformal>, ass; pighead; hardnose <nonformal>, hardhead, hard-liner; standpat *and* **standpatter, stickler; intransigent,** maverick; dogmatist,

bigot, fanatic, purist; **diehard, bitter-ender**

VERBS **7 balk, stickle;** hold one's ground, not budge, **stand pat** <nonformal>, **not yield an inch,** stick to one's guns; hold out; not take 'no' for an answer; die hard; cut off one's nose to spite one's face; **persevere** 360.2,7

ADJS **8 obstinate, stubborn, pertinacious, restive; willful, selfwilled,** strong-willed, hardheaded, **headstrong; dogged, tenacious, perserving; bullheaded, pigheaded, mulish** <nonformal>, stubborn as a mule; set, **set in one's ways,** stiffnecked; sullen, sulky; balky, balking; unregenerate, uncooperative; bigoted, intolerant 979.1 i, overzealous, fanatic, dogmatic, opinionated 969.22

9 unyielding, unbending, inflexible, hard, hard-line, firm, stiff, rigid, rigorous, stuffy; rockribbed; **adamant,** adamantine; unmoved, unaffected; **immovable; unalterable,** unchangeable, immutable; **uncompromising,** intransigent, irreconcilable, hard-shell *and* hard-core <both nonformal>; implacable, **relentless,** unrelenting; stern, grim, dour; flinty, steely

10 obdurate, tough, **hard,** hardbitten, hard-nosed *and* hardboiled <both nonformal>

11 perverse, contrary, wrongheaded, wayward, froward, difficult, cantankerous, feisty, ornery <nonformal>; sullen, sulky; irascible 110.19

12 ungovernable, unmanageable, uncontrollable, indomitable, intractable, refractory; incorrigible, unreconstructed; unsubmissive, indocile; irrepressible; recidivist, recidivistic; **recalcitrant,** contumacious; obstreperous, **unruly, restive,** wild, fractious; beyond control, out of hand; **resistant, resisting** 453.5; **defiant** 454.7

13 unpersuadable, deaf, blind; closed-minded; dogmatic 969.22

ADVS **14 obstinately, stubbornly,**
pertinaciously; willfully, head-
strongly; **doggedly,** tenaciously;
bullheadedly, pigheadedly, mul-
ishly

**15 unyielding, unbending, in-
flexibly, adamantly,** obdurately,
firmly, stiffly, rigidly, rigorously;
unalterably, unchangeably, im-
mutably, immovably, unregener-
ately; uncompromisingly, intran-
sigently, irreconcilably; implaca-
bly, inexorably, relentlessly, unrelentingly; sternly, grimly, dourly

16 perversely, contrarily, contrariwise, waywardly, wrong-
headedly, frowardly, cantankerously, feistily, sullenly, sulkily

**17 ungovernably, unmanageably,
uncontrollably,** indomitably, intractably; incorrigibly; unsubmissively; irrepressibly; contumaciously; obstreperously, restively, fractiously

362 IRRESOLUTION

NOUNS **1 irresolution, indecision,**
unsettledness, irresoluteness, **indecisiveness**; mugwumpery,
fence-sitting, fence-straddling;
ambivalence; dubiety, dubiousness, **uncertainty** 970; **instability, inconstancy,** changeableness 853; capriciousness, mercuriality, fickleness 364.3; change of
mind, second thoughts, tergiversation 363.1

2 vacillation, fluctuation, oscillation, **wavering,** wobbling, waffling <nonformal>, **shilly-
shallying,** blowing hot and cold;
equivocation 344.4

3 hesitation, hesitancy, hesitating, holding back, dragging one's
feet; falter, faltering, shilly-
shallying; diffidence, tentativeness

**4 weak will, weak-mindedness;
weakness,** faintheartedness,
frailty, infirmity; wimpiness or
wimpishness <nonformal>,
spinelessness; fear 127; cowardice 491; **pliability** 1045.2

**5 vacillator, shillyshallyer, wa-
verer**; mugwump, fence-sitter,

fence-straddler; **wimp** <nonfor-
mal>, weakling, jellyfish,
Milquetoast

VERBS **6 not know one's own
mind,** not know where one
stands, **be of two minds,** have
mixed feelings; stagger, stumble,
boggle

**7 hesitate, pause, falter, hang
back,** hover; shilly-shally, **hem
and haw;** wait to see how the
wind blows; jib, stick at, stickle;
think twice about, wrinkle one's
brow; debate, deliberate, see both
sides of the question, balance,
weigh one thing against another,
consider both sides of the question; come down squarely in the
middle, sit on or straddle the
fence, fall between two stools;
yield, back down 433.7; retreat,
withdraw 163.6, wimp or chicken
or cop out <all nonformal>; pull
back, drag one's feet; **flinch, shy
away from, shy** 902.7, back off
<nonformal>; fear; not face up
to, hide one's head in the sand

8 vacillate, waver, waffle
<nonformal>, **fluctuate,** oscil-
late, wobble, teeter, dither, **shilly-
shally,** back and fill, keep or leave
hanging in midair; blow hot and
cold 364.4; **equivocate** 344.7;
change one's mind, tergiversate;
vary, **alternate** 853.5; shift,
change horses in midstream,
change 851.5

ADJS **9 irresolute, unresolved; undecided, indecisive, undetermined,** unsettled; dubious,
uncertain 970.15; at loose ends;
of two minds, ambivalent;
changeable, mutable 853.6; capricious, mercurial, fickle 364.6;
mugwumpish, fence-sitting,
fence-straddling

10 vacillating, vacillatory, waffling
<nonformal>, oscillatory, wob-
bly, **wavering, fluctuating,**
oscillating, **shilly-shallying**

11 hesitant, hesitating; faltering;
shilly-shallying; diffident, tentative, timid, cautious; scrupling;
jibbing, sticking, straining, stickling

12 weak-willed, weak-minded,
weak-kneed, **weak,** wimpy *or*
wimpish <nonformal>, fainthearted, **frail, faint, infirm;**
spineless; without a will of one's
own, unable to say 'no'; **chicken**
and chicken-hearted *and* chicken-
livered <all nonformal>, cowardly 491.10; like putty, **pliable**
1045.9

ADVS **13 irresolutely, unde-**
cidedly, indecisively, undeter-
minedly; uncertainly; hesitantly,
hesitatingly, falteringly; waveringly, vacillatingly

363 CHANGING OF MIND

NOUNS **1 reverse, reversal,** flip
and flip-flop *and* U-turn <all non-
formal>, turnabout, turnaround,
about-face; tergiversation, ter-
giversating; **change of mind;**
second thoughts, better thoughts,
afterthoughts

2 apostasy; treason, misprision
of treason, betrayal, turning traitor, changing one's stripes, ratting
<nonformal>, going over, siding
with the enemy; **defection;** bolting, secession, breakaway; **de-**
sertion 370.2; **recidivism,** recidivation, relapse, backsliding
394.2; faithlessness, **disloyalty**
645.5

3 recantation, withdrawal, dis-
avowal, denial, reneging, **un-**
saying, repudiation, retrac-
tion; disclaimer, disownment,
disowning, abjuration, **renuncia-**
tion, renouncement, forswearing; expatriation

4 timeserver, temporizer, oppor-
tunist; mugwump; chameleon

5 apostate, turncoat, renegade,
defector, tergiversator, tergiver-
sant; **deserter,** turntail, quisling,
fifth columnist, collaborationist,
collaborator, **traitor** 357.10;
strikebreaker; **bolter, seceder,**
secessionist, **separatist,** schismatic; **backslider,** recidivist;
convert, proselyte

6 change one's mind *or* **song** *or*
tune *or* **note,** sing a different
tune, dance to another tune;

come round, do an about-face, do
a flip-flop *or* U-turn <nonfor-
mal>; have second thoughts, be
of another mind; bite one's
tongue

7 apostatize *or* apostacize, go
over, change sides, switch, switch
over, change one's allegiance, **de-**
fect; turn one's coat; desert *or*
leave a sinking ship; secede,
break away, bolt; desert

8 recant, retract, repudiate,
withdraw, take back, renege,
welsh <nonformal>, **abjure, dis-**
avow, disown; deny, disclaim;
renounce, forswear, eat one's
words, eat one's hat, eat crow, eat
humble pie; **back down** *or* **out**

9 be a timeserver, temporize,
change with the times; sit on *or*
straddle the fence

ADJS **10 timeserving, trimming,**
temporizing; supple, neither fish
nor fowl

11 apostate, renegade, tergiver-
sant; **treasonous, treasonable,**
traitorous; collaborating; faithless, **disloyal** 645.20

12 repudiative; schismatic; **sep-**
aratist, secessionist, breakaway
<nonformal>; **opportunistic,**
mugwumpish, fence-straddling,
fence-sitting

364 CAPRICE

NOUNS **1 caprice, whim,** humor,
whimsy, freak; **fancy,** fantasy,
conceit, notion, crazy idea, fantastic notion, harebrained idea,
brainstorm, **vagary; fad, craze,**
passing fancy; quirk, crotchet,
crank, kink; bee in one's bonnet
<nonformal>

2 capriciousness, caprice, **whim-**
sicalness, whimsy, whimsicality;
fancifulness, freakishness;
crankiness, crotchetiness, quirkiness; **moodiness;** petulance
110.6; **arbitrariness**

3 fickleness, flightiness, skittishness, inconstancy, **lightness,**
levity; volatility, mercurialness;
mood swing; faddishness, faddism; **changeableness** 853;
unpredictability 970.1; unre-

liability, undependability 645.4;
frivolousness 921.7

VERBS **4 blow hot and cold,** keep
off and on, **fluctuate** 853.5, vacillate 362.8; act on impulse

ADJS **5 capricious, whimsical,**
freakish, humorsome, vagarious;
fanciful, notional, fantastic,
crotchety, kinky, harebrained,
cranky, flaky <nonformal>,
quirky; wanton, wayward, vagrant; **arbitrary, unreasonable,**
motiveless; **moody, temperamental,** prima-donnaish; petulant 110.22

6 fickle, flighty, skittish, **light;**
coquettish, flirtatious, toying;
inconstant, changeable 853.7;
vacillating 362.10; volatile, mercurial; faddish; **scatterbrained**
984.16, unpredictable; **impulsive**

ADVS **7 capriciously, whimsically,**
fancifully, at one's own sweet will
<nonformal>; **flightily, lightly;**
arbitrarily, unreasonably, without
rhyme or reason

365 IMPULSE

NOUNS **1 impulse;** blind impulse,
instinct, urge, drive; vagrant
impulse; reflex, knee jerk; gut
response *or* reaction <nonfor-
mal>; **notion, fancy; sudden
thought,** flash, inspiration,
brainstorm

**2 impulsiveness, impetuous-
ness,** impetuosity; **hastiness,**
suddenness; **precipitateness,**
precipitancy; hair-trigger; **recklessness, rashness** 493; impatience 135

3 thoughtlessness, heedlessness
983.1, **carelessness,** inconsiderateness; **negligence** 102.2

**4 unpremeditation, unde-
liberateness, spontaneity,
spontaneousness;** snap judgment *or* decision

**5 improvisation, extemporiza-
tion,** improvising, **impromptu,
ad-lib,** ad-libbing *and* playing by
ear <both nonformal>, **ad hoc
measure;** extemporaneousness;
temporary measure *or* arrange-

ment, **stopgap, makeshift,** jury-
rig <naut>; **cannibalization**

6 improviser, extemporizer, ad-
libber <nonformal>; cannibalizer

VERBS **7 act on the spur of the
moment,** obey one's impulse, let
oneself go; shoot from the hip
<nonformal>, be too quick on the
trigger *or* the uptake *or* the draw;
blurt out, come out with, let slip
out, say the first thing that comes
into one's head *or* to one's mind

8 improvise, extemporize, talk
off the top of one's head <nonfor-
mal>, speak off the cuff, think on
one's feet, make it up as one goes
along, play it by ear <nonfor-
mal>, throw away *or* depart from
the prepared text, **ad-lib** <nonfor-
mal>, **do offhand,** wing it
<nonformal>, vamp, fake
<nonformal>, play by ear
<nonformal>; **dash off, strike
off,** knock off, toss off *or* out;
make up, whip up, **cook up,** slap
up *or* together *and* throw *or* slap
together <all nonformal>, cobble
up; jury-rig; cannibalize

ADJS **9 impulsive, impetuous,
hasty,** overhasty, quick, sudden;
quick on the draw *or* trigger *or*
uptake, hair-trigger; **precipitate,**
headlong; **reckless, rash** 493.7;
impatient 135.6

**10 unthinking, unreasoning,
unreflecting,** uncalculating,
**thoughtless, inadvertent, heed-
less, careless,** inconsiderate; unguarded; arbitrary, capricious 364.5

**11 unpremeditated, uncalcu-
lated, spontaneous, unde-
signed, unstudied;** unintentional, unintended, inadvertent,
unwilled, **indeliberate; involuntary,** reflexive, knee-jerk <nonfor-
mal>, automatic, goose-step,
lockstep; gut <nonformal>,
unconscious; **unconsidered,**
unadvised, snap, casual, offhand, throwaway <nonformal>;
ill-considered, ill-advised

**12 extemporaneous, extempor-
ary,** extempore, **impromptu,**
unrehearsed, **improvised,** im-
provisatory; **ad-lib; ad-hoc,**

stopgap, makeshift, jury-rigged; **offhand,** off the top of one's head *and* off-the-cuff <both nonformal>, **spur-of-the-moment, quick and dirty** <nonformal>

ADVS 13 **impulsively, impetuously,** hastily, suddenly, quickly, **precipitately,** headlong; **recklessly, rashly** 493.10

14 **on impulse, on the spur of the moment; without premeditation,** unpremeditatedly; unthinkingly, thoughtlessly, heedlessly, carelessly, inconsiderately, unadvisedly; unintentionally, inadvertently

15 **extemporaneously,** extempore, **impromptu, ad lib, offhand;** at *or* on sight; by ear, off the top of one's head *and* off the cuff <both nonformal>; at short notice

366 LEAP

NOUNS 1 **leap, jump, hop, spring, skip, bound,** bounce; **pounce; hurdle; vault;** leapfrog; handspring

2 **caper,** dido <nonformal>, **gambol, frisk,** cavort; **prance**

3 **leaping, jumping,** bouncing, bounding, hopping, capering, cavorting, prancing, skipping, **springing,** saltation; **vaulting; hurdling;** leapfrogging

4 **jumper,** leaper, hopper; **vaulter; hurdler;** jumping jack; jumping bean

VERBS 5 **leap, jump, vault, spring, skip, hop, bound,** bounce; upspring; leap over, jump over, etc; overleap, overjump, overskip; leapfrog; **hurdle,** clear, negotiate; **pounce,** pounce on *or* upon

6 **caper, cut capers,** cut a dido <nonformal>, cavort, **gambol, frisk,** flounce, **trip, skip,** bob, bounce, jump about; **romp; prance**

ADJS 7 **leaping, jumping,** springing, hopping, skipping, prancing, bouncing, bounding

367 PLUNGE

NOUNS 1 **plunge, dive, pitch, drop, fall;** free-fall; header

<nonformal>; **swoop, pounce,** stoop; nose dive, power dive; bungee jump

2 **submergence, submersion, immersion,** engulfment, **inundation,** burial; **dipping, ducking,** dunking <nonformal>, sinking; **dip, duck;** baptism

3 **diving,** plunging; skydiving; bungee jumping; scuba diving, snorkeling

4 **diver,** plunger; high diver; bungee jumper; parachute jumper, sky diver, smoke jumper; skin diver, snorkel diver, scuba diver, frogman

5 <diving equipment> diving bell, diving chamber, bathysphere, diving chamber, bathyscaphe, benthoscope, aquascope; submarine 180.9; diving boat; scuba or self-contained underwater breathing apparatus, Aqua-Lung <trademark>; Scuba

VERBS 6 **plunge, dive, pitch, plummet, drop, fall;** skydive; bungee jump; free-fall; plump, plunk, plop; swoop, swoop down, stoop, **pounce,** pounce on *or* upon; nose-dive, make *or* take a nose dive; parachute, sky-dive; skin-dive; sound; take a header <nonformal>

7 **submerge, immerse, sink,** bury, engulf, **inundate,** deluge, drown, overwhelm, whelm; **dip, duck, dunk** <nonformal>; baptize

8 **sink, scuttle,** send to the bottom; **founder, go down,** sink like lead, go down like a stone

ADJS 9 **submersible,** immersible, sinkable

368 AVOIDANCE

NOUNS 1 **avoidance, shunning; forbearance,** refraining; hands-off policy, **nonintervention,** noninvolvement, neutrality; **evasion;** side-stepping, **circumvention;** prevention, forestalling; **escape** 369; evasive action, the runaround <nonformal>; zigzag, slip, dodge, duck, side step, shy; sidetracking; evasiveness, elusiveness; **equivocation** 344.4, fudging

2 **shirking, slacking,** goldbricking <nonformal>, soldiering, goofing *and* goofing off *and* fucking off <all nonformal>; clockwatching; **malingering; dodging,** ducking; truancy

3 **shirker, slacker,** soldier *or* old soldier, **goldbricker,** goldbrick <nonformal>; clock watcher; **malingerer;** truant

4 **flight,** exit, quick exit, making oneself scarce *and* getting the hell out <both nonformal>, bolt, disappearing act <nonformal>, hasty retreat; **running away, decampment;** skedaddle *and* skedaddling *and* scramming <all nonformal>; **elopement; disappearance** 34; French leave, absence without leave *or* AWOL; **desertion** 370.2; hegira

5 **fugitive, runaway, bolter,** skedaddler <nonformal>; **absconder, eloper; refugee, evacuee,** boat person, *émigré* <Fr>; **displaced person** *or* DP, stateless person; **escapee** 369.5; illegal immigrant, wetback <nonformal>

VERBS 6 **avoid, shun, fight shy of, shy away from, keep away from, circumvent,** keep clear of, avoid like the plague, **steer clear of** <nonformal>, keep *or* get out of the way of, **give a wide berth,** keep remote from; make way for, give place to; **keep one's distance,** keep at a respectful distance, keep *or* stand *or* hold aloof; give the cold shoulder to <nonformal>, have nothing to do with, **have no truck with** <nonformal>; not meddle with, let alone, let well enough alone, keep hands off, not touch with a tenfoot pole; turn away from, turn one's back upon, slam the door in one's face

7 **evade, elude, get out of,** skirt, **get around** <nonformal>, circumvent; give one the runaround; ditch *and* shake *and*

shake off <all nonformal>, give the runaround *or* the slip <nonformal>; lead one a chase *or* merry chase; escape 369.6–8

8 **dodge, duck; take evasive action,** zig-zag; throw off the trail; shy, shy off *or* away; swerve, sheer off; pull clear; pull back, shrink, recoil 902.6, 7; **sidestep,** step aside; parry, fence, ward off; have an out *or* escape hatch; shift, put off; **hedge,** pussyfoot <nonformal>, be *or* sit on the fence, beat around *or* about the bush, hem and haw, beg the question, tapdance <nonformal>, dance around, equivocate 344.7

9 **shirk, slack, lie** *or* **rest upon one's oars,** not pull one's weight; **lie down on the job** <nonformal>; soldier, **goof off** *and* dog it <both nonformal>, **goldbrick** <nonformal>; **malinger; get out of,** sneak *or* slip out of, dodge, duck

10 **flee, fly, take flight, run, cut and run** <nonformal>, **run off** *or* **away,** run away from, bug out <nonformal>, **decamp,** pull up stakes, **take to one's heels,** make off, **depart** 188.6, do the disappearing act, make a quick exit, **beat a retreat** *or* **a hasty retreat, turn tail; run for it, bolt, run for one's life;** make a run for it; advance to the rear, make a strategic withdrawal; **take French leave,** go AWOL; **desert; abscond, elope,** run away with; skip *or* jump bail

11 <nonformal terms> **beat it, blow, scram,** lam, **take it on the lam,** take a powder *or* runout powder, make tracks, cut and run, peel out, **split, skip,** skip out, duck out, duck and run, vamoose, **clear out,** make oneself scarce, get the hell out, make a break for it

12 **slip away, steal away, sneak off,** shuffle off, slink off, slide off, slither off, skulk away, mooch off *and* duck out <both nonformal>, slip out of

13 **not face up to,** hide one's head

in the sand, not come to grips
with, put off, procrastinate, temporize

ADJS **14 avoidable, escapable;** pre-
ventable

15 evasive, elusive; shifty, slippery, slippery as an eel; shirking,
malingering

16 fugitive, runaway, in flight, on
the lam <nonformal>

369 ESCAPE

NOUNS **1 escape; getaway** *and*
break *and* breakout <all nonfor-
mal>; **deliverance; delivery,**
riddance, **release,** setting-free,
freeing, **liberation, extrication,
rescue; leakage,** leak; jailbreak,
break, breakout; evasion 368.1;
flight 368.4

2 narrow escape, hairbreadth escape, **close call** *or* **shave**
<nonformal>, **near miss,** close
or tight squeeze <nonformal>,
squeaker <nonformal>

3 bolt-hole, escape hatch, fire escape, life net, lifeboat, life raft,
life buoy, lifeline

4 loophole, way out, escape
hatch, escape clause; pretext 376;
alternative, choice 371

5 escapee, escaper, evader; escape
artist; escapologist; **fugitive**
368.5; escapist

VERBS **6 escape,** make *or* effect
one's escape; **get away, make a
getaway** <nonformal>; **free oneself,** deliver oneself, gain one's
liberty, **get free, get clear of,** bail
out, **get out, get out of; break
loose,** cut loose, break away,
break one's bonds *or* chains, slip
the collar; **jump** *and* **skip** <both
nonformal>; **break jail** *or*
prison, escape prison, fly the
coop <nonformal>; leap over
the wall; evade 368.7; flee
368.10

7 get off, go free, win freedom, go
at liberty, **go scot free,** escape
with a whole skin, walk *and* beat
the rap <both nonformal>; **get
away with** <nonformal>, get by,
get by with, get off easy *or* lightly,
get away with murder <nonfor-

mal>, **get off cheap;** cop a plea
and cop out <nonformal>

8 scrape *or* squeak through,
squeak by, escape with *or* by
the skin of one's teeth, have a
close call *or* close shave <non-
formal>

9 slip away, give one the slip, slip
through one's hands *or* fingers;
slip *or* sneak through; **slip out of,**
slide out of, crawl *or* creep out of,
sneak out of, wiggle *or* squirm *or*
shuffle *or* wriggle *or* worm out
of, find a loophole

10 find vent, issue forth, come
forth, exit, **emerge, issue,** debouch, erupt, break out, break
through, come out, run out, **leak
out,** ooze out

ADJS **11 escaped, loose,** on the
loose, disengaged, well out of;
fled, flown, fugitive, runaway;
free as a bird, scot-free, at large,
free

370 ABANDONMENT

NOUNS **1 abandonment, forsaking, leaving;** jettison, jettisoning,
throwing overboard *or* away *or*
aside, casting aside; **withdrawal,**
evacuation, pulling out; cessation
856; disuse, desuetude

2 desertion, defection; dereliction; **secession,** bolt, breakaway,
walkout; betrayal 645.8; schism,
apostasy 363.2

3 <giving up> **relinquishment,
surrender, resignation, renouncement,** renunciation, abdication, waiver, abjuration,
ceding, cession, handing over,
standing *or* stepping down, **yielding, forswearing; withdrawing,
dropping out** <nonformal>

4 derelict, castoff; jetsam, flotsam, **flotsam and jetsam;
rubbish, junk,** trash, refuse,
waste, waste product; **dump,**
dumpsite, garbage dump, landfill,
sanitary landfill, junkheap, junkpile, scrap heap; waif, throwaway,
orphan, dogie <nonformal>;
castaway; foundling; wastrel, reject, **discard** 390.3

VERBS **5 abandon, desert, for-**

sake; **quit, leave,** leave behind, take leave of, depart from, absent oneself from, turn one's back upon, say goodbye to, walk away, **walk** or **run out on** <nonformal>, **leave flat** and leave high and dry or holding the bag or in the lurch <all nonformal>, throw to the wolves <nonformal>; **withdraw, back out, drop out** <nonformal>, pull out; **go back on, go back on one's word;** beg off, renege; **vacate,** evacuate; quit cold and leave flat <both nonformal>; jilt, throw over <nonformal>; maroon; **jettison; junk,** deep-six <nonformal>, **discard** 390.7; let fall into disuse

6 **defect, secede, bolt,** break away; pull out <nonformal>, sell out and sell down the river <both nonformal>, **betray** 645.14; turn one's back on; apostatize

7 **give up, relinquish, surrender, yield,** yield up, waive, **forgo, resign, renounce,** throw up, abdicate, **abjure, forswear, give up on, have done with,** give up as a bad job, cede, hand over, lay down, wash one's hands of, **write off,** drop, drop all idea of, drop like a hot potato; **cease** 856.6, **desist from,** leave off, give over; hold or stay one's hand, acknowledge defeat, **throw in the towel** or **sponge** 433.8

ADJS 8 **abandoned, forsaken, deserted,** left; disused; **derelict,** castaway, jettisoned; marooned; junk, junked, discarded 390.11

371 CHOICE

NOUNS 1 **choice, selection, election,** preference, decision, **pick, choosing,** free choice; co-optation; **will,** volition, free will 430.6,7; first choice; the pick 998.7

2 **option, discretion, pleasure;** possible choice, alternative

3 **dilemma,** Scylla and Charybdis, the devil and the deep blue sea; Hobson's choice, **no choice,** zero option; limited choice, affirmative action

4 **adoption, embracement,** espousal; affiliation

5 **preference, predilection,** proclivity, bent, affinity, prepossession, predisposition, partiality, inclination, leaning, tilt, penchant, bias, tendency, taste; prejudice; druthers <nonformal>; style, one's cup of tea <nonformal>, type, bag and thing <both nonformal>; way of life, lifestyle

6 **vote,** voting, **suffrage,** franchise, enfranchisement, voting right, right to vote; **voice, say;** representation; **poll,** polling, canvass, canvassing, counting heads or noses, exit poll; **ballot,** secret ballot, Australian ballot; **plebiscite, referendum;** yeas and nays; voice vote, *viva voce* vote; show of hands, proxy, deciding vote; write-in vote, write-in; graveyard vote; cumulative voting, preferential voting, proportional representation; **straw vote** or **poll**

7 **selector,** chooser, optant, elector, **voter; electorate**

8 **nomination, designation,** naming, proposal

9 **election, appointment;** political election

10 **selectivity,** selectiveness, picking and choosing; **choosiness** 495.1; eclecticism; **discrimination** 943

11 **eligibility, qualification, fitness, suitability,** acceptability, worthiness, desirability; eligible

12 **elect,** elite, the chosen

VERBS 13 **choose, elect,** pick, go with <nonformal>, opt, opt for, co-opt, make or take one's choice, have one's druthers <nonformal>, use or take up or exercise one's option; **shop around** <nonformal>, pick and choose

14 **select,** make a selection; **pick,** handpick, **pick out, single out,** smile on, give the nod <nonformal>, jump at, seize on; **decide between, choose up sides** <nonformal>, cull, glean, winnow, sift; separate the wheat from

the chaff, separate the sheep from
the goats

15 adopt; approve, ratify, pass,
carry, endorse, sign off on
<nonformal>; **take up, go in for**
<nonformal>; accept, take on up
on <nonformal>, **embrace,** espouse; affiliate

16 decide upon, determine upon,
settle upon, fix upon, resolve
upon; make or take a decision,
make up one's mind

17 prefer, favor, like better or
best, prefer to, set before or
above; **had** or **have rather,** had
rather or sooner, had or would as
soon; think proper, see or think
fit, think best, please; tilt or incline or lean or tend toward,
have a bias or partiality or penchant

18 vote, cast one's vote, ballot,
cast a ballot; have a say or a voice;
exercise one's suffrage or
frachise, stand up and be
counted; **poll,** canvass

19 nominate, name, designate;
put up, propose, submit, name
for office; run, run for office

20 elect, vote in, place in office; **appoint**

21 put to choice, offer, present, set
before

ADJS **22 elective;** voluntary; **optional,** discretional; **alternative**

23 selective; eclectic; elective, electoral; appointive, constituent;
exclusive, discriminating 943.7;
choosy <nonformal>, particular
495.9

24 eligible, qualified, fit, fitted,
suitable, acceptable, admissible,
worthy, desirable; enfranchised

25 preferable, of choice or preference, **better,** preferred, **to be
preferred,** more desirable, favored

26 chosen, selected, picked; select, elect; handpicked; **adopted,**
accepted, embraced, espoused,
approved, ratified; **elected;** appointed; **nominated,** designated

ADVS **27 at choice, at will,** at one's
pleasure, at one's discretion, at

the option of, if one wishes; on
approval; **optionally**

28 preferably, by choice or **preference; rather than,** sooner than,
rather, before

372 REJECTION

NOUNS **1 rejection, repudiation;
renouncement** 370.3; disownment, disavowal, **recantation**
363.3; **exclusion,** exception
772.1; **disapproval, nonacceptance,** nonapproval, declination,
refusal 442; contradiction, **denial** 335.2; passing by or up
<nonformal>, discounting, dis-
missal, disregard 983.1; throwing
out or away, chucking and chucking out <both nonformal>;
discard 390.3; turning out or
away, rebuff 907.2; **spurning,**
kiss-off and brush-off <both non-
formal>, scouting, despising,
contempt 157; scorn, disdain

VERBS **2 reject, repudiate,** abjure,
forswear, **renounce** 370.7, **disown, disclaim, recant;** except,
exclude 772.4, close the door on,
leave out in the cold, cut out,
blackball, blacklist; **disapprove,
decline, refuse** 442.3; contradict, **deny** 335.4; pass by or up
<nonformal>, waive, wave aside,
brush aside, refuse to consider,
discount, **dismiss; disregard**
983.2; **discard** 390.7; push aside,
repulse, repel, slap down
<nonformal>, rebuff 907.2, send
packing; turn one's back on;
spurn, scout, **disdain,** scorn,
turn up one's nose at, look down
one's nose at, raise one's eyebrows at, **despise** 157.3

ADJS **3 rejected, repudiated; re-
nounced,** forsworn, **disowned;
denied,** refused; excluded, excepted; **disapproved, declined;**
ignored, discounted, **dismissed,**
dismissed out of hand; **discarded;** repulsed, rebuffed;
spurned, scouted, **disdained,
scorned, despised**

4 rejective; renunciative, abjura-
tory; dismissive; contemptuous,
despising, **scornful,** disdainful

373 CUSTOM, HABIT

NOUNS **1 custom, convention,**
use, **usage, wont, way,** time-
honored practice, **tradition,**
folkway, manner, **practice, ob-**
servance, ritual, **mores; social**
convention 579; **fashion** 578;
manners, etiquette 580.3; way of
life, lifestyle; **generalization**
863.1, labeling, stereotyping

2 standard usage, standard behavior, proper thing, what is
done

3 culture, society, civilization;
trait, culture trait; **folkways,**
mores, system of values, **ethos,**
culture pattern; cultural lag; culture conflict; acculturation

4 habit, custom, second nature;
use, **usage,** wont, **way,** practice,
praxis; **stereotype; pattern, habit**
pattern; stereotyped behavior;
force of habit; creature of habit

5 rule, norm, procedure, **com-**
mon practice, the way things are
done, form, prescribed or set
form; matter of course; standard
operating procedure or SOP

6 routine, round, beaten path or
track; **rut, groove; treadmill;** the
grind or the daily grind <nonfor-
mal>; **red tape, bureaucracy**

7 customariness, accustomed-
ness, **habitualness; inveteracy,**
inveterateness, fixedness; commonness, prevalence 863.2

8 habituation, accustoming;
conditioning, seasoning, training; **familiarization,** breaking-in
<nonformal>, orientation; **do-**
mestication, taming, breaking;
acclimation, acclimatization; **in-**
urement, hardening; adjustment,
accommodation 866.1

9 addiction 87.1; **addict** 87.2

VERBS **10 accustom, habituate,**
wont; **condition,** season, **train;**
familiarize, break in <nonfor-
mal>, orient, orientate; **domesti-**
cate, tame, break, housebreak;
inure, harden, case harden;
adapt, adjust, accommodate
787.7; acculturate

11 become a habit, take root, be-

come fixed, **grow on one,** take
hold of one, take one over

12 be used to, be wont, wont,
make a practice of; get used to,
take to, accustom oneself to,
make a practice of

13 get in a rut, be in a rut, follow
the beaten path or track

ADJS **14 customary, wonted;** traditional, time-honored; familiar, everyday, ordinary, **usual;**
established, received, accepted;
set, prescribed, prescriptive; **nor-**
mative, normal; standard,
regular, stock, regulation; prevalent, prevailing, widespread,
obtaining, accepted, popular, **cur-**
rent 863.12; **conventional** 579.5

15 habitual, regular, frequent,
constant, persistent; repetitive,
recurring, recurrent; stereotyped;
knee-jerk <nonformal>, automatic 962.14; **routine,** well-
worn, beaten; trite, hackneyed
117.9

16 accustomed, wont, wonted,
used to; conditioned, trained,
seasoned; experienced, **famil-**
iarized, broken-in, oriented,
orientated; acclimatized; inured,
hardened, case-hardened;
adapted, adjusted, accommo-
dated; housebroken

17 used to, familiar with, conversant with, **at home in** or **with,** no
stranger to, an old hand at

18 habituated; in the habit of; in a
rut

19 confirmed, inveterate,
chronic, established, long-
established, **fixed, settled,**
rooted, thorough; **deep-rooted,**
deep-seated; ingrained, fast,
dyed-in-the-wool; implanted, in-
culcated, instilled; **set in one's**
ways

ADVS **20 customarily,** conventionally, accustomedly, wontedly;
normally, **usually; as is the cus-**
tom

21 habitually, regularly, routinely,
persistently, repetitively, recur-
ringly; **inveterately, chronically;**
by force of habit, as is one's
wont

374 UNACCUSTOMEDNESS

NOUNS **1 unaccustomedness, newness,** unwontedness, disaccustomedness, unusedness, unhabituatedness; shakiness <nonformal>; **unfamiliarity;** inexperience 414.2; ignorance 929

VERBS **2 disaccustom, cure, break off,** stop, **wean**
 3 break the habit, cure oneself of, wean oneself from, break the pattern; **give up,** leave off, **abandon,** drop, stop, discontinue, kick *and* shake <both nonformal>, throw off, rid oneself of; get on the wagon, swear off 668.8

ADJS **4 unaccustomed, new, unused, unwonted;** unseasoned, untrained, unhardened; shaky <nonformal>; unhabituated, **not in the habit of;** rusty; unweaned; **unused to, unfamiliar with,** unacquainted with, unconversant with, unpracticed, new to, a stranger to; inexperienced 414.17; ignorant 929.12

375 MOTIVATION, INDUCEMENT

NOUNS **1 motive, reason, cause;** matter, score, consideration; **ground, basis** 885.1; sake; **aim, goal** 380.2; **ideal,** principle, **ambition,** aspiration, inspiration, guiding light *or* star, lodestar; calling, vocation
 2 motivation, moving, **actuation, prompting, stimulation,** animation, triggering, setting in motion, getting under way; direction; **influence** 893
 3 inducement, solicitation, **persuasion;** exhortation, preaching; **selling,** salesmanship, huckstering; jawboning *and* arm-twisting <both nonformal>; **lobbying; coaxing,** wheedling, cajolery, conning, snow job *and* smoke and mirrors <both nonformal>, blandishment, sweet talk *and* soft soap <both nonformal>, soft sell <nonformal>; **allurement** 377
 4 incitement, instigation, stimulation, arousal, excitement, agitation, inflammation, fomentation, stirring-up, whipping-up, rabble-rousing; **provocation,** irritation, exasperation; pep talk
 5 urging, pressure, pressing, pushing; **encouragement; insistence,** instance; **goading, prodding,** spurring, pricking, needling
 6 urge, urgency; **pressure, drive,** push; sudden *or* rash impulse; constraint, exigency
 7 incentive, inducement, encouragement, invitation, provocation, incitement; stimulus, stimulation; carrot; reward, payment 624; **profit** 472.3; bait, **lure** 377.2; bribe 378.2; sweetening *and* sweetener <both nonformal>, interest, percentage
 8 goad, spur, prod, sting, **gadfly;** whip, lash, whiplash, gad <nonformal>
 9 inspiration, infusion; fire, spark; **animation, exhilaration;** afflatus, divine afflatus; genius, animus, moving spirit; muse
 10 prompter, mover, prime mover, motivator, impeller, energizer, galvanizer, inducer, **actuator, animator,** moving spirit; **encourager,** abettor, **inspirer,** spark plug <nonformal>; persuader; **stimulator, gadfly;** tempter 377.3; coaxer, wheedler, cajoler, pleader
 11 instigator, inciter; provoker, catalyst; **agitator, fomenter,** inflamer; **rabble-rouser, demagogue; firebrand, incendiary; seditionist,** seditionary; **troublemaker,** mischief-maker, ringleader

VERBS **12 motivate, move,** set in motion, **actuate, impel,** propel; **stimulate,** energize, galvanize, **animate, spark;** promote, foster; force, compel 424.4
 13 prompt, provoke, evoke, elicit, call up, summon up, muster up, **inspire;** bring about, **cause**
 14 urge, press, push, work on <nonformal>, twist one's arm <nonformal>; **sell; insist,** push

for, **importune, nag, pressure, high-pressure,** throw one's weight around, jawbone *and* build a fire under <both nonformal>; **lobby; coax,** wheedle, cajole, blandish, sweet-talk *and* soft-soap <both nonformal>, **exhort,** advocate, put in a good word; insist upon

15 **goad, prod,** poke, nudge, **spur,** prick, sting, needle; whip, lash; pick on, nibble away at

16 **urge on** *or* **along, egg on** <nonformal>; **goad on, spur on,** drive on, whip along; cheer on, root on <nonformal>

17 **incite, instigate, put up to** <nonformal>; **foment, agitate, arouse, excite, stir up,** work up, whip up; rally; **inflame,** incense, **fire,** heat up, impassion; **provoke,** pique; nettle; lash into a fury *or* frenzy; add fuel to the flame, fan, fan the flame

18 **kindle, fire, spark, spark off, trigger, trigger off, touch off,** set off, **enflame,** set on fire

19 **rouse, arouse, waken, awaken,** wake up, turn on <nonformal>, charge *or* psych *or* pump up <nonformal>, stir, **stir up, pique**

20 **inspire,** inspirit; fire, **fire one's imagination;** animate, exhilarate, enliven; **infuse, infect,** inoculate, imbue

21 **encourage, hearten, embolden,** pat on the back, stroke <nonformal>; **invite; abet,** aid and abet, countenance; **foster, nurture,** nourish

22 **induce, prompt, move one to, influence, sway, dispose, lead one to; lure; tempt;** enlist, procure, interest in, get to do

23 **persuade, prevail on** *or* **upon, sway,** convince, lead to believe, **bring round,** bring to one's senses; **win, win over,** win around; **talk over, talk into,** argue into, out-talk <nonformal>; hook <nonformal>, con *and* do a snow job on <both nonformal>, sell *and* sell one on <both nonformal>, **charm, captivate;** wear down, overcome one's resistance,

twist one's arm <nonformal>; **bribe** 378.3, grease *or* oil *or* cross one's palm <nonformal>

24 **persuade oneself, make oneself easy about,** make sure of, make up one's mind; be persuaded

ADJS 25 **motivating, motivational, motive, moving, animating, actuating, impelling, driving; urgent, pressing, driving;** compelling

26 **inspiring, inspirational,** inspiriting; infusive; animating, exhilarating, enlivening

27 **provocative, provoking,** piquant, **exciting, rousing, stirring, stimulating,** stimulative, energizing, electric, galvanizing; **encouraging, alluring**

28 **incitive,** inciting; **instigative,** instigating; **agitative; inflammatory, incendiary,** fomenting

29 **persuasive,** persuading; wheedling, cajoling; hortatory

30 **moved, motivated, prompted, impelled, actuated;** inclined, of a mind to, with half a mind to

31 **inspired, fired,** afire, on fire

376 PRETEXT

NOUNS 1 **pretext, pretense, pretension, show; front,** facade, **sham** 354.3; **excuse,** apology, protestation; **occasion,** mere occasion; put-off <nonformal>; handle, peg to hang on, leg to stand on; **subterfuge,** refuge, device, stratagem, feint, **trick** 356.6; smoke screen, **screen, cover, blind;** guise, semblance; mask, cloak, veil; **cosmetics,** gloss, varnish, whitewash <nonformal>; **cover,** cover-up, cover story, alibi; band-aid

2 **claim,** profession, allegation

VERBS 3 make a pretext of, take as an excuse, **pretend,** make a pretense of; put up a front *or* false front; **allege, claim,** profess, purport, avow

4 **hide under,** take cover under, wrap oneself in, cloak oneself

with, take refuge in; **cover,** cover up, gloss over

ADJS **5 pretexted, pretended, alleged, claimed, professed, purported,** avowed; **ostensible, specious;** so-called, in name only

ADVS **6 ostensibly, allegedly,** purportedly, professedly, avowedly; under the pretext of, **as a pretext,** as an excuse

377 ALLUREMENT

NOUNS **1 allurement, allure, enticement, inveiglement,** invitation, come-hither <nonformal>, blandishment, cajolery; inducement 375.7; **temptation; seduction; beguilement,** beguiling; **fascination, captivation,** enthrallment, entrapment, snaring; **enchantment,** witchery, bewitchment; **attraction, interest, charm, glamour, appeal,** magnetism; charisma; star quality

2 attractiveness, allure, impressiveness, **seductiveness, winsomeness; sexiness,** sex appeal

3 lure, charm, **come-on** <nonformal>, attention-getter *or* -grabber, **attraction, draw,** crowd-pleaser, headliner; hook *and* gimmick <both nonformal>, drawing card; **decoy; bait,** baited hook; **snare,** trap; **endearment** 562; honeyed words; forbidden fruit

4 tempter, seducer, enticer, inveigler, **charmer,** enchanter, tantalizer, teaser; coquette, flirt; Don Juan; **temptress,** enchantress, seductress, **siren; vampire,** vamp <nonformal>, *femme fatale* <Fr>

VERBS **5 lure,** allure, **entice, seduce, inveigle, decoy, lead on;** come on to *and* give the come-on *and* give a come-hither look <all nonformal>, flirt with, flirt; **woo;** coax, cajole, blandish; **ensnare;** draw in, suck in *and* rope in <both nonformal>; bait, bait the hook

6 attract, interest, appeal, engage, impress, catch one's eye, command one's attention, rivet

one, take *or* tickle one's fancy; **invite,** summon, beckon; **tempt, tantalize, titillate,** tickle, **tease,** whet the appetite, make one's mouth water, dangle before one

7 fascinate, captivate, charm, spellbind, cast a spell, **beguile, intrigue, enthrall,** infatuate, **enrapture, transport, enravish, entrance, enchant, bewitch;** carry away, sweep off one's feet, turn one's head; hypnotize, mesmerize

ADJS **8 alluring, fascinating, captivating, riveting, charming, glamorous, enchanting,** spellbinding, **entrancing,** ravishing, **intriguing, enthralling, bewitching; attractive, interesting, appealing,** sexy <nonformal>, engaging, eye-catching, fetching, winning, winsome; exciting; charismatic; **seductive,** seducing, **beguiling, enticing, inviting,** come-hither <nonformal>; flirtatious, coquettish; coaxing, cajoling, blandishing; **tempting, tantalizing,** teasing, titillating, tickling; **provocative;** appetizing, mouth-watering, piquant; **irresistible;** hypnotic

ADVS **9 alluringly, fascinatingly,** captivatingly, charmingly, enchantingly, entrancingly, beguilingly, glamorously, bewitchingly; attractively, engagingly, winsomely; **enticingly, seductively,** with bedroom eyes <nonformal>; **temptingly,** provocatively; **tantalizingly,** teasingly; irresistibly; hypnotically

378 BRIBERY

NOUNS **1 bribery,** subornation, **corruption, graft**

2 bribe, bribe money, gratuity, payoff <nonformal>, boodle <nonformal>; hush money <nonformal>; protection

VERBS **3 bribe,** throw a sop to; grease *and* **grease the palm** *or* **hand** <all nonformal>; **purchase;** buy *and* **buy off** *and* pay off <all nonformal>; suborn, **cor-**

rupt, tamper with; reach *and* get at *and* get to <all nonformal>; **fix, take care of**

ADJS **4 bribable,** corruptible; approachable; fixable; on the take <nonformal>; **venal, corrupt,** bought and paid for, in one's pocket

379 DISSUASION

NOUNS **1 dissuasion,** talking out of <nonformal>, remonstrance, admonition, **warning,** caveat, **caution,** cautioning; intimidation, **determent,** deterrence, scaring *or* frightening off

2 deterrent; discouragement, disincentive, chilling effect; damper, **wet blanket,** cold water

VERBS **3 dissuade, talk out of** <nonformal>; remonstrate, expostulate, admonish, cry out against; **warn, warn off** *or* **away, caution; intimidate,** scare *or* frighten off, daunt

4 disincline, indispose; deter, repel, turn from, turn away *or* aside; divert, deflect; distract, put off *and* turn off <both nonformal>; **discourage; pour** *or* **dash** *or* **throw cold water on,** damp, dampen, demotivate, **cool, chill,** quench, blunt; take the starch out of, take the wind out of one's sails.

ADJS **5 dissuasive,** dissuading, disinclining, **discouraging; deterrent,** off-putting; intimidating

380 INTENTION

NOUNS **1 intention, intent,** mindset, **aim,** effect, meaning, view, **point, purpose,** function; sake; **design, plan, project,** idea, notion; **quest,** pursuit; **proposal,** prospectus; **resolve,** resolution, mind, will; **motive** 375.1; determination 359.1; desideratum, **ambition,** aspiration, **desire** 100; striving

2 objective, object, aim, end, goal, end in view; end in itself; **target,** butt, bull's-eye; quarry, prey, game; *raison d'être* <Fr>

3 intentionality, deliberation, deliberateness; express inten-

tion, **premeditation, calculation, calculatedness,** forethought

VERBS **4 intend, purpose, plan,** purport, **mean,** think, **propose; resolve,** determine 359.7; project, **design,** destine; **aim,** draw a bead on, set one's sights on, go for, drive at, aspire to *or* after; **desire** 100.14, 18

5 contemplate, meditate; envisage, envision, **have in mind, have in view;** have every intention, have a mind *or* notion, have half a mind *or* notion

6 plan, plan on, figure on, plan for *or* out, count on, figure out, calculate, calculate on, reckon, reckon *or* bargain on, bargain for, bank on *or* upon, make book on <nonformal>

7 premeditate, calculate, preresolve, predetermine, work out beforehand; plan; plot, scheme

ADJS **8 intentional, intended,** proposed, **projected, designed, meant, purposeful,** purposive, **willful, voluntary, deliberate;** deliberated; considered, studied, advised, **calculated, contemplated, envisaged,** envisioned, **conscious,** knowing, witting; planned

9 premeditated, predeliberated, predetermined, **aforethought**

ADVS **10 intentionally, purposely,** purposefully, purposively, pointedly, **on purpose,** with a view *or* an eye to, **deliberately, designedly, willfully, voluntarily,** of one's own accord *or* one's own free will; **wittingly, consciously, knowingly;** advisedly, **calculatedly,** premeditatedly, **with premeditation, with intent, by design,** with one's eyes open; with malice aforethought, in cold blood

381 PLAN

NOUNS **1 plan, scheme, design,** method, **program,** device, contrivance, conception, enterprise, **idea, notion;** rationalization, systematization; **planning,** calcu-

lation, figuring; **master plan**, the
picture *and* the big picture <both
nonformal>; approach, attack,
plan of attack; **arrangement**, system, disposition, layout, setup,
lineup; **schedule**, timetable;
deadline; **schema**; blueprint,
guideline, guidelines; methodology; tactics, **strategy**, game
plan <nonformal>; contingency
plan; **intention** 380; forethought,
foresight 960

2 **project, projection, scheme;
proposal**, prospectus, proposition; **scenario, game plan**
<nonformal>

3 **diagram, plot, chart, blueprint**, graph; flow diagram, flow
chart; **table; design, pattern**,
cartoon; **sketch, draft, drawing;
outline, delineation**, skeleton,
figure, profile; elevation, projection; **map**

4 **policy**, polity, principles; **procedure**, plan of action; creed
952.3; **platform**; position paper

5 **intrigue**, web of intrigue, **plot,
scheme**, stratagem, finesse;
counterplot; **conspiracy**, confederacy, cabal; **complicity, collusion, connivance; artifice** 415.3;
contrivance, contriving; **scheming**, schemery; finagling <non-
formal>, **machination**, manipulation, **maneuvering**, engineering; frame-up <nonformal>;
wire-pulling <nonformal>

6 **planner, designer**, deviser, projector; entrepreneuer; organizer,
promoter, developer, engineer; expediter, facilitator; **policymaker,
decision-maker; architect, tactician, strategist**

7 **schemer, plotter**, finagler
<nonformal>, Machiavellian;
intriguer, cabalist; **conspirer,
conspirator, coconspirator, conniver;** maneuverer, operator
<nonformal>, opportunist, ex-
ploiter; wire-puller <nonfor-
mal>

VERBS 8 **plan, devise, contrive,
design**, frame, shape, cast, concert, lay plans; organize, rationalize, systematize, schematize,

configure, pull together; **arrange**,
make arrangements, set up, work
up, work out; **schedule;** program; **calculate**, figure; **project**,
make a projection, plan ahead

9 **plot, scheme, intrigue**, be up to
something; **conspire, connive**,
collude, cabal; **hatch**, cook up
<nonformal>, brew, concoct,
hatch a plot; **maneuver**, operate
<nonformal>, engineer, rig, wan-
gle <nonformal>, frame *or* frame up
<both nonformal>; counterplot

10 **plot; map**, chart 159.11, **blueprint; diagram**, graph; **sketch**,
sketch out; map out, plot out, **lay
out**, set out, mark out

11 **outline, delineate**, brief;
sketch, draft, trace; rough in,
rough out

ADJS 12 **planned, devised, designed**, shaped, **blueprinted,
contrived**; organized, ratio-
nalized, systematized; worked
out, calculated; **projected;
scheduled**, in the works, in the
pipeline <nonformal>, on the calendar, on the docket, on the
carpet; tactical, **strategic**

13 **scheming, calculating, designing, contriving, plotting, intriguing; manipulative; oppor-
tunistic;** Machiavellian, Byzantine; **conniving**, conspiring, collusive

14 schematic, diagrammatic

382 PURSUIT

NOUNS 1 **pursuit**, pursuance;
quest, seeking, hunting, searching; **following**, follow-up;
tracking, trailing, tracking down,
dogging, shadowing, stalking;
chase, hot pursuit

2 **hunting**, gunning, shooting,
sport; **hunt, chase**, coursing;
blood-sport; stalking

3 **fishing; angling**

4 **pursuer, chaser**, follower;
hunter, **seeker**

5 **hunter, huntsman**, sportsman,
Nimrod; huntress, sportswoman;
stalker; courser; trapper; gamekeeper; beater; falconer

6 **fisher,** fisherman, angler
7 **quarry, game, prey,** venery, victim; kill
VERBS 8 **pursue, follow,** follow up, **go after,** take out *or* off after <nonformal>, go in pursuit of; **chase, give chase;** hound, dog; **quest,** quest after, **seek,** seek out, hunt, **search** 937.29, 30
9 **hunt,** hunt down, chase, run, sport; engage in a blood sport; shoot, gun; course; ride to hounds; **track,** trail; **stalk;** hound, dog; hawk, falcon; fowl; flush, start; drive
10 **fish,** go fishing, **angle;** cast one's hook *or* net; shrimp, whale, clam; reel in
ADJS 11 **pursuing,** pursuant, following; **questing, seeking, searching** 937.37; **in pursuit,** in hot pursuit, in full cry; hunting, fishing, piscatorial

383 ROUTE, PATH

NOUNS 1 **route, path, way, itinerary, course,** track, run, line, road; trajectory; circuit, tour, orbit; walk, beat, round; path of least resistance, primrose path, garden path; shortcut
2 **path, track, trail, pathway,** footpath; walkway; **sidewalk, walk;** boardwalk; promenade, esplanade, mall; towpath; bridle path; bicycle path; beaten track *or* path, rut, groove
3 **passageway, pass, passage, defile; avenue, artery; corridor, aisle, alley, lane; channel, conduit** 239.1; opening, aperture; access, inlet 189.5; exit, outlet 190.9; gallery, arcade, portico, colonnade, cloister, ambulatory; tunnel; junction, interchange, **intersection** 170.2
4 **byway, bypath,** byroad, side street; **bypass, detour,** roundabout way; back road, back street
5 **road,** highway, roadway, right-of-way; **street**
6 **pavement,** paving; macadam, blacktop, asphalt, tarmac; concrete; cobblestone; gravel; washboard; curb, curbing; gutter

7 **railway, railroad,** rail, line, track; junction; terminus, terminal, the end of the line; roadway, roadbed, embankment; bridge, trestle
8 **cableway,** ropeway, wireway, wire ropeway, cable *or* rope railway, funicular *or* funicular railway
9 **bridge, span, viaduct**

384 MANNER, MEANS

NOUNS 1 **manner, way,** wise, **means, mode,** modality, **fashion, style,** tone; **method,** methodology, **system;** algorithm <MS math>; **approach,** attack, tack; **technique, procedure, process,** proceeding, course, practice; *modus operandi* <L>, mode of operation *or* MO; **routine**
2 **means, ways and means,** means to an end; **wherewithal;** funds 728.14; **resources,** capital 728.15; bankroll <nonformal>; stock in trade, stock, supply 386; power base, constituency, backing, support; devices; method
3 **instrumentality, agency;** machinery, **mechanism,** modality; gadgetry <nonformal>; **expedient,** recourse, resort, device 994.2
4 **instrument, tool, implement, appliance,** device; contrivance, mechanism; **vehicle, organ; agent** 576; medium, mediator, intermediary, liaison, go-between 576.4; expediter, facilitator; midwife, servant, slave, handmaid, handmaiden; **cat's-paw, puppet, dummy, pawn,** creature, minion, stooge <nonformal>; stalking horse; dupe 358
VERBS 5 **use, utilize,** adopt, effect; **approach, attack;** proceed, practice, go about; routinize
6 **find means, find a way,** provide *or* have the wherewithal; get by hook or by crook, obtain by fair means or foul; beg, borrow, or steal
7 **be instrumental, serve,** serve one's purpose, come in handy,

stand in good stead, fill the bill; act in the interests of, **promote, advance, forward, assist,** facilitate; mediate, go between

ADJS 8 modal; **instrumental, implemental; useful,** handy, employable, **serviceable; helpful,** conducive, favoring, promoting, facilitating; subservient, ministering; mediating, intermediary

ADVS 9 **how, in what way** or **manner**; to what extent; at what price; after this fashion, in this way, along these lines; **thus, so,** just so; on the lines of

10 **anyhow, anyway,** in any way, **by any means, by any manner of means;** in any event, at any rate, leastways <nonformal>, in any case; **nevertheless, nonetheless, however, regardless;** at all, nohow <nonformal>

11 **somehow, in some way,** in some way or other, by some means, **somehow or other,** in one way or another, in some such way, after a fashion; no matter how, **by hook or by crook,** by fair means or foul

12 herewith, therewith, wherewith, wherewithal; whereby, thereby, hereby

385 PROVISION, EQUIPMENT

NOUNS 1 **provision,** providing; **equipment, accouterment,** outfitting; **supply,** supplying; **furnishing;** chandlery, **retailing, selling** 734.2; **logistics;** procurement 472.1; provisioning, victualing, catering; resupply, replenishment, reinforcement; **preparation** 405

2 **provisions, supplies** 386.1; **merchandise** 735

3 **accommodations,** facilities; **lodgings; room and board, bed and board; subsistence,** keep

4 **equipment,** matériel, munitions; **furniture, furnishings; fixtures, fittings, appointments, accouterments, appurtenances; appliances,** utensils, **conveniences; outfit, apparatus, rig,** machinery; stock-in-

trade; paraphernalia, **gear, stuff** <nonformal>, impedimenta <pl>, **tackle;** armament, munition

5 **harness,** caparison, trappings, **tack,** tackle

6 **provider, supplier;** patron; **purveyor,** provisioner, **caterer,** victualer, sutler; chandler, retailer, merchant 730.2; commissary, quartermaster, storekeeper

VERBS 7 **provide, supply,** find, dish up and rustle up <both nonformal>, **furnish;** accommodate; invest, endow, fund, subsidize; donate, give, afford, contribute, kick in <nonformal>, yield, present 478.12; make provision or due provision for; prepare 405.6; support, maintain, keep; replenish, restock, recruit

8 **equip, furnish, outfit, gear, prepare, fit,** fit up or out, **rig,** rig up or out, **turn out,** appoint, accouter; arm, munition

9 **provision,** provender, cater, victual; **board,** feed; forage; **purvey,** sell 734.8

10 **accommodate;** house, lodge 225.10; **put up**

11 **make a living,** earn a living or livelihood, **make** or **earn one's keep**

12 **support oneself,** make one's way; **make ends meet, keep body and soul together, keep the wolf from the door,** keep one's head above water; **survive, subsist, cope, eke out,** scrape along, get by

ADJS 13 **provided, supplied, furnished,** provisioned, catered; **equipped, fitted,** fitted out, outfitted, accoutered; staffed, manned; readied, **prepared** 405.16

14 **well-provided, well-supplied, well-furnished,** well-stocked; **well-equipped,** well-appointed

386 STORE, SUPPLY

NOUNS 1 **store, hoard, treasure,** treasury; plenty, plenitude, abundance, cornucopia; **collection, accumulation, amassment,** budget, **stockpile; backlog;** repertoire; stock-in-trade; **inventory, stock;** lock, stock, and barrel; **stores, supplies, provisions,** rations; larder, commissary; munitions; matériel

2 **supply, fund, resource, resources; means, assets,** liquid assets, **capital,** capitalization, cash flow, stock in trade; venture capital; grist for the mill; holdings, property 471

3 **reserve, reserves,** resource; **stockpile, cache,** backup, something to fall back on, **nest egg, savings;** ace in the hole <nonformal>, a card up one's sleeve

4 **source of supply,** source, staple, resource; well, fountain, fount, wellspring; mine, **gold mine, bonanza;** quarry, lode, vein; cornucopia

5 **storage, stowage;** preservation, conservation, safekeeping, warehousing; storage space, shelfroom; custody, guardianship 1007.2

6 **storehouse, storeroom,** stock room, **depository, repository,** reservoir, depot, supply depot, supply base, warehouse; entrepôt; dock; attic, cellar, basement; closet, cupboard; wine cellar; **treasury,** exchequer; bank, vault 729.12, strongroom, strongbox; **archives, library;** armory, arsenal, dump; vat, tank; **locker,** hutch; bookcase, stack

7 **garner, granary,** grain bin, elevator, grain elevator, **silo;** mow, haymow, hayloft, hayrick; crib

8 **larder, pantry;** root cellar; dairy

9 **museum; gallery,** art gallery; salon

VERBS 10 **store, stow; lay in,** lay in a supply or stock or store, store away, stow away, **put away, lay away,** put or lay by, lay down, salt down or away and sock away and squirrel away <all nonformal>; **deposit,** reposit, lodge; **cache,** stash <nonformal>; **bank,** coffer; warehouse

11 **store up, stock up, lay up,** put up, **save up, heap up,** pile up,

build up a stock or an inventory; **accumulate, collect, amass, stockpile; hoard,** treasure, save, squirrel, squirrel away; hide, secrete 346.7

12 **reserve, save, conserve, keep,** retain, husband, husband one's resources, keep or hold back, withhold; **keep in reserve;** sequester, put in escrow; **preserve** 397.7; **set or put aside,** put or lay or set by; save up, keep as a nest egg, **save for a rainy day,** provide for or against a rainy day

13 **have in store** or reserve, have to fall back upon, have something laid by, have something laid by for a rainy day

ADJS 14 **stored, accumulated,** amassed, laid up; **stockpiled;** backlogged; **hoarded**

15 **reserved, preserved, saved,** retained, held, withheld, held back, kept or held in reserve; spare

ADVS 16 **in store,** in stock, in supply, **on hand**

17 **in reserve,** back, aside, by

387 USE

NOUNS 1 **use, employment,** utilization, **usage; exercise, exertion;** hard use, hard or rough usage; **application;** expenditure, exhausting, dissipation, **consumption** 388

2 **usage, treatment, handling,** management; stewardship, custodianship, guardianship

3 **utility, usefulness, usability, use,** avail, **serviceability, helpfulness,** applicability, availability, **practicability,** practicality, **effectiveness,** efficacy, efficiency

4 **benefit, use, service, avail, profit, advantage,** point, percentage and mileage <all nonformal>; interest, behalf; **value, worth**

5 **function, use, purpose, role,** end use, operation; work, office

6 **functionalism, utilitarianism;** pragmatism; functional design

7 <law terms> usufruct, imperfect usufruct, perfect usufruct, right of use, user

8 utilization, using, making use of, using as a means or tool; **employment,** employing; **management,** manipulation, operation, **exploitation,** mobilizing

9 user, employer; **consumer,** enjoyer

VERBS **10 use, utilize, make use of; employ,** practice, ply, work, manipulate, operate, **wield; have** or **enjoy the use of;** exercise, **exert**

11 apply, put to use or **good use,** carry out, **put into practice** or **operation,** put in force, enforce

12 treat, handle, manage, **deal with, cope with,** take on, tackle <nonformal>, contend with

13 spend, consume, expend, **pass,** employ, **put in;** give to or give over to, devote or consecrate or dedicate to; while away; dissipate, **exhaust, use up**

14 avail oneself of, make use of, resort to, put to use or **good use,** have recourse to, **turn to,** look to, betake oneself to; revert to, fall back on or upon; convert or turn to use, press or enlist into service, impress, **call upon,** call or bring into play, recruit, muster

15 take advantage of, avail oneself of, make the most of, make good use of, **turn to use** or **profit** or **account** or **good account,** turn to advantage or good advantage, use to advantage; **profit by, benefit from,** reap the benefit of; **exploit, capitalize on, make capital of,** make a good thing of <nonformal>, make hay <nonformal>, **trade on,** cash in on <nonformal>; make the best of, make a virtue of necessity

16 <take unfair advantage of> **exploit, take advantage of, use, use for one's own ends;** sucker and play for a sucker <both nonformal>; **manipulate,** work on, stroke, play on or upon; play both ends against the middle; **impose upon,** presume upon; use ill, abuse, misuse 389.4; milk, bleed, bleed white <nonformal>; suck the blood of or from, suck dry;

feather one's nest <nonformal>, **profiteer**

17 avail, be of service, serve, **suffice, do, answer** or **serve one's purpose,** serve one's need, fill the bill and do the trick <both nonformal>; **stand one in good stead,** be handy; advantage, be of advantage or service to; **profit, benefit,** pay and pay off <both nonformal>

ADJS **18 useful,** of service, **serviceable;** good for; **helpful,** of help 449.21; **advantageous, to one's advantage** or **profit, profitable,** beneficial 998.12; **practical, functional, utilitarian,** of general utility or application; fitting, expedient 994.5; well-used, well-thumbed

19 using, exploitive, exploitative, manipulative

20 handy, convenient; available, accessible, **ready, at hand,** to hand, **on hand,** on tap, on deck <nonformal>, at one's call or beck and call, at one's fingertips, at one's disposal; versatile, adaptable; quick and dirty <nonformal>

21 effectual, effective, efficacious, operative

22 valuable, of value, **profitable,** yielding a return, well-spent, **worthwhile,** rewarding; remunerative

23 usable, utilizable; applicable; reusable; exploitable; compliant 433.12

24 used, employed, applied; secondhand 841.18

25 in use, in practice, in force, in effect, in service, in operation

ADVS **26 usefully,** to good use; **profitably, advantageously, to advantage,** to good effect; effectually, effectively, efficiently; serviceably, **practically;** handily, conveniently

388 CONSUMPTION

NOUNS **1 consumption, consuming, using** or **eating up;** absorption, assimilation, **expenditure,** expending, spending; squandering, wastefulness 486.1; **depletion**, exhausting, **exhaustion**, impoverishment; **waste**, wasting away, erosion, attrition

2 **consumable, consumable item** *or* **goods;** nonrenewable *or* non-recyclable item *or* resource; **throwaway,** disposable goods *or* item

VERBS 3 **consume, spend, expend, use up;** absorb, assimilate, digest, **eat up,** gobble, gobble up; burn up; **finish,** finish off; **exhaust, deplete,** impoverish, drain; suck dry, bleed white <nonformal>; erode; waste away; **throw away,** squander 486.3

4 **be consumed, be used up,** waste; **run out, give out,** peter out <nonformal>; run dry, dry up

ADJS 5 **used up, consumed;** irreplaceable; nonrenewable, non-recyclable, **nonreusable; spent,** exhausted, effete, dissipated, depleted, impoverished, drained, worn-out; worn away, eroded; **wasted** 486.9

6 **consumable, expendable**; replaceable; disposable, throwaway

389 MISUSE

NOUNS 1 **misuse, misusage, abuse; misemployment, misapplication; mishandling,** mismanagement; breach of public trust, maladministration; diversion, defalcation, misappropriation, conversion, **embezzlement,** peculation, pilfering; profanation, violation, pollution, desecration, debasement; malpractice, abuse of office, misconduct, malfeasance, misfeasance

2 **mistreatment, ill-treatment, maltreatment, ill-use, abuse; molesting, molestation,** child abuse *or* molestation; **violation,** atrocity, cruel and unusual punishment

3 **persecution,** oppression, harrying, hounding, tormenting, bashing <nonformal>, harassment, victimization; **witch-hunting,** red-baiting <nonformal>, McCarthyism

VERBS 4 **misuse, misemploy, abuse, misapply; mishandle,** mismanage; divert, misappropriate, embezzle, pilfer, peculate; pervert, prostitute; profane, violate, pollute, foul, foul one's own nest, desecrate, defile, debase

5 **mistreat, maltreat, ill-treat, ill-use, abuse, molest;** outrage, do violence to; mishandle, manhandle; buffet, **savage,** manhandle, maul

6 <nonformal terms> screw, screw over, shaft, stiff

7 **persecute,** oppress, **torment,** victimize, play cat and mouse with, **harass,** get *or* keep after, harry, hound, beset

ADVS 8 on one's back *and* on one's case <both nonformal>

390 DISUSE

NOUNS 1 **disuse,** desuetude; **non-use, nonemployment; abstinence, abstention; obsolescence,** obsoleteness; superannuation, retirement

2 **discontinuance,** cessation; **abdication,** renunciation, abjuration; waiver, nonexercise; abeyance, suspension, back burner *and* cold storage <all nonformal>

3 **discard, discarding,** jettison, deep six <nonformal>, disposal, dumping, **waste disposal; scrapping, junking** <nonformal>; removal, elimination 772.2; **rejection** 372; **reject,** throwaway; **refuse** 391.4

VERBS 4 **cease to use; abdicate, relinquish; discontinue, disuse,** quit, give up, lay off <nonformal>, **phase out,** put behind one, leave off, come off <nonformal>, desist, desist from, have done with; renounce, abjure

5 **not use, do without,** dispense with, **let alone,** hold off; **abstain, refrain,** forgo, forbear, waive; keep *or* hold back, reserve, sock *or* squirrel away, tuck away, put under the mattress, hoard; have up one's sleeve

6 **put away,** lay away, **put aside,**

put *or* lay *or* set by; stow, store 386.10; **pigeonhole, shelve,** put on the shelf, put in mothballs; **table,** lay on the table; put on hold *or* on the back burner <nonformal>, postpone, delay 845.8

7 discard, reject, throw away, throw out, chuck *or* chuck away *and* shit-can *and* eighty-six <all nonformal>, cast off *or* away *or* aside; **get rid of,** get quit of, rid oneself of, shrug off, **dispose of,** slough, **dump, ditch** <nonformal>, **jettison, throw** *or* **heave** *or* **toss overboard,** deep-six <nonformal>, throw out the window; throw over, jilt; part with, give away; throw to the wolves, write off, walk away from, **abandon** 370.5; remove, **eliminate** 772.5

8 scrap, junk <nonformal>, consign to the scrap heap; superannuate, retire, put out to pasture

9 obsolesce, fall into disuse; be superseded

ADJS **10 disused, abandoned,** deserted, **discontinued,** done with; out, **out of use; outworn,** worn-out, not worth saving; **obsolete,** obsolescent, superannuated; superseded, out-of-date, outmoded; retired, pensioned off; on the shelf; antiquated, old-fashioned

11 discarded, rejected, **castoff,** castaway

12 unused, unutilized, **unemployed,** unexercised; in abeyance, suspended; waived; **unspent,** unexpended; held back, held out, put by, put aside, held in reserve, to spare, extra, reserve; stored 386.14; untouched, unhandled; untapped; **new,** pristine, fresh off the assembly line, in mint condition

391 USELESSNESS

NOUNS **1 uselessness,** inutility; **needlessness;** unserviceability, **unusability,** disrepair; unhelpfulness; unsuitability, unfitness; otioseness, otiosity; **superfluousness** 992.4

2 futility, vanity, emptiness, hollowness; **fruitlessness,** bootlessness, unprofitability, otiosity, worthlessness; triviality, nugaciousness; unproductiveness 890; **ineffectuality,** ineffectiveness, inefficacy 19.3; **impotence** 19.1; **pointlessness,** meaninglessness, purposelessness, aimlessness, fecklessness; inanity, fatuity; vicious circle *or* cycle; **rat race** <nonformal>

3 labor in vain, labor lost; **wildgoose chase;** waste of breath, waste of time, wasted effort, wasted breath

4 refuse, waste, waste matter, sludge; **offal; leavings, scraps; garbage,** hogwash <nonformal>; bilgewater; **dregs** 256.2; **offscourings,** scourings, rinsings; parings, shavings; **scum;** chaff, stubble, husks; deadwood; rags, bones, shard, potsherd; slag

5 rubbish, rubble, trash, junk <nonformal>, riffraff, **scrap, debris,** litter

6 trash pile, junkpile <nonformal>, scrap heap, dustheap; **junkyard** <nonformal>, **dump,** dumpsite, landfill, sanitary landfill, toxic waste dump

7 wastepaper basket, wastebasket; litter basket; garbage bag, garbage can

VERBS **8 be useless, be futile, make no difference, cut no ice; die aborning; labor in vain, go on a wild-goose chase,** go around in circles, spin one's wheels *and* bang one's head against a brick wall <both nonformal>, tilt at windmills, bay at the moon, waste one's effort *or* breath, beat *or* flog a dead horse, carry coals to Newcastle, look for a needle in a haystack, lock the barn door after the horse is stolen

ADJS **9 useless,** of no use, no go <nonformal>; **aimless,** meaningless, **purposeless, pointless,** feckless; **unavailing,** of no avail; ineffective, **ineffectual** 19.15; impotent 19.13; **superfluous** 992.17

10 needless, unnecessary, unes-

sential, nonessential, **unneeded, uncalled-for;** unrecognized

11 **worthless, valueless, good-for-nothing,** no-account <nonformal>, dear at any price, not worth a dime *or* a red cent *or* a hill of beans *or* shit <nonformal>, not worth mentioning *or* speaking of, not worth a rap *or* a continental *or* a damn, not worth the pains *or* the trouble, of no earthly use; trivial, penny-ante <nonformal>, nugatory, nugacious; **junk** and **junky** <both nonformal>; **cheap,** shoddy, trashy, **shabby**

12 **fruitless,** profitless, otiose, **unprofitable,** unremunerative; **unrewarding;** abortive; barren, sterile, unproductive 890.4

13 **vain, futile,** hollow, empty, idle; absurd; inane, fatuous

14 **unserviceable, unusable,** unworkable; out of order, out of whack *and* on the blink *and* on the fritz <all nonformal>, in disrepair; **unhelpful;** inapplicable; nonfunctional, otiose

ADVS 15 **uselessly; needlessly;** fruitlessly; **futilely, vainly;** to no purpose, **aimlessly, pointlessly,** fecklessly

392 IMPROVEMENT

NOUNS 1 **improvement, betterment,** change for the better; melioration, **amelioration; mend, amendment; progress,** progression, headway; breakthrough; **advance,** advancement; **promotion, furtherance; rise,** ascent, **lift, uplift,** uptick <nonformal>, upswing; **increase** 251, upgrade; **enhancement, enrichment; restoration,** revival, recovery

2 **development, refinement,** elaboration, **perfection;** embellishment; maturation, ripening

3 **cultivation, culture, refinement, polish,** civility; **civilization;** acculturation; socialization; enlightenment, education 927.4

4 **revision, emendation, amendment, correction, corrigenda, rectification;** editing, redaction; **polishing,** touching up, putting on the finishing touches, finishing, perfecting, tuning, fine-tuning

5 **reform, reformation;** regeneration 857.2; **transformation; conversion** 857; revisionism; utopianism; progressiveness, progressivism; extremism, radicalism 611.4; revolution 859

6 **reformer,** meliorist; gradualist, revisionist; utopian; progressive; radical, extremist 611.12; revolutionary 859.3

VERBS 7 <get better> **improve, grow better,** meliorate, ameliorate; **look up** *or* **pick up** *or* **perk up** <all nonformal>; **develop,** shape up; **advance, progress, make progress, make headway, gain,** gain ground, go forward, get ahead, come along *and* come along nicely <both nonformal>; make strides *or* rapid strides, take off *and* skyrocket <both nonformal>, make up for lost time

8 **rally,** come round, **take a favorable turn,** take a turn for the better; come a long way <nonformal>; **recuperate, recover** 396.20

9 **improve, better,** change for the better; improve upon, **mend, amend,** emend; meliorate, **ameliorate; advance, promote,** foster, favor, nurture; **lift,** elevate, **uplift,** raise, boost <nonformal>; upgrade; gentrify; **enhance, enrich,** fatten; make one's way, better oneself; **reform,** put *or* set straight; turn over a new leaf, mend one's ways, straighten out, go straight <nonformal>; get it together *and* get one's ducks in a row <both nonformal>; **civilize,** acculturate, socialize; enlighten, edify; **educate**

10 **develop,** elaborate; embellish; **cultivate;** come of age, come into its own, mature, ripen, evolve

11 **perfect, touch up,** finish, put on the finishing touches, polish, fine-tune <nonformal>, **brush up,**

furbish, spruce up, freshen, brighten up, polish, polish up, shine <nonformal>; retouch; **revive, renovate** 396.17, 17; **repair, fix** 396.14; retrofit

12 **revise,** redact, **revamp, rewrite, rework,** work over; **emend, amend, rectify; edit,** blue-pencil

ADJS 13 **improved, bettered;** changed for the better, ameliorated, enhanced, enriched; beautified, embellished; gentrified; **reformed; transformed,** transfigured; **cultivated,** cultured, **refined,** polished, civilized; **educated** 927.18

14 **better,** better off, better for, all the better for

15 **improving, bettering;** meliorative, ameliorative; progressive, progressing, advancing; mending, **on the mend;** on the rise or upswing or upbeat or upgrade <nonformal>

16 **emendatory, corrective;** reformative; **reformist,** progressive, melioristic; revisionist; utopian; radical 611.20; revolutionary 859.5

17 **improvable,** ameliorable, corrigible, revisable, perfectible; **emendable** 396.25

393 IMPAIRMENT

NOUNS 1 **impairment, damage, injury, harm,** mischief, **hurt, detriment,** sickening; **worsening;** incapacitation; encroachment, inroad, infringement 214.1; **disrepair, dilapidation; breakdown, collapse,** crash and crack-up <both nonformal>; **malfunction,** glitch <nonformal>; bankruptcy; ruination; sabotage; mayhem, mutilation, crippling, hobbling, hamstringing, maiming; destruction 395

2 **corruption, pollution, contamination,** vitiation, **defilement,** fouling; **poisoning;** infection, festering, suppuration; **perversion,** prostitution, misuse 389; adulteration

3 **deterioration, decadence, degradation, debasement;**

degeneration, degenerateness, effeteness; depravation, depravedness; **retrogression, regression;** devolution, involution; downward mobility; **decline,** comedown, **descent,** downtick <nonformal>, downtrend, downturn, depreciation, **decrease** 252, **drop, fall, plunge,** free-fall, falling-off, lessening, slippage, slump, lapse, fading, dying, failing, failure, wane, ebb

4 **waste,** wastage, **consumption;** withering, wasting away, atrophy, wilting; emaciation 270.6

5 **wear,** use, hard wear; **wear and tear; erosion, weathering,** ravages of time

6 **decay, decomposition, disintegration, dissolution,** degradation, biodegradation, **corruption, spoilage, dilapidation; corrosion,** oxidation, rust; mildew, mold 1000.2; degradability, biodegradability

7 **rot, rottenness, foulness, putridness,** rancidness, rankness, **putrefaction,** putrescence, spoilage, decay, decomposition; dry rot, wet rot

8 **wreck, ruins, ruin, total loss;** hulk, carcass, skeleton; wreck of one's former self; rattletrap

VERBS 9 **impair, damage, injure, harm, hurt,** irritate; **worsen,** deteriorate, put or set back, aggravate, exacerbate; **weaken; dilapidate;** add insult to injury, rub salt in the wound

10 **spoil, mar,** botch, **ruin,** wreck, blight, **play havoc with; destroy** 395.10

11 <nonformal terms> **screw up, foul up,** fuck up, bitch up, **blow,** louse up, queer, snafu, snarl up, bugger, bugger up, gum up, ball up, bollix, bollix up, **mess up,** hash up, muck up; play hell with; upset the apple cart, cook, sink, shoot down in flames; **total**

12 **corrupt, debase, degrade,** degenerate, **deprave, debauch, defile,** violate, desecrate, deflower, ravish, ravage, despoil;

contaminate, pollute, vitiate, poison, infect, taint; pervert, warp, twist, distort; prostitute, misuse 389.4; **cheapen,** devalue; coarsen, vulgarize, drag in the mud; adulterate, alloy, water down

13 <inflict an injury> **injure, hurt;** draw blood, wound; **traumatize;** stab, stick, pierce, puncture; cut, incise, slit, slash, gash, scratch; abrade, eat away at, chafe, fret, gall, bark, skin; craze, check; lacerate, claw, tear, rip, rend; run; frazzle, fray; burn, scorch, scald; mutilate, maim, rough up <nonformal>, make mincemeat of, maul, batter, savage; sprain, strain, wrench; bloody; **blemish** 1003.4; **bruise, contuse;** buffet, batter, bash <nonformal>, maul, pound, beat, beat black and blue; give a black eye

14 **cripple, lame,** maim; **hamstring,** hobble; wing; emasculate, castrate; incapacitate, **disable** 19.9

15 **undermine,** sap, mine, honeycomb; sabotage, throw or toss a monkey-wrench in the works <both nonformal>, subvert

16 **deteriorate, sicken, worsen, get or grow worse, degenerate; retrogress,** retrograde, regress, relapse; let oneself go, let down, slacken; be the worse for wear and have seen better days <both nonformal>

17 **decline, sink, fail, fall,** slip, fade, die, wane, ebb, subside, lapse, **run down,** go down, **go downhill, fall away, fall off,** slide, slump, hit a slump, take a nose dive <nonformal>, go into a tailspin, take a turn for the worse; hit the skids <nonformal>; hit or touch bottom, hit rock bottom

18 **languish, pine, droop, flag, wilt; fade,** fade away; **wither, shrivel,** shrink, diminish, wither or die on the vine, **dry up,** desiccate, wizen, wrinkle, sear

19 **waste, waste away, wither away,** atrophy, erode away, emaciate, pine away; dribble away

20 **wear, wear away, wear down, wear off;** abrade, fret, whittle away, rub off; fray, frazzle, tatter; **wear out;** weather, erode

21 **corrode, erode,** eat, gnaw, eat into, gnaw at the root of; canker; **oxidize, rust**

22 **decay, decompose, disintegrate;** go or fall into decay, go or fall to pieces, break up; **spoil,** corrupt, canker, **go bad; rot, putrefy,** putresce; fester, suppurate, rankle <nonformal>; **mortify,** gangrene; molder, rot away, rust away; mildew

23 **break, break up,** fracture, **come apart, fall to pieces, fall apart, disintegrate;** burst, rupture; crack, split, fissure; spring a leak, come apart at the seams, come unstuck <nonformal>

24 **break down, founder, collapse;** crash <nonformal>, cave or fall in, come crashing or tumbling down, topple; totter, sway

25 **get out of order, malfunction,** get out of gear; get out of joint; go wrong

26 <nonformal terms> **get out of whack,** get out of kilter, get out of commission, **go on the blink or fritz, go haywire,** go kerflooey, give out, **break down,** conk out

ADJS 27 **impaired, damaged, hurt, injured, harmed; deteriorated, worsened,** cut to the quick, aggravated, exacerbated, irritated, embittered; **worse,** worse off, the worse for; lacerated, mangled, cut, split, rent, torn, slit, slashed, mutilated, chewed-up; **broken** 801.24, **shattered, smashed,** in bits, in pieces, in shards; cracked, chipped, crazed, checked; burned, scorched, scalded; **damaging, injurious,** traumatic, degenerative

28 **spoiled** or spoilt, **marred,** botched, blighted, **ruined,** wrecked; **destroyed** 395.28

29 <nonformal terms> queered, screwed up, fouled up, loused up

30 **crippled,** game <nonformal>, bad, handicapped, maimed; **lame, halt,** halting, limping;

hamstrung; **disabled, incapaci-tated;** emasculated, castrated

31 worn, well-worn, worn-down, the worse for wear, dog-eared; worn to the stump, worn to the bone; **worn ragged,** worn to rags; **threadbare,** bare

32 shabby, shoddy, seedy, scruffy, **tacky** <nonformal>, dowdy, tatty, ratty; raggedy, raggedy-ass <non-formal>, **ragged, tattered, torn; frayed, frazzled;** in rags, in tatters, in shreds; **out at the el-bows, down-at-the-heel** or **-heels**

33 dilapidated, ramshackle, de-crepit, **tumbledown, broken-down, run-down,** in ruins, ru-ined, derelict, the worse for wear; **battered,** beaten up, **beat-up** <nonformal>

34 weatherworn, weather-beaten, weathered, weather-scarred; eroded; **faded,** washed-out, bleached, blanched, etiolated

35 wasted, atrophied, shrunken; **withered,** sere, shriveled, wilted, wizened, dried-up, desiccated; wrinkled; **emaciated** 270.20; starved, skin and bones

36 worn-out, used up <nonfor-mal>, worn to a frazzle, frazzled; **exhausted, tired,** fatigued, pooped <nonformal>, **spent,** ef-fete, played out, jaded, emptied; **run-down,** dragged-out <nonfor-mal>, laid low, at a low ebb, in a bad way, on one's last legs

37 in disrepair, out of order, mal-functioning, inoperative; out of tune, out of gear; out of joint; **broken** 801.24

38 <nonformal terms> **out of whack** or **kilter** or sync or com-mission, on the fritz, on the blink, kerflooey, haywire

39 putrefactive, rotting; **septic;** saprophytic

40 decayed, decomposed; spoiled, corrupt, peccant, bad, **gone bad; rotten,** rotting, pu-trid, **putrefied, foul;** putrescent, **mortified,** necrotic, gangrenous; ulcerated, festering, suppurating; rotten to the core

41 tainted, off; stale; sour, soured, turned; **rank, rancid,** strong <nonformal>, **high,** gamy

42 blighted, blasted, ravaged; fly-blown, wormy, maggoty; **moth-eaten, worm-eaten; moldy,** moldering, **mildewed,** smutty, smutted; **musty, fusty**

43 corroded, eroded, eaten; **rusty,** rust-worn

44 corrupting, corruptive; cor-roding; eroding, **damaging, injurious** 999.12

45 deteriorating, worsening, dis-integrating, coming unstuck, crumbling, cracking, going to pieces; **decadent, degenerate,** effete; **retrogressive,** retrograde, regressive, from better to worse; **declining, sinking, failing,** wan-ing, subsiding, **slipping,** sliding, slumping; **languishing, pining,** drooping, flagging, wilting; **wast-ing,** fading, **withering,** shriveling

46 on the wane, on the decline, on the downgrade, on the skids <nonformal>; tottering, on the way out

47 degradable, biodegradable, decomposable, putrefiable, putrescible

ADVS **48** out of the frying pan into the fire, from better to worse; for the worse

394 RELAPSE

NOUNS **1 relapse, lapse; rever-sion, regression** 858.1; **reverse, reversal,** devolution, **setback; return,** recurrence, renewal; throwback, atavism

2 backsliding; fall, fall from grace; recidivism, recidivation; apostasy 363.2

3 backslider, recidivist, rever-sionist; apostate 363.5

VERBS **4 relapse, lapse, back-slide, slip back,** sink back, **fall back, return to, revert to,** recur to, yield again to, fall again into, recidivate; revert, **regress** 858.4; **fall, fall from grace**

ADJS **5 relapsing, lapsing, back-sliding;** recrudescent; **regressive** 858.7; apostate 363.11

395 DESTRUCTION

NOUNS **1 destruction, ruin, ruina-**
tion, rack and ruin; perdition,
damnation; **wreck**; devastation,
ravage, havoc, holocaust, firestorm, carnage, shambles,
slaughter, bloodbath, **desola-**
tion; waste, consumption;
decimation; **dissolution,**
disintegration, disruption, undoing; vandalism, depredation,
spoliation, despoliation, despoilment; the road to ruin

2 end, fate, doom, death, death
knell, bane, deathblow, quietus,
cutoff

3 fall, downfall, prostration;
overthrow, overturn, upset, up-
heaval; convulsion, **subversion,**
sabotage

4 debacle, disaster, cataclysm,
catastrophe; breakup; break-
down, collapse; crash,
smashup, crack-up <nonfor-
mal>; **wreck,** wrack; cave-in,
cave; washout; total loss

5 demolition, wreckage, leveling,
razing, flattening; **dismantle-**
ment, disassembly

6 extinction, extermination,
elimination, eradication, extirpation; deracination, uprooting;
annihilation, snuffing out; abo-
lition; annulment, **nullification,**
voiding, **negation; liquidation,**
purge; suppression; choking,
suffocation, stifling, strangulation

7 obliteration, erasure, efface-
ment, blotting out, wiping out;
cancellation, cancel; deletion

8 destroyer, ruiner, wrecker,
bane; vandal, hun; exterminator,
annihilator; **iconoclast;** nihilist;
bomber, dynamiter; arsonist

9 eradicator, expunger; **eraser,**
rubber

VERBS **10 destroy,** deal or unleash
destruction, nuke <nonformal>;
ruin, play or raise hob with;
throw into disorder, upheave;
wreck, wrack, shipwreck; damn,
seal the doom of, **condemn,** confound; **devastate, desolate,**

waste, **lay waste, ravage,** wreak
havoc, despoil, depredate; vandalize; **decimate;** gut, gut with
fire, incinerate, vaporize

11 do for, fix <nonformal>, settle,
sink, cook one's goose and cut one
down to size and cut one off at
the knees and pull the plug on
and pull the rug out from under
<all nonformal>, dish, scuttle,
put the kibosh on and put the
skids under <both nonformal>,
do in, **undo,** poleax, torpedo,
knock out, zap and shoot down
and shoot down in flames <all
nonformal>; break the back of;
make short work of; **defeat** 412.6

12 put an end to, make an end of,
end, finish, finish off <nonfor-
mal>, deal a deathblow to,
dispose of, get rid of, do in, do
away with; cut off, take off, be the
death of, sound the death knell of;
put out of the way, **slaughter,** off
and waste and blow away <all
nonformal>, kill off, strike down,
kill 308.13

13 abolish, nullify, void, abrogate,
annihilate, annul, repeal, revoke,
negate, invalidate, **undo, cancel,**
bring to naught, put or lay to rest

14 exterminate, eliminate, eradi-
cate, deracinate, **extirpate,**
annihilate; wipe out <nonfor-
mal>; out, uproot, pull or pluck
up by the roots, strike at the root
of; **liquidate, purge;** remove,
sweep away, wash away

15 extinguish, quench, snuff out,
put out, stamp or trample out,
trample underfoot; **smother,**
choke, stifle, strangle, suffocate;
silence; **suppress, quash, quell,**
put down

16 obliterate, expunge, efface,
erase, blot, sponge, **wipe out,**
wipe off the map, rub out, **blot**
out, sponge out, wash away; cancel, strike out, rule out; blue-
pencil; **delete** or dele, kill

17 demolish, wreck, total and rack
up <both nonformal>, undo, un-
make, **dismantle, disassemble;**
take apart, tear apart, tear
asunder, rend, take or **pull** or

pick or **tear to pieces,** tear to shreds or rags or tatters; sunder, cleave, **split; disintegrate, fragment,** make mincemeat of, reduce to rubble, atomize, pulverize, **smash,** shatter 801.13

18 **blow up,** blast, blow to pieces or bits or smithereens or kingdom come; self-destruct

19 **raze,** rase, **fell, level,** flatten, smash, prostrate, raze to the ground; steamroller, bulldoze; **pull down, tear down, take down,** bring down, bring down about one's ears, bring crashing down, break down, throw down, cast down, beat down, knock down or over; cut down, chop down

20 **overthrow, overturn; upset, subvert,** throw over; undermine, **sap, weaken**

21 **overwhelm,** whelm, swamp, engulf; inundate

22 <be destroyed> **fall,** come tumbling or crashing down, topple, bite the dust <nonformal>; **break up,** crumble, disintegrate, go or fall to pieces; go down the tube or tubes <nonformal>; self-destruct

23 **perish, expire, succumb, die, cease, end,** come to an end, go, pass, **pass away, vanish, disappear,** fade away, run out, come to nothing or naught, be no more, be done for

24 **go to ruin, go to rack and ruin,** go wrong, **go to the dogs** or **pot** <nonformal>, go to seed, go to hell in a handbasket <nonformal>, go to the deuce or devil <nonformal>, go to hell <nonformal>, go to glory <nonformal>

25 **drive to ruin, force to the wall,** drive to the dogs <nonformal>

ADJS 26 **destructive; ruinous; disastrous, calamitous, cataclysmic,** cataclysmal, **catastrophic;** fatal, fateful, baneful; **deadly;** consuming, withering; **devastating, desolating,** ravaging, wasting; subversive; nihilist, nihilistic; suicidal, self-destructive; fratricidal, internecine

27 **exterminative, annihilative,**

eradicative, extirpative; all-devouring, all-consuming

28 **ruined, destroyed, wrecked, blasted, undone,** down-and-out, broken, bankrupt; **devastated, desolated, ravaged,** blighted, wasted; gone to wrack and ruin

29 <nonformal terms> **shot, done for,** done in, finished, kaput; gone to pot, gone to the dogs, gone to hell in a handbasket, belly up, kerflooey, dead in the water, washed up, all washed up, history, **dead meat, down the tube** or **tubes,** zapped, nuked, tapped out, wiped out

396 RESTORATION

NOUNS 1 **restoration, restitution, reestablishment, redintegration, reinstatement,** reversion, reconstitution, recomposition; **rehabilitation,** redevelopment, reconversion, reactivation, reenactment; improvement 392

2 **reclamation, recovery, retrieval,** salvage; redemption, salvation

3 **revival,** revivification, **renewal,** resurrection, resuscitation, reanimation, resurgence, recrudescence; **refreshment 9;** renaissance, renascence, **rebirth,** new birth; **rejuvenation,** rejuvenescence, new lease on life; **regeneration,** regenesis, palingenesis

4 **renovation, renewal;** refreshment; **redecorating; reconditioning,** refurbishment, refurbishing; face-lifting or face-lift; slum clearance, urban renewal

5 **reconstruction, re-creation, remaking, rebuilding,** refashioning; reassembly; reformation; restructuring, perestroika

6 **reparation, repair,** repairing, **fixing, mending,** making or setting right; maintenance; **overhaul,** overhauling; troubleshooting <nonformal>; **rectification, correction, remedy; redress,** making or setting right, amends, compensation, **recompense**

7 **cure, curing, healing, remedy**
86; **therapy** 91

8 **recovery, rally, comeback**
<nonformal>, return; **recupera-
tion, convalescence**

9 **restorability, reparability,** re-
mediability, redeemability,
salvageability

10 **mender, fixer,** restorer, renova-
tor, **repairman, repairwoman,
serviceman, servicewoman;
troubleshooter** <nonformal>;
mechanic; tinker, tinkerer; cobbler; salvager

VERBS 11 **restore, put back, replace, return;** reestablish, re-
integrate, **reinstate; reinstall,**
reinvest, reinstitute, reconstitute,
recompose, **rehabilitate,** redevelop; reconvert, reactivate;
refill, replenish; give back
481.4

12 **redeem, reclaim, recover, retrieve;** ransom; rescue; salvage;
recycle; win back, **recoup**

13 **remedy, rectify, correct, right,**
patch up, emend, amend, **redress, put right,** set right, put or
set to rights, put or set straight,
make all square; pay reparations,
give satisfaction, requite, restitute, recompense, compensate,
remunerate

14 **repair, mend, fix,** fix up
<nonformal>, doctor <nonfor-
mal>, put in repair, put in shape,
set to rights, put in order or condition; **condition, recondition,**
put in commission, ready; **service, overhaul;** fiddle, fiddle
around; cobble; sew up, darn

15 **cure,** work a cure, **remedy,
heal, restore to health,** heal up,
give a new or fresh lease on life,
make well, fix up, pull through,
set on one's feet; snatch from the
jaws of death

16 **revive,** revivify, **renew; reanimate, regenerate, rejuvenate,
revitalize,** breathe new life into;
refresh 9.2; **resuscitate,** bring
to; **resurrect,** bring back, call
back, recall to life, raise from the
dead; rewarm, warm up or over;
rekindle, relight

17 **renovate, renew; recondition,**
revamp, refurbish; refresh, face-
lift

18 **remake,** reconstruct, remodel,
reconstitute, **rebuild,** refashion,
reassemble

19 **recuperate, gain strength,** renew one's strength, catch one's
breath, **get better; improve**
392.7; **rally, pick up,** perk up and
brace up <both nonformal>, take
a new or fresh lease on life; **take a
favorable turn,** turn the corner,
be out of the woods, take a turn
for the better; **convalesce;** sleep
it off

20 **recover, rally, revive, get well,
get over, pull through,** come
back <nonformal>, make a comeback <nonformal>; get back in
shape <nonformal>, be oneself
again, feel like a new person; **survive,** weather the storm; **come
to,** show signs of life; come up
smiling and bounce back <both
nonformal>, get one's second
wind; come or pull or snap out of
it <nonformal>

21 **heal, heal over,** close up, scab
over, cicatrize, granulate; heal or
right itself; **knit, set**

ADJS 22 **tonic, restorative, restitutive;** remedial, **curative** 86.39

23 **recuperative; convalescent;**
buoyant, resilient, elastic

24 **renascent,** redivivus, redux,
resurrected, revived, reborn, resurgent, recrudescent, phoenixlike

25 **remediable, curable;** medica-
ble, treatable; **correctable,**
rectifiable, corrigible; **improvable; reparable,** repairable,
mendable, fixable; salvageable,
retrievable, recyclable, redeemable; renewable

397 PRESERVATION

NOUNS 1 **preservation, conservation, saving, salvation,** salvage,
keeping, safekeeping, maintenance, upkeep, support; conser-
vationism; nature conservation or
conservancy

2 **food preservation; curing,** salt-

ing, pickling, marinating, corning; **drying,** dry-curing, jerking; **smoking,** kippering; **refrigeration,** freezing; irradiation; **canning;** bottling

3 **embalming,** mummification; taxidermy, stuffing

4 **preservative;** salt, brine, vinegar, formaldehyde, embalming fluid

5 **preserver,** conservator, keeper, safekeeper; taxidermist; rescuer, deliverer, savior; **conservationist,** preservationist; **ranger, forest ranger,** fire warden, game warden

6 **life preserver,** life jacket, Mae West <nonformal>; life buoy; water wings; breeches buoy; lifeboat; lifeline; safety belt; **parachute;** ejection seat *or* ejector seat, ejection capsule

7 **preserve, reserve, reservation; park;** wilderness preserve; **refuge, sanctuary** 1008.1; museum, library 558, archives 549.2

VERBS 8 **preserve, conserve, save,** spare; **keep,** keep safe, keep inviolate *or* intact; **guard, protect** 1007.18; **maintain, sustain,** uphold, support, **keep up,** keep alive

9 **preserve,** cure, season, salt, brine, marinate or marinade, pickle, corn

10 **embalm,** mummify; stuff; tan

11 **put up,** do up; **can;** bottle, jar, pot

ADJS 12 **preservative,** conservative, conservatory; custodial, curatorial; **conservational,** conservationist; preserving, conserving, saving, keeping; **protective** 1007.23

13 **preserved,** conserved, **kept,** saved, spared; protected 1007.21; **untainted, unspoiled;** intact, all in one piece, undamaged 1001.8; **well-preserved, well-kept,** in a good state of preservation

398 RESCUE

NOUNS 1 **rescue, deliverance, saving; extrication, release, freeing, liberation** 431; **bailout;**

salvation, salvage, **redemption,** ransom; **recovery, retrieval**

2 **rescuer,** lifesaver, lifeguard; savior 592.2; lifeboat

VERBS 3 **rescue,** come to the rescue, **deliver, save, redeem,** ransom, **salvage; recover, retrieve** 481.6; **free,** set free, **release, extricate, liberate** 431.4; snatch from the jaws of death; save one's bacon *and* save one's neck *or* ass *and* bail one out <all nonformal>

ADJS 4 **rescuable, savable;** redeemable; **deliverable, extricable;** salvageable

399 WARNING

NOUNS 1 **warning, caution,** caveat, **admonition; notice,** notification; **word to the wise,** enough said; **hint,** broad hint, little birdy <nonformal>; tip-off <nonformal>; **lesson,** object lesson, **example; alarm** 400; ultimatum; **threat** 514

2 **forewarning, premonition;** advance warning *or* notice; presentiment, hunch *and* funny feeling <both nonformal>, **foreboding; portent**

3 **warning sign, premonitory sign, danger sign; symptom; precursor** 815; **omen** 133.3,6; **handwriting on the wall;** straw in the wind; gathering clouds, clouds on the horizon; falling barometer *or* glass; storm *or* stormy petrel, **red light,** red flag; death's-head, skull and crossbones; **high sign** <nonformal>, **warning signal, alert,** red alert; siren, klaxon, tocsin

4 **warner,** admonisher, monitor; prophet *or* messenger of doom, Cassandra, Jeremiah; **lookout, lookout man; sentinel, sentry; signalman,** flagman; lighthouse keeper

VERBS 5 **warn, caution, advise, admonish; give warning,** give fair warning, utter a caveat, have a word with one, say a word to the wise; tip *and* tip off <both nonformal>; notify, put on notice, give notice, give advance notice *or*

advance word; issue an ultimatum; **threaten** 514.2; **alert,**
warn against, put on one's guard,
warn away *or* off; **give the high
sign** <nonformal>; **put on alert,**
cry havoc, sound the alarm 400.3

6 forewarn, precaution; tell in advance, give advance notice; **portend, forebode**

ADJS **7 warning, cautionary; monitory,** admonitory, admonishing;
exemplary, deterrent

**8 forewarning, premonitory;
portentous,** foreboding 133.17;
precautionary

400 ALARM

NOUNS **1 alarm,** alarum, **alert;** hue
and cry; **red light,** amber light,
caution signal; **alarm button,**
panic button <nonformal>;
beeper, buzzer; tocsin, alarm
bell; SOS, Mayday, upside-down
flag; storm warning; foghorn;
burglar alarm; fire alarm; **lighthouse,** beacon

2 false alarm, cry of wolf; flash in
the pan *and* dud <both nonfor-
mal>

VERBS **3 alarm, alert, arouse,** put
on the alert; **warn** 399.5; **sound
the alarm,** give *or* raise *or* beat *or*
turn in an alarm, ring *or* sound
the tocsin, cry havoc, raise a hue
and cry; give a false alarm, **cry
wolf;** frighten *or* scare out of
one's wits *or* to death, **frighten,**
startle 131.8

ADJS **4 alarmed, aroused;** alerted;
frightened to death *or* out of one's
wits, **frightened; startled** 131.13

401 HASTE
    <rapidity of action>

NOUNS **1 haste, hurry, scurry,
rush, race,** dash, scamper,
scramble, hustle <nonformal>,
bustle, flurry, helter-skelter

2 hastiness, hurriedness, quickness, swiftness, expeditiousness,
alacrity, promptness 330.3; **speed**
174.1,2; **precipitousness,** pre-
cipitance *or* precipitancy;
suddenness, abruptness; **impetuousness** 365.2, impetuosity,

impulsiveness, **rashness** 493;
eagerness, zealousness, **overeagerness, overzealousness**

3 hastening, hurrying, speeding,
quickening, **acceleration;** fast-
forward

VERBS **4 hasten,** haste, **hurry, accelerate, speed,** speed up, **hurry
up, rush,** quicken, hustle <non-
formal>, bustle; **dispatch, expedite; whip,** whip along, spur,
urge 375.14,16; push, press;
crowd, stampede; **hurry on,** hasten on, drive on, push on, press
on; **hurry along,** rush along,
speed along, **speed on its way;
push through,** railroad through
<nonformal>

**5 make haste, hasten, hurry,
hurry up, race, run, rush,
chase, tear, dash,** spurt, **scurry,
scamper, scramble, hustle**
<nonformal>, **bustle;** bestir one-
self, move quickly 174.9; hurry
on, dash on, press *or* push on,
crowd; break one's neck *or* fall all
over oneself <both nonformal>;
lose no time, not lose a moment;
dash off; make fast work of, make
up for lost time; do on the run *or*
on the fly

6 <nonformal terms> **step on it,
snap to it,** hop to it, hotfoot, bear
down on it, shake it up, **get moving** *or* **going,** get a move on, get
cracking <chiefly Brit>, get the
lead out of one's ass, give it the
gun, hump, hump it, hump oneself, tear ass, **get a hustle** *or*
move *or* **wiggle on,** not spare the
horses

7 rush into, plunge into, dive
into, plunge, plunge ahead *or*
headlong; **not stop to think,** go
off half-cocked <nonformal>,
leap before one looks

8 be in a hurry, be under the gun
<nonformal>, have no time to
lose *or* spare, not have a moment
to spare, hardly have time to
breathe, work against time *or* the
clock, work under pressure, have
a deadline

ADJS **9 hasty, hurried, quick,** flying, **expeditious,** prompt 330.18;

quick-and-dirty <nonformal>, **immediate,** instant, on the spot; onrushing, **swift, speedy; urgent;** feverish; **cursory,** passing, superficial; spur-of-the-moment, last-minute

10 **precipitate,** precipitant; **sudden,** abrupt; **impetuous, impulsive, rash;** headlong, breakneck; breathless, panting

11 **hurried, rushed,** pushed, pressed, crowded, **pressed for time,** hard-pressed; on the double

ADVS 12 **hastily, hurriedly, quickly; expeditiously,** promptly, with dispatch; apace, hand over fist, **immediately,** instantly, in a second or split second or jiffy, at once, as soon as possible or ASAP; **swiftly, speedily,** on or at fast-forward; with great or all haste, in a mad rush, at fever pitch; furiously, feverishly, in a sweat or lather; **helter-skelter,** pellmell; slapdash, cursorily, superficially, on the run or fly, on the spur of the moment

13 **posthaste;** express; by fax

14 **in a hurry, in haste,** in all haste; in short order; against the clock

15 **precipitately,** precipitantly, slap-bang; **suddenly,** abruptly; **impetuously, impulsively, rashly; headlong,** headfirst, head over heels

402 LEISURE

NOUNS 1 **leisure, ease, convenience,** freedom; retirement, semiretirement; rest, repose 20; **free time, spare time,** odd moments, idle hours; time to spare or burn or kill, time on one's hands, time at one's disposal; one's own sweet time <nonformal>; downtime

2 **leisureliness, unhurriedness;** inactivity 331; **slowness** 175; deliberateness, deliberation

VERBS 3 **have time,** have time enough, have time to spare, nave plenty of time, be in no hurry

4 **take one's leisure,** take one's ease, **take one's time, take one's**

own sweet time <nonformal>, do at one's leisure or convenience or pleasure; lead the life of Riley <nonformal>

ADJS 5 **leisure, leisured;** idle, unoccupied, free, open, spare; retired, semiretired

6 **leisurely, unhurried,** laid-back <nonformal>, relaxed; deliberate; inactive 331.17

ADVS 7 **at leisure, at one's leisure, at one's convenience,** when one gets around to it, when one has a minute to spare, when one has a moment to call one's own

403 ENDEAVOR

NOUNS 1 **endeavor,** effort, striving; **all-out effort,** best effort, old college try <nonformal>; **exertion** 725; determination, resolution 359; **enterprise** 330.7

2 **attempt, trial, effort, essay; endeavor, undertaking;** approach, move; coup, stroke 328.3, step; gambit, offer, **bid;** experiment; trial and error

3 <nonformal terms> **try, whack, fling, shot, crack,** bash, belt, go, stab, lick, rip, ripple, cut, hack, smack

4 **one's best, one's level best, one's utmost,** one's damndest or darndest <nonformal>, one's best effort, the best one can, the best one knows how, all one can do, one's all <nonformal>

VERBS 5 **endeavor, strive, struggle,** strain, sweat, sweat blood, labor, get one's teeth into, come to grips with, make an all-out effort, move heaven and earth, **exert oneself,** apply oneself, use some elbow grease <nonformal>; resolve, be determined 359.8

6 **attempt, try, essay;** try one's hand or wings; **undertake** 404.3, **approach,** come to grips with, engage, take the bull by the horns; venture, chance; **make an attempt** or **effort,** lift a finger or hand

7 <nonformal terms> **tackle, take on, make a try, give a try,** take a shot or stab or crack or try or

whack at; try on for size, **go for it,** go for the brass ring, **have a fling** or go at, **make a stab at**

8 **try to,** try and <nonformal>, **attempt to, endeavor to,** strive to, seek to, study to, aim to, venture to, dare to

9 **try for, strive for,** strain for, struggle for, contend for, make a play for <nonformal>

10 **see what one can do,** see what can be done, see if one can do, do what one can; try anything once; **try one's hand,** try one's luck; feel one's way, test the waters

11 **make a special effort,** go out of one's way, take special pains, **put oneself out,** fall or bend or lean over backward <all nonformal>, fall all over oneself, trouble oneself, **go to the trouble,** take trouble, **take pains,** redouble one's efforts

12 **try hard, push** <nonformal>, **put one's back to** or **into,** put one's heart into, try until one is blue in the face, die trying, **try and try;** exert oneself 725.9

13 **do one's best** or **level best, do one's utmost,** try one's best or utmost, **do all** or **everything one can,** do the best one can, **do the best one knows how,** do all in one's power; **strain every nerve; give it one's all;** be on one's mettle, **die trying**

14 <nonformal terms> **knock oneself out, break one's neck,** break or bust one's balls, bust a gut, bust one's ass or hump, do it or break a leg, do it or bust a gut, do or try one's damndest or darndest, go all out, go for broke, shoot the works, give it all one's got, give it one's best shot, go for it

15 **make every effort, spare no effort** or **pains, go to great lengths,** go through fire and water, not rest, not relax, move heaven and earth, leave no stone unturned, leave no avenue unexplored

ADJS 16 **trial, tentative, experimental; venturesome, willing;** determined, resolute 359.11; **utmost, damndest**

ADVS 17 **out for,** out to, **on the make** <nonformal>

18 **at the top of one's bent,** as far as possible

404 UNDERTAKING

NOUNS 1 **undertaking, enterprise, operation,** work, **venture, project,** proposition and deal <both nonformal>; **program, plan** 381; **affair, business, matter, task** 724.2, concern, interest; **initiative,** effort, attempt 403.2; **action** 328.3; **engagement, contract, obligation, commitment** 436.2

2 **adventure, mission;** quest; expedition

VERBS 3 **undertake, assume,** accept, **take on, take upon oneself,** take upon one's shoulders, take up, **tackle,** attack; obligate or commit oneself; **put** or **set** or **turn one's hand to, engage in, devote oneself to, apply oneself to,** address oneself to; associate oneself with, **come aboard** <nonformal>; busy oneself with 724.11; **take up, go in** or **out for** <nonformal>, **enter on** or **upon,** proceed to, embark in or upon, **venture upon,** get going, get under way; set about, go about; **go** or **swing into action, set to, turn to, fall to; pitch into** <nonformal>, plunge into, **launch into** or **upon;** go at, set at, have at <nonformal>, knuckle or buckle down to; put or lay one's shoulder to the wheel; take the bull by the horns; **endeavor, attempt**

4 **have in hand, have one's hands in,** have on one's hands or shoulders

5 **be in progress** or **process,** be in the works or hopper or pipeline <nonformal>, **be under way**

6 **bite off more than one can chew** <nonformal>, overextend or overreach oneself, have too many irons in the fire, have too much on one's plate

ADJS 7 **undertaken, assumed,** accepted, **taken on** <nonformal>; **ventured,** attempted, chanced; **in hand, in progress** or **process,** on one's plate, in the works or hopper or pipeline <nonformal>, on the agenda, **under way**

8 **enterprising,** venturesome, keen, eager

405 PREPARATION

NOUNS 1 **preparation,** preparing, prep and prepping <both nonformal>, **readying,** getting or making ready; warm-up, getting in shape or condition; mobilization; **run-up; prearrangement** 964, lead time, advance notice, warning, alerting; **planning** 381.1; trial, dry run, **tryout** 941.3; **provision, arrangement;** preparatory or preliminary act or measure or step; **preliminary, preliminaries;** clearing the decks <nonformal>; **grounding,** basic training, familiarization, briefing; prerequisite; **spadework,** groundwork, foundation 900.6

2 **fitting,** fit; **conditioning;** adaptation, adjustment, tuning; **qualification,** enablement; **equipment, furnishing** 385.1

3 <a preparation> **concoction,** decoction, brew, **confection;** composition, mixture 796.5

4 **preparedness, readiness; fitness, suitability;** condition, trim; **qualification,** credentials, record, track record <nonformal>; **competence** or competency, **ability, capability, proficiency,** mastery; ripeness, maturity, seasoning, tempering

5 **preparer**; trainer, coach, instructor, mentor, teacher; **trailblazer, pathfinder; forerunner** 815.1

VERBS 6 **prepare, make** or **get ready,** prep <nonformal>, **ready, fix** <nonformal>; **arrange; make preparations** or **arrangements,** clear the decks <nonformal>, clear for action; mobilize, marshal, deploy, marshal or deploy one's forces or resources; **prearrange; plan; try out** 941.8; fix

up <nonformal>, put in or into shape; dress; treat, pretreat, process; cure, tan

7 **make up, get up, fix up** and rustle up <both nonformal>; **concoct,** decoct, brew; **compound, compose, put together, mix;** make

8 **fit, condition, adapt, adjust,** tune, attune, put in tune or trim or working order; **qualify; equip, furnish** 385.7,8

9 **prime, load,** charge, cock, set; wind, wind up; steam up, get up steam, warm up

10 **prepare to, get ready to,** get set for <nonformal>; be about to, be on the point of

11 **prepare for, provide for,** make arrangements or dispositions for, look to, look out for, see to, **make provision** or **due provision for;** provide against, forearm, **provide for** or **against a rainy day;** lay in provisions, lay up a store, keep as a nest egg, lay by, husband one's resources, salt or squirrel something away; set one's house in order

12 **prepare the way, pave the way,** smooth the path or road, **clear the way,** open the way, open the door to; **break the ice; blaze the trail; prepare the ground,** cultivate the soil, sow the seed; do the spadework, lay the groundwork or foundation

13 **prepare oneself,** brace oneself, **get ready, get set** <nonformal>, put one's house in order, strip for action, get into shape or condition, roll up one's sleeves, limber up, warm up, flex one's muscles, gird up one's loins, get into harness; **run up to,** build up to, gear up, tool up

14 **be prepared, be ready,** stand by, stand ready, hold oneself in readiness, keep one's powder dry

15 <be fitted> **qualify, measure up,** meet the requirements, have the credentials or qualifications or prerequisites; be up to and be just the ticket and fill the bill <all nonformal>

ADJS **16 prepared, ready,** prepped <nonformal>, in readiness, all ready, good and ready; psyched or pumped up <nonformal>, eager, keen, champing at the bit; alert, vigilant 339.13; **ripe, mature; set** and **all set** <both nonformal>, on the mark <nonformal>; about to, fixing to <nonformal>; **prearranged; primed,** loaded, cocked, **loaded for bear** <nonformal>; familiarized, briefed, informed; groomed, coached; ready for anything; in the saddle; armed and ready, in arms, **armed** 460.14; mobilized; **provided, equipped** 385.13; dressed; **readied,** available 221.12

17 fitted, adapted, adjusted, suited; qualified, fit, competent, able, capable, proficient; checked out <nonformal>; well-qualified, well-suited

18 prepared for, ready for, set or all set for <nonformal>; loaded for, primed for; up for <nonformal>; equal to, up to

19 ready-made; prefabricated, prefab <nonformal>, preformed; ready-to-wear, off-the-rack; cut-and-dried or cut-and-dry

20 preparatory, preparative; prerequisite; provident, provisional

ADJS, ADVS **21 in readiness, in store, in reserve;** in anticipation

22 in preparation, in course of preparation, **in progress** or **process,** under way, **going on, in production,** on stream, under construction, **in the works** or hopper or pipeline <nonformal>, on the way, **in the making, in hand,** in the oven; under revision; brewing, forthcoming

23 afoot, on foot, afloat, astir

406 UNPREPAREDNESS

NOUNS **1 unpreparedness, unreadiness,** lack of preparation; vulnerability 1005.4; improvisation, ad lib <nonformal>; **unfitness, unsuitability, unqualifiedness,** lack of credentials, poor track record <nonformal>; **disqualification,** incompetence or incompetency, incapability

2 improvidence, thriftlessness, unthriftiness; shiftlessness, fecklessness, thoughtlessness, heedlessness; hastiness 401.2; negligence 340.1

3 <raw or original condition> **naturalness,** inartificiality; **natural state,** nature, **state of nature,** nature in the raw; pristineness, intactness, virginity; natural man; artlessness 416

4 undevelopment, nondevelopment; **immaturity,** immatureness, callowness, **rawness, unripeness, greenness; unfinish, unrefinement, uncultivation; crudity,** crudeness, **rudeness, coarseness,** roughness, the rough; **oversimplification,** simplism, reductionism

5 raw material; crude; ore, rich ore, rich vein; **diamond in the rough; virgin soil**

VERBS **6 be unprepared** or **unready,** not be ready; go off half-cocked <nonformal>; be taken unawares or aback, be blindsided <nonformal>, be caught napping, be caught with one's pants down <nonformal>, be surprised; **extemporize,** improvise, ad-lib and play by ear <both nonformal>

7 make no provision, take no thought of tomorrow, seize the day, live for the day, live from hand to mouth

ADJS **8 unprepared, unready,** unprimed; surprised, caught napping, caught with one's pants down <nonformal>, taken by surprise, taken aback, taken unawares, blindsided <nonformal>, caught off balance, caught off base <nonformal>; **unarranged,** unorganized, haphazard; makeshift, rough-and-ready, **extemporaneous,** improvised, ad-lib and off the top of one's head <both nonformal>; impromptu, snap <nonformal>; **unmade,** unhatched, unplanned, unpremeditated; hasty, precipitate 401.10

9 **unfitted, unfit,** ill-fitted, **unsuited, unadapted, unqualified,** disqualified, incompetent, incapable; **unequipped, unfurnished,** unarmed, ill-equipped, ill-furnished, **unprovided**

10 **raw, crude; uncooked;** underdone, rare

11 **immature, unripe,** underripe, unripened, **raw, green,** callow, wet behind the ears, unfledged, unseasoned; half-grown, adolescent, juvenile, puerile, boyish, girlish; half-baked <nonformal>; half-cocked <nonformal>

12 **undeveloped, unfinished,** unformed; unfashioned, unworked, unprocessed; **underdeveloped;** backward, arrested, stunted; **crude, rude, coarse, unpolished, unrefined; uncultivated, uncultured; rough,** roughhewn, **in the rough; rudimentary,** rudimental; embryonic, in embryo, fetal; **oversimple, simplistic,** reductive

13 <in the raw or original state> **natural, native, in a state of nature,** in the raw; artless 416.5; virgin, virginal, pristine, untouched, unsullied

14 **fallow,** untilled, uncultivated, unsown

15 **improvident, prodigal; thriftless, unthrifty;** hand-to-mouth; **shiftless, feckless, thoughtless, heedless;** happy-go-lucky; negligent 340.10

407 ACCOMPLISHMENT
<act of accomplishing; entire performance>

NOUNS 1 **accomplishment, achievement, fulfillment, performance, execution,** implementation, **discharge, dispatch, consummation, realization, attainment,** production, fruition; **success** 409; track record or track <nonformal>; done deal <nonformal>; mission accomplished

2 **completion, finish, conclusion, end,** ending, **termination,**

close, windup <nonformal>, rounding off or out, topping off, wrap-up, finalization; **perfection,** culmination 1001.3; ripeness, maturity, maturation

3 **finishing touch,** final touch, last touch, last stroke, icing the cake, the icing on the cake; capstone, crown; climax 198.2

VERBS 4 **accomplish, achieve, effect, effectuate, consummate, do, execute, produce, deliver, make,** enact, **perform, discharge, fulfill, realize, attain; work,** work out; **dispatch, dispose of,** knock off <nonformal>, polish off <nonformal>, take care of <nonformal>, **deal with,** put away, make short work of; succeed, manage 409.12; come through and do the job <both nonformal>, **do** or **turn the trick** <nonformal>

5 **bring about, bring to pass; implement, carry out, carry through; bring off, carry off, pull off** <nonformal>; **put through,** get through, **put over** or **across** <nonformal>

6 **complete, perfect, finish, finish off, conclude, terminate, end,** bring to a close, carry to completion; **get through, get done;** get through with, get it over with, **finish up;** clean up and wind up and button up and sew up and wrap up and mop up <all nonformal>, close up or out; put the lid on and call it a day <both nonformal>; **round off** or **out, wind up** <nonformal>, **top off;** top out, crown, cap 198.9; climax, culminate; put the finishing touches or strokes on, lick or whip into shape, finalize, put the icing on the cake

7 **do to perfection, do up brown** <nonformal>, **do to a turn,** do to a T or to a frazzle <nonformal>, do oneself proud <nonformal>, use every trick in the book, leave no loose ends, leave nothing hanging; go to all lengths, go the whole way, go the limit and go whole hog and go all out and

shoot the works *and* go for broke
<all nonformal>

8 ripen, mature, maturate;
bloom, blossom, flourish; come
to fruition, bear fruit; **mellow;**
grow up, reach maturity; come *or*
draw to a head; bring to a head

ADJS **9 completing, finishing,** con-
summative, culminating, conclusive, **concluding,** fulfilling,
finalizing, crowning; ultimate,
last, final, terminal

**10 accomplished, achieved,
effected,** effectuated, imple-
mented, **consummated, executed, discharged, fulfilled,
realized, attained; dispatched,
disposed of,** set at rest; wrought

11 completed, done, finished,
concluded, terminated, **ended,**
finished up; signed, sealed, and
delivered; cleaned up *and* wound
up *or* sewn up *and* wrapped up
and mopped up <all nonformal>;
washed up <nonformal>,
through, done with; all over
with, all said and done, all over
but the shouting

**12 complete, perfect, consum-
mate,** polished; exhaustive,
thorough 793.10; fully realized

13 ripe, mature, matured, seasoned; blooming; **mellow,** full-
grown, fully developed

ADVS **14 to completion,** to the end,
to the limit; to a turn, to a T
<nonformal>, to a frazzle
<nonformal>

408 NONACCOMPLISHMENT

NOUNS **1 nonaccomplishment,
nonachievement, nonperformance, noncompletion,**
nonconsummation, nonfulfillment, unfulfillment; nonfeasance, omission; **neglect** 340;
loose ends, rough edges; endless
task, Sisyphean toil; **disappointment** 132; **failure** 410

VERBS **2** neglect, leave undone
340.7, fail 410.8-10,13; be disappointed 132.4

ADJS **3 unaccomplished, un-
achieved, unperformed,** unex-
ecuted, undischarged, unfulfilled,

unconsummated, unrealized, un-
attained; **unfinished, uncompleted, undone;** open-ended;
neglected 340.14; **disappointed**
132.5

409 SUCCESS

NOUNS **1 success, successfulness,**
fortunate outcome; **prosperity**
1009; accomplishment 407; **victory** 411

2 sure success, foregone conclusion, sure-fire proposition
<nonformal>; **winner** *and* **natu-
ral** <both nonformal>; shoo-in
and **sure thing** *and* sure bet *and*
cinch *and* lead-pipe cinch <all
nonformal>

3 great success, triumph, brilliant success; **stardom; success
story;** brief success, nine days'
wonder, flash in the pan, fad; best
seller

4 <nonformal terms> **smash, hit,**
smash hit, boffo, showstopper,
howling *or* roaring success, one
for the book, wow, sensation,
overnight sensation

5 score, hit, bull's-eye; goal,
touchdown; grand slam; strike;
hole in one; home run, homer
<nonformal>

6 <successful person> **winner,**
star, success, superstar <nonfor-
mal>; phenom *and* comer <both
nonformal>; **victor** 411.2

VERBS **7 succeed, prevail,** be successful, be crowned with success,
meet with success, deliver, come
through *and* make a go of it
<both nonformal>; **go, come off,**
go off; **prosper** 1009.7; do *or*
work wonders, go to town *or* go
great guns <both nonformal>;
make a hit <nonformal>, click
and connect <both nonfor-
mal>, **catch on** *and* take <both nonfor-
mal>, catch fire, have legs
<nonformal>; **go over** *and* go
over big *or* with a bang <all non-
formal>; win one's spurs *or*
wings, get one's credentials; pass
with flying colors

**8 achieve one's purpose, gain
one's end** *or* **ends,** attain one's

objective, reach one's goal, bring it off, pull it off *and* hack it *and* swing it <all nonformal>; make one's point; play it *or* handle it just right <nonformal>

9 **score a success,** score, hit the mark, ring the bell <nonformal>, break the bank *or* make a killing <both nonformal>, hit the jackpot <nonformal>

10 **make good, come through, achieve success,** make a success, **make it** <nonformal>, hit one's stride, **make one's mark, give a good account of oneself,** do all right by oneself *and* **do oneself proud,** make out like a bandit <all nonformal>; **advance, progress,** make headway, **get on,** come on <nonformal>, **get ahead** <nonformal>; go places, **go far;** rise, **rise in the world,** work one's way up, move up in the world, claw *or* scrabble one's way up, mount the ladder of success, pull oneself up by one's bootstraps; **arrive,** get there <nonformal>; come out on top; **be a success,** have it made *or* wrapped up <nonformal>, have the world at one's feet, eat *or* live high on the hog <nonformal>; **make a noise in the world** <nonformal>, cut a swath, set the world on fire; make a breakthrough

11 **succeed with,** crown with success; **make a go of it; accomplish,** compass, **achieve** 407.4; **bring off, carry off, pull off** <nonformal>, **put through,** bring through; **put over** *or* **across** <nonformal>; get away with it <nonformal>

12 **manage, contrive, succeed in; make out, get on** *or* **along** <nonformal>, go on; **scrape along,** worry along, get by, **manage somehow; make it** <nonformal>, **make the grade,** cut the mustard *and* hack it <both nonformal>; **swing** <nonformal>, put over <nonformal>, put through

13 **win through, win out** <nonfor-mal>, come through <nonformal>, rise to the occasion, beat the system <nonformal>; **triumph** 411.3; **weather the storm,** live through, keep one's head above water; come up fighting *or* smiling, not know when one is beaten, persevere 360.2

ADJS 14 **successful,** succeeding, crowned with success; **prosperous,** fortunate 1009.14; **triumphant;** ahead of the game, out in front, on top, sitting on top of the world *and* sitting pretty <both nonformal>, on top of the heap <nonformal>; surefire

ADVS 15 **successfully,** swimmingly <nonformal>; beyond all expectation, beyond one's fondest dreams, from rags to riches, with flying colors

410 FAILURE

NOUNS 1 **failure, unsuccessfulness;** no go <nonformal>; futility, uselessness 391; **defeat** 412; losing game, **no-win situation;** nonaccomplishment 408; **bankruptcy** 625.3

2 <nonformal terms> **flop,** flopperoo, **bust, fizzle,** lemon, clinker, dud, non-starter, **loser, washout,** turkey, bomb

3 **collapse, crash,** comedown, breakdown, derailment, **fall,** pratfall <nonformal>, stumble, tumble, **downfall;** nose dive *and* tailspin <both nonformal>; deflation, bursting of the bubble, letdown, **disappointment** 132

4 **miss,** near-miss; **slip, slipup** <nonformal>, slip 'twixt cup and lip; **error, mistake** 974.3

5 **abortion, miscarriage,** abortive attempt, vain attempt; wild-goose chase, merry chase; **misfire, flash in the pan,** malfunction, glitch <nonformal>; **dud** <nonformal>; **flunk** <nonformal>, **washout** <nonformal>

6 **fiasco, botch,** botch-up, bungle, hash, mess, muddle, bollix *and* bitch-up *and* screw-up *and* fuckup <all nonformal>

7 <unsuccessful person> **failure,**
flash in the pan
8 <nonformal terms> **loser, non-
starter,** born loser, **flop,** washout,
dud, also-ran, bum, bust, turkey
VERBS **9 fail,** be unsuccessful, not
work *and* not come off <both
nonformal>, come to grief, **lose,**
not make the grade, be found
wanting, not come up to the
mark; not pass, **flunk** *and* **flunk
out** <both nonformal>; labor in
vain 391.8; come away empty-
handed; tap out <nonformal>, go
bankrupt 625.7
10 <nonformal terms> **lose out,
not make it,** not hack it, not get
to first base, drop the ball, **flop,**
fall flat on one's ass, lay an egg, go
over like a lead balloon, draw a
blank, bomb; fold, fold up; take it
on the chin, take the count; crap
out; strike out, fan, whiff
11 sink, founder, go down, go under <nonformal>; **slip,** go downhill, be on the skids <nonformal>
12 fall, fall down <nonformal>,
fall *or* drop by the wayside, fall
flat, fall flat on one's face; fall
down on the job <nonformal>;
**fall short, fall through; fall
dead; collapse; crash**
13 come to nothing, hang up *and*
get nowhere <both nonformal>;
poop out <nonformal>; fail miserably *or* ignominiously; **fizzle**
and **fizzle out** *and* peter out *and*
poop out <all nonformal>; **misfire,** flash in the pan, hang fire;
**blow up, blow up in one's face,
explode, end** *or* **go up in smoke**
14 miss, miss the mark; slip, slip
up <nonformal>; goof <nonfor-
mal>, blunder, **err** 974.9; **botch,
bungle** 414.11,12; run around in
circles, spin one's wheels
15 miscarry, abort, be stillborn; **go
amiss,** go astray, **go wrong,** take
a wrong turn, derail
16 stall, stick, die, go dead, **conk
out** <nonformal>, run out of gas
or steam, come to a dead stop
17 flunk *or* **flunk out** <both nonfor-
mal>; **fail,** bust *and* wash out
<both nonformal>

ADJS **18 unsuccessful,** failing; **unfortunate** 1010.14; **abortive,**
miscarried, stillborn; fruitless,
no-win <nonformal>; futile, useless 391.9; lame, **ineffectual,**
ineffective, inefficacious, of no
effect; malfunctioning
ADVS **19 unsuccessfully, without
success;** fruitlessly, ineffectually,
ineffectively, lamely; to little *or* no
purpose, **in vain**

411 VICTORY

NOUNS **1 victory, triumph, conquest;** a feather in one's cap
<nonformal>; total victory, grand
slam; **championship,** crown,
laurels, cup, trophy, belt, blue ribbon, first prize; raised arms;
victory lap; **winning,** win
<nonformal>; knockout *or* KO
<nonformal>; walkover *and*
walkaway <both nonformal>,
pushover *and* picnic <both non-
formal>; romp *and* shellacking
<both nonformal>; landslide vic-
tory, landslide; Pyrrhic victory;
moral victory; **success** 409; ascendancy 417.6; mastery 612.2
**2 victor, winner; conqueror, van-
quisher,** subjugator; top dog
<nonformal>; hero, conquering
hero; champion, champ *and*
number one <both nonformal>;
easy winner, sure winner, shoo-in
<nonformal>; runner-up
VERBS **3 triumph, prevail, be victorious,** come out ahead, come
out on top <nonformal>, clean
up; **win, gain, capture, carry;**
win out <nonformal>; **win
through,** carry off *or* away; **win**
or **carry** *or* **gain the day,** finish
in front, make a killing <nonfor-
mal>; get *or* have the last laugh;
win the prize, win the palm *or*
laurels, take the cake <nonfor-
mal>, win one's spurs *or* wings;
win by a fluke <nonformal>; **win
by a nose** *and* nose out *and* edge
out <all nonformal>; **succeed;**
break the record
4 win hands down *and* win going
away <both nonformal>, win in a
canter *and* walk *and* waltz <all

nonformal>, romp *or* breeze *or* waltz home <all nonformal>, **walk off** *or* **away with,** waltz off with <nonformal>, **walk over** <nonformal>; have it all one's way; **take** *or* **carry by storm,** sweep aside all obstacles, carry all before one, make short work of

5 **defeat** 412.6, **triumph over, prevail over,** best, get the best of <nonformal>, **beat** <nonformal>, **get the better** *or* **best of; surmount, overcome**

6 **gain the ascendancy,** come out on top <nonformal>, **get the advantage, gain the upper** *or* **whip hand,** dominate the field, get the edge on *or* jump on *or* drop on <nonformal>, get a leg up on <nonformal>, get a stranglehold on

ADJS 7 **victorious, triumphant,** triumphal, **winning, prevailing;** conquering, vanquishing, overcoming; ahead of the game, ascendant, in the ascendant, in ascendancy, sitting on top of the world *and* sitting pretty <both nonformal>, dominant 612.18; successful; flushed with success *or* victory

8 **undefeated, unbeaten, unvanquished, unconquered,** unsubdued, unquelled, unbowed

ADVS 9 **triumphantly, in triumph;** by a mile

412 DEFEAT

NOUNS 1 **defeat; beating,** drubbing, thrashing; clobbering *and* hiding *and* lathering *and* whipping *and* lambasting *and* trimming *and* licking <all nonformal>, trouncing; **vanquishment, conquest, conquering,** mastery, subjugation; **overthrow,** overturn; **fall, downfall,** collapse, smash, crash, **undoing, ruin,** debacle; **destruction** 395; deathblow, quietus; Waterloo

2 **discomfiture, rout, repulse,** rebuff; **frustration; checkmate,** check, balk; **reverse,** reversal, **setback**

3 **utter defeat,** crushing defeat, smashing defeat, decisive defeat; no contest; **smearing** *and* **pasting** *and* creaming *and* **clobbering** *and* **shellacking** *and* whomping :all nonformal>; **shutout**

4 **ignominious defeat,** abject defeat, inglorious defeat, disastrous defeat, utter rout

5 **loser**; the vanquished; good loser, sport *or* **good sport** <nonformal>; poor sport, poor loser; **underdog, also-ran;** fall guy <nonformal>; victim 96.11

VERBS 6 **defeat, worst, best, get the better** *or* **best of,** be too much for, be more than a match for; **outdo,** outmaneuver, outclass, outshine; **triumph over;** deal a deathblow to; undo, ruin, destroy 395.10; beat by a nose *and* nose out *and* edge out <all nonformal>

7 **overcome,** surmount; **overpower; overthrow, overturn; upset,** trip, trip up, send flying *or* sprawling; silence, floor, deck; kick the habit <nonformal>

8 **overwhelm,** snow under <nonformal>, overbear, deal a crushing *or* smashing defeat; **discomfit, rout, put to rout,** put to flight, scatter, stampede, panic; confound

9 <nonformal terms> **clobber, trim, skin alive, beat,** skunk, drub, massacre, lick, whip, thrash, trim, hide, cut to pieces, run rings *or* circles around, throw for a loss, lather, trounce, **lambaste,** skin alive; fix, settle, settle one's hash, make one say 'uncle,' do in, lick to a frazzle, beat all hollow, beat one's brains out, cook one's goose, make mincemeat of, mop up the floor with, sandbag, smear, paste, cream, **shellac,** whup, whop, whomp

10 **conquer, vanquish,** quell, **suppress, put down, subdue, subjugate,** master; **reduce,** prostrate, fell, **flatten, break, smash, crush, humble,** bend, **bring one to his knees;** trample in the dust,

ride or run roughshod over; have
one's way with

11 **thwart, frustrate,** dash, check,
checkmate 1011.15

12 **lose,** lose out <nonformal>, lose
the day, come off second best, **get**
or have the worst of it, meet
one's Waterloo; fall, succumb,
bow, go down, go under, **bite or**
lick the dust, take the count
<nonformal>; throw in the towel,
say 'uncle'; have enough

ADJS **13 lost,** unwon

14 **defeated, worsted, bested,**
outdone; beaten, discomfited,
put to rout, **routed,** scattered,
stampeded, panicked; con-
founded; **overcome, over-**
thrown, overpowered, over-
whelmed, overmastered; fallen,
down; floored, silenced; **undone,**
done for <nonformal>, **ruined,**
kaput and on the skids <both
nonformal>

15 <nonformal terms> beat, clobbered, licked, whipped,
trimmed, sandbagged, done in,
lathered, creamed, shellacked,
trounced, lambasted; thrown for
a loss

16 **shut out,** skunked and blanked
and whitewashed <all nonfor-
mal>, scoreless, not on the
scoreboard

17 **conquered, vanquished,**
quelled, suppressed, put down,
subdued, subjugated, mastered;
reduced, prostrated, **flattened,**
smashed, **crushed,** broken; **hum-**
bled, brought to one's knees

18 **irresistible, overpowering,**
overcoming, overwhelming,
overmastering

413 SKILL

NOUNS 1 **skill,** skillfulness, **expert-**
ness, expertise, proficiency,
craft, **cleverness; dexterity,**
dexterousness; **adroitness,**
adeptness, deftness; **compe-**
tence, capability, capacity,
ability, efficiency; **facility,**
prowess; grace, style, finesse;
tact, tactfulness, diplomacy;
savoir-faire <Fr>; **artistry;**

artfulness; **craftsmanship,**
workmanship; **know-how** and
savvy and bag of tricks <all non-
formal>; **technique, touch,**
technical brilliance, technical
mastery, **virtuosity,** bravura, wizardry; brilliance 919.2; cunning
415; **ingenuity,** resourcefulness,
wit; **mastery, command,** control,
grip

2 **agility, nimbleness, spryness,**
lightness

3 **versatility, ambidexterity,**
many-sidedness, all-roundedness
<nonformal>; **adaptability,** flex-
ibility; broad-gauge, many hats;
Renaissance man or woman

4 **talent, flair, gift, endowment,**
genius, instinct, **faculty; power,**
ability, capability, capacity, potential; caliber; **forte,** specialty,
long suit, strong point; **equip-**
ment, qualification; talents,
powers, parts; the goods and the
stuff and the right stuff and what
it takes <all nonformal>

5 **aptitude,** inborn or innate aptitude, aptness, flair; **bent, turn,**
propensity, **leaning,** inclination,
tendency; capacity for, gift for, genius for; an eye for, an ear for, a
hand for, a way with

6 **knack, art, hang, trick,** way;
touch, feel

7 **art, science, craft; skill; tech-**
nique, technical knowledge
or skill, technical know-how
<nonformal>; **mechanics,** mech-
anism; method

8 **accomplishment, acquire-**
ment, attainment; finish

9 **experience, practice,** practical
knowledge or skill, hands-on experience <nonformal>, field-
work; background, seasoning,
tempering; **worldly wisdom,**
blaséness, **sophistication;**
sagacity 919.4

10 **masterpiece, masterwork,** *chef*
d'œuvre <Fr>; **master stroke;**
feat, *tour de force* <Fr>

11 **expert, adept,** proficient; **artist,**
craftsman, artisan, journeyman;
technician; seasoned or experienced hand; shark or sharp and

no slouch *and* tough act to follow
<all nonformal>; **professional,
pro** <nonformal>; **jack-of-all-
trades,** handy man; **authority,**
maven <nonformal>; **consultant,** attaché, technical adviser;
pundit, savant 928.3; connoisseur; marksman, crack shot, dead
shot

12 talented person, talent, man *or*
woman of parts, gifted person,
prodigy, natural <nonformal>,
genius, intellectual prodigy, mental giant; rocket scientist *and*
brain surgeon <both nonformal>;
child prodigy, wunderkind, whiz
kid *and* boy wonder <both non-
formal>

13 master, past master; world-
class performer, **good hand,**
skilled *or* practiced hand; **prodigy; wizard,** magician; **virtuoso;
genius;** mastermind; sage 920.1

14 <nonformal terms> **ace, star,
superstar, crackerjack,** great,
all-time great, whiz, flash, hot
stuff, pisser, pistol, world-beater,
the one who wrote the book

15 champion, champ <nonfor-
mal>, title-holder; **record
holder;** laureate; **prizewinner;**
hall of famer

16 veteran, vet <nonformal>, **old
pro** <nonformal>; **old hand, old-
timer** <nonformal>; old campaigner, war-horse *or* old war-
horse <nonformal>; salt *and* old
salt *and* old sea dog <all nonfor-
mal>; shellback <nonformal>

**17 sophisticate, man of the
world;** slicker *and* city slicker
<both nonformal>; man-about-
town; **cosmopolitan,** cosmopolite, citizen of the world

VERBS 18 excel in *or* **at, shine in**
or **at** <nonformal>, be master of;
write the book <nonformal>,
have a good command of, feel
comfortable with, be at home in;
have a gift *or* **flair** *or* **talent** *or*
bent *or* **faculty for,** be a natural
and be cut out <both nonfor-
mal>, **have a good head for,**
have an ear for, have an eye for, be
born for, show aptitude *or* talent

for; have the knack *or* touch, have
a way with, have a lot going for
one <nonformal>, be able to do it
blindfolded *or* standing on one's
head <nonformal>; have something *or* plenty on the ball
<nonformal>

**19 know backwards and for-
wards, know one's stuff** *or*
know one's onions <both non-
formal>, **know the ropes** *and*
know all the ins and outs <both
nonformal>, know from A to Z,
know like the back of one's hand
or a book, know all the tricks *or*
moves, know all the tricks of the
trade; **know what's what, know
a thing or two, know what it's
all about, know the score** *and*
know all the answers <both non-
formal>; **know one's way about,**
know the ways of the world, have
been around the block <nonfor-
mal>, have been through the mill
<nonformal>, have cut one's wis-
dom teeth *or* eyeteeth <nonfor-
mal>, **not be born yesterday;** get
around <nonformal>

20 exercise skill, handle oneself
well, **strut one's stuff** *and* hotdog
and grandstand *and* showboat
<all nonformal>; play one's cards
well

21 be versatile, double in brass *and*
wear more than one hat <both
nonformal>

**ADJS 22 skillful, good, expert,
proficient; dexterous, adroit,
deft, adept, coordinated,** well-
coordinated, **apt, handy; clever,**
cute *and* slick *and* slick as a whistle <all nonformal>; fancy,
graceful, stylish; some *or* quite
some *or* quite a *or* every bit a <all
nonformal>; **masterly, masterful;** magisterial; authoritative,
professional; crack *or* crackerjack
<both nonformal>; whiz-kid
<nonformal>; **virtuoso,** bravura;
brilliant 919.14; cunning 415.12;
tactful, diplomatic, statesmanlike; **ingenious,** resourceful;
**artistic; workmanlike, well-
done**

23 agile, nimble, spry, sprightly,

fleet, light, graceful, nimble-footed, sure-footed; nimble-fingered

24 competent, capable, able, efficient, qualified, fit, fitted, suited, worthy; equal to, up to; up to snuff <nonformal>; well-qualified, well-suited

25 versatile, ambidextrous, two-handed, **all around** <nonformal>, broad-gauge, **well-rounded, many-sided; adaptable,** adjustable, flexible

26 skilled, accomplished; practiced; professional, career; trained, coached, prepared, primed, finished; initiated, initiate; conversant

27 skilled in, proficient in, adept in, versed in, **good at,** expert at, **handy at, a hand** *or* **good hand at,** master of, strong in, at home in; **up on,** well up on, well-versed 927.20

28 experienced, practiced, mature, ripe, **seasoned,** tried, tried and true, **veteran;** sagacious 919.16; **worldly, worldly-wise,** wise in the ways of the world, knowing, **sophisticated,** cosmopolitan, blasé, dry behind the ears, not born yesterday

29 talented, gifted, endowed, with a flair; born for, made for, cut out for <nonformal>

30 well-laid, well-devised, well-designed, well-planned; **well-reasoned,** well-thought-out; **cunning, clever**

ADVS **31 skillfully, expertly, proficiently,** well; **cleverly,** ingeniously, resourcefully; cunningly 415.13; **dexterously, adroitly, deftly, adeptly,** aptly, handily; nimbly, spryly; **competently, capably, ably,** efficiently; **masterfully;** brilliantly, superbly; **artistically,** artfully; with finesse

414 UNSKILLFULNESS

NOUNS **1 unskillfulness, inexpertness, unproficiency, uncleverness;** unintelligence 921; **undexterousness, undeftness;** inefficiency; **incompetence** *or* incompetency, **inability, incapability, incapacity,** inadequacy; ineffectiveness, **ineffectuality; mediocrity; inaptitude,** inept-ness, maladroitness; thought-lessness, inattentiveness; maladjustment; rustiness <nonformal>

2 inexperience; rawness, greenness, callowness, unreadiness, immaturity; ignorance 929; **unfamiliarity,** unacquaintance; **amateurishness,** unprofessionalism

3 clumsiness, awkwardness, bumblingness, **maladroitness, unhandiness,** heavy-handedness, ham-handedness <nonformal>; **ungainliness,** uncouthness, **ungracefulness,** gracelessness, inelegance; **gawkiness,** gawkishness; **lubberliness, oafishness,** loutishness, boorishness; **cumbersomeness, ponderousness; unwieldiness, unmanageability**

4 bungling, blundering, boggling, **fumbling, botching; sloppiness, carelessness** 340.2; too many cooks

5 bungle, blunder, botch, flub, boner *and* bonehead play <both nonformal>, boggle, boo-boo *and* screw-up *and* fuck-up <all nonformal>; **fumble, muff,** fluff, miscue <nonformal>; **slip,** trip, stumble; **hash** *and* **mess** <both nonformal>; off day; **error, mistake** 974.3

6 mismanagement, mishandling, misdirection, misguidance, misconduct, **misgovernment,** misrule; maladministration; malfeasance, malpractice, misfeasance, wrongdoing 655; nonfeasance, omission; **negligence,** neglect 340.6; inexpedience *or* inexpediency 995

7 incompetent, incapable; mediocrity, duffer *and* hacker <both nonformal>, no great shakes, no prize package, no brain surgeon, no rocket scientist

8 bungler, blunderer, blunderhead, bumbler, **fumbler,**

botcher; bull in a china shop, ox; lout, oaf, gawk, boor, **clown,** slouch; clodhopper, yokel; **clod, dolt,** blockhead 923.4; blind leading the blind

9 <nonformal terms> **goof,** goofball, goofus, foul-up, fuck-up, screw-up, bonehead, dub, klutz, **butterfingers,** stumblebum, duffer, lummox, **slob,** lump, dub; rube, hick

VERBS 10 **not know how,** not have the knack, not have it in one <nonformal>; not be up to <nonformal>; not be versed

11 **bungle, blunder,** bumble, boggle, **muff,** muff one's cue or lines, **fumble,** be all thumbs; **flounder,** muddle, lumber; stumble, **slip,** trip, trip over one's own feet, get in one's own way, miscue; commit a *faux pas,* commit a gaffe; blunder on or upon or into; be not one's day; **botch,** mar, **spoil, butcher, murder;** play havoc with

12 <nonformal terms> **goof, pull a boner,** lay an egg, put or stick one's foot in it, drop the ball; **blow,** blow it, **mess up,** flub, flub the dub, **make a mess** or **hash of,** foul up, fuck up, goof up, bollix up, **screw up, louse up, gum up,** gum up the works, bugger, bugger up, play the deuce or devil or hell or merry hell with; go at it ass-backwards; put one's foot in one's mouth

13 **mismanage, mishandle, misconduct,** misdirect, misguide, **misgovern, misrule;** maladminister

14 not know what one is about, make an ass of oneself, **make a fool of oneself,** not know on which side one's bread is buttered, not know one's ass from one's elbow or a hole in the ground, kill the goose that lays the golden egg, cut one's own throat, dig one's own grave, **play with fire,** burn one's fingers, jump out of the frying pan into the fire, lock the barn door after the horse is stolen, **count one's**

chickens before they are hatched, buy a pig in a poke, **put the cart before the horse,** run before one can walk

ADJS 15 **unskillful,** artless, **inexpert, unproficient, unclever;** inefficient; **undexterous, undeft; inept,** hopeless, half-assed *and* clunky <both nonformal>, **poor;** mediocre, pedestrian; thoughtless, inattentive

16 **unskilled, unaccomplished, untrained,** unschooled, uninitiated, **unprepared,** unprimed, unfinished, unpolished; **untalented, ungifted, unendowed; amateurish,** unprofessional, unbusinesslike

17 **inexperienced,** unversed, unconversant, **unpracticed;** undeveloped, unseasoned; **raw, green,** green as grass, callow, unfledged, immature, wet behind the ears, not dry behind the ears, **untried;** unskilled in, unversed in, unconversant with, unaccustomed to, unused to, unfamiliar or unacquainted with, new to, a stranger to, a novice at; ignorant 929.12

18 **out of practice,** out of training, soft <nonformal>, out of shape or condition, stiff, **rusty;** gone to seed *and* over the hill *and* not what one used to be <all nonformal>, losing one's touch, slipping

19 **incompetent, incapable, unable, inadequate, unequipped, unqualified,** out of one's depth, outmatched, **unfit, unfitted,** not equal or up to, not cut out for <nonformal>; ineffective, **ineffectual**

20 **bungling, blundering,** bumbling, fumbling; **clumsy, awkward, uncoordinated,** maladroit, unhandy, heavy-handed, **all thumbs;** stiff; **ungainly,** uncouth, **ungraceful,** graceless, inelegant, *gauche* <Fr>; **gawky,** gawkish; **lubberly, loutish, oafish,** boorish, clownish, lumpish; **sloppy, careless** 340.11; **ponderous, cumbersome,** lumbering, hulking; **unwieldy**

21 botched, bungled, fumbled, muffed, spoiled, **butchered,** murdered; mismanaged, **misdirected, misguided;** impolitic, ill-considered, ill-advised

22 <nonformal terms> **goofed-up, bobbled, messed-up, fouled-up, fucked-up, screwed-up, bollixed-up, loused-up,** gummed-up, snafued; clunky, half-assed; ass-backwards

ADVS **23 unskillfully, inexpertly, unproficiently, uncleverly;** inefficiently; **incompetently, incapably,** inadequately; **undeftly; ineptly,** poorly

24 clumsily, awkwardly; bunglingly, blunderingly; maladroitly, unhandily; **ungracefully,** gracelessly, inelegantly, uncouthly; **ponderously, cumbersomely,** lumberingly, hulkingly

415 CUNNING

NOUNS **1 cunning, craft, craftiness, artfulness, art, artifice, wiliness,** wiles, guile, **slyness,** insidiousness, **foxiness,** slipperiness, shiftiness, trickiness; gamesmanship *and* one-upmanship <both nonformal>; **canniness, shrewdness,** sharpness, acuteness, astuteness, **cleverness** 413.1; **resourcefulness, ingeniousness, wit,** inventiveness, readiness; subtlety, subtleness, fine Italian hand, finesse; **sophistry** 935; satanic cunning; sneakiness, **stealthiness, stealth** 345.4; cageyness <nonformal>, wariness 494.2

2 Machiavellianism; politics, diplomacy

3 stratagem, artifice, craft, wile, strategy, **device, contrivance, expedient, design, scheme, trick,** gimmick <nonformal>, **ruse, red herring, shift,** tactic, **maneuver, stroke,** master stroke, **move, coup,** gambit, **ploy, dodge; game,** racket *and* grift <both nonformal>; **plot,** conspiracy, **intrigue;** method in one's madness; **subterfuge,** blind; chicanery, deceit, trickery 356.4

4 machination, manipulation, wire-pulling <nonformal>; influence, behind-the-scenes influence *or* pressure; **maneuvering,** maneuvers; **tactics,** devices, expedients, gimmickry <nonformal>

5 circumvention, getting round; **evasion,** elusion, the slip <nonformal>; the runaround *and* buck-passing *and* passing the buck <all nonformal>; **frustration, foiling, thwarting** 1011.3; **outwitting,** outsmarting, **outmaneuvering**

6 sly dog <nonformal>, **fox,** reynard, dodger, smooth *or* cool customer <nonformal>, smooth *or* sweet talker, smoothie <nonformal>, charmer; **trickster,** shyster <nonformal>, shady character, Philadelphia lawyer <nonformal>; horse trader; **swindler** 357.3

7 strategist, tactician; maneuverer, manipulator, wire-puller <nonformal>; **intriguer**

8 Machiavellian; diplomat, politician 610; influence peddler; powerbroker, kingmaker; power behind the throne, gray eminence

VERBS **9 live by one's wits;** finesse; twist and turn, zig and zag; have something up one's sleeve, have an out *or* a way out *or* an escape hatch; **trick, deceive** 356.14

10 maneuver, manipulate, pull strings; **contrive,** angle <nonformal>, **jockey;** play games <nonformal>; **plot, scheme, intrigue; finagle, wangle**

11 outwit, outfox, outsmart, outguess, outfigure, **outmaneuver,** outgeneral, outflank, outplay; get the better *or* best of, go one better; play one's trump card; **circumvent, evade,** stonewall <nonformal>, **elude, frustrate, foil,** give the slip *or* runaround <nonformal>; pass the buck <nonformal>; pull a fast one <nonformal>, steal a march on; make a fool of, make a sucker *or* patsy of <nonformal>; throw a curve <nonformal>, **deceive, victimize** 356.18

ADJS **12 cunning, crafty, artful, wily,** guileful, **sly,** insidious, **shifty,** arch, **smooth, slick** *and* slick as a whistle <both nonformal>, **slippery,** snaky, serpentine, **foxy,** vulpine, feline; **canny, shrewd,** sharp, razor-sharp, astute, **clever;** resourceful, ingenious, inventive, ready; subtle; **tricky,** gimmicky <nonformal>; **Machiavellian,** diplomatic; strategic, tactical; crazy like a fox <nonformal>, too clever by half; sneaky, **stealthy** 345.12; cagey <nonformal>, wary 494.9; **scheming, designing; manipulative; deceitful**

ADVS **13 cunningly, craftily, artfully,** guilefully, insidiously, shiftily, smoothly, slick <nonformal>; **slyly,** on the sly; **cannily, shrewdly,** astutely, **cleverly;** subtly; cagily <nonformal>, warily 494.13

416 ARTLESSNESS

NOUNS **1 artlessness, ingenuousness, guilelessness; simplicity,** simpleness, plainness; simplemindedness; **unsophistication,** unsophisticatedness; *naïveté* <Fr>; **innocence;** trustfulness, trustingness, unguardedness, unwariness; **openness,** openheartedness, sincerity, **candor** 644.4; **integrity;** directness, bluffness, bluntness, outspokenness

2 naturalness; state of nature; unspoiledness; **unaffectedness,** unaffectation, **unassumingness,** unpretentiousness; genuineness

3 simple soul, unsophisticate, **ingenue, innocent, child, babe,** newborn babe, babe in the woods, lamb, dove; child of nature; primitive; **yokel,** rube *and* hick <both nonformal>; oaf, lout 923.5; dupe 358

VERBS **4** wear one's heart on one's sleeve, look one in the face

ADJS **5 artless, simple,** plain, **guideless; ingenuous; unsophisticated, naive;** childlike, born yesterday; **innocent;** trustful, trusting, unguarded, unwary,

unreserved, confiding; **open,** openhearted, sincere, candid, **frank** 644.17; direct, bluff, blunt, outspoken

6 natural; in the state of nature; primitive, primal, pristine, unspoiled, untainted, uncontaminated; **unaffected, unassuming, unpretending,** unpretentious; **genuine,** unartificial, unadorned, unvarnished, unembellished; homespun; **pastoral, rural,** arcadian, bucolic

ADVS **7 artlessly, ingenuously, guilelessly;** simply, plainly; naturally, genuinely; openly

417 AUTHORITY

NOUNS **1 authority, prerogative, right, power,** faculty, competence *or* competency; **mandate;** royal prerogative; legal *or* lawful *or* rightful authority, legitimacy; **the say** *and* **the say-so** <both nonformal>; divine right; absolute power, absolutism 612.9

2 authoritativeness, authority, power, magisterialness, **potency** *or* potence, **strength,** might, mightiness, clout <nonformal>

3 authoritativeness, masterfulness, lordliness, magisterialness; **arbitrariness,** peremptoriness, **imperiousness,** highhandedness, dictatorialness, overbearingness, domineering, authoritarianism

4 prestige, authority, influence; pressure, **weight,** weightiness, moment, **consequence;** eminence, **stature,** rank, seniority, preeminence, priority, precedence; **greatness** 247; **importance, prominence** 996.2

5 governance, authority, jurisdiction, control, command, power, rule, reign, dominion, sovereignty, empire, **sway;** government 612; **control, grip,** claws, **clutches**

6 dominance, dominion, domination; preeminence, supremacy, superiority 249; **ascendance** *or* **ascendancy; upper** *or* **whip hand, sway; sovereignty,**

suzerainty, **overlordship;** primacy, **predominance,** hegemony; preponderance; balance of power; eminent domain

7 **mastership,** masterhood, masterdom, **mastery; leadership, headship, lordship;** hegemony; supervisorship, directorship 573.4; hierarchy, nobility, aristocracy, **ruling class** 575.15; chair, chairmanship

8 **sovereignty, royalty, majesty,** empire, **emperorship; kingship,** kinghood; queenship, queenhood; sultanate; caliphate; the throne, the Crown, the purple

9 **scepter, rod, staff,** wand, baton, mace, truncheon; crosier, crook; caduceus; gavel; mantle; portfolio

10 <seat of authority> **saddle** <nonformal>, **helm, driver's seat** <nonformal>; seat, **chair,** bench; seat of power; dais

11 **throne,** royal seat

12 <acquisition of authority> **accession; succession; usurpation,** arrogation, assumption, seizure; anointment, anointing, consecration, coronation; **delegation,** deputation, assignment, **appointment; election; authorization,** empowerment

VERBS 13 **possess** or **wield authority, have power,** have the right, have the say or say-so <nonformal>, have the whip hand, wear the crown, hold the prerogative, have the mandate; exercise sovereignty; be vested or invested, carry authority, have clout <nonformal>, have what one says go, have one's own way; show one's authority, crack the whip, throw one's weight around and ride herd <both nonformal>; **rule** 612.14, **control;** supervise 573.10

14 **take command, take charge, take over,** take the helm, take the reins of government, get the power into one's hands, gain or get the upper hand, take the lead; ascend or mount or succeed to the throne; **assume command,** assume, **usurp,** arrogate, seize; usurp or seize the throne or crown or mantle; seize power, execute a *coup d'état*

ADJS 15 **authoritative,** clothed or vested or invested with authority, **commanding, imperative; governing, controlling, ruling** 612.18; **preeminent, supreme, superior** 249.12; **powerful, potent;** dominant, ascendant, hegemonic; **influential, prestigious, weighty,** momentous, consequential, eminent, substantial, considerable; great 247.6; important, prominent; ranking, senior; authorized, empowered, duly constituted, competent; **official,** *ex officio* <L>; authoritarian; absolute, autocratic; **totalitarian**

16 **imperious,** imperial, **masterful,** authoritative, aristocratic, **lordly, magisterial;** arrogant 141.9; **arbitrary, peremptory,** imperative; **dictatorial, authoritarian; bossy** <nonformal>, **domineering, high-handed, overbearing;** autocratic, **despotic, tyrannical;** tyrannous, oppressive 98.24; repressive; strict, severe 425.6

17 **sovereign; regal, royal, majestic,** purple; **kinglike, kingly; imperial;** monarchic or monarchical, monarchal; dynastic

ADVS 18 **authoritatively,** by virtue of office; **commandingly, imperatively; powerfully, potently,** mightily; **influentially, weightily,** momentously, consequentially; **officially,** *ex cathedra* <L>

19 **imperiously, masterfully,** magisterially; **arbitrarily, peremptorily; autocratically, dictatorially, high-handedly, domineeringly, overbearingly, despotically, tyrannically**

20 **by authority of,** in the name of, in or by virtue of

21 **in authority, in power, in charge, in control, in command,** at the reins, **at the helm,** at the wheel, **in the saddle** or driver's seat <nonformal>, on the throne

418 LAWLESSNESS
<absence of authority>

NOUNS **1 lawlessness; licentiousness,** license, unrestraint 430.3; indiscipline, insubordination, mutiny, disobedience 327; permissiveness; **irresponsibility,** unaccountability; interregnum, power vacuum

2 anarchy, anarchism; **disorderliness, unruliness, disorder,** disruption, disorganization, confusion, **turmoil, chaos; nihilism;** lynch law, mob rule *or* law, mobocracy; **law of the jungle**

3 anarchist; nihilist; mutineer, rebel 327.5

VERBS **4 reject** *or* **defy authority; take the law in one's own hands;** do *or* go as one pleases, indulge oneself; be a law unto oneself, answer to no man

ADJS **5 lawless; licentious, ungoverned,** undisciplined, unrestrained; permissive; insubordinate, mutinous, disobedient 327.8; **uncontrolled,** uncurbed, unbridled, unchecked, rampant, untrammeled; **irresponsible,** wildcat; willful, headstrong, heady

6 anarchic, anarchical, anarchistic; **unruly, disorderly,** disorganized, **chaotic; nihilistic**

ADVS **7 lawlessly;** anarchically, chaotically

419 PRECEPT

NOUNS **1 precept,** prescript, **prescription, teaching; instruction, direction, charge,** commission, **injunction,** dictate; **order,** command 420

2 rule, law, canon, maxim, dictum, moral; **norm, standard;** formula, form; moral precept; commandment; **tradition;** ordinance, imperative, **regulation; principle,** tenet, convention; **guideline,** ground rule, rubric, protocol, working rule; guiding principle, golden rule; **code**

3 formula, recipe; prescription; formulary

ADJS **4 preceptive,** didactic, instructive, moralistic, **prescriptive;** prescribed, mandatory, hard-and-fast, binding; standard, regulation, official, authoritative, statutory, rubrical; **normative; conventional;** traditional

420 COMMAND

NOUNS **1 command, commandment, order,** command decision, **bidding,** behest, imperative, **dictate,** dictation, **will, pleasure,** say-so <nonformal>, word; **authority** 417

2 injunction, charge, commission, **mandate**

3 direction, directive, instruction, rule, regulation; prescript, prescription, **precept** 419

4 decree, fiat, **edict; law** 673.3; **rule, ruling,** dictum; **ordinance; proclamation,** pronouncement, pronunciamento, **declaration,** ukase; **bull;** diktat

5 summons, bidding, beck, call, calling, **beck and call; convocation,** convoking; evocation, invocation; requisition

6 court order, injunction, legal order

7 process server, summoner

VERBS **8 command, order, dictate, direct, instruct,** mandate, **bid, enjoin, charge,** commission; issue a writ *or* an injunction; **decree, rule, ordain,** promulgate; give an order, issue a command, say the word; call the shots *or* tune *or* signals *or* play <nonformal>; order about *or* around; **speak, proclaim, declare,** pronounce 352.12

9 prescribe, require, demand, dictate, impose, lay down, set, fix, appoint, make obligatory *or* mandatory; decide once and for all, carve in stone, set in concrete <nonformal>; authorize 443.11

10 lay down the law, put one's foot down <nonformal>, read the riot act, lower the boom <nonformal>, set the record straight

11 summon, call, demand; call for, send for *or* after; **cite, summons**

<nonformal>, **subpoena,** serve; page; convoke, convene; muster, invoke, conjure; order up, summon up, muster up, call up, conjure up; evoke, call forth, summon forth; recall, call in; requisition

ADJS **12 mandatory,** mandated, **imperative, compulsory,** prescriptive, **obligatory;** dictated, imposed, required; decisive, final, peremptory, absolute, eternal, written, hard-and-fast, carved in stone, set in concrete <nonformal>, ultimate, conclusive, binding, irrevocable

13 commanding, imperious, imperative, peremptory; **directive, instructive; mandating,** dictating, compelling, obligating, **prescriptive,** preceptive; **authoritative** 417.15

ADVS **14 commandingly, imperatively,** peremptorily

15 by order or **command,** as ordered or required, to order; compulsorily

421 DEMAND

NOUNS **1 demand, claim, call; requisition,** requirement, order; strong or heavy demand, draft, drain, levy, tax, taxing; imposition, impost, tribute, duty, contribution; exorbitant or extortionate demand, exaction, extortion, blackmail; **ultimatum,** nonnegotiable demand; notice, warning 399

2 stipulation, provision, proviso, condition; **terms;** exception, reservation; **qualification** 958

3 <nonformal terms> **catch, Catch-22,** kicker, zinger, snag, joker; strings attached; ifs, ands, and buts

4 insistence, exigence, importunity, importunateness, **demandingness,** pertinacity; pressure, **urgency, exigency** 996.4; **persistence** 360.1

VERBS **5 demand, ask, ask for,** make a demand; **call for,** call on or upon one for; cry or cry out for, clamor for; **claim, require;** levy,

impose, impose on one for; **exact, extort,** squeeze; blackmail; **requisition,** make or put in requisition, **confiscate; order,** put in or place an order; deliver or issue an ultimatum; warn 399.5

6 claim, pretend to, lay claim to, stake a claim <nonformal>, assert or vindicate a claim or right or title to; **challenge**

7 stipulate, set conditions or terms; **qualify** 958.3

8 insist, insist on or **upon,** stick to <nonformal>, set one's heart or mind upon; **take one's stand upon,** put or lay it on the line <nonformal>, make no bones about it; stand upon one's rights, **put one's foot down** <nonformal>; brook no denial, not take no for an answer; **maintain, contend,** assert; urge, press 375.14; **persist** 360.2

ADJS **9 demanding, exacting,** exigent; draining, taxing, exorbitant, extortionate; **insistent, importunate,** urgent, pertinacious, pressing, clamorous; persistent

10 claimed, spoken for; requisitioned

ADVS **11 demandingly, exactingly,** exigently; exorbitantly, extortionately; **insistently, importunately, urgently,** pressingly, clamorously

12 on demand, at demand, **on call,** upon presentation

422 ADVICE

NOUNS **1 advice, counsel, recommendation, suggestion;** proposal; advocacy; **direction, instruction,** guidance, briefing; **exhortation,** enjoinder, expostulation, remonstrance; **sermons,** sermonizing, preaching, preachiness; **admonition,** caution, caveat, **warning** 399; **idea,** thought, opinion 952.6; **consultancy, consultation,** parley 541.6; **counseling**

2 piece of advice, **word of advice, word to the wise, hint, broad hint, flea in the ear** <nonformal>, **tip** <nonformal>, a few

words of wisdom, one's two cents'
worth <nonformal>

3 **adviser, counsel, counselor,
consultant,** expert, maven
<nonformal>; instructor, guide,
mentor, nestor; confidant; admonisher, monitor, Dutch uncle;
teacher 571; meddler, buttinsky
and yenta *and* kibitzer *and* backseat driver <all nonformal>

4 **advisee,** counselee; client

VERBS 5 **advise, counsel, recommend, suggest, advocate,** propose, submit; prescribe; give a
piece of advice, give a hint *or*
broad hint, hint at, intimate, insinuate, put a flea in one's ear
<nonformal>, have a word with
one; meddle, kibitz <nonformal>;
confer, consult with 541.11

6 **admonish, exhort,** expostulate,
remonstrate, preach; **enjoin,
charge;** caution, issue a caveat,
wag one's finger <nonformal>;
warn away, warn off, **warn**
399.5,6; move, prompt, **urge,
incite, encourage, induce,
persuade** 375.23; **implore**
440.11

7 **take** *or* **accept advice, follow
advice,** go along with <nonfor-
mal>, buy *or* buy into <nonfor-
mal>; **be advised by;** have at
one's elbow, take one's cue from

ADJS 8 **advisory; consultative;** instructive; **admonitory,** monitory,
cautionary, **warning** 399.7; **ex-
postulatory,** expostulative,
remonstrative; exhortative, ex-
hortatory, hortative, hortatory,
didactic, moralistic, sententious

423 COUNCIL

NOUNS 1 **council,** conclave, deliberative *or* advisory body, **assembly;** chamber, house; **board,**
court, bench; **full assembly,**
plenum, plenary session; **congress,** diet, synod, senate;
legislature 613; **cabinet,** divan,
council of ministers, council of
state; kitchen cabinet; junta, directory; Sanhedrin; privy council;
brain trust <nonformal>, inner
circle; council of war; syndicate,

association 617; **conference**
541.6; **assembly** 769.2; **tribunal**
595

2 **committee,** subcommittee,
standing committee; ad hoc committee; committee of one

3 **forum, conference,** discussion
group, buzz session <nonfor-
mal>, **round table, panel;** open
forum, colloquium, symposium;
powwow <nonformal>

4 ecclesiastical council, chapter,
conclave, conference, congregation, consistory, convention,
convocation, presbytery, session,
synod, vestry; parochial council;
diocesan conference, diocesan
court; provincial court, plenary
council; ecumenical council; con-
ciliarism

ADJS 5 **conciliar,** council, coun-
cilmanic, aldermanic; **consultative, deliberative, advisory;**
synodic

ADVS 6 **in council, in conference,
in consultation, in a huddle**
<nonformal>, in conclave; **in ses-
sion**

424 COMPULSION

NOUNS 1 **compulsion, obligation;
command** 420; **necessity** 962;
inevitability 962.7; **irresistibility, compulsiveness; forcing,**
enforcement; **constraint;** restraint 428

2 **force; brute force,** naked force,
main force, physical force; the
law of the jungle; **tyranny** 612.10;
steamroller <nonformal>

3 **coercion,** intimidation, scare
tactics, arm-twisting <nonfor-
mal>, **duress;** strong-arm tactics
<nonformal>, a pistol *or* gun to
one's head, the sword, the mailed
fist, the boot in the face, the big
stick, the club; **pressure, high
pressure,** high-pressure
methods; **violence** 671

VERBS 4 **compel, force, make;
constrain, bind,** tie, tie one's
hands; **restrain** 428.7; enforce,
drive, impel; dragoon, use force
upon, force one's hand, hold a
gun to one's head

5 **oblige, necessitate, require,** exact, demand, **dictate,** impose; brook no denial; admit of no option

6 **press; bring pressure to bear upon, put pressure on,** bear down on, bear hard upon

7 **coerce,** use violence, ride roughshod, intimidate, bully, bludgeon; hijack, shanghai, dragoon

8 <nonformal terms> **twist one's arm, arm-twist, twist arms,** knock or bang heads together, strong-arm, steamroller, bulldoze, **pressure,** high-pressure, lean on, squeeze; put the screws on or to, get one over a barrel or under one's thumb, hold one's feet to the fire, put the heat on

9 **be compelled, be coerced,** have to 962.10; be stuck with <nonformal>, can't help but

ADJS 10 **compulsory, compulsive, compelling;** pressing, driving, imperative, imperious; constraining; **restraining** 428.11; **irresistible**

11 **obligatory, compulsory,** imperative, mandatory, dictated, **binding; inevitable** 962.15

12 **coercive, forcible;** steamroller and bulldozer and sledgehammer and strong-arm <all nonformal>

ADVS 13 **compulsively,** compulsorily, **compellingly,** imperatively, imperiously

14 **forcibly, by force,** by main force; by force of arms, at gunpoint, with a gun to one's head, at the point of a gun, at the point of the sword or bayonet

15 **obligatorily,** compulsorily, by stress of, under press of; under the lash or gun; of necessity

425 STRICTNESS

NOUNS 1 **strictness, severity, harshness, stringency, hard line; discipline,** strict or tight or rigid discipline, regimentation; **austerity, sternness,** grimness, **toughness** <nonformal>; **belt-tightening;** Spartanism; authoritarianism; **meticulousness** 339.3

2 **firmness, rigor, rigorousness,** rigidity, stiffness, **hardness,** obduracy, obdurateness, **inflexibility,** inexorability, unyieldingness, unbendingness, **relentlessness; uncompromisingness;** stubbornness, obstinacy 361; fundamentalism, orthodoxy

3 **firm hand, iron hand,** heavy hand, strong hand, tight hand, tight rein; tight or taut ship

VERBS 4 **hold or keep a tight hand upon,** keep a firm hand on, keep a tight rein on, rule with an iron hand, knock or bang heads together <nonformal>; regiment, discipline; run a tight or taut ship, ride herd, keep one in line; go out of one's way, go the extra mile <nonformal>

5 **deal hardly or harshly with,** bear hard upon, **take a hard line,** not pull one's punches <nonformal>

ADJS 6 **strict, exacting,** exigent, demanding, not to be trifled with, **stringent;** disciplined, spit-and-polish; **severe, harsh,** dour, unsparing; **stern, grim, austere,** rugged, **tough** <nonformal>; Spartan; **hard-line,** authoritarian 417.16; **meticulous** 339.12

7 **firm, rigid, rigorous,** stiff, **hard,** iron, steel, hard-shell, obdurate, **inflexible,** ironhanded, inexorable, dour, **unyielding,** unbending, **relentless,** unrelenting, procrustean; **uncompromising;** stubborn, obstinate 361.8; fundamentalist, orthodox; ironbound, rockbound, ironclad <nonformal>; straitlaced, hidebound

ADVS 8 **strictly, severely, stringently, harshly; sternly,** grimly, **austerely**

9 **firmly, rigidly, rigorously,** stiffly, stiff, obdurately, **inflexibly,** inexorably, unbendingly; **uncompromisingly, relentlessly,** unrelentingly; ironhandedly, with an iron hand

426 LAXNESS

NOUNS 1 **laxness, laxity, slackness, looseness;** loosening, relaxation; imprecision, careless-

ness, remissness, negligence
340.1; indifference 102; weakness
16; impotence 19

2 unstrictness, undemanding-
ness; leniency 427; **permissiveness,** overindulgence, **softness;
flexibility,** pliancy

VERBS **3 hold a loose rein, give
free rein to, give one his head,**
give rope enough to; permit all *or*
anything

ADJS **4 lax, slack, loose,** relaxed;
imprecise, sloppy <nonformal>,
careless, slipshod; remiss, negligent 340.10; indifferent 102.6;
weak 16.12; impotent 19.13; untrammeled, unrestrained

5 unstrict, undemanding, **unexacting; unsevere, unharsh;**
lenient 427.7; **permissive,** overindulgent, **soft;** easy, easygoing,
laid-back <nonformal>; **flexible,**
pliant, yielding

427 LENIENCY

NOUNS **1 leniency,** lenity; **clemency, mercifulness,** mercy, **humaneness,** humanity, pity,
compassion 145.1; **mildness,
gentleness,** tenderness, softness;
easiness, easygoingness; laxness
426; **forebearance,** patience 134;
tolerance 978.4

**2 compliance, complaisance,
agreeableness;** affability, graciousness, generousness,
decency, amiability; kindness,
kindliness, **benevolence** 143

3 indulgence, humoring, obliging; gratification; **pampering,
coddling,** mollycoddling, **spoiling; permissiveness,** overindulgence; sparing the rod

4 spoiled child *or* **brat,** mama's
boy, mollycoddle, sissy

VERBS **5 be easy on,** ease up on,
handle with kid gloves, slap one's
wrist, spare the rod; **tolerate,**
bear with 134.5

6 indulge, humor, oblige; favor,
please, gratify, satisfy, **cater to;
give way to,** yield to, let one have
his own way; **pamper, coddle,**
mollycoddle, **spoil;** spare the rod

ADJS **7 lenient, mild, gentle,** mild-

mannered, tender, humane, compassionate, **clement;** soft, moderate, **easy,** easygoing; lax 426.4;
forebearing, forbearant; accepting, **tolerant** 978.11

**8 indulgent, compliant, ob-
liging, accommodating,
agreeable,** amiable, gracious,
affable, decent, kind, kindly,
benign, benevolent 143.15;
hands-off <nonformal>, permissive, overindulgent

**9 indulged, pampered, coddled,
spoiled,** spoiled rotten <nonfor-
mal>

428 RESTRAINT

NOUNS **1 restraint, constraint; inhibition;** injunction, enjoinder,
interdict; **control, curb, check,**
rein, arrest; **retardation,** deceleration; retrenchment, curtailment; self-control 359.5; **hindrance** 1011; rationing; restraint
of trade, monopoly, protection,
protectionism; clampdown *and*
crackdown <both nonformal>,
proscription; **prohibition** 444

**2 suppression, repression; sub-
dual,** quelling, shutting *or* closing
down, smashing, crushing; quashing, squashing *and* squelching
<both nonformal>; smothering,
stifling, suffocating, strangling,
throttling; **censorship,** bleeping
or bleeping out <nonfor-
mal>

**3 restriction, limitation, con-
finement;** Hobson's choice, no
choice, zero option; circumscription 210; stint, cramping, cramp;
qualification 958

4 shackle, restraint, **restraints,
fetter, hamper,** trammel, **manacle, bonds,** irons, chains; stranglehold; **handcuffs;** stocks, bilbo,
pillory; **tether,** leash; **rein;** hobble; straitjacket; **muzzle, gag**

5 lock, bolt, bar, safety catch; barrier 1011.5

6 restrictionist, protectionist, monopolist; censor

VERBS **7 restrain, constrain, control, govern,** contain, keep under
control, put under restraint; **in-**

hibit; enjoin, clamp *or* crack down on <nonformal>, proscribe, prohibit 444.3; **curb, check, arrest, bridle,** rein; **retard,** decelerate; **cool** *and* **cool off** *and* **cool down** <all nonformal>; retrench, curtail; hold, **hold in,** keep, withhold, hold up <nonformal>, **keep from; hold back, keep back,** set back; **hold in, keep in,** pull in, rein in; **hold** *or* **keep in check,** hold at bay, tie one's hands; keep a tight hand on; restrain oneself, not go too far, not go off the deep end <nonformal>

8 **suppress, repress,** stultify; **keep down,** hold down; **close** *or* shut down; **subdue, quell, put down,** smash, **crush; quash, squash** *and* **squelch** <both nonformal>; **extinguish,** quench, stanch, dash *or* pour cold water on, drown, kill; **smother, stifle,** suffocate, asphyxiate, strangle, throttle, choke off, **muzzle, gag;** sit on *and* sit down on *and* slap *or* smack down <all nonformal>; jump on *and* crack down on *and* clamp down on <all nonformal>, put *or* keep the lid on <nonformal>; bottle up, cork, cork up

9 **restrict, limit, narrow, confine,** tighten; ground; circumscribe 210.4; keep in *or* within bounds, keep from spreading, localize; **cage in,** hem, hem in, box, box in *or* up; **cramp,** stint

10 **bind, restrain, tie,** tie up, **strap,** leash, fasten, secure, make fast; **hamper, trammel;** rope; **chain; shackle, fetter, manacle, put in irons; handcuff, tie one's hands;** tie hand and foot, hogtie <nonformal>; straitjacket; hobble, fetter; tether, moor, anchor; tie down, pin down, peg down; get a stranglehold on; **bridle**

ADJS 11 **restraining, constraining; inhibiting,** inhibitive; **suppressive, repressive,** stultifying; controlling, on top of <nonformal>

12 **restrictive,** restricting, **narrowing, limiting, confining,** cramping; censorial

13 **restrained, constrained, inhibited,** pent up; controlled, curbed, bridled; **under restraint,** in check; grounded, out of circulation; retarded, arrested, in remission

14 **suppressed, repressed; subdued,** quelled, smashed, crushed; quashed; smothered, stifled, suffocated; censored

15 **restricted, limited, confined;** circumscribed 210.6, hemmed in, hedged in *or* about, boxed in; **shut-in;** cramped

16 **bound, tied,** bound hand and foot, hampered, trammeled, shackled, handcuffed, fettered, manacled, tethered; **in bonds,** in irons *or* chains

429 CONFINEMENT

NOUNS 1 **confinement,** lockup, caging, penning, impounding, **restraint,** restriction; check, **restraint, constraint** 428.1

2 **quarantine, isolation,** cordoning off, segregation, separation, sequestration, seclusion; walling in *or* up *or* off

3 **imprisonment, jailing,** incarceration, internment, immurement; **detention, captivity,** duress, durance, durance vile; preventive detention

4 **commitment,** committal, consignment; mittimus <law>; institutionalization

5 **custody,** custodianship, **keeping, care, change, ward,** hold, protective *or* preventive custody; protection, safekeeping 1007.1

6 **arrest,** pinch *and* bust *and* collar <all nonformal>; **capture, apprehension, seizure**

7 **place of confinement,** close quarters, not enough room to swing a cat; limbo, hell, purgatory; **cage; enclosure,** pen, coop 212.3

8 **prison,** correctional facility, minimum- *or* maximum-security facility, **penitentiary,** pen <nonformal>, penal institution, bastille; **jail,** jailhouse, lockup; **military prison, guardhouse,**

stockade, brig; dungeon,
oubliette, black hole; **reformatory,** reform school; **prison camp,** internment camp, detention camp, labor camp, gulag, **concentration camp;** solitary confinement, the hole <nonformal>; **cell,** prison or jail cell; **detention cell,** lockup; tank <nonformal>; cellblock, cellhouse; death house or row; penal settlement or colony

9 <nonformal terms> **slammer, slam, jug,** can, coop, cooler, hoosegow, stir, clink, pokey; **joint,** big house, brig, tank

10 **jailer,** correction officer; **keeper, warder,** prison guard, **turnkey,** bull and screw <both nonformal>; **warden;** custodian, guardian 1007.6; **guard** 1007.9

11 **prisoner, captive; convict,** con <nonformal>; **jailbird** <nonformal>; **detainee; internee; prisoner of war** or POW; political prisoner, prisoner of conscience; lifer <nonformal>; trusty; parolee; ex-convict; chain gang

VERBS 12 **confine, shut in,** shut away, coop in, hem in, fence in or up, wall in or up, rail in; **shut up, coop up, pen up,** bottle up, cork up, seal up, **impound;** pen, coop, cloister, immure, cage, cage in; **enclose** 212.5; **hold, keep in,** hold or keep in custody, **detain,** keep in detention, constrain, ground, **restrain,** hold in restraint; check, inhibit 428.7; restrict 428.9; shackle 428.10

13 **quarantine, isolate,** segregate, separate, seclude; **cordon, cordon off,** seal off, rope off; wall off

14 **imprison, incarcerate, intern,** immure; **jail,** jug <nonformal>, throw into jail; throw in prison, clap in jail or prison, send up the river <nonformal>; **lock up,** put or keep under lock and key; hold captive, hold prisoner; hold under house arrest

15 **arrest,** make an arrest, put under arrest, pick up; catch flat-footed; catch with one's pants down or hand in the till <nonformal>, catch one in the act or red-handed or in flagrante delicto, catch or have one dead to rights; run down, run to earth, **take captive, take prisoner, apprehend, capture,** seize, **take into custody**

16 <nonformal terms> **bust, pinch,** make a pinch, nab, pull in, **run in,** collar

17 **commit,** send to jail, send up and send up the river <both nonformal>; commit to an institution, institutionalize

18 **be imprisoned, do** or **serve time** <nonformal>; pay one's debt to society

ADJS 19 **confined,** in confinement, **shut-in,** pent, **pent-up,** under restraint; impounded; grounded, out of circulation; **detained;** restricted 428.15; cloistered, enclosed 212.10

20 **quarantined,** isolated, segregated, separated; cordoned, cordoned or sealed or roped off

21 **jailed, imprisoned, incarcerated, interned,** immured; **in prison,** in stir <nonformal>, in captivity, **behind bars,** locked up, under lock and key, in durance vile

22 **under arrest, in custody,** under or in detention; under house arrest

430 FREEDOM

NOUNS 1 **freedom, liberty; license;** run and the run of <both nonformal>; **civil liberty,** the Four Freedoms <F D Roosevelt>: freedom of speech and expression, freedom of worship, freedom from want, freedom from fear; constitutional freedom; academic freedom

2 **right, rights, civil rights,** civil liberties, constitutional rights, legal rights; **unalienable rights, human rights,** natural rights

3 **unrestraint, unconstraint; unreserve,** irrepressibleness, irrepressibility, uninhibitedness, exu-

berance 109.4; **immoderacy, intemperance,** incontinence, unruliness; **abandon,** abandonment, **licentiousness,** wantonness, riotousness, wildness; permissiveness, **laxness** 426

4 **latitude, scope, room,** range, way, field, maneuvering room, room to swing a cat <nonformal>; **margin,** clearance, **space,** open space, elbowroom, breathing space, **leeway** <nonformal>, wide berth; **tolerance; free scope,** full scope, **free hand,** free play; **carte blanche,** blank check; no holds barred; rope, long rope or tether; rope enough to hang oneself

5 **independence, self-determination, self government,** self-direction, **autonomy,** home rule; self-containment, self-sufficiency; **individualism,** rugged individualism; **self-reliance,** self-dependence

6 **free will,** free choice, **discretion,** option, choice, say, say-so and druthers <both nonformal>; **full consent**

7 **own free will, own account, own accord, own hook** and own say-so <both nonformal>, own discretion, own choice, **own initiative,** personal initiative, own responsibility, own volition, own authority, own power; own way, own sweet way <nonformal>; law unto oneself

8 **exemption,** exception, **immunity; release,** discharge; **franchise, license,** charter, patent, liberty; diplomatic immunity, congressional or legislative immunity; privilege; permission 443

9 **noninterference, nonintervention; isolationism; laissez-faireism,** deregulation; liberalism, free enterprise, free competition; free trade

10 **liberalism,** libertarianism; broad-mindedness, open-mindedness, toleration, tolerance; libertinism, **freethinking,** free thought; liberalization, **liberation** 431

11 **freeman,** freewoman; citizen, free citizen; emancipated or manumitted slave, freedman, freedwoman

12 **free agent, independent, free lance; individualist,** rugged individualist; free spirit; **liberal,** libertarian, libertine, freethinker; free trader; **nonpartisan,** neutral, mugwump; isolationist

VERBS 13 **liberalize,** ease; **free, liberate** 431.4

14 **exempt, free, release,** discharge, **let go** and **let off** <both nonformal>, set at liberty, spring <nonformal>; **excuse,** spare, except; **dispense,** give dispensation from; dispense with; remit; absolve 601.4

15 **give a free hand, give one his head; give the run of** <nonformal>, give the freedom of; give one leeway <nonformal>; give one scope or space or room; **give rein** or **free rein to,** give one rope; **give one carte blanche, give one a blank check**

16 **not interfere, leave** or **let alone, let be,** leave or let well enough alone, let sleeping dogs lie; **keep hands off,** not involve oneself, not get involved, let it ride <nonformal>, let nature take its course; live and let live, leave one to oneself, leave one in peace; mind one's own business; **decontrol, deregulate**

17 <nonformal terms> **get off one's back** or **one's case** or **one's tail,** get out of one's face or hair, **butt out, back off,** leave be, get lost, take a walk

18 **be free,** feel free, feel free as a bird; **go at large,** breathe the air of freedom; **have free scope,** have one's druthers <nonformal>, have a free hand, have the run of <nonformal>; be at home, feel at home; be exonerated, go or get off scot-free, walk

19 **let oneself go,** let loose and cut loose and let one's hair down <all nonformal>, **give way to,** let it all hang out <nonformal>; go all out, pull out all the stops; run wild,

have one's fling, sow one's wild oats

20 **stand on one's own two feet, shift for oneself, fend for oneself,** strike out for oneself, look out for number one <nonformal>; **go it alone, be one's own man,** play a lone hand <nonformal>, **paddle one's own canoe** <nonformal>; make *or* pay one's own way; ask no favors, ask no quarter; **be one's own boss** <nonformal>, answer only to oneself; **go one's own way**; do on one's own, do on one's own initiative, do on one's own hook *or* say-so <nonformal>, do in one's own sweet way <nonformal>; **have a will of one's own,** have one's own way, do what one likes *or* wishes *or* chooses, **do as one pleases, suit oneself;** free-lance, be a free agent

ADJS 21 **free; at liberty, at large,** on the loose, **loose,** disengaged, detached, unattached, uncommitted, uninvolved, clear, in the clear, easygoing, footloose, footloose and fancy-free, free and easy; free as air, free as a bird, free as the wind; scot-free; **freeborn; freed, liberated, emancipated,** released, uncaged, sprung <nonformal>

22 **independent,** self-dependent; free-spirited, freewheeling, freestanding; **self-determined,** self-directing; **individualistic; selfgoverning, autonomous,** sovereign; stand-alone, self-reliant, self-sufficient, self-contained; nonpartisan, neutral, **nonaligned**

23 **free-acting,** free-moving; freehanded; **free-spoken,** outspoken, **plain-spoken, open, frank,** direct, candid, blunt 644.17

24 **unrestrained, unconstrained, unforced,** uncoerced; unmeasured, **uninhibited, unsuppressed, unrepressed, unreserved,** exuberant 109.14; **uncurbed, unchecked, unbridled,** unmuzzled; **unreined; uncontrolled,** unsubdued, ungoverned,

unruly; out of control; **abandoned,** intemperate, immoderate, **incontinent, licentious,** loose, wanton, rampant, riotous, wild; irrepressible; lax 426.4

25 **nonrestrictive,** unrestrictive; **permissive,** hands-off <nonformal>; indulgent 427.8; lax 426.4; **liberal,** libertarian; broadminded, open-minded, tolerant; unbigoted 978.8; libertine; freethinking

26 **unhampered, untrammeled, unhandicapped, unimpeded,** unhindered, unobstructed; clear, unencumbered, unburdened

27 **unrestricted, unconfined, uncircumscribed,** unbounded; **unlimited,** limitless, illimitable; unqualified, **unconditional,** without strings, no strings attached; **absolute,** perfect, unequivocal, full, plenary; openended, open, **wide-open** <nonformal>; deregulated

28 **unbound,** untied, **unfettered,** unshackled, unchained; unmuzzled, ungagged

29 **unsubject,** unenslaved, **unenthralled;** unvanquished, unconquered, unquelled, **untamed,** unbroken, undomesticated

30 **exempt, immune;** exempted, **released, excused,** excepted, let off <nonformal>, spared; **privileged, licensed,** favored, chartered; **unliable,** irresponsible, unaccountable, unanswerable

31 **quit, clear, free, rid; free of, clear of, quit of, rid of, shut of,** shed of <nonformal>

ADVS 32 **freely,** free; **without restraint,** without stint, **unreservedly,** with abandon; outright

33 **independently, alone, by oneself,** all by one's lonesome <nonformal>, **on one's own** *and* **on one's own hook** <both nonformal>, on one's own initiative; **on one's own account** *or* **responsibility,** on one's own say-so <nonformal>; **of one's own free will, of one's own accord,** of

one's own volition, at one's own
discretion

431 LIBERATION

NOUNS **1 liberation, freeing,** setting free, setting at liberty; **deliverance, delivery; rescue** 398;
emancipation, manumission;
enfranchisement; women's liberation; gay liberation; women's or
gay or men's lib <nonformal>

2 release, freeing, unhanding,
loosing, unloosing; unbinding,
unshackling, unfettering, un-
manacling, **unleashing,** unchain-
ing, untethering, unhobbling, un-
harnessing, unyoking, unbri-
dling; unmuzzling, ungagging;
unlocking, unlatching, unbolting,
unbarring; unpenning, uncaging;
discharge, dismissal; parole; demobilization

3 extrication, freeing, releasing;
**disengagement, disentangle-
ment,** untangling, unsnarling,
unraveling, unknotting, dis-
embroilment; breaking out or
loose

VERBS **4 liberate, free, deliver, set
free,** set at liberty; **emancipate,**
manumit, disenthrall; enfranchise

**5 release, unhand, let go, let
loose, turn loose,** cast loose, let
go free; **discharge, dismiss;** let
out on bail, grant bail to, go bail
for <nonformal>; parole, put on
parole; release from prison,
spring <nonformal>; demobilize

6 loose, loosen, cut loose or free;
unbind, untie, unstrap, unbuckle, unlash; **unfetter, un-
shackle,** unmanacle, unchain,
untie one's hands; **unleash,** un-
tether, unhobble; unharness,
unyoke, unbridle

7 extricate, free, release, clear,
get out; **disengage,** disentangle,
untangle, unsnarl, unravel, dis-
entwine, disembroil; dislodge;
break out or loose, cut loose, tear
loose

8 free oneself from, deliver oneself from, **get free of,** get quit of,
get rid of, get out of, extricate

oneself, get out of a jam <non-
formal>; **throw off, shake off;**
break out, bust out <nonfor-
mal>, **escape** 369.6; wriggle
out of

9 go free, go scot free, go at liberty, **get off,** get off scot-free, beat
the rap and walk <both nonfor-
mal>

ADJS **10 liberated, freed, emancipated, released;** delivered, res-
cued, ransomed, redeemed;
extricated, unbound, untied, unshackled

432 SUBJECTION

NOUNS **1 subjection, subjugation;**
domination 612.2; **restraint,
control** 428.1; **bondage, captivity; thrall, thralldom,** enthrallment; **slavery,** enslavement; **servitude,** compulsory or involuntary servitude, servility; **serfdom,**
serfhood, **vassalage;** helotry;
peonage; feudalism; absolutism,
tyranny 612.9,10; disenfranchise-
ment

2 subservience or subserviency,
subordination, inferiority; back
seat and second fiddle and hind
tit <all nonformal>; **service**

3 dependence or dependency,
tutelage

4 subdual, quelling, crushing,
trampling down, reduction, **humbling, humiliation; breaking,
taming,** domestication; **suppression** 428.2

5 subordinate, junior, secondary,
inferior; underling, low man on
the totem pole <nonformal>,
flunky, gofer <nonformal>;
strong right arm, **right-hand
man** 616.7; **servant, employee**
577

6 dependent, charge, ward, client, protégé, encumbrance;
pensioner; ward of the state; foster child; dependency, client
state, satellite or satellite state,
puppet government

7 subject, vassal, liege; **captive;
slave,** servant, chattel, **bondsman,** bondman, **bondslave,**
thrall; indentured servant; la-

borer, esne; bondwoman, bonds-
woman, bondmaid; odalisque,
concubine; galley slave; **serf,**
helot; churl; **peon**

VERBS **8 subjugate, subject, subordinate; dominate** 612.15; dis-
enfranchise, divest or deprive of
freedom; **enslave,** enthrall, hold
in thrall, make a chattel of; take
captive, lead into captivity; **hold
in subjection,** hold in bondage,
hold captive, hold in captivity;
hold down, keep down; **keep or
have under one's thumb,** have
tied to one's apron strings, hold in
leash, keep at one's beck and call;
vassalize, make dependent or
tributary; peonize

**9 subdue, master, quell, crush,
reduce,** beat down, **break,** overwhelm; trample on or down,
trample underfoot, trample in the
dust; **suppress** 428.8; make one
give in or say 'uncle' <nonfor-
mal>, **conquer** 412.10; kick
around <nonformal>, tyrannize
612.16; unman 19.12; bring low,
bring to terms, humble, humiliate, take down a notch or peg,
bend, **bring one to his knees,**
bend to one's will

10 have subject, twist or turn or
wind around one's little finger,
make lie down and roll over, have
eating out of one's hand, **lead by
the nose,** make a puppet of; use
as a doormat, treat like dirt under
one's feet

11 domesticate, tame, break, bust
<nonformal>, break in, break to
harness; housebreak

12 depend on, be at the mercy of,
be the plaything or puppet of, be
putty in the hands of; eat out of
one's hands; play second fiddle,
suck hind tit <nonformal>, take a
back seat

ADJS **13 subject, dependent,** tributary, client; **subservient, subordinate, inferior;** servile; liege;
vassal, feudal

**14 subjugated, enslaved, en-
thralled, in thrall, captive;**
disenfranchised, **oppressed,
suppressed** 428.14; **in subjec-**

tion, in bondage, in captivity,** in
slavery, in chains; under the heel;
in one's power, in one's hands or
clutches, in one's pocket, **under
one's thumb,** at one's mercy, at
one's beck and call, at one's feet,
at one's pleasure; **subordinated,**
playing second fiddle; at the bottom of the ladder, sucking hind tit
<nonformal>

15 subdued, quelled, crushed,
broken, reduced, humbled, humiliated, brought to one's knees,
brought low, made to grovel;
tamed, domesticated, broken to
harness

16 downtrodden, kept down or under, ground down, overborne,
trampled, **oppressed; abused;**
henpecked, browbeaten, led by
the nose, tied to one's apron
strings, kicked around <nonfor-
mal>, regimented, tyrannized;
slavish, servile, submissive
433.12; unmanned 19.19; treated
like dirt under one's feet

433 SUBMISSION

NOUNS **1 submission,** submittal,
**yielding; compliance, acquies-
cence, acceptance;** going along
with <nonformal>, **assent** 332;
consent 441; **obedience** 326;
subjection 432; **resignation,** stoicism; **deference,** homage,
obeisance; **passivity, unasser-
tiveness,** passiveness, supineness, nonresistance, nondissent,
quietude; **cowardice** 491

2 surrender, capitulation; renunciation, abandonment, relinquishment, **cession;** giving up or
in, backing off or down <nonfor-
mal>, retreat

**3 submissiveness, docility, trac-
tability,** pliancy, pliability, flexibility, malleability, plasticity, facility; agreeability; subservience,
servility 138

**4 manageability, governability,
controllability,** corrigibility;
tameness; milquetoast, Caspar
Milquetoast

**5 meekness, gentleness, tame-
ness, mildness,** mild-mannered-

ness, peaceableness; **self-abnegation, humility** 137

VERBS **6 submit, comply, take, accept,** go along with <nonformal>, suffer, bear, brook, **acquiesce,** be agreeable, accede, **assent** 332.8; **consent** 441.2; relent, **succumb,** resign, resign oneself; take one's medicine, face the music; **bite the bullet; knuckle down** *or* **under,** take it, swallow it; jump through a hoop, dance to another's tune; take it lying down; put up with it, grin and bear it, make the best of it, take the bitter with the sweet, shrug off, **live with it;** obey 326.2

7 yield, cede, give way, give ground, back down, give up, give in, cave in <nonformal>, have no fight left

8 surrender, give up, capitulate, acknowledge defeat, **cry quits,** say 'uncle' <nonformal>, **throw in the towel** *or* **sponge** <nonformal>, show *or* wave the white flag, lower *or* haul down *or* strike one's flag *or* colors, pull in one's horns <nonformal>, come to terms; renounce, abandon, relinquish, **cede,** give over, hand over

9 submit to, yield to, defer to, bow to, give way to, knuckle under to, succumb to

10 bow down, bow, bend, stoop, crouch, **bow one's head,** bend the neck; genuflect; **bow to,** bend to, knuckle to <nonformal>, bend *or* bow to one's will; kneel to, **bend the knee to, fall on one's knees before, fall at one's feet,** throw oneself at the feet of, prostrate oneself before, **truckle to,** cringe to; **kowtow,** bow and scrape, grovel, do obeisance *or* homage; kiss ass <nonformal>

11 eat dirt, eat crow, eat humble pie, lick the dust, kiss the rod

ADJS **12 submissive, compliant,** complying, **acquiescent,** consenting 441.4; **assenting,** accepting, agreeable; subservient, abject, **obedient** 326.3; servile; **resigned,** uncomplaining; unassertive; **passive,** supine,

unresisting, long-suffering, nondissenting

13 docile, tractable, unmurmuring, **yielding,** pliant, pliable, flexible, malleable, moldable, like putty in one's hands

14 manageable, governable, controllable, corrigible, restrainable, untroublesome; domitable, tamable; milk-toast *or* milquetoast

15 meek, gentle, mild, mild-mannered, peaceable, pacific, quiet; **subdued, chastened, tame,** tamed, broken, housebroken, domesticated; lamblike, gentle as a lamb; humble

16 deferential, obeisant; subservient, obsequious, servile 138.13; on one's belly, on one's knees, on bended knee

ADVS **17 submissively, compliantly,** agreeably; **obediently** 326.6; **resignedly,** uncomplainingly, with resignation; **passively,** supinely, unresistingly, unresistantly

18 docilely, tractably, yieldingly, pliantly, pliably, malleably, flexibly

19 meekly, gently, tamely, mildly, peaceably, pacifically, quietly, like a lamb

434 OBSERVANCE

NOUNS **1 observance,** observation; **keeping,** adherence, heeding; compliance, conformance, conformity, accordance; **faith,** faithfulness, fidelity; **respect, deference** 155.1; **performance, practice,** execution, discharge, carrying out *or* through; dutifulness 641.2, fulfillment, satisfaction

VERBS **2 observe, keep, heed, follow,** keep the faith; regard, defer to, **respect** 155.4, **comply with,** conform to; **abide by,** adhere to; **live up to,** practice what one preaches, **be faithful to,** keep faith with, do the right thing by; **fulfill,** fill, meet, satisfy; **make good,** keep one's word *or* promise, be as good as one's word

3 perform, practice, do, execute, discharge, carry out *or* through, do one's duty 641.10, fulfill one's role, discharge one's function

ADJS **4 observant,** respectful 155.8, regardful, mindful, **faithful,** devout, devoted, true, loyal, constant; dutiful 641.13, duteous; as good as one's word; **practicing,** active; compliant, conforming; punctual, punctilious, scrupulous, meticulous, conscientious 339.12

435 NONOBSERVANCE

NOUNS **1 nonobservance,** nonadherence; nonconformity, **nonconformance, noncompliance;** apostasy; inattention, indifference, **disregard** 983.1; laxity 426.1; **nonfulfillment, nonperformance,** nonfeasance, **dereliction, delinquency,** omission, default, slight, oversight; **negligence; neglect** 340; abandonment 370

2 violation, infraction, breach; **infringement, transgression, trespass,** contravention; offense 674.4; breach of promise, breach of contract, breach of trust *or* faith, bad faith, breach of privilege; breach of the peace

VERBS **3 disregard,** lose sight of, pay no regard to; **neglect** 340.6; renege, abandon 370.5; defect 857.13

4 violate, break, breach; infringe, transgress, trespass, contravene, trample on *or* upon, trample underfoot, do violence to, make a mockery of, outrage; **defy,** flout, set at naught; take the law into one's own hands; break one's promise, break one's word

ADJS **5 nonobservant,** unobservant; nonconforming, unconforming, noncompliant, uncompliant; inattentive, **disregardful** 983.6; **negligent** 340.10; unfaithful, untrue, unloyal, inconstant, lapsed, renegade 857.20/363.11

436 PROMISE

NOUNS **1 promise, pledge,** troth, plight, faith, parole, **word, word of honor,** solemn declaration *or* word; **oath, vow; assurance, guarantee,** warranty; entitlement

2 obligation, commitment, agreement, engagement, undertaking; **understanding,** gentlemen's agreement; tacit *or* unspoken agreement; **contract** 437.1; designation, committal, earmarking

3 betrothal, betrothment, espousal, **engagement,** troth, marriage contract *or* vow, plighted troth *or* faith *or* love; banns, banns of matrimony; prenuptial agreement *or* contract

VERBS **4 promise,** give *or* make a promise, hold out an expectation; **pledge,** plight, troth, **vow; give one's word,** pledge one's word, **give one's word of honor,** plight one's troth, pledge one's honor; cross one's heart and hope to die <nonformal>, **swear;** vouch, **warrant, guarantee, assure;** underwrite

5 commit, engage, undertake, obligate, bind, **agree to,** be answerable for, take on oneself, be responsible for, go bail for, bind oneself to; have an understanding; enter into a gentlemen's agreement; take the vows *or* marriage vows; shake hands on; contract; designate, commit, earmark

6 be engaged, affiance, betroth, troth, plight one's troth, **contract,** promise in marriage; publish the banns

ADJS **7 promissory,** votive; under *or* upon oath, on one's word, on one's word of honor, on the Book

8 promised, pledged, bound, committed, obligated; sworn, warranted, **guaranteed,** assured, underwritten; contracted 437.12; **engaged, plighted, affianced, betrothed,** intended

ADVS **9** on one's honor *or* word *or*

word of honor or parole; solemnly

437 COMPACT

NOUNS **1 compact, pact, contract,
covenant,** convention, accord,
agreement, stipulation; adjustment, accommodation; **understanding, arrangement, bargain, deal** <nonformal>; **settlement; labor contract, union
contract** 727.3; cartel, consortium; protocol; bond, binding
agreement, ironclad agreement;
gentleman's or gentlemen's agreement; promise 436

  2 treaty, international agreement,
concord, concordat, cartel, convention, capitulation; **alliance,
league;** nonaggression pact,
mutual-defense treaty

  3 signing, signature, sealing, closing, conclusion, solemnization;
handshake

  **4 execution, completion; trans-
action; carrying out, discharge,
fulfillment,** prosecution, effectuation; enforcement; observance
434

VERBS **5 contract,** compact, **covenant, bargain, agree, engage,**
undertake, commit, make a deal
<nonformal>, stipulate, agree to,
bargain for, contract for; **promise** 436.4; subcontract, outsource

  6 treat with, negotiate, bargain,
make terms, sit down with, sit
down at the bargaining table

  7 sign, shake hands or shake
<nonformal>, affix one's John
Hancock <nonformal>, seal, formalize, make legal and binding,
solemnize; agree on terms, come
to an agreement 332.10; strike a
bargain 731.18; plea-bargain

  8 arrange, settle; adjust, fine-
tune, accommodate, reshuffle, rejigger <nonformal>, **compose,**
fix, make up, straighten out, put
or set straight, work out, sort out
and square away <both nonfor-
mal>; **conclude,** close, **close
with,** settle with

  9 execute, complete, transact,
promulgate, **make; discharge,**

fulfill, render, administer; **carry
out,** carry through, put through,
prosecute; effect, effectuate, set
in motion, implement; enforce,
put in force; **abide by, honor, live
up to,** adhere to, live by, **observe**
434.2

ADJS **10** contractual, covenantal,
conventional

  **11 contracted, covenanted,
agreed upon, bargained for,**
stipulated; engaged, undertaken;
promised 436.8; arranged, settled; **signed,** sealed; signed sealed
and delivered

ADVS **12 contractually, as agreed
upon, as promised,** as contracted for, by the terms of the
contract

438 SECURITY

<thing given as a pledge>

NOUNS **1 security, surety,** indemnity, **guaranty, guarantee, warranty, insurance,** warrant, assurance; **obligation** 436.2, full
faith and credit

  2 pledge, gage; undertaking; **earnest,** earnest money; escrow;
pawn, hock <nonformal>; **bail,**
bond; replevin, recognizance;
hostage, surety

  3 collateral, collateral security or
warranty; deposit, stake, forfeit;
caution money, caution; margin

  4 mortgage, mortgage deed, deed
of trust, lien, security agreement;
hypothecation; chattel mortgage;
adjustable-rate mortgage or
ARM, variable-rate mortgage or
VRM, fixed-rate mortgage; equity
loan; reverse equity

  5 lien, tax lien, mechanic's lien;
mortgage bond

  6 guarantor, warrantor, guaranty,
guarantee; mortgagor; insurer;
underwriter; sponsor, surety;
bondsman, bailsman

  7 warrantee, mortgagee; insuree,
policyholder

  8 guarantorship, **sponsorship,**
sponsion

VERBS **9 secure, guarantee, guaranty, warrant, assure, insure,**
ensure, bond, **certify; sponsor,**

be sponsor for, sign for, sign one's
note, **back,** stand behind or back
of, stand up for; **endorse;** sign,
cosign, **underwrite,** undersign,
subscribe to; confirm, attest

10 **pledge, deposit, stake,** post,
put in escrow, **put up,** put up as
collateral, lay out or down; **pawn,
hock** and **put in hock** <both non-
formal>; mortgage, hypothecate,
bond; **put up** or **go bail,** bail out

ADJS 11 **secured,** covered, **guaranteed, warranted, insured,** en-
sured, **assured;** certain, sure
969.13

12 **pledged,** staked, in escrow, **put
up,** put up as collateral; on deposit, at stake; as earnest;
pawned, in pawn, **in hock**
<nonformal>

13 **in trust,** held in trust, fiduciary;
in escrow

439 OFFER

NOUNS 1 **offer,** offering, presentation, **bid,** submission; **advance,
overture,** approach, invitation;
preliminary approach, feeling-
out, **feeler** <nonformal>; **coun-
teroffer, counterproposal**

2 **proposal, proposition, suggestion; motion,** resolution; sexual
advance or approach or overture,
indecent proposal, pass <nonfor-
mal>; request 440

3 **ultimatum,** last or final word or
offer, firm bid or price, sticking
point

VERBS 4 **offer, proffer, present,**
tender, offer up, **put up, submit,
extend, hold out,** hold forth,
place in one's way, put or place at
one's disposal

5 **propose, submit; suggest,** recommend, **advance,** commend to
attention, **propound, pose, put
forward,** put or set forth, put it
to, put or set or lay or bring before, dish up and come up with
<both nonformal>; put a bee in
one's bonnet, put ideas into one's
head; **bring up, broach, moot,**
introduce, launch, start, kick off
<both nonformal>; **move, make a
motion;** postulate 950.12

6 **bid,** bid for, make a bid

7 **make advances,** approach,
make an overture, throw or fling
oneself at one <nonformal>; **solicit, importune**

8 <nonformal terms> **proposition, come on to,** hit on, put or
make a move on, make a pass,
george, **make a play for,** play
footsie with, pitch

9 **urge upon, press upon,** push
upon, force upon, thrust upon;
press, ply; insist

10 **volunteer, come** or **step forward, offer** or **present oneself,**
be at one's service, not wait to be
asked, not wait for an invitation,
need no prodding

440 REQUEST

NOUNS 1 **request,** asking; the
touch <nonformal>; desire, wish;
petition, address; **application;
requisition;** demand 421

2 **entreaty, appeal, plea, bid,**
suit, call, cry, clamor, beseeching;
supplication, prayer, imploring,
adjuration, imprecation; **invocation**

3 **importunity,** importunateness,
urgency, pressure, high pressure
and hard sell <both nonformal>;
urging, pressing, plying; but-
tonholing; **teasing,** pestering,
plaguing, nagging, nudging
<nonformal>; **coaxing,** whee-
dling, blandishment

4 **invitation, invite** and **bid** <both
nonformal>, bidding, **call,** calling, **summons**

5 **solicitation, canvass, canvassing; suit,** addresses; **courting,
wooing**

6 **beggary,** mendicancy; **begging,**
scrounging; mooching and bumming and panhandling <all
nonformal>

7 **petitioner, supplicant,** suitor;
solicitor 730.7; **applicant,** claimant; **aspirant,** seeker, wannabee
<nonformal>; **candidate,** pos-
tulant; bidder

8 **beggar, mendicant,** scrounger,
cadger; **bum** and **moocher** and
panhandler <all nonformal>;

schnorrer <Yiddish>; hobo,
tramp 178.3; loafer 331.8; mendicant friar
VERBS **9 request, ask,** make a request, **beg leave; desire,** wish,
wish for, crave; **ask for,** order, put
in an order for, call for; **requisition,** put in a requisition; make
application, **apply for,** file for,
put in for; demand 421.4
10 petition, present a petition, sign
a petition; **pray,** sue; **apply to,
call on** *or* **upon**
11 entreat, implore, beseech, beg,
crave, **plead, appeal, pray, supplicate;** adjure; invoke, **call on** *or*
upon, appeal to, cry to, run to;
go cap *or* hat in hand to; go down
on one's knees to, fall on one's
knees to, go on bended knee to,
throw oneself at the feet of; **plead
for,** clamor for, cry for, cry out
for
12 importune, urge, press, pressure <nonformal>, prod, apply *or*
exert pressure, push, **ply;** dun;
beset, buttonhole, besiege; work
on <nonformal>, **tease,** pester,
plague, nag, make a pest *or* nuisance of oneself, try one's
patience, bug <nonformal>,
nudge; **coax,** wheedle, cajole,
blandish, flatter, soft-soap
<nonformal>
**13 invite, ask, call, summon,
call in,** extend *or* issue an invitation, request the presence of,
request the pleasure of one's company
14 solicit, canvass; court, woo,
pop the question <nonformal>;
seek, bid for, look for; **fish for,**
angle for
15 beg, **scrounge, cadge; mooch**
and **bum** *and* **panhandle** <all
nonformal>; **hit** *and* hit up *and*
touch *and* put the touch on *and*
make a touch <all nonformal>;
pass the hat <nonformal>
ADJS **16 supplicatory, suppliant,**
supplicant, supplicating; **peti-
tionary; begging,** mendicant,
cadging, scrounging, mooching
<nonformal>; on one's knees
17 imploring, entreating, be-

seeching, **begging, pleading,
appealing,** adjuratory
18 importunate; teasing, pesky
<nonformal>, pestering, plagu-
ing, nagging; **coaxing,** wheedling, cajoling, flattering, soft-
soaping <nonformal>; **insistent,
demanding, urgent**
19 invitational, inviting, invitatory

441 CONSENT

NOUNS **1 consent, assent, agreement,** acceptance, approval, approbation, sanction, **endorsement,** ratification, backing; affirmation; **leave, permission** 443;
willingness, readiness, promptness, eagerness, unloathness,
tacit *or* unspoken *or* silent *or* implicit consent, **connivance;
acquiescence, compliance;** submission 433
VERBS **2 consent, assent,** give consent, be amenable, be persuaded,
accede to, **nod, nod assent; accept, play** *or* **go along** <nonfor-
mal>, **agree to, sign off on**
<nonformal>, go along with
<nonformal>; be in accord with,
be in favor of, take kindly to, **approve of,** hold with; **approve,**
give one's blessing to, **okay** *or* **OK**
<nonformal>; sanction, **endorse,
ratify; wink at, connive at; be
willing,** turn a willing ear; deign,
condescend; have no objection;
permit 443.9
**3 acquiesce, comply, comply
with,** fall in with, take one up on
<nonformal>, be persuaded,
come around, come over, see
one's way clear to; **submit** 433.6,9
ADJS **4 consenting, assenting,** affirmative, amenable, persuaded,
approving, agreeing, favorable,
consentient; sanctioning, endors-
ing, ratifying; **acquiescent,
compliant;** submissive 433.12;
willing, agreeable, content;
ready, eager, nothing loath, ungrudging; permissive 443.14
ADVS **5 consentingly, assentingly,**
affirmatively, approvingly, favorably, positively, agreeably; willingly 324.8

·442 REFUSAL

NOUNS 1 **refusal, rejection,** turn-
down; thumbs-down <nonfor-
mal>; nonacceptance; **declining,**
declination, disclaimer;
repudiation 372.1; disagreement, dissent 333; recantation
363.3; contradiction 335.2; negation, abnegation, nix <nonfor-
mal>; unwillingness 325; disobedience 327; noncompliance,
nonobservance 435; withholding,
holding back, deprivation

2 **repulse, rebuff,** peremptory *or*
flat *or* point-blank refusal; kiss-
off *and* slap in the face *and* kick in
the teeth <all nonformal>; short
shrift

VERBS 3 **refuse, decline,** refuse
consent, **reject, turn down**
<nonformal>; not hold with; **say
no,** vote negatively *or* in the negative, side against, disagree, beg to
disagree, dissent 333.4; shake
one's head; vote down, **turn
thumbs down on;** turn one's
back on, turn a deaf ear to, set
oneself against, be unmoved, resist persuasion; stand aloof, not
lift a finger, have nothing to do
with, wash one's hands of; hold
out against; put *or* set one's foot
down, refuse point-blank; decline
politely *or* with thanks, beg off; **repudiate,** disallow, disclaim 372.2

4 **deny, withhold;** grudge, begrudge; deprive one of

5 **repulse, rebuff, repel,** slap one
in the face *and* kick one in the
teeth <all nonformal>, give one
short shrift, shut *or* slam the door
in one's face, turn one away; slap
or smack one down <nonfor-
mal>; refuse to receive, not be at
home to, cut, **snub** 157.5

ADJS 6 **unconsenting,** nonconsent-
ing, **negative; unwilling** 325.5;
uncompliant, uncomplying, uncooperative; disobedient; deaf to,
not willing to hear of

443 PERMISSION

NOUNS 1 **permission, leave, allowance; consent** 441; **license,**
liberty 430.1; **okay** *and* **OK** *and*
nod *and* **go-ahead** *and* **green
light** *and* **go sign** *and* **thumbs-up**
<all nonformal>; charter, dispen-
sation, release, waiver; variance

2 **sufferance, tolerance,** toleration, **indulgence;** winking, overlooking, connivance; permissiveness

3 **authorization, authority, sanction, licensing,** countenance,
warrant, warranty, fiat; empowerment, entitlement; enfranchisement; ratification 332.4;
legalization, legitimation, de-
criminalization

4 **carte blanche,** blank check
<nonformal>, **full authority,** full
power, free hand, open mandate

5 **grant, concession;** charter,
franchise, liberty, diploma, patent

6 **permit, license, warrant;** nihil
obstat, imprimatur

7 **pass, passport, safe-conduct,**
safeguard, protection; visa; **clearance;** bill of health, clean bill of
health

8 **permissibility,** permissibleness,
allowableness; admissibility,
admissibleness; **validity,** legitimacy, lawfulness, licitness

VERBS 9 **permit, allow, admit, let,**
give permission, give leave, make
possible; **allow** *or* **permit of;** give
or leave room for, open the door
to; consent 441.2; **grant,** accord;
okay *and* **OK** *and* **give the nod** *or*
go-ahead *or* **green light** <all
nonformal>, say *or* give the word
<nonformal>; dispense, release,
waive

10 **suffer, countenance, tolerate,
condone,** brook, endure, stomach, bear, bear with, put up with,
stand for, go along with <both
nonformal>; indulge 427.6; shut
one's eyes to, **wink at,** blink at;
leave the door *or* way open to

11 **authorize, sanction, warrant;**
legitimize, validate, legalize; empower, entitle; **license; privilege;**
charter, franchise; accredit, certificate, certify; ratify 332.12;
legalize, legitimate, legitimize

12 give carte blanche, give a blank check <nonformal>, give full power *or* authority, give free rein, give a free hand, leave alone; open the floodgates, remove all restrictions

13 may, can, have permission, **be permitted** *or* **allowed**

ADJS **14 permissive,** permitting, allowing; consenting 441.4; obliging, **tolerant;** suffering, **indulgent, lenient 427.7;** hands-off <nonformal>; lax 426.4

15 permissible, allowable, admissible; justifiable, sanctionable; licit, **lawful, legitimate, legal,** legitimized, legalized

16 permitted, allowed; tolerated; unprohibited, unregulated, unchecked

17 authorized, empowered, entitled; **warranted, sanctioned; licensed, privileged;** chartered; franchised; accredited, certificated

ADVS **18 permissively,** admissively; **tolerantly, indulgently**

19 permissibly, allowably; by one's leave; lawfully, legitimately, legally

444 PROHIBITION

NOUNS **1 prohibition, forbidding; ruling out, disallowance,** denial, rejection 372; refusal 442; **repression, suppression 428.2; ban, embargo, enjoinder, injunction, proscription,** inhibition, **interdict,** interdiction; **index;** taboo; law, statute 673.3; forbidden fruit, contraband; zoning, restrictive convenant; **forbidden ground** *or* **territory,** no-man's land <nonformal>

2 veto; line-item veto, pocket veto; **thumbs-down** <nonformal>

VERBS **3 prohibit, forbid; disallow, rule out** *or* **against;** deny, **reject** 372.2; say no to, **refuse** 442.3; **bar,** debar, preclude, exclude, shut *or* close the door on, **prevent** 1011.14; **ban, outlaw; repress, suppress** 428.8; **enjoin,**

issue an injunction against; **proscribe,** inhibit, **interdict;** put on the Index; embargo, **lay** *or* **put an embargo on; taboo**

4 not permit *or* **allow, not have, not suffer** *or* **tolerate,** not endure, not stomach, not bear, not bear with, **not countenance,** not brook, not put up with, not go along with <nonformal>; not stand for <nonformal>, put one's foot down on <nonformal>

5 veto, decide *or* rule against, **turn thumbs down on** <nonformal>, kill

ADJS **6 prohibitive,** prohibitory, **forbidding;** inhibitory, **repressive, suppressive** 428.11; proscriptive, interdictory; **preventive** 1011.19

7 prohibited, forbidden, barred; vetoed; unpermissible, not permitted *or* allowed, **unallowed;** disallowed, ruled out, contraindicated; beyond the pale, off limits, out of bounds; unauthorized, **unsanctioned,** unlicensed; banned, **outlawed,** contraband; taboo; **illegal,** unlawful, illicit

445 REPEAL

NOUNS **1 repeal, revocation;** reneging, welshing <nonformal>, **rescinding,** rescission, **reversal, striking down, abrogation,** cessation, reversal; suspension; **waiver, setting aside; countermand;** annulment, nullification, **invalidation,** voidance, vacation; **cancellation,** canceling, cancel, write-off; **abolition; recall,** retraction, recantation 363.3

VERBS **2 repeal, revoke, rescind, reverse, strike down, abrogate;** renege, welsh <nonformal>; suspend; **waive, set aside; countermand; abolish,** do away with; **cancel,** write off; **annul,** nullify, **invalidate,** void, vacate, declare null and void; **overrule,** override; **recall,** retract, recant

ADJS **3 repealed, revoked, rescinded,** struck down, set aside; **invalid,** void, **null and void**

446 PROMOTION

NOUNS **1 promotion, preferment, advancement, advance,** elevation, upgrading, jump, step up; **raise, boost** <nonformal>; kicking upstairs <nonformal>; exaltation, aggrandizement; graduation, passing

VERBS **2 promote, advance,** elevate, upgrade, jump; kick upstairs <nonformal>; **raise;** exalt, aggrandize; pass, graduate

447 DEMOTION, DEPOSAL

NOUNS **1 demotion,** downgrading, debasement; abasement, humbling, humiliation; **reduction,** bump *and* bust <both nonformal>; stripping of rank

2 deposal, deposition, removal, displacement, supplanting, replacement, deprivation, **ousting,** unseating; **cashiering, firing** <nonformal>, **dismissal** 908.5; forced resignation; kicking upstairs <nonformal>; **superannuation,** pensioning off, putting out to pasture, **retirement,** the golden handshake *or* parachute <nonformal>; **suspension;** impeachment; purge, **liquidation; overthrow; disbarment,** disbarring; defrocking, unchurching; expulsion, excommunication 908.4

VERBS **3 demote, degrade,** downgrade, debase, abase, humble, humiliate, **lower, reduce,** bump *and* bust <both nonformal>; strip of rank

4 depose, remove from office, send to the showers *and* give the gate <both nonformal>, divest *or* deprive of office, **remove,** displace, supplant, replace; **oust; suspend; cashier,** drum out, strip of rank, **break,** bust <nonformal>; **dismiss** 908.19; **purge, liquidate; overthrow; retire,** superannuate, pension, pension off, put out to pasture, give the golden handshake *or* parachute <nonformal>; kick upstairs <nonformal>; **unseat,**
unsaddle; **disbar;** defrock, unchurch; read out of; **expel, excommunicate** 908.17

448 RESIGNATION, RETIREMENT

NOUNS **1 resignation, withdrawal, retirement,** pensioning, pensioning off, golden handshake *or* parachute <nonformal>, superannuation, emeritus status; **abdication;** deposal 447; relinquishment 370.3

VERBS **2 resign, quit,** leave, **vacate,** withdraw from; **retire,** superannuate, be superannuated, be pensioned *or* pensioned off, be put out to pasture, get the golden handshake *or* parachute <nonformal>; relinquish, give up 370.7; retire from office, step aside, give up one's post, hang up one's spurs <nonformal>; **tender** *or* **hand in one's resignation; abdicate,** renounce the throne; pension off 447.4

ADJS **3 retired,** in retirement, superannuated, pensioned off, emeritus, emerita <fem>

449 AID

NOUNS **1 aid, help, assistance, support, succor, relief, comfort,** ease, remedy; **service, benefit** 387.4; ministration, office, good offices; therapy 91; protection 1007; **bailout** <nonformal>, **rescue** 398

2 assist, helping hand, hand, lift; leg up <nonformal>; **support group,** self-help group, 12-step group

3 support, maintenance, sustainment, sustenance, subsistence, provision, meal ticket <nonformal>; **keep, upkeep; livelihood, living,** daily bread; **nurture, fostering,** nurturance, nourishment, mothering, parenting, rearing, foster-care, **care, caring,** tender loving care *or* TLC <nonformal>; manna; subsidy, endowment; **support services, social services**

4 patronage, fosterage, tutelage, sponsorship, backing, auspices, aegis, coattails <nonformal>, **championing, championship;** interest, advocacy, **backing;** countenance, **favor, goodwill,** charity, **sympathy**

5 furtherance, helping along, advancement, promotion, facilitation, easing *or* smoothing of the way, greasing of the wheels, expediting, rushing; special *or* preferential treatment

6 self-help, self-improvement; independence 430.5

7 helper, assistant 616.6; benefactor 592; facilitator

8 reinforcements, support, relief, reserves

9 facility, accommodation, appliance, convenience, amenity, appurtenance; advantage

10 helpfulness; utility, **usefulness** 387.3; **advantageousness,** profitability

VERBS **11 aid, help, assist,** comfort, **succor,** relieve, **ease,** doctor, remedy; be of some help; do good, **benefit, avail** 998.10; **favor, befriend; give help,** render assistance, offer aid, come to the aid of, rush to the assistance of, lend aid, **give** *or* **lend a hand** *or* **helping hand,** hold out a helping hand; take by the hand, take in tow; **give a leg up** *or* lift *or* boost <nonformal>; **save,** redeem, bail out <nonformal>, **rescue** 398.3; protect 1007.18; put on one's feet; give new life to, resuscitate, rally, reclaim, revive, **restore** 396.11,15; see one through

12 support, lend support; maintain, sustain, keep; uphold, hold up, bear, **bear up;** reinforce, undergird, bolster, **bolster up,** buttress, shore up, prop up; **finance,** fund, subsidize; pick up the tab *or* check <nonformal>

13 back, back up, stand behind, stand back of *or* in back of, get behind; **stand by, stick up for** <nonformal>, **champion; second, take the part of,** take up the cause of, take under one's wing,

go to bat for <nonformal>, **side with,** associate oneself with, align oneself with, come down *or* range oneself on the side of, find time for

14 abet, aid and abet, encourage, hearten, embolden; advocate, hold a brief for <nonformal>, countenance, **endorse, lend oneself to,** lend one's support to, plump for <nonformal>, lend one's name to, give one's support to, give moral support to, hold one's hand, make one's cause one's own, weigh in for <nonformal>; **favor, go for** <nonformal>, smile upon, shine upon

15 patronize, sponsor, take up

16 foster, nurture, nourish, mother, care for, lavish care on, feed, parent, rear, sustain, cultivate, **cherish;** pamper, coddle; **nurse,** suckle; spoon-feed

17 be useful, further, forward, advance, promote, stand in good stead, encourage, **boost** <nonformal>, **facilitate,** speed, expedite, quicken, hasten, lend wings to; contribute to

18 serve, lend *or* **give oneself, work for, labor in behalf of; minister to,** cater to; pander to

19 oblige, accommodate, favor, do a service

ADJS **20 helping,** assisting, serving; **assistant, auxiliary,** subservient, subsidiary, ancillary, accessory; fostering, nurtural; care, caring, care-giving

21 helpful, useful; profitable, salutary, good for, **beneficial** 998.12; therapeutic; **serviceable, useful** 387.18; **contributory,** contributing, conducive, **constructive, positive;** at one's service, at one's command, at one's beck and call

22 favorable, propitious; kind, kindly, **well-disposed,** well-intentioned, well-meant, **well-meaning;** benevolent, beneficent, benign; friendly, amicable, neighborly; cooperative

23 self-helpful, self-helping, self-improving

ADVS **24 helpfully; beneficially,**
favorably, profitably, advantageously, to advantage; **usefully**

450 COOPERATION

NOUNS **1 cooperation, collaboration,** synergy, synergism; **consensus, commonality; com-
munity,** harmony, concord, fellowship, solidarity, concert,
teamwork; pulling *or* working
together, joining of forces, pool-
ing of resources, joining of hands;
reciprocity; joint effort, common
effort, collective *or* united action,
mass action; job-sharing; co-
agency; symbiosis, commen-
salism; **cooperativeness,** collab-
orativeness, *esprit de corps* <Fr>;
ecumenism, ecumenicalism; **collusion,** complicity

**2 affiliation, alliance, align-
ment, association,** combination,
union, unification, **coalition,** fusion, merger, coalescence,
amalgamation, **league, federation, confederation,** confederacy, consolidation, integration;
partnership, cahoots <nonfor-
mal>; **collegialism, collegiality;
fraternity,** fraternization; sorority; **fellowship,** sodality;
comradeship, camaraderie

VERBS **3 cooperate, collaborate,**
do business *and* **play ball** <both
nonformal>, concur; **join,** band,
league, **associate, affiliate,** ally,
combine, unite, fuse, merge, coalesce, amalgamate, federate,
confederate, consolidate; be in
league, **go into partnership
with,** go partners <nonformal>,
go *or* be in cahoots with; **join together,** club together, league
together, band together; **work together,** get together *and* team up
and buddy up <all nonformal>,
work as a team, act in concert,
**pull together; hold together,
hang together,** keep together,
stand together, stand shoulder
to shoulder; put *or* get heads together; **close ranks,** make common cause, throw in together

<nonformal>; reciprocate; **con-
spire,** collude

**4 side with, unite with; join, join
with,** join up with *and* get together with *and* team up with <all
nonformal>; **throw in with**
<nonformal>, **go along with;
line up with** <nonformal>, align
oneself with, stand in with; **join
hands with,** be hand in glove
with, go hand in hand with; act
with, **go in with;** cast in one's lot
with, join one's fortunes with,
stand shoulder to shoulder with,
be cheek by jowl with, sink or
swim with, stand or fall with;
close ranks with, make common
cause with, pool one's interests
with

ADJS **5 cooperative, cooperating,
hand in glove; collaborative,**
synergic, synergistic; **fellow;**
concurrent, concurring, concerted, **in concert; consensus,**
consensual, in agreement, of like
mind; harmonious, concordant,
common, communal, collective;
mutual, reciprocal; **joint, combined** 804.5; symbiotic; uncom-
petitive, noncompetitive, ecumenical; **conniving, collusive**

ADVS **6 cooperatively,** concurrently; in consensus, consen-
sually; **jointly, conjointly,**
concertedly, in concert with;
harmoniously, concordantly;
communally, collectively, **together;** as one, with one voice,
unanimously, as one man; **side
by side, hand in hand, hand in
glove, shoulder to shoulder,
back to back**

**7 in cooperation, in collabora-
tion, in partnership, in cahoots**
<nonformal>, **in collusion,** in
league

451 OPPOSITION

NOUNS **1 opposition,** opposing,
crossing, bucking <nonformal>,
standing against; **resistance** 453;
noncooperation; contention
457; **rejection** 372, refusal; refusal 442; **contradiction,**
challenge, contravention, re-

buttal, denial, impugnment;
crosscurrent, undercurrent, undertow

2 **hostility, antagonism, antipathy,** enmity, bad blood, inimicalness; **contrariness, contrariety,** orneriness <nonformal>,
repugnance *or* repugnancy, perverseness, **obstinacy** 361; fractiousness, refractoriness, recalcitrance 327.2; uncooperativeness,
negativeness, **obstructionism;
friction, conflict, collision,**
cross-purposes, dissension, disaccord 456; rivalry, competition
457.2

VERBS 3 **oppose, counter, cross,**
go *or* act in opposition to, **go
against, run counter to,** fly in
the face of, fly in the teeth of;
make waves <nonformal>, **protest** 333.5; set one's face *or* heart
against; be *or* play at cross-
purposes, **obstruct,** sabotage;
**take issue with, take one's
stand against,** lift *or* raise a hand
against, declare oneself against,
vote against, vote nay, veto; make
a stand against; join the opposition; not put up with, not abide,
not be content with; counteract,
countervail 899.6; **resist,** withstand 453.3

4 **contend against,** militate
against, **contest, combat, battle,
clash with, clash, fight against,
strive against,** struggle against,
take on <nonformal>, grapple
with, close with, go the the mat
with <nonformal>, **fight, buck**
<nonformal>, **counter;** buffet,
beat against, breast *or* stem the
tide *or* current *or* flood, buffet the
waves; rival, compete with *or*
against, vie with *or* against; fight
back, **resist, offer resistance**
453.3

5 **confront, affront,** go eyeball-to-
eyeball *or* one-on-one with
<nonformal>, **meet head-on**

6 **contradict,** cross, contravene,
controvert, rebut, **gainsay;** challenge, contest; **belie,** be contrary
to, come in conflict with, negate
335.3; **reject** 372.2

7 **be against,** be agin <nonfor-
mal>; discountenance 510.11;
not hold with; have a bone to pick

ADJS 8 **oppositional, opponent,
opposing, opposed;** confrontational, confrontive; at odds, at
loggerheads; **adverse, adversary,**
adversarial, antithetical, repugnant, **set** *or* **dead set against;
contrary, counter; negative;
opposite,** death on; cross; **contradictory;** unfavorable, unpropitious 133.17; **hostile, antagonistic,** unfriendly, enemy, inimical, alien, antipathetic;
fractious, refractory, recalcitrant
327.10; uncooperative, **obstructive;** ornery <nonformal>,
perverse, obstinate 361.8; **conflicting, clashing,** dissentient;
rival, competitive

ADVS 9 **in opposition, in confrontation,** eyeball-to-eyeball *and*
one-on-one <both nonformal>,
head-on, **at variance, at cross-
purposes, at odds,** at issue, at
war with, up in arms, at daggers
drawn; contrariwise, counter,
cross, athwart; against the tide *or*
wind *or* grain

452 OPPONENT

NOUNS 1 **opponent, adversary,
antagonist, assailant, foe, enemy,** archenemy; opposite camp,
opposite *or* opposing side, **the
opposition,** the loyal opposition;
combatant 461

2 **competitor, contestant, contender,** player, entrant; **rival,**
arch-rival; the field; finalist, semi-
finalist, etc

3 **oppositionist,** opposer; obstructionist, naysayer; **objector,
protester,** dissident, dissentient;
resister; disputant, litigant,
plaintiff, defendant; quarreler,
scrapper <nonformal>, wrangler,
brawler; die-hard, bitter-ender,
last-ditcher, intransigent

453 RESISTANCE

NOUNS 1 **resistance,** withstanding,
countering; **defiance** 454; **opposing, opposition** 451; **stand;**

repulsion, repulse, rebuff; **objection, protest,** remonstrance, **dispute,** challenge, **demur; complaint;** dissentience, **dissent** 333; reaction, **counteraction** 899; revolt 327.4; recalcitrance or recalcitrancy, fractiousness, refractoriness 327.2; **reluctance** 325.1; **obstinacy** 361; passive resistance, noncooperation; uncooperativeness, negativism

VERBS **2 resist, withstand; stand; endure** 134.5; **stand up, bear up, hold up, hold out; defy** 454.3, tell one where to get off <nonformal>, throw down the gauntlet; bear up against; **repel, repulse,** rebuff

3 offer resistance, fight back, bite back, show fight, stand or hold one's ground, **withstand, take one's stand,** make a stand, square off and put up one's dukes <both nonformal>, **stand up to,** stand up against; **confront,** meet head-on, fly in the face of, **face up to,** face down; **object, protest,** remonstrate, **dispute,** challenge, **complain,** exclaim at; **dissent** 333.4; make waves <nonformal>; kick out against, recalcitrate; put up a fight or struggle <nonformal>, not take lying down, hang tough and tough it out <both nonformal>; **revolt** 327.7; **oppose** 451.3; **contend with** 457.18; **strive against** 451.4

4 stand fast, stand or **hold one's ground,** make a resolute stand, **hold one's own,** remain firm, **stick to one's guns, stick it out** <nonformal>, **hold out,** not back down, not give up, not submit, **never say die; fight to the last ditch,** die hard, sell one's life dearly

ADJS **5 resistant, resistive,** resisting, up against, **withstanding,** repellent; **unyielding,** unsubmissive 361.12; rebellious 327.11; **objecting, protesting,** disputatious, complaining, dissentient, dissenting 333.6; recalcitrant, fractious, refractory

327.10; **reluctant** 325.6; uncooperative; up in arms, on the barricades, not lying down

454 DEFIANCE

NOUNS **1 defiance,** defying; **daring, audacity,** boldness, bold front, brashness, brassiness <nonformal>, brazenness, bravado, insolence; **arrogance** 141; **sauciness, cheekiness** <nonformal>, pertness, impudence, impertinence; bumptiousness, cockiness; **contempt,** contemptuousness, derision, **disdain,** disregard; **risk-taking,** tightrope walking

2 challenge, dare, double dare; fighting words; gage, gauntlet, glove, chip on one's shoulder, invitation to combat, call to arms; war cry, war whoop, battle cry, rebel yell

VERBS **3 defy,** bid defiance, hurl defiance, shout or scream defiance; **dare,** double-dare; **challenge,** throw or fling down the gauntlet or glove or gage, knock the chip off one's shoulder, cross swords; beard the lion in his den, look in the eye, stare down, **confront, affront,** say right to one's face, go eyeball-to-eyeball or one-on-one with <nonformal>; give one the finger; **ask for it** <nonformal>, ask or look for trouble, make something of it <nonformal>; **brave** 492.11

4 flout, slight, treat with contempt, fly in the teeth or face of, **snap one's fingers at; thumb one's nose at; disdain, despise, scorn** 157.3; laugh at, laugh in one's face; hold in derision, scout, scoff at, **deride** 508.8

5 show or **put up a bold front,** bluster, strut, crow, look big

6 take a dare, accept a challenge, **take one up on** and **call one's bluff** <both nonformal>; **start something,** take up the gauntlet

ADJS **7 defiant,** defying, challenging; **daring, bold,** brash, brassy <nonformal>, brazen, **auda-**

cious, insolent; arrogant 141.9; saucy, cheeky <nonformal>, pert, impudent, impertinent; bumptious, cocky; **contemptuous,** disdainful, derisive

ADVS **8 in defiance of,** in the teeth of, in the face of, under one's very nose

455 ACCORD
<*harmonious relationship*>

NOUNS **1 accord,** accordance, **concord, harmony; rapport;** good vibrations <nonformal>, good vibes <nonformal>, good karma; amity 587.1; **sympathy,** empathy, identity, feeling of identity, **fellowship,** kinship, togetherness, **affinity; agreement, understanding, like-mindedness, congruence;** congeniality, **compatibility; oneness,** unity, unison, union; **community,** communion, community of interests; solidarity, team spirit, esprit; mutuality, reciprocity; ties of affection; happy family; peace 464; **love,** charity, brotherly love; correspondence 787.1

VERBS **2 get along,** harmonize, **agree with, agree, get along with,** cotton to *or* hit it off with <both nonformal>, **be in harmony with,** be in tune with, blend in with, go hand in hand with, **be at one with;** be on the same wavelength <nonformal>; **sympathize,** empathize, identify with, respond to, understand one another, enter into the ideas *or* feelings of; **accord,** correspond 787.6

ADJS **3 in accord, harmonious, in harmony,** congruous, congruent, in tune, attuned, **in rapport,** amicable 587.15,18; **sympathetic,** simpatico <nonformal>, empathic, empathetic, **understanding; like-minded,** of the same mind, of one mind, together; concordant, corresponding 787.9; agreeable, congenial, **compatible; peaceful** 464.9

456 DISACCORD
<*unharmonious relationship*>

NOUNS **1 disaccord, discord,** discordance, **unharmoniousness,** disharmony, inharmony, incongruence, incompatibility, incompatibleness; culture gap, generation gap, gender gap; **conflict,** open conflict *or* war, **friction,** rub; jar, **jarring,** jangle, clash, clashing; touchiness, strained relations, **tension;** bad blood; **unpleasantness; contention** 457; **enmity** 589

2 disagreement, difficulty, misunderstanding, difference, difference of opinion, **variance,** division, dividedness; crosspurposes; polarization; **disparity** 788.1

3 dissension, dissent, dissidence, flak <nonformal>; bickering, infighting, partisanship, partisan spirit; **divisiveness; quarrelsomeness;** litigiousness; pugnacity, bellicosity, combativeness, **aggressiveness,** contentiousness, belligerence; feistiness <nonformal>, **touchiness, irritability,** shrewishness, irascibility 110.2

4 falling-out, breach of friendship, parting of the ways, bust-up <nonformal>; **alienation, estrangement, disaffection,** disfavor; **breach, break, rupture, schism, split, rift,** cleft, **disunity, disunion, disruption,** separation, cleavage, divergence, division, dividedness; house divided against itself; open rupture, breaking off of negotiations

5 quarrel, dustup, **dispute, argument,** polemic, lovers' quarrel, **controversy,** altercation, **fight, squabble, contention,** strife, **tussle,** bicker, wrangle, snarl, **tiff, spat,** fuss; **breach of the peace; fracas,** donnybrook; imbroglio; sharp words, war of words, logomachy; **feud,** blood feud, vendetta; brawl 457.5

6 <nonformal terms> **row, rumpus,** ruckus, ruction, brannigan, shindy, set-to, run-in, **scrap, hassle,** rhubarb; knock-down-and-drag-out fight

7 bone of contention, apple of discord, sore point, tender spot, rub, beef <nonformal>; **bone to pick**

VERBS **8 disagree, differ,** hold opposite views, **be at variance,** not get along, be at cross-purposes; misunderstand one another; **conflict, clash,** collide, jostle, jangle, jar; live a cat-and-dog life

9 have a bone to pick with, have a beef with <nonformal>

10 fall out, have a falling-out, **break with, split,** separate, **diverge,** divide, agree to disagree, **part company,** come to or reach a parting of the ways

11 quarrel, dispute, fight, squabble, tiff, spat, **bicker, wrangle,** spar, have words, set to; cross swords, **feud, battle; brawl; be quarrelsome** or contentious, be thin-skinned, be touchy or sensitive, get up on the wrong side of the bed

12 <nonformal terms> **row, scrap, hassle,** make or kick up a row; mix it up, lock horns, bump heads

13 pick a quarrel, look for trouble, pick a bone with; have a chip on one's shoulder; add insult to injury

14 sow dissension, stir up trouble, make or borrow trouble; **alienate, estrange,** separate, **divide, disunite,** disaffect, **come between;** **irritate, provoke,** aggravate; **set at odds,** set at variance, **set against,** pit against, set at one's throat; add fuel to the fire or flame, fan the flame, light the fuse, stir the pot <nonformal>

ADJS **15 disaccordant, unharmonious,** inharmonious, out of tune, unsynchronized, out of sync <nonformal>, **discordant,** dissident, dissentient, **disagreeing, differing; conflicting,** clashing, colliding; like cats and dogs; **divided,** faction-ridden, fragmented

16 at odds, at variance, at log-gerheads, at cross-purposes; at war, at swords' points, up in arms

17 partisan, polarizing, **divisive,** factional, factious; **quarrelsome,** bickering, disputatious, wrangling, polemical; litigious, pugnacious, combative, **aggressive,** bellicose, belligerent; feisty <nonformal>, touchy, irritable, shrewish, **irascible** 110.19

457 CONTENTION

NOUNS **1 contention, contest,** combat, **fighting, conflict, strife, war, struggle,** blood on the floor; fighting at close quarters, infighting; **warfare** 458; **hostility,** enmity 589; **quarrel, altercation, controversy,** dustup, polemic, debate, **argument, dispute, disputation;** litigation; words, war of words, logomachy; **fighting,** scrapping and hassling <both nonformal>; **quarreling, bickering, wrangling, squabbling;** contentiousness, disputatiousness, litigiousness, **quarrelsomeness** 456.3; **competitiveness**

2 competition, rivalry, vying, emulation, jockeying <nonformal>; cutthroat competition; **sportsmanship, gamesmanship,** one-upmanship, **competitive advantage**

3 contest, engagement, encounter, match, matching, meet, meeting, derby, pissing match <nonformal>, **trial, test; close contest,** closely fought contest, horse race and crapshoot <all nonformal>; tournament, tourney; rally; **game** 743.9; **games,** gymkhana; cookoff

4 fight, battle, fray, affray, combat, action, conflict; gun battle; **clash; brush, skirmish,** scrimmage; tussle, **scuffle, struggle,** scramble, shoving match; exchange of blows, clash of arms; **quarrel** 456.5; pitched battle; battle royal; **fistfight,** punch-out and duke-out <both nonformal>; **hand-to-hand fight,** stand-up fight <nonformal>; tug-of-war; dogfight, cockfight; street fight, rumble <nonformal>; **internal struggle,** internecine struggle

5 **free-for-all, knock-down-and-drag-out** <nonformal>, **brawl,** melee, **fracas,** riot

6 **death struggle, life-or-death struggle, struggle** *or* **fight to the death,** all-out war, total war, last-ditch fight

7 **duel,** monomachy, satisfaction, **affair of honor**

8 **fencing, swordplay;** swordsmanship

9 **boxing** 754, **fighting,** manly art of self-defense, **fisticuffs, pugilism, prize-fighting,** the fights <nonformal>, the ring; **boxing match, prizefight,** spar, bout; infighting, the clinches <nonformal>; savate

10 **wrestling,** rassling <nonformal>, grappling, *sumo* <Japanese>; **martial arts**

11 **racing, track; horse racing** 757, the turf, the sport of kings

12 **race;** derby; **horse race; automobile race; heat, lap**

VERBS 13 **contend, contest,** jostle; **fight, battle, combat, war, declare** *or* **go to war,** take up arms, put up a fight <nonformal>; wage war; **strive, struggle,** scramble, go for the brass ring; **tussle, scuffle; quarrel** 456.11,12; clash, collide; **wrestle,** rassle <nonformal>, grapple, go to the mat with; **come to blows,** close, **mix it up** *and* go toe-to-toe <both nonformal>, exchange blows, **box,** spar, give and take; **cross swords, fence,** thrust and parry; **joust, tilt, tourney; duel,** fight a duel, give satisfaction; feud; skirmish; fight the good fight; **brawl,** broil; **riot**

14 **raise one's hand against;** make war on; take up the cudgels; square off <nonformal>; have at; jump; lay on, lay about one; **pitch into** *and* **sail into** *and* light into *and* lay into *and* rip into <all nonformal>, strike the first blow, draw first blood; **attack** 459.15

15 **encounter, go up against,** run afoul of; close with, fight hand-to-hand

16 **engage, take on** <nonformal>, go up against, close with, put on the gloves with; **join issue** *or* **battle, do** *or* **give battle,** engage in battle *or* combat

17 **contend with, engage with, fight with, strive with, struggle with,** wrestle with, grapple with, tilt with, **cross swords with;** exchange shots, shoot it out with <nonformal>; **lock horns** *and* **bump heads** <both nonformal>; **tangle with** *and* **mix it up with** <both nonformal>; have it out, fight *or* battle it out, settle it; **fight** *or* **go at it hammer and tongs** *or* **tooth and nail,** fight it out, duke it out <nonformal>, ask and give no quarter, make blood flow freely, fight to the death

18 **compete, contend, vie,** jockey <nonformal>; **compete with** *or* **against, vie with, challenge,** enter into competition, give a run for one's money, **meet;** test one another; **rival,** emulate, outvie; keep up with the Joneses

19 **race,** race with, run a race; horse-race, boat-race

20 **contend for, strive for, struggle for, fight for,** vie for; hold out for, make a point of

21 **dispute, contest,** take issue with; **fight over, quarrel over, wrangle over, squabble over**

ADJS 22 **contending,** contesting; **contestant,** disputant; striving, struggling; fighting, battling, warring; **warlike; quarrelsome** 456.17

23 **competitive,** competing, **vying,** rivaling, **rival,** in competition; **cutthroat**

458 WARFARE

NOUNS 1 **war, warfare, warring, warmaking, combat, fighting;** armed conflict, armed combat, military operations, resort to arms, force of arms, bloodshed; **state of war, hostilities,** belligerence *or* belligerency, open war *or* warfare *or* hostilities; **hot war, shooting war;** total war, **all-out war; wartime; battle** 457.4; **attack** 459; **war zone, theater of operations**

2 **the sword,** arbitrament of the sword, appeal to arms

3 **battle array,** order of battle, **disposition, deployment, marshaling;** echelon

4 **campaign,** war, **drive, expedition; crusade,** holy war, jihad

5 **operation,** action; **movement; mission; operations; strategy, tactics; battle**

6 **military science,** art *or* rules *or* science of war; war, **arms; generalship;** chivalry

7 **declaration of war,** challenge; defiance 454

8 **call to arms, call-up,** call to the colors, **rally; mobilization; muster;** conscription, recruitment; **rallying cry,** slogan, watchword, catchword, exhortation; **battle cry,** war cry, rebel yell; banzai, gung ho, go for broke; **bugle call,** trumpet call, clarion call

9 **service, military service;** military obligation; selective service; reserve status

10 **militarization,** activation, **mobilization;** war *or* wartime footing, national emergency; **war effort, war economy;** martial law, suspension of civil rights; garrison state, military dictatorship; remilitarization, reactivation; arms race; war clouds, war scare

11 **warlikeness,** ferocity, fierceness; **hard line; combativeness, contentiousness; hostility, antagonism;** aggression, **aggressiveness;** belligerence *or* belligerency, **pugnacity, bellicosity, truculence,** fight <nonformal>; chip on one's shoulder <nonformal>; militancy, **militarism;** saber rattling; **chauvinism, jingoism,** hawkishness <nonformal>, **warmongering; quarrelsomeness** 456.3

12 <rallying devices and themes> battle flag, banner, colors, bloody shirt, atrocity story, enemy atrocities; martial music, war song, battle hymn, national anthem; national honor, face; expansionism, manifest destiny; independence, self-determination

13 war-god, Mars, Ares, Odin *or* Woden *or* Wotan, Tyr *or* Tiu *or* Tiw; war-goddess, Athena, Minerva, Bellona, Enyo, Valkyrie

VERBS 14 **war, wage war, make war, carry on war** *or* **hostilities,** engage in hostilities; battle, **fight;** spill *or* shed blood

15 **make war on,** levy war on; **attack** 459.15,17; **declare war, challenge,** throw *or* fling down the gauntlet; defy 454.3; open hostilities, plunge the world into war; launch a holy war on, go on a crusade against

16 **go to war,** breach the peace, take up the gauntlet, **go on the warpath, rise up in arms, take** *or* **resort to arms,** take up arms, take up the cudgels *or* sword; take the field

17 **campaign,** undertake operations, go on a crusade

18 **serve,** do duty; fulfill one's military obligation, wear the uniform; **soldier,** see *or* do active duty; **bear arms,** carry arms; see action *or* combat

19 **call to arms, call up,** call to the colors, **rally; mobilize; muster,** levy; **conscript, recruit;** sound the call to arms, beat the drums

20 **militarize, activate, mobilize,** go on a wartime footing, gird *or* gird up one's loins; reactivate, remilitarize, take out of mothballs *and* retread <both nonformal>

ADJS 21 **warlike, militant,** fighting, warring, battling; **martial, military,** soldierly, soldierlike; **combative, contentious; belligerent, pugnacious, truculent, bellicose,** scrappy <nonformal>, full of fight; **aggressive,** offensive; fierce, ferocious, savage, bloody, bloodthirsty, sanguinary; **unpeaceful,** unpeaceable, unpacific; **hostile, antagonistic,**

enemy, inimical; unfriendly
589.9; **quarrelsome** 456.17

22 **militaristic, warmongering,**
saber-rattling; **chauvinistic,
jingoistic,** jingo; **hard-line,
hawkish** <nonformal>, of the
war party

23 **embattled, engaged,** in combat; **arrayed, deployed,** in battle
array, in the field; **militarized;
armed** 460.14; war-ravaged, war-
torn

ADVS 24 **at war, up in arms;** in the
thick of the fray *or* combat; at
swords' points

459 ATTACK

NOUNS 1 **attack, assault; offense,
offensive; aggression; onset,
onslaught; strike;** surgical
strike, first strike, preventive war;
charge, rush; **drive, push**
<nonformal>; **sally, sortie;** infil-
tration; frontal attack *or* assault,
head-on attack, flank attack;
mass attack, kamikaze attack;
banzai attack *or* charge, suicide
attack *or* charge; hit-and-run attack; breakthrough; **counterattack, counteroffensive; pre-
emptive strike; blitzkrieg, blitz;**
atomic *or* thermonuclear attack,
first-strike capacity, megadeath,
overkill

2 **surprise attack,** surprise, **sneak
attack** <nonformal>; stab in the
back

3 **thrust, pass, lunge, swing,** cut,
stab, jab; feint

4 **raid, foray; invasion, incursion; air raid, air strike; tank** *or*
armored attack, panzer attack

5 **siege, besiegement, beleaguerment;** encirclement, envelopment; blockading, blockade; vertical envelopment; pincer movement

6 **storm,** storming, taking by
storm, overrunning

7 **bombardment, bombing, air
bombing;** strafing

8 **gunfire, fire, firing, shooting,**
fireworks *or* gunplay <both non-
formal>; gunfight, shoot-out;
firepower, offensive capacity

9 **volley, salvo,** burst, spray, **fusillade, cannonade,** cannonry,
broadside, enfilade; **barrage, artillery barrage**

10 **stabbing,** piercing; **knifing,** bay-
oneting; the sword; **impalement,
transfixion**

11 **stoning,** lapidation

12 **assailant,** assailer, **attacker;** as-
saulter, mugger <nonformal>;
aggressor; invader, raider

13 **zero hour,** H hour; D-day, target
day

VERBS 14 **attack, assault, assail,**
harry, assume *or* take the offensive; **strike, hit, pound;** go at,
come at, have at, **launch out
against;** fall on *or* upon, set on
or **upon, descend on** *or* upon,
come down on, swoop down on;
pounce upon; **lift** *or* **raise** *or* **lift a
hand against,** take up arms *or*
the cudgels against; **lay hands
on,** lay a hand on, bloody one's
hands with; gang up on; surprise,
ambush; blitz

15 <nonformal terms> **pitch into,
light into, lambaste,** pile into,
sail into, wade into, lay into, plow
into, tie into, rip into; **let one
have it,** let one have it with both
barrels; **land on,** land on like a
ton of bricks, climb all over, crack
down on, lower the boom on, tee
off on; **mug,** jump, bushwhack,
sandbag; **go for, go at;** blindside,
sucker-punch; **take a swing** *or*
crack *or* **swipe** *or* **poke** *or* punch
or **shot at**

16 **lash out at, strike out at,** let fly
at, strike out at; **strike at,** hit at,
poke at, thrust at, **swing at,**
swing on, make a thrust *or* pass
at, lunge at, flail at, flail away at,
take a fling at; cut and thrust;
feint

17 **launch an attack,** mount an attack, **push, thrust,** mount *or*
open an offensive, **drive; advance against** *or* **upon, march
upon** *or* against, bear down
upon; **infiltrate; strike;** flank;
press the attack, follow up the attack; **counterattack**

18 **charge,** rush, **rush at, fly at,**

make a dash *or* rush at; go full tilt at, ride full tilt against; **jump off,** go over the top <nonformal>

19 **besiege, lay siege to,** encompass, surround, **encircle,** envelope, invest, set upon on all sides, close the jaws of the pincers *or* trap; **blockade; beset, beleaguer, harry, harass,** press one hard; soften up

20 **raid,** foray, make a raid; **invade,** make an inroad; escalade, scale, scale the walls, board; storm, take by storm, overwhelm, inundate

21 **pull a gun on,** draw a gun on; **get the drop on** *and* **beat to the draw** <both nonformal>

22 **pull the trigger, fire upon,** fire at, **shoot at,** take a pop at <nonformal>, take *or* fire a shot at, blaze away at <nonformal>; **open fire,** commence firing, open up on <nonformal>; aim at, take aim at, zero in on, take dead aim at, draw a bead on; **snipe,** snipe at; **bombard, blast, strafe, shell,** cannonade, mortar, barrage, blitz; pepper, fusillade, fire a volley; rake, enfilade; **torpedo; shoot**

23 **bomb,** drop a bomb, lay an egg <nonformal>; dive-bomb, glide-bomb, skip-bomb, pattern-bomb

24 **mine,** plant a mine, trigger a mine

25 **stab, stick** <nonformal>, **pierce,** plunge in; **run through, impale,** spit, **transfix; spear,** lance, bayonet, saber, sword, put to the sword; **knife,** dagger, stiletto

26 **gore,** horn, tusk

27 **pelt, stone,** pellet; brickbat *or* egg <both nonformal>

28 **hurl at, throw at, cast at,** heave at, chuck at <nonformal>, fling at, toss at, fire at, let fly at; hurl against

ADJS 29 **attacking,** assailing, assaulting, charging, thrusting, advancing; **invading,** invasive, incursive

30 **offensive, combative,** on the offensive *or* attack; **aggressive**

ADVS 31 **under attack, under fire;** under siege

460 DEFENSE

NOUNS 1 **defense, guard,** ward; **protection** 1007; self-defense, self-protection, self-preservation; the defensive; covering one's ass *or* rear-end <nonformal>; defenses, psychological defenses; bunker atmosphere *or* mentality

2 **military defense, national defense,** defense capability; **civil defense;** radar defenses, distant early warning *or* DEW Line; antimissile, antiballistic-missile system *or* ABM; strategic defense initiative *or* Star Wars

3 **armor;** armor plate; panoply, harness; **mail,** chain mail, chain armor; bulletproof vest; **battle-gear; protective covering, thick skin,** carapace, shell 295.15; spines, needles

4 **fortification,** work, defense work, **bulwark, rampart, fence, barrier** 1011.5; **enclosure** 212.3

5 **entrenchment, trench,** ditch; **moat; dugout; bunker; foxhole;** tunnel, fortified tunnel; undermining, sap; mine

6 **stronghold,** hold, safehold, fasthold, strong point, **fastness,** keep, ward; **bastion, citadel, castle,** tower, tower of strength, strong point; **fort, fortress,** post; **bunker, pillbox,** blockhouse, barricades; acropolis; martello tower, martello; **bridgehead, beachhead**

7 **defender, champion, advocate; upholder; guardian angel, supporter** 616.9; vindicator, apologist; **protector** 1007.5; **guard** 1007.9; paladin

VERBS 8 **defend, guard, shield,** screen, secure, guard against; defend tooth and nail *or* to the death *or* to the last breath; **safeguard, protect** 1007.18; stand by the side of; **advocate, champion** 600.10; **defend oneself,** cover one's ass *or* rear-end <nonformal>, CYA *or* cover your ass <nonformal>

9 **fortify; arm; armor,** armor-plate; **man;** garrison, man the trenches *or* barricades; **barricade, blockade;** bulwark, wall, palisade, fence; entrench, **dig in;** mine

10 **fend off, ward off, stave off, hold off, fight off,** beat off, parry, fend, counter; **hold** *or* **keep at bay; hold the fort, hold the line,** stop, check, block, hinder, obstruct; **repel, repulse, rebuff, drive back,** push back; go on the defensive, fight a holding *or* delaying action

ADJS 11 **defensive, guarding,** screening; **protective** 1007.23

12 **fortified;** castellated, crenellated

13 **armored,** armor-plated; panoplied, in harness; mailed, ironclad

14 **armed,** heeled *and* carrying *and* gun-toting <all nonformal>; **in arms,** bearing *or* wearing *or* carrying arms, under arms; **well-armed, armed to the teeth; garrisoned,** manned

15 **defensible, defendable, tenable**

ADVS 16 **defensively, in defense,** in self-defense; **on the defensive;** with one's back to the wall

461 COMBATANT

NOUNS 1 **combatant, fighter, battler,** scrapper <nonformal>; **contestant, contender, competitor, rival;** disputant, wrangler, squabbler; tussler, scuffler; brawler, rioter; feuder; **belligerent,** militant; gladiator; jouster, tilter; **knight;** swordsman, blade, sword; **tough,** rowdy, **ruffian,** thug, **hoodlum, hood** <nonformal>, hooligan, streetfighter, bully; gorilla *and* goon *and* plug-ugly <all nonformal>; hatchet man *and* enforcer <both nonformal>, strong-arm man

2 **boxer, pugilist,** pug *or* palooka <both nonformal>; **street fighter,** scrapper, pit bull

3 **wrestler,** rassler *and* grunt-and-groaner <both nonformal>, grappler, scuffler, matman

4 **bullfighter,** toreador; banderillero, picador, matador

5 **militarist, warmonger,** war hawk, **hawk** <nonformal>; **chauvinist, jingo,** jingoist

6 **military man** *or* **woman, serviceman, servicewoman; soldier, warrior,** brave, fighting man, legionary, hoplite, **man-at-arms; cannon fodder;**

7 <common soldiers> GI, GI Joe, dough *and* John Dogface <both nonformal>, doughboy, Yank; Tommy Atkins *or* Tommy *or* Johnny <all Brit>; redcoat; poilu <Fr>; Aussie, digger <both Australian>; jock <Scots>; Fritz, Heinie, Hun, Kraut <German soldier>; Janissary <Turkish soldier>; sepoy <India>; askari <Africa>

8 **enlisted man,** noncommissioned officer 575.19; **common soldier, private,** buck private <nonformal>; private first class *or* pfc

9 **infantryman, foot soldier; rifleman; sharpshooter; sniper**

10 <nonformal terms> **grunt, dogface,** footslogger, paddlefoot, doughfoot, blisterfoot, crunchie, line doggie, groundpounder

11 **artilleryman, gunner; bomber,** bombardier

12 **cavalryman,** mounted infantryman, **trooper**

13 **tanker,** tank corpsman, tank crewman

14 **engineer,** combat engineer, pioneer, Seabee; sapper, sapper and miner

15 **elite troops,** special troops, shock troops, storm troops, elite corps; rapid deployment force *or* RDF; commandos, rangers, Special Forces, Green Berets, marines, paratroops

16 **irregular,** casual; **guerrilla,** partisan; **bushfighter,** bushwhacker <nonformal>; underground, resistance, maquis; underground *or* resistance fighter

17 **mercenary, hireling,** free lance, **soldier of fortune,** adventurer;

gunman, gun, hired gun, hired killer, professional killer

18 **recruit, rookie** <nonformal>, **conscript, draftee, inductee, selectee, enlistee,** boot <nonformal>; **raw recruit,** tenderfoot; awkward squad <nonformal>

19 **veteran, vet** <nonformal>, campaigner, old campaigner, old soldier, war-horse <nonformal>

20 **defense forces, services, the service, armed forces, armed services,** fighting machine; **the military,** the military establishment

21 **branch, branch of the service, corps; service, arm of the service**

22 <military units> **unit, organization, outfit** <nonformal>; **army,** corps, **division; regiment, battle group, company,** troop, brigade, legion, phalanx, cohort, **platoon,** section, **battery; combat team,** combat command; **task force; squad;** cadre

23 **army,** this man's army <nonformal>, **soldiery, forces, troops, host,** array, legions; ranks, rank and file; **standing army, regular army,** regulars, professional *or* career soldiers; the line, troops of the line; ground forces, ground troops; storm troops; **airborne troops,** paratroops; ski troops; mountain troops; occupation force

24 militia, organized militia, national militia

25 **reserves,** auxiliaries, **second line of defense,** army reserves

26 **volunteers, enlistees,** volunteer army, volunteer navy

27 **navy,** naval forces, **first line of defense; fleet,** flotilla, argosy, armada, squadron, escadrille, division, task force, task group; mosquito fleet; merchant marine, merchant navy, merchant fleet; naval reserve; coast guard

28 **marines,** sea soldiers, Marine Corps; **leathernecks** *and* devil dogs *and* gyrenes <all nonformal>

29 **air force,** air arm; strategic air

force, tactical air force; squadron, escadrille, flight, wing

30 **war-horse, charger,** courser, trooper

462 ARMS

NOUNS 1 **arms, weapons,** instruments of destruction, **military hardware,** matériel, **weaponry, armament, munitions, ordnance,** munitions of war; musketry; missilery; small arms; side arms; conventional weapons, nonnuclear weapons; **nuclear weapons,** atomic weapons, thermonuclear weapons, A-weapons; biological weapons; weapons of mass destruction; arms industry, arms maker, military-industrial complex

2 **armory, arsenal,** magazine, dump; ammunition depot, ammo dump <nonformal>; park, gun park, artillery park; atomic arsenal, thermonuclear arsenal

3 **ballistics, gunnery,** musketry, artillery; rocketry, missilery; archery

4 **fist, clenched fist; brass knuckles;** knucks *and* brass knucks <both nonformal>, knuckles, knuckle-dusters; **club,** blunt instrument

5 **sword, blade,** good *or* trusty sword; steel, **cold steel; knife; dagger; axe**

6 **arrow, shaft, dart, bolt;** quarrel; arrowhead, barb; flight, volley

7 **bow,** longbow; **bow and arrow;** crossbow

8 **spear,** throwing spear, javelin

9 **sling, slingshot;** throwing-stick, spear-thrower, atlatl; **catapult,** arbalest, trebuchet

10 **gun, firearm;** shooting iron *and* gat *and* rod *and* heater *and* piece <all nonformal>; stun gun; automatic, BB gun, Browning automatic rifle, burp gun <nonformal>, carbine, derringer, handgun, machine gun, musket, pistol, repeater, revolver, rifle, Saturday night special, sawed-off shotgun, shotgun, six-gun *or* six-shooter <nonformal>, sub-

machine gun, Thompson sub-
machine gun or tommy gun
<nonformal>, Uzi submachine
gun

11 artillery, cannon, ordnance, Big
Bertha, howitzer; field artillery;
heavy artillery; siege artillery;
breakthrough weapons; moun-
tain artillery, coast artillery, antiaircraft artillery, flak <nonfor-
mal>; battery

12 antiaircraft gun or AA gun, ack-
ack <nonformal>, pom-pom
<nonformal>

13 ammunition, ammo <nonfor-
mal>, **powder and shot**

14 explosive, high explosive; cellu-
lose nitrate, cordite, dynamite,
gelignite, guncotton, gunpowder,
nitroglycerin, plastic explosive or
plastique, powder, trinitrotoluene
or trinitrotoluol or TNT

15 fuse, detonator; cap, blasting
cap, percussion cap, mercury fulminate, fulminating mercury;
electric detonator or exploder;
detonating powder; **primer,**
priming; primacord

16 charge, load; blast; warhead,
payload

17 cartridge, shell; ball cartridge

18 missile, projectile, bolt; brickbat, stone, rock, Irish confetti
<nonformal>; boomerang; bola;
ballistic missile, cruise missile,
Exocet missile, surface-to-air
missile or SAM, surface-to-
surface missile, Tomahawk missile; **rocket** 1072.2-6,14; **torpedo**

19 shot; ball, cannonball; **bullet,**
slug, pellet; dumdum bullet, expanding bullet, explosive bullet,
manstopping bullet, manstopper,
copkiller or Teflon bullet <trade-
mark>; tracer bullet, tracer;
shell, high-explosive shell,
shrapnel

20 bomb, bombshell; antipersonnel
bomb, atomic bomb or atom
bomb or A-bomb, atomic warhead, blockbuster, depth charge
or depth bomb or ash can <non-
formal>, fire bomb or incendiary
bomb or incendiary, grenade,

hand grenade, hydrogen bomb or
H-bomb, letter bomb, Molotov
cocktail, napalm bomb, neutron
bomb, nuclear warhead, pipe
bomb, plastic or plastique bomb,
plutonium bomb, smart bomb,
stench or stink bomb, time bomb;
clean bomb, dirty bomb; **mine**

21 launcher, bazooka; rocket
launcher, grenade launcher,
hedgehog, **mortar**

463 ARENA

NOUNS **1 arena, scene of action,
site,** scene, setting, background,
field, ground, terrain, sphere,
place, locale, milieu, precinct,
purlieu; course, range; **theater,**
stage, stage set or setting, scenery; **platform; forum,** marketplace, public square; **amphitheater,** circus, **hippodrome,
coliseum,** colosseum, **stadium,
bowl; hall, auditorium;** gymnasium, gym <nonformal>; **lists,**
tiltyard, tilting ground; floor, **pit,**
cockpit; **ring,** prize ring, boxing
ring, canvas, wrestling ring, mat,
bull ring; parade ground; athletic
field, field, playing field; stamping
ground, turf, bailiwick 893.4

2 battlefield, battleground, battle site, **field, field of battle;** field
of slaughter, killing ground or
field, shambles; **battlefront, the
front,** front line, **line,** firing line,
line of battle; combat zone; **theater, theater of operations,**
theater of war; zone of communications; no-man's-land; demilitarized zone or DMZ; jump area or
zone, landing beach

3 campground, camp, encampment, bivouac

464 PEACE

NOUNS **1 peace; peacetime,** the
storm blown over; **harmony,** accord 455

**2 peacefulness, tranquillity, se-
renity, calmness, quiet,** peace
and quiet, quietude, quietness,
quiet life, restfulness; order, orderliness, law and order

3 peace of mind, peace of heart,

peace of soul *or* spirit, peace of God; ataraxia

4 **peaceableness, unpugnaciousness,** nonaggression; dovishness <nonformal>, **pacifism;** peaceful coexistence; **nonviolence;** meekness

5 **noncombatant,** nonbelligerent, nonresister; **civilian,** citizen

6 **pacifist,** peacenik <nonformal>, **peace lover, dove;** peacemaker, bridgebuilder; peacemonger; **conscientious objector**

VERBS 7 **keep the peace,** remain at peace, wage peace; forswear violence, beat one's swords into plowshares; pour oil on troubled waters; defuse

8 refuse to shed blood, keep one's sword in its sheath

ADJS 9 **pacific, peaceful, peaceable; tranquil, serene;** idyllic, pastoral; halcyon, soft, piping, **calm, quiet,** restful, **untroubled,** orderly, **at peace;** peacetime

10 **unbelligerent, unhostile, unpugnacious, uncontentious,** unmilitant, **nonaggressive,** noncombative, nonmilitant; noncombatant, civilian; **antiwar, pacific, peaceable,** peace-loving, dovish <nonformal>; meek, lamblike 433.15; **pacifistic,** pacifist; **nonviolent;** conciliatory 465.12

465 PACIFICATION

NOUNS 1 **pacification, peacemaking, conciliation, propitiation, placation, appeasement, mollification; calming, soothing;** détente, relaxation of tension, easing of relations; mediation 466; peace-keeping force

2 **peace offer,** parley; peace feelers; **peace offering,** propitiatory gift; **olive branch; white flag,** flag of truce; calumet, peace pipe, **pipe of peace;** hand of friendship, outstretched hand; **cooling off, cooling-off period**

3 **reconciliation,** *rapprochement* <Fr>, making up *and* kissing and making up <both nonformal>

4 **adjustment,** accommodation, resolution, compromise, arrangement, settlement, terms; consensus building, consensus seeking

5 **truce, armistice, peace; pacification,** treaty of peace, suspension of hostilities, **cease-fire,** stand-down, breathing spell, cooling-off period; temporary arrangement; hollow truce; demilitarized zone, buffer zone, neutral territory

6 **disarmament,** reduction of armaments; unilateral disarmament; **demilitarization,** deactivation, disbanding, disbandment, **demobilization,** mustering out, reconversion, decommissioning; civilian life

VERBS 7 **pacify, conciliate, placate, propitiate, appease, mollify; calm, settle, soothe,** tranquilize 670.7; smooth over *or* out, smooth one's feathers; allay; pour oil on troubled waters, take the edge off of, take the sting out of; cool <nonformal>, defuse; clear the air

8 **reconcile, bring to terms, bring together,** reunite, heal the breach; bring about a détente; **harmonize,** restore harmony; **iron** *or* **sort out,** adjust, settle, compose, accommodate, settle differences, resolve, compromise; **patch things up,** fix up <nonformal>, patch up a friendship *or* quarrel, smooth it over

9 **make peace,** cease hostilities, cease fire, stand down; **cool it** *and* **chill out** <both nonformal>, **bury the hatchet, smoke the pipe of peace;** negotiate a peace; make a peace offering, hold out the olive branch, hoist *or* show *or* wave the white flag

10 **make up** *and* **kiss and make up** *and* make it up <all nonformal>, **shake hands,** come round, come together, come to an understanding, **come to terms,** let bygones be bygones, forgive and forget, put it all behind one, settle *or* compose one's differences, meet halfway

11 **disarm,** lay down one's arms, turn in one's weapons, turn

swords into plowshares; **demilitarize,** deactivate, **demobilize, disband,** decommission

ADJS **12 pacific, conciliatory, propitiatory, placative,** placatory, mollifying, appeasing; **pacifying, soothing** 670.15, appeasable

13 pacifiable, placable, appeasable, propitiable

ADVS **14 pacifically, peaceably;** with no hard feelings

466 MEDIATION

NOUNS **1 mediation,** mediating, intermediation, **intercession; intervention,** interposition, stepping in, involvement; interventionism

2 arbitration, arbitrament, compulsory arbitration, binding arbitration; nonbinding arbitration

3 mediator, intermediator, intermediate, **intermediary; medium; intercessor,** interceder; ombudsman; **intervener,** intervenor; **go-between, middleman** 576.4; connection <nonfor­mal>; front *and* front man <both nonformal>; deputy, agent 576; **spokesman, spokeswoman,** spokesperson, spokespeople; **mouthpiece; negotiator**

4 arbitrator, arbiter, impartial arbitrator, third party, unbiased observer; **moderator; umpire, referee, judge;** magistrate 596.1

5 peacemaker, make-peace, reconciler; **pacifier; conciliator,** propitiator; **appeaser**

VERBS **6 mediate,** intermediate, **intercede,** go between; **intervene,** interpose, step in, involve oneself, use one's good offices; butt in *and* put one's nose in <both nonformal>; represent 576.14; **negotiate,** bargain, **treat with,** make terms, meet halfway; **arbitrate,** moderate; **umpire, referee,** judge

7 settle, arrange, compose, patch up, adjust, straighten out; make peace 465.9

ADJS **8 mediatory,** mediating,

going *or* coming between; intermediary, intermediate, **middle,** intervening, interlocutory; **intercessory,** intercessional

467 NEUTRALITY

NOUNS **1 neutrality, neutralism;** noncommitment, noninvolvement; **independence, nonpartisanism, unalignment, nonalignment;** fence-sitting *or* -straddling; **evasion, cop-out** <nonformal>, abstention; **impartiality** 649.4

2 indifference; passiveness 329.1; apathy 94.4

3 middle course *or* **way; middle ground,** neutral ground *or* territory, center; meeting ground, interface; gray area, penumbra; **middle of the road,** sitting on *or* straddling the fence <nonfor­mal>; medium, **happy medium;** mean, **golden mean;** moderation, moderateness 670.1; compromise 468

4 neutral, neuter; **independent, nonpartisan;** fence-sitter *or* -straddler; unaligned *or* nonaligned nation, third force

VERBS **5 remain neutral,** hold no brief, **keep in the middle of the road, straddle** *or* **sit on the fence** *and* sit out *and* sit on the sidelines <all nonformal>; **evade,** evade the issue, duck the issue *and* waffle *and* **cop out** <all non­formal>, abstain

6 steer a middle course, hold *or* keep a middle course, strike *or* preserve a balance, **strike** *or* **keep a happy medium,** steer between *or* avoid Scylla and Charybdis

ADJS **7 neutral,** neuter; noncommitted, uncommitted, noninvolved, uninvolved; **indifferent;** passive 329.6; apathetic 94.13; neither one thing nor the other; even, half-and-half, fifty-fifty <nonformal>; **on the fence** *or* **sidelines** <nonformal>, **in the middle of the road,** centrist, moderate, midway; **independent, nonpartisan; unaligned,**

nonaligned, third-force; **impartial** 649.10

468 COMPROMISE
<mutual concession>

NOUNS **1 compromise,** adjustment, accommodation, settlement, give-and-take; bargain, deal <nonformal>, arrangement, understanding; **concession,** giving way, yielding; surrender, cop-out <nonformal>

VERBS **2 compromise,** reach a compromise, compose, accommodate, adjust, settle, make an adjustment *or* arrangement, **make a deal** <nonformal>, come to an understanding, strike a bargain, do something mutually beneficial; plea-bargain; strike a balance, **meet halfway,** split the difference, give and take; steer a middle course 467.6; **make concessions,** give way, yield, wimp *or* chicken out <nonformal>; **surrender** 433.8, sidestep, duck responsibility *and* cop out *and* punt <all nonformal>

469 POSSESSION

NOUNS **1 possession,** possessing; **owning,** having title to; nine points of the law, *de facto* possession, *de jure* possession, lawful *or* legal possession; property rights, proprietary rights; **title;** squatting, **squatter's right; claim, legal claim,** lien; **occupancy,** occupation; **hold, holding, tenure; tenancy, lease,** leasehold, sublease; freehold, alodium; dependency, colony, mandate; preoccupation, preoccupancy; bird in hand; **property** 471

2 ownership, title, proprietorship, proprietary, **property right** *or* rights; **dominion, sovereignty** 417.5; landholding, land tenure

3 monopoly, monopolization; **corner** *and* cornering *and* a corner on <all nonformal>

VERBS **4 possess, have, hold,** have and hold, possess outright *or* free and clear, **occupy, fill, enjoy,** boast; be possessed of, have in hand, have in one's grip *or* grasp, have in one's possession; **command,** have at one's command *or* pleasure *or* disposition *or* disposal, have going for one <nonformal>; claim; **squat,** claim squatter's right

5 own, have title to, have for one's own *or* very own, have to one's name, call one's own

6 monopolize, hog *and* grab all of *and* gobble up <all nonformal>, take it all, have all to oneself, have exclusive possession of *or* exclusive rights to; tie up; **corner** *and* get a corner on *and* corner the market <all nonformal>

7 belong to, pertain to, appertain to; vest in

ADJS **8 possessed, owned,** held; in fee simple, **free and clear; own,** of one's own; **in one's possession, in hand,** in one's grip *or* grasp, at one's command *or* disposal; on hand, by one, in stock, in store

9 possessing, having, holding, having and holding, **occupying, owning; in possession of, possessed of,** master of; tenured; endowed with, blessed with; worth; propertied, property-owning, landed, landowning, landholding

10 possessive, possessory, **proprietary**

11 monopolistic, monopolist, monopolizing, hogging *or* hoggish <both nonformal>

ADVS **12 free and clear, outright;** bag and baggage

470 POSSESSOR

NOUNS **1 possessor, holder,** keeper, enjoyer

2 proprietor, proprietary, **owner;** titleholder, deedholder; proprietress; **master, mistress, lord; landlord, landlady;** lord of the manor; squire, country gentleman; householder; beneficiary

3 landowner, landholder, property owner, propertied *or* landed person, man of property, free-

holder; landed gentry, slum-
lord, rent gouger; absentee landlord

4 tenant, occupant, incumbent,
resident; lodger, roomer, paying
guest; **renter, lessee,** leaseholder;
squatter; homesteader

5 trustee, fiduciary; depository,
depositary

471 PROPERTY

NOUNS **1 property, properties,
possessions, holdings,** goods,
chattels, **effects,** what one can
call one's own, what one has to
one's name, all one owns *or* has,
one's all; household possessions
or effects, lares and penates; ac-
quisitions, receipts 627; **inheritance** 479.2

2 belongings, appurtenances,
trappings, paraphernalia, appointments, accessories, perquisites, appendages; **things,**
material things, mere things;
consumer goods; **personal effects**

**3 impedimenta, luggage, dun-
nage, baggage,** bag and baggage,
traps, apparatus, gear, outfit

4 estate, interest, equity, stake,
part, percentage; **right, title**
469.1, **claim,** holding; trust;
vested interest; easement; limitation; settlement

5 freehold, estate of freehold

6 real estate, realty, real property,
land, land and buildings; **land,
lands,** property, grounds, acres;
lot, lots, parcel, plot; manor

7 assets, means, resources, total
assets *or* resources; stock, stock-
in-trade; **worth,** net worth, what
one is worth; circumstances,
funds 728.14; wealth 618; **material assets,** tangible assets,
tangibles; intangible assets, in-
tangibles; current assets, fixed
assets, frozen assets, liquid assets, net assets; assessed valuation

ADJS **8 propertied,** proprietary;
landed

9 real; manorial; feudal

10 freehold, leasehold

472 ACQUISITION

NOUNS **1 acquisition,** getting, getting hold of <nonformal>, coming by, **attainment,** winning;
accession; addition 253; **procurement,** procurance; **earnings,**
making, pulling *or* dragging *or*
knocking down <nonformal>,
moneymaking, moneygrubbing

2 collection, gathering, gleaning,
bringing together, assembling,
putting *or* piecing together, **accumulation, amassment,** grubbing

3 gain, profit, percentage <non-
formal>, **take** *and* piece *and* slice
and rakeoff *and* skimmings <all
nonformal>; **gains, profits,
earnings, winnings, return, returns, proceeds, bottom line**
<nonformal>; **income** 624.4; **re-
ceipts** 627; **fruits,** pickings,
gleanings; **booty, spoils** 482.11;
pelf, lucre, filthy lucre; perquisite,
perk *or* perks; **pile** *and* bundle
and cleanup *and* killing *and* mint
<all nonformal>; net *or* neat
profit, clean *or* clear profit, net;
gross profit, gross; paper profits;
capital gains; interest, dividends;
hoard, store 386; wealth 618

4 profitableness, profitability,
remunerativeness, bang for the
buck <nonformal>

5 yield, output, production; **proceeds,** produce, product; **crop,
harvest,** fruit, vintage; bumper
crop

6 find, finding, **discovery; trove;**
treasure trove, buried treasure;
windfall, windfall profit, found
money, money in the bank, **bonus, gravy** <nonformal>

7 godsend, boon, blessing;
manna, manna from heaven,
loaves and fishes, gift from on
high

VERBS **8 acquire, get, gain, obtain, secure, procure; win,**
score; **earn,** make; **reap, harvest;**
take, capture; **net;** come *or*
enter into possession of, **come
into, come by,** come in for, be
seized of; draw, derive

9 <nonformal terms> **grab, latch**

or glom on to, corral, bag, get *or* lay hold of, rake in *or* up *or* off, skim *or* skim off, catch, collar, cop, dig up, grub up, round up, drum up, get hold of, get *or* lay one's hands *or* mitts on, get one's fingers *or* hands on, get one's hooks into, snag, snaffle, grub up, scratch together, hook, land, throw together, nab, pick up, nail, scare *or* scrape up; take home, pull *or* drag down

10 take possession, appropriate, take up, take over, move in *or* move in on <nonformal>, annex

11 collect, gather, glean, pick, pluck, cull, **take up,** pick up, get *or* gather in, bring *or* get together; scrape together; heap up, amass, assemble, accumulate 386.11

12 profit, make *or* **draw** *or* **realize** *or* **reap profit, come out ahead, make money;** rake it in *and* coin money *and* make a bundle *or* pile *or* killing *or* mint *and* clean up <all nonformal>; **capitalize on,** commercialize, make capital out of, **cash in on** *and* make a good thing of <both nonformal>, turn to profit *or* account, **realize on,** make money by, turn a penny *or* an honest penny; **gross, net; realize, clear;** kill two birds with one stone, turn to one's advantage; make a fast *or* quick buck <nonformal>

13 be profitable, pay, repay, pay off <nonformal>, yield a profit, be worthwhile *or* worth one's while, be a good investment

ADJS **14 obtainable, attainable, available,** accessible

15 acquisitive, acquiring; grasping, graspy, hoggy *and* grabby <both nonformal>; **greedy** 100.27

16 gainful, productive, **profitable, remunerative, remuneratory, lucrative,** fat, **paying,** well-paying, high-yield; advantageous, worthwhile; moneymaking, breadwinning

ADVS **17 profitably, gainfully,** remuneratively, lucratively, **at a profit,** in the black; to advantage, to profit, to the good

473 LOSS

NOUNS **1 loss, losing, privation,** getting away, losing hold of; **deprivation, bereavement,** taking away, stripping, dispossession, robbery; divestment, denudation; **sacrifice, forfeit, forfeiture,** giving up *or* over, denial; **expense, cost, debit;** detriment, injury, damage; **destruction, ruin,** perdition, total loss, dead loss; losing streak <nonformal>; **loser** 412.5

2 waste, wastage, **exhaustion, depletion,** sapping, depreciation, dissipation, diffusion, **wearing, wearing away, erosion,** leaching away; molting, shedding, casting *or* sloughing off; **using, using up, consumption, expenditure, drain;** stripping, clear-cutting; impoverishment, shrinkage; leakage, evaporation; decrement, decrease 252

3 losses, losings; red ink; net loss

VERBS **4 lose,** incur loss, **suffer loss,** undergo privation *or* deprivation, be bereaved *or* bereft of, meet with a loss; kiss good-bye <nonformal>; let slip through one's fingers; **forfeit,** default; **sacrifice; miss,** wander from; **mislay,** misplace; **lose everything,** go broke *and* lose one's shirt *and* take a bath *or* to the cleaners *and* tap out <all nonformal>

5 waste, deplete, depreciate, dissipate, wear away, erode, consume, drain, **shrink,** dribble away; **molt, shed,** cast *or* slough off; squander 486.3

6 go to waste, come to nothing, come to naught, go up in smoke *and* go down the drain <both nonformal>; go to pot <nonformal>, go to seed; dissipate, scatter to the winds

ADJS **7 lost, gone;** forfeit; by the board, out the window *and* down the drain *or* tube <all nonformal>; **nonrenewable;** wasted, consumed, depleted, dissipated, diffused, **expended; worn away, eroded,** used up, shrunken;

stripped, clear-cut; squandered 486.9; irretrievable 125.15

8 bereft, bereaved, divested, denuded, **deprived of,** shorn of, parted from, stripped of, robbed of; **out of,** wanting, lacking; cut off, cut off without a cent; out-of-pocket; **penniless, destitute, broke** *and* cleaned out *and* tapped out *and* wiped out <all nonformal>

ADVS **9 at a loss, unprofitably**; in the red <nonformal>

474 RETENTION

NOUNS **1 retention, keeping, holding, maintenance, preservation;** keeping *or* holding in, **bottling** *or* corking up <nonformal>, locking in, suppression, repression, inhibition; **tenacity** 802.3

2 hold, purchase, grasp, grip, clutch, clamp, clinch, clench; cling, clinging; toehold, foothold, footing; **clasp, hug, embrace,** bear hug; firm hold, tight grip, iron grip, death grip

3 <wrestling holds> half nelson, full nelson, stranglehold, toehold, hammerlock, headlock, scissors, bear hug

4 clutches, claws, talons; nails, fingernails; **pincers; tentacles; fingers,** digits, hooks <nonformal>; **hands,** paws *and* meathooks *and* mitts <all nonformal>; **jaws,** mandibles; **teeth,** fangs

VERBS **5 retain, keep, save,** save up, pocket <nonformal>; **maintain, preserve;** keep *or* hold in, **bottle** *or* cork up <both nonformal>, suppress, repress, inhibit, keep to oneself; persist in

6 hold, grip, grasp, clutch, clip, **clinch, clench; clasp, hug, embrace; cling, cling to,** cleave to, stick to, adhere to; **hold on to,** hold fast *or* tight, hang on to, keep a firm hold upon; **hold on, hang on** <nonformal>, hang on for dear life; keep hold of; **seize** 480.14

7 hold, keep, harbor, have and hold, hold on to; **cherish,** fondle;

foster, nurture, nurse; embrace, hug, cling to

ADJS **8 retentive,** keeping, holding, gripping, grasping; **tenacious,** clinging; viselike; anal

9 prehensile, raptorial; fingered, digital; clawed, taloned, jawed, toothed, fanged

ADVS **10 for keeps** <nonformal>, **for good,** for good and all, for always

475 RELINQUISHMENT

NOUNS **1 relinquishment, release,** dispensation; **disposal,** disposition, riddance, getting rid of, dumping 390.3; **renunciation,** forgoing, forswearing, swearing off, abjuration, **abandonment** 370; retraction 363.3; **surrender,** turning over, **yielding;** sacrifice

2 waiver, quitclaim

VERBS **3 relinquish, give up, surrender, yield,** cede, hand *or* turn over; loose one's grip on; spare; resign, vacate; drop, **waive,** dispense with; **forgo,** get along without, abjure, **renounce,** swear off; walk away from, **abandon** 370.5; disgorge, throw up; have done with, wash one's hands of; **part with,** rid oneself of, get rid of, see the last of, dump 390.7; kiss goodbye *or* off <nonformal>; **sacrifice;** sell off

4 release, let go, let loose of, unhand, unclutch, unclasp, relax one's grip *or* hold

ADJS **5 relinquished,** released, disposed of; waived, dispensed with; abjured, **abandoned** 370.8; **surrendered,** ceded, yielded; sacrificed

476 PARTICIPATION

NOUNS **1 participation, partaking, sharing,** having a part *or* share *or* voice, contribution, association; **involvement,** engagement; complicity; **voting** 609.18; **suffrage** 609.17; **power-sharing**

2 communion, community, communal effort *or* enterprise, **cooperation; collectivity,** collectivism, collective farm, kibbutz, kolkhoz; **democracy**

3 communization, communalization, socialization

4 participator, participant, partaker, player, sharer; party, **a party to,** accomplice, accessory; partner

VERBS **5 participate, take part, partake, contribute,** involve *or* engage oneself; **have *or* take a hand in,** get in on, have a finger in the pie, have a part in, be an accessory to, be implicated in, be a party to, be a player in; **participate in,** partake of *or* in, **take part in,** take an active part in, **join, join in,** figure in, make oneself part of, play *or* perform a part in, play a role in, get in the act <nonformal>; **join up,** sign on, enlist; climb on the bandwagon; **have a voice in,** help decide, **vote,** be enfranchised; **enter into;** make the scene <nonformal>; sit in, sit on; pull an oar

6 share, share in, come in for a share, **go shares,** be partners in, have a stake in, have a percentage *or* piece of <nonformal>, **divide with, divvy up with** <nonformal>; **go fifty-fifty** *and* go even steven <all nonformal>, **share and share alike;** do one's share *or* part, pull one's weight; cooperate 450.3

7 communize, communalize, socialize, collectivize, nationalize

ADJS **8 participating, participative,** participant, participatory; involved, engaged, **in *or* in on** <nonformal>; implicated, accessory; **sharing**

9 communal, common, general, public, collective, popular, social, societal; **mutual,** reciprocal, associated, **joint, in common,** share and share alike; **cooperative** 450.5; power-sharing, profit-sharing

477 APPORTIONMENT

NOUNS **1 apportionment, apportioning, portioning, division, partition,** partitioning, parceling, budgeting, rationing, **dividing, sharing,** splitting, cutting, slicing, cutting the pie *and* divvying up <both nonformal>

2 distribution, dispersion, **disposal,** disposition; dole, passing around; **dispensation,** administration, issuance; disbursal, disbursement, paying out; redistribution

3 allotment, assignment, appointment, setting aside, **earmarking,** tagging; appropriation; **allocation;** misallocation

4 dedication, commitment, devotion, consecration

5 portion, share, interest, part, piece, bit, segment; **bite** *and* **cut** *and* **slice** *and* **chunk** *and* slice of the pie *or* melon *and* piece of the action <all nonformal>, **lot, allotment, proportion, percentage,** measure, quantum, **quota,** moiety, mess, helping; contingent; dividend; **commission,** rake-off <nonformal>; **lion's share,** bigger half; modicum; **allowance, ration, budget; load;** fate, destiny 963.2

VERBS **6 apportion, portion, parcel, partition, part, divide,** share; share with, cut *or* deal one in <nonformal>, share and share alike; divide with; divide into shares, **share out *or* around,** divide up, divvy *or* divvy up *or* out <nonformal>, **split,** split up, carve, cut, slice, carve up, slice up, cut up, cut *or* slice the pie *or* melon <nonformal>; divide *or* split fifty-fifty

7 proportion, proportionate, **prorate**

8 parcel out, portion out, measure out, spoon *or* ladle *or* dish out, **deal out, dole out, hand out,** give out, hand around, pass around; dole, deal; **distribute,** disperse; **dispense,** issue, administer; disburse, pay out

9 allot, assign, appoint, set; allocate, schedule; **set apart *or* aside, earmark,** tag, mark out for; set off, mark off; reserve, restrict to, restrict 210.5; **ordain, destine, fate**

10 **budget, ration;** allowance, put on an allowance

11 **dedicate, commit, devote, consecrate,** set apart

ADJS 12 **apportioned,** portioned out, parceled, allocated, etc; **apportionable,** allocable, appropriable, dispensable, severable

13 **proportionate,** proportional; prorated, *pro rata* <L>; half; fifty-fifty *or* even steven <all nonformal>, half-and-half, equal; **distributive; respective,** particular, per capita

ADVS 14 **proportionately, in proportion,** *pro rata* <L>; **distributively; respectively;** share and share alike, in equal shares; fifty-fifty *and* even steven <both nonformal>

478 GIVING

NOUNS 1 **giving, donation; endowment, presentation; award,** awarding; grant, granting; conferral; investiture; **delivery,** deliverance, surrender; **concession,** communication, impartment; **contribution,** subscription; tithing; accommodation, supplying, provision 385; **offer** 439; **liberality** 485

2 **commitment, consignment,** assignment, **delegation,** relegation, commendation, remanding, **entrustment**

3 **charity,** almsgiving; **philanthropy** 143.4

4 **gift, present,** presentation, **offering;** tribute, **award;** freebie *and* gimme <both nonformal>; peace offering

5 **gratuity, largess, bounty,** liberality; perquisite; consideration, **tip,** sweetener, inducement; **premium, bonus,** something extra, **gravy** <nonformal>, lagniappe; baker's dozen; honorarium; incentive pay; bribe 378.2

6 **donation; contribution, subscription; alms,** pittance, **charity, dole, handout** <nonfor-

mal>; **offering,** offertory, votive offering, collection; tithe

7 **benefit,** benefaction, benevolence, **blessing, favor, boon,** grace; manna, manna from heaven

8 **subsidy,** subvention, subsidization, support, tax benefit *or* write-off; **grant,** grant-in-aid, bounty; **allowance, stipend,** allotment; **aid,** assistance; **help;** scholarship, fellowship; honorarium; **welfare,** public assistance, relief, aid to dependent children; guaranteed annual income; alimony; annuity; pension, old-age insurance, retirement benefits; unemployment insurance

9 **endowment,** investment, **settlement,** foundation; **dowry; dower,** widow's dower

10 **bequest,** bequeathal, **legacy;** inheritance 479.2; **will, testament,** last will and testament

11 **giver, donor,** bestower, grantor, awarder, imparter; fairy godmother, sugar daddy <nonformal>; **contributor, subscriber,** supporter, backer, financer, angel <nonformal>; subsidizer; patron, patroness; tither; almsgiver; **philanthropist** 143.8

VERBS 12 **give, present, donate,** slip <nonformal>; **bestow, confer, award, allot, render,** bestow on; **grant,** accord, **allow,** vouchsafe, yield, afford, make available; **tender,** proffer, offer, extend, come up with <nonformal>; **issue, dispense,** administer; **distribute; give out, deal out, dole out, mete out, hand** or dish out <nonformal>, shell out <nonformal>; make a present of; **give generously,** give the shirt off one's back; be generous *or* liberal with, give freely; give in addition *or* as lagniappe, give into the bargain

13 **deliver, hand, pass,** reach, forward, render, put into the hands of; transfer; **hand over,** give over, fork over <nonformal>, **pass over, turn over,** come across with <nonformal>; hand out, give out,

pass out, distribute, circulate;
hand in, give in; **surrender,** resign

14 **contribute, subscribe, chip in**
and kick in *and* pony up *and* pay
up <all nonformal>, give one's
share *or* fair share; put oneself
down for, pledge; contribute to,
give to, **donate to;** put something
in the pot, sweeten the kitty

15 **furnish, supply, provide, afford,** provide for; **make available to,** put one in the way of;
heap upon, lavish upon

16 **commit, consign, assign, delegate,** relegate, confide, commend,
remit, remand; **entrust,** trust

17 **endow,** invest, vest; endow with,
favor with, bless with, grace with;
settle on *or* **upon; dower**

18 **bequeath, will,** will and bequeath, **leave, devise, will to,**
hand on, pass on, transmit; **make
a will**

19 **subsidize, finance,** bankroll
<nonformal>, fund; **aid, assist,
support, help,** pick up the check
or tab *and* spring for *and* pop for
<all nonformal>; pension, pen-
sion off

20 **thrust upon, force upon, press
upon,** push upon, ram *or* cram
down one's throat

21 **give away,** dispose of, part with,
sacrifice, spare

ADJS 22 philanthropic, eleemosynary, **charitable** 143.15; generous
to a fault, **generous** 485.4

23 **giveable,** presentable; bequeathable, devisable; fundable

24 **given,** allowed, accorded,
granted, vouchsafed, bestowed,
etc; gratuitous 634.5; God-given,
providential

25 donative, contributory; testate,
testamentary; intestate

26 **endowed,** invested; dower,
dowry, dotal; subsidiary, stipendiary, pensionary

ADVS 27 as a gift, gratis, on one, on
the house, free

479 RECEIVING

NOUNS 1 **receiving, reception, receipt, getting, taking;** acquisi-

tion 472; **assumption, acceptance;** admission; **reception** 187

2 **inheritance, heritage, patri-
mony, birthright, legacy,
bequest,** reversion; entail; **succession,** line of succession;
primogeniture; **heritable; heir-
loom**

3 **recipient, receiver,** taker, ac-
quirer, obtainer, procurer; payee;
addressee, consignee; trustee;
hearer, viewer, beholder, audience, listener, looker, spectator;
the receiving end

4 **beneficiary, donee, grantee;
assignee, assign; devisee,
legatee;** stipendiary; pensioner,
pensionary; annuitant

5 **heir,** inheritor; **heiress; heir apparent; heir presumptive;** legal
heir; **successor,** next in line

VERBS 6 **receive, get, gain, secure,** have, come by, be in receipt
of, be on the receiving end; **obtain, acquire** 472.8,9; **admit,
accept, take,** take off one's
hands; **take in** 187.10; assume,
take on, take over; **derive, draw,**
draw *or* derive from; have an income of, drag down *and* pull
down *and* rake in <all nonfor-
mal>, have coming in, take home

7 **inherit,** be heir to, **come into,**
come in for, come by, fall *or* step
into; step into the shoes of, succeed to

8 **be received, come in,** come to
hand, pass *or* fall into one's
hands; **accrue,** accrue to

ADJS 9 **receiving,** on the receiving
end; **receptive**

10 **received, accepted, admitted,
recognized, approved**

480 TAKING

NOUNS 1 **taking,** possession, taking possession, taking away;
claiming, staking one's claim; **acquisition** 472; **reception** 479.1;
theft 482

2 **seizure, seizing, grab,** grab-
bing, snatching; **kidnapping,
abduction,** forcible seizure;
power grab <nonformal>, coup,
coup d'état; hold 474.2; **catch,**

catching; **capture,** collaring
<nonformal>; **apprehension; arrest,** taking into custody; picking
up *and* taking in *and* running in
<all nonformal>; dragnet

3 **sexual possession**; sexual assault, ravishment, **rape,** violation, date rape *or* acquaintance
rape, serial rape *or* gang bang
<nonformal>; statutory rape;
deflowerment

4 **appropriation, taking over,
takeover** <nonformal>, **adoption, assumption, usurpation,**
arrogation; requisition; preoccupation, prepossession, preemption; **conquest,** occupation,
subjugation, enslavement, colonization

5 **attachment, annexation; confiscation,** sequestration; impoundment; **commandeering,
impressment;** expropriation,
collectivization; levy; garnishment; execution; eminent
domain, right of eminent domain

6 **deprivation, deprival,** privation, bereavement; relieving;
curtailment; disentitlement

7 **dispossession,** expropriation;
reclaiming, repossessing, **repossession,** foreclosure; **eviction** 908.2; **disinheritance,**
disownment

8 **extortion, shakedown** <nonformal>, **blackmail,** bloodsucking;
protection racket

9 **rapacity,** rapaciousness, ravenousness, **predaciousness**;
pillaging, looting

10 **take, catch, bag,** seizure, **haul;**
booty 482.11

11 **taker;** partaker; **catcher, captor,**
capturer

12 **extortionist,** extortioner, **blackmailer,** racketeer, shakedown
artist <nonformal>, **bloodsucker,** leech, **vampire; predator; vulture,** shark; profiteer

VERBS 13 **take,** possess, take possession; **get,** get into one's possession; pocket, palm; draw off,
drain off; skim *and* skim off *and*
take up front <all nonformal>;
claim, stake one's claim; partake;

acquire 472.8,9; **receive** 479.6;
steal 482.13

14 **seize,** take *or* get hold of, **lay
hold of,** catch *or* grab hold of,
glom *or* latch on to <nonformal>,
get *or* **lay hands on,** put one's
hands on; get one's fingers *or*
hands on; **grab, grasp, grip,
grapple, snatch,** snatch up, nail
<nonformal>, **clutch,** claw,
clinch, clench; **clasp, hug, embrace;** pillage, loot; take by
storm; **kidnap, abduct,** snatch
<nonformal>; shanghai; throttle

15 **possess sexually,** take; **rape,**
commit rape, commit date *or* acquaintance rape, ravish, violate,
assault sexually, have one's will
of; deflower

16 **seize on** *or* **upon,** fasten upon;
spring *or* pounce upon, jump
<nonformal>, swoop down upon;
catch at, snatch at, snap at,
scramble for

17 **catch, take,** catch flatfooted,
land *and* nail <both nonformal>,
hook, **snag, snare,** spear; ensnare, enmesh, entangle; tangle,
foul; **net,** mesh; **bag,** sack; **trap,**
entrap

18 **capture, apprehend, collar**
<nonformal>, run down, run to
earth, **nab** <nonformal>, grab
<nonformal>, take prisoner; **arrest,** place *or* put under arrest,
take into custody; pick up *or* take
in *or* run in <all nonformal>

19 **appropriate, adopt, assume,
usurp,** arrogate; requisition; **take
possession of,** arrogate to oneself, take up, **take over, help
oneself to,** dip one's hands into;
take all of, hog <nonformal>, monopolize, sit on; preoccupy,
prepossess, preempt; **conquer,**
overrun, occupy, subjugate, enslave, colonize

20 **attach, annex; confiscate,** sequester, sequestrate, impound;
commandeer, press, **impress;**
expropriate, nationalize, collectivize; exercise the right of
eminent domain; replevin; garnishee, garnish

21 **take from,** take away from, **de-**

prive of, do out of <nonformal>, relieve of, disburden of; **deprive, bereave, divest;** tap, milk, mine, drain, bleed, curtail; cut off

22 **wrest,** wring, wrench, **rend,** rip; **extort, exact,** squeeze, **shake down** <nonformal>, **blackmail,** play the badger game <nonformal>; **force from, wrest from, wrench from, wring from, tear from, rip from, rend from,** snatch from, pry loose from

23 **dispossess,** expropriate, foreclose; **evict** 908.15; **disinherit, disown,** cut out of one's will, **cut off,** cut off without a cent

24 **strip,** strip bare *or* clean, **fleece** <nonformal>, **shear,** denude, skin <nonformal>, flay, **despoil, divest,** pick clean, pick the bones of; **milk; bleed, bleed white;** exhaust, drain, suck dry; **impoverish,** beggar; clean out *and* take to the cleaners <both nonformal>; eat out of house and home

ADJS 25 **taking, catching;** confiscatory; **thievish** 482.21

26 **rapacious, ravenous,** ravening, vulturine; **wolfish,** lupine, predacious, **predatory,** raptorial; **bloodsucking,** parasitic; **extortionate; grasping,** grabby <nonformal>, **insatiable** 100.27

481 RESTITUTION

NOUNS 1 **restitution, restoration,** restoring, giving back, sending back, remitting, remission, **return;** extradition; repatriation; recommitment, remandment

2 **reparation, recompense,** paying back, squaring <nonformal>, repayment, reimbursement, refund, remuneration, **compensation, indemnification;** retribution, atonement, redress, satisfaction, **amends,** making good, **requital**

3 **recovery; retrieval; recuperation,** recoup, recoupment; **retake,** recapture; **repossession,** reoccupation, **reclamation,** reclaiming; **redemption,** ransom, salvage; replevin; **revival, restoration** 396

VERBS 4 **restore, return, give back,** restitute, hand back; take back, bring back; put the genie back into the bottle, put the toothpaste back into the tube; **remit;** repatriate; extradite; remand

5 **make restitution,** make reparation, **make amends,** make up for, atone, give satisfaction, redress, **recompense,** square <nonformal>, repay, reimburse, refund, remunerate, **compensate, requite,** indemnify, make up for; pay damages, pay reparations; pay conscience money

6 **recover, regain, retrieve,** recuperate, **recoup, get back; redeem,** ransom; **reclaim; repossess,** reoccupy; **retake,** recapture; replevin; revive, renovate, **restore** 396.11,15

ADJS 7 **restitutive, restorative;** compensatory, retributive; reversionary; redemptive

ADVS 8 **in restitution,** in reparation, in recompense, in compensation, in return for, in retribution, in requital, in atonement

482 THEFT

NOUNS 1 **theft, thievery, stealing,** thieving, **purloining;** swiping *and* lifting *and* snatching *and* snitching *and* pinching <all nonformal>; **appropriation,** liberation *and* annexation <both nonformal>; **pilfering,** pilferage, **filching,** scrounging <nonformal>; abstraction; shoplifting; poaching; **graft; embezzlement** 389.1; **fraud, swindle** 356.8

2 **larceny,** petit *or* petty larceny, grand larceny, aggravated larceny

3 **theft, robbery;** banditry, highway robbery; **armed robbery, holdup, mugging;** purse snatching; **pocket picking; hijacking;** cattle rustling; **extortion** 480.8

4 <nonformal terms> **heist, stickup,** job, stickup job, bag job, boost, burn, knockover, **ripoff**

5 **burglary,** burglarizing, housebreaking, **breaking and entering,** break-in, unlawful entry; second-story work <nonformal>

6 **plundering, pillaging, looting, sacking,** freebooting, ransacking, rifling, **despoliation,** despoilment; rapine, spoliation, depredation, **raiding,** ravaging, rape, ravishment; **pillage, plunder,** sack; banditry; **marauding,** foraging; raid, foray

7 **piracy, buccaneering, privateering, freebooting; air piracy,** airplane hijacking, skyjacking

8 **plagiarism,** plagiarizing, **piracy,** literary piracy, appropriation, cribbing; infringement of copyright

9 **abduction, kidnapping, snatching** <nonformal>; **shanghaiing,** impressment

10 **grave-robbing,** body-snatching <nonformal>

11 **booty,** spoil, **spoils, loot, swag** <nonformal>, ill-gotten gains, **plunder,** prize, haul, take, stolen goods, hot goods <nonformal>; **boodle** and squeeze and **graft** <all nonformal>; perquisite, pork barrel, public trough; public till

12 **thievishness,** taking ways <nonformal>, light fingers, sticky fingers; kleptomania

VERBS 13 **steal, thieve, purloin, appropriate, take,** snatch, palm, **make off with,** walk off with, run off or away with, have one's hand in the till; **pilfer, filch;** shoplift; poach; rustle; **embezzle** 389.4; defraud, swindle; **extort** 480.22

14 **rob,** commit robbery; pick pockets, jostle; hold up

15 **burglarize,** commit burglary; crack a safe

16 <nonformal terms> **swipe, pinch,** bag, **lift,** hook, crib, **cop,** nip, snitch, snare, boost, borrow, burn, clip, **rip off; heist, knock off** or **over; stick up; mug;** roll

17 **plunder, pillage, loot, sack,** ransack, rifle, spoil, spoliate, depredate, prey on or upon, **raid,** ravage, ravish, raven, sweep, gut; **fleece** 480.24; maraud, foray, forage

18 **pirate,** buccaneer, privateer, freeboot

19 **plagiarize, pirate,** borrow and crib <both nonformal>, appropriate; **pick one's brains**

20 **abduct,** spirit away, **carry off** or **away; kidnap,** snatch <nonformal>, hold for ransom; skyjack; **shanghai,** impress

ADJS 21 **thievish, thieving, larcenous, light-fingered, sticky-fingered;** kleptomaniacal; piratical; fraudulent

22 **plunderous, plundering, looting,** pillaging, ravaging, marauding; predatory, predacious

23 **stolen,** pilfered, purloined; pirated, plagiarized; hot <nonformal>

483 THIEF

NOUNS 1 **thief, robber,** purloiner, **crook** <nonformal>; larcenist; **pilferer, filcher;** sneak thief; prowler; snoplifter; poacher; **grafter;** jewel thief; **swindler,** con man 357.3,4; land-grabber; grave robber, body snatcher, ghoul; embezzler, white-collar thief

2 **pickpocket,** cutpurse, dip <nonformal>; **purse snatcher**

3 **burglar,** yegg and cracksman <both nonformal>; housebreaker, cat burglar, second-story worker; **safecracker,** safeblower; pete blower or pete man or peterman <all nonformal>

4 **bandit, brigand; gangster** and mobster <both nonformal>; racketeer; **thug, hoodlum** 593.4

5 **robber, holdup man** and stickup man <both nonformal>; highwayman, highway robber, footpad; **mugger** <nonformal>, sandbagger; train robber; bank robber, **hijacker** <nonformal>

6 **plunderer, pillager, looter, marauder,** rifler, sacker, spoiler, despoiler, **raider,** forager, ravisher, ravager

7 **pirate, corsair, buccaneer, privateer,** sea rover, rover, picaroon; viking, sea king; air pirate, airplane hijacker, skyjacker

8 cattle thief, rustler and **cattle rustler** <both nonformal>

9 **plagiarist,** plagiarizer, cribber <nonformal>, **pirate,** literary pirate

10 **abductor, kidnapper; shang-haier,** snatcher *and* baby-snatcher <both nonformal>

484 PARSIMONY

NOUNS 1 **parsimony,** parsi-moniousness; frugality 635.1; **stinting, pinching, scrimping,** skimping, cheeseparing

2 **niggardliness,** penuriousness, **meanness,** shabbiness, sordid-ness

3 **stinginess, ungenerosity, illib-erality, cheapness, chintziness** *and* tightness *and* narrowness <all nonformal>, closeness, closefistedness, tightfistedness, **miserliness,** penny-pinching, hoarding; **avarice** 100.8

4 **niggard, tightwad** *and* **cheap-skate** <both nonformal>, **miser,** hard man with a buck <nonfor-mal>, **skinflint,** scrooge, penny pincher, churl

VERBS 5 **stint, scrimp, skimp, scamp,** scant, **pinch,** starve; **pinch pennies,** rub the print off a dollar bill; live on nothing; grudge, begrudge

6 **withhold,** hold back, hold out on <nonformal>

ADJS 7 **parsimonious, sparing,** cheeseparing, **stinting, scamp-ing, scrimping,** skimping; frugal 635.6; penny-wise, penny-wise and pound-foolish

8 **niggardly,** niggard, pinchpenny, penurious, **grudging, mean,** mingy, shabby, sordid

9 **stingy, illiberal, ungenerous, chintzy, miserly, cheap** *and* **tight** *and* narrow <all nonfor-mal>, **near, close, closefisted,** tightfisted; pinching, **penny-pinching; avaricious** 100.27

ADVS 10 **parsimoniously,** stint-ingly, scrimpingly, skimp-ingly

11 **niggardly, stingily,** illiberally, ungenerously, tightfistedly; meanly

485 LIBERALITY

NOUNS 1 **liberality,** freeness; **gen-erosity,** generousness, **unselfish-ness, munificence,** largess; bountifulness, bounteousness, **bounty;** hospitality, welcome, graciousness; **openhandedness,** freehandedness, open *or* free hand; open-heartedness, big-heartedness; open heart, big *or* large *or* great heart, heart of gold; **magnanimity** 652.2

2 **cheerful giver,** free giver; Lady Bountiful

VERBS 3 **give freely,** give cheer-fully, give with an open hand, give with both hands, loosen *or* untie the purse strings; **spare no ex-pense,** spare nothing, let money be no object; **heap upon,** lavish upon, shower down upon; give the coat *or* shirt off one's back, **give until it hurts;** not hold back

ADJS 4 **liberal, free,** free with one's money, free-spending; **generous, munificent,** princely, handsome; **unselfish,** ungrudging; **unspar-ing, unstinting,** unstinted; **bountiful,** bounteous, **lavish,** profuse; hospitable, gracious; **openhanded,** freehanded; **giv-ing;** openhearted, **bighearted; magnanimous** 652.6

ADVS 5 **liberally, freely; gener-ously, munificently,** hand-somely; **unselfishly,** ungrudg-ingly; **unsparingly, unstintingly; bountifully,** bounteously, **lav-ishly,** profusely; hospitably, graciously; **openhandedly,** free-handedly; openheartedly, big-heartedly; with open hands, with both hands, without stint

486 PRODIGALITY

NOUNS 1 **prodigality, over-liberality,** overgenerousness; profligacy, **extravagance,** pound-foolishness, recklessness; inconti-nence, intemperance 669; lavish-ness, profuseness, profusion; **wastefulness, waste; dissipa-tion, squandering;** conspicuous consumption *or* waste

2 **prodigal, wastrel,** waster, **squanderer; spendthrift,** spender, big-time spender <nonformal>; prodigal son

VERBS 3 **squander, lavish,** slather, blow <nonformal>; **dissipate,** scatter to the winds; **run through,** go through; **throw away,** throw one's money away, throw money around, **spend money like water,** hang the expense, spend as if money grew on trees, spend money as if it were going out of style, throw money around, spend like a drunken sailor; gamble away; seize the day, live for the day, let tomorrow take care of itself

4 **waste, consume, spend, expend, use up, exhaust;** lose; spill, pour down the drain or rathole; cast pearls before swine, kill the goose that lays the golden egg, throw out the baby with the bath water

5 **fritter away,** fool away, fribble away, dribble away, drivel away, **trifle away,** piss away <nonformal>; diddle away <nonformal>; idle away, while away

6 **misspend, throw good money after bad,** throw out the baby with the bathwater

7 **overspend,** spend more than one has; overdraw one's account, live beyond one's means, have champagne tastes on a beer budget

ADJS 8 **prodigal, extravagant, lavish,** profuse, **overliberal,** overgenerous, overlavish, **spendthrift, wasteful,** profligate, dissipative; incontinent, intemperate 669.7; penny-wise and pound-foolish; easy come, easy go

9 **wasted, squandered, dissipated,** consumed, spent; **gone to waste;** down the drain or rathole <nonformal>; misspent

487 CELEBRATION

NOUNS 1 **celebration,** celebrating; **observance,** formal or solemn or ritual observance, **solemniza-**tion; **commemoration,** remembrance, memory; jubilee; red-letter day, **holiday** 20.4; anniversaries; **festivity** 743.3,4; **revel** 743.6; rejoicing 116; **ceremony,** rite 580.4; religious rites 701; ovation, triumph; **tribute;** testimonial banquet or dinner; toast; roast; **salute;** salvo; flourish of trumpets, fanfare

VERBS 2 **celebrate, observe, keep, mark, honor; commemorate,** memorialize; **solemnize,** hallow, mark with a red letter; jubilate; **make merry;** kill the fatted calf; sound a fanfare, beat the drum, fire a salute

ADJS 3 **celebrative,** celebratory, celebrating; **commemorative,** commemorating; memorial

ADVS 4 **in honor of, in commemoration of,** in memory or remembrance of, to the memory of

488 HUMOROUSNESS

NOUNS 1 **humorousness, funniness,** hilarity, hilariousness; wittiness 489.2; **drollness,** drollery; **whimsicalness; ludicrousness, ridiculousness, absurdity,** absurdness, eccentricity, incongruity, bizarreness; richness, pricelessness <nonformal>

2 **comicalness,** comicality; farcicalness, **farcicality,** slapstick quality, broadness

3 bathos; anticlimax, comedown

ADJS 4 **humorous, funny, amusing; witty** 489.15; **droll, whimsical,** quizzical; **laughable,** risible, good for a laugh; **ludicrous, ridiculous, hilarious, absurd,** quaint, eccentric, incongruous, bizarre

5 <nonformal terms> **funny haha,** priceless, too funny for words, rich, hysterical

6 **comic** or **comical; farcical,** slapstick, broad; **burlesque** 508.14; tragicomic

ADVS 7 **humorously, amusingly,** funnily, **laughably;** wittily 489.18; drolly, whimsically, quizzically; **comically,** farcically, broadly; **ludicrously,** ridiculously, **absurdly,** quaintly, eccentrically, incongruously, bizarrely

489 WIT, HUMOR

NOUNS **1 wit, humor,** pleasantry; Attic wit *or* salt; ready wit, quick wit, nimble wit; **comedy** 704.6; black humor, sick humor, gallows humor; **satire,** sarcasm, irony; **parody, lampoon,** travesty, **caricature, burlesque**; **farce**; **slapstick,** slapstick humor, broad humor

2 wittiness, humorousness 488, **funniness; facetiousness,** pleasantry, **jocularity,** jocosity; **joking,** japery, joshing <nonformal>; pungency, saltiness; keenwittedness, quick-wittedness, nimble-wittedness

3 drollery, drollness; **whimsicality,** whimsicalness, humorsomeness, antic wit

4 waggishness, waggery; roguishness 322.2; **playfulness,** sportiveness, **levity, frivolity,** flippancy, merriment 109.5; **prankishness**

5 buffoonery, clowning, harlequinade; **clownishness,** buffoonishness; **foolery, tomfoolery**; horseplay; shenanigans *and* monkey tricks *and* monkeyshines <all nonformal>; **banter** 490

6 joke, jest, gag *and* one-liner <both nonformal>, **wheeze,** jape; **fun, sport, play**; yarn, **funny story,** good story; dirty story *or* joke, blue story *or* joke; shaggy-dog story; sick joke <nonformal>; ethnic joke; belly laugh, rib tickler, sidesplitter, thigh-slapper, howler, wow, scream, riot, panic; visual joke, sight gag <nonformal>; **point,** punch line, gag line, tag line

7 witticism, pleasantry; crack *and* smart crack *and* **wisecrack** <all nonformal>; **quip,** conceit; **mot, bon mot,** one-liner *and* zinger <both nonformal>; epigram, aphorism, apothegm; flash of wit, scintillation; **sally,** flight of wit; **repartee,** retort, riposte, snappy comeback <nonformal>; quips and cranks; **gibe, dirty** *or* **nasty crack** <nonformal>; persiflage 490.1

8 wordplay, play on words, paronomasia; **pun,** punning; anagram, logogram, logogriph; acrostic, double acrostic; palindrome; spoonerism; malapropism

9 old joke, old wheeze *or* turkey, **trite joke**; **chestnut** *and* corn *and* **corny joke** *and* oldie <all nonformal>; twice-told tale, warmed-over cabbage <nonformal>

10 prank, trick, practical joke, antic, caper, frolic; **monkeyshines** *and* **shenanigans** <both nonformal>

11 sense of humor, risibility, funny bone

12 humorist, wit, funnyman, comic, life of the party; **joker,** jokester, gagman <nonformal>, **jester, quipster, wisecracker** *and* gagster <both nonformal>; wag; zany, madcap, cutup <nonformal>; **prankster; comedian,** stand-up comic *or* comedian, banana <nonformal>; **clown** 707.10; punster, punner; epigrammatist; satirist; burlesquer, caricaturist, parodist, lampooner; gag writer <nonformal>, jokesmith

VERBS **13 joke, jest, wisecrack** *and* crack wise <both nonformal>, **quip,** jape, josh <nonformal>, **kid** *or* **kid around** <both nonformal>; **make a funny** <nonformal>; **crack a joke,** get off a joke, tell a good story; pun, play on words; scintillate, sparkle; **make fun of,** gibe at, mock, scoff at, poke fun at, make the butt of one's humor, be merry with; ridicule 508.8

14 trick, play a practical joke, play tricks *or* pranks, **play a joke** *or* **trick on,** make merry with; **clown around**; pull one's leg <nonformal>

ADJS **15 witty, amusing; humorous** 488.4,5, **comic, comical,** farcical 488.6; **funny; jocular, joking, jesting, jocose, tongue-in-cheek; facetious,** joshing <nonformal>, **whimsical, droll**; smart, clever, brilliant, scintillating, sparkling, sprightly; keen, sharp, rapier-like, pungent, pointed, biting, mordant; satiric, **satirical, sarcastic, ironic**; salty, salt, Attic; **keen-witted, quick-witted, nimble-witted**

16 **clownish,** buffoonish

17 **waggish;** roguish 322.6; **playful, sportive; prankish,** pranksome; tricky

ADVS 18 **wittily, humorously; jocularly, jocosely; facetiously; whimsically, drolly**

19 **in fun, in sport, in play, in jest,** jokingly, jestingly, with tongue in cheek; for fun, for sport

490 BANTER

NOUNS 1 **banter, badinage, persiflage, pleasantry, fooling, fooling around, kidding** *and* **kidding around** <both nonformal>, **raillery, sport,** good-natured banter, harmless teasing; ridicule 508; exchange, give-and-take; **byplay**

2 **bantering, twitting, chaffing, joking, jesting,** japing, **fooling, teasing,** hazing

3 <nonformal terms> **kidding,** joshing, jiving, fooling around; **ribbing,** ragging, razzing, **roasting**

4 **banterer, chaffer, twitter; kidder** *and* josher <both nonformal>

VERBS 5 **banter, twit, chaff, joke, jest,** jape, **tease**

6 <nonformal terms> **kid,** jolly, josh, fool around, jive, rub, put on; **razz, roast,** ride, needle

ADJS 7 **bantering, chaffing, twitting; kidding** *and* **joshing etc** <all nonformal>, **fooling, teasing,** quizzical

491 COWARDICE

NOUNS 1 **cowardice, cowardliness; fear** 127; **faintheartedness,** chickenheartedness; **yellowness,** lily-liveredness <nonformal>, **weak-kneedness;** weakness, softness; unmanliness,

unmanfulness; timidness, **timidity,** timorousness

2 **uncourageousness, unvaliantness; plucklessness, spunklessness** *and* gritlessness *and* gutlessness <all nonformal>

3 **dastardliness, pusillanimity, poltroonery,** poltroonishness, baseness, **cravenness;** desertion under fire, bugout *and* skedaddling <both nonformal>

4 **cold feet** <nonformal>, weak knees, **faintheart,** chicken heart, **yellow streak** <nonformal>

5 **coward,** jellyfish, **weakling,** weak sister <nonformal>, milksop, milquetoast, mouse, **sissy, wimp** <nonformal>, baby, **big baby, chicken** <nonformal>; **yellow-belly** *and* lily-liver *and* chicken-liver <all nonformal>; fraid-cat *and* **fraidy-cat** *and* scaredy-cat <all nonformal>

6 **dastard, craven, poltroon,** recreant, arrant coward

VERBS 7 **dare not; have a yellow streak** <nonformal>, **have cold feet** <nonformal>

8 **lose one's nerve, get cold feet** <nonformal>; falter, funk <nonformal>, **chicken** <nonformal>; put one's tail between one's legs, back out, funk out <nonformal>, **wimp** *or* **chicken out** <both nonformal>; turn tail, bug out *and* skedaddle <both nonformal>, **run scared** <nonformal>, scuttle

9 **cower, quail, cringe, crouch, skulk, sneak, slink**

ADJS 10 **cowardly; afraid, fearful** 127.32,34; timid, timorous, overtimid, rabbity *and* mousy <both nonformal>; **fainthearted,** weak-hearted, chicken-hearted; lily-livered *and* chicken-livered *and* milk-livered <all nonformal>; **yellow** *and* yellow-bellied *and* with a yellow streak <all nonformal>; **weak-kneed, chicken** <nonformal>, afraid of one's shadow; weak, soft; **wimpy** *or* wimpish <nonformal>, unmanly, unmanful, sissified; milksoppish; panicky, panic-prone, funking *and* funky <both nonformal>;

daunted, dismayed, unmanned, cowed, intimidated

11 uncourageous, unvaliant, un-valorous, unheroic, ungallant, **unintrepid, undaring;** un-soldierly; **pluckless, spunkless** *and* gritless <both nonformal>, **gutless** <nonformal>

12 dastardly; hit-and-run; **pol-troonish; pusillanimous,** base, craven

13 cowering, quailing, cringing; skulking, sneaking, slinking, sneaky, slinky

ADVS **14 cravenly,** poltroonishly, **cowardly, uncourageously,** unvalorously, **unvaliantly,** ungallantly; plucklessly, spunk-lessly <nonformal>, spiritlessly, heartlessly; faintheartedly, chick-enheartedly; wimpishly

492 COURAGE

NOUNS **1 courage,** courageous-ness, **nerve,** pluck, **bravery,** brave-ness, ballsiness *and* gutsiness *or* guttiness <all nonformal>, **bold-ness, valor,** valorousness, val-iancy, **gallantry,** conspicuous gal-lantry, gallantry under fire *or* beyond the call of duty, gallant-ness, **intrepidity,** intrepidness, **prowess,** virtue; doughtiness, stalwartness, stoutness, stout-heartedness, lionheartedness; **heroism;** chivalry, chivalrous-ness; martial spirit, soldierly virtues; **manliness,** manfulness, **manhood,** virility, machismo; Dutch courage <nonformal>

2 valiance, greatheartedness; knightliness

3 fearlessness, dauntlessness, **un-dauntedness, unfearfulness,** unapprehensiveness; **confi-dence** 969.5

4 <nonformal terms> **balls, guts,** intestinal fortitude, spunk, brass balls, cojones, moxie, **backbone,** chutzpah

5 daring, derring-do, deeds of derring-do; **bravado,** bravura; **audacity,** audaciousness; **ven-turousness,** venturesomeness, risk-taking; **adventurousness,** adventuresomeness, enterprise; foolhardiness 493.3

6 fortitude, hardihood, hardi-ness; **pluckiness; spunkiness** *and* grittiness *and* nerviness <all nonformal>, mettlesomeness; **gameness,** gaminess; grit, **stamina,** toughness, **mettle, heart,** spirit, stout heart; **resolu-tion** 359, resoluteness, tenacity, pertinacity, bulldog courage

7 exploit, feat, deed, enterprise, achievement, adventure, bold stroke, heroic act *or* deed

8 <brave person> **hero, heroine;** brave, stalwart, gallant, valiant, man *or* woman of courage *or* met-tle, a man, good soldier; the brave; decorated hero; lion, **tiger,** bulldog

9 encouragement, heartening, inspiration, inspiriting, embold-ening, assurance, pat on the back

VERBS **10 dare, venture, make bold to,** make so bold as to, **have the nerve, have the guts** *or* the balls <nonformal>, have the courage of one's convictions, be a man

11 brave, face, confront, look one in the eye, say to one's face, **face up to, meet head-on** *or* boldly, stand up to *or* against, go eyeball-to-eyeball *or* one-on-one with <nonformal>; speak up, speak out, stand up and be counted; not flinch *or* shrink from, bite the bul-let <nonformal>, present a bold front; head into, face up, come to grips with, grapple with; face the music <nonformal>; **brazen,** brazen out *or* through; put one's head in the lion's mouth, fly into the face of danger, take the bull by the horns, go through fire and water, throw caution to the wind, run the gauntlet, take one's life in one's hands, put one's ass *or* life on the line <nonformal>

12 outbrave, outdare; outface, face down, face out; **outbrazen,** brazen out; **outstare,** stare down

13 steel oneself, get up nerve, nerve oneself, muster *or* summon up *or* gather courage, screw up

one's nerve *or* courage, stiffen
one's backbone <nonformal>

14 take courage, take heart, pluck
up courage; **brace** *or* **buck up**
<nonformal>

15 keep up one's courage, bear up,
keep one's chin up <nonformal>, **keep a stiff upper lip**
<nonformal>, take what comes;
hang in *or* hang in there *or* hang
tough *or* stick it out <all nonformal>, stick to one's guns

16 encourage, hearten, embolden, nerve, pat on the back,
assure, reassure, bolster, support, cheer on, root for; **inspire,**
inspirit; buck *or* brace up
<nonformal>; make a man of;
cheer 109.7

ADJS **17 courageous, plucky,
brave, bold, valiant, valorous,
gallant, intrepid,** doughty,
hardy, stalwart, stout, stout-
hearted, lionhearted, bold as a
lion; **heroic; chivalrous,** soldierly, soldierlike; **manly,** manful,
virile, macho

**18 resolute, tough, game; spir-
ited,** red-blooded, **mettlesome;**
tenacious, pertinacious

19 <nonformal terms> **ballsy,**
gutsy, gutty, stand-up, dead game,
gritty, spunky, nervy

**20 unafraid, unfearing, unfear-
ful; unapprehensive; confident**
969.21; **fearless, dauntless,**
dreadless; **unfrightened,** un-
scared, unterrified; **untimid,**
untimorous

21 undaunted, undismayed,
uncowed, unintimidated, unabashed, unawed; **unflinching,
unshrinking,** unquailing, un-
cringing, unwincing, unblinking

22 daring, audacious, overbold;
**adventurous, venturous, ven-
turesome,** adventuresome,
enterprising; foolhardy 493.9

ADVS **23 courageously, bravely,
boldly, heroically, valiantly,** val-
orously, **gallantly, intrepidly,**
doughtily, stoutly, stalwartly;
pluckily, spunkily <nonformal>,
gutsily <nonformal>, **resolutely,
gamely,** tenaciously, per-

tinaciously, bulldoggishly, **fear-
lessly; daringly,** audaciously;
chivalrously, knightly; like a man

493 RASHNESS

NOUNS **1 rashness, brashness,
incautiousness,** overboldness,
imprudence, indiscretion,
injudiciousness, improvidence;
unwariness, unchariness; overconfidence, overweeningness;
impudence, insolence 142; **gall**
and brass *and* cheek *and* chutzpah <all nonformal>; hubris;
temerity, temerariousness;
heroics

2 recklessness, devil-may-
careness; heedlessness, **carelessness** 340.2; **impetuousness**
365.2, impetuosity, hotheadedness; **haste** 401, **hastiness,**
overeagerness, overzealousness,
overenthusiasm; **furiousness,**
wantonness, wildness; **precipitateness**

3 foolhardiness, harebrained-
ness; **audacity,** audaciousness;
more guts than brains <nonfor-
mal>; forwardness, boldness,
presumption, presumptuousness; **daring,** daredeviltry, fire-
eating; playing with fire, flirting
with death, courting disaster,
stretching one's luck, going for
broke <nonformal>, brinkmanship; adventurousness

4 daredevil, madcap, wild man,
hellcat, harumscarum *and* fire-
eater <both nonformal>; **adventurer,** adventuress

VERBS **5** be rash, be reckless, sail
too near the wind, go out of one's
depth, take a leap in the dark, buy
a pig in a poke, count one's
chickens before they are hatched,
lean on a broken reed, put all
one's eggs in one basket; go out
on a limb <nonformal>, leave
oneself wide open <nonformal>,
drop one's guard, stick one's neck
out *and* ask for it <both nonfor-
mal>

6 court danger, go in harm's way,
tempt fate *or* **the gods** *or* **Providence,** play a desperate game,

ride for a fall; play with fire, flirt with death, stretch one's luck, put one's head in a lion's mouth, beard the lion in his den, play Russian roulette, working without a net; **risk all,** go for broke *and* shoot the works <both nonformal>

ADJS **7 rash, brash, incautious,** overbold, **imprudent, indiscreet,** injudicious, improvident; **unwary, unchary;** overcareless; overconfident, oversure, overweening, **impudent,** insolent, brazenfaced, brazen; hubristic; temerarious

8 reckless, devil-may-care; careless 340.11; **impetuous,** hotheaded; **hasty** 401.9, hurried, overeager, overzealous, overenthusiastic; **furious,** desperate, mad, wild, wanton; **headlong, breakneck;** slapdash

9 foolhardy, harebrained, madcap, **wild; audacious;** forward, bold, **presumptuous; daring,** daredevil, fire-eating, deathdefying; adventurous

ADVS **10 rashly, brashly, incautiously, imprudently, indiscreetly,** injudiciously, improvidently; **unwarily, uncharily;** overconfidently, overweeningly, **impudently,** insolently, **brazenly,** hubristically, temerariously

11 recklessly, happen what may; heedlessly, **carelessly** 340.18; **impetuously,** hotheadedly; **hastily,** hurriedly, overeagerly, overzealously, overenthusiastically; **furiously,** wildly, wantonly, **madly,** like mad *or* crazy *and* like there was no tomorrow <all nonformal>; **precipitately; headlong,** headfirst, **head over heels;** slapdash, slam-bang <nonformal>; helter-skelter

12 foolhardily, daringly, audaciously, presumptuously, harebrainedly

494 CAUTION

NOUNS **1 caution, cautiousness;** slowness to act *or* commit oneself

or make one's move; **care, heed, solicitude; carefulness, heedfulness,** mindfulness, thoroughness; paying mind *or* attention; **guardedness;** uncommunicativeness 344; **gingerliness, tentativeness,** hesitation, hesitancy, unprecipitateness; wait-and-see attitude *or* policy; **prudence, circumspection, discretion; coolness, judiciousness** 919.7; calculation, **deliberateness,** deliberation, prior consultation; **safeness,** safety first, no room for error; **hedge, hedging,** hedging one's bets, cutting one's losses

2 wariness, chariness, cageyness *and* **leeriness** <both nonformal>; **suspicion,** suspiciousness; **distrust,** distrustfulness, mistrust, mistrustfulness

3 precaution; forethought, foresight; providence, forearming; precautions, steps, measures; **safeguard,** protection 1007, preventive measure, safety net, safety valve; **insurance**

4 overcaution, overcautiousness, overcarefulness

VERBS **5 be cautious, be careful;** think twice, give it a second thought; make haste slowly, take it easy *or* slow <nonformal>; take one step at a time, go step by step, feel one's way; pussyfoot, tiptoe, walk on eggs *or* eggshells *or* thin ice; pull *or* draw in one's horns

6 take precautions, take steps *or* **measures; prepare** *or* **provide for** *or* **against,** forearm; **guard against, make sure against,** make sure; **play safe** <nonformal>, keep on the safe side; leave no stone unturned, overlook no possibility, leave no room *or* margin for error, leave nothing to chance, consider every angle; **look before one leaps;** see how the land lies *or* the wind blows, see how the cat jumps <nonformal>; clear the decks, batten down the hatches, have an anchor to windward; **hedge,** hedge

one's bets, cut one's losses; keep
something for a rainy day

7 beware, take care, have a care,
take heed; keep at a respectful
distance, keep out of harm's way;
mind, mind one's business; **be on
one's guard,** be on the watch *or*
lookout; **look out, watch out**
<nonformal>; **look sharp,** keep
one's eyes open, keep one's eye
peeled <nonformal>, **watch
one's step** <nonformal>, look
over one's shoulder; stop, look,
and listen; not stick one's neck
out <nonformal>, not go out on a
limb <nonformal>, not expose
oneself, **keep a low profile,** lie
low, stay in the background,
blend with the scenery; not blow
one's cover <nonformal>; hold
one's tongue 51.5

ADJS **8 cautious, careful,** heedful,
mindful, regardful, **thorough;
prudent, circumspect,** slow to
act *or* commit oneself *or* make
one's move, noncommittal, uncommitted; sly, crafty, scheming;
discreet, politic, judicious
919.19; unadventurous, unenterprising, undaring; **gingerly;
guarded,** on guard, on one's
guard; uncommunicative 344.8;
tentative, hesistant, unprecipi-
tate, cool; **deliberate;** safe, on the
safe side, leaving no stone unturned, overlooking no possibility, leaving no room *or* margin for
error

9 wary, chary, cagey <nonfor-
mal>, **leery** <nonformal>, **suspicious, distrustful,** shy

10 precautionary; preventive,
prophylactic; **forethoughtful,**
forethoughted, **foresighted;
provident**

11 overcautious, overcareful,
overwary

ADVS **12 cautiously, carefully,**
heedfully, mindfully; **prudently,
circumspectly, discreetly,** judiciously; **gingerly,** guardedly, with
caution, with care

13 warily, charily, cagily <nonfor-
mal>; **askance,** suspiciously,
distrustfully

495 FASTIDIOUSNESS

NOUNS **1 fastidiousness, particularity,** particularness; **scrupulousness,** scrupulosity;
punctiliousness, punctilio, spit
and polish; **meticulousness,
conscientiousness; taste** 496;
sensitivity, discrimination 943;
selectiveness, selectivity, picki-
ness <nonformal>, choosiness;
strictness 339.3, **perfectionism,
purism; puritanism, priggishness, prudishness, prissiness**
<nonformal>, propriety, strait-
lacedness

2 finicalness, finickiness, finical-
ity; **fussiness,** persnicketiness
<nonformal>; squeamishness,
queasiness

3 nicety, niceness, **delicacy,** deli-
cateness, daintiness, exquisiteness, fineness, refinement, **subtlety**

4 overfastidiousness, **overscrupulousness, overpartic-
ularity, overconscientious-
ness,** overmeticulousness; **over-
criticalness,** hairsplitting; overrefinement, oversubtlety; over-
squeamishness, oversensitivity,
hypersensitivity

5 exclusiveness, exclusivity, se-
lectness, selectiveness, selectivity;
cliquishness, clannishness;
snobbishness, snobbery, snobbism

6 perfectionist, stickler, nitpicker
<nonformal>, captious critic
945.7

7 fussbudget, fusspot <nonfor-
mal>, fuss, fusser, **fuddy-duddy**
<nonformal>

VERBS **8 be hard to please,** want
everything just so, **fuss,** fuss over;
pick and choose; **turn up one's
nose,** look down one's nose, disdain, scorn, spurn

ADJS **9 fastidious, particular,
scrupulous, meticulous, conscientious,** exacting, precise,
punctilious, spit-and-polish; **sensitive, discriminating** 943.7,
discriminative; **selective,** picky
<nonformal>, choosy; critical;

strict 339.12, perfectionistic, puristic; puritanic, puritanical,
priggish, prudish, prissy, proper,
strait-laced, censorious, judgmental

10 **finical, finicky,** finicking; **fussy,**
fuss-budgety <nonformal>;
squeamish, persnickety <nonfor-
mal>, difficult, hard to please

11 **nice, dainty, delicate,** fine, refined, exquisite, **subtle**

12 **overfastidious,** queasy, **over-
particular, overscrupulous,
overconscientious,** over-
meticulous, **overnice,** over-
precise; **overcritical,** hypercriti-
cal, ultracritical, hairsplitting;
overrefined; oversqueamish, over-
sensitive, hypersensitive; **compulsive**

13 **exclusive,** selective, **select,**
elect, elite; **cliquish,** clannish;
snobbish, snobby

ADVS 14 **fastidiously, particularly,
scrupulously, meticulously,
conscientiously,** critically, punctiliously; discriminatingly,
selectively; **finically,** finickily;
fussily; squeamishly, queasily

496 TASTE, TASTEFULNESS

NOUNS 1 **taste, good taste,** discernment *or* appreciation of excellence, preference for the best;
tastefulness, quality, excellence,
elegance, grace, gracefulness,
graciousness; **refinement,** finesse, **polish, culture, cultivation,** refined *or* cultivated *or* civilized taste; delicacy, daintiness,
**subtlety, sophistication; dis-
crimination** 943, fastidiousness
495; acquired taste

2 sound critical judgment, civi-
lizedness; niceness, nicety

3 **decorousness, decorum,** decency, propriety, **seemliness,**
fitness, appropriateness, suitability, meetness, felicity; gentility, genteelness; civility, urbanity 504.1

4 **restraint, understatement,** unobtrusiveness, quietness, quiet
taste; simplicity 499.1

5 **aesthetic** *or* **artistic taste,** virtu-

osity, **expertise**; dilettantism; epicurism, epicureanism; gastronomy; aesthetics

6 **aesthete,** person of taste, lover
of beauty

7 **connoisseur; judge, critic, expert,** authority, maven <nonfor-
mal>, arbiter, arbiter of taste,
tastemaker, trend-setter; **epicure,**
epicurean; **gourmet, gourmand,**
good *or* refined palate; virtuoso;
dilettante, amateur

ADJS 8 **tasteful, in good taste,** in
the best taste; excellent, of quality, of the best, of the first water;
aesthetic, artistic, pleasing, well-
chosen, choice; classic *or* classical, restrained, understated,
unobtrusive, quiet, subdued, simple, unaffected 499.7

9 **elegant,** graceful, gracile; **refined, polished, cultivated,**
civilized; **cultured;** delicate,
dainty, **subtle, sophisticated,
discriminating** 943.7, fastidious
495.9

10 **decorous,** decent, proper, right,
right-thinking, **seemly, becoming,** fitting, appropriate, suitable,
meet, happy, felicitous; genteel;
civil, urbane 504.14

ADVS 11 **tastefully, with taste,** in
good taste, in the best taste; elegantly, gracefully; decorously,
genteelly, properly, seemly, becomingly; quietly, unobtrusively;
simply 499.10

497 VULGARITY

NOUNS 1 **vulgarity,** vulgarness,
commonness; **inelegance** *or* inelegancy, **indelicacy, impropriety,
indecency, indecorum,** indecorousness, unseemliness, inappropriateness, unsuitable-
ness, unsuitability; **untasteful-
ness,** tastelessness, tackiness
<nonformal>; low *or* bad *or* poor
taste; vulgar taste, bourgeois
taste, philistinism; popular taste,
pop culture *and* pop <both non-
formal>; campiness, camp, high
or low camp; kitsch

2 **coarseness, grossness, rudeness, crudeness,** crudity,

crassness, **earthiness;** ribald-
ness, ribaldry; raunchiness
<nonformal>, **obscenity** 666.4;
loudness <nonformal>, **gaudiness** 501.3

3 **unrefinement, uncouthness,
uncultivation;** impoliteness, incivility; **barbarism,** barbarousness, barbarity, philistinism; **savagery; brutality,** brutishness,
bestiality, **mindlessness;**
troglodytism

4 **boorishness, churlishness,
loutishness,** cloddishness, yokelism; ruffianism, rowdyism, hooliganism

5 **commonness, commonplaceness; lowness, baseness,
meanness; ignobility,** plebeian-
ism

6 **vulgarian,** vulgar or ill-bred fellow, guttersnipe <nonformal>;
Babbitt, Philistine, bourgeois; upstart; cad, **boor,** churl, clown,
lout, yahoo, redneck <nonfor-
mal>, peasant, yokel; rough,
ruffian, roughneck <nonfor-
mal>, **rowdy,** hooligan

7 **barbarian, savage,** animal,
brute; troglodyte

8 **vulgarization,** coarsening; popu-
larization

VERBS 9 vulgarize, coarsen; popularize; **pander**

ADJS 10 **vulgar, inelegant, indelicate, indecorous, indecent, improper, unseemly,** unbecoming,
inappropriate, unsuitable, **ungenteel,** undignified; **untasteful,**
tasteless, in bad or poor taste,
tacky and chintzy and Mickey
Mouse <all nonformal>; **offensive**

11 **coarse, gross, rude, crude,**
crass, raw, rough, **earthy;** ribald;
obscene 666.9; meretricious,
loud <nonformal>, **gaudy** 501.20

12 **unrefined, unpolished, uncouth,** unkempt, uncombed;
**uncultivated, uncultured; un-
civilized;** impolite, uncivil, ill-
bred 505.6; **wild,** untamed; **barbarous,** barbaric, barbarian;
outlandish; primitive; **savage,
brutal,** brutish, bestial, animal,

mindless; troglodytic; wild-and-
woolly, rough-and-ready

13 **boorish, churlish, loutish,** redneck <nonformal>, cloddish,
clownish; rowdy, **rowdyish, ruffianly,** roughneck <nonformal>,
hooliganish, raffish

14 **common, commonplace, ordinary;** plebeian; homespun;
general, public, popular, pop
<nonformal>; vernacular; Phi-
listine, bourgeois; campy, kitschy

15 **low, base, mean, ignoble,** vile,
scurvy, sorry, scrubby, beggarly;
low-minded, base-minded

ADVS 16 **vulgarly, uncouthly, inelegantly,** indelicately, indecorously, indecently, improperly,
unseemly, untastefully, offensively; **coarsely, grossly, rudely,
crudely,** crassly, roughly; ribaldly

498 ORNAMENTATION

NOUNS 1 **ornamentation, ornament; decoration,** decor; **adornment, embellishment,** embroid-
ery, elaboration; garnish, garni-
ture; flourish; emblazonry; illumination; **color; arrangement;**
table setting or decoration; window dressing; **interior decoration** or decorating, interior design; **redecoration, refurbishment** 396.4

2 **ornateness, elegance, fanci-
ness, elaborateness;** ostentation 501; richness, luxuriousness,
luxuriance; **floweriness,** floridness; **gaudiness, flashiness**
501.3; flamboyance or flamboyancy, chi-chi; **overelegance,**
overornamentation; cluttered-
ness; baroqueness, baroque,
rococo, arabesque, chinoiserie

3 **finery,** frippery, gaudery, gaiety,
bravery, trumpery, folderol, trickery, trappings, festoons, superfluity; **frills,** bells and whistles
and gimmickry and Mickey
Mouse and glitz <all nonformal>,
frillery, frilliness; froufrou; gingerbread; **tinsel,** gilt, gilding

4 **trinket,** gewgaw, **knickknack** or
nicknack, **gimcrack, bauble,** bibelot, gaud; bric-a-brac

5 jewelry, bijouterie, ice <nonformal>; costume jewelry, glass, paste, junk jewelry <nonformal>

6 jewel, bijou, **gem,** stone; rhinestone; pin, brooch, stickpin; cufflink, tie clasp *or* clip; **ring,** band, wedding band, signet ring, school *or* class ring, earring, nose ring; bracelet, wristlet, wristband, armlet, anklet; chain, necklace; locket; beads, wampum; bangle; charm; fob; crown, coronet, diadem, tiara

7 motif, figure, detail; pattern, theme, design; **background,** setting, foil, **style,** ornamental *or* decorative style, national style, **period style**

VERBS **8 ornament, decorate, adorn, dress, trim, garnish,** array, **deck,** bedeck, bedizen; prettify, **beautify; redecorate,** refurbish, redo; gimmick *or* glitz <nonformal>; **embellish, furbish,** embroider, enrich, grace, set off *or* out, paint, color, blazon, emblazon; **dress up; spruce up** *and* gussy up *and* doll up *and* fix up <all nonformal>, **primp up,** prink up, trick up *or* out, deck out; primp, prink, prank, preen; smarten, smarten up, dandify

9 figure, filigree; **spangle, bespangle;** bead; tinsel; jewel; bejewel; ribbon; beribbon; flounce; flower, garland, wreathe; feather, plume; flag; illuminate; paint 35.13; engrave

ADJS **10 ornamental, decorative,** adorning, embellishing

11 ornamented, adorned, decorated, embellished, bedecked, decked out, tricked out, garnished, trimmed, bedizened; figured; flowered; festooned; wreathed; spangled, bespangled; jeweled, bejeweled; beaded; studded; plumed, feathered; beribboned

12 ornate, elegant, fancy, fine, chichi; picturesque; **elaborate,** overornamented, overornate, overelegant, etc, labored; **ostentatious** 501.18; **rich, luxurious,** luxuriant; **flowery,** florid; flamboyant, fussy, frilly, frilled, flouncy, gingerbread *or* gingerbready; **overelegant,** overelaborate, overwrought, overornamented, busy; cluttered; **baroque,** rococo, arabesque; gimmicked- *or* glitzed- *or* sexed-up <nonformal>

499 PLAINNESS
<unaffectedness>

NOUNS **1 plainness, simplicity** 797, **simpleness, ordinariness, commonness, commonplaceness,** prosaicness, prosiness, matter-of-factness; **purity,** chasteness, classic *or* classical purity

2 naturalness, inartificiality; **unaffectedness,** unassumingness, **unpretentiousness;** directness, straightforwardness; innocence, naiveté

3 unadornment, unembellishment, unornamentation; **no frills,** no nonsense, back-to-basics; **uncomplexity, unsophistication,** unadulteration; bareness, baldness, nakedness, nudity, undress

4 inornateness, unelaborateness, unfanciness, unfussiness; **austerity,** severity, starkness

VERBS **5 simplify** 797.4; chasten, restrain, purify; put in words of one syllable, spell out

ADJS **6 simple** 797.6, **plain, ordinary, nondescript, common, commonplace, prosaic,** prosy, **matter-of-fact, homely, homespun,** everyday, workaday, common- *or* garden-variety; pure, **pure and simple,** chaste

7 natural, native; **inartificial,** unartificial; **unaffected, unpretentious,** unpretending, unassuming, unfeigning, direct, straightforward, honest, candid; innocent, naive

8 unadorned, undecorated, unornamented, unembellished, unvarnished, untrimmed; back-to-basics, no-frills, no-nonsense; back-to-nature; **uncomplex,** uncomplicated, **unsophisticated,**

unadulterated; **undressed,** undecked, unarrayed; bare, bald, blank, naked, nude

9 **inornate,** unornate, **unelaborate,** unfancy, unfussy; austere, monkish, cloistral, severe, stark, Spartan

ADVS 10 **plainly, simply,** ordinarily, commonly, commonplacely, prosaically, matter-of-factly

11 **unaffectedly, naturally,** unpretentiously, unassumingly, directly, straightforwardly

500 AFFECTATION

NOUNS 1 **affectation, affectedness; pretension, pretense, airs,** putting on airs; **show, false show,** mere show; front, false front <nonformal>, **facade, image,** public image; **hypocrisy** 354.6; phoniness <nonformal>, sham 354.3; artificiality, unnaturalness; airs and graces; stylishness, mannerism

2 **mannerism, trick of behavior, quirk,** habit, peculiarity, idiosyncrasy, trademark

3 **posing, pose, posturing,** attitudinizing; peacockery, peacockishness

4 **foppery, foppishness, dandyism,** conceit

5 **overniceness,** overpreciseness, **overrefinement, elegance,** exquisiteness, preciousness, preciosity; purism, formalism, formality, pedantry, precisionism; euphuism; euphemism

6 **prudery, prudishness, prissiness, priggishness, primness, smugness, stuffiness** <nonformal>, **strait-lacedness,** stiffneckedness, hidebound, narrowness, sanctimony, sanctimoniousness, **puritanism,** puritanicalness; **false modesty,** overmodesty, demureness

7 **phony** and **fake** and **fraud** <all nonformal> 354.13; **pretender,** actor, playactor <nonformal>, performer; paper tiger, hollow man, man of straw, empty suit <nonformal>

8 **poser, poseur, posturer,** attitudinarian, attitudinizer

9 **dandy, fop,** coxcomb, macaroni, gallant, dude and swell and sport <all nonformal>, exquisite, blood, fine gentleman, puppy, jackanapes, clotheshorse, fashion plate; beau, Beau Brummel, spark, blade, ladies' man, ladykiller <nonformal>; man-about-town, boulevardier

10 **fine lady,** grande dame <Fr>; belle, toast

11 **prude, prig,** puritan, bluenose, goody-goody <nonformal>; Victorian

VERBS 12 **affect, assume, put on,** assume or put on airs, **pretend, simulate, counterfeit, sham, fake** <nonformal>, **feign,** make a show of, play, playact <nonformal>, act or play a part, put up a front <nonformal>, dramatize, lay it on thick <nonformal>, overact, ham and ham it up and emote <all nonformal>, tug at the heartstrings

13 **pose, posture, attitudinize,** peacock, strike a pose, strike an attitude, pose for effect

14 **mince,** mince it; **simper,** smirk, bridle

ADJS 15 **affected, pretentious,** la-di-da; **mannered; artificial, unnatural,** insincere; theatrical, stagy, histrionic; overdone, overacted, hammed up <nonformal>

16 **assumed, put-on, pretended,** simulated, **phony** and **fake** and **faked** <all nonformal>, feigned, counterfeited; spurious, sham; hypocritical

17 **foppish, dandified,** dandy, coxcombical, conceited

18 <affectedly nice> **overnice,** precious, exquisite, **overrefined, elegant,** mincing, simpering, namby-pamby; **goody-goody** <nonformal>; puristic, formalistic, pedantic, precisionistic, euphuistic, euphemistic

19 **prudish, priggish, prim, prissy, smug, stuffy** <nonformal>, **overmodest,** demure, **strait-laced,** stiff-necked, hide-bound, narrow,

censorious, sanctimonious, **puritanical,** Victorian

ADVS **20 affectedly, pretentiously;** elegantly, mincingly; for effect, for show

21 prudishly, priggishly, primly, smugly, strait-lacedly, stiffneckedly, puritanically

501 OSTENTATION

NOUNS **1 ostentation,** ostentatiousness; **pretentiousness, pretension, pretense;** loftiness

2 pretensions; airs, lofty airs, highfalutin *or* highfaluting ways <nonformal>, side, swank <nonformal>

3 showiness, flashiness, flamboyance, panache, dash, jazziness <nonformal>, glitter, glare, dazzle, dazzlingness; extravaganza; **gaudiness,** glitz *and* gimmickry *and* razzmatazz *and* razzledazzle <all nonformal>, **tawdriness,** meretriciousness; **garishness,** loudness <nonformal>, **blatancy,** shamelessness, brazenness, luridness, extravagance, sensationalism, obtrusiveness, vulgarness, crudeness

4 display, show, demonstration, manifestation, **exhibition, parade; pageantry,** pageant, **spectacle;** blazon, flourish, flaunt, flaunting; daring, éclat, bravura, flair; dash *and* splash *and* splurge <all nonformal>; **exhibitionism,** showing-off; theatrics, histrionics, dramatics, staginess; false front, **sham** 354.3

5 grandeur, grandness, grandiosity, **magnificence, splendor,** splendiferousness, resplendence, brilliance, glory; nobility, proudness, **state, stateliness, majesty;** impressiveness, imposingness; **sumptuousness, elegance, elaborateness, lavishness, luxuriousness;** ritziness *or* poshness *or* plushness *or* swankness *or* swankiness <all nonformal>; **luxury**

6 pomp, circumstance, pride, **state,** solemnity, formality; **pomp and circumstance;** heraldry

7 pompousness, pomposity, pontification, **stuffiness** <nonformal>, **self-importance,** inflation; grandiloquence, turgidity, orotundity

8 swagger, strut, swank <nonformal>, bounce; swaggering, strutting; swash, **swashbucklery;** peacockishness, peacockery

9 stuffed shirt <nonformal>; bloated aristocrat

10 strutter, swaggerer, swash, swasher, **swashbuckler,** peacock

11 show-off <nonformal>, **exhibitionist,** flaunter; **grandstander** *or* grandstand player *or* hot dog *or* **hotshot** *or* showboat <all nonformal>

VERBS **12 put** *or* **thrust oneself forward,** step to the front *or* fore, step into the limelight, take center stage, make oneself conspicuous

13 cut a dash, make a show, put on a show, cut a swath, **cut** *or* **make a figure;** make a splash *or* a splurge <nonformal>; **splurge** *and* splash <both nonformal>; shine, glitter, glare, dazzle

14 give oneself airs, put on airs, put on, put on the dog <nonformal>, put up a front <nonformal>, look big, **swank** <nonformal>; pontificate

15 strut, swagger, prance, stalk, peacock, swashbuckle

16 show off <nonformal>, **grandstand** *and* hotdog *and* showboat <all nonformal>, play to the gallery <nonformal>, please the crowd; parade one's wares <nonformal>, strut one's stuff <nonformal>, go through one's paces, show what one has

17 flaunt, vaunt, **parade, display, demonstrate,** manifest, make a great show of, **exhibit,** air, flash *and* sport <both nonformal>; advertise; **flourish,** brandish, wave; dangle before the eyes; emblazon, blazon forth; trumpet, trumpet forth

ADJS **18 ostentatious, preten-**

tious; **ambitious,** vaunting, **lofty, highfalutin** and highfaluting <both nonformal>, **high-flown,** high-flying; **high-toned,** tony <nonformal>, **fancy,** classy <nonformal>, flossy <nonformal>

19 **showy, flaunting, flashy,** snazzy, flashing, glittering, **jazzy** and **glitzy** and gimmicky and splashy and splurgy <all nonformal>; exhibitionistic, bravura; **gay,** jaunty, rakish, **dashing;** gallant, brave, daring; **sporty** or dressy <both nonformal>; **frilly, flouncy,** frothy, chichi

20 **gaudy, tawdry;** gorgeous, colorful; **garish, loud** <nonformal>, **blatant, flagrant,** shameless, **brazen,** lurid, extravagant, sensational, **spectacular,** glaring, flaring, flaunting, screaming <nonformal>, obtrusive, vulgar, crude; meretricious, tacky <nonformal>

21 **grandiose, grand, magnificent, splendid,** splendiferous, **glorious,** superb, fine, fancy, swell <nonformal>; **imposing, impressive,** larger-than-life, awe-inspiring, awesome; **noble, proud, stately, majestic,** princely; **sumptuous, elegant, elaborate, luxurious,** extravagant, deluxe; plush and posh and ritzy and swank and swanky <all nonformal>; palatial; barbaric

22 **pompous, stuffy** <nonformal>, **self-important,** pontifical; **inflated, swollen,** bloated, tumid, turgid, flatulent, gassy <nonformal>, stilted; grandiloquent, **bombastic** 545.9

23 **strutting, swaggering; swashbuckling;** peacockish, peacocky; too big for one's britches

24 **theatrical, theatric, stagy, dramatic, histrionic**

ADVS 25 **ostentatiously, pretentiously, loftily;** with flourish of trumpet, with flying colors

26 **showily, flauntingly,** flashily, with a flair, glitteringly; gaily, jauntily, **dashingly;** gallantly, bravely, daringly

27 **gaudily, tawdrily; garishly, blatantly, flagrantly,** shamelessly, **brazenly,** luridly, sensationally, **spectacularly,** glaringly, obtrusively

28 **grandiosely, grandly, magnificently, splendidly,** splendiferously; nobly, proudly, majestically; imposingly, impressively; **sumptuously, elegantly,** elaborately, luxuriously, **extravagantly;** palatially

29 **pompously, pontifically,** stuffily <nonformal>, **self-importantly;** stiltedly; **bombastically** 545.12

502 BOASTING

NOUNS 1 **boasting, bragging,** vaunting; **boastfulness, braggadocio; boast, brag,** vaunt; side, bombast, bravado, blowing-off or blowing or tooting one's own horn <all nonformal>; bluster, swagger 503.1; vanity, conceit 140.4; heroics

2 <nonformal terms> **big talk,** fine talk, fancy talk, tall talk, highfalutin or highfaluting, **hot air,** gas, bunk, bunkum, **bullshit;** tall story, fish story

3 **self-approbation,** self-praise, self-applause, self-vaunting, self-advertising, self-adulation, self-glorification, self-dramatization, self-promotion; **vainglory,** vaingloriousness

4 **crowing,** exultation, elation, triumph, jubilation; **gloating**

5 **braggart, boaster,** brag, braggadocio, hector, fanfaron; **blowhard** and big mouth and bullshit artist and hot-air artist and gasbag and windbag and big bag of wind <all nonformal>; blusterer 503.2

VERBS 6 **boast, brag,** vaunt, flourish, puff, advertise oneself, **blow one's own trumpet, toot one's own horn,** sing one's own praises; bluster, swagger 503.3

7 <nonformal terms> **blow,** blow off, mouth off, **blow hard, talk big,** blow off and toot or blow one's own horn, **bullshit,** shoot the shit, lay it on thick

8 flatter oneself, congratulate oneself, hug oneself, shake hands with oneself, **pat oneself on the back**; think one's shit doesn't stink <nonformal>

9 exult, triumph, glory, jubilate; **crow** *or* crow over, crow like a rooster *or* cock; **gloat,** gloat over

ADJS **10 boastful, boasting, braggart, bragging,** big-mouthed <nonformal>, vaunting, vaporing; vain, conceited 140.11; **vainglorious**

11 self-approving, self-praising, self-adulatory, self-glorifying, self-congratulatory, self-applauding, self-praising, self-advertising, self-promoting

12 inflated, swollen, windy *and* gassy <both nonformal>, **bombastic, high-flown, highfalutin** *and* highfaluting <both nonformal>, **pretentious,** extravagant

13 crowing, exultant, exulting, elated, jubilant, **triumphant, flushed; gloating**

ADVS **14 boastfully,** boastingly, braggingly, vauntingly; **self-approvingly,** self-praisingly, etc

15 exultantly, exultingly, elatedly, jubilantly, triumphantly, in triumph; **gloatingly**

503 BLUSTER

NOUNS **1 bluster,** blustering, hectoring, bullying, **swagger; bravado,** rant, rodomontade; fuss, bustle, fluster, flurry; bluff, bluster and bluff; intimidation 127.6; **boastfulness** 502.1

2 blusterer, swaggerer, swashbuckler, fanfaron, bravo, **bully,** bullyboy, cock of the walk; ranter, raver, hector; **braggart** 502.5

VERBS **3 bluster,** hector; **swagger,** swashbuckle; bully; bounce, vapor; roister; sputter, splutter; rant, rage, rave, rave on, storm; bluff, put up a bluff <nonformal>; intimidate; shoot off one's mouth, sound off, **brag** 502.6

ADJS **4 blustering,** blustery, blusterous, hectoring, **bullying, swaggering,** swashing, swashbuckling, boisterous, roisterous,

roistering, rollicking; ranting, raging, raving, storming; tumultuous; noisy

504 COURTESY

NOUNS **1 courtesy,** courteousness, common courtesy, **politeness, civility,** agreeableness, urbanity, comity, affability; **graciousness; thoughtfulness, considerateness** 143.3, **tactfulness,** tact, consideration, **solicitousness, solicitude; respect,** respectfulness, deference; civilization

2 gallantry, gallantness, **chivalry,** chivalrousness; courtliness, politeness

3 mannerliness, manners, good manners, excellent *or* exquisite manners, good *or* polite behavior; *savoir-faire* <Fr>; correctness, **etiquette** 580.3

4 good breeding, breeding; refinement, finish, polish, **culture, cultivation;** gentility, genteelness, elegance

5 suavity, suaveness, smoothness, smugness, blandness; **unctuousness,** oiliness, smarminess <nonformal>; **glibness,** slickness <nonformal>, fulsomeness; sweet talk, fair words, sweet *or* honeyed words *or* tongue, incense; soft soap *and* butter <both nonformal>

6 courtesy, civility, amenity, urbanity, attention, act of courtesy *or* politeness, graceful gesture; courtliness

7 amenities, courtesies, civilities, graces; formalities, ceremonies, rites, rituals, observances

8 regards, compliments, respects; best wishes, one's best, good wishes, best regards, kind *or* kindest regards, love; greetings 585.3; remembrances

9 gallant, cavalier, chevalier, **knight**

10 kind remembrances; compliments of the season

VERBS **11 mind one's manners,** mind one's P's and Q's <nonformal>; keep a civil tongue in one's head; observe etiquette, observe *or* follow protocol

12 extend courtesy, do the honors, pay one's respects, make one's compliments, pay attentions to, wait on *or* upon

13 give one's regards *or* **compliments** *or* love, give one's best regards, give one's best, send one's regards *or* compliments *or* love; wish one joy, wish one luck, bid Godspeed

ADJS **14 courteous, polite, civil, urbane, gracious,** graceful, agreeable, affable, fair; obliging, accommodating; **thoughtful, considerate,** tactful, solicitous; respectful, deferential, attentive

15 gallant, chivalrous; courtly; formal, ceremonious

16 mannerly, well-mannered, good-mannered, **well-behaved,** well- *or* fair-spoken; **correct**

17 well-bred, well-brought-up; cultivated, cultured, polished, refined, genteel

18 suave, smooth, smug, bland, **glib, unctuous,** oily, soapy *and* buttery <both nonformal>, fulsome, ingratiating, disarming; fine-spoken, fair-spoken, soft-spoken, smooth-tongued, honey-tongued

ADVS **19 courteously, politely, civilly,** urbanely, mannerly; **gallantly, chivalrously;** courtly; **graciously,** with a good grace; complacently; out of consideration *or* courtesy; obligingly, accommodatingly; respectfully, attentively, deferentially

505 DISCOURTESY

NOUNS **1 discourtesy,** discourteousness; **impoliteness,** unpoliteness; **rudeness, incivility,** inurbanity, **ungraciousness, ungallantness, unmannerliness, ill breeding,** conduct unbecoming a gentleman, caddishness; inconsiderateness, unsolicitude, tactlessness, **insensitivity; grossness, crassness,** gross *or* crass behavior, **boorishness, vulgarity,**

coarseness, crudeness, offensiveness, loutishness

2 disrespect, disrespectfulness 156.1; **insolence** 142

3 gruffness, brusqueness, curtness, shortness, sharpness, abruptness, bluntness, brashness; **harshness**; truculence, aggressiveness; **surliness,** crustiness, beastliness, churlishness

ADJS **4 discourteous,** uncourteous, **impolite,** unpolite; **rude, uncivil, ungracious, ungallant,** uncourtly, unaccommodating; disrespectful; **insolent**

5 unmannerly, unmannered, mannerless, **ill-mannered, ill-behaved**

6 ill-bred, ungenteel, caddish; **ungentlemanly; unladylike; vulgar, boorish, unrefined** 497.12, **inconsiderate, unsolicitous, tactless, insensitive; gross,** offensive, crass, **coarse, crude,** loutish

7 gruff, brusque, curt, short, sharp, snippy <nonformal>, abrupt, **blunt,** brash; **harsh;** truculent, aggressive; **surly,** crusty, beastly, churlish

ADVS **8 discourteously, impolitely, rudely,** uncivilly, ungraciously, ungallantly, caddishly; inconsiderately, unsolicitously, tactlessly, insensitively

9 gruffly, brusquely, curtly, shortly, sharply, snippily <nonformal>, abruptly, bluntly, brashly; harshly, crustily, churlishly, **boorishly,** nastily

506 RETALIATION

NOUNS **1 retaliation, reciprocation,** exchange, give-and-take; **retort, reply,** return, comeback <nonformal>; counterblow, recoil, boomerang, backlash

2 reprisal, requital, retribution; recompense, compensation 338, **reward,** comeuppance <nonformal>, desert, deserts, **just deserts,** what's coming to one *and* a dose of one's own medicine <both nonformal>; **revenge** 507; **punishment** 604

3 tit for tat, measure for measure, like for like, blow for blow, a game two can play, **an eye for an eye,** a tooth for a tooth, law of retaliation, *lex talionis* <L>

VERBS **4 retaliate, retort,** counter, **strike back,** hit back at <nonformal>, give in return; **reciprocate,** give and take; **get** *or* **come back at** <nonformal>, turn the tables upon

5 requite, make retribution, get satisfaction, recompense, make restitution, indemnify, reward, redress, make amends, **repay,** pay, **pay back; give one his comeuppance** <nonformal>, give one his desserts *or* just desserts, serve one right, give one what is coming to him <nonformal>

6 give in kind, match, give as good as one gets; repay in kind, **give one a dose of one's own medicine** <nonformal>; return the like, return the compliment; return like for like, **return evil for evil;** return blow for blow, **give one tit for tat,** give as good as one gets, give measure for measure, give *or* get an eye for an eye and a tooth for a tooth

7 get even with <nonformal>, even the score, **settle** *or* **settle up with, settle** *or* **square accounts** *and* settle the score *and* fix <all nonformal>, pay off old scores, pay back in full measure; fix one's wagon <nonformal>, **take revenge** 507.4; **punish** 604.10,11

ADJS **8 retaliatory,** retaliative; **retributive,** retributory; compensatory, reciprocal; punitive

ADVS **9 in retaliation, in exchange,** in reciprocation; **in return,** in reply; **in requital, in reprisal,** in retribution; **in revenge**

507 REVENGE

NOUNS **1 revenge, vengeance, avengement,** sweet revenge, getting even, evening of the score; **wrath; retaliation, reprisal** 506.2; vendetta, feud, blood feud

2 revengefulness, vengefulness, vindictiveness, rancor, irreconcilableness, implacability

3 avenger, vindicator; revanchist

VERBS **4 revenge, avenge, take** *or* **exact revenge,** have one's revenge; **retaliate, even the score, get even with** 506.4-7

5 harbor revenge; have accounts to settle; brood over; dwell on *or* upon, keep the wound open

6 reap *or* **suffer** *or* **incur vengeance** *or* revenge; sow the wind and reap the whirlwind

ADJS **7 revengeful, vengeful,** avenging; **vindictive; punitive; wrathful,** rancorous, irreconcilable, unappeasable, implacable, unwilling to forgive and forget, unwilling to let bygones be bygones; **retaliatory** 506.8

508 RIDICULE

NOUNS **1 ridicule, derision, mockery, raillery,** chaffing; panning *and* razzing *and* roasting *and* ragging <all nonformal>, **scoffing, jeering, sneering,** snickering, sniggering, smirking, grinning, leering, levity, flippancy, smart-aleckiness *and* joshing <both nonformal>, fooling, japery, twitting, taunting, hooting, catcalling; **banter** 490

2 gibe, scoff, jeer, flout, mock, **taunt, twit,** quip, jest, jape, foolery; **insult** 156.2; scurrility, caustic remark; **cut,** cutting remark, verbal thrust; short answer, comeback <nonformal>, parting shot, Parthian shot

3 boo, booing, hoot, catcall; Bronx cheer *and* **raspberry** *and* razz <all nonformal>; **hiss, hissing,** the bird <nonformal>

4 scornful laugh *or* smile, snicker, snigger, **smirk,** sardonic grin, leer, **sneer,** snort

5 sarcasm, irony, cynicism, satire, invective, innuendo; causticity 144.8

6 burlesque, lampoon, parody, satire, farce, mockery, imitation, takeoff <nonformal>, **travesty, caricature**

7 **laughingstock,** derision, mockery, **figure of fun,** jest, joke, **butt,** target, **goat** <nonformal>, **fair game,** victim, dupe, fool, monkey

VERBS 8 **ridicule, deride,** ride <nonformal>, make a laughingstock *or* a mockery of; roast <nonformal>, **insult** 156.5; **make fun** *or* **game of, poke fun at,** put one on *and* pull one's leg <both nonformal>; **laugh at,** laugh in one's face, snicker *or* snigger at; hold in derision, hoot down; point at, point the finger of scorn; pillory

9 **scoff, jeer,** gibe, **mock, revile, rail at,** chaff, **twit, taunt,** jape, flout, scout; jab, jab at, dig at, take a dig at; **pooh-pooh; sneer at,** curl one's lip

10 **boo, hiss, hoot,** catcall, give the raspberry *or* Bronx cheer <nonformal>, give the bird <nonformal>

11 **burlesque, lampoon, satirize, parody, caricature,** travesty, hit *or* take off on

ADJS 12 **ridiculing, derisive,** derisory; **mocking,** railing, chaffing; panning *and* razzing *and* roasting *and* ragging <all nonformal>, **scoffing,** jeering, sneering, snickering, sniggering, smirky, smirking, grinning, leering, snorting, flippant, smart, smart-alecky *and* smart-ass *and* wise-ass <all nonformal>; twitting, taunting, hooting, catcalling, hissing, bantering, kidding, teasing

13 **satiric, satirical;** sarcastic, **ironic, ironical, sardonic, cynical,** Rabelaisian; caustic

14 **burlesque, farcical, broad,** slapstick; parodic, caricatural, macaronic, doggerel

ADVS 15 **derisively, mockingly, scoffingly,** jeeringly, sneeringly

509 APPROVAL

NOUNS 1 **approval, approbation; sanction,** acceptance, countenance, **favor; admiration, esteem, respect** 155; endorsement, vote, adherence, blessing, seal of approval, nod, stamp of approval

2 **applause,** plaudit, **acclaim, acclamation; popularity; cheer** 116.2; burst of applause; **round of applause, hand, big hand; ovation,** standing ovation

3 **commendation,** good word, acknowledgment, recognition, appreciation; boost *and* buildup <both nonformal>; **puff,** promotion; **blurb** *and* **plug** *and* hype <all nonformal>

4 **recommendation; advocacy,** advocating; **reference, credential,** voucher, **testimonial;** character reference, good character

5 **praise; laudation; glorification,** glory, exaltation, **honor; eulogy; encomium,** accolade, kudos, panegyric; paean; **tribute,** homage; congratulation 149.1; flattery 511; overpraise, idolizing, idolatry, deification, apotheosis, adulation, lionizing, hero worship

6 **compliment,** complimentary *or* flattering remark, stroke <nonformal>; **bouquet** *and* posy <both nonformal>

7 **praiseworthiness, laudability,** laudableness, meritoriousness, exemplariness, admirability

8 commender, eulogist, eulogizer; **praiser,** lauder, extoller, encomiast, panegyrist; **booster** <nonformal>, puffer, promoter; plugger *and* tout *and* touter <all nonformal>; **applauder; claque;** rooter *and* fan *and* buff <all nonformal>, adherent; **flatterer** 138.3, 511.4

VERBS 9 **approve, approve of,** think well of, take kindly to; **sanction, accept; admire, esteem, respect** 155.4; endorse, bless, sign off on <nonformal>; **countenance;** uphold; **favor,** be in favor of, view with favor, take kindly to

10 **applaud, acclaim, hail; clap;** give a hand *or* big hand, hear it for <nonformal>; **cheer** 116.6; root for <nonformal>, cheer on

11 **commend, speak well** *or*

highly of, speak warmly of, have *or* say a good word for; boost *and* give a boost to <both nonformal>, puff, promote; plug *and* tout *and* hype; pour *or* spread *or* lay it on thick <all nonformal>; **recommend, advocate,** put in a word *or* good word for, support, back, lend one's name *or* support *or* backing to, make a pitch for <nonformal>

12 praise, talk one up <nonformal>; **laud; eulogize,** panegyrize, pay tribute, salute, hand it to one <nonformal>; **extol, glorify,** magnify, exalt, bless; puff, puff up; boast of, brag about <nonformal>, make much of; celebrate, emblazon, sound the praises of, ring one's praises, sing the praises of, trumpet; praise to the skies; flatter 511.5; overpraise, praise to excess, idolize, deify, apotheosize, adulate, lionize, hero-worship; put on a pedestal

13 espouse, associate oneself with, take up, take for one's own; **campaign for, crusade for,** take up the cudgels for, push for <nonformal>; carry the banner of; beat the drum for; fight the good fight for; devote *or* dedicate oneself to, sacrifice oneself for

14 compliment, pay a compliment, give a bouquet <nonformal>, say something nice about; hand it to *and* have to hand it to <nonformal>, pat on the back, take off one's hat to, congratulate 149.2

15 meet with approval, find favor with, **pass muster,** do credit to; redound to the honor of

ADJS **16 approbatory, approbative, commendatory, complimentary, laudatory,** eulogistic, panegyric, **appreciative, appreciatory; admiring, regardful, respectful** 155.8; flattering 511.8

17 approving, favorable, favoring, well-disposed, well-inclined, backing, **advocating;** promoting; touting *and* puffing *and* hyping <all nonformal>

18 uncritical, uncriticizing, **un-**censorious, unreproachful; overpraising, overappreciative, excessive in one's praise, idolatrous, adulatory, lionizing, hero-worshiping, fulsome

19 approved, favored, backed, advocated, supported; favorite; **accepted,** received, admitted; **recommended,** highly touted <nonformal>, **admired** 155.11, **applauded,** well-thought-of, **acclaimed; popular**

20 praiseworthy, worthy, **commendable,** estimable, **laudable,** admirable, meritorious, creditable; exemplary, model, unexceptionable, **good** 998.12,13

510 DISAPPROVAL

NOUNS **1 disapproval, disapprobation,** disfavor, disesteem, disrespect 156; dim view, poor *or* low opinion, adverse judgment; **displeasure, distaste, dissatisfaction,** discontentment, discontentedness, disgruntlement, **unhappiness;** disillusion, disillusionment, disenchantment, disappointment; disagreement, **opposition** 451; rejection, thumbs-down, exclusion, ostracism, blackballing, blackball, ban; **complaint, protest,** objection, **dissent** 333

2 deprecation, denigration; **ridicule** 508; depreciation, disparagement 512; **contempt** 157

3 censure, reprehension, stricture, reprobation, **blame, denunciation,** decrying, bashing *and* trashing <both nonformal>, impeachment, arraignment, indictment, **condemnation,** damnation, fulmination, anathema; castigation, flaying, skinning alive <nonformal>, excoriation; pillorying

4 criticism, flak <nonformal>, bad notices, bad press, animadversion, **aspersion,** stricture, obloquy; **knock** *and* **slam** *and* **rap** *and* hit <all nonformal>, home thrust; niggle, cavil, quibble, exception, nit <nonformal>; **censoriousness,** reproachfulness; **faultfinding,** taking exception, carping, caviling, pettifogging, quibbling, captiousness, niggling, nitpicking, pestering, nagging; hairsplitting

5 **reproof,** reproval, reprobation; **rebuke, reprimand, reproach,** reprehension, **scolding, chiding,** rating, **upbraiding,** objurgation; **admonishment, admonition; correction,** castigation, chastisement, spanking, rap on the knuckles; **disrecommendation,** low rating, adverse report

6 <nonformal terms> piece of one's mind, **talking-to,** speaking-to, roasting, **raking-over,** raking over the coals, dressing-down; **bawling-out,** cussing-out, **calling-down,** going-over, chewing-out, reaming-out, reaming, ass-chewing, what-for

7 **berating,** tongue-lashing; **revilement, vilification,** blackening, **execration, abuse, vituperation,** invective, contumely, cutting *or* bitter words; **tirade, diatribe,** jeremiad, philippic; **attack, assault,** onslaught; **abusiveness; acrimony**

8 **reproving look,** dirty *or* nasty look <nonformal>, black look, frown, scowl

9 **faultfinder,** basher <nonformal>; **critic** 945.7, **nitpicker** <nonformal>, belittler, censor, censurer, carper, caviler, quibbler, pettifogger; **scold,** common scold; kvetch, **complainer** 108.3

VERBS 10 **disapprove, disapprove of,** raise an objection, side against; **disfavor, view with disfavor, raise one's eyebrows, frown at** *or* **on,** look askance at, make a wry face at, grimace at, **turn up one's nose at,** shrug one's shoulders at; **take a dim view of** <nonformal>, not think much of, think ill of, think little of, not take kindly to, hold no brief for *and* not sign off on <both nonformal>; not go for <nonformal>; not want *or* have any part of, wash one's hands of, dissociate oneself from; **object to,** take

exception to; **oppose** 451.3, set one's face *or* heart against; **reject,** categorically reject, disallow, not hear of; **turn thumbs down on** <nonformal>, vote down, veto, exclude, ostracize, blackball, ban; **dissent from, protest, object** 333.4,5; turn over in one's grave

11 **discountenance,** not countenance, **not tolerate,** not brook, not condone, not abide, not endure, not put up with, **not stand for** <nonformal>

12 **deprecate,** not be able to say much for, denigrate, **fault,** find fault with, put down <nonformal>, pick on, pick holes in, pick to pieces; **ridicule** 508.8; **depreciate, disparage** 512.8; **hold in contempt,** disdain, **despise** 157.3

13 **censure,** reprehend; **blame,** lay *or* cast blame upon; **bash** *and* trash *and* rubbish <all nonformal>; **reproach,** impugn; **condemn,** damn; damn with faint praise; fulminate against, anathematize; **denounce, accuse** 599.7,9, **decry,** impeach, arraign, indict, call to account, inveigh against, cry out against, raise one's voice against, raise a hue and cry against; reflect upon, cast reflection upon, complain against; throw a stone at, cast *or* throw the first stone

14 **criticize; pan** *and* **knock** *and* **slam** <all nonformal>, snipe at, strike out at, tie into *and* tee off on *and* rip into *and* open up on <all nonformal>

15 **find fault,** take exception, faultfind, pick holes, cut up, **pick** *or* **pull** *or* **tear to pieces; tear down, carp, cavil,** quibble, **nitpick,** pettifog

16 **nag,** niggle, **carp at, fuss at, fret at, pick at** <nonformal>, peck at, nibble at, **pester, henpeck, pick on** <all nonformal>, bug *and* hassle <nonformal>

17 **reprove, rebuke, reprimand,** reprehend, **scold, chide, admonish, upbraid,** objurgate, take a hard line with; **lecture,** read a

lecture to; **correct,** rap on the knuckles, **chastise,** spank, turn over one's knees; **take to task,** call to account, bring to book, call on the carpet, read the riot act, give one a tongue-lashing, tonguelash

18 <nonformal terms> **call down** or **dress down, speak** or **talk to, tell off,** tell a thing or two, pin one's ears back, **give a piece** or **bit of one's mind, rake** or **haul over the coals,** let one have it, let one have it with both barrels, come down on or down hard on, jump on or all over or down one's throat; give one a hard time or what for; **bawl out, chew out,** chew ass, ream, ream out, cuss out, lambaste, give a going-over, tell where to get off; give the devil, give hell

19 berate, jaw <nonformal>, **tongue-lash, rail at,** rag, fulminate against, bark or yelp at; **revile, vilify,** blacken, **execrate, abuse,** vituperate

20 <criticize or reprove severely> **attack, assail; castigate, flay,** skin alive <nonformal>, lash, slash, **excoriate,** fustigate, scarify, scathe, **roast** <nonformal>, scorch, blister, trounce

ADJS **21 disapproving, disapprobatory,** unapproving, turned-off, **displeased, dissatisfied,** less than pleased, discontented, disgruntled, indignant, **unhappy;** disillusioned, disenchanted, disappointed; **unfavorable, opposed** 451.8, **opposing,** against, agin <nonformal>, dead set against, death on, down on, **dissenting** 333.6; **uncomplimentary**

22 condemnatory, censorious, denunciatory, reproachful, priggish, judgmental; deprecatory; **derisive, ridiculing, scoffing** 508.12; **depreciative, disparaging** 512.13; **contemptuous** 157.8; reviling, vilifying, blackening, execrating, abusive, vituperative

23 critical, faultfinding, carping, picky <nonformal>, caviling, quibbling, pettifogging, captious, cynical; nagging, niggling; overcritical, hairsplitting

24 unpraiseworthy, illaudable; uncommendable; objectionable, exceptionable, unacceptable, beyond the pale

25 blameworthy, much at fault; **reprehensible,** censurable, reproachable, reprovable; **culpable,** impeachable, indictable

ADVS **26 disapprovingly, askance, unfavorably;** reproachfully; captiously

511 FLATTERY

NOUNS **1 flattery, adulation; praise** 509.5; **blandishment,** palaver, **cajolery,** wheedling; **blarney** and bunkum and **soft soap** <all nonformal>, eyewash <nonformal>; strokes and stroking and ego massage <all nonformal>, sweet talk, pretty lies, sweet nothings; **compliment** 509.6; ass-kissing <nonformal>, fawning, sycophancy 138.2

2 unction; unctuousness, oiliness; slobber, gush, smarminess <nonformal>; insincerity 354.5

3 overpraise, overestimation; idolatry 509.5

4 flatterer, adulator; **cajoler, wheedler; backslapper;** asskisser <nonformal>, brownnoser, **sycophant** 138.3

VERBS **5 flatter,** adulate; **cajole, wheedle, blandish,** palaver; slaver or slobber over; **praise, compliment** 509.14, praise to the skies; scratch one's back, kiss ass <nonformal>, fawn upon 138.9

6 <nonformal terms> **soft-soap,** butter, honey, **butter up;** stroke <nonformal>, massage the ego <nonformal>; **blarney,** jolly, pull one's leg; lay it on <nonformal>, pour or spread or lay it on thick or with a trowel <nonformal>, overdo it; string along, kid along

7 overpraise, overlaud; overesteem, overestimate, overdo it,

protest too much; idolize 509.12,
put on a pedestal

ADJS **8 flattering, adulatory; complimentary** 509.16; **blandishing, cajoling, wheedling,** soft-
soaping <nonformal>; **mealymouthed,** oily-tongued; fulsome,
slimy, slobbery, gushing, protesting too much, smarmy <nonfor-
mal>, insinuating, oily, **unctuous,** smooth, bland; insincere;
**fawning, sycophantic, obse-
quious**

512 DISPARAGEMENT

NOUNS **1 disparagement, faultfinding, depreciation, detraction,** deprecation, derogation,
bad-mouthing *and* running down
and putting down <all nonfor-
mal>, **belittling;** sour grapes;
slighting, minimizing, faint
praise, decrying, decrial; **disapproval** 510; **contempt** 157;
indignity, disgrace

2 defamation, defamation of
character, injury to one's reputation; **vilification,** revilement,
defilement, denigration; **smear,**
character assassination, name-
calling, smear campaign; **muckraking, mudslinging**

3 slander, scandal, libel, traduce-
ment; calumny, calumniation;
backbiting, cattiness *and* bitchiness <both nonformal>

4 aspersion, slur, **remark, reflection, insinuation,** suggestion,
innuendo, whispering campaign

5 lampoon, send-up <nonformal>,
lampoonery, **satire, burlesque**
508.6; poison pen, hatchet job

6 disparager, depreciator, de-
crier, detractor, basher *and*
trasher <both nonformal>, belittler, debunker, deflater, derogator,
hatchet man; **slanderer,** libeler,
defamer, backbiter; calumniator,
traducer; **muckraker, mud-
slinger; cynic**

7 lampooner, lampoonist, **satirist,** pasquinader

VERBS **8 disparage, depreciate,
belittle,** slight, make little of,
degrade, debase, **run down**

<nonformal>, **put down** <non-
formal>; **discredit,** bring into
discredit, disgrace; detract from,
cut down to size <nonformal>;
decry, cry down; speak ill of;
speak slightingly of, not speak
well of; disapprove of 510.10;
hold in contempt 157.3; bring
down, bring low

9 defame, malign, bad-mouth
and poor-mouth <both nonfor-
mal>; **asperse, cast aspersions
on,** cast reflections on, damage
one's good name, give one a black
eye <nonformal>; **slur,** do a number *or* a job on <nonformal>, tear
down

**10 vilify, revile, defile, sully, soil,
smear,** smirch, besmirch, tarnish, **blacken,** denigrate, blacken
one's good name, give a black eye
<nonformal>; **call names,** give a
bad name, stigmatize 661.9;
muckrake, throw mud at, mud-
sling, drag through the mud;
engage in personalities

11 slander, libel; calumniate, tra-
duce; stab in the back, speak ill of
behind one's back

12 lampoon, satirize, pasquinade;
parody, send up <nonformal>;
burlesque 508.11

ADJS **13 disparaging, derogatory,**
derogative, **depreciatory,** deprecatory, slighting, belittling,
minimizing, pejorative, backbiting, catty *and* bitchy <both
nonformal>, contumelious, derisive, derisory, ridiculing 508.12;
snide, insinuating; **defamatory,**
vilifying, **slanderous, scandalous, libelous;** calumniatory;
abusive, scurrilous

513 CURSE

NOUNS **1 curse, malediction,**
damnation, denunciation, imprecation, execration; blasphemy;
anathema, fulmination, excommunication; ban, proscription;
hex, evil eye, whammy <nonfor-
mal>

2 vilification, abuse, revilement,
vituperation, invective, opprobrium, obloquy, contumely,

calumny, scurrility; **disparagement** 512

3 cursing, cussing <nonformal>, **swearing, profanity,** foul *or* profane *or* obscene *or* blue *or* bad *or* strong *or* indelicate language, vulgar language, vile language, colorful language, billingsgate, ribaldry, **dirty language** <nonformal>, **obscenity,** scatology, coprology, **filthy language, filth**

4 oath, curse; cuss *or* cuss word *and* dirty word *and* four-letter word *and* **swearword** <all nonformal>, naughty word, **expletive, epithet,** dirty name <nonformal>, obscenity

VERBS **5 curse, damn,** darn, **confound,** blast, anathematize, execrate, imprecate; excommunicate; put a curse on; blaspheme; hex, give the evil eye, throw a whammy <nonformal>

6 curse, swear, cuss <nonformal>, execrate, take the Lord's name in vain; swear like a trooper; **talk dirty** <nonformal>, use strong language

7 vilify, abuse, revile, vituperate, call names; **swear at,** damn, cuss out <nonformal>

ADJS **8 cursing, maledictory,** imprecatory, **damnatory,** denunciatory; **abusive,** vituperative, contumelious; calumniatory; execratory, fulminatory; **scurrilous;** blasphemous, **profane, foul, foulmouthed, vile, dirty** <nonformal>, **obscene,** scatological, coprological; ribald, Rabelaisian, raw, risqué

9 cursed, accursed, **damned, damn, damnable,** goddamned, goddamn, **execrable**

10 <euphemisms> **darned,** danged, **confounded,** deuced, blessed, **blasted,** dashed, blamed, goshdarn, doggone *or* doggoned, dadburned; **blankety-blank**

514 THREAT

NOUNS **1 threat, menace,** knife poised at one's throat, sword of Damocles; imminent threat, powder keg, timebomb; **foreboding; warning** 399; saber-rattling, muscle-flexing, bulldozing, scare tactics, **intimidation** 127.6, armtwisting <nonformal>; denunciation; veiled *or* implied threat, idle *or* hollow *or* empty threat

VERBS **2 threaten, menace,** bludgeon, bulldoze, put the heat *or* screws *or* squeeze on <nonformal>, lean on <nonformal>; hold a pistol to one's head, terrorize, **intimidate,** twist one's arm <nonformal>; utter threats against, shake one's fist at; hold over one's head; denounce; **lower,** spell *or* mean trouble, look threatening, loom, loom up; **be imminent** 839.2; **forebode** 133.11; **warn** 399.5

ADJS **3 threatening, menacing,** minatory; **lowering; imminent** 839.3; **ominous,** foreboding 133.17; denunciatory, abusive; fear-inspiring, **intimidating,** muscle-flexing, saber-rattling, bulldozing, browbeating, bullying, hectoring, blustering, terrorizing

ADVS **4** under duress *or* threat, under the gun, at gunpoint *or* knifepoint

515 FASTING

NOUNS **1 fasting,** abstinence from food; starvation; hunger strike

2 fast, lack of food; spare *or* meager diet; short rations, starvation diet, bread and water, bare subsistence

3 fast day; Lent; Yom Kippur; Ramadan

VERBS **4 fast,** go hungry; eat sparingly

ADJS **5 fasting,** uneating, unfed; **Lenten**

516 SOBRIETY

NOUNS **1 sobriety, soberness;** temperance 668

VERBS **2 sober up;** sleep it off; dry out

ADJS **3 sober,** in one's right mind, in possession of one's faculties; clearheaded; **unintoxicated, un-**

inebriated, untipsy; cold *or* stone sober <nonformal>, **sober as a judge;** dry, straight, temperate 668.9

4 unintoxicating; nonalcoholic, soft

517 SIGNS, INDICATORS

NOUNS **1 sign,** telltale sign, sure sign, tip-off <nonformal>, **index,** indicant, **indicator,** measure; tip of the iceberg; **symptom; mark, earmark,** hallmark, **badge,** device, banner, stamp, signature, seal, trait, **characteristic,** peculiarity, idiosyncrasy, **property;** image, **representation; insignia** 647

2 symbol, emblem, icon, token, type; **allegory; symbolism, symbology,** iconology; **symbolization; ideogram,** logogram, pictogram; **logo** <nonformal>, logotype; **totem**

3 indication, signification, identification, differentiation, denotation, **designation,** denomination; characterization, highlighting; **specification,** naming, pointing, fingering <nonformal>, picking out, selection; indicativeness; **meaning** 518; hint, suggestion 551.4; **expression, manifestation** 348; show, showing, disclosure 351

4 pointer, index, **lead; direction, guide;** index finger; **arrow; needle,** compass needle; **signpost,** guidepost, direction post; milepost

5 mark, marking; watermark; **scratch,** engraving, **score,** gash, blaze; **scar,** cicatrix, scarification, cicatrization; **brand, earmark; stigma; stain, discoloration** 1003.2; blemish, macula, **spot,** blotch, splotch; mottle, dapple; **dot,** point; tittle, jot; **speck, speckle,** fleck; **freckle,** lentigo, mole; **birthmark,** strawberry mark, port-wine stain, nevus; caste mark; **check,** checkmark; prick, puncture; tattoo

6 line, score, **stroke,** slash, virgule, diagonal, **dash, stripe,**

strip, streak, striation; squiggle; hairline; delineation; **underline,** underlining, underscore, underscoring; hatching, crosshatching, hachure

7 print, imprint, impress, impression; dent, indent, indentation, indention, concavity; **stamp,** seal, signet; colophon; **fingerprint,** thumbmark, dactylograph; **footprint,** footstep, step, vestige; **bump,** boss, stud, pimple, lump, excrescence, convexity, embossment

8 track, trail, path, course, line, wake; spoor, signs, traces, **scent**

9 clue, cue, key, tip-off <nonformal>, telltale, smoking gun <nonformal>, straw in the wind; **trace, vestige, spoor,** scent, whiff; catchword, key word; **evidence** 956; **hint, intimation, suggestion** 551.4

10 marker, mark; landmark; bench mark; **milestone,** milepost; cairn, menhir; **lighthouse,** lightship, tower; watchtower, pharos; **buoy; monument** 549.12

11 identification, identification mark; **badge,** identification badge, identification tag, dog tag <military>, **identity card** *or* **ID card** *or* **ID; card,** business card, calling card, visiting card; signature, monogram, calligram; credentials; **criminal identification,** forensic tool; fingerprint 517.7

12 password, watchword, countersign; token; open sesame; secret grip; shibboleth

13 label, tag; ticket, tally; **stamp, sticker; seal,** signet; cachet; stub, counterfoil; **token,** check; **brand, brand name, trade name; trademark; hallmark**; plate, bookplate, colophon, *ex libris* <L>, logotype *or* logo;

14 gesture, gesticulation; motion, movement; carriage, bearing, posture, poise, pose, stance, way of holding oneself; body language, kinesics; shrug; charade, dumb show, **pantomime;** dactylology, deaf-and-dumb alphabet; hand signal

15 signal, sign; high sign *and* the wink *and* the nod <all nonformal>; tone of one's voice; nod; nudge, elbow in the ribs, poke, kick, touch; **alarm 400; beacon; flare;** signal bell, bell, **police whistle; foghorn; traffic signal,** traffic light; heliograph; signal flag; **semaphore;** telecommunications

16 call, summons; whistle; **bugle call,** trumpet call; **reveille, taps; battle cry,** war cry, war whoop, rebel yell

VERBS **17 signify, betoken,** stand for, identify, differentiate, speak of, talk, **indicate,** be indicative of, be an indication of, connote, denominate, be symptomatic *or* diagnostic of, **characterize, mark,** highlight, be the mark *or* sign of, **denote, mean** 518.8; testify, give evidence; **show, express, display, manifest** 348.5, **hint,** suggest 551.10, reveal, **disclose** 351.4; entail, involve 771.4

18 designate, specify; denominate, denote; stigmatize; **symbolize, stand for,** typify, be taken as; **point to,** refer to, advert to, allude to, make an allusion to; pick out, select; **point out,** put *or* lay one's finger on, finger <nonformal>

19 mark, make a mark; pencil, chalk; mark out, demarcate, delimit, define; **mark off, check, check off,** tick off; punctuate; point; **dot, spot,** blotch, splotch, dash, **speck, speckle,** fleck, freckle; mottle, dapple; blemish; **brand,** stigmatize; **stain, discolor** 1003.6; stamp, seal, punch, impress, imprint, **print, engrave; score, scratch,** gash, scar, scarify, cicatrize; nick, notch 289.4; **blaze,** blaze a trail; **line, seam,** trace, **stripe, streak, striate;** hatch; **underline, underscore;** prick, puncture, riddle, pepper

20 label, tag, tab, ticket; stamp, seal; **brand, earmark;** hallmark; bar-code

21 gesture, gesticulate; motion; beckon, wiggle the finger at; wave the arms, wig-wag; shrug; pantomime, mime, ape, take off

22 signal, signalize, sign, give a signal, make a sign; speak; flash; **give the high sign** *or* **the nod** *or* a high five <all nonformal>; nod; nudge, poke, kick, dig one in the ribs, touch; wink, glance, raise one's eyebrows; **wave,** wave the hand, **flag,** flag down; **unfurl a flag,** hoist a banner, break out a flag; **show one's colors; salute,** dip; hail; sound an alarm, raise a cry; beat the drum, sound the trumpet

ADJS **23 indicative,** indicatory; connotative, indicating, signifying, signalizing; **significant,** significative, meaningful; symptomatic, diagnostic; evidential, **designative,** denotative, denominative, naming; **suggestive,** implicative; **expressive,** demonstrative; representative; identifying; individual, peculiar, idiosyncratic; **emblematic, symbolic,** emblematical, symbolical; typical; figurative, metaphorical; ideographic; semiotic, semantic

24 marked, designated, flagged; monogrammed, individualized, personal

25 gestural, gesticulatory; pantomimic, **in pantomime,** in dumb show

518 MEANING

NOUNS **1 meaning, significance, signification,** point, **sense,** idea, **purport, import,** where one is coming from <nonformal>; **reference, referent;** intension, extension; **denotation;** lexical meaning; emotive *or* affective meaning, undertone, overtone, coloring; relevance, bearing, **relation,** pertinence *or* pertinency; **substance,** gist, pith, spirit, essence, name of the game *and* meat and potatoes *and* bottom line <all nonformal>; **drift,** tenor; sum and substance; **literal meaning, true meaning, un-**

adorned meaning; **secondary meaning, connotation** 519.2; more than meets the eye, what is read between the lines; effect, force, impact, consequence, response; implied meaning, **implication** 519.2; syntactic *or* structural meaning, grammatical meaning; symbolic meaning; metaphorical *or* transferred meaning; range *or* span of meaning, scope

2 **intent, intention, purpose, aim, object, design**

3 **explanation, definition,** construction, sense-distinction, **interpretation** 341

4 **acceptation,** accepted *or* received meaning; **usage,** acceptance

5 **meaningfulness,** expressiveness, pregnancy; **significance;** intelligibility; pithiness, meatiness, sententiousness

6 <units> sign, symbol, significant, significant, type, token, icon

7 **semantics,** semiotic, semiotics; lexicology

VERBS 8 **mean, signify, denote, connote,** import, spell, have the sense of, be construed as, have the force of; **stand for, symbolize; imply,** suggest, argue, breathe, bespeak, **indicate; refer to; mean something,** mean a lot, have impact, come home, hit one where one lives *and* hit one close to home <both nonformal>

9 **intend,** have in mind, seek to communicate

ADJS 10 **meaningful, significant; denotative, connotative,** denotational, connotational, intensional, extensional, associational; **referential; symbolic, metaphorical,** figurative, allegorical; extended; intelligible, interpretable, definable; **suggestive,** indicative, **expressive; pregnant,** loaded *or* laden *or* fraught *or* heavy with significance; **pithy, meaty,** sententious, substantial, full of substance; pointed

11 **meant,** implied 519.7, **intended**

12 **semantic,** semiotic; **symbolic,** **verbal,** phrasal, lexical; structural

ADVS 13 **meaningfully,** meaningly, **significantly;** suggestively, indicatively; **expressively**

519 LATENT MEANINGFULNESS

NOUNS 1 **latent meaningfulness, latency,** delitescence; **potentiality,** virtuality; dormancy 173.4

2 **implication, connotation, import,** latent *or* underlying *or* implied meaning, more than meets the eye, what is read between the lines; meaning 518; **suggestion,** allusion; coloration, tinge, undertone, overtone, undercurrent, intimation, nuance, innuendo; **code word,** weasel word; **hint** 551.4; **inference, supposition,** presupposition, assumption, presumption; metaphorical sense; subsidiary sense, **subtext;** cryptic *or* hidden *or* esoteric *or* arcane meaning, occult meaning; **symbolism, allegory**

VERBS 3 **be latent, underlie, lie under the surface, lurk,** lie beneath, lie dormant, smolder; make no sign, escape notice

4 **imply, implicate, involve,** import, connote, entail 771.4; mean 518.8; **suggest,** lead one to believe, bring to mind; **hint, insinuate, infer, intimate** 551.10; **allude to;** allegorize; **suppose, presuppose,** assume, presume, take for granted; mean to say *or* imply *or* suggest

ADJS 5 **latent, lurking,** lying low, delitescent, **hidden** 346.11, obscured, obfuscated, veiled, muffled, covert, occult, cryptic; esoteric; **underlying, under the surface,** submerged; **between the lines;** hibernating, sleeping, dormant 173.14; **potential,** unmanifested, virtual, possible

6 **suggestive, allusive,** allusory, **indicative, inferential; insinuating,** insinuative; ironic; **implicative,** implicatory, implicational; referential

7 **implied,** implicated, involved;

meant, indicated; **suggested, intimated, insinuated, hinted; inferred, supposed,** assumed, presumed, presupposed; hidden, arcane, esoteric, **cryptic**

8 **tacit, implicit, implied, understood**

9 **unexpressed, unsaid, unspoken, unuttered,** undeclared, wordless, silent; **unmentioned,** untalked-of, **untold,** unsung, unproclaimed, unpublished; unwritten, unrecorded

10 **symbolic,** allegorical, figurative, **metaphoric,** metaphorical

ADVS 11 **latently; potentially,** virtually

12 **suggestively, allusively, inferentially,** insinuatingly

13 **tacitly, implicitly,** unspokenly, wordlessly, silently

520 MEANINGLESSNESS

NOUNS 1 **meaninglessness, senselessness,** nonsensicality; **insignificance; noise,** static, empty sound, talking to hear oneself talk; inanity, emptiness, nullity; purposelessness, aimlessness, futility; dead letter

2 **nonsense, stuff and nonsense,** pack of nonsense, **folderol, balderdash, rubbish,** trash, vaporing, fudge; **humbug,** hocus-pocus; claptrap, fustian, rodomontade, bombast, absurdity 922.3; **twaddle,** fiddle-faddle, fiddlesticks, **blather, babble, gabble, blabber, gibber, jabber,** prate, **prattle,** palaver, rigmarole *or* rigamarole, drivel, drool; **gibberish,** jargon, mumbo jumbo, **double-talk,** gobbledygook <nonformal>; glossolalia, speaking in tongues

3 <nonformal terms> **bullshit,** shit, crap, horseshit, horsefeathers, bull, poppycock, bosh, applesauce, bunkum, bunk, garbage, guff, jive, bilge, piffle, a crock *or* a crock of shit, claptrap, tommyrot, rot, hogwash, malarkey, hokum, hooey, bushwa, blah, baloney, blarney, tripe, hot air, gas, wind

VERBS 4 **be meaningless, mean nothing,** signify nothing, not mean a thing; not make sense; **not register,** not ring any bells

5 **talk nonsense, twaddle, piffle, blather, blabber, babble, gabble, jabber, gibber,** prate, **prattle,** rattle; talk through one's hat; gas *and* bull *and* **bullshit** *and* throw the bull *and* shoot off one's mouth *and* shoot the bull <all nonformal>; **drivel,** vapor, run off at the mouth <nonformal>; speak in tongues

ADJS 6 **meaningless, senseless,** importless; **insignificant;** empty, inane, null; garbled, scrambled; **purposeless, aimless,** designless, **without rhyme or reason**

7 **nonsensical,** silly; **foolish, absurd;** rubbishy, trashy

ADVS 8 **meaninglessly,** unmeaningly, **senselessly, nonsensically;** insignificantly; **purposelessly,** aimlessly

521 INTELLIGIBILITY

NOUNS 1 **intelligibility, comprehensibility, apprehensibility, understandability,** scrutability, penetrability, fathomableness, decipherability

2 **clearness, clarity; plainness, distinctness,** explicitness, clearcutness, definition; **lucidity,** limpidity, pellucidity, crystallinity, perspicuity, transpicuity, transparency; **simplicity,** straightforwardness, directness, literalness; unmistakableness, unequivocalness, unambiguousness; **coherence,** consistency, structure; plain language, plain style, plain English, plain speech, unadorned style

3 **legibility,** decipherability, **readability**

VERBS 4 **be understandable, make sense;** be plain *or* clear, be obvious, be self-evident, be self-explanatory; **speak for itself,** speak volumes, have no secrets

5 <be understood> **get over** *or* **across** <nonformal>, **register**

<nonformal>, **penetrate, sink in,** soak in; dawn on

6 make clear, make it clear, **let it be understood,** make oneself understood, get or put over or across <nonformal>; **simplify,** put in plain words or plain English, put in words of one syllable, spell out <nonformal>; elucidate, **explain,** explicate, **clarify** 341.10; de-mystify; **decode, decipher;** make available to all, popularize, vulgarize

7 understand, comprehend, apprehend, know, conceive, realize, appreciate, have no problem with, savvy <nonformal>, make sense out of, make something of; **fathom, follow; grasp, seize,** grasp or seize the meaning, **take in, catch on,** get the meaning of, get the hang of; **master, learn** 570.6-15, 551.14; **assimilate, absorb, digest**

8 <nonformal terms> **read one loud and clear,** read one, dig, get the idea, be with one, be with it, get the message, get into or through one's head or thick head, get it, catch or get the drift, have it down pat, see where one is coming from, hear loud and clear, hear what one is saying, have a fix on, know like the back or palm of one's hand, know inside out

9 perceive, see, discern, make out, descry; see the light, see daylight <nonformal>, wake up to, tumble to <nonformal>; **see through,** see to the bottom of, penetrate, see into, plumb; see at a glance, see with half an eye; get or have someone's number and read someone like a book <both nonformal>

ADJS **10 intelligible, comprehensible, apprehensible,** graspable, **knowable,** cognizable, scrutable, **fathomable,** decipherable, penetrable, interpretable; **understandable,** easily understood, easy to understand; readable; articulate

11 clear, crystal-clear, clear as crystal, clear as day, clear as the nose on one's face; **plain, distinct; definite,** defined, well-defined, **clear-cut,** clean-cut; **direct, literal;** simple, **straightforward; explicit, express; unmistakable, unequivocal,** unambiguous, unconfused; **loud and clear** <nonformal>; **lucid,** pellucid, limpid, crystal-clear, crystalline, perspicuous, transpicuous, **transparent,** translucent, luminous; **coherent,** consistent

12 legible, decipherable, readable; uncoded, clear

ADVS **13 intelligibly, understandably, comprehensibly;** articulately; **clearly, lucidly,** limpidly, pellucidly, perspicuously, **simply, plainly, distinctly,** definitely; **coherently; explicitly, expressly; unmistakably, unequivocally,** unambiguously; in plain terms or words, in plain English, in no uncertain terms, in words of one syllable

14 legibly, decipherably, readably, fairly

522 UNINTELLIGIBILITY

NOUNS **1 unintelligibility, incomprehensibility,** unknowability, inscrutability, impenetrability, unfathomableness, numinousness; **incoherence,** unconnectedness, ramblingness; inarticulateness; **ambiguity** 539

2 abstruseness, reconditeness; knottiness; **complexity,** intricacy, **complication** 798.1; **hardness, difficulty;** profundity

3 obscurity, obscurantism, obfuscation, mumbo jumbo <nonformal>; perplexity; **unclearness,** unclarity, opacity; **vagueness,** indistinctness, indeterminateness, fuzziness, shapelessness, amorphousness; murkiness, murk, mistiness, mist, fogginess, fog, darkness, dark

4 illegibility, unreadability; indecipherability; scribble, scrawl

5 unexpressiveness, inexpressiveness, **expressionlessness,** impassivity; uncommunicativeness; straight face, dead pan <nonformal>, poker face <nonformal>

6 inexplicability, indefinability, undefinability; **enigmaticalness,** mystery, strangeness, weirdness

7 <something unintelligible> Greek, double Dutch; gibberish, babble, jargon, garbage, gobbledygook, noise, Babel; scramble, jumble, garble; argot, cant, slang, secret language, code, cipher, cryptogram; glossolalia, gift of tongues

8 enigma, mystery, puzzle, puzzlement; Chinese puzzle; **problem**; question, question mark, sixty-four dollar question <nonformal>; **perplexity;** knot, crux; **puzzler,** poser, brain twister *or* teaser <nonformal>; mindboggler; **tough nut to crack;** tough proposition <nonformal>

9 riddle, conundrum, charade, rebus; logogriph, anagram; riddle of the Sphinx

VERBS **10 be incomprehensible, not make sense,** go over one's head, be beyond one, lose one, need explanation *or* clarification *or* translation, be Greek to, pass comprehension *or* understanding; **baffle, perplex** 970.13, speak in riddles; speak in tongues; babble, gibber, ramble, drivel

11 not understand, be unable to comprehend, not have the first idea, not get <nonformal>, be unable to get into *or* through one's head *or* thick skull; be out of one's depth, be at sea, be lost; **not know what to make of,** not make head or tail of; not see the wood for the trees; go over one's head, escape one; give up, pass <nonformal>

12 make unintelligible, scramble, jumble, garble; **obscure,** obfuscate, mystify, shadow; **complicate** 798.3

ADJS **13 unintelligible, incomprehensible, ununderstandable,** unknowable, incognizable; **unfathomable, inscrutable,** impenetrable, numinous; **ambig-**

uous; incoherent, unconnected, rambling; **inarticulate; past comprehension,** beyond one's comprehension, beyond understanding; Greek to one

14 hard to understand, difficult, hard, beyond one, **over one's head,** beyond *or* out of one's depth; intricate, **complex,** perplexed, **complicated** 798.4; **scrambled,** jumbled, **garbled; obscure,** obscured, obfuscated

15 obscure, vague, indistinct, indeterminate, fuzzy, shapeless, amorphous; unclear, opaque, muddy, **clear as mud** *and* clear as ditch water <both nonformal>; **dark,** dim, shadowy; **murky,** cloudy, foggy, fogbound, hazy, misty, nebulous

16 recondite, abstruse, abstract, transcendental; **profound, deep; hidden** 346.11; arcane, **esoteric, occult; secret** 345.11

17 enigmatic, enigmatical, cryptic, sphinxlike; **perplexing, puzzling**

18 inexplicable, unexplainable, uninterpretable, undefinable, indefinable, funny, **unaccountable; insolvable,** unsolvable, insoluble, inextricable; mysterious, mystical, shrouded *or* wrapped in mystery

19 illegible, unreadable, unclear; indecipherable

20 inexpressive, unexpressive, impassive; uncommunicative; **expressionless; vacant, empty, blank;** glazed-over, wooden; deadpan, poker-faced <nonformal>

ADVS **21 unintelligibly, incomprehensibly,** ununderstandably

22 obscurely, vaguely, indistinctly, indeterminately; **unclearly,** unplainly; illegibly

23 reconditely, abstrusely; esoterically, occultly

24 inexplicably, unexplainably, undefinably, **unaccountably, enigmatically; mysteriously**

25 expressionlessly, vacantly, blankly, emptily, woodenly, glassily, fishily

523 LANGUAGE

NOUNS 1 **language**, speech, tongue, spoken language; **talk, parlance, locution**, phraseology, **idiom, lingo** <nonformal>; dialect; system of oral communication, individual speech, competence; **usage; language type; language family, subfamily, language group;** world language, universal language

2 **dead language,** ancient language, lost language; classical language; vernacular

3 **mother tongue,** native language, vernacular

4 **standard language,** standard dialect; national language; educated speech; literary language, written language; **Standard English, the King's** or **Queen's English**

5 **nonformal language** or **speech, spoken language, colloquial language** or **speech,** vernacular; **slang;** colloquialism, colloquial usage; nonformal English, conversational English, colloquial English

6 **substandard** or nonstandard language or **speech;** vernacular language or speech, **vernacular,** demotic language or speech, vulgate, vulgar tongue, common speech; uneducated speech, illiterate speech; substandard usage

7 **dialect,** idiom; class dialect; regional or local dialect; subdialect; folk speech or dialect, patois; **provincialism, localism, regionalism**

8 <idioms> Anglicism, Briticism, Englishism; Americanism, Yankeeism; Irishism, Hibernicism; Canadianism, Scotticism, Germanism, Russianism, Latinism, etc

9 **jargon, lingo** <nonformal>, **slang, cant, argot, patois, patter, vernacular;** gobbledygook, mumbo jumbo, gibberish; **nonformal:** taboo language, vulgar language; scatology; double-speak

10 <jargons> Academese, economese, sociologese, legalese, telegraphese, journalese, officialese, Pentagonese, Washingtonese, technobabble, psychobabble; Yinglish, Franglais, Spanglish; Eurojargon

11 **lingua franca,** jargon, **pidgin,** trade language; auxiliary language, interlanguage; creolized language, creole language, creole; koine; pidgin English, talkeetalkee; Esperanto

12 **linguistics,** linguistic science; glottology; linguistic analysis; linguistic terminology, metalanguage; **philology;** paleography; bowwow theory, dingdong theory, pooh-pooh theory

13 **linguist,** linguistician, linguistic scholar; philologist, philologian; **grammarian,** grammatist; **etymologist,** etymologer; **lexicologist; lexicographer,** glossographer; phonetician, phonetician, phonologist, orthoepist; dialectician; semanticist, semasiologist

14 **polyglot,** linguist, **bilingual,** trilingual, multilingual

15 **colloquializer;** jargonist, jargonizer; slangster

VERBS 16 **speak, talk,** use language, communicate orally or verbally; colloquialize, vernacularize; jargon, jargonize, cant; patter

ADJS 17 **linguistic,** lingual, glottological; descriptive, structural, psycholinguistic, sociolinguistic, metalinguistic; **philological;** lexicological, lexicographic, lexicographical; syntactic, syntactical, **grammatical;** grammatic, semantic 518.12; phonetic 524.31, phonemic, phonological; morphological; graphemic, paleographic, paleographical

18 **vernacular, colloquial, conversational, unliterary, nonformal,** demotic, spoken, vulgar, vulgate; unstudied, familiar, common, everyday; **substandard,** nonformal, uneducated

19 **jargonish; slang,** slangy; taboo; scatological; rhyming slang

20 idiomatic; dialect, dialectal; provincial, regional, local

524 SPEECH
<utterance>

NOUNS **1 speech, talk,** the power *or* faculty of speech, talking, speaking, **discourse,** oral communication, vocal *or* voice communication, communication; **palaver, prattle, gab** <nonformal>; rapping *and* yakking *and* yakkety-yak <all nonformal>; **words, accents;** chatter 540.3; conversation 541; elocution 543.1; **language** 523

2 the verbal or oral faculty, the spoken word

3 utterance, speaking; speech act, linguistic act *or* behavior; string, utterance string, sequence of phonemes; **voice, tongue;** word of mouth, parol; vocable, **word** 526

4 remark, statement, earful *and* crack *and* one's two cents' worth <all nonformal>, **word,** say, **saying, utterance, observation, reflection, expression; note,** thought, **mention; assertion,** allegation, affirmation, pronouncement, position, dictum; **declaration;** interjection, exclamation; question 937.10; answer 938; address, greeting, apostrophe; sentence, phrase; subjoinder

5 articulateness, facility of speech; **eloquence** 544

6 articulation, uttering, phonation, voicing, giving voice, **vocalization; pronunciation, enunciation,** utterance; **delivery, attack**

7 intonation, inflection, modulation; tone, pitch

8 manner of speaking, way of saying, mode of expression; **tone of voice, voice, tone;** voice quality, vocal style, **timbre**

9 accent, regional accent, brogue, twang, burr, drawl, broad accent; **foreign accent**

10 pause, juncture, open juncture, close juncture

11 accent, accentuation; **empha-** sis, stress, word stress; ictus, beat, rhythmical stress; rhythm, rhythmic pattern, **cadence**

12 vowel quantity, quantity, mora

13 speech sound, phone, phonetic unit; puff of air, aspiration; articulation, manner of articulation; **stop,** plosive, explosive, mute, check, occlusive, **affricate, liquid,** lateral, **nasal;** voice, voicing; sonority; aspiration, palatalization, labialization, glottalization; surd, voiceless sound; sonant, voiced sound; **consonant; semivowel,** glide, transition sound; vocalic; **vowel; diphthong,** triphthong; **syllable; phoneme;** modification, assimilation, dissimilation; **allophone**

14 phonetics; phonology; orthoepy

15 phonetician, phonetist, phoneticist; orthoepist

16 ventriloquism, ventriloquy; **ventriloquist**

17 talking machine, sonovox, voder, vocoder

18 talker, speaker, sayer, utterer, patterer; **chatterbox** 540.4; conversationalist 541.8

19 vocal or speech organ, articulator; tongue, apex, tip, blade, dorsum, back; vocal cords or bands, vocal processes, vocal folds; voice box, larynx, Adam's apple

VERBS **20 speak, talk; patter** *or* **gab** *or* wag the tongue <all nonformal>; mouth; chatter 540.5; converse 541.9; declaim 543.10

21 <nonformal terms> **yak,** yap, yakkety-yak, gab, spiel, chin, jaw, shoot off one's face *or* mouth, shoot *or* bat the breeze, beat one's gums, bend one's ear, make chin music, rattle away, talk a blue streak, talk someone's ear *or* head off, spout off, sound off

22 speak up, speak out, speak one's piece *or* **one's mind, pipe up, open one's mouth,** open one's lips, say loud and clear, say out loud, sound off, raise one's voice, break silence, find one's tongue; take the floor; put in a word, get in a word edgewise; **have one's say,** put in one's two

cents <nonformal>, get a load off
one's mind <nonformal>, give
vent *or* voice to, pour one's heart
out

23 say, utter, breathe, sound,
voice, vocalize, **articulate, enunciate, pronounce,** ; whisper;
express, give expression, verbal-
ize, put in words, find words to
express; **word,** formulate, put
into words, couch, phrase 532.4;
present, deliver; **emit, let out,**
come out with, put *or* set forth,
pour forth; chorus, chime; **tell,
communicate** 343.6,7; **convey,
impart, disclose** 351.4

24 state, declare, assert, aver, affirm, asseverate, allege; **say,** make
a statement, send a message; **announce,** tell the world; **relate,
recite;** quote; proclaim, nuncu-
pate

**25 remark, comment, observe,
note; mention,** let drop *or* fall,
say by the way, make mention of;
refer to, allude to, touch on, make
reference to, call attention to;
muse, reflect; opine <nonfor-
mal>; interject; blurt, blurt out,
exclaim

26 <utter in a certain way> murmur, mutter, mumble, whisper,
breathe, buzz, sigh; gasp, pant;
exclaim, yell 59.6,8; sing, lilt, warble, chant, coo, chirp; pipe, flute;
squeak; cackle, crow; bark, yelp,
yap; growl, snap, snarl; hiss, sibilate; grunt, snort; roar, bellow,
blare, trumpet, bray, blat, bawl,
thunder, rumble, boom; scream,
shriek, screech, squeal, squawk,
yawp, squall; whine, wail, keen,
blubber, sob; drawl, twang

27 address, speak to, talk to, beg
the ear of; **appeal to,** invoke;
apostrophize; **approach; buttonhole,** take by the lapel; take
aside, talk to in private, closet
oneself with; **accost, call to, hail,**
greet, salute, speak

**28 pass one's lips, escape one's
lips,** fall from the lips

29 inflect, modulate, intonate

ADJS **30 speech; language, linguistic,** lingual; **spoken,** ut-

tered, **said,** vocalized, **voiced,
verbalized, pronounced,
sounded, articulated, enun-
ciated;** vocal; **oral, verbal, unwritten,** nuncupative, parol

31 phonetic; phonic; articulatory,
acoustic; intonated; pitched,
pitch, tonal

32 speaking, talking; articulate,
talkative 540.9; **eloquent** 544.8,
well-spoken; plain-speaking,
plain-spoken, **outspoken,** free-
speaking, free-spoken, loud-
speaking, soft-speaking, soft-
spoken; English-speaking, etc

33 ventriloquial, ventriloquistic

ADVS **34 orally, vocally, verbally,
by word of mouth;** from the lips
of, from his own mouth

525 IMPERFECT SPEECH

NOUNS **1 speech defect,** speech
impediment; dysphasia, dysphra-
sia; dyslalia, dyslogia; **broken
speech,** cracked *or* broken voice,
broken tones *or* accents; indistinct *or* blurred *or* muzzy speech;
loss of voice, aphonia; **nasaliza-
tion, twang,** nasal twang, talking
through one's nose; **falsetto;
shake, quaver,** tremor; **lisp,** lisping; hiss, sibilation; **croak;** crow;
harshness, dysphonia, hoarseness 58.2

2 inarticulateness, inarticulacy;
thickness of speech

3 stammering, stuttering, hesitation, faltering; stammer, stutter

4 mumbling, muttering, maundering, droning, drone; mumble,
mutter; jabber, jibber, gibber, gabble; susurration; mouthing

5 mispronunciation, misspeak-
ing, cacoepy; **corruption,** language pollution

6 aphasia, agraphia; aphrasia;
aphonia, loss of speech, hysterical aphonia, stage fright, mutism,
muteness 51.2

VERBS **7 speak poorly,** talk incoherently, be unable to put two
words together; have an impediment in one's speech; speak
thickly; **croak; lisp; shake, quaver; drawl;** mince, clip one's

words; lose one's voice, get stage fright, freeze <nonformal>

8 **stammer, stutter**; hesitate, falter, halt, stumble; hem, haw, **hem and haw**

9 **mumble, mutter,** maunder; drone, drone on; swallow one's words, speak drunkenly or incoherently; jabber, gibber, gabble; splutter, sputter; blubber, sob; whisper, susurrate; murmur; mouth

10 nasalize, whine, **speak through one's nose,** twang

11 mispronounce, misspeak, missay, **murder the King's or Queen's English**

ADJS 12 <imperfectly spoken> inarticulate, indistinct, blurred; **mispronounced; shaky,** shaking, **quavering,** tremulous, titubant; **drawling; lisping; throaty, guttural,** thick, velar; stifled, choked, choking, strangled; **nasal, twangy,** breathy, adenoidal, snuffling; croaking, hawking; harsh, dysphonic, hoarse 58.15

13 **stammering, stuttering,** halting, hesitating, faltering, stumbling; **aphasic;** aphrasic; aphonic, dumb, **mute** 51.12

526 WORD

NOUNS 1 **word,** free form, **term,** expression, locution, lexeme; verbalism, vocable, utterance, articulation; **usage;** syllable, polysyllable; homonym, homophone, homograph; monosyllable; synonym; metonym; antonym

2 **root,** etymon; eponym; derivative, derivation; cognate; doublet

3 **morphology,** morphemics; **morpheme;** morph, allomorph; accidence; **inflection,** conjugation, declension; paradigm; derivation, word-formation; root, radical; theme, stem; word element, combining form; **affix, suffix, prefix,** infix

4 **word form,** formation, construction; back formation; clipped word; spoonerism; **compound;** acronym, acrostic; paronym, conjugate

5 **technical term**; jargon word; jargon 523.9,10

6 **barbarism, corruption, vulgarism, impropriety,** taboo word, dirty word and four-letter word <both nonformal>; **colloquialism, slang, localism** 526.6

7 **loan word,** borrowing, borrowed word, paronym

8 **neologism,** neology, neoterism; **coinage; nonce word;** ghost word or name

9 **catchword,** catch phrase, shibboleth, slogan, cry; **pet expression,** byword, cliché; **buzzword,** vogue word, fad word, in-word; euphemism, **code word**

10 long word, jawbreaker or jawtwister and two-dollar or five-dollar word <all nonformal>, polysyllable; sesquipedalian, sesquipedalia; grandiloquence 545

11 hybrid word, **hybrid;** macaronicism, macaronic; hybridism; blendword, blend, portmanteau word, portmanteau, **counterword**

12 **archaism,** antiquated word or expression; obsoletism

13 **vocabulary, lexis, words, word stock,** wordhoard, stock of words; phraseology; **thesaurus,** Roget's; lexicon

14 **lexicology; lexicography**; onomastics 527.1, toponymics; **meaning** 518, semantics, semasiology

15 **etymology, derivation, origin,** semantic history; historical linguistics, comparative linguistics; eponymy; folk etymology

16 echoic word, onomatopoeic word; onomatopoeia; bowwow theory

17 **neologist, word-coiner,** neoterist; phraser, phrasemaker, phrasemonger

ADJS 18 **verbal,** vocabular, vocabulary

19 lexical, lexicological; lexigraphic, **lexicographical,** lexicographic; etymological, derivational; onomastic, onomatologic;

echoic, onomatopoeic; conjugate, paronymous, paronymic

20 neological, neoteric

21 morphological, morphemic; morphophonemic

527 NOMENCLATURE

NOUNS **1 nomenclature, termi-nology,** orismology; onomastics; toponymics, toponymy, place-names, place-naming; antono-masia; polyonymy; **taxonomy,** classification, binomial nomen-clature, binomialism, Linnaean method

2 naming, calling, denomina-tion, appellation, designation, designating, styling, terming, def-inition, identification; **christen-ing,** baptism; dubbing; nick-naming

3 name, appellation, appellative, **denomination, designation, style, cognomen,** full name; proper name *or* noun; moniker *and* handle <both nonformal>; **ti-tle,** honorific; **label, tag; epithet,** byword; **scientific name,** trino-men, trinomial name, binomen, binomial name; eponym; name-sake; secret name, cryptonym, euonym

4 first name, forename, **Christian name, given name,** baptismal name; **middle name**

5 surname, last name, family name, cognomen, byname; **maiden name;** married name; patronymic, matronymic

6 <Latin terms> praenomen, no-men, agnomen, cognomen

7 nickname, sobriquet, byname, cognomen; epithet, agnomen; **pet name,** diminutive, hypocoristic

8 alias, pseudonym, anonym, **as-sumed name,** false *or* fictitious name; **pen name, nom de plume;** stage name, professional name

9 misnomer, wrong name

10 signature, sign manual, **auto-graph, hand, John Hancock** <nonformal>; subscription; countersignature, countersign; endorsement; visa; monogram, cipher, device; seal, sigil, signet

VERBS **11 name, denominate,** nominate, **designate, call, term, style, dub;** specify; define, iden-tify; **title,** entitle; **label, tag; nickname; christen,** bap-tize

12 misname, misnomer, **miscall**

13 be called, be known by *or* as, go by, **go by the name of,** go under the name of, bear the name of; go under an assumed *or* a false name, have an alias

ADJS **14 named, called,** yclept <old>, **styled, titled,** denomi-nated, **known as,** known by the name of, designated, termed, dubbed, identified as; christened, baptized

15 nominal, cognominal; **titular, in name only,** nominative, for-mal; **so-called;** would-be; **self-called, self-styled;** honorific; ag-nominal, epithetic, epithetical; hypocoristic, diminutive; **alias,** a k a [also known as]

16 denominative, nominative, appellative; eponymous, ep-onymic

17 terminological, nomenclatural, orismological; onomastic; topo-nymic, toponymous; taxonomic, classificatory, Linnaean

528 ANONYMITY

NOUNS **1 anonymity, anonymous-ness, namelessness; incognito;** cover, cover name; code name; anonym

2 what's-its-name *and* **what's-his-name** *and* what's-his-face *and* what's-her-name *and* **what-you-may-call-it** *and* what-you-may-call-'em *and* what-d'ye-call-'em *and* what-d'ye-call-it *and* whatzit <all nonformal>; such-and-such; **so-and-so,** certain person, Mr X; you-know-who

ADJS **3 anonymous, anon; name-less, unnamed,** unidentified, un-designated, unspecified, innomi-nate, without a name, **unknown;** undefined; unacknowledged; **in-cognito;** cryptonymic

529 PHRASE

NOUNS **1 phrase, expression, locution, utterance,** usage, term, verbalism; **word-group,** construction; syntactic structure; **clause; sentence; paragraph; idiom;** turn of phrase *or* expression, manner *or* way of speaking

2 diction, phrasing

3 phraser, phrasemaker, phrasemonger, phraseman

ADJS **4 phrasal,** phrase; phrasey

5 in set phrases *or* terms, in round terms

530 GRAMMAR

NOUNS **1 grammar,** rules of language, linguistic structure, syntactic structure; **traditional grammar, school grammar; structural grammar; transformational grammar, transformational generative grammar; parsing,** grammatical analysis; **morphology** 526.3; **phonology** 524.14

2 syntax, structure, syntactic structure, word order, word arrangement; syntactic analysis; surface structure, shallow structure, deep structure, underlying structure; **function, subject, predicate, complement, object,** direct object, indirect object; **modifier,** qualifier, appositive, attributive

3 part of speech, function class; **adjective,** adjectival, attributive; **adverb,** adverbial; **preposition; participle,** present participle, past participle, perfect participle; **conjunction,** subordinating conjunction, coordinating conjunction, conjunctive adverb, copulative; **interjection, particle**

4 verb, transitive verb, intransitive verb, deponent verb, defective verb; finite verb; linking verb, copula; verbal; **infinitive; auxiliary verb,** modal auxiliary; phrasal verb; verb phrase

5 noun, pronoun, substantive, hypostasis; verbal noun, gerund; noun phrase

6 article, definite article, indefinite article

7 person; first person; second person, proximate; third person; fourth person, obviative

8 number; singular, dual, trial, plural

9 case; nominative; object *or* objective case, accusative, dative, possessive case, genitive

10 gender, masculine, feminine, neuter

11 mood, mode; indicative, subjunctive, imperative, conditional, potential, obligative, optative, jussive

12 tense; present; historical present; **past,** preterit *or* preterite; aorist; imperfect; future; **perfect,** present perfect, future perfect; past perfect, **pluperfect;** progressive tense

13 aspect; perfective, imperfective, inchoative, iterative

14 voice; active voice, passive voice; reflexive

15 punctuation, punctuation marks; diacritical mark; reference mark, reference; point, tittle; stop, end stop

VERBS **16** grammaticize; **parse,** analyze; inflect, **conjugate, decline; punctuate,** mark, point; parenthesize, hyphenate, bracket; diagram, notate

ADJS **17 grammatical, syntactical,** formal, structural; correct, well-formed; **functional;** substantive, nominal, pronominal; verbal, transitive, intransitive; linking, copulative; attributive, adjectival, adverbial, participial; prepositional, post-positional; conjunctive

531 UNGRAMMATICALNESS

NOUNS **1 ungrammaticalness,** bad *or* faulty grammar, faulty syntax; lack of agreement, faulty reference, misplaced *or* dangling modifier, shift of tense, shift of structure, faulty subordination, faulty comparison, faulty coordination, faulty punctuation, lack of parallelism, sentence frag-

ment, comma fault, comma
splice

2 solecism, ungrammaticism,
misusage, missaying, misconstruction, barbarism, infelicity; corruption; antiphrasis,
malapropism 974.7

VERBS **3** solecize, commit a solecism, use faulty *or* inadmissible
or inappropriate grammar, murder the King's *or* Queen's English

ADJS **4 ungrammatic, ungrammatical,** solecistic, **incorrect,**
barbarous; faulty, erroneous
974.16; infelicitous, improper
788.7; careless, slovenly, slipshod
809.15; loose, imprecise 974.17

532 DICTION

NOUNS **1 diction,** verbiage, wordusage, **usage,** choice of words,
formulation, way of putting *or*
couching; **rhetoric,** speech, talk
<nonformal>; **language,** dialect,
parlance, locution, expression,
grammar 530; **idiom;** composition

2 style; mode, manner, vein; fashion, way; **rhetoric; manner of
speaking,** mode of expression,
literary style, style of writing,
command of language *or* idiom,
expression of ideas; feeling for
words *or* language, way with
words, sense of language; gift of
gab <nonformal>; blarney *or* the
blarney <nonformal>; linguistic
finesse; personal style; mannerism, trick, pecularity; affectation;
inflation, exaggeration, grandiloquence 545; the grand style; **stylistics,** stylistic analysis

3 stylist, master of style; rhetorician; mannerist

VERBS **4 phrase, express,** find a
phrase for, give expression to,
word, state, **frame,** conceive,
style, couch, **put in** *or* **into
words,** clothe in words, couch in
terms, find words to express; put,
present, set out; **formulate;** paragraph

ADJS **5 phrased,** expressed,
worded, formulated, styled, put,
presented, couched; stylistic

533 ELEGANCE
<of language>

NOUNS **1 elegance,** elegancy;
grace, gracefulness; **taste,** tastefulness, good taste; **correctness,**
seemliness, **propriety,** aptness;
refinement, precision, exactitude, lapidary quality, finish; **discrimination,** choice; **restraint;
polish, finish,** terseness, neatness; smoothness, flow, **fluency;
felicity,** felicitousness, **ease;** clarity, lucidity, limpidity, pellucidity,
perspicuity; distinction, dignity;
purity, chastity, chasteness;
plainness, straightforwardness,
directness, **simplicity,** naturalness, unaffectedness, unadorned
simplicity, gracility; classicism;
well-rounded *or* well-turned periods; fittingness, appropriateness

2 harmony, proportion, symmetry, **balance,** equilibrium, order,
measuredness; rhythm; **euphony,** sweetness, beauty

3 <affected elegance> **affectation,**
affectedness, studiedness, **pretentiousness, mannerism,** manneredness, artifice, artfulness,
artificiality, unnaturalness; **euphuism; preciousness,** preciosity; euphemism; purism;
overelegance, overelaboration,
overrefinement

4 purist, classicist, plain stylist

5 euphuist; phrasemaker, phrasemonger

ADJS **6 elegant, tasteful, graceful,
polished,** finished, round, terse;
neat, trim, **refined, exact,** lapidary; **restrained; clear,** lucid,
limpid, pellucid, perspicuous;
simple, unaffected, natural, unlabored, fluent, flowing, **easy;
pure,** chaste, **plain,** straightforward, direct, unadorned, gracile;
classic, classical

**7 appropriate, fit, fitting, proper,
correct, seemly,** comely; **felicitous,** happy, **apt, well-chosen;
well-put,** well-expressed, inspired

8 harmonious, balanced, symmetrical, orderly, ordered, measured; **euphonious,** euphonic, sweet; **smooth,** tripping, smooth-sounding, fluent, flowing

9 <affectedly elegant> **affected,** euphuistic; elaborate, elaborated; **pretentious, mannered, artificial, unnatural,** studied; precious, overrefined, overelegant, overelaborate

534 INELEGANCE
<of language>

NOUNS 1 **inelegance,** inelegancy; infelicity; **clumsiness,** clunkiness *and* klutziness <both nonformal>, leadenness, heavy-handedness, ham-handedness, heaviness, stiltedness, **ponderousness,** unwieldiness; sesquipedalianism; turgidity, bombasticness, pompousness 545.1; **gracelessness,** ungracefulness; **tastelessness,** bad taste, **impropriety,** indecorousness, unseemliness; incorrectness, impurity; **vulgarity,** vulgarism, barbarism, barbarousness, **coarseness, unrefinement,** roughness, grossness, rudeness, crudeness, uncouthness; poor diction; cacophony, harshness; slipshod construction, ill-balanced sentences; lack of finish *or* polish

ADJS 2 **inelegant, clumsy, clunky** *and* **klutzy** <both nonformal>, heavy-handed, heavy-footed, ham-handed, graceless, ungraceful, infelicitous, unfelicitous; **tasteless,** in bad taste; **incorrect, improper; indecorous, unseemly,** uncourtly, undignified; **unpolished, unrefined;** impure, unclassical; **vulgar,** barbarous, barbaric, rude, **crude, uncouth,** outlandish; low, gross, **coarse,** doggerel; cacophonous, uneuphonious, harsh, ill-sounding

3 **stiff, stilted, formal, labored,** ponderous, elephantine, lumbering, leaden, heavy, unwieldy, sesquipedalian, inkhorn, turgid, bombastic, pompous 545.8;

forced, awkward, cramped, halting; crabbed

535 PLAIN SPEECH

NOUNS 1 **plain speech,** plain speaking, plain-spokenness, plain style, unadorned style, gracility, **plain English,** plain words, vernacular, household words, words of one syllable; **plainness,** simpleness, simplicity; soberness, restrainedness; severity, austerity; spareness, leanness, bareness, starkness, unadornedness, naturalness, unaffectedness; **directness, straightforwardness,** calling a spade a spade, mincing no words, making no bones about it <nonformal>; unimaginativeness, prosaicness, matter-of-factness, prosiness; homespun; **candor,** frankness, openness

VERBS 2 **speak plainly,** waste no words, **call a spade a spade,** come to the point, lay it on the line, not beat about the bush, mince no words, make no bones about it *and* talk turkey <both nonformal>

ADJS 3 **plain-speaking,** simple-speaking; **plain,** common; **simple,** unadorned, unvarnished, pure; sober, severe, austere, ascetic, spare, lean, bare, stark, Spartan; **natural, unaffected;** direct, straightforward, woman-to-woman, man-to-man, one-on-one; commonplace, homely, homespun; **candid,** up-front <nonformal>, plain-spoken, frank, open; **prosaic,** prosy; unpoetical, unimaginative, dull, dry, **matter-of-fact**

ADVS 4 **plainly, simply,** naturally, unaffectedly, matter-of-factly; in plain words, plain-spokenly, **in plain English,** in words of one syllable; **directly,** point-blank, to the point; candidly, frankly

536 FIGURE OF SPEECH

NOUNS 1 **figure of speech, figure, image,** trope, turn of expression, ornament, device, flourish; purple passage; imagery, figurative

language; figured or florid or flowery style, euphuism
VERBS **2** metaphorize; similize; personify; symbolize
ADJS **3 figurative; metaphorical;** allusive; mannered, figured, ornamented, **flowery** 545.11
ADVS **4 figuratively; metaphorically;** symbolically; **figuratively speaking,** so to say or speak, in a manner of speaking, **as it were**

537 CONCISENESS

NOUNS **1 conciseness,** concision, briefness, **brevity;** shortness, compactness; **curtness,** brusqueness, **crispness, terseness;** taciturnity 344.2, reserve 344.3; **pithiness,** succinctness, pointedness, sententiousness
2 laconicness, laconism, economy of language
3 aphorism, epigram 973.1; **abridgment** 557
4 abbreviation, shortening, clipping, cutting, pruning, truncation; ellipsis, aposiopesis, contraction, syncope, apocope, elision, crasis, syneresis <all rhetoric>
VERBS **5 be brief, come to the point,** get to the bottom line or the nitty-gritty <nonformal>, **make a long story short,** cut the shit <nonformal>, waste no words, put it in few words; shorten, condense, **abbreviate** 268.6
ADJS **6 concise, brief, short; condensed, compressed,** tight, close, compact; **curt,** brusque, **crisp, terse,** summary; taciturn 344.9; reserved 344.10; **pithy, succinct; laconic; abridged, abbreviated,** vest-pocket, synopsized, shortened, clipped, cut, pruned, contracted, truncated, docked; elliptic; sententious, epigrammatic, gnomic, aphoristic[al], **pointed,** to the point
ADVS **7 concisely, briefly,** standing on one leg; laconically; **curtly,** brusquely, **crisply, tersely,** summarily; **pithily, succinctly,** point-

edly; **sententiously, aphoristically,** epigrammatically
8 in brief, in short, for short; in substance, in outline; **in a nutshell; in a word,** in two words, in a few words, without wasting or mincing words; **to be brief,** to come to the point, to cut the matter short, **to make a long story short**

538 DIFFUSENESS

NOUNS **1 diffuseness,** diffusiveness, diffusion; shapelessness, **formlessness** 263, amorphousness, unstructuredness; obscurity 522.3
2 wordiness, verbosity, verbiage; **prolixity, long-windedness;** flow of words; **profuseness,** profusiveness, profusion; **effusiveness,** effusion, gush, gushing; outpour, tirade; logorrhea, verbal diarrhea, diarrhea of the mouth, **talkativeness 540; copiousness, exuberance,** extravagance, prodigality, fertility, fecundity, rankness, productivity, abundance, overflow; superfluity, superabundance, overflow, inundation; **redundancy,** pleonasm, repetitiveness, reiteration, iteration, tautology; repetition for effect or emphasis
3 discursiveness, digressiveness, aimlessness; rambling, maundering, meandering, wandering
4 digression, departure, deviation, **discursion,** excursion, excursus, sidetrack
5 circumlocution, roundaboutness, circuitousness; deviousness, obliqueness, **indirection;** periphrasis
6 amplification, expatiation, enlargement, expansion, dilation, dilating; **elaboration, laboring; development,** explication, unfolding, fleshing-out, detailing
VERBS **7 amplify, expatiate, dilate, expand,** enlarge, **enlarge on,** expand on, **elaborate;** detail, particularize; **develop,** fill in, flesh out, evolve, unfold; work out, explicate; descant

8 **protract, extend, spin out,**
string out, draw out, stretch out,
go on about, **drag out,** drive
into the ground <nonformal>;
pad, fill out; perorate; **speak at
length;** chatter, talk one to death
540.5, 6

9 **digress,** wander, **get off the
subject, wander from the subject,** get sidetracked, ramble,
maunder, stray; depart, **deviate,**
turn aside, jump the track; **go off
on a tangent,** go up blind alleys

10 circumlocute <nonformal>, say
in a roundabout way, talk in circles, **go round about,** go around
and around, **beat around** or
about the bush; periphrase

ADJS 11 **diffuse,** diffusive; **formless** 263.4, unstructured; **profuse,** profusive; **effusive,** gushing, gushy; copious, exuberant,
extravagant, prodigal, fecund,
teeming, prolific, abundant, overflowing; **redundant,** pleonastic,
repetitive, reiterative, iterative,
tautologous

12 **wordy, verbose; talkative**
540.9; **prolix,** windy <nonfor-
mal>, **long-winded; protracted,**
extended, lengthy, **long-drawn-
out,** spun-out, endless, unrelenting; padded

13 **discursive, aimless,** loose; **rambling, maundering, wandering,**
peripatetic, roving; excursive, **digressive,** deviative, **desultory;** by
the way

14 **circumlocutory,** circumlocu-
tional, **roundabout, circuitous,**
oblique, indirect; periphrastic

15 **expatiating,** dilative, enlarging,
amplifying, expanding; **developmental**

ADVS 16 **at length,** ad nauseam
<L>, in full, in detail

539 AMBIGUITY

NOUNS 1 **ambiguity,** ambiguous-
ness; **equivocalness; double
meaning;** punning, paronomasia; double entendre; twilight
zone, gray area; six of one and
half dozen of the other; inexplicit-
ness, uncertainty 970; irony, con-

tradiction, oxymoron; levels of
meaning, richness of meaning

2 <ambiguous word or expres-
sion> **ambiguity,** equivoque;
equivocation, double entendre;
portmanteau word; weasel word;
squinting construction; pun
489.8

VERBS 3 equivocate, weasel

ADJS 4 **ambiguous, equivocal;**
two-edged, either-or, betwixt and
between; bittersweet, mixed; in-
explicit, uncertain 970.15; ironic;
obscure, mysterious, funny, enigmatic 522.17

540 TALKATIVENESS

NOUNS 1 **talkativeness, loquacity,**
loquaciousness; loose tongue, big
mouth <nonformal>; gabbiness
and windiness and gassiness <all
nonformal>; **garrulousness,**
garrulity; **long-windedness,
prolixity, verbosity** 538.2; **vol-
ubility, fluency, glibness; gift of
gab** <nonformal>; openness, candor, frankness 644.4; effusion,
gush, slush; gushiness, **effusiveness;** flow or spate of words;
communicativeness 343.3; gregariousness, sociability

2 **logomania, logorrhea, diarrhea of the mouth, verbal
diarrhea**

3 **chatter, jabber,** gibber, **babble,
prating, prattle, palaver,** chat,
gabble, gab <nonformal>, blab,
blabber, blather, clatter, cackle;
twaddle, **prittle-prattle, tittle-
tattle,** mere talk, idle talk or chatter; **guff** and **gas** and **hot air** and
yak and yakkety-yak <all nonfor-
mal>; **gossip**

4 **chatterer, chatterbox, babbler,
jabberer, prater, prattler, gab-
bler, gabber** <nonformal>,
blabberer, blabber, blatherer,
word-slinger, blab, rattle; magpie,
jay; **windbag** and gasbag and hot-
air artist <all nonformal>; idle
chatterer, talkative person, **big** or
great talker <nonformal>

VERBS 5 **chatter, chat, prate, prattle, patter,** palaver, **babble, gab**
<nonformal>, **gabble,** tittle-

tattle, **jabber,** gibber, **blab, blabber, blather,** clatter, twaddle, rattle, clack, dither, spout or **spout off** <nonformal>, pour forth, **gush,** have a big mouth <nonformal>, love the sound of one's own voice; **jaw** and **gas** and yak and **yakkety-yak** and run off at the mouth and beat one's gums <all nonformal>, **shoot off one's mouth** or **face** <nonformal>; reel off; **talk on, go on** <nonformal>, run on, rattle on; ramble on; talk oneself hoarse, talk till one is blue in the face; **talk too much; gossip;** talk nonsense 520.5

6 <nonformal terms> **talk one to death, talk one's head** or **ear off,** talk one deaf and dumb

7 **outtalk,** outspeak, **talk down;** filibuster

8 be loquacious or garrulous, be a windbag or gasbag <nonformal>; have a big mouth <nonformal>

9 **talkative, loquacious, talky,** big-mouthed <nonformal>, overtalkative, garrulous, chatty; gossipy; gabby and windy and gassy <all nonformal>; **longwinded, prolix, verbose** 538.12; **voluble, fluent; glib,** flip <nonformal>, smooth; candid, frank 644.17; **effusive,** gushy, expansive, **communicative;** gregarious, sociable

10 **chattering, prattling, prating,** jabbering, gibbering, babbling, blabbing, blathering

ADVS 11 **talkatively, loquaciously,** garrulously; **volubly, fluently,** glibly; effusively, gushingly

541 CONVERSATION

NOUNS 1 **conversation,** conversing, rapping <nonformal>; colloquy; **exchange;** verbal intercourse, give-and-take, rapping <nonformal>, **repartee,** backchat; **discourse; communion, intercourse, communication** 343

2 the art of conversation, colloquial discourse

3 **talk, palaver, speech, words;** confabulation, **confab** <nonformal>; **chinfest** and **chinwag** and **talkfest** and **bull session** <all nonformal>; **dialogue; interview**

4 **chat,** friendly chat or talk, **little talk,** causerie, **visit** <nonformal>, *tête-à-tête* <Fr>, **heart-to-heart talk** or heart-to-heart; pillow-talk

5 **chitchat,** chitter-chatter, tittletattle, **small talk,** table talk, idle chat, gossip

6 **conference, congress, convention, parley, palaver, confab** <nonformal>, confabulation, **conclave, powwow, huddle** <nonformal>, **consultation, meeting;** session, sitting, sitdown <nonformal>, séance; exchange of views; **council,** council of war; **discussion; interview, audience; news conference,** press conference; high-level talk, summit, summit conference; summitry; negotiations, bargaining session; confrontation, eyeball-to-eyeball encounter <nonformal>; teleconference

7 **discussion, debate,** debating, **deliberation, nonformalogue,** exchange of views, canvassing, ventilation, airing, review, **treatment, consideration,** investigation, **examination, study, analysis;** dialectic; buzz session <nonformal>, rap session <nonformal>; **panel,** panel discussion, open discussion, symposium, colloquium, conference, seminar; **forum,** open forum, town meeting

8 **conversationalist;** talker, discourser, confabulator; conversational partner; interlocutor; parleyer, palaverer; dialogist

VERBS 9 **converse, talk together, talk** or **speak with,** converse with, strike up a conversation, **commune with,** communicate with, take counsel with, **have a talk with,** have a word with, chin <nonformal>, **chew the rag** or **fat** <nonformal>, **shoot the breeze** <nonformal>, hold or carry on or join in or engage in a conversation; confabulate, con-

fab <nonformal>; **bandy words;
communicate** 343.6,7

10 **chat, visit** <nonformal>, pass
the time of day, touch base with,
have a friendly *or* cozy chat; **have
a little talk,** have a heart-to-heart
talk, let one's hair down; be clos-
eted with, make conversation *or*
talk, engage in small talk; **prattle,**
tittle-tattle; **gossip**

11 **confer,** hold a conference, parley, palaver, powwow, sit down
together, meet around the conference table, **go into a huddle**
<nonformal>, deliberate, coun-
sel, **put heads together; confer
with,** sit down with, **consult
with, advise with, discuss with,
take up with,** reason with; **discuss,** talk over; **consult,** refer
to, call in; **compare notes,** exchange observations *or* views;
have conversations; negotiate,
bargain

12 **discuss, debate, reason, deliberate,** deliberate upon, exchange
views *or* opinions, talk, **talk over,
hash over** <nonformal>, rap
<nonformal>, comment upon,
discourse about, **consider, treat,**
deal with, take up, **go into, examine,** investigate, talk out,
analyze, sift, **study,** canvass, review, controvert, ventilate, air,
thresh out, reason the point,
consider pro and con; **kick
or knock around** <nonfor-
mal>

ADJS 13 conversational, colloquial,
confabulatory, interlocutory;
communicative; chatty, cozy

ADVS 14 conversationally, collo-
quially; *tête-à-tête* <Fr>

542 SOLILOQUY

NOUNS 1 **soliloquy; monologue;**
aside; apostrophe

2 **soliloquist,** soliloquizer; **monologist**

VERBS 3 **soliloquize,** monologize;
talk to oneself, say to oneself,
think out loud *or* aloud; say aside;
do all the talking, monopolize the
conversation

ADJS 4 soliloquizing; apostrophic

543 PUBLIC SPEAKING

NOUNS 1 **public speaking, declamation, speechmaking,
speaking,** speechification <non-
formal>, lecturing, speeching;
after-dinner speaking; **oratory,**
platform oratory *or* speaking; the
soap box; **elocution; rhetoric,**
art of public speaking; **eloquence** 544; forensics, **debating;
preaching,** Bible-thumping
<nonformal>, the pulpit, homile-
tics; demagogism, demagogy,
demagoguery, rabble-rousing;
pyrotechnics

2 **speech,** speechification <non-
formal>, **talk, oration, address,**
declamation, harangue; public
speech *or* address; campaign
speech, stump speech; **tirade,**
screed, **diatribe,** jeremiad, philippic, invective; funeral oration,
eulogy; allocution, exhortation;
recitation, recital, reading; salu-
tatory; valediction, valedictory;
pep talk <nonformal>; pitch,
sales talk 734.5; talkathon, filibuster; peroration; debate

3 **lecture,** prelection, **discourse;
sermon,** homily; preachment,
preaching; **evangelism,** television *or* TV evangelism; travel-
ogue

4 **speaker, talker, public
speaker, speechmaker,** speech-
ifier <nonformal>, spieler <non-
formal>; after-dinner speaker;
spokesman, spokeswoman;
demagogue, rabble-rouser; de-
claimer, ranter, tub-thumper
<nonformal>, haranguer; vale-
dictorian, salutatorian; panelist,
debater

5 **lecturer,** prelector, discourser;
reader; **preacher;** sermonizer,
hellfire preacher; **evangelist,**
television *or* TV evangelist; **expositor,** expounder

6 **orator, public speaker,** platform orator *or* speaker; rhetorician, rhetor; silver-tongued orator, **spellbinder; soapbox orator,** stump orator

7 **elocutionist; recitationist,** re-

citer, diseur, diseuse; reader; improvisator

8 rhetorician, rhetor, elocutionist; speech-writer

VERBS **9 make a speech, give a talk, deliver an address,** speechify <nonformal>, **speak, talk, discourse; address;** stump <nonformal>, go on the stump; take the floor

10 declaim, hold forth, **orate,** spout <nonformal>, spiel <nonformal>, mouth; **harangue, rant,** tub-thump, perorate, rodomontade; **recite,** read; debate; rabble-rouse

11 lecture, deliver a lecture; **preach,** Bible-thump and preachify <both nonformal>, **sermonize**

ADJS **12 declamatory, elocutionary, oratorical, rhetorical,** forensic; eloquent 544.8; demagogic

544 ELOQUENCE

NOUNS **1 eloquence, rhetoric, silver tongue,** fecundity; **articulateness;** gift of gab <nonformal>, **glibness,** smoothness, slickness; **felicitousness,** felicity; **oratory** 543.1; expression, **expressiveness,** command of words, gift of gab <nonformal>, vividness, graphicness; pleasing or effective style; **meaningfulness** 518.5

2 fluency, flow; **smoothness, facility, ease; grace,** gracefulness; **elegance** 533

3 vigor, force, power, strength, vitality, drive, sinew, vigorousness, forcefulness, effectiveness, impressiveness, pizzazz and punch and clout <all nonformal>; incisiveness, trenchancy, cuttingness, poignancy, bite, mordancy; strong language

4 spirit, pep <nonformal>, liveliness, raciness, sparkle, vivacity, dash, verve, vividness; pungency

5 vehemence, passion, impassionedness, enthusiasm, **ardor, fervor,** fervency, fire, fieriness

6 loftiness, elevation, sublimity;

grandeur, **nobility,** stateliness, majesty, gravity, *gravitas* <L>, solemnity, **dignity**

VERBS **7 have the gift of gab** <nonformal>; **spellbind;** shine

ADJS **8 eloquent, silver-tongued,** silver; well-spoken, **articulate,** fecund; **glib, smooth,** smooth-tongued, **slick; felicitous;** facile, slick as a whistle <nonformal>, spellbinding

9 fluent, flowing, tripping; **smooth,** pleasing, facile, **easy, graceful, elegant** 533.6

10 expressive, graphic, vivid, suggestive, imaginative; well-turned; **meaningful** 518.10

11 vigorous, strong, **powerful, forceful,** forcible, vital, driving, sinewy, punchy and full of piss and vinegar and zappy <all nonformal>, **striking, telling, effective,** impressive; incisive, trenchant, cutting, biting, piercing, poignant, penetrating, slashing, mordant, acid, corrosive; sensational

12 spirited, lively, peppy and gingery <both nonformal>, racy, sparkling, vivacious; pungent

13 vehement, emphatic, **passionate, impassioned,** enthusiastic, **ardent,** fiery, **fervent,** burning, glowing, warm; urgent, stirring, exciting, stimulating, provoking

14 lofty, elevated, sublime, grand, majestic, noble, stately, grave, solemn, dignified; serious, weighty; moving, inspiring

ADVS **15 eloquently; fluently,** smoothly, glibly; **expressively,** vividly, graphically; **meaningfully** 518.13; **vigorously,** powerfully, forcefully, spiritedly; tellingly, strikingly, effectively, impressively; **vehemently, passionately,** ardently, fervently, glowingly, in glowing terms

545 GRANDILOQUENCE

NOUNS **1 grandiloquence,** magniloquence, **pompousness,** pomposity, orotundity; **rhetoric,** mere rhetoric; big or tall talk <nonformal>; grandioseness, grandiosity;

loftiness, stiltedness; fulsomeness; **pretentiousness,** pretension, **affectation** 533.3; ostentation; **flamboyancy,** showiness,
flashiness, gaudiness, meretriciousness, **glitz** <nonformal>,
garishness; sensationalism, luridness; **inflation, inflatedness,**
turgidity, flatulence *or* flatulency,
tumidity; sententiousness, pontification; platitudinous ponderosity, pompous prolixity; convolution, tortuousness, ostentatious
complexity

2 **bombast, fustian,** highfalutin
<nonformal>, **rant,** rodomon-
tade; **hot air** <nonformal>; balderdash, gobbledygook <nonfor-
mal>

3 **high-sounding words; sesquipedalian word,** two- dollar *or*
five-dollar word <nonformal>,
jawbreaker, jawtwister, mouthful; sesquipedalianism, sesqui-
pedality

4 **ornateness, floweriness,** floridness, floridity, lushness, luxuriance; flourish, **purple patches** *or*
passages, fine writing; **ornament,** ornamentation, **adornment, embellishment, em-
broidery, frill,** figure, **figure of
speech** 536

5 **phrasemonger,** rhetorician;
phrasemaker, fine writer, word-
spinner; euphuist; pedant

VERBS 6 **talk big** <nonformal>,
pontificate, blow <nonformal>,
vapor; inflate, bombast, lay *or*
pile it on <nonformal>, lay it on
thick *and* lay it on with a trowel
<both nonformal>; smell of the
lamp

7 **ornament, decorate, adorn,
embellish, embroider,** enrich;
festoon, weight down with ornament; **gild,** gild the lily, trick out,
varnish; paint in glowing colors,
tell in glowing terms; elaborate,
convolute, involve

ADJS 8 **grandiloquent,** magnilo-
quent, **pompous, orotund; grandiose;** fulsome; lofty, elevated,
tall <nonformal>, **stilted; pretentious, affected** 533.9; over-

done, overwrought; **showy,
flashy, ostentatious,** gaudy,
glitzy <nonformal>, meretricious, flamboyant, flaming,
flaunting, garish; lurid, sensational; **high-flown, high-falutin**
<nonformal>; **high-sounding,
big-sounding,** sonorous; **rhetorical,** declamatory; **pedantic;** sententious; convoluted, tortuous,
labyrinthine, overelaborate, over-
involved; euphuistic

9 **bombastic,** fustian, **inflated,
swollen,** swelling, turgid, tumid,
tumescent, flatulent, windy *and*
gassy <both nonformal>; over-
adorned, fulsome

10 sesquipedalian, polysyllabic,
jawbreaking *and* jawtwisting
<both nonformal>

11 **ornate,** purple <nonformal>,
colored, **fancy;** adorned, **embellished, embroidered,** lavish,
decorated, festooned, overcharged, overloaded, befrilled;
flowery, florid, lush, luxuriant;
figured, **figurative** 536.3

ADVS 12 **grandiloquently,** magnil-
oquently, **pompously,** grandiosely, fulsomely, loftily, stiltedly,
pretentiously; **ostentatiously,**
showily; **bombastically,** turgidly,
tumidly, flatulently, windily
<nonformal>

13 **ornately,** fancily; **flowerily,** flor-
idly

546 LETTER

NOUNS 1 **letter, written character,
character, sign, symbol;** diacri-
tic, diacritical mark; lexigraphic
character *or* symbol; ideographic
symbol; pictographic symbol; cipher, device; monogram; **writing**
547

2 <phonetic and ideographic sym-
bols> phonogram; phonetic symbol; logogram, logograph; word
letter; ideogram, ideograph, phonetic; pictograph, pictogram;
hieroglyphic, hieroglyph; rune,
runic character or symbol; cuneiform, character; wedge, arrowhead; shorthand 547.8; hiero-
glyphics

3 **writing system, script, letters; alphabet, ABC's; phonetic alphabet,** International Phonetic Alphabet *or* IPA; **syllabary;** paleography

4 **spelling,** orthography; phonetic spelling *or* respelling, phonetics; spelling reform; spelling bee, spelldown; bad spelling, cacography

5 **lettering,** initialing; **inscription,** epigraph, graffito; alphabetization; transliteration, romanization, pin-yin, Wade-Giles system; transcription

VERBS 6 **letter, initial, inscribe,** character, mark; **capitalize; alphabetize;** transliterate, transcribe

7 **spell**; spell *or* respell phonetically; spell out, write out, trace out; spell down; syllabify, syllabicate

ADJS 8 **literal, lettered; alphabetic, alphabetical;** abecedarian; large-lettered, majuscule, majuscular, uncial; **capital,** capitalized, upper-case; small-lettered, minuscule, minuscular, lower-case; lexigraphic, ideographic, pictographic; transliterated, transcribed

547 WRITING

NOUNS 1 **writing,** inscription, lettering; engrossment; pen, **pen-and-ink;** pen *or* pencil <nonformal>; **typing, typewriting;** stroke of the pen; secret writing, cryptography 345.6; **alphabet, writing system** 546.3

2 **authorship, writing,** wordsmanship, **composition,** the art of composition; **creative writing,** literary art, verbal art, literary composition, literary production; **expository writing;** technical writing; journalism, rewriting; artistry, literary power, literary artistry, literary talent *or* flair, skill with words *or* language, facility in writing, ready pen; **writer's itch;** automatic writing; writer's cramp

3 **handwriting, hand, script,** fist <nonformal>, chirography, **calligraphy; manuscript; autograph,** holograph; **penmanship;** stylography; graphology; paleography

4 handwriting style; printing, handprinting, block letter, lettering; stationery

5 <good writing> **calligraphy,** fine writing, **good hand,** fine hand, good fist <nonformal>

6 <bad writing> **cacography, bad hand,** poor fist <nonformal>, cramped *or* crabbed hand, botched writing, childish scrawl, illegible handwriting

7 **scribbling; scribble,** scrabble, **scrawl, scratch;** hen tracks *and* hen scratches <both nonformal>, pothooks and hangers

8 **stenography, shorthand,** brachygraphy, tachygraphy; speedwriting

9 **letter, written character** 546.1; **alphabet, writing system** 546.3; punctuation 530.15, 18–20

10 <written matter> **writing, the written word; piece;** piece of writing, text, screed; **copy, matter;** the written word; **composition, work,** opus, production, literary production, lucubration, brainchild; **document** 549.5,8; **paper,** parchment, scroll; **script; penscript, typescript; manuscript** *or* MS *or* Ms *or* ms, holograph, autograph; **draft,** recension, **version;** transcription, transcript, fair copy, engrossment

11 <ancient manuscript> **codex;** scroll; palimpsest; papyrus, parchment

12 **literature, letters, belles lettres,** humane letters, republic of letters; **work, literary work, text, literary text; works, complete works,** oeuvre, canon, **literary canon, author's canon; classics,** ancient literature; medieval literature, Renaissance literature, etc; contemporary literature; underground literature; erotic literature, erotica; pornographic literature, pornography, porn *and* hard porn *and* soft porn

<all nonformal>, obscene literature, scatological literature; kitsch

13 writer, scribbler <nonformal>, **penman,** penwoman; pen or pencil pusher <nonformal>, wordslinger, **inkslinger** <nonformal>; **scribe, scrivener, amanuensis, secretary, clerk; copyist,** copier, transcriber; chirographer, calligrapher

14 writing expert, graphologist, handwriting expert; paleographer

15 author, writer, scribe <nonformal>, composer, inditer; authoress, penwoman; **creative writer,** literary artist, literary craftsman, belletrist, man of letters, literary man; wordsmith, word painter; free lance, freelance writer; ghostwriter, ghost <nonformal>; prose writer; **short story writer;** storyteller; **novelist;** diarist; **newspaperman; annalist; poet** 720.13; **dramatist,** humorist 489.12; scriptwriter; **essayist;** monographer; reviewer, critic, literary critic, music critic, art critic, drama critic, dance critic; columnist; pamphleteer; copywriter, advertising writer; encyclopedist, bibliographer

16 hack writer, hack, literary hack, **scribbler** <nonformal>, **potboiler** <nonformal>

17 stenographer, tachygrapher; stenotypist

18 typist; printer

VERBS **19 write, pen, pencil; scribe;** inscribe, scroll; take pen in hand; **put in writing,** put in black and white; **draw up, draft, write out,** make out; **write down, record** 549.16; take down in shorthand; **type; transcribe,** copy out, engross, make a fair copy, copy; **rewrite, revise, edit,** recense, make a recension

20 scribble, scrabble, **scratch, scrawl,** make hen tracks or hen or chicken scratches <nonformal>, doodle

21 write, author, **compose, indite,** formulate, produce, prepare;

dash off, knock off or out <nonformal>, pound or crank or grind or churn out; free-lance; collaborate, coauthor; ghostwrite, ghost <nonformal>; novelize; scenarize; pamphleteer; editorialize

ADJS **22 written,** penned, penciled; **inscribed;** engrossed; **in writing, in black and white,** on paper; calligraphic; manuscript, autograph, autographic, holograph, holographic, holographical, in one's own hand; **longhand,** in longhand, in script; **shorthand,** in shorthand; italic, italicized; cursive, running, flowing; typewritten; printed

23 scribbled, scrabbled, **scratched, scrawled; scribbly, scratchy, scrawly**

24 literary, belletristic; classical

25 auctorial, authorial

26 alphabetic, ideographic, etc 546.8

27 stenographic; shorthand

28 clerical, secretarial

548 PRINTING

NOUNS **1 printing,** publishing, publication; **photoengraving; letterpress, typography; gravure;** rotogravure; **lithography,** photolithography; photo-offset; xerography; silk-screen printing; color printing; photography 714; **graphic arts, printmaking** 713.1

2 composition, typesetting, setting, composing; photosetting, photocomposition; imposition; justification; computerized typesetting; layout, dummy

3 print, imprint, stamp, impression, impress, letterpress; reprint, reissue; offprint; offcut; offset

4 copy, manuscript, typescript; **camera-ready copy; matter**

5 proof, proof sheet; galley, **galley proof;** page proof, color proof, reproduction or repro proof, blueprint, blue <nonformal>; author's proof; revise

6 type, print, stamp, letter; type size; font; face, typeface; roman, sans serif, script, italic, black letter; case, typecase; point, pica; en, em

7 space, spacing, patent space, justifying space, justification space

8 printing surface, plate, printing plate

9 **presswork,** makeready; **press, printing press**; rotary press, web press, rotogravure press; bed, platen, web

10 **printed matter; reading matter, text**; advertising matter

11 **press,** print shop; **publishing house; pressroom,** composing room

12 **printer; compositor, typesetter,** typographer, Linotyper; keyboarder; stereotyper, stereotypist, electrotyper; apprentice printer, devil, printer's devil; **pressman**

13 **proofreader,** reader, copyholder; **copyreader,** copy editor

VERBS 14 **print; imprint, impress, stamp**; engrave; run, run off, strike; **publish, issue, put in print, bring out, put out, get out**; put to press, put to bed, see through the press

15 autotype, electrotype

16 **compose,** set, set in print; **make up,** impose; justify, overrun; pi

17 **copy-edit; proofread,** read, read or correct copy

18 <be printed> go to press, come off press, come out, appear in print

ADJS 19 **printed, in print**; typeset

20 **typographic, typographical; boldface,** bold-faced; **lightface,** light-faced; **upper-case, lower-case**

549 RECORD

NOUNS 1 **record, recording,** documentation, written word; **chronicle, annals,** history, story; roll, **rolls; account; register, registry,** roster, scroll, catalog, inventory, table, list 870; letters, correspondence; **vestige, trace,** memorial, token, relic, remains

2 **archives,** public records, government archives, government papers, presidential papers, historical documents, historical records, memorabilia; biographical records, biographical material, papers; parish rolls or register or records

3 registry, registry office; archives, files; chancery

4 **memorandum, memo** <nonformal>, memoir, *aide-mémoire* <Fr>, memorial; **reminder** 988.6; **note, notation,** annotation, jotting, docket, marginal note, marginalia, scholium, scholia, adversaria, footnote; **entry,** register, **registry,** item; **minutes**

5 **document,** official document, legal document, **instrument,** writ, **paper,** parchment, scroll, roll, **writing,** script; holograph, chirograph; **papers,** ship's papers; docket, **file,** personal file, **dossier**

6 **certificate,** certification, **ticket; authority,** authorization; **credential, voucher, warrant,** warranty, testimonial; note; **affidavit,** sworn statement, notarized statement, deposition, witness, attestation; **visa; bill of health,** clean bill of health; **diploma,** sheepskin <nonformal>; birth certificate, death certificate

7 **report, bulletin, brief, statement, account,** accounting; account rendered; **minutes,** the record, proceedings, transactions, acta; **yearbook,** annual; **returns,** census report or returns, election returns, tally

8 <official documents> state paper, white paper; blue book, green book, white book, yellow book; gazette, official journal, Congressional Record

9 <registers> genealogy, pedigree, studbook; Social Register, blue book; directory; Who's Who

10 <recording media> bulletin board; scoresheet, scorecard, scoreboard; **tape,** magnetic tape, videotape, ticker tape; **computer disk,** diskette, floppy disk or floppy, hard disk, disk cartridge; memory; compact disc or CD; phonograph record, disc or disk,

platter <nonformal>; film, motion-picture film; slip, card, index card, filing card; library catalog, catalog card; microcard, microfiche, microdot, microfilm; **file** 870.3

11 <record books> **notebook, pocketbook,** blankbook; **memorandum book,** memo book <nonformal>, commonplace book, adversaria; **blotter,** police blotter; docket, court calendar; **calendar,** engagement book, agenda; **tablet,** writing tablet; pad, **scratch pad; scrapbook, album; diary, journal; log,** ship's log, **logbook; account book, ledger,** daybook; **cashbook;** Domesday Book; yearbook, annual; guestbook, guest register, register

12 monument, memorial; necrology, obituary, **memento,** remembrance, testimonial; cup, trophy, prize, ribbon, plaque; **marker;** inscription; **tablet,** stone, boundary stone, memorial stone; **pillar,** stele *or* stela, shaft, column; cross; war memorial; arch, memorial arch. triumphal arch; memorial statue, bust; monolith, obelisk, **pyramid; tomb,** grave 309.16; **gravestone, tombstone;** memorial tablet, brass; headstone, footstone; mausoleum; cenotaph; cairn, mound, barrow, cromlech, dolmen, megalith, menhir; **shrine,** reliquary, tope, stupa

13 recorder, registrar 550.1

14 registration, register, registry; recording; enrollment, matriculation, enlistment; **listing, tabulation, cataloging,** indexing; chronicling; **entry,** insertion, entering, posting; **inscription; booking, logging**

VERBS **15 record,** place upon record; **inscribe,** enscroll; **register, enroll,** matriculate, check in; impanel; poll; **file,** index, **catalog,** calendar, **tabulate, list,** docket; **chronicle;** put in the minutes *or* on the record, spread on the record; commit to *or* preserve in an archive; **write,** commit *or* reduce to writing, put in writing, put in black and white, put on paper; **write out; make out,** fill out; **write up;** chalk up; **write down, mark down, jot down, put down, set down, take down; note,** note down, make a note; **post; enter,** make an entry, insert, write in; **book, log;** put on tape, tape, tape-record; record, cut; videotape

ADJS **16 recording,** registrational; certificatory

17 recorded, registered; inscribed, written down; **filed,** indexed, enrolled, **entered,** logged, booked, posted; documented; **on record,** on file, on the books; official, legal, of record

18 documentary, archival; epigraphic, inscriptional; necrological, obituary; testimonial

550 RECORDER

NOUNS **1 recorder; registrar,** register; archivist; librarian; **clerk,** penpusher <nonformal>, filing clerk; town *or* municipal clerk; county clerk; bookkeeper, accountant; **scribe,** scrivener; **secretary,** amanuensis; **stenographer** 547.17; scorekeeper, scorer, official scorer, timekeeper; engraver, stonecutter

2 annalist, genealogist, chronicler; historian

551 INFORMATION

NOUNS **1 information,** info <nonformal>, **facts, data, knowledge** 927; public knowledge, open secret, common knowledge; factual information, hard information; **evidence, proof** 956; **enlightenment,** light; sidelight; **acquaintance,** familiarization, briefing; **instruction** 568.1; **intelligence; the dope** *and* the goods *and* **the scoop** <all nonformal>; transmission, **communication** 343; **report, word,** message, presentation, account, **statement,** mention; white paper, white book, blue book; dispatch, bulletin, communiqué, handout <nonformal>, fact sheet, release; publicity, promotional material, broadside; **notice,** notification; announcement, publication 352; directory, guidebook 574.10

2 inside information, private *or* confidential information; **the lowdown** *and* **inside dope** *and* **hot tip** <all nonformal>; insider; pipeline <nonformal>; privileged information, classified information

3 tip *and* tip-off *and* **pointer** <all nonformal>, clue, cue; steer <nonformal>; **advice;** whisper, **word to the wise,** word in the ear, bug in the ear <nonformal>, bee in the bonnet <nonformal>; warning, caution, monition, alerting, sound bite

4 hint, gentle hint, **intimation, indication, suggestion, mere** *or* **faint suggestion, suspicion, inkling,** whisper, **glimmer, glimmering; cue, clue,** index, **symptom, sign,** spoor, track, scent, sniff, whiff, telltale, tip-off <nonformal>; **implication, insinuation, innuendo;** broad hint, gesture, signal, nod, wink, look, nudge, kick, prompt

5 informant, informer, source, teller, enlightener; **adviser,** monitor; **reporter,** notifier, **announcer,** annunciator; spokesperson, spokespeople, spokeswoman, spokesman, press secretary, press officer, information officer, mouthpiece; communicator, communicant, publisher; **authority,** witness, expert witness; **tipster** <nonformal>, **tout** <nonformal>; newsmonger, gossipmonger; **information medium** *or* **media, mass media,** print media, electronic media, the press, radio, television; channel, the grapevine; information network, network; information center; public relations officer

6 informer, betrayer, doublecrosser <nonformal>; **snitch** *and* snitcher <both nonformal>; whistle-blower <nonformal>;

tattler, tattletale, telltale, talebearer; blab *or* blabberer *or* blabbermouth <all nonformal>; **squealer** *and* **stool pigeon** *and* stoolie *and* **fink** *and* rat <all nonformal>; **spy** 576.9

7 information *or* communication theory; data storage *or* retrieval, EDP *or* electronic data processing

VERBS **8 inform, tell, speak on** *or* **for,** apprise, **advise, advertise, give word,** mention to, **acquaint, enlighten,** familiarize, brief, verse, give the facts, give an account of, give by way of information; **instruct; let know, have one to know, give** *or* **lead one to believe** *or* **understand;** tell once and for all; notify, give notice *or* notification, serve notice; **communicate** 343.6,7; bring *or* send *or* leave word; **report** 552.11; **disclose** 351.4; put in a new light, shed new *or* fresh light upon

9 post *and* **keep one posted** <both nonformal>; wise up *and* clue *or* fill in *and* bring up to speed *or* date *and* put in the picture <all nonformal>

10 hint, intimate, suggest, insinuate, imply, indicate, adumbrate, give *or* drop *or* throw out a hint, give an inkling of, **hint at; leak,** let slip out; allude to, make an allusion to; **prompt,** put onto; put in *or* into one's head, put a bee in one's bonnet

11 tip *and* tip off *and* **give one a tip** <all nonformal>, alert; **give a pointer to** <nonformal>; **let in on**; put next to *and* **put on to** *and* put on to something hot <all nonformal>; **confide,** confide to, entrust with information, give confidential information, mention privately *or* confidentially, whisper, buzz, breathe, **put a bug in one's ear** <nonformal>

12 inform on *or* **against, betray; tattle;** turn informer; testify against, **bear witness against;** turn state's evidence

13 <nonformal terms> **sell one out** *or* **down the river,** tell on, blab, snitch, squeal, sell out, sing, rat, stool, fink, finger, put the finger on, blow the whistle, spill one's guts, spill the beans, squawk

14 learn, come to know, be informed or **apprised of, get wise to** <nonformal>, **get hep to** and **next to** and **on to** <all nonformal>; become conscious or aware of, awaken to, tumble to <nonformal>, open one's eyes to

15 know 927.12, be informed or apprised, have the facts, be in the know <nonformal>, **come to one's knowledge,** reach one's ears; be told, **hear, overhear,** hear tell of <nonformal>; get wind of; **know well** 927.13; have inside information, know where the bodies are buried <nonformal>

16 keep informed, keep posted <nonformal>, **keep up on,** keep up to date or au courant, keep abreast of the times; **keep track of,** keep watch on, keep tabs on <nonformal>, keep an eye on

ADJS **17 informed** 927.18–20; informed of, in the know 927.16, clued-in or clued-up <nonformal>

18 informative, informational; **instructive, enlightening;** educative, educational; advisory, monitory; **communicative**

19 telltale, tattletale, kiss-and-tell

ADVS **20** from information received, according to reports or rumor, as a matter of general information, from what one can gather, as far as anyone knows

552 NEWS

NOUNS **1 news, tidings, intelligence, information, word,** advice; newsworthiness; a nose for news; **journalism,** reportage, coverage, news coverage; **the press,** the fourth estate, the press corps, print journalism, electronic journalism, broadcast journalism, broadcast news, radio journalism, television journalism; **news medium** or **media,** newspaper, newsletter, newsmagazine, radio, television; press box, press gallery; yellow press, tabloid press

2 good news, good word, **glad tidings;** bad news

3 news item, piece of news; **article, story,** piece; copy; scoop and beat <both nonformal>, exclusive; breaking story, newsbreak; follow-up, sidebar; spot news; outtake; sound bite

4 message, dispatch, word, communication, communiqué, advice, press release, release; **letter** 553.2; **telegram** 347.14

5 bulletin, news report, **flash**

6 report, rumor, unverified or unconfirmed report, **hearsay, scuttlebutt** and latrine rumor <both nonformal>; **talk, whisper, buzz, rumble,** cry; **common talk, talk of the town,** topic of the day, cause célèbre <Fr>; **grapevine; canard**

7 gossip, gossiping, gossipmongering, newsmongering, back-fence gossip <nonformal>; **talebearing; tattle,** tittle-tattle, chitchat, **talk,** idle talk, small talk; piece of gossip, groundless rumor, tale, story

8 scandal, dirt <nonformal>, **malicious gossip;** juicy morsel, tidbit, choice bit of dirt <nonformal>; **scandalmongering;** gossip column; character assassination, **slander** 512.3; whispering campaign

9 newsmonger, rumormonger, scandalmonger, gossip, gossipmonger, gossiper, yenta <Yiddish>, quidnunc, **busybody,** tabby <nonformal>; **talebearer,** taleteller, telltale, **tattletale** <nonformal>, tattler, tittletattler; gossip columnist; reporter, newspaperman

10 <secret news channel> **grapevine; pipeline;** a litle birdie

VERBS **11 report,** give a report, give an account of, tell, relate; write up, make out or write up a report; gather the news; dig up dirt <nonformal>; bring word, tell the news, break the news, give tidings of; bring glad tidings, give the good word; announce 352.12; put around, spread, **rumor** 352.10; clue in <nonformal>, **inform** 551.8

12 **gossip,** talk over the back fence <nonformal>; **tattle,** tittle-tattle; **talk;** retail gossip, **dish the dirt** <nonformal>

ADJS 13 **newsworthy,** front-page, newsy; reportorial

14 **gossipy,** gossiping, newsy; **talebearing,** taletelling

15 **reported, rumored,** whispered; rumored about, talked about, whispered about, bruited about, bandied about; **in the news, in circulation, in the air, going around,** going about, **current, rife,** afloat, on all tongues, on the street, all over town; made public 352.17

ADVS 16 reportedly, allegedly, as they say, as it is said, **as the story goes,** as the fellow says <nonformal>, it is said

553 CORRESPONDENCE

NOUNS 1 **correspondence, letter writing,** written communication, exchange of letters; personal correspondence, business correspondence; mailing, mass mailing

2 **letter, epistle, message, communication, dispatch, missive;** personal letter, business letter; **note, line,** chit; **reply, answer, acknowledgment**

3 **card, postcard, postal card;** picture postcard

4 **mail, post, postal services,** letter bag; mailing list; junk mail <nonformal>; direct mail, direct-mail advertising or selling, mail-order selling; mail solicitation; fan mail

5 **postage;** stamp, postage stamp; frank; postmark, cancellation; postage meter

6 **mailbox;** letter drop, mail drop; mailing machine or mailer; mailbag

7 **postal service, postal system;** post office or PO, mailboat;

mailman, postman; mail clerk, post-office or postal clerk; postal union

8 **correspondent, letter writer,** writer, communicator; pen pal <nonformal>; addressee

9 **address,** name and address, **destination;** zone, postal zone, zip code or zip, postal code <Canada>; letterhead, billhead; drop

VERBS 10 **correspond,** correspond with, **communicate with, write, write to,** write a letter, **drop a line** <nonformal>; use the mails; keep up a correspondence, exchange letters

11 **reply, answer, acknowledge;** reply by return mail

12 **mail, post,** dispatch, send; airmail

13 **address, direct,** superscribe

ADJS 14 epistolary; **postal,** post; letter; mail-order, direct-mail; mail-in; mailable

554 BOOK

NOUNS 1 **book, volume, tome;** publication, writing, **work, opus, production; title;** trade book; **textbook,** schoolbook; **reference book; novel; best seller; children's book;** prayer book, psalter, psalmbook; **classic,** magnum opus, standard work, definitive work

2 **publisher,** book publisher; publishing house, press, small press, vanity press; **editor;** packager; **printer,** book printer; **bookbinder; bookdealer, bookseller;** book manufacturer, press

3 **book, printed book, bound book,** bound volume; **hardcover, hardbound book; paperback,** paper-bound book

4 volume, tome; folio

5 **edition,** issue; volume, number; **printing,** impression; series, set, boxed set, collection, library; library edition; **trade edition;** school edition

6 **rare book,** early edition; first edition; manuscript, scroll, codex; incunabulum

7 **compilation,** omnibus; symposium; collection, miscellany; collected works, selected works, complete works, canon; **miscellanea,** analects; chrestomathy; **anthology;** *Festschrift* <Ger>; quotation book; scrapbook

8 **handbook, manual,** vade mecum, gradus; **cookbook;** field guide; travel book, **guidebook** 574.10

9 **reference book; encyclopedia; concordance; catalog;** *catalogue raisonné* <Fr>; **directory; atlas, gazetteer;** source book, casebook; **language reference book; dictionary,** lexicon, wordbook; **thesaurus, Roget's,** storehouse *or* treasury of words

10 **textbook, text, schoolbook, manual,** manual of instruction; **primer,** abecedarium; hornbook; gradus, exercise book, workbook; **grammar, reader;** spelling book, speller, casebook

11 **booklet, pamphlet, brochure, chapbook, leaflet, folder, tract;** circular 352.8

12 **makeup, design;** front matter, text, back matter; page, leaf, folio; flyleaf, endpaper, signature; recto, verso; copyright page, imprint, colophon; dedication, inscription; acknowledgments, preface, foreword, introduction; table of contents; errata; bibliography; index

13 part, section, book, volume; article; serial

14 bookbinding, bibliopegy

15 <bookbinding styles> Aldine, Arabesque, Byzantine, Canevari, cottage, dentelle, Etruscan, fanfare, Grolier, Harleian, Jansenist, Maioli, pointillé, Roxburgh

16 **bookstore, bookshop,** *librairie* <Fr>; **bookstall,** bookstand; **book club**

17 **bookholder, bookrest, book end; bookcase,** bookrack, bookstand, **bookshelf;** stack, bookstack; **portfolio**

18 **booklover,** bibliophile, bibliolater, book collector, bibliomaniac;

bookworm, bibliophage; bookstealer, biblioklept

19 **bibliology,** bibliography

ADJS 20 bibliological, bibliographical

555 PERIODICAL

1 **periodical, serial, journal,** gazette; **magazine;** pictorial; review; organ, **house organ; trade journal,** trade magazine; daily, weekly, biweekly, bimonthly, monthly, quarterly; annual, yearbook

2 **newspaper,** news, **paper,** sheet *or* rag <both nonformal>, **gazette,** daily newspaper, daily, weekly newspaper, weekly; newspaper of record; **tabloid,** extra, special edition

3 **the press,** journalism, **the fourth estate;** print medium, the print media, print journalism, the print press, the public print; **wire service,** newswire; **publishing,** newspaper publishing, magazine publishing; **the publishing industry, communications,** mass media, the communications industry

4 **journalist, newspaperman, newspaperwoman, newsman, newswoman,** newspeople, inkstained wretch, newswriter, gentleman *or* representative of the press; **reporter,** newshawk *and* newshound <both nonformal>; leg man <nonformal>; investigative reporter; **cub reporter; correspondent, foreign correspondent,** war correspondent, special correspondent, stringer; publicist; rewriter, **rewrite man; editor, copy editor; copyreader;** editorial writer; **columnist; photographer, news photographer,** photojournalist; paparazzo

ADJS 5 **journalistic,** journalese <nonformal>; **periodical,** serial; **editorial; reportorial**

556 TREATISE

NOUNS 1 **treatise,** treatment, tractate, tract; examination, survey, discourse, discussion, disquisition, descant, exposition, screed; homily; memoir; dissertation; **thesis; essay,** theme; pandect; **study,** lucubration; **paper,** research paper, term paper; **sketch,** outline; **monograph; note;** prolegomenon; **article**

2 **commentary; comment, remark; criticism,** critique, analysis; **review,** critical review, **report,** notice, **write-up** <nonformal>; **editorial**

3 **discourser,** expositor, descanter; symposiast, discussant; **essayist; writer, author** 547.15

4 **commentator;** expositor, expounder; annotator, scholiast; **critic; reviewer,** book reviewer; **editor;** editorial writer, editorialist; news analyst; publicist

VERBS 5 **write upon,** touch upon, **discuss, treat, treat of, deal with,** take up, handle, go into, inquire into, survey; discourse, descant; **comment upon,** remark upon; **criticize, review, write up**

ADJS 6 dissertational, disquisitional; expository, expositive; essayistic; monographic; critical

557 ABRIDGMENT

NOUNS 1 **abridgment,** compendium, **condensation,** short version, condensed version, abbreviation, brief, digest, **abstract,** epitome, **précis, capsule,** capsulization, encapsulation, sketch, thumbnail sketch, **synopsis,** conspectus, syllabus, **survey, review,** overview, pandect, bird's-eye view; **outline,** skeleton, draft

2 **summary, résumé, recapitulation, recap** <nonformal>, rundown, run-through; **summation;** sum and substance, **wrapup** <nonformal>; pith, meat, gist, core, essence, main point 996.6

3 **excerpt, extract, selection,** extraction, excerption, snippet; passage, selected passage; **clip** <nonformal>, film clip, outtake, sound bite <nonformal>

4 **excerpts, extracts, gleanings,** cuttings, clippings, snippets; **anthology;** fragments; analects; **miscellany,** miscellanea; **collection**

VERBS 5 **abridge, shorten** 268.6, **condense, cut, clip; summarize,** synopsize, wrap up <nonformal>; **outline, sketch,** sketch out, hit the high spots; capsule, capsulize, encapsulate; **put in a nutshell**

ADJS 6 **abridged,** condensed; shortened, clipped; nutshell, compendious, **brief** 268.8

ADVS 7 in brief, in summary, in sum, in a nutshell 537.8

558 LIBRARY

1 **library,** book depository; learning center; media center, media resource center, information center; **public library; special library; circulating library, lending library; book wagon, bookmobile;** bookroom, athenaeum; reading room; **national library**

2 **librarianship; library science,** information science, library services

3 **librarian,** professional librarian, library professional; **director, head librarian, chief librarian**

4 **bibliography; index; publisher's catalog,** publisher's list, backlist; **library catalog,** computerized catalog, on-line catalog, integrated online system; CD-ROM workstation

559 RELATIONSHIP BY BLOOD

NOUNS 1 **blood relationship,** consanguinity, common descent *or* ancestry, biological *or* genetic relationship, **kinship,** kindred, **relation, relationship;** propinquity; cognation; filiation; affiliation; alliance, connection, **family connection** *or* tie; motherhood, maternity; fatherhood, paternity; patrilineage, matrilineage; brotherhood, brother-

ship, fraternity; sisterhood, sister-
ship; **ancestry** 560

2 kinfolk *and* **kinfolks** <both
nonformal>, **kinsmen, kinsfolk,
kindred, kin,** kith and kin, **family, relatives, relations, people,**
folks <nonformal>, connections;
blood relation *or* **relative,** flesh,
blood, flesh and blood; cognate;
agnate, enate; kinsman, kins-
woman, sib, sibling; german; next
of kin; collateral relative, collateral; distaff *or* spindle side; sword
or spear side; **tribesman,** tribes-
people, clansman *or* -woman; **ancestry** 560, **posterity** 561

3 brother, bub *and* bubba *and* bro
and bud *and* buddy <all nonfor-
mal>, frater; brethren 700.1;
sister, sis *and* sissy <both nonfor-
mal>; kid brother *or* sister; blood
brother *or* sister, brother- *or*
sister-german; half brother *or*
sister, foster brother *or* sister,
stepbrother *or* stepsister; **aunt,**
auntie <nonformal>; **uncle,** unc
and uncs *and* nuncle <all nonfor-
mal>, **nephew, niece; cousin,**
cousin-german; first cousin, second cousin, etc; cousin once
removed, cousin twice removed,
etc; country cousin; great-uncle,
granduncle; great-granduncle;
great-aunt, grandaunt; great-
grandaunt; grandnephew, grand-
niece; **father, mother; son,
daughter** 561.2

**4 race, people, folk, family,
house, clan, tribe, nation;** patri-
clan, matriclan, gens, phyle,
phratry, totem; **lineage,** line,
blood, strain, stock, stem, species, stirps, **breed,** brood, kind;
plant *or* animal kingdom, class,
order, etc 808.5; **ethnicity,** tribal-
ism, clannishness

5 family, brood, nuclear family,
extended family, one-parent *or*
single-parent family; **house,
household,** hearth, hearthside,
ménage, people, **folk,** homefolk,
folks *and* homefolks <both non-
formal>; **children,** issue, descendants, progeny, **offspring,** get,
kids <nonformal>

ADJS 6 related, kindred, akin;
consanguineous, consanguine, by
or of the blood; **biological,** genetic; **natural, birth,** by birth;
cognate, agnate, enate; sib, sibling; allied, affiliated; german;
germane; collateral; foster; patri-
lineal, matrilineal; patroclinous,
matroclinous; patrilateral, ma-
trilateral; avuncular; intimately
or closely related, remotely *or* dis-
tantly related

**7 racial, ethnic, tribal, national,
family,** clannish, totemic, **lineal;
ethnic;** phyletic, phylogenetic,
genetic; gentile, gentilic

560 ANCESTRY

NOUNS 1 ancestry, progenitorship;
parentage, parenthood; grand-
parentage, grandfatherhood,
grandmotherhood

2 paternity, fatherhood; natural
or birth *or* biological fatherhood;
fatherliness, paternalness; adoptive fatherhood

3 maternity, motherhood; natural *or* birth *or* biological motherhood; motherliness, maternal-
ness; adoptive motherhood; surrogate motherhood

**4 lineage, line, bloodline, de-
scent,** descendancy, line of
descent, ancestral line, succession, **extraction,** derivation,
birth, **blood,** breed, **family,**
house, **strain, stock,** race, stirps,
seed; direct line, phylum;
branch, stem; filiation, affiliation; side, father's side, mother's
side; enate, agnate, cognate; male
line; female line; consanguinity,
common ancestry 559.1

5 genealogy, pedigree, genealogical tree, **family tree,** tree

**6 heredity, heritage, inheri-
tance, birth;** patrocliny,
matrocliny; endowment, inborn
capacity *or* tendency *or* susceptibility *or* predisposition;
inheritability, heritability; **ge-
netics,** eugenics; **gene,** factor,
inheritance factor, determiner,
determinant; **character,** dominant *or* recessive character, allele

or allelomorph; germ cell, germ
plasm; **chromosome;** chromatin,
chromatid; genetic code; DNA,
RNA, replication

**7 ancestors, antecedents, prede-
cessors, fathers, forefathers,
forebears,** progenitors; **grand-
parents,** grandfathers; patri-
archs, elders

8 parent, progenitor, ancestor,
procreator, begetter; natural *or*
birth *or* biological parent; step-
parent; adoptive parent; surrogate parent

9 father, sire, genitor, paternal ancestor, pater <nonformal>, the
old man <nonformal>; patriarch,
paterfamilias; stepfather; foster
father, adoptive father; birth
father

10 <nonformal terms> **papa,** pa,
pappy, **pop,** pops, **dad, daddy,**
daddyo, big daddy, the old
man

11 mother, maternal ancestor, matriarch, materfamilias; stepmother; foster mother, adoptive
mother; birth mother

12 <nonformal terms> **mama,** the
old woman, **ma, mom, mommy,**
mummy, mumsy

13 grandfather, grandsire; old man
304.2; great-grandfather

14 <nonformal terms> **grandpa,**
grampa, gramps, grandpappy,
granddad, granddaddy, grand-
dada, pop, grandpop

15 grandmother, grandam; great-
grandmother

16 <nonformal terms> **grandma,**
old woman 304.3; **granny,**
grammy, gammer

ADJS **17 ancestral,** patriarchal;
parental, parent; **paternal,** fa-
therly, fatherlike; **maternal,**
motherly, motherlike; grand-
motherly; grandfatherly

18 lineal, family, genealogical; enate, agnate, cognate; direct, in a
direct line

19 hereditary, patrimonial, **inherited, innate;** genetic;
patroclinous, matroclinous

20 inheritable, heritable, heredita-
ble

561 POSTERITY

NOUNS **1 posterity, progeny, issue, offspring,** fruit, seed, brood,
breed, family; **descent,** succession; lineage 560.4, blood,
bloodline; **descendants,** heirs,
inheritors, sons, **children, kids**
<nonformal>, little ones, hos-
tages to fortune, youngsters; new
or young *or* rising generation

2 <of animals> **young, brood,** get,
spawn, spat, fry; **litter,** farrow
<of pigs>; clutch, hatch

**3 descendant; offspring, child,
scion; son,** son and heir, a chip
off the old block, sonny; **daughter,** heiress; grandchild, grand-
son, granddaughter; stepchild,
stepson, stepdaughter; foster
child

4 <derived or collateral descen-
dant> **offshoot,** offset, **branch,**
sprout, shoot, filiation

5 bastard, illegitimate, whoreson,
child born out of wedlock *or* without benefit of clergy *or* on the
wrong side of the blanket, natural
or love child; illegitimacy, bastardy, bar *or* bend sinister

6 sonship, sonhood; daughtership,
daughterhood

ADJS **7 filial,** sonlike; **daughterly,**
daughterlike

562 LOVEMAKING, ENDEARMENT

NOUNS **1 lovemaking,** dalliance,
amorous dalliance, billing and
cooing; **fondling, caressing,**
hugging, kissing; cuddling, snug-
gling, nestling, nuzzling; bundling; sexual intercourse 75.7

2 <nonformal terms> **making
out, necking, petting,** spooning,
smooching, canoodling, pitching
woo, sucking face, swapping spit

3 embrace, hug, squeeze, fond
embrace, embracement, clasp,
enfoldment, bear hug <nonfor-
mal>

4 kiss, buss, smack, smooch
<nonformal>, **osculation;**
French kiss, soul kiss

5 endearment; caress, pat; sweet

talk, soft words, honeyed words, sweet nothings; blandishments, artful endearments; love call, mating call, wolf whistle

6 <terms of endearment> **darling, dear,** deary, **sweetheart, sweetie, sweet,** sweets, sweetkins, **honey,** hon, honeybun, honeybunch, honey child, sugar, love, lover, precious, precious heart, pet, petkins, babe, **baby, doll,** baby-doll, cherub, angel, chick, duck, ducks, lamb, lambkin, snookums

7 **courtship, courting, wooing;** court, suit, suing, amorous pursuit, addresses; gallantry; serenade

8 **proposal,** marriage proposal, offer of marriage, popping of the question; engagement 436.3

9 **flirtation, flirtiness, coquetry,** dalliance; flirtatiousness, coquettishness, coyness; goo-goo eyes <nonformal>, amorous looks, coquettish glances, come-hither look; bedroom eyes <nonformal>

10 **philandering,** lady-killing <nonformal>; lechery, licentiousness, unchastity 665

11 **flirt, coquette,** gold digger *and* vamp <both nonformal>; strumpet, whore 665.14,16

12 **philanderer,** woman chaser, **ladies' man,** heartbreaker; masher, lady-killer, wolf, skirt chaser, man on the make *and* make-out artist <both nonformal>; libertine, lecher, seducer 665.12, Casanova, Don Juan

13 **love letter,** billet-doux, mash note <nonformal>; valentine

VERBS 14 **make love,** bill and coo; dally, toy, trifle, make time; sweet-talk <nonformal>, whisper sweet nothings; go steady, keep company; copulate

15 <nonformal terms> **make out, neck,** pet, spoon, smooch, canoodle, pitch woo, suck face, swap spit

16 **caress, pet,** pat; feel *or* feel up <nonformal>, **fondle,** dandle; chuck under the chin

17 **cuddle, snuggle, nestle,** nuzzle; lap; bundle

18 **embrace, hug, clasp, press, squeeze** <nonformal>, fold, **enfold,** put *or* throw one's arms around, take to *or* in one's arms

19 **kiss, osculate,** smack, smooch <nonformal>; blow a kiss

20 **flirt, coquet; philander,** gallivant, play the field <nonformal>, run *or* play around, sow one's oats; **make eyes at, ogle,** eye, make goo-goo eyes at <nonformal>; play hard to get

21 **court, woo,** sue, press one's suit, **pay court** *or* **suit to,** cozy up to <nonformal>, pay attention to, fling oneself at, throw oneself at the head of; **pursue,** follow; chase <nonformal>; set one's cap for <nonformal>; serenade; spark <nonformal>, squire

22 **propose, pop the question** <nonformal>, ask for one's hand; become engaged

ADJS 23 amatory, amative; sexual 75.28,29; **flirtatious,** flirty; **coquettish,** coy, come-hither

563 MARRIAGE

NOUNS 1 **marriage, matrimony, wedlock, married status,** holy matrimony, holy wedlock, match, splicing <nonformal>, union, matrimonial union, alliance, marriage sacrament, sacrament of matrimony, bond of matrimony, wedding knot, conjugal bond *or* tie *or* knot, nuptial bond *or* tie *or* knot; married state, wedded state, wedded bliss, weddedness; cohabitation; bed, marriage bed, bridebed; intermarriage, mixed marriage, interfaith marriage, interracial marriage; miscegenation; misalliance

2 **marriageability,** nubility, ripeness

3 **wedding, marriage,** marriage ceremony, nuptial mass; church wedding, civil wedding, civil ceremony; banns; **nuptials;** wedding song, marriage song, nuptial song, prothalamium, epithalamium, hymeneal; wedding veil;

bridal suite; **honeymoon;** forced marriage, shotgun wedding; elopement

4 wedding party; wedding attendant, usher; **best man; bridesmaid,** maid *or* matron of honor

5 newlywed; bridegroom, groom; bride, blushing bride; war bride, GI bride <nonformal>; honeymooner

6 spouse, mate, partner, consort, **better half** <nonformal>

7 husband, married man, man, benedict, old man <nonformal>

8 wife, married woman, wedded wife, squaw, woman, lady, matron, old lady *and* old woman *and* little woman *and* ball and chain <all nonformal>, **better half** <nonformal>, **helpmate,** helpmeet, rib, wife of one's bosom; wife in name only; wife in all but name, concubine, common-law wife

9 married couple, wedded pair, happy couple, **man and wife,** husband and wife, man and woman, one flesh; newlyweds, **bride and groom**

10 harem, seraglio, serai; zenana, purdah

11 monogamist, monogynist; **bigamist;** digamist; trigamist; **polygamist,** polygynist, polyandrist

12 matchmaker, marriage broker, matrimonial agent, *shadchen* <Yiddish>

13 <god> Hymen; <goddesses> Hera, Teleia; Juno, Pronuba; Frigg

VERBS **14** <join in marriage> **marry,** wed, nuptial, **join, unite, hitch** *and* **splice** <both nonformal>, couple, match, match up, make *or* arrange a match, join together, **unite in marriage,** join *or* unite in holy wedlock, tie the knot, make one; give away, give in marriage; marry off, find a mate for, find a husband *or* wife for

15 <get married> **marry, wed,** mate, couple, espouse, wive, **take to wife, get hitched** *or* **spliced** <both nonformal>, tie the knot, become one, be made one, give

one's hand to, lead to the altar, take for better or for worse; remarry, rewed; intermarry, interwed, miscegenate

16 honeymoon, go on a honeymoon

17 cohabit, live together, live as man and wife, share one's bed and board

ADJS **18 matrimonial, marital, conjugal, connubial, nuptial,** wedded, married, hymeneal; epithalamic; **spousal;** husbandly, uxorious; wifely, uxorial

19 monogamous, monogynous, monandrous; **bigamous,** digamous; **polygamous,** polygynous, polyandrous; morganatic

20 marriageable, nubile, of age, of marriageable age

21 married, wedded, one, mated, matched, coupled, paired, hitched *and* spliced <both nonformal>

564 RELATIONSHIP BY MARRIAGE

NOUNS **1 marriage relationship,** marital affinity; connection, family connection, marriage connection

2 in-laws <nonformal>, relatives-in-law

3 stepfather, stepmother; stepbrother, stepsister

ADJS **4 affinal,** affined, by marriage

565 CELIBACY

NOUNS **1 celibacy, singleness,** single *or* unmarried *or* unwed state *or* condition; **bachelorhood,** bachelordom; **spinsterhood,** maidenhood, maidenhead, **virginity,** maiden *or* virgin state; **monasticism;** misogamy, misogyny; sexual abstinence *or* abstention, continence 664.3

2 celibate; monk, monastic, priest, nun; misogamist, misogynist; unmarried, single <nonformal>

3 bachelor, bach <nonformal>, confirmed bachelor, **single man**

4 single *or* unmarried woman, spinster, spinstress, **old maid,**

maid, maiden, bachelor girl, single girl, single woman, lone woman, maiden lady; **virgin,** cherry <nonformal>; vestal, vestal virgin

VERBS **5 be unmarried, be single, live alone,** enjoy single blessedness, **bach** *and* **bach it** <both nonformal>, keep bachelor quarters, keep one's freedom

ADJS **6 celibate; monastic,** monachal, **monkish;** misogamic, misogynous; sexually abstinent *or* continent, abstinent, abstaining

7 unmarried, unwedded, unwed, single, spouseless, wifeless, husbandless; **bachelorly,** bachelorlike; **spinsterly,** spinsterish, spinsterlike; **old-maidish;** maiden, maidenly; virgin, virginal

566 DIVORCE, WIDOWHOOD

NOUNS **1 divorce,** civil divorce, **separation,** legal separation, separate maintenance; interlocutory decree; dissolution of marriage; annulment, decree of nullity; broken marriage, broken home

2 divorcé, divorced person, divorced man, divorced woman, *divorcée* <Fr>; grass widow, grass widower

3 widowhood; widowerhood; weeds, widow's weeds

4 widow, widow woman <nonformal>; dowager; **widower,** widowman <nonformal>

VERBS **5 divorce, separate,** part, split up <nonformal>, unmarry, obtain a divorce, come to a parting of the ways, untie the knot, sue for divorce, file suit for divorce; grant a divorce, grant a final decree; grant an annulment, annul a marriage, put asunder

6 widow, bereave

ADJS **7** widowly, widowish, widowlike; **widowed,** widowered; **divorced;** separated, legally separated

567 SCHOOL

NOUNS **1 school, educational institution,** teaching institution, academic institution, teaching and research institution, **institute, academy,** seminary; alternative school; magnet school

2 preschool, nursery school; day nursery, **day-care center,** crèche; playschool; **kindergarten**

3 elementary school, grade school, the grades; **primary school; grammar school**

4 secondary school, middle school, **academy,** lyceum; **high school; junior high school,** junior high <nonformal>, intermediate school; **senior high school,** senior high <nonformal>; **preparatory school,** prep school <nonformal>, seminary; Latin school

5 college, university, institution of higher education *or* learning, degree-granting institution; graduate school, coeducational school; academe, academia, the groves of Academe, **the campus,** the halls of learning *or* ivy, ivied halls; alma mater

6 service school, service academy, military academy, naval academy

7 art school, performing arts school, music school, conservatory, school of the arts, dance school

8 religious school, parochial school, church-related school, church school; Sunday school

9 reform school, reformatory, correctional institution, industrial school, training school

10 schoolhouse, school building; little red schoolhouse; classroom building; hall; campus

11 schoolroom, classroom; recitation room; lecture room *or* hall; auditorium; theater, amphitheater

12 governing board, board; board of education, school board

ADJS **13 scholastic, academic,** institutional, **school,** classroom; **collegiate; university;** preschool; interscholastic, intercollegiate; intramural

568 TEACHING

NOUNS **1 teaching, instruction, education, schooling, tuition; edification, enlightenment,** illumination; tutelage; tutoring, coaching; spoon-feeding; direction, guidance; **pedagogy,** didacticism; catechization; computer-aided instruction, programmed instruction; self-teaching, self-instruction; information 551; reeducation 857.4; **school** 567; **formal education,** coursework, schoolwork

2 inculcation, indoctrination, catechization, inoculation, **implantation, impression, instillment,** impregnation, **infusion,** imbuement; absorption and regurgitation; conditioning, brainwashing; reindoctrination 857.5

3 training, preparation, readying <nonformal>, **conditioning, grooming,** cultivation, development, improvement; **discipline; upbringing, bringing-up, rearing, raising, breeding, nurture,** nurturing, fostering; **practice,** rehearsal, **exercise, drill,** drilling; **apprenticeship,** in-service training, on-the-job training; work-study; military training; basic training; manual training, sloyd; vocational training or education

4 preinstruction; **priming,** cramming <nonformal>

5 elementary education; initiation, introduction; rudiments, grounding, first steps, elements, **ABC's, basics;** reading, writing, and arithmetic, **three R's;** primer, abecedarium

6 instructions, directions, orders; briefing

7 lesson, teaching, instruction, lecture, harangue, **discourse,** disquisition, exposition, **talk,** homily, **sermon,** preachment; **recitation,** recital; **assignment, exercise,** task, homework; **moral,** moral lesson; object lesson

8 study, branch of learning; **discipline,** subdiscipline; **field,** **specialty,** area; **course,** course of study, **curriculum; subject; major, minor;** requirement or required course, elective course, core curriculum; refresher course; summer-session course, intersession course; gut course <nonformal>; **seminar,** proseminar

9 physical education, physical culture, gymnastics, calisthenics, eurythmics

VERBS **10 teach, instruct,** give instruction, give lessons in, **educate, school; edify, enlighten,** illumine; **direct, guide;** get across, **inform** 551.8; **show,** show the ropes, demonstrate; give an idea of; set right; improve one's mind, broaden the mind; sharpen the wits, open the eyes or mind; teach a lesson, give a lesson to; **ground,** teach the rudiments or elements or basics; catechize; teach an old dog new tricks

11 tutor, coach; prime, cram <nonformal>, cram with facts, stuff with knowledge

12 inculcate, indoctrinate, catechize, **instill, infuse,** imbue, impregnate, **implant,** impress; **impress upon the mind or memory,** beat into, beat or knock into one's head, drum into one's head or skull; **condition, brainwash, program**

13 train; drill, exercise; practice, rehearse; keep in practice, keep one's hand in; **prepare,** ready, **condition, groom,** fit, put in tune, form, **lick into shape** <nonformal>, **rear, raise, bring up,** bring up by hand, **breed; cultivate,** develop, improve; **nurture, foster,** nurse; **discipline,** take in hand; put through the mill or grind <nonformal>; break, break in, housebreak; apprentice

14 preinstruct, pre-educate; **initiate,** introduce

15 give instructions, give directions; **brief,** give a briefing

16 expound; explain 341.10; **lec-**

ture, **discourse,** harangue, hold forth, give or read a lesson; **preach,** sermonize; **moralize,** point a moral

17 **assign,** give or make an assignment; give homework, set a task; lay out a course

ADJS 18 **educational,** educative, educating, teaching, **instructive,** instructional, **tuitional; cultural, edifying, enlightening,** illuminating; informative; didactic; preceptive; self-teaching, autodidactic; lecturing, preaching, hortatory, homiletic; initiatory, introductory; **disciplinary;** coeducational

19 **scholastic, academic, schoolish, pedantic; scholarly; pedagogical;** graduate, professional, postgraduate; interdisciplinary, cross-disciplinary; curricular

20 extracurricular; nonscholastic, noncollegiate

569 MISTEACHING

NOUNS 1 **misteaching,** misinstruction; **misguidance,** misdirection, misleading; sophistry 935; perversion, corruption; mystification, obscuration, obfuscation, obscurantism; **misinformation,** misknowledge; the blind leading the blind

2 **propaganda;** indoctrination; brainwashing; **propagandist,** agitprop; **disinformation**

VERBS 3 **misteach,** misinstruct, miseducate; **misinform;** misadvise, **misguide,** misdirect, **mislead;** pervert, corrupt; mystify, obscure, obfuscate

4 **propagandize,** carry on a propaganda; indoctrinate; **disinform,** brainwash

ADJS 5 **mistaught,** misinstructed; **misinformed;** misadvised, **misguided,** misdirected, **misled**

6 misteaching, misinstructive, miseducative, **misinforming; misleading,** misguiding, misdirecting; obscuring, mystifying, obfuscatory; propagandistic, indoctrinational; disinformational

570 LEARNING

NOUNS 1 **learning,** intellectual acquisition or attainment, stocking the mind, mental cultivation, improving or broadening the mind; **mastery,** mastery of skills; **self-education,** self-instruction; **knowledge, erudition** 927.5; education 568.1; memorization 988.4

2 **absorption,** assimilation, taking-in, getting, getting the hang of <nonformal>, soaking-up, digestion

3 **study, studying,** application; **reading, perusal;** brushing up, boning up <nonformal>, **review;** contemplation 930.2; **inspection** 937.3; **engrossment; brainwork, headwork,** lucubration; exercise, **practice, drill;** grind and grinding and boning <all nonformal>, **cramming** and cram <both nonformal>

4 **studiousness, scholarliness,** scholarship; bookishness, diligence 330.6

5 **teachableness, teachability, educability; aptness, aptitude,** quickness, **readiness; receptivity,** mind like a blotter, ready grasp, quick mind, quick study; **willingness, motivation,** hunger or thirst for learning; docility, **malleability,** moldability, facility, **impressionability,** susceptibility; brightness, cleverness, **intelligence** 919

VERBS 6 **learn,** get, get into one's head, get through one's thick skull <nonformal>; **gain knowledge,** pick up information, gather or collect or glean knowledge or learning; improve or broaden the mind; **find out, ascertain, discover,** find, determine; **become informed,** gain knowledge or understanding of, acquire information or intelligence about, **learn about, find out about;** acquaint oneself with, become acquainted with; be informed 551.14

7 **absorb, acquire, take in,** get by

osmosis, **assimilate, digest, soak up,** drink in; **soak in, seep in**

8 **memorize** 988.17, get by rote; fix in the mind 988.18

9 **master,** attain mastery of, make oneself master of, **gain command of, become adept in,** become familiar or conversant with, become versed or well-versed in, **get up in** or on, gain a thorough knowledge of, **learn all about, get down pat** <nonformal>, get down cold <nonformal>, get to the bottom or heart of; **get the hang** or **knack of; learn the ropes,** learn the ins and outs

10 **learn by experience,** learn by doing, **live and learn,** learn the hard way <nonformal>; teach or school oneself; **learn a lesson,** be taught a lesson

11 **be taught, receive instruction,** be tutored, pursue one's education, attend classes, go to or attend school, matriculate, enroll, register; **train,** prepare oneself, ready oneself, go into training; serve an apprenticeship; apprentice oneself to; **study with,** read with, sit at the feet of, learn from, have as one's master; monitor, audit

12 **study,** apply oneself to, crack a book and hit the books <both nonformal>; **read, peruse,** go over, read up or read up on, have one's nose in a book <nonformal>; **review; contemplate** 930.12; **examine** 937.23; **pore over**; be highly motivated, hunger or thirst for knowledge; bury oneself in, wade through, plunge into; **dig** and **grind** and **bone** and bone up on <all nonformal>; lucubrate, **burn the midnight oil;** make a study of; **practice, drill**

13 **browse, scan, skim, dip into,** thumb through, run over or through, glance or run the eye over or through, have a look at, hit the high spots

14 **study up, get up,** study up on, read up on, get up on; **review,**

brush up, polish up <nonformal>, **cram** or cram up <nonformal>, **bone up** <nonformal>

15 **study to be, study for; specialize in, go in for**; major in, minor in

ADJS 16 educated, **learned** 927.21,22; self-taught, self-instructed, autodidactic

17 **studious,** devoted to studies, **scholarly,** academic, professorial; owlish; pedantic; bookish 927.22; diligent 330.22

18 **teachable, instructable, educable,** trainable; **apt,** quick, **ready; receptive, willing,** motivated; hungry or thirsty for knowledge; docile, **malleable, moldable,** pliable, **impressionable,** formable; bright, clever, **intelligent** 919.12

571 TEACHER

NOUNS 1 **teacher, instructor, educator,** preceptor, **mentor; master; pedagogue; schoolteacher, schoolmaster; professor, academic;** guide 574.7, docent; rabbi, pandit, pundit, guru

2 <woman teachers> instructress, educatress, mistress; schoolmistress; schoolma'am or schoolmarm; governess

3 <academic ranks> professor, associate professor, assistant professor, instructor, tutor, associate, assistant, lecturer

4 teaching fellow, teaching assistant

5 **tutor; coach; private instructor**

6 **trainer, handler, groomer;** drillmaster; **coach,** athletic coach

7 **lecturer,** lector, **preacher,** homilist

8 **principal,** headmaster, headmistress; president, chancellor, vice-chancellor, rector, provost, master; dean

9 **faculty,** staff <Brit>, faculty members

10 instructorship, teachership, preceptorship

ADJS 11 **pedagogic, pedagogical,** preceptorial, tutorial; **teacherish,** teacherlike, **schoolteacher-**

ish, schoolmasterish; school-marmish <nonformal>; **professorial**, academic, tweedy; pedantic 927.22

572 STUDENT

NOUNS **1 student, pupil, scholar,** learner, **trainee**; tutee; inquirer; self-taught person, autodidact; auditor; **reader**, great reader

2 disciple, follower, apostle; convert, proselyte 857.7; **discipleship**, pupilage, tutelage

3 schoolchild, school kid <nonformal>; **schoolboy,** school lad; **schoolgirl;** preschool child, preschooler, nursery school child; kindergartner, grade schooler; secondary schooler, prep schooler, preppie <nonformal>, high schooler; schoolmate, schoolfellow, fellow student, classmate

4 special *or* exceptional student, gifted student; special education *or* special ed <nonformal> student; learning disabled *or* LD student; learning impaired student; slow learner, underachiever; handicapped *or* retarded student; emotionally disturbed student; culturally disadvantaged student

5 college student, collegian, collegiate, university student, college boy *or* girl; co-ed <nonformal>; seminarian, seminarist; *yeshiva bocher* <Yiddish>

6 undergraduate, undergrad <nonformal>, cadet, midshipman; underclassman, **freshman,** plebe, **sophomore; upperclassman, junior, senior**

7 <Brit terms> commoner, pensioner, sizar

8 graduate, grad <nonformal>; **alumnus,** alumni, alumna, alumnae; **graduate student,** grad student <nonformal>, master's degree candidate, doctoral candidate; **postgraduate,** postgrad <nonformal>; degrees; college graduate, college man *or* woman

9 novice, novitiate, **tyro,** abecedarian, **beginner** 817.2, entrant, **neophyte, tenderfoot** *and*

greenhorn <both nonformal>, freshman, **fledgling;** catechumen, initiate, debutant; newcomer 773.4; ignoramus 929.8; **recruit, raw recruit,** inductee, **rockie** *and* yardbird <both nonformal>, boot; **probationer,** probationist, postulant; **apprentice**

10 nerd *and* grind *or* greasy grind <all nonformal>; bookworm 928.4

11 class, grade; track; year

ADJS **12 studentlike,** schoolboyish, schoolgirlish; **collegiate,** college-bred; sophomoric; autodidactic; **studious** 570.17; **learned, bookish** 927.22; exceptional, gifted, special

13 probationary, probational, on probation

573 DIRECTION, MANAGEMENT

NOUNS **1 direction, management, managing,** handling, **running** <nonformal>, **conduct;** governance, **command, control, chiefdom, government** 612; **authority** 417; **regulation,** ordering; manipulation; **guidance, lead, leading;** steering, **navigation,** pilotage, conning, the conn, the helm, the wheel

2 supervision, superintendence, heading, heading up *and* **bossing** *and* running <all nonformal>; **surveillance,** oversight, eye; **charge, care, auspices, jurisdiction; responsibility,** accountability 641.2

3 administration, executive function *or* role, command function, say-so *and* last word <both nonformal>; **decision-making; disposition,** disposal, **dispensation**

4 directorship, leadership, managership, directorate, chairmanship, presidency, generalship, captainship; dictatorship, sovereignty 417.8; superintendence *or* **superintendency**; stewardship, custody, guardianship, shepherding

5 helm, conn, rudder, tiller, wheel,

steering wheel; **reins,** reins of government

6 **domestic management, housekeeping,** homemaking, ménage; home economics

7 **efficiency engineering,** scientific management, bean-counting <nonformal>, industrial engineering; efficiency expert; time and motion study, time-motion study, time study

VERBS 8 **direct, manage, regulate, conduct, carry on, handle, run** <nonformal>; **control, command, head, govern** 612.12, **boss** and head up and **mastermind** and quarterback and call the signals <all nonformal>; **order, prescribe;** lay down the law, make the rules, call the shots or tune <nonformal>; **head,** head up, skipper <nonformal>; **lead,** take the lead, lead on; manipulate, maneuver, engineer; take command 417.14; be responsible for

9 **guide, steer, drive, run** <nonformal>; herd, shepherd; channel; **pilot,** take the helm, be at the helm or wheel or tiller or rudder, hold the reins, **be in the driver's seat** <nonformal>

10 **supervise, superintend, boss, oversee,** overlook, ride herd on <nonformal>, stand over, keep an eye on or upon, keep in order; take care of 1007.19

11 **administer; officiate; preside,** preside over; chair, occupy the chair

ADJS 12 **directing, directive; managing, managerial; commanding, controlling, governing** 612.18; regulating, regulative, regulatory; **head, chief**

13 **supervising, supervisory,** overseeing, **superintendent, boss; in charge** 417.21

14 **administrative, administrating;** ministerial, **executive; officiating, presiding**

ADVS 15 in the charge of, in the hands of, in the care of; **under the auspices of,** under the aegis of; in one's charge, on one's

hands, under one's care, under one's jurisdiction

574 DIRECTOR

NOUNS 1 **director, governor,** rector, **manager, administrator, conductor;** person in charge, responsible person; impresario, producer; deputy, agent 576

2 **superintendent; supervisor, foreman,** monitor, **head,** headman, **boss,** chief, taskmaster; **overseer,** overlooker; inspector, surveyor; proctor; **straw boss** <nonformal>; slave driver; controller, comptroller, auditor

3 **executive,** officer, official; **president,** prexy <nonformal>, chief executive officer; provost, prefect, warden, archon; policy-maker, agenda-setter; **chairman of the board; chancellor,** vice-chancellor; vice-president or VP or veep <nonformal>; secretary; treasurer; dean; executive officer, executive director; **management,** the administration 574.11

4 **steward,** seneschal; major-domo, butler, housekeeper; master of ceremonies or MC and emcee <both nonformal>; proctor, attorney; guardian, custodian 1007.6; curator, librarian

5 **chairman,** chairwoman, **chair,** speaker, presiding officer

6 **leader;** pacemaker, pacesetter; bellwether, Judas goat; standard-bearer, torchbearer; **leader of men,** born leader, charismatic leader or figure; messiah; forerunner 815.1; ringleader 375.11; choirmaster 710.18

7 **guide; shepherd,** herd, herdsman, drover, cowherd, goatherd, etc; tour guide, tour director or conductor, cicerone, courier, dragoman; **pilot, helmsman,** coxswain; automatic pilot; pointer, guidepost 517.4

8 **guiding star, polestar,** polar star, lodestar, Polaris, **North Star**

9 **compass,** magnetic compass, gyrocompass, gyroscopic compass

10 **directory, guidebook,** hand-

book, Baedeker; city directory, business directory; telephone directory, telephone book, phone book <nonformal>, classified directory, Yellow Pages; **bibliography;** catalog, index, handlist, checklist, finding list; itinerary, road map, roadbook; gazetteer, reference book

11 **directorate,** directory, **management, the administration,** the brass *and* top brass <both nonformal>; the executive, executive arm *or* branch; middle management; **cabinet; board,** governing board *or* body, board of directors, board of trustees, board of regents; steering committee, executive committee; cadre, executive council; infrastructure; council 423

575 MASTER

NOUNS 1 **master, lord, lord and master,** overlord, seigneur, paramount, lord paramount, liege, liege lord, patroon; **chief, boss,** sahib <India>; employer; husband, man of the house, master of the house, paterfamilias; patriarch, elder; teacher, rabbi, guru; church dignitary, ecclesiarch

2 **mistress,** governess, madam; **matron, housewife,** homemaker, lady of the house, chatelaine; housemother; abbess, mother superior; great lady, first lady; matriarch, dowager

3 **chief,** principal; **master,** dean, doyen, doyenne; high priest <nonformal>; **leader** 574.6; important person, personage 996.8

4 <nonformal terms> **top dog,** boss man, big boy, Big Daddy, big cheese, kingpin, kingfish, honcho *or* head honcho, top banana, big enchilada, himself, herself; queen bee, Big Momma

5 **figurehead,** nominal head, dummy, lay figure, front man *and* front <both nonformal>, stooge <nonformal>, puppet, creature

6 **governor, ruler; captain, master, commander,** commandant, commanding officer, chatelain,

chatelaine; **director, manager, executive** 574.3

7 **head of state, chief of state; premier, prime minister, chancellor,** grand vizier; doge; **president,** chief executive

8 **potentate, sovereign, monarch, ruler, prince,** dynast, **crowned head, emperor, king,** majesty, royalty, royal personage; grand duke; paramount, lord paramount, suzerain, overlord; **chief, chieftain,** high chief; prince consort 608.7

9 <rulers> **caesar,** kaiser, **czar;** Dalai Lama; **pharaoh;** pendragon; **mikado;** shogun, tycoon; khan; shah; negus; bey; **sheikh;** sachem, sagamore

10 <Muslim rulers> sultan, Grand Turk, grand seignior

11 **sovereign queen, sovereign princess, princess, queen, empress,** czarina; rani, maharani <both India>; grand duchess; queen consort

12 **regent,** protector, prince regent, queen regent

13 <regional governors> **governor,** governor-general, lieutenant governor; **viceroy,** exarch, proconsul, khedive, vizier; nabob <India>; eparch; palatine; tetrarch; hospodar; dey, bey *or* beg, satrap; provincial

14 **tyrant, despot,** warlord; **autocrat,** autarch; oligarch; omnipotent *or* all-powerful ruler; **dictator,** pharaoh, caesar, czar; usurper, arrogator; **oppressor, hard master, slave driver,** Simon Legree; **martinet, disciplinarian,** stickler

15 **the authorities, the powers that be,** ruling class *or* classes, **the Establishment,** the power elite, **the power structure; they,** them; the inner circle; the ins *and* the in-group *and* those on the inside <all nonformal>; **management, the administration; top brass** <nonformal>; higher-ups *and* the people upstairs *or* in the front office <all nonformal>; **the top** <nonfor-

mal>, the corridors of power; hierarchy; ministry; **bureaucracy, officialdom;** directorate 574.11

16 official, officer, officiary, functionary, apparatchik; **public official,** public servant; officeholder; government *or* public employee; **civil servant; bureaucrat,** mandarin; petty tyrant

17 <public officials> **minister,** secretary, undersecretary, cabinet minister, cabinet member; chancellor; archon; magistrate; syndic; commissioner; commissar; city manager, mayor, lord mayor, burgomaster; headman; **councilman,** councilwoman, councillor, city councilman, elder, city father, alderman, selectman; supervisor; legislator 610.3

18 commissioned officer, officer; top brass *and* the brass <both nonformal>; **commander in chief,** generalissimo; general of the army, general of the air force, five-star general <nonformal>, **marshal,** field marshal; general officer, **general,** four-star general <nonformal>; lieutenant general, three-star general <nonformal>; major general, two-star general <nonformal>; brigadier general, one-star general <nonformal>; field officer; **colonel,** chicken colonel <nonformal>; lieutenant colonel; **major;** company officer; **captain; lieutenant,** shavetail <nonformal>; warrant officer, chief warrant officer; **commander,** commandant, the Old Man <nonformal>; **commanding officer** *or* CO, old man <nonformal>; executive officer, exec <nonformal>; chief of staff; aide, aide-de-camp *or* ADC; officer of the day *or* OD; staff officer; senior officer, junior officer

19 Army noncommissioned officer, noncom *or* NCO <nonformal>; sergeant, sarge <nonformal>; sergeant major of the Army, command sergeant major, sergeant major, first sergeant, master sergeant, sergeant first class, technical sergeant, staff sergeant, sergeant, specialist seven, platoon sergeant; **Air Force noncommissioned officer,** chief master sergeant of the Air Force, chief master sergeant, senior master sergeant, master sergeant, technical sergeant, staff sergeant, sergeant, airman first class

20 Navy *or* **naval officer; fleet admiral, admiral,** vice admiral, rear admiral, **commodore, captain, commander,** lieutenant commander, **lieutenant,** lieutenant junior grade, ensign; warrant officer; Navy *or* naval noncommissioned officer, master chief petty officer of the Navy, master chief petty officer, senior chief petty officer, chief petty officer, petty officer first class, petty officer second class, petty officer third class; **Marine Corps noncommissioned officer,** sergeant major of the Marine Corps, sergeant major, master gunnery sergeant, first sergeant, master sergeant, gunnery sergeant, staff sergeant, sergeant, corporal, lance corporal

21 <heraldic officials> herald, king of arms, king at arms, earl marshal

576 DEPUTY, AGENT

NOUNS **1 deputy, proxy, representative, substitute, alternate,** backup *and* stand-in <both nonformal>, alter ego, **surrogate,** understudy, pinch hitter <nonformal>, utility man *or* woman, the bench <nonformal>; second in command, executive officer; exponent, advocate, pleader, champion; **lieutenant;** vicar, vicar general; amicus curiae; **puppet,** dummy, creature, cat's-paw, figurehead

2 delegate, legate; **commissioner; messenger,** herald, **emissary, envoy; minister**

3 agent, instrument, implement, implementer; expediter, facilitator; **tool; steward** 574.4; **functionary; official** 575.16; clerk, **secretary;** amanuensis; factor, consignee; puppet, cat's-paw; dupe 358

4 go-between, middleman, intermediary, medium, intermediate, **internuncio,** broker; connection <nonformal>, **contact; negotiator;** arbitrator, mediator 466.3

5 spokesman, spokeswoman, spokesperson, spokespeople, official spokesman or -woman or -person, press officer, speaker, **voice,** mouthpiece <nonformal>; reporter

6 diplomat, diplomatist, diplomatic agent; **emissary, envoy, legate, minister,** foreign service officer; **ambassador,** ambassadress, ambassador-at-large; envoy extraordinary, plentipotentiary, **minister plenipotentiary;** nuncio, internuncio, apostolic delegate; resident, minister resident; chargé d'affaires, chargé; secretary of legation; **attaché,** commercial attaché, military attaché, **consul,** consul general, vice-consul, consular agent; career diplomat

7 foreign office, foreign service, diplomatic service; diplomatic mission, diplomatic staff or corps; **embassy, legation;** consular service

8 vice-president, vice-chairman, vice-governor

9 secret agent, operative, cloak-and-dagger operative, **undercover man; spy,** espionage agent; counterspy, double agent; **spotter; scout,** reconnoiterer; **intelligence agent or officer;** spymaster; spy-catcher <nonformal>, counterintelligence agent

10 detective, operative, investigator, sleuth; police detective, **plainclothesman;** private detective or dick, private investigator or PI; hotel detective, house dick <nonformal>, store detective; narcotics agent, narc <nonformal>; FBI agent or G-man <nonformal>; treasury agent or T-man <nonformal>; Federal or fed <nonformal>

11 <nonformal terms> **dick,** gumshoe, hawkshaw, sleuthhound, flatfoot; eye, private eye; skip tracer

12 secret service, intelligence service, intelligence, military intelligence, naval intelligence; **counterintelligence**

13 <group of delegates> **delegation, deputation, commission, mission;** committee, subcommittee

VERBS **14 represent, act for,** act on behalf of, substitute for, appear for, speak for, be the voice of, give voice to, be the mouthpiece of <nonformal>, hold the proxy of, hold a brief for, act in the place of, serve in one's stead, pinch-hit for <nonformal>; understudy, double for and stand in for and back up <all nonformal>; front for <nonformal>; deputize, commission

ADJS **15 deputy,** deputative; **acting,** representative

16 diplomatic, ambassadorial, consular, ministerial, plenipotentiary

ADVS **17 by proxy,** indirectly; in behalf of 861.12

577 SERVANT, EMPLOYEE

NOUNS **1 retainer,** dependent, follower; myrmidon, yeoman; vassal, liege, liege man; inferior, **underling, subordinate; minion,** creature, hanger-on, lackey, flunky, stooge <nonformal>; peon, serf, slave 432.7

2 servant, servitor, help; **domestic,** domestic help, domestic servant, house servant; live-in help, day help; **menial,** drudge; scullion

3 employee; pensioner, **hireling, mercenary,** myrmidon; hired man, hired hand, man or girl Friday, right-hand man, assistant 616.6; worker 726

4 man, manservant, serving man, **boy,** houseboy, houseman; butler; valet, gentleman, gentleman's gentleman; driver, chauffeur; gardener

5 attendant, usher, squire, yeoman; errand boy *or* girl, gofer <nonformal>, office boy *or* girl, copyboy; page, footboy; bellboy, bellman, bellhop; cabin boy, purser; printer's devil; caddie; bootblack; orderly; **cabin** *or* **flight attendant, steward, stewardess, hostess,** airline stewardess *or* hostess

6 lackey, flunky, liveried servant; **footman**

7 waiter, waitress; carhop; counterman, soda jerk <nonformal>; busboy; headwaiter, *maître d'hôtel* <Fr>, maître d' <nonformal>; hostess; wine steward, sommelier; bartender, barkeeper *or* barkeep; barman

8 maid, maidservant, girl, servant girl, serving girl, wench, hired girl; au pair girl, amah <China>; live-in maid, live-out maid; **handmaid,** handmaiden; **lady's maid,** abigail, soubrette; chaperon; duenna; parlormaid; kitchenmaid; cook; housemaid, chambermaid, upstairs maid; nursemaid 1007.8

9 factotum, man of all work; maid of all work

10 major-domo, steward, butler, chamberlain, seneschal; **housekeeper**

11 staff, personnel, employees, help, hired help, the help, **crew, gang,** men, force

12 service, servanthood; **employment, employ; ministry, ministration, attendance;** serfdom, peonage, slavery 432.1

VERBS **13 serve, work for,** serve one's every need; minister to, pander to, do service to; **help** 449.11; **care for,** do for <nonformal>, **look after,** wait on hand and foot, take care of; **wait, wait on** *or* **upon, attend,** tend, attend on *or* upon, dance attendance upon; drudge 725.14

ADJS **14 serving, ministering,** waiting, **attending,** attendant; in one's pay *or* employ; helping 449.20; **menial, servile**

578 FASHION

NOUNS **1 fashion, style, mode, vogue,** trend, prevailing taste; ton, bon ton; custom 373; convention 579.1,2; the swim <nonformal>; height of fashion; the new look; high fashion, *haute couture* <Fr>

2 fashionableness, ton, bon ton, **stylishness, modishness,** voguishness; **popularity,** prevalence, currency 863.2

3 smartness, chic, elegance; style-consciousness, clothesconsciousness; **spruceness, nattiness,** neatness, trimness, sleekness, **dapperness,** jauntiness; sharpness *and* spiffiness *and* classiness *and* niftiness <all nonformal>; swankness *and* **swankiness** <both nonformal>; foppery, foppishness, coxcombry, dandyism; hipness <nonformal>

4 the rage, the thing, the last word <nonformal>, **the latest thing,** the in thing *and* the latest wrinkle <both nonformal>

5 fad, craze, rage; wrinkle <nonformal>; novelty 840.2; faddishness, faddism; **faddist;** the bandwagon

6 society, fashionable society, **polite society, high society,** high life, *beau monde, haut monde* <both Fr>; best people, people of fashion, right people; world of fashion; **smart set** <nonformal>; the Four Hundred, **upper crust** <nonformal>; **cream of society,** *crème de la crème* <Fr>, elite, carriage trade; café society, jet set, beautiful people, in-crowd, the glitterati <nonformal>; drawing room, salon; social register

7 person of fashion, man-about-town, man *or* woman of the world; leader *or* arbiter of fashion, tastemaker, trendsetter, tonesetter, *arbiter elegantiae* <L>; ten best-dressed, fashion plate, clotheshorse, sharpy <nonformal>, Beau Brummel; fop, dandy 500.9; **socialite; clubwoman,** clubman; jet setter; swinger

<nonformal>; **debutante,** sub-debutante, deb *and* subdeb <both nonformal>

VERBS **8 catch on,** become popular, **become the rage,** catch *or* take fire

9 be fashionable, be the style, be the rage, be the thing; cut a figure in society <nonformal>, set the fashion *or* style *or* tone; dress to kill

10 follow the fashion, get in the swim <nonformal>, get *or* climb *or* jump on the bandwagon <nonformal>, join the parade, follow the crowd, go with the tide *or* current *or* flow; keep in step, do as others do; keep up, **keep up appearances,** keep up with the Joneses

ADJS **11 fashionable, in fashion, smart, in style, in vogue; all the rage,** all the thing; **popular,** prevalent, current 863.12; **up-to-date,** up-to-the-minute, switched-on *and* hip *and* with-it <all nonformal>, trendy <nonformal>, newfashioned, modern, new 840.9,10,12-14; **in the swim;** sought-after, much sought-after

12 stylish, modish, voguish, vogue; dressy <nonformal>

13 chic, smart, elegant; style-conscious, clothes-conscious; **well-dressed,** well-groomed, all dressed up, dressed to kill, dressed to the teeth, dressed to the nines, well-turned-out; **spruce, natty,** neat, trim, sleek, smug, trig; **dapper,** dashing, jaunty; sharp *and* spiffy *and* classy *and* nifty *and* snazzy <all nonformal>; **swank** *or* **swanky** <nonformal>, posh <nonformal>, ritzy <nonformal>, swell <nonformal>; genteel; cosmopolitan, sophisticated

14 ultrafashionable, ultrastylish, ultrasmart; chichi; foppish, dandified

15 trendy <nonformal>, **faddish,** faddy <nonformal>

16 socially prominent, in society, high-society, elite; café-society, jet-set; lace-curtain; silk-stocking

ADVS **17 fashionably, stylishly, modishly,** in the latest style *or* mode

18 smartly, dressily, chicly, elegantly, exquisitely; **sprucely, nattily,** neatly, trimly, sleekly; **dapperly,** jauntily, dashingly; foppishly, dandyishly

579 SOCIAL CONVENTION

NOUNS **1 social convention, convention,** conventional usage, what is done, what one does, **social usage, form, formality; custom** 373; **conformism, conformity** 866; **propriety, decorum,** decorousness, correctness, decency, seemliness, good form, etiquette 580.3; **conventionalism, conventionality**

2 the conventions, the proprieties, the mores, accepted *or* sanctioned conduct, what is done, civilized behavior; **dictates of society**

3 conventionalist; conformist 866.2

VERBS **4 conform,** observe the proprieties, play the game, follow the rules 866.4, fall in *or* into line

ADJS **5 conventional, decorous,** orthodox, **correct,** right, **right-thinking, proper,** decent, seemly, meet; **accepted, recognized,** acknowledged, received, admitted, approved, being done; *comme il faut, de rigueur* <both Fr>; **traditional, customary**

ADVS **6 conventionally,** decorously, orthodoxly; **customarily, traditionally;** correctly, properly, as is proper, *comme il faut* <Fr>; according to custom, according to the dictates of society

580 FORMALITY

NOUNS **1 formality, form, formalness; ceremony,** ceremonial, **ceremoniousness; the red carpet; ritual,** rituality; formalization, stylization; **stiffness, stiltedness,** primness, prissiness, rigidness, starchiness, **dignity,** gravity, weight, staidness, **solem-**

nity 111; **pomp** 501.6; pomposity 501.7

2 formalism, ceremonialism, ritualism; legalism; pedantry, pedanticism; precisianism, preciseness, preciousness, preciosity; purism; punctiliousness, punctilio, scrupulousness

3 etiquette, social code, rules *or* code of conduct; **formalities,** social conduct, what is done, what one does; **manners,** good manners, exquisite manners, **politeness,** comity, civility 504.1; **amenities,** civilities, **social graces, mores, proprieties;** decorum, good form; **courtliness,** elegance 533; **protocol,** diplomatic code; punctilio, point of etiquette; convention, social usage; table manners

4 <ceremonial function> **ceremony,** ceremonial; **rite, ritual, formality; solemnity, service, function,** office, **observance,** performance; **exercise; celebration,** solemnization; **liturgy,** religious ceremony; **rite of passage;** convocation; commencement, commencement exercises; graduation, graduation exercises; baccalaureate service; inaugural, inauguration; initiation; empty formality *or* ceremony, mummery

VERBS **5 formalize,** ritualize, solemnize, **celebrate,** dignify; **observe;** conventionalize, stylize

6 stand on ceremony, observe the formalities, follow protocol

ADJS **7 formal,** formulary; formalistic; legalistic; pedantic; stylized, conventionalized; extrinsic, outward, impersonal 767.3; surface, **superficial, nominal** 527.15

8 ceremonious, ceremonial; redcarpet; ritualistic, ritual; hieratic, sacerdotal, liturgic; **grave, solemn** 111.3; **pompous** 501.22; **stately** 501.21; well-mannered 504.16; **conventional,** decorous 579.5

9 stiff, stilted, prim, prissy, rigid, starchy, starched

10 punctilious, scrupulous, precise, precisian, precious, puristic; by-the-book; exact. **meticulous** 339.12; **orderly, methodical** 806.6

ADVS **11 formally,** in due form; **ceremoniously, ritually,** ritualistically; **solemnly** 111.4; *pro forma* <L>, **as a matter of form;** by the book

12 stiffly, stiltedly, starchly, primly, rigidly

581 INFORMALITY

NOUNS **1 informality, unceremoniousness; casualness,** offhandedness, **ease, easiness; relaxedness;** affability, graciousness, cordiality, sociability 582; Bohemianism, unconventionality 867.2; **familiarity; naturalness,** simplicity, plainness, homeliness, homeyness, folksiness <nonfor­mal>, common touch, **unaffectedness,** unpretentiousness 499.2; unconstraint, unconstrainedness, looseness; irregularity

VERBS **2 not stand on ceremony,** let one's hair down <nonformal>, be oneself, be at ease, come as you are; relax

ADJS **3 informal, unceremonious; casual, offhand,** offhanded, unstudied, easygoing, free and easy; **relaxed;** affable, gracious, cordial, sociable; Bohemian, unconventional 867.6; **familiar; natural,** simple, plain, homely, homey, down-home *and* folksy <both nonformal>; **unaffected, unassuming** 499.7; unconstrained, loose; irregular; unofficial

ADVS **4 informally, unceremoniously,** without ceremony; **casually,** offhand, offhandedly; familiarly; **naturally,** simply, plainly; **unaffectedly, unassumingly** 499.11; unconstrainedly, unofficially

582 SOCIABILITY

NOUNS **1 sociability,** sociableness, fitness for society, socialmindedness, **gregariousness, affability,** compatibility, geniality, **conge-**

niality; hospitality 585; clubbishness, clubbiness; intimacy, familiarity; amiability, **friendliness** 587.1; **communicativeness** 343.3; social grace, civility, urbanity, courtesy 504

2 **camaraderie,** comradeship, **fellowship, good-fellowship;** consorting, hobnobbing, hanging *and* hanging out <both nonformal>

3 **conviviality, joviality, jollity,** gaiety, heartiness, cheer, good cheer, festivity, partying, merrymaking, merriment, revelry

4 **social life, social intercourse,** social activity, **intercourse, communication, communion, fellowship, community,** collegiality, commerce, congress, converse, conversation, social relations

5 **social circle** *or* **set,** social class, one's crowd *or* set, clique, coterie, crowd <nonformal>; **association** 617

6 **association,** affiliation, bonding, social bonding, **fellowship, companionship, company, society;** fraternity, **fraternization;** membership, participation, partaking, sharing, cooperation 450

7 **visit, social call,** call; visiting, visitation; round of visits; social round, social whirl, mad round

8 **appointment, engagement, date** <nonformal>, double date *and* blind date <both nonformal>; arrangement, interview; engagement book

9 **rendezvous, tryst, assignation, meeting;** trysting place, meeting place, place of assignation; assignation house; love nest <nonformal>

10 **social gathering, social,** social affair, social hour, hospitality hour, affair, gathering, get-together <nonformal>; **reception,** at home, salon, levee, soiree; reunion, family reunion; wake

11 **party, entertainment, festivity** 743.3,4

12 <nonformal terms> **brawl,** bash, blast, clambake, wingding, blowout, shindig, shindy

13 **tea,** afternoon tea, five-o'clock tea, high tea

14 **bee,** quilting bee, raising bee, husking bee, cornhusking, corn shucking, husking

15 **debut, coming out** <nonformal>, presentation

16 <sociable person> joiner, mixer *and* **good mixer** <both nonformal>, good company, life of the party, bon vivant; man-about-town, playboy, social lion

VERBS 17 **associate with,** consort with, hobnob with, fall in with, go around with, **mingle with, mix with, touch** *or* **rub elbows** *or* **shoulders with; fraternize,** join in fellowship; **keep company with,** walk hand in hand with; **join; flock together**

18 <nonformal terms> **hang with,** hang out *or* around with, run with, chum, chum together, pal, pal with, pal around with, run around with, run with

19 **visit,** make *or* pay a visit, **call on** *or* **upon, drop in,** stop in, look in, look one up, see, stop off <nonformal>, drop *or* stop by, drop around *or* round; leave one's card; exchange visits

20 have *or* give a party, entertain

21 <nonformal terms> **throw a party; party,** live it up, have a ball, ball, kick up one's heels, whoop it up

ADJS 22 **sociable, social,** social-minded, fond of society, **gregarious, affable; companionable,** companionate, compatible, genial, **congenial;** hospitable 585.11; clubby <nonformal>, clubbish; **communicative** 343.10; amiable, **friendly;** civil, urbane, courteous 504.14

23 **convivial,** boon, free and easy, hail-fellow-well-met; **jovial, jolly,** hearty, festive, gay

24 **intimate, familiar,** cozy, chatty; man-to-man, woman-to-woman

ADVS 25 **sociably,** socially, gregariously, affably; companionably, arm in arm, hand in hand

583 UNSOCIABILITY

NOUNS **1 unsociability,** unsociableness; **ungregariousness,** uncompanionability; ungeniality, **uncongeniality;** incompatibility; **unfriendliness** 589.1; **uncommunicativeness** 344; sullenness, moroseness; self-sufficiency, self-containment; autism, catatonia; bashfulness 139.4

2 aloofness, standoffishness, offishness, withdrawnness, **remoteness,** distance, detachment; **coolness,** coldness, frigidity, chill, chilliness, iciness, frostiness; cold shoulder; inaccessibility, unapproachability

3 seclusiveness; exclusiveness, exclusivity

VERBS **4 keep to oneself,** keep oneself to oneself, not mix or mingle, enjoy or prefer one's own company, stay at home, shun companionship, be a poor mixer, **stand aloof,** hold oneself aloof or apart, keep one's distance, keep at a distance, keep in the background, retire, creep into a corner, seclude oneself; have nothing to do with 586.5, be unfriendly, not give one the time of day

ADJS **5 unsociable,** unsocial; **ungregarious; uncompanionable,** ungenial, uncongenial; incompatible, socially incompatible; **unfriendly** 589.9; **uncommunicative** 344.8; sullen, morose; close; self-sufficient, self-contained; autistic, catatonic; bashful 139.12

6 aloof, standoffish, offish, standoff, **distant, remote,** withdrawn, removed, detached; **cool,** cold, cold-fish, frigid, chilly, icy, frosty; seclusive; exclusive; inaccessible, unapproachable; tight-assed <nonformal>

584 SECLUSION

NOUNS **1 seclusion, retirement, withdrawal, retreat,** recess; renunciation or forsaking of the world; **sequestration,** quarantine, separation, detachment,

apartness; segregation, apartheid, Jim Crow; **isolation;** ivory tower, ivory-towerishness; **privacy, secrecy;** privatization; isolationism

2 hermitism, eremitism, anchoritism, anchoretism, cloistered monasticism

3 solitude, solitariness, **aloneness,** loneness, singleness; **loneliness, lonesomeness**

4 forlornness, desolation; friendlessness, homelessness, rootlessness; helplessness, defenselessness; abandonment, desertion

5 recluse, loner, solitary; **shut-in,** invalid, bedridden invalid; cloistered monk or nun; **hermit,** eremite, anchorite; hermitess, anchoress; **ascetic;** stylite, pillarist, pillar saint; desert saints, desert fathers; outcast, pariah 586.4; **stay-at-home, homebody;** isolationist

6 retreat 1008.5, **hideaway, cell, ivory tower,** lair, sanctum, sanctum sanctorum, inner sanctum

VERBS **7 seclude oneself, go into seclusion, retire, go into retirement,** retire from the world, abandon or forsake the world, lead a cloistered life, sequester or sequestrate oneself, be or remain incommunicado, shut oneself up, live alone, live apart, retreat to one's ivory tower; rusticate; take the veil; cop out <nonformal>, drop out of society

ADJS **8 secluded, seclusive, retired, withdrawn; isolated,** shut off, insular, **separate,** separated, **apart,** detached, removed; segregated, quarantined; **remote, out-of-the-way,** in a backwater, out-of-the-world; **unfrequented,** unvisited, off the beaten track; untraveled

9 private, reclusive; ivory-towered

10 recluse, reclusive, sequestered, cloistered, sequestrated, shut up or in; hermitlike, hermitic, eremitic; anchoritic; stay-at-home, domestic; homebound

11 solitary, alone; in solitude, by

oneself, all alone; **lonely, lone-some, lone;** lonely-hearts

12 forlorn, lorn; **abandoned, for-saken, deserted, desolate,** godforsaken <nonformal>, friendless, homeless; helpless, defenseless; outcast 586.10

ADVS **13 in seclusion, in retire-ment,** in retreat, in solitude; in privacy, in secrecy

585 HOSPITALITY, WELCOME

NOUNS **1 hospitality,** receptive-ness; freedom of the house; **cor-diality,** amiability, graciousness, **friendliness,** neighborliness, ge-niality, bonhomie, **generosity,** liberality, openheartedness, warmth, warmness, warmheart-edness

2 welcome, welcoming, **recep-tion;** cordial *or* warm *or* hearty welcome, the glad hand <nonfor-mal>, **open arms; embrace, hug;** welcome mat

3 greetings, salutations; regards

4 greeting, salutation, salute; **hail, hello,** how-do-you-do; ac-cost, address; nod, bow, bob; curtsy 155.2; wave; handshake, handclasp; open arms, embrace, hug, kiss; smile, nod of recogni-tion

5 host, mine host; hostess, recep-tionist, greeter; landlord 470.2

6 guest, visitor, visitant; **caller,** company; invited guest, invitee; frequenter, habitué, haunter; uninvited guest, gate-crasher <nonformal>; moocher *and* free-loader <both nonformal>

VERBS **7 receive, admit,** accept, take in, let in, open the door to; **be at home to,** have the latchstring out, put out the wel-come mat, keep an open house, keep the home fires burning

8 entertain, entertain guests; host, preside, do the honors <nonformal>; give a party, throw a party <nonformal>

9 welcome, make welcome, bid one welcome, make one feel wel-come *or* at home *or* like one of the family, give one the freedom of

the house, hold out the hand, ex-tend the right hand of friendship; give the glad hand <nonformal>; **embrace, hug, receive** *or* **wel-come with open arms;** give a warm reception to, roll out the red carpet, give the red-carpet treatment, receive royally

10 greet, hail, accost, address; **sa-lute,** make one's salutations; **bid** *or* **say hello;** exchange greetings; **give one's regards** 504.13; shake hands, give one some skin *and* give a high *or* a low five <all non-formal>, press the flesh <non-formal>, squeeze one's hand; nod to, bow to; curtsy 155.6; take one's hat off to, uncover; kiss, greet with a kiss, kiss hands *or* cheeks

ADJS **11 hospitable, receptive,** welcoming; **cordial,** amiable, gracious, **friendly,** neighborly, genial, hearty, open, openhearted warm, warmhearted; **generous,** liberal

12 welcome, wanted, desired, wished-for; **agreeable,** desirable; **grateful,** gratifying, pleasing

ADVS **13 hospitably, with open arms**

586 INHOSPITALITY

NOUNS **1 inhospitality,** unrecep-tiveness; **uncordialness,** ungra-ciousness, **unfriendliness,** un-neighborliness; nonwelcome, nonwelcoming

2 unhabitability, uninhabitability, unlivability

3 ostracism, thumbs down; **ban-ishment** 908.4; **proscription, ban; boycott; blackball,** black-balling, blacklist; **rejection** 442.1

4 outcast, social outcast, outcast of society, **castaway, derelict; pariah, untouchable;** leper; out-caste; **outlaw; expellee, evictee; displaced person** *or* **DP; exile, expatriate,** man without a coun-try; *persona non grata* <L>

VERBS **5 have nothing to do with,** have no truck with <nonformal>, steer clear of <nonformal>, **spurn, turn one's back upon,**

not give one the time of day
<nonformal>; refuse to receive,
not be at home to; shut the door
upon

6 **ostracize,** turn thumbs down;
reject 442.3; **exile, banish**
908.17; **proscribe, ban, outlaw**
444.3; **boycott, blackball,** blacklist

ADJS 7 **inhospitable; unreceptive,**
closed; **uncordial,** ungracious,
unfriendly, unneighborly

8 **unhabitable, uninhabitable,**
unlivable, unfit to live in, not fit
for man or beast

9 **unwelcome, unwanted; un-**
agreeable, undesirable, unacceptable; **uninvited,** unasked,
unbidden

10 **outcast, cast-off, castaway,**
derelict; outlawed 444.7; **re-**
jected, disowned; abandoned,
forsaken

587 FRIENDSHIP

NOUNS 1 **friendship, friendliness;**
amicability, amicableness, amity; **amiability,** amiableness, **con-**
geniality; neighborliness; sociability 582; **affection, love** 104;
loving kindness, kindness 143

2 **fellowship, companionship,**
comradeship, boon companionship; camaraderie, male bonding;
brotherhood, fraternity, frater-
nalism, sodality, confraternity;
sisterhood, sorority; brotherli-
ness, sisterliness; community of
interest

3 **good terms, good understand-**
ing, good footing, friendly
relations; **harmony,** sympathy,
rapport 455.1; **favor, goodwill,**
good graces, regard, respect,
mutual regard, the right side of
<nonformal>; an in <nonformal>

4 **acquaintance,** close acquaintance; **introduction,** presentation

5 **familiarity, intimacy,** intimate
acquaintance, closeness, nearness, inseparability; affinity,
special affinity, mutual affinity;
chumminess <nonformal>, palsi-
ness <nonformal>

6 **cordiality, geniality,** heartiness,
bonhomie, ardency, warmth,
affability, warmheartedness;
hospitality 585

7 **devotion, devotedness;** dedication, commitment; fastness,
steadfastness, firmness, constancy, staunchness; true-
blueness

8 cordial friendship, warm or
ardent friendship, devoted
friendship, bosom friendship,
beautiful friendship, fast or firm
friendship, staunch friendship

VERBS 9 **be friends,** have the
friendship of, have the ear of; be
old friends or friends of long
standing, go way back; **know, be**
acquainted with; associate with;
cotton to and hit it off <both non-
formal>, hobnob with, fraternize
with; be close friends with, be
best friends, be inseparable; **be**
on good terms, enjoy friendly relations with; keep on good terms,
have an in with <nonformal>

10 **befriend, make friends with,**
gain the friendship of, **strike up a**
friendship, take up with <non-
formal>, shake hands with; **get**
acquainted, make acquaintance
with; win friends, win friends and
influence people

11 <nonformal terms> be buddy-
buddy or palsy-walsy with,
click, have good or great chemistry, team up; **get next to, get**
palsy or **palsy-walsy with,** get
cozy with, cozy or snuggle up to,
get close to, get chummy with,
buddy or pal up with

12 **cultivate,** cultivate the friendship of, **court,** pay court to, seek
the company of, **run after** <non-
formal>, **shine up to,** make up
to <nonformal>, play up to and
suck up to <both nonformal>;
make advances, approach,
break the ice

13 **get on good terms with, get**
into favor, win the regard of, **get**
in the good graces of, get in
good with, get in with or on the
in with and get next to <all non-
formal>, **get on the right side of**

<nonformal>; stay friends with, keep in with <nonformal>

14 introduce, present, acquaint, give an introduction, do the honors <nonformal>

ADJS **15 friendly**; **amicable, peaceable**; **harmonious** 455.3; **amiable, congenial**, pleasant, agreeable, favorable, well-disposed, well-intentioned, well-meaning, well-meant; **brotherly**, fraternal; sisterly; neighborly, neighborlike; sociable; **kind** 143.13

16 cordial, genial, hearty, ardent, warm, warmhearted, affable; hospitable 585.11

17 friends with, friendly with; **acquainted**

18 on good terms, on a good footing, on friendly *or* amicable terms, **on speaking terms**, on a first-name basis; **in good with**, in with *and* on the in with *and* in <all nonformal>; **in favor, in one's good graces**, on the right side of <nonformal>

19 familiar, intimate, close, near, inseparable, on familiar *or* intimate terms; one-on-one, man-to-man, woman-to-woman; hand-in-hand; **thick, thick as thieves** <nonformal>

20 chummy <nonformal>; pally *and* palsy *and* palsy-walsy *and* buddy-buddy <all nonformal>

21 devoted, dedicated, committed, **fast**, steadfast, constant, faithful, staunch; **tried and true**, true-blue

ADVS **22 amicably**, friendly; **amiably, congenially**, pleasantly, agreeably, favorably; **cordially, genially**, heartily, ardently, warmly, with open arms; familiarly, intimately; arm in arm, hand in hand

588 FRIEND

NOUNS **1 friend, acquaintance**, close acquaintance; confidant, confidante; **intimate**, familiar, **close friend**, intimate *or* familiar friend; **bosom friend**, inseparable friend, **best friend**; alter ego;

brother, fellow, fellow creature, neighbor; **sympathizer**, well-wisher, partisan, advocate, backer, **supporter** 616.9; casual acquaintance; pickup <nonformal>; lover 104.12; live-in lover, significant other

2 good friend, best friend, **devoted friend**, warm *or* ardent friend, **faithful friend**, trusted friend, constant friend, staunch friend, fast friend; **friend in need**, friend indeed

3 companion, fellow, comrade, amigo <nonformal>, **associate** 616, confrere, consort, **colleague, partner, crony**, old crony; girlfriend <nonformal>; **roommate**; bunkmate; bedfellow, bedmate; **schoolmate**, classmate, school chum, fellow student *or* pupil; **playmate**; **teammate**; workmate; shipmate; messmate; comrade in arms

4 <nonformal terms> **pal, buddy**, bosom buddy, asshole buddy, goombah, pally, palsy-walsy, pardner, sidekick, **chum**

5 boon companion; good fellow, *bon vivant* <Fr>

589 ENMITY

NOUNS **1 enmity, unfriendliness**, inimicality; **uncordiality**, ungeniality, disaffinity, incompatibility, incompatibleness; **tension**; coolness, coldness, chilliness, chill, frost, iciness; inhospitality 586, unsociability 583

2 disaccord 456; ruffled feelings, strained relations, alienation, **disaffection, estrangement** 456.4

3 hostility, antagonism, repugnance, antipathy, spitefulness, spite, malice, malevolence, malignity, **hatred, hate** 103; **conflict, contention** 457, collision, clash, **friction**; quarrelsomeness 456.3; belligerence

4 animosity, animus; **ill will**, ill feeling, bitter feeling, **hard feelings**, no love lost; **bad blood**, blood feud, vendetta; **bitterness**,

sourness, **rancor,** acrimony, virulence, venom, vitriol

5 **grudge, spite,** bone to pick;
peeve *and* pet peeve <both non-
formal>

6 **enemy, foe, adversary, antagonist;** bitter enemy; sworn enemy;
public enemy; archenemy; the
opposition; **bane** 395.8, bête
noire

VERBS 7 **antagonize,** set against,
set at odds, set at each other's
throat; aggravate, exacerbate,
heat up, **provoke,** envenom,
embitter, infuriate, madden;
alienate, estrange 456.14; be
alienated *or* estranged, draw *or*
grow apart

8 **bear ill will,** bear malice, have
it in for <nonformal>, hold it
against, be down on <nonfor-
mal>; **bear** *or* **harbor** *or* **nurse a
grudge,** have a bone to pick with;
no love is lost between; pick a
quarrel; **hate** 103.5

ADJS 9 **unfriendly, inimical, un-
amicable; uncordial,** ungenial,
incompatible; strained; tense; unharmonious; cool, cold, chill,
chilly, frosty, icy; inhospitable
586.7; unsociable 583.5

10 **hostile, antagonistic,** repugnant, antipathetic, snide, spiteful,
malicious, malevolent, malignant, hateful, full of hate *or*
hatred; virulent, **bitter,** rancorous, caustic, venomous,
vitriolic; conflicting, clashing,
colliding; quarrelsome 456.17;
provocative, off-putting; belligerent

11 **alienated, estranged,** disaffected, separated, divided,
disunited, torn; irreconcilable

12 **at outs, on the outs** <nonfor-
mal>, **at odds,** at loggerheads, at
cross-purposes, at sixes and sevens, at each other's throat, at
swords points

13 **on bad terms,** not on speaking
terms; in bad with <nonformal>,
in bad odor with, on one's shitlist
<nonformal>

ADVS 14 **unamicably,** inimically;
uncordially, unamiably, un-

genially; coolly, coldly, chillily,
frostily; **hostilely, antagonistically**

590 MISANTHROPY

NOUNS 1 **misanthropy,** mis-
anthropism, people-hating, antisocial sentiments *or* attitudes;
unsociability 583; **man-hating;
woman-hating,** misogyny; **sexism,** sex discrimination, male *or*
female chauvinism

2 **misanthrope,** misanthropist,
people-hater; **man-hater;
woman-hater,** misogynist; **sexist,** male *or* female chauvinist

ADJS 3 **misanthropic,** people-
hating, **antisocial;** unsociable
583.5; **man-hating; woman-
hating,** misogynistic; **sexist,**
male- *or* female-chauvinistic

591 PUBLIC SPIRIT

NOUNS 1 **public spirit,** social consciousness *or* responsibility; **citizenship, good citizenship;**
altruism

2 **patriotism,** love of country;
nationalism, ultranationalism;
chauvinism, jingoism; flag-
waving; saber-rattling

3 **patriot;** nationalist; ultrana-
tionalist; **chauvinist, jingo,**
jingoist; flag waver, superpatriot,
hundred-percenter; hawk

ADJS 4 **public-spirited, civic; pa-
triotic; nationalistic;** ultrana-
tionalistic; superpatriotic, flag-
waving, **chauvinist, chauvinistic,** jingoist, jingoistic; hawkish

592 BENEFACTOR

NOUNS 1 **benefactor,** benefactress,
benefiter; ministering angel;
Samaritan, **good Samaritan;
helper,** assister, help, aid, helping
hand; Johnny-on-the-spot <non-
formal>; angel <nonformal>,
patron, backer 616.9, angel *and*
cash cow <both nonformal>;
good person 659

2 **savior, redeemer,** deliverer, **lib-
erator,** rescuer, freer, **emancipa-
tor,** manumitter

VERBS 3 **benefit, aid,** assist, succor; befriend, take under one's wing; back, support; save one's neck *or* skin

ADJS **4 benefitting, aiding, befriending, assisting; backing, supporting; saving, redemptive, redeeming; liberating, freeing, emancipative, emancipating, manumitting**

ADVS **5 by one's good offices,** with one's support, on one's shoulders *or* coattails

593 EVILDOER

NOUNS **1 evildoer, wrongdoer, malefactor,** public enemy, **sinner, villain,** transgressor, delinquent; bad *or* bad guy *and* baddy *and* meany <all nonformal>; **criminal,** outlaw, felon, **crook** <nonformal>, lawbreaker, perpetrator, perp <nonformal>, gangster *and* mobster <both nonformal>, racketeer, thief; **bad person** 660

2 troublemaker, mischiefmaker; agitator 375.11

3 ruffian, rowdy, thug, desperado, cutthroat, mad dog; gunman; bully; devil, hellcat, hellraiser

4 <nonformal terms> **roughneck, tough,** bruiser, bozo, ugly customer, **hoodlum, hood, hooligan,** gorilla, ape, plug-ugly, strong-arm man, muscle man, **goon;** gun, gunsel, trigger man, torpedo, hatchet man; holy terror, ugly customer

5 savage, barbarian, brute, beast, animal, tiger, shark, hyena; wild man; cannibal, maneater; **wrecker, vandal,** destroyer

6 monster, fiend, demon, devil, devil incarnate; **vampire, harpy, ghoul;** werewolf; ogre, ogress

7 witch, hag, vixen, hellcat, shedevil, virago, termagant, grimalkin, beldam, she-wolf, tigress, wildcat, siren, fury

594 JURISDICTION
<administration of justice>

NOUNS **1 jurisdiction,** legal authority *or* power *or* right, the confines of the law; civil *or* criminal jurisdiction, common-law *or* equitable jurisdiction

2 judiciary, judicial *or* legal *or* court system, judicature, court; criminal-justice system; **justice,** the wheels of justice, judicial process

3 magistracy, magistrateship; **judgeship,** justiceship

4 bureau, office, department; secretariat, ministry, commissariat; bailiwick

VERBS **5 administer justice,** administer; preside; **sit in judgment** 598.17; **judge** 945.8

ADJS **6 jurisdictional; judicatory,** judicative, **juridic *or* juridical; judicial, judiciary;** magisterial

595 TRIBUNAL

NOUNS **1 tribunal, forum, board,** curia; judicature, judiciary 594.2; council 423; inquisition

2 court, law court, court of law *or* **justice,** legal tribunal, judicature

3 <ecclesiastical courts> Papal Court, Curia, Rota, Sacra Romana Rota

4 military court, court-martial; naval court, captain's mast

5 seat of justice, judgment seat; bench

6 courthouse, court; courtroom; jury box; witness stand, dock

ADJS **7 tribunal, judicial,** judiciary, court; appellate

596 JUDGE, JURY

NOUNS **1 judge, magistrate, justice,** adjudicator; **justice of the peace** *or* **JP;** arbiter, arbitrator, moderator; umpire, referee; critic 945.7

2 <historical> tribune, praetor, ephor, archon

3 <Muslim> mullah, ulema, hakim, mufti, cadi

4 Chief Justice, Associate Justice, Justice of the Supreme Court

5 Pontius Pilate, Solomon, Minos, Rhadamanthus, Aeacus

6 jury, panel, jury of one's peers, twelve men in a box; inquest; jury

panel, jury list; hung *or* dead-
locked jury

7 juror, juryman, jurywoman,
talesman; foreman; grand-
juryman; petit-juryman

597 LAWYER

NOUNS **1 lawyer, attorney,
attorney-at-law,** barrister, **counselor,** counselor-at-law, **counsel,**
legal counsel, **solicitor, advocate, pleader;** member of the
bar, officer of the court; pettifogger, Philadelphia lawyer; friend at
court, amicus curiae; sea lawyer,
latrine *or* guardhouse lawyer
<nonformal>, legalist

2 jurist; member of a court-
martial

3 <nonformal terms> **shyster,
mouthpiece, ambulance
chaser,** fixer, legal eagle

4 bar, legal profession, members
of the bar; representation, counsel; **practice,** legal practice,
criminal practice, corporate practice, etc; pro bono practice; **law
firm**

VERBS **5 practice law**; be admitted
to the bar

ADJS **6 lawyerly,** lawyerlike; representing, of counsel

598 LEGAL ACTION

NOUNS **1 lawsuit, suit**; counter-
suit; **litigation, prosecution, action, legal action,** proceedings,
legal process; legal remedy; **case,
court case,** cause, legal case; **judicial process**

**2 summons, subpoena; writ,
warrant**

**3 arraignment, indictment, im-
peachment; complaint, charge**
599.1; presentment; information;
bill of indictment, true bill; **bail**
438.2

4 jury selection, impanelment,
venire

5 trial, jury trial, trial by jury,
hearing, inquiry, inquisition,
inquest; court-martial; **examination,** cross-examination; mistrial;
change of venue

6 pleadings; plea, pleading, argu-

ment; **defense**; demurrer; refutation 957.2; rebuttal 938.2

7 declaration, statement, allegation, statement of facts; **deposition,** affidavit; claim; complaint;
bill, bill of complaint

8 testimony; evidence 956; **argument,** presentation of the case;
resting of the case; **summing up,**
summation, charge to the jury,
charging of the jury

9 judgment, decision, landmark
decision; **verdict, sentence**
945.5; acquittal 601; condemnation 602

10 appeal, appeal motion, appeal
to a higher court; writ of error;
certiorari, writ of certiorari

11 litigant, litigator; party, party
to a suit; injured *or* aggrieved
party, **plaintiff** 599.5; **defendant**
599.6; witness, accessory, accessory before *or* after the fact; panel

VERBS **12 sue, litigate, prosecute,
bring suit, go to law,** seek justice
or legal redress, **bring action
against,** prosecute a suit against,
institute legal proceedings
against; take to court, bring into
court, hale *or* haul *or* drag into
court, bring before a jury, bring
to justice, bring to trial, **put on
trial,** take before the judge

13 summons, issue a summons,
subpoena

14 arraign, indict, impeach, present a true bill, prefer *or* file a
claim; **prefer charges** 599.7

15 select *or* **impanel a jury,** impanel, panel

16 call to witness, bring forward,
put on the stand; swear in 334.7;
take oath; take the stand, testify

17 try, try a case, **hear,** sit on;
charge the jury, deliver one's
charge to the jury; **judge, sit in
judgment**

18 plead, enter a plea *or* **pleading,**
argue at the bar; **plead** *or* **argue
one's case,** present one's case,
make a plea, tell it to the judge
<nonformal>; rest, rest one's
case; sum up one's case; throw
oneself on the mercy of the court

19 bring in a verdict, pass *or* **pro-**

nounce sentence 945.13; acquit 601.4; convict 602.3; penalize 603.4

ADJS **20** litigious, litigant; lawyerly; litigable, actionable, prosecutable; prosecutorial; **moot**, sub judice; unactionable, unprosecutable, unlitigable, frivolous, without merit

599 ACCUSATION

NOUNS **1 accusation,** finger-pointing <nonformal>, **charge, complaint,** count, **blame, imputation,** reproach, taxing; **accusing, bringing of charges,** bringing to book; **denunciation,** denouncement; **impeachment, arraignment, indictment,** bill of indictment, true bill; **allegation**; **imputation,** ascription; **insinuation, implication, innuendo,** veiled accusation, unspoken accusation; information, bill of particulars; charge sheet; specification; prosecution, suit, lawsuit 598.1

2 incrimination, inculpation, citation, impugnment; attack, assault; **censure** 510.3

3 recrimination, retort, countercharge

4 trumped-up charge, false witness; **put-up job** and **frame-up** and **frame** <all nonformal>

5 accuser, accusant; incriminator, impugner; informer 551.6; impeacher, indictor; **plaintiff, complainant,** claimant, appellant, petitioner, libelant, **party,** party to a suit; **prosecutor**

6 accused, defendant, respondent, codefendant, corespondent, libelee, suspect, prisoner

VERBS **7 accuse,** bring accusation; **charge, press charges, prefer** or **bring charges**; complain, **lodge a complaint**; **impeach, arraign, indict,** bring in or hand up an indictment, return a true bill, **cite**; book; **denounce**; **finger** and point the finger at and **put** or lay the finger on <all nonformal>, **inform on** or **against** 551.12,13; **impute,** ascribe; allege, insinu-

ate, imply; bring to book; task, take to task or account; **reproach**; report, put on report

8 blame, blame on or upon <nonformal>, hold against, **put** or **place** or **lay the blame on,** cast blame upon, place or fix the blame or responsibility for; fasten on or upon, pin or hang on <nonformal>

9 accuse of, charge with, saddle with, lay at one's door, bring home to, throw in one's teeth, throw up to one, throw in the face of

10 incriminate, inculpate, implicate, involve; cry out against, raise one's voice against; attack, assail, impugn; **censure** 510.13; throw a stone at, cast or throw the first stone

11 recriminate, countercharge

12 trump up a charge, bear false witness; frame and frame up and set up <all nonformal>

ADJS **13 accusing, accusatory,** accusatorial, accusative; imputative, denunciatory; recriminatory; prosecutorial; **condemnatory**

14 incriminating, incriminatory; inculpative, inculpatory

15 accused, charged, blamed, tasked, reproached, **denounced, impeached, indicted, arraigned; under a cloud** or a cloud of suspicion; incriminated, inculpated, implicated, involved; **cited,** impugned; under attack, under fire

600 JUSTIFICATION

NOUNS **1 justification, vindication; clearing,** clearing of one's name or one's good name, clearance, purging, **exculpation** 601.1; failure to indict; explanation, rationalization; reinstatement, restoration, **rehabilitation**

2 defense, plea, pleading; argument; answer, reply, response, riposte; **refutation** 957.2, **rebuttal** 938.2; demurrer; denial, objection, exception; **special**

pleading; self-defense, plea of self-defense

3 apology, apologia, apologetic

4 excuse, cop-out and **alibi** and **out** <all nonformal>; lame excuse, poor excuse, likely story; escape hatch, way out

5 extenuation, mitigation, palliation, softening; extenuative, palliative; **whitewash, whitewashing,** decontamination; gloss, varnish, color, putting the best color on; qualification, allowance; extenuating circumstances

6 warrant, reason, good reason, **cause,** call, **right, basis, ground, grounds,** substance

7 justifiability, vindicability, defensibility; excusability, remissibility, veniality; warrantableness, allowableness, admissibility, reasonableness, legitimacy

8 justifier, vindicator; defender, pleader; **advocate,** proponent, **champion; apologist;** whitewasher

VERBS **9 justify, vindicate,** do justice to, make justice or right prevail; **warrant,** account for, show sufficient grounds for, give good reasons for; **rationalize,** explain; cry sour grapes; get off the hook <nonformal>, **exculpate** 601.4; **clear,** clear one's name or one's good name, purge, destigmatize, reinstate, restore, rehabilitate

10 defend, offer in defense, **support, uphold, sustain, maintain,** assert; **answer,** reply, respond, riposte, counter; refute 957.5, **rebut** 938.5; **plead for,** offer as a plea, plead one's case or cause, put up a front or a brave front; **advocate,** champion, go to bat for <nonformal>, espouse, join or associate oneself with, stand or stick up for, speak up for, contend for, speak for, argue for, put in a good word for

11 excuse, alibi <nonformal>, give as an excuse, cover with excuses, **explain,** offer an explanation; **apologize for,** make apology for;

crawl or worm or squirm out of, have an out or alibi or story <all nonformal>

12 extenuate, mitigate, palliate, soften, lessen, diminish, **ease,** mince; **soft-pedal;** slur over, ignore, give the benefit of the doubt, not hold it against one, **explain away, gloss or smooth over,** put a good face upon, varnish, **white-wash,** color, put the best color or face on, show to best advantage; **allow for,** make allowance for; give the Devil his due

ADJS **13 justifying;** vindicatory; refuting 957.6; **excusing,** excusatory; **apologetic; extenuating,** extenuative, **palliative**

14 justifiable, vindicable, defensible; excusable, pardonable, forgivable, expiable, remissible; venial; **condonable,** dispensable; **warrantable,** allowable, admissible, reasonable, legitimate; innocuous, unobjectionable, inoffensive

601 ACQUITTAL

NOUNS **1 acquittal,** acquittance; **exculpation; exoneration, absolution, vindication, remission,** purgation, purging; **clearing,** clearance, quietus; **pardon, excuse, forgiveness, free pardon; discharge, release, dismissal;** quashing of the charge or indictment

2 exemption, immunity, impunity; **amnesty,** nolle prosequi; stay

3 reprieve, respite, grace

VERBS **4 acquit, clear, exculpate, exonerate, absolve,** give absolution; **vindicate,** justify; **pardon, excuse, forgive;** remit, grant remission; amnesty, grant or extend amnesty; **discharge, release, dismiss, free, set free,** let off <nonformal>, let go; quash the charge or indictment, withdraw the charge; **exempt,** grant immunity, exempt from; shrive, purge; wipe the slate clean; **whitewash**; destigmatize; non-pros

5 **reprieve,** respite, give *or* grant a reprieve

602 CONDEMNATION

NOUNS 1 **condemnation, damnation, doom,** guilty verdict, verdict of guilty; proscription, excommunication, anathematizing; **denunciation; censure** 510.3; **conviction; sentence, judgment,** rap <nonformal>
2 attainder; bill of attainder
VERBS 3 **condemn, damn, doom; denounce; censure** 510.13; **convict,** find guilty; proscribe, excommunicate, anathematize; blacklist; pronounce judgment 945.13; **sentence,** pronounce sentence, pass sentence on; penalize 603.4
4 **stand condemned,** be convicted, be found guilty
ADJS 5 **condemnatory, damnatory,** denunciatory, proscriptive; **censorious**

603 PENALTY

NOUNS 1 **penalty,** penalization, penance; **sanctions,** punitive measures; **punishment** 604; **reprisal** 506.2, retaliation 506; the devil to pay
2 **handicap,** disability, **disadvantage** 1011.6
3 **fine,** mulct, **damages,** punitive damages, compensatory damages; escheat, escheatment
VERBS 4 **penalize,** put *or* impose *or* inflict a penalty *or* sanctions on; **punish** 604.10; **handicap**
5 **fine,** mulct, estreat; award damages
ADVS 6 **on pain of, on** *or* **under penalty of**

604 PUNISHMENT

NOUNS 1 **punishment, chastisement, chastening, correction, discipline, castigation,** infliction, scourge, what-for <nonformal>; **retribution,** retributive justice, nemesis; punishment that fits the crime, well-deserved punishment; **penalty,** penal retribution; cruel and unusual punishment; judgment; **just desserts, desserts**
2 <forms of punishment> penal servitude, jailing, imprisonment, incarceration, confinement; torture, torment, martyrdom; tar-and-feathering, the rack, impalement, dismemberment; strappado
3 **slap,** smack, whack, whomp, **cuff, box,** buffet, belt; blow 901.4; **rap on the knuckles,** box on the ear, slap in the face; slap on the wrist
4 **corporal punishment, whipping, beating, thrashing, spanking, flogging,** flagellation, scourging, flailing, trouncing, belaboring; **lashing, lacing,** horse-whipping, strapping, belting; **switching; clubbing,** cudgeling, caning, fustigation, bastinado; pistol-whipping; battery
5 <nonformal terms> **licking,** larruping, walloping, whaling, lathering, **hiding, tanning, dressing-down; paddling**
6 <old nonformal terms> strap oil, hazel oil, hickory oil
7 **capital punishment, execution; hanging,** the gallows, the rope *or* noose; **lynching,** necktie party <nonformal>, vigilante justice; **crucifixion; electrocution,** the chair <nonformal>; gassing, the gas chamber; lethal injection; **decapitation,** beheading, the guillotine; **strangling,** strangulation, garrote; **shooting,** firing squad; **burning,** burning at the stake; **poisoning,** hemlock; stoning; defenestration
8 **punisher,** discipliner, chastiser, chastener; **executioner,** executionist; **hangman; lyncher;** electrocutioner; **beheader;** strangler, garroter; sadist, torturer
9 **penologist;** jailer 429.10
VERBS 10 **punish, chastise, chasten, discipline, correct, castigate, penalize; take to task,** bring *or* call to account; settle *or* square accounts; **give one his desserts** *or* **just desserts;** inflict upon, visit upon; teach *or* give

one a lesson; make an example of; pillory

11 <nonformal terms> **attend to,** do for, take care of, **give it to**; pay, pay out, **fix, settle,** fix one's wagon, settle one's hash, settle the score, **give one his come-uppance**; lower the boom, come down on or down hard on, throw the book at; **give what-for,** give a going-over, let one have it, light into, lay into, mop or wipe up the floor with, have one's hide

12 **slap,** smack, whack, **cuff, box,** buffet; strike 901.13; box the ears, give a rap on the knuckles

13 **whip,** give a whipping or beating or thrashing, **beat, thrash, spank, flog,** scourge, flagellate, flail, whale; **smite,** thump, trounce, baste, **pummel, drub, buffet, belabor,** lay on; **lash, lace,** stripe; horsewhip; **strap,** belt; **switch,** birch; **club, cudgel,** cane, truncheon, fustigate, bastinado; pistol-whip

14 **thrash soundly, batter,** bruise

15 <nonformal terms> **beat up,** rough up, clobber, work over, lick, larrup, wallop, whop, beat one's brains out, whale, whale the tar out of, beat or kick the shit out of, **beat black and blue, knock one's lights out, nail,** welt, lather, **hide,** tan, **tan one's hide,** dress down, **kick ass,** knock heads together; **paddle; lambaste, clobber,** take it out of one's hide or skin

16 **torture**; put on the rack; dismember, tear limb from limb; draw and quarter, break on the wheel, tar and feather, ride on a rail, keelhaul, impale

17 **execute, put to death,** inflict capital punishment; **electrocute,** burn and fry <nonformal>; send to the gas chamber; **behead, decapitate,** guillotine; **crucify; shoot; burn at the stake; strangle,** garrote; stone; defenestrate

18 **hang; string up** <nonformal>; gibbet, bring to the gallows; **lynch;** hang, draw, and quarter

19 **be hanged,** suffer hanging, **swing,** dance upon nothing, kick the air or wind or clouds

20 **be punished, suffer, suffer the consequences** or **penalty,** get it and **catch it** <both nonformal>, get or catch it in the neck <nonformal>, catch hell or the devil <nonformal>, get or take a licking or shellacking <nonformal>; **get one's desserts** or **just desserts** 639.6; get it coming and going <nonformal>, sow the wind and reap the whirlwind; have or get one's knuckles rapped

21 **take one's punishment,** take the consequences, **take one's medicine** or what is coming to one, swallow one's medicine, pay the piper, face the music <nonformal>, make one's bed and lie on it; take the rap <nonformal>

22 **deserve punishment, have it coming** <nonformal>, be in for it, be heading for a fall

ADJS 23 **punishing, chastising,** chastening, corrective, disciplinary; retributive; **penal, punitive;** castigatory

605 INSTRUMENTS OF PUNISHMENT

NOUNS 1 **whip, lash, scourge,** strap, thong, rawhide, cowhide, belt, razor strap; knout; bullwhip, bullwhack; horsewhip; crop; quirt; cat, cat-o'-nine-tails

2 **rod, stick, switch; paddle,** ruler, ferule; birch, rattan; cane; club

3 <devices> **pillory, stocks;** cucking stool, ducking stool, trebuchet; whipping post, wooden horse, treadmill, crank

4 <instruments of torture> **rack,** wheel, Iron Maiden of Nuremberg; screw, thumbscrew; boot, iron heel; Procrustean bed

5 <instruments of execution> **scaffold; block,** guillotine, ax, maiden; **stake; cross; gallows,** gallows-tree, gibbet, tree, drop; **hangman's rope, noose,** rope, halter, hemp; **electric chair,** the chair <nonformal>, hot seat

<nonformal>; **gas chamber,** lethal chamber, death chamber

606 THE PEOPLE
<the population>

NOUNS 1 **the people, the populace, the public,** the general public; **the population,** the citizenry, the polity, the body politic; **the community, the commonwealth, society,** the society, the social order *or* fabric, the nation; commoners, *demos* <Gk>; **common people, ordinary people** *or* **folk, persons, folk, folks,** gentry; plain people *or* folks, the rank and file; Tom, Dick, and Harry; the salt of the earth, Everyman, Everywoman, the man *or* woman in the street, the common man, you and me, John Doe, Joe Six-pack <nonformal>, the third estate; **the upper class; the middle class; the lower class**

2 **the masses,** *hoi polloi* <Gk>, the many, **the multitude,** the crowd, **the mob,** the horde, **the majority,** the mass of the people, the herd, the great unwashed, **the vulgar** *or* **common herd**

3 **rabble,** rabblement, rout, canaille, ragtag <informal>, **ragtag and bobtail;** rag, tag, and bobtail; **riffraff, trash,** chaff, **rubbish,** dregs, **scum, scum of the earth, dregs** *or* **scum of society,** swinish multitude, vermin, cattle

4 **the underprivileged,** the disadvantaged, the poor, ghetto-dwellers, slum-dwellers, welfare cases, underclass, depressed class, poverty subculture, the wretched of the earth, outcasts, the homeless, the dispossessed, the powerless, the unemployable, the lumpenproletariat

5 **common man, commoner,** little man, **little fellow, average man,** ordinary man, **man in the street,** one of the people, man of the people, Everyman; **plebeian; proletarian;** ordinary *or* average Joe *and* Joe Doakes *and* Joe Six-pack <all nonformal>, John Doe, Jane Doe

6 **peasant, countryman,** country-woman, **provincial,** tiller of the soil; **peon,** fellah; **farmer 1067.5, hick** *and* yokel *and* rube *and* hay-seed *and* shit-kicker <all nonformal>, **bumpkin,** country bumpkin, clod, **clodhopper** <nonformal>, hillbilly <nonformal>, **boor,** clown, lout

7 **upstart, parvenu,** adventurer; *nouveau riche* <Fr>, *arriviste* <Fr>, **newrich; social climber,** climber, name-dropper, status seeker

ADJS 8 **populational,** population; **demographic;** national, societal; **popular,** public, mass, grass-roots, **common,** commonplace, **plain, ordinary, lowly,** low, mean, base; **humble,** homely; **lowborn,** baseborn, earthborn, earthy, plebeian; third-estate; ungenteel, shabby-genteel; **vulgar, rude,** coarse; **parvenu, upstart,** risen from the ranks, jumped-up <nonformal>; **newrich,** *nouveau-riche* <Fr>

607 SOCIAL CLASS AND STATUS

NOUNS 1 **class, social class, economic class,** social grouping, status group, social category, order, grade, caste, estate, rank; **status, social status, economic status,** socioeconomic status *or* background, standing, footing, prestige, rank, ranking, place, station, position, level, degree, stratum; **social structure, hierarchy,** social system, class structure, class distinction, status system, power structure, ranking, stratification, ordering, social scale, gradation, division, social inequality, inequality, haves and have-nots; **social bias, class conflict,** class identity, class difference, class prejudice, class struggle, class politics; **mobility, social mobility,** upward mobility, downward mobility, vertical mobility

2 **upper class, upper classes, aristocracy,** second estate, ruling

class, ruling circles, elite, elect, the privileged, the classes, the better sort, upper circles, upper cut *and* upper crust *and* crust *and* cream <all nonformal>, upper-income group *or* higher-income group, gentry; **high society,** the Four Hundred, bon ton; nobility, gentry 608

3 aristocracy, aristocratic status, high status, high rank, quality, high estate, gentility, social distinction, social prestige; **birth,** high birth, distinguished ancestry *or* descent *or* heritage *or* blood, **blue blood**

4 aristocrat, patrician, Brahmin, blue-blood, thoroughbred, member of the upper class, socialite, swell *and* upper-cruster <both nonformal>, grand dame, dowager; **gentleman, lady,** person of breeding

5 middle class, lower middle class, upper middle class, bourgeoisie, educated class, professional class, middle-income group, white-collar workers, salaried workers; suburbia; Middle America, silent majority

6 bourgeois, white-collar worker 726.2, salaried worker; pillar of society, solid citizen

7 lower class, lower classes, workers, working class, working people, proletariat, toilers, toiling class *or* classes, low-income group, wage-earners, hourly worker, blue-collar workers

8 the underclass, the underprivileged

9 worker 726.2, **workman, working man, working woman,** proletarian, laborer, laboring man, toiler, stiff *and* working stiff <both nonformal>, artisan, mechanic, industrial worker, factory worker

ADJS **10 upper-class, aristocratic,** patrician, **upscale;** gentle, genteel; ladylike, quite the lady; **wellborn, well-bred, blue-blooded; thoroughbred,** purebred, pure-blooded, full-blooded; **highborn,** highbred; born to the

purple, born with a silver spoon in one's mouth; **high-society,** socialite, hoity-toity <nonformal>; posh; **middle-class, bourgeois,** suburban; **working class, blue collar,** proletarian, lower-class, born on the wrong side of the tracks; **class-conscious; mobile, socially mobile,** upwardly mobile, downwardly mobile, vertically mobile, déclassé

608 ARISTOCRACY, NOBILITY, GENTRY
<noble rank or birth>

NOUNS **1 aristocracy, nobility,** titled aristocracy, hereditary nobility, noblesse, **aristocracy; elite,** upper class, elect, the classes, **upper classes** *or* circles, upper cut *and* **upper crust** <both nonformal>, the Four Hundred, high society, high life, *haut monde* <Fr>; old nobility; **peerage;** royalty

2 nobility, nobleness, aristocracy; gentility, genteelness; quality, rank, distinction; birth, high *or* noble birth, ancestry, high *or* honorable descent; blood, **blue blood;** royalty 417.8

3 gentry, gentlefolk, gentlefolks, gentlepeople, better sort; lesser nobility; landed gentry, squirearchy

4 nobleman, noble, gentleman; peer; aristocrat, patrician, Brahmin, **blue blood,** thoroughbred, silk-stocking, lace-curtain, swell *and* upper-cruster <both nonformal>; **grandee,** magnate; **lord;** seignior, seigneur, *hidalgo* <Sp>; **duke,** marquis, **earl, count,** viscount, **baron, baronet;** squire; esquire; palsgrave, waldgrave, margrave, landgrave

5 knight, cavalier, chevalier, *caballero* <Sp>; **knight-errant;** baronet, knight baronet

6 noblewoman, peeress, gentlewoman; lady, dame; **duchess,** grand duchess, marchioness, viscountess, **countess, baroness**

7 prince, atheling, sheikh, sherif, khan, emir, crown prince, heir apparent; heir presumptive; prince consort; prince regent; **king**

8 **princess,** *infanta* <Sp>; crown princess; **queen** 575.11

9 <rank or office> lordship, ladyship; dukedom, marquisate, earldom, barony

ADJS 10 **noble,** of rank, high, exalted; **aristocratic, patrician; gentle,** genteel, of gentle blood; gentlemanly, gentlemanlike; ladylike, quite the lady; ducal, archducal; princely, princelike; **regal** 417.17, kingly, kinglike; queenly, queenlike; titled

11 **wellborn, well-bred, blueblooded,** well-connected; **thoroughbred,** purebred, pureblooded, full-blooded; **highborn;** born to the purple

609 POLITICS

NOUNS 1 **politics,** polity, the art of the possible; practical politics, *Realpolitik* <Ger>; **party** or **partisan politics, partisanism; politicization;** power politics; machine politics, bossism <nonformal>; confrontation or confrontational politics; **interest politics,** single-issue politics, interest-group politics, pressure-group politics; consensus politics; petty politics, peanut politics <nonformal>; pork-barrel politics

2 **political science,** poli-sci <nonformal>, **politics, government, civics;** political philosophy, political theory; political economy, comparative government, international relations, public administration; political geography, geopolitics

3 **statesmanship, statecraft,** political or governmental leadership, national leadership; kingcraft, queencraft

4 **policy, polity,** public policy; line, **party line,** party principle or doctrine or philosophy, **position,** bipartisan policy; noninterference, nonintervention, laissez-faireism; free enterprise; go-slow policy; planned economy, managed currency, price supports, pump-priming <nonformal>; autarky, economic self-sufficiency; free trade; protection, protectionism; bimetallism; strict constructionism; sectionalism, states' rights, nullification

5 **foreign policy, foreign affairs;** world politics; **diplomacy;** shirt-sleeve diplomacy; shuttle diplomacy; dollar diplomacy; gunboat diplomacy; brinkmanship; **nationalism, internationalism;** expansionism, imperialism, manifest destiny, colonialism, neo-colonialism; spheres of influence; balance of power; containment; deterrence; militarism, preparedness; the big stick <nonformal>; isolationism, neutralism, coexistence, peaceful coexistence; détente; compromise, appeasement; peace offensive; good-neighbor policy; open-door policy, open door

6 program; Square Deal <Theodore Roosevelt>, New Deal <Franklin D Roosevelt>

7 **platform,** party platform, **program; plank; issue;** keynote address, keynote speech; position paper

8 **political convention, convention;** conclave, powwow <nonformal>; national convention, quadrennial circus <nonformal>; state convention; constitutional convention

9 **caucus,** legislative or congressional caucus

10 **candidacy, running, running for office,** throwing or tossing one's hat in the ring <nonformal>

11 **nomination,** direct nomination, petition nomination; acceptance speech

12 **electioneering,** campaigning, politicking <nonformal>; **stumping** and **whistle-stopping** <both nonformal>; **rally,** clambake <nonformal>; fund-raising dinner

13 **campaign,** all-out campaign, hard-hitting campaign; **canvass,**

solicitation; front-porch campaign; grass-roots campaign; **whistle-stop campaign** <nonformal>; TV *or* media campaign; campaign commitments *or* promises; campaign fund, campaign contribution; campaign button

14 **smear campaign,** mudslinging campaign, negative campaign; **whispering campaign;** muckraking, **mudslinging** *and* **dirty politics** *and* **dirty tricks** *and* dirty pool <all nonformal>, character assassination

15 **election,** general election, by-election; congressional election; presidential election; **primary,** primary election; direct primary, open primary, closed primary, preference primary, presidential primary, runoff primary; caucus 609.9; runoff, runoff election; disputed *or* contested election; referendum; close election, horse race *and* toss-up <both nonformal>

16 **election district, precinct, ward, borough;** congressional district; safe district; swing district <nonformal>; gerrymander, gerrymandered district; silk-stocking district *or* ward

17 **suffrage, franchise, the vote,** right to vote; universal suffrage, manhood suffrage, woman *or* female suffrage; suffragism; suffragist, woman-suffragist, suffragette; one man one vote

18 **voting,** going to the polls, casting one's ballot; preferential voting; proportional representation *or* PR; absentee voting; proxy voting; voting machine; election fraud, ballot-box stuffing; **vote** 371.6

19 **ballot, slate, ticket,** proxy <nonformal>; straight ticket, split ticket; Australian ballot; Massachusetts ballot; Indiana ballot; absentee ballot; sample ballot; party emblem

20 **polls,** poll, polling place; voting booth, polling booth; ballot box; voting machine

21 **returns,** election returns, **poll,** count, official count; **recount;** landslide, tidal wave

22 **electorate,** electors; **constituency,** constituents; electoral college

23 **voter, elector, balloter;** registered voter; fraudulent voter, ballot-box stuffer; proxy

24 **political party, party,** major party, minor party, third party, splinter party; party in power, opposition party, loyal opposition; **fraction, camp; machine,** political *or* party machine; city hall; one-party system, two-party system, multiple-party system

25 **partisanism,** partisanship, partisanry

26 **nonpartisanism, independence;** mugwumpism

27 **partisan, party member,** party man *or* woman; regular, stalwart, loyalist; wheelhorse, party wheelhorse; heeler, ward heeler, **party hack;** party faithful

28 **nonpartisan, independent, neutral, mugwump,** undecided *or* uncommitted voter; swing vote

29 **political influence, wire-pulling** <nonformal>; **social pressure, public opinion, special-interest pressure,** group pressure; **influence peddling; lobbying; logrolling,** back scratching

30 **wire-puller** <nonformal>; **influence peddler,** power broker, fixer <nonformal>; logroller

31 **pressure group,** interest group, special-interest group, political action committee *or* PAC, single-issue group; **special interest;** vested interest; minority interests, ethnic vote, black vote, Jewish vote, Italian vote, etc; **Black Power,** White Power, Polish Power, etc

32 **lobby,** legislative lobby, special-interest lobby; **lobbyist,** registered lobbyist, lobbyer

33 **front, movement,** coalition; popular front, communist front, etc; grass-roots movement, ground swell, the silent majority

34 <political corruption> **graft,** boodling <nonformal>; pork-

barrel legislation; political intrigue

35 spoils of office; graft, boodle <nonformal>; slush fund <nonformal>; campaign fund, campaign contribution; public trough <nonformal>; spoils system; cronyism, nepotism

36 political patronage, patronage, favors of office, pork and **pork barrel** <both nonformal>, plum, melon <nonformal>

37 political or **official jargon; officialese** and federalese and Washingtonese and gobbledygook <all nonformal>; bafflegab <nonformal>; political doubletalk, doublespeak, bunkum <nonformal>; pussyfooting

VERBS **38 politick** <nonformal>, politicize; mend one's fences <nonformal>; caucus; gerrymander

39 run for office, run; **throw** or **toss one's hat in the ring** <nonformal>, announce for, enter the arena

40 electioneer, campaign; stump and stump the country and take to the hustings and hit the campaign trail and **whistle-stop** <all nonformal>; **canvass,** go to the voters or electorate, solicit votes, ring doorbells; shake hands and kiss babies

41 support, back and **back up** <both nonformal>, come out for, **endorse;** follow the party line; **get on the bandwagon** <nonformal>; **nominate, elect, vote** 371.18,20

42 hold office, hold or occupy a post, fill an office, be the incumbent, be in office

ADJS **43 political;** governmental, civic; geopolitical; statesmanlike; diplomatic

44 partisan, party; bipartisan, biparty, two-party

45 nonpartisan, independent, neutral, **on the fence**

610 POLITICIAN

NOUNS **1 politician,** politico, political leader, professional politi-

cian; party leader, party boss <nonformal>; machine or clubhouse politician, **political hack; pol** <nonformal>; old campaigner, war-horse; reform politician, reformer

2 statesman, stateswoman, solon, public man or woman, national leader; elder statesman

3 legislator, lawmaker, solon, lawgiver; **congressman,** congresswoman, Member of Congress; **senator; representative;** Speaker of the House; majority leader, minority leader; floor leader; whip, party whip; state senator, assemblyman, assemblywoman, freeholder, councilman, alderman, city father

4 <petty politician> **two-bit politician** <nonformal>, political dabbler; **hack, party hack**

5 <corrupt politician> **dirty** or **crooked politician** <both nonformal>; **grafter,** boodler <nonformal>; influence peddler 609.30

6 <political intriguer> strategist, wheeler-dealer <nonformal>; operator and finagler and **wirepuller** <all nonformal>; **logroller,** pork-barrel politician; Machiavellian; behind-the-scenes operator, gray eminence, *éminence grise* <Fr>, power behind the throne, kingmaker <nonformal>, **powerbroker** 893.6

7 <political leader> **boss** <nonformal>, higher-up or man higher up <nonformal>; keynoter <nonformal>, policy maker; standard-bearer; ringleader 375.11; **big shot** <nonformal> 996.9

8 henchman, cohort, hanger-on, buddy and sidekick <both nonformal>; **ward heeler** <nonformal>; hatchet man

9 candidate, aspirant, hopeful and political hopeful and wannabee <all nonformal>, office seeker or hunter, baby kisser <nonformal>; running mate; head of the ticket or slate; **dark horse;** favorite son; presidential timber; defeated candidate, also-ran *and* dud <both nonformal>

10 **campaigner,** electioneer, **stumper** <nonformal>, whistle-stopper <nonformal>, stump speaker *or* orator <nonformal>

11 **officeholder,** public servant, public official, **incumbent;** hold-over, lame duck; new broom <nonformal>; president-elect; ins

12 **political worker, committee-man,** committeewoman, precinct captain, precinct leader, district leader; party chairman, state chairman, national chairman

VERBS 13 go into politics; **run,** get on the ticket; **campaign,** stump

ADJS 14 **statesmanlike,** states-manly

611 POLITICO-ECONOMIC PRINCIPLES

NOUNS 1 **conservatism, conser-vativeness, rightism;** standpat-tism <nonformal>, unprogres-siveness, backwardness; **ultra-conservatism, reaction,** arch-conservative, die-hardism <nonformal>

2 **moderatism, moderateness;** middle of the road, moderate po-sition, **center,** centrism; non-alignment

3 **liberalism, progressivism; left, left wing**

4 **radicalism, extremism;** radical-ization; ultraconservatism 611.1; extreme left, extreme left wing, left-wing extremism; New Left, Old Left; **anarchism, nihilism;** extreme rightism, radical right-ism, know-nothingism; extreme right, extreme right wing; social Darwinism; laissez-faireism 329.1; **royalism, monarchism**

5 **communism, Bolshevism, Marxism,** Marxism-Leninism, Trotskyism, Stalinism, Maoism, Castroism, revisionism; dialecti-cal materialism; dictatorship of the proletariat; **Communist Party;** iron curtain 1011.5

6 **socialism,** collective ownership, collectivization, public owner-ship; **collectivism;** creeping socialism; state socialism; uto-pian socialism; Marxian socialism, Marxism 611.5; **na-tionalization**

7 **welfarism,** welfare statism; womb-to-tomb security, cradle-to-grave security; social welfare; social security, social insurance; old-age *and* survivors insurance; unemployment compensation, unemployment insurance; work-men's compensation; health insurance, Medicare, Medicaid, **socialized medicine;** public as-sistance, **welfare, relief,** welfare payments, aid to dependent chil-dren *or* ADC, old-age assistance, aid to the blind, aid to the per-manently and totally disabled; guaranteed income, guaranteed annual income; welfare state; welfare capitalism

8 **capitalism,** capitalistic system, **free enterprise,** private enter-prise, free-enterprise economy, free-enterprise system, free econ-omy; *laissez-faire* <Fr>, laissez-faireism; private sector; private ownership; state capitalism; **indi-vidualism,** rugged individualism

9 **conservative, rightist, right-winger;** standpat *and* stand-patter <both nonformal>; hard hat; social Darwinist; ultracon-servative, arch-conservative, ex-treme right-winger, **reactionary,** diehard; **royalist, monarchist,** Tory, imperialist; **right, right wing; radical right**

10 **moderate, centrist,** middle-of-the-roader <nonformal>; inde-pendent; center

11 **liberal, progressive, leftist, left-winger;** welfare stater; **left**

12 **radical, extremist; revolution-ary,** revolutionist; subversive; left-wing extremist, **red** <nonfor-mal>; **anarchist,** nihilist; pink *and* parlor pink *and* pinko <all nonformal>; lunatic fringe

13 Communist, Bolshevist; Bol-shevik, Red and commie and bolshie <all nonformal>; Marxist, Leninist

14 **socialist,** collectivist; social

democrat; state socialist; utopian socialist

15 capitalist; coupon-clipper <nonformal>

VERBS **16 politicize;** democratize, socialize; nationalize 476.7; deregulate, privatize, denationalize; radicalize

ADJS **17 conservative, right-wing,** right of center; old-line, die-hard, unreconstructed, standpat <nonformal>, unprogressive, nonprogressive; ultraconservative, **reactionary**

18 moderate, centrist, middle-of-the-road <nonformal>, independent

19 liberal, liberalistic, bleeding-heart <nonformal>; **progressive; leftist, left-wing,** on the left, left of center

20 radical, extreme, extremist; revolutionary, revolutionist; subversive; ultraconservative 611.17; extreme left-wing, **red** <nonformal>; anarchistic, nihilistic; pink <nonformal>

21 Communist, communistic, Red <nonformal>; **Marxist,** Leninist, Marxist-Leninist, Trotskyite *or* Trotskyist, Stalinist, Maoist, Castroite; revisionist

22 socialist, socialistic; social-democratic

23 capitalist, capitalistic, bourgeois, individualistic, nonsocialistic, free-enterprise, private-enterprise

612 GOVERNMENT

NOUNS **1 government,** governance, **discipline, regulation; direction, management, administration,** oversight, **supervision** 573.2; **regime,** regimen; **rule, sway, sovereignty, reign;** empire; social order, civil government, political government; form *or* system of government, polity

2 control, mastery, mastership, command, power, jurisdiction, dominion, domination; hold, grasp, grip; iron hand, clutches; helm, reins of government

3 the government, the authori-

ties; **the powers that be,** national government, central government, the Establishment; the corridors of power, government circles; Uncle Sam, Washington

4 <kinds of government> **federal government,** federation; **constitutional government; republic,** commonwealth; **democracy,** representative government, representative democracy, direct *or* pure democracy, town-meeting democracy; **parliamentary government;** social democracy, welfare state; mob rule, tyranny of the majority, mobocracy <nonformal>; minority government; aristocracy, hierarchy, oligarchy; feudal system; monarchy, constitutional monarchy; dictatorship, tyranny, autocracy, autarchy; triumvirate; **totalitarian government** *or* regime, police state; **fascism, communism; military government,** militarism, garrison state; martial law; regency; hierocracy, theocracy; gerontocracy; technocracy, meritocracy; **autonomy, self-government,** self-rule, self-determination, home rule; dominion rule, colonial government, colonialism, neocolonialism; provisional government; coalition government

5 matriarchy, matriarchate, gynarchy, gynocracy, gynecocracy; petticoat government

6 <nonformal terms> foolocracy, gunocracy, mediocracy, moneyocracy

7 supranational government, supergovernment, **world government,** United Nations 514

8 <principles of government> constitutionalism, rule of law, parliamentarism; monarchism, royalism; feudalism; imperialism; fascism, neofascism, Nazism, national socialism; statism; collectivism, communism 611.5, socialism 611.6; federalism; centralism; pluralism

9 absolutism, dictatorship, des-

potism, tyranny, autocracy, autarchy, monarchy, absolute monarchy; **authoritarianism;** totalitarianism; one-man rule, one-party rule; benevolent despotism, paternalism

10 **despotism, tyranny, fascism,** domination, oppression; heavy hand, high hand, iron hand, iron heel *or* boot; big stick; **terrorism,** reign of terror; thought control

11 **officialism, bureaucracy; red-tapeism** *and* red-tapery *and* **red tape** <all nonformal>

VERBS 12 **govern, regulate; wield authority** 417.13; **command,** captain, **head, lead,** be at the head of; **preside over,** chair; **direct, manage, supervise, administer;** discipline; stand over

13 **control, hold in hand,** have in one's power, gain a hold upon; hold the reins, call the shots *or* tune *and* be in the driver's seat *or* saddle <all nonformal>; have control of, **have under control, have in hand** *or* **well in hand;** be master of the situation, have it all one's own way, hold all the aces <nonformal>; pull the strings

14 **rule, sway, reign,** have the sway, wear the crown, sit on the throne; rule over, overrule

15 **dominate, predominate,** preponderate, prevail; **have the ascendancy, have the upper** *or* **whip hand,** get under control; **master,** have the mastery of; dictate, lay down the law; **rule the roost** *and* crack the whip *and* ride herd <all nonformal>; take the lead; **lead by the nose, twist** *or* **turn around one's little finger; keep under one's thumb,** bend to one's will

16 **domineer, lord it over;** browbeat, order around, henpeck <nonformal>, intimidate, bully, cow, bulldoze <nonformal>, walk over, walk all over; castrate, unman; daunt, terrorize; **tyrannize,** push *or* kick around <nonformal>; **grind,** grind down, break, **oppress,** suppress, re-

press, weigh heavy on; keep under, keep down, beat down, clamp down on <nonformal>; overbear, overmaster, overawe; override, ride over, trample *or* stamp *or* tread upon, **trample** *or* **tread underfoot,** keep down, **ride roughshod over;** hold *or* keep a tight hand upon, rule with an iron hand *or* fist; enslave, subjugate 432.8; compel, coerce 424.7

ADJS 17 **governmental,** gubernatorial; **political, civil,** civic; **official,** bureaucratic; democratic, republican, fascist, fascistic, oligarchic, oligarchical, aristocratic, theocratic, **federal,** federalist, **constitutional,** parliamentary; monarchic *or* monarchical; autocratic, absolute; **authoritarian;** despotic, **dictatorial; totalitarian;** pluralistic; paternalistic, patriarchical; matriarchical; autonomous, self-governing

18 **governing, controlling, regulating,** regulative, regulatory, **commanding; ruling, reigning, sovereign,** regnant; **master, chief,** general, **boss, head; dominant, predominant,** preponderant, preponderate, prevalent, **leading, paramount, supreme,** number one <nonformal>, hegemonic; ascendant, in the ascendant, in ascendancy; at the head; in charge 417.21

19 **executive, administrative;** official, bureaucratic; **supervisory, directing, managing** 573.12

ADVS 20 **under control, in hand,** well in hand; **in one's power,** under one's control

613 LEGISLATURE, GOVERNMENT ORGANIZATION

NOUNS 1 **legislature,** legislative body; **parliament, congress, assembly,** general assembly, legislative assembly, **national assembly, chamber of deputies,** diet, court; unicameral legislature, bicameral legislature; legislative chamber, **upper** chamber *or* house, **lower chamber** *or* **house**; state legislature, state assembly; provincial legislature, provincial parliament; city council, city board, board of aldermen; representative town meeting, town meeting

2 United States Government, Federal Government

3 **cabinet,** ministry, **council,** advisory council, council of state, privy council, divan; shadow cabinet; kitchen cabinet

4 **capitol, statehouse; courthouse;** city hall

5 **legislation, lawmaking; enactment,** constitution, passage, passing; **resolution;** act 673.3

6 <legislative procedure> introduction, first reading, committee consideration, tabling

7 **veto,** executive veto, qualified *or* limited veto, suspensive *or* suspensory veto, item veto, pocket veto; veto power

8 **referendum,** constitutional referendum; **mandate; plebiscite;** initiative; recall

9 **bill,** omnibus bill; **clause, proviso; rider; calendar, motion**

VERBS 10 **legislate,** make *or* enact laws, **enact, pass,** ordain; **put through, jam** *or* **steamroller** *or* **railroad through** <nonformal>; table, pigeonhole; take the floor, get the floor, have the floor; yield the floor; **filibuster; logroll; veto, pocket, kill; decree** 420.8

ADJS 11 **legislative,** lawmaking; deliberative; **parliamentary, congressional;** senatorial; bicameral, unicameral

614 UNITED NATIONS, INTERNATIONAL ORGANIZATIONS

NOUNS 1 **United Nations** *or* **UN;** League of Nations

2 <United Nations organs> Secretariat; General Assembly; Security Council; Trusteeship Council; International Court of Justice; **United Nations agency,** Economic and Social Council *or* ECOSOC, ECOSOC commission

3 international organization, non-UN international organization

615 COMMISSION

NOUNS 1 **commission,** commissioning, **delegation,** devolution, devolvement, vesting, investing, investment, investiture; **deputation;** commitment, entrusting, entrustment, **assignment,** consignment; **errand, task, office; care, responsibility,** purview, jurisdiction; **mission,** legation, embassy; **authority** 417; **authorization,** empowerment, power to act, full power, plenipotentiary power, delegated authority; **warrant,** license, **mandate, charge, trust; agency;** regency, regentship; trusteeship, executorship; **proxy, power of attorney**

2 **appointment, assignment,** designation, **nomination,** naming, selection; **ordainment,** ordination; posting, transferral

3 **installation, instatement,** induction, **inauguration,** investiture, taking office; **accession;** coronation

4 **engagement, employment, hiring, appointment,** recruitment, recruiting; executive recruiting, executive search; reservation, booking

5 executive search agency *or* firm; executive recruiter, executive development specialist; **headhunter** *and* body snatcher *and* flesh peddler *and* talent scout <all nonformal>

6 **rental, rent; lease,** let; hire, hiring; sublease; **charter;** lend-lease

7 **enlistment, enrollment; conscription, draft, drafting, induction,** impressment, press; call, draft call, call-up, summons; call to the colors, letter from Uncle Sam <nonformal>; **recruitment,** recruiting; **muster,** mustering, levy, levying; mobilization; selective service, compulsory military service

8 indenture, binding over; **apprenticeship**

9 **assignee, appointee,** selectee,

nominee, candidate; licensee, licentiate; deputy, agent 576

VERBS **10 commission, authorize, empower,** accredit; **delegate,** devolve, devolve upon, vest, invest; depute, **deputize; assign, commit, charge, entrust,** give in charge; license, charter, warrant; detail, detach, post, transfer, send out, send on a mission

11 appoint, assign, designate, **nominate,** name, select; **ordain**

12 install, instate, induct, **inaugurate,** invest, put in, place, **place in office;** crown, enthrone, anoint

13 be instated, take office, accede; take or mount the throne; attain to

14 employ, hire, give a job to, take on <nonformal>, recruit, headhunt <nonformal>, **engage,** sign up or on <nonformal>; retain; sign up for <nonformal>, **reserve,** book

15 rent, lease, let, hire, job, **charter; sublease, sublet**

16 rent out, rent; lease; hire out, hire; charter; **sublease, sublet;** lend-lease, lease-lend; lease-back; farm, farm out; job

17 enlist, enroll, sign up or on <nonformal>; **conscript, draft, induct,** press, impress, commandeer; detach, detach for service; summon, call up, call to the colors; **mobilize,** call to active duty; recruit, muster, levy, raise, muster in; join 617.14

18 indenture, article, bind, bind over; **apprentice**

ADJS **19 commissioned, authorized, accredited;** delegated, deputized, appointed

20 employed, hired, hireling, paid, mercenary; rented, leased, let; sublet, subleased; chartered

21 indentured, articled; **apprenticed, apprentice**

ADVS **22 for hire,** for rent, to let, to lease

616 ASSOCIATE

NOUNS **1 associate, confederate, colleague,** fellow member, **companion, fellow,** bedfellow, **crony,** consort, cohort, compatriot, confrere, **ally,** adjunct; comrade in arms, **comrade** 588.3

2 partner, pardner <nonformal>, copartner, buddy <nonformal>, **sidekick** <nonformal>; **mate; business partner,** general partner, special partner, silent partner

3 accomplice, cohort, confederate, fellow conspirator, coconspirator, partner in crime; **accessory,** accessory before the fact, accessory after the fact; **abettor**

4 collaborator; coauthor; **collaborationist**

5 coworker, workmate, fellow worker, buddy <nonformal>; **teammate, yokefellow,** yokemate

6 assistant, helper, auxiliary, **aid,** aide, paraprofessional; **help, helpmate, helpmeet;** deputy, **agent** 576; **attendant, second,** acolyte; **servant, employee** 577; adjutant, aide-de-camp; lieutenant, executive officer; supporting actor or player; supporting instrumentalist, sideman

7 right-hand man or woman, **right hand, man** or gal Friday, second self, alter ego, confidant

8 follower, disciple, adherent, votary; **man, henchman,** camp follower, hanger-on, satellite, lackey, flunky, stooge <nonformal>, jackal, minion, myrmidon; yes-man <nonformal>, sycophant 138.3; puppet, cat's-paw; dummy, figurehead

9 supporter, upholder, sustainer; support, **mainstay, standby** <nonformal>, stalwart; **abettor, seconder,** second; endorser, sponsor; **backer, promoter,** angel <nonformal>, rabbi <nonformal>; **patron; champion,** defender, apologist, **advocate,** exponent, **protagonist; wellwisher,** sympathizer; **partisan,** sectary, votary; **fan** and buff <both nonformal>, aficionado, **admirer**

617 ASSOCIATION

NOUNS **1 association, society, body; alliance, coalition,** league, union; council; **bloc, axis**; **partnership; federation, confederation,** confederacy, grouping, assemblage 769; **combination,** combine; **unholy alliance, gang** *and* **ring** *and* mob <all nonformal>; machine, **political machine**; economic community, common market, customs union; credit union; cooperative, consumer cooperative; **group,** corps, band 769.3

2 **community, society, commonwealth;** body; **kinship group, clan,** moiety, totemic group, gens, caste, subcaste; **family,** extended family, nuclear family; order, **class, social class** 607, economic class; colony, settlement; **commune,** ashram

3 **fellowship,** sodality; **society,** guild, order; **brotherhood, fraternity,** fraternal order; **sisterhood, sorority; club**; secret society, **cabal**

4 **party, interest, camp, side;** interest group, pressure group, ethnic group; minority group; silent majority; **faction, sect,** wing, **caucus,** splinter group, offshoot; **political party** 609.24

5 **school, sect; denomination, communion,** church; **persuasion; disciples, followers,** adherents

6 **clique, coterie, set, circle,** ring, cabal, **clan,** group; **crew** *and* mob *and* **crowd** *and* **bunch** *and* outfit <all nonformal>; cell; cadre, inner circle; charmed circle; ingroup; elite, elite group; **old-boy network**

7 **team, outfit,** squad, string; varsity, first team, first string; bench, reserves, second team, second string, third string; platoon; complement; **cast,** company

8 **organization,** establishment, **foundation, institution, institute**

9 **company, firm, business firm, concern, house; business, industry, enterprise,** business establishment, commercial enterprise; **trust, syndicate, cartel,** combine, pool, consortium; combination in restraint of trade; trade association

10 **branch, organ, division,** wing, arm, offshoot, **affiliate; chapter,** lodge; **local;** branch office

11 **member,** affiliate, insider, initiate, one of us, cardholder, card-carrying member; **enrollee,** enlistee; **associate, fellow;** brother, sister; comrade; member in good standing, dues-paying member; charter member; clubman, clubwoman; fraternity man, fraternity *or* frat brother, sorority woman; sorority sister; joiner <nonformal>; pledge

12 **membership,** members, associates, affiliates, body of affiliates, constituency

13 **partisanism,** partisanship, **partiality; factionalism, sectionalism,** faction; **cliquism,** cliquishness; **clannishness;** exclusiveness, exclusivity; ethnocentricity; *esprit de corps* <Fr>; the old college spirit

VERBS 14 **join,** join up <nonformal>, **enter, go into,** swell the ranks of; **enlist, enroll, affiliate, sign up** *or* **on** <nonformal>, take up membership, take out membership; associate oneself with; affiliate with, team up with; insinuate oneself into; **combine, associate** 804.4

15 **belong,** hold membership, be a member, subscribe, hold *or* carry a card, be in <nonformal>

ADJS 16 **associated, corporate,** incorporated; **combined** 804.5; non-profit, not-for-profit

17 **associational, social, society, communal;** organizational; coalitional; sociable

18 **cliquish, clannish;** ethnocentric; exclusive

19 **partisan,** party; **partial,** interested; **factional, sectional,** sectarian, sectary, denominational

ADVS 20 **in association, conjointly** 450.6

618 WEALTH

NOUNS 1 **wealth, riches, opulence** *or* opulency 990.2, **luxurious-**

ness 501.5; **prosperity, affluence,** comfortable *or* easy
circumstances, independence;
money, lucre, gold, mammon;
**substance, property, posses-
sions; assets** 728.14; **fortune,
treasure;** full *or* well-lined *or* bottomless *or* fat purse, deep pockets
<nonformal>; money to burn
<nonformal>; high income, six-
figure income; high tax bracket

2 **large sum,** good sum, tidy sum
and **pretty penny, king's ransom;** cool million, billion, etc

3 <nonformal terms> **bundle, big
bucks,** megabucks, big money,
serious money, gobs, heaps,
heavy lettuce, important money,
potful, mint, barrel, raft, **loads,**
pile, wad, nice hunk of change

4 <rich source> **mine, gold mine,**
bonanza, mother lode, Eldorado,
Golconda, gravy train <nonfor-
mal>; rich uncle; cash cow
<nonformal>

5 **the golden touch,** Midas touch

6 **the rich, the wealthy,** the-well-
to-do

7 **rich man** *or* **woman,** wealthy
man *or* woman, **moneyed man**
or **woman,** man *or* woman of
wealth, **man** *or* **woman of means**
or **substance,** fat cat <nonfor-
mal>, deep pocket *and* moneybags *and* Mr Moneybags <all
nonformal>, coupon-clipper,
nabob; capitalist, plutocrat,
bloated plutocrat; **millionaire,**
multimillionaire, millionairess,
multibillionaire, multimillion-
airess, billionaire

8 Croesus, Midas, Plutus, Dives
VERBS 9 enrich, richen

10 **grow rich, get rich,** fill *or* line
one's pockets, **make** *or* **coin
money,** have the golden touch,
make a fortune, make one's pile
<nonformal>; **strike it rich;**
come into money; do all right by
oneself *and* rake it in <both non-
formal>

11 **have money, be loaded** *and*
have deep pockets <both nonfor-
mal>, have the wherewithal, have
independent means; **afford**

12 **live well,** live high on the hog
<nonformal>, **live in clover,** live
in the lap of luxury; have all the
money in the world, have money
to burn <nonformal>

13 worship mammon, worship the
golden calf
ADJS 14 **wealthy, rich, affluent,
moneyed** *or* **monied, well-to-do,
well-off, well-situated, prosperous,** comfortable, well provided for, fat, **flush,** flush with
money, worth a great deal, rich as
Croesus; independently wealthy;
luxurious 501.21; **opulent** 990.7;
privileged, born with a silver
spoon in one's mouth

15 <nonformal terms> **loaded,
well-heeled, filthy rich,** in the
money *or* dough, **well-fixed,** made
of money, **rolling in money,** rolling in it, disgustingly rich, rich-
rich, lousy rich

619 POVERTY

NOUNS 1 **poverty,** impecunious-
ness, impecuniosity; **straits,**
difficulties, **hardship** 1010.1;
financial distress *or* embarrassment, **embarrassed** *or* **reduced**
or **straitened circumstances,**
tight squeeze, crunch <nonfor-
mal>, cash *or* credit crunch
<nonformal>; cash-flow short-
age; insolvency, light purse;
unprosperousness; genteel poverty; vows of poverty

2 **indigence, penury, penniless-
ness,** penuriousness; **pauperism, impoverishment,** grinding
poverty, chronic pauperism; **beggary,** beggarliness, mendicancy;
homelessness; **destitution, privation, deprivation; neediness,
want,** need, lack, pinch, gripe,
necessitousness, **homelessness;
hand-to-mouth existence,** bare
subsistence, wolf at the door,
empty purse *or* pocket

3 **the poor, the needy,** the have-
nots <nonformal>, the down-
and-out, **the disadvantaged,** the
underprivileged, the distressed,
the underclass; the urban poor,
ghetto-dwellers, barrio-dwellers;

welfare rolls, welfare clients, welfare families; the homeless, the ranks of the homeless; the other America; depressed area; underdeveloped nation, third world

4 poor man, down-and-out *or* down-and-outer, **pauper,** indigent; homeless person, bag woman *or* lady, shopping-bag lady, homeless *or* street person; **beggar** 440.8; welfare client; charity case; bankrupt 625.4

VERBS **5 be poor,** be hard up <nonformal>, have seen better days, be on one's uppers, be pinched *or* strapped, **be in want; starve,** not know where one's next meal is coming from, **live from hand to mouth; not have a penny,** not have one dollar to rub against another; go on welfare

6 impoverish, reduce, **pauperize, beggar;** eat out of house and home; **bankrupt** 625.8

ADJS **7 poor,** hard up <nonformal>, impecunious, **unmoneyed; unprosperous;** in reduced circumstances; **straitened, in straitened circumstances,** feeling the pinch, strapped, **financially embarrassed** *or* distressed, **pinched,** feeling the pinch, squeezed, at the end of one's rope, on the edge *or* ragged edge <nonformal>; short, **short of money** *or* **funds** *or* **cash,** out-of-pocket; unable to make ends meet, unable to keep the wolf from the door; poor as a church mouse; land-poor

8 indigent, poverty-stricken; needy, necessitous, **in need, in want,** disadvantaged, deprived, underprivileged; **beggared,** beggarly, mendicant; **impoverished, pauperized;** bereft; stripped, fleeced; **down at heels,** on one's uppers, out at the heels, in rags; on welfare

9 destitute, down-and-out, in the gutter; **penniless,** out of funds, without a penny to bless oneself with, without one dollar to rub against another; insolvent, in the red, **bankrupt** 625.11; homeless

10 <nonformal terms> **broke, dead broke,** busted, **flat, flat broke,** flat on one's ass, down for the count, stone *or* stony broke, **strapped,** beat; down to one's last penny *or* cent, cleaned out, tapped out, Tap City, wiped out, without a pot to piss in

620 LENDING

NOUNS **1 lending, loaning;** moneylending, lending at interest; **usury,** loan-sharking *and* shylocking <both nonformal>; **interest,** interest rate, the price of money; points, mortgage points

2 loan, advance, accommodation

3 lender, loaner; loan officer; commercial banker; **moneylender;** banker 729.10; **usurer,** shylock *and* loan shark <both nonformal>; **pawnbroker;** mortgagee, mortgage holder

4 lending institution, savings and loan association *or* thrift *or* thrift institution *or* savings institution; savings and loan *or* thrift industry; finance company, loan office, mortgage company; commercial bank, **bank** 729.13; **credit union; pawnshop, pawnbroker, hock shop** <nonformal>

VERBS **5 lend, loan, advance,** accommodate with; loan-shark <nonformal>; negotiate a loan

ADJS **6 loaned, lent**

ADVS **7 on loan,** on security; in advance

621 BORROWING

NOUNS **1 borrowing,** moneyraising; touching *or* hitting *or* hitting-up <all nonformal>; installment buying, installment plan; debt, debtor 623.4

2 adoption, appropriation, taking, derivation, assumption; imitation, simulation, copying, mocking; a leaf from someone else's book; plagiarism, pastiche; infringement, pirating

VERBS **3 borrow,** get on credit *or* trust, get on the cuff <nonformal>; get a loan, float *or* negotiate a loan, **raise money; touch** *and* **hit up** *and* hit one for *and* put the arm *or* bite *or* touch on <all nonformal>; pawn 438.10

4 **adopt, appropriate,** take, assume, take a leaf from someone's book, derive from; **imitate,** simulate, copy, mock, steal one's stuff <nonformal>; plagiarize, steal; pirate, infringe

622 FINANCIAL CREDIT

NOUNS 1 **credit, trust;** tax credit, investment credit; credit line, line of credit; installment plan, consumer credit, store credit; **credit standing, credit rating,** rating, Dun and Bradstreet rating, solvency 729.6; credit squeeze, insolvency; credit bureau; credit union

2 **account,** charge account; bank account, savings account, checking account; expense account

3 **credit instrument; letter of credit;** deposit slip, certificate of deposit; negotiable instruments 728.11; **credit card,** plastic, gold card, charge card, charge plate; smart card, supersmart card

4 **creditor;** mortgagee, mortgageholder; credit man; bill collector, collection agent; dunner

VERBS 5 **credit, credit with; credit to one's account**

6 **give** *or* **extend credit** *or* **a line of credit;** sell on credit, trust; carry, carry on one's books

7 **receive credit, charge,** charge to one's account, keep an account with, buy on credit, buy on the cuff <nonformal>, buy on time; go in hock for <nonformal>; have one's credit good for

ADJS 8 **credited,** of good credit, **well-rated**

ADVS 9 **to one's account,** to the account of

10 **on credit, on account, on trust, on the cuff** <nonformal>; on terms, on good terms, on easy terms, in installments, on time

623 DEBT

NOUNS 1 **debt, indebtedness, obligation, liability,** financial commitment, **dues,** score, pledge, amount due, outstanding debt; **bill, bills,** chits <nonformal>, **charges;** borrowing 621; maturity; bad debts, uncollectibles; **national debt,** public debt; deficit, national deficit

2 **arrears,** back debts, back payments; **deficit,** default; cash *or* credit crunch <nonformal>; bounced *or* bouncing check, rubber check <nonformal>; deficit financing

3 **interest, premium, price, rate;** interest rate, **prime rate,** bank rate, the price of money; discount rate; **usury** 620.1, excessive *or* exorbitant interest; points, mortgage points; simple interest, compound interest

4 **debtor,** borrower; mortgagor

VERBS 5 **owe, be indebted,** be obligated for, be financially committed, be bound to pay

6 **go in debt,** get into debt, plunge into debt, incur a debt, go in hock <nonformal>, be overextended, **run up a bill** *or* a score *or* an account *or* a tab; run *or* show a deficit, operate at a loss; borrow

7 **mature, accrue, fall due**

ADJS 8 **indebted, in debt,** plunged in debt, in difficulties, embarrassed, in the hole *and* in hock <both nonformal>, in the red, encumbered, mortgaged, mortgaged to the hilt, tied up, involved; deep in debt, burdened with debt, up to one's ears in debt <nonformal>; cash poor

9 **chargeable, obligated, liable,** pledged, responsible, answerable for

10 **due, owed, owing, payable,** receivable, **outstanding, unpaid,** in arrears

624 PAYMENT

NOUNS 1 **payment, paying,** paying off, paying up <nonformal>, payoff; **defrayment,** defrayal; paying out, **disbursal** 626.1; **discharge, settlement, clearance, liquidation, amortization,** retirement, satisfaction; **debt service, inter-**

est payment; **remittance;** installment, installment plan, layaway plan; down payment, deposit, earnest money, binder; **cash,** hard cash, spot cash, cash payment, cash on the barrelhead <nonformal>; pay-as-you-go; prepayment; **postponed** or **deferred payment;** payment in kind

2 reimbursement, recoupment, restitution; **refund;** kickback <nonformal>; payback, **repayment** 481.2

3 recompense, remuneration, compensation; requital, **retribution, reparation, redress,** satisfaction, **atonement, amends,** restitution 481; **blood money; indemnity,** indemnification; price, consideration; **reward;** honorarium; damages

4 pay, payment, remuneration, compensation, financial package, pay and allowances, financial remuneration; rate of pay; **salary, wage, wages, income, earnings,** hire; real wages, purchasing power; payday, pay check, pay envelope; take-home pay, net income or wages or pay or earnings, taxable income; living wage; minimum wage, base pay; portal-to-portal pay; severance pay, wage scale; guaranteed annual income, negative income tax; fixed income; wage freeze, wage rollback, wage reduction, wage control; guaranteed annual wage; overtime pay; combat pay, flight pay; back pay; strike pay; **payroll**

5 fee, stipend, allowance, emolument, tribute; **reckoning,** account, bill; assessment; initiation fee; retainer; hush money, blackmail; blood money

6 <extra pay or allowance> **bonus, premium, fringe benefit,** bounty, perquisites, perks <nonformal>, gravy <nonformal>, lagniappe; **tip** 478.5; overtime pay

7 dividend; royalty; **commission,** rake-off and cut <both nonformal>

8 <the bearing of another's expense> **treat,** standing treat, picking up the check or tab <nonformal>; subsidy 478.8

9 payer, remunerator, recompenser; paymaster, purser, bursar, cashier, treasurer 729.11; **taxpayer**

VERBS **10** pay, render, tender; **recompense, remunerate, compensate, reward,** indemnify, satisfy; salary, fee; remit; pay in installments, pay on, pay in

11 repay, pay back, **reimburse,** recoup; **requite, atone, make amends,** make good, make up for, make restitution, make reparation 481.5; pay in kind, pay one in his own coin, give tit for tat; **refund,** kick back <nonformal>

12 settle with, reckon with, pay out, **settle** or **square accounts with,** get square with, **get even with;** even the score <nonformal>, pay old debts, clear the board

13 pay in full, pay off, pay up <nonformal>, **discharge, settle,** square, **clear, liquidate, amortize,** retire, honor; satisfy; meet one's obligations or commitments, redeem, redeem one's pledge or pledges, have a mortgage-burning party, settle or square accounts; pay the bill

14 pay out, fork out or over <nonformal>, **shell out** <nonformal>; **expend** 626.5

15 pay over, hand over; **ante up,** put up; put down, show the color of one's money

16 <nonformal terms> **kick in, fork over,** pony up, pay up, cough up, come across, come across with, plank down, plunk down, grease the palm, cross one's palm with

17 pay cash, pay spot cash, pay cash down, pay cash on the barrelhead <nonformal>, plunk down the money and put one's money on the line <both nonformal>; pay as you go; pay cash on delivery or pay COD

18 pay for, pay or stand the costs,

bear the expense or **cost,** pay the piper <nonformal>; **finance, fund** 729.15; **defray,** defray expenses; pay the bill, **foot the bill** and pick up the check or tab and spring or pop for <all nonformal>; pay one's way; pay one's share, chip in <nonformal>, go Dutch <nonformal>

19 **treat,** treat to, **stand treat,** go treat, pick up the check or tab <nonformal>, set up, blow to <nonformal>; stand drinks; maintain, support 449.12; subsidize 478.19

20 **be paid, draw wages,** be salaried, work for wages, **earn,** get an income, pull down and drag down <both nonformal>

ADJS 21 **paying, remunerative, re-muneratory; compensating,** compensatory; **rewarding;** lucrative, moneymaking, profitable; repaying, satisfying, reparative

22 **paid, paid-up, discharged, set-tled, liquidated,** paid in full; **spent, expended;** salaried, waged, hired

23 **unindebted, out of debt,** above water, out of the red <nonformal>, **clear,** free and clear; solvent 729.17

ADVS 24 **in compensation,** in recompense, for services rendered, **in reward,** in reparation, in retribution, in restitution, in exchange for, **in amends,** in atonement, to atone for

25 **cash,** cash on the barrelhead <nonformal>; **cash down, money down;** cash on delivery or **COD;** on demand, on call; pay-as-you-go

625 NONPAYMENT

NOUNS 1 **nonpayment, default, delinquency,** failure to pay; repudiation; bad debt, uncollectible

2 **moratorium,** grace period; **write-off,** cancellation

3 **insolvency, bankruptcy,** receivership, Chapter 11, **failure; crash,** collapse, bust <nonformal>; run on a bank; insufficient funds, overdrawn account,

bounced or bouncing check, kited check

4 **insolvent,** insolvent debtor; **bankrupt,** failure; **loser,** heavy loser

5 **defaulter,** delinquent; **welsher** <nonformal>; tax evader, tax dodger or cheat <nonformal>

VERBS 6 **not pay;** repudiate, stop payment; **default, welsh** <nonformal>; **underpay;** bounce or kite a check <nonformal>

7 **go bankrupt, go broke** <nonformal>, go into receivership, become insolvent or bankrupt, **fail,** break, bust <nonformal>, crash, collapse, **fold, fold up,** belly up and go up and go belly up and **go under** <all nonformal>, shut one's doors, go out of business, **be ruined,** go to the wall, go to pot <nonformal>, go to the dogs; take a bath and be taken to the cleaners and be cleaned out and lose one's shirt and tap out <all nonformal>

8 **bankrupt, ruin, break;** put out of business, drive to the wall, scuttle, sink; impoverish 619.6

9 **declare a moratorium; write off, forgive, cancel,** wipe the slate clean; wipe out

ADJS 10 **defaulting,** nonpaying, **delinquent;** in arrears

11 **insolvent, bankrupt,** in receivership, in the hands of receivers, belly-up <nonformal>, broken, **broke** <nonformal>, **ruined,** failed, out of business, unable to meet one's obligations, on the rocks; destitute 619.9

12 **unpaid, unremunerated,** uncompensated, unrecompensed, **unrewarded;** underpaid

13 **unpayable,** irredeemable, inconvertible

626 EXPENDITURE

NOUNS 1 **expenditure, spending,** expense, disbursal, **disburse-ment;** costing, costing-out; **pay-ment** 624; deficit spending; **use** 387; **consumption** 388

2 spendings, disbursements, payments, outgo, outflow, **outlay**

3 expenses, costs, charges, disbursals, **liabilities; expense, cost;** budget item, line item; **overhead,** general expenses; expense account, swindle sheet <nonformal>; business expenses, overhead, out-of-pocket expenses; direct costs, indirect costs; material costs; labor costs; unit cost; replacement cost

4 spender, expender, expenditor, disburser

VERBS **5 spend, expend, disburse, pay out,** fork out *or* over <nonformal>, shell out <nonformal>, **lay out;** go to the expense of; **pay** 624.10; loosen *or* untie the purse strings *and* throw money around <both nonformal>, go on a spending spree, splurge, spend money like a drunken sailor *and* spend money as if it were going out of style <both nonformal>, go *or* run through, **squander** 486.3; **invest,** sink money in <nonformal>; throw money at the problem; **incur costs** *or* **expenses; use** 387.13; **consume**

6 be spent, burn a hole in one's pocket

7 afford, bear, stand, support, endure, undergo, meet the expense of, swing

627 RECEIPTS

NOUNS **1 receipts, income, revenue, profits, earnings, returns, proceeds, take;** credit, credits; gains 472.3; gate receipts, gate, box office; net receipts, net; gross receipts, gross; **dividend** 738.7, dividends, payout, payback; royalties, commissions; receivables; **yield, output** 892.2, bang for the buck <nonformal>, fruits, first fruits

2 <written acknowledgment> **receipt, acknowledgment, voucher; receipt in full,** release, discharge

VERBS **3 receive** 479.6, **pocket, acquire** 472.8,9; acknowledge receipt of, receipt, mark paid

4 yield, bring in, afford, pay, pay off <nonformal>, **return; gross; net**

628 ACCOUNTS

NOUNS **1 accounts; outstanding accounts,** uncollected *or* unpaid accounts; **accounts receivable,** receipts, assets; **accounts payable,** expenditures, liabilities; **budget,** budgeting; costing out

2 account, reckoning, tally, rendering-up, score; balance, trial balance

3 statement, bill, itemized bill, **account, reckoning, check,** score *or* tab <both nonformal>; **dun; invoice**

4 account book, ledger, journal, daybook; **register,** registry, **record book,** books; inventory, catalog; **log,** logbook; **cashbook; bankbook,** passbook

5 entry, item, line item, minute, note

6 accounting, accountancy, bookkeeping, audit, auditing

7 accountant, bookkeeper; clerk, registrar, recorder; cost accountant; certified public accountant *or* CPA; **auditor,** bank examiner; comptroller *or* controller

VERBS **8 keep accounts, keep books,** render accounts; **credit, debit;** charge off, write off; capitalize; **balance,** balance accounts, balance the books; close the books, close out

9 take account of, take stock; inventory; audit, examine *or* inspect the books

10 falsify accounts, garble accounts, cook *or* doctor accounts <nonformal>, salt; surcharge

11 bill, send a statement; **invoice;** call, call in, demand payment, **dun**

ADJS **12** accounting, bookkeeping; budget, budgetary

629 TRANSFER OF PROPERTY OR RIGHT

NOUNS **1 transfer,** transference; **conveyance,** conveyancing; **giv-**

ing 478; **delivery,** deliverance; **assignment; consignment;** conferment, conferral, settling, settlement; **sale** 734; transmission, transmittal; disposition, deaccession, deaccessioning; demise; alienation, abalienation; amortization; deeding; **exchange,** barter, trading

2 devolution, succession, reversion

VERBS 3 **transfer, convey, deliver; give** 478.12–14,16,21; **hand over, turn over, pass over; assign, consign;** cede, surrender; bequeath 478.18; **sell** 734.8,11,12, sell off, deaccession; **make over, sign over,** sign away; transmit; **hand down, hand on, pass on,** devolve upon; amortize; **deed,** deed over, give title to; **exchange,** barter, trade, trade away

4 **change hands,** change ownership; devolve, pass on, descend

ADJS 5 **transferable, conveyable,** negotiable; **assignable,** consignable; bequeathable; heritable

630 PRICE, FEE

NOUNS 1 **price, cost, expense,** expenditure, **charge,** damage *and* score *and* tab <all nonformal>; **quotation,** quoted price, price tag *and* **ticket** *and* **sticker** <all nonformal>; **price list**

2 **worth, value,** rate; face value; face; par value; market value; street value; money's worth, value received; bang for the buck <nonformal>

3 **valuation, evaluation,** pricing, price determination, **assessment, appraisal,** estimation

4 **price index,** business index; wholesale price index; consumer price *or* retail price index; cost-of-living index; rising prices, **inflation,** inflationary spiral

5 **price controls,** price-fixing; managed prices, fair trade, fair-trade agreement; **price supports;** price freeze

6 **fee, dues, toll, charge, charges, demand, exaction; fare,** carfare; user fee; airport fee; license fee;

admission fee, admission; cover charge

7 freightage, freight, haulage, carriage, cartage, drayage; poundage, tonnage

8 **rent, rental;** ground rent, wayleave rent

9 **tax, taxation, duty, tribute,** taxes, **assessment, revenue enhancement, levy, toll, impost,** imposition; tax code, tax law; **tithe; tax burden;** bracket *or* tax-bracket creep; progressive taxation, graduated taxation; regressive taxation; tax withholding; tax return; tax evasion *or* avoidance; tax haven *or* shelter; **tax deduction, deduction; tax write-off,** tax relief; tax exemption, tax-exempt status; tax base; taxable income *or* goods *or* land *or* property

10 **tax collector,** taxman; internal revenue agent; assessor, **tax assessor;** revenuer; **customs agent; customs;** customhouse

VERBS 11 **price,** set *or* name a price, fix the price of; place a value on, **value, evaluate, appraise, assess, rate;** quote a price; control the price of; mark up, mark down, **discount;** reassess

12 **charge, demand, ask,** require; overcharge, undercharge; **exact, assess, levy, impose; tax,** slap a tax on <nonformal>, subject to a tax *or* fee *or* duty, collect a tax *or* duty on; tithe; prorate, assess *pro rata;* charge for

13 **cost, sell for, fetch, bring,** bring in; **come to,** run to *or* into, **amount to,** mount up to, come up to, total up to

ADJS 14 **priced, valued,** assessed, appraised, rated; **worth,** valued at; good for

15 **chargeable, taxable,** assessable, dutiable, leviable, declarable; tithable

16 tax-free, nontaxable, nondutiable, tax-exempt; deductible, tax-deductible; duty-free

ADVS 17 **at a price;** to the amount

of, to the tune of *and* in the neighborhood of <both nonformal>

631 DISCOUNT

NOUNS 1 **discount, cut, deduction,** slash, abatement, reduction, price reduction, price-cutting, price-cut, rollback <nonformal>; underselling; **rebate**; write-off, charge-off; **depreciation; allowance,** concession; **refund,** kickback <nonformal>; **premium,** percentage

VERBS 2 **discount, cut, deduct,** abate; **take off,** write off, charge off; **depreciate;** reduce; sell at a loss; **allow,** make allowance; rebate, **refund,** kick back <nonformal>

ADVS 3 **at a discount,** at a reduction, at a reduced rate, below par, below *or* under cost

632 EXPENSIVENESS

NOUNS 1 **expensiveness, costliness, dearness,** stiffness *or* **steepness** <both nonformal>, priceyness; **richness, sumptuousness, luxuriousness**

2 **preciousness, dearness, value,** high *or* great value, **worth,** extraordinary worth, **valuableness; pricelessness, invaluableness**

3 **high price,** big price tag *and* big ticket *and* big sticker price <all nonformal>, **fancy price,** steep *or* stiff price <nonformal>, a pretty penny *or* an arm and a leg <both nonformal>, exorbitant *or* unconscionable *or* extortionate price; inflationary prices, rising *or* soaring *or* spiraling prices, soaring costs; sellers' market; **inflation,** cost *or* cost-push inflation *or* cost-push, inflationary trend *or* pressure, inflationary spiral; reflation; stagflation

4 **exorbitance, extravagance,** excess, **excessiveness,** inordinateness, immoderateness, immoderation, unreasonableness, outrageousness, preposterousness; unconscionableness

5 **overcharge,** surcharge; gouging

or price-gouging; **extortion,** extortionate price; **holdup** *and* armed robbery *and* highway robbery <all nonformal>; profiteering

VERBS 6 **cost much,** cost a pretty penny *or* an arm and a leg <nonformal>, **run into money;** be overpriced, price out of the market

7 **overprice,** set the price tag too high; **overcharge,** surcharge, overtax; **hold up** *and* **soak** *and* **stick** *and* **sting** *and* **clip** <all nonformal>, **make pay through the nose, gouge;** victimize, swindle 356.18; exploit, skin <nonformal>, **fleece,** put the screws to <nonformal>, bleed, bleed white; profiteer

8 **overpay,** overspend, pay too much, pay more than it's worth, **pay dearly, pay through the nose,** be had *or* taken <both nonformal>

9 **inflate,** heat *or* heat up the economy; reflate

ADJS 10 **precious, dear, valuable,** worthy, rich, golden, worth a pretty penny <nonformal>, worth its weight in gold, good as gold; **priceless, invaluable,** inestimable, not to be had for love or money, not for all the tea in China

11 **expensive, dear, costly, high, high-priced,** premium, at a premium; big ticket <nonformal>, **fancy** *and* stiff *and* steep <all nonformal>, pricey; beyond one's means, not affordable, more than one can afford; upmarket, upscale <nonformal>; rich, sumptuous, posh <nonformal>, **luxurious** 501.21, gold-plated

12 **overpriced,** grossly overpriced, **exorbitant, excessive, extravagant, inordinate, immoderate,** unwarranted, unreasonable, unconscionable, outrageous, preposterous, out of bounds, out of sight <nonformal>, **prohibitive; extortionate,** cutthroat, **gouging, usurious,** exacting; **inflationary,** spiraling, skyrocketing

ADVS 13 **dear, dearly;** at great cost,

at a premium, at heavy cost, at great expense

14 **preciously, valuably,** worthily; pricelessly, invaluably, inestimably

15 **expensively,** richly, sumptuously, luxuriously

16 **exorbitantly, excessively,** grossly, **extravagantly, inordinately,** unduly, unreasonably, unconscionably, outrageously, preposterously; **extortionately,** usuriously, gougingly

633 CHEAPNESS

NOUNS **1 cheapness, inexpensiveness,** affordability, reasonableness, modestness; drug *or* glut on the market

2 **low price, nominal price,** reasonable price, modest *or* manageable price, sensible price, moderate price; low *or* nominal *or* reasonable charge; bargain prices, budget prices, rock-bottom prices; buyers' market; small price tag *and* low sticker price *and* low tariff <all nonformal>; **reduced price,** cut price, sale price

3 **bargain, buy** <nonformal>, **good buy, steal** <nonformal>; money's worth

4 **cheapening, depreciation, devaluation,** reduction, lowering; deflation, cooling *or* cooling off of the economy; **buyers' market; decline,** plummeting, plunge, dive, **nosedive** *and* slump *and* sag <all nonformal>, free fall; **price cut** *or* **reduction,** cut, slash, **markdown**

VERBS **5 be cheap,** cost little, not cost anything *and* cost nothing *and* next to nothing <all nonformal>; **buy dirt cheap** *or* for a song *or* for peanuts <all nonformal>, buy at a bargain; get one's money's worth

6 **cheapen, depreciate, devaluate,** lower, reduce, **mark down, cut prices, cut,** slash, shave, trim, pare, underprice; deflate, cool *or* cool off the economy; beat down; fall in price; **fall,** decline,

plummet, dive, nosedive <nonformal>, drop, crash, plunge, sag, slump; break

ADJS **7 cheap, inexpensive,** unexpensive, **low, low-priced,** frugal, reasonable, sensible, manageable, modest, moderate, affordable, to fit the pocketbook, budget, easy, economy, economical; nominal, token; worth the money, well worth the money; cheap at half the price

8 **dirt cheap,** cheap as dirt, **a dime a dozen,** bargain-basement, five-and-ten, dime-store

9 reduced, cut, cut-price, slashed, marked down; cut-rate

ADVS **10 cheaply, cheap; inexpensively,** reasonably, moderately, nominally; for a song <nonformal>, at a low price, at budget prices, at a sacrifice; at cost *or* cost price, at wholesale; at reduced rates

634 COSTLESSNESS
<absence of charge>

NOUNS **1 costlessness, freeness,** expenselessness, no charge; free ride <nonformal>; freebie <nonformal>; labor of love; **gift** 478.4

2 **complimentary ticket, pass,** comp <nonformal>, free pass, paper <nonformal>, Annie Oakley <nonformal>; discount ticket, twofer <nonformal>

3 **freeloader,** free rider, pass holder

VERBS **4 give, present** 478.12, comp <nonformal>; freeload, sponge

ADJS **5 gratuitous, gratis, free, free of charge,** for free, **for nothing,** free for nothing, free for the asking, for love, free as air; freebie <nonformal>; without charge, free of cost *or* expense; no charge; unpaid-for; **complimentary, on the house, comp** <nonformal>, given 478.24; eleemosynary, charitable 143.15

ADVS **6 gratuitously, gratis, free, free of charge,** for nothing, for the asking, at no charge, without charge, on the house

635 THRIFT

NOUNS **1 thrift, economy, thriftiness,** sparingness, unwastefulness, **frugality,** frugalness; tight purse strings; parsimony, **parsimoniousness** 484.1; false economy; carefulness, care, chariness, canniness; **prudence,** providence; **husbandry,** good management *or* stewardship, custodianship, prudent administration; **austerity,** austerity program, belt-tightening; economic planning

2 economizing, economization; **cost-effectiveness; saving,** scrimping, skimping <nonformal>, scraping, sparing; **retrenchment, curtailment,** cutback, rollback, slowdown, cooling off *or* down, low growth rate

3 economizer, saver, string-saver

VERBS **4 economize, save,** make economies; **scrimp, skimp** <nonformal>, **scrape; manage,** husband one's resources; live frugally, get along on a shoestring, get by on little; keep *or* stay within one's means *or* budget, live within one's income, make ends meet, stay ahead of the game; put something aside, **save up,** save for a rainy day, have a nest egg

5 retrench, cut down, cut *or* pare down expenses, **curtail expenses; cut corners, tighten one's belt,** cut back, roll back, slow down

ADJS **6 economical, thrifty, frugal,** unwasteful, conserving, **saving,** economizing, spare, **sparing; prudent,** prudential, provident; careful, chary, canny; scrimping, skimping <nonformal>; pennywise; **parsimonious** 484.7; **cost-effective, cost-efficient; efficient**

ADVS **7 economically, thriftily, frugally; cost-effectively, cost-efficiently;** prudently, providently; carefully, charily, cannily; sparingly

636 ETHICS

NOUNS **1 ethics, principles,** standards, norms, principles of behavior; **morals,** moral principles; code, ethical *or* moral code, **ethic,** ethical system, value system; **norm,** behavioral norm; moral climate, **ethos;** Ten Commandments, decalogue

2 ethical *or* moral philosophy, ethonomics

3 morality, morals, morale; virtue 653; ethicality

4 amorality, unmorality; amoralism

5 conscience, grace, **sense of right and wrong;** ethical self, superego; **voice of conscience,** still small voice within, guardian *or* good angel; clear *or* clean conscience; social conscience; twinge of conscience 113.2

ADJS **6 ethical, moral,** moralistic; ethological

637 RIGHT

NOUNS **1 right,** rightfulness, rightness; what is right *or* proper, what should be, what ought to be, the right *or* proper thing to do, what is done

2 propriety, decorum, decency, good behavior *or* conduct, correctness, properness, decorousness, goodness, seemliness; fitness, appropriateness, suitability 994.1; normality; proprieties, decencies; **righteousness** 653.1

ADJS **3 right,** rightful; fit, suitable 994.5; **proper, correct, decorous,** good, decent, seemly, **due, appropriate,** fitting, condign, **right and proper,** as it should be, as it ought to be; in the right; normative, normal, rightminded, right-thinking, **righteous**

ADVS **4 rightly, rightfully,** right; **by rights,** by right, **as is right** *or* **only right; properly,** correctly, as is proper *or* fitting, **duly, appropriately,** fittingly, condignly, **in justice,** in equity; in all conscience

638 WRONG

NOUNS **1 wrong,** wrongfulness, wrongness; **impropriety, indecorum;** incorrectness, improperness, indecorousness, unseemliness; unfitness, inappropriateness, unsuitability 995.1; infraction, violation, delinquency, criminality, illegality, unlawfulness; abnormality, deviance, aberrance; sinfulness, wickedness, unrighteousness; **dysfunction,** malfunction; maladjustment; malfeasance, malpractice

2 abomination, horror; scandal, disgrace, shame, pity, atrocity, profanation, desecration, violation, sacrilege, infamy, ignominy

ADJS **3 wrong, wrongful; improper, incorrect, indecorous,** undue, unseemly; unfitting, inappropriate, unsuitable 995.5; delinquent, criminal, illegal, unlawful; fraudulent; abnormal, deviant, aberrant; **dysfunctional; evil, sinful, wicked, unrighteous;** not the thing, not done; **off-base** and **out-of-line** and **off-color** <all nonformal>; abominable, terrible, scandalous, disgraceful, shameful, shameless, atrocious, sacrilegious, infamous, ignominious

ADVS **4 wrongly, wrongfully,** wrong; **improperly,** incorrectly, indecorously

639 DUENESS

NOUNS **1 dueness, entitlement,** deservedness, just or justifiable expectation, expectations, outlook, prospect, prospects; **justice** 649

2 due, one's due, what one is entitled to, what one has earned, what is coming to one, acknowledgment, cognizance, recognition, credit, crediting; **right**

3 desserts, just desserts, due reward or punishment, **comeuppance** <nonformal>, all that is coming to one; retaliation 506, vengeance 507.1

VERBS **4 be due,** be one's due, be

entitled to, have a rightful claim to or upon, **have coming,** come by honestly

5 deserve, merit, earn, **be worthy of,** be deserving, richly deserve

6 get one's desserts, get one's comeuppance and get his or hers <all nonformal>, get what is coming to one; serve one right; reap the fruits or benefit of, come into one's own

ADJS **7 due, owed, owing,** payable, redeemable, coming, **coming to**

8 rightful, condign, appropriate, proper; fit, becoming 994.5; **fair, just** 649.8

9 warranted, justified, entitled, worthy; **deserved, merited,** richly deserved, well-earned

10 due, entitled to; deserving, meriting, meritorious, worthy of; attributable, ascribable

ADVS **11 duly,** rightfully, condignly, as is one's due

640 UNDUENESS

NOUNS **1 undueness, undeservedness,** unentitlement, unmeritedness; disentitlement; invalid claim or title, empty claim or title; **inappropriateness** 995.1; **impropriety** 638.1; **excess** 992

2 presumption, assumption, **imposition; license, undue liberty,** liberties, familiarity, presumptuousness, hubris; lawlessness 418; injustice 650

3 usurpation, arrogation, unlawful seizure, **appropriation,** assumption, adoption, infringement, encroachment, trespass, trespassing

4 usurper, arrogator, pretender

VERBS **5 not be entitled to,** have no right or title to, have no claim upon, not have a leg to stand on

6 presume, assume, venture, hazard, dare, pretend, attempt, **make bold** or so bold, make free, **take the liberty,** take upon oneself, go so far as to

7 presume on or **upon, impose on** or **upon,** encroach upon, obtrude upon; **take liberties,** overstep one's rights or bounds or prerogatives, make free with, abuse one's rights, abuse a privilege; **inconvenience**, bother, trouble, cause to go out of one's way

8 <take to oneself unduly> **usurp, arrogate**, seize, grab *and* latch on to <both nonformal>, **appropriate**, assume, adopt, take over, arrogate *or* accroach to oneself, pretend to, infringe, encroach, invade, trespass; play God

ADJS 9 **undue, unowed, unowing**, not outstanding; **undeserved, unmerited**, unearned; **unwarranted, unjustified**, unprovoked; unentitled, undeserving, unworthy; preposterous, outrageous

10 **inappropriate** 995.5; **excessive** 992.16

11 **presumptuous, presuming**; hubristic 493.7

641 DUTY

<moral obligation>

NOUNS 1 **duty, obligation, onus, burden**, mission, imperative, bounden duty, proper *or* assigned task, what ought to be done, where the buck stops <nonformal>, deference, respect 155, allegiance, loyalty, homage; devotion, dedication, **commitment**; self-commitment, self-imposed duty; **business** 724, function, province, place 724.3; ethics 636; line of duty; call of duty

2 **responsibility**, incumbency; **liability, accountability**, accountableness, answerability, amenability; **responsibleness, dutifulness**, duteousness, devotion *or* dedication to duty, sense of duty *or* obligation

VERBS 3 **should, ought to**, had best, had better

4 **behoove, become**, befit, be bound, be obliged *or* obligated, be under an obligation; **owe it to**

5 **be the duty of, be incumbent on** *or* **upon**, be his *or* hers to, duty calls one to

6 **be responsible for, answer for, be liable for**, be answerable *or* accountable for; be on the hook

for *and* take the heat *or* rap for <all nonformal>

7 **be one's responsibility**, be one's mission, **rest with**, lie upon, devolve on, rest on the shoulders of, fall to one *or* to one's lot

8 **incur a responsibility**, become bound to

9 **take** *or* **accept the responsibility, take upon oneself**, take upon one's shoulders, commit oneself; **answer for**; sponsor, be sponsor for; do at one's risk *or* peril; **take the blame**, be in the hot seat *or* on the spot *and* take the heat *or* rap for <all nonformal>

10 **do one's duty**, perform *or* fulfill *or* discharge one's duty, do what one has to do, pay one's dues <nonformal>, **do what is expected**, do the right thing, do justice to, **do** *or* **act one's part**, play one's proper role; do one's bit *or* part

11 **meet an obligation**, satisfy one's obligations; **acquit oneself, make good**, redeem one's pledge

12 **obligate, oblige, require**, make incumbent *or* imperative, tie, **bind**, pledge, commit, saddle with, put under an obligation; call to account, hold responsible *or* accountable *or* answerable

ADJS 13 **dutiful, duteous**; moral, ethical; conscientious, scrupulous, observant; obedient 326.3; deferential, respectful 155.8

14 **incumbent on** *or* **upon**, chargeable to, behooving

15 **obligatory, binding, imperative**, mandatory; **necessary**, required 962.13

16 **obliged, obligated, under obligation; bound, duty-bound**, in duty bound, pledged, committed, saddled, beholden, bounden; **obliged to**, beholden to, **indebted to**

17 **responsible, answerable; liable, accountable**, amenable, chargeable, on one's head, at one's doorstep, on the hook <nonformal>; responsible for

ADVS **18 dutifully, duteously, in
the line of duty,** as in duty
bound; beyond the call of duty

642 PREROGATIVE

NOUNS **1 prerogative, right, due**;
authority; faculty; **claim,** proper
claim, demand, **interest, title,**
pretension; birthright; natural
right, presumptive right, inalienable right; divine right; property
right; conjugal right

**2 privilege, license, liberty, free-
dom, immunity;** franchise,
patent, copyright, grant, warrant,
blank check, carte blanche; favor,
indulgence, **special favor,** dispensation

3 human rights, rights of man;
constitutional rights, rights of citizenship, **civil rights** 430.2, civil
liberties; rights of minorities, minority rights; gay rights, gay
liberation

4 women's rights, rights of
women; **feminism, women's liberation,** women's lib <nonfor-
mal>, women's movement, sisterhood

**5 women's rightist, feminist,
women's liberationist,** women's
liberation advocate or activist,
women's libber and libber <both
nonformal>

VERBS **6** have or claim or assert a
right, exercise a right; defend a
right

643 IMPOSITION

<a putting or inflicting upon>

NOUNS **1 imposition, infliction,**
charging, taxing, tasking; burdening, weighting down, freighting,
loading down, heaping on or
upon; **exaction, demand** 421;
unwarranted demand, obtrusiveness, presumptuousness 142.1;
inconvenience, trouble, bother;
inconsiderateness 144.3

2 administration, bestowal; application, meting out, prescribing;
forcing, forcing on or upon

3 charge, duty, tax, task; **burden,**
weight, freight, cargo, load, onus

VERBS **4 impose, impose on or**

upon, **inflict on or upon, put on
or upon,** enjoin; **put, place, set,
lay,** put down; **levy, exact, demand** 421.4; **tax,** task, **charge,**
burden with, weight down with,
yoke with, **fasten upon,** saddle
with; subject to

5 inflict, wreak, do to, bring,
bring upon, bring down upon,
bring on or down on one's head,
visit upon

6 administer, give, bestow; ap-
ply, put on or upon, lay on or
upon, dose with, mete out, prescribe; **force, force upon,**
impose by force, strongarm
<nonformal>, force down one's
throat

**7 impose on or upon, take ad-
vantage of** 387.16; **presume
upon** 640.7; **deceive,** play or
work on, put over or across
<nonformal>; palm or pass or
fob off on, foist on; shift the
blame, **pass the buck** <nonfor-
mal>

ADJS **8 imposed, inflicted,** heaped
on; burdened with, stuck with
<nonformal>; exacted

644 PROBITY

NOUNS **1 probity, honesty, integrity, rectitude, uprightness,** up-
standingness, **virtue, righteousness, goodness; decency;
honor,** worthiness, reputability;
unimpeachability, irreproach-
ableness, blamelessness; stainlessness, pureness, purity; re-
spectability; high principles, high
ideals, high-mindedness; **character,** good or sterling character,
moral strength; **fairness,** justice
649

**2 conscientiousness, scrupu-
lousness,** scrupulosity, **scruples,**
punctiliousness, meticulousness;
scruple, point of honor, punctilio;
qualm 325.2; twinge of conscience 113.2; overconscientious-
ness, overscrupulousness; fastidiousness 495

3 honesty, veracity, veraciousness, **truthfulness,** truth, truth-
speaking; truth-loving; credibility

4 candor, candidness, frankness, plain dealing; sincerity, genuineness; ingenuousness; artlessness 416; **openness,** openheartedness; **unreserve,** unrestraint; **forthrightness, directness, straightforwardness; outspokenness,** plainspokenness, plain speaking; **bluntness,** bluffness, brusqueness

5 undeceptiveness, undeceitfulness, guilelessness

6 trustworthiness, reliability, dependability, dependableness; responsibility 641.2; incorruptibility, inviolability

7 fidelity, faithfulness, loyalty, faith; **constancy, steadfastness,** staunchness, firmness; good faith; **allegiance, fealty, homage;** bond, tie; attachment, adherence, adhesion; devotion, devotedness

8 person or **man** or **woman of honor,** man of his word, woman of her word; gentleman; **honest man,** good man; **lady, real lady; honest woman, good woman;** salt of the earth; square or straight shooter and straight arrow <all nonformal>; true blue; trusty, faithful

VERBS **9 keep faith, keep one's word** or **promise,** show good faith, be as good as one's word, one's word is one's bond, play by the rules, acquit oneself, make good; practice what one preaches

10 shoot straight <nonformal>, **put one's cards on the table,** level with one <nonformal>

11 speak or **tell the truth,** paint in its true colors; tell the truth, the whole truth, and nothing but the truth

12 be frank, speak plainly, speak out, speak one's mind, **call a spade a spade,** tell it like it is

ADJS **13 honest, upright, upstanding,** erect, **righteous, virtuous, good,** clean, squeaky-clean <nonformal>, **decent; honorable, reputable,** estimable, creditable, worthy, noble, sterling; unimpeachable, irreproachable, blameless, immaculate, spotless, stainless, unstained, unspotted, unblemished, untarnished, unsullied, undefiled, pure; **respectable; ethical, moral; principled, high-principled,** high-minded, right-minded; uncorrupt, uncorrupted, inviolate; **law-abiding; fair, just** 649.8

14 straight, square, foursquare, straight-arrow <nonformal>, honest and aboveboard; **fair and square; square-dealing,** straight-shooting, up-and-up, **on the up-and-up** and **on the level** and on the square <all nonformal>; **aboveboard, open and aboveboard;** bona fide, goodfaith; authentic, all wool and a yard wide, veritable, genuine; honest as the day is long

15 conscientious; scrupulous, careful 339.10; punctilious, meticulous, strict, nice; fastidious 495.9; overconscientious, overscrupulous

16 honest, veracious, truthful, true, true to one's word; truthtelling, truth-speaking

17 candid, frank, sincere, open, genuine, ingenuous; **open-**hearted, transparent, open-faced; artless 416.5; **straightforward, direct,** up-front and straight <both nonformal>, **forthright,** downright, straight-out <nonformal>; **unreserved,** unrestrained, unconstrained, unchecked; unguarded, uncalculating; free; **outspoken, plain-spoken,** freespeaking; explicit, unequivocal; **blunt,** bluff, brusque; heart-to-heart

18 undeceptive, undeceitful, undissembling, uncalculating; **guileless;** unassuming, unflattering; unaffected, unfeigned, undisguised, unvarnished, untrimmed

19 trustworthy, trusty, reliable, dependable, responsible, straight <nonformal>, to be trusted, **to be depended** or **relied upon,** to be reckoned on, as good as one's word; tried, true,

tried and true, tested, proven;
incorruptible, inviolable
20 **faithful, loyal,** devoted; **true,
true-blue,** true to one's colors;
constant, steadfast, unswerving,
steady, consistent, stable, unfailing, staunch, firm, solid
ADVS 21 **honestly, uprightly, honorably,** upstandingly, erectly, **vir-
tuously, righteously, decently,**
reputably; unimpeachably, irre-
proachably, blamelessly, immaculately, purely; high-mindedly,
morally; **conscientiously, scrupulously,** punctiliously, meticulously, fastidiously 495.14
22 **truthfully, truly,** veraciously; to
tell the truth, to speak truthfully;
in truth, with truth
23 **candidly, frankly, sincerely,**
genuinely, in all seriousness, from
the heart, in all conscience; in
plain words *or* English, straight
from the shoulder, not to mince
words, without equivocation, all
joking aside *or* apart; **openly,**
openheartedly, **unreservedly,**
unrestrainedly, **forthrightly,
directly, straightforwardly,**
outspokenly, **plainly,** plain-
spokenly, **bluntly,** bluffly,
brusquely
24 **trustworthily, reliably, dependably, responsibly;** unde-
ceitfully, guilelessly; incorrupt-
ibly
25 **faithfully, loyally,** devotedly;
constantly, steadfastly, steadily,
responsibly, consistently, unfailingly, unswervingly, staunchly,
firmly; in *or* with good faith, *bona
fide* <L>

645 IMPROBITY

NOUNS 1 **improbity, dishonesty,**
dishonor; **unscrupulousness;
corruption,** corruptness; **crookedness,** criminality, feloniousness, **fraudulence,** underhandedness, unsavoriness, fishiness
and shadiness <both nonfor-
mal>, shiftiness, slipperiness, deviousness, evasiveness, trickiness
2 **knavery, roguery, rascality,
villainy;** chicanery 356.4;

knavishness, roguishness, villainousness; **baseness, vileness,**
degradation, moral turpitude
3 **deceitfulness; falseness** 354;
perjury, untruthfulness 354.8,
credibility gap; **insincerity,**
uncandidness, unfrankness,
disingenuousness; sharp practice
356.4; fraud 356.8; artfulness,
craftiness 415.1; intrigue
4 **untrustworthiness, unreliability, undependability,**
irresponsibility
5 **infidelity, unfaithfulness,**
faithlessness; **inconstancy,
unsteadfastness,** fickleness;
disloyalty; falsity, falseness; disaffection, dereliction; bad faith;
breach of promise, breach of
trust *or* faith, barratry
6 **treachery,** treacherousness;
perfidy, perfidiousness, two-
facedness; **duplicity, double-
dealing,** foul play, dirty work *and*
dirty pool *and* dirty trick <all
nonformal>
7 **treason,** misprision of treason,
high treason; lese majesty, sedition; collaboration, fraternization
8 **betrayal,** letting down <nonfor-
mal>, **double cross** *and* sellout
<both nonformal>, kiss of death,
stab in the back
9 **corruptibility, venality,** brib-
ability, purchasability
10 criminal 660.10, perpetrator,
perp <nonformal>, scoundrel
660.3, traitor 357.10, deceiver
357
VERBS 11 <be dishonest> live by
one's wits; deceive; cheat; falsify;
lie; sail under false colors
12 **be unfaithful,** not keep faith *or*
troth, **go back on** <nonformal>,
fail, break one's word *or* promise,
renege, go back on one's word
<nonformal>, break faith, per-
jure oneself; forsake, desert
370.5; pass the buck <nonfor-
mal>
13 **play one false; stab one in the
back,** knife one <nonformal>;
bite the hand that feeds one; play
dirty pool <nonformal>; move

the goalposts *and* change the
rules <both nonformal>

14 betray, double-cross *and* two-
time <both nonformal>, **sell out**
and sell down the river <both
nonformal>, turn in; **mislead,**
lead one down the garden path;
inform on 551.12

15 act the traitor, go over to the
enemy, sell out <nonformal>;
collaborate, fraternize

ADJS **16 dishonest, dishonorable;
unconscientious,** conscienceless, unconscionable, shameless,
without shame *or* remorse, **unscrupulous, unprincipled,**
unethical, immoral, amoral; **corrupt,** rotten; **crooked, criminal,**
felonious, **fraudulent,** underhanded; shady <nonformal>, up
to no good, unsavory, dark, sinister, insidious, indirect, slippery,
devious, tricky, shifty, evasive;
fishy <nonformal>, questionable,
suspicious, doubtful, dubious

**17 knavish, roguish, scampish,
rascally, scoundrelly,** villainous,
base, vile; **infamous, notorious**

18 deceitful; falsehearted; **insincere,** uncandid, unfrank, disingenuous; artful, crafty 415.12;
calculating, scheming; **tricky**

**19 untrustworthy, unreliable, un-
dependable,** fly-by-night, irresponsible, not to be trusted, not
to be depended *or* relied upon

20 unfaithful, faithless; **inconstant, unsteadfast,** fickle; **disloyal,** unloyal; false, **untrue,** not
true to; disaffected, recreant, derelict

21 treacherous, perfidious,
falsehearted; **shifty,** slippery,
tricky; **double-dealing; two-
faced**

22 traitorous, turncoat, double-
crossing *and* two-timing <both
nonformal>, betraying; **treasonable,** treasonous; Trojan-horse

23 corruptible, venal, bribable,
purchasable, on the pad <nonfor-
mal>, mercenary, hireling

ADVS **24 dishonestly, dishonorably; unscrupulously,** unconscientiously; **crookedly,** crimi-

nally, feloniously, **fraudulently,**
underhandedly, insidiously, deviously, shiftily, evasively, fishily
<nonformal>, suspiciously, dubi-
ously, by fair means or foul; **deceitfully;** roguishly, villainously;
basely, vilely; infamously, notoriously

25 perfidiously, falseheartedly; **un-
faithfully,** faithlessly; **treacherously;** traitorously

646 HONOR
<token of esteem>

NOUNS **1 honor,** distinction, glory,
credit

2 award, reward, prize; blue ribbon; consolation prize; booby
prize; sweepstakes; jackpot

3 trophy, laurels, palm, crown,
wreath, garland, **feather in one's
cap** <nonformal>; **cup,** loving
cup; **belt,** championship belt,
black belt, brown belt, etc; banner, flag

4 citation, eulogy, mention, honorable mention, kudos, **accolade,
tribute, praise** 511.1

5 decoration, order, ornament;
ribbon; blue ribbon, *cordon bleu*
<Fr>; cordon; garter; star, gold
star

6 medal, military honor, order,
medallion; military medal, service medal, war medal, soldier's
medal

7 scholarship, fellowship

VERBS **8 honor, do honor,** give *or*
pay *or* render honor to, **recognize; cite; decorate,** pin a medal
on; crown; hand it to *or* take off
one's hat to one <nonformal>,
pay tribute, praise 511.5; give
credit where credit is due; roll out
the red carpet

ADJS **9 honored, distinguished;**
laureate

10 honorary, honorific, honorable

ADVS **11 with honor,** with distinction; *cum laude, magna cum
laude, summa cum laude*

647 INSIGNIA

NOUNS **1 insignia, regalia,** ensign,
emblem, badge, symbol; badge

of office, mark of office; wand, **mace, staff, baton;** livery, uniform, mantle, dress; cockade; brassard; figurehead; eagle; cross 170.4, skull and crossbones, fleur-de-lis; medal, **decoration** 646.5; **heraldry,** armory, blazonry

2 <heraldry terms> heraldic device, achievement, bearings, coat of arms, arms, armorial bearings, armory

3 <royal insignia> regalia; scepter, rod, rod of empire; orb; crown, royal crown, coronet, tiara, diadem; seal, signet, great seal, privy seal

4 <ecclesiastical insignia> tiara, triple crown; miter, crosier, crook, pastoral staff

5 <military insignia> chevron, stripe; star, bar, eagle, chicken <nonformal>, oak leaf; shoulder patch, patch; aviation badge *or* wings; parachute badge, submarine badge; service stripe, hash mark <nonformal>; epaulet

6 **flag, banner, standard,** guidon; **pennant,** pennon, burgee, **streamer; bunting; national flag, colors; ensign**

648 TITLE
<appellation of dignity or distinction>

NOUNS 1 **title, honorific, honor,** title of honor; **handle** <nonformal>; courtesy title

2 <honorifics> Excellency, Eminence, Reverence, Grace, Honor, Worship, Your *or* His *or* Her Excellency; Lord, My Lord

3 Sir, sire, sirrah; Esquire; Master, Mister 76.7; mirza, effendi, sirdar, emir, khan, sahib

4 Mistress, madame 77.8

5 <ecclesiastical titles> Reverend, His Reverence, His Grace; Monsignor; Holiness, His Holiness; Dom, Brother, Sister, Father, Mother; Rabbi

6 **degree, academic degree; bachelor,** baccalaureate, bachelor's degree; **master,** master's degree; **doctor,** doctorate, doctor's degree

ADJS 7 **titular,** titulary; honorific; honorary

8 the Noble, the Most Noble, the Most Excellent

649 JUSTICE

NOUNS 1 **justice, justness; equity,** equitableness, level playing field <nonformal>; **evenhandedness,** measure for measure, give-and-take; balance, equality 789; **right, rightness,** meetness, properness, propriety, what is right; justification, **justifiableness,** justifiability, defensibility; poetic justice; retributive justice, nemesis; summary justice, drumhead justice, rude justice; scales of justice; lawfulness, legality 673

2 rightfulness, warrantedness

3 **fairness,** fair-mindedness, candor; the fair thing, the right *or* proper thing; level playing field, **square deal** *and* **fair shake** <both nonformal>; **fair play,** cricket <nonformal>; sportsmanship

4 **impartiality,** detachment, **dispassion,** loftiness, Olympian detachment, **dispassionateness, disinterestedness,** disinterest; **neutrality** 467; selflessness, unselfishness 652

5 <personifications> Justice, Justitia, blind *or* blindfolded Justice

VERBS 6 **be just, be fair,** do the fair thing, do the handsome thing <nonformal>, do right, do it fair and square, do the right thing by; **do justice to,** see justice done, redress a wrong *or* an injustice, remedy an injustice, shoot straight with *and* **give a square deal** *or* **fair shake** <all nonformal>; give the Devil his due; give and take; bend *or* lean over backwards, go the extra mile <nonformal>

7 **play fair, play the game** <nonformal>, be a good sport; judge on its own merits

ADJS 8 **just, fair,** square, **fair and square, even,** evenhanded; **right, rightful;** justifiable, justified, warranted, defensible; **due** 639.7,10, deserved, merited; meet, right and proper, fit, **proper, good,** as it should *or* ought to be; lawful, legal 673.10

9 fair-minded; **sporting,** sportsmanlike; square-dealing *and* square-shooting <both nonformal>

10 **impartial, impersonal, evenhanded,** equitable, **dispassionate, disinterested,** detached, objective, lofty; **unbiased,** uninfluenced, unswayed; **neutral** 467.7; selfless, unselfish 652.5

ADVS 11 **justly, fairly,** fair, in a fair manner; rightly, duly, deservedly, meetly, properly; **equitably, equally, evenly**; justifiedly, justifiably; **impartially, impersonally, dispassionately, disinterestedly,** without fear or favor

12 **in justice,** in equity, in reason, in all conscience, in all fairness, **to be fair,** as is only fair *or* right

650 INJUSTICE

NOUNS 1 **injustice, unjustness; inequity,** inequitableness; inequality 790, inequality of treatment; **wrong, wrongness,** improperness, **impropriety;** what should not be, what ought not *or* must not be; unlawfulness, illegality 674

2 **unfairness; unsportsmanlikeness;** foul, a hit below the belt, dirty pool <nonformal>

3 **partiality, onesidedness; bias,** leaning, inclination, tendentiousness; undetachment, interest, involvement, **partisanism,** partisanship; unneutrality; **slant,** angle, spin <nonformal>; **favoritism,** preference, nepotism; unequal *or* preferential treatment, discrimination, inequality

4 **injustice, wrong, injury,** grievance, disservice; raw *or* rotten deal *and* bad rap <all nonformal>; mockery *or* miscarriage of justice; great wrong, grave *or* gross injustice; atrocity, outrage

5 **unjustifiability,** indefensibility; **inexcusability,** unconscionableness, **unpardonability,** unforgivableness

VERBS 6 not play fair, hit below the belt, give a raw deal *or* rotten deal *or* bad rap <nonformal>

7 **do one an injustice, wrong,** do wrong by, **do one a wrong,** do a disservice; do a great wrong, do a grave *or* gross injustice, commit an atrocity *or* outrage

8 **favor,** prefer, show preference, **play favorites,** treat unequally, discriminate; **slant,** angle

ADJS 9 **unjust, inequitable, unbalanced, discriminatory, uneven, unequal** 790.4; **wrong, wrongful; undue** 640.9, unmeet, undeserved, unmerited; unlawful, illegal 674.6

10 **unfair,** not fair; **unsporting, unsportsmanlike,** not done; **dirty** <nonformal>, foul, below the belt

11 **partial, interested,** involved, **partisan, one-sided,** undetached, interested, unobjective, **undispassionate, biased,** tendentious, warped, slanted

12 **unjustifiable, unwarrantable,** unallowable, unreasonable, indefensible; **inexcusable,** unconscionable, **unpardonable, unforgivable,** inexpiable, irremissible

ADVS 13 **unjustly, unfairly;** wrongfully, wrongly, undeservedly; inequitably, unevenly; partially, one-sidedly, undispassionately; **unjustifiably, unwarrantably,** unallowably, unreasonably, indefensibly; inexcusably, unconscionably, unpardonably, unforgivably, inexpiably, irremissibly

651 SELFISHNESS

NOUNS 1 **selfishness, self-seeking,** self-serving, **self-indulgence,** hedonism; self-advancement, self-promotion; **careerism; narcissism, self-love, self-consideration,** self-solicitude, self-sufficiency, self-absorption, ego trip, self-occupation; self-containment, self-isolation; remoteness 583.2; **self-interest;** self-esteem, self-admiration 140.1; **self-**

centeredness, **self-obsession, narcissism, egotism** 140.3; **avarice, greed,** graspingness, grabbiness <nonformal>, acquisitiveness, possessiveness; **individualism** 430.5, private *or* personal desires, private *or* personal aims

2 **ungenerousness, unmagnanimousness, illiberality,** meanness, smallness, paltriness, pettiness; **niggardliness, stinginess** 484.3

3 **self-seeker,** self-pleaser; member of the me generation; **narcissist, egotist** 140.5; fortune hunter, name-dropper; self-server, careerist; monopolist, hog, road hog; dog in the manger; **individualist,** loner *and* lone wolf <both nonformal>

VERBS 4 **please oneself,** gratify oneself; be *or* go on an ego trip <both nonformal>, be full of oneself; indulge *or* pamper *or* coddle oneself, look after one's own interests, know which side one's bread is buttered on, take care of *or* look out for number one *or* numero uno <nonformal>

ADJS 5 **selfish, self-seeking, self-serving,** self-advancing, self-promoting, **self-indulgent,** hedonistic, self-sufficient; **self-interested,** self-occupied, self-absorbed, wrapped up in oneself, self-contained, remote 583.6; self-admiring 140.8; **self-centered, self-obsessed, narcissistic, egotistical** 140.10; **avaricious, greedy,** grasping, grabby <nonformal>, acquisitive; **individualistic**

6 **ungenerous, illiberal,** unchivalrous, mean, small, little, paltry, mingy, petty; **niggardly, stingy** 484.9

ADVS 7 **selfishly, for oneself,** in one's own interest, from selfish *or* interested motives

652 UNSELFISHNESS

NOUNS 1 **unselfishness, selflessness;** self-subordination, self-abasement, self-effacement; **humility** 137; modesty 139; self-

neglect; **self-renunciation; self-denial,** self-abnegation; **self-sacrifice,** sacrifice, self-devotion, devotion, dedication, commitment, consecration; disinterestedness; unacquisitiveness; **altruism** 143.4

2 **magnanimity, generosity,** openhandedness, **liberality,** liberalness; **bigness, bigheartedness,** big heart, greatness of heart; noble-mindedness, **high-mindedness, idealism; benevolence** 143.4; **nobleness,** nobility, greatness, **loftiness,** elevation, exaltation, sublimity; chivalry, chivalrousness; heroism

VERBS 3 not have a selfish bone in one's body, think only of others; be generous to a fault; put oneself out, go out of the way, lean over backwards; sacrifice, make a sacrifice; subject oneself, subordinate oneself, abase oneself

4 observe the golden rule, do unto others as you would have others do unto you

ADJS 5 **unselfish, selfless;** self-abasing, self-effacing; **altruistic** 143.15, **humble; unpretentious, modest** 139.9; **self-denying,** self-abnegating; **self-sacrificing,** sacrificing, devoted, dedicated, committed, consecrated, unsparing of self, disinterested; unacquisitive

6 **magnanimous,** great-spirited; **generous,** generous to a fault, openhanded, **liberal; big, bighearted,** great of heart; noble-minded, **high-minded, idealistic; benevolent** 143.15, **noble,** princely, handsome, great, high, elevated, **lofty,** exalted, sublime; chivalrous; heroic

ADVS 7 **unselfishly, altruistically,** forgetful of self

8 **magnanimously, generously,** openhandedly, **liberally; bigheartedly; nobly,** handsomely, chivalrously

653 VIRTUE
<moral goodness>

NOUNS 1 **virtue, virtuousness, goodness, righteousness,** rectitude, the straight and narrow, the right thing; probity 644; **morality,** moral fiber *or* rectitude *or* virtue, morale; **saintliness; godliness** 692.2

2 right conduct or behavior, the straight and narrow way

3 purity, immaculateness, spotlessness; **uncorruptness; unsinfulness, sinlessness; chastity** 664; guiltlessness, innocence 657

4 cardinal virtues, natural virtues; prudence, justice, temperance, fortitude; theological virtues *or* supernatural virtues; faith, hope, charity *or* love

VERBS **5 be good,** do no evil, do the right thing; walk the straight path, follow the straight and narrow; fight the good fight

ADJS **6 virtuous, good, moral; upright, honest** 644.13,14,16; **righteous,** just, straight, right-minded, right-thinking; **angelic,** seraphic; **saintly,** saintlike; **godly** 692.9

7 chaste, immaculate, spotless, pure 664.4; **clean,** squeaky-clean <nonformal>; guiltless, **innocent** 657.6

8 uncorrupt, uncorrupted; **unsinful,** sinless; **unwicked,** unerring; undegenerate, undepraved, undemoralized

654 VICE
   <moral badness>

NOUNS **1 vice,** viciousness; criminality, **wrongdoing** 655; **immorality, evil; amorality** 636.4; **unvirtuousness; unrighteousness, ungodliness,** unsaintliness; **uncleanness, impurity, unchastity** 665, fallen state; waywardness, wantonness, prodigality; delinquency; backsliding, recidivism; **evil nature, carnality** 663.2

2 vice, weakness, weakness of the flesh, **flaw,** moral flaw *or* blemish, **frailty, infirmity; failing,** failure; weak point, foible; bad habit; **fault, imperfection** 1002

3 iniquity, evil, bad, wrong,

villainy, knavery, reprobacy, **abomination, atrocity, infamy,** shame, disgrace, scandal, unforgivable *or* cardinal *or* mortal sin, **sin** 655.2

4 wickedness, badness, naughtiness, **evilness, viciousness, sinfulness, iniquitousness; baseness,** rankness, **vileness,** nefariousness, **heinousness,** villainousness, flagitiousness; fiendishness, hellishness; deviltry

5 turpitude, moral turpitude; corruption, corruptness, rottenness, moral pollution, lack *or* absence of moral fiber; **decadence** *or* decadency, debasement, **degradation,** demoralization; **degeneracy,** degenerateness, degeneration, reprobacy, **depravity,** depravedness; **dissoluteness, profligacy;** abandonment, abandon

6 obduracy, hardheartedness, hardness, callousness, heartlessness, hardness of heart, heart of stone

7 sewer, gutter, pit, sink; den of iniquity, fleshpots; the pits <nonformal>; Sodom, Gomorrah, Babylon; **brothel** 665.9

VERBS **8 do wrong, sin** 655.5; misbehave

9 go wrong, stray, go astray, **err,** deviate, leave the straight and narrow, step out of line; **fall, lapse,** slip, trip; **degenerate; go to the bad** 395.24; **relapse,** recidivate, backslide 394.4

10 corrupt; sully, soil, defile; demoralize, vitiate

ADJS **11 vice-prone,** vicious, **steeped in vice; immoral,** unmoral; **amoral,** nonmoral; unethical

12 unvirtuous, virtueless; **unrighteous, ungodly,** unsaintly; **unclean, impure,** spotted, flawed, blemished, **unchaste** 665.23; fleshly, carnal 663.6, wayward, wanton, prodigal; erring, **fallen, lapsed;** frail, weak; peccable; **relapsing, backsliding,** recidivistic; of easy virtue 665.26

13 diabolic, diabolical, devilish,

demonic, **satanic; fiendish; hellish, infernal**

14 corrupt, corrupted, morally polluted, rotten, tainted, contaminated, vitiated; warped, perverted; **decadent,** debased, degraded, reprobate, **depraved, debauched, dissolute, degenerate,** profligate, abandoned, gone to the dogs, steeped in iniquity, rotten to the core

15 evil-minded, evilhearted, **blackhearted; base-minded,** lowminded; dirty <nonformal>

16 wicked, evil, vicious, bad, naughty, wrong, sinful, iniquitous, peccant, reprobate; **base, low, vile,** foul, rank, arrant, nefarious, **heinous,** villainous, criminal, up to no good, flagitious; abominable, atrocious, monstrous, unspeakable, execrable, damnable; shameful, disgraceful, scandalous, **infamous, unpardonable,** unforgivable; **improper,** reprehensible, blameworthy, unworthy

17 hardened, hard, casehardened, obdurate, inured, indurated; **callous,** calloused, **seared; hardhearted,** heartless; **shameless,** conscienceless, unblushing, **brazen**

18 irreclaimable, irredeemable, unredeemable, unregenerate, **irreformable,** incorrigible; **lost**

ADVS **19 wickedly, evilly, sinfully, iniquitously,** peccantly, **viciously;** basely, vilely, foully, rankly, arrantly, flagrantly, flagitiously

655 WRONGDOING

NOUNS **1 wrongdoing, evildoing, wickedness, misbehavior** 322, **misconduct,** misfeasance, malfeasance, **malpractice; sin; crime, criminality,** feloniousness; viciousness, **vice** 654; misprision, misprision of treason *or* felony

2 misdeed, misdemeanor, misfeasance, malfeasance, malefaction, criminal *or* guilty *or* sinful act, **offense,** injustice, injury, **wrong, iniquity, evil,** peccancy; tort; **error, fault,** breach; **impropriety,** venial sin, **indiscretion,** peccadillo, misstep, trip, slip, lapse; **transgression,** trespass; **sin; cardinal** *or* **deadly** *or* **mortal sin,** unpardonable *or* unforgivable *or* inexpiable sin; sin of commission; sin of omission, nonfeasance, omission, failure, dereliction, delinquency; **crime, felony;** capital crime; whitecollar crime; computer crime; war crime, crime against humanity, genocide; **outrage, atrocity,** enormity

3 original sin, fall from grace, fall, fall of man, fall of Adam *or* Adam's fall, sin of Adam

VERBS **4 do wrong,** misdemean oneself, **misbehave** 322.4, **err,** offend; **sin,** commit sin; **transgress,** trespass

ADJS **5 wrongdoing, evildoing,** malfeasant; **wrong,** iniquitous, **sinful, wicked** 654.16; **criminal,** felonious; crime-ridden

656 GUILT

NOUNS **1 guilt, guiltiness; criminality,** peccancy; **culpability,** reprehensibility, blameworthiness; answerability, much to answer for; censurability, reproachability, reprovability, inculpation, implication, involvement, complicity, impeachability, indictability, arraignability; bloodguilt, redhandedness, dirty hands, bloody hands; much to answer for; **ruth,** ruefulness, remorse, guilty conscience; onus, burden

VERBS **2 be guilty,** look guilty, look like the cat that swallowed the canary, blush, stammer; have on one's hands, have much to answer for; be caught in the act *or* flatfooted *or* redhanded, be caught with one's pants down *or* with one's hand in the till *or* with one's hand in the cookie jar <nonformal>

ADJS **3 guilty,** peccant, **criminal, to blame, at fault,** on one's head; **culpable,** reprehensible, censurable, reproachable, reprovable, inculpated, implicated, involved, impeachable, indictable, arraignable; red-handed, bloodguilty; caught in the act *or* flatfooted *or* red-handed, caught with one's pants down *or* with one's hand in the till *or* with one's hand in the cookie jar <nonformal>

ADVS **4 red-handed, in the act,** in the very act, *in flagrante delicto* <L>

5 guilty, shamefacedly, sheepishly

657 INNOCENCE

NOUNS **1 innocence; guiltlessness,** faultlessness, blamelessness, **sinlessness; spotlessness,** unblemishedness; **purity,** immaculateness, immaculacy, impeccability; clean hands, clean slate, clear conscience, nothing to hide

2 childlikeness 416.1; lamblikeness; unacquaintance with evil, uncorruptedness, incorruptness, pristineness, undefiledness

3 inculpability, unblamability, **unblameworthiness,** irreproachability, impeccability, unexceptionableness, **irreprehensibility,** irreprehensibleness, uncensurableness, unimpeachability

4 innocent, baby, babe, babe in arms, newborn babe, infant, babe in the woods, child, lamb, angel

VERBS **5** have clean hands, have a clear conscience, look as if butter would not melt in one's mouth

ADJS **6 innocent;** unfallen, unlapsed, prelapsarian; **unguilty,** not guilty, **guiltless, faultless, blameless,** reproachless, **sinless,** with clean hands; in the clear; without reproach; innocent as a lamb, lamblike, angelic, childlike 416.5; untouched by evil, uncorrupted, pristine, undefiled

7 spotless, stainless, taintless, unblemished, unspotted, **untainted, unsoiled, unsullied, undefiled; pure, clean, immaculate,** impeccable, pure as driven snow, squeaky-clean <nonformal>

8 inculpable, unblameworthy, **irreproachable,** irreprovable, **irreprehensible,** unimpeachable, unobjectionable, unexceptionable, above suspicion

ADVS **9 innocently, guiltlessly, unguiltily; unknowingly,** unconsciously; unawares

658 ATONEMENT

NOUNS **1 atonement, reparation, amends,** making amends, **restitution, propitiation, expiation, redress, recompense,** setting right, making right *or* good, making up, squaring, redemption, reclamation, satisfaction; indemnification; compromise; expiatory offering, peace offering

2 apology, excuse, regrets; acknowledgment, penitence, contrition, confession 351.3; abject apology

3 penance, penitence, repentance; penitential act, **mortification,** flagellation; **asceticism** 667, **fasting** 515; **purgation,** purgatory; **sackcloth and ashes;** hair shirt

VERBS **4 atone, atone for, propitiate, expiate,** restitute, recompense, redress, redeem, repair, satisfy, **make amends, make reparation** *or* **compensation** *or* **expiation** *or* **restitution,** make good *or* right, set right, **make up for,** square things, pay one's dues <nonformal>; wipe the slate clean; set one's house in order; live down

5 apologize, beg pardon, ask forgiveness, beg indulgence, express regret; take back; get *or* fall down on one's knees

6 do penance, flagellate oneself, mortify oneself, mortify one's flesh, shrive oneself, purge oneself, cleanse oneself of guilt, wear a hair shirt, wear sackcloth *or* sackcloth and ashes; receive absolution

ADJS **7 atoning, propitiatory, expiatory,** restitutive, restitutional, redressing, recompensing, compensatory, righting, squaring; redemptive, redeeming; **apolo-**

getic, **apologetical;** repentant,
repenting; **penitential,** purgative, purgatorial; cleansing, purifying; ascetic

659 GOOD PERSON

NOUNS **1** good person, fine person,
worthy, prince, man *or* woman after one's own heart; **good fellow,**
capital fellow, **good sort,** right
sort; real person, real man *or*
woman, mensch <nonformal>;
gentleman, perfect gentleman, a
gentleman and a scholar; **lady,**
perfect lady, **gem,** jewel, pearl,
diamond; diamond in the rough;
honest man 644.8

2 <nonformal terms> **good guy,**
brick, good egg, stout fellow, nice
guy, Mr Nice Guy, good Joe, no
slouch, doll, living doll, pussycat,
sweetheart, sweetie

3 **good** *or* **respectable citizen,** exemplary citizen, good neighbor,
burgher, taxpayer, **pillar of society,** pillar of the church, salt of
the earth

4 **paragon, ideal,** beau ideal, nonpareil, person to look up to, **good
example, role model,** shining
example; exemplar, epitome;
model, pattern, standard,
norm, mirror; **standout,** a man
among men, a woman among
women

5 **hero, god, demigod,** phoenix;
heroine, goddess, demigoddess;
idol

6 holy man; guru; saint, angel 679

660 BAD PERSON

NOUNS **1** bad person, bad man *or*
woman *or* child, disreputable person, unworthy, disreputable, **undesirable,** *persona non grata*
<L>, bad news <nonformal>; bad
example

2 **wretch, beggar; bum** *and* bummer *and* lowlife <all nonformal>;
devil, **poor devil,** poor creature;
sad case, sad sack <nonformal>;
**good-for-nothing, good-for-
naught, no-good** <nonformal>,
ne'er-do-well, wastrel, worthless
fellow; **derelict,** Bowery bum,

tramp, hobo, beachcomber,
drifter, drunkard, vagrant, stiff
and bindlestiff <both nonfor-
mal>; human wreck

3 **rascal,** rogue, knave, **scoundrel,**
villain, blackguard, **scamp, scalawag** <nonformal>, rapscallion,
devil; shyster; sneak

4 mean *or* miserable wretch, beggarly fellow, skid-row bum

5 **reprobate,** recreant, **miscreant,**
bad egg <nonformal>; **scape-
grace,** black sheep; lost soul, lost
sheep, backslider, recidivist,
fallen angel; degenerate, pervert;
profligate, **lecher** 665.11; trollop,
whore 665.14,16; **pimp** 665.18

6 <nonformal terms> **asshole,
prick, bastard, son of a bitch** *or*
SOB, **jerk, horse's ass,** creep,
motherfucker, dork, **shit,** turd,
shithead, shitface, fart, **louse,
meanie, heel, shitheel, rat,
stinker,** pill, bugger, dirtbag,
dork, sleaze, sleazoid, sleazebag;
hood, hooligan 593.4

7 beast, **animal; cur,** dog, hound,
mongrel; **reptile,** viper, serpent,
snake; vermin, varmint <nonfor-
mal>; **swine,** pig; **skunk;** worm

8 cad, bounder *and* rotter
<nonformal>

9 **wrongdoer, malefactor, sinner,**
transgressor, delinquent; **culprit,
offender; evil person, evildoer**
593

10 **criminal, felon, perpetrator,
crook** *and* perp <both nonfor-
mal>, public enemy, **lawbreaker,**
scofflaw; **gangster** *and* mobster
and wiseguy <all nonformal>,
racketeer; swindler 357.3; thief
483; thug 593.3; **desperado; outlaw,** fugitive, **convict,** jailbird;
gallows bird <nonformal>; **traitor,** betrayer, Judas, two-timer
<nonformal>, **deceiver** 357

11 **the underworld,** gangland,
organized crime, organized
crime family, the rackets, the
mob, the syndicate, the Mafia,
Cosa Nostra; **gangsterism; gangster,** gangleader, capo, soldier

12 **the wicked,** the bad, the evil, the
unrighteous, the reprobate; sons

or children of the devil, children of darkness; **scum of the earth,** dregs of society

661 DISREPUTE

NOUNS **1 disrepute, ill repute,** bad repute, evil repute *or* reputation, ill fame, unsavory reputation, **bad name,** bad odor, bad report, ill report, bad character; **disesteem, dishonor, discredit; disfavor,** ill-favor; disapprobation 510.1

2 disreputability, disreputableness, **notoriety;** unsavoriness, **unrespectability; shamefulness**

3 baseness, lowness, meanness, crumminess <nonformal>, pettiness, paltriness, smallness, littleness, pokiness, **shabbiness, shoddiness, squalor,** scruffiness; **abjectness, wretchedness,** despicableness, contemptibleness, abominableness, execrableness, obnoxiousness; **vulgarity,** tastelessness, crudity, crudeness, tackiness *and* chintziness <both nonformal>; **vileness** 98.2, foulness, rankness, fulsomeness, grossness, heinousness, **atrociousness,** monstrousness, enormity; degradation, debasement, depravity

4 infamy, infamousness; **ignominy,** ignominiousness; ingloriousness, **ignobility,** odium, obloquy, opprobrium; loss of honor *or* name *or* repute *or* face; degradation, **demotion** 447

5 disgrace, scandal, humiliation; shame, dirty shame <nonformal>, crying shame; **reproach,** a disgrace to one's name

6 stigma, onus; **brand,** badge of infamy; **slur,** reproach, censure, reprimand, imputation, aspersion, reflection, stigmatization; pillorying; **black eye** <nonformal>, black mark; **disparagement** 512; **stain, taint, tarnish,** blur, **smirch,** smudge, **smear,** spot, blot, blot on one's escutcheon; mark of Cain

VERBS **7 incur disgrace,** incur dishonor *or* discredit, get a black eye <nonformal>, be shamed, earn a bad name, fall into disrepute; lose one's good name, **lose face,** lose countenance, **lose caste; disgrace oneself,** lower oneself, demean oneself, degrade *or* debase oneself, get one's hands dirty, sully *or* lower oneself, derogate, stoop, descend, fall from one's high estate, foul one's own nest; **scandalize,** put one's good name in jeopardy; compromise oneself; raise eyebrows, cause tongues to wag

8 disgrace, dishonor, discredit, reflect discredit upon, bring into discredit, reproach; **shame, put to shame,** hold up to shame; hold up to public scorn *or* public ridicule, pillory, bring shame upon, **humiliate** 137.4; **degrade, debase** 447.3, defrock, unfrock, bring low

9 stigmatize, brand; stain, besmirch, smirch, tarnish, taint, blot, **blacken, smear,** bespatter, **sully,** soil, defile, vilify, **slur,** cast a slur upon; disapprove 510.10; **disparage, defame** 512.9; censure, reprimand, **give a black eye** <nonformal>, give a black mark; give a bad name, give a dog a bad name; expose; pillory, gibbet; burn *or* hang in effigy; **skewer,** impale, crucify

ADJS **10 disreputable, discreditable, dishonorable,** unsavory, shady, **seamy, sordid; unrespectable, ignoble, ignominious, infamous,** inglorious; notorious; unpraiseworthy; derogatory 512.13

11 disgraceful, shameful, pitiful, deplorable, opprobrious, sad, sorry; degrading, debasing, demeaning, beneath one, beneath one's dignity, unbecoming, unworthy of one; cheap, gutter; **humiliating; scandalous,** shocking, outrageous

12 base, low, low rent *and* low ride *and* low-down *and* cotton-picking <all nonformal>, **mean,** crummy <nonformal>, poor, petty, paltry, small, little, **shabby, shoddy, squalid,** scrubby, scummy,

scurvy, scruffy, mangy <nonformal>, measly *and* cheesy <both nonformal>, poky, beggarly, **wretched, miserable,** abject, **despicable, contemptible,** abominable, execrable, obnoxious, **vulgar,** tasteless, crude, **tacky** *and* chintzy <both nonformal>; **disgusting, odious** 98.18, vile, foul, **dirty,** rank, fulsome, gross, flagrant, grave, arrant, nefarious, heinous, reptilian, **atrocious,** monstrous, unspeakable, unmentionable; degraded, debased, depraved

13 **in disrepute,** in bad repute, in bad odor; **in disfavor,** in discredit, **in bad** <nonformal>, out of favor; **in disgrace,** in Dutch *and* **in the doghouse** <both nonformal>, under a cloud; scandal-plagued *or* -ridden; stripped of reputation, disgraced, discredited, dishonored, shamed, unable to show one's face; **in trouble**

14 **unrenowned,** nameless, inglorious, **unnotable, unnoted,** unnoticed, unremarked, **undistinguished, unfamed,** uncelebrated, unsung, unpopular; **unknown,** little known, obscure, unheard-of

ADVS 15 **disreputably, discreditably, dishonorably, unrespectably, ignobly, ignominiously, infamously,** ingloriously

16 **disgracefully, scandalously,** shockingly, deplorably; **shamefully,** to one's shame

17 **basely, meanly, shabbily, shoddily, wretchedly, miserably,** abjectly, **despicably, contemptibly,** abominably, execrably, **odiously** 98.26, **vilely,** flagrantly, nefariously, heinously, **atrociously,** monstrously

662 REPUTE

NOUNS 1 **repute, reputation; name,** character; **fame, renown, kudos,** report, **glory;** éclat, **celebrity, popularity,** recognition, a place in the sun; popular acceptance *or* favor, vogue; **acclaim,**

public acclaim, réclame, **publicity; notoriety,** talk of the town; **exposure**

2 **reputability,** reputableness; good reputation, good name, **good** *or* **high repute,** good track record <nonformal>, good odor, face, fair name, name to conjure with

3 **esteem,** estimation, **honor, regard, respect,** approval, approbation, favor, **credit,** points *and* Brownie points <both nonformal>

4 **prestige, honor; dignity; rank, standing,** stature, high place, position, station, face, **status**

5 **distinction, mark, note; importance, consequence,** significance; **notability, prominence, eminence, preeminence, greatness,** conspicuousness; **stardom;** elevation, exaltation, exaltedness, loftiness; nobility, grandeur, sublimity; excellence 998.1

6 **illustriousness, luster,** brilliance, radiance, splendor, resplendency, refulgency, **glory,** nimbus, halo, aura, envelope; charisma, mystique, glamour, numinousness, magic

7 <posthumous fame> **memory, remembrance,** blessed *or* sacred memory, legend; **immortality,** undying fame, secure place in history; immortal name

8 **glorification, ennoblement, exaltation,** elevation, magnification, aggrandizement; enshrinement; beatification, canonization, sanctification; **deification, apotheosis**

9 **celebrity,** man *or* woman of note, person of note *or* consequence, **notable, notability, luminary, great man** *or* **woman,** worthy, name, **big name,** figure, public figure, **somebody; important person, VIP** *and* **standout** <both nonformal>, personage 996.8, million; cynosure, model, ideal type, **idol,** popular idol, tin god *or* little tin god <nonformal>; lion, social lion; hero, heroine, folk hero; **star, superstar,** hot

stuff <nonformal>; cult figure; **immortal;** luminaries, galaxy, constellation

VERBS **10 be somebody,** be something, **impress; figure,** make or cut a figure, make a splash <nonformal>, **make a noise in the world,** make or leave one's mark; live, **flourish; shine,** glitter, gleam, glow

11 gain recognition, be recognized, **make a name** or make a name for oneself, come into one's own, come to the fore, come into vogue; **burst onto the scene,** become an overnight celebrity, come onto the scene <nonformal>, come out of the woods or out of nowhere or out of left field <all nonformal>; make points or Brownie points <nonformal>

12 honor, confer or bestow honor upon; **dignify,** adorn, grace; **distinguish,** confer distinction on, give credit where credit is due

13 glorify, glamorize; **exalt,** elevate, raise, uplift, **ennoble,** aggrandize, magnify; immortalize, enshrine, hand one's name down to posterity, make legendary; beatify, canonize, sanctify; **deify,** apotheosize; **lionize**

14 reflect honor, lend credit or distinction, redound to one's honor, give one a reputation

ADJS **15 reputable,** highly reputed, **estimable, esteemed,** much or highly esteemed, **honorable,** honored; **meritorious,** worth one's salt, noble, worthy, creditable; respected, highly respectable; revered, venerable, venerated; **well-thought-of,** highly regarded, held in esteem, in good odor, in favor, in high favor; prestigious

16 distinguished, distingué; **noted, notable,** marked, of note; **famous,** famed, honored, **renowned, celebrated, popular,** acclaimed, much acclaimed, sought-after, hot and world-class <both nonformal>, **notorious,**

well-known, best-known, on everyone's tongue or lips, talked-of, talked-about; far-famed; fabled, legendary, mythical

17 prominent, conspicuous, outstanding, much in evidence, in the limelight <nonformal>; **important,** consequential, significant

18 eminent, high, exalted, elevated, lofty, sublime, held in awe, awesome; immortal; **great,** big <nonformal>, **grand;** excellent 998.12,13,15, mighty, high and mighty <nonformal>; glorified, ennobled, magnified, aggrandized; immortalized, enshrined; beatified, canonized, sainted, sanctified; **idolized, godlike, deified,** apotheosized

19 illustrious, lustrous, glorious, brilliant, radiant, splendid, resplendent, bright, shining; charismatic, glamorous, numinous, magical

ADVS **20 reputably, estimably, honorably,** nobly, respectably, worthily, creditably

21 famously, notably, notedly, notoriously, popularly; **prominently, eminently,** conspicuously, outstandingly; **illustriously**

663 SENSUALITY

NOUNS **1 sensuality,** sensualness, sensualism; **voluptuousness,** luxuriousness, luxury; **unchastity** 665; **pleasure-seeking; self-indulgence, hedonism;** epicureanism; pleasure principle, **instant gratification;** sensuousness 24.1

2 carnality, carnal-mindedness; **fleshliness,** flesh; animal or carnal nature, the flesh, the beast, fallen state or nature, lapsed state or nature, postlapsarian state or nature; **animality, animalism, bestiality,** beastliness, brutishness, **brutality;** coarseness, grossness; swinishness; **earthiness**

3 sensualist, voluptuary, pleasure-seeker, sybarite, **hedo-**

nist, *bon vivant* <Fr>; epicure, epicurean; gourmet, gourmand

VERBS **4** sensualize, carnalize, coarsen, brutify; *carpe diem* <L, seize the day>, live for the moment

ADJS **5 sensual,** sensualist; **voluptuous,** luxurious; **unchaste** 665.23, **hedonistic, pleasure-seeking,** pleasure-bent, luxury-loving, hedonic, epicurean, sybaritic; sensory, sensuous

6 carnal, carnal-minded, **fleshly,** bodily, physical; fallen, lapsed, postlapsarian; animal; **brutish, brutal,** brute; **bestial,** beastlike; coarse, gross; swinish; orgiastic; **earthy,** unspiritual, nonspiritual, material, materialistic

664 CHASTITY

NOUNS **1 chastity, virtue,** virtuousness, honor; **purity,** cleanliness; whiteness, snowiness; **immaculacy,** immaculateness, spotlessness, stainlessness, taintlessness, unblemishedness, unsulliedness, undefiledness, untarnishedness; uncorruptness; sexual innocence, innocence 657

2 decency, seemliness, propriety, decorum; modesty, shame, pudicity, pudency

3 continence or continency; abstemiousness, abstinence 668.2; celibacy; **virginity,** maidenhood, maidenhead; marital fidelity or faithfulness

ADJS **4 chaste, virtuous; pure,** purehearted, pure in heart; **clean; immaculate, spotless,** stainless, snowy, pure as driven snow; **unsoiled, unsullied, undefiled,** untarnished, unstained, unspotted, untainted, unblemished; sexually innocent, innocent 657.6,7

5 decent, modest, decorous, delicate, elegant, proper, becoming, seemly

6 continent; abstemious, abstinent 668.10; celibate; virginal, **virgin,** maidenly, vestal

7 undebauched, undissipated, undissolute

665 UNCHASTITY

NOUNS **1 unchastity,** unchasteness; unvirtuousness; **impurity,** uncleanness, sulliedness; **indecency** 666

2 incontinence, uncontinence; unrestraint 430.3

3 profligacy, dissoluteness, licentiousness, license, unbridledness, wildness, rakishness, gallantry, **libertinism; dissipation, debauchery;** venery, wenching, whoring, womanizing

4 wantonness, waywardness; looseness, laxity, loose morals, easy virtue, whorishness, **promiscuity,** sleeping around <nonformal>

5 lasciviousness, lechery, lecherousness, lewdness, bawdiness, **dirtiness,** salaciousness, **carnality,** animality, **sexuality, sexiness, lust, lustfulness;** obscenity 666.4; **prurience,** sexual itch, concupiscence, libidinousness, randiness, horniness <nonformal>, lubricity, lubriciousness, **sensuality,** eroticism; satyriasis, gynecomania; nymphomania; erotomania

6 seduction, betrayal; violation, abuse; **debauchment, defilement,** ravishment, fate worse than death; priapism; defloration, deflowering; **rape,** sexual or criminal assault; date or acquaintance rape

7 <illicit sexual intercourse> **adultery,** criminal congress or cohabitation, extramarital or premarital sex, extramarital or premarital relations. extracurricular sex or relations <nonformal>, **fornication; incest;** cuckoldry

8 prostitution, harlotry, street-walking; soliciting, solicitation; whoremongering, whoremastery, pimping, pandering

9 brothel, house of prostitution, house of assignation, house of joy or ill repute or ill fame, **whorehouse,** massage parlor, disorderly house, **cathouse, bordello,** bagnio, dive, den of iniq-

uity, crib, joint; red-light district,
tenderloin

10 **libertine, swinger** <nonformal>, **profligate, rake, roué,**
womanizer, cocksman <nonformal>, debauchee, **wolf** <nonformal>, woman chaser, skirt chaser
<nonformal>, gay deceiver, gallant, philanderer, lady-killer,
Lothario, Don Juan, Casanova

11 **lecher, satyr, goat,** old goat,
dirty old man; whoremaster

12 **seducer, betrayer,** deceiver;
debaucher, ravisher, ravager,
violator, despoiler, defiler; **rapist**

13 **adulterer, cheater, fornicator;**
adulteress

14 **strumpet, trollop, wench,**
hussy, slut, jade, baggage; tart
and **chippy** *and* **floozy** <all nonformal>, bitch, drab, trull, harridan, Jezebel, wanton, whore
<nonformal>, **loose woman,**
easy lay <nonformal>, woman
of easy virtue; nymphomaniac,
nympho <nonformal>; nymphet

15 **demimonde,** demimondaine;
courtesan, adventuress, **seductress,** femme fatale, vampire,
vamp, temptress; hetaera, houri,
harem girl, odalisque; Jezebel

16 **prostitute, harlot, whore,** call
girl *and* B-girl <both nonformal>,
scarlet woman, painted woman,
fallen woman, **streetwalker,** hustler *and* **hooker** <both nonformal>, meretrix; white slave

17 **mistress,** woman, **kept woman,**
paramour, concubine, doxy; live-
in lover <nonformal>

18 **procurer, pimp,** pander *or* panderer; **bawd; gigolo,** fancy man;
procuress, **madam** <nonformal>;
white slaver

VERBS 19 **be promiscuous,** sleep
around *and* swing <both nonformal>; **debauch, wanton,** chase
women, womanize, whore, sow
one's wild oats; **philander; dissipate** 669.6; **fornicate, cheat,**
commit adultery, get a little on
the side <nonformal>

20 **seduce, betray, deceive,** lead
astray, lead down the garden *or*
the primrose path; **debauch,**

ravish, ravage, despoil, ruin;
deflower; **defile,** soil, sully; **violate,** abuse; **rape**

21 **prostitute oneself,** streetwalk;
pimp, procure, pander

22 **cuckold;** wear horns, wear the
horn

ADJS 23 **unchaste, unvirtuous,** unvirginal; **impure, unclean; indecent** 666.5; soiled, sullied, defiled, tainted

24 **incontinent,** uncontinent; **orgiastic;** intemperate 669.7;
unrestrained

25 **profligate, licentious,** unbridled, untrammeled, uninhibited, free; **dissolute, dissipated,**
debauched, abandoned; **wild,**
fast, gallant, rakish

26 **wanton, wayward; loose,** lax,
slack, loose-moraled, of loose
morals, of easy virtue, easy
<nonformal>, **light,** whorish,
promiscuous

27 freeloving; **adulterous,** illicit,
extramarital, premarital; incestuous

28 **prostituted, whorish, harlot,**
scarlet, fallen, meretricious,
streetwalking, hustling <nonformal>, on the streets, in the life

29 **lascivious, lecherous, sexy, salacious, carnal, sexual, lustful,**
hot, horny *and* sexed-up *and* hot
to trot <all nonformal>; prurient,
itching, itchy <nonformal>; concupiscent, libidinous, randy,
horny <nonformal>; lubricious;
lewd, bawdy, adult, X-rated,
hard, pornographic, porno <nonformal>, **dirty, obscene** 666.9;
erotic, **sensual,** fleshly; goatish,
satyric, priapic; nymphomaniacal

666 INDECENCY

NOUNS 1 **indecency, indelicacy,**
inelegance, **indecorousness,** indecorum, **impropriety** 638.1,
inappropriateness, unseemliness,
indiscretion, indiscreetness; **unchastity** 665

2 **immodesty,** unmodestness, impudicity; exhibitionism; **shamelessness; brazenness** 142.2,
brassiness, pertness, forward-

ness, boldness, bumptiousness; **flagrancy,** notoriousness, scandalousness

3 **vulgarity** 497, **uncouthness, coarseness, crudeness, grossness,** raunchiness <nonformal>; **earthiness,** frankness; **spiciness, raciness**

4 **obscenity, dirtiness, ribaldry, pornography,** porno *and* porn <both nonformal>, hard *or* hardcore pornography, soft *or* softcore pornography, salacity, **smut, dirt, filth; lewdness, bawdiness,** salaciousness, **smuttiness, foulness, filthiness,** vileness, offensiveness; scurrility; erotic art *or* literature, pornographic art *or* literature; blue movie *and* dirty movie *and* porno film *and* skin flick <all nonformal>, adult movie, stag film <nonformal>, X-rated movie; **dirty talk, scatology** 523.9

ADJS 5 **indecent, indelicate, inelegant, indecorous, improper, unseemly, unbecoming,** indiscreet

6 **immodest;** exhibitionistic; **shameless,** unembarrassed, unabashed, unblushing, **brazen,** brazenfaced; **forward,** bold, pert, bumptious; **flagrant,** notorious, scandalous

7 **risqué,** risky, **racy,** salty, spicy, **off-color,** suggestive, scabrous

8 **vulgar, uncouth, coarse, gross,** rank, raw, broad, low, foul, gutter; **earthy,** frank

9 **obscene, lewd, adult, bawdy,** ithyphallic, **ribald, pornographic, salacious,** sultry <nonformal>, lurid, **dirty, smutty,** raunchy <nonformal>, blue, impure, unchaste, unclean, **foul, filthy, nasty,** vile, fulsome, offensive, not fit for mixed company; scurrilous; **foulmouthed;** Rabelaisian

667 ASCETICISM

NOUNS 1 **asceticism, austerity, self-denial,** self-abnegation, **rigor; puritanism,** eremitism, anchoritism, monasticism; mor-

tification, self-mortification, maceration, flagellation; **abstinence** 668.2; belt-tightening, fasting 515; voluntary poverty, mendicantism

2 **ascetic, puritan; abstainer** 668.4; anchorite, **hermit** 584.5; yogi; dervish, fakir, flagellant; mendicant

VERBS 3 deny oneself; abstain, tighten one's belt; flagellate oneself, wear a hair shirt

ADJS 4 **ascetic, austere,** self-denying, self-abnegating, **rigorous, rigoristic; puritanical,** eremitic, anchoritic; **abstinent** 668.10; mendicant, discalced, barefoot, wedded to poverty; flagellant

668 TEMPERANCE

NOUNS 1 **temperance,** temperateness, **moderation,** moderateness; golden mean, via media; sobriety, frugality, forbearance, abnegation; renunciation, renouncement, forgoing; denial, **self-denial;** restraint, **self-restraint; self-control,** self-mastery, **discipline,** self-discipline

2 **abstinence,** abstention, **abstemiousness,** refrainment, avoidance, eschewal, denying *or* refusing oneself, passing up <nonformal>; **total abstinence, teetotalism;** the pledge; sexual abstinence, celibacy 565; chastity 664; Stoicism; vegetarianism; plain living, spare diet, simple diet; Lenten fare; fast 515.2,3; **continence** 664.3; **asceticism** 667

3 **prohibition,** prohibitionism

4 **abstainer,** abstinent; **teetotaler,** teetotalist; vegetarian; **ascetic** 667.2; nonsmoker, nondrinker, etc

5 **prohibitionist, dry** <nonformal>

VERBS 6 **restrain oneself,** constrain oneself, curb oneself, **avoid excess; limit oneself, restrict oneself; control oneself,** control one's appetites, contain oneself, discipline oneself, exercise self-control *or* self-restraint, keep oneself under control, know when one has had enough, **deny** *or* refuse oneself, **say no** *or* just say no; live plainly *or* simply *or* frugally; mortify oneself, mortify the flesh; eat to live, not live to eat; eat sparingly

7 **abstain,** abstain from, refrain, **refrain from, forbear, forgo,** spare, withhold, hold back, **avoid, shun,** eschew, **pass up** <nonformal>, **keep from,** have nothing to do with, take no part in, have no hand in, **let alone,** let well enough alone, **deny oneself,** do without, go without, make do without, keep hands off

8 **swear off, renounce,** forswear, **give up,** abandon; take the pledge, get on the wagon <nonformal>; **kick** *and* kick the habit <both nonformal>, dry out

ADJS 9 **temperate, moderate,** sober, frugal, restrained, **sparing,** stinting, measured

10 **abstinent, abstemious;** teetotal, sworn off, on the wagon <nonformal>; sexually abstinent, celibate, chaste; Stoic; vegetarian; Spartan, Lenten; **continent** 664.6; **ascetic**

11 prohibitionist, antisaloon, dry <nonformal>

ADVS 12 **temperately, moderately, sparingly,** stintingly, frugally, in moderation, within bounds

669 INTEMPERANCE

NOUNS 1 **intemperance,** intemperateness, **indulgence, self-indulgence; overindulgence,** overdoing; **unrestraint,** unconstraint; **immoderation,** immoderacy, immoderateness; inordinateness; **excess, excessiveness,** too much; prodigality, extravagance; crapulence *or* crapulency, crapulousness; **incontinence** 665.2; **swinishness, gluttony** 672; **drunkenness** 88.1

2 **dissipation, licentiousness; riotous living,** high living <nonformal>, killing pace, burning the candle at both ends; **debauchery,** debauchment; **carousal** 88.5, carousing; **debauch, orgy,** saturnalia

3 **dissipater,** high liver <nonformal>; nightowl <both nonformal>; **playboy,** partyer, partygoer, party girl

VERBS 4 **indulge,** indulge oneself, indulge one's appetites, deny oneself nothing; **give oneself up to,** give free rein to; live high on the hog <nonformal>, live off the fat of the land; indulge in, luxuriate in, wallow in; roll in

5 **overindulge, overdo, carry to excess,** carry too far, go whole hog <nonformal>, not know when to stop, spread oneself too thin; live above *or* beyond one's means

6 **dissipate, debauch, wanton, carouse,** run riot, live hard *or* fast, burn the candle at both ends, keep up a killing pace, sow one's wild oats, have one's fling, **party** <nonformal>

ADJS 7 **intemperate, indulgent, self-indulgent; overindulgent,** overindulging, unfrugal, **immoderate,** inordinate, **excessive,** too much, prodigal, extravagant, unlimited; crapulous, crapulent; undisciplined, uncontrolled, unbridled, unconstrained, uninhibited, **unrestrained; incontinent** 665.24; **swinish, gluttonous** 672.6; bibulous

8 **licentious, dissipated, riotous, dissolute, debauched;** free-living, high-living <nonformal>

9 **orgiastic,** saturnalian, corybantic

ADVS 10 **intemperately,** prodigally, **immoderately,** inordinately, excessively, **in** *or* **to excess,** to extremes, beyond all bounds *or* limits, without restraint; high, high on the hog <nonformal>

670 MODERATION

NOUNS 1 **moderation,** moderateness; **restraint,** constraint, control; **judiciousness,** prudence; steadiness, evenness, balance, equilibrium, **stability** 854; **temperateness,** temperance, sobriety; self-abnegation, self-restraint, self-control, self-denial; abstinence, continence, abnegation; **mildness,** lenity, gentleness; calmness, serenity, tranquillity, repose, calm, cool <nonformal>; nothing in excess; **happy medium, golden mean,** middle way *or* path; **conservatism** 852.3; **nonviolence,** pacifism; impartiality, neutrality; ecumenism

2 modulation, **abatement,** remission, **mitigation,** diminution, defusing, de-escalation **reduction,** lessening, falling-off; **relaxation,** relaxing, slackening, **easing,** letup *and* letdown <both nonformal>; **alleviation,** assuagement, allayment, palliation, leniency; **tempering, softening,** subdual; **deadening, dulling,** damping, blunting; drugging, narcotizing, sedating, sedation; **pacification, tranquilization,** tranquilizing, mollification, **quieting,** lulling, **soothing, calming,** hushing

3 **moderator, mitigator,** modulator, stabilizer, assuager; **mediator, bridge-builder,** wiser head; **alleviator,** alleviative, palliative, lenitive; **pacifier, soother,** comforter, peacemaker, mollifier; **drug,** anodyne, **tranquilizer,** calmative; **sedative** 86.12; balm, salve; cushion, shock absorber

4 **moderate,** middle-of-the-roader, **centrist,** neutral, compromiser; **conservative** 852.4

VERBS 5 **be moderate, keep within bounds;** practice self-control *or* self-denial, live within one's means, do nothing in excess, strike a balance, strike *or* keep a happy medium, keep to the middle way; keep the peace, practice nonviolence; not rock the boat *and* not make waves *or* static <all nonformal>; cool it *and* keep one's cool <both nonformal>, keep one's head *or* temper; be conservative 852.6

6 **moderate, restrain,** constrain, control, **keep within bounds;**

modulate, mitigate, defuse, abate, weaken, **diminish, reduce,** de-escalate, slacken, lessen, slow down; **alleviate,** assuage, allay, lighten, palliate, extenuate, **temper; soften, subdue,** tame, hold in check, keep a tight rein, chasten, play down, downplay, de-emphasize, tone down; lower the voice; **drug,** narcotize, sedate, tranquilize, deaden, dull, blunt, take the edge off; smother, suppress, stifle; **damp, dampen,** bank the fire, throw cold water on, throw a wet blanket on; sober, sober up; clear the air

7 **calm,** calm down, **stabilize, tranquilize, pacify,** mollify, appease; **quiet,** hush, still, rest, compose, **lull, soothe,** gentle; cool, **subdue,** quell; ease, steady, smooth, smooth over, smooth down, even out; keep the peace, pour oil on troubled waters

8 **cushion,** absorb the shock, **soften the blow,** break the fall, deaden, damp *or* dampen, soften, suppress, neutralize, offset; show pity *or* mercy *or* consideration *or* sensitivity

9 **relax,** unbend, ease, **ease up,** ease off, **let up,** let down; abate, mitigate; **slacken,** slack; loose, **loosen;** unstring

ADJS 10 **moderate, temperate,** sober; **mild,** soft, bland, **gentle,** tame; gentle as a lamb; nonviolent, peaceable, peaceful; **judicious, prudent**

11 **restrained,** constrained, limited, controlled, **stable,** in hand; tempered, **softened, subdued,** chastened

12 **unexcessive,** unextreme, unextravagant, **conservative;** reasonable

13 **equable,** even, low-key *or* low-keyed, **cool,** even-tempered, level-headed, dispassionate; tranquil, reposeful, serene, calm 173.12

14 **mitigating,** assuaging, abating, **diminishing, reducing, alleviating, relaxing, easing;** tempering,

softening, chastening, **subduing**; deadening, dulling, blunting, damping, cushioning

15 **tranquilizing**, pacifying, mollifying, appeasing; cooling-off; **calming**, lulling, gentling, hushing, stilling; **soothing**, restful; dreamy, drowsy

16 **palliative, alleviative**, lenitive, **calmative, narcotic, sedative**, demulcent, anodyne

ADVS 17 **moderately, in moderation**, restrainedly, within reason, within bounds, in balance; **temperately**, soberly, prudently, judiciously; calmly, coolly, evenly, steadily, equably, tranquilly, serenely; conservatively

671 VIOLENCE
<vehement action>

NOUNS 1 **violence, vehemence, virulence, venom, furiousness, force, rigor**, harshness, inclemency, **severity, intensity**, acuteness, **sharpness; acrimony** 17.5; fierceness, ferociousness, viciousness, savagery, destructiveness, **destruction, vandalism; terrorism, barbarity, brutality, atrocity**, inhumanity, killer instinct, murderousness, mercilessness, mindlessness, animality, brutishness; **rage, anger** 152

2 **turbulence, turmoil**, chaos, **fury, furor, rage, frenzy, passion**, fanaticism, zealousness, zeal, tempestuousness, tumultuousness, **tumult, uproar**, racket, cacophony, pandemonium, hubbub, **commotion, disturbance, agitation**, bluster, embroilment, brouhaha, fuss, **row, rumpus**, ruckus <nonformal>, **ferment**, seething, ebullition, fomentation

3 **unruliness, disorderliness**, obstreperousness; **riot, rioting;** looting, pillaging, plundering, rapine; wilding <nonformal>; laying waste, sacking; scorched earth; **attack** 459, **assault**, onslaught, battering; **rape, violation; killing** 308, butchery, massacre, slaughter

4 **storm, tempest,** squall, **tornado, cyclone, hurricane,** typhoon, storm-center, tropical storm, eye of the storm *or* hurricane; stormy weather, rough weather, foul weather; rainstorm 316.2; thunderstorm 316.3; windstorm 318.12; **snowstorm** 1022.8; **firestorm**

5 **upheaval, convulsion,** cataclysm, catastrophe, disaster; **fit,** spasm, **paroxysm;** climax; **earthquake,** quake, temblor, diastrophism, epicenter, shockwave; tidal wave, tsunami

6 **outburst, outbreak, eruption,** eructation, belch, spew; **burst;** meltdown; **torrent,** rush, gush, spate, cascade, spurt, jet, rapids, volcano

7 **explosion, discharge, blowout,** blowup, detonation, fulmination, **blast, burst, report** 56.1; flash, flash point, flare-up, fulguration; bang, boom 56.4; backfire

8 **concussion, shock, impact,** crunch, smash; percussion, repercussion

9 <violent person> **hothead,** hotspur; **devil, demon, fiend, brute,** hellion, hell-raiser; **beast,** wild beast, mad dog, wolf, monster, savage; **rapist, mugger, killer;** hit man <nonformal>, contract killer, hired killer, hired gun; **fury,** virago, vixen, termagant, she-wolf, tigress, witch; firebrand, revolutionary 859.3, **terrorist,** incendiary, bomber, guerrilla

10 <nonformal terms> **goon, gorilla,** ape, muscle man, plug-ugly, cowboy, bimbo, bozo, bruiser, tough guy, tough, hoodlum, hood, gunsel, tough *or* ugly customer

VERBS 11 **rage, storm, rant, rave,** roar; **rampage, tear,** tear around; **destroy, wreck,** wreak havoc, ruin; sow disorder; **terrorize,** sow terror, vandalize, barbarize, brutalize; **riot,** loot, burn, pillage, sack, lay waste; **slaughter, butcher; rape,** violate; **attack, assault,** batter, savage, mug, maul, hammer; go for the jugular

12 seethe, boil, fume, foam, simmer, stew, ferment, stir, churn

13 erupt, burst forth or **out, break out, blow out** or **open,** eruct, belch, **vomit,** spout, spew, disgorge, **discharge,** eject, throw or hurl forth

14 explode, blow up, burst, go off, go up, blow out, blast; **detonate, fulminate; touch off,** trigger, trip, set off; **discharge;** backfire; melt down

15 run amok, go berserk, go on a rampage, cut loose, run riot, run wild

ADJS **16 violent, vehement, virulent, venomous, severe, rigorous, furious, fierce, intense,** sharp, acute, keen, piercing; **destructive;** rough, bruising, tough <nonformal>; **drastic,** extreme, outrageous, excessive, unconscionable, intemperate, immoderate; acrimonious 17.14

17 unmitigated, unsoftened, untempered, unquelled; unabated; unmixed, unalloyed; **total**

18 turbulent, tumultuous, raging, chaotic, hellish, anarchic, **storming,** stormy, **tempestuous, frenzied, wild, wild-eyed, frantic, furious,** insensate, **mad,** demented, insane, raging, enraged, raving, slavering; **angry; blustering,** blustery; **uproarious,** riproaring <nonformal>

19 unruly, disorderly, obstreperous; **unbridled; riotous,** wild, rampant; **terroristic,** anarchic, nihilistic, revolutionary 859.5

20 boisterous, rampageous, rambunctious <nonformal>, wild, rollicking, **rowdy,** rough, harumscarum <nonformal>; roughand-tumble, knock-down-and-drag-out <nonformal>

21 savage, fierce, ferocious, vicious, murderous, mindless, brutal, brutish, **bestial,** mindless, insensate, monstrous, inhuman, ruthless, merciless, bloody, sanguinary; feral; **wild,** untamed, undomesticated; **barbarous,** barbaric; **uncivilized**

22 fiery, heated, inflamed, scorching, red-hot, white-hot; **fanatic, zealous,** hard-core, hard-line, ardent, passionate; **hotheaded**

23 convulsive, cataclysmic, disastrous, upheaving; seismic; **spasmodic,** paroxysmal

24 explosive, bursting, detonating, fulminating, fulminant; **volcanic,** eruptive

ADVS **25 violently, vehemently, virulently, venomously, rigorously, severely, fiercely, drastically; furiously,** wildly, **like mad,** like fury <nonformal>

26 turbulently, tumultuously, riotously, uproariously, stormily, tempestuously, **frenziedly, frantically, furiously, ragingly, enragedly, madly; angrily** 152.33

27 savagely, fiercely, ferociously, atrociously, viciously, murderously, brutally or brutishly, mindlessly, bestially, barbarously, inhumanly, ruthlessly, mercilessly; **tooth and nail**

672 GLUTTONY

NOUNS **1 gluttony, greed,** greediness, voraciousness, ravenousness, crapulence or crapulency, rapacity, insatiability; omnivorousness; **piggishness, hoggishness,** swinishness; **overindulgence, overeating;** eating disorder, bulimia, bulimia nervosa; **intemperance** 669

2 epicureanism, gourmandise; gastronomy

3 glutton, trencherman, trencherwoman, gobbler, gorger, **gourmand,** gourmandizer, gormand, gormandizer; animal, **hog** and **pig** and chow hound <all nonformal>

VERBS **4 gluttonize,** gormandize, **indulge one's appetite,** live to eat; **gorge,** glut, cram, **stuff,** batten, guzzle, **devour,** raven, bolt, gobble, gulp, **wolf,** gulp or bolt or wolf down, eat like a horse, stuff oneself and eat one's head off and fork or shovel it in <all nonfor-

mal>, eat one out of house and
home

**5 overeat, overgorge, overin-
dulge, make a pig** *or* **hog of oneself, pig out** <nonformal>; stuff
oneself

ADJS **6 gluttonous, greedy,** voracious, ravenous, rapacious, insatiable, bulimic; **piggish, hoggish;**
crapulous, crapulent; intemperate 669.7; omnivorous; **gorging,**
cramming, glutting, stuffing, guzzling, wolfing, bolting, **gobbling,
gulping**

7 overfed, overgorged, overin-
dulged

ADVS **8 gluttonously, greedily,** voraciously, ravenously; **piggishly,
hoggishly**

673 LEGALITY

NOUNS **1 legality, legitimacy, lawfulness, legitimateness, licitness,** validity, applicability; **jurisdiction** 594; **constitutionality,**
constitutional validity; legal process, legal form, **due process;
justice** 649

**2 legalization, legitimation, le-
gitimatization, decriminaliza-
tion;** money-laundering; validation; authorization, sanction; legislation, enactment

3 law, statute, rubric, **canon; ordinance; act, enactment, measure,** legislation; **rule, ruling;
prescript,** prescription; **regulation; dictate,** dictation; form, formula, formality; standing order;
bylaw; **edict, decree** 420.4; **bill**

4 law, legal system, system of
laws, legal branch *or* specialty

5 code, digest, pandect, **body of
law,** legal code, code of laws; **codification; civil code, penal code;**
Justinian Code; Napoleonic code;
lawbook, statute book, compilation; Blackstone

6 constitution; constitutional
amendment; Bill of Rights

**7 jurisprudence, law; forensic
science;** criminology

VERBS **8 legalize, legitimize,** legitimatize, legitimate, **decriminal-
ize;** launder money; validate; **au-**

thorize, sanction; constitute, ordain, put in force; prescribe, formulate; regulate; **decree; legislate, enact; enforce; litigate**
598.12

9 codify, digest; compile, publish

ADJS **10 legal, legitimate,** legit *and*
kosher <both nonformal>, **licit,
lawful,** within the law; **actionable,** litigable, justiciable; **en-
forceable,** legally binding; **judicial,** juridical; **authorized, sanctioned,** valid, applicable; **constitutional; legislative, lawmaking; just** 649.8

11 jurisprudent, jurisprudential;
legalistic; forensic; nomistic,
nomothetic; criminological

ADVS **12 legally, legitimately, lic-
itly, lawfully,** by law, *de jure* <L>,
in the eyes of the law

674 ILLEGALITY

NOUNS **1 illegality, unlawfulness,
illicitness, lawlessness;** imper-
missibility, **unconstitutionality;
outlawry; anarchy,** breakdown
or paralysis of authority, anomie

2 illegitimacy, illegitimateness,
illegitimation; **bastardy,** bastard-
ism

3 lawbreaking, violation, breach
or violation of law, infringement,
contravention, infraction, **transgression,** trespass; **criminality,**
delinquency; flouting *or* making a
mockery of the law

4 offense, wrong, illegality; **violation** 435.2; **wrongdoing** 655;
crime, felony; misdemeanor;
tort

VERBS **5 break** *or* **violate the law,**
contravene, infract, violate 435.4,
transgress, trespass, disobey the
law, flout the law, make a mockery of the law, fly in the face of the
law, snap one's fingers at the law,
circumvent the law, disregard the
law, **take the law into one's own
hands,** twist the law to one's own
purposes; commit a crime; live
outside the law

ADJS **6 illegal, unlawful, illegitimate, illicit,** lawless, wrongful,
fraudulent, **against the law; un-**

authorized, impermissible, unwarranted, unofficial; unstatu-
tory; unconstitutional; flawed,
irregular, contrary to law; actionable, chargeable, justiciable, litigable; criminal, felonious; outlaw, outlawed; contraband,
bootleg, black-market; under-the-
table; unregulated, unchartered;
anarchic, anomic

7 illegitimate, spurious, false;
bastard, misbegot, misbegotten,
born out of wedlock, without
benefit of clergy

ADVS 8 illegally, unlawfully, ille-
gitimately, illicitly; criminally,
feloniously; in violation of law

675 RELIGIONS, CULTS, SECTS

NOUNS 1 religion, religious belief
or faith, belief, faith, teaching,
doctrine, creed, credo, theology
676, orthodoxy 687; system of
beliefs; tradition

2 cult, ism; cultism; mystique

3 sect, religious order, denomination, persuasion, faction,
church, communion, commu-
nity, group, fellowship, affiliation,
order, school, party, society, body,
organization; branch; offshoot;
schism, division

4 sectarianism, denominational-
ism; schismatism; syncretism,
eclecticism

5 theism; monotheism; polythe-
ism; ditheism; tritheism; pantheism; anthropotheism, anthropomorphism; anthropolatry; zo-
otheism; deism

6 animism, animistic religion or
cult; voodooism, voodoo, jujuism, obeahism; shamanism; fetishism, totemism; nature worship, naturism; primitive religion

7 Christianity, Christianism,
Christendom; Roman or Western
Christianity; Judeo-Christian religion or tradition or belief; fundamentalism, Christian fundamentalism

8 Catholicism, Catholicity; Roman Catholicism; Catholic

Church, Roman Catholic
Church; Eastern Rites

9 Orthodoxy; Eastern Orthodox
Church, Holy Orthodox Catholic Apostolic Church, Greek Orthodox Church, Russian Orthodox Church

10 Protestantism, Reformation-
ism; Evangelicalism; dissent 333;
apostasy 363.2; new theology

11 Anglicanism; High-Churchism,
Low-Churchism; Anglo-Catholi-
cism; Church of England, Established Church

12 Judaism; Orthodox Judaism,
Conservative Judaism, Reform
Judaism, Reconstructionism

13 Islam, Muslimism; Sufism,
Sunnism, Shiism; Black Muslimism; Muslim fundamentalism,
militant Muslimism

14 Christian Science; New
Thought, Higher Thought, Practi-
cal Christianity, Mental Science,
Divine Science Church

15 religionist, religioner; believer
692.4; cultist

16 theist; monotheist; polytheist;
ditheist, dualist; tritheist; tetra-
theist; pantheist; zootheist; deist

17 Christian, Nazarene, Nazarite;
Christian sectarian

18 sectarian, sectary, denomina-
tionalist, schismatic

19 Catholic, Roman Catholic , papist <nonformal>; Eastern-Rite
Christian

20 Protestant, Reformationist,
Evangelical; dissenter 333.3;
apostate 363.5

21 Jew, Hebrew, Israelite; Orthodox or Conservative or Reform
Jew, Reconstructionist; Hasid

22 Mormon, Latter-day Saint

23 Muslim, Moslem, Islamite;
Shiite, Shia; Sunni, Sunnite, Sufi;
dervish; Black Muslim; Muslim
fundamentalist or militant

24 Christian Scientist, Christian
Science Practitioner

ADJS 25 religious, theistic; mono-
theistic; polytheistic, ditheistic,
tritheistic; pantheistic; anthropomorphic, anthropotheistic; de-
istic

491 675.26-677.17

26 **sectarian,** sectary, **denominational,** schismatic
27 **nonsectarian, undenomina-
tional, nondenominational;** in-
terdenominational
28 **Protestant,** Reformed, Evangelical; Lutheran, Calvinist;
dissentient 333.6; apostate
363.11
29 **Catholic; Roman Catholic**
30 **Jewish, Hebrew,** Judaic, Israelite, Israelitic; Orthodox, Conservative, Reform, Reconstructionist; Hasidic
31 **Muslim, Islamic,** Moslem,
Muhammadan, Mohammedan;
Shiite, Sunni, Sunnite
32 <Oriental> Buddhist;
Brahmanic; Vedic, Vedantic;
Confucian; Taoist, Shintoist;
Zoroastrian, Parsee

676 THEOLOGY

NOUNS 1 **theology, religion, divinity;** theologism; doctrinism, doc-
trinalism
2 **doctrine, dogma** 952.2; **creed,**
credo; articles of faith; Apostles'
Creed, Nicene Creed; Catechism
3 **theologian,** theologician; **divine;** scholastic, schoolman;
theological or divinity student,
theologue; canonist
ADJS 4 **theological, religious; divine;** doctrinal, doctrinary; can-
onic or canonical

677 DEITY

NOUNS 1 **deity, divinity,** divineness; **godliness,** godlikeness;
godhood, godhead, godship, Fatherhood; heavenliness; **transcendence**
2 **God;** Jehovah; Yahweh, Adonai,
Elohim <all Heb>; **Allah;** the
Great Spirit, Manitou
3 <Hinduism> **Brahma,** the Supreme Soul, the Essence of the
Universe; **Atman,** the Universal
Ego or Self; **Vishnu,** the Preserver; **Siva,** the Destroyer, the
Regenerator
4 <Buddhism> **Buddha,** the
Blessed One, the Teacher, **the
Lord Buddha,** bodhisattva

5 <Zoroastrianism> Ahura
Mazda, Ormazd, Mazda, the Lord
of Wisdom
6 <Christian Science> **Mind, Divine Mind,** Spirit, Soul Principle,
Life, Truth, Love
7 **world spirit** or **soul,** universal
life force, **world-self,** infinite
spirit, supreme soul or principle,
oversoul, nous, Logos
8 **Nature, Mother Nature**
9 **Godhead, Trinity;** Trimurti,
Hindu trinity or triad
10 **Christ**
11 **the Word, Logos,** the Word
Made Flesh, **the Incarnation,** the
Hypostatic Union
12 **God the Holy Ghost, the Holy
Ghost, the Holy Spirit,** the Spirit
of God, the Spirit of Truth, the
Comforter, the Consoler, the Intercessor
13 <divine functions> creation,
preservation, dispensation; **providence, divine providence,** dealings or dispensations of providence
14 <functions of Christ> salvation,
redemption; atonement, propitiation; mediation, intercession;
judgment
15 <functions of the Holy Ghost>
inspiration, unction, regeneration, sanctification, comfort, consolation, grace, witness
ADJS 16 **divine,** heavenly, celestial,
empyrean; **godly, godlike** 692.9;
transcendent, superhuman, supernatural; self-existent; Christ-
like, redemptive, propitiatory,
mediatory, intercessional; incarnate; messianic
17 **almighty, omnipotent,** all-
powerful; creative, making, shaping; **omniscient,** all-wise, all-
knowing; **infinite,** boundless, unbounded, unlimited, undefined,
omnipresent, ubiquitous; eternal,
everlasting, timeless, perpetual,
immortal, permanent; immutable, unchanging, changeless; supreme, sovereign, highest; holy,
hallowed, sacred, numinous; glorious, radiant, luminous; majestic; good, just, loving, merciful

678 MYTHICAL AND POLYTHEISTIC GODS AND SPIRITS

NOUNS **1 the gods,** the immortals; the major deities, the greater gods; the minor deities, the lesser gods; **pantheon; spirits,** animistic spirit, manitou

2 god; deity, divinity, immortal, heathen god, pagan deity *or* divinity; **goddess; idol,** false god

3 godling; demigod, half-god, hero; cult figure; demigoddess, heroine

4 god, goddesses; Greek and Roman deities; Norse and Germanic deities; Celtic deities; Hindu deities; avatars of Vishnu; Egyptian deities; Semitic deities; Chinese deities; Japanese deities; specialized *or* tutelary deities

5 spirit, intelligence, supernatural being; **genius,** demon; **specter** 987; **evil spirits** 680

6 elemental, elemental spirit; sylph; gnome, earth-spirit; salamander; undine, water-sprite

7 fairyfolk, elfenfolk, **the little people** *or* **men,** denizens of the air; **fairyland**

8 fairy, sprite, fay; elf, brownie, pixie, gremlin; imp, goblin 680.8; **gnome,** dwarf; **sylph,** sylphid; **banshee; leprechaun;** fairy queen

9 nymph; nymphet; **dryad,** hamadryad, wood nymph; tree nymph; oread, mountain nymph; meadow *or* flower nymph; glen nymph

10 water god, water spirit *or* **sprite** *or* **nymph;** undine; **naiad; mermaid,** sea-maiden, siren; Thetis; **merman,** man fish

11 forest god, sylvan deity, field spirit, fertility god, **faun, satyr;** Pan

12 familiar spirit, familiar; **genius, good genius,** daemon, demon, totem; **guardian, guardian spirit, guardian angel,** angel, good angel, ministering angel, **fairy godmother; tutelary** *or* **tutelar god** *or* **genius** *or*

spirit; **household gods;** penates, lares and penates; ancestral spirits; manes

13 Santa Claus, Santa, Saint Nicholas, Saint Nick, Kriss Kringle, Father Christmas

14 mythology, mythicism; **legend, lore, folklore,** mythical lore; fairy lore, fairyism; mythologist

ADJS **15 mythic, mythical, mythological; fabulous, legendary;** folkloric

16 divine, godlike

17 fairy, fairylike, fay; sylphlike; **elfin,** elfish, elflike; gnomish, gnomelike; pixieish

18 nymphic, nymphal, nymphean, nymphlike

679 ANGEL, SAINT

NOUNS **1 angel,** celestial, celestial *or* heavenly being; messenger of God; **seraph,** seraphim; **cherub, cherubim;** archangel; recording angel; **saint,** beatified soul, canonized mortal; patron saint; martyr; redeemed *or* saved soul

2 heavenly host, host of heaven, choir invisible, angelic host, heavenly hierarchy,

3 <celestial hierarchy of Pseudo-Dionysius> seraphim, cherubim, thrones; dominations or dominions, virtues, powers; principalities, archangels, angels

4 Azrael, angel of death, death's bright angel; Abdiel, Chamuel, Gabriel, Jophiel, Michael, Raphael, Uriel, Zadkiel

5 the Madonna; the Immaculate Conception; Mariology; Mariolatry

ADJS **6 angelic, seraphic, cherubic; heavenly, celestial; saintly, sainted,** beatified, canonized; martyred; saved, redeemed, glorified

680 EVIL SPIRITS

NOUNS **1 evil spirits, demons, demonkind,** powers of darkness, host of hell, denizens of hell, inhabitants of Pandemonium, souls in hell, damned spirits, lost souls

2 devil, diable <Fr>, diablo <Sp>

3 Satan, Satanas

4 Beelzebub, Belial, Eblis, Azazel

5 <gods of evil> Set, Typhon, Loki; Nemesis

6 demon, fiend, devil, Satan, dybbuk, bad or evil or unclean spirit; hellion <nonformal>, hellhound, she-devil; cacodemon, incubus, succubus; jinni, genie, genius; evil genius; ghoul, Lilith, Baba Yaga, vampire, the undead

7 imp, pixie, sprite, elf, puck, poltergeist, gremlin, bad fairy; little or young devil; erlking

8 goblin, hobgoblin, hob, ouphe

9 bugbear, bugaboo, bogey; booger, bugger, booger-man, bogeyman, boogeyman; bête noire

10 Fury, avenging spirit; the Furies, the Eumenides

11 changeling, elf child; shapeshifter

12 werefolk, were-animals; werewolf, lycanthrope

13 devilishness, fiendishness; horns, the cloven hoof, the Devil's pitchfork

14 Satanism, diabolism, devilworship, demonism, devilry, diablerie, demonry; demonianism; black magic; Black Mass; sorcery 690; demonolatry, demon or devil worship; demonology, demonography; devil lore

15 Satanist, Satan-worshiper, diabolist, devil-worshiper, demonist; demoniast; demonologist; demonolater, demon worshiper; sorcerer 690.5

VERBS 16 demonize, devilize, diabolize; possess, obsess; bewitch, bedevil

ADJS 17 demoniac or demoniacal, demonic, demonish; devilish, devil-like; satanic, diabolic, diabolical; hellish 682.8; fiendish, fiendlike; ghoulish; foul, unclean, damned; inhuman

18 impish, puckish, elfish, elvish; mischievous 322.6

681 HEAVEN
<abode of the deity and blessed dead>

NOUNS 1 better world, eternity, glory, Paradise

2 the hereafter, the afterworld, the afterlife 838.2, life after death

3 Holy City, Zion, New Jerusalem, Heavenly or Celestial City, City Celestial, Heavenly City of God, City of God

4 heaven of heavens, seventh heaven, the empyrean, throne of God, God's throne, celestial throne, the great white throne

5 <Christian Science> bliss, harmony, spirituality, the reign of Spirit, the atmosphere of Soul

6 <Mormon> celestial kingdom, terrestrial kingdom, telestial kingdom

7 <Muslim> Alfardaws, Assama; Falak al aflak

8 <Hindu, Buddhist, and Theosophical> nirvana; Buddhafield; devaloka, land of the gods; kamavachara, kamaloka; devachan; samadhi

9 <mythological> Olympus, Mount Olympus; Elysium, Elysian fields; fields of Aalu; Islands or Isles of the Blessed, Happy Isles, Fortunate Isles or Islands; Avalon; garden of the Gods, garden of the Hesperides, Bower of Bliss; Tir-na-n'Og, Annwfn

10 <Norse> Valhalla, Asgard, Fensalir, Glathsheim, Vingolf, Valaskjalf, Hlithskjalf, Thruthvang or Thruthheim, Bilskirnir, Ydalir, Sökkvabekk, Breithablik, Folkvang, Sessrymnir, Noatun, Thrymheim, Glitnir, Himinbjorg, Vithi

11 <removal to heaven> apotheosis, resurrection, translation, gathering, ascension, the Ascension; assumption, the Assumption; removal to Abraham's bosom

ADJS 12 heavenly, heavenish; paradisal, paradisaic, paradisaical, paradisiac, paradisiacal, paradisic, paradisical; celestial, supernal, ethereal; **unearthly,** unworldly; **otherworldly,** extraterrestrial, extramundane, transmundane, transcendental; Elysian, Olympian; blessed, beatified, beatific *or* beatifical, glorified, in glory; from on high

ADVS 13 **celestially,** paradisally, supernally, ethereally; in heaven, in Abraham's bosom, *in sinu Abraham* <L>, on high, among the blest, in glory

682 HELL

NOUNS 1 hell, Hades, perdition, Pandemonium, **inferno,** the pit, **the bottomless pit,** the abyss, **nether world,** lower world, underworld, infernal regions, abode *or* world of the dead, abode of the damned, place of torment, the grave, shades below; **purgatory; limbo**

2 **hellfire,** fire and brimstone, lake of fire and brimstone, everlasting fire *or* torment

3 <mythological> Hades, Orcus, Tartarus, Avernus, Acheron

4 <rivers of Hades> Styx, Stygian creek; Acheron, River of Woe; Cocytus, River of Wailing

5 <deities of the nether world> Pluto, Orcus, Hades *or* Aides *or* Aidoneus, Dis *or* Dis pater, Charon

VERBS 6 **damn,** doom, send *or* consign to hell, cast into hell, doom to perdition, condemn to hell *or* eternal punishment

7 go to hell *or* to the devil, be damned, go the other way *or* to the other place <nonformal>

ADJS 8 **hellish, infernal,** sulfurous, brimstone, fire-and-brimstone; chthonic, chthonian; pandemonic, pandemoniac; devilish; purgatorial, hellborn

ADVS 9 **hellishly, infernally,** in hell, in hellfire, below, in torment

683 SCRIPTURE

NOUNS 1 **scripture, scriptures, sacred writings** *or* **texts, bible;** canonical writings *or* books

2 **Bible, Holy Bible, Scripture, the Scriptures, Holy Scripture,** Holy Writ, the Book, the Good Book, the Book of Books, the Word, the Word of God; Vulgate, Septuagint, Douay Bible, Authorized *or* King James Version, Revised Version, American Revised Version; Revised Standard Version; Jerusalem Bible; Testament; canon

3 **Old Testament,** Tenach; Hexateuch, Octateuch; Pentateuch, Chumash, Five Books of Moses, **Torah,** the Law, the Jewish *or* Mosaic Law, Law of Moses; the Prophets, Nebiim, Major *or* Minor Prophets; the Writings, Hagiographa, Ketubim; Apocrypha, noncanonical writings

4 **New Testament; Gospels,** Evangels, the Gospel, Good News, Good *or* Glad Tidings; Synoptic Gospels, Epistles, Pauline Epistles, Catholic Epistles, Johannine Epistles; Acts, Acts of the Apostles; Apocalypse, Revelation

5 **Talmud,** Mishnah, Gemara; Masorah

6 **Koran,** Alkoran *or* Alcoran; Avesta, **Zend-Avesta;** Granth, Adigranth; Tripitaka, agama; Tao Tĕ Ching; Analects of Confucius; the Eddas; Arcana Caelestia; **Book of Mormon;** Science and Health with Key to the Scriptures

7 <Hindu> **the Vedas, Veda,** Rig-Veda, Yajur-Veda, Sama-Veda, Atharva-Veda, sruti; Brahmana, Upanishad, Aranyaka; Samhita; shastra, Smriti, Purana, Tantra, Agama; Bhagavad-Gita

8 <Buddhist> Vinaya Pitaka, Sutta Pitaka, Abhidamma Pitaka; Dhammapada, Jataka; The Diamond-Cutter, The Lotus of the True Law, Prajna-Paramita Sutra, Pure Land Sutras

9 **revelation, divine revelation; inspiration;** afflatus, divine inspiration; theophany, epiphany; **mysticism,** direct *or* immediate intuition *or* communication, mystical experience, mystical intuition, contemplation, ecstasy;

prophecy, prophetic revelation, apocalypse

ADJS **10 scriptural, Biblical,** Old-Testament, New-Testament, Gospel, Mosaic, Yahwist, Elohist; **revealed, revelational;** prophetic, apocalyptic; **inspired;** evangelic, evangelical; gospel; apostolic, apostolical; textual; canonical

11 Talmudic, Mishnaic, Gemaric, Masoretic; rabbinic

12 epiphanic, mystic, mystical

13 Koranic; Avestan; Eddic; Mormon

14 Vedic; tantrist

684 PROPHETS, RELIGIOUS FOUNDERS

NOUNS **1 prophet** 961.4; Old Testament prophets

2 <Christian founders> **evangelist, apostle, disciple,** saint; Matthew, Mark, Luke, John; Paul; Peter; **the Fathers, fathers of the church**

3 Martin Luther, John Calvin, John Wycliffe, Jan Hus, John Wesley, John Knox, George Fox <Protestant reformers>; Emanuel Swedenborg <Church of the New Jerusalem>; Mary Baker Eddy <Christian Science>; Joseph Smith <Church of Jesus Christ of Latter-day Saints>

4 Buddha, Gautama Buddha <Buddhism>; Mahavira or Vardhamana or Jina <Jainism>; Muhammad or Mohammed <Islam>; Confucius <Confucianism>; Lao-tzu <Taoism>; Zoroaster or Zarathustra <Zoroastrianism>; Nanak <Sikhism>

685 SANCTITY
<sacred quality>

NOUNS **1 sanctity,** sanctitude; **sacredness, holiness,** hallowedness, numinousness; sacrosanctness; heavenliness, transcendence, divinity, divineness 677.1; venerableness, **venerability, blessedness;** awesomeness; **inviolability;** ineffability, unutter-

ability, inenarrableness; godliness 692.2

2 the sacred, the holy, the holy of holies, the numinous, the ineffable, the unutterable, the unspeakable, the transcendent

3 sanctification, hallowing; purification; beatitude; blessing; **glorification,** exaltation; **consecration,** devotion, setting apart; sainting, canonization; enshrinement; **sainthood, beatification; blessedness; grace,** state of grace; justification, justification by faith, justification by works

4 redemption, salvation, conversion, regeneration, reformation, adoption; **rebirth, new birth, second birth;** circumcision, spiritual cleansing

VERBS **5 sanctify, hallow; purify,** wash one's sins away; **bless,** beatify; **glorify,** exalt; **consecrate,** dedicate, set apart; **beatify, saint, canonize;** enshrine

6 redeem, regenerate, reform, convert, save

ADJS **7 sacred, holy,** numinous, **sacrosanct, religious, spiritual,** heavenly, divine; **venerable,** awful; inviolable, **inviolate; ineffable,** unutterable

8 sanctified, hallowed; blessed, consecrated, devoted, dedicated, set apart; **glorified, exalted; saintly,** sainted, beatified, canonized

9 redeemed, saved, converted, reborn, born-again; circumcised, spiritually purified or cleansed

686 UNSANCTITY

NOUNS **1 unsanctity,** unsanctitude; **unsacredness, unholiness,** unhallowedness; profaneness; unregenerateness, reprobation; **worldliness,** secularity, secularism

2 the profane, the unholy; the temporal, the secular, **the worldly,** the fleshly, the mundane

ADJS **3 unsacred, unholy,** unhallowed, unsanctified, unblessed; profane, **secular, temporal, worldly,** fleshly, mundane;

unsaved, unredeemed, unregenerate, reprobate

687 ORTHODOXY

NOUNS **1 orthodoxy; soundness,** soundness of doctrine, right belief *or* doctrine; **authoritativeness,** authenticity, canonicity; traditionalism; the truth, religious truth, gospel truth

2 the faith, true faith, apostolic faith, primitive faith; old-time religion, faith of our fathers

3 the Church, the true church; apostolic church; universal church; church militant, church triumphant

4 true believer, orthodox Christian; Sunni Muslim; Orthodox Jew; textualist, textuary; canonist; fundamentalist; the orthodox

5 strictness, strict interpretation, scripturalism, evangelicalism; hyperorthodoxy, puritanism, puritanicalness, purism; staunchness; straitlacedness, stiff-neckedness, hideboundness; hard line <nonformal>; **bigotry** 979.1; **dogmatism** 969.6; **fundamentalism,** literalism, precisianism; bibliolatry

6 bigot 979.5; **dogmatist** 969.7

ADJS **7 orthodox;** of the true faith, **sound,** firm, faithful, true, true-blue, right-thinking; **evangelical; scriptural,** canonical; traditional; literal, textual; **authoritative,** authentic, accepted, received, approved; correct, right, proper

8 strict, evangelical; puritanical, purist *or* puristic, straitlaced; staunch; hidebound, hardline <nonformal>; **bigoted** 979.10; **dogmatic** 969.22; **fundamentalist,** precisianist *or* precisianistic, literalist *or* literalistic

688 UNORTHODOXY

NOUNS **1 unorthodoxy, heterodoxy; unsoundness; unauthoritativeness,** unauthenticity, uncanonicity; **nonconformity** 867

2 heresy, false doctrine, **misbelief; fallacy, error** 974

3 infidelity; atheism, unbelief 695.5

4 paganism, heathenism; pagandom, heathendom; allotheism; animism; idolatry 697

5 heretic, misbeliever; heresiarch; nonconformist 867.3; antinomian

6 gentile; non-Christian; **non-Jew,** goy; non-Muslim, non-Muhammadan, kaffir; non-Mormon; infidel; unbeliever 695.11

7 pagan, heathen; allotheist; animist; idolater 697.4

VERBS **8 misbelieve, err,** stray, deviate, wander, go astray, stray from the path, go wrong, fall into error; serve Mammon

ADJS **9 unorthodox, heterodox, heretical; unsound; unscriptural,** uncanonical, apocryphal; **unauthoritative,** unauthentic, unaccepted, unreceived, unapproved; **fallacious,** erroneous 974.16; antinomian

10 infidel; atheistic, unbelieving 695.19; **unchristian;** gentile, uncircumcised; non-Muslim, non-Islamic; non-Mormon

11 pagan, paganish, paganistic; **heathen, heathenish;** allotheistic; animist; idolatrous 697.7

689 OCCULTISM

NOUNS **1 occultism, esoterics,** esoterism; cabalism, cabala *or* kabala; yoga; **theosophy,** anthroposophy; anagogics; anagoge; mystery; mystification, hocus-pocus, mumbo jumbo; mysticism 683.9

2 supernaturalism, preternaturalism, **transcendentalism; the supernatural**

3 metaphysics, hyperphysics, transphysical science

4 psychics; parapsychology, psychical research; metapsychics, metapsychism

5 spiritualism, spiritism; mediumism; necromancy; séance, sitting; spirit 987.1

6 psychic *or* psychical phenomena, spirit manifestation; mate-

rialization; poltergeistism, poltergeist; telekinesis, psychokinesis,
telesthesia, teleportation; levitation; automatism, psychography,
automatic *or* trance *or* spirit writing

7 **ectoplasm**; aura, emanation, effluvium

8 **extrasensory perception** *or*
ESP; **clairvoyance,** second sight,
sixth sense; intuition 933; foresight 960; premonition 133.1;
clairaudience, crystal vision,
metapsychosis

9 **telepathy, mental telepathy,
mind reading,** thought transference, telepathic transmission

10 **divination** 961.2; **sorcery** 690

11 **occultist,** mystic, mystagogue,
cabalist, supernaturalist, tran-
scendentalist; adept, mahatma;
yogi; theosophist, anthroposoph-
ist

12 **parapsychologist; metapsy-
chist; metaphysician,** meta-
physicist

13 **psychic; spiritualist, medium,**
ecstatic, automatist, psycho-
graphist; necromancer

14 **clairvoyant;** clairaudient; psy-
chometer

15 **telepathist, mental telepathist, mind reader**

16 **diviner** 961.4; **sorcerer** 690.5

17 astral body, astral, linga sharira,
design body, subtle body

18 <seven principles of man, the-
osophy> spirit, atman; mind,
manas; soul, buddhi; life principle, vital force, prana; astral body,
linga sharira; physical *or* dense *or*
gross body, sthula sharira; principle of desire, kama

19 **spiritualization,** etherealization; **dematerialization,** imma-
terialization, unsubstantialization;
disembodiment

VERBS 20 **spiritualize;** etherealize;
dematerialize, immaterialize;
disembody

21 hold a séance *or* sitting; call up
spirits 690.11

22 **telepathize, read one's mind**

ADJS 23 **occult, esoteric, esoteri-
cal, mysterious,** mystic, mysti-

cal, anagogical; metaphysical;
cabalistic; **paranormal, supernatural** 869.15; theosophical, an-
throposophical

24 **psychic, psychical, spiritual;
spiritualistic; clairvoyant,**
second-sighted, **telepathic; extrasensory;** telekinetic, psycho-
kinetic; automatist

690 SORCERY

NOUNS 1 **sorcery, necromancy,
magic,** sortilege, **wizardry,**
theurgy, rune, glamour; **witch-
craft,** spellbinding, spellcasting;
witchery, enchantment; **voodooism, voodoo,** juju, jujuism, obeah, obeahism; shamanism; fetishism; vampirism; thauma-
turgy; alchemy; **divination** 961.2;
spell, charm 691

2 **black magic,** the black art; **diabolism, demonism,** Satanism

3 <practices> magic circle; ghost
dance; witches' meeting *or* Sabbath; ordeal by battle *or* fire *or*
water *or* lots

4 **conjuration,** evocation, invocation; **exorcism;** exsufflation; **incantation** 691.4

5 **sorcerer, necromancer, wizard,** theurgist; warlock, male
witch; thaumaturge, thaumatur-
gist; alchemist; **conjurer; diviner**
961.4; dowser, water witch *or* diviner; diabolist

6 **magician,** mage, magus,
magian; Merlin; prestidigitator,
illusionist 357.2

7 **shaman,** shamanist; **voodoo,
witch doctor,** obeah doctor,
medicine man; witch-hunter,
witch-finder; exorcist, exorciser

8 **sorceress,** shamaness; **witch,**
witchwoman <nonformal>, **hex,
hag,** lamia; coven, witches' coven

9 **bewitcher, enchanter,
charmer, spellbinder; enchantress, siren,** vampire

VERBS 10 sorcerize, shamanize;
make *or* work magic, wave a
wand, rub the ring *or* lamp

11 **conjure, conjure up,** evoke, invoke, raise, summon, call up; **call
up spirits,** conjure *or* conjure up

spirits, summon spirits, raise ghosts, evoke from the dead

12 exorcise, lay; lay ghosts, **cast out devils;** unspell

13 cast a spell, bewitch 691.9

ADJS **14** sorcerous, necromantic, **magic, magical,** numinous, thaumaturgic, thaumaturgical, miraculous, wizardlike, wizardly; alchemical, alchemistic; shaman, shamanic, shamanistic; witchlike; voodoo; incantatory, incantational; talismanic

691 SPELL, CHARM

NOUNS **1 spell,** magic spell, **charm,** glamour; hand of glory; evil eye, whammy <nonformal>; **hex, jinx, curse;** exorcism

2 bewitchment, witchery, bewitchery; enchantment, entrancement, fascination, captivation; illusion, maya; bedevilment; **possession, obsession**

3 trance, ecstasy, mystic transport; meditation, contemplation; **rapture;** yoga trance; hypnosis 22.7

4 incantation, conjuration, magic words; hocus-pocus, abracadabra, mumbo jumbo; open sesame

5 charm, amulet, talisman, fetish, phylactery; **voodoo,** juju, obeah, mumbo jumbo; **goodluck charm, lucky piece,** rabbit's-foot, four-leaf clover; love charm, philter; scarab; veronica, sudarium; swastika, fylfot

6 wish-bringer; wand, magic wand; Aladdin's lamp, magic ring, magic carpet, seven-league boots; wishing well, wishing stone; **wishbone,** wishing bone

VERBS **7 cast a spell, spellbind; entrance,** put in a trance; **hypnotize, mesmerize**

8 charm, enchant, fascinate, captivate, glamour

9 bewitch, witch, **hex, jinx;** voodoo; **possess, obsess;** bedevil, demonize, hagride; cast the evil eye

10 put a curse on, put a hex on, put a juju on, put obeah on, give the evil eye

ADJS **11 bewitching, witching;** illusory, illusive, illusionary; **charming, enchanting, entrancing, spellbinding, fascinating,** glamorous

12 enchanted, charmed; spellbound; fascinated, captivated; **hypnotized, mesmerized;** under a spell, in a trance

13 bewitched, witched; hagridden; **possessed,** taken over, obsessed

692 PIETY

NOUNS **1 piety, piousness,** pietism; **religion, faith; religiousness, religiosity,** religiousmindedness; theism; love of God, adoration; **devoutness,** devotion, devotedness, worship 696, worshipfulness, cultism; faithfulness, dutifulness, observance, churchgoing, conformity 866; **reverence,** veneration; discipleship

2 godliness, godlikeness; **sanctity,** sanctitude; odor of sanctity; **righteousness, holiness,** goodness; **spirituality,** spiritualmindedness; **purity,** pureness, pureness of heart; **saintliness;** saintship, sainthood; heavenliness; **unworldliness,** otherworldliness

3 zeal, zealousness, zealotry; **evangelism, revival,** evangelicalism, revivalism; pentecostalism, charismatic movement; charismatic gift, gift of tongues, glossolalia; **overreligiousness, religiosity,** overpiousness, overrighteousness, **overzealousness;** fundamentalism, militance, **fanaticism** 925.11; **sanctimony** 693

4 believer, receiver; God-fearing man, pietist, religionist, saint, theist; **devotee,** devotionalist, votary; **zealot,** fundamentalist, militant; **churchgoer;** pillar of the church; communicant; **convert,** proselyte, neophyte, catechumen; **disciple,** follower, servant, faithful servant; **fanatic**

5 the believing, the faithful, the righteous, the good; the elect, the chosen, the saved; the children of God, the children of light; Christendom, the Church 687.3

VERBS **6 be pious, be religious; have faith,** trust in God, love God, fear God; witness, bear witness, affirm, **believe** 952.10; keep the faith, let one's light shine, walk humbly with one's God; be observant

7 be converted, get religion <nonformal>, receive or accept Christ, stand up for Jesus; be born again, see the light

ADJS **8 pious,** pietistic; **religious,** religious-minded; **devout,** devoted, worshipful, prayerful, cultish, cultist; **reverent,** reverential, venerational, adoring, solemn; faithful, dutiful; affirming, witnessing, believing 952.21; **observant, practicing**

9 godly, godlike; God-fearing; righteous, holy, good; **spiritual,** spiritual-minded; **pure,** pure-hearted, pure in heart; **saintly,** saintlike; **angelic, angelical;** heavenly; **unworldly,** unearthly, otherwordly, not of this world

10 regenerate, regenerated, **converted, redeemed, saved,** reborn, **born-again;** sanctified 685.8

11 zealous; overreligious, overpious, overrighteous, **overzealous; fanatical** 925.32; sanctimonious 693.5

693 SANCTIMONY

NOUNS **1 sanctimony, sanctimoniousness; pietism,** piety, **piousness,** false piety; religiosity; **self-righteousness;** pharisaicalness; **falseness, insincerity, hypocrisy** 354.6; affectation 500; **cant,** mummery; unctuousness, oiliness, mealymouthedness

2 lip service, mouth honor, mouthing; formalism, solemn mockery

3 pietist, religionist, **hypocrite,** religious hypocrite, canting hypocrite, pious fraud, whited sepulcher, **pharisee;** bleeding heart <nonformal>; **canter,** ranter, snuffler, sniveler; dissembler, dissimulator; affecter; poser 500.8; **lip server,** lip worshiper, formalist; Pharisee, scribes and Pharisees; Pecksniff

VERBS **4 be sanctimonious, be hypocritical;** cant, snuffle, snivel; render or pay lip service

ADJS **5 sanctimonious,** sanctified, **pious, pietistic, pietistical,** self-righteous, pharisaical, **holier-than-thou; false, insincere, hypocritical** 354.32; affected 500.15; canting, sniveling, unctuous, mealymouthed

694 IMPIETY

NOUNS **1 impiety, impiousness; irreverence,** undutifulness; apostasy, recreancy; backsliding, recidivism, lapse, fall or lapse from grace; **atheism, irreligion; unsanctity** 686

2 sacrilege, blasphemy, blaspheming, impiety; **profanity,** profaneness; sacrilegiousness, blasphemousness; **desecration, profanation**

3 sacrilegist, blasphemer; apostate, recreant; backslider, recidivist; **atheist**

VERBS **4 desecrate, profane,** dishonor, unhallow, commit sacrilege

5 blaspheme; vilify, abuse 513.7; curse, swear 513.6; take in vain; taint, pollute, contaminate

ADJS **6 impious, irreverent,** undutiful; **profane; sacrilegious, blasphemous;** recreant, backsliding, recidivist or recidivistic, lapsed, fallen, lapsed or fallen from grace; atheistic, **irreligious** 695.17; **unsacred** 686.3

695 NONRELIGIOUSNESS

NOUNS **1 nonreligiousness, unreligiousness; undevoutness;** lukewarm piety; indifference 102; **laicism,** unconsecration; **deconsecration, secularization,** laicization

2 secularism, worldliness, earthliness, earthiness, mundaneness; **unspirituality,** carnality; materialism, Philistinism

3 **ungodliness,** godlessness, **unrighteousness, irreligion, unholiness;** impiety 694; **wickedness, sinfulness** 654.4

4 **unregeneracy, reprobacy,** gracelessness

5 **unbelief, disbelief** 954.1; infidelity, infidelism, faithlessness; **atheism;** nullifidianism

6 **agnosticism; skepticism, doubt, incredulity;** scoffing 508.1

7 **freethinking, latitudinarianism; humanism**

8 antireligion, antichristianity

9 **iconoclasm,** iconoclasticism, image breaking

10 **irreligionist; worldling,** earthling; **materialist;** iconoclast, idoloclast; anti-Christian, antichrist

11 **unbeliever, disbeliever,** nonbeliever; **atheist, infidel, pagan, heathen;** nullifidian; **gentile** 688.6

12 **agnostic; skeptic, doubter, doubting Thomas,** scoffer

13 **freethinker, latitudinarian;** humanist

VERBS 14 **disbelieve,** doubt 954.6; scoff 508.9; **laicize,** deconsecrate, **secularize,** desacralize

ADJS 15 **nonreligious, unreligious,** having no religious preference; **undevout,** undutiful, nonobservant, nonpracticing; lukewarm, indifferent 102.6; unconsecrated, **deconsecrated, secularized**

16 **secularist, secularistic,** worldly, **earthly,** earthy, **mundane,** temporal; **unspiritual, profane,** carnal, **secular;** humanistic; **materialistic,** material, Philistine

17 **ungodly,** godless, **irreligious, unrighteous, unholy;** impious 694.6; **wicked, sinful** 654.16

18 **unregenerate, unconverted,** godless, reprobate, **lost, damned;** lapsed, fallen

19 **unbelieving, disbelieving, faithless; infidel; pagan, hea-**

then; atheistic, atheist; nullifidian

20 **agnostic; skeptic, skeptical, doubtful, dubious, incredulous**

21 **freethinking, latitudinarian**

22 **antireligious;** antiscriptural; **iconoclastic**

696 WORSHIP

NOUNS 1 **worship,** worshiping, **adoration, devotion, homage, veneration, reverence;** cult, cultism; prostration; idolatry 697

2 **glorification,** glory, **praise,** laudation, laud, exaltation, magnification

3 **paean,** laud; hosanna, hallelujah, alleluia; **hymn,** hymn of praise, **doxology, psalm, anthem,** canticle; **chant,** versicle; mantra; response, responsory, report, answer; antiphon, antiphony; offertory, hymnody, hymnology, psalmody

4 **prayer, supplication, invocation,** impetration, entreaty, petition, suit, orison, obsecration, obtestation, rogation, **devotions;** silent prayer, meditation, contemplation, communion; intercession; **grace, thanks, thanksgiving;** litany; breviary, canonical prayers; collect; chaplet; rosary, beads, beadroll; prayer wheel *or* machine

5 **benediction, blessing,** benison; laying on of hands

6 **propitiation,** appeasement 465.1; atonement 658

7 **oblation, offering, sacrifice, immolation,** incense; libation; votive offering; human sacrifice, hecatomb; self-sacrifice, self-immolation; sutteeism; scapegoat, suttee; offertory, collection

8 **divine service,** service, public worship, liturgy 701.3

9 **worshiper,** adorer, venerator, votary, communicant, celebrant; churchgoer; suppliant, supplicant, supplicator, petitioner; revivalist, evangelist; congregation; **idolater** 697.4

VERBS 10 **worship, adore, reverence, venerate, revere,** honor, pay homage to, lift up the heart, bow down and worship, humble oneself before; **idolize** 697.5

11 **glorify, praise, laud, exalt, extol,** magnify, bless, celebrate; praise God, praise *or* glorify the Lord; sing praises, sing the praises of, sound *or* resound the praises of

12 **pray, supplicate,** invoke, petition, make supplication, *daven* <Yiddish>; **implore, beseech** 440.11; offer a prayer, commune with God; **say one's prayers;** tell one's beads, recite the rosary; **say grace, give** *or* **return thanks**

13 **bless, give one's blessing,** give benediction, confer a blessing upon; cross, make the sign of the cross over *or* upon; lay hands on

14 **propitiate,** make propitiation; appease 465.7; **offer sacrifice,** sacrifice, make sacrifice to

ADJS 15 **worshipful,** worshiping; **adoring,** adorant; **devout,** devotional; **reverent,** reverential; **venerative;** at the feet of; **prayerful, supplicatory,** supplicant, suppliant, precatory, precative, imploring, on bended knee; prostrate before; blessing, benedictory, benedictional; propitiatory

697 IDOLATRY

NOUNS 1 **idolatry,** idolism, **idol worship;** heathenism, paganism; image worship, iconolatry; **fetishism; demonism,** demon *or* devil worship, Satanism; hero worship; idolomancy

2 **idolization,** fetishization; **deification,** apotheosis

3 **idol; fetish,** totem, joss; **graven image, golden calf;** sacred cow

4 **idolater,** idolatress, idolizer, idolist, idol worshiper, image-worshiper; fetishist, totemist; demon *or* devil worshiper, demonolater

VERBS 5 **idolatrize,** idolize, idol; fetishize, fetish; **make an idol of,** deify, apotheosize

6 **worship idols,** worship the golden calf

ADJS 7 **idolatrous, idol worship-**ing; idolistic, fetishistic, totemistic; heathen, pagan

698 THE MINISTRY

NOUNS 1 **the ministry, pastorate,** pastoral care, **the Church,** the cloth, the pulpit; **priesthood,** priestship; apostleship; call, vocation, sacred calling; holy orders; rabbinate

2 ecclesiasticalism, ecclesiology, priestcraft

3 **clericalism,** sacerdotalism; priesthood; episcopalianism

4 **monasticism, monkhood;** celibacy 565

5 ecclesiastical office, church office, dignity

6 **papacy, pontificate,** the Vatican, Apostolic See, See of Rome, the Church

7 hierarchy, hierocracy; theocracy

8 **diocese, see,** archdiocese, bishopric, archbishopric; province; synod, conference; **parish**

9 **benefice,** living, **incumbency;** curacy, cure *or* care of souls; prelacy, vicarage

10 **holy orders, orders** 699.4; calling, election, nomination, appointment, preferment, induction, institution, installation, investiture; conferment, presentation; **ordination,** ordainment, consecration, canonization

VERBS 11 **be ordained, take holy orders,** take orders, take vows; **take the veil,** wear the cloth

12 **ordain,** frock, **canonize, consecrate**

ADJS 13 **ecclesiastic, ecclesiastical, churchly; ministerial, clerical,** sacerdotal, **pastoral; priestly;** episcopal, episcopalian; archiepiscopal; primatal, primatical; canonical; capitular, capitulary; **evangelistic;** rabbinic, rabbinical; priest-ridden

14 **monastic, monasterial, monkish;** conventual

15 **papal, pontific, pontifical,** apostolic; **popish** *or* papist *or* papish <all nonformal>

16 **hierarchical,** hierarchal; theocratic

17 ordained; in orders, in holy orders, of the cloth

699 THE CLERGY

NOUNS **1 clergy, ministry,** the cloth; clerical order, clericals; **priesthood;** presbytery; prelacy; rabbinate

2 clergyman, clergywoman, man *or* woman of the cloth, **divine, ecclesiastic, churchman, cleric,** clerical; clerk, clerk in holy orders; **minister, minister of the Gospel, parson, pastor, rector,** curate, man *or* woman of God, reverend <nonformal>; **chaplain;** military chaplain, padre <nonformal>

3 preacher, sermoner, sermonizer, sermonist, homilist; preaching friar; televison *or* TV preacher, telepreacher <nonformal>

4 holy orders, priest *or* presbyter, deacon *or* diaconus; acolyte *or* acolytus, exorcist, reader *or* lector; ordinand, candidate for holy orders

5 priest, father, padre, cassock, presbyter; curé, parish priest; confessor, father confessor, spiritual father, holy father; penitentiary

6 evangelist, revivalist, evangel; **missionary,** missioner; television *or* TV evangelist, televangelist <nonformal>

7 benefice-holder, beneficiary, **incumbent;** resident, residentiary

8 church dignitary, ecclesiarch, ecclesiast, hierarch

9 <Mormon> deacon, teacher, priest, elder

10 <Jewish> rabbi, rabbin; chief rabbi

11 <Muslim> imam, qadi, sheikh, mullah

12 <Hindu> Brahman, pujari, purohit, pundit, guru

13 <Buddhist> bonze, bhikku, poonghie

14 <pagan> Druid, Druidess; flamen

15 religious; monk, monastic; brother, lay brother; cenobite, conventual; **mendicant, friar;**

pilgrim, palmer; stylite, pillar saint; beadsman; prior; abbot; hermit 584.5; ascetic 667.2; celibate 565.2

16 religious orders

17 nun, sister, clergywoman, conventual; abbess, prioress; **mother superior,** the reverend mother, holy mother; canoness; novice, postulant

700 THE LAITY

NOUNS **1 the laity, lay persons,** laymen, laywomen, nonclerics, seculars; brothers, sisters, brethren, sistren <nonformal>; people; flock, fold, sheep; **congregation,** parishioners, churchgoers, assembly; *minyan* <Heb>; **parish,** society; class

2 layman, laic, secular, churchman, **parishioner,** church member; brother, sister, lay brother, lay sister; laywoman, churchwoman; catechumen; communicant

ADJS **3 lay,** laic *or* laical; **nonecclesiastical,** nonclerical, nonministerial, nonpastoral, nonordained; **secular,** secularist; secularistic; temporal, popular, civil; congregational

701 RELIGIOUS RITES

NOUNS **1 ritualism,** rituality, **ceremonialism, formalism,** liturgism; **cult,** cultism; sacramentalism, sacramentarianism; ritualization, **solemnization,** solemn observance, **celebration**

2 ritualist, ceremonialist, liturgist, **formalist,** formularist; sacramentalist, sacramentarian

3 rite, ritual, rituality, **liturgy,** holy rite; order of worship; **ceremony, ceremonial; observance,** ritual observance; **formality,** solemnity; **form,** formula, formulary, form of worship *or* usage; prescribed form; service, function, duty, office, practice; **sacrament,** sacramental, mystery; ordinance; institution

4 seven sacraments, mysteries: baptism, confirmation, the Eucharist, penance, extreme unction, holy orders, matrimony

5 **unction,** sacred unction, sacramental anointment, chrism *or* chrisom, chrismation, chrismatory; **extreme unction, last rites,** viaticum

6 **baptism,** baptizement; **christening; immersion,** total immersion; **sprinkling,** aspersion, aspergation; affusion, infusion; baptistery, **font; confirmation,** bar *or* bas mitzvah <both Jewish>

7 **Eucharist, Lord's Supper, Last Supper, Communion,** Holy Communion, **the Sacrament,** the Holy Sacrament; intinction; consubstantiation; transubstantiation; consecrated elements, bread and wine, body and blood of Christ; Host, wafer, loaf, bread, altar bread, consecrated bread

8 **Mass,** Eucharistic rites; **the Liturgy,** the Divine Liturgy; **parts of the Mass**

9 **sacred object** *or* **article; ritualistic manual,** Book of Common Prayer, breviary, canon, haggadah <Jewish>, missal, prayer book, siddur <Jewish>

10 **psalter, psalmbook;** Psalm Book, Book of Common Order; Book of Psalms, the Psalter, the Psaltery

11 **holy day,** holytide; feast, fast; Sabbath; Lord's day; saint's day; ecclesiastical calendar

12 Christian holy days; Jewish holy days

13 <Muslim holy days> Ramadan <MS month>, Bairam, Muharram

VERBS 14 **celebrate, observe, keep, solemnize;** celebrate Mass; communicate, administer Communion; receive the Sacrament, partake of the Lord's Supper; attend Mass

15 **minister, officiate,** do duty, **perform a rite,** perform service *or* divine service; administer a sacrament, administer the Eucharist, etc; anoint, chrism; confirm, impose, lay hands on

16 **baptize, christen;** dip, immerse; sprinkle, asperge

17 **confess,** make confession, receive absolution; **shrive,** hear confession; **absolve,** administer absolution; administer extreme unction

ADJS 18 **ritualistic, ritual; ceremonial, ceremonious; formal,** formulary; **liturgic, liturgical; sacramental;** eucharistic, baptismal; paschal

702 ECCLESIASTICAL ATTIRE

NOUNS 1 **canonicals,** clericals <nonformal>, robes, cloth; **vestments,** vesture; liturgical garments, ceremonial attire; pontificals, pontificalia, episcopal vestments

2 **robe,** frock, mantle, gown, cloak

3 **staff,** pastoral staff, **crosier, cross,** cross-staff, crook, paterissa

ADJS 4 **vestmental,** vestmentary

703 RELIGIOUS BUILDINGS

NOUNS 1 **church,** bethel, **meetinghouse, house of God,** place of worship, house of worship *or* prayer; conventicle; **mission;** basilica; **cathedral;** collegiate church

2 **temple; tabernacle; synagogue,** *shul* <Yiddish>; **mosque,** masjid; pagoda; pantheon

3 **chapel,** side chapel, sacrament chapel, oratory, oratorium; chantry; sacrarium

4 **shrine,** holy place, dagoba, naos; sacrarium, delubrum; tope, stupa; reliquary

5 **sanctuary, holy of holies, sanctum, sanctum sanctorum,** adytum, sacrarium

6 **cloister, monastery, house, abbey,** friary; priory, priorate; lamasery; **convent, nunnery**

7 **parsonage,** pastorate, **church house;** presbytery, **rectory,** vicarage, deanery; chapter house

8 bishop's palace; **Vatican;** Lambeth Palace

9 <church interior> vestry, sacristy, sacrarium, diaconicon *or*

diaconicum; baptistery; apse, chancel, choir, cloisters, confessional, crypt, nave, porch, presbytery, spire *or* steeple, transept; organ loft

10 <church furnishings> piscina; stoup, holy-water stoup *or* basin; baptismal font; reredos; chancel screen; altar cloth, cerecloth, chrismal; communion *or* sacrament cloth, corporal, oblation cloth; baldachin; kneeling stool; *prie-dieu* <Fr>; prayer rug *or* carpet *or* mat

11 <vessels> cruet; chalice; ciborium, pyx; chrismal, chrismatory; monstrance, ostensorium; reliquary; font, holy-water font

12 **altar; Lord's table, Communion table,** chancel table; altar desk, missal stand; credence, prothesis, predella; retable, retablo; altarpiece, altar rail, altar stair; altar facing *or* front, frontal; altar slab, altar stone, mensal

13 **pulpit, rostrum,** ambo; **lectern,** desk, reading desk

14 <seats> **pew; stall;** mourners' bench, anxious bench *or* seat, penitent form; amen corner; sedilia

ADJS 15 **churchly, ecclesiastical;** churchlike, templelike; tabernacular; synagogical, synagogal; pantheonic

16 **claustral, cloistered; monastic, monasterial; coventual,** conventicular

704 SHOW BUSINESS, THEATER

NOUNS 1 **show business,** show biz <nonformal>, the entertainment industry; **the theater, the footlights, the stage, the boards,** the bright lights, Broadway, the Great White Way; avant-garde theater, experimental theater, theater of the absurd, guerrilla theater, street theater; **drama,** legitimate stage *or* theater, off Broadway, off-off-Broadway; musical theater; dinner theater; regional theater; repertory drama *or* theater, stock; summer stock, straw

hat *or* straw hat circuit <nonformal>; **vaudeville,** variety; **burlesque; circus**

2 **dramatics;** dramatization; **theatrics, theatricalism,** theatricality, staginess; theatricals, amateur theatricals; **histrionics;** dramatic *or* histrionic *or* Thespian art; **melodramatics,** sensationalism; **dramaturgy,** dramatic structure, dramatic form; dramatic irony, tragic irony

3 **theatercraft, stagecraft,** scenecraft; **showmanship**

4 **stage show, show; play,** stage play, piece, vehicle, work; **hit** *or* hit show <nonformal>, success; failure, **flop** *and* bomb *and* turkey <all nonformal>

5 **tragedy,** tragic drama; tragic flaw; tragic muse

6 **comedy;** comic relief, comedy relief; comic muse; sock, cap and bells, motley, slapstick

7 **act, scene, number, turn,** bit *and* shtick <both nonformal>, routine <nonformal>; curtain raiser; **prologue,** epilogue; **entr'acte,** intermezzo, intermission, interlude; **finale;** curtain call, curtain; song and dance; burlesque act, striptease; stand-up comedy act; sketch, skit

8 **acting, playing,** playacting, performing, **performance; representation, portrayal, characterization,** projection; **impersonation,** personation, miming, mimicking, mimesis; pantomiming, mummery; ham *and* hamming *or* hamming up <all nonformal>, overacting; stage presence; stage directions, **business,** stage business; stunt *and* gag <both nonformal>; hokum *or* hoke <nonformal>; buffoonery, slapstick; patter; stand-up comedy

9 **repertoire, repertory;** stock

10 **role, part,** piece <nonformal>; cue, **lines,** side; cast; **character,** personage; lead, starring *or* lead *or* leading role, fat part, leading man, leading woman *or* lady, hero, heroine; antihero; title role,

protagonist, principal character; supporting role, supporting character; ingenue, romantic lead; soubrette; villain, heavy <nonformal>, antagonist; bit, bit part, minor role; walk-on; top banana, second banana; **actor** 707.2

11 engagement, booking; **run; stand,** one-night stand or one-nighter; **circuit,** vaudeville circuit, borscht circuit; **tour, bus-and-truck, production tour;** date

12 theatrical performance, **performance, show, presentation, production,** entertainment, stage presentation or performance; bill; **exhibit, exhibition;** benefit performance, benefit; personal appearance, flesh show <nonformal>; showcase, tryout; premiere, premier performance, debut; farewell performance, swan song <nonformal>

13 production, mounting, staging, putting on; stage management; **direction;** blocking; **rehearsal,** dress rehearsal, walk-through, run-through, final dress, run-through or run

14 theater, playhouse, house, odeum; **auditorium; opera house,** opera; **hall,** music hall, concert hall; **amphitheater;** circle theater, arena theater, theater-in-the-round; vaudeville theater; burlesque theater; **little theater,** community theater; outdoor theater; Greek theater; children's theater; Elizabethan theater; showboat; dinner theater

15 auditorium; parquet, orchestra; **orchestra circle,** parquet circle, parterre; **dress circle; box,** box seat, **loge;** proscenium boxes, parterre boxes; balcony, gallery; **peanut gallery** and paradise <both nonformal>

16 stage, the boards; thrust stage, theater-in-the-round; apron; proscenium stage, proscenium arch, proscenium; orchestra, pit, orchestra pit; **bandstand,** shell, band shell; **wings;** dressing room, greenroom; flies; board, light-

board, switchboard; prompter's box; curtain, safety curtain, asbestos curtain, fire curtain; stage door

17 <stage requisites> **property, prop;** costume 5.9; makeup, greasepaint; spirit gum

18 lights, instruments; **footlights,** foots <nonformal>; **limelight,** spotlight or spot <nonformal>, arc light, arc, klieg or kleig light; color filter, medium, gelatin or gel; dimmer

19 setting, stage setting, stage set, set; location, locale

20 scenery, decor; **scene;** screen, **flat;** batten; side scene, **wing;** border; tormentor, **teaser;** transformation, transformation scene; flipper; counterweight; **curtain,** hanging; **drop,** drop scene, drop curtain, scrim, cloth; **backdrop;** tab, tableau curtain

21 playbook, script, text, **libretto;** prompt-book; book; **score; scenario,** continuity, shooting script; lines, actor's lines, cue, sides; stage direction; prompt book

22 dramatist; playwright, dramaturge; play doctor <nonformal>; **scriptwriter, scenario writer,** scenarist, **screenwriter; gagman,** joke writer, jokesmith; **librettist;** tragedian, comedian; farcist, farcer; melodramatist; **choreographer**

23 theater man; showman, exhibitor, **producer, impresario; director,** auteur; stage director, **stage manager;** set designer; costume designer, costumer, wardrobe master or mistress; dresser; makeup man or artist; prompter; callboy; playreader; ringmaster; barker, spieler <nonformal>

24 stage technician, stagehand, sceneshifter; flyman; carpenter; **electrician;** scene painter

25 agent, actor's agent, tenpercenter <nonformal>; **booking agent;** advance agent, advance man; publicity man or agent

26 patron, patroness; **backer, angel** <nonformal>

27 playgoer, theatergoer; spectator 917, audience 48.6; movie-
goer, **motion-picture fan** <non-
formal>; first-nighter; standee;
claqueur <Fr>, hired applauder;
pass holder, deadhead <nonfor-
mal>

VERBS **28 dramatize;** melodrama-
tize; **present, stage, produce,
mount, put on,** put on the stage;
put on a show; try out, preview;
premiere; **open,** open a show; set
the stage; ring up the curtain,
ring down the curtain; **star, feature** <nonformal>, bill, **headline,** give top billing to; succeed,
make *or* be a hit *and* have legs
<all nonformal>; fail, flop *and*
bomb *and* bomb out <all nonfor-
mal>

29 act, perform, play, playact,
tread the boards; appear, **appear
on the stage;** act like a trouper;
register; emotionalize, emote
<nonformal>; pantomime,
mime; patter; sketch; troupe,
barnstorm <nonformal>; steal
the show, upstage, steal the spotlight; **debut,** make one's debut *or*
bow, come out; act as foil, stooge
<nonformal>, be straight man
for; **star,** play the lead, get
top billing, have one's name in
lights

**30 enact, act out; represent, de-
pict, portray;** act *or* play *or*
perform a part *or* role, take a part,
act *or* play the part of; create a
role *or* character; **impersonate,**
personate; play opposite, support

31 overact, overdramatize, chew
up the scenery <nonformal>;
ham *and* ham it up <both non-
formal>; **mug** <nonformal>,
grimace; spout, rant, roar, declaim; milk a scene; **underact,**
throw away <nonformal>

32 rehearse, practice, go through,
walk *or* run through, go over; go
through one's part, read one's
lines; study one's part; be a fast
or slow study

ADJS **33 dramatic, dramaturgic,
dramaturgical; theatric, theat-**
rical, **histrionic, thespian;**
scenic; **stagy; spectacular;
melodramatic;** ham *or* hammy
<nonformal>; overacted, over-
played, milked <nonformal>;
underacted, underplayed, thrown
away; **operatic;** ballet, balletic;
legitimate; stellar, all-star; stage-
struck, starstruck; stageworthy,
actor-proof

34 tragic, heavy; buskined

35 comic, light; tragicomical, **farcical, slapstick;** camp *or* campy
<nonformal>

ADVS **36 on the stage** *or* boards,
before an audience, before the
footlights; **in the limelight** *or*
spotlight; onstage; downstage,
upstage; backstage, off stage,
behind the scenes

705 DANCE

NOUNS **1 dancing,** terpsichore,
dance; the light fantastic; **choreography;** dance drama, choreo-
drama; **hoofing** <nonformal>

2 dance, hop <nonformal>, **shindig** <nonformal>; **ball;** masked
ball, masque, mask, masquerade
ball, masquerade, fancy-dress
ball, cotillion; promenade, **prom**
<nonformal>, formal <nonfor-
mal>; square dance, barn dance;
mixer, stag dance; dinner-dance,
tea dance, *thé dansant* <Fr>

3 dancer, terpsichorean, **hoofer**
<nonformal>, tap dancer, clog
dancer, etc; **ballet dancer;
ballerina,** danseuse; **modern
dancer;** *corps de ballet* <Fr>;
chorus girl, chorine, chorus boy
or man; chorus line; taxi dancer;
topless dancer; burlesque dancer,
strip-teaser, stripper <nonfor-
mal>; choreographer

4 ballroom, dance hall; dance
palace; casino

VERBS **5 dance, trip the light fantastic,** trip, skip, hop, foot, **hoof**
<nonformal>, clog, tap-dance;
shake, shimmy, shuffle; waltz,
one-step, two-step, foxtrot, etc;
choreograph

ADJS **6 dancing, dance, terpsichorean;** balletic; choreographic

706 MOTION PICTURES

NOUNS **1 motion pictures, movies, the movies, the pictures,** moving pictures, films, the film, the cinema, the screen, the big screen, the silver screen, the flicks *and* the flickers <both nonformal>; **motion picture, movie, picture, film,** flick *and* flicker <both nonformal>; picture show, motion-picture show, moving-picture show, photoplay; **sound film,** silent film; cinéma vérité; magic realism; **documentary film** *or* **movie,** docudrama; **feature,** feature film, feature-length film, main attraction; **motion-picture genre** *or* **type**; TV film *or* movie, made-for-television movie *or* film; **short,** short subject; preview, sneak preview; **B-movie,** B-picture, Grade B movie, low-budget picture; **educational film** *or* **movie,** training film, promotional film; **underground film** *or* **movie,** avant-garde film, art film; **cartoon,** animated cartoon, animation; **rated movie** *or* **film,** rating system, rating

2 script, screenplay, shooting script, storyboard, scenario, treatment, original screenplay; **dialogue,** book; **role,** lead, romantic lead, stock character, ingenue, soubrette, cameo, bit, silent bit

3 motion-picture studio, movie studio, film studio, dream factory <nonformal>, lot, back lot, sound stage, location; **set, motion-picture set, film set,** properties *or* props; **film company,** production company; **producer,** filmmaker, moviemaker; **director,** screenwriter *or* scriptwriter *or* scenarist, editor *or* film editor, **actor, actress, film actor, film actress,** player, star, starlet, character actor, featured player, supporting actor *or* actress, supporting player, bit player, extra; **crew,** film crew

4 motion-picture photography, photography, cinematography, camera angle, camera position, **shot, take,** footage, retake; screen test; **special effects,** rear-screen projection, mechanical effects, optical effects; **color photography,** black-and-white, color, colorization; **cameraman** *or* **camerawoman, motion-picture cameraman** *or* **camerawoman,** cinematographer

5 motion-picture editing, editing, cutting; **transition,** fade, fade-out/fade-in, dissolve

6 motion-picture theater, movie theater, cinema <Brit>, movie palace, dream palace <nonformal>, drive-in theater *or* movie; **screen,** movie screen, motion-picture screen, silver screen

VERBS **7 film, shoot,** cinematize; colorize

ADJS **8 motion-picture, movie, film,** cinema, cinematic; colorized; animated

707 ENTERTAINER

NOUNS **1 entertainer,** performer; artist, artiste; impersonator, female impersonator; **vaudevillian;** dancer 705.3, hoofer <nonformal>; song and dance man; chorus girl, show girl, chorine <nonformal>; chorus boy *or* man; burlesque queen <nonformal>; **stripteaser,** exotic dancer, ecdysiast; stripper <nonformal>; belly dancer; go-go dancer; geisha, geisha girl; **magician,** conjurer, prestidigitator, sleight-of-hand artist; mummer; singer, musician 710; performance artist

2 actor, actress, player, stage player *or* performer, playactor, thespian, trouper; child actor; mummer; pantomime, pantomimist; monologist, diseur, diseuse, reciter; mime, mimer, mimic; strolling player; barnstormer <nonformal>; character actor *or* actress, character; **villain,** antagonist, **bad guy** *or* **heavy** <both nonformal>; juvenile, ingenue; soubrette; foil, stooge <nonformal>, straight man; matinee idol <nonformal>; romantic lead

3 circus artist *or* performer; trapeze artist, aerialist; high-wire artist, tightrope walker, equilibrist; acrobat, tumbler; bareback rider; juggler; lion tamer, sword swallower; snake charmer; clown; ringmaster

4 **motion-picture actor,** movie actor; **movie star,** film star; starlet

5 **ham** *or* ham actor <both nonformal>

6 **lead,** leading man *or* lady, principal, **star,** superstar, headliner; headline *or* feature attraction; costar; **hero, heroine,** protagonist; juvenile lead; **prima donna,** diva, singer 710.13; première danseuse, prima ballerina

7 **supporting actor** *or* **actress; support,** supporting cast; **supernumerary,** super <nonformal>, spear-carrier <nonformal>, **extra;** bit player; walk-on; figurant, figurante; **understudy, stand-in,** standby, substitute, swing

8 **tragedian,** tragedienne

9 **comedian,** comedienne, **comic, funnyman;** farcist, farcer; stand-up comic *or* comedian <nonformal>; slapstick comedian

10 **buffoon, clown, fool, jester, zany, motley fool,** wearer of the cap and bells; harlequin

11 **cast,** cast of characters, characters, *dramatis personae* <L>; **company,** acting company, **troupe;** repertory company, stock company; ensemble, chorus, *corps de ballet* <Fr>; circus troupe

708 MUSIC

NOUNS **1** **music,** harmonious sound

2 **melody,** melodiousness, **tunefulness,** musicality; **tune, tone,** musical sound, musical quality, tonality; sweetness, dulcetness, mellifluence, mellifluousness

3 **harmony, concord,** concordance, concert, accordance, **accord,** diapason; synchronism,

synchronization; **attunement,** tune; chime, chiming; unison, homophony, monody; **euphony;** music of the spheres; harmonics 709

4 **air,** aria, **tune, melody,** line, melodic line, refrain, note, **song,** solo, solo part, soprano part, treble, lay, descant, lilt, **strain,** measure; canto, cantus

5 **piece,** opus, **composition,** production, work; **score; arrangement,** adaptation, orchestration, harmonization, setting; **form**

6 **classical music;** serious music, longhair music <nonformal>, symphonic music; semiclassical music

7 **popular music,** pop music, popular song *or* air *or* tune, **ballad;** hit, song hit, hit tune

8 **dance music,** ballroom music, **dances;** syncopated music, **syncopation; ragtime** *or* rag

9 **jazz;** hot jazz, Dixieland, Basin Street; **swing,** jive <nonformal>; bebop, bop <nonformal>; avant-garde jazz; boogie *or* boogie-woogie

10 **rock-and-roll, rock music,** rock'n'roll, rock, hard rock, acid rock, folk rock, country rock

11 **folk music,** folk songs, ethnic music, ethnomusicology; folk ballads; country music, hillbilly music; country-and-western music, old-time country music; bluegrass; the blues, country blues

12 **march,** martial *or* military music; military march; processional march, recessional march; funeral march; wedding march

13 **vocal music, song; singing,** caroling, warbling, lyricism, vocalism, **vocalization;** bel canto, coloratura, bravura; choral singing; folk singing; croon, crooning; yodel, yodeling; scat, scat singing; solmization, solfeggio

14 **song,** lay, *Lied* <Ger>, *chanson* <Fr>, carol, **ditty,** canticle, lilt; **ballad,** ballade

15 **solo; aria;** operatic aria

16 <Italian terms for arias> arietta, arioso; aria buffa

17 **sacred music, church music,** liturgical music; **hymn,** hymnody, hymnology; **psalm,** psalmody; **chorale,** choral fantasy, anthem; motet; **oratorio;** passion; **mass;** requiem mass, requiem, missa solemnis; offertory, offertory hymn; **cantata;** doxology, introit, canticle, paean; recessional

18 **part music,** polyphonic music, part song, part singing; ensemble music, ensemble singing; **duet,** duo; **trio,** terzet; **quartet; quintet; sextet,** sestet; **septet; octet;** cantata, lyric cantata; madrigal; **chorus** 710.16, chorale, glee club, choir; choral singing

19 **round, rondo,** rondeau, **roundelay,** catch, troll; **fugue,** canon

20 **polyphony,** polyphonism; **counterpoint; plainsong,** Gregorian chant

21 monody, monophony, homophony

22 **part,** melody *or* voice part, **voice** 709.5, **line;** descant, canto, cantus, plain song, plain chant; soprano, tenor, treble, alto, contralto, baritone, bass; **accompaniment**

23 **response,** answer; echo; antiphon, antiphony, antiphonal chanting *or* singing

24 **passage, phrase,** strain, part, motive, motif, theme, subject, figure; leitmotiv; **movement;** statement, exposition, development, variation; division; period, musical sentence; section; **measure;** figure; **verse, stanza;** burden, bourdon; **chorus, refrain,** response; **ornament** 709.18, cadence 709.23, resolution; **coda,** tailpiece; intermezzo, interlude; bridge, bridge passage

25 <fast, slow, etc passages> presto, prestissimo; allegro, allegretto; scherzo, scherzando

26 **overture, prelude, introduction,** voluntary, descant, vamp; curtain raiser

27 **impromptu, extempore, improvisation, interpolation;** cadenza; **ornament** 709.18, flourish, grace note, appoggiatura, mordent; **run,** melisma; vamp; lick, hot lick, riff

28 **score,** musical score, **music,** musical notation, written music, copy, draft, transcription, version, edition, arrangement; part; orchestral score, short score; tablature; opera score, opera; **libretto;** sheet music; **songbook,** songster; hymnbook, hymnal

29 **staff;** line, ledger line; bar, bar line; space, degree; brace

30 **execution, performance; rendering,** rendition, **touch, expression;** fingering; intonation; glissando

31 **musicianship;** musical talent, musicality; virtuosity; ear for music; musical sense, sense of rhythm; absolute *or* perfect pitch

32 musical occasion; choral service, service of lessons and carols, service of song, sing <nonformal>, singing, community singing *or* sing, songfest; hootenanny <nonformal>; **festival,** music festival; opera festival; folk-music festival, jazz festival, rock festival; jam session <nonformal>

33 **performance, program,** musical program; **concert,** symphony concert, chamber concert; popular concert, pops *and* pop concert <both nonformal>; promenade concert; band concert; **recital;** service of music; concert performance <of an opera>; **medley,** potpourri; swan song, farewell performance

34 **musical theater, music theater, lyric theater,** musical stage, lyric stage; **music drama,** lyric drama; **opera,** grand opera, light opera; comic opera; **operetta; musical comedy; musical;** Broadway musical; **ballet;** dance drama; **song-and-dance act;** minstrel show

VERBS **35 harmonize,** be in tune *or* concert, chord, **accord,** synchronize, **chime, blend,** blend in;

tune, attune, sound in tune; assonate; musicalize

36 tune, tune up, attune, **put in tune;** voice; string; tone up, tone down

37 strike up, strike up a tune, **strike up the band,** break into music, pipe up, **burst into song**

38 sing, vocalize, carol, descant, lilt, belt out *and* tear off <both nonformal>; **warble,** trill, tremolo, quaver, shake; **chirp,** chirrup, **twitter;** pipe, whistle; **chant; intone,** intonate; **croon; hum; yodel;** chorus, sing in chorus; **hymn;** sing the praises of; minstrel; ballad; **serenade;** solmizate

39 play, perform, execute, render, do; interpret; make music; concertize; accompany; play by ear; play at, pound out *and* saw away at <both nonformal>

40 strum, thrum, pluck, plunk, **pick,** twang, sweep the strings

41 fiddle <nonformal>, play violin *or* the violin

42 blow a horn, sound the horn, sound, blow, wind, **toot,** tootle, pipe; bugle, carillon, clarion, fife, flute, trumpet, whistle; bagpipe; lip, tongue, double-tongue, triple-tongue

43 syncopate, play jazz, swing, jive <nonformal>, rag <nonformal>

44 beat time, keep time, tap out the rhythm; count, count the beats; beat the drum, **drum 55.4,** play the drums, thrum, beat, thump, pound; tomtom; ruffle; beat *or* sound a tattoo

45 conduct, direct, lead, wield the baton

46 compose, write, arrange, score, set, set to music, put to music; **harmonize; orchestrate; instrument; adapt,** make an adaptation; transcribe, transpose

ADJS **47 musical, musically inclined,** musicianly, with an ear for music; virtuoso, virtuosic; **music-loving,** philharmonic

48 melodious, melodic; **musical; tuneful,** tunable; fine-toned, **pleasant-sounding,** agreeable-sounding, pleasant, appealing, agreeable, catchy, singable; **euphonious, lyric, lyrical; lilting,** songlike; **sweet, dulcet,** sweet-sounding; honeyed, mellifluent, mellifluous; rich, mellow; sonorous, canorous; sweet-voiced, golden-voiced, silver-voiced, silver-tongued, golden-tongued

49 harmonious, harmonic, symphonious; harmonizing, **chiming,** blending, blended; **concordant,** consonant, accordant, according, **in accord,** in concord, in concert; synchronous, synchronized, in sync <nonformal>, **in tune,** tuned, attuned; in unison, in chorus

50 vocal, singing; **choral,** choric; operatic; hymnal; psalmic; psalmodic; sacred, liturgical; treble, soprano, tenor, alto, falsetto; coloratura, lyric, bravura, dramatic, heroic; baritone; bass

51 instrumental, orchestral, symphonic, concert; syncopated, jazzy, rock, swing

52 polyphonic, contrapuntal

709 HARMONICS, MUSICAL ELEMENTS

NOUNS **1 harmonics,** harmony; melodics; rhythmics; musicality; music, **music theory,** theory; musicology; musicography

2 harmonization; orchestration, instrumentation; arrangement, setting, adaptation, transcription; chordal progression; phrasing, modulation, intonation, suspension, solution, resolution

3 tone, tonality 50.3

4 pitch, tuning, tune, **tone, key, note,** register, tonality; pitch range, tessitura; temperament

5 voice; soprano, mezzo-soprano, dramatic soprano, lyric soprano, coloratura soprano; boy soprano; male soprano, castrato; alto, contralto; tenor, lyric tenor, operatic tenor, heldentenor *or* heroic tenor *or* Wagnerian tenor; countertenor *or* male alto; baritone, light *or* lyric baritone; **bass,** basso, basso profundo, lyric bass; treble, falsetto

6 scale, gamut, register, compass, range, diapason; diatonic scale, chromatic scale, whole-tone scale; octave scale, pentatonic scale; twelve-tone scale

7 sol-fa, tonic sol-fa, do-re-mi; solmization

8 <diatonic series> tetrachord, chromatic tetrachord, enharmonic tetrachord, Dorian tetrachord; hexachord

9 octave, ottava <Ital>, eighth; ottava alta <Ital>

10 mode, octave species; major mode, minor mode

11 form, arrangement, pattern, model, design; song *or* lied form; **sonata form**

12 notation, character, mark, symbol, signature, sign

13 clef; C clef, soprano clef

14 note, musical note, notes of a scale; **tone** 50.2; **sharp, flat, natural; accidental;** breve; whole note, semibreve; half note, minim; quarter note, crotchet; eighth note, quaver; sixteenth note, semiquaver; thirty-second note, demisemiquaver; sixty-fourth note, hemidemisemiquaver

15 key, key signature, tonality, sharps and flats; **keynote,** tonic; tonic key; major, minor, major *or* minor key, tonic major *or* minor

16 harmonic, harmonic tone, overtone

17 chord; major *or* minor chord, tonic chord, dominant chord

18 ornament, grace, arabesque, embellishment; **flourish,** roulade, flight, run; passage, division 708.24; florid phrase *or* passage; coloratura; incidental, incidental note; grace note; rubato; mordent; cadence, cadenza

19 trill; tremolo; quaver, quiver, tremble, tremor, flutter, falter, shake; **vibrato**

20 interval, degree, step, note, tone

21 rest, pause; breve rest, semibreve rest, half rest, minim, quarter rest, eighth rest, sixteenth rest, thirty-second rest, sixty-fourth rest

22 rhythm, beat, meter, measure, lilt, swing; prosody, metrics; rhythmic pattern *or* phrase

23 cadence *or* cadency, authentic cadence, plagal cadence

24 tempo, time, beat, timing; simple time *or* measure, compound time *or* measure; mixed times; **syncopation,** syncope; **ragtime,** rag <nonformal>; waltz time; three-four *or* three-quarter time, andante tempo, march tempo; largo; presto

25 accent, accentuation, rhythmical accent *or* accentuation, ictus, emphasis

26 beat, throb, pulse, pulsation; downbeat, upbeat, offbeat

ADJS **27 tonal,** tonic; chromatic; semitonic

28 rhythmic, rhythmical, cadent, cadenced, **measured, metric, metrical;** in rhythm; beating, throbbing, pulsing, pulsating

29 syncopated; ragtime; jazz; jazzy *and* jazzed *and* jazzed up <all nonformal>, hot, swingy <nonformal>

ADVS **30 in time,** in tempo 709.24, *a tempo* <Ital>

710 MUSICIAN

NOUNS **1 musician, music maker,** professional musician; performer, interpreter, artiste, artist, concert artist, **virtuoso,** virtuosa; maestro; **soloist,** duettist; street musician

2 popular *or* pop musician; **jazz musician, jazzman; rock** *or* **rock'n'roll musician**

3 player, instrumentalist; bandman, bandsman; orchestral musician; symphonist; concertist; accompanist

4 wind player, wind-instrumentalist, horn player; bassoonist, bugler, clarinetist, cornetist, fifer, oboist, piccoloist, saxophonist, trombonist; trumpeter, trumpet major; fluegelhornist; flutist *or* flautist

5 string musician, strummer, picker <nonformal>, thrummer, twanger; banjoist, banjo-picker

<nonformal>, citharist, guitarist,
guitar-picker <nonformal>, classical guitarist, folk guitarist, lute
player, lutenist, lutist, lyrist,
mandolinist; violinist, fiddler
<nonformal>; bass violinist,
bassist, bass player, contrabass-
ist; violoncellist, cellist; violist;
harpist, harper; zitherist,
psalterer

6 **xylophonist, marimbaist, vibist**
or **vibraphonist**

7 **pianist,** piano player, ivory
tickler <nonformal>; keyboard
player *or* keyboardist; harpsi-
chordist, clavichordist, mono-
chordist; accordionist, concer-
tinist

8 **organist,** organ player

9 organ-grinder, hurdy-gurdy man

10 **drummer, percussionist,** tym-
panist, kettle-drummer; taborer

11 **cymbalist;** bell-ringer, **caril-
loneur,** campanologist, campan-
ist

12 **orchestra, band, ensemble,**
combo <nonformal>, group;
strings, woodwind *or* woodwinds,
brass *or* brasses, string *or* woodwind *or* brass section, string *or*
woodwind *or* brass choir; desks

13 **singer, vocalist,** vocalizer, voice,
songster, songbird, warbler, car-
oler, cantor; songstress, chan-
teuse, song stylist, canary <non-
formal>; chanter, chantress; lie-
der singer, opera singer, diva,
prima donna; improvisator; rap
singer; blues singer, torch singer
<nonformal>; crooner, rock *or*
rock-and-roll singer; yodeler;
country singer, folk singer; psalm
singer, hymner; **singing voice,
voice** 709.5

14 **minstrel, ballad singer,**
balladeer, **bard,** rhapsodist;
wandering *or* strolling minstrel,
troubadour, minnesinger, jongleur; street singer; serenader;
folk singer, folk-rock singer;
country-and-western singer

15 **choral singer,** choir member,
chorister, choralist; choirman,
choirboy; chorus girl

16 **chorus, chorale, choir,** choral

group, choral society, oratorio society, chorale, men's *or* women's
chorus, male chorus, mixed
chorus, ensemble, voices; **glee
club,** singing club *or* society;
choral symphony

17 **conductor,** leader, symphonic
conductor, **music director,** director; **orchestra leader, band
leader, bandmaster**

18 **choirmaster,** choral director *or*
conductor, song leader; precen-
tor, cantor, chorister

19 **concertmaster,** first violinist;
first chair

20 **composer, scorer, arranger,**
musicographer; melodist, melo-
dizer; **orchestrator;** symphonist;
ballad maker, balladeer, ballad-
ist; madrigalist; lyrist; hymnist,
hymnographer, hymnologist;
contrapuntist; song writer, song-
smith, tunesmith; lyricist, librettist; musicologist

21 **music lover, music fan** *and*
music buff <both nonformal>,
musicophile; concertgoer, oper-
agoer

22 <patrons> the Muses, the Nine,
sacred Nine

23 **songbird, songster,** warbler;
nightingale; canary, cuckoo, lark,
song sparrow, thrush

711 MUSICAL INSTRUMENTS

1 **musical instrument**; electronic
instrument, synthesizer, Moog
synthesizer <trademark>

2 **string** *or* **stringed instrument**;
strings

3 **harp, lyre**

4 plucked stringed instrument

5 **viol** *or* violin; Stradivarius, Strad
<nonformal>; Amati, Cremona,
Guarnerius; bow, fiddlestick;
bridge, sound hole, soundboard,
fingerboard, tuning peg, scroll

6 **wind instrument,** wind; **horn,**
pipe, tooter; mouthpiece, embouchure, lip, chops <nonformal>;
valve, bell, reed, key, slide

7 **brass wind, brass** *or* brass-wind
instrument; brasses

8 **woodwind,** wood *or* woodwind
instrument; woods; reed instru-

ment, **reed; double reed; single-reed instrument,** single reed

9 **bagpipe** or bagpipes, pipes, doodlesack; chanter, drone; pipe bag

10 **mouth organ,** mouth harp, harp, French harp <nonformal>, **harmonica,** harmonicon; jaws or Jew's harp, mouth bow; kazoo

11 **accordion; concertina;** squeeze box <nonformal>; mellophone

12 keyboard instrument, **piano, harpsichord, clavichord, player piano**

13 **organ,** keyboard wind instrument

14 **hurdy-gurdy,** vielle, **barrel organ,** hand organ, grind organ, street organ

15 **music box,** musical box; orchestrion, orchestrina

16 **percussion instrument**, percussion, **drum;** drumstick, jazz stick, tymp stick

17 **keyboard,** fingerboard; console, **keys,** manual, claviature; piano keys, ivories <nonformal>, eighty-eight <nonformal>, organ manual; pedals

18 **carillon,** chimes 711.18; electronic carillon

19 **organ stop, stop,** rank, register

20 string, chord, steel string, wound string, nylon string; fiddlestring, catgut; horsehair; music wire, piano wire

21 plectrum, plectron, pick

22 <aids> metronome, rhythmometer; tone measurer, monochord, sonometer; tuning fork, tuning bar, diapason; pitch pipe, tuning pipe; mute; music stand, music lyre; baton, conductor's baton, stick <nonformal>

712 VISUAL ARTS

NOUNS 1 **visual arts; art, artwork,** the arts; **fine arts; design,** designing; art form; abstract art, representative art; **graphic arts** 713; **arts and crafts;** primitive art, cave art; folk art; calligraphy; commercial art, applied art; sculpture 715; ceramics 742; pho-

tography 714; etching, engraving 713.2; decoration 498.1; artist 716

2 *beaux arts* <Fr>; arts of design

3 **craft, manual art,** industrial art, **handicraft,** craftwork; industrial design; woodcraft, woodwork, metalcraft

4 <act or art of painting> **painting,** coloring; the brush

5 <art of drawing> **drawing, draftsmanship, sketching, delineation; black and white,** charcoal; mechanical drawing, drafting; freehand drawing

6 scenography, ichnography

7 **artistry, art, talent,** artistic skill, artistic flair; artiness *and* artycraftiness *and* artsy-craftiness <all nonformal>; artistic quality

8 **style;** genre; **school,** movement; the grand style

9 **treatment; technique,** draftsmanship, brushwork, painterliness; **composition, design,** arrangement; grouping, balance; **color,** values; atmosphere, tone; shadow, shading; **line;** perspective

10 **work of art, object of art,** objet d'art, art object, art work, piece, **work, study, design, composition;** creation, brainchild; **masterpiece,** *chef d'œuvre* <Fr>, masterwork, old master, classic; museum piece, grotesque; statue; mobile, stabile; nude, still life; pastiche; artwork; bric-a-brac; kitsch

11 **picture; image, likeness, representation,** tableau; photograph 714.3; **illustration,** illumination; miniature; copy, reproduction; print, color print; engraving 713.2, stencil, block print; abstraction; mural, fresco, wall painting; cyclorama, panorama; montage, collage, assemblage; still life; tapestry, mosaic, stained glass, **icon,** altarpiece, diptych, triptych

12 **scene, view, scape; landscape;** seascape; diorama; exterior, interior

13 **drawing; delineation;** line

drawing; **sketch, draft; black and white,** chiaroscuro; **charcoal, crayon, pen-and-ink,** pencil drawing, charcoal drawing, pastel painting; silhouette; vignette; rough copy, cartoon, **study,** design; silver-print drawing, tracing

14 **painting, canvas; oil painting,** oil; **watercolor,** water, aquarelle, wash, wash drawing; finger painting; tempera, egg tempera; gouache

15 **portrait, portraiture, portrayal;** head; profile; silhouette, shadow figure; miniature

16 **cartoon, caricature; comic strip;** comic section, comics, funny paper *and* funnies <both nonformal>; comic book; animated cartoon

17 **studio,** *atelier* <Fr>; **gallery** 386.9

18 <art equipment> palette; easel; paintbox; art paper, drawing paper; sketchbook, sketchpad; canvas

VERBS 19 **portray, picture, depict, limn,** draw *or* paint a picture; **paint** 35.13; brush, brush in; color, tint; spread *or* lay on a color; **daub** <nonformal>; **draw, sketch, delineate, draft;** draw in, pencil in; dash off, scratch <nonformal>; doodle; design; diagram; cartoon; copy, trace; stencil; hatch, crosshatch, shade

ADJS 20 **artistic,** painterly; **arty** *or* arty-crafty *or* artsy-craftsy <nonformal>; **art-minded,** art-conscious; **aesthetic; tasteful; beautiful; decorative, ornamental** 498.10; **well-composed,** well-grouped, well-arranged; of consummate art; in the grand style

21 **pictorial, graphic, picturesque;** picturable; photographic 714.17; monochrome, polychrome; freehand

713 GRAPHIC ARTS

NOUNS 1 **graphic arts, graphics; printmaking; painting; drawing; relief-carving; photography** 714; **printing** 548; graphic artist 716.8

2 **engraving,** graving, enchasing, **tooling,** chiseling, incising, incision, lining, scratching, slashing, scoring; **inscription; marking;** hatching, cross-hatching; etch, etching; stipple, stippling; photoengraving 548.1

3 **lithography,** planography, artist lithography; chromolithography; photolithography; offset lithography 548.1

4 stencil printing; silk-screen printing, serigraphy; monotype; decal, decalcomania

5 **print,** numbered print, imprint, impression, first impression, impress; negative; color print; **etching; lithograph; block, block print,** linoleum-block print, wood engraving, **woodprint,** xylograph, **cut, woodcut,** woodblock; vignette

6 **plate,** steel plate, copperplate, chalcography; zincograph; stone, lithographic stone; printing plate 548.8

7 **proof,** artist's proof, remarque proof

8 **engraving tool, graver,** burin, style, etching point, etching needle; etching ball; etching ground *or* varnish; **die,** punch, stamp, intaglio, seal

VERBS 9 **engrave, grave, tool, enchase, incise, sculpture, inscribe, mark,** line, crease, score, scratch, scrape, cut, carve, chisel; groove, furrow 290.3; stipple; hatch, crosshatch; lithograph; print 548.14

10 **etch,** eat, eat out, corrode, bite, bite in

ADJS 11 **engraved, graven,** graved; tooled, enchased, inscribed, incised, marked, lined, creased, cut, carved, glyphic, **sculptured;** grooved, furrowed 290.4; **printed, imprinted, impressed, stamped**

12 glyptic, glyptical, lapidary, lapidarian; xylographic, wood-block; lithographic; aquatint

714 PHOTOGRAPHY

NOUNS **1 photography**, picture-taking; **cinematography,** motion-picture photography; color photography; **3-D,** three-dimensional photography; photofinishing; photogravure; radiography, X-ray photography

2 photographer 716.5, shutter-bug <nonformal>, press photographer, lensman

3 photograph, photo <nonformal>, **picture,** shot <nonformal>; **snapshot,** snap <nonformal>; candid photograph; still, still photograph; photomural; montage, photomontage; aerial photograph; facsimile *or* fax transmission; telephotograph, Telephoto <trademark>, Wirephoto <trademark>; photomicrograph, microphotograph; electron micrograph; **portrait;** pinup <nonformal>, cheesecake *and* beefcake <both nonformal>; police photograph, **mug** *or* mug shot <nonformal>; rogues' gallery; photobiography

4 tintype *or* ferrotype, ambrotype, **daguerreotype,** calotype *or* talbotype, collotype, photocollotype, autotype, vitrotype

5 print, photoprint, positive; glossy, matte, semi-matte; **enlargement, blowup;** photocopy, Photostat <trademark>, photostatic copy, Xerox <trademark>, Xerox copy; microcopy; blueprint; **slide,** transparency, lantern slide; contact printing, projection printing; photogravure; hologram

6 shadowgraph, shadowgram, skiagraph

7 spectrograph, spectrogram; spectroheliogram

8 <motion pictures> **shot; take, retake;** close-up, long shot, medium shot, full shot, group shot, deuce shot, matte shot, process shot, boom shot, travel shot, tracking shot, follow-focus shot, pan shot *or* panoramic shot, rap shot, reverse *or* reverse-angle shot, wild shot, zoom shot; motion picture; kinescope

9 exposure, time exposure; shutter speed; f-stop, lens opening; film rating, **film speed,** film gauge, ASA exposure index; exposure meter, light meter

10 film; negative; printing paper, photographic paper; **plate;** dry plate; vehicle; motion-picture film, panchromatic film, monochromatic film, black-and-white film, color film, color negative film, color reversal film; microfilm; sound-on-film, sound film; sound track, soundstripe; roll, cartridge; frame; emulsion, dope, backing

11 camera, Kodak <trademark>; motion-picture camera

12 projector; motion-picture projector, cineprojector, vitascope; **slide projector,** magic lantern, stereopticon; slide viewer

13 processing solution; developer, soup <nonformal>; fixer, fixing bath, sodium thiosulfate *or* sodium hyposulfite *or* hypo; stop bath, short-stop, short-stop bath

VERBS **14 photograph, shoot** <nonformal>, take a photograph, **take a picture, snap,** snapshot, snapshoot; **film,** get *or* capture on film; **mug** <nonformal>; daguerreotype, talbotype, calotype; Photostat <trademark>; xerox; microfilm; pan; **X-ray,** radiograph

15 process; develop; print; blueprint; **blow up, enlarge**

16 project, show, screen

ADJS **17 photographic,** photo; **photogenic;** photosensitive, photoactive; panchromatic; telephoto; tintype; three-dimensional, 3-D

715 SCULPTURE

NOUNS **1 sculpture, sculpturing; modeling; statuary; stonecutting;** gem-cutting, masonry; **carving,** bone-carving, cameo carving, scrimshaw, whittling, woodcarving *or* xyloglyphy; embossing, **engraving** 713.2, **chas-**

ing, founding, casting, molding, plaster casting, lost-wax process; sculptor 716.6

2 <sculptured piece> **sculpture; glyph; statue;** marble, bronze, terra cotta; mobile, stabile; cast 784.6; found object, *objet trouvé* <Fr>

3 **relief,** relievo; **embossment,** boss; half relief; high relief; low relief, bas-relief; sunk relief, **intaglio;** glyph, anaglyph; glyptograph; **mask;** plaquette; **medallion; medal; cameo,** cameo glass, sculptured glass; cut glass

4 <tools, materials> chisel, point, mallet, modeling tool, spatula; cutting torch, welding torch, soldering iron; solder; modeling clay, Plasticine <trademark>, sculptor's wax; plaster

VERBS 5 **sculpture,** sculp *or* sculpt <nonformal>; **carve,** chisel, cut, grave, engrave, chase; weld, solder; **model, mold;** cast, found

ADJS 6 **sculptural,** sculpturesque; statuary; **statuesque,** statuelike; **monumental,** marmoreal

7 **sculptured,** sculpted; **molded, modeled, carved,** chiseled; **graven;** in relief, in high *or* low relief; glyphic, glyptic, anaglyphic, anaglyptic; embossed, chased, hammered

716 ARTIST

NOUNS 1 **artist,** *artiste* <Fr>, creator; maker; master, **old master;** dauber, daubster; copyist; **craftsman, artisan** 726.6

2 **limner,** delineator, depicter, picturer, portrayer, imager; **illustrator;** illuminator; calligrapher; commercial artist

3 **draftsman, sketcher, delineator;** drawer, architectural draftsman; crayonist, charcoalist, pastelist; **cartoonist, caricaturist**

4 **painter; colorist; oil painter,** oil-colorist; **watercolorist;** aquarellist; genre painter, historical painter, landscapist, miniaturist, portrait painter, portraitist, marine painter, still-life painter; pavement artist

5 **photographer,** lensman, **cameraman; cinematographer;** shutterbug <nonformal>; daguerreotypist; radiographer, X-ray technician

6 **sculptor,** sculptress; figurer, **modeler,** molder, wax modeler, clay modeler; graver, chaser, carver; stonecutter, mason, wood carver, whittler; ivory carver, bone carver, shell carver; gem carver, glyptic *or* glyptographic artist

7 **ceramist, ceramicist, potter;** tile painter, majolica painter; glassblower, glass cutter; enamelist, enameler

8 **printmaker,** graphic artist; **engraver,** graver, burinist; inscriber, carver; **etcher; lithographer,** chromolithographer; serigrapher, silk-screen artist; gem engraver, glyptographer, lapidary; wood engraver, xylographer; pyrographer, xylopyrographer; zincographer

9 **designer, stylist,** styler; costume designer, dress designer, *couturier* <Fr>, *couturière* <Fr fem>

10 **architect,** civil architect; landscape architect; city *or* urban planner, urbanist

11 **decorator,** ornamentalist; **interior decorator** *or* designer; window decorator *or* dresser

717 ARCHITECTURE, DESIGN

NOUNS 1 **architecture,** architectural design, building design; **architectural science,** architectural engineering, structural engineering, building technology; **architectural style; architectural specialty;** landscape architecture

2 **architectural element; ornamentation,** architectural ornamentation; **type of construction**

3 **architect;** landscape architect; city *or* urban planner, urbanologist

4 **design, styling,** patterning,

planning, shaping; **design specialty**

5 **designer, stylist,** styler

ADJS 6 **architectural, design, designer**

718 LITERATURE

NOUNS 1 **literature, letters, belles lettres,** humane letters, republic of letters; **work, literary work, text, literary text; works, complete works, oeuvre, canon, literary canon, author's canon; classics;** underground literature; folk literature; travel literature; erotica; pornography, porn *and* hard porn *and* soft porn <all nonformal>

2 **authorship, writing, composition; creative writing,** versewriting, short-story writing, novel-writing, playwriting, drama-writing; essay-writing; **expository writing;** artistry, literary power, literary talent *or* flair, facility in writing; **writer's itch**

3 **writer, scribbler** <nonformal>, **penman, pen;** word-slinger, **inkslinger** <nonformal>

4 **author, writer;** penwoman; **creative writer,** belletrist, man of letters, literary man; wordsmith; collaborator; **short story writer;** storyteller; **novelist;** diarist; **newspaperman; annalist; poet** 720.13; **dramatist; essayist;** reviewer, critic; compiler, encyclopedist, bibliographer

5 **hack writer,** hack, **penny-a-liner, scribbler** <nonformal>, **potboiler** <nonformal>

VERBS 6 **write,** author, pen, **compose, indite,** formulate; dash off, knock off *or* out <nonformal>, pound *or* crank *or* grind *or* churn out; free-lance; collaborate; ghostwrite, ghost <nonformal>

ADJS 7 **literary,** belletristic; classical

8 auctorial, authorial

719 HISTORY

NOUNS 1 **history,** the record of the past; historical research; **annals, chronicles,** chronology; chronicle, record 549; **historiography; oral history; biography, memoir, life, life story;** life and letters; hagiology, hagiography; **autobiography, memoirs; journal, diary; profile, biographical sketch;** necrology, martyrology; historiography; **the past 836; record, recording** 549

2 the historical discipline, the investigation of the past

3 **story, tale, yarn, account, narrative,** narration, chronicle; **anecdote,** anecdotage; **epic,** epos, **saga**

4 **historian,** historiographer; **chronicler,** annalist; **biographer,** Boswell; autobiographer; diarist, Pepys

VERBS 5 **chronicle,** historify; historicize; immortalize; **record** 549.16

6 **narrate, tell, relate, recount,** report, **recite**

ADJS 7 **historical, historic;** historiographical; **chronicled; traditional, legendary;** biographical, autobiographic, autobiographical; hagiographical, martyrological; necrological

8 **narrative,** narrational; **fictional**

ADVS 9 **historically;** according to *or* by all accounts

720 POETRY

NOUNS 1 **poetry,** poesy, **verse, song, rhyme**

2 **poetics,** versification, versemaking; **poetic language; poetic license, poetic justice**

3 **bad poetry,** doggerel; poesy; nonsense verse, amphigory; macaronic verse

4 **poem, verse, rhyme;** verselet, versicle

5 **book of verse, collection, anthology;** poesy

6 **metrics, prosody, versification; scansion**

7 **meter, measure; rhythm, cadence,** movement, lilt, jingle, swing; sprung rhythm; **accent, beat; foot, metrical foot; iambic pentameter, dactylic hexameter**

8 rhyme; consonance, assonance; alliteration

9 <poetic divisions> measure, strain; syllable; line; verse; stanza

10 Muse; poetic genius, poesy, afflatus, fire of genius, **creative imagination** 985.2, **inspiration** 919.8

11 poet, poetess; ballad maker, balladmonger; **bard, minstrel, jongleur, troubadour;** laureate, **poet laureate; lyric poet**

12 bad poet; rhymester, rhymer; versemonger; **poetaster**

VERBS **13 poetize, versify, sing;** elegize; poeticize

14 rhyme, assonate, alliterate; **scan;** jingle

ADJS **15 poetic, poetical; lyrical; narrative**

16 metric, metrical, prosodic, prosodical; rhythmic, rhythmical, measured

17 rhyming; assonant; alliterative; lilting

ADVS **18 poetically, lyrically; metrically, rhythmically,** in measure; musically

721 PROSE

NOUNS **1 prose;** expository prose; prose rhythm; prose style

2 prosaism, prosaicism, prosaicness, unpoeticalness; matter-of-factness; unimaginativeness 986; **plainness;** insipidness, flatness, vapidity; **dullness** 117

VERBS **3 prose,** write prose *or* in prose; pedestrianize

ADJS **4 prose;** unversified, nonmetrical

5 prosaic, prosy, prosing; plain, **common, commonplace, ordinary,** unembellished, mundane; **matter-of-fact, unromantic, unidealistic,** pedestrian, **unimaginative** 986.5; insipid, vapid; **dull** 117.6

722 FICTION

NOUNS **1 fiction,** narrative literature; **narration,** recital, recounting; **storytelling**

2 narration, narrative, relation,

recital, recounting, recountal; **storytelling**

3 story, short story, tale, narrative, yarn, account, narration, chronicle, relation, version; **novel**

4 <story elements> plot, fable, argument, story, line, story line, subplot, secondary plot, mythos; structure

5 narrator, relator, reciter, recounter, raconteur <Fr>; anecdotist; storyteller

VERBS **6 narrate, tell, relate, recount,** report, **recite;** fictionalize; mythify, mythologize, allegorize

ADJS **7 fictional,** fictionalized; **novelistic,** novelized; **legendary, fabulous; allegorical;** romantic

8 narrative, narrational; anecdotal; epic

723 CRITICISM OF THE ARTS

NOUNS **1 criticism,** criticism of the arts, esthetic *or* artistic criticism, critical commentary; **art criticism**

2 review, critical notice, commentary

3 literary criticism, literary analysis *or* evaluation *or* interpretation *or* exegetics *or* hermeneutics, poetics; **critical approach** *or* **school; literary theory**

4 critic, exegete, explicator

VERBS **5 criticize,** critique, evaluate, explicate

ADJS **6 critical,** evaluative, exegetical, explicative

724 OCCUPATION

NOUNS **1 occupation, work, job, employment, activity, function,** enterprise, **work, affairs; affair, matter, concern, interest;** commerce 731

2 task, work, stint, job, chore; assignment, charge, mission, commission, **duty**

3 function, office, duty, job, province, **role; capacity**

4 <sphere of work or activity> **field, sphere,** bailiwick, turf <nonformal>, discipline, orbit, realm, arena, domain; **specialty**

5 position, job, situation, **office,**

post, place, station, **appointment**, engagement, gig <nonformal>; incumbency, tenure

6 **vocation, occupation, business, work, line, line of work, walk of life, calling,** mission, **profession, practice, pursuit, specialty, trade,** racket *and* game <both nonformal>; **career; craft**

7 **avocation, hobby,** sideline

8 **professionalism,** professional standing *or* status

9 **nonprofessionalism, amateurism,** amateur status

VERBS 10 **occupy, engage, busy, employ,** occupy oneself, busy oneself, go about one's business, devote oneself

11 **busy oneself with, do,** occupy *or* engage oneself with; **engage in, take up,** devote oneself to; **be about, be doing**

12 **work,** be employed, **ply one's trade;** do *or* transact business

13 **officiate, function, serve; perform as, act as,** act *or* play one's part, **do duty**

14 **hold office,** fill an office, occupy a post

ADJS 15 **occupied, busy,** working; materialistic 695.16; workaday; **commercial** 731.21

16 **occupational, vocational,** functional; **professional**

17 **avocational,** hobby, amateur, nonprofessional

ADVS 18 **professionally,** vocationally; as a profession

725 EXERTION

NOUNS 1 **exertion, effort, energy,** elbow grease; **endeavor** 403; **trouble, pains**

2 **strain,** straining, **stress,** stressfulness, **stress and strain,** taxing, **tension**

3 **struggle, fight, battle, tussle,** scuffle, wrestle

4 **work, labor, employment, industry, toil,** sweat of one's brow; **drudgery, sweat; makework,** tedious *or* tiresome work, grind <nonformal>; **manual labor,** stitch of work <nonformal>; **workload**

5 **hard work** *or* **labor, backbreaking work; hard job** 1012.2; **laboriousness, toilsomeness, strenuousness, arduousness**

6 **exercise** 84; **practice, drill, workout;** yoga

7 exerciser; horizontal bar, parallel bars, horse

VERBS 8 **exert, exercise, ply, put forth;** practice

9 **exert oneself,** use some elbow grease <nonformal>, spread oneself; go all out <nonformal>; **do one's best; apply oneself, buckle** *or* **knuckle** <nonformal>

10 **strain, tense, stress, stretch, tax,** press, rack; **pull, tug,** haul, **heave**

11 **struggle, strive, contend, fight, battle,** buffet, scuffle, tussle, wrestle, hassle <nonformal>

12 **work, labor;** do a lick of work, earn one's keep

13 **work hard; scratch** *and* **hustle** *and* **sweat** <all nonformal>, **slave, sweat and slave** <nonformal>, **work day and night, burn the midnight oil;** lucubrate

14 **drudge, grind** *and* **dig** <both nonformal>, **grub, toil, plod, slog, peg, plug** <nonformal>, **keep one's nose to the grindstone**

15 **set to work, get rolling, get busy, get down to business** *or* **work,** roll up one's sleeves, **fall to, buckle** *or* **knuckle down to** <nonformal>, **turn to, set to** *or* **about; get on the job** <nonformal>; **go to it** *and* **get with it** *and* **get cracking** <all nonformal>; **attack, tackle** <nonformal>; **plunge into; pitch in** *or* **into** <nonformal>

16 **task, work, busy,** keep busy, **sweat** <nonformal>, **drive, tax; overwork**

ADJS 17 **laboring, working; struggling, striving;** straining; **drudging, toiling,** slaving, **plodding**

18 **laborious, toilsome, arduous, strenuous; heavy, backbreaking; labored, intensive**

ADVS 19 **laboriously, arduously, toilsomely, strenuously, hard,** with might and main; **hammer and tongs, tooth and nail,** heart and soul; **industriously** 330.27

726 WORKER, DOER

NOUNS 1 **doer, agent, performer, worker, practitioner; producer, maker,** creator, fabricator, **author, agent; executor, operator**

2 **worker, laborer, toiler**; proletarian; **workman, workingman; workwoman, workingwoman**; factory worker; **commuter**; office worker, **white-collar worker; jobholder, wage earner,** salaried worker; **breadwinner; hand, workhand; laborer, unskilled laborer**; agricultural worker

3 **drudge, hack, plodder, slave, workhorse;** grind <nonformal>; slave labor, sweatshop labor

4 **professional**; pro *and* old pro <both nonformal>, seasoned professional

5 **amateur, nonprofessional, layman,** laic

6 **skilled worker, journeyman,** mechanic; **craftsman, handicraftsman; artisan,** artificer; **maker; wright; technician; master**

7 engineer, professional engineer; technician

8 smith; farrier <Brit>, forger

727 UNIONISM, LABOR UNION

NOUNS 1 **unionism,** trade unionism, labor unionism; **unionization; collective bargaining; arbitration**

2 **labor union,** trade union; organized labor; **craft union; industrial union; local**

3 **union shop, closed shop;** open shop; nonunion shop; **labor contract, union contract**

4 **unionist, labor unionist, trade unionist, union member**; shop steward; business agent

5 **strike, walkout** *or* tie-up <both nonformal>, **job action;** work stoppage, sit-down strike, wildcat strike; **slowdown; boycott; lockout**

6 **striker;** sitdown striker; holdout <nonformal>

7 <strike enforcer> picket; goon <nonformal>

8 strikebreaker, scab and rat and fink <all nonformal>

VERBS 9 **organize, unionize;** bargain, bargain collectively; arbitrate; submit to arbitration

10 **strike, go on strike, go out, walk, walk out;** slow down; sit down; **boycott;** picket; **lock out**

11 **break a strike; scab** *and* **rat** *and* **fink** <all nonformal>

728 MONEY

NOUNS 1 **money, currency, legal tender, medium of exchange, cash,** hard cash, cold cash; **silver;** dollars; **the wherewithal;** lucre; **filthy lucre** <nonformal>, the almighty dollar, root of all evil, mammon; **hard currency,** soft currency

2 <nonformal terms> **dough, bread, jack, kale,** scratch, sugar, change, mazuma, gelt, coin, spondulics, wampum, moolah, boodle, **sugar,** simoleons, shekels, **bucks,** green stuff, cabbage, loot

3 **wampum,** peag, sewan, roanoke; cowrie

4 **specie,** hard money; coin; **gold piece**

5 **paper money; bill**; note; **bank note**

6 <nonformal terms> **folding money, green stuff,** the long green, lettuce, greenbacks

7 <US denominations> mill; cent, penny, copper, red cent <nonformal>; five cents, nickel; ten cents, dime; twenty-five cents, quarter, two bits <nonformal>; fifty cents, half-dollar, four bits <nonformal>; dollar, dollar bill; **buck** *and* skin <both nonformal>; silver dollar; two-dollar bill, two-spot <nonformal>; five-dollar bill; fiver and five-spot and fin <all nonformal>; ten-dollar bill; tenner and ten-spot and sawbuck

<all nonformal>; twenty-dollar bill, double sawbuck <nonformal>; fifty-dollar bill, half a C <nonformal>; hundred-dollar bill; C and C-note and century and bill <all nonformal>; five hundred dollars, half grand <nonformal>, five-hundred-dollar bill, half G <nonformal>; thousand dollars, G and grand <both nonformal>, thousand-dollar bill, G-note and yard and big one <all nonformal>

8 <British denominations> mite; farthing; halfpenny or ha'penny, bawbee <Brit nonformal>, mag or meg <both Brit nonformal>; penny; pence, p; new pence, np; two-pence or tuppence; three-pence or thrippence, threepenny bit or piece; fourpence, fourpenny, groat; sixpence, tanner <Brit nonformal>, teston; shilling, bob <Brit nonformal>

9 **foreign money, foreign exchange**

10 **counterfeit,** funny or phony or bogus money <nonformal>, queer <nonformal>; **forgery,** bad check, rubber check and bounced check and kite <all nonformal>

11 **negotiable instrument** or **paper,** commercial paper, paper, bill; **bill of exchange; check, money order; promissory note, note, IOU**

12 **token, counter,** slug; **scrip, coupon; check, ticket**

13 **sum,** amount of money; round sum, lump sum

14 **funds, finances, moneys, assets,** resources, **pecuniary resources, means, fund, kitty** <nonformal>

15 **capital, fund; risk** or **venture capital;** capitalization

16 **money market,** supply of short-term funds; tight money, cheap money; **borrowing** 621; **lending** 620

17 **bankroll;** roll or wad <both nonformal>

18 **cash, ready money** or **cash,** cash in hand, **liquid assets, cash flow;** treasury

19 **petty cash, pocket money, pin money, change,** chicken feed <nonformal>

20 precious metals; gold, yellow stuff <nonformal>; nugget, gold nugget; silver, copper

21 standard of value, gold standard, silver standard

22 <science of coins> **numismatics,** numismatology; numismatist, numismatologist

23 monetization; issuance, circulation

24 **coining,** coinage, mintage, striking, stamping

25 coiner, minter, mintmaster, moneyer

VERBS 26 monetize; **issue, circulate;** devalue

27 discount, discount notes

28 **coin, mint; counterfeit, forge**

29 **cash,** cash in <nonformal>, liquidate

ADJS 30 **monetary, pecuniary, financial;** fiscal

31 convertible, liquid, negotiable

729 FINANCE, INVESTMENT

NOUNS 1 **finance, finances, money matters; high finance,** investment banking, international banking; the gnomes of Zurich

2 **financing, funding, backing, sponsorship, patronization; stake** and **grubstake** <both nonformal>; subsidy 478.8; **capitalizing**

3 **investment, venture, risk.** plunge <nonformal>, speculation; **divestment,** disinvestment

4 **banking,** money dealing; investment banking

5 **financial condition; credit rating**

6 **solvency,** soundness; creditworthiness

7 **crisis,** financial crisis; dollar crisis, dollar gap

8 **financier,** moneyman, **capitalist;** investor

9 **financer, backer, sponsor, patron, supporter,** angel <nonformal>, **fundraiser**

10 banker, money dealer, money-monger; money broker

11 treasurer, bursar, **cashier; paymaster**

12 treasury, treasure-house; depository, repository; **strongbox, safe, coffer, locker, chest; vault, till;** bursary; **public treasury**

13 bank, banking house, **central bank**

14 purse, wallet, pocketbook, bag, handbag, billfold, money belt, **pocket;** purse strings

VERBS **15 finance, back, fund, sponsor, patronize, support,** capitalize, bankroll <nonformal>; **stake** or **grubstake**

16 invest; risk, venture; invest in, put money in, pour money into; plunge <nonformal>, speculate 737.23

ADJS **17 solvent, sound,** creditworthy; **able to pay,** good for

18 insolvent, unsound, indebted 623.8

730 BUSINESSMAN, MERCHANT

NOUNS **1 businessman,** businesswoman, businessperson, businesspeople; entrepreneur; magnate, tycoon <nonformal>, baron; **industrialist,** captain of industry

2 merchant, merchandiser, marketer, **trader,** trafficker, **dealer,** monger; **tradesman,** tradeswoman; **storekeeper, shopkeeper; wholesaler,** jobber, middleman; **distributor; retailer; dealership, distributorship**

3 salesman, seller, salesperson, salesclerk; **saleswoman,** saleslady, salesgirl; **clerk; agent, sales agent**

4 traveling salesman, traveler, commercial traveler, knight of the road; detail man

5 vendor, peddler, huckster, hawker; sidewalk salesman

6 solicitor, canvasser

7 <nonformal terms> tout, touter, **pitch-man** or **-woman** or person, **ballyhoo man**

8 auctioneer, auction agent

9 broker, note broker, bill broker <Brit>, discount broker

10 ragman, old-clothesman; **junkman,** junk dealer

11 tradesmen, tradespeople, tradesfolk, **merchantry**

ADJS **12 business, commercial,** mercantile

731 COMMERCE, ECONOMICS

NOUNS **1 commerce, trade, traffic,** intercourse, **dealing, dealings; business,** the marketplace; **market,** marketing; **industry** 725.4

2 trade, trading, doing business, trafficking; bartering, **exchange;** horse trading, **dealing, deal-making,** wheeling and dealing <nonformal>; **buying and selling; wholesaling, retailing**

3 negotiation, bargaining, haggling, dickering, chaffering, hammering out a deal

4 transaction, deal, business deal

5 bargain, deal <nonformal>, dicker; **trade, swap** <nonformal>; horse trade <nonformal>

6 custom, patronage, trade; **goodwill,** good name

7 economy, economic system, free-enterprise economy, market economy, socialist or socialistic economy, collectivized economy

8 standard of living; real wages, take-home pay; **cost of living**

9 business cycle, economic cycle, business fluctuations; prosperity; **recession, depression; growth,** economic growth, **economic expansion; trade cycle; monetary cycle; inflation,** deflation, stagflation

10 economics, economic science, the dismal science; classical economics; Keynesian economics, Keynesianism; supply side economics

11 economist, economic expert

12 commercialism, mercantilism; industrialism

13 commercialization; industrialization

VERBS **14 trade, deal, traffic, truck, buy and sell, do business; barter; exchange, swap** <nonformal>, **swap horses** and **horse-trade** <both nonformal>; **ply one's trade** 724.12

15 deal in, trade in, traffic in, handle, carry; **sell**

16 trade with, deal with, traffic with, do business with, have dealings with; shop at, **patronize,** take one's business or trade to

17 bargain, drive a bargain, negotiate, haggle, chaffer, **deal, dicker,** make a deal, hack out or work out or hammer out a deal; drive a hard bargain

18 strike a bargain, make a deal, shake on it <nonformal>; **come to terms** 332.10; be a go and be a deal <both nonformal>

19 put on a business basis or footing

20 <adjust the economy> cool or cool off the economy; heat or heat up the economy

ADJS **21 commercial, business, trade,** trading, **mercantile,** merchant; mercantilistic

22 economic; socio-economic

732 ILLICIT BUSINESS

NOUNS **1** illicit business, illegitimate business, illegal operations, shady dealings, **racket** <nonformal>; **the rackets** <nonformal>, the syndicate, **organized crime, Mafia,** Cosa Nostra; **black market,** gray market; **drug** or **narcotics traffic; prostitution; pimping**

2 smuggling, contraband; gunrunning

3 contraband, smuggled goods; narcotics, drugs; stolen goods or property, hot goods <nonformal>

4 racketeer; Mafioso; **black marketeer,** gray marketeer; bootlegger; pusher and dealer <both nonformal>, drug pusher <nonformal>; **drug lord**

5 smuggler, runner; mule <nonformal>

6 fence, receiver of stolen goods, bagman, bagwoman

VERBS **7** <deal in illicit goods> push <nonformal>; **sell under the counter; blackmarket;** fence <nonformal>

8 smuggle, run, sneak

733 PURCHASE

NOUNS **1 purchase, buying, purchasing; shopping, marketing;** comparison shopping; window-shopping; impulse buying; shopping spree; **buying up, cornering; buying** or **purchasing power; consumerism**

2 option, first option, first refusal

3 market, public; **clientele, customers, patronage, custom,** trade; carriage trade

4 customer, client; patron, regular; **prospect;** mark or sucker <both nonformal>

5 buyer, consumer; shopper; browser

6 decoy, shill <nonformal>

VERBS **7 purchase, buy,** procure, make a deal for, blow oneself to <nonformal>; **buy up, corner,** monopolize

8 shop, market, go shopping, go marketing; **shop around; browse;** impulse-buy

9 bid, make a bid, make an offer; shill <nonformal>; bid up

ADJS **10 purchasing, buying,** in the market; cliental

11 bought, store-bought, purchased

734 SALE

NOUNS **1 sale; wholesale, retail; market, demand**

2 selling, merchandising, marketing; wholesaling, jobbing; **retailing; vending, peddling, hawking, huckstering;** hucksterism; sales campaign, sales promotion; **salesmanship**

3 sale, closing-out sale, going-out-of-business sale

4 auction, auction sale; Dutch auction; **auction block, block**

5 sales talk, sales pitch, patter; **pitch** or spiel or ballyhoo <all nonformal>

6 sales resistance, consumer or buyer resistance

7 salability, salableness, commerciality

VERBS **8 sell, merchandise, market,** move, make a sale; **sell out,** close out; **retail; wholesale;** dump, unload, flood the market with

9 vend, dispense, **peddle, hawk, huckster**

10 put up for sale, put up, offer for sale

11 auction, auction off, auctioneer, sell at auction, **put on the block**

12 be sold, sell, bring, realize, sell for

ADJS **13 sales, marketing, merchandising, retail,** wholesale

14 salable, marketable, retailable, merchandisable; in demand

15 unsalable, nonsalable, **unmarketable;** on one's hands, not moving, unbought, unsold

ADVS **16 for sale,** to sell, up for sale; marked down

17 at auction, by auction, **on the block**

735 MERCHANDISE

NOUNS **1 merchandise, commodities, wares, goods; items,** oddments; **consumer goods,** consumer items; **stock, stock-intrade; inventory; line; luxury goods**

2 commodity, ware, vendible, **product, article, item,** article of commerce *or* merchandise

3 dry goods, soft goods; textiles; yard goods

4 hard goods, durables, durable goods; appliances 385.4; **hardware; housewares,** home furnishings

5 furniture 229, furnishings, home furnishings

6 notions, sundries, novelties, knickknacks

7 groceries, food items, edibles; **produce**

736 MARKET
<place of trade>

NOUNS **1 market, mart, store, shop,** boutique; **retail store;** **wholesale house, discount store, discount house, outlet store; general store, department store; co-op; variety store, dime store; ten-cent store; trading post; supermarket**

2 marketplace, mart, market, open market; shopping center, shopping plaza *or* **mall; bazaar, fair,** flea market

3 booth, stall, stand; newsstand, kiosk

4 vending machine, coin machine, **automat**

5 salesroom, showroom

6 counter, shopboard <old>

737 STOCK MARKET

NOUNS **1 stock market, the market, Wall Street**

2 active market, brisk market

3 inactive market, slow market

4 rising market, bull market, bullishness

5 declining market, bear market, bearishness; **slump, crash**

6 rigged market, manipulated market

7 stock exchange, exchange, Wall Street, **stock market, board;** ticker

8 financial district, Wall Street, the Street

9 stockbrokerage, brokerage, brokerage house

10 stockbroker, broker, registered representative

11 speculator, plunger, arbitrager *or* arbitrageur; inside trader

12 bear, short, short seller

13 bull, long

14 stockholder, shareholder; bondholder

15 stock company, joint-stock company

16 trust, investment company

17 pool, bear pool, bull pool

18 stockbroking, brokerage, stockbrokerage, jobbing

19 trading; speculation; venture; arbitrage, arbitraging; **buyout, takeover; leverage**

20 **manipulation, rigging; raid, corner,** wash sale
21 option, stock option, right, put, call
22 **panic,** bear panic, rich man's panic
VERBS 23 **trade, speculate,** venture, operate, **play the market; arbitrage; plunge,** take a flier <nonformal>
24 **sell,** liquidate; **sell short**
25 manipulate the market
26 corner, get a corner on, corner the market

738 SECURITIES

NOUNS 1 **securities, stocks and bonds,** investment securities
2 stock, shares <Brit>, equity
3 **share, lot;** round lot; odd lot
4 **stock certificate**; street certificate; **coupon**
5 bond; nominal rate
6 issue, issuance; flotation
7 **dividend;** regular dividend; special dividend; **interest** 623.3; **return, yield**
8 assessment, Irish dividend
9 **price, quotation;** bid-and-asked prices, **par**
10 margin
11 <commodities> spots, spot grain, etc; futures
VERBS 12 **issue, float,** put on the market; issue stock
13 **declare a dividend,** cut a melon <nonformal>
ADVS 14 dividend off, ex dividend; dividend on, cum dividend

739 WORKPLACE

NOUNS 1 **workplace,** worksite, **workshop, shop;** shop floor, workspace; **bench; work station; desk; workroom;** studio, *atelier* <Fr>; **establishment, facility; company, corporation;** financial institution, stock exchange 737, **bank** 729; **market, store** 736; **restaurant, eating place** 8.17
2 hive, hive of industry, bee hive
3 **plant, factory, works,** manufacturing plant; **power plant**

1031.18; **machine shop; mill, yard; factory district**
4 **foundry,** metalworks; steelworks, steel mill
5 repair shop, fix-it shop <nonformal>
6 **laboratory, lab** <nonformal>
7 **office, study,** den, carrel; **embassy**

740 WEAVING

NOUNS 1 **weaving,** weave, warp and woof *or* weft, texture; **fabric, web; interweaving, interlacing, intertwining,** intertwinement; **lacing, twining, braiding,** plaiting
2 **braid,** plait, **wreath,** wreathwork
3 **warp; woof, weft,** filling; shoot, pick
4 weaver, interlacer
5 **loom;** hand loom; knitting machine
VERBS 6 **weave,** loom, tissue; **interweave, interlace, intertwine; lace,** enlace; **twine,** entwine; **braid,** plait, **wreathe, knit**
ADJS 7 **woven,** loomed, textile; **interwoven, interlaced, intertwined, laced,** fretted, knit; **twined,** entwined; **braided,** plaited
8 **weaving, twining; intertwining, interlacing**

741 SEWING

NOUNS 1 **sewing, needlework,** stitchery; **fancywork**
2 **sewer, needleworker, seamstress, tailor**
3 **sewing machine,** sewer
VERBS 4 **sew, stitch,** needle; stitch up, sew up; **tailor**

742 CERAMICS

NOUNS 1 **ceramics, pottery;** potting
2 **ceramic ware, ceramics; pottery, crockery; china, porcelain**
3 <materials> clay; potter's clay or earth
4 **potter's wheel,** wheel; kick wheel, power wheel

5 **kiln, oven, stove, furnace;** pyrometric cone

VERBS 6 pot, shape, **throw, throw** a pot; **fire**

ADJS 7 **ceramic,** earthen, clay, china, porcelain

743 AMUSEMENT

NOUNS 1 **amusement, entertainment, diversion,** solace, **recreation, relaxation; pastime; mirth** 109.5; **pleasure, enjoyment** 95

2 **fun;** funmaking, **play, sport; good time,** big time *and* **high time** *and* high old time <all nonformal>

3 **festivity, merrymaking, merriment, gaiety, jollity, joviality, conviviality,** whoopee *and* hoopla <both nonformal>; **revelry**

4 **festival, festivity,** festive occasion, **fete, gala, blowout** <nonformal>, **jamboree** <nonformal>; **high jinks; feast, banquet** 8.9; **fair,** carnival

5 **frolic, play,** romp, rollick, frisk, gambol, caper

6 **revel, lark, escapade,** ploy; **celebration** 487; **party** 582.11; **spree, bout, fling,** wingding <nonformal>

7 round of pleasure, mad round, whirl

8 **sports** 744; **athletics;** athleticism

9 **game;** card game; **play; contest** 457.3; **event, meet; bout, match**

10 **tournament,** tourney, **field day;** rally; **regatta**

11 **playground;** playing field; **gymnasium,** gym <nonformal>; **court; playroom** 197.12

12 **swimming pool, pool,** swimming hole

13 **entertainment; entertainment industry, show business,** show biz <nonformal>; **theater; cabaret, tavern, roadhouse; nightclub,** discothèque *or* disco <nonformal>; **resort** 228.27

14 **park,** public park, **amusement park, theme park**

15 merry-go-round, carousel, roundabout, ride

16 **toy, plaything;** bauble, gewgaw, trinket; **doll; dollhouse,** doll carriage; **hobbyhorse,** rocking horse; **hula hoop; top; jack-in-the-box;** jacks, pick-up sticks; **blocks; checkerboard,** chessboard; **marble**

17 **chessman,** man, piece; **bishop, knight, king, queen, pawn, rook** *or* castle

18 **player, frolicker, funmaker,** funster, gamboler; **pleasure-seeker, playboy** <nonformal>; **reveler, celebrant, merrymaker, carouser**

19 athlete, jock <nonformal>, player

20 master of ceremonies, MC *or* emcee <both nonformal>

VERBS 21 **amuse, entertain, divert,** exhilarate; **relax,** loosen up; **delight, tickle, titillate; make one laugh, strike one as funny**

22 **amuse oneself,** get one's kicks *or* jollies <both nonformal>; **relax,** loosen up; **have fun, have a good time,** have a ball *and* have lots of laughs <both nonformal>

23 **play, sport, disport;** frolic, rollick, gambol, frisk, romp, caper, cut capers <nonformal>; **cut up** <nonformal>

24 **make merry, revel, roister,** lark <nonformal>, **blow** *or* **let off steam;** cut loose, **kick up one's heels; paint the town red** <nonformal>; **celebrate** 487.2; **go on a spree, carouse;** sow one's wild oats, have one's fling

25 let oneself go, let loose, let go

ADJS 26 **amused,** entertained; **delighted,** tickled, tickled pink *or* to death <nonformal>

27 **amusing, entertaining, diverting,** beguiling; **fun,** more fun than a barrel of monkeys <nonformal>; **delightful,** titillating

28 **festive, festal; merry, gay, jolly, jovial, joyous, joyful,** convivial, gala, hilarious; **on the town, out on the town**

29 **playful, sportive,** sportful; **frolicsome**

30 sporting, sports; athletic

ADVS **31 in fun, for fun,** for the fun of it; for kicks *and* for laughs <both nonformal>

744 SPORTS

NOUNS **1 sport, sports, athletics,** athletic competition, contest; **ball game; track and field** 755; **gymnastics; outdoor sport; winter sport; combat sport,** martial art; **decathlon; triathlon,** biathlon; **bicycling, weightlifting, bodybuilding**

VERBS **2 play, compete;** practice, train, work out; try out, go out for; follow

745 BASEBALL

NOUNS **1 baseball, ball,** the national pastime; **organized baseball, league,** loop, circuit, **major league,** big league, **minor league,** the minors *and* bush leagues <both nonformal>; **farm team,** farm club, farm system; **ball park, ball field; stands, grandstand,** bleachers; **diamond; home plate, the plate; base line, line,** base path; **base, bag,** sack; **infield; outfield**

2 baseball team, team, nine, squad, **club,** ball club; **starting lineup, lineup batting order; starter, regular; manager, pilot, coach**

3 game, ball game; umpire; pitch; strike zone; balk; count, balls and strikes, full count; **foul ball, foul; base on balls, walk;** error, passed ball; **out,** strikeout, force-out, double play; **catch,** shoestring catch, pitch-out; **base runner,** pinch-runner; **run; inning**

4 statistics, averages, stats and numbers <nonformal>

VERBS **5 play,** play ball; **umpire,** call balls and strikes; **pitch, throw,** dust the batter off; **relieve,** put out the fire <nonformal>; **bat, be up,** step up to the plate; **hit,** belt *and* clout *and* connect <all nonformal>; **fly,** hit a fly; **ground,** bounce, lay down a bunt; sacrifice, hit a sacrifice fly; **hit,** get a base hit; **hit a home run, homer; single, double, triple; walk, get a free ride** *or* free pass <both nonformal>; **strike out,** go down *or* out on strikes

746 FOOTBALL

NOUNS **1 football, ball; organized football, college football,** conference, league; conference championship, post-season game, national championship *or* mythical national championship; **professional football,** pro football <nonformal>; **stadium,** bowl, domed stadium, dome; **field, gridiron; line**

2 football team, eleven, team, squad; starting lineup, offensive team *or* platoon, defensive team *or* platoon, kicking team; **ball,** football, pigskin *and* oblate spheroid <both nonformal>; **line, linemen, backfield,** back, tailback, flanker back, running back, blocking back, linebacker, safety; **pass receiver, receiver,** wide receiver

3 game, strategy, game plan, ball control

4 statistics, averages, stats <nonformal>

VERBS **5 play,** kick, kick off, run, scramble, pass, punt; complete a pass, catch a pass; **block, tackle,** double-team, blindside, sack, blitz, red-dog; **lose possession,** fumble, give up the ball; **score,** get on the scoreboard

747 BASKETBALL

NOUNS **1 basketball; organized basketball, college basketball; professional basketball,** pro basketball <nonformal>; **tournament,** competition, championship; **basketball court, court**

2 basketball team, five, team, squad; **basketball player,** hoopster

3 basketball game, game, play, strategy, defense, offense; **official, referee,** umpire; **foul,**

violation, infraction; **play, strategy,** fast break, passing game; **jump; pass,** assist, bounce pass; **tactics, action,** dribble, fake, hand-off, ball control; **shot, score, basket** or **field goal**

VERBS **4 play,** play basketball, play ball, **dribble,** pass, **guard, shoot, score,** sink one and can and swish <all nonformal>; **foul,** commit a foul or violation

748 TENNIS

NOUNS **1 tennis,** lawn tennis, singles, doubles, mixed doubles; **tournament,** tennis competition, match; **tennis ball, ball, tennis racket; tennis court, court,** grass surface or grass, all-weather court, clay court

2 game; official, umpire, linesmen, line umpires or linesmen; **play, stroke, shot**

VERBS **3 play tennis, play,** serve, return, drive, volley, smash, lob, fault, make an unforced error; **score** or **make a point,** break service

749 HOCKEY

NOUNS **1 hockey,** ice hockey; **professional hockey, amateur hockey; competition,** Stanley Cup; **rink,** hockey rink, boards, blue line, red line, goal line, crease, goal and net and cage

2 hockey team, team, skaters, squad, bench; line, forward line; **defense**

3 game, match; **referee,** linesman, goal judge, timekeepers, scorer; **foul, play,** stick handling, checking, passing, shooting; **pass, check; offense,** breakout; **shot,** slap shot, wrist shot; power play; **score,** hat trick; **period**

4 field hockey, banty or bandy, hurley or hurling

5 team, attack, outside left, inside left, center forward, inside right, outside right, defense

6 game, match; umpire, timekeeper; team

VERBS **7 play, skate,** pass, check, block, stick-handle or puck-

handle, give-and-go, break out, shoot, score, clear, freeze the puck, ice or ice the puck

750 BOWLING

NOUNS **1 bowling,** kegling <nonformal>, tenpin bowling or tenpins, candlepin bowling, duckpin bowling, fivepin bowling, rubberband duckpin bowling; amateur bowling, league bowling; **professional bowling,** pro bowling <nonformal>; **tournament,** competition, match-play tournament, round-robin tournament; **alley, lane,** gutter, foul line

2 game or string, frame; **delivery, approach,** follow-through, gutter ball; **pocket, strike** or ten-strike; **spare,** split; **score,** perfect game or 300 game

3 lawn bowling, lawn bowls, bowls; **bowling green,** green; **ball,** bowl; **team,** side, rink

751 GOLF

NOUNS **1 golf,** the royal and ancient; **professional golf,** pro golf <nonformal>, tour; **amateur golf,** club; **tournament,** championship, title, cup; **golf course,** course, links

2 golfer, player, scratch golfer or player, dub and duffer and hacker <all nonformal>, twosome, threesome, foursome

3 round, match, stroke play, match play, medal play; **official,** referee; **play, stroke, shot; score,** eagle, double eagle, birdie, par, bogey, double bogey, hole-in-one and ace

VERBS **4 play, shoot,** tee up, tee off, drive, hit, draw, fade, pull, push, hook, slice, top, sky, loft, dunk, putt, can <nonformal>, hole out, sink, eagle, double eagle, birdie, par, bogey, double bogey

752 SOCCER

NOUNS **1 soccer,** football; **league,** college soccer; **tournament,** championship, cup; **professional soccer,** pro soccer; **soccer field,**

field, soccer pitch, pitch, goal
line, touch line, halfway line,
goal area, goal, goalpost, corner
area

2 team, squad, side, midfielder,
goalkeeper *or* goaltender *or*
goalie

3 game, match; official, referee,
linesman; **play,** kick, throw-in,
goal kick, corner kick, save; **rule,**
law; **foul; penalty,** caution, red
card; **goal,** score, point, bonus
point; **period,** quarter, overtime
period

VERBS **4 play,** kick, kick off, trap,
pass, dribble, screen, head, center, clear, mark, tackle, save

753 SKIING

NOUNS **1 skiing,** downhill skiing,
Nordic skiing, cross-country skiing; **organized skiing,** competition skiing; **competition, championship,** cup, race; **slope,** ski
slope, ski run, mogul; **ski lift, lift,**
rope tow, chair lift; **race course,**
downhill course, slalom course;
ski-jump, ramp

2 skier, cross-country skier, ski-
jumper, downhill racer

3 race, downhill race, slalom, giant slalom, cross-country race;
technique, style, **position,** tuck
and egg, sitting position, flight
position; **maneuver, turn**

VERBS **4 ski,** run, schuss, traverse,
turn, check

754 BOXING

NOUNS **1 boxing, prizefighting,**
fighting, pugilism, noble *or* manly
art of self-defense, the ring; **amateur boxing, professional
boxing,** club fighting; Marquess
of Queensbury rules; **boxing
ring, ring,** prize ring, canvas

2 boxer, fighter, pugilist,
prizefighter, pug <nonformal>,
slugger; **weight;** division; **manager; trainer; handler;** second,
sparring partner

3 fight, match, bout; official,
referee, judge, timekeeper;
strategy, fight-plan, style, foot-
work, **offense, punch,** blow;

defense, feint, clinching; **foul;
win, knockout** *or* **KO,** technical
knockout *or* TKO, decision;
round

VERBS **4 fight, box,** punch, spar,
mix it up <nonformal>, clinch,
slip a punch, duck, feint, slug,
maul, go down for the count

755 TRACK AND FIELD

NOUNS **1 track, track and field;
games,** competition, cup; **stadium, arena,** oval, field house;
track, lane, finish line, **infield;**
lap, victory lap

2 track meet, meet, games,
program; **running event; field
event; all-around event,** decathlon, heptathlon, pentathlon; triathlon; **race walking,** the walk,
heel-and-toe racing

756 AUTOMOBILE RACING

NOUNS **1 automobile racing, auto
racing, car racing; racing association; race,** competition,
championship; **track,** speedway,
dirt track; **car, racing car,** racer;
racing engine; supercharger,
turbocharger; **tires, racing tires,**
shoes <nonformal>, slicks; **body,**
spoiler, roll bar; **wheel,** wire
wheel *or* wire, magnesium wheel
or mag; **fuel, racing fuel,** meth-
anol, nitromethane *or* nitro

**2 race driving, racing driver,
driver,** fast driver *or* leadfoot
<nonformal>, slow driver *or*
balloon foot, novice driver *or*
yellowtail

3 race, driving, start, flying start,
paced start; **position,** inside position, pole *or* pole position; **track,**
turn, curve, hairpin, switchback,
banked turn, corner, drift,
straightaway *or* chute, pit, pit
area; **signal,** black flag, white
flag, checkered flag; **lap,** pace
lap, victory lap

VERBS **4 drive, race,** start, jump,
rev, accelerate, slow down, back
off, stroke it, draft, fishtail

ADVS **5 at top speed,** flat-out, full-
bore, ten-tenths ride the rail,
spin, spin out, crash, t-bone

757 HORSE RACING

NOUNS **1 horse racing, the turf,** the sport of kings; **flat racing; harness racing,** trotting, pacing; **Triple Crown,** Kentucky Derby, Preakness Stakes, Belmont Stakes; **racetrack, track,** racecourse, turf, oval, course, strip; rail, inside rail, infield, paddock; turf track, steeplejack course; gate *and* barrier

2 jockey, jock, rider, money rider; apprentice jockey, bug <nonformal>; **railbird** <nonformal>, turf-man; **racehorse, pony,** thoroughbred, standardbred, mount, trotter, pacer, quarter horse, bangtail *and* filly *and* gee-gee <all nonformal>; **sire, dam,** stallion, stud, stud horse, brood mare, gelding; **horse,** three-year-old, two-year-old, colt, filly, foal, maiden, yearling; **favorite,** chalk, choice, odds-on favorite; runner, front-runner, pacesetter; **nag** *and* hayburner *and* plater *and* selling plater <all nonformal>

3 horse race, race; race meeting, race card, scratch sheet; **starters,** field; **start, break,** off; easy race, romp, shoo-in, armchair ride, hand ride; **finish,** dead heat, photo finish; **dishonest race,** boat race *and* fixed race <both nonformal>

4 statistics, records, chart, **form, racing form,** past performance, **track record,** dope *or* tip *or* tout sheet <nonformal>; **betting;** pari-mutuel 759.4

VERBS **5 race, run; start, break, be off;** make a move, drive, extend; fade, come back; ride out, run wide; **win,** romp *or* breeze in; **place, show,** be in the money; be out of the money

ADJS **6 winning, in the money;** losing, out of the money; out in front

758 CARDPLAYING

NOUNS **1 cardplaying,** shuffling, dealing; **card game,** game; gambling 759, gambling games

2 card, playing card, pasteboard; **deck, pack; suit; face card; king,** cowboy *and* sergeant from K Company <both nonformal>; **queen,** queen of spades, Black Maria *and* Maria *and* slippery Anne <all nonformal>; **jack,** knave, one-eyed jack; **joker; ace,** bull *and* bullet *and* seed *and* spike <all nonformal>

3 bridge, auction bridge, contract bridge, rubber bridge, duplicate *or* tournament bridge; **bridge player,** partner, dummy, North and South, East and West; **suit,** major suit, minor suit, trump suit, trump *or* trumps; **call, bid;** pass; **hand; play,** lead, **trick,** quick trick *or* honor trick; **score,** grand slam, little slam *or* small slam, game, rubber

VERBS **4 shuffle,** make up the pack, fan *and* wash <both nonformal>; cut; **deal**

759 GAMBLING

NOUNS **1 gambling, playing, betting, action,** wagering, hazarding, gaming, taking *or* giving *or* laying odds; **speculation, play;** drawing *or* casting lots, tossing a coin

2 gamble, chance, risk, risky thing, hazard; gambling *or* gambler's chance, betting proposition, bet, **luck of the draw,** roll *or* throw of the dice, turn of the wheel, turn of the cards, toss of a coin, toss; heads or tails; pig in a poke; shot in the dark; potshot, random shot; **speculation, venture,** flier *and* plunge <both nonformal>; calculated risk

3 bet, wager, stake, hazard, lay; cinch bet *or* sure thing; long shot; **ante;** parlay

4 betting system; pari-mutuel, off-track betting *or* OTB

5 pot, jackpot, pool, stakes, kitty; bank; office pool

6 gambling odds, odds, price; **short odds, long odds,** long shot; even chance, small chance, no chance 971.10; **handicapper,** odds maker, pricemaker

7 game of chance, friendly game; card games

8 dice, bones *and* rolling bones *and* ivories <all nonformal>, **craps,** crap shooting, crap game, floating crap game; **false** *or* crooked *or* loaded dice

9 <throw of dice> **throw, cast, rattle, roll, shot**

10 poker, draw poker *or* five-card draw, stud poker *or* stud, five-card stud *or* seven-card stud; **straight poker; poker hand;** bad hand *or* cards; **openers,** raise *or* kick *or* bump *or* pump *or* push

11 blackjack *or* **twenty-one**; deal, card count, blackjack *or* natural; card-counting

12 roulette, American roulette, European roulette; wheel, American wheel, European wheel

13 cheating, angle, con *and* grift *and* scam *and* sting <all nonformal>; deception 356

14 lottery, drawing, sweepstakes; **raffle; state lottery; numbers game** *or* **policy**

15 bingo, slow death <nonformal>, keno, lotto

16 <gambling device> wheel of fortune; cage, birdcage; pinball machine; slot machine, the slots, one-armed bandit <nonformal>; **layout** *or* green cloth, gambling table, craps table, roulette table

17 pari-mutuel, pari-mutuel machine; totalizator, totalizer, tote *and* tote board <both nonformal>, odds board

18 chip, check, counter, bean <nonformal>

19 casino, gambling house, house, betting parlor, gambling den, gambling hall; illegal gambling house, clip joint *and* deadfall *and* flat joint *and* wire joint *and* wolf trap <all nonformal>; **handbook, book,** bookie joint <nonformal>, horse room, off-track betting parlor, OTB

20 bookmaker, bookie <nonformal>; **tout**

21 gambler, player, sport; **bettor,** wagerer, punter; high roller, plunger; low roller, piker *and* tin-

horn *and* tinhorn gambler <all nonformal>; **professional gambler; skillful gambler, sharp, shark,** sharper, river gambler *and* dice gospeller *and* sharpie <all nonformal>; **cardsharp** *or* cardshark, cardsharper; **card counter**; crap shooter <nonformal>; compulsive gambler; **spectator, kibitzer**

22 cheater, cheat, bunco artist *and* grifter *and* hustler *and* rook *and* worker <all nonformal>; **dupe, victim,** john *and* lamb *and* mark *and* monkey *and* patsy *and* **sucker** <all nonformal>

VERBS **23 gamble,** game, play, **try one's luck; speculate; run** *or* **bank a game; cast lots;** cut the cards *or* deck; shoot craps, roll the bones <nonformal>; play the ponies <nonformal>

24 chance, risk, hazard, venture, wager, take a flier <nonformal>; **gamble on,** take a gamble on; **take a chance, chance it; take** *or* **run the risk; take chances,** tempt fortune; **leave** *or* **trust to chance** *or* **luck;** buy a pig in a poke

25 bet, wager, gamble, hazard, stake, punt, lay, **make a bet, lay a wager,** give *or* take *or* lay odds, make book, get a piece of the action <nonformal>; **bet on** *or* **upon, back;** play *or* follow the ponies <nonformal>; parlay; **ante, ante up; cover, call,** fade; **check, sandbag** <nonformal>, **pass,** stand pat

26 cheat, pluck *and* skin *and* rook <all nonformal>

ADJS **27 speculative, uncertain** 970.15; **hazardous, risky** 1005.10, dicey <nonformal>; **lucky,** hot *and* red hot *and* on a roll <all nonformal>; **unlucky,** cold <nonformal>

760 EXISTENCE

NOUNS **1 existence, being;** subsistence, entity, noumenon; **occurrence,** presence; **materiality** 1050, **substantiality** 762; **life** 306

2 **reality, actuality,** empirical *or* demonstrable *or* objective existence; **truth** 972; **authenticity**

3 **fact,** the truth of the matter; **matter of fact; bare fact,** naked fact, **simple fact,** simple *or* sober truth; **cold fact,** hard fact, **stubborn fact, brutal fact,** the nitty-gritty *and* the bottom line <both nonformal>; **actual fact, self-evident fact,** axiom, postulate, premise; **accepted fact,** established fact; **demonstrable fact, circumstance** 765; **salient fact**

4 **the facts,** the particulars, the details, the specifics, **the data;** the dope *and* the scoop *and* the score <all nonformal>

5 self-existence, uncreated being

6 **mere existence,** simple existence, **vegetable existence, vegetation**

7 <philosophy of being> ontology, metaphysics, existentialism

VERBS 8 **exist, be,** be in existence; breathe, **live** 306.7; subsist, stand, obtain, hold, prevail; **occur**

9 **live on,** continue to exist, persist, last, stand the test of time, endure 826.6

10 **vegetate,** merely exist, just be, pass the time

11 **exist in, consist in,** subsist in, lie in, **inhere in,** be present in, be a quality of

12 **become,** come to be, get to be, turn out to be; turn into 857.17; grow 860.5; be changed

ADJS 13 **existent, existing,** in existence, de facto; **subsistent,** subsisting; **being,** in being; **living** 306.11; **present, extant, prevalent, current**

14 self-existent, self-existing

15 **real, actual,** factual, veritable, for real <nonformal>, de facto, **hard; absolute, positive; self-evident,** axiomatic; accepted, conceded, stipulated, given; **established, inescapable, indisputable, undeniable; demonstrable,** provable; empirical, ob-

jective; **true** 972.12; **authentic; substantial** 762.6

ADVS 16 **really, actually; factually; genuinely,** veritably, **truly; in reality,** in actuality, in fact, de facto; positively, absolutely

761 NONEXISTENCE

NOUNS 1 **nonexistence,** nonsubsistence; **nonbeing,** unbeing; **nothingness,** nullity; vacancy, deprivation, emptiness, inanity, vacuity 222.2; vacuum, void 222.3; nonoccurrence; **unreality,** nonreality

2 **nothing, nil, naught, aught;** zero, cipher; nothing whatever

3 <nonformal terms> zilch, zip, zippo, nix, goose egg

4 **none,** not any, none at all, not a one, not a blessed one <nonformal>, never a one, ne'er a one; **not a bit**

VERBS 5 **not exist,** not occur, not be found, be absent *or* lacking *or* wanting

6 **cease to exist** *or* **be,** be annihilated, be destroyed, **be wiped out,** be extirpated, be eradicated; **go, vanish,** be no more, leave no trace; **vanish, disappear** 34.2, evaporate; **perish, expire,** pass away, **die** 307.19

7 **annihilate** 395.13, **exterminate** 395.14, eradicate, extirpate, **eliminate,** liquidate, **wipe out, stamp out**

ADJS 8 **nonexistent,** unexistent, nowhere to be found; **minus, missing,** lacking, wanting; **null, void,** vacuous; **negative**

9 **unreal,** unrealistic; **immaterial** 1051.7; **unsubstantial** 763.5; **imaginary, imagined, fantastic, fanciful, fancied** 985.19-22; illusory

10 **uncreated, unmade,** unborn, unbegotten, unconceived, unproduced

11 **no more, extinct, defunct, dead** 307.30, expired, passed away; perished, annihilated; gone, all gone

ADVS 12 **none, no,** not at all, in no way, to no extent

762 SUBSTANTIALITY

NOUNS **1 substantiality**, substantialness; materiality 1050; **substance, body**, mass; **solidity**, density, concreteness, **tangibility**, palpability; **sturdiness, stability, strength**, durability

2 substance, stuff, fabric, material, matter 1050.2, medium; **elements**, constituents, ingredients, components, building blocks

3 something, thing; being, **entity**, unit, individual; **person**, persona, personality; **creature**; **organism**, life form, living thing, life; **object** 1050.4

4 embodiment, incarnation, materialization, substantiation

VERBS **5 embody**, incarnate, **materialize**, concretize, body forth, lend substance to, reify

ADJS **6 substantial**, substantive; **solid, concrete; tangible**, sensible, palpable; **material** 1050.9; **real** 760.15; **created**

7 sturdy, stable, **solid**, sound, firm, steady, tough, stout, **strong**, rugged; **durable**, enduring; **hard, dense**, unyielding; **well-made**, well-built; **well-founded**, well-established, well-grounded; **massive**

ADVS **8 substantially**, essentially, materially

763 UNSUBSTANTIALITY

NOUNS **1 unsubstantiality**, insubstantiality; **immateriality** 1051; **intangibility**, impalpability; **thinness, tenuousness**, attenuation, ethereality; **fragility, frailness; flimsiness** 16.2; **transience** 827, **ephemerality**, ephemeralness

2 thing of naught, nullity, zero; **nonentity, nobody** <nonformal>, nonperson; **trifle** 997.5; nothing 761.2

3 spirit, air, **thin air**, ether, **bubble, shadow**, mere shadow; illusion 975; phantom 987.1

VERBS **4 spiritualize, disembody**, dematerialize; etherealize, **at-**

tenuate, weaken, enervate, sap

ADJS **5 unsubstantial**, insubstantial; intangible, impalpable; **immaterial** 1051.7; **bodiless**, incorporeal; **transient** 827.7, ephemeral, fle .ting, fugitive

6 thin, tenuous, evanescent, rarefied; **ethereal**, airy, vaporous, gaseous; **chimerical**, gossamer; dreamlike, **illusory, unreal**; fatuous, fatuitous, inane; **imaginary**, fanciful 985.20

7 fragile, frail 1048.4; **flimsy**, shaky, **unsound**, infirm 16.15

8 baseless, groundless, ungrounded, **without foundation**, unfounded, built on sand

764 STATE

NOUNS **1 state**, modality; **status, situation**, status quo, standing, footing, location, bearings, spot; **rank**, estate, station, **standing; condition**, circumstance 765; **case, lot; predicament, plight**, pass

2 the state of affairs, how things stand, how things are, **the way things are**, the way things go, the way the cookie crumbles, **how it is**, the lay of the land

3 good condition, bad condition; adjustment, fettle, form, order, repair, **shape** <nonformal>, trim

4 mode, manner, way, tenor, vein, fashion, style, thing and bag <both nonformal>; **form**, shape, guise, complexion, make-up; **role**

VERBS **5 be in** or **have** a certain state, **fare; enjoy** or **occupy** a certain position; **get on** or **along**, come on or along <nonformal>; **manage** <nonformal>, **contrive, make out** <nonformal>; **turn out**

ADJS **6** conditional, modal, formal, situational, statal

7 in condition or **order** or repair or **shape; out of order**, out of commission and **out of kilter** or kelter and out of whack <all nonformal>

765 CIRCUMSTANCE

NOUNS 1 **circumstance, occurrence, occasion, event** 830, **incident; condition** 764.1

2 **circumstances,** terms of reference, **environment** 209, context, frame, setting, surrounding conditions; **the picture,** full particulars

3 **particular, instance, item, detail,** point, matter, article, ingredient, factor, facet, aspect; **respect, regard,** angle

4 circumstantiality, particularity

5 **circumstantiation,** itemization, particularization, specification, spelling-out, detailing

VERBS 6 **itemize, specify,** particularize, **spell out, detail,** anatomize; **analyze** 800.6; **cite,** instance, adduce, document; **substantiate**

ADJS 7 **circumstantial,** conditional, provisional; **incidental,** adventitious, **accidental, chance,** fortuitous

8 environmental, contextual, attending, attendant, limiting

9 **detailed, minute, full, particular,** meticulous, fussy, finicky or finicking or finical, picayune

ADVS 10 **thus, thusly** <nonformal>, **so,** just so, like this, like that, just like that; similarly 783.18, precisely

11 **accordingly, in that case, in that event, at that rate,** that being so, **under the circumstances,** as matters stand, **therefore** 887.7, **consequently; as the case may be; by the same token,** equally

12 **circumstantially,** conditionally, provisionally

13 **fully, in full, in detail,** specifically, particularly, completely 793.14, **at length**

766 INTRINSICALITY

NOUNS 1 **intrinsicality, inwardness; inbeing,** immanence; **innateness, inherence,** indigenousness; **subjectivity,** internal reality

2 **essence, substance,** essential nature, quiddity; **quintessence, epitome,** embodiment, incarnation; **essential,** principle, postulate, axiom; **gist,** gravamen, **nub** <nonformal>, **core, pith,** meat; **heart**

3 <nonformal terms> **meat and potatoes,** nuts and bolts, the nitty-gritty, the guts, the name of the game, the bottom line

4 **nature, character, quality; constitution,** composition, **characteristics,** constituents; **build,** body-build, somatotype; **temperament,** temper, fiber, **disposition,** spirit; **way, habit,** tenor, cast, hue, tone, grain, vein, streak, stripe, mold, brand, stamp; **kind** 808.3, **sort, type,** ilk; **property, characteristic** 864.4; **tendency** 895

5 **inner nature,** true being, essential nature, what makes one tick <nonformal>, vital principle; **spirit, soul, heart, breast, bosom, inner person,** heart of hearts, bottom or cockles of the heart; **vital principle,** life force

VERBS 6 **inhere,** indwell; run in the blood, run in the family, inherit

ADJS 7 **intrinsic,** internal, **inner,** inward; **inherent,** implicit, immanent; inalienable, unchallengeable, irreducible, qualitative; **ingrained;** infixed, implanted, deep-seated; **subjective,** esoteric, private, secret

8 **innate, inborn,** born, congenital; **native, natural,** indigenous; **constitutional,** bodily, physical, organic; **inbred, genetic, hereditary,** inherited, in the blood, rooted; **instinctive,** instinctual, atavistic, primal

9 **essential, fundamental; primary,** primitive, primal, elemental, bare-bones and nofrills and bread-and-butter <all nonformal>, original, **basic, gut** <nonformal>, underlying; **substantive,** material

ADVS 10 **intrinsically, inherently,** innately; **inwardly, immanently;**

naturally, congenitally, genetically, by birth, by nature
11 essentially, fundamentally, primarily, basically; at bottom, at
heart; in essence, at the core; substantially, materially, most of all

767 EXTRINSICALITY

NOUNS 1 extrinsicality, extraneousness, otherness, discreteness; objectivity, impersonality
2 nonessential, unessential, carrying coals to Newcastle; accessory, extra, collateral; appendage, appurtenance, supplement,
addition, addendum, adjunct
254; subsidiary, subordinate,
secondary; contingency, incidental, accidental, mere chance; superfluity, superfluousness; fifth
wheel <nonformal>
ADJS 3 extrinsic, external, outly-
ing; extraneous, foreign; objective, impersonal
4 unessential, nonessential, unnecessary, superfluous; accessory, extra, collateral, auxiliary;
adventitious, adscititious; additional, supplementary, supple-
mental; secondary, subsidiary,
subordinate; incidental, circumstantial, contingent; accidental,
chance, fortuitous, aleatory; indeterminate, unpredictable,
capricious

768 ACCOMPANIMENT

NOUNS 1 accompaniment; synchronism, simultaneity 835, simultaneousness; coincidence,
concurrence; parallelism
2 company, association, society,
community; companionship,
fellowship
3 attendant, concomitant, corollary, accessory, appendage;
adjunct 254
4 accompanier, accompanist;
attendant, companion, fellow,
mate, consort, partner
5 escort, conductor, usher, shepherd; guide, cicerone; squire;
chaperon, duenna; bodyguard,
guard, convoy; companion, sidekick <nonformal>

6 attendance, following, cortege, retinue, entourage, suite,
train, body of retainers
VERBS 7 accompany, keep one
company, keep company with,
go or travel or run with, go along
with, attend, wait on or upon;
associate with, consort with,
hang around with and hang out
with and hang with <all nonfor-
mal>; combine 804.3, associate,
flock or band or herd together
8 escort, conduct, have in tow
<nonformal>, marshal, usher,
shepherd, guide, lead; convoy,
guard; squire, attend, wait on or
upon
ADJS 9 accompanying, attending,
attendant, concomitant, accessory, collateral; combined 804.5,
associated, coupled, paired; fellow, twin, joint, joined 799.13;
simultaneous, concurrent, coincident
ADVS 10 hand in hand or glove,
arm in arm, side by side, cheek
by jowl, shoulder to shoulder
11 together, collectively, mutually, jointly, in conjunction, in a
body, in association; simultaneously, coincidentally,
concurrently

769 ASSEMBLAGE

NOUNS 1 assemblage, assembly,
collection, gathering, ingather-
ing, congregation; concourse,
confluence, convergence; mobilization, call-up, muster; comparison 942
2 assembly <of persons>, gathering, forgathering, congregation, congress, conference, convocation, concourse, meeting,
get-together <nonformal>; convention, synod, council, conclave; caucus; rally; session,
séance; panel, symposium, colloquium; party, festivity 743.4,
fete, soiree, reception, dance,
ball, shindig and brawl <both
nonformal>; rendezvous, date,
assignation
3 company, group, network,
party, band, knot, gang, crew,

complement, cast, outfit, **body,** corps; **team,** squad, string; covey, bevy; posse, contingent; **party, faction,** movement, wing, persuasion; coterie, salon, clique, **set;** junta, cabal

4 **throng, multitude, horde,** host, panoply, legion; flock, cluster, galaxy; **crowd,** press, crush, flood, spate, deluge, mass; **mob,** rabble

5 <animals> flock, bunch, pack, colony, host, troop, army, herd

6 <birds, insects> flock, flight, swarm, cloud

7 **bunch, group,** grouping, crop, **cluster, clump,** knot; **batch, lot,** slew <nonformal>, **mess** <nonformal>

8 **bundle, pack, package,** packet, **parcel,** sack, bag, poke <nonformal>, **roll,** bolt; quiver, sheaf; bouquet, nosegay, posy

9 **accumulation,** cumulation, gathering, **amassment,** congeries; agglomeration, conglomeration; **aggregation,** aggregate; **mass, lump,** gob <nonformal>, chunk *and* hunk <both nonformal>, wad

10 **pile, heap, stack; mound, hill;** molehill, anthill; bank, embankment, dune

11 **collection,** collectibles; **holdings,** fund, treasure; corpus, **body,** data; compilation, anthology, treasury; chrestomathy

12 **set, suit, suite, series,** outfit <nonformal>

13 **miscellany; assortment, medley, variety, mixture** 796; hodgepodge, conglomerate, **conglomeration; sundries, odds and ends**

14 <a putting together> assembly, assemblage

15 **collector,** gatherer, accumulator, connoisseur, fancier, enthusiast, pack rat *and* magpie <both nonformal>

VERBS 16 **come together, assemble, congregate, collect,** come from far and wide; **unite** 799.5; muster, **meet, gather, forgather,** mass; **merge,** converge, fuse; **throng, crowd,** swarm, teem, hive, surge, seethe; **be crowded,** be mobbed, burst at the seams, be full to overflowing; **cluster,** bunch, bunch up, clot; **huddle,** go into a huddle, close ranks; **couple,** copulate, link

17 **convene, meet,** hold a meeting *or* session, sit; **convoke,** summon, call together

18 <bring or gather together> assemble, gather; drum up, muster, rally, mobilize

19 **pile, pile on, heap, stack,** heap *or* pile *or* stack up; mound, hill; bank, bank up; rick; pyramid; drift

20 **bundle,** bundle up, **package, pack,** bag, truss up; bale; wrap, **wrap up**

ADJS 21 **assembled, collected, gathered;** congregated; **combined** 804.5; **joined** 799.13; joint, leagued 804.6; **accumulated,** cumulate, massed, **amassed;** heaped, stacked, piled; **clustered,** bunched, lumped, clumped, knotted

22 **crowded, packed, crammed;** bumper-to-bumper <nonformal>, jam-packed; **compact,** firm, solid, dense, close; **teeming, swarming, crawling,** bristling, populous

23 **cumulative,** accumulative, total, overall

770 DISPERSION

NOUNS 1 **dispersion** *or* **dispersal,** scattering, diffraction; **distribution, spreading,** broadcasting, **broadcast, spread, dissemination,** propagation, dispensation; **radiation,** divergence 171; **diffusion; dilution,** attenuation, thinning-out, watering-down, weakening; **evaporation,** dissipation

2 **decentralization,** deconcentration

3 **disbandment,** dispersion *or* dispersal, diaspora, separation, parting; breakup, split-up <nonformal>; **demobilization,** deactivation, **release;** dissolution, disintegration 805

VERBS 4 **disperse, scatter,** diffract; **distribute, broadcast, sow,** disseminate, propagate, publish 352.10; **diffuse, spread,** strew, bestrew; **radiate,** diverge 171.5; splay, branch *or* fan *or* spread out; **issue, deal out,** retail, dispense

5 **dissipate, dispel,** attenuate, dilute, thin, water down, weaken; **evaporate,** volatilize

6 **sprinkle,** besprinkle, **spatter,** splatter; **dot,** spot, speck, speckle, stud; **pepper,** powder, dust

7 decentralize, deconcentrate

8 **disband, disperse, scatter, separate, part,** break up, split up; part company, go separate ways; **demobilize,** deactivate, muster out, **release,** detach, discharge; dismiss 908.18; **dissolve,** disintegrate 805.3

ADJS 9 **dispersed, scattered, distributed,** dissipated, disseminated, strewn, broadcast, **spread; widespread,** diffuse, sparse; **diluted,** thinned, thinned-out, watered, watered-down; **sporadic**

10 **sprinkled,** spattered, splattered, splashed, **peppered,** spotted, dotted, powdered, dusted, specked, speckled, **studded**

11 dispersive, **scattering, spreading, distributive,** disseminative, diffusive, dissipative

ADVS 12 **scatteringly, dispersedly,** diffusely, sparsely, **sporadically,** *passim* <L>, **here and there;** in places, **in spots** <nonformal>

771 INCLUSION

NOUNS 1 **inclusion, comprisal, comprehension,** coverage, incorporation, embodiment, assimilation, reception; **membership,** participation, eligibility, legitimation, legitimization; **power-sharing,** enfranchisement; **completeness** 793, **inclusiveness, comprehensiveness,** exhaustiveness; **whole** 791

2 **entailment, involvement, implication;** assumption, presumption, presupposition

VERBS 3 **include, comprise, con-**
tain, comprehend,** hold, **take in; cover,** occupy, take up, fill; **complete** 793.6; **embrace,** encompass, incorporate, assimilate, embody, envisage; **legitimize,** legitimatize; **share power,** enable, enfranchise, cut in *and* deal in *and* give a piece of the action <all nonformal>

4 <include as a necessary circumstance or consequence> entail, involve, implicate, imply, assume, presume

ADJS 5 **included, comprised,** comprehended, envisaged, embraced, encompassed, subsumed; **involved** 897.3

6 **inclusive, including, containing, comprising, covering, embracing,** encompassing, incorporating, envisaging

7 **comprehensive, sweeping, complete** 793.9; **whole** 791.9; **all-comprehensive,** all-inclusive 863.14; **overall,** universal, global, wall-to-wall <nonformal>, **total,** blanket, omnibus, across-the-board

772 EXCLUSION

NOUNS 1 **exclusion, barring,** debarment, preclusion, exception, omission; **restriction, circumscription,** demarcation; **rejection,** repudiation; **ban,** bar, taboo, injunction; boycott, lockout; inadmissibility, exclusivity

2 **elimination, riddance,** culling, winnowing-out, shakeout, eviction, bum's rush <nonformal>; **severance** 801.2; **removal,** detachment, disjunction 801.1; **ejection,** expulsion, suspension; **deportation, exile,** expatriation, ostracism; **liquidation, purge**

3 **exclusiveness, narrowness; insularity,** snobbishness, parochialism; **segregation, separation, separationism,** division; **isolation,** insulation, seclusion; quarantine; racial segregation, apartheid; **out-group; outsider,** the other, they; **foreigner, alien** 773.3, outcast 586.4; *persona non grata* <L>

VERBS **4 exclude, bar,** debar, lock out, **shut out, keep out,** close the door on, cut off, preclude; **reject, repudiate,** blackball *and* turn thumbs down on <both nonformal>, ostracize; **ignore,** turn a blind eye, turn a deaf ear, tune out; **ban,** prohibit, proscribe, taboo, **leave out,** pass over, ignore; **blockade,** embargo

5 eliminate, get rid of, rid oneself of, **get quit of, dispose of, remove,** eject, expel, give the bum's rush <nonformal>, throw over *or* overboard <nonformal>; **deport, exile,** outlaw, expatriate; **weed out,** pick out; **cut out,** elide; eradicate; **purge, liquidate**

6 segregate, separate, cordon off; **isolate,** insulate, seclude; **set apart,** keep apart; **quarantine,** put in isolation; **set aside,** lay aside, put aside, keep aside; **sort** *or* **pick out,** cull out, sift, screen, sieve, bolt, winnow out; thresh, thrash, gin

ADJS **7 excluded, barred,** debarred, precluded, **shut-out, left-out,** left out in the cold <nonformal>, passed-over; not in the picture <nonformal>; **ignored; banned,** prohibited, proscribed, tabooed; **expelled,** ejected, **purged,** liquidated; deported, exiled; **blockaded,** embargoed

8 segregated, separated, cordoned-off, divided; isolated, insulated, secluded; **set apart,** sequestered; **quarantined; ghettoized**

9 exclusive, excluding, exclusory; seclusive, inadmissible, prohibitive, preventive, restrictive; select, selective; narrow, insular, parochial, ethnocentric, xenophobic, snobbish

773 EXTRANEOUSNESS

NOUNS **1 extraneousness, foreignness;** alienation; **extrinsicality** 767; **exteriority** 206; nonconformity

2 intruder, foreign intruder *or* intrusion, interloper, encroacher; **impurity,** blemish 1003; speck

258.7, spot, macula, blot; mote, splinter *or* sliver, **weed,** misfit 788.4; oddball 869.4

3 alien, stranger, foreigner, outsider, not one of us, not our sort, the other, outlander, barbarian; **exile,** outcast, outlaw, refugee, émigré, displaced person *or* DP

4 newcomer, new arrival; Johnny-come-lately <nonformal>; **tenderfoot,** greenhorn; settler, emigrant, immigrant; recruit, rookie <nonformal>; **intruder, squatter**

ADJS **5 extraneous, foreign, alien,** strange, exotic; unearthly, extraterrestrial 1070.26; exterior, **external;** extrinsic 767.3; ulterior, outlandish; barbarian, barbarous, barbaric

ADVS **6 abroad,** in foreign parts; oversea, **overseas**

774 RELATION

NOUNS **1 relation, relationship, connection;** relatedness, connectedness, **association** 617, **affiliation,** bond, union, alliance, **tie,** tie-in <nonformal>, link, linkage, liaison, **addition** 253, adjunct 254, **combination** 804, assemblage 769; **contrariety** 778, **disagreement** 788; **positive** *or* **good relation, affinity, rapport,** mutual attraction, sympathy, accord 455; **closeness,** propinquity, **proximity,** approximation, contiguity, nearness 223, intimacy; **relations, dealings,** transactions, intercourse; **similarity** 783

2 relativity, contingency; **relativism,** indeterminacy, uncertainty; **interrelation, correlation** 776

3 kinship, common source *or* stock *or* descent *or* ancestry, consanguinity, blood relationship 559; affinity 564.1

4 relevance, pertinence, pertinency, cogency, relatedness, **appositeness;** applicability, appropriateness; **connection, bearing,** interest

VERBS **5 relate to,** refer to, **apply to, bear on** *or* **upon, concern, involve,** touch, affect, interest;

pertain, pertain to, appertain to,
belong to; agree, agree with, correspond to; have to do with, have
connection with, link with, connect, tie in with <nonformal>
6 relate, associate, connect, interconnect, ally, link, link up,
weld, bind, tie, couple, bracket,
equate, identify; bring to bear
upon, apply; parallel, draw a parallel; interrelate, correlate 776.4
ADJS 7 relative, comparative; rela-
tivistic, indeterminate, variable;
connective, linking, associative;
relating, pertaining, pertinent
8 approximate, approximating,
approximative, proximate; near,
close 223.14; comparable, commensurable; proportional, proportionate; correlative; like, ho-
mologous, similar 783.10
9 related, connected; linked,
coupled, knotted, wedded, married or married up, conjugate,
bracketed, bound, yoked, spliced,
joined 799.13; associated, affiliated, allied, interrelated,
interlinked, involved, implicated,
overlapping, correlated; parallel,
collateral; congenial, compatible
10 kindred, akin, related, cognate,
connate, consanguine or consanguineous, genetically related,
related by blood 559.6
11 relevant, pertinent, appertain-
ing, germane, apposite, cogent,
material, applicable, pertaining,
belonging, involving, appropriate, apropos, to the point
ADVS 12 relatively, comparatively,
proportionately, to some extent;
relevantly, pertinently, appos-
itely, germanely

775 UNRELATEDNESS

NOUNS 1 unrelatedness; irrelevance, irrelevancy, inappositeness, immateriality, inapplicabil-
ity; unconnectedness, separateness, dissociation, disassociation
2 misconnection, mismatch,
mismatching, misalliance; misapplication, misapplicability
3 an irrelevance or irrelevancy,
something else again and a whole

different story and a whole different ball game <all nonformal>
VERBS 4 not concern, not involve,
not imply, not implicate, not entail, have nothing to do with, cut
no ice and make no never mind
<both nonformal>
5 foist, drag in 213.6; impose on
643.7
ADJS 6 unrelated, unconnected,
unallied, unlinked, unassociated, unaffiliated or disaffiliated;
separated, segregated, apart,
other, independent, bracketed;
isolated, insular; foreign, alien,
strange, exotic, outlandish; extraneous 767.3
7 irrelevant; impertinent, inapposite, ungermane, uncogent,
inapplicable, immaterial; wide of
or away from the point, beside
the point, wide of the mark,
beside the question, off the
subject, nothing to do with the
case; unessential, extraneous,
extrinsic 767.3
8 farfetched, remote, distant,
out-of-the-way, strained, forced;
imaginary 985.19; improbable
968.3
ADVS 9 irrelevantly, inappositely,
ungermanely, uncogently; without reference or regard

776 CORRELATION

<reciprocal or mutual
relation>

NOUNS 1 correlation; reciprocation, reciprocity, reciprocality,
relativity 774.2; mutuality, community; common denominator;
proportionality; equilibrium,
balance, symmetry 264; correspondence, equivalence
2 interrelation, interrelationship;
interconnection, interlocking,
interlinkage, interdependence,
interdependency
3 interaction, intercourse, intercommunication, interplay;
meshing, intermeshing, mesh,
engagement; complementation,
complementary relation; interweaving, interlacing, intertwining 740.1; interchange 862, tit

for tat, *quid pro quo* <L>; **concurrence** 898, **cooperation** 450; codependency

4 **correlate,** correlative; **correspondent,** analogue, counterpart; reciprocator, reciprocatist

VERBS 5 **correlate; interrelate, interconnect,** interlink, intercouple, interlock

6 **interact, interplay;** mesh, intermesh, engage, fit like a glove, dovetail; **interweave,** interlace, intertwine; **interchange; cooperate**

7 **reciprocate, correspond,** correspond to, respond to, answer, answer to; **complement; cut both ways**

ADJS 8 **correlative,** correlational; **correlated; interrelated, interconnected,** interlocked, intercoupled, interdependent

9 **interacting,** interactive; dovetailed; **cooperative,** cooperating 450.5

10 **reciprocal,** reciprocative, tit-for-tat, seesaw; **corresponding,** correspondent, answering, analogous, tantamount, equivalent, coequal; **complementary**

11 **mutual, common, joint, communal,** shared, sharing; respective, two-way

ADVS 12 **reciprocally,** back and forth, backward and forward, alternately, to and fro; vice versa

13 **mutually, commonly, jointly;** respectively

777 SAMENESS

NOUNS 1 **sameness, identity,** identicalness, two peas in a pod; **coincidence,** correspondence, congruence; **equivalence, equality** 789; **synonymousness,** synonymity, synonymy; **oneness, unity,** homogeneity

2 **identification,** likening, coalescence, union, fusion, merger, blending, synthesis

3 **the same, selfsame,** one and the same, a distinction without a difference, the same difference <nonformal>; **equivalent** 783.3; **synonym; duplicate,** twin, very

image, look-alike, dead ringer <nonformal>, the image of, the picture of, spitting image *and* spit and image <both nonformal>, **exact counterpart, copy** 784.1,3-5, replica, facsimile, carbon copy

VERBS 4 **coincide, correspond,** agree, chime with, match, tally, go hand in glove with, twin

5 **identify,** make one, **unify,** unite, join, combine, coalesce, synthesize, merge, blend, meld, fuse 804.3

6 **reproduce,** copy, reduplicate, **duplicate,** ditto <nonformal>, clone

ADJS 7 **identical; same, selfsame, one and the same,** all the same; **indistinguishable,** without distinction, without difference, undifferentiated; **alike, all alike, like** 783.10, like peas in a pod; **duplicate,** twin; **homogeneous**

8 **coinciding,** coincident; **corresponding,** congruent; **synonymous, equivalent,** six of one and half a dozen of the other <nonformal>; **equal** 789.7, coequal, coextensive

ADVS 9 **identically,** synonymously, **alike;** correspondingly, congruently; **equally** 789.11, coequally, coextensively, coterminously; on the same footing; **likewise,** just the same

778 CONTRARIETY

NOUNS 1 **contrariety, oppositeness, opposition** 451; **antithesis, contrast,** contraindication, contradistinction; **antagonism,** oppugnance, oppugnancy, **hostility,** perversity, nay-saying, inimicalness, **antipathy; confrontation,** showdown, standoff, Mexican standoff <nonformal>, collision, cross-purposes 456.2, conflict; polarity; discrepancy, inconsistency, **disagreement** 788

2 **the opposite, the contrary, the antithesis, the reverse,** the other way round *or* around, the inverse, the converse; **the other side,** the other side of the coin, the flip side

<nonformal>; the direct *or* polar opposite; countercheck *or* counterbalance *or* counterpoise; **opposite pole,** counterpoint; opposite number <nonformal>; **antonym**

3 <contrarieties when joined or coexisting> self-contradiction, **paradox** 788.2, oxymoron, **irony,** equivocation, **ambiguity**

VERBS **4 go contrary to, run counter to,** counter, **contradict,** contravene, controvert, fly in the face of; **oppose,** be opposed to; **conflict with,** come in conflict with, oppugn, conflict, clash; contrast with, **offset,** set off, counterbalance, countervail; **counteract,** juxtapose in opposition

5 reverse, transpose 205.5, flip <nonformal>

ADJS **6 contrary;** contrarious, perverse, **opposite,** antithetical, **contradictory; converse, reverse,** obverse, inverse; **adverse,** adversarial, **opposing, opposed,** oppositional; dead against; **antagonistic,** repugnant, oppugnant, perverse, contrarious, ornery <nonformal>, hostile, combative, bellicose, belligerent, inimical, antipathetical, discordant; discrepant, conflicting, clashing, at cross-purposes, **confrontational,** confrontive, eyeball to eyeball *and* toe-to-toe <both nonformal>, at loggerheads; countervailing, counterbalancing, compensating

7 diametric, diametrical, diametrically opposite, at opposite poles, in polar opposition, antipodal *or* antipodean

8 self-contradictory, **paradoxical,** oxymoronic, **ironic;** equivocal, **ambiguous**

ADVS **9** contrarily, contrariwise, counter, conversely, inversely, **vice versa,** topsy-turvy, upside down, **on the other hand, on** *or* **to the contrary,** at loggerheads, quite the contrary, otherwise 779.11, **oppositely,** just the opposite *or* reverse; against the grain; perversely

779 DIFFERENCE

NOUNS **1 difference,** otherness, separateness, discreteness, distinctness, **distinction;** unlikeness, **dissimilarity** 786; **variation,** variance, variegation, variety, **mixture** 796, **heterogeneity, diversity; deviation; disparity,** inequality 790; **discrepancy,** inconsistency, incongruity, nonconformity, **strangeness** 869, unorthodoxy 688, incompatibility, irreconcilability; **disagreement, dissent** 333, discordance, dissonance; **contrast,** opposition, **contrariety** 778; a far cry

2 margin, differential; distinction; **nicety, subtlety, subtle distinction,** fine point; shade *or* particle of difference, **nuance; seeming difference,** distinction without a difference

3 a different thing, a different story <nonformal>, **something else,** something else again <nonformal>, another tune, horse of a different color; **nothing of the kind,** no such thing, **quite another thing; other, another,** whole nother thing *and* different ball game *and* whole different ball game <all nonformal>

4 differentiation, discrimination, distinction; demarcation, limiting, drawing the line; **separation, separateness,** discreteness 801.1, division, disjunction, segregation, severance; **modification, alteration, change** 851, variation, diversification; **particularization,** individuation, specialization

VERBS **5 differ, vary,** diverge, stand apart; **deviate from,** diverge from, depart from; **disagree with,** conflict with, contrast with, clash with; bear no resemblance to 786.2, not square with, not accord with

6 differentiate; distinguish, make a distinction, discriminate; separate, sever, segregate, divide; **demarcate,** mark out *or* off, set off, set apart, draw a line, set limits; **modify,** vary, diversify, **change** 851.5,6; **particularize,** individualize, individuate, personalize, specialize, atomize, analyze; split hairs, chop logic

ADJS **7 different,** differing; unlike, not like, **dissimilar** 786.4; **distinct,** distinguished, differentiated, discriminated, discrete, disjoined 801.21; **various,** variant, varied, heterogeneous, motley, assorted, variegated, diverse, divers, **diversified** 782.4; **several,** many; **divergent,** deviative, diverging, deviating; **disparate,** unequal 790.4; **discrepant,** inconsistent, inconsonant, incongruous, incongruent, incompatible, irreconcilable; **disagreeing,** in disagreement; **at odds,** at variance, clashing, discordant, dissonant, out of tune; **contrasting,** poles apart, worlds apart; **contrary** 778.6; **discriminable,** separable, severable

8 other, another, other than or from; not the same, not that sort, of another sort; **unique,** one of a kind, rare, **special,** peculiar, *sui generis* <L, of its own kind>, in a class by itself

9 differentiative, differentiating, differential; **distinguishing,** discriminating, discriminative, discriminatory, characterizing, individualizing, individuating, personalizing; **distinctive,** contrastive, peculiar, idiosyncratic

ADVS **10 differently,** diversely, variously; distinguishingly

11 otherwise, in other ways, **in other respects; on the other hand;** contrarily 778.9

780 UNIFORMITY

NOUNS **1 uniformity, evenness,** equability; **steadiness,** stability 854, steadfastness, firmness, constancy, persistence, perseverance, continuity, **consistency;** unity, **homogeneity,** monolithism; **equanimity,** equilibrium, serenity, tranquility, calm, calmness, cool <nonformal>

2 regularity, constancy, invari-

ability, even tenor or pace, smoothness, clockwork regularity; **sameness** 777, **monotony,** the same old thing <nonformal>, the daily round or routine, the treadmill

VERBS **3 persist, prevail,** persevere, run true to form or type; drag on or along

4 make uniform; regulate, regularize, normalize, stabilize, damp; **even, equalize,** harmonize, balance; **level,** level out or off, smooth, smooth out, even, even out, flatten; **homogenize, assimilate,** standardize

ADJS **5 uniform, equable,** equal, **even; level,** flat, smooth; **regular, constant,** steadfast, persistent, continuous; **unvaried,** unruffled, unbroken, seamless, undiversified, undifferentiated, unchanged; invariable, unchangeable, immutable; **unvarying,** undeviating, unchanging, steady, stable; **ordered,** balanced, measured; **orderly,** methodical, systematic, mechanical, automatic; **consistent,** consonant, **alike,** all of a piece, of a piece, monolithic

6 same, wall-to-wall, back-to-back; **monotonous, humdrum,** unrelieved, repetitive, drab, gray, as usual; tedious, boring

ADVS **7 uniformly, evenly;** monotonously, in a rut or groove, routinely, unrelievedly

8 regularly; constantly, steadily, continually; **invariably,** without exception, all the time, week in week out, year in year out, day in day out; methodically, systematically; **always** 828.11; like clockwork

781 NONUNIFORMITY

NOUNS **1 nonuniformity, unevenness, irregularity,** choppiness, **disorder** 809; **difference** 779; inequality; **inconstancy, inconsistency,** variability, changeability, mutability, capriciousness, **instability, unsteadiness; variation, deviation,** deviance, divergence, differentiation, ramification; versatility, **diversity,** diversification; **nonconformity,** unconformity, **unorthodoxy; pluralism,** variegation, variety, motleyness; multiculturalism

VERBS **2 diversify, vary,** variegate 47.7, waver, mutate; **differentiate,** diverge, ramify; **differ** 779.5; **disunify,** break up, break down, fragment, **analyze** 800.6

ADJS **3 nonuniform,** ununiform, **uneven, irregular,** ragged, jagged, rough, disorderly, unsystematic; **different** 779.7, unequal, unequable; **inconstant, inconsistent, variable,** varying, **changeable,** changing, mutable, capricious, impulsive, mercurial, erratic, spasmodic, sporadic, **unstable, unsteady;** deviating, divergent; **diversified; nonconformist,** unorthodox; **pluralistic,** variegated, various, motley 47.9,12; multicultural, multiracial

ADVS **4 nonuniformly,** unequally, **unevenly, irregularly, inconsistently,** unsteadily, erratically, by fits and starts, capriciously, impulsively, sporadically; unsystematically, chaotically, helterskelter; every which way <nonformal>, here, there and everywhere

782 MULTIFORMITY

NOUNS **1 multiformity,** multifariousness, **variety, diversity,** diversification, variation, proteanism, heterogeneity; everything but the kitchen sink <nonformal>

VERBS **2 diversify, vary,** change form, change shape, cover the spectrum, **variegate** 47.7

ADJS **3 multiform,** diversiform, variable, versatile; **protean;** manifold, multifarious; polymorphous, polymorphic

4 diversified, varied, assorted, heterogeneous; **various,** many and various, diverse, sundry, **several, many**

ADVS **5 variously, severally,** sundrily, multifariously, diversely, manifoldly

783 SIMILARITY

NOUNS **1 similarity, likeness, sameness; resemblance,** semblance; **analogy, correspondence,** conformity, accordance, agreement, comparability, comparison, **parallelism, parity; approximation,** approach, closeness, nearness; assimilation, likening, **simile, metaphor; simulation, imitation,** copying, aping, mimicking

2 kinship, affinity, family resemblance, generic or genetic resemblance; connateness

3 likeness, the likes of <nonformal>; **analogue, parallel;** cognate; **counterpart, complement, correspondent; approximation,** rough idea, sketch; correlate, correlative; **close imitation** or copy or facsimile or replica; **close match, match-up, fellow, mate;** soul mate, **companion, twin;** alter ego; a chip off the old block; **look-alike**

4 close or **striking resemblance, faint** or **remote resemblance,** mere hint

5 set, group, matching pair or set

6 <of words or sounds> assonance, alliteration, rhyme

VERBS **7 resemble,** be like, bear resemblance; **look like,** favor <nonformal>, mirror; **take after,** sound like; **have all the earmarks of,** have every appearance of; **approximate,** approach, come close; **compare with,** stack up with <nonformal>; **correspond, match, parallel;** imitate 336.5, **simulate**

8 similarize, approximate, assimilate

9 assonate, alliterate, rhyme

ADJS **10 similar, like, alike, resembling,** favoring <nonformal>, **on the order of; simulated,** imitated, **mock,** synthetic

11 analogous, comparable; **corresponding,** equivalent; **parallel, matching,** cast in the same mold

12 such as, suchlike, so

13 akin, connate, cognate, correlative; brothers *or* sisters under the skin

14 approximating, approximate; **near, close;** nearly the same

15 very like, mighty like, remarkably like, **ridiculously like, for all the world like,** as like as can be; faintly *or* remotely like

16 lifelike, true to life; realistic, natural

17 <of words or sounds> assonant, assonantal, alliterative

ADVS **18 similarly,** correspondingly, **like, likewise, in like manner,** in kind; **thus** 765.10

19 so to speak, in a manner of speaking, **as it were**

784 COPY

NOUNS **1 copy, representation, facsimile, image, likeness** 783.3, **resemblance,** semblance; **imitation** 336.3, **counterfeit** 354.13

2 reproduction, duplication

3 duplicate, duplication, double, reproduction, replica, repro <nonformal>, facsimile, **counterpart;** a chip off the old block

4 transcript, transcription; transfer, tracing, rubbing, **carbon copy;** microfiche, fiche

5 print, offprint; **impression,** impress; **reprint,** proof; **facsimile,** fax <nonformal>; **photograph,** photocopy

6 cast, casting; mold, **molding,** die, stamp, seal

7 reflection; shadow, silhouette, outline 211.2; **echo**

VERBS **8 copy, reproduce,** replicate, **duplicate;** clone; **transcribe;** mimeograph, facsimile, fax <nonformal>; **microcopy,** microfilm

ADVS **9** in duplicate, in triplicate, etc

785 MODEL
<thing copied>

NOUNS **1 model, pattern, standard, criterion,** paradigm; **original,** *locus classicus* <L>; **type, prototype, archetype, precedent**

2 example, exemplar; **representative,** exponent; **exemplification, instance, case,** case in point

3 sample, specimen; piece, taste, swatch

4 ideal, ideal type, acme; cynosure, apotheosis, idol; **shining example, hero, superhero; model,** role model, paragon, epitome

5 artist's model, dressmaker's model, photographer's model, mannequin

6 mold, form 262, template, matrix; **die**

VERBS **7 set an example,** set the pace; **exemplify,** epitomize, **emulate**

ADJS **8 model, exemplary,** paradigmatic, normative, classic

9 prototypal, prototypical, archetypal, archetypical

786 DISSIMILARITY

NOUNS **1 dissimilarity; dissimilitude, unresemblance; unlikeness; disparity,** diversity, divergence, **contrast, difference** 779; incommensurableness, incommensurability; **disguise**

VERBS **2 not resemble, bear no resemblance,** not look like, **not compare with; differ** 779.5

3 disguise, dissimilate, camouflage; vary 851.6

ADJS **4 dissimilar, unlike, unalike,** unidentical; **disparate,** diverse, **contrasting, different** 779.7; nonuniform 781.3

5 nothing like, not a bit alike, **nothing of the sort,** something else, something else again <nonformal>, quite another thing; not that you would know it *and* **far from it;** way out

6 uncomparable, incomparable; incommensurable, incommensurate

ADVS **7 dissimilarly, differently** 779.10, disparately

787 AGREEMENT

NOUNS **1 agreement, accord** 455; **concord,** concordance; **har-**

mony, **cooperation** 450, **consonance, unison,** chorus; **correspondence,** coincidence; congeniality, compatibility, affinity; **conformity, congruity; consistency, assent** 332

2 **understanding,** entente; consortium; **compact** 437

3 <general agreement> consensus, consentaneity

4 **adjustment, adaptation, compromise,** arbitration; **regulation, coordination,** accommodation, reconciliation

5 **fitness, suitability, appropriateness,** propriety, **aptness, relevance** 774.4, appositeness, applicability

VERBS 6 **agree, accord** 455.2, **harmonize, concur** 332.9, go along with <nonformal>, **cooperate** 450.3, **correspond, conform,** coincide, parallel, **match,** tally, jibe <nonformal>; **be consistent,** cohere; **assent** 332.8, see eye to eye, **go together**

7 <make agree> **harmonize,** coordinate, bring into line, accord; **adjust, set, accommodate, reconcile,** synchronize; adapt, adjust to, key to; **rectify,** set right, make plumb; **tune,** attune

8 **suit,** fit, fit like a glove, **qualify, do,** do the job *and* do the trick *and* fill the bill *and* cut the mustard <all nonformal>

ADJS 9 **agreeing, in agreement; in accord, concurring, in harmony,** in accordance, **likeminded, unanimous** 332.15; **harmonious, concordant,** consonant; **consistent, coinciding** 777.8, coincident, **congruous,** congruent; **agreeable,** compatible; **synchronized,** synchronous

10 **apt, apposite, appropriate, suitable;** applicable, relevant; **fitting, suiting,** becoming; **fit, suited,** adapted; **right,** just right, **pat,** happy, just what the doctor ordered <nonformal>

ADVS 11 **in step, in unison,** in chorus, **in line, in conformity, in keeping,** hand in glove; **unani-** mously, **as one, with one voice, harmoniously,** in synchronization, in sync <nonformal>, **by consensus**

788 DISAGREEMENT

NOUNS 1 **disagreement, discord; disaccord** 456, disaccordance; **disharmony, jarring,** clashing; **difference** 779, **variance,** divergence; **disparity,** discrepancy, **opposition** 451, **conflict,** controversy; **dissent** 333, contradiction

2 **inconsistency, incongruity,** asymmetry; **incompatibility,** irreconcilability, incommensurability; paradox, oxymoron, **ambiguity** 539.2

3 **unfitness, inappropriateness, unsuitability,** impropriety; **inaptness, inappositeness, irrelevance** *or* irrelevancy; abnormality, anomaly; **maladjustment**

4 **misfit, nonconformist,** individualist, oddball <nonformal>; **freak,** anomaly

VERBS 5 **disagree, differ** 779.5, not see eye-to-eye, **disaccord** 456.8, **conflict,** clash, **jar,** jostle, square off; **mismatch,** mismate; **dissent** 333.4, **negate** 335.3, **contradict,** counter

ADJS 6 **disagreeing, differing** 779.7, **discordant** 456.15; **inharmonious,** divergent, variant; **at odds,** at daggers drawn, at crosspurposes; **hostile,** antagonistic; **jarring,** grating; **contradictory, contrary; disagreeable,** uncongenial

7 **inappropriate, inapt,** inapposite, **irrelevant,** malapropos; **unsuited, unfitted,** ill-fitted; **maladjusted,** mismatched; **unfit,** inept; **unsuitable, unbecoming,** unseemly; **unseasonable, untimely,** ill-timed; **out of place**

8 **inconsistent, incongruous, inconsonant,** incoherent, **incompatible,** irreconcilable; **absurd; abnormal,** anomalous

9 **nonconformist,** individualistic, inner-directed, perverse; **unorthodox,** heterodox, heretical

789 EQUALITY

NOUNS **1 equality, parity, identity**
777.1; **correspondence,** parallelism; **likeness, balance,** equipoise, **equilibrium; justice** 649,
equity

   **2 equating, equation; equaliz-
ing;** coordination, adjustment;
even break *and* fair shake <both
nonformal>

   3 the same 777.3; **tie, draw,
standoff** *and* Mexican standoff
and dead heat <all nonformal>,
impasse; six of one and half a
dozen of the other

   4 equal, match, mate, **like,
equivalent, peer,** colleague

VERBS **5 equal, match, rival, correspond,** be tantamount to; **keep
pace with, keep step with, run
abreast; amount to,** come down
to; **measure up to,** stack up with
<nonformal>; **balance, parallel;
tie, draw,** knot

   6 equalize; equate; even, make
both ends meet; **balance,** strike
a balance, poise, balance out;
compensate, make up
for

ADJS **7 equal, equalized,** like,
alike, even, level, on a par, at
parity, proportionate; on terms of
equality, **on even** *or* **equal terms,**
on even ground; on a level playing
field, in the same boat; **square,**
quits, zero-sum; **fifty-fifty;** nip
and tuck, **drawn, tied,** neck-and-
neck <nonformal>, too close to
call

   8 equivalent, tantamount, coordinate; **identical** 777.7; **all one,**
all the same, neither here nor
there

   **9 balanced, poised, on an even
keel**

   10 equisized, equidimensional

ADVS **11 equally, correspondingly,
proportionately,** equivalently,
evenly; identically 777.9; to the
same degree; to all intents and
purposes, other things being
equal

   12 to a standoff <nonformal>, to a
tie *or* draw

790 INEQUALITY

NOUNS **1 inequality, disparity,
unevenness, contrariety** 778,
difference 779; **irregularity,**
heterogeneity; **disproportion,**
asymmetry; **unbalance,** imbalance, tippiness; **inadequacy,**
insufficiency, shortcoming;
odds, handicap; **injustice,** inequity

VERBS **2 unequalize,** disproportion

   3 unbalance, overcompensate,
throw off balance, upset, skew

ADJS **4 unequal,** disparate, **uneven; irregular** 781.3; **out of
proportion,** mismatched *or* ill-
matched, ill-sorted; **inadequate,**
insufficient

   5 unbalanced, ill-balanced, off-
balance, listing, heeling, leaning,
canted; **lopsided, unstable,** unsteady

ADVS **6 unequally,** disparately, dis-
proportionately

791 WHOLE

NOUNS **1 whole, totality, entirety;
unity, integrity, wholeness;** oneness

   2 total, sum, sum total, sum and
substance

   **3 all, the whole, the entirety, ev-
erything,** all the above *or* all of
the above <both nonformal>;
package, set, complement; **the
lot, the ensemble; be-all,** be-all
and end-all

   4 <nonformal terms> **whole
bunch, whole mess, whole kit
and caboodle,** whole megillah,
**whole shooting match, whole
deal, whole shebang,** whole
nine yards

   5 wholeness, totality, **completeness** 793, **unity, fullness,** comprehensiveness; universality

   6 major part, best part, better
part

VERBS **7 make a whole, integrate,**
unite

   **8 total, amount to, come to, run
to** *or* **into,** mount up to, add up
to, tote *or* tote up to <nonfor-

mal>, aggregate; **number, comprise**, encompass

ADJS **9** <not partial> **whole, total, entire,** aggregate, **one,** one and indivisible; **inclusive,** all-inclusive, **exhaustive,** comprehensive

10 intact, untouched, undamaged 1001.8, all in one piece <nonformal>, unimpaired, virgin, pristine

11 undivided, uncut; **undiminished,** complete

12 unabridged, uncondensed, unexpurgated

ADVS **13** <not partially> **wholly, entirely,** all; **totally,** from soup to nuts <nonformal>, from A to Z; **altogether,** in its entirety; **as a whole, in the aggregate,** in in bulk; **collectively, corporately,** lock, stock, and barrel; hook, line, and sinker

14 on the whole, in the long run, over the long haul, all in all, on balance, **by and large, in the main, mainly, mostly, chiefly,** substantially, essentially, effectually, **for the most part**

792 PART

NOUNS **1 part, portion, fraction;** percentage; **division** 801.1; **share,** quota; **section,** sector, **segment;** quarter, quadrant; **item,** detail, particular; **subdivision,** subset, subgroup; **cross section,** sampling; **component** 795.2, **adjunct** 254; **remainder** 256

2 <part of writing> section, front or back matter, prologue, epilogue, foreword, preface, introduction, afterword, text, chapter, verse, article

3 piece, particle, bit, scrap 248.3, bite, **fragment, morsel, crumb,** shard; **cut,** snip, snippet, chip, slice; **tatter, shred,** stitch; **splinter,** sliver; **shiver, smithereen** <nonformal>; **lump,** gob <nonformal>, **hunk, chunk; stump,** butt-end, fag-end, tail-end; modicum 248.2

4 member, organ; appendage;

limb; branch, twig, sprig, spray; **off-shoot,** ramification, spur

5 dose, portion

VERBS **6 separate,** apportion, distribute, cut up, slice up, divide 801.18

ADJS **7 partial; fractional,** sectional; **fragmentary**

ADVS **8 partly, partially,** part, **in part**

9 piece by piece, bit by bit, little by little, inch by inch, drop by drop; **piecemeal, by degrees**

793 COMPLETENESS

NOUNS **1 completeness, totality; wholeness** 791.5, **entirety; unity, integrity,** intactness; solidity, solidarity; **thoroughness,** exhaustiveness, comprehensiveness, pervasiveness

2 fullness; amplitude, plenitude; plethora; saturation, satiety, congestion

3 full measure, fill; load, capacity, complement, charge; the whole bit <nonformal>

4 completion, fulfillment, consummation, culmination, **accomplishment** 407, closure

5 limit, end 819, **extremity, acme,** apogee, climax, **maximum, peak,** summit, **pinnacle,** crown, top; **utmost,** utmost extent

VERBS **6** <make whole> **complete,** bring to completion or fruition, mature; **fill in, fill out,** eke or eke out, **make up,** make good, **accomplish**

7 fill, charge, load, lade, freight, weight; **stuff, wad,** pad, **pack,** crowd, **cram,** jam, chock; **fill up,** fill to the brim, surfeit

8 <be thorough> **go to all lengths, go all out, go the limit** <nonformal>, go the whole way, **go the whole hog** <nonformal>, **see it through** <nonformal>; leave nothing undone, use every trick in the book <nonformal>; **move heaven and earth, leave no stone unturned**

ADJS **9 complete, whole, total,** global, **entire,** intact, solid; **full,**

full-fledged, full-scale; full-grown, mature; **uncut,** unexpurgated

10 **thorough, thoroughgoing,** exhaustive, intensive, A-to-Z, comprehensive, omnibus, radical, sweeping; **pervasive,** ubiquitous, omnipresent, **universal; unmitigated, unqualified, unconditional, all-out,** wholesale, whole-hog <nonformal>; **out-and-out, through-and-through,** outright, downright; **consummate,** unmitigated, egregious, dyed-in-the-wool; **utter, absolute, total; sheer, pure, plain**

11 **full, replete,** plenary; **brimful,** brimming; **chock-full; jam-full, jam-packed, overcrowded; packed, crammed; swollen** 259.13, **saturated,** satiated; congested; surfeited

12 **fraught, laden, loaded, charged,** burdened

13 **completing, fulfilling,** filling; **complementary**

ADVS 14 **completely, totally,** globally, **entirely, wholly, fully,** integrally, **altogether, exhaustively,** comprehensively; lock, stock, and barrel <nonformal>; **unconditionally,** with no strings attached; **thoroughly,** inside out <nonformal>

15 **absolutely, perfectly, quite,** clean, sheer, plumb <nonformal>

16 **utterly, to the utmost,** all the way, **all out,** hammer and tongs <nonformal>, **to the full, to the limit,** to the nth degree *or* power, **to a fare-thee-well,** all hollow <nonformal>

17 **throughout, all over,** overall, **inside and out, through and through;** through thick and thin, **from the ground up,** to the death; **at full length;** head and shoulders, heart and soul; **in every respect,** in all respects; **on all counts**

18 **from beginning to end, from start to finish, from first to last, from A to Z,** from soup to nuts <nonformal>, from cover to cover; **from top to bottom, from head to foot; from stem to stern,** fore and aft

794 INCOMPLETENESS

NOUNS 1 **incompleteness,** incompletion; **deficiency,** defectiveness, imperfection, **inadequacy; immaturity,** callowness; **sketchiness,** patchiness

2 <part lacking> deficiency, want, lack, need, deficit, defect, shortage

VERBS 3 **lack** 991.7, want, want for; fall short 910.2; be arrested, underdevelop, undergrow

ADJS 4 **incomplete, uncompleted, deficient,** defective, unfinished, imperfect, **inadequate; undeveloped,** underdeveloped, stunted, **immature,** callow, infant, arrested, embryonic, **wanting, lacking,** needing, missing, **partial;** in default, in arrears; **in short supply,** scanty; **short; sketchy**

5 **mutilated,** garbled, hashed, **mangled, butchered,** docked, hacked, lopped, truncated, castrated

ADVS 6 **incompletely, partially,** by halves, by *or* in half measures, in *or* by bits and pieces; **deficiently**

795 COMPOSITION

<manner of being composed>

NOUNS 1 **composition, constitution, construction, formation,** fabrication, fashioning; **embodiment,** incarnation; **make, makeup; assembly,** assemblage, synthesis; **combination** 804; **compound** 796.5; **junction** 799.1; **mixture** 796

2 **component, constituent, ingredient,** makings *and* fixings <both nonformal>, **element, factor, part** 792, part and parcel; appurtenance, adjunct 254; **feature**

VERBS 3 **compose, constitute,** fabricate; **incorporate,** embody; **form, organize,** structure; **enter into, make, make up, build,** assemble, put *or* piece together;

consist of, form a part of, combine or unite in; consist, be constituted of, contain; synthesize; combine 804.3; join 799.5; mix

ADJS 4 composed of, formed of, made of, consisting of; composing, comprising, constituting, including, containing, embodying, subsuming

5 component, constituent, modular, integrant, integral; formative, elementary

796 MIXTURE

NOUNS 1 mixture, blending; admixture, composition, mingling, commingling, intermingling, interlarding; eclecticism, syncretism; pluralism, multiculturalism, ethnic or racial or cultural diversity; fusion, integration, coalescence; merger, combination 804

2 imbuement, impregnation, infusion, suffusion, infiltration, instillation, pervasion, penetration; saturation

3 adulteration, corruption, contamination, pollution, doctoring <nonformal>; dilution, cutting <nonformal>; debasement

4 crossbreeding, crossing, interbreeding, miscegenation; hybridism, hybridization

5 compound, mixture, admixture, intermixture, composite, blend, concoction, combination, marriage; amalgam, alloy

6 hodgepodge; medley, miscellany, mélange, pastiche, conglomeration, assortment, assemblage, jumble, mix, mishmash, mess, can of worms <nonformal>, salmagundi, potpourri, omnium-gatherum, odds and ends, everything but the kitchen sink <nonformal>, broad spectrum

7 <slight admixture> tinge, tincture, touch, dash, smack, trace, vestige, soupçon, suggestion, whiff

8 hybrid, crossbreed, cross, half-breed, half-caste; mongrel; mulatto

9 mixer, blender, beater, agitator, food processor

VERBS 10 mix, admix, intermix, mingle, commingle, intermingle, interlace, interweave, intertwine, interlard; blend; amalgamate, integrate, alloy, coalesce, fuse, merge, meld, concoct; combine 804.3; jumble, throw or toss together; homogenize, emulsify

11 imbue, infuse, suffuse, instill, impregnate, permeate, pervade, penetrate, leaven; tinge, tincture, saturate, steep, decoct, brew

12 adulterate, corrupt, contaminate, debase, pollute, denature, tamper with, doctor and doctor up <both nonformal>; fortify, spike <nonformal>, lace; dilute, cut <nonformal>

13 hybridize, crossbreed, cross, interbreed

ADJS 14 mixed, mingled, amalgamated; combined 804.5; composite, compound, complex, multifaceted; conglomerate, pluralistic, heterogeneous, varied, miscellaneous, motley, patchy; scrambled, jumbled, thrown together; ambiguous, ambivalent, ironic; eclectic

15 hybrid, mongrel, interbred, crossbred, crossed, cross; half-breed, half-caste

16 miscible, mixable, assimilable, integrable

797 SIMPLICITY

<freedom from mixture or complexity>

NOUNS 1 simplicity, purity, plainness, no frills; unadulteration, unsophistication, unspoiledness, intactness; singleness, integrity, homogeneity

2 simplification, refinement, purification, distillation; disentanglement, disinvolvement

3 oversimplification, oversimplicity, oversimplifying; simplism, reductivism

VERBS **4 simplify,** streamline, **re-duce,** reduce to essentials; purify, refine, distill

5 disinvolve, disembroil, **disentangle,** untangle, **unscramble, unsnarl, unravel,** ravel; **unclutter,** clarify

ADJS **6 simple, plain,** bare-bones *and* no-frills <both nonformal>; **single,** homogeneous, of a piece; **pure, essential,** elementary; **primary,** primal, primitive, **irreducible, fundamental,** basic; undifferentiated, monolithic; **austere,** chaste, unadorned, uncluttered, spare, stark, severe

7 unmixed, unmingled, unblended, **uncombined,** uncompounded; unleavened; **unadulterated,** intact, virgin, uncorrupted, unsophisticated; **clear,** clarified, **distilled**

8 uncomplicated, uninvolved, straightforward

9 simplified, streamlined, stripped down

10 oversimplified; simplistic, reductive

ADVS **11 simply, plainly, purely;** merely, barely; **singly, solely,** only, **alone,** exclusively, just

798 COMPLEXITY

NOUNS **1 complexity, complication, involvement,** tortuousness, **entanglement,** perplexity, **intricacy,** subtlety

2 complex, tangle, mess *and* snafu *and* fuck-up <all nonformal>; Gordian knot; **maze,** Chinese puzzle, **labyrinth; wilderness, jungle,** morass, quagmire; can of worms

VERBS **3 complicate, involve, perplex,** ramify; **confound, confuse,** muddle, **mix up,** screw up *and* foul up *and* fuck up *and* snafu *and* louse up <all nonformal>, implicate; **tangle,** entangle, **snarl, snarl up,** tie in knots

ADJS **4 complex, complicated,** many-faceted, ramified, **confused, involved,** implicated, **intricate,** involuted, convoluted;

mixed up, screwed up *and* loused up *and* fouled up *and* fucked up <all nonformal>; **tangled, snarled,** twisted, **labyrinthine, devious,** Byzantine

5 inextricable, irreducible, unknottable, unsolvable

799 JOINING

NOUNS **1 joining, junction, connection, union,** bonding, connectedness *or* connectivity, tie-up *and* tie-in <both informal>; **combination** 804; conglomeration, **aggregation,** agglomeration, congeries; **coupling,** copulation, **bracketing,** yoking, splicing; **linking,** linkage, **concatenation,** articulation; **meeting,** confluence, convergence

2 interconnection, interlinking; interassociation

3 fastening, attachment, annexation; **binding,** bonding, splicing

4 joint, juncture, union, connection, link, **coupling;** articulation <anatomy and botany>; **pivot, hinge;** boundary, interface

VERBS **5 put together, join,** conjoin, **unite,** bond, **connect,** associate, **assemble,** accumulate; **join up,** come aboard <nonformal>; **gather,** mobilize, marshal, **collect; combine** 804.3; **couple,** pair, tie the knot <nonformal>; **link,** link up, splice, bracket; **concatenate,** articulate, agglutinate; **put together,** piece together, lump together; **include,** encompass, embrace, comprise

6 interconnect, interjoin, interlink, interlock

7 fasten, fix, attach, affix, annex; **secure,** anchor, moor; **make fast**

8 hook, hitch; **clasp,** hasp, clip, snap; **wedge,** jam, stick; batten, batten down; **hinge,** joint, articulate

9 bind, tie, brace, truss, **lash, splice, gird,** cinch; **tie up,** bind up, do up; **wrap,** bundle; **bandage,** swathe, swaddle

10 yoke, hitch up, hook up; harness, harness up

11 <be joined> join, connect, unite,

meet, meet up, link up, merge,
converge, come together

ADJS **12 joint, combined,** joined,
conjoint, cooperative; concurrent, coincident

13 joined, united, connected,
copulate, **coupled,** tight-knit,
bracketed, associated, integrated,
**merged, collected; associated,
allied,** banded together; hand-in-
hand, hand-in-glove; **wedded,**
matched, married, paired, yoked,
mated; **tied, bound,** knotted,
spliced, lashed

14 fast, fastened, fixed, secure,
bonded, jammed, wedged,
seized up

15 inseparable, impartible, **indivisible,** indissoluble, inalienable,
bound up in *or* with

16 joining, connecting, meeting;
communicating, connective;
conjunctive, copulative, linking,
bridging

17 jointed, articulate

ADVS **18 jointly,** corporately, **together; in common,** mutually, in
concord; **all together,** in unison,
in harmony

19 securely, firmly, fast, tight; **in-
separably**

800 ANALYSIS

NOUNS **1 analysis,** analyzation,
breakdown, breaking down,
breaking up; **division, subdivision,** segmentation

2 itemization, enumeration, detailing, breakout

3 classification, categorization,
sorting, taxonomy, grouping;
weighing, evaluation, gauging,
assessment, appraisal, **judgment**
945

4 outline, plan, scheme, schema;
diagram, blueprint; catalog,
catalogue raisonné <Fr>

5 analyst, analyzer, examiner
937.16; taxonomist

VERBS **6 analyze, break down,**
anatomize, dissect; **divide, subdivide,** segment

7 itemize, enumerate, detail,
break out; **outline,** schematize

8 classify, categorize, catalog,

sort, group, winnow, thrash out;
evaluate, judge, gauge 945.9

ADJS **9 analytical,** analytic; classificatory, enumerative

ADVS **10** analytically

801 SEPARATION

NOUNS **1 separation, disjunction,**
delinkage, disarticulation, **disconnection,** disconnectedness,
discontinuity, disassociation, segregation; **parting,** alienation, estrangement, **removal,** sequestration, abstraction; **subtraction**
255; **division,** subdivision, partition, compartmentalization; **dislocation, separateness,** discreteness

2 severance, sunderance, scis-
sion, fission, cleavage; **cutting,**
slitting, slashing, **splitting,** slicing; **rending, tearing,** laceration

3 disruption, dissolution, revolution 859; **disintegration** 805,
fragmentation; **bursting, scattering,** dispersal, diffusion

4 break, breach, burst, **rupture,
fracture; crack,** cleft, **fissure,
cut, split,** slit; **slash,** slice

5 dissection, analysis 800

6 disassembly, dismantlement,
dismemberment, undoing; **stripping,** stripping away *or* down, divestiture, divestment

7 separator, sieve, centrifuge

VERBS **8 separate, divide, disjoin,
disunite,** dissociate, **disjoint,**
disarticulate, **disconnect;** part,
cut the knot, **divorce,** estrange;
alienate, segregate, sequester,
cut off *or* out *or* loose *or* adrift;
withdraw, leave, depart, take
one's leave; subtract 255.9; delete
255.12; **expel,** eject, cast off *or*
out

9 come apart, spring apart, come
undone, come apart at the seams,
come *or* **drop** *or* fall to pieces,
disintegrate, go to pieces, fall
apart at the seams, fragmentize,
pulverize, unravel

10 detach, remove, disengage,
doff; **unfasten, undo, free, release,** liberate, unleash, unfetter;

unloosen, unhook, unhitch, **untie,** unbind

11 **sever, dissever,** amputate; **cleave, split,** fissure; sunder, cut in two; **cut,** incise, carve, **slice,** pare, prune, **chop, hew,** hack, **slash; tear, rend,** rive, rend asunder

12 **break, burst,** breach; **fracture, rupture; crack,** split, check, fissure

13 **shatter, splinter,** shiver, fragmentize, break to or into smithereens <nonformal>; **smash,** crush, crunch, squash; **disrupt,** demolish; **scatter,** disperse, diffuse; **fragment,** fission, atomize; **pulverize** 1049.9, grind, mince, make mincemeat of

14 **tear** or **rip apart, pick** or **rip** or **tear to pieces, shred,** rip to shreds; **dismember,** tear limb from limb, draw and quarter; **mangle,** lacerate, mutilate

15 **disassemble,** tear down; **dismantle, demolish**

16 **disjoint,** unjoint, **unhinge,** disarticulate, **dislocate**

17 dissect, analyze 800.6

18 **apportion, portion,** partition, compartmentalize, segment; **divide,** divvy and divvy up <both nonformal>, **parcel, split,** split up

19 **part company, part, separate,** split up, **disperse,** break up, **go separate ways,** diverge

ADJS 20 **separate, distinct, discrete; unjoined, unconnected, unattached,** unassociated; **apart,** asunder, **in two; isolated,** insular, detached, free-standing, autonomous; **independent,** stand-alone <nonformal>; **subdivided,** partitioned, compartmentalized

21 **separated,** disjointed, **disconnected,** disengaged, **disunited, divided,** divorced, **alienated,** estranged, **segregated,** sequestered, cloistered; **scattered,** dispersed

22 **unfastened, unbound, undone, loose, free,** loosened, clear; **untied, unbound,** unfet-

tered, unhitched; **unanchored,** adrift, afloat, free-floating

23 **severed, cut,** cleaved, cleft, cloven, riven, hewn, sheared; **splintered,** shivered, cracked, **split, rent, torn;** quartered, **dismembered**

24 **broken, ruptured, shattered,** fragmentized, fragmentary, fragmented, in smithereens <nonformal>

25 **separating, dividing,** parting, distancing

26 **separable,** severable, **divisible,** cleavable, partible; **fissionable,** fissile, scissile

ADVS 27 **separately,** piecemeal; **apart,** adrift, asunder, **in two,** in twain

28 **disjointedly,** sporadically, spasmodically, discontinuously, by fits and starts

29 **to pieces, to bits, to smithereens** <nonformal>, to tatters, to shreds

802 COHESION

NOUNS 1 **cohesion,** cohesiveness, **coherence, adherence, adhesion, sticking,** inseparability; agglutination; concretion, solidification, congelation, coagulation; **conglomeration,** agglomeration, consolidation; **clustering**

2 **consistency** 787.1, connection, **connectedness;** continuity, **consecutiveness** 811.1

3 **tenacity,** tenaciousness, **adhesiveness,** cohesiveness; **tightness,** snugness; **tackiness, viscidity,** consistency, viscosity; **stick-to-itiveness** <nonformal>, toughness, **stubbornness, obstinacy** 361, bullheadedness

4 <something adhesive or tenacious> adhesive, adherent, adherer; bulldog, barnacle, leech

5 **conglomeration, conglomerate,** agglomerate, agglomeration, cluster, bunch, mass

VERBS 6 **cohere, adhere, stick, cling, cleave,** hold; **persist,** stay; cling to, embrace, clinch; **stick together, hang** or **hold together;** grow together; **solidify, set,** conglomerate, agglomerate; **congeal**, coagulate, **clot; cluster,** bunch

7 be consistent 787.6, connect

8 **hold fast, stick close,** stick like glue, stick like a wet shirt *or* wet T-shirt *or* second skin

9 **stick together, cement, bind, colligate, paste, glue,** agglutinate; **weld,** fuse, **solder,** braze

ADJS 10 **cohesive,** cohering, coherent; adhering, **sticking, clinging,** inseparable, cleaving, holding together; **cemented,** agglutinative, agglutinated, conglutinated; **concrete, condensed, solidified, set, congealed,** clotted, coagulated; conglomerated, **compacted, consolidated,** agglomerated; **clustered**

11 **consistent** 787.9, **connected;** continuous 811.8, **serial,** uninterrupted, sequential, **consecutive** 811.9; **joined** 799.13

12 **adhesive, adherent,** retentive; **tenacious, sticky, tacky, viscid,** glutinous; **persistent,** tough, **stubborn, obstinate** 361.8, bullheaded

803 NONCOHESION

NOUNS 1 **noncohesion,** incoherence, inconsistency, discontinuity 812, untenacity; **separateness,** discreteness, aloofness; **disjunction** 801.1, dismemberment; **dislocation; dissolution, chaos** 809.2, anarchy, **disorder** 809; **scattering,** dispersion *or* dispersal

2 **looseness, slackness, laxness,** laxity

VERBS 3 **loosen, slacken, relax;** slack off; ease off, let up; **loose, free,** unleash; **disjoin,** dismember; **sow confusion,** open Pandora's box; **scatter,** disperse

ADJS 4 **incoherent, inconsistent, uncohesive, unadhesive,** nonadherent, **untenacious, unconsolidated,** tenuous; **disordered** 809.12, **chaotic, anarchic; discontinuous** 812.4, discrete, aloof

5 **loose, slack, lax, relaxed,** easy, sloppy; **shaky, rickety; flapping,** drooping, dangling

804 COMBINATION

NOUNS 1 **combination,** combo <nonformal>; **union, unification,** coupling, linking; **incorporation,** aggregation, agglomeration, congeries; **amalgamation, consolidation,** assimilation, integration, inclusion, ecumenism; **junction** 799.1; conjunction; **alliance,** affiliation, **association** 617, **merger,** tie-up <nonformal>; **federation, confederation,** confederacy; **fusion,** blending, melding; coalescence, coalition; **synthesis,** syncretism; **conspiracy,** cabal, junta; **agreement** 787; **addition** 253

2 **mixture** 796, **compound** 796.5

VERBS 3 **combine, unite, unify,** couple, link, yoke; **incorporate, amalgamate, consolidate, integrate,** solidify, coalesce, put *or* lump together; **connect, join** 799.5; **mix; add** 253.4; **merge,** meld, **blend, fuse,** conflate; **encompass,** comprise; **synthesize,** syncretize; syndicate

4 **ally, affiliate, associate; federate, confederate,** federalize, centralize; **join forces,** join *or* unite with, join *or* come together, tie up *or* in with <nonformal>, **throw in with** <nonformal>, go *or* be in cahoots <nonformal>, **pool one's interests, join fortunes with,** make common cause with; **marry, wed, couple, yoke,** yoke together, link; **band together,** bunch up <nonformal>; team with, **team up with** <nonformal>, couple, pair, double up, buddy up <nonformal>; **conspire**

ADJS 5 **combined, united, amalgamated, incorporated, consolidated, integrated,** assimilated, **joined** 799.13, joint 799.12, conjoint; **merged,** blended, fused; **mixed; synthesized,** syncretized, eclectic

6 **leagued, allied, affiliated,** affiliate, **associated,** associate, corpo-

rate; **in league,** in cahoots <nonformal>, in with; **conspiratorial;** teamed, coupled, paired, yoked, linked

7 **combining, uniting,** incorporating; merging, blending, fusing; combinative, combinatory; associative

805 DISINTEGRATION

NOUNS 1 **disintegration, decomposition, dissolution, decay,** resolution, disorganization, fragmentation, atomization; **ruination, destruction** 395; **erosion,** corrosion, dilapidation, ravages of time; **disjunction** 801.1; **incoherence** 803.1; **impairment** 393

2 dissociation; catalysis

VERBS 3 **disintegrate, decompose, decay,** dissolve, disorganize, **break up** 395.22, go to rack and ruin 395.24, **come** or **fall to pieces; erode,** corrode, wear or waste away, molder, crumble

4 <chemical terms> dissociate; catalyze, dialyze, hydrolyze, electrolyze, photolyze

ADJS 5 **disintegrative,** decomposing, disintegrating, disruptive, disjunctive; **destructive, ruinous** 395.26; **erosive,** corrosive; **dilapidated,** disintegrated, ruinous, shacky, worn-out, moldering, ravaged, totaled <nonformal>

806 ORDER

NOUNS 1 **order, arrangement** 807; **organization** 807.2; **disposition,** deployment; **formation, structure, configuration,** array, makeup, layout; **peace,** quiet, quietude, **tranquillity; regularity,** uniformity 780; symmetry, **harmony,** order

2 **continuity,** logical order; **degree** 245; **hierarchy, gradation,** subordination, place; **sequence** 814

3 **orderliness, trimness, tidiness, neatness;** good shape <nonformal>, apple-pie order <nonformal>; **discipline,** method, methodology, system

VERBS 4 **order, arrange** 807.8, get

it together <nonformal>, **organize, regulate;** dispose, deploy, marshal; **form,** configure, structure, get one's ducks in a row <nonformal>, put one's house in order; **pacify,** cool off or down <nonformal>, **tranquilize; regularize,** harmonize; **systematize,** normalize, standardize, routinize

5 **form, take form, take shape,** crystallize, **shape up; fall** or **drop into place,** fall into line; come together, rally round

ADJS 6 **orderly,** ordered, **regular, well-regulated, well-ordered, methodical, formal,** uniform 780.5, **systematic,** symmetrical, **harmonious; arranged** 807.14

7 **in order, in trim,** to rights and in apple-pie order <both nonformal>; **in condition,** in kilter <nonformal>, **in shape,** in good shape <nonformal>, **in good form,** in fine fettle; **in repair,** in commission, in working order; up to snuff <nonformal>

8 **tidy, trim, natty, neat,** spruce, smart, **shipshape; well-kept,** well-cared-for, well-groomed

ADVS 9 **methodically, systematically, regularly,** uniformly, harmoniously, like clockwork

10 **in order, in turn, in sequence, in succession;** step by step, by stages

807 ARRANGEMENT

<*putting in order*>

NOUNS 1 **arrangement, ordering,** structuring, shaping, forming; **disposition, disposal, deployment,** placement, marshaling, **arraying; distribution,** allocation, apportionment; **formation,** formulation, **configuration,** form, array; regimentation; **order** 806

2 **organization, methodization,** codification, regularization, rationalization; **adjustment,** harmonization, fine-tuning; **systematization,** coordination

3 **grouping, classification** 808, categorization, taxonomy; **gradation,** subordination, **ranking,**

placement; **sorting,** screening, triage, culling

4 table, code, digest, index, inventory, census

5 **arranger, organizer,** coordinator; **sorter,** sifter, **sieve, screen**

6 <act of making neat> cleanup, red-up <nonformal>; tidy-up

7 **rearrangement, reorganization,** reconstitution, **reordering, restructuring,** shake-up <nonformal>; **redeployment,** realignment

VERBS 8 **arrange,** order 806.4, **put** or **get** or **set in order,** right, get one's ducks in a row <nonformal>; **put** or **set to rights, get it together** <nonformal>, **pull it together,** whip into shape <nonformal>

9 **dispose, distribute, fix, place,** set out, allocate, **compose, marshal,** rally, array; **line up,** form up; **allot, apportion,** parcel out

10 **organize, systematize,** rationalize, regularize; **harmonize,** synchronize, **tune,** tune up; **regularize,** routinize, standardize; **regulate,** adjust, coordinate; **plan,** codify

11 **classify** 808.6, **group,** categorize; **grade,** gradate, rank, subordinate; **sort,** assort; **separate;** collate; **sift,** sieve, **screen**

12 tidy, **tidy up, put in trim,** trim up, **straighten up, clean up,** police and police up <both nonformal>, groom, spruce and spruce up <both nonformal>, **clear up,** clear the decks

13 **rearrange, reorganize,** reconstitute, **reorder, restructure,** reshuffle, tune up, fine-tune; **shake up,** shake out; reallocate, realign

ADJS 14 **arranged, ordered, disposed,** configured, composed, constituted, aligned, arrayed, marshaled, grouped, ranked, **graded;** organized, **regularized,** standardized, **systematized; classified** 808.8, categorized, **sorted,** assorted; **orderly** 806.6

15 **organizational,** formational, structural

808 CLASSIFICATION

NOUNS 1 **classification, categorization, pigeonholing, sorting, grouping; grading,** stratification, ranking; division, subdivision; **cataloging,** codification, rationalization, filing; **taxonomy, arrangement** 807

2 **class, category, head, order, division, group,** grouping; **section,** heading, rubric, **label,** title; **grade,** rank, rating, status, stratum, station, position; **caste,** clan, **subdivision**

3 **kind, sort, ilk, type,** breed of cat <nonformal>, **variety, species, genus, nature, character,** persuasion, the like or likes of <nonformal>; **stamp, brand,** feather, kidney; **make,** cast, form, mold

4 **hierarchy,** class structure, power structure, pyramid, establishment, pecking order; domain, realm, **kingdom**

5 kingdom; subkingdom, phylum

VERBS 6 **classify,** designate; **categorize,** type, **pigeonhole,** place, **group, arrange** 807.8, range; **order** 806.4, rank, rate, **grade; sort,** assort; **divide, analyze** 800.6, subdivide, break down; **catalog,** tabulate, rationalize, **index,** codify

ADJS 7 **classificational,** classificatory; **categorical, taxonomic** or **taxonomical;** ordinal; **typical,** typal; **special,** characteristic, particular, peculiar, distinctive, varietal

8 **classified, cataloged, pigeonholed,** indexed, sorted, assorted, **graded, grouped,** ranked, rated, stratified

ADVS 9 **any kind** or sort, **of any description, at all**

809 DISORDER

NOUNS 1 **disorder, disorderliness, disarrangement, disorganization;** discomposure, **dishevelment, disarray,** discomfiture, disconcertedness; **irregularity,** randomness, unsymmetry or nonsymmetry, **disproportion,** disharmony; indiscriminateness, haphazardness; **randomness,** vagueness, trendlessness; **disruption** 801.3, destabilization; **incoherence** 803.1; untogetherness <nonformal>; disintegration 805

2 **confusion, chaos,** anarchy, misrule, license; **Babel,** cognitive dissonance; **muddle,** morass, **mix-up** and foul-up and fuck-up and snafu and screw-up <all nonformal>, pretty kettle of fish, nice piece of work

3 **jumble, scramble, tumble, snarl-up, mess,** holy or unholy or god-awful mess <nonformal>, **turmoil,** welter, mishmash, hash, farrago; **clutter, litter, hodge-podge** 796.6, rat's nest

4 **commotion, hubbub, Babel, tumult,** turmoil, **uproar, racket,** riot, **disturbance, rumpus** <nonformal>, ruckus and ruction <both nonformal>, **fracas, hassle,** rampage; **ado,** to-do <nonformal>, stir <nonformal>, **fuss,** brouhaha; **row** and hassle <both nonformal>, **brawl,** free-for-all <nonformal>, donnybrook, embroilment, melee, **roughhouse, rough-and-tumble**

5 **pandemonium, hell, bedlam,** Babel, confusion of tongues; **cacophony**

6 slovenliness, **slipshodness,** carelessness, negligence; **untidiness, messiness** <nonformal>, **sloppiness, shabbiness,** tawdriness, shoddiness, tackiness <nonformal>, grubbiness <nonformal>, blowziness; **slatternliness,** sluttishness; **squalor,** sordidness

7 **slob** <nonformal>, **slattern, sloven,** frump <nonformal>; drab, **slut, trollop; pig,** swine; **litterbug**

VERBS 8 lapse into disorder, come apart at the seams, come unstuck or unglued <nonformal>, disintegrate 805.3

9 **disorder, disarrange** 810.2, **disorganize,** dishevel; **confuse** 810.3, sow confusion, **muddle, discompose** 810.4, **upset,** destabilize

10 **riot, roister,** roil, carouse; **create a disturbance, make a commotion,** make trouble, cause a stir or commotion, **cut loose, run wild,** go on a rampage, go berserk

11 <nonformal terms> **kick up a row, raise the devil,** raise a rumpus or a storm, raise a ruckus, raise Cain, **raise hell, carry on, cut up, roughhouse**

ADJS 12 unordered, **orderless, disordered, unorganized, random, unarranged, unmethodical, unsystematic,** nonsystematic; disarticulated, **incoherent** 803.4; **formless,** amorphous, inchoate, shapeless; **irregular, haphazard,** desultory, **erratic,** sporadic, spasmodic, fitful, indiscriminate, capricious, random, dispersed, undirected, **aimless,** straggly; gratuitous

13 **disorderly, in disorder,** disordered, **disorganized, disarranged, discomposed,** dislocated; **upset, disturbed,** perturbed, unsettled, disconcerted; **turbulent,** turbid; **out of order,** out of place, misplaced, shuffled; **out of kilter** or **kelter** <nonformal>, **out of whack** <nonformal>; **cockeyed** <nonformal>, awry, amiss, askew

14 **disheveled, mussed up** <nonformal>, messed up <nonformal>, **rumpled,** ruffled, snarled

15 **slovenly, slipshod, careless, loose, slack,** negligent; **untidy, unsightly, unkempt; messy** <nonformal>, **sloppy** <nonformal>, **shabby,** shoddy, grubby <nonformal>, **frowzy, blowzy,** tacky <nonformal>; **slatternly, sluttish, frumpish,** frumpy, bedraggled; down at the heel, out at the heels, out at the elbows, tattered; **squalid,** sordid; dilapidated, ruinous

16 **confused, chaotic,** anarchic, **muddled, jumbled,** helter-skelter <nonformal>, in a mess; **topsy-turvy,** ass-backwards <nonformal>; **mixed up, balled** or **bollixed up** <nonformal>,

screwed up <nonformal>, mucked up <nonformal>, **fouled up** <nonformal>

ADVS **17 in disorder, in disarray, in confusion,** in a muddle, in a mess; helter-skelter <nonformal>, willy-nilly <nonformal>, **all over the place**

18 haphazardly, unsystematically, unmethodically, irregularly, desultorily, **erratically,** capriciously, indiscriminately, **sloppily** <nonformal>, **carelessly,** randomly, **fitfully;** sporadically, spasmodically, **by fits and starts; at random, hit or miss**

19 chaotically, anarchically, turbulently, **riotously; confusedly, aimlessly,** planlessly

810 DISARRANGEMENT
<bringing into disorder>

NOUNS **1 disarrangement, derangement,** convulsion, dislocation; **disorganization; discomposure,** perturbation; **disorder** 809

VERBS **2 disarrange; disorder, disorganize,** dislocate, **disarray; dishevel,** rumple, ruffle; mess and **mess up** <both nonformal>; **litter, clutter**

3 confuse, muddle, jumble, confound, garble, scramble; **shuffle; mix up,** snarl up, **ball or bollix up** <nonformal>, **foul up and screw up** and muck up <all nonformal>

4 discompose, throw into confusion, **upset, unsettle, disturb,** trip up, perturb, throw <nonformal>, agitate, convulse, embroil; **psych** and spook and bug <all nonformal>

ADJS **5 disarranged** 809.13, **confused** 809.16, **disordered** 809.12

811 CONTINUITY
<uninterrupted sequence>

NOUNS **1 continuity, uninterruption, uninterruptedness,** unrelievedness, monotony, **uniformity** 780; seamlessness, jointlessness, gaplessness, smoothness; **consecutiveness, endlessness,** ceaselessness; **constancy** 846.2, equilibrium, stability 854

2 series, succession, run, **sequence,** course, gradation; **continuum; connection, concatenation, chain,** articulation, reticulation, nexus; **train,** range, rank, **file, line, string,** thread, queue, **row; round, cycle,** rotation, routine, the daily grind <nonformal>, recurrence, periodicity; gamut, spectrum, scale

3 procession, train, column, line, string, cortege; cavalcade, caravan, motorcade; **parade,** pomp

VERBS **4 continue, connect, concatenate, join** 799.5, link or link up, **string together**

5 align, line, line up, string out, rank, array, range, get or put in a row

6 line up, get in or get on line, queue

7 file, defile, file off; parade

ADJS **8 continuous,** continued, **continual,** continuing; **uninterrupted, unintermittent,** unrelieved, monotonous; **connected, joined** 799.13, linked, concatenated, articulated; **unbroken, uniform** 780.5, homogeneous, undifferentiated, back-to-back <nonformal>, seamless, jointless, gapless; unremitting; **incessant, constant,** steady, stable, **ceaseless,** unceasing, **endless,** unending, never-ending, **interminable,** perennial

9 consecutive, successive, back-to-back <nonformal>; **sequential;** linear

ADVS **10 continuously, continually; uninterruptedly; without cease,** without a break, back-to-back, seamlessly, **connectedly,** cumulatively; unceasingly, **endlessly,** ad infinitum <L>, **interminably,** repetitively, monotonously, unrelievedly

11 consecutively, progressively, sequentially, successively, **in succession,** one after the other, **in turn;** step by step; **serially,** in a series, **in a line**

812 DISCONTINUITY
<interrupted sequence>

NOUNS **1 discontinuity,** discontinuance; **incoherence** 803.1, **disconnectedness,** disconnection, discreteness, **disjunction** 801.1; **nonuniformity** 781; irregularity, **intermittence**

 2 interruption, suspension, break, gap, hiatus, caesura; **interval, pause, intermission**

VERBS **3 discontinue, interrupt** 856.10, **break,** break off, **disjoin; disarrange** 810.2; intermit 850.2

ADJS **4 discontinuous, incoherent** 803.4, **disconnected,** unconnected, decoupled, **broken; interrupted,** suspended; disjunctive, discrete; **intermittent, fitful** 850.3; choppy, jerky, spasmodic

ADVS **5 discontinuously, disconnectedly, haphazardly** 809.18, randomly, occasionally, infrequently, intermittently, fitfully, **by fits and starts;** willy-nilly, **here and there,** sporadically, patchily

813 PRECEDENCE
<in order>

NOUNS **1 precedence**, antecedence; **priority,** preference, urgency; **superiority** 249; **dominion** 417.6; **precursor** 815; prelude 815.2

VERBS **2 precede,** antecede, **come first,** come or go before, **go in advance, head,** head up <nonformal>, front, **lead** 165.2, take precedence, have priority

 3 <place before> **prefix, preface,** premise, prelude, prologize, preamble, introduce

ADJS **4 preceding,** precedent, **prior,** antecedent, **leading** 165.3; **preliminary,** precursory, prefatory, preparatory, inaugural; **first, foremost, chief** 249.14

 5 former, foregoing; aforesaid, aforementioned

ADVS **6 before** 216.12; above, *supra* <L>

814 SEQUENCE

NOUNS **1 sequence, succession, consecutiveness,** following; descent, lineage; **series** 811.2; **order,** order of succession; **priority; progression, continuity** 811; **continuation,** extension

VERBS **2 succeed, follow, ensue,** come or go after, **come next; inherit,** take the mantle of

 3 <place after> suffix, append, subjoin

ADJS **4 succeeding, successive, following, ensuing,** sequential, **subsequent,** consequent; proximate, **next**

815 PRECURSOR

NOUNS **1 precursor, forerunner,** front-runner; pioneer, frontiersman, bushwhacker; pathfinder, trailblazer or trailbreaker, guide; **leader** 574.6; **herald,** messenger, harbinger; **predecessor,** forebear, **ancestor; vanguard, avantgarde,** innovator, groundbreaker

 2 curtain raiser, run-up and walk-up <both nonformal>, opening gun or shot; **opening episode, prelude, preamble, preface,** prologue, foreword, introduction; frontispiece; **preliminary,** front matter; **innovation, breakthrough** <nonformal>

VERBS **3 go before, pioneer,** blaze or break the trail, break new ground; guide; **lead** 165.2, lead or show the way; **precede** 813.2; herald, usher in

ADJS **4 preceding** 813.4; preliminary, pioneering, trailblazing, inaugural; **advanced,** avant-garde

816 SEQUEL

NOUNS **1 sequel,** sequitur, **consequence** 886.1; **continuation,** continuance, **follow-up** or **follow-through** <nonformal>; **supplement,** addendum, appendix, postlude, **epilogue,** conclusion, peroration, codicil; parting or Parthian shot

 2 afterpart, afterpiece; wake, trail, train

3 **aftermath,** afterglow, after-image, aftereffect, aftertaste; **afterbirth,** placenta

4 **successor, replacement,** backup, stand-in; **descendant,** posterity, **heir,** inheritor

VERBS 5 **succeed,** come next, come after; **follow through,** carry through

817 BEGINNING

NOUNS 1 **beginning, commencement, start,** running or flying start, **outset,** outbreak, **onset; creation, foundation, establishment, establishing, institution, origin,** origination, establishment, setting in motion; **launching, opening;** fresh start, new departure; **opening wedge,** cutting edge

2 **beginner, neophyte, tyro;** newcomer 773.4, Johnny-come-lately <nonformal>; entrant, **novice,** novitiate, probationer; **recruit,** rookie <nonformal>; **apprentice,** trainee; freshman 572.6; tenderfoot, greenhorn

3 **first,** first ever, primary, **initial; initiation,** gambit, **first step,** openers, starters, first blush, first glance, first impression

4 **origin,** origination, **genesis, inception,** inchoation; **divine creation,** creationism; **birth,** bearing, parturition, pregnancy, nativity; **infancy**

5 **inauguration,** installation, induction, **introduction,** initiation; **launching,** unveiling, debut, coming out <nonformal>; opener <nonformal>, curtain raiser; maiden speech, inaugural address

6 **basics, essentials, rudiments, elements, nuts and bolts** <nonformal>; **principles,** first steps, **outlines, primer,** hornbook, **ABC's,** abecedarium

VERBS 7 **begin, commence, start; start up, kick in** <nonformal>; **start in, start off, start out, set out,** set to or about, go or swing into action, get to or down to, **turn to,** fall to, pitch in <nonfor-mal>, **go ahead,** let her rip <nonformal>, get the show on the road <nonformal>, start the ball rolling <nonformal>

8 **make a beginning,** make a move <nonformal>, **start up,** get going <nonformal>, get off the ground <nonformal>, **get under way,** set up shop; set a course, **get squared away** <nonformal>; **get off to a good start,** make a dent; get in on the ground floor <nonformal>; **break in, warm up,** get one's feet wet <nonformal>

9 enter, **enter on** or **upon** or **into, embark on** or **upon,** take a crack or whack or shot at <nonformal>; **debut,** make one's debut

10 **initiate, originate, create,** invent; **precede** 813.2, **take the initiative, take the first step,** pioneer 815.3; **lead,** lead the way; head up <nonformal>, stand at the head; **break the ice,** take the plunge, break ground

11 **inaugurate,** institute, **found, establish,** set up <nonformal>; **install,** induct; **introduce,** broach, raise; **launch,** float; **usher in; set on foot,** turn on, kick-start and jump-start <both nonformal>, start up, start going

12 **open,** open up, breach, open the door to; open fire

13 **originate,** be born, come into the world, **become,** come to be, see the light of day, rise, **arise, come forth, issue,** spring or crop up; burst forth, erupt

14 **engender, beget, procreate** 78.8; **give birth to,** bear, birth, bring to birth; father, mother, sire

ADJS 15 **beginning, initial; incipient,** inceptive, **introductory,** inchoative, inchoate; inaugural; **prime,** primal, **primary,** primeval; **original, first,** first ever; aboriginal, autochthonous; **elementary,** elemental, **fundamental; rudimentary; ancestral; formative, creative,** procreative; embryonic, fetal, gestatory, parturient, pregnant; **natal,** nascent

16 **preliminary, prefatory,** preludial, proemial; entry-level,

door-opening; prepositive, pre-
fixed
17 first, foremost, front
ADVS **18 first, firstly, at first,** for
openers *or* starters <nonformal>,
in the first place, first and foremost; **principally,** mainly, chiefly,
most of all; **primarily,** initially;
**originally, in the beginning, at
the start,** at first glance *or* first
blush, at the outset; from the
ground up, **from scratch** <non-
formal>, **from the word 'go'**
<nonformal>**19**

818 MIDDLE

NOUNS **1 middle,** median, **midst;**
thick of things; **center** 208.2;
heart, core, kernel; **mean** 246;
interior 207.2; **waist,** waistline;
equator; diameter
2 mid-distance, middle distance;
equidistance; half, moiety; **middle ground,** middle of the road
VERBS **3** seek the middle, bisect; average 246.2
ADJS **4 middle, medial,** median,
mediocre, average, **medium**
246.3, **mean,** mid; **midmost,**
middlemost; **central** 208.11,
core, nuclear; **intermediate,** intermediary; equidistant, equatorial; centrist, moderate, middle-
of-the-road
ADVS **5 midway, halfway, in the
middle,** betwixt and between
<nonformal>; half-and-half, nei-
ther here nor there; medially, mediumly; *in medias res* <L>; **in the
midst of**

819 END

NOUNS **1 end,** end point, **termination, terminus, terminal,** terminating, **expiration,** discontinuation, closeout, **cessation** 856,
ceasing, **conclusion, finish,
finis, finale,** the end, quietus,
stoppage, windup *and* payoff
<both nonformal>, curtains
<nonformal>, end of the road *or*
line <nonformal>; decease, taps,
death 307; **last,** last gasp *or*
breath, last hurrah <nonformal>;
goal, destination, finish line, tape

and wire <both nonformal>; denouement, catastrophe, resolution; last *or* final words, peroration, dying words, envoi, epilogue; **fate, destiny,** doom; **effect**
886; **happy ending**
2 extremity, extreme; limit 793.5,
ultimacy, definitiveness, **boundary,** jumping-off place, **pole; tip,**
point; tail, **tail end,** butt end, tag
end; bottom of the barrel <non-
formal>
3 close, closing, cessation; **home-
stretch,** last stage
4 finishing stroke, end-all, quietus, **deathblow,** *coup de grâce*
<Fr>, kiss of death; finishing *or*
crowning touch
VERBS **5 end, terminate,** close the
books on, phase out *or* down, **finish, conclude,** finish *or* wind up
<nonformal>; **put an end to,** put
or lay to rest, **make an end of,**
bring to an end, bring to a close
or halt, end up; bring down *or*
drop the curtain; put the lid on
<nonformal>, fold up <nonfor-
mal>, wrap *and* wrap up <both
nonformal>, sew up <nonfor-
mal>; call off <nonformal>; **dispose of,** polish off <nonformal>;
put the kibosh on <nonformal>,
put the skids under <nonfor-
mal>; **stop, cease** 856.6; **kill**
308.13, extinguish, waste *and*
take out *and* zap <all nonfor-
mal>, **give the quietus,** knock
out <nonformal>, kayo *or* KO
<both nonformal>, shoot down
and shoot down in flames <both
nonformal>, wipe out <nonfor-
mal>; **cancel, delete,** expunge,
censor
**6 come to an end, draw to a
close, expire, die** 307.19, come
to rest; lapse, become void *or* extinct *or* defunct, run its course,
pass, **pass away,** die away, be no
more
7 complete 793.6, perfect, finish
off, put the last *or* final *or* finishing touches on
ADJS **8 ended, at an end, terminated, concluded, finished,
complete** 793.9, perfected, set-

tled, decided, set at rest; **over, all over,** all up <nonformal>; **done,** done with, over with, over and done with; wound up <nonformal>, washed up <nonformal>; all over but the shouting <nonformal>; **dead** 307.30, **defunct,** extinct; **finished,** defeated, out of action; **canceled, deleted,** expunged, censored

9 <nonformal terms> **belly-up, dead meat,** kaput, shot, done for, SOL *or* shit out of luck, shot down in flames, wasted, zapped, wiped out, washed up, down the tubes, totaled

10 **ending, closing, concluding, finishing, ultimate,** definitive, terminating, crowning, capping

11 **final, terminal,** definitive, **conclusive; last,** last-ditch <nonformal>, eventual, farthest, extreme, limiting, **endmost, ultimate**

ADVS 12 **finally,** in fine; **ultimately, eventually, as a matter of course; lastly,** last, **at last,** at long last; **in conclusion, in sum**

13 **to the end, to the bitter end, all the way,** to the last gasp, **to a finish,** till hell freezes over <nonformal>

820 TIME

NOUNS 1 **time, duration,** continuity 811, term; tense 530.12; **period** 823, time frame; time warp; **chronology** 831.1

2 Time, Father Time, Cronus, Kronos

3 hourglass of time, sands of time, ravages of time

4 **passage of time, course of time, lapse of time,** sweep of time, march *or* step of time, flight of time

VERBS 5 **elapse,** lapse, **pass, expire,** run its course, run out, go *or* pass by; **flow,** tick away *or* by *or* on, run, roll *or* press on, flit, fly, slip, glide; **continue** 811.4, last, **endure**

6 **spend time, pass time, put in time,** employ *or* use time, kill time <nonformal>, consume time, take time, while away the

time; race with *or* against time, buy time, work against time, run out of time, make time stand still

ADJS 7 **temporal, chronological;** lasting, continuous

ADVS 8 **when, at which time,** at which moment *or* instant, on which occasion, **upon which, whereupon,** at which, in which time, whenever

9 **at that time,** on that occasion, at the same time as, concurrently, simultaneously, contemporaneously

10 in the meantime, meanwhile 825.5; at a stretch

11 **then,** thereat, thereupon, **at that time,** at that moment *or* instant, on that occasion; **again,** at another time, anon

12 **whenever,** whensoever, **at whatever time,** anytime, no matter when

821 TIMELESSNESS

NOUNS 1 **timelessness,** datelessness, eternity 828.1,2; time out of time, stopping time

2 <a time that will never come> Greek calends *or* kalends, when hell freezes over

ADJS 3 **timeless, dateless**

ADVS 4 **never, not ever,** at no time, on no occasion, not at all; **nevermore;** never in the world, never in all one's born days <nonformal>

5 without date, *sine die* <L>, openended

822 INFINITY

NOUNS 1 **infinity,** infinitude, the be-all and end-all; **boundlessness, limitlessness, endlessness; immeasurability,** unmeasurability, immensity, incalculability, innumerability, incomprehensibility; measurelessness, numberlessness; inexhaustibility; universality; **all-inclusiveness; eternity** 828.1,2, **perpetuity** 828, forever

VERBS 2 **have no limit** *or* **bounds,** be without end, **go on and on,** go on forever

ADJS **3 infinite, boundless, endless, limitless**; unbounded, uncircumscribed, **unlimited,** without bound, without limit or end, no end of or to; illimitable; **interminable; immeasurable,** incalculable, incomprehensible, unfathomable; **unmeasured,** unmeasurable, immense, unplumbed, without measure or number or term; inexhaustible; **all-inclusive, universal** 863.14; **perpetual, eternal** 828.7

ADVS **4 infinitely,** boundlessly, limitlessly, **interminably; immeasurably,** incalculably, incomprehensibly; **endlessly,** without end or limit; ad infinitum <L>, to infinity; **forever, eternally** 828.10, in perpetuity

823 PERIOD
<portion or point of time>

NOUNS **1 period, point, juncture,** stage; **interval,** lapse of time, time frame, timespan, stretch; **time,** while, **moment,** minute, instant, hour, day, **season; spell** 824

2 <periods> **moment, second,** millisecond, microsecond, nanosecond; **minute,** hour, **day, week;** fortnight; **month,** moon, lunation; **quarter; semester,** trimester, term, session, academic year; **year, decade, century; millennium**

3 term, time, duration, **tenure;** spell 824

4 age, generation, time, day, date, cycle; **eon**

5 era, epoch, age

824 SPELL
<period of duty, etc>

NOUNS **1 spell,** fit, stretch, go <nonformal>

2 turn, bout, round, inning, time, whack and go <both nonformal>; opportunity, chance; **relief, spell;** one's turn

3 shift, tour, tour of duty, stint, bit, **watch, trick,** time, **turn,** relay; day shift, night shift, swing shift, graveyard shift <nonformal>; lobster trick; split shift; flextime; **overtime**

4 term, time; **tenure; enlistment, hitch** <nonformal>, tour; prison term, stretch <nonformal>

VERBS **5 take one's turn,** have a go <nonformal>; **take turns,** alternate; **time off, spell** <nonformal>, **relieve,** cover, **fill in for,** take over for; put in one's time, work one's shift; **stand one's watch** or **trick,** keep a watch; hold office; **enlist,** sign up; re-enlist; do a hitch <nonformal>, do a tour of duty; serve or do time

825 INTERIM
<intermediate period>

NOUNS **1 interim, interval, interlude, intermission,** pause, break, **time-out,** recess, coffee break, interruption; **lull,** quiet spell, plateau, letup, relief, vacation, holiday, time off; downtime; **respite** 20.2; **intermission;** interregnum

2 meantime, meanwhile, while, the while

VERBS **3 intervene; pause,** break, **recess,** declare a recess; call a halt or break or intermission; **call time** or time-out; take a break <nonformal>

ADJS **4 interim, temporary,** tentative, provisional

ADVS **5 meanwhile, meantime, in the meanwhile** or **meantime,** in the interim; between acts or halves, between now and then; till or until then; in the intervening time, at the same time, for a time or season

826 DURATION

NOUNS **1 durability, endurance,** duration, durableness, abidingness, perdurability; **continuance,** maintenance, **steadfastness,** constancy, **stability** 854, **persistence, permanence** 852, standing, long standing; **longevity,** long-livedness; **antiquity, age; survival,** survivability, viability; **service life,** useful life, shelf life; **perpetuity** 828

2 protraction, prolongation, continuation, extension, drawing- *or* stretching- *or* spinning-out, lingering; procrastination 845.5

3 length of time, distance of time, vista *or* stretch *or* desert of time, corridor *or* tunnel of time

4 long time, long while; **age** *and* **ages** <both nonformal>, **eon, century, eternity,** years, **years on end,** month of Sundays <nonformal>

5 lifetime, life, life expectancy, lifespan, all the days of one's life; **generation, age;** all one's born days <nonformal>

VERBS **6 endure, last** *or* **last out, abide,** dwell, perdure, **continue,** run, **go on,** carry on, keep on, stay the course, go the distance, grind *or* plug away; live, **live on,** continue to be, subsist, exist, tarry; **persist;** hang in *and* hang in there *and* hang tough <all nonformal>; **remain, stay,** keep, prevail, hold out; **survive,** defy *or* defeat time; live to fight another day; **survive,** live through; wear well

7 linger on, linger, tarry, **go on and on, wear on,** crawl, creep, **drag on,** drag along

8 outlast, outstay, last out, outwear, **outlive, survive**

9 protract, prolong, continue, **extend, lengthen,** lengthen out, **draw out, spin out,** stretch out; dawdle, procrastinate, temporize, drag one's feet

ADJS **10 durable,** perdurable, **lasting, enduring, abiding, continuing,** remaining, **stable** 854.12, **persistent,** perennial; inveterate; **steadfast, constant,** intransient, immutable, **permanent** 852.7, perennial, **long-lasting,** of long duration *or* standing; **long-lived,** tough, hardy, vital; **ancient,** aged, antique; **perpetual** 828.7

11 protracted, prolonged, extended, lengthened; **long,** timeconsuming, interminable, marathon, **lingering,** languishing;

drawn- *or* stretched- *or* dragged-*or* spun-out, **long-drawn-out;** long-winded, prolix, verbose 538.12

12 daylong, nightlong, weeklong, monthlong, yearlong

13 lifelong, livelong, lifetime, for life

ADVS **14 for a long time, long, for long, interminably,** persistently, protractedly, enduringly; **forever and a day, forever and ever, for years on end, for days on end, etc;** morning, noon, and night; hour after hour, day after day, month after month, year after year; day in day out, month in month out, year in year out; till hell freezes over <nonformal>, till the cows come home <nonformal>, from now till doomsday, from here to eternity, till the end of time; since time began, time out of mind, time immemorial

827 TRANSIENCE

<short duration>

NOUNS **1 transience** *or* transiency, **impermanence** *or* impermanency, transitoriness, **mutability, instability,** fleetingness, **momentariness; ephemerality,** ephemeralness, short duration; evanescence, volatility, fugacity, **short-livedness; mortality,** death, perishability; **expedience** 994

2 brevity, briefness; swiftness 174, fleetness

3 short time, little while, instant, moment 829.3, span, spurt, **short spell;** no time, less than no time; bit *or* **little bit,** a breath, the wink of an eye; **two shakes** *and* two shakes of a lamb's tail <both nonformal>

4 transient; sojourner; passerby; **wanderer; vagabond,** drifter, derelict, homeless person, tramp, hobo, bum <nonformal>

5 ephemeron, ephemera, ephemeral

VERBS **6** <be transient> **flit, fly,** fleet; pass, **pass away, vanish, evaporate,** dissolve, evanesce, disappear, fade, melt, sink; vanish like a dream, **go up in smoke**

ADJS **7 transient, transitory; temporary,** temporal; **impermanent,** unenduring; frail, brittle, fragile, insubstantial; changeable 853.6, **mutable, unstable,** inconstant 853.7; capricious, fickle, impulsive, impetuous; **short-lived, ephemeral,** fly-by-night, evanescent, volatile, **momentary; passing,** fleeting, flitting, flying, fading; fugitive, fugacious; perishable, mortal, corruptible; here today and gone tomorrow; **expedient** 994.5

8 brief, short, quick, brisk, swift, fleet, speedy; meteoric, short-term

ADVS **9 temporarily,** for the moment, **for the time being,** for a time, awhile

10 transiently, impermanently, transitorily, fleetingly, flittingly, **briefly, shortly,** quickly, **for a little while,** for a short time; **momentarily,** for a moment; **in an instant** 829.7

828 PERPETUITY
<endless duration>

NOUNS **1 perpetuity; eternity,** infinite duration; **everlastingness, permanence** 852, duration 826, perdurability, indestructibility; **constancy,** stability, immutability, **ceaselessness,** incessancy; timelessness 821; **endlessness, interminability; infinity** 822

2 forever, an eternity, time without end

3 immortality, eternal life, **deathlessness,** imperishability; eternal youth, fountain of youth

4 perpetuation, preservation, immortalization

VERBS **5 perpetuate, preserve,** keep fresh *or* alive, **eternalize, immortalize**

6 last *or* endure forever, **go on forever,** go on and on, **have no end,** have no limits *or* bounds

ADJS **7 perpetual, everlasting,** everliving, permanent 852.7, perdurable, indestructible; **eternal,** sempiternal, **infinite** 822.3; dateless, ageless, timeless, immemorial; **endless,** never-ending, **interminable; continual,** continuous, steady, **constant, ceaseless,** nonstop, unceasing, **incessant,** unremitting, uninterrupted

8 perennial, evergreen, ever-new, ever-young

9 immortal, everlasting, **deathless,** undying, **imperishable,** incorruptible; **unfading**

ADVS **10 perpetually,** in perpetuity, **everlastingly, eternally, permanently** 852.9, perennially, perdurably, indestructibly, **constantly,** continually, steadily, **ceaselessly,** unceasingly, **incessantly, endlessly,** unendingly, **interminably,** without end; **infinitely,** *ad infinitum* <L> 822.4

11 always, all along, all the time, all the while, at all times; **invariably,** without exception

12 forever, forevermore, for ever and ever, forever and a day <nonformal>, now and forever; **ever, evermore,** ever and again; **for good,** for keeps <nonformal>, for all time; **to the end of time,** till time runs out, till doomsday; till hell freezes over <nonformal>, till the cows come home <nonformal>

13 for life, while one draws breath, in all one's born days <nonformal>; **till death,** till death do us part

829 INSTANTANEOUSNESS
<imperceptible duration>

NOUNS **1 instantaneousness,** momentariness, **immediateness** *or* immediacy; simultaneity 835

2 suddenness, abruptness, precipitateness, precipitancy; **unexpectedness**

3 instant, moment, second, split second, half a second, minute, **trice,** twinkle, **twinkling, twinkling** *or* **twinkle of an eye, wink,** bat of an eye <nonformal>, **flash,** breath, twitch; two shakes of a lamb's tail *and* **jiffy** *and* half a jiffy <all nonformal>

ADJS **4 instantaneous,** instant, momentary, **immediate**; lightning-swift; simultaneous

5 sudden, abrupt, precipitant, **precipitate; hasty,** headlong, impulsive, impetuous; speedy, swift, quick; **unexpected** 131.10, unanticipated, unpredicted, unforeseen; **surprising** 131.11, startling, electrifying

ADVS **6 instantly,** instanter, momentarily, **instantaneously, immediately, right off the bat** <nonformal>

7 quickly, in an instant, in a trice, in a second, in a moment, in a jiffy *or* half a jiffy <nonformal>, in a flash, in a wink <nonformal>, **in a twinkling, in the twinkling of an eye, as quick as a wink,** as quick as greased lightning <nonformal>, in two shakes of a lamb's tail <nonformal>, before you can say 'Jack Robinson' <nonformal>; **in no time,** in less than no time, in short order; at the drop of a hat, like a shot; with the speed of light

8 at once, then and there, now, **right now, right away, right off,** straightaway, forthwith, **without delay,** in a hurry <nonformal>; **simultaneously,** in the same breath; **all at once**

9 suddenly, all of a sudden, all at once: abruptly, sharp; precipitately, precipitantly, impulsively, impetuously, hastily; **unexpectedly** 131.14, out of a clear blue sky; on short notice, without notice *or* warning, without further ado, unawares, **surprisingly** 131.15, like a bolt from the blue

830 EVENT

NOUNS **1 event, eventuality,** effect 886, issue, aftermath, consequence; **realization,** materialization, coming to be *or* pass, incidence

2 event, occurrence, incident, episode, experience, adventure, happening, happenstance, **phenomenon,** matter of fact, circumstance, **occasion,** turn of events; **nonevent**

3 affair, concern, matter, thing, interest, **business, transaction,** proceeding, doing; cause célèbre

4 affairs, concerns, matters, circumstances, **dealings, proceedings,** goings-on <nonformal>; course of events, the way things go, march of events; order of the day; **conditions, state of affairs**

VERBS **5 occur, happen** 971.11, eventuate, **take place,** go on, **transpire,** be realized, **come off** <nonformal>, **come about,** come true, **come to pass,** pass, **befall,** betide; **be found**

6 turn up, show up <nonformal>, **come along,** come one's way, cross one's path, **crop up,** spring up, pop up <nonformal>, arise, approach, materialize, present itself

7 turn out, result 886.5

8 experience, have, know, feel, taste; **encounter, meet,** meet with, run up against <nonformal>; **undergo, go through,** pass through, be subjected to, be exposed to, **endure, suffer,** sustain

ADJS **9 happening, occurring, current, actual,** passing, taking place, **going on,** ongoing <nonformal>, **prevalent, prevailing,** in the wind, afloat, afoot, under way, in hand, **on foot;** incidental, circumstantial, accompanying; accidental; occasional; resultant; eventuating

10 eventful, momentous, stirring, bustling

11 eventual, coming, final, last, **ultimate; contingent,** collateral, secondary, indirect

ADVS **12 eventually, ultimately, finally, in the end, after all is said and done, in the long run, over the long haul;** in the course of things, in the natural way of things, as the tree falls, the way the cookie crumbles <nonformal>, as things turn out

831 MEASUREMENT OF TIME

NOUNS **1 chronology,** timekeep-ing, timing, clocking, horology, **chronometry;** watch- *or* clock-making; **dating,** carbon-14 dat-ing, dendrochronology

2 time of day, time 820, **the time; hour,** minute

3 standard time, civil time, zone time

4 date, point of time, time, day

5 epact, annual epact

6 timepiece, timekeeper, **timer, chronometer;** horologe, horolo-gium; **clock,** Big Ben, **watch,** turnip <nonformal>; hourglass, sundial

7 almanac, The Old Farmer's Al-manac

.**8** calendar, calends; calendar stone, chronogram

9 chronicle, chronology, regis-ter, registry, record; **annals,** journal, diary; time sheet, time book, **log,** daybook; datebook; **timetable,** schedule, timeline, time chart; time scale; time study, motion study, time and motion study

10 chronologist, chronologer, chronographer, horologist, horol-oger; watchmaker *or* clockmaker; timekeeper, timer; **chronicler,** annalist, diarist; calendar maker; calendarist

VERBS **11 time, fix** *or* **set the time; keep time,** mark time, beat time; **clock** <nonformal>

12 punch the clock *and* punch in *and* punch out *and* **time in** *and* **time out** <all nonformal>; ring in, ring out; clock in, clock out

13 date, be dated, date at *or* from, bear the date of; fix *or* set the date, make a date; **predate,** back-date, antedate; **postdate; up-date,** bring up to date

14 chronologize, chronicle, calen-dar, intercalate

ADJS **15 chronologic<al>,** tempo-ral, timekeeping; **chronomet-ric<al>,** chronographic *or* chronographical, horologic *or* horological, metronomic *or* metronomical, calendric *or* cal-endrical, intercalary *or* interca-lated; dated

ADVS **16 o'clock,** of the clock, by the clock

832 ANACHRONISM

<*false estimation or knowledge of time*>

NOUNS **1 anachronism,** chrono-logical error, **mistiming, misdat-ing,** postdating, antedating; para-chronism, metachronism, pro-chronism; prolepsis, anticipation

VERBS **2 mistime, misdate;** ante-date, postdate; lag

ADJS **3 anachronous** *or* **anach-ronistic,** parachronistic, meta-chronistic, prochronistic; **mis-timed, misdated;** antedated, postdated; ahead of time, **before-hand, early; behindhand, late,** unpunctual, tardy; **overdue,** past due; **dated,** out-of-date

833 PREVIOUSNESS

NOUNS **1 previousness, earliness** 844, **antecedence,** priority, **ante-riority, precedence,** precession; *status quo ante* <L>, earlier state; preexistence; **anticipation,** pre-dating, antedating; **past time** 836

2 antecedent, precedent, premise; forerunner, **precursor** 815, an-cestor

VERBS **3 be prior,** come on the scene *or* appear earlier, **precede, antecede,** come *or* go before, set a precedent; **herald,** usher in, proclaim, announce; **anticipate,** antedate, predate; **preexist**

ADJS **4 previous, prior, early** 844.7, **earlier, former, preceding** 165.3, foregoing, above, anterior, **anticipatory,** antecedent; **pre-existent**

5 prewar, antebellum, before the war; prerevolutionary; prelap-sarian, before the Fall; antedilu-vian, before the Flood; prehis-toric 836.10; precultural

ADVS **6 previously, hitherto, here-tofore; before, early** 844.11, **ear-lier,** ere, ere then; already, yet; be-fore all; **formerly** 836.13

834 SUBSEQUENCE
<later time>

NOUNS **1 subsequence,** posteriority, **succession, ensuing, following** 166, sequence, supervenience, supervention; lateness 845; remainder 256, hangover <nonformal>

2 sequel 816, **follow-up,** sequelae, **aftermath; consequence, effect** 886; **posterity; successor; lineage,** dynasty, family

VERBS **3 come** or **follow** or **go after, follow, follow on** or **upon, succeed,** replace, take the place of, displace, overtake, supervene; **ensue,** issue, emanate, attend, **result;** tread on the heels of, dog the footsteps of; **step into** or **fill the shoes of,** assume the robe of

ADJS **4 subsequent, after, later,** after-the-fact, *ex post facto* <L>, posterior, **following, succeeding,** successive, sequent, ensuing, attendant

5 posthumous, afterdeath; **postprandial,** after-dinner; **post-war,** after the war; **postdiluvian,** after the flood, postlapsarian, after the Fall

ADVS **6 subsequently, after, afterwards,** after that, after all, **later, next,** since; **thereafter, then;** in the process or course of time; at a subsequent or later time; *ex post facto* <L>; hard on the heels

7 after which, on or **upon which, whereupon,** wherefore, on, upon; hereinafter

835 SIMULTANEITY

NOUNS **1 simultaneity** or **simultaneousness,** coincidence, concomitance or concomitancy; **coexistence; contemporaneousness** or contemporaneity; unison; **synchronism,** synchronization; isochronism

2 contemporary, coeval, concomitant

3 tie, dead heat, draw, wash <nonformal>

VERBS **4 coincide,** concur; **coexist; synchronize,** isochronize, be in time, keep time; **accompany** 768.7, **agree 787.6,** match, go along with, go hand in hand, keep pace with, keep in step

ADJS **5 simultaneous, concurrent,** concomitant; **tied,** neck-and-neck; coexistent, coexisting; **contemporaneous,** contemporary; coterminous, conterminous; isochronous, isochronal; accompanying 768.9, collateral

6 synchronous, synchronized, synchronic or synchronal, in sync <nonformal>; **in time**

ADVS **7 simultaneously, concurrently; together,** all together, **at the same time,** at one and the same time, in chorus, with one voice, in unison, in the same breath; **synchronously,** isochronously, in phase, **in sync** <nonformal>

836 THE PAST

NOUNS **1 the past,** past times, times past, water under the bridge, **days** or **times gone by, bygone times** or **days, yesterday, yesteryear;** recent past, just or only yesterday; **history;** dead past, dead hand of the past

2 old or **olden times,** early times, **old** or **olden days, days of old, days of yore,** good old days, the way it was, auld lang syne <Scots>, **the long ago,** time out of mind, days beyond recall

3 antiquity, ancient times, time immemorial, ancient history, remote time, dim or **distant past;** ancientness 841

4 memory 988, **remembrance, recollection, reminiscence, fond remembrance, retrospection,** musing on the past, looking back; **reliving,** reexperiencing; revival 396.3

5 <grammatical terms> past tense, preterit, perfect tense, past perfect tense

VERBS **6 pass,** be past, **be a thing of the past,** slip by or away, be gone, fade, be dead and gone, have run its course, have had its day; **disappear** 34.2; **die** 307.19

ADJS **7 past, gone,** by, **gone-by, by-gone, over,** departed, passed away, elapsed, lapsed, vanished, faded, irrecoverable, not coming back; **dead** 307.30, dead as a dodo, expired, extinct, dead and buried, defunct, deceased; **passé, obsolete,** has-been, dated, antique, **antiquated**

  8 reminiscent 988.22, **retrospective, remembered** 988.23, **recollected; relived, reexperienced; restored, revived**

  9 <grammatical terms> past, preterit or preteritive, pluperfect, past perfect

10 former, past, **previous,** late, recent, **once, onetime, erstwhile,** quondam; **prior** 833.4; **ancient, immemorial,** primeval, prehistoric; **old**

11 foregoing, aforegoing, **preceding** 813.4; last, latter

12 back, backward; retrospective, retroactive

ADVS **13 formerly, previously; earlier, before,** before now, erenow, **hitherto, heretofore, in the past,** in times past; then; **yesterday,** only yesterday, recently; **historically**

14 once, once upon a time, one day, one fine morning

15 ago, since, gone by; back, back when; backward, to or into the past; **retrospectively,** retroactively

16 long ago, a long while or time ago, some time ago or since, ages ago, **years ago; in times past,** in times gone by, in the good old days; **of old, of yore,** in ancient times, in the olden times, **in days of yore,** in the memory of man, time out of mind

17 since, ever since, until now; **since long ago, long since, from time immemorial,** from time out of mind, since time began, since Hector was a pup and since God knows when <both nonformal>

837 THE PRESENT

NOUNS **1 the present,** present time, the here and now; **now,** the present hour or moment, this instant or second or moment, **the present day or time or hour or minute, etc; the present age; today,** this day, **this day and age; this point, now,** nowadays, **the time being; the times,** our times, these days; **contemporaneousness or** contemporaneity; **newness** 840, modernity; the Now Generation, the me generation

ADJS **2 present, immediate,** current, extant, existent, **existing,** topical; **present-day,** present-time, **modern** 840.13, modern-day; **contemporary,** contemporaneous; up-to-date, up-to-the-minute, **new** 840.7

ADVS **3 now, at present, at this point,** at this juncture, **at this time,** at this moment or instant, at the present time; **today, in this day and age,** in our time, **nowadays; tonight;** here, **here and now,** just now, as of now, as things are; for the time being

  4 until now, hitherto, till now, **hereunto,** heretofore, until this time, **up to now,** up to the present, to this day, to the present moment, to this very instant, **so far,** thus far, **as yet, to date,** yet

838 THE FUTURE

NOUNS **1 the future,** futurity, what is to come, imminence 839, subsequence 834, eventuality 830.1, **hereafter, time to come,** years to come, etc; **tomorrow,** the morning after; **immediate or near future,** immediate prospect, offing; **distant future,** remote future; **by-and-by,** the sweet by-and-by <nonformal>; **prospect,** outlook, anticipation, expectation, extrapolation, foresight, prevision, prevenience, envisagement, prophecy, divination, clairvoyance; the womb of time

  2 destiny 963.2, **fate,** doom, karma, kismet, what is fated or destined, what is in the books; **the hereafter,** a better place; **the afterworld, the next world,** the world to come, **the beyond,** the great beyond, the great unknown, **the grave,** abode of the dead, eternal home; **afterlife, postexistence, life to come,** life after death

3 **doomsday,** day of reckoning; **Judgment Day,** Day of Judgment, the Judgment; eschatology, **last days**

4 **futurity;** ultimateness, eventuality, finality

5 **advent, coming, approach of time**

VERBS 6 **come,** come on, **approach,** near, **draw on** *or* **near;** be fated *or* destined *or* doomed, be in the cards; **loom,** threaten, stare one in the face, be imminent 839.2; **predict,** envision, envisage, previse, foretell, prophesy; **anticipate, expect,** hope for, look forward to, **project,** think ahead, extrapolate

7 **live on,** postexist, survive, get by *or* through

ADJS 8 **future, later,** hereafter; **coming, forthcoming, imminent** 839.3, approaching, **prospective; eventual** 830.11, ultimate, **to come; projected,** plotted, planned, desired, **predicted,** prophesied, foreseen, anticipated, previsional, prevenient, envisioned, envisaged, extrapolated; determined, fatal, destined, doomed

ADVS 9 **in the future, afterward** *or* afterwards, **later,** at a later time, anon; **by and by,** in the sweet by-and-by <nonformal>; **tomorrow; in the near** *or* **immediate future,** just around the corner, **imminently** 839.4, **soon, before long;** probably, predictably, hopefully

10 in future, **hereafter,** hereinafter, **henceforth, henceforward, thenceforth,** thenceforward, from this time forward, from this day on, from this *or* that time, from then on, **from here** *or* **now**

on, **from now on in** <nonformal>, from this moment on

11 **in time, in due time,** in due course, all in good time, **in the fullness of time,** in the course of time, **eventually** 830.12, **ultimately,** in the long run

12 **sometime, someday, some of these days,** one of these days, sometime or other, **sooner or later,** when all is said and done

839 IMMINENCE
<future event>

NOUNS 1 **imminence** *or* **imminency,** forthcomingness; **forthcoming, approach, loom;** immediate *or* near future

VERBS 2 **be imminent, impend, overhang,** hang over, **loom,** hang over one's head, hover, **threaten, menace,** lower; **come** *or* **draw on,** draw near *or* nigh, **approach, loom up, near,** be on the horizon, be in the offing, **confront, loom,** stare one in the face, breathe down one's neck

ADJS 3 **imminent, impending, overhanging,** hanging over one's head, waiting, lurking, **threatening, looming,** lowering, **menacing; brewing,** gathering; **coming, forthcoming, upcoming, to come,** about to be, about *or* going to happen, **approaching, nearing,** looming; **near, close,** immediate, **at hand,** near at hand, close at hand; **in the offing,** on the horizon, **in prospect,** just around the corner, in store, **in the wind;** on the lap of the gods, in the cards <nonformal>

ADVS 4 **imminently,** impendingly; **any time,** any time now, any day; **to be expected,** as may be

840 NEWNESS

NOUNS 1 **newness,** freshness, dewiness, mint condition, virginity, intactness, immaturity, callowness; **recentness,** recency; **novelty,** newfangledness; originality 337.1; **uncommonness,** strangeness

2 **novelty, innovation,** new-

fangled contraption <nonformal>, **new** *or* **latest wrinkle** <nonformal>, **the last word** <nonformal>; what's happening *and* what's in *and* the in thing *and* where it's at <all nonformal>; vanguard, **avant-garde**

3 **modernity**; modernism; modernization; space age

4 **modern**; modernist; modern *or* rising *or* new generation; neonate, fledgling, stripling, upstart, parvenu; Young Turk

VERBS 5 **innovate, invent,** coin, mint, inaugurate; **renew,** renovate 396.17

6 **modernize,** streamline; update, **bring up to date,** keep *or* stay current, move with the times

ADJS 7 **new,** young, **fresh,** fresh as a daisy; **unused, firsthand, original;** untried, untouched; virgin, virginal, intact, maiden, maidenly; green, vernal; pristine, evergreen; **immature,** undeveloped, raw, callow, unfledged

8 **fresh, additional, further,** other, another; **renewed**

9 **new-made,** new-mown, newminted, new-coined, in mint condition, mint; **newfound;** newborn, neonatal, new-fledged

10 <nonformal terms> **brand-new, spanking new; just out; hot,** hottest, hot off the griddle, hot off the press; newfangled

11 **novel, original, unique, different;** unfamiliar, unheard-of; **first, first ever** 817.15

12 **recent, late,** newly come, of yesterday; latter, later

13 **modern, contemporary, present-day,** present-time, latterday, space-age, neoteric, fashionable, modish, **up-to-date, up-to-the-minute, in,** abreast of the times; **advanced,** progressive, forward-looking, **avant-garde;** ultramodern, ahead of its time, far out, way out; postmodern

14 **state-of-the-art, newest, latest,** up-to-the-minute, most recent, newest of the new, farthest out

ADVS 15 **newly,** freshly, **anew,**

from the ground up, from scratch <nonformal>, **afresh, again**

16 **now, recently, lately, of late,** not long ago, a short time ago, the other day, only yesterday

841 OLDNESS

NOUNS 1 **oldness, age;** elderliness, seniority, senior citizenship, senility, **old age** 303.5; **ancientness, antiquity;** venerableness, great *or* hoary age; old order; **primitiveness,** primordialism, aboriginality; atavism

2 **tradition, custom, immemorial usage;** ancient wisdom, ways of the fathers; traditionalism; myth, mythology, legend, lore, folklore, folktale, folk motif; racial memory

3 **antiquation, superannuation,** staleness, disuse; **old-fashionedness; old-fogyishness,** stodginess

4 antiquarianism; classicism, medievalism

5 **antiquarian,** antiquary; dry-as-dust; **archaeologist;** classicist, medievalist; archaist

6 **antiquity, antique,** archaism; **relic; remains,** survival, vestige, ruin *or* ruins; **fossil;** petrification, petrified wood, petrified forest; **artifact**

7 **ancient,** man *or* woman of old, **prehistoric mankind;** preadamite, antediluvian; anthropoid, humanoid, protohuman, prehuman, missing link, hominid; **primitive, aboriginal,** aborigine, bushman, autochthon; **caveman,** cave dweller, troglodyte

8 <antiquated person> back number <nonformal>; dodo *and* old dodo <both nonformal>; fossil *and* antique *and* relic <all nonformal>; **mossback** <nonformal>, longhair *and* square <both nonformal>, **mid-Victorian,** antediluvian; has-been; **fogy, old fogy, fuddy-duddy** <nonformal>; granny <nonformal>, **old woman,** matriarch; **old man,** pa-

triarch, elder, old-timer <nonformal>, Methuselah

VERBS **9 age,** grow old 303.10, grow *or* have whiskers; **antiquate,** fossilize, date, **superannuate,** outdate; obsolesce, molder, rust, fade, perish; become obsolete *or* extinct; be a thing of the past

ADJS **10 old, age-old,** old-time; **ancient, antique,** venerable, hoary; dateless, timeless, ageless; **immemorial,** old as the hills; **elderly** 303.16

11 primitive, primeval, primordial; atavistic; **aboriginal,** autochthonous; ancestral, patriarchal; **prehistoric,** protohistoric; prehuman, protohuman, humanoid

12 traditional; mythological, heroic; **legendary,** unwritten, oral, handed down; **prescriptive, customary,** conventional, recognized, acknowledged, received; **hallowed, time-honored,** immemorial; **venerable,** hoary; **longstanding, of long standing,** long-established, inveterate

13 antiquated, grown old, **superannuated, antique, old,** old-world; antediluvian; **fossil,** fossilized, petrified

14 stale, fusty, musty, rusty, dusty, moldy, mildewed; **worn, timeworn; moth-eaten,** moldering, gone to seed, dilapidated

15 obsolete, passé, extinct, gone out, gone-by, dead, past, run out, **outworn**

16 old-fashioned, dated, out, out-of-date, outdated, outmoded, out of style *or* fashion, **unfashionable, behind the times,** old hat *and* back-number *and* has-been <all nonformal>

17 old-fogyish, old-fogy; fuddy-duddy; **stuffy, stodgy; aged** 303.16, senile, bent with age

18 secondhand, used, worn, previously owned, pawed-over; hand-me-down <nonformal>

19 older, senior, elder, dean; **oldest,** eldest; first-born, firstling

20 archaeological, paleological;

antiquarian; paleolithic, eolithic, neolithic, mezzolithic

ADVS **21** anciently 836.16

842 TIMELINESS

NOUNS **1 timeliness, seasonableness, opportuneness,** convenience; **expedience** *or* **expediency,** meetness, fitness, appropriateness, suitability; **favorableness, propitiousness,** auspiciousness, felicitousness; **ripeness,** expectancy

2 opportunity, chance, time, occasion; opening, scope, space; level playing field, fair game, fair shake *and* even break <both nonformal>; **opportunism;** equal opportunity, affirmative action; a leg up, stepping-stone, rung of the ladder

3 good opportunity, good chance, golden opportunity, the chance of a lifetime; suitable occasion, proper occasion, **good time,** high time; propitious moment

4 crisis, critical point, crunch, climax, climacteric; **turning point,** hinge, cusp; **emergency, exigency,** convergence of events, critical juncture, crossroads; **pinch,** clutch <nonformal>, rub, strait, extremity; **emergency**

5 crucial moment, critical moment, decisive moment, defining moment, turning point, climax, **moment of truth,** crunch *and* when push comes to shove <both nonformal>; **psychological moment,** right moment; nick of time, eleventh hour; **zero hour**

VERBS **6 be timely,** suit *or* befit the occasion, come *or* fall just right

7 take *or* **seize the opportunity,** use the occasion; take the bit in the teeth, take the bull by the horns, bite the bullet, **make one's move,** cross the Rubicon; **commit oneself,** drive an entering wedge

8 improve the occasion, turn to good account, avail oneself of, **take advantage of,** profit by, **cash in** *or* **capitalize on;** take time by the forelock, seize the opportunity, *carpe diem* <L, seize the day>, make hay while the sun shines; strike while the iron is hot; get going *and* get off the dime <both nonformal>

ADJS **9 timely, well-timed, seasonable, opportune, ill-timed,** convenient; **expedient,** meet, fit, fitting, befitting, suitable, appropriate; **favorable, propitious,** auspicious, providential, heaven-sent

10 critical, crucial, pivotal, climactic, decisive; pregnant, loaded, charged; exigent, emergent

11 incidental, occasional, casual, accidental; parenthetical, by-the-way

ADVS **12 opportunely, seasonably, propitiously,** auspiciously, in proper time *or* season, in due time, in the fullness of time, **in good time**; in the nick of time, just in time, at the eleventh hour

13 incidentally, by the way, by the by; while on the subject, speaking of, apropos; **in passing**; parenthetically; for example

843 UNTIMELINESS

NOUNS **1 untimeliness, unseasonableness,** inopportuneness, inconvenience; **inexpedience,** irrelevance *or* irrelevancy; **awkwardness,** inappropriateness, impropriety, unsuitability; **unfavorableness,** unfortunateness, inauspiciousness, unpropitiousness, infelicity; **intrusion,** interruption; **prematurity** 844.2; **lateness** 845

2 wrong time, bad time, wrong *or* bad *or* poor timing; evil hour, unlucky day *or* hour

VERBS **3 ill-time, mistime; lack the time,** have other *or* better things to do, be otherwise occupied, be preoccupied, have other fish to fry <nonformal>

4 talk out of turn, put one's foot in one's mouth <nonformal>, intrude, butt in *and* stick one's nose in <both nonformal>, **go off half-cocked** <nonformal>, open one's big mouth <nonformal>

5 miss an opportunity, miss the chance, miss out, miss the boat, miss one's turn, lose the opportunity, allow the occasion to go by, let slip through one's fingers, be left at the starting gate, be caught looking <nonformal>, lock the barn door after the horse is stolen

ADJS **6 untimely, unseasonable, inopportune, ill-timed,** mistimed, ill-considered, out of phase *or* time *or* sync; **inconvenient,** unhandy; **inappropriate,** irrelevant, improper, out of line, **inexpedient,** unfitting, unbefitting, untoward, intrusive; **unfavorable,** infelicitous, inauspicious, **unpropitious,** misfortuned; **premature** 844.8; **late** 845.16

ADVS **7 inopportunely, unseasonably,** inconveniently, inexpediently; **unpropitiously,** inauspiciously, unfortunately

844 EARLINESS

NOUNS **1 earliness,** early hour, time to spare; **head start,** running start, ground floor, very beginning, preliminaries; **anticipation, foresight,** prevision, prevenience; advance notice, lead time, a stitch in time, readiness

2 prematurity, prematureness; **untimeliness** 843; **precociousness,** forwardness; precipitation, rush, impulse, impulsiveness

3 promptness, promptitude, punctuality, readiness; instantaneousness 829, immediacy, decisiveness, **alacrity, quickness** 174.1, swiftness, expeditiousness, dispatch

4 early bird <nonformal>, early riser, first on the scene; **precursor** 815

VERBS **5 be early,** be ahead of time, be up and stirring, be ready and waiting, be off and running; gain time

6 anticipate, foresee, see the handwriting on the wall, pave the way for; **forestall, get ahead of,** get a head start, steal a march on, beat someone to the punch *or* the draw <nonformal>; **jump the gun,** go off half-cocked <nonformal>

ADJS **7 early,** bright and early <nonformal>, **beforetime,** in good time; foresighted, **anticipative** *or* **anticipatory,** prevenient, previsional

8 premature, too early, too soon; untimely; precipitate, hasty 829.5, **overhasty,** too quick on the draw *or* trigger *or* uptake <nonformal>; **unprepared,** unripe, impulsive; unpremeditated, ill-considered, **half-cocked** *and* **half-baked** <both nonformal>, uncrystallized; **precocious, forward, advanced,** born before one's time

9 prompt, punctual, immediate, instant, instantaneous 829.4, speedy, swift, expeditious, **ready,** Johnny-on-the-spot <nonformal>

10 earlier, previous 833.4

ADVS **11 early, bright and early, beforehand, beforetime,** early on, precociously, **ahead of time,** in anticipation, **with time to spare**

12 in time, in good time, soon enough, time enough, early enough; just in time, **in the nick of time,** just under the wire, without a minute to spare

13 prematurely, too soon, untimely, before its *or* one's time; **precipitately,** impulsively, in a rush, **overhastily;** at half cock <nonformal>

14 punctually, precisely, exactly, sharp; **on time, on the dot** <nonformal>

15 promptly, without delay, directly, **immediately,** immediately if not sooner <nonformal>, **instantly** 829.6, instanter, **at once,** right off, **right away,** straightaway, **forthwith, quickly,** swiftly, speedily, **summarily,** decisively, expeditiously, apace; no sooner said than done

16 soon, presently, directly, shortly, before long, ere long, in a while, **in a little while, after a** while, by and by, anon, betimes, in due course, at the first opportunity; in a moment *or* minute

845 LATENESS

NOUNS **1 lateness, tardiness, belatedness, unpunctuality;** eleventh hour, last minute, high time; unreadiness, unpreparedness

2 delay, stoppage, logjam <nonformal>, obstruction, tie-up *and* bind <both nonformal>, **block,** blockage; **retardation,** slowdown *and* slow-up <both nonformal>, time lag, dragging one's feet *and* foot-dragging <both nonformal>; **detention,** suspension, holdup <nonformal>, **obstruction, hindrance; wait, halt, stay, stop,** down-time, break, pause, respite; reprieve, stay of execution; moratorium

3 waiting, cooling one's heels <nonformal>, **tarrying; lingering, dawdling,** dillydallying

4 postponement, deferment *or* **deferral,** prorogation, tabling, holding up; **prolongation,** protraction, continuation; **adjournment,** adjournment sine die

5 procrastination, hesitation 362.3; **temporization, a play for time, stall** *and* tap-dancing <both nonformal>; **dilatoriness,** remissness, slackness, laxness

6 latecomer, late arrival, Johnny-come-lately; slow starter, dawdler; late bloomer *or* developer; late riser

VERBS **7 be late, not be on time,** be overdue, miss the boat; **stay late,** stay up late *or* into the small hours, burn the midnight oil, keep late hours; keep banker's hours

8 delay, retard, detain, slacken, lag, drag one's feet *and* stonewall <both nonformal>, slow down, **hold up** <nonformal>, **stop,** arrest, impede, **block,** throw a monkey wrench in the works <nonformal>, confine; tie up with red tape

9 postpone, delay, defer, put off, give one a rain check <nonfor-

mal>, prorogue, put on hold *or* ice *or* the back burner <all nonformal>, **suspend,** hang fire; protract, drag *or* stretch out <nonformal>, **prolong, extend,** spin *or* string out, prorogue; **hold over,** lay over, stand over, **put aside,** lay *or* set *or* push aside, **table,** pigeonhole, **shelve,** put on ice <nonformal>

10 **be left behind,** be outdistanced, make a slow start, be left at the post *or* starting gate

11 **procrastinate,** be dilatory, hesitate, let something slide, hang fire; **temporize, play for time,** drag one's feet <nonformal>, hold off <nonformal>; **stall, stall for time,** tap-dance <nonformal>; filibuster

12 **wait, delay, stay, bide one's time; take one's time,** mark time; **tarry, linger, loiter,** dawdle, dally, dillydally; stick around <nonformal>; **hold on** <nonformal>, sit tight <nonformal>, hold one's breath; hold everything *and* hold your horses *and* hold your water *and* keep your shirt on <all nonformal>; **wait and see,** see how the cookie crumbles *or* the ball bounces <nonformal>; wait for something to turn up; **await** 130.8

13 wait impatiently, tear one's hair *and* sweat it out *and* champ *or* chomp at the bit <all nonformal>

14 be kept waiting, be stood up <nonformal>, be left; **cool one's heels** <nonformal>

15 overstay, overtarry

ADJS 16 **late, belated, tardy,** slow, slow on the draw *or* uptake *or* trigger <all nonformal>, **overdue, long-awaited, untimely; unpunctual,** unready; **delayed,** detained, **held up** <nonformal>, **retarded, arrested,** blocked, **hung up** <nonformal>, obstructed, jammed, congested; **postponed, in abeyance,** put off, **on hold** *or* put on hold <nonformal>, on the back burner *or* put on the back burner <nonformal>

17 **dilatory, delaying;** last off the

mark; **procrastinating; obstructive,** obstructionist; **lingering,** loitering, lagging, dillydallying, **slow,** sluggish, laggard, footdragging; easygoing, **lazy, lackadaisical; remiss,** lax

18 later 834.4; last-minute, eleventh-hour, deathbed

ADVS 19 **late, behind, belatedly,** backward, slow, **behind time;** late in the day, at the last minute, at the eleventh hour, in the nick of time, under the wire

20 **tardily, slow, slowly,** sluggishly, lackadaisically, leisurely, lingeringly

846 FREQUENCY

NOUNS 1 **frequency; commonness,** prevalence, **common occurrence,** routineness; **incidence**

2 **constancy, continualness,** steadiness, **regularity,** incessancy, ceaselessness, continuity 811; perpetuity 828; repetition 848; **rapidity** 174.1; rapid *or* quick fire, tattoo, **staccato; vibration,** pulsation, **oscillation** 915

VERBS 3 **be frequent,** have a high incidence, recur 849.5; vibrate, oscillate 915.10

ADJS 4 **frequent, recurrent, oftrepeated; common,** of common occurrence, **prevalent,** routine, habitual, ordinary, everyday

5 **constant, continual** 811.8, **perennial; steady,** sustained, **regular; incessant, ceaseless, unceasing,** unremitting, relentless, unrelenting, uninterrupted, unbroken; **perpetual** 828.7; repeated 848.12; **rapid, staccato;** pulsating, vibrating, **oscillating** 915.15

ADVS 6 **frequently, commonly,** ordinarily, routinely, habitually; **often, oftentimes; repeatedly** 848.16, **again and again, time after time;** most often *or* frequently, in many instances, **many times,** many a time, more often than not; **in quick** *or* **rapid succession;** as often as you wish *or* like, whenever you wish *or* like

7 constantly, continually 811.10, **steadily, regularly,** as regular as clockwork, unvaryingly, uninterruptedly, **incessantly,** unceasingly, **ceaselessly,** perennially, all the time, at all times, without letup *or* break *or* intermission; **perpetually, always** 828.11; **rapidly;** all year round, every day, every hour, every moment; **night and day,** day and night; **morning, noon, and night; day in day out,** month in month out, year in year out

847 INFREQUENCY

NOUNS **1 infrequency,** seldomness; **rarity, scarcity, scarceness,** rareness, **uncommonness,** uniqueness; **sparsity** 884.1; **slowness** 175

ADJS **2 infrequent, rare,** scarce, scarcer than hens' teeth, **uncommon,** unique, unusual, few and far between, **sparse** 884.5; one-shot, once in a lifetime; **slow** 175.10

3 occasional, casual, incidental; odd, sometime, off-and-on, out-of-the-way, **part-time**

ADVS **4 infrequently, seldom, rarely, uncommonly, scarcely** *or* **hardly ever,** only now and then, off-and-on; **sparsely** 884.8

5 occasionally, on occasion, **sometimes, at times,** at odd times, every so often <nonformal>, at various times, **now and then,** now and again, **once in a while,** every once in a while <nonformal>, every now and then, every now and again, once or twice, **from time to time;** only occasionally, only when the spirit moves, only when necessary, at infrequent intervals, once in a blue moon <nonformal>; irregularly, sporadically

6 once, one-time, just this once, once and for all *or* always

848 REPETITION

NOUNS **1 repetition, reproduction,** duplication 873; **recurrence,** return, reincarnation, re-birth, reappearance, renewal, resumption; regurgitation, rehearsal; **quotation; imitation** 336; plagiarism 621.2; **reexamination,** second *or* another look

2 iteration, reiteration, recapitulation, retelling, recounting, recountal, **recital, rehearsal, restatement,** rehash <nonformal>; review, summary, précis, résumé, summing up; reassertion, reaffirmation; elaboration; **copy** 784

3 redundancy, tautology, tautologism, pleonasm; padding, expletive

4 repetitiousness, repetitiveness, stale *or* unnecessary repetition; **monotony,** monotone, drone; **tedium** 118, the daily round *or* grind; **humdrum; rhyme, alliteration; repeated sounds** 55

5 repeat, bis, ditto <nonformal>, echo; **refrain,** chant, undersong, chorus, bob

6 encore, reprise; replay, replaying

VERBS **7 repeat, redo, reproduce, duplicate** 873.3, reduplicate, double, redouble, **echo, parrot,** reecho; **rattle off,** reel off, regurgitate; come again *and* run it by again <both nonformal>, repeat oneself, **quote,** repeat verbatim, repeat like a broken record; **copy, imitate** 336.5; plagiarize 621.4,336.5; **reexamine,** take *or* have another look

8 iterate, reiterate, rehearse, recapitulate, recount, rehash <nonformal>, **recite, retell,** retail, **restate,** reword, review, summarize, précis, resume, encapsulate; do *or* say over again, **go over** *or* **through,** practice, go over the same ground, fight one's battles over again; **tautologize,** pad, fill; **reaffirm,** reassert

9 dwell on *or* **upon,** insist upon, **harp on,** beat a dead horse, labor, belabor, hammer away at, sing the same old tune, play the same old record; **thrash** *or* **thresh over,** cover the same ground

10 din, ding; drum 55.4, beat, ham-

mer, pound; **din in the ear,** din
into, drum into, say over and over

11 <be repeated> **repeat, recur,** reoccur, **come again,** come up
again, resurface, reenter, **return,
reappear, resume;** resound, reverberate, echo; revert, turn *or* go
back; happen over and over

ADJS 12 **repeated,** reproduced; **duplicated,** reduplicated; regurgitated, recited by rote; **echoed,**
reechoed, parroted; **quoted,** plagiarized; **iterated, reiterated;** re-
told, **twice-told;** warmed up *or*
over

13 **recurrent,** recurring, **returning,** reappearing, revenant, ubiquitous, frequent, incessant, continuous 811.8, year-to-year,
month-to-month, week-to-week,
etc

14 **repetitious,** repetitive, repeat-
ing; **duplicative,** reduplicative;
imitative 336.9, parrotlike; echoing, reechoing, echoic; **iterative,
reiterative,** reiterant; **tautological** *or* **tautologous, redundant**

15 **monotonous,** monotone; **tedious;** harping, labored; **humdrum; rhymed, rhyming, alliterative**

ADVS 16 **repeatedly, often, frequently, recurrently, every time
one turns around,** with every
other breath, **again and again,
over and over,** over and over
again, many times over, time and
again, **time after time, ad nauseam;** year in year out, week in
week out, etc; **many times,** many
a time; every now and then, every
once in a while

17 again, over, over again, once
more

849 REGULARITY OF RECURRENCE

NOUNS 1 **regularity,** clockwork
regularity, predictability, punctuality, **steadiness, evenness,
unvariableness, methodical-
ness; repetition** 848; **uniformity**
780; **constancy** 846.2

2 **periodicity;** undulation, **pulsation; intermittence** *or* intermit-

tency, alternation; rhythm
709.22, meter, beat; **oscillation**
915; **recurrence,** reappearance,
return, **cyclicalness,** cyclicality

3 **round, revolution, rotation,
cycle,** circle, wheel, **circuit; beat,**
upbeat, downbeat, **pulse;** course,
series, **bout, turn,** spell 824

4 **anniversary, commemoration;**
immovable feast, annual holiday;
centennial, centenary; bicentennial, bicentenary; tercentennial,
tercentenary; quincentennial,
quincentenary; **wedding anniversary, birthday,** birthdate, natal day; **religious holiday,** holy
day

VERBS 5 <occur periodically> **recur, reoccur, return, repeat**
848.7, reappear, **come again,**
come up again, resurface, reenter,
come round *or* **around; rotate,
revolve,** turn, circle, wheel, cycle,
roll around, go around, go
round; **intermit,** alternate, **come
and go;** undulate 915.11; **oscillate** 915.10, **pulse, pulsate**
915.12

ADJS 6 **regular, systematic,** methodical, regular as clockwork;
uniform 780.5; **constant** 846.5

7 **periodic** *or* periodical, **cyclic** *or*
cyclical, serial; measured, steady,
even, **rhythmic** *or* rhythmical
709.28; **recurrent,** recurring; **intermittent,** alternate, every other

8 **momentary, hourly; daily,** diur-
nal, quotidian, circadian; **weekly;**
fortnightly; **monthly,** menstrual,
catamenial; **yearly, annual;** centennial, centenary, secular

ADVS 9 **regularly, systematically,
methodically,** like clockwork,
steadily; at stated times, at fixed
or established periods; **uniformly**
780.7; **constantly** 846.7

10 **periodically, recurrently, sea-
sonally,** cyclically, epochally;
rhythmically, synchronously,
hourly, daily, etc

11 **alternately, by turns, in turns,
in rotation,** turn about, **turn
and turn about,** reciprocally,
one after the other; to and fro;
off and on

850 IRREGULARITY OF RECURRENCE

NOUNS **1 irregularity,** unmethodicalness; **inconstancy, unevenness, unsteadiness, variability,**
capriciousness, unpredictability,
whimsicality, eccentricity; **fitful-
ness,** jerkiness, fits and starts,
patchiness, spottiness, choppiness, discontinuity 812; **intermittence, fluctuation; nonuniformity** 781

VERBS **2 intermit, fluctuate,** go by
fits and starts

ADJS **3 irregular,** unsystematic, unmethodical; **inconstant, unsteady, uneven, unrhythmical;
variable, capricious, erratic,**
off-again-on-again, eccentric;
wobbly, staggering, lurching, careening; **fitful, spasmodic** or
spasmodical, **jerky,** herky-jerky
<nonformal>; **sporadic,** patchy,
spotty, choppy, **broken, disconnected, discontinuous** 812.4;
nonuniform 781.3; **intermittent, desultory, fluctuating, wavering,** wandering, rambling

ADVS **4 irregularly,** unsystematically, unmethodically; **inconstantly, unsteadily, unevenly,**
uncertainly; **variably,** capriciously, unpredictably, whimsically, eccentrically, erratically;
**intermittently, disconnectedly,
discontinuously** 812.5; **nonuniformly** 781.4; **brokenly, desultorily,** in snatches; **by fits and
starts, fitfully, sporadically,
jerkily, spasmodically;** off and
on, at irregular intervals

851 CHANGE

NOUNS **1 change, alteration,
modification; variation,** diversity, diversification; **deviation,** diversion, **divergence; switch,
switchover, changeover,** turn,
turnabout, about-face, **reversal;**
apostasy, defection, change of
heart; **shift,** transition, **modulation; conversion, renewal,** revival, revivification; remaking, restructuring, *perestroika* <Russ>;

adaptation, **adjustment,** accommodation; **reform,** reformation,
improvement, amelioration,
betterment, change for the better; **social mobility,** vertical mobility, horizontal mobility, upward or downward mobility; **continuity** 811; **degeneration, deterioration,** worsening, change for
the worse, disorder 809; changeableness 853;

2 revolution, break, break with
the past, sudden change, catastrophic change, **upheaval,** overthrow, **quantum jump** or **leap,**
sea change; **discontinuity** 812

3 transformation, trans-
mogrification; **translation;
metamorphosis; mutation,**
transmutation, permutation; **mu-
tant,** sport; **transfiguration** or
transfigurement; metathesis, **displacement,** metastasis; **transubstantiation;** transmigration, reincarnation; metabolism, anabolism, catabolism

4 innovation, introduction, invention; **breakthrough,** leap,
quantum leap

5 transformer, transmogrifier, **innovator;** precursor 815; **agent,**
catalytic agent, catalyst; the
winds of change; **leaven,** yeast,
ferment; **modifier**

VERBS **6 be changed, change, undergo a change,** dance to a different tune <nonformal>; **alter,**
mutate, modulate, **vary,** checker,
diversify; **deviate, diverge,** take a
new turn, turn the corner, **shift,**
veer, tack, come round or around,
swerve, warp; change horses in
midstream; **revive,** feel like a new
person; **improve,** meliorate, mitigate; **degenerate, deteriorate,
worsen;** hit bottom, bottom out
<nonformal>

7 change, work or **make a
change, alter; mutate; modify;**
adapt; modulate, accommodate,
fine-tune, **qualify; vary, diversify; convert, renew, recast, revamp** <nonformal>, change over,
revive; rebuild, reconstruct, restructure; realign; **reform, im-**

prove, meliorate, mitigate; **revolutionize,** subvert, overthrow, break up; give a twist to, turn the tide, turn the tables; turn over a new leaf; **about-face,** do an about-face, flip-flop <nonformal>

8 **transform, transfigure, transmute,** transmogrify; **translate;** metamorphose; metabolize

9 **innovate,** make innovations, invent, discover, make a breakthrough, make a quantum leap, **pioneer** 815.3, **revolutionize**

ADJS 10 **changed, altered, modified,** qualified, **transformed,** transmuted, **metamorphosed;** divergent; **converted, renewed,** revived, **rebuilt; reformed,** improved, **better; degenerate, worse,** unmitigated; subversive, **revolutionary;** changeable 853.6,7

11 **innovational,** innovative

12 **metamorphic, metabolic,** anabolic, catabolic

852 PERMANENCE

NOUNS 1 **permanence** or permanency, **immutability, changelessness,** invariability; **unchangeableness,** unchangeability; **fixedness, constancy,** steadfastness, firmness, solidity, persistence or persistency, faithfulness, **lastingness, abidingness, endurance,** duration, inveteracy; durability 826; **perpetualness** 828.1; **stability** 854; **unchangeability** 854.4; **immobility,** stasis, **rigidity; quiescence,** torpor, coma

2 **maintenance, preservation** 397, **conservation**

3 **conservatism, conservativeness,** resistance to change, unprogressiveness, backwardness, old-fashionedness; ultraconservatism, arch-conservatism

4 **conservative**; ultraconservative, arch-conservative, **diehard,** standpatter <nonformal>, **old fogy,** stick-in-the-mud <nonformal>, **rightist, right-winger** 611.9

VERBS 5 **remain, endure** 826.6, last, stay, persist, bide, abide, stand, hold, subsist; be ever the same

6 **be conservative,** oppose change; stand pat and stand still <both nonformal>; **let things take their course,** leave things as they are, stick with it and let it ride <both nonformal>, let well enough alone, do nothing; stop or turn back the clock

ADJS 7 **permanent, changeless, unchanging, immutable,** unvarying; **unchanged,** unchangeable, **unaltered,** inalterable, inviolate, intact; **constant, persistent,** sustained, fixed, steadfast, like the Rock of Gibraltar; unchecked, unfailing, unfading; **lasting, enduring,** abiding, remaining, staying, continuing; **durable** 826.10; **perpetual** 828.7; **unchangeable** 854.17; **immobile, static,** stationary, frozen, **rigid; quiescent,** torpid

8 **conservative, preservative,** old-line, **diehard,** standpat <nonformal>; **backward,** backward-looking, old-fashioned, **unprogressive,** unreconstructed, stuck-in-the-mud; ultraconservative, **old-fogyish; right-wing** 611.17

ADVS 9 **permanently,** abidingly, steadfastly, unwaveringly; enduringly, **perpetually,** invariably, **forever, always** 828.11; statically, inflexibly

10 **as is, as usual;** at a standstill

853 CHANGEABLENESS

NOUNS 1 **changeableness, changeability, alterability,** convertibility; **mutability,** impermanence, **transience,** transitoriness, mobility, motility, plasticity, malleability, fluidity; **resilience, adaptability,** adjustability, **flexibility,** suppleness; **nonuniformity** 781

2 **inconstancy, instability,** changefulness, **unsteadiness,** unsteadfastness, rootlessness; **uncertainty,** undependability, inconsistency, unreliability; **vari-**

ability, variation; unpredictability, irregularity 850.1; **desultoriness,** waywardness, wantonness; freakishness, freakery; impulsiveness, mercuriality, moodiness, whimsicality, **capriciousness, fickleness** 364.3

3 changing, fluctuation, vicissitude, **variation, shiftingness;** alternation, oscillation, **vacillation; mood swings; wavering,** shifting, teetering, tottering; **exchange**

4 <comparisons> Proteus, kaleidoscope, chameleon

VERBS **5 change, fluctuate, vary; shift; alternate, vacillate,** oscillate, blow hot and cold <nonformal>; ebb and flow, wax and wane; go through phases, waver, wobble, flounder, teeter, totter, **seesaw, teeter-totter; exchange,** trade, play musical chairs

ADJS **6 changeable, alterable,** alterative, modifiable; mutable, permutable, transient, **transitory; variable,** checkered, kaleidoscopic; **movable,** mobile, motile; **resilient, adaptable,** adjustable, **flexible,** supple, able to roll with the punches *or* bend without breaking; protean, proteiform

7 inconstant, changeable, changeful, changing, shifting, uncertain, inconsistent; **shifty,** unreliable, undependable; **unstable, unfixed,** infirm, restless, **unsettled, unsteady,** indecisive, irresolute, blowing hot and cold <nonformal>; **variable;** whimsical, **capricious, fickle** 364.6, off-again-on-again; **erratic, eccentric,** freakish; volatile, mercurial, moody, flighty, impulsive, impetuous; **fluctuating,** alternating, **vacillating, wavering,** flickering, guttering; irregular, spasmodic 850.3; **desultory,** rambling, roving, vagrant, wanton, wayward; **unrestrained, undisciplined,** irresponsible

ADVS **8 changeably, variably, inconstantly,** shiftingly, uncertainly, **unsteadily,** unsteadfastly,

capriciously, erratically, waveringly; **impulsively, impetuously,** precipitately

854 STABILITY

NOUNS **1 stability, firmness, soundness, substantiality, solidity; security,** secureness; **rootedness,** fastness; reliability 969.4; **steadiness,** steadfastness; **imperturbability,** unflappability <nonformal>, steady *or* unshakable nerves, unshakableness, stolidness *or* stolidity, **cool** <nonformal>, *sang-froid* <Fr>; **equilibrium, balance,** homeostasis; steady state; aplomb

2 fixity, fixedness, fixation; **establishment, stabilization,** confirmation, entrenchment; inveteracy, **deep-seatedness**

3 immobility, immovability, unmovability, immovableness; **firmness,** solidity, rigidity, **inflexibility** 1044.3; inertia, inertness; immobilization

4 unchangeableness, unchangeability, immutability, inconvertibility; lastingness, **permanence** 852; irrevocability, **irreversibility;** irretrievability; intransmutability

5 indestructibility, imperishability, immortality, **deathlessness;** invulnerability, impregnability; ineradicability, indelibility

6 <comparisons> rock, Rock of Gibraltar, bedrock

VERBS **7 stabilize; firm, firm up** <nonformal>; **steady, balance,** counterbalance; **immobilize,** freeze, retain; **transfix,** pin *or* nail down <nonformal>

8 secure, make sure *or* secure, chain, tether; **wedge, jam, seize; make fast, fasten,** fasten down; **anchor,** moor; batten *and* batten down; **confirm,** ratify

9 fix, define, set, **settle; establish,** found, ground, lodge, seat, **entrench; root;** ingrain, implant, engraft, embed; **print,** imprint, **stamp,** inscribe, **etch,** engrave, impress; **dye in the wool;** stereotype

10 <become firmly fixed> **root,
take root,** strike root; **stick,** stick
fast; seize, seize up, freeze; **catch,
jam,** lodge, foul

11 **stand fast,** stand firm, **stand
pat** <nonformal>, stay put <nonformal>, hold fast, not budge,
stand or **hold one's ground,**
hold one's own, dig in one's heels,
take one's stand, **stick to one's
guns; hold out,** stick or tough it
out and hang tough <all nonformal>, stay the course; **hold up;
weather,** weather the storm, ride
it out; be imperturbable, be unflappable and not bat an eye
and keep one's cool <all non-
formal>

ADJS 12 **stable, substantial, firm,
solid, sound;** solid as a rock,
built on bedrock; **fast, secure;
steady,** unwavering, steadfast;
**balanced; well-balanced; im-
perturbable,** unflappable <non-
formal>, unshakable, **cool** <non-
formal>, impassive, stolid, stoic;
without a nerve in one's body, unflinching; **reliable** 969.17, predictable

13 **established,** stabilized, **en-
trenched,** vested; **well-
established,** well-founded, **well-
grounded,** on bedrock; long-
established; **confirmed, inveterate; settled, set;** well-settled, in
place; **rooted, deep-rooted,
deep-seated,** deep-dyed; **infixed,
ingrained,** implanted, engrafted,
embedded, ingrown, inwrought;
engraved, etched, graven, embossed; **dyed-in-the-wool**

14 **fixed,** anchored; **set, settled,
stated;** staple

15 **immovable,** unmovable, **immobile,** unmoving, **irremovable,**
stationary, frozen, at a standstill,
on dead center; **firm, unyielding,**
adamant, adamantine, rigid, **inflexible** 1044.12

16 **stuck, fast,** stuck fast, **fixed,
transfixed, caught,** fastened,
tied, tethered, anchored, moored,
inextricable; **jammed,** impacted,
congested, packed, wedged;
seized, seized up, frozen

17 **unchangeable,** changeless, unchanged, unchanging, unvarying,
unvariable, **unalterable,** unaltered, **immutable,** unmodifia-
ble; **constant, invariable,** undeviating, undeflectible; **permanent** 852.7; irrevocable, indefeasible, **irreversible,** nonreversible;
irretrievable, unrestorable, non-
returnable

18 **indestructible, imperishable,**
incorruptible; **deathless,** immortal, undying; **invulnerable, invincible,** inexpugnable, impregnable; **ineradicable,** indelible,
ineffaceable; **inextinguishable,**
unquenchable

855 CONTINUANCE

<continuance in action>

NOUNS 1 **continuance, continuation, ceaselessness,** unremit-
tingness, **continualness** 811.1;
**prolongation, extension, pro-
traction, perpetuation,** spinning
or stringing out; **survival** 826.1,
holding on, hanging on or in;
maintenance; progress, progression; **persistence, perseverance** 360; **endurance** 826.1,
stamina, staying power; **continuity** 811; **repetition** 848

2 **resumption, recommence-
ment,** revival, recrudescence,
renewal, reappearance; **fresh
start,** new beginning

VERBS 3 **continue** 811.4, keep or
stay with it, keep or stay at it,
carry on; **remain, abide, stay,**
tarry, linger; **go on, keep on,**
keep going, carry on, see it
through, hold steady, plug away
<nonformal>, grind away or on,
put one foot in front of the other;
never cease, cease not; **endure**
826.6

4 **sustain, protract, prolong, extend,** perpetuate, lengthen;
maintain, retain, preserve; **keep
up,** keep going, keep alive, **survive** 826.6

5 **persist, persevere,** keep at it
360.2, stick it out, never say die,
see it through, hang in and hang
tough and not know when one is

licked <all nonformal>; survive, get along, get on; go on, go on with, press on; persevere, iterate, reiterate, **harp**, chew one's ear off *and* run off at the mouth <both nonformal>, beat a dead horse

6 resume, recommence, renew, reestablish; **revive,** resuscitate, recrudesce; **return to,** go back to, begin again, make a new beginning, make a fresh start, have another shot *or* crack *or* go <nonformal>

ADJS **7 continuing, abiding** 826.10; staying, remaining; **continuous** 811.8, **ceaseless, unceasing,** unending, incessant, unremitting, sustained, indefatigable, **persistent; repetitious, repetitive** 848.14; **resumed,** recommenced

856 CESSATION

NOUNS **1 cessation, discontinuance,** discontinuation; **desistance,** surcease, **ceasing,** ending, termination; **close,** shutdown; sign-off; **relinquishment,** abandonment

2 stop, stoppage, **halt, stay, arrest,** check, cutoff <nonformal>; stand, **standstill;** dead stop, screaming *or* grinding *or* shuddering halt; **end,** ending, final whistle, checkmate; **tie,** stalemate, deadlock, wash *and* toss-up <both nonformal>, standoff *and* Mexican standoff <both nonformal>; **terminal,** end of the line, terminus

3 pause, rest, break, caesura, recess, **intermission,** interlude; **respite,** letup <nonformal>; **interruption, suspension,** break in the action, cooling-off period; **postponement** 845.4; **remission;** abeyance, lapse; truce, cease-fire, stand-down; **vacation, holiday,** leisure

4 <grammatical terms> pause, juncture, boundary

5 <legislatures> cloture, clôture <Fr>; cloture by compartment

VERBS **6 cease, discontinue, end, stop, halt,** terminate, close the

books, abort, cancel, scratch *and* scrub <both nonformal>, hold, **quit; desist, refrain,** leave off, **have done with;** cut it out *and* drop it *and* knock it off <all nonformal>, relinquish, abandon; **come to an end** 819.6

7 stop, halt, stop in one's tracks, stop dead, **stall; bring up, pull up, fetch up; stop short,** bring up short, come to a screaming *or* grinding *or* shuddering halt, stop on a dime <nonformal>, come to a full stop, grind to a halt; **stick,** jam, hang fire, seize, seize up, freeze; run into a brick wall

8 <stop work> **lay off, knock off** <nonformal>, call it a day <nonformal>, call it quits <nonformal>; **strike,** walk out, call a strike, go *or* go out on strike

9 pause, rest, take it easy <nonformal>; **relax,** rest on one's oars; **recess; take a break,** take ten

10 interrupt, suspend, break, break off, take a break <nonformal>

11 put a stop to, call a halt to, blow the whistle on <nonformal>, **put an end to** 819.5; **stop, stay, halt, arrest, check;** block, brake, stem the tide *or* current; pull up, put on the brakes; **bring to a standstill,** bring to a close *or* halt, freeze, bring up short, **stop dead** *or* dead in one's tracks, set one back on his heels, stop cold; checkmate, stalemate, deadlock

12 turn off, shut off, shut down; **phase out,** taper off, wind up *or* down; **kill, cut,** switch off

857 CONVERSION
<change to something different>

NOUNS **1 conversion,** reconversion, **change-over;** convertibility; **change** 851, sea change, **transformation,** transmutation; **transition,** transit, **switch** *and* **switchover** <both nonformal>, **shift; reversal,** about-face *and* flip-flop <both nonformal>; **relapse,** lapse; **breakthrough; growth,** development; **resolu-**

tion 939.1; **assimilation,** assumption; alchemy

2 **new start, new beginning,** fresh start, clean slate; **reformation, reform, regeneration, revival, reclamation,** redemption, recrudescence, **rebirth,** renascence, **change of heart**

3 apostasy, renunciation, **defection, desertion,** treason, abandonment

4 **rehabilitation,** reconditioning, recovery, restoration; **reeducation; repatriation**

5 **indoctrination; brainwashing;** alienation, corruption

6 **conversion,** proselytization, evangelization

7 **convert, proselyte,** catechumen, disciple

8 **apostate, defector,** turncoat, traitor, **renegade**

9 **converter, proselyter,** proselytizer, **missionary, apostle, evangelist**

10 <instruments> philosopher's stone, melting pot, crucible

VERBS 11 **convert,** reconvert; **change over,** switch *and* switch over <both nonformal>, **shift; do over,** make over; **change, transform** 851.5,8, transmute; **change into, turn into, become,** naturalize; **make,** render; **reverse,** do an about-face; change one's tune

12 **re-form,** remodel, refashion, recast; regroup, redeploy; **renew;** be reborn, be born again, feel like a new person; get it together *and* get one's act together *and* get one's ducks in a row <all nonformal>; **regenerate, reclaim,** redeem, amend, set straight; **reform, rehabilitate,** restore self-respect; mend *or* change one's ways, **turn over a new leaf**

13 **defect,** renege, wimp *or* chicken *or* cop out <nonformal>, desert, apostatize, turn against, turn traitor; desert a sinking ship; lapse, relapse

14 **rehabilitate,** reclaim; **reeducate,** reinstruct; **repatriate**

15 **indoctrinate, brainwash,** reindoctrinate; subvert, alienate

16 **convince, persuade,** wean, **win over;** proselyte, **proselytize,** evangelize

17 be converted into, **turn into** *or* to, become 760.12, **change into,** grow into, **develop** *or* evolve into, merge *or* blend *or* melt into, shift into, settle into, come round to

ADJS 18 **convertible,** transmutable, **transformable, transitional,** modifiable

19 **converted, changed, transformed;** assimilated; **reformed,** regenerated, born-again

20 **apostate, treasonable, traitorous, renegade**

858 REVERSION
<change to a former state>

NOUNS 1 **reversion,** retroversion, **retrogression,** retrocession, relapse 394, **regression, backsliding,** lapse, slipping back, recidivism; **reverse, reversal,** turnabout, about-face, flip-flop <nonformal>, **turn; return,** returning; **reclamation, rehabilitation,** redemption; **reinstatement,** restitution, restoration

2 **throwback,** atavism

3 **returnee, repeater;** prodigal son, lost lamb; recidivist, two-time loser <nonformal>; backslider

VERBS 4 **revert, regress, retrogress,** retrocede, **reverse, return;** backslide, slip back, recidivate, relapse 394.4

5 **turn back, change back, go back, hark back,** cry back, break back, **turn;** do an about-face *and* flip-flop *and* do a flip-flop <all nonformal>; put the toothpaste back into the tube; go back to square one <nonformal>

6 **revert to, return to,** go back to; hark back to

ADJS 7 **reversionary, regressive,** recessive, **retrogressive, retrograde;** reactionary; recidivist *or* recidivistic, lapsarian; atavistic

859 REVOLUTION
<sudden or radical change>

NOUNS **1 revolution, radical change, violent change,** sweeping change, clean slate, square one <nonformal>, tabula rasa; quantum leap or jump; **overthrow,** overturn, upset, convulsion, spasm, subversion, coup d'état; **cataclysm, catastrophe,** debacle; **revolution; revolt** 327.4

  2 revolutionism, revolutionariness, anarchism, syndicalism, terrorism

  3 revolutionist, revolutionary; rebel 327.5; anarchist, syndicalist, terrorist 671.9; subversive; red

VERBS **4 revolutionize, make a radical change,** make a clean sweep; **overthrow, overturn,** upset; revolt 327.7

ADJS **5 revolutionary;** transilient; cataclysmic, catastrophic; **radical,** sweeping 793.10; **insurrectionary** 327.11

  6 revolutionist, revolutionary, anarchic or anarchical, syndicalist, terrorist or terroristic

860 EVOLUTION

NOUNS **1 evolution, evolving,** evolvement; **development, growth,** rise, incremental change, developmental change, natural growth or development; flowering, blossoming; ripening, coming of age, maturation 303.6; accomplishment 407; **advance,** advancement, furtherance; **progress,** progression; **elaboration,** enlargement, amplification, **expansion**

  2 unfolding, unfoldment, unrolling, unfurling, unwinding; revelation, gradual revelation

  3 <biological terms> genesis; phylogeny, phylogenesis

  4 evolutionism, theory of evolution; **Darwinism,** Darwinianism, organic evolution, survival of the fittest; Lamarckism or Lamarckianism, Lysenkoism

VERBS **5 evolve; develop, grow,** wax; **progress, advance,** come a long way; accomplish 407.4; ripen, mellow, mature 303.9, maturate; degenerate

  6 elaborate, develop, work out, enlarge on or upon, amplify, **expand,** expand on or upon, detail, flesh out, **pursue,** spell out <nonformal>

  7 unfold, unroll, unfurl, unwind, unreel, uncoil

ADJS **8 evolutionary,** evolutionist; **evolving, developing, unfolding; maturing; progressing, advancing;** degenerative; genetic, phylogenetic, ontogenetic

861 SUBSTITUTION
<change of one thing for another>

NOUNS **1 substitution, exchange, change,** switch, subrogation; **surrogacy;** vicariousness, **representation,** deputation, **delegation; agency, power of attorney; supplanting,** successsion; **replacement,** displacement; superseding, supersession; tit for tat, quid pro quo <L>

  2 substitute, substitution, replacement, backup, secondary, utility player; **change, exchange; ersatz,** phony and fake <both nonformal>, counterfeit, imitation 336, copy 784; surrogate; **alternate,** alternative, next best thing; **successor; proxy,** dummy, ghost; vicar, agent, representative; **deputy** 576; locum tenens; **relief,** fill-in, **stand-in, understudy, pinch hitter** or runner <nonformal>; double; **equivalent,** equal; ringer <nonformal>; ghostwriter; **analogy, metaphor, symbol, sign**

  3 scapegoat, goat <nonformal>, fall guy and patsy <nonformal>, **whipping boy**

VERBS **4 substitute, exchange, change,** take or ask or offer in exchange, switch, **put in the place of,** give place to; **pass off,** pawn or foist or fob off; rob Peter to pay Paul

  5 substitute for, subrogate; **act**

for, stand in for, fill in for, change places with, swap places with <nonformal>, step into or fill the shoes of, pinch-hit <nonformal>; **relieve,** cover for; ghost, ghost-write; **represent** 576.14; **supplant, supersede,** succeed, **replace,** displace, **take the place of**

6 <nonformal terms> **cover up for,** front for; **take the rap for,** take the fall for, be the goat or patsy or fall guy

7 **delegate, deputize, commission,** give the nod to <nonformal>, designate an agent or a proxy

ADJS 8 **substitute, alternate, alternative,** other, token, dummy, utility; ad hoc, provisional; **vicarious,** ersatz, mock, phony and fake and bogus <all nonformal>, counterfeit, imitation 336.8; **proxy;** makeshift, **spare,** stopgap, temporary, provisional

9 **substitutional,** substitutive; **substituted**

10 **replaceable,** supersedable, expendable

ADVS 11 **instead, rather**; in its stead or place; in one's place, in one's shoes; by proxy; as an alternative

862 INTERCHANGE
<double or mutual change>

NOUNS 1 **interchange, exchange**; **transposition,** transposal; mutual support; **cooperation** 450; alternation; **interplay, tradeoff, compromise, reciprocation** 776.1, reciprocity, mutuality; **give-and-take,** quid pro quo <L>, measure for measure, **tit for tat,** an eye for an eye; **retaliation**; cross fire

2 **trading, swapping** <nonformal>; trade, swap <nonformal>, **switch;** barter 731.2; logrolling, back scratching, pork barrel

3 **interchangeability,** standardization; convertibility, commutability

VERBS 4 **interchange, exchange**; alternate; **transpose;** convert,

commute, permute; **trade, swap** <nonformal>, **switch;** bandy about; **reciprocate, trade off,** compromise, keep a balance; **give and take,** give tit for tat, give as good as one gets, return the compliment or favor, pay back, compensate, **requite,** return; **retaliate,** get back at, get even with; logroll, scratch each other's back, **cooperate** 450.3

ADJS 5 **interchangeable, exchangeable,** changeable, standard; equivalent; **even,** equal; **convertible,** commutable, permutable; retaliatory, equalizing; **reciprocative** or **reciprocating, reciprocatory, reciprocal; mutual,** give-and-take; **exchanged, transposed, swapped** <nonformal>, **interchanged**

ADVS 6 **interchangeably, exchangeably;** in exchange, in return; **even, evenly; reciprocally,** mutually; **in turn,** each in its turn, turn and turn about

863 GENERALITY

NOUNS 1 **generality, universality,** inclusiveness 771.1; ecumenicity or ecumenicalism; catholicity; **internationalism,** cosmopolitanism; **generalization,** universalization, globalization, ecumenization, internationalization

2 **prevalence, commonness,** commonality, usualness, **currency; extensiveness,** rifeness, rampantness; **normality,** habitualness

3 **average, run, run of the mill;** any Tom, Dick, or Harry; Everyman; common or average man, the man in the street, John Q Public, John or Jane Doe, ordinary Joe, Joe Six-pack; girl next door; everyman, everywoman

4 **all, everyone, everybody, each and everyone, one and all,** all comers and all hands and every man Jack and every mother's son <all nonformal>, every living soul, **all the world, whole, totality** 791.1; **everything,** all manner of things; you name it and what

have you *and* all the above <all nonformal>

5 **any, anything,** either; **anybody, anyone**

6 **whatever, whatsoever, what, whichever**

7 **whoever,** whoso, **whosoever, whomever,** no matter who

8 <idea or expression> **generalization, abstraction**; glittering generality; **truism, platitude, conventional wisdom,** commonplace; **cliché,** bromide, trite *or* hackneyed expression

VERBS 9 **generalize, universalize,** catholicize, ecumenicize; **broaden, widen, expand,** extend, spread; deal in generalities; **label,** stereotype

10 **prevail, predominate, obtain,** dominate, reign, rule; be in force *or* effect; be the rule *or* fashion

ADJS 11 **general, generalized, nonspecific,** generic, **indefinite,** vague, nebulous, undifferentiated, bland, neutral

12 **prevalent, prevailing, common,** popular, **current,** running; reigning, **ruling, predominant,** predominating, **dominant; rife, rampant,** pandemic, epidemic; **ordinary, normal, average, usual,** routine, standard, stereotyped

13 **extensive, broad, wide,** diffuse, **sweeping; cross-disciplinary,** interdisciplinary; widespread, **far-reaching,** far-ranging, **far-flung,** wide-ranging; **wholesale, indiscriminate**

14 **universal,** cosmic, galactic, planetary, world-wide, **global; total,** holistic; catholic, **all-inclusive, all-embracing,** all-encompassing; nonsectarian, nondenominational, ecumenical; **cosmopolitan,** international; **national**

15 **every, all,** any, whichever, whichsoever; **each,** each one; every one, each and every, **one and all**

16 **trite, commonplace,** hackneyed, platitudinous, stereotyped

ADVS 17 **generally, in general; generally speaking, broadly,** broadly speaking, **roughly,** roughly speaking; **usually, as a rule, ordinarily, commonly, normally,** routinely, as a matter of course; **by and large,** altogether, overall, **all things considered,** taking one thing with another, on balance, **all in all,** taking all in all, **on the whole,** as a whole, **in the long run,** for the most part, for better or worse; **prevailingly, predominantly, mostly,** chiefly, mainly

18 **universally,** galactically, cosmically; **everywhere, all over,** the world over, internationally; in every instance, without exception, **invariably** 19

864 PARTICULARITY

NOUNS 1 **particularity, individuality, singularity, differentiation,** distinctiveness, uniqueness; **personality,** personal identity; soul; **selfness,** self-identity; oneness 871.1, wholeness, integrity; **nonconformity** 867; **individualism,** particularism

2 **specialty, specialness,** specificality, **specificness,** definiteness

3 **the specific, the particular,** the concrete, the individual, the unique

4 **characteristic, peculiarity, singularity,** particularity, specialty, individualism, **character,** nature, **trait,** quirk, saving grace, redeeming feature, mannerism, keynote, trick, **feature,** lineament; **mark, earmark,** hallmark, index; **brand,** cast, stamp, cachet, seal, mold, cut, figure, shape, configuration; **idiosyncrasy; quality, property, attribute**

5 **self, ego; oneself, I,** number one <nonformal>, yours truly <nonformal>; inner self, inner man; subliminal *or* subconscious self; superego, better self, ethical self; other self, alter ego

6 **specification, designation, stipulation,** singling-out, featuring, highlighting, focusing on, de-

nomination; **allocation,** attribution

7 particularization, specialization; localization; itemization 765.5

8 characterization, distinction, **differentiation;** definition, description

VERBS **9 particularize, specialize; individualize,** personalize; **descend to particulars,** get down to brass tacks *or* to cases <nonformal>, get down to the nittygritty <nonformal>; **itemize** 765.6, detail, spell out

10 characterize, distinguish, differentiate, define, describe; mark, earmark, mark out, demarcate, **set apart**; set the tone *or* mood, set the pace; **be a feature** *or* **trait of**

11 specify, specialize, **designate, stipulate,** determine, highlight, focus on, mention, select, **fix,** set, assign, pin down; **name,** denominate, state, mark, **indicate, signify**

ADJS **12 particular, special, especial, specific, express,** precise, **concrete; singular, individual; personal,** private, intimate, inner, solipsistic; **fixed, definite, defined,** distinct, different, different as night and day, absolute; **distinguished,** noteworthy, **exceptional, extraordinary**

13 characteristic, peculiar, singular, quintessential, intrinsic, unique, **distinctive,** marked, distinguished, notable; idiosyncratic, **in character, true to form**

14 this, this and no other, this one

ADVS **15 particularly, specially, especially, specifically, expressly,** concretely, exactly, precisely, **in particular,** to be specific; **definitely, distinctly; minutely,** in detail, item by item, singly, separately

16 personally, privately, idiosyncratically, **individually; in person,** in the flesh; as for me, **for my part, as far as I am concerned**

17 characteristically, peculiarly,

singularly, intrinsically, **uniquely,** markedly, **distinctively**

18 namely, nominally, **that is to say, to wit**

19 each, apiece; severally, respectively, each to each

865 SPECIALTY

<object of special attention or preference>

NOUNS **1 specialty, line, pursuit, pet subject, business, line of business, field,** area, main interest; **vocation** 724.6; **forte, métier, strong point,** long suit; **way,** manner, **style,** type; **lifestyle,** way of life; cup of tea *and* bag *and* thing *and* weakness <all nonformal>

2 special, feature, main feature; **leader,** lead item

3 specialist, expert, authority, connoisseur, maven <nonformal>; **pundit,** critic; amateur, dilettante; fan, buff, **freak** *and* nut <both nonformal>, aficionado

VERBS **4 specialize, feature; narrow, restrict,** limit, confine; specialize in, **go in for,** be strong in, follow, pursue, **make one's business;** do one's thing <nonformal>

ADJS **5 specialized**; down one's alley <nonformal>, cut out for one; technical; **restricted, limited,** confined; **featured,** feature; **expert, authoritative**

866 CONFORMITY

NOUNS **1 conformity; conformance,** conformation; **compliance,** acquiescence, obedience, **orthodoxy;** strictness; **accordance,** accord, **correspondence,** harmony, agreement, **uniformity** 780; **consistency,** congruity; **accommodation,** adaptation, malleability, flexibility, adjustment; reconciliation, reconcilement; **conventionality** 579.1

2 conformist, sheep, parrot, yesman, organization man; **conventionalist,** Babbitt, Philistine, **bourgeois,** Middle American, plastic person *and* clone *and* square <all nonformal>; model child; **formalist,** perfectionist, precisianist *or* precisian; pedant

VERBS **3 conform, comply, correspond; adapt,** adjust, **accommodate,** bend, meet, suit, fit, shape; **comply with,** agree with, tally with, observe, follow, bend, yield, take the shape of; **adapt to,** adjust to, gear to, **accommodate to** *or* **with; reconcile,** settle, compose; **make conform,** shape, force into a mold; straighten, rectify, **discipline**

4 follow the rule, toe the mark, do it by the book <nonformal>, play the game <nonformal>; go through channels; **fit in, follow the crowd,** swim *or* go with the stream *or* tide *or* current, get on the bandwagon, follow the beaten path, **get** *or* **stay in line,** fall in *or* into line, fall in with; **keep in step,** walk in lockstep

ADJS **5 conformable, adaptable; compliant,** pliant, malleable, flexible, plastic, acquiescent, submissive, tractable, obedient

6 conformist, conventional 579.5, bourgeois, cloned *and* clonish *and* cookie-cutter <all nonformal>; **orthodox,** traditionalist *or* traditionalistic; kosher; **formalistic,** legalistic, precisianistic, compulsive; pedantic, stuffy *and* hidebound <both nonformal>, uptight <nonformal>; in accord, in keeping, in line, in lockstep; **corresponding,** accordant, concordant

ADVS **7** conformably, in conformity, **obediently, pliantly,** malleably, complaisantly, **compliantly,** submissively; **conventionally,** traditionally; **compulsively;** pedantically

8 according to rule, according to regulations; **according to Hoyle** *and* **by the book** *and* by the numbers <all nonformal>

867 NONCONFORMITY

NOUNS **1 nonconformity,** nonconformism, **inconsistency,** incongruity; originality 337.1; **nonconformance; nonobservance,**

noncompliance, dissent 333, **protest** 333.2, disagreement, contrariety, recalcitrance, refractoriness; **deviation** 869.1, deviationism

2 unconventionality, unorthodoxy 688, revisionism, heterodoxy, heresy, originality, counterculture

3 nonconformist, original, eccentric, gonzo <nonformal>, maverick <nonformal>, dropout, Bohemian; **misfit,** square peg in a round hole, fish out of water; **dissenter** 333.3; **heretic** 688.5

VERBS **4 not conform,** nonconform, not comply; **get out of line** *and* **rock the boat** *and* make waves <all nonformal>; **leave the beaten path, go out of bounds,** break step, break bounds; **dissent** 333.4, **protest** 333.5

ADJS **5 nonconforming,** unadaptable, unadjustable; **uncompliant,** unsubmissive; **nonobservant;** contrary, recalcitrant, refractory; **deviant,** deviationist; **dissenting** 333.6, **dissident**

6 unconventional, unorthodox, eccentric, gonzo <nonformal>, heterodox, heretical; unfashionable; offbeat <nonformal>, way out *and* far out *and* kinky *and* out in left field <all nonformal>, **out-of-the-way; original,** maverick, Bohemian, counterculture; **nonformal,** free and easy <nonformal>

7 out of line, out of keeping, out of step, out of turn <nonformal>

868 NORMALITY

NOUNS **1 normality,** typicality, normalcy, **naturalness;** propriety, **regularity; order** 806

2 usualness, ordinariness, commonness, commonplaceness, mediocrity; **generality** 863, **prevalence,** currency

3 the normal, the usual, the ordinary, the common, the commonplace, the normal order of things; common *or* garden variety, the run of the mill

4 rule, law, principle, standard,

criterion, canon, code, maxim, prescription, guideline, rulebook; **norm, model,** rule of behavior, ideal, ideal type, specimen type, exemplar; **rule** *or* **law of nature,** natural *or* universal law; **form, formula,** prescribed *or* set form; standing order, standard operating procedure; **hard-and-fast rule**

5 normalization, standardization, regularization; codification, formalization

VERBS **6 normalize, standardize, regularize; codify,** formalize

7 do the usual thing, make a practice of, carry on

ADJS **8 normal, natural; general** 863.11; typical, unexceptional; **normative,** prescribed, model, ideal, desired; realistic; **orderly** 806.6

9 usual, regular; customary, habitual, accustomed, wonted, **normative,** prescriptive, conventional; **common, commonplace, ordinary, average, everyday,** familiar, vernacular, stock; **prevailing, predominating,** popular; **universal** 863.14

ADVS **10 normally, naturally; normatively,** prescriptively, **regularly; typically,** ordinarily, customarily, habitually, generally; mostly, chiefly, mainly; **as a rule,** as a matter of course; **as usual; as may be expected**

869 ABNORMALITY

NOUNS **1 abnormality; unnaturalness,** strangeness; **anomaly,** anomalousness; **aberration,** aberrance *or* aberrancy; **atypicality,** atypicalness; **irregularity, deviation,** divergence, **difference** 779; **eccentricity,** unpredictableness, randomness; **monstrosity; subnormality; inferiority** 250; **superiority** 249; **derangement** 810.1

2 unusualness, uncommonness, unwontedness, exceptionality; **rarity,** rareness, **uniqueness; prodigiousness,** wondrousness; **incredibility** 954.3, inconceivability, **impossibility** 966

3 oddity, queerness, curiousness, quaintness, **peculiarity, absurdity** 966.1, singularity; **strangeness,** outlandishness; bizarreness; **freakishness, grotesqueness,** monstrousness, monstrosity, malformation, deformity, teratism

4 <odd person> oddity, character <nonformal>, type, **case** <nonformal>, natural, original, odd fellow, queer specimen; **oddball** *and* **weirdo** <both nonformal>, queer duck; **rare bird,** *rara avis* <L>; eccentric 926.3; **freak** *and* **screwball** *and* **crackpot** *and* **kook** <all nonformal>; **fanatic, crank,** zealot; **outsider, alien,** foreigner; **alien,** extraterrestrial, Martian, little green man, visitor from another planet; pariah, loner, lone wolf, solitary, hermit; hobo, tramp; maverick; **outcast,** outlaw, scapegoat; **nonconformist** 867.3

5 <odd thing> oddity, curiosity, wonder; abnormality, anomaly; rarity, improbability, exception

6 monstrosity, monster, miscreation, abortion, teratism, abnormal *or* defective birth, abnormal *or* defective fetus; **freak**

7 supernaturalism, supranaturalism, **preternaturalism,** superhumanity; **the paranormal;** numinousness; **unearthliness,** unworldliness, **otherworldliness;** the supernatural, **the occult,** the supersensible; **paranormality;** supernature, supranature; **mystery,** mysteriousness

8 miracle, sign, signs and portents, prodigy, wonder, wonderwork; fantasy, enchantment

ADJS **9 abnormal, unnatural; anomalous; irregular,** eccentric, erratic, **different** 779.7; **aberrant,** stray, straying, wandering; formless, shapeless, amorphous; **subnormal**

10 unusual, uncustomary, unwonted, **uncommon, unfamiliar,** atypical; **rare, unique,** *sui*

generis <L, of its own kind>; **out of the ordinary,** out of this world, **off the beaten track,** offbeat, breakaway; unexpected, undreamed-of

11 odd, queer, peculiar, absurd 966.7, **singular, curious, oddball** <nonformal>, weird *and* kooky *and* freaky *and* freaked-out <all nonformal>, quaint, **eccentric,** gonzo <nonformal>; **strange, outlandish,** off-the-wall <informal>, surreal; **weird,** unearthly

12 fantastic, fanciful, antic, **unbelievable** 954.10, **impossible, incredible,** incomprehensible, unimaginable, inconceivable

13 freakish; monstrous, deformed, malformed, misshapen, **misbegotten,** teratogenic; **grotesque, bizarre**

14 extraordinary, exceptional, remarkable, noteworthy, **wonderful, marvelous,** fabulous, mythical, legendary; **stupendous,** stupefying, prodigious, portentous, phenomenal; indescribable, unspeakable, ineffable

15 supernatural, supranatural, **preternatural; supernormal,** hypernormal, preternormal; **paranormal; superhuman,** preterhuman, unhuman, nonhuman; **supramundane,** extramundane, extraterrestrial; **unearthly, unworldly, otherworldly, eerie,** fey; psychical, **spiritual, occult; transcendental; mysterious,** arcane, esoteric

16 miraculous, wondrous, prodigious; magical, enchanted, bewitched

ADVS **17 unusually, uncommonly, incredibly, unnaturally,** abnormally, **uncustomarily,** unexpectedly; **rarely, seldom**

18 extraordinarily, exceptionally, remarkably, wonderfully, marvelously, prodigiously, fabulously, ineffably, phenomenally

19 oddly, queerly, peculiarly, singularly, curiously, strangely, outlandishly, **fantastically; gro-** tesquely, **monstrously; eerily, mysteriously**

870 LIST

NOUNS **1 list, enumeration, itemization,** listing, shopping list *and* laundry list *and* wish list *and* hit list *and* shit list *and* drop-dead list <all nonformal>, items, **schedule, register,** registry; **inventory,** repertory, tally; **checklist**

2 table, contents, table of contents

3 catalog; *catalogue raisonné* <Fr>; **card catalog, bibliography, file**

4 dictionary, word list, **lexicon, glossary, thesaurus,** Roget's, **vocabulary,** terminology

5 bill, statement, account, ledger

6 roll, roster, scroll; **roll call,** muster, **census,** nose *or* head count <nonformal>, **poll,** questionnaire; jury list *or* panel; **calendar,** docket, **agenda; program,** dramatis personae, lineup

7 index, listing, tabulation; **cataloging, itemization; registration,** registry, enrollment

VERBS **8 list, enumerate, itemize, tabulate, catalog,** tally; **register,** post, enter, **enroll, book; file,** pigeonhole; **index;** inventory; calendar; **schedule,** program

ADJS **9 listed, enumerated, entered, itemized, cataloged,** tallied; filed, **indexed, tabulated; scheduled,** programmed; put on the agenda

871 ONENESS
<state of being one>

NOUNS **1 oneness, unity, singleness,** singularity, **individuality,** identity; **particularity** 864; **uniqueness;** intactness, inviolability, purity, simplicity 797, irreducibility; **integrity; unification,** integration, fusion, combination 804; **solidification,** solidity, **indivisibility, wholeness** 791.5; uniformity 780

2 aloneness, loneness, **loneliness, lonesomeness,** soleness, singleness; **privacy,** solitariness, **solitude;** detachment, seclusion, sequestration, **withdrawal, alienation,** standing *or* moving *or* keeping apart, **isolation;** celibacy

3 one, I, unit; monad; one and only

4 individual, single, unit, **integer, entity,** singleton, **item,** article, point, module; persona, soul, body, warm body <nonformal>; **individuality**

VERBS **5 unify,** make one; **unite** 804.3

6 stand alone, keep apart, keep to oneself, withdraw, alienate *or* seclude *or* sequester *or* isolate oneself

ADJS **7 one, single, singular, individual, sole, unique, solitary, lone; integral,** indivisible, irreducible, monadic, monistic, unitary, undivided, solid, wholecloth, seamless, uniform 780.5, simple 797.6, whole 791.9

8 alone, solitary, solo; **isolated,** insular, apart, separate, alienated, withdrawn, aloof, standoffish, detached, removed; **lone, lonely, lonesome; private,** reserved, reticent, **friendless,** rootless, companionless, **unaccompanied,** unescorted, unattended; **unaided,** unassisted, unabetted; **single-handed,** solo

9 sole, unique, singular, absolute, unrepeated, **alone,** lone, **only, one and only;** odd, unpaired; celibate

10 unitary, integrated, integral; **unified,** united

11 unipartite, one-piece; unilateral, one-sided; unidimensional, unidirectional; unipolar, **univalent, univocal**

12 unifying, uniting; combining, combinative 804.5,7, combinatory; connective, connecting; conjunctive 799.16; coalescing

ADVS **13 singly, individually,** particularly, severally, one by one, one at a time; **singularly; alone,** *per se* <L>; **by oneself,** on one's own, under one's own steam, **single-handedly,** solo, **unaided**

14 solely, exclusively, only, merely, **purely,** simply; **entirely,** wholly, totally; **integrally, indivisibly**

872 DOUBLENESS

NOUNS **1 doubleness, duality,** dualism, **twoness;** twofoldness; polarity; coupling, yoking; **doubling,** duplication 873, twinning, bifurcation; **dichotomy,** bisection 874; halving; **duplicity,** twofacedness, hypocrisy; **irony,** ambiguity, equivocation, **ambivalence**

2 two; couple, pair, matching pair, twosome, duo, duet, brace, yoke; **match,** mates; **couplet,** doublet

3 deuce; pair, doubleton; **craps** *and* **snake eyes** <both crapshooting>

4 twins, identical twins, fraternal twins, look-alikes, dead ringers <nonformal>

VERBS **5 double,** duplicate, replicate; **halve,** bifurcate, dichotomize, bisect; team, **yoke,** span; **mate, match,** couple, conjugate; **pair,** pair off, pair up, team up, buddy up <nonformal>

ADJS **6 two; dual, double,** duplex, duplicated, replicated; **dualistic;** bipartisan, bilateral, two-sided; dichotomous; bifurcated, bisected, split down the middle *or* fifty fifty <nonformal>; **twofaced,** duplicitous, hypocritical

7 both, the two, the pair; for two, tête-à-tête

8 coupled, paired, yoked, matched, matched up, mated, paired off, paired up, teamed up, buddied up <nonformal>; **bracketed**

873 DUPLICATION

NOUNS **1 duplication, reduplication,** replication; **reproduction, doubling;** twinning, gemination; **repetition** 848, iteration, reiteration, echoing; **imitation** 336, parroting; **copying** 336.1; **duplicate** 784.3

2 repeat, encore, repeat performance; echo

VERBS **3 duplicate,** ditto <nonfor-

mal>; **double,** double up; ; **reduplicate, reproduce,** replicate, redouble; **repeat** 848.7; **copy**

ADJS **4 double, doubled, duplicate,** duplicated, reproduced,
replicated, cloned, twinned, gem-
inate

ADVS **5 doubly; twofold,** as much
again, twice as much; twice, two
times

  6 secondly, second, secondarily,
in the second place

  7 again, once more, once again,
over again; **anew,** afresh, new,
freshly, newly

874 BISECTION

NOUNS **1 bisection,** halving; **dichotomy, halving, division, in
half** or **by two,** splitting or dividing or cutting in two; subdivision;
bifurcation, ramification, branching

  2 half, moiety; hemisphere, semicircle, **fifty percent;** half-and-
half and fifty-fifty <both nonfor-
mal>

  3 bisector, diameter, equator, halfway mark, divider, partition
213.5, boundary 211.3

VERBS **4 bisect, halve,** transect,
subdivide; cleave, fission, **divide**
or **split** or **cut in two,** share and
share alike, go Dutch <nonfor-
mal>, **dichotomize;** bifurcate,
fork, ramify, branch

ADJS **5 half, part, partly, partial,**
halfway

  6 halved, bisected, divided; bifurcated, forked, branched; **split,**
cloven, cleft

  7 bipartite, bicuspid, bicameral,
binocular, binomial, biped, bi-
petalous, bisexual

ADVS **8 in half, in two,** down the
middle; apart, asunder

875 THREE

NOUNS **1 three, trio, threesome,**
troika; **triad,** trilogy, **trinity; trip-
let,** tercet; tripod, trivet; **triangle,**
tricorn, trimester, trinomial, triptych, trireme, triumvirate; triple
crown, triple threat; trey and
threespot <both cards>

  2 threeness, tripleness; trinity

ADJS **3 three, triple,** triplex, trinal;
triadic<al>; triform; **triangular,**
deltoid

876 TRIPLICATION

NOUNS **1 triplication,** triplicity,
trebleness, **threefoldness;** triplicate

VERBS **2 triplicate, triple, treble,
multiply by three;** cube

ADJS **3 triple,** triplicate, **treble,
threefold,** triplex, trinal; three-
ply

  4 third, tertiary

ADVS **5 triply, trebly; threefold;
thrice,** three times

  6 thirdly, in the third place

877 TRISECTION

NOUNS **1 trisection,** tripartition,
trichotomy

  2 third, tierce, third part, one-
third

VERBS **3 trisect, divide in three,**
trichotomize; trifurcate

ADJS **4 tripartite,** trisected, **three-
parted,** trichotomous; three-
sided, trilateral; **three-
dimensional;** three-forked,
three-pronged, trifurcate; trident
trifid; tricuspid; three-footed, tri-
pedal; trifoliate, trifloral, tri-
florous, tripetalous, triarch; tri-
merous; three-cornered, tricor-
nered, tricorn; **triangular,** triangulate, deltoid

878 FOUR

NOUNS **1 four,** tetrad, quatern, quaternary, **quartet, quadruplet,
foursome;** quadrennium; tetral-
ogy; quadrille, square dance;
quatrefoil or quadrifoil; tetra-
gram, tetragrammaton; quadrangle, quad <nonformal>, rect-
angle; tetrahedron; tetragon,
square; quadrinomial; quadra-
ture; quadrilateral

  2 fourness, quaternity, quadru-
plicity

VERBS **3 square, quadrate,** form
òr make four; form fours or
squares; **cube, dice**

ADJS **4 four;** foursquare; quaternary, quartile, quadratic; tetrad; quadrinomial; **quadruped,** four-legged; tetravalent; quadrilateral 278.9

879 QUADRUPLICATION

NOUNS **1 quadruplication,** quadruplicature
VERBS **2 quadruple, quadruplicate,** multiply by four; biquadrate, quadruplex
ADJS **3 quadruplicate, quadruple, quadruplex, fourfold,** four-ply, tetraploid, quadrigeminal

880 QUADRISECTION

NOUNS **1 quadrisection,** quadripartition, **quartering**
2 fourth, quarter, fourth part, two bits <nonformal>; quartern
VERBS **3 divide by four** or **into four; quadrisect**
ADJS **4 quadrisected, quartered;** quadripartite, quadriform; quadrifoliate, quadrigeminal, quadriplanar, quadrivial, quadrifurcate, quadrumanous
5 fourth, quarter
ADVS **6 fourthly,** in the fourth place; quarterly

881 FIVE AND OVER

NOUNS **1 five,** V; **quintet, fivesome,** quintuplets, quints <nonformal>, pentad; **five dollars,** fiver and fin and finniff and five bucks <all nonformal>; pentagon, pentagram; pentameter, pentastich; Pentateuch; pentathlon
2 six, half a dozen, sextet, sestet, sextuplets; hexagon, hexahedron, hexagram, star of David; hexameter, hexastich; hexapod
3 seven, heptad; septet, heptad; heptagon, heptahedron; heptameter, heptastich; Septuagint, Heptateuch
4 eight; octad; octagon, octahedron; octave; octachord; octet, octameter
5 nine; ennead; nonagon; novena
6 ten, X; **decade;** decagon, decahedron; decagram, decigram, decaliter, deciliter, decameter, decimeter; decapod; decasyllable; de-

cemvir, decemvirate; Ten Commandments or Decalogue
7 <eleven to ninety> **eleven; twelve, dozen,** boxcar and boxcars <both crapshooting>, duodecimo; **teens; thirteen,** baker's dozen; **fourteen,** fortnight; **fifteen,** quindecennial; ; **twenty, score; twenty-four,** two dozen; **twenty-five,** quarter of a century; **forty,** twoscore; **fifty,** L, half a hundred; **sixty,** sexagenary; Sexagesima; sexagenarian, threescore; **seventy,** septuagenarian, threescore and ten; **eighty,** octogenarian, fourscore; **ninety,** nonagenarian, four-score and ten
8 hundred, century, C; centennial, centenary; centenarian; centigram, centiliter, centimeter; hecatomb; centipede; centurion; <144> gross; <150> sesquicentennial, sesquicentenary; <200> bicentenary, bicentennial; <300> tercentenary, tercentennial, etc
9 five hundred, D; five C's <nonformal>
10 thousand, M, chiliad; **millennium;** G and grand and yard <all nonformal>; millepede; milligram, milliliter, millimeter, kilogram or kilo, kiloliter, kilometer; kilocycle, kilohertz; **ten thousand,** myriad
11 million; ten million
12 billion, thousand million, milliard
13 trillion, quadrillion, quintillion, sextillion, septillion, octillion, nonillion, decillion, duodecillion, tredecillion, quattuordecillion, quindecillion, sexdecillion, septendecillion, octodecillion, novemdecillion, vigintillion
14 <division into five or more parts> quinquesection, quinquepartition, sextipartition, etc; decimation, decimalization; fifth, sixth, etc; **tenth, tithe,** decima
VERBS **15** <divide by five, etc> quinquesect; decimalize
16 <multiply by five, etc> fivefold, sixfold, etc; quintuple, quintuplicate; sextuple, sextuplicate; centuple, centuplicate

ADJS **17 fifth,** quinary; **fivefold, quintuple,** quintuplicate; quinquennial; pentad, pentavalent, quinquevalent

18 sixth, senary; **sixfold, sextuple;** sexpartite, hexadic, sextipartite, hexapartite; hexagonal, hexahedral, hexangular; hexad, hexavalent; sextuplex, hexastyle; sexennial

19 seventh, septimal; **sevenfold, septuple,** septenary; heptagonal, heptahedral, heptangular

20 eighth, octonary; **eightfold, octuple;** octal, octaploid; octagonal, octahedral, octangular; octosyllabic

21 ninth, novenary, nonary; **ninefold, nonuple**

22 tenth, denary, **decimal,** tithe; **tenfold, decuple;** decagonal, decahedral; decasyllabic

23 eleventh, undecennial, undecennary

24 twelfth, duodenary, duodenal; duodecimal

25 thirteenth, fourteenth, etc

26 twentieth, vicenary, vicennial, vigesimal

27 sixtieth, sexagesimal, sexagenary

28 seventieth, septuagesimal, septuagenary

29 hundredth, centesimal, **centennial,** centenary, centurial; **hundredfold, centuple,** centuplicate

30 thousandth, millenary, **millennial; thousandfold**

882 PLURALITY
<more than one>

NOUNS **1 plurality;** a certain number; **several,** some, a few 884.2, more; compositeness, nonuniqueness; **pluralism** 781.1, variety

2 majority, plurality, the greater number, **most,** preponderance *or* preponderancy, **bulk, mass;** lion's share

3 pluralization

4 multiplication, proliferation, **increase** 251; duplication 873

VERBS **5 pluralize;** raise to more than one

6 multiply, proliferate, **increase** 251.4,6, duplicate 873.3

ADJS **7 plural,** pluralized, more, several, severalfold; **some,** certain; not singular, composite, nonunique; **pluralistic** 781.3, various; many, numerous 883.6

8 multiple, multiplied, multifold, **manifold** 883.6; **increased** 251.7

9 majority, most, the greatest number

ADVS **10 in the majority;** and others, et al, et cetera 253.14; plurally

883 NUMEROUSNESS

NOUNS **1 numerousness, multiplicity,** manifoldness, multitudinousness, multifariousness, rifeness, profuseness, profusion; **plenty, abundance** 990.2; **countlessness,** infinitude

2 <indefinite number> **a number,** a certain number, **a few, several,** passel <nonformal>; eleventeen *and* umpteen <both nonformal>

3 <large number> **multitude, throng** 769.4; numbers, quantities, lots 247.4, flocks, **scores;** an abundance of, all kinds *or* sorts of, no end of, quite a few, tidy sum; any number of, **large amount; host, army,** fistful *and* slew *and* shitload *and* shithouse full <all nonformal>; legion, clutter; **swarm, flock** 769.5, flight, cloud, hail, bevy, covey, bunch 769.7

4 <immense number> **a myriad,** a thousand, **a thousand and one,** a million, a billion, a quadrillion, a nonillion, etc 881.13; a zillion *or* jillion <nonformal>; googol, googolplex

VERBS **5 teem with,** overflow with, **abound with,** bristle with, **swarm with,** throng with, **crawl with,** be alive with, **have coming out of one's ears** <nonformal>; clutter, overwhelm, overflow; multiply 882.6

ADJS **6 numerous, many, manifold,** not a few; **very many,** full many; **multitudinous,** multifarious, **myriad,** thousand, mil-

lion, billion; zillion *and* jillion
<both nonformal>

7 several, divers, **sundry,** various;
fivish, sixish, etc; some five or six,
etc; upwards of

8 abundant, copious, plenteous,
plentiful 990.7

9 teeming, swarming, crowding,
thronging, overflowing, overcrowded, overwhelming, bursting, **crawling, alive with,** lousy
with <nonformal>, populous,
prolific, proliferating, jam-
packed, thronged, studded, bristling, rife, lavish, prodigal, **profuse,** in profusion, thick, **thick
with**

10 innumerable, numberless,
unnumbered, **countless,** un-
counted, untold, incalculable, immeasurable, measureless, inexhaustible, infinite, without end *or*
limit, more than you can shake a
stick at <nonformal>; **astronomical,** galactic; millionfold,
trillionfold, etc

11 and many more, and heaven
knows what

ADVS **12 numerously,** multi-
tudinously, **profusely,** copiously,
**abundantly, prodigally; innu-
merably,** countlessly, infinitely,
incalculably, inexhaustibly, immeasurably; **no end** <nonfor-
mal>

884 FEWNESS

NOUNS **1 fewness,** infrequency,
sparsity, sparseness, **scarcity,
paucity, scantiness, meagerness,** niggardliness, restricted-
ness; scrimpiness *and* skimpiness
<both nonformal>; **rarity,** exi-
guity; smallness 258.1

2 a few, too few, mere *or* piddling,
only a few, **small number,** limited *or* piddling number, not
enough to matter, not enough to
shake a stick at, **handful, scattering,** sprinkling, trickle

3 minority, least; the minority, the
few

ADJS **4 few, not many;** scarcely any,
precious few, to be counted on
one's fingers

5 sparse, scant, **scanty,** exiguous,
infrequent, scarce as hen's teeth
<nonformal>, piddling, **meager;**
miserly, niggardly, tight; chintzy
and chinchy *and* stingy <all non-
formal>, skimping *and* scrimping
<both nonformal>; **scattered,**
sprinkled, spotty, **few and far
between; rare,** seldom seen

6 fewer, less, smaller, not so much
or many

7 minority, least

ADVS **8 sparsely, scantily, meagerly,** exiguously, piddlingly; stingily *and* scrimpily *and* skimpily
<all nonformal>, thinly; **scarcely,**
rarely, infrequently; **scatteringly,**
scatteredly, spottily, in dribs and
drabs <nonformal>, **here and
there**

885 CAUSE

NOUNS **1 cause, occasion,** antecedents, **grounds, basis,** element, principle, factor; **determinant;** causation, causality; etiol-
ogy

2 reason, reason why, rationale,
underlying reason, **explanation,
the why,** the wherefore, **the why
and wherefore;** stated cause,
pretext, pretense, excuse

3 immediate cause, proximate
cause, trigger, spark; **domino effect,** ripple effect, slippery slope;
ultimate cause, immanent cause,
remote cause, first cause; **final
cause, end,** end in view, teleol-
ogy; provocation, **last straw,**
straw that broke the camel's back

4 author, agent, **originator,** gener-
ator, begetter, producer, **creator,**
mover; **parent, mother, father,**
sire; **prime mover;** instigator,
catalyst

5 source, origin, genesis, **derivation, rise, beginning,** conception, inception, **head;** prove-
nance, provenience, background;
root

6 fountainhead, headwater,
mainspring, wellspring, well-
head, well, **spring, fountain,**
fount, font

7 vital force *or* **principle,** *élan*

vital <Fr>; **egg,** ovum 305.12,
germ, spermatozoon 305.11,
nucleus 305.7, **seed; embryo**
305.14; bud 310.21; loins; **womb,**
matrix, uterus
8 **birthplace, breeding place,**
breeding ground, hatchery; **hotbed;** incubator, brooder; **nest,**
nidus; **cradle**
9 <a principle or movement>
cause, principle, interest, issue,
lifework; reason for being, *raison
d'être* <Fr>; **movement,** activity;
drive, campaign, crusade
VERBS 10 **cause,** lie at the root of;
bring about, bring to pass, effectuate, **effect,** realize; **impact,**
impact on, influence; **occasion,
make, create, engender,** generate, **produce; originate;** give occasion to, **give rise to,** spark, trigger; **give birth to, beget,** bear,
bring forth, author, **father,** sire,
sow the seeds of; gestate, **conceive; set on foot;** found, establish, inaugurate, institute
11 **induce,** lead, procure, **effect,
bring on, call forth, elicit,
evoke, provoke,** inspire, influence, instigate, egg on, **motivate;**
open the door to; suborn
12 **determine,** decide, have the last
word; **necessitate,** entail, require; contribute to, lead to; **advance, forward,** influence; **spin
off**
ADJS 13 **causal,** causative; chicken-
and-egg <nonformal>; **at the
bottom of,** behind the scenes;
formative, determinative, decisive, pivotal; etiological
14 **original, primary,** primal, primitive, pristine, primeval, aboriginal, **elementary,** elemental, **basic,** basal, **rudimentary,** crucial,
central, **fundamental;** embryonic, germinal, seminal, pregnant; **generative**

886 EFFECT

NOUNS 1 **effect, result,** resultant,
consequence, consequent, sequel, sequela, sequelae; event,
eventuality, eventuation, **upshot,
outcome,** scenario; **outgrowth,**

spin-off, offshoot, aftermath,
legacy; **product** 892, **fruit,** first
fruits, crop, harvest; derivative,
derivation, by-product
2 **impact,** force, **repercussion,** reaction; backwash, backlash, response; mark, imprint, impression
3 **aftereffect, aftermath,** after-
shock, afterimage, afterglow;
track; domino effect
VERBS 4 **result, ensue, issue, follow,** attend, accompany; **turn
out, come out,** fall out, redound,
work out, pan out <nonformal>,
fare; turn out to be, prove to be;
develop, unfold; **eventuate,** terminate, end; **end up,** wind up
5 **result from,** originate in *or*
from, **come from,** come out of,
grow out of, follow from *or* on,
proceed from, issue from, ensue
from, emanate from, flow from,
derive from, rise *or* arise from,
spring from, stem from, sprout
from, bud from, germinate from;
spin off; depend on, hinge *or*
pivot *or* turn on
ADJS 6 **resultant, resulting, following, ensuing; consequent,**
consequential, sequent, sequential; necessitated, entailed, required; **final**
ADVS 7 **consequently, as a result,**
as a consequence, in consequence, necessarily, of necessity,
inevitably, as a matter of course,
it follows that; **therefore; accordingly** 765.11; **finally**
CONJS 8 **resulting from,** coming
from, arising from, in consequence of; **owing to, due to;** attributable to, dependent *or* contingent on; **caused by,** occa-
sioned by, **at the bottom of**

887 ATTRIBUTION
<assignment of cause>

NOUNS 1 **attribution, assignment,**
assignation, **ascription, imputation,** attachment, **charge,
blame; indictment; responsibility; credit,** honor; derivation from, connection with; eti-
ology

2 **acknowledgment,** citation, tribute; **reference; by-line,** credit line

VERBS 3 **attribute, assign, ascribe, impute,** give, place, put, apply, attach, refer

4 **attribute to, ascribe to, impute to,** assign to, **lay to,** apply to, refer to, point to; **pin on,** pinpoint <nonformal>, fix on or upon, attach to, accrete to, connect with, **saddle on,** place upon, saddle with; blame, **blame for,** blame on, put the blame on, place the blame or responsibility for, indict, **fix the responsibility for,** put the finger on and finger <both nonformal>, **charge to,** lay to one's charge, lay at the door of, bring home to; acknowledge, confess; **credit with;** put words in one's mouth

5 **trace to,** follow the trail to; **derive from,** trace the origin or derivation of

ADJS 6 **attributable, assignable, ascribable, imputable,** explicable; owing, **due,** derivative, derivational; **charged,** alleged, imputed, putative; **credited, attributed**

ADVS 7 **hence, therefore,** therefor, **wherefore,** whence, then, thence, *ergo* <L>; **consequently** 886.7; **accordingly** 765.11; **because of that,** for that, for that reason, in consideration of something, from or for that cause, **on that account,** on that ground; **because of this, on this account,** for this reason; thus; on or at someone's doorstep

8 **why,** how is it that, **wherefore, what for,** for which, **on what account,** on account of which, for what or whatever reason

888 OPERATION

NOUNS 1 **operation, functioning, action, performance, working, work,** workings; agency; operations; **management** 573, **direction, conduct, running, carrying-on** or **-out,** execution, oversight; **handling,** manipulation; responsibility 641.2; **occupation** 724

2 **process, procedure,** proceeding, course; **act,** step, measure, initiative, maneuver, motion

3 **workability, operability,** manageability, maneuverability; **practicability, feasibility,** viability

4 **operator,** operative, operant; **handler,** manipulator; **manager** 574.1, **executive** 574.3; functionary, agent; driver

VERBS 5 **operate, function, run, work; manage, direct** 573.8, **conduct; carry on** or **out** or **through,** perform; **handle,** manipulate, maneuver; deal with, take care of; occupy oneself with 724.10; be responsible for 641.6

6 **operate on, act on** or **upon, work on, affect, influence,** bear on, impact on; focus or concentrate on; bring to bear on

7 <be operative> **operate, function, work, act, perform, go, run;** be effective, go into effect, have effect, take effect, militate

8 **function as,** work as, **act as,** act or play the part of, have the function or role or job or mission of

ADJS 9 **operative, operational, functional, practical; effective,** effectual, efficient, efficacious

10 **workable, operable, performable,** manageable, negotiable, maneuverable; **practicable, feasible,** practical, viable

11 **operating, operational, working, functioning,** operant, functional, running, **going,** ongoing; **in operation,** in action, **in practice, in force,** in play, at work; **in process,** in the works, in the pipeline <nonformal>, in hand

12 operational, functional; **managerial** 573.12

889 PRODUCTIVENESS

NOUNS 1 **productiveness, productivity; fruitfulness, fertility,** fecundity; **pregnancy; luxuriance, exuberance,** bountifulness, plentifulness, plenteousness, **abundance** 990.2, superabundance, copiousness

2 proliferation, multiplication, fructification, teeming; **reproduction** 78, **production** 891

3 fertilization, enrichment, fecundation; insemination, impregnation 78.4

4 fertilizer, top dressing; manure, muck, night soil, dung, guano, compost, leaf mold, humus, bone meal

5 <goddesses of fertility> Demeter, Ceres, Isis

6 <comparisons> rabbit, Hydra, warren

VERBS **7 produce, be productive, proliferate,** fructify, be fruitful, **multiply,** engender, beget, teem; **reproduce** 78.7,8

8 fertilize, enrich, fatten, feed; fructify, fecundate; inseminate, impregnate 78.10; dress, top-dress, manure

ADJS **9 productive, fruitful,** fecund; **fertile, pregnant,** seminal, **rich,** flourishing, thriving; **prolific, teeming,** swarming, bursting, plenteous, **plentiful,** copious, generous, bountiful, **abundant** 990.7, **luxuriant, exuberant, lush,** superabundant; creative

10 bearing, yielding, producing; fructiferous

11 fertilizing, enriching, richening, fattening, fecundatory, fructificative, **seminal,** germinal

890 UNPRODUCTIVENESS

NOUNS **1 unproductiveness,** ineffectualness 19.3; **unfruitfulness, barrenness,** nonfruition, aridity, dearth, famine; sterileness, **sterility, infertility,** infecundity; **birth control, contraception,** family planning, planned parenthood; abortion; impotence 19

2 wasteland, waste, desolation, barren or **barrens,** barren land; **desert,** Sahara, badlands, dust bowl, salt flat, Death Valley; **wilderness,** wild, wilds

VERBS **3** be unproductive, **come to nothing,** come to naught, fizzle or peter out <nonformal>; **lie fallow**

ADJS **4 unproductive,** nonproductive or nonproducing; **infertile, sterile,** unfertile, **unfruitful,** infecund, unprolific; **impotent,** gelded 19.19; **ineffectual** 19.15; **barren, desert, arid,** sere, exhausted, drained, leached, sucked dry, wasted, gaunt, **waste, desolate,** jejune; **childless,** without issue; fallow, unplowed, unsown, untilled, uncultivated; celibate

5 uncreative, nongerminal, unpregnant; uninventive, unoriginal, derivative

891 PRODUCTION

NOUNS **1 production, creation, making, origination, invention, conception,** originating, engenderment, genesis; **devising,** hatching, fabrication, **concoction, contriving,** contrivance; **authorship; generation** 78.6; improvisation

2 production, manufacture or **manufacturing, making, producing,** devising, design, fashioning, formulation; processing, conversion; casting, **shaping,** molding; machining, milling, finishing; **assembly,** composition, elaboration; **workmanship, craftsmanship, skill** 413; **construction, building,** erection, architecture; **fabrication,** prefabrication; **mining,** extraction, smelting, **refining; growing,** cultivation, **raising,** harvesting

3 industrial production, industry, mass production, assembly-line production; production line, assembly line; **cottage industry;** piecework

4 establishment, foundation, constitution, **organization,** inauguration, **inception, setting-up,** realization, effectuation

5 performance, execution, doing, accomplishment, achievement, productive effort, realization, fructification, effectuation, operation 888; overproduction, glut; underproduction, scarcity; **productiveness** 889

6 **bearing, yielding, birthing; fruition**

7 **producer, maker,** craftsman; **manufacturer,** industrialist; **creator, author,** mother, **father,** sire; **ancestors** 560.7; **precursor** 815; **originator,** initiator, mover, prime mover, motive force, instigator; **founder,** organizer, founding father, founding partner, cofounder; **inventor,** discoverer, deviser; **builder,** artificer, **architect,** planner, **conceiver,** designer, **shaper;** facilitator, animator; **grower,** raiser; **apprentice, journeyman, master,** past master

VERBS 8 **produce, create, make, manufacture, form,** formulate, elaborate, fashion, **fabricate,** configure, extrude, frame; **construct, build,** erect, rear; compose, write, devise, design, concoct, compound; **put together, assemble,** piece together, patch together, improvise 365.8; **make to order,** custom-make, custom-build

9 **process,** convert 857.11; mill, machine; carve, chisel; **mine,** extract, pump, smelt, **refine; raise,** rear, **grow,** cultivate, harvest

10 **establish, found,** constitute, institute, install, form, **set up, organize,** equip, endow, inaugurate, realize

11 **perform, do,** execute, **accomplish, achieve** 407.4, **deliver,** realize, engineer, effectuate, **bring about,** bring to fruition; massproduce, industrialize; overproduce; underproduce; **be productive** 889.7

12 **originate, invent, conceive,** discover, **make up, devise, contrive,** concoct, fabricate, hatch *or* cook up, strike out; improvise, make do with; dream up, **design,** plan; **generate, develop,** mature, **evolve;** breed, engender, beget, spawn, hatch; bring forth, give rise to; procreate 78.8

13 **bear, yield, produce,** furnish; **bring forth,** usher into the world; fruit, **bear fruit,** fructify

ADJS 14 **productional, creational;**

manufacturing, industrial, smokestack

15 **constructional, structural; architectural,** architectonic

16 **creative, originative,** causative, **productive** 889.9, **constructive,** formative; inventive; generative 78.16

17 **produced, made, caused, brought about;** effectuated, executed

18 **made,** man-made; **manufactured,** created, crafted, formed, shaped, molded, cast, forged, machined, milled, fashioned, **built, constructed,** fabricated; **well-made,** well-built, wellconstructed; **homemade,** homespun, **handmade,** handcrafted, handicrafted; machine-made; **processed; assembled; custommade,** custom-built, made to order; **ready-made,** ready-to-wear, off-the-shelf, off-the-rack; prefabricated, prefab <nonformal>

19 **invented,** originated, **conceived,** discovered; fabricated; **made-up,** made out of whole cloth

20 **manufacturable, producible**

ADVS 21 **in production;** in the works; in the pipeline; on-line

892 PRODUCT

NOUNS 1 **product,** end product; **work, handiwork, artifact; creation; offspring,** fruit of one's loins; **result, effect** 886, issue, outcome; **invention,** origination, coinage, brainchild; **concoction,** composition; **masterwork, masterpiece,** crowning achievement

2 **production,** produce, proceeds, net, **yield, output,** throughput; **crop,** harvest, return

3 **extract, distillation,** essence; **by-product,** spin-off, outgrowth, offshoot; **residue,** leavings, waste, waste product, lees, dregs

4 <amount made> make, making; batch, lot, run

893 INFLUENCE

NOUNS 1 **influence; power** 18, force, clout <nonformal>, po-

tency, **say,** the last word, say-so
<nonformal>; veto power; **pres-
tige,** favor, good feeling, credit,
esteem, repute, personality, leadership, charisma, magnetism,
charm, enchantment; **weight,**
moment, consequence; **authority**
417, domination, hold; **sway**
612.1, reign, rule; **mastery,** ascendancy, supremacy, dominance, predominance; upper
hand, whip hand, trump card;
leverage, purchase; **persuasion**
375.3

2 favor, interest; connections,
inside track <nonformal>

3 influence, intrigues, deals,
schemes, **games,** ploys; **wires
and strings** *and* ropes <all non-
formal>; **wire-pulling** <nonfor-
mal>; **influence peddling;**
lobbying

4 sphere of influence, orbit, ambit; bailiwick, vantage, **territory,**
turf, constituency, **power base**

5 influenceability, movability;
persuadability, persuasibility,
open-mindedness, accessibility,
receptiveness, responsiveness,
amenableness; **suggestibility,**
susceptibility, impressionability,
malleability

6 <influential person or thing>
influence; person *or* **woman** *or*
man of influence, a presence, a
palpable presence, a mover and
shaker <nonformal>, a person to
be reckoned with; heavyweight,
very important person *or* VIP
<nonformal>; wheeler-dealer
<nonformal>; **wire-puller** <non-
formal>; **powerbroker; power
behind the throne,** gray eminence, *éminence grise* <Fr>,
friend at court, kingmaker; **influence peddler,** lobbyist; Svengali,
Rasputin; **pressure group,**
special-interest group, single-
issue group, PAC *or* political action committee; lobby; the Establishment, powers that be 575.15;
key, key to the city, access, open
sesame

VERBS **7 influence,** make oneself
felt, **affect, sway,** bias, bend, in-

cline, dispose, predispose, **move,**
prompt, lead; slant, impart spin;
induce, persuade 375.23, jawbone *and* twist one's arm *and*
hold one's feet to the fire <all non-
formal>, work *or* bend to one's
will; lead by the nose <nonfor-
mal>, wear down, soften up

8 <exercise influence over> **govern** 612.12, **rule, control** 612.13,
order, **regulate,** direct, guide; **determine,** decide, dispose; have
veto power over, call the shots
and be in the driver's seat *and*
wear the pants <all nonformal>

9 exercise *or* **exert influence, use
one's influence, bring pressure
to bear upon,** lean on <nonfor-
mal>, **work on,** throw one's
weight around; lead on, magnetize; **approach,** make advances
or overtures, make up to *or* get
cozy with <both nonformal>;
pull strings *or* **wires** *or* **ropes;**
lobby

**10 have influence, be influential,
carry weight, weigh, tell, count,**
cut ice, have a lot to say about
<nonformal>; have pull *or* drag
or leverage <nonformal>; have a
way with one, charm the birds
out of the trees, charm the pants
off one <nonformal>, be persuasive; have the inside track <non-
formal>

11 have influence *or* **power** *or* a
hold over, have pull *or* clout with
<nonformal>; **lead by the nose,
twist** *or* **turn** *or* **wind around
one's little finger,** have in one's
pocket; hypnotize, mesmerize,
dominate 612.15

12 gain influence, get in with
<nonformal>, ingratiate oneself
with; make peace, **mend fences;**
gain a footing, take hold; gain a
hearing, make one's voice heard,
make one sit up and take notice;
get control of, get the inside track
<nonformal>, gain a hold upon;
turn the tables

ADJS **13 influential, powerful**
18.12, potent, to be reckoned
with; **effective,** effectual, efficacious, telling; **weighty,** mo-

mentous, important, consequential, substantial, **prestigious,** estimable, authoritative, reputable; **persuasive, winning,** magnetic, charming, charismatic

14 <in a position of influence> **well-connected,** near the seat of power; **dominant** 612.18, **predominant,** preponderant, ruling, swaying, prevailing, in the driver's seat <nonformal>; **ascendant,** in the ascendant

15 **swayable, movable; persuadable,** persuasible, open-minded, pervious, accessible, receptive, responsive, amenable; **under one's thumb,** in one's pocket; coercible, bribable; **plastic, pliant,** pliable, malleable; **suggestible, susceptible, impressionable,** weak 16.12

894 ABSENCE OF INFLUENCE

NOUNS 1 **lack of influence** or **power** or **force,** powerlessness, impotence 19, impotency; **ineffectiveness,** inefficacy, ineffectuality; unpersuasiveness, lack of magnetism or charisma; **weakness** 16, wimpiness or wimpishness <nonformal>

2 **uninfluenceability,** unmovability; **unpersuadability,** impersuasibility, imperviousness, unresponsiveness; unsuggestibility, **unsusceptibility,** unimpressionability; **obstinacy** 361

ADJS 3 **uninfluential, powerless,** impotent 19.13; **weak** 16.12, wimpy or wimpish <nonformal>; **ineffective,** ineffectual, inefficacious; **of no account,** lightweight

4 **uninfluenceable, unswayable, unmovable; unpliable,** unyielding, inflexible; **unpersuadable** 361.13, unreceptive, unresponsive, unamenable; impervious; **unsuggestible,** unimpressionable; invulnerable; **obstinate** 361.8

5 **uninfluenced, unmoved, unaffected, unswayed**

895 TENDENCY

NOUNS 1 **tendency, inclination, leaning,** penchant, susceptibility; liability 896, readiness, willingness, eagerness, aptness, aptitude, **disposition, proclivity, propensity,** predisposition, **predilection,** affinity, prejudice, **liking,** delight, soft spot; **yen,** hunger, thirst; **bent, turn, bias,** slant, tilt, spin <nonformal>, cast, warp, twist; probability 967

2 **trend, drift, course, current,** movement, motion, run, **tenor,** tone, **set,** direction, the general tendency or drift, the way the wind blows, **the way things go**

VERBS 3 **tend,** have a tendency, **incline,** be disposed, **lean, trend,** have a penchant, set, **go,** head, lead, point, verge, turn, warp, tilt, bias, bend to; **conduce,** contribute, serve, redound to

ADJS 4 **tending;** tendentious or tendential; **leaning, inclining; mainstream,** mainline

896 LIABILITY

NOUNS 1 **liability, likelihood** or **likeliness; probability** 967, contingency, chance 971, eventuality 830.1; **possibility** 965; **responsibility** 641.2; **indebtedness** 623.1, financial commitment

2 **susceptibility, liability, openness, exposure; vulnerability** 1005.4

VERBS 3 **be liable; be subjected** or **subjected to,** be a pawn of, lie under; **expose oneself to, lay** or **leave oneself open to; gamble,** stand to lose or gain, stand a chance, **run the chance** or **risk,** let down one's guard or defenses; **admit of,** open the possibility of; **owe,** be indebted for

4 **incur, contract, invite,** welcome, run, **bring on, bring down,** bring down upon oneself; **be responsible for** 641.6

ADJS 5 **liable, likely, prone; probable; responsible,** answerable; **in debt, indebted,** financially burdened, overextended; **exposed,**

susceptible, at risk, overex-
posed, like a sitting duck, vulnerable
6 liable to, subject to, standing
to, dependent on; susceptible or
prone to, open or vulnerable or
exposed to, in danger of, within
range of, at the mercy of; capable
of, ready for; likely to, apt to
895.67

897 INVOLVEMENT

NOUNS 1 involvement, implication, entanglement, engagement, embarrassment; relation
774; inclusion 771; absorption
982.3
VERBS 2 involve, implicate, tangle, entangle, embarrass, enmesh, draw in, drag into, catch
up in, make a party to; interest,
concern; absorb 982.13
3 be involved, partake, participate, interest oneself, have a
role
ADJS 4 involved, implicated; interested, concerned, a party to;
included 771.5
5 involved in, implicated in, en-
meshed in, caught up in, tied up
in, wrapped up in, dragged into;
deeply involved, up to one's neck
or ears in, head over heels in, absorbed in 982.17, immersed in

898 CONCURRENCE

NOUNS 1 concurrence, collaboration, combined effort or operation, united or concerted action,
concert, synergy; cooperation
450; agreement 787; coincidence, synchronism; concomitance, accompaniment 768;
union, junction 799.1, conjunction, combination 804, association; conspiracy, collusion, cahoots <nonformal>; accordance
455.1, concordance, correspondence; symbiosis, parasitism
VERBS 2 concur, collaborate, syn-
ergize; cooperate 450.3; conspire, collude, connive, be in cahoots <nonformal>; combine
804.3, unite, associate 804.4,
conjoin; harmonize; coincide,

synchronize; accord 455.2, correspond, agree 787.6
3 go along with, go hand in hand
with, be hand in glove with; keep
pace with
ADJS 4 concurrent, concurring;
collaborative, collective, synergistic; cooperative 450.5; conspiratorial, collusive; united,
joint, conjoint, combined,
concerted; coincident, synchronous, coordinate; concomitant, accompanying 768.9;
meeting, uniting, combining; accordant, agreeing 787.9, concordant, harmonious; symbiotic,
parasitic
ADVS 5 concurrently, jointly, conjointly, concertedly, in harmony
or unison with, synchronously,
together; with one accord, with
one voice; shoulder to shoulder,
cheek by jowl

899 COUNTERACTION

NOUNS 1 counteraction, counterworking; opposition 451, confutation, contradiction; antagonism, repugnance; antipathy,
conflict, friction, interference,
collision; backlash, recoil, backfire; resistance, recalcitrance, dissent 333, revolt 327.4, perverseness, crankiness, crotchetiness,
orneriness <nonformal>; swimming upstream; contrariety 778
2 neutralization, nullification,
annulment, cancellation, voiding, invalidation, vitiation; offsetting, countervailing
3 counteractant, counteractive,
counteragent; counterirritant;
antidote, remedy, preventive,
prophylactic; neutralizer, nulli-
fier, offset
4 counterforce, countervailing
force; counterpoise, counterweight; crosscurrent, undercurrent
5 countermeasure, counterattack; counterblow, counterfire;
counterrevolution, counterin-
surgency; counterterrorism;
counterculture; retort, comeback

VERBS **6 counteract,** counter, counterattack, countervail; **oppose,** antagonize, **run counter to,** go *or* **work against,** fly in the face of, beat against, militate against; **resist,** lift a hand against, defend oneself; **dissent,** dissent from; **cross,** confute, **contradict,** contravene, oppugn, **conflict,** interfere *or* conflict with, come in conflict with, **clash,** collide, meet head-on, lock horns; go against the grain; swim upstream *or* against the tide

7 neutralize, nullify, annul, cancel, negate, invalidate, vitiate, void, frustrate, stultify, thwart, undo; **offset, counterbalance** 338.5; buffer

ADJS **8** counteractive, **counteracting, counterworking, counterproductive,** countervailing; **opposing,** oppositional; **antagonistic,** hostile, antipathetic, inimical, oppugnant, repugnant, **conflicting, clashing;** reactionary; resistant, recalcitrant, nonconformist, perverse, cranky, crotchety, ornery <nonformal>

9 neutralizing, nullifying, stultifying, annulling, negating, invalidating, vitiating, voiding; **balanced,** in poise, **zero-sum; offsetting,** counterbalancing, countervailing

ADVS **10** counteractively, antagonistically, opposingly, **in opposition to, counter to**

900 SUPPORT

NOUNS **1 support, backing, aid** 449; **upholding, upkeep,** carriage, **sustaining; reinforcement,** backup; **infrastructure; moral support;** security blanket <nonformal>; **power base, constituency, party; approval** 509; **assent, concurrence** 332; **reliance** 952.1

2 supporter, support; upholder, bearer, carrier, sustainer, maintainer; **advocate** 616.9; **stay, prop,** fulcrum, **bracket, brace,** bracer, guy, guywire *or* guyline, shroud; buttress, shoulder, arm, good right arm; **mainstay,** backbone, spine; **reinforcement,** strengthener, stiffener

3 <mythology> Atlas, Hercules, Telamon

4 buttress, buttressing; abutment, shoulder; **bulwark,** rampart; **embankment,** bulkhead, piling; **breakwater,** seawall, **jetty; pier,** buttress pier; flying buttress; **beam**

5 footing, foothold, toehold, hold, perch, **purchase** 905; **standing;** footrest

6 foundation, base, basis, footing, ground, groundwork, seat, fundament; **substructure,** substratum; infrastructure; **understructure,** undergirding, underpinning, bearing wall; *terra firma* <L>; rock bottom, bedrock; hardpan; riprap; **fundamental** 996.6, **principle, premise** 956.1

7 foundation stone, footstone; **cornerstone, keystone,** headstone, first stone, quoin

8 base, pedestal; stand; shaft 273, **upright, column, pillar, post,** stanchion, pier, piling, banister, balustrade, colonnade, caryatid; **trunk,** stem, **stalk,** pedicel, peduncle

9 sill, groundsel

10 frame, infrastructure, chassis, **skeleton; mounting,** mount, **backing, setting**

11 handle, hold, grip, grasp, haft, helve

12 scaffold, scaffolding; stage, staging

13 platform; stage, dais, floor; **rostrum, podium, pulpit,** speaker's platform, **soapbox** <nonformal>; hustings, **stump; terrace,** deck; **balcony, gallery**

14 shelf, ledge, shoulder; mantel, mantelpiece

15 table, board, **stand; bench,** workbench; **counter,** bar, buffet; **desk,** writing table, **secretary,** escritoire; **lectern,** ambo, reading desk

16 trestle, horse; sawhorse, buck *or* sawbuck; trestle table; A-frame

17 seat, chair; saddle

18 sofa, **bed; couch;** bedstead; **litter, stretcher,** gurney
19 **bedding; mattress,** paillasse, pallet; sleeping bag; pad, mat, rug; litter, bedstraw; **pillow,** cushion, bolster

VERBS 20 **support, bear,** carry, **hold, sustain, maintain, bolster, reinforce,** give *or* furnish *or* lend support; go to bat for <nonformal>; **hold up, bear up,** bolster up, buoy up, back up; **uphold; brace, prop,** buttress; **shore up; underlie,** be at the bottom of, form the foundation of; cradle; **subsidize;** subvene; **approve** 509.9
21 **rest on, stand on, lie on, lean on,** abut on; **straddle,** bestraddle, stride, bestride

ADJS 22 **supporting, supportive, bearing; holding,** maintaining, sustaining; bracing, propping, shoring, bolstering, buttressing
23 **supported, borne,** buoyed-up, **upheld, sustained,** maintained; **braced,** guyed, propped, shored up, bolstered, buttressed; based *or* founded *or* grounded on

ADVS 24 **on, across, astride, astraddle,** on the back of; pickaback *or* piggyback

901 IMPULSE, IMPACT
<driving and striking force>

NOUNS 1 **impulse,** impulsion, impellent; **drive,** driving force *or* power; **motive power, power** 18; clout <nonformal>; **impetus; momentum;** moment; propulsion 903.1
2 **thrust, push, shove,** boost <nonformal>; **pressure; stress;** press; **prod, poke, punch, jab,** dig, nudge; **bump,** jog, joggle, jolt; **jostle,** hustle
3 **impact, collision, clash, encounter,** meeting, impingement, **bump, crash;** sideswipe <nonformal>; smash *and* crunch <both nonformal>; **shock, brunt; concussion,** percussion; **thrusting, ramming,** bulling, **bulldozing;** onslaught 459.1
4 **hit, blow, stroke, knock, rap,**

pound, slam, bang, crack, **whack, smack, thwack,** smash, dash, swipe, swing, **punch, poke, jab,** dig, drub, thump, pelt, cut, chop, dint, slog; **drubbing, drumming,** tattoo, fusillade; **beating** 604.4
5 <nonformal terms> **sock,** bang, bash, bat, belt, bonk, bust, clip, clout, duke, swat, plunk, larrup, paste, lick, biff, clump, clunk, clonk, wallop, whop, bonk, slam, slug
6 **punch,** boxing punch, blow
7 **tap, rap, pat,** dab, chuck, touch, tip; love-tap; **snap, flick, flip,** fillip, flirt
8 **slap, smack,** flap; **box, cuff,** buffet; **spank**
9 **kick,** boot; punt
10 **stamp,** stomp <nonformal>

VERBS 11 **impel, set going,** put *or* set in motion, give momentum; **drive, move,** animate, actuate; **thrust,** power; drive *or* whip on; goad; **propel**
12 **thrust, push, shove,** boost <nonformal>; press, stress, **bear,** bring pressure to bear upon; **ram,** tamp, crowd, cram; **drive, force,** run; **prod, goad, poke, punch, jab,** dig, nudge; **bump,** jog, joggle, jolt, shake, rattle; **jostle,** hustle, hurtle; elbow, shoulder; **butt,** run *or* bump *or* butt against, bump up against
13 **collide,** be on a collision course, **clash,** meet, encounter, impinge; **bump, hit, strike, knock, bang; run into, bump into,** bang into, **crash into, impact,** smash into; rear-end; **hit against,** strike against, knock against; hurtle, hurt; **carom; sideswipe** <nonformal>; **crash,** smash, whomp
14 **hit, strike, knock,** knock down *or* out, smite; **poke, punch, jab,** thwack, **smack,** clap, crack, swipe, **whack;** take a punch at, throw one at <nonformal>, deal *or* fetch a blow, let have it; **thump**
15 <nonformal terms> **belt,** bat, clout, bang, slam, bash, biff, paste, wham, whop, clump, bonk, wallop, clip, cut, plunk, swat,

soak, sock, slog, slug, clunk,
clonk
16 **pound, beat, hammer, maul,
knock, rap, bang,** thump, **drub,**
buffet, **batter,** pummel, pelt,
baste, lambaste
17 <nonformal terms> **clobber,**
knock for a loop, knock cold,
punch out, rough up, slap down,
smack down, sandbag, work over,
deck, wallop, larrup
18 **tap, rap, pat,** chuck; **snap, flick,
flip,** tickle, flirt, whisk, **graze,**
brush
19 **slap, smack,** flap; **box, cuff,**
buffet; **spank**
20 **club,** cudgel, blackjack, sandbag
21 **kick,** boot, kick about or around;
knee
22 **stamp,** stomp <nonformal>,
trample, drub
ADJS 23 **impelling,** impellent; impulsive, **moving,** motive, animating, actuating, **driving**
24 concussive, percussive, crashing,
smashing

902 REACTION

NOUNS 1 **reaction, response,** feedback; reply, answer 939.1, **rise**
<nonformal>; **reflex,** reflection,
reflex action; reflux, refluence;
action and reaction; retroaction,
revulsion; knee-jerk and knee-jerk
response <both nonformal>
2 **recoil, rebound,** resilience, repercussion; **bounce, bound,
spring,** bounce-back; **repulse,
rebuff; backlash, kick,** a kick
like a mule <nonformal>; **backfire, boomerang;** ricochet,
carom
3 <a drawing back or aside> **retreat,** recoil, fallback, pullout,
pullback, contingency plan; evasion, avoidance, sidestepping;
flinch, wince, cringe; **side step,**
shy; **dodge, duck** <nonformal>
4 **reactionary,** reactionist, recalcitrant
VERBS 5 **react, respond,** reply, answer, riposte; take the bait; go off
half-cocked
6 **recoil, rebound,** resile; **bounce,
bound, spring;** spring or fly

back, bounce or bound back,
snap back; **kick,** kick back, kick
like a mule <nonformal>; **backfire, boomerang;** backlash, lash
back; ricochet, carom
7 **pull** or **draw back,** retreat, recoil, fade, **fall back,** hang back,
give ground; **shrink, flinch,
wince, cringe,** blink, quail; **shy,**
shy away, evade, avoid, sidestep,
weasel, weasel out, cop out <non-
formal>; **dodge, duck** <nonfor-
mal>; give a wide berth
8 get a reaction, get a response,
evoke a response, ring a bell,
strike a responsive chord, hit a
nerve, get a rise out of <nonfor-
mal>
ADJS 9 **reactive,** reacting; **responsive,** respondent; **quick on the
draw** or **trigger** or **uptake; reactionary;** retroactive; **reflex,**
reflexive, knee-jerk <nonfor-
mal>
10 recoiling, rebounding, **resilient;
bouncing,** bouncy, bounding,
springing, springy
ADVS 11 **on the rebound,** on the
bounce; on the spur of the moment, off the top of the head

903 PUSHING, THROWING

NOUNS 1 **pushing, propulsion,
propelling, shoving,** butting;
drive, thrust, motive power, driving force; **push, shove;** shunt,
impulsion 901.1
2 **throwing, projection,** ejaculation, flinging, slinging, **pitching,
tossing,** casting, hurling, lob-
bing, chucking, heaving; **shooting,** gunnery, gunning, musketry
3 **throw, toss, fling, sling, cast,
hurl,** chuck, lob, **heave, pitch,
toss,** peg <nonformal>; **flip**
4 **shot,** discharge; ejection 908;
detonation 56.3; gunfire; **salvo,
volley,** fusillade, tattoo, spray
5 **projectile,** ejecta, ejectamenta;
missile
6 **propeller,** prop <nonformal>;
propellant, propulsor, driver;
screw, wheel, paddle wheel; tur-
bine; fan, impeller, rotor
7 **thrower, pitcher,** hurler,

chucker, **heaver, tosser,** flinger, slinger; bowler

8 shooter, shot; **gunner,** gun, **gunman; rifleman,** musketeer; Nimrod, hunter 382.5; trapshooter; archer, toxophilite; **marksman, markswoman, sharpshooter,** sniper

VERBS **9 push, propel,** impel, **shove,** thrust 901.11; **drive, move;** sweep along; butt, bunt; shunt

10 throw, fling, sling, pitch, toss, cast, hurl, heave, chuck, chunk *and* peg <both nonformal>, lob, fire, burn, launch, let fly, let loose; catapult; **flip,** snap, jerk; bowl; pass; serve

11 project, jaculate

12 shoot, fire, let fly, **discharge,** eject 908.13; detonate 56.8; shoot at 459.22, gun for <nonformal>; strike, hit, plug <nonformal>; shoot down, fell, drop; **riddle, pepper,** pelt, pump full of lead <nonformal>; snipe, pick off; torpedo; potshot, take a potshot;

13 start, start up, crank up, give a push *or* shove <nonformal>, jump-start, kick-start, **put** *or* **set in motion, set on foot,** set going *or* agoing, start going

ADJS **14 propulsive,** propulsory, **propellant,** propelling; **motive; driving, pushing, shoving**

15 projectile, ejaculatory; **ballistic**

16 jet-propelled, rocket-propelled

904 PULLING

NOUNS **1 pulling, traction, drawing,** draft, dragging, heaving, tugging, towing; towage; **hauling,** haulage, drayage

2 pull, draw, heave, haul, tug, strain, drag

3 jerk, yank <nonformal>, quick *or* sudden pull; **twitch,** tweak, pluck, hitch, wrench, snatch, start, bob; **flip,** flick, flirt, flounce; jig, **jiggle;** jog, joggle

VERBS **4 pull, draw, heave, haul,** lug, **tug, tow,** take in tow; **drag,** man-haul, snake <nonformal>; troll, trawl

5 jerk, yank <nonformal>;

twitch, tweak, pluck, snatch, hitch, wrench, snake <nonformal>; **flip,** flick, flirt, flounce; **jiggle;** jog, joggle

ADJS **6 pulling, drawing,** tractional, tractive, hauling, tugging, towing, towage; man-hauled

905 LEVERAGE, PURCHASE
    <mechanical advantage applied to moving or raising>

NOUNS **1 leverage; pry,** prize <nonformal>

2 purchase, hold, advantage; **foothold,** toehold, footing; traction

3 fulcrum, axis, pivot, bearing, rest, resting point

4 lever; pry, prize <nonformal>; **bar,** pinch bar, **crowbar,** crow, wrecking bar, ripping bar, claw bar; **jimmy;** boom, spar, beam, outrigger

5 arm; forearm; wrist; elbow; upper arm, biceps

6 tackle, purchase

7 windlass; capstan <nautical>; **winch,** crab; reel

VERBS **8 get a purchase,** get leverage; **pry,** prize, **lever;** pry *or* prize out; **jimmy,** crowbar, pinchbar

9 reel in, wind in, bring in, draw in, pull in, crank in, trim, tighten, tauten; windlass, winch, reel

906 ATTRACTION
    <a drawing toward>

NOUNS **1 attraction,** traction 904.1, attractiveness; mutual attraction; pulling power, **pull,** drag, draw, tug; magnetism 1031.7; gravity, gravitation; capillarity, capillary attraction; **affinity; allurement** 377

2 attractor, attractant; cynosure, focus, center of attraction *or* attention; crowd-pleaser, charismatic figure; **lure** 377.2

3 magnet, electromagnet, solenoid, magnetic needle; lodestone, magnetite

VERBS **4 attract, pull, draw,** drag, tug; **magnetize,** be magnetic; **lure**

ADJS **5** attracting, drawing, pulling, dragging, tugging; **attractive, magnetic;** charismatic; **alluring**

ADVS **6** attractively; magnetically; charismatically

907 REPULSION

<*a thrusting away*>

NOUNS **1 repulsion, repelling;** mutual repulsion, polarization; disaffinity; ejection 908

2 repulse, rebuff; dismissal, cold shoulder, snub, spurning, brush-off, cut; kiss-off <nonformal>; turn-off <nonformal>; refusal; discharge 908.5

VERBS **3 repulse, repel, rebuff, turn back,** drive *or* push *or* thrust back; drive away, chase off *or* away; send off *or* away, **send packing,** dismiss; snub, cut, brush off, drop; kiss off <nonformal>; spurn, refuse; **ward off,** hold off, keep off, fend off, keep at arm's length; slap down <nonformal>; eject 908.13, discharge 908.19

ADJS **4 repulsive,** repellent, **repelling;** diamagnetic

ADVS **5** repulsively, repellently

908 EJECTION

NOUNS **1 ejection, expulsion, discharge,** extrusion, obtrusion, **ousting, ouster,** removal, kicking *or* booting *or* chucking out <all nonformal>; the boot *and* the bounce *and* the bum's rush *and* the old heave-ho <all nonformal>; defenestration; **rejection** 372; jettison

2 eviction, ousting, dispossession; **ouster**

3 depopulation; devastation, desolation

4 banishment, relegation, exclusion 772; **excommunication; disbarment,** unfrocking, defrocking; **expatriation, exile;** ostracism, ostracization, thumbs-down, blackballing, silent treatment, cold shoulder; **deportation, extradition;** rustication; degradation, **demotion** 447, stripping; deprivation

5 dismissal, discharge; firing *and* canning <both nonformal>, **cashiering,** drumming out, dishonorable discharge; **layoff,** removal, furloughing; suspension; **retirement;** the bounce; the boot *and* the gate *and* the ax <all nonformal>; walking papers <nonformal>; pink slip <nonformal>; deposal 447

6 evacuation, voidance, voiding; **elimination,** removal; **clearance, clearing;** unfouling, freeing; scouring *or* cleaning out, unclogging; exhausting, venting, depletion; **unloading,** off-loading; draining, drainage; **excretion,** defecation 12.2,4

7 disgorgement, expulsion, ejaculation, **discharge,** emission; **eruption, blowout, outburst;** outpour

8 vomiting, disgorgement, regurgitation, emesis, the heaves <nonformal>; **retching,** heaving, gagging; nausea; **vomit,** vomitus, puke *and* barf <both nonformal>

9 belch, burp <nonformal>, belching, wind, gas, eructation; **hiccup**

10 fart <nonformal>, **flatulence** *or* flatulency, flatus, gas, wind

11 ejector, expeller; **ouster; bouncer** *and* chucker <both nonformal>

12 dischargee, expellee; ejectee; evictee

VERBS **13 eject, expel, discharge,** extrude, obtrude, exclude, **reject,** cast, remove; **oust, bounce** <nonformal>, **put out, turn out; throw out,** cast out, chuck out, toss out, heave out; kick *or* boot out <nonformal>; give the bum's rush *or* give the old heave-ho *or* throw out on one's ear <all nonformal>; defenestrate; jettison, throw overboard, discard, junk, throw away; **be rid of,** see the last of

14 drive out, run out, chase out, chase away, run off, **rout out;** drum out, read out; freeze out <nonformal>, send packing;

hunt out; smoke out, drive into the open

15 evict, oust, dislodge, dispossess, put out, turn out, turn out of house and home, throw into the street

16 depopulate; devastate, desolate

17 banish, expel, cast out, relegate, ostracize, exclude, blackball, spurn, turn thumbs down on, snub, cut, give the cold shoulder, give the silent treatment; excommunicate; exile, expatriate, deport, extradite; outlaw, ban, proscribe; rusticate

18 dismiss, send off or away, turn off or away, bundle off, hustle out, send packing, send about one's business; bow out, show the door; give the gate or the air <nonformal>

19 dismiss, discharge, expel, cashier, drum out, separate involuntarily, lay off, suspend, furlough, turn off, turn out, release, displace, strike off the rolls, give the pink slip ; unfrock, defrock; depose, disbar 447.4; bust <nonformal>; retire; pension off, superannuate, put out to pasture

20 <nonformal terms> fire, can, sack, bump, bounce, give one the sack or the ax or the boot or the gate or the air or one's walking papers

21 do away with, exterminate, annihilate; purge, liquidate; shake off, dispel; throw off, cast off; eliminate, get rid of 772.5; throw away 390.7

22 evacuate, void; eliminate, remove; empty, empty out, deplete, exhaust, vent, drain; clear, purge, unclog, flush out, blow, blow out, make a clean sweep, clear the decks; defecate 12.13

23 unload, unpack, unburden, discharge, dump

24 let out, give vent to, emit, exhaust, evacuate, let go; exhale, expire, breathe out, blow, puff; smoke, reek; open the floodgates

25 disgorge, debouch, discharge, exhaust, expel, ejaculate, send out or forth; erupt, eruct, blow

out; pour out or forth, pour, decant; spew, squirt, spurt

26 vomit, spew, disgorge, regurgitate, throw up, bring up, be sick; retch, heave, gag; be seasick

27 <nonformal terms> puke, upchuck, oops, toss one's cookies, barf

28 belch, burp <nonformal>, eruct, eructate; hiccup

29 fart <nonformal>, cut a fart <nonformal>, let or break wind

ADJS 30 ejective, expulsive, ejaculative, emissive, extrusive; vomitory; eructative; flatulent; rejected 372.3, rejective

909 OVERRUNNING

NOUNS 1 overrunning, overpassing; overrun, overpass; overspreading, overgrowth; inundation, overwhelming; seizure, taking 480; overflowing 238.6; surplus, excess 992

2 infestation; invasion, swarming, teeming, ravage, plague; overrunning, overswarming, overspreading

3 overstepping, transgression, trespass, intrusion, encroachment, infraction, infringement

VERBS 4 overrun, overgo, overpass, overreach, go beyond; overshoot, overshoot the mark; superabound, exceed, overdo 992.10

5 overspread, spread over; overgrow, run riot, swarm over, teem over

6 infest, beset, swarm, ravage; overrun, overswarm, overspread; crawl with, swarm with

7 run over, overrun; ride over, override, run down, ride down; trample, step on, walk on or over, trample underfoot, ride roughshod over; inundate, whelm, overwhelm

8 pass, go or pass by, get ahead of; bypass; pass over, cross, ford; step over

9 overstep, transgress, trespass, intrude, go too far, encroach, infringe, invade, advance upon; usurp

ADJS **10 overrun, overspread,**
overpassed, overgrown; inundated, overwhelmed

11 infested, teeming; lousy, pe-
diculous; wormy, grubby

910 SHORTCOMING
<motion or action short of>

NOUNS **1 shortcoming,** falling
short, **shortfall; shortage,** short
measure, deficit; **inadequacy**
794.1; insufficiency 991; **default,**
defalcation; **arrears; inferiority**
250; **failure** 410

VERBS **2 fall short, run short,** stop
short, not reach; not measure up,
not hack it *and* not make the
grade *and* not make the cut <all
nonformal>, not make it, not
make out; **be found wanting,** not
fill the bill, not suffice; decline,
lag, lose ground, slump, collapse,
fall away, run out of gas *or* steam;
lose out, fail 410.9

3 fall through, fall down, **fall to
the ground,** fall flat, **collapse,**
break down; get bogged down,
get mired down, get hung up,
come to nothing, go up in smoke;
fizzle *or* peter *or* poop out <non-
formal>; fall *or* drop by the wayside

4 miss, miscarry, go amiss, go
astray, **miss the mark,** miss by a
mile <nonformal>; **miss out,**
miss the boat

ADJS **5 short of,** short, not all *or*
what it is cracked up to be; **deficient, inadequate** 794.4; **insufficient** 991.9; **inferior** 250.6; **lacking**

ADVS **6 behind, in arrears** *or* arrear

7 amiss, astray, beside the mark,
below the mark, in vain, vainly,
fruitlessly

911 ELEVATION
<act of raising>

NOUNS **1 elevation, raising, lifting; rearing,** escalation, **erection;** upraising, **uplifting; uplift,**
upheaval, upthrust; **exaltation;**
apotheosis, deification; beatification, canonization; enshrinement, assumption

2 lift, boost *and* **hike** <both non-
formal>, heave

3 lifter, erector; crane, derrick;
jack; hoist, hydraulic lift; forklift

4 elevator; escalator, moving stairway

VERBS **5 elevate, raise, rear,** esca-
late, up, boost *and* hike <both
nonformal>; **erect, heighten,
lift, hoist,** heist <nonformal>,
heft, heave; **upraise, uplift,** uphold; upheave, upthrow, upcast

6 exalt, elevate; deify, apotheosize;
beatify, canonize; enshrine; put
on a pedestal

7 give a lift, give a boost, give a
leg up <nonformal>, **help up**

8 pick up, take up, pluck up,
gather up; draw up, fish up, haul
up, drag up; dredge, dredge up

ADJS **9 raised, lifted, elevated;** upraised, **uplifted,** upcast; **reared,**
upreared; **exalted, lofty;** deified,
apotheosized; canonized, sainted,
beatified; enshrined, sublime

10 elevating, lifting; **uplifting;**
erectile

912 DEPRESSION
<act of lowering>

NOUNS **1 depression, lowering;
sinking;** ducking, pushing *or*
thrusting under, down-thrusting,
detrusion, pushing *or* pulling *or*
hauling down; diminution; debasement, degradation

2 downthrow, downcast; **overthrow,** overturn 205.2; **precipitation,** fall, downfall

3 crouch, stoop, bend, squat;
bow, genuflection, kneeling, kow-
towing, salaam, obeisance,
curtsy; prostration, supination;
crawling, groveling

VERBS **4 depress, lower,** debase,
de-escalate, **sink,** bring low, reduce; take down a peg <nonfor-
mal>; thrust *or* press *or* push
down, detrude

5 fell, drop, bring down, take
down a peg, lay low; **raze,** raze
to the ground; **level; cut down,**
chop down, mow down; **knock
down,** send headlong, **floor,** deck
and lay out <both nonformal>,

bowl down *or* **over** <nonformal>; **trip up, topple, tumble; prostrate,** supinate; **throw,** throw *or* fling *or* cast down, **precipitate**

6 **overthrow,** overturn 205.6; depose 447.4

7 **drop, let go of,** let drop *or* fall

8 **crouch, duck,** cringe, **cower; stoop, bend, stoop down, squat,** squat down, hunker down <nonformal>; hunch down, hunch over

9 **bow, bend, kneel,** genuflect, **curtsy,** make a reverence *or* an obeisance, salaam; **kowtow,** prostrate oneself; crawl, grovel

10 **sit down,** seat oneself

11 **lie down, recline** 201.5; prostrate, supinate; prostrate oneself; hit the dirt <nonformal>

ADJS 12 **depressed, lowered,** debased, reduced, **fallen;** sunk, **sunken,** submerged; downcast, downthrown; prostrated, prostrate 201.8; low, at a low ebb

913 CIRCUITOUSNESS

NOUNS 1 **circuitousness,** circuity; **roundaboutness,** indirection, meandering, **deviation** 164; deviousness, **digression,** circumlocution 538.5; **circling, wheeling,** circulation, rounding, **orbiting; spiraling;** circumambulation, circumflexion, circumnavigation; convolution 281

2 **circuit, round,** revolution, **circle,** full circle, **cycle,** orbit, ambit; **beat,** rounds, **walk,** tour, turn, lap

3 **detour, bypass, roundabout way,** circuit, the long way around, digression, deviation

VERBS 4 **go roundabout,** meander, deviate, take the long way around, twist and turn; **detour,** make a detour, **go around,** go out of one's way, **bypass;** deviate 164.3; digress 538.9; **talk in circles;** equivocate 935.9, shillyshally

5 **circle, circuit,** move in a circle, **circulate; go round** *or* **around;** come full circle, return to the

starting point; cycle; go around in circles, chase one's tail; **compass,** encompass, encircle, surround; skirt, flank; circumambulate; circumnavigate, girdle

6 **turn, go around, round,** turn *or* round a corner

ADJS 7 **circuitous, roundabout, out-of-the-way, devious, oblique, indirect,** meandering; **deviating,** digressive, discursive; evasive 368.15; vacillating 362.10; **circular** 280.11, **round;** spiral, helical

8 circumambient, circumambulatory

ADVS 9 **circuitously, deviously, obliquely, indirectly, roundabout,** in a roundabout way, by a side door

914 ROTATION

NOUNS 1 **rotation, revolution,** roll, **gyration, spin,** circulation; **turning, whirling,** swirling, **spinning,** wheeling, reeling; **spiraling;** swiveling, pivoting, swinging; **rolling,** trolling, bowling

2 **whirl,** wheel, reel, **spin, turn,** round; spiral, helix; pirouette; **swirl,** twirl, **eddy;** vortex, **whirlpool,** maelstrom; rat race; **whirlwind** 318.14

3 revolutions, revs <nonformal>

4 **rotator, rotor; roller;** whirler, whirligig, **top; merry-go-round,** carousel; **wheel,** disk

5 **axle, axis; pivot, swivel, spindle,** arbor; fulcrum 900.2; pin, pintle; **hub,** nave; mandrel; gimbal; **hinge**

6 axle box, journal

7 **bearing,** ball bearing, journal bearing, roller bearing, thrust bearing, bushing

8 <science of rotation> trochilics, gyrostatics

VERBS 9 **rotate, revolve, spin, turn,** turn round *or* around **spiral, gyrate;** circle, circulate; **swivel, pivot, wheel,** swing; pirouette, turn a pirouette

10 **roll,** trundle, troll, **bowl;** roll up, **furl**

11 whirl, whirligig, twirl, **wheel, reel, spin;** swirl, eddy

12 <move around in confusion> **seethe, mill,** mill around *or* about, stir, roil, moil, be turbulent

13 <roll about in> **wallow, welter,** grovel, roll, flounder, tumble

ADJS **14 rotating, revolving, turning,** gyrating; **whirling, swirling,** twirling, **spinning,** wheeling, **reeling; rolling,** trolling, bowling

15 rotary, rotational, rotatory; vertiginous; spiral, helical, gyrational, gyroscopic; whirligig; cyclonic, tornadic

ADVS **16 round, around,** round about, **in a circle; round and round,** in circles; in a whirl, in a spin; head over heels; clockwise, counterclockwise, anticlockwise

915 OSCILLATION
<motion to and fro>

NOUNS **1 oscillation, vibration,** vibrancy; libration, nutation; **fluctuation,** vacillation, wavering 362.2; **frequency,** frequency band *or* spectrum; resonance, resonant *or* resonance frequency; **periodicity** 849.2

2 waving, wave motion, **undulation,** undulancy; **brandishing, flourishing,** flaunting, shaking; brandish, flaunt, flourish; wave 238.14

3 pulsation, pulse, beat, throb; beating, throbbing; staccato, drumming 55.1; **rhythm, tempo** 709.24; **palpitation,** flutter, arrhythmia, pitter-patter, pit-a-pat; fibrillation; **heartbeat**

4 wave, wave motion, **ray; light** 1024; **radio wave** 1033.11; **sound wave** 50.1; seismic wave, **shock wave; tidal wave,** tsunami; amplitude, crest, trough; **surf,** roller, curler, comber, whitecap; wavelength; frequency, frequency band *or* spectrum; resonance, resonant *or* resonance frequency; period

5 alternation, reciprocation; coming and going, to-and-fro, back-and-forth, ebb and flow, ups and downs; sine wave; **seesawing,** teetering, tottering, **teeter-tottering**

6 swing, swinging, **sway,** swag; **rock, lurch, roll, reel,** careen; wag, waggle; wave, waver

7 seismicity, seismism; seismology

8 <instruments> oscilloscope, oscillograph, oscillometer

9 oscillator, vibrator; pendulum, pendulum wheel; metronome; swing; seesaw, teeter-totter, teeterboard; rocker, rocking chair

VERBS **10 oscillate, vibrate,** librate, nutate; pendulate; **fluctuate,** vacillate, waver, wave; resonate; **swing, sway,** swag, dangle; **reel, rock, lurch, roll,** careen, toss, pitch; **wag,** waggle; **wobble,** wamble; **bob,** bobble

11 wave, undulate; brandish, flourish, flaunt, shake, swing, wield; **flap, flutter;** wag, wigwag

12 pulsate, pulse, beat, throb; palpitate, go pit-a-pat; beat time, beat out; drum 55.4

13 alternate, reciprocate, swing, **go to and fro, come and go,** ebb and flow, wax and wane, back and fill; **seesaw,** teeter, **teeter-totter;** zigzag

14 <move up and down> pump, shake, bounce

ADJS **15 oscillating,** oscillatory; **vibrating,** vibratory, harmonic; libratory; nutational; **periodic,** pendular, pendulous; **fluctuating,** fluctuant; wavering; vacillating; resonant

16 waving, undulating, undulatory, undulant

17 swinging, swaying, dangling, **reeling, rocking, lurching,** careening, **rolling,** tossing, pitching

18 pulsating, pulsing, beating, throbbing, palpitating, pit-a-pat, staccato; rhythmic 709.28

19 alternate, reciprocal; sinewave; **back-and-forth, to-and-fro,** up-and-down, seesaw

20 seismatical, seismological, seismographic

ADVS **21 to and fro, back and forth,** backward and forward, **in and out, up and down,** seesaw,

from side to side, off and on,
round and round

916 AGITATION
<irregular motion>

NOUNS **1 agitation, perturbation;
frenzy, excitement** 105; **trepida-
tion** 127.5, **fidgets** *and* **jitters** *and*
ants in the pants <all nonfor-
mal>, antsiness *and* jitteriness
<both nonformal>, jumpiness,
nervousness, twitter, upset; **unrest, malaise, unease,** restlessness; fever, feverishness, febrility;
disquiet, disquietude, inquietude, discomposure; **stir, churn,
ferment,** foment; seething,
ebullition, boiling; turbidity,
fume, **disturbance, commotion,**
moil, **turmoil, turbulence** 671.2,
swirl, tumult, hubbub, fuss, row,
to-do, bluster, fluster, flurry, hoo-
ha *and* flap <both nonformal>,
brouhaha, hurly-burly; maelstrom; **disorder** 809

2 shaking, quaking, palsy, **quivering, quavering, shivering,
trembling,** tremulousness, **shuddering, vibration;** jerkiness, fits
and starts, spasms; the shakes
and the shivers *and* the cold
shivers <all nonformal>, chattering

3 shake, quake, quiver, quaver,
falter, **tremor, tremble, shiver,
shudder,** twitter, dither; **wobble;
shock, jolt,** jar, jostle; **bounce,**
bump; **jerk, twitch,** tic, grimace,
rictus

4 flutter, flitter, **flicker, waver,**
dance; **sputter, splutter; palpitation,** throb, pit-a-pat, pitter-patter

5 twitching, jerking; fidgets,
fidgetiness

6 spasm, convulsion, cramp, **paroxysm,** throes; **orgasm,** sexual
climax; **seizure, fit,** ictus; epilepsy; apoplexy

7 wiggle, wriggle; wag, waggle;
writhe, **squirm**

8 flounder, flounce, stagger, totter,
stumble, falter; wallow, welter;
roll, rock, reel, lurch, careen,
swing, sway; toss, tumble,
pitch, plunge

9 <instruments> agitator, shaker

VERBS **10 agitate, shake, disturb,
perturb,** perturbate, **disquiet,
discompose, upset, trouble, unsettle, stir,** swirl, flurry, flutter,
fret, ruffle, rumple, ripple, ferment, convulse; **churn,** whip,
whisk, beat, paddle; **excite**
105.11; **stir up,** cause a stir;
disarrange 810.2

**11 shake, quake, vibrate; trem-
ble, quiver, quaver, shudder,
shiver,** chatter; shake in one's
boots *or* shoes, quake *or* shake *or*
tremble like a leaf, have the jitters
or the shakes <nonformal>, have
ants in one's pants <nonformal>;
shock, jolt, jar, jostle, hustle,
jounce, **bounce**

12 flutter, flitter, **flicker,** gutter, **waver,** dance; **sputter, splutter;
flap,** beat, slat; **palpitate,** throb,
go pit-a-pat

13 twitch, jerk; itch; **jig, jiggle;
fidget,** have the fidgets

**14 wiggle, wriggle; writhe,
squirm;** have ants in one's
pants <nonformal>

15 flounder, flounce, **stagger,** totter, stumble, falter, blunder; **wallow, welter; roll, rock, reel,
lurch,** careen, career, **swing,
sway; toss, tumble,** thrash
about, **pitch, plunge,** toss and
turn; **seethe**

ADJS **16 agitated, disturbed, perturbed, disquieted, discomposed, troubled, upset, ruffled,**
flustered, unsettled; stirred up,
all worked up, all shook up <nonfor-
mal>; fidgety *and* jittery *and*
antsy <all nonformal>, jumpy,
nervous, restless, **uneasy,** unquiet, unpeaceful; **turbulent**

17 shaking, vibrating, chattering;
**quivering, quavering, quaking,
shivering, shuddering, trembling, tremulous,** palsied;
shaky, quivery, trembly; wobbly

**18 fluttering, flickering, waver-
ing,** guttering, dancing; sputtering, spluttering, sputtery; fluttery,
flickery, unsteady, desultory

19 jerky, twitchy *or* twitchety, jerking, **twitching, fidgety, jumpy;**

spastic, spasmodic, orgasmic, convulsive

20 **jolting, joggling,** jouncy, **bouncy, bumpy,** choppy, rough; **jarring,** bone-bruising

21 **wriggly,** wriggling, creepy-crawly <nonformal>; **wiggly,** wiggling; squirmy, squirming; writhy, writhing, antsy <nonformal>

ADVS 22 **agitatedly, restlessly,** uneasily, unpeacefully, nervously, feverishly; **excitedly**

23 **shakily,** quiveringly, **tremblingly,** tremulously; waveringly, unsteadily, desultorily; **jerkily,** spasmodically, fitfully, by fits and starts

917 SPECTATOR

NOUNS 1 **spectator, observer; looker, onlooker, watcher,** gaper, goggler, **viewer,** beholder, perceiver; **witness, eyewitness; bystander,** passerby; sidewalk superintendent; kibitzer; **viewer**

2 **attender** 221.5, attendee; theatergoer; **audience** 48.6, house, crowd, gate, fans

3 **sightseer, tourist,** rubberneck *or* **rubbernecker** <nonformal>

4 **sight-seeing,** rubbernecking <nonformal>; **tour**

VERBS 5 **witness, see** 27.12, look on, eye, **ogle, gape;** take in, **look at, watch;** attend 221.8

6 **sight-see,** take in the sights; **rubberneck** <nonformal>; go on a tour

ADJS 7 onlooking; sight-seeing, rubberneck <nonformal>

918 INTELLECT
<mental faculty>

NOUNS 1 **intellect, mind;** mental *or* intellectual faculty, **reason, rationality,** power of reason, ratio, **intelligence,** mentality, mental capacity, **understanding,** reasoning, intellection; **brain, brains,** brainpower, smarts *and* gray matter <both nonformal>

2 **wits, senses, faculties,** parts, capacities, intellectual gifts *or* talents; consciousness 927.2

3 **inmost mind,** inner recesses of the mind; subconscious, subconscious mind

4 **psyche, spirit, soul, heart, mind,** anima; shade, shadow, manes; spiritual being, inner man; **ego,** the self

5 **life principle,** vital principle, **vital force;** essence *or* substance of life; divine spark

6 **brain** 2.13, seat *or* organ of thought; sensorium; encephalon; gray matter; noodle *or* noggin *or* bean <all nonformal>

ADJS 7 **mental, intellectual, rational, reasoning, thinking,** noetic, conceptual; intelligent 919.12; psychic, psychical, psychological; spiritual; cerebral

919 INTELLIGENCE, WISDOM
<mental capacity>

NOUNS 1 **intelligence, understanding, comprehension,** apprehension, intellectual grasp, intellectual power, brainpower; ideation, conception; rationality, reasoning *or* deductive power, ratiocination; **sense, wit,** natural *or* native wit; **intellect** 918; **intellectuality;** capacity, mental capacity, **mentality,** reach *or* compass *or* scope of mind

2 **smartness, braininess,** smarts *and* savvy <both nonformal>, **brightness, brilliance, cleverness,** mental alertness, **sharpness, keenness,** acuity; **mental ability *or* capability,** gifts, **talent, flair, genius;** quickness, adroitness, dexterity; ready wit, quick wit, sprightly wit

3 **shrewdness, artfulness, cunning,** canniness, **craft, craftiness,** wiliness, guilefulness, slickness <nonformal>, **slyness,** animal cunning, low cunning; **subtlety;** insinuation, insidiousness, deviousness

4 **sagacity,** sagaciousness, **astuteness, acumen; foresight,** providence; **farsightedness; discernment, insight,** acuteness, acuity; perspicacity, perspicaciousness,

perspicuity, perspicuousness; incisiveness, trenchancy, cogency;
percipience *or* percipiency, **perception**

5 **wisdom,** wiseness, sageness, sa-
pience; erudition 927.5; **profundity,** profoundness, depth; **conventional wisdom,** received wisdom

6 **sensibleness, reasonableness,**
reason, rationality, sanity, **soundness; practicality; sense,** good
or common sense, **horse sense**
<nonformal>; **levelheadedness,**
balance, coolheadedness, coolness

7 **judiciousness, judgment,** cool
judgment, soundness of judgment; **prudence,** providence,
policy, polity; circumspection,
circumspectness, reflectiveness,
thoughtfulness; discretion, discreetness; **discrimination**

8 **genius,** spirit, soul; demon,
daemon; **inspiration,** afflatus;
fire of genius; **creativity**

9 <intelligent being> **intelligence,
intellect,** head, brain, mentality,
consciousness

VERBS 10 **have all one's wits
about one,** have all one's marbles
<nonformal>, have one's head
screwed on right <nonformal>;
have method in one's madness;
use one's head, get *or* keep one's
wits about one; know what's what

11 be brilliant, **scintillate,** sparkle,
coruscate

ADJS 12 **intelligent;** conceptual,
conceptive; **knowing, understanding, reasonable, rational,
sensible, bright;** strong-minded

13 **clear-witted,** clearheaded, clear-
sighted; **wide-awake, alert,** on
the ball <nonformal>

14 **smart, brainy** <nonformal>,
bright, brilliant, scintillating;
clever, apt, **gifted,** talented;
sharp, keen; **quick,** adroit, dexterous; **sharp-witted, quick-
witted,** quick-thinking, nimble-
witted, quick on the trigger *or* uptake <nonformal>; sharp as a
tack <nonformal>; not born yesterday <nonformal>

15 **shrewd, artful, cunning, knowing, crafty, wily,** guileful, canny,
slick, sly, smart as a fox, crazy like
a fox <nonformal>; **subtle;** insidious, devious, Byzantine, calculating

16 **sagacious, astute; understanding, discerning,** penetrating, incisive, acute, trenchant, cogent,
piercing; **foresighted,** provident;
farsighted, farseeing; **perspicacious,** perspicuous; **perceptive,
percipient**

17 **wise, sage,** sapient, **knowing;
learned** 927.21; **profound,** deep;
wise as an owl; wise beyond one's
years

18 **sensible, reasonable, rational,
logical; practical,** pragmatic;
philosophical; **levelheaded,**
coolheaded, **sound, sane,** sober,
sober-minded

19 **judicious,** judgmatic, **prudent,**
politic, provident, **considerate,**
circumspect, **thoughtful,** reflective; **discreet;** discriminating;
well-advised, enlightened

ADVS 20 **intelligently, under-
standingly,** knowingly; **reasonably,** rationally; **smartly, cleverly; shrewdly,** cunningly;
wisely, sagaciously, astutely; **judiciously, prudently,** discreetly,
circumspectly

920 WISE PERSON

NOUNS 1 **wise man, wise woman,
sage; master, mistress,** authority, mastermind, oracle; **philosopher,** lover of wisdom; rabbi;
doctor; mahatma, guru, rishi; elder statesman; illuminate; seer;
mentor; **intellect,** man of intellect; mandarin, **intellectual** 928;
savant, **scholar** 928.3

2 Solomon, Socrates, Plato, Mentor, Confucius

3 the wise, the intelligent, the sensible

4 Seven Wise Men of Greece,
Seven Sages, Seven Wise Mas-
ters

5 Magi, Three Wise Men

6 **wiseacre,** wisenheimer <non-
formal>, wise guy, smart ass

<nonformal>; wise man of
Gotham, wise man of Chelm

921 UNINTELLIGENCE

NOUNS **1 unintelligence,** unwiseness, intellectual *or* mental weakness; **senselessness, witlessness, mindlessness,** slackwitted-
ness, slackmindedness; **irrationality; ignorance** 929; **foolishness** 922; incapacity, ineptitude

2 unperceptiveness, imperceptiveness, impercipience *or* imper-
cipiency, **incomprehension;
blindness; unawareness,** unconsciousness; **shortsightedness**

3 stupidity, stupidness, **dumbness** <nonformal>, **doltishness,**
cloddishness, **asininity;** oafishness, loutishness; **density,** denseness, opacity; grossness, crassness, boorishness; **dullness, obtuseness,** bovinity, cowishness,
slowness, lethargy, stolidity; **dim-
wittedness, dull-wittedness,**
slow-wittedness; **thick-
wittedness;** wrongheadedness

4 <nonformal terms> **block-
headedness,** klutziness, goofiness, chuckleheadedness, meat-
headedness, fatheadedness,
boneheadedness, knuckleheaded-
ness

5 muddleheadedness, addlehead-
edness

6 empty-headedness, airheaded-
ness *and* bubbleheadedness
<both nonformal>; **vacuity,** vac-
uousness, blankness, hollowness,
inanity, vapidity, jejunity

**7 superficiality, shallowness,
unprofundity,** lack of depth;
shallow-mindedness; **frivolousness,** flightiness, volatility, dizziness <nonformal>

8 feeblemindedness, weak-
mindedness; mushiness <nonfor-
mal>

9 mental deficiency, mental retardation, amentia, mental defectiveness; **arrested development,** retardation, backwardness; **simplemindedness,** simpleness; **idiocy, imbecility,** half-

wittedness; cretinism; Down's
syndrome; insanity 925

10 senility, caducity, senectitude,
decline; **childishness, second
childhood, dotage, dotardism;**
anility; senile dementia, Alzhei-
mer's disease

11 puerility, immaturity, **childishness; infantilism**

VERBS **12 be stupid,** not have all
one's marbles; not see an inch beyond one's nose, not have enough
sense to come in out of the rain;
lose one's mind *or* marbles

ADJS **13 unintelligent, unthinking, unreasoning, irrational,**
unwise, **not bright; senseless,**
insensate; **mindless, witless,
reasonless, brainless;** foolish
922.8; **ignorant** 929.12

14 undiscerning, unperceptive,
impercipient, insensible, uncomprehending; **shortsighted,** myopic, nearsighted; **blind,** blind as a
bat; blinded, blindfolded

15 stupid, dumb, dullard, **doltish,**
blockish, cloddish, lumpish,
oafish, asinine, lamebrained;
dense, thick <nonformal>,
opaque; bovine, cowish; un-
teachable, ineducable

16 dull, dopey <nonformal>, **obtuse,** dim, slow, **slow-witted,
dim-witted, dull-witted, thickwitted,** thick-headed

17 <nonformal terms> **block-
headed,** woodenheaded, chow-
derheaded, chuckleheaded,
lunkheaded, muttonheaded,
meatheaded, fatheaded; dead
from the neck up; featherheaded,
airheaded, bubbleheaded, out to
lunch, not playing with a full
deck

18 muddleheaded, mixed-up,
muddled, addled, addleheaded,
addlepated, addlebrained; dizzy
<nonformal>, muzzy

19 empty-headed; vacuous, vacant, inane, vapid, jejune, airheaded *and* bubbleheaded <both
nonformal>; **rattlebrained;** scatterbrained 984.16

**20 superficial, shallow, unpro-
found;** shallow-witted; **frivolous,**

dizzy <nonformal>, flighty, light, frothy, fluffy, **featherbrained, birdbrained**

21 feebleminded, weak-minded, soft in the head

22 mentally deficient, mentally defective, mentally handicapped, retarded, **mentally retarded,** backward, arrested, subnormal, not right in the head, **not all there** <nonformal>; **simpleminded,** simple; **half-witted,** half-baked <nonformal>; **idiotic, moronic, imbecile,** imbecilic, cretinous; crackbrained, cracked, crazy; babbling, driveling, slobbering, drooling, blithering

23 senile, decrepit, doddering, doddery; **childish,** childlike, in one's second childhood, **doting**

24 puerile, immature, **childish; infantile; babyish**

ADVS **25 unintelligently, stupidly;** foolishly

922 FOOLISHNESS

NOUNS **1 foolishness, folly,** foolheadedness, **stupidity, asininity; inanity, fatuity,** fatuousness; ineptitude; **silliness; frivolousness,** frivolity, giddiness; triviality, nugacity, desipience; **nonsense,** tomfoolery, poppycock; **senselessness, insensateness, witlessness, thoughtlessness; idiocy, imbecility; craziness, madness,** lunacy, **insanity; eccentricity;** screwiness and nuttiness and wackiness and goofiness and daffiness and battiness and sappiness <all nonformal>; **clownishness, buffoonery,** clowning

2 unwiseness, unwisdom, **injudiciousness, imprudence; indiscretion,** thoughtlessness, lack of sensitivity; **unreasonableness, unsoundness, unsensibleness,** senselessness, **irrationality, unreason,** inadvisability; gullibility; inexpedience 995; unintelligence 921

3 absurdity, absurdness, **ridiculousness;** ludicrousness 488.1; **nonsense,** nonsensicality, stuff and nonsense, horseshit and bullshit <both nonformal>; **preposterousness, outrageousness**

4 <foolish act> **folly, stupidity,** act of folly, absurdity, dumb thing to do <nonformal>; **imprudence, indiscretion;** blunder 974.5

5 stultification; infatuation; trivialization

VERBS **6 be foolish; act** or **play the fool; fool,** tomfool <nonformal>, **trifle; fool** or **horse around** <nonformal>, clown around); **make a fool of oneself,** invite ridicule, play the buffoon; **lose one's head, take leave of one's senses,** go haywire

7 stultify, infatuate, turn's one's head, befool; gull, dupe; **make a fool of,** make a monkey of and play for a sucker and put on <all nonformal>

ADJS **8 foolish, stupid, dumb** <nonformal>, **asinine;** buffoonish; **silly,** apish, dizzy <nonformal>; **fatuous,** fatuitous, inept, **inane, senseless, witless, thoughtless,** insensate, brainless; **idiotic,** moronic, imbecile, imbecilic; **crazy, mad,** daft, **insane;** infatuated, besotted, credulous, gulled, beguiled, doting; sentimental, maudlin; dazed

9 <nonformal terms> **screwy, nutty,** cockeyed, wacky, goofy, daffy, loony, batty, sappy, kooky, flaky, damn-fool, out of it, out to lunch, dorky, dippy, dizzy, loony, dopey, loopy

10 unwise, injudicious, **imprudent,** unpolitic, impolitic, **counterproductive;** indiscreet; unthinking, unreflecting, unreflective; **unreasonable, unsound, unsensible,** senseless, insensate, reasonless, **irrational,** reckless, inadvisable; inexpedient 995.5; **ill-advised, ill-considered,** illjudged, ill-devised, on the wrong track, unconsidered; shortsighted, myopic; self-defeating

11 absurd, nonsensical, insensate, ridiculous, laughable, ludicrous 488.4; **foolish, crazy;** preposterous, cockamamie <nonformal>, fantastic, wild, weird, **outrageous,** incredible, extravagant, **bizarre**

12 foolable, gullible; naive, artless, guileless, impressionable; malleable

ADVS **13 foolishly, stupidly,** idiotically; **unwisely,** injudiciously, imprudently, indiscreetly; myopically, blindly, senselessly, unreasonably, thoughtlessly, witlessly, insensately, unthinkingly; absurdly, ridiculously

923 FOOL

NOUNS **1 fool, damn fool,** perfect fool; **ass,** jackass, stupid ass; zany, **clown, buffoon;** figure of fun; **lunatic** 925.15; **ignoramus** 929.8

2 stupid person, dolt, dunce, clod, **dullard,** yahoo, thickwit, **dope, nitwit,** dimwit, half-wit, lamebrain

3 <nonformal terms> **chump, boob,** booby, sap, klutz, dingbat, dingdong, ding-a-ling, **ninny, nincompoop,** jerk, asshole, goof, schlemiel, gonzo, dumbo, nerd, twerp, yo-yo

4 <nonformal terms> **blockhead, airhead,** bubblehead, dum-dum, dumbo, dumb cluck, dumbbell, dumb bunny, bonehead, jughead, numskull, lunkhead, chucklehead, knucklehead, chowderhead, noodlehead, pinhead, peabrain, fathead, blubberhead, muddlehead, addlebrain, puddinghead, mushhead, dunderhead

5 oaf, lout, boor, **gawk, lummox,** yokel, rube, hick, hayseed, bumpkin, clod, clodhopper

6 silly

7 scatterbrain, rattlebrain, rattlehead, rattlepate, **harebrain,** featherbrain, **flibbertigibbet**

8 idiot; imbecile, moron, half-wit, natural-born fool, mental defective, defective; **simpleton**

9 dotard, senile; fogy, **old fogy,** fuddy-duddy, old fart

924 SANITY

NOUNS **1 sanity, saneness, soundness of mind,** right mind <nonformal>, senses, reason, **rationality,** reasonableness, lucidity, balance; **mental health;** mental hygiene; mental balance; a sound mind in a sound body; contact with reality; knowing right from wrong

VERBS **2 come to one's senses,** sober up, recover one's balance *or* equilibrium, get things into proportion; see in perspective; have all one's marbles <nonformal>

3 bring to one's senses, bring to reason

ADJS **4 sane, rational,** reasonable, sensible, **lucid,** wholesome, clearheaded, balanced, **sound,** of sound mind, right in the head, **in one's right mind,** in possession of one's faculties *or* senses, together *and* all there <both nonformal>; in touch with reality

925 INSANITY, MANIA

NOUNS **1 insanity, lunacy, madness, craziness, daftness,** abnormality; loss of contact with reality; dementia, mental sickness, **criminal insanity; mental illness, mental disease;** brain damage; **mania;** alienation, aberration, mental disturbance, **derangement,** distraction, disorientation, mental disorder, unbalance, mental instability, **unsoundness of mind; sick mind,** disturbed *or* troubled *or* clouded mind, disordered mind *or* reason; senselessness, witlessness, irrationality; possession

2 <nonformal terms> **nuttiness,** craziness, daffiness, battiness, screwiness, goofiness, wackiness, dottiness, balminess; bats in the belfry, a screw loose

3 psychosis, psychopathy, psychopathology, psychopathic condition; **neurosis**

4 schizophrenia, dementia praecox, mental dissociation

5 depression, melancholia, depressive psychosis

6 **rabies, hydrophobia,** lyssa, canine madness

7 **frenzy, furor,** fury, maniacal excitement, fever, **rage; seizure,** attack, acute episode, episode, **fit,** paroxysm, spasm, **convulsion; amok,** homicidal mania

8 **delirium,** deliriousness, brainstorm; incoherence, wandering, raving, ranting; exhaustion delirium or infection

9 delirium tremens

10 <nonformal terms> the DT's, the horrors, the shakes

11 **fanaticism, rabidness, overzealousness,** zealotry, bigotry; extremism, excessiveness

12 **mania, craze, infatuation, enthusiasm,** passion, fascination, rage, furor; manic psychosis; megalomania

13 **obsession,** prepossession, preoccupation, **hang-up** <nonformal>, **fixation,** tic, complex, fascination; **compulsion,** morbid drive, obsessive compulsion; **monomania,** ruling passion, fixed idea, one-track mind; **possession**

14 **insane asylum,** asylum, mental institution, mental home, bedlam; **bughouse** and nuthouse and **loonybin** and **booby hatch** and funny farm <all nonformal>; mental hospital, psychiatric hospital or ward

15 **lunatic, madman, madwoman,** non compos; demoniac; **maniac,** raving lunatic; homicidal maniac, psychopathic killer

16 <nonformal terms> **nut,** nutcase, loony, crazy, psycho, crackpot, screwball, weirdo, kook, flake, crackbrain, fruitcake, wacko, sicko

17 **psychotic,** psycho <nonformal>, mental case, **psychopath,** psychopathic case; psychopathic personality; paranoiac, paranoid; schizophrenic, schizoid; manic-depressive; megalomaniac

18 **fanatic,** infatuate, **bug** <nonformal>, **nut** <nonformal>, **buff** and **fan** <both nonformal>, freak <nonformal>, devotee, **zealot, enthusiast; monomaniac**

19 psychiatry, alienism

VERBS **20** **be insane, be out of one 's mind,** not be in one's right mind, not be right in the head, **not be all there** <nonformal>; have bats in the belfry and have a screw loose, not have all one's buttons or marbles <nonformal>, not play with a full deck <nonformal>; **wander, ramble; rave,** rage, **rant,** have a fit; run amok, go berserk

21 **go mad, take leave of one's senses,** lose one's mind or senses, **crack up,** go off one's head <nonformal>

22 <nonformal terms> **go crazy, go bats,** go nuts, go out of one's gourd or skull, go off one's nut or rocker, go off the track, go off the deep end, flip one's lid or wig, go ape, go bananas, blow one's mind, freak out, flip out, have a screw loose, have bats in one's belfry, have rocks in one's head, lose one's marbles

23 addle the wits, **affect one's mind, go to one's head**

24 **madden, craze, unbalance,** unhinge, **derange,** distract, frenzy, shatter, **drive insane** or mad or **crazy,** put or send out of one's mind, drive up the wall <nonformal>

25 **obsess, possess,** beset, infatuate, **preoccupy,** be uppermost in one's thoughts, have a thing about <nonformal>; **fixate; drive,** compel, impel

ADJS **26** **insane, mad,** mad as a hatter, mad as a march hare, **stark-staring mad,** maddened, **sick,** crazed, **lunatic,** moonstruck, **daft, non compos mentis,** non compos, **unsound,** of unsound mind, **demented, deranged,** deluded, disoriented, unhinged, **unbalanced,** unsettled, distraught, crackbrained, sick or soft in the head, not in one's right mind, **touched,** touched in the head, **out of one's mind,** out of one's senses *or* wits, bereft of reason, irrational, senseless, witless; hallucinated; manic; queer in the head, odd, strange, off

27 <nonformal terms> **crazy, nutty,** daffy, dotty, dippy, crazy as a coot, loony, goofy, wacky, flaky, kooky, potty, batty, ape, out to lunch, bats, nuts, nutty as a fruitcake, screwy, screwball, bananas, loopy, bughouse, cuckoo, freaked-out, off-the-wall, haywire, off one's nut *or* rocker, nobody home, psycho, cracked, not right in the head, tetched, off one's head, out of one's head, out of one's gourd *or* skull, not all there, not tightly wrapped, off the wall

28 **psychotic, psychopathic, psychoneurotic, mentally ill,** mentally sick; disturbed, neurotic; schizophrenic; depressive; manic; manic-depressive; paranoiac, **paranoid;** catatonic

29 **possessed, pixilated, bedeviled,** demonized, demonic, demonical

30 **rabid, maniac** *or* **maniacal,** raving mad, **frenzied, frantic,** frenetic; **mad, wild, furious, violent; beside oneself,** like one possessed; **raving, raging,** ranting; frothing *or* foaming at the mouth; **amok, berserk,** running wild

31 **delirious,** out of one's head <nonformal>, off; **giddy,** light-headed; **wandering, rambling, raving, ranting,** babbling, incoherent

32 **fanatic, fanatical, rabid; overzealous, overenthusiastic,** bigoted; **extreme,** extremist, extravagant, inordinate; **unreasonable, irrational; wild-eyed**

33 **obsessed, possessed,** prepossessed, **infatuated,** preoccupied, fixated, **hung up** <nonformal>, gripped

34 **obsessive,** obsessional; **obsessing, possessing, preoccupying,** gripping, holding; driving, impelling, **compulsive, compelling**

ADVS 35 madly, insanely, crazily; deliriously; fanatically, rabidly, etc

926 ECCENTRICITY

NOUNS 1 **eccentricity, idiosyncrasy, queerness, oddity, peculiarity,** strangeness, singularity, freakishness, quirkiness, crotchetiness, dottiness, crankiness; whimsicality; abnormality, anomaly, deviancy, divergence, aberration; **nonconformity,** unconventionality 867.2

2 **quirk, twist,** kink, crank, mannerism, **crotchet,** conceit, whim, bee in one's bonnet <nonformal>

3 **eccentric,** erratic, character; odd person 869.4; **nonconformist** 867.3, recluse 584.5

4 freak, crackpot, screwball, weirdo, kook, oddball, flake, odd fellow, crank, bird, wacko

ADJS 5 **eccentric, erratic,** idiosyncratic, **queer,** queer in the head, **odd, peculiar,** fey, singular, anomalous; unnatural, abnormal, divergent, deviative, deviant; unconventional 867.6; **crotchety,** quirky, dotty, whimsical, twisted; solitary, reclusive, antisocial

6 <nonformal terms> **kooky, goofy,** kinky, loopy, goofus, screwy, screwball, nutty, wacky, flaky, oddball, wacko, out to lunch, nobody home

927 KNOWLEDGE

NOUNS 1 **knowledge,** ken; **command,** reach; **acquaintance, familiarity,** intimacy; **information,** data, database, datum; **certainty, sure** *or* **certain knowledge** 969; **intelligence; experience, know-how, expertise**

2 **cognizance;** cognition, noesis; **recognition, realization; perception,** insight, illumination, dawning; **consciousness, awareness,** mindfulness, note, notice; altered state of consciousness *or* ASC

3 **understanding, comprehension, apprehension,** intellection, prehension; conception, conceptualization, ideation; **grasp,** mental grasp, grip, **command,** mastery; precognition, foreknowl-

edge 960.3, clairvoyance 689.8

4 learning, enlightenment, education, schooling, instruction, edification, illumination; sophistication; store of knowledge

5 scholarship, erudition, learnedness, reading, letters; **intellectuality,** intellectualism; **literacy; culture, literary culture, high culture,** book learning, booklore; **bookishness, pedantry;** bibliomania, bibliolatry, bibliophilism

6 profound knowledge, total command *or* mastery; specialized *or* special knowledge; expertise, proficiency 413.1; **encyclopedic knowledge,** polymathy, polyhistory, pansophy; **omniscience,** all-knowingness

7 slight knowledge 929.6

8 tree of knowledge

9 lore, body of knowledge, corpus, body of learning, store of knowledge; **canon;** bibliography; encyclopedia

10 science, art, study, discipline; field, field of inquiry, concern, province, domain, area, arena, sphere, branch *or* field of study, academic discipline; **technology, technics,** high technology, high-tech *or* hi-tech <nonformal>; social science, natural science; applied science, pure science, experimental science

11 scientist; technologist; savant, **scholar** 928.3; authority, expert, maven <nonformal>; intellectual

VERBS **12 know, perceive, apprehend,** recognize, discern; conceive, conceptualize; **realize, appreciate, understand, comprehend,** fathom; have, possess, **grasp,** seize, have hold of; have knowledge of, be informed, be apprised of, have a good command of, have information about, be acquainted with, be conversant with, be cognizant of, be conscious *or* aware of

13 know well, know full well, have a good *or* thorough knowledge of, be well-informed, **be up on** <nonformal>, be master of, be thoroughly grounded in, **have**

down pat *or* **cold** <both nonformal>, have at one's fingertips, **know by heart** *or* rote, **know like a book,** know like the back of one's hand, know backwards and forwards, **know inside out, know one's stuff** *and* know one's onions <both nonformal>, know a thing or two, know one's way around; be expert in; **know the ropes,** know all the ins and outs, know the score <nonformal>, know all the answers <nonformal>; know what's what

14 learn <acquire knowledge> 570.6,9–11

ADJS **15 knowing,** knowledgeable, informed; **cognizant, conscious, aware, sensible; mindful, comprehending,** apprehending; **perceptive,** insightful, percipient, perspicacious; **shrewd, sagacious, wise** 919.17; omniscient, all-knowing

16 cognizant of, aware of, conscious of, mindful of, sensible to *or* **of, appreciative of,** no stranger to; privy to, in the know <nonformal>, behind the scenes; **wise to** <nonformal>, hep to *and* on to <both nonformal>; streetwise; apprised of, informed of

17 <nonformal terms> **hep, hip, with it,** into, groovy; clued in, in the know, trendy

18 informed, enlightened, instructed, versed, educated, schooled, **taught;** posted, briefed, primed, trained; **up on,** abreast of, *au courant* <Fr>

19 versed in, informed in, up on, strong in, at home in, master of, proficient in, **familiar with,** at home with, **conversant with, acquainted with,** intimate with

20 well-informed, well-posted, **well-grounded, well-versed, well-read,** widely read

21 learned, erudite, educated, cultured, cultivated, lettered, civilized, **scholarly; profound,** deep, abstruse; **encyclopedic,** polymath

22 book-learned, literary, bookish, book-minded; book-loving, bibliophilic; **pedantic,** scholastic, inkhorn; **bluestocking**

23 **intellectual; highbrow** <nonformal>; elitist

24 **self-educated,** self-taught, autodidactic

25 **knowable,** cognizable, **understandable, comprehensible,** apprehensible, graspable, discernible, conceivable, perceptible, ascertainable, discoverable

26 **known, recognized,** ascertained, conceived, grasped, apprehended, perceived, discerned, **understood, comprehended,** realized; pat *and* **down pat** <both nonformal>

27 **well-known,** well-understood, well-recognized, **widely known,** commonly known; **familiar,** household, **common, current; proverbial;** public, notorious; talked-about, **on everyone's tongue** *or* **lips;** commonplace, trite 117.9, hackneyed, platitudinous

28 **scientific; technical, technological;** high-tech *or* hi-tech <nonformal>; **scholarly**

ADVS 29 **knowingly, consciously, wittingly,** intelligently, studiously, learnedly, eruditely

30 to one's knowledge, **to the best of one's knowledge,** as far as one knows

928 INTELLECTUAL

NOUNS 1 **intellectual, intellect,** member of the intelligentsia; brainworker, thinker; **brain** *and* rocket scientist *and* brain surgeon <all nonformal>; **pundit, Brahmin, mandarin,** egg-head <nonformal>; **highbrow** <nonformal>

2 **intelligentsia,** literati, illuminati; intellectual elite; clerisy; literati

3 **scholar;** student 572; **learned man,** man of learning, **savant,** pundit; genius 413.12; polymath, **mine of information, walking encyclopedia;** literary man, **man of letters;** philologist, philologue; philomath; philosopher;

academician, schoolman; classicist, humanist

4 **bookworm,** bibliophage; **grind** <nonformal>; **booklover, bibliophile,** bibliolater, bibliolatrist; bibliomaniac

5 **pedant; formalist, precisionist,** precisian, purist, **bluestocking**

6 **dilettante, half scholar,** sciolist, **dabbler,** dabster, amateur, trifler, smatterer

929 IGNORANCE

NOUNS 1 **ignorance, unknowingness,** nescience; knowledge-gap; empty-headedness, vacuousness, vacuity, inanity; tabula rasa; **unintelligence** 921; **unacquaintance, unfamiliarity; greenness,** callowness, unripeness, **inexperience** 414.2; innocence, ingenuousness, simpleness, simplicity; pristine ignorance; know-nothingism, obscurantism; agnosticism

2 unknowing, lack of information

3 **incognizance, unawareness, unconsciousness, insensibility,** unwittingness; deniability; incomprehension; **unmindfulness;** mindlessness

4 **unenlightenment, benightedness,** darkness; savagery, barbarism, paganism, heathenism

5 **unlearnedness, inerudition,** ineducation; **unscholarliness; illiteracy,** functional illiteracy; **unintellectuality,** Philistinism

6 **slight knowledge,** vague notion, imperfect knowledge, a little learning, glimmering, **smattering of knowledge,** smattering of ignorance, **half-learning,** sciolism; **superficiality,** shallowness; **dilettantism**

7 **the unknown,** the unknowable, the unfamiliar, the incalculable; **matter of ignorance,** riddle, enigma, mystery, puzzle 970.3; *terra incognita* <L>; frontiers of knowledge

8 **ignoramus, know-nothing;** puddinghead, dunce, fool 923; **illiterate; lowbrow** <nonformal>;

greenhorn, tenderfoot, neophyte, novice; **dilettante,** dabbler 928.6; **middlebrow** <nonformal>

VERBS **9 be ignorant, know nothing,** know from nothing <nonformal>; wallow in ignorance; **not know what's what,** not know what it is all about, not know the score <nonformal>, not be with it <nonformal>; not know the time of day, not know beans, not know one's ass from one's elbow <nonformal>, not know enough to come in out of the rain, **not know up from down,** not know which way is up

10 be in the dark, grope in the dark

11 not know, know not, know not what, know nothing of, have no idea *or* notion *or* conception, **not have the first idea, not have the least *or* remotest idea,** not have the foggiest <nonformal>, **not pretend to say,** not take upon oneself to say; not know the half of it; half-know, scratch the surface, know a little

ADJS **12 ignorant,** nescient, **unknowing,** uncomprehending, **know-nothing;** simple, **dumb** <nonformal>, empty-headed, vacuous, inane, **unintelligent** 921.13; **ill-informed, uninformed, unenlightened,** unilluminated; **unacquainted, unconversant,** unversed, uninitiated, **unfamiliar,** strange to; **inexperienced** 414.17; **green,** callow, ingenuous, gauche, awkward, naive, unripe, raw

13 unaware, unconscious, insensible, unknowing, incognizant; mindless, witless; **unmindful,** unwitting, unsuspecting; unperceiving, imperceptient; unaware of, out of it <nonformal>, not with it <nonformal>; **blind to, deaf to,** dead to, a stranger to; **off one's guard,** caught napping

14 unlearned, inerudite, uneducated, unschooled, untutored, unbriefed, unedified; hoodwinked, deceived; **illiterate,** functionally illiterate, unlettered;

unscholarly, unstudious; **unliterary, unread,** unbookish; **uncultured,** uncultivated, unrefined, Philistine; barbarous, pagan, heathen; **unintellectual; lowbrow** <nonformal>

15 half-learned, half-baked <nonformal>, half-cocked *and* half-assed <both nonformal>, sciolistic; **shallow, superficial;** sophomoric; **dilettante,** dilettantish, smattering, dabbling, amateur, amateurish

16 benighted, dark, in darkness, in the dark

17 unknown, unheard-of, unapprehended, unsuspected; unascertained; unidentified, unclassified, uncharted, unfathomed, unplumbed, virgin, untouched; undisclosed, undivulged, sealed; **unfamiliar,** strange, incalculable, **unknowable,** incognizable, undiscoverable; enigmatic 522.17, mysterious, puzzling

ADVS **18 ignorantly, unknowingly,** unwittingly, witlessly, **unawares;** for aught one knows, not that one knows

930 THOUGHT
    <exercise of the intellect>

NOUNS **1 thought, thinking, cogitation,** cerebration, ideation, noesis, intellectualization, ratiocination; using one's head *or* noodle <nonformal>; **reasoning** 934; **brainwork, headwork,** mental labor *or* effort, mental *or* intellectual exercise; **way of thinking,** habit of thought *or* mind; heavy thinking, straight thinking; conception, conceptualization; excogitation, thinking out *or* through; **idea** 931

2 consideration, contemplation, reflection, speculation, meditation, musing, rumination, deliberation, lucubration, **pondering,** turning over in the mind, looking at from all angles; lateral thinking

3 thoughtfulness, reflectiveness; **pensiveness,** reverie, musing, melancholy; **preoccupation, ab-**

sorption, **engrossment,** brown study; **concentration**

4 thoughts, mind's content; secret thoughts, one's heart of hearts; **train of thought,** sequence of thought or ideas; **stream of consciousness; association,** association of ideas

5 mature thought, developed thought, ripe idea; **afterthought,** second thought or thoughts; **reconsideration,** reappraisal, revaluation, review

6 introspection, self-consultation, subjective inspection or speculation

7 food for thought, something to get one's teeth into

VERBS **8 think, cogitate,** cerebrate, put on one's thinking cap <nonformal>, intellectualize, ideate, conceptualize; **reason** 934.15; **use one's head,** use or exercise the mind, have something on one's mind, have a lot on one's mind

9 think hard, rack one's brains, cudgel one's brains, work one's head to the bone, do some heavy thinking; sweat or stew over <nonformal>, hammer away at; **puzzle over**

10 concentrate, concentrate on or upon, attend closely to, brood on, **focus on** or **upon,** bring the mind to bear upon; get to the point; gather or collect one's thoughts, focus or fix one's thoughts, marshal one's thoughts or ideas

11 think about, cogitate, **apply the mind to,** put one's mind to, apply oneself to, turn the mind or thoughts to, **give thought to, trouble one's head about,** occupy the mind with; think through or out, puzzle out, sort out, excogitate

12 consider, contemplate, speculate, reflect, study, ponder, weigh, deliberate, debate, meditate, muse, brood, ruminate, digest; introspect; fall into a brown study, retreat into one's mind or thoughts; **toy with, play**

with, play around with, flirt with the idea

13 think over, ponder over, brood over, muse over, mull over, reflect over, deliberate over, meditate over, ruminate over, chew over, turn over in the mind, deliberate upon, meditate upon, muse on or upon

14 take under consideration, entertain, take under advisement, **think it over; sleep upon**

15 reconsider, re-examine, review; reappraise, revaluate, rethink; view in a new light, have second thoughts

16 think of, seize on; **entertain the idea of,** entertain thoughts of; **have in mind, contemplate, consider, have under consideration;** take it into one's head; **bear in mind, keep in mind;** harbor an idea, cherish or foster or nurse or nurture an idea

17 <look upon mentally> **contemplate, look upon, view, regard,** see, view with the mind's eye, **envisage,** envision, **visualize** 985.15

18 occur to, come to mind, rise to mind, come into one's head, impinge on one's consciousness, pass through one's mind, dawn upon one, **enter one's mind, cross one's mind,** flash across the mind; **strike,** strike one, grab one <nonformal>, **suggest itself,** present itself, give one pause

19 impress, make an impression, strike, grab <nonformal>, hit; seize one's mind, sink or penetrate into the mind, **sink in** <nonformal>

20 occupy the mind or **thoughts,** engage the thoughts, fasten itself on the mind, seize the mind, fill the mind, take up one's thoughts; **preoccupy,** occupy, **absorb, engross,** obsess the mind; be uppermost in the mind; have in or on one's mind, **have on the brain** <nonformal>, have constantly in one's thoughts

ADJS **21 cognitive, thought,** conceptual, conceptualized, ideative,

noetic, **mental; rational** 934.18,
logical, ratiocinative; **thoughtful,
contemplative, reflective, speculative, deliberative, meditative, ruminative,** ruminant; **pensive,** wistful; introspective; sober,
serious, deepthinking; concen-
trating

22 absorbed or engrossed in
thought, **absorbed, engrossed,**
introspective, rapt, **wrapped in
thought, lost in thought,** abstracted, immersed in thought,
buried in thought, engaged in
thought, occupied, **preoccupied**

ADVS **23** thoughtfully, contem-
platively, reflectively, medita-
tively, ruminatively; **pensively,**
wistfully

24 on one's mind, on the brain
and on one's chest <both nonfor-
mal>, in the thoughts; in the
heart, in one's innermost
thoughts

931 IDEA

NOUNS **1 idea; thought, notion,
concept,** conception, fancy; **perception, sense, impression,**
mental impression, **mental image,** mental picture; **sentiment,**
apprehension; reflection, observation; **opinion** 952.6; supposition, **theory** 950

2 <philosophy> noumenon; universal concept or conception; Platonic idea or form, archetype,
prototype, model, exemplar, transcendent idea or essence, innate
idea; complex idea, simple idea;
percept; supreme principle of
pure reason, transcendent non-
empirical concept; the Absolute,
the Absolute Idea, the Self-
determined, the realized ideal;
logical form or category; **idealism** 1051.3

3 abstract idea, abstraction, generality, abstract

4 main idea, leading or principal
idea, fundamental or basic idea,
guiding principle, crowning principle

5 novel idea, new or **latest wrin-**

kle <nonformal>, new slant or
twist or take <nonformal>

**6 good idea, great idea; bright
thought, insight; brainchild** and
brainstorm <both nonformal>,
inspiration

7 absurd idea, brainstorm <non-
formal>

8 ideology, system of ideas, system of theories; world view; philosophy; **ethos**

ADJS **9** ideational, ideal, **conceptual, notional,** fanciful; **intellectual;** theoretical 950.13; **ideological**

10 ideaed, notioned

932 ABSENCE OF THOUGHT

NOUNS **1 thoughtlessness; vacuity,** vacancy, **emptiness of
mind, empty-headedness,**
blankness; fatuity, inanity, foolishness 922; **nirvana,** calm or
tranquillity of mind; **oblivion,**
forgetfulness, amnesia; passivity,
apathy; blank mind, tabula rasa

VERBS **2 not think, make the
mind a blank,** let the mind lie
fallow; **not think of,** be unmindful of; **not enter one's mind** or
head, be far from one's thoughts;
pay no attention or mind

**3 get it off one's mind, get it off
one's chest** <nonformal>, clear
the mind; **put it out of one's
thoughts,** dismiss from the mind
or thoughts

ADJS **4 thoughtless, thoughtfree,**
incogitant **unthinking,** unreasoning; unintellectual; **vacuous,**
vacant, **empty-headed,** fatuous,
inane 921.19; tranquil; oblivious

5 unthought-of, undreamed-of,
unconceived, unconceptualized;
unimagined

933 INTUITION, INSTINCT

NOUNS **1 intuition, intuitiveness,
sixth sense;** intuitive knowledge,
direct perception or apprehension, knowledge without thought
or reason, flash of insight; intuitive understanding, spontaneous
sense; **revelation,** epiphany; **insight,** inspiration, aperçu; antici-

pation, a priori knowledge; second sight, precognition 960.3, clairvoyance 689.8

2 **instinct,** native *or* natural tendency, **impulse,** blind *or* unreasoning impulse, vital impulse; **libido, id**; archetype, archetypal pattern *or* idea; collective unconscious, race memory; **reflex,** spontaneous reaction, unthinking response, knee-jerk

3 **hunch** <nonformal>, sense, **presentiment, premonition,** intimation, foreboding; suspicion, **impression,** intuition, intuitive impression, **feeling,** vague feeling *or* idea, feeling in one's bones

VERBS 4 **intuit, sense, feel, feel** *or* **know in one's bones** <nonformal>, have a funny feeling <nonformal>, **get** *or* **have the impression, have a hunch** <nonformal>, know instinctively

ADJS 5 **intuitive,** sensing, feeling; second-sighted, precognitive 960.7, clairvoyant

6 **instinctive, inherent, innate**; **involuntary, automatic,** spontaneous, impulsive; **instinctual**

ADVS 7 **intuitively; instinctively,** automatically, spontaneously, **instinctually**

934 REASONING

NOUNS 1 **reasoning, reason,** logical thought, rationalizing, ratiocination; the divine faculty; **rationalism, rationality**; sweet reason, reasonableness; demonstration, proof 956; specious reasoning, sophistry 935; philosophy 951

2 **logic**; **dialectics,** dialectic, dialecticism; art of reason, science of discursive thought; formal logic, material logic; modern *or* epistemological logic, pragmatic *or* instrumental *or* experimental logic; psychological logic; symbolic *or* mathematical logic

3 <methods> a priori reasoning, a fortiori reasoning, a posteriori reasoning; **deduction, deductive reasoning,** syllogism, syllogistic reasoning; **induction, inductive**

reasoning; **inference; generalization,** particularization; synthesis, analysis; hypothesis and verification

4 **argumentation, argument, controversy, dispute, disputation, polemic, debate; contention, wrangling, bickering,** hubbub 53.3, bicker, rhubarb *and* hassle <both nonformal>; war of words, verbal engagement *or* contest, logomachy; academic disputation, defense of a thesis; pilpul, casuistry; polemics; litigation

5 **argument; case, plea,** pleading, brief; **reason, consideration; refutation; pros and cons**; talking point; **dialogue,** dialectic

6 syllogism; prosyllogism; mode

7 **premise, proposition, position, assumption,** presupposition, **hypothesis, thesis, theorem, statement,** affirmation, assertion, foundation; **postulate, axiom, postulation**; major premise, minor premise

8 **conclusion** 945.4

9 **reasonableness, logicalness,** logicality, **rationality, sensibleness, soundness,** justifiability, admissibility; cogency; **sense,** common sense, **logic, reason**; plausibility 967.3

10 **good reasoning, right thinking,** sound reasoning; **cogency**; sound evidence, strong point

11 **reasoner,** ratiocinator, **thinker; rationalist**; rationalizer; synthesizer; **logician**; dialectician; syllogist, syllogizer; sophist 935.6; philosopher 951.6

12 **arguer, controversialist, disputant, debater,** advocate, wrangler, Philadelphia lawyer <nonformal>, guardhouse lawyer <nonformal>, casuist; polemic, polemicist; logomachist; apologist

13 **contentiousness,** litigiousness, **quarrelsomeness,** argumentativeness, disputatiousness, testiness, feistiness <nonformal>, combativeness; ill humor 110

14 side, interest

VERBS **15 reason;** rationalize, provide a rationale; intellectualize; bring reason to bear, put two and two together; **deduce, infer, generalize; synthesize, analyze; theorize,** hypothesize; philosophize; syllogize

16 argue, dispute, logomachize, polemicize, moot, **bandy words, chop logic, plead,** pettifog <nonformal>, cross swords, lock horns, **contend, contest,** spar, **bicker, wrangle,** hassle <nonformal>, have it out; thrash out; **put up an argument** <nonformal>; take sides; argue to no purpose; **quibble, cavil** 935.9

17 be reasonable, be logical, make sense, stand to reason, be demonstrable, be irrefutable; hold water <nonformal>; have a leg to stand on

ADJS **18 reasoning, rational**; analytic, analytical

19 argumentative, argumental, dialectic, dialectical, controversial, **disputatious, contentious, quarrelsome,** litigious, combative, testy, feisty <nonformal>, ill-humored 110.18, polemic, polemical, logomachical, pro and con

20 logical, reasonable, rational, cogent, sensible, sane, sound, well-thought-out, justifiable, admissible; credible 952.24; plausible 967.7; well-argued, **well-founded, well-grounded**

21 reasoned, advised, considered, calculated, meditated, contemplated, deliberated, studied, weighed, thought-out

22 dialectic, dialectical; syllogistic, syllogistical, inductive, deductive, inferential, synthetic, analytic, analytical, discursive; a priori, a posteriori; categorical, hypothetical, conditional

23 deducible, derivable, inferable; sequential

ADVS **24 reasonably, logically, rationally, sensibly,** sanely, soundly; syllogistically, analytically; **in reason,** within reason, **within bounds,** within the bounds of possibility, as far as possible

935 SOPHISTRY
<specious reasoning>

NOUNS **1 sophistry,** sophism, **casuistry,** subtlety, oversubtlety; **false** or **specious reasoning, rationalization,** sophistical reasoning, special pleading; **fallacy,** fallaciousness; **speciousness,** superficial or apparent soundness, plausibleness, plausibility; **insincerity, disingenuousness; equivocation;** fudging and waffling <both nonformal>; perversion, distortion, misapplication; vicious circle, circularity; reduction, trivialization

2 illogicalness, illogicality, **unreasonableness, irrationality, reasonlessness, senselessness, unsoundness,** invalidity, inconclusiveness; **inconsistency,** incongruity

3 <specious argument> **sophism,** sophistry, mere rhetoric, philosophism, solecism; claptrap, empty words, doubletalk, doublespeak; bad case, weak point, flaw in an argument; **fallacy,** logical fallacy; *argumentum ad hominem, argumentum ad baculum, argumentum ad captandum, argumentum ad captandum vulgus* <all L>, *petitio principii* <L>, begging the question, **circular argument,** undistributed middle, *non sequitur* <L>, *post hoc ergo propter hoc* <L>

4 quibble, quodlibet, **cavil;** quip, quirk, dodge

5 quibbling, caviling, captiousness, nit-picking, **bickering; logic-chopping, hairsplitting;** subterfuge, chicanery, pettifoggery; **equivocation,** tergiversation, prevarication, **evasion, hedging, pussyfooting** <nonformal>, **sidestepping,** dodging, parrying

6 sophist, sophister, **casuist;** paralogist

7 quibbler, caviler, pettifogger, hairsplitter, nitpicker; **equivoca-**

tor, Jesuit, prevaricator, tergiversator; **hedger**

VERBS **8** reason speciously, paralogize, reason in a circle; explain away, rationalize; not have a leg to stand on

9 quibble, cavil, bicker, split hairs, nitpick; **equivocate,** mystify, obscure, prevaricate, tergiversate, doubletalk, doublespeak, tap-dance <nonformal>, **shuffle, dodge,** shy, **evade,** sidestep, pussyfoot <nonformal>, evade the issue; **beat about** or **around the bush, beg the question;** pick holes in, pick to pieces

ADJS **10 sophistical,** sophistic, casuistic, Jesuitical, **fallacious, specious,** plausible, superficially or apparently sound; deceptive, illusive, empty; oversubtle, **insincere, disingenuous**

11 illogical, unreasonable, irrational, reasonless, senseless, without rhyme or reason; unscientific, unphilosophical; **invalid,** faulty, flawed, paralogical, fallacious; inconclusive, inconsequential; **inconsistent,** incongruous, unconnected; contradictory, **self-contradictory,** oxymoronic

12 unsound, unsubstantial, insubstantial, flimsy, unrigorous, inconclusive, unsustained

13 baseless, groundless, ungrounded, **unfounded, unsupported,** unsustained, **without foundation; untenable, unsupportable,** unsustainable; **unwarranted,** idle, empty, vain

14 quibbling, caviling, equivocatory, captious, nitpicky <nonformal>, bickering; picayune, petty, trivial; hedging, pussyfooting <nonformal>; **evasive; hairsplitting,** logic-chopping

ADVS **15 illogically, unreasonably, irrationally, reasonlessly, senselessly;** baselessly, groundlessly; untenably

936 TOPIC

NOUNS **1 topic, subject, matter, subject matter, concern,** focus of attention, discrete matter, category; **theme,** burden, **text,** motif, motive, business at hand, **case, question, problem, issue; point,** point in question, gist 996.6; rubric; substance, essence, material part, basis

2 caption, title, heading, head, rubric; **headline; subhead, subheading,** subtitle; legend, motto, epigraph

VERBS **3** focus on, have regard to, distinguish, lift up, set forth, specify, zero in on <nonformal>; **headline;** subtitle, subhead

ADJS **4 topical, thematic**

937 INQUIRY

NOUNS **1 inquiry,** inquiring, probing, **inquest** 307.18; inquisition; inquiring mind; analysis 800

2 examination, exam <nonformal>, **test, quiz;** oral examination, viva voce examination; **audition, hearing**

3 examination, inspection, scrutiny; survey, review, perusal, once over and look-see <both nonformal>, **study,** scan, runthrough; visitation; quality control; confirmation, cross-check

4 investigation, research, inquiry into; data-gathering, gathering or amassing evidence; **probe,** exhaustive study; police inquiry or investigation, criminal investigation, detective work, detection, sleuthing; witch-hunt, fishing expedition, Inquisition

5 preliminary or tentative examination; cursory inspection, once-over-lightly <nonformal>

6 checkup, check; physical examination, **physical,** physical checkup; self-examination; testing, drug testing, alcohol testing, random testing

7 re-examination, review, reappraisal, revaluation

8 reconnaissance; reconnoitering, reconnoiter, **scouting**

9 surveillance, shadowing, tailing <nonformal>, stakeout <nonformal>; **spying, espionage, intelligence,** military intelligence, cloak-and-dagger work <nonformal>; counterespionage, counterintelligence

10 question, query, inquiry, interrogation, interrogatory; **problem, issue, topic** 936, bone of contention, question *or* point at issue, **moot point,** question mark; **burning question;** feeler, trial balloon; catechism, catechizing

11 interview, press conference

12 questioning, interrogation, querying; pumping, probing, inquiring; **quiz, examination;** challenge, dispute; catechizing, catechization; Socratic method *or* induction

13 grilling, inquisition; **the third-degree** <nonformal>; direct examination, **cross-examination**

14 canvass, survey, inquiry, questionnaire; poll, **public-opinion poll,** opinion poll *or* survey

15 search, quest, hunt, stalking, dragnet, posse, search party; **rummage, ransacking,** turning upside down; **forage;** exploration, probe; **body search**

16 inquirer, asker, prober, questioner, interrogator; **quizzer,** examiner, catechist; inquisitor, inquisitionist; **cross-examiner; pollster,** opinion sampler; **interviewer; detective** 576.10; **secret agent** 576.9

17 examiner, tester; inspector, scrutinizer, scrutator; **monitor,** reviewer; **investigator**

18 seeker, hunter, searcher; rummager, ransacker; digger, delver; **researcher, fact finder**

19 examinee, examinant

VERBS **20 inquire, ask, question, query; make inquiry,** institute *or* pursue *or* conduct *or* carry on an inquiry, ask after, inquire after, ask about, ask questions; inquire of, put a question to, pose *or* set *or* propose *or* propound a question

21 interrogate, question, query, quiz, test, examine; catechize; **pump,** pump for information, pick the brains of; draw one out

22 grill, put on the grill <nonformal>; put the pressure on *and* put the screws to *and* go over <all nonformal>; **cross-examine, cross-question;** give *or* put through the third degree <nonformal>

23 investigate, sift, **explore, look into,** peer into, **search into, go into, delve into,** dig into, poke into, pry into; **probe, sound, plumb, fathom; check into, check on, check out;** poke about, cast about *or* around

24 examine, inspect, scrutinize, survey, canvass, **look at,** peer at, **observe, scan, peruse, study; look over,** give the once-over <nonformal>; go over, run over, pass over, pore over; **monitor, review; take stock of,** size *or* size up; **check, check out, check over** *or* **through; check up on**

25 make a close study of, scrutinize, examine thoroughly, **go deep into,** look closely at; go over with a fine-tooth comb, subject to close scrutiny

26 examine cursorily, give a once-over-lightly <nonformal>, **scan, skim, skim over** *or* **through, glance at,** give the once-over <nonformal>, pass over lightly, **dip into, touch upon,** touch upon lightly *or* in passing, **hit the high spots; thumb through,** leaf *or* flick through

27 re-examine, recheck, **reconsider,** reappraise, reevaluate, rethink, **review,** revise, take another look; go back over

28 reconnoiter, case <nonformal>, scout, **scout out,** spy, **spy out,** peep; **watch,** put under surveillance, stake out <nonformal>; bug <nonformal>

29 canvass, survey, make a survey; **poll,** conduct a poll, sample

30 seek, hunt, quest, pursue, go in search of, try to find; **look up, hunt up; look for,** look around *or* about for, look for high and low, **search for,** seek for, **hunt for,** cast *or* beat about for; **fish for, angle for,** go on a fishing expedition; **ask for,** inquire for; **gun for,** go gunning for

31 search, hunt, explore; research; **hunt through, search through, look through, go through;** dig, delve, burrow, root, pick over, poke, pry; poke around, nose around; beat the bushes

32 grope, grope for, **feel for,** fumble, poke around, grope in the dark; **feel** *or* **pick one's way**

33 ransack, rummage, rake, scour, comb; rifle; **look everywhere, look high and low, look all over,** turn upside down, turn inside out, **leave no stone unturned**

34 search out, hunt out, spy out, scout out, **ferret out,** fish out, pry out, dig out, root out

35 trace, stalk, track, trail; follow, follow up, shadow, tail <nonformal>, have *or* keep an eye on; **smell** *or* **sniff out;** follow a clue; **trace down, hunt down, track down, run down, run to earth**

ADJS **36 inquiring, questioning, querying,** quizzing; **quizzical, curious; interrogatory; inquisitorial,** inquisitional; catechetical

37 examining; testing, trying, **tentative; inspectional; investigative;** heuristic; **exploratory,** explorative, explorational; analytic, analytical

38 searching, probing, prying, nosy <nonformal>; poking, digging, fishing; looking for, **out for,** on the lookout for, **in the market for**

ADVS **39 in question, at issue,** in debate *or* dispute, **under consideration, under advisement,** under investigation, under surveillance; **before the house, on the docket, on the agenda, on the table, on the floor**

938 ANSWER

NOUNS **1 answer, reply, response**; respondence; riposte; **uptake** <nonformal>, **retort, rejoinder, comeback** <nonformal>, back talk; **repartee,** clever reply *or* retort, snappy comeback <nonfor-

mal>; **acknowledgment;** antiphon; **echo,** reverberation 54.2

2 rebuttal, counterstatement, counterclaim, countercharge; **rejoinder,** rebutter; refutation

3 answerer, replier, responder, **respondent**

VERBS **4 answer, reply, respond,** say in reply; **retort,** riposte; come back at <nonformal>, answer back *and* talk back *and* shoot back <all nonformal>; **react; acknowledge,** make *or* give acknowledgement; echo, reecho, reverberate 54.7

5 rebut, make a rebuttal; counterclaim, countercharge; confute, refute

ADJS **6 answering, replying, responsive,** respondent; antiphonal; echoing, echoic, reechoing 54.11; confutative, refutative

ADVS **7 in answer, in reply, in response, in rebuttal**

939 SOLUTION

<answer to a problem>

NOUNS **1 solution, resolution, answer, reason, explanation** 341.4; **finding,** conclusion, determination, judgment; **outcome, upshot,** denouement, **result,** end result; **solving, working-out,** resolving, **clearing up,** cracking; unscrambling, unraveling, sorting out, untwisting, untangling, disentanglement; **decipherment, deciphering, decoding,** decryption; interpretation 341; **happy ending** *or* outcome, the answer to one's prayers, light at the end of the tunnel

VERBS **2 solve, resolve,** find the solution *or* answer, **clear up, work out, find out, figure out,** dope *and* dope out <both nonformal>; **straighten out, iron out,** sort out, puzzle out; **unriddle,** riddle, unscramble, untangle, disentangle, untwist, **unravel,** ravel; **decipher, decode,** crack; **make out,** interpret 341.9; **answer, explain** 341.10; unlock, find a clue to; **get to the bottom** *or* **heart of, fathom,** plumb; hit upon a solution, hit the nail on the head, hit it on the nose <nonformal>; guess, divine, guess right

ADJS **3 solvable,** soluble, **resolvable,** capable of solution, workable; explicable, ascertainable; **decipherable,** decodable

940 DISCOVERY

NOUNS **1 discovery, finding, detection,** spotting, catching sight of; **locating, location; disclosure, exposure,** revelation, **uncovering, unearthing,** exhumation, bringing to light *or* view; **find,** strike, lucky strike; serendipity; **learning, finding out,** determining

VERBS **2 discover, find,** get; strike, hit; put *or* lay one's hands on, **locate** 159.10; **hunt down,** search out, track down, **run down, run** *or* **bring to earth;** trace; **learn, find out,** become cognizant *or* conscious of, become aware of; discover *or* find out the hard way

3 come across, run across, meet with, fall in with, **encounter, run into,** bump into <nonformal>; **come on** *or* **upon, hit on** *or* **upon,** light on *or* upon; **chance on** *or* **upon,** happen on *or* upon *or* across, **stumble on** *or* **upon,** *or* **across** *or* **into,** trip over, bump up against, blunder upon

4 uncover, unearth, dig up, disinter, exhume, excavate; **disclose, expose, reveal,** crack wide open, **bring to light; turn up;** worm out, ferret out

5 detect, spot <nonformal>, **see, lay eyes on,** catch sight of, **spy,** discern, **perceive, make out, recognize**

6 scent, sniff, smell, get a whiff of <nonformal>, **get wind of;** sniff *or* smell out, nose out; be on the right scent, be near the truth

7 catch; catch napping, catch off-guard, catch asleep at the switch; **catch red-handed,** catch in *flagrante delicto,* **catch with one's pants down** <nonformal>

8 <detect the hidden nature of> **see through, penetrate,** see in its true colors, read between the lines; open the eyes to, tumble to, catch on to, wise up to <nonformal>; **be on to, be wise to, have one's number,** have dead to rights <nonformal>

9 turn up, show up; hang out <nonformal>; materialize, **come to light**

ADJS **10** on the right scent, **on the right track,** on the trail of; **hot** *and* **warm** <both nonformal>; **discoverable, detectable,** disclosable, exposable, locatable, **discernible**

941 EXPERIMENT

NOUNS **1 experiment, experimentation;** experimental method; **trial;** running it up the flagpole <nonformal>, trying it on *or* out <nonformal>; **trial and error,** cut and try <nonformal>; empiricism, pragmatism; **rule of thumb;** controlled experiment, **control;** experimental design; experimental proof *or* verification

2 test, trial, try; essay; assay; determination; **proof,** verification; touchstone, standard, criterion 300.2; acid test, litmus *or* litmus-paper test; ordeal, crucible; probation; **feeling out, sounding out**

3 tryout, workout, **rehearsal,** practice; pilot program; **dry run; trial run,** practical test; shakedown, shakedown cruise, bench test; flight test, test flight

4 feeler, probe, sound, sounder; **trial balloon,** barometer; straw vote

5 laboratory, lab <nonformal>; **proving ground;** think tank <nonformal>

6 experimenter, experimentist

7 subject, experimental subject, sample; laboratory animal, **guinea pig**

VERBS **8 experiment, research, run an experiment; test, try,** essay, cut and try <nonformal>, **test** *or* **try out;** run it up the flagpole and see who salutes <nonformal>; put to the test, **put to** the proof, **prove, verify,** validate, substantiate, confirm; **give a try,** give it a go <nonformal>, take a stab <nonformal>; sample, taste; assay; **road-test,** shake down; experiment *or* practice upon; try it on

9 **sound out, feel out, sound,** get a reading *or* sense, probe, **feel the pulse,** read; **put out a feeler,** send up a trial balloon; **see which way the wind blows,** see how the land lies, test the waters; take a straw vote

10 **stand the test, stand up, hold up, pass muster,** get by <nonformal>, make it *and* hack it *and* cut the mustard <all nonformal>

ADJS 11 **experimental, test, trial;** testing, proving, trying; probative, probatory; **tentative,** provisional; empirical; trial-and-error, cut-and-try; heuristic

12 **tried, well-tried, tested, proved,** verified, confirmed, tried and true

ADVS 13 **experimentally,** by trial and error, by hit and miss, by guess and by God

14 **on trial,** under examination, **on** *or* **under probation,** under suspicion, **on approval**

942 COMPARISON

NOUNS 1 **comparison,** examining side by side, matching, matchup, comparative judgment *or* estimate; **likening,** comparing, **analogy;** weighing, balancing; opposing, opposition, **contrast; relation** 774; correlation 776; simile, similitude, metaphor, allegory, figure *or* trope of comparison

2 **collation,** point-by-point comparison; **verification, confirmation, checking**

3 **comparability,** comparableness; **commensurability;** ratio, proportion, balance; **similarity** 783

VERBS 4 **compare, liken,** liken to, compare with; **make** *or* **draw a comparison; analogize; relate** 774.6; **draw a parallel; match;** examine side by side, view to-

gether, hold up together; weigh *or* measure against; **contrast, oppose,** set in opposition, set off against, set in contrast, **put** *or* **set over against,** set *or* place against, counterpose; compare and contrast; **weigh,** balance

5 **collate,** compare point by point; **verify, confirm, check, cross-check**

6 **compare notes,** put heads together <nonformal>

7 **be comparable, compare, compare to** *or* **with,** admit of comparison, be worthy of comparison, be fit to be compared; **measure up to, come up to,** match up with, stack up with <nonformal>, hold a candle to <nonformal>; **match, parallel,** vie, vie with, rival; **resemble** 783.7

ADJS 8 **comparative, relative** 774.7, **comparable,** commensurate, commensurable, parallel, matchable, **analogous; correlative; similar** 783.10

9 **incomparable,** incommensurable; apples and oranges; **unlike, dissimilar** 786.4

ADVS 10 **comparatively, relatively;** comparably; dollar for dollar, pound for pound, etc

943 DISCRIMINATION

NOUNS 1 **discrimination;** seeing *or* making distinctions; **criticalness; finesse,** refinement, delicacy; niceness of distinction, nicety, subtlety; **tact, tactfulness,** feel, feeling, sense, **sensitivity** 24.3, **sensibility** 24.2; intuition, instinct 933; taste, aesthetic *or* artistic judgment; palate, fine *or* refined palate; ear, good ear, educated ear; eye, good eye; connoisseurship, savvy <nonformal>, selectiveness, fastidiousness 495

2 **discernment,** critical discernment, penetration, **perception,** perceptiveness, **insight,** perspicacity; **flair; judgment,** acumen 919.4; analysis 800

3 **distinction,** contradistinction; **distinguishment, differentia-**

tion 779.4, winnowing, shakeout, separation, segregation, demarcation; subtle *or* fine distinction, **nuance,** shade of difference; hairsplitting

VERBS **4 discriminate, distinguish,** draw *or* make distinctions, **separate,** separate out, analyze 800.6, subdivide, **segregate, differentiate,** set off, **set apart,** sift, winnow, screen, screen out, sort, classify; **pick out, select** 371.14; separate the sheep from the goats, separate the men from the boys, separate the wheat from the chaff; **draw the line,** fix *or* set a limit; **split hairs,** draw *or* make a fine *or* overfine distinction

5 be discriminating, discriminate, exercise discrimination; **be tactful**; pick and choose; use advisedly

6 distinguish between, make *or* **draw a distinction,** see nuances *or* shades of difference, know which is which, know what's what <nonformal>, know one's ass from one's elbow <nonformal>

ADJS **7 discriminating, discriminate,** discriminative, selective; discriminatory; **tactful, sensitive;** appreciative, appreciatory; **critical; distinguishing;** fine, delicate, subtle, refined; fastidious 495.9

8 discerning, perceptive, perspicacious, insightful; **astute, judicious** 919.19

9 discriminable, distinguishable, separable, differentiable, contrastable, opposable

ADVS **10 discriminatingly,** discriminately, discriminately; with finesse; **tactfully; tastefully**

944 INDISCRIMINATION

NOUNS **1 indiscrimination,** indiscriminateness, unselectiveness, **uncriticalness, unparticularness;** unfastidiousness; **casualness,** promiscuousness, **promiscuity; indiscretion,** indiscreetness, **imprudence** 922.2; un-

tactfulness, tactlessness, **insensitivity,** insensibility 25; **generality** 863, catholicity

2 indistinction, indistinctness, vagueness 32.2; **indefiniteness** 970.4; uniformity 780; **indistinguishableness**; a distinction without a difference

VERBS **3 confound, confuse, mix,** mix up, muddle, jumble, **blur,** blur distinctions

4 use loosely, use unadvisedly

ADJS **5 undiscriminating, indiscriminate,** indiscriminative, unselective; wholesale, **general** 863.11, **blanket; uncritical,** undemanding; **unparticular,** unfastidious; unsubtle; **casual, promiscuous; indiscreet,** undiscreet, **imprudent; untactful,** tactless, insensitive

6 indistinguishable, undistinguishable, indiscernible, **indistinct, without distinction,** undifferentiated, **alike,** six of one and half a dozen of the other <nonformal>; **indefinite;** faceless, impersonal; standard, interchangeable, stereotyped, uniform 780.5

945 JUDGMENT

NOUNS **1 judgment,** adjudication, judicature; judgment call <nonformal>; **resolution** 359; **choice** 371; **discrimination** 943

2 criticism; censure 510.3; **approval** 509; **critique,** review, critical notice; literary criticism, art criticism, etc

3 estimate, estimation; view, opinion 952.6; **assessment,** assessing, **appraisal,** appreciation, reckoning, **stocktaking,** valuation, **evaluation,** value judgment, gauging, ranking, **rating;** measurement 300; comparison 942

4 conclusion, deduction, inference, consequence, consequent, corollary; induction

5 verdict, decision, determination, finding, holding; **decree, ruling, pronouncement,** deliverance; **award,** action, **sentence; condemnation,** doom; dictum

6 **judge,** adjudicator; arbiter
596.1; referee, umpire
7 **critic;** connoisseur; literary
critic; social critic, muckraker;
caviler, carper, faultfinder; **censor,** censurer; **reviewer, commentator;** scholiast
VERBS 8 **judge,** exercise judgment;
make a judgment call <nonfor-
mal>; adjudge, adjudicate; **consider, regard,** hold, **deem, esteem,** count, **account,** think
of; **suppose, presume** 950.10,
opine, give *or* express an opinion,
put in one's two cents <nonfor-
mal>
9 **estimate;** reckon, call, guess,
figure <nonformal>; **assess, appraise, gauge, rate, rank, value,
evaluate,** place *or* set a value on,
weigh, appreciate; size up <non-
formal>, **measure** 300.11
10 **conclude,** draw a conclusion,
come to *or* **arrive at a conclusion;** find, hold; deduce, derive,
extract, **gather,** collect, glean,
fetch; **infer,** draw an inference;
reason; put two and two together
11 **decide, determine; find,** hold,
ascertain; **resolve** 359.7, **settle,**
fix; **make up one's mind**
12 **sit in judgment,** hold court;
hear, give a hearing to; **try**
598.17; **referee, umpire,** officiate
13 **pass judgment, pronounce
judgment,** deliver judgment; return a verdict, hand down a verdict, **bring in a verdict, find,** find
for *or* against; pronounce on, act
on, **pronounce,** report, **rule,** decree, order; **sentence,** pass sentence, hand down a sentence
14 **criticize,** critique; **censure**
510.13; **approve** 509.9; **review;**
moralize upon; pontificate
15 **rank, rate,** count, be regarded,
be thought of
ADJS 16 **judicial, judiciary,** judicative, judgmental; **judicious**
919.19; **evaluative; critical; approbatory** 509.16
ADVS 17 **all things considered, on
the whole, taking one thing
with another,** on balance; other
things being equal, taking into ac-

count, considering, after all, this
being so; on the one hand, on the
other hand, having said that

946 PREJUDGMENT

NOUNS 1 **prejudgment; precon-
ception, presumption, supposition, presupposition, prepossession; predilection,** predisposition; **predetermination,** premature judgment; an ax to grind,
prejudice 979.3
VERBS 2 **prejudge; preconceive,
presuppose, presume; be predisposed;** judge beforehand *or*
prematurely, judge before the evidence is in, have one's mind made
up; **jump to a conclusion,** go off
half-cocked
ADJS 3 **prejudged, preconceived,
presumed, presupposed;** predetermined, judged beforehand *or*
prematurely; **predisposed**

947 MISJUDGMENT

NOUNS 1 **misjudgment,** error in
judgment, warped judgment;
**miscalculation, misreckoning,
misestimation,** misperception,
wrong impression; **misreading,**
misconstruction, **misinterpretation** 342; **inaccuracy, error** 974;
injudiciousness 922.2
VERBS 2 **misjudge, miscalculate,
misestimate,** misperceive, get a
wrong impression, misconjec-
ture; **misread,** misconstrue, misread the situation *or* case; **misinterpret** 342.2; fly in the face of
facts

948 OVERESTIMATION

NOUNS 1 **overestimation,** overestimate, **overreckoning, overrat-
ing,** overappraisal; **overstatement, exaggeration** 355
VERBS 2 **overestimate, over-
reckon,** overcalculate, over-
count, see more than is there;
overrate, overesteem, **overvalue,**
make too much of, put on a pedestal, idealize; overreact to; **overstate, exaggerate** 355.3; pump
up *and* make a big deal *or* Federal
case <all nonformal>

ADJS **3 overestimated, overrated,**
puffed up, pumped up <nonformal>, overvalued; **exaggerated**
355.4

949 UNDERESTIMATION

NOUNS **1 underestimation,** underestimate, **underrating,** undervaluation, misprizing; **belittlement, depreciation,** deprecation, **minimization,** disparagement 512

VERBS **2 underestimate,** misestimate, **underrate, undervalue,**
underprize; **misprize; make little of,** attach little importance to,
not do justice to, sell short, think
little of, make *or* think nothing of,
see less than is there, make light
of, shrug off; **depreciate, deprecate,** minimize, belittle, badmouth *and* poor-mouth *and* put
down *and* run down <all nonformal>, take someone for a fool;
disparage 512.8

ADJS **3 underestimated, underrated,** undervalued, on the low
side; unvalued, unprized, misprized

950 THEORY, SUPPOSITION

NOUNS **1 theory,** theorization; **hypothesis,** hypothesizing; **speculation**; doctrinairism; analysis,
explanation, abstraction

2 theory, explanation, proposal,
proposition; **hypothesis,** working hypothesis

3 supposition, supposal; presupposition, presupposal; **assumption, presumption, conjecture,
inference, surmise, guesswork;
postulate,** postulation; **proposition, thesis, premise** 934.7; **axiom** 973.2

4 guess, conjecture, speculation,
guesswork, surmise, educated
guess; guesstimate *and* hunch
and shot *and* stab <all nonformal>; rough guess, wild guess,
shot in the dark <nonformal>

5 <vague supposition> **suggestion, suspicion, inkling, hint,
sense, feeling, feeling in one's
bones, intuition** 933, intima-

tion, **impression, notion,** hunch
and sneaking suspicion <both
nonformal>, vague idea, hazy
idea, **idea** 931

6 suppositiousness, presumptiveness

7 theorist, theorizer, theoretician; speculator; doctrinaire;
synthesizer; armchair philosopher

8 supposer, surmiser, **conjecturer, guesser**

VERBS **9 theorize, hypothesize,
speculate,** espouse a theory

**10 suppose, assume, presume,
surmise, suspect, infer, understand, gather, conclude, deduce, consider, fancy,** conceive,
believe, deem, think, be afraid
<nonformal>; **presuppose;** provisionally accept, take one up on
<nonformal>, take it as given, say
or assume for argument's sake

11 conjecture, guess, talk off the
top of one's head <nonformal>,
venture a guess, go out on a limb
<nonformal>

12 postulate, predicate, posit, set
forth, lay down, assert; pose, advance, **propose, propound** 439.5

ADJS **13 theoretical, hypothetical;
speculative, conjectural;** intuitive 933.5; merely theoretical, academic, moot; impractical, armchair

14 supposed, suppositive, **assumed, presumed, conjectured, inferred,** understood,
deemed, **reputed,** putative, alleged; **presumptive;** taken for
granted, stipulated; **postulated**

15 supposable, presumable, assumable

ADVS **16 theoretically, hypothetically,** ideally; **in theory,**
in the abstract, on paper

17 supposedly, presumably, presumptively, reputedly; suppositiously; **seemingly**

18 conjecturally; as a guess, as an
approximation

951 PHILOSOPHY

NOUNS **1 philosophy;** philosophical inquiry *or* investigation,

philosophical speculation; philosophic system, school of thought;
philosophic doctrine, philosophic
theory; sophistry 935

2 Platonic philosophy, Platonism,
philosophy of the Academy

3 materialism; idealism 1051.3

4 monism, philosophical unitar-
ianism; pantheism, cosmotheism

5 pluralism; dualism, mind-matter
theory

6 **philosopher; thinker,** speculator; metaphysician, cosmologist;
sophist 935.6

VERBS **7 philosophize,** reason
934.15, probe

ADJS **8 philosophical,** philosophic,
sophistical 935.10

9 absurdist, acosmistic, aesthetic

10 Aristotelian, Peripatetic

952 BELIEF

NOUNS **1 belief,** credence, credit;
**confidence, assurance; cer-
tainty** 969; **reliance, dependence,** stock *and* store <both
nonformal>; reception, acquiescence; full faith and credit; suspension of disbelief; **credulity**
953

2 **a belief, tenet, dogma,** precept,
principle, principle *or* **article of
faith,** canon, maxim, axiom; **doctrine**

3 **system of belief; religion, faith**
675.1; **school, cult, ideology,**
world view; political faith *or* belief *or* philosophy; **creed, credo;**
articles of faith, stated belief; gospel; catechism

4 **statement of belief** *or* **principles, manifesto,** position paper;
solemn declaration

5 **conviction, persuasion, certainty; firm belief,** moral certainty, staunch belief, mature
judgment *or* belief, fixed opinion,
steadfast faith

6 **opinion, sentiment, feeling,
sense, impression,** reaction, **notion, idea, thought,** mind, thinking, **way of thinking, attitude,**
stance, posture, position, mindset, **view,** point of view, eye, sight,
lights, observation, **conception,**

concept, conceit, **estimation,** estimate, consideration, **theory**
950, assumption, presumption,
conclusion, judgment 945, personal judgment; **point of view**
977.2; public opinion, public belief, general belief, prevailing belief *or* sentiment, common belief,
community sentiment, popular
belief, conventional wisdom, climate of opinion; ethos; mystique

7 profession, confession, declaration, **profession** *or* **confession**
or **declaration of faith**

**8 believability, persuasiveness,
credibility, credit, trustworthiness, plausibility,** tenability, ; **reliability** 969.4

9 believer, truster; true believer;
ideologist, ideologue

VERBS **10 believe, credit, trust,
accept,** buy <nonformal>; give
credit *or* credence to, take
credit *or* credence to, take stock
in *or* set store by <nonformal>,
take to heart; accept implicitly,
believe without reservation, take
for granted, take as gospel truth
<nonformal>, take on faith, take
on trust *or* credit, pin one's faith
on; take at face value; **take one's
word for,** take at one's word; **buy**
and **buy into** <both nonformal>,
swallow 953.6; **be certain** 969.9

**11 think, opine, be of the opinion,
be persuaded, be convinced;
have the idea, suppose, assume, presume, judge** 945.8,
guess, surmise, suspect, have
an inkling, be under the impression, have a sense *or* the sense,
imagine, fancy, daresay; **deem,
esteem, hold, regard, consider,
maintain,** reckon, estimate

12 state, assert, swear, swear to
God <nonformal>, declare, **affirm,** vow, avow, asseverate, profess, express the belief; depose,
make an affidavit *or* a sworn
statement

**13 hold the belief, have the opin-
ion,** entertain a belief *or* an opinion, take as an article of faith; foster *or* nurture *or* cherish a belief;
get it into one's head, form a conviction

14 be confident, have confidence, **be satisfied, be convinced, be certain,** be secure in the belief, **feel sure, rest assured;** doubt not, **have no doubt,** have no misgivings *or* qualms, have no reservations, have no second thoughts

15 believe in, have faith in, have confidence in, place reliance in, put oneself in the hands of, **trust in,** have childlike faith in; give *or* get the benefit of the doubt

16 rely on *or* **upon, depend on** *or* **upon,** place reliance on, **count on, bank on** *or* **upon** <nonformal>; **trust to, swear by,** take one's oath upon; **bet on** *and* gamble on *and* lay money on *and* bet one's bottom dollar on <all nonformal>

17 trust, confide in, rely on, depend on, place trust *or* confidence in, have confidence in, **trust in** 952.15, trust utterly *or* implicitly, take one's word, take at one's word

18 convince; convert, win over, lead one to believe, bring to one's senses, **persuade, lead to believe, give to understand; satisfy, assure;** put one's mind at rest on; bring *or* drive home to; cram down one's throat *and* beat into one's head <both nonformal>

19 convince oneself, persuade oneself, sell oneself <nonformal>, satisfy oneself on that point, make up one's mind

20 find credence, be believed, be accepted, be received; carry conviction; have the ear of, gain the confidence of

ADJS **21 belief,** principled; **believing, undoubting, undoubtful;** God-fearing, pious, **devout; convinced, confident,** positive, dogmatic, secure, **persuaded,** sold on, **satisfied, assured; sure, certain** 969.13,20

22 trusting, trustful, confiding, unsuspecting, unsuspicious; childlike, innocent, guileless, naive 416.5; **knee-jerk, credulous** 953.8

23 believed, credited, held, trusted, accepted; undoubted, unquestioned, undisputed

24 believable, credible; tenable, plausible; fiduciary; reliable 969.17; unimpeachable, unexceptionable, **unquestionable** 969.15

25 fiducial, fiduciary, convictional

26 convincing, well-founded, **persuasive,** assuring, satisfactory, confidence-building; decisive, absolute, conclusive, determinative

27 doctrinal, preceptive, canonical, dogmatic, confessional, mandatory, of faith

ADVS **28 believingly, undoubtingly,** without doubt *or* question, unquestioningly; **trustingly;** piously, devoutly; **with confidence,** on faith

29 in one's opinion, to one's mind, to one's way of thinking, in one's estimation, according to one's lights, **as one sees it, to the best of one's belief**

953 CREDULITY

NOUNS **1 credulity, credulousness,** inclination to believe, willingness to believe; **blind faith,** unquestioning belief, knee-jerk response <nonformal>; uncritical acceptance, hasty *or* rash conviction; **trustfulness, trustingness, unsuspiciousness;** infatuation, dotage

2 gullibility, dupability, deceivability, persuadability; **simpleness,** simplicity, **ingenuousness, unsophistication; greenness, naïveté**

3 superstition, superstitiousness; **old wives' tale;** tradition, lore, folklore

4 trusting soul; dupe 358; sucker *and* patsy *and* easy mark *and* pushover <all nonformal>

VERBS **5 be credulous,** accept unquestioningly; **believe anything,** be uncritical, be a dupe, think the moon is made of green cheese, buy a pig in a poke

6 <nonformal or nonformal terms> kid oneself; fall for, swallow, swallow anything; swallow hook, line, and sinker; eat up, lap up, devour, gulp down, gobble up or down, buy into, bite, nibble, take the bait, tumble for, be taken in, be a sucker or a patsy or an easy mark

7 be superstitious; knock on wood, keep one's fingers crossed

ADJS **8 credulous, knee-jerk** <nonformal>, easily taken in; **undoubting** 952.21; **trustful, trusting; unsuspicious, unsuspecting;** overcredulous, overtrusting, overconfiding; infatuated, doting; **superstitious**

9 gullible, dupable, deceivable, foolable, deludable, exploitable, victimizable, seduceable; soft, easy <nonformal>, **simple; ingenuous, unsophisticated, green, naive** 416.5

954 UNBELIEF

NOUNS **1 unbelief, disbelief,** discredit; refusal or inability to believe; **incredulity** 955; **unpersuadedness,** lack of conviction; **denial** 335.2, **rejection** 372; atheism, **agnosticism** 695.6

2 doubt, doubtfulness, dubiousness, dubiety; **reservation, question; skepticism; suspicion,** suspiciousness, wariness, leeriness, **distrust, mistrust, misdoubt; misgiving,** self-doubt, diffidence; apprehension 127.4; **uncertainty** 970; shadow of doubt

3 unbelievability, unbelievableness, **incredibility, implausibility,** inconceivability, untenableness; **doubtfulness, questionableness**

4 doubter, doubting Thomas; scoffer, skeptic, cynic, poohpooher, nay-sayer, unbeliever 695.11

VERBS **5 disbelieve, not believe,** refuse to admit, not buy <nonformal>, take no stock in and set no store by <both nonformal>; **discredit,** refuse to credit or give credence to; gag on, **not swallow** 955.3; negate, scoff at, poohpooh; **reject** 372.2

6 doubt, be doubtful, be dubious, be skeptical, have one's doubts, harbor or entertain doubts or suspicions, half believe, **take with a grain of salt, distrust, mistrust; be uncertain** 970.9; **suspect,** smell a rat <nonformal>; **question,** query, **challenge, contest, dispute,** greet with skepticism, keep one's eye on, raise a question, awake a doubt or suspicion; **doubt one's word**

7 be unbelievable, be incredible, be hard to swallow, defy belief, strain one's credulity, **stagger belief;** undermine one's faith; boggle the mind, fill with doubt

ADJS **8 unbelieving, disbelieving; incredulous** 955.4; **heretical** 688.9; **irreligious** 695.17

9 doubting, doubtful, in doubt, dubious; questioning; skeptical; distrustful, mistrustful, untrustful; suspicious, suspecting, wary, leery; **agnostic; uncertain**

10 unbelievable, incredible, unthinkable, **implausible,** inconceivable, **hard to believe,** tall <nonformal>; **defying belief,** passing belief; **mind-boggling,** preposterous, absurd, ridiculous, unearthly, ungodly; **doubtful, dubious,** doubtable, dubitable; **questionable,** problematic, **unconvincing,** open to doubt or suspicion; **suspicious,** suspect

11 under a cloud, unreliable

12 doubted, questioned, disputed, contested, moot; **distrusted,** mistrusted; **suspect,** suspected, **under suspicion,** under a cloud; **discredited,** exploded, rejected, **disbelieved**

ADVS **13 unbelievingly,** doubtingly, **doubtfully, dubiously,** questioningly, **skeptically,** suspiciously; **with a grain of salt**

14 unbelievably, incredibly, implausibly, inconceivably

955 INCREDULITY

NOUNS **1 incredulity, incredulousness,** tough-mindedness, hardheadedness, **inconvincibility,** unpersuasibility; **suspicious-**

ness, suspicion, wariness, leeriness, guardedness, caution; **skepticism** 954.2

2 **ungullibility, undupability, undeceivability; sophistication**

VERBS 3 **refuse to believe, not allow oneself to believe,** be slow to believe *or* accept; **disbelieve** 954.5; **be skeptical** 954.6; **not swallow,** not go for *and* not fall for <both nonformal>, not be taken in by; **not accept, not buy** *or* **buy into** <nonformal>, **reject** 372.2

ADJS 4 **incredulous, hard of belief,** disposed to doubt, disinclined to believe, unwilling to accept; **inconvincible,** unconvincible, unpersuadable; **suspicious, suspecting,** wary, leery, cautious, guarded; **skeptical** 954.9

5 **ungullible, undupable, undeceivable, unfoolable, undeludable; sophisticated, wise, hardheaded,** practical, realistic, tough-minded; nobody's fool, not born yesterday

956 EVIDENCE, PROOF

NOUNS 1 **evidence, proof; reason to believe; ground, grounds, facts, data,** premises; **fact, datum; indication, manifestation, sign, symptom,** mark, token; documentation; **clue;** exhibit

2 **testimony, attestation, witness;** testimonial; **statement, declaration, assertion,** asseveration, affirmation 334, **disclosure** 351, profession, word; **deposition,** sworn evidence *or* testimony; affidavit, sworn statement

3 **proof, demonstration,** ironclad proof, incontrovertible proof; **determination, establishment, settlement; conclusive evidence,** smoking gun <nonformal>; open-and-shut case; burden of proof, onus; the proof of the pudding

4 **confirmation, substantiation,** affirmation, attestation, **authentication, validation,** certifica-

tion, **verification; corroboration, support,** bolstering, reinforcement, undergirding, strengthening; **documentation**

5 **citation, reference,** quotation; **exemplification,** instance, example, case, case in point, particular, item

6 **witness, eyewitness,** spectator; **bystander,** passerby; **deponent, testifier,** attestant, attester, attestator, voucher, swearer; **informant,** informer

7 **provability, demonstrability,** determinability; confirmability, supportability, verifiability

VERBS 8 **evidence, evince,** furnish evidence, **show, go to show, mean,** testify to; **demonstrate, illustrate,** exhibit, manifest, set forth; **attest; indicate, signify,** signalize, **denote, betoken, point to,** give indication of; **connote, imply, suggest,** involve; **speak for itself,** speak volumes

9 **testify, attest, give evidence, give** *or* **bear witness; disclose** 351.4; **vouch, depose,** depone, **warrant, swear,** avow, **affirm,** avouch, aver, asseverate, **certify, give one's word**

10 **prove, demonstrate, show,** prove true; **establish, determine, ascertain,** remove all doubt; **settle,** settle the matter; **set at rest;** nail down <nonformal>; **prove one's point,** make one's case, make out a case; follow as a matter of course

11 **confirm,** affirm, **attest,** warrant, **substantiate, authenticate, validate, certify,** ratify, **verify; corroborate, bear out,** support, buttress, **sustain,** fortify, bolster, reinforce, undergird, strengthen; **document**

12 **adduce,** produce, **advance, present,** bring to bear, **offer, bring forward,** bring on; rally, marshal, deploy, array; call to *or* put in the witness box

13 **cite, name,** call to mind; **instance,** cite cases *or* a case in point, itemize, particularize; **exemplify, illustrate,** demonstrate;

document; **quote,** quote chapter and verse
14 **refer to,** direct attention to, **appeal to,** invoke; make reference to
15 **have evidence** *or* **proof,** have a case, **have something on** <nonformal>; **have the goods on** <nonformal>
ADJS 16 **evidential,** evidentiary, **factual, significant, indicative,** probative; implicit, suggestive; material, weighty; **conclusive,** determinative, **decisive,** incontrovertible, indisputable, irrefutable, absolute; documented, documentary; **valid, admissible**
17 **demonstrative,** demonstrating; apodictic
18 **confirming,** confirmatory; substantiating, **verifying; corroborating, corroborative,** supportive, **supporting**
19 **provable, demonstrable,** apodictic, **confirmable,** supportable, sustainable, **verifiable**
20 **proved, proven, demonstrated,** shown; **established, settled, determined,** nailed down <nonformal>; **confirmed, substantiated, authenticated, certified, validated, verified; corroborated,** borne out
21 **unrefuted,** uncontroverted, uncontradicted, **undenied**
ADVS 22 **evidentially,** on the evidence, as attested by; **in confirmation, in corroboration of, in support of;** dead to rights *and* with a smoking gun *and* with one's pants down <all nonformal>
23 **to illustrate,** to prove the point, as a case in point, by way of example, **for example, for instance,** to cite an instance

957 DISPROOF

NOUNS 1 **disproof,** disproving, disproval, **invalidation,** negation ; exposure, exposé
2 **refutation, confutation, rebuttal, answer,** crushing rejoinder, squelch; discrediting; **contradiction,** controversion, **denial** 335.2
3 **conclusive argument, knockdown argument,** sockdolager <nonformal>; **clincher** *or* crusher *or* **settler** *and* squelcher <all nonformal>
VERBS 4 **disprove, invalidate,** discredit, prove the contrary, give the lie to; **negate; expose, show up; explode,** blow sky-high, **puncture,** deflate, **shoot** *or* **poke full of holes, cut to pieces, cut the ground from under; knock the bottom out of** <nonformal>, cut the ground from under one's feet, have the last word, put *or* lay to rest
5 **refute, confute, confound, rebut,** parry, **answer conclusively,** dispose of; **overthrow,** overturn, overwhelm, undermine; crush, smash all opposition; silence, stop the mouth of; take the wind out of one's sails; **contradict,** controvert, **deny** 335.4
ADJS 6 **refuting, confuting,** contradictory, contrary 335.5
7 **disproved, invalidated,** negated, discredited, belied; **exposed,** shown up; **punctured,** deflated, **exploded; refuted,** confuted, confounded; **upset, overthrown,** overturned; **contradicted,** impugned
8 **unproved, undemonstrated; untried,** untested; **unestablished,** unsettled, **undetermined,** unascertained; **unconfirmed, unsubstantiated, unauthenticated,** unvalidated, **unverified; uncorroborated,** unsustained, **unsupported, groundless, unfounded** 935.13; **inconclusive,** indecisive; **moot**
9 **unprovable, undemonstrable,** unsubstantiatable, **unsupportable,** unconfirmable, unsustainable, unverifiable
10 **refutable,** confutable

958 QUALIFICATION

NOUNS 1 **qualification, limitation, limiting, restriction,** circumscription, **modification;** specification; **allowance, concession,** cession, grant; grain of

salt; **reservation, exception,**
waiver, exemption; **exclusion;**
mental reservation, crossing
one's fingers; extenuating circumstances

2 **condition, provision, proviso,**
stipulation; specification, limitation, boundary condition;
contingency, circumstance 765;
catch and **joker** and **kicker** <all
nonformal>; **requisite, prerequisite,** obligation; escape clause,
escape hatch; **terms,** provisions;
small or fine print and fine print
at the bottom <all nonformal>

VERBS 3 **qualify, limit,** hedge,
modify, restrict, circumscribe,
set limits or conditions, box in
<nonformal>; **temper, season,**
leaven, soften, modulate, moderate, assuage, **mitigate,** palliate,
abate

4 **make conditional, condition;**
attach a condition or proviso,
stipulate; make a point of; **have**
a catch and have a joker or kicker
and have a string attached <all
nonformal>; cross one's fingers
behind one's back

5 **allow for, make allowance for,**
make room for, open the door to,
take into account or **consideration, consider;** allow, **grant, concede,** admit exceptions; **relax,** relax the condition, **waive, set**
aside, ease, pull one's punches
<nonformal>; disregard, **discount,** leave out of account; take
with a grain of salt

6 **depend; depend on** or **upon,**
hang on or **upon, rest on** or
upon, stand on or upon, be based
on, be bounded or limited by, be
predicated on, **be contingent** or
conditional on; hinge on or
upon, turn on or **upon, revolve**
on or **upon**

ADJS 7 **qualifying, modifying,** altering; **limiting, limitational, restricting,** limitative, restrictive,
bounding; **extenuating,** extenuatory, **mitigating,** mitigatory,
modulatory, palliative

8 **conditional, provisional,** provi-

sory; **specified, stipulated; temporary,** expedient

9 **contingent, dependent, depending;** contingent on, **dependent on, depending on,** predicated on, based on, turning on;
hedged or hedged about by;
boxed in <nonformal>; **subject**
to, incidental to

10 **qualified, modified, conditioned, limited, restricted,**
hedged about; **tempered, seasoned,** leavened, **mitigated,**
modulated

ADVS 11 **conditionally, provisionally, with qualifications,**
with a string or catch or joker or
kicker to it <all nonformal>; with
a grain of salt; **temporarily,** for
the time being

959 NO QUALIFICATIONS

NOUNS 1 **unqualifiedness, unconditionality, unreservedness,** uncircumscribedness; **absoluteness,** definiteness, explicitness

ADJS 2 **unqualified, unconditional, unrestricted,** unhampered, **unlimited,** uncircumscribed, unmitigated, **categorical, unreserved**; unadulterated,
intact; **implicit,** unhesitating; **explicit, express, unequivocal,** unmistakable; **peremptory,** indisputable; **without exception,** admitting no exception; **positive,**
absolute, flat, definitive, decisive, conclusive; **complete, entire, whole, total,** global; **utter,**
out-and-out, straight-out <nonformal>

ADVS 3 <nonformal terms> **no ifs,**
ands, or buts; no strings attached, no holds barred; downright, what you see is what you
get

960 FORESIGHT

NOUNS 1 **foresight, prevision,**
divination 961.2, forecast; **prediction** 961; **foreglimpse; prospect; anticipation,** envisagement; **foresightedness; farsightedness**; sagacity, discretion, provision, readiness, prudence 919.7

2 forethought, premeditation;
caution 494; lead time, advance
notice

3 foreknowledge, precognition,
prescience, presage, presentiment, foreboding; clairvoyance
689.8

4 foretaste

VERBS **5 foresee**, see ahead, **anticipate**, envision, envisage, **look
forward to**, look or pry or peep
into the future; **predict** 961.9

6 foreknow, know beforehand,
precognize; **have a presentiment, have a premonition**
133.11; see the handwriting on
the wall, intuit 933.4

ADJS **7 foreseeing, foresighted;
foreknowing, precognizant**,
precognitive, prescient; divinatory 961.11; anticipatory; **farseeing, farsighted**, sagacious, providential, prudent 919.19; intuitive
933.5; clairvoyant

8 foreseeable 961.13; foreseen
961.14; intuitable

ADVS **9** with foresight; against the
time when, for a rainy day

961 PREDICTION

NOUNS **1 prediction, foretelling**,
forecasting, **prognosis**, prognostication, presaging; **prophecy**, prophesying, vaticination;
soothsaying; forecast, promise;
apocalypse; prospectus; foresight
960; presentiment, foreboding;
omen 133.3,6; **guesswork**, speculation; **probability** 967; improbability 968

2 divination, divining; **augury**,
haruspication; **fortunetelling**,
crystal gazing, palm-reading,
palmistry; crystal ball; sorcery
690; clairvoyance 689.8

3 dowsing, witching, water witching; **divining rod** or stick, dowsing rod; dowser, water witch

**4 predictor, foreteller, prog-
nosticator**, seer, prefigurer; **forecaster**; prophet, soothsayer; **diviner**; augur; psychic 689.13; **for-
tuneteller**; crystal gazer; palmist;
haruspex, astrologer 1070.23;
prophet of doom, Cassandra

5 <nonformal terms> **dopester,
tipster, tout**

6 sibyl; Pythia

7 oracle; Delphic or Delphian oracle

8 predictability, divinability, **cal-
culability, foreseeability**

VERBS **9 predict, foretell, soothsay**, prefigure, **forecast, prophesy, prognosticate**, vaticinate,
forebode, presage, read the future; **foresee** 960.5; call the turn
and call one's shot <both nonfor-
mal>; **divine; tell fortunes**; read
palms, read tea leaves, cast a
horoscope; **guess**, speculate; **bet,
bet on, gamble**

10 portend, foretoken 133.12

ADJS **11 predictive; foretelling**,
forewarning, forecasting; **prophetic**, apocalyptic, apocalypti-
cal; vatic, vaticinal, mantic,
sibylline; **divinatory, oracular,**
auguring; **foreseeing** 960.7; presaging; **prognostic**, prognostica-
tive

12 ominous, premonitory, foreboding 133.17

**13 predictable, divinable, fore-
tellable, calculable; foreseeable, foreknowable**, precogniz-
able; **probable** 967.6; improbable
968.3

14 predicted, prophesied, presaged, **foretold, forecast**, foreshown; foreseen, foreglimpsed,
foreknown

962 NECESSITY

NOUNS **1 necessity**, entailment;
obligation; compulsion, duress
424.3

**2 requirement, requisite; neces-
sity, need, want**, occasion; **call
for, demand**, demand for; **prerequisite; must**, must item; **essential**, indispensable; necessities, essentials, bare necessities

3 needfulness, requisiteness; **es-
sentiality**, essentialness; **indis-
pensability**, indispensableness

**4 urgent need, dire necessity;
exigency** or exigence, **urgency**,
imperativeness, immediacy, pressure; case of need or emergency,

matter of life and death; **predicament** 1012.4

5 involuntariness, instinctiveness; compulsiveness; **instinct,** impulse 365; blind impulse *or* instinct

6 choicelessness, no choice, no alternative, **Hobson's choice**; six of one and half a dozen of the other, distinction without a difference

7 inevitability, inevitableness, **unavoidableness,** necessity, inescapableness, ineluctability; irrevocability, indefeasibility; relentlessness, inexorability, inflexibility; fatefulness, **certainty,** sureness; act of God, unavoidable casualty; **predetermination, fate** 963.2

VERBS **8 necessitate, oblige,** dictate, **constrain;** insist upon, **compel** 424.4

9 require, need, want, be in need of, be hurting for <nonformal>, stand in need of, not be able to do without; **call for,** cry for, cry out for, clamor for; **demand,** ask, claim, exact

10 be necessary, be one's fate; be a must <nonformal>; be under the necessity of; be obliged, **must, have to, need to,** have need to; **cannot help but,** cannot do otherwise

11 have no choice *or* **alternative,** have one's options reduced *or* closed, have no option but, cannot choose but; be pushed to the wall, be driven into a corner; take it or leave it *and* like it or lump it <both nonformal>

ADJS **12 necessary, obligatory, compulsory,** mandatory; **exigent, urgent,** necessitous, importunate, **imperative**

13 requisite, needful, required, needed, wanted, called for, indicated; **essential, vital, indispensable,** irreplaceable; prerequisite

14 involuntary, instinctive, automatic, mechanical, reflexive, knee-jerk <nonformal>, conditioned; **unconscious,** unthink-

ing; **unwitting,** unintentional, against one's will; **compulsive;** forced; **impulsive** 365.9

15 inevitable, unavoidable, necessary, **inescapable,** unpreventable, undeflectable, ineluctable, irrevocable, indefeasible; relentless, inexorable, unyielding, inflexible; **certain,** fateful, **sure,** sure as death and taxes; **destined, fated** 963.9

ADVS **16 necessarily, needfully,** requisitely; **of necessity,** from necessity, perforce; **willy-nilly,** whether one will or not; come what may; compulsorily

17 if necessary, if need be, if worst comes to worst; for lack of something better

18 involuntarily, instinctively, automatically, mechanically, reflexively; **unconsciously,** without premeditation; **unwittingly; compulsively; unwillingly** 325.8

19 inevitably, unavoidably, inescapably, come hell or high water <nonformal>, ineluctably; irrevocably, indefeasibly; relentlessly, inexorably; fatefully, **certainly, surely**

963 PREDETERMINATION

NOUNS **1 predetermination, predestination, preordination;** foregone conclusion, par for the course <nonformal>; **necessity** 962

2 fate, fortune, lot, cup, **portion,** karma, kismet; **destiny,** destination, **end,** final lot; **doom,** will of Heaven; **inevitability** 962.7; the handwriting on the wall; wheel of fortune *or* chance; astral influences, stars, planets, constellation, astrology 1070.20

3 Fates, Fata <L>, **Parcae, Moirai** <Gk>

4 determinism, fatalism, predeterminism; predestinarianism

5 determinist, fatalist, necessitarian, necessarian

VERBS **6 predetermine, predecide; predestine, preordain**

7 destine, predestine, ordain,

fate, appoint; have in store for;
doom, foredoom

ADJS **8 determined, predetermined, predecided, predestined, preordained**

9 destined, fated, fateful, ordained, in the cards, marked,
in store; **doomed,** foredoomed

10 deterministic, fatalistic, necessitarian, necessarian

964 PREARRANGEMENT

NOUNS **1 prearrangement**; premeditation, plotting, planning,
scheming; **reservation**

2 <nonformal terms> **put-up job,**
stacked deck, cold deck, boat
race, tank job; **frame-up,** frame,
setup

**3 schedule, program, bill, calen-
dar,** docket, slate; **batting order,
lineup, roster; prospectus; order of the day, agenda;** protocol;
laundry list *and* wish list <both
nonformal>

VERBS **4 prearrange,** preconcert;
premeditate, plot, plan, scheme;
reserve

5 <nonformal terms> **fix, rig,**
cook up; **stack the cards,** cold-
deck; frame, set up; **throw,** go in
the tank

6 schedule, line up <nonformal>,
slate, book, calendar, docket,
budget, put on the agenda

ADJS **7 prearranged,** precontrived,
preconcerted, cut out; premeditated, schemed; cut-and-dried,
cut-and-dry

8 <nonformal terms> **fixed,
rigged, put-up,** packed, stacked,
cooked; **in the bag,** on ice, sewed
up; **framed, framed-up,** set-up

9 scheduled, slated, booked,
billed, booked-in

965 POSSIBILITY

NOUNS **1 possibility, the realm of
possibility, conceivability,** imag-
inability; **probability, likelihood**
967; what can be done, the possible, the attainable, the feasible;
potential, potentiality, virtuality; contingency, eventuality;
chance, prospect; outside

chance <nonformal>, off chance,
remote possibility, ghost of a
chance; hope, outside hope, small
hope; **good possibility, good
chance**

**2 practicability, practicality, fea-
sibility; workability,** operability,
negotiability; **viability,** viable-
ness; **achievability, attainability;** surmountability

3 accessibility, access, **approachability, openness; penetrability,** perviousness; **ob-
tainability, availability,** se-
curableness

VERBS **4 be possible, have** or
stand a chance or **good chance,
bid fair to**

5 enable, clear the path for,
smooth the way for, open the
door to, open up the possibility of

ADJS **6 possible,** within the bounds
or realm or range of possibility, in
one's power, in one's hands, humanly possible; **probable, likely**
967.6; **conceivable, imaginable,
thinkable;** plausible 967.7; **potential**

**7 practicable, practical, fea-
sible; workable,** realizable, operable, negotiable, bridgeable; **viable; achievable, attainable;** sur-
mountable

**8 accessible, approachable,
reachable,** within reach; **open,**
open to; **penetrable,** pervious;
**obtainable, attainable, avail-
able,** procurable, securable, easy
to come by

ADVS **9 possibly, conceivably,**
imaginably, feasibly; within the
realm of possibility; **perhaps;
maybe,** for all one knows

**10 by any possibility, by any
chance,** by any means, **by any
manner of means;** in any possible way, **at any cost, at all;** on the
off chance, by merest chance

11 if possible, if humanly possible,
God willing

966 IMPOSSIBILITY

NOUNS **1 impossibility,** the realm
of the impossible, **inconceivability,** what can never be,

what cannot happen, hopelessness, **no chance** 971.10; **self-contradiction,** absurdity, paradox, oxymoron, logical impossibility

2 **impracticability, impracticality, unfeasibility; unworkability,** inoperability; **unachievability, unattainability;** insurmountability, **insuperability**

3 **inaccessibility; unapproachability,** unreachableness; **impenetrability,** imperviousness; **unobtainability, unattainability, unavailability**

VERBS 4 **be impossible, not have a chance,** be a waste of time; **contradict itself,** be a logical impossibility; fly in the face of reason

5 **attempt the impossible,** try for a miracle, look for a needle in a haystack, make a silk purse out of a sow's ear *or* change the leopard's spots *or* get blood from a turnip

6 **make impossible, rule out,** disqualify, **bar,** prohibit, put out of reach

ADJS 7 **impossible, not possible,** contrary to reason, at variance with the facts; **inconceivable, unimaginable, unthinkable, not to be thought of, out of the question;** hopeless; **absurd,** ridiculous, preposterous; **self-contradictory,** paradoxical, oxymoronic, logically impossible

8 **impracticable, impractical, unpragmatic, unfeasible; unworkable,** inoperable; **unachievable, unattainable;** insurmountable, unsurmountable, **insuperable; beyond one's depth,** too much for

9 **inaccessible,** unaccessible; **unapproachable; unreachable,** beyond reach, out of reach; **impenetrable,** impervious; **unobtainable, unattainable, unavailable,** unsecurable; **not to be had for love or money**

ADVS 10 **impossibly, inconceiva-**

bly, unimaginably, unthinkably; not at any price

967 PROBABILITY

NOUNS 1 **probability, likelihood; chance, odds; expectation, outlook,** prospect; favorable prospect, fair expectation; **good chance** 971.8; presumption; tendency; reasonable ground *or* presumption; possibility 965

2 mathematical probability, statistical probability, statistics

3 **plausibility; reasonability** 934.9; **credibility** 952.8

VERBS 4 **be probable, seem likely,** offer the expectation, have a good chance; **promise,** be promising, **bid fair to,** be in the cards, lead one to expect; **make probable,** smooth the way for; increase the chances

5 **think likely, daresay,** venture to say; **presume**

ADJS 6 **probable, likely, liable, apt,** in the cards, odds-on; **promising, hopeful;** foreseeable, **predictable; presumable,** presumptive; **statistical,** actuarial

7 **plausible; reasonable** 934.20; credible 952.24; **conceivable** 965.6

ADVS 8 **probably, in all probability** *or* **likelihood,** likely, **most likely, very likely; doubtlessly,** doubtless, **no doubt,** indubitably; **presumably,** presumptively

968 IMPROBABILITY

NOUNS 1 **improbability, unlikelihood,** unlikeliness; **doubtfulness,** dubiousness, **questionableness; implausibility,** incredibility 954.3; bare possibility, faint likelihood, poor prospect, a ghost of a chance, fat chance <nonformal>; **small chance** 971.9

VERBS 2 **be improbable, not be likely,** strain one's credulity, go beyond reason, go beyond the bounds of reason *or* probability, be far-fetched

ADJS 3 **improbable, unlikely,** unpromising, logic-defying; **doubt-**

ful, dubious, **questionable,** more than doubtful; **implausible,** incredible 954.10; unexpected, unpredictable

969 CERTAINTY

NOUNS 1 **certainty, certitude, sureness, surety, assurance, assuredness; positiveness, absoluteness, definiteness,** dead or moral or absolute certainty; unequivocalness, unambiguity, univocality; **infallibility,** inerrancy, **necessity,** predetermination, predestination, **inevitability** 962.7; **truth** 972; **proved fact**

2 <nonformal terms> **sure thing,** dead certainty, dead-sure thing, sure bet, lead-pipe cinch, dead cinch, lock, shoo-in, open-and-shut case

3 **unquestionability, undeniability, indisputability,** incontrovertibility, **irrefutability,** unimpeachability; **doubtlessness, questionlessness; demonstrability; reality,** actuality 760.2

4 **reliability, dependability, dependableness, validity, trustworthiness;** predictability; **soundness,** solidity, staunchness, steadiness, **steadfastness;** secureness, **security;** invincibility 15.4; **authoritativeness, authenticity**

5 **confidence,** conviction, belief 952, **sureness, assurance, assuredness,** surety, security, certitude; **faith;** trust 952.1; **positiveness, cocksureness; self-confidence, self-assurance, self-reliance;** poise 106.3; courage 492; **overconfidence, oversureness,** hubris; pride 136, arrogance 141, pomposity 501.7, self-importance 140.1

6 **dogmatism,** pontification, **positiveness, opinionatedness**

7 **dogmatist,** doctrinaire, bigot

8 **ensuring, assurance;** reassurance; **certification;** ascertainment, **determination,** establishment; **verification, corroboration,** substantiation, validation; **confirmation**

VERBS 9 **be certain, be confident,** feel sure, rest assured, **have no doubt,** doubt not; **bet on** and gamble on and bet one's bottom dollar on and bet the ranch on <all nonformal>; **go without saying**

10 **dogmatize,** pontificate, proclaim

11 **make sure, make certain,** make no mistake; **assure, ensure,** insure, **certify; ascertain, get a fix** or **lock on** <nonformal>; **find out,** get at, see to it, see that; **determine,** decide, **establish,** lock in and nail down and clinch and cinch <all nonformal>, set at rest; **reassure**

12 **verify, confirm,** audit, **collate,** validate, **check, double-check,** cross-check, check and double-check

ADJS 13 **certain, sure; positive, absolute, definite,** apodictic; decisive, conclusive; unequivocal, unmistakable, unambiguous; **necessary,** ineluctable, predetermined, predestined, **inevitable** 962.15; **true** 972.12

14 <nonformal or nonformal terms> dead sure, sure as death and taxes, sure as can be, sure as shooting, sure as God made little green apples, as sure as I live and breathe

15 **obvious, patent, unquestionable, unexceptionable, undeniable, self-evident,** axiomatic; indubitable, unarguable, indisputable, incontestable, **irrefutable,** incontrovertible, irrefragable, unanswerable, unimpeachable, absolute; **demonstrable,** verifiable, confirmable; well-founded, well-established, well-grounded; factual, **real,** actual 760.15

16 **undoubted, unquestioned, undisputed, uncontested,** unchallenged, uncontroversial; **doubtless, questionless,** beyond a shadow of doubt, beyond question

17 **reliable, dependable, sure,** surefire <nonformal>, **trustwor-**

thy, **trusty, to be depended** or
**relied upon; secure, solid,
sound, firm,** fast, **stable, substantial,** staunch, steady, **steadfast, faithful, unfailing**

18 **authoritative, authentic, official;** ex cathedra; approved, accepted, received, pontific; straight
from the horse's mouth

19 **infallible, inerrable,** inerrant,
unerring

20 **assured; determined, decided,
ascertained; settled, established,** fixed, set, stated, secure;
certified, attested, guaranteed,
warranted, proved; wired and
open-and-shut and nailed down
and in the bag <all nonformal>

21 **confident, sure,** secure, **assured,** determined; **convinced,**
persuaded, positive, **cocksure;
unhesitating,** unfaltering, unwavering; **undoubting** 952.21;
**self-confident, self-assured,
self-reliant; overconfident,
oversure,** overweening, hubristic; arrogant 141.9, pompous
501.22, self-important 140.8

22 **dogmatic, dogmatical,
positive,** peremptory, pontifical, oracular; **opinionated,**
conceited 140.11; doctrinaire;
bigoted

ADVS 23 **certainly, surely, assuredly, positively, absolutely, definitely,** decidedly; decisively, distinctly, unequivocally, unmistakably; **for certain,** and no mistake
<nonformal>; **most certainly,**
most assuredly; **indeed;** truly; **of
course,** as a matter of course; **by
all means,** by all manner of
means; at any rate, at all events;
no two ways about it; no ifs, ands,
or buts

24 **surely, sure, to be sure,** sure
enough, for sure <nonformal>;
sure thing <nonformal>

25 **unquestionably, without question, undoubtedly, beyond the
shadow of a doubt, beyond a
reasonable doubt, indubitably,
admittedly, undeniably,** unarguably, indisputably, incontestably, incontrovertibly, irre-

futably, irrefragably; **doubtlessly,**
doubtless, **no doubt, without
doubt**

26 **without fail,** unfailingly, **come
what may,** come hell or high water <nonformal>; rain or shine,
sink or swim

970 UNCERTAINTY

NOUNS 1 **uncertainty, incertitude,
unsureness; unpredictability,**
unaccountability; **indetermination,** indeterminacy; **relativity,**
relativism, contingency; **randomness, chance, luck; indecision,**
indecisiveness; **hesitation, hesitancy; suspense,** suspensefulness; **fickleness, capriciousness, erraticness, changeableness** 853; **vacillation, irresolution** 362

2 **doubtfulness, dubiousness,
doubt,** dubiety; **questionableness, disputability,** deniability;
disbelief 954.1

3 **bewilderment,** disconcertedness, **embarrassment, confoundment,** discomposure, **confusion; perplexity, puzzlement,
bafflement,** predicament, plight,
quandary, dilemma, horns of a
dilemma; fix and jam and pickle
and scrape and stew <all nonformal>; **disturbance, upset,
bother**

4 **vagueness, indefiniteness, indecisiveness,** indefinableness,
unclearness, indistinctness,
haziness, fogginess; **obscurity,**
obscuration; **looseness, laxity,
inexactness,** imprecision;
broadness, generality; amorphousness, shapelessness, inchoateness, incoherence

5 **equivocalness,** equivocality,
ambiguity 539

6 **unreliability, undependability,
untrustworthiness,** treachery;
unsureness, insecurity, unsoundness, infirmity, insolidity,
instability, insubstantiality, **unsteadfastness,** unsteadiness;
precariousness, hazard, riskiness, moment of truth, tightrope
walking, perilousness, ticklish-

ness; **unauthoritativeness,** unauthenticity

7 **fallibility,** errancy, liability to
error

8 <an uncertainty> **gamble,
guess,** guesstimate *and* ballpark
figure <nonformal>; **chance, wager; toss-up** <nonformal>, **touch
and go;** contingency; **question,
open question;** undecided issue,
loose end; **gray area,** borderline
case; pig in a poke; leap in the
dark

VERBS 9 **be uncertain, feel unsure; doubt,** have one's doubts,
question, agonize over; **wonder,**
wonder whether; not be able to
make head or tail of; be at sea; be
at one's wit's end, **not know
which way to turn,** be of two
minds, be at sixes and sevens, go
around in circles; go off in all directions at once

10 **hang in doubt,** think twice; **falter,** dither, **hesitate, vacillate**
362.8

11 **depend,** be contingent *or* conditional on, hang on; **hang, hang
in the balance,** be touch and go,
**hang in suspense; hang by a
thread,** hang by a hair

12 **bewilder, disconcert,** discompose, **upset,** perturb, **disturb,
dismay;** abash, **embarrass, put
out, bother,** keep one on tenterhooks

13 **perplex, baffle, confound,**
daze, addle, muddle, **mystify,
puzzle,** nonplus; keep one guess-
ing

14 <nonformal terms> **stump,** buffalo, bamboozle, stick, floor, beat
the shit out of

15 **make uncertain, obscure,
muddle, confuse** 984.7

ADJS 16 **uncertain, unsure; doubting,** agnostic, **skeptical,** uncon-
vinced, unpersuaded; **unpredictable,** unforeseeable, incalculable,
uncountable; unverifiable, unprovable, unconfirmable; **equivocal,** imprecise, ambiguous;
fickle, capricious, whimsical,
erratic, variable, wavering,
changeable 853.6; **hesitant,** hes-

itating; **indecisive, irresolute**
362.9

17 **doubtful; in doubt;** dubitable,
**dubious, questionable, prob-
lematical, problematical, speculative,** conjectural; **debatable,**
moot, arguable, disputable, **controversial,** refutable, deniable;
suspicious, suspect; open to
question *or* doubt

18 **undecided, undetermined, unsettled,** unfixed, unestablished;
pending, depending, contingent,
conditional; **open,** in question, at
issue, **in the balance, up in the
air,** up for grabs <nonformal>, **in
suspense**

19 **vague, indefinite, indecisive,
indeterminate,** indeterminable,
**undetermined; random,
chance,** chancy <nonformal>,
hit-or-miss; indefinable, undefined, ill-defined, **unclear, indistinct,** fuzzy, **obscure, confused,
hazy,** shadowy, misty, foggy,
murky, blurred, blurry, veiled;
loose, lax, inexact, inaccurate,
imprecise; unspecified; **broad,
general,** sweeping; amorphous,
shapeless; inchoate, disordered,
chaotic, incoherent

20 **unreliable, undependable, untrustworthy, unsure,** not to be
relied on; **insecure, unsound,
infirm, unstable,** insubstantial,
unsteadfast, unsteady, desultory; **precarious,** perilous, risky,
ticklish; shifty, slippery as an eel;
provisional, tentative, temporary

21 **unauthoritative, unauthentic,
unofficial,** apocryphal; **uncer-
tified, unverified,** uncorroborated, unauthenticated, unvalidated; **undemonstrated, unproved**

22 **fallible, errable,** errant, liable
or open to error

23 **unconfident, unsure, un-
assured, insecure**

24 **bewildered, dismayed,** distracted, distraught, abashed, **disconcerted, embarrassed,** discomposed, **put-out, disturbed,
upset,** perturbed, **bothered,** all
hot and bothered <nonformal>;

confused 984.12; going around in circles, like a chicken with its head cut off <nonformal>; **in a fix** or stew or pickle or jam <nonformal>; **lost, adrift, at sea,** off the track, disoriented
25 **in a dilemma,** on the horns of a dilemma; **perplexed, confounded, mystified, puzzled, nonplussed, baffled,** bamboozled <nonformal>, buffaloed <nonformal>; **at a loss, at one's wit's end,** fuddled, addled, muddled, dazed; **on tenterhooks,** in suspense
26 <nonformal terms> **beat,** stuck, stumped, thrown, buffaloed
27 **bewildering, confusing, distracting, disconcerting,** discomposing, **dismaying, embarrassing,** disturbing, **upsetting,** perturbing, bothering; **perplexing, baffling, mystifying, mysterious, puzzling; problematic** or problematical
ADVS **28 uncertainly, unsurely; doubtfully, dubiously;** at sea, on the horns of a dilemma, at sixes and sevens; perplexedly, disconcertedly, confusedly
29 **vaguely, indefinitely,** indefinably, **indistinctly,** indecisively, **obscurely; broadly, generally**

971 CHANCE
<absence of assignable cause>

NOUNS **1 chance,** happenstance; **luck;** serendipity, dumb luck <nonformal>, rotten and tough luck <both nonformal>; **fortune,** fate, **destiny; fortuity, randomness,** fortuitousness, adventitiousness, uncertainty 970, casualness, crazy quilt, patternlessness; break <nonformal>, the breaks <nonformal>, the luck of the draw, fall or throw of the dice, the way things fall, the way the cards fall, how they fall, the way the cookie crumbles or the ball bounces <both nonformal>; **probability** 967, law of averages; random sample, **risk, risktaking, chancing, gamble** 759; **opportunity** 842.2

2 Chance, Fortune, Lady or Dame Fortune
3 **purposelessness, causelessness,** randomness, **unpredictability** 970.1, **aimlessness**
4 **haphazard, random;** potluck
5 **vicissitudes,** ins and outs, **ups and downs,** feast and famine; **chain of circumstances,** vicious circle, **domino effect**
6 <chance event> **happening,** happenstance; **fortuity, accident,** casualty, hazard; contingency; **fluke** <nonformal>, freak occurrence or accident; lucky shot, long shot, one in a million
7 **even chance,** even break and fair shake <both nonformal>, level playing field, touch and go; **half a chance,** fifty-fifty; toss, **toss-up**
8 **good chance, sporting chance;** odds-on chance, **likelihood, possibility** 965, probability 967; **sure bet,** sure thing and dollars to doughnuts <both nonformal>
9 **small chance,** dark horse, **poor prospect** or prognosis, **unlikelihood, improbability** 968, not half a chance; **off chance, outside chance** <nonformal>, **remote possibility,** a ghost of a chance, **fighting chance** <nonformal>; long shot <nonformal>, hundred-to-one shot <nonformal>
10 **no chance,** not a snowball's chance in hell <nonformal>, not a prayer; **impossibility** 966, hopelessness
VERBS **11 chance,** happen by chance, hazard, **happen** 830.5, come or happen along, **turn up,** pop up <nonformal>, **befall**
12 **risk,** take a chance, push or press one's luck, put one's money where one's mouth is <nonformal>, **gamble, bet** 759.19; risk one's neck and shoot the works and go for broke <all nonformal>; **predict** 961.9, prognosticate, make book <nonformal>
13 have a chance or an opportunity, **stand a chance, bid fair to,** admit of; be in the running <nonfor-

mal>; have *or* take a chance at,
have a fling *or* shot at <nonfor-
mal>; be a dark horse
14 not have *or* stand a chance, not
have a prayer, not stand a snowball's chance in hell <nonfor-
mal>; **be out of the running**
ADJS **15 chance;** chancy <nonfor-
mal>, **risky** <nonformal>; **fortuitous, accidental; lucky,** fortunate, serendipitous; **casual,** adventitious, contingent, iffy <non-
formal>; **causeless,** uncaused;
unexpected 131.10, **unpredictable,** unforeseeable, **unforeseen**
**16 purposeless, causeless, aim-
less,** unmotivated, mindless;
haphazard, random, inexplicable, promiscuous, indiscriminate,
leaving much to chance
17 unintentional, unintended, **un-
meant, unplanned; unpremeditated,** unguided; **unwitting, unthinking,** unconscious, involuntary
18 impossible 966.7; improbable
968.3
ADVS **19 by chance, by accident,
accidentally, casually,** incidentally, by coincidence, **unpredictably, fortuitously, out of a clear
blue sky; as it chanced, as luck
would have it,** as the case may
be; somehow, in some way, in
some way or other, for some reason
**20 purposelessly, aimlessly; hap-
hazardly, randomly,** inexplicably, unaccountably, promiscuously, indiscriminately, **at random**
**21 unintentionally, without de-
sign, unwittingly**

972 TRUTH

<conformity to fact or reality>

NOUNS **1 truth, trueness, verity,**
veridicality, simple *or* unadorned
truth; **unerroneousness, un-
falseness,** unfallaciousness; **objective truth, actuality,** historic-
ity; **fact, actuality, reality** 760.2,
the real world; truthfulness, veracity 644.3
2 a truth, a self-evident truth, an

axiomatic truth, an axiom; a
premise, a given
3 the truth, the truth of the matter, the case; the unvarnished
truth, the unadorned truth, the
naked truth; the absolute truth,
the unalloyed truth, the hard
truth, gospel truth; the truth, the
whole truth, and nothing but the
truth
4 <nonformal terms> **what's
what,** like it is, where it's at, the
honest-to-God truth, the real
thing, the genuine article, the real
McCoy, chapter and verse, the
gospel truth, the lowdown
**5 accuracy, correctness, right-
ness, rigor, rigorousness, exactness, exactitude; preciseness,
precision;** pinpoint accuracy;
faultlessness, perfection,
flawlessness, impeccability, unimpeachability; **faithfulness,
fidelity;** literalness, the letter;
strictness, severity, rigidity; subtlety, refinement; **meticulousness** 339.3
6 validity, soundness, solidity,
justness; authority, **authoritativeness; cogency,** persuasiveness
7 genuineness, authenticity,
bona fides, **legitimacy; realness,
realism, naturalism,** naturalness, truth to nature, **lifelike-
ness,** slice of life, true-to-lifeness,
verisimilitude; **literalness,** liter-
ality; **unspuriousness,** un-
speciousness, artlessness, unaffectedness; **honesty, sincerity**
VERBS **8 be true;** square with the
facts; **prove true, prove out;**
hold true, hold good, hold water <nonformal>, hold *or* stick
together <nonformal>, **hold up,**
wash <nonformal>, **stand up,**
stand the test, **hold,** remain valid;
be truthful
9 seem true, ring true, sound true,
carry conviction, have the ring
of truth
10 be right, be correct, get it
straight; add up; **hit the nail on
the head,** hit the bull's-eye
11 be accurate, dot one's i's and

cross one's t's, be precise; make precise, particularize

12 **come true, come about, turn out, come to pass** *or* **to be,** happen as expected

ADJS 13 **true, truthful; unerroneous,** in conformity with the facts *or* the evidence *or* reality, on the up-and-up <nonformal>; gospel, **hard,** cast-iron; **real, veritable,** objective, in conformity with the facts *or* the evidence *or* the data *or* reality, **factual, actual** 760.15, effectual, **historical; certain,** unquestionable 969.15; **ascertained, proved, proven, verified,** validated, **certified,** demonstrated, confirmed, determined, established, attested, substantiated, **authenticated,** corroborated; **veracious** 644.16

14 **valid, sound, well-grounded, well-founded,** hard, solid, substantial; consistent, self-consistent, logical; **good, just,** sufficient; **cogent, weighty, authoritative**

15 **genuine, authentic,** veridical, **real, natural, realistic, naturalistic, true to nature, lifelike,** true to life, veristic; **literal,** letter-perfect; verbatim, **word-for-word; legitimate,** rightful, lawful; **bona fide,** card-carrying <nonformal>, **good,** sure-enough <nonformal>, **sincere, honest;** candid, honest-to-God <nonformal>; **inartificial, unsynthetic; undisguised, uncounterfeited, unpretended, unaffected, unassumed; unassuming, simple,** unfeigning; **unfictitious,** unconcocted, uninvented, unimagined; **original;** unexaggerated, undistorted, unflattering, unvarnished, uncolored, unqualified; **unadulterated** 797.7; **pure,** simon-pure; **sterling,** all wool and a yard wide <nonformal>

16 **accurate, correct, right,** proper, just; all right *or* OK *or* okay <all nonformal>, dead right, on target *and* on the money *and* on the nose <all nonformal>; **faultless,** flawless, impeccable, unimpeach-

able, unexceptionable; **absolute, perfect; meticulous** 339.12

17 **exact, precise,** express; **faithful;** direct; **unerring,** undeviating, constant; **infallible,** inerrant, inerrable; **strict, rigorous,** rigid; **nice,** delicate, subtle, **fine,** refined

ADVS 18 **truly, really, verily,** veritably, **in truth, actually,** historically, objectively, impersonally, rigorously, strictly, unquestionably, **in reality, in fact,** in point of fact, as a matter of fact, to tell the truth, with truth; **indeed; certainly; indubitably, undoubtedly** 969.25

19 **genuinely, authentically, really,** naturally, **legitimately, honestly,** veridically; warts and all; with all one's heart and soul

20 **accurately, correctly,** rightly, properly, straight; **perfectly, faultlessly,** flawlessly, impeccably, unimpeachably, unexceptionably; **just right**

21 **exactly, precisely,** to a T, expressly; **just, dead,** right, straight, even, square, **plumb,** directly, squarely, point-blank; verbatim, **literally,** word for word, word for word and letter for letter, in the same words, to the letter; **faithfully, strictly, rigorously,** rigidly; **definitely, positively, absolutely; in every respect,** in all respects

22 **to be exact, to be precise,** strictly, technically, strictly **speaking,** by the book

23 **to a nicety,** to a T, within an inch

973 WISE SAYING

NOUNS 1 **maxim, aphorism, apothegm, epigram, dictum, adage, proverb, saw, saying,** witticism, catchphrase, mot, motto, moral; **precept,** sutra; wise saying *or* expression, sententious expression *or* saying; **conventional wisdom, common knowledge; ana, analects, proverbs, wisdom, wisdom literature, collected sayings**

2 axiom, truth, postulate, **truism,** self-evident truth; theorem; **proposition; principle; formula; rule, law, dictum;** golden rule

3 platitude, cliché, saw, old saw, commonplace, banality, bromide, **chestnut** <nonformal>, tired phrase, trite saying, hackneyed *or* stereotyped saying, **familiar tune** *or* **story, old song** *or* **story,** twice-told tale; prosaism; old joke 489.9

4 motto, slogan, catchword, catchphrase, tag line; **device;** epithet; inscription, epigraph

VERBS **5** aphorize, epigrammatize, coin a phrase

ADJS **6 aphoristic, proverbial,** epigrammatic, **axiomatical; sententious, pithy,** gnomic, pungent, succinct, terse; formulaic; **cliché,** banal, tired, trite, **platitudinous** 117.9

ADVS **7 proverbially, as the saying goes,** as they say, as the fellow says <nonformal>, as it has been said

974 ERROR

NOUNS **1 error, erroneousness; untrueness,** untruthfulness, **untruth; wrongness, wrong; falseness, falsity; fallacy, fallaciousness,** self-contradiction; fault, **faultiness,** defectiveness; **sin** 655, sinfulness, peccancy, flaw; misfeasance; errancy, aberrancy, **deviancy; heresy,** unorthodoxy, heterodoxy; perversion, **distortion; mistaking,** misconstruction; **delusion, illusion** 975; **misinterpretation** 342

2 inaccuracy, inaccurateness, **incorrectness, uncorrectness, inexactness,** inexactitude, **unpreciseness,** imprecision, laxity, unrigorousness; negligence; approximation; **deviation;** uncertainty 970

3 mistake, error; fault; misconception, misapprehension, misunderstanding; misstatement, misquotation; **misprint, typographical error,** typo <nonformal>; **misjudgment, mis-**

calculation 947.1; misuse; miscarriage

4 slip, slipup *and* miscue <both nonformal>; **lapse, oversight,** omission, inadvertence *or* inadvertency; **misstep,** false *or* wrong step; false note; **slip of the tongue; slip of the pen**

5 blunder, faux pas, gaffe, solecism; indiscretion 922.4; **botch, bungle** 414.5

6 <nonformal terms> **goof, booboo,** muff, flub, blooper, boot, bobble, boner, bonehead play *or* trick; howler, screamer; fuck-up, screw-up, foul-up, snafu, louse-up; pratfall

7 grammatical error, solecism, missaying, mispronunciation; **bull,** fluff, **malapropism,** malaprop; spoonerism; catachresis

VERBS **8 not hold water** *and* not hold together <both nonformal>, not stand up, not square, not add up, **not hold up,** not wash <nonformal>

9 err, go wrong, go amiss, go astray, get out of line, stray, **deviate,** wander; **lapse, slip, slip up,** trip, stumble; **miscalculate** 947.2

10 be wrong, mistake oneself, be mistaken, be in error, be at fault, be out of line, be off the track, be in the wrong, have another think coming <nonformal>; receive a false impression, be misled, be misguided; deceive oneself, delude oneself; labor under a false impression

11 bark up the wrong tree, back the wrong horse

12 misdo; misuse, misapply; mismanage; miscall, miscount, misdeal, misplay; misprint, misquote, misread, misspell

13 mistake, make a mistake; misidentify; misunderstand, misapprehend, misconceive, **misinterpret** 342.2; **confuse** 810.3

14 blunder, make a blunder, make a faux pas, make a misstep; **misspeak,** misspeak oneself, trip over one's tongue; have egg on one's face <nonformal>; **botch, bungle** 414.11

15 <nonformal terms> **make** or
pull a boner or boo-boo or
blooper; goof, fluff, foozle, boot,
bobble, blow, blow it; fuck-up,
screw-up, foul-up, louse-up; put
one's foot in it or in one's mouth;
muff or blow or fluff one's lines,
fall flat on one's face or ass

ADJS **16 erroneous, untrue, not
right;** unfactual, **wrong; false,
fallacious,** self-contradictory; **illogical** 935.11; **unproved** 957.8;
faulty, flawed, defective, **at fault;**
wide of the mark, beside the
mark; amiss, awry, deviant, devi-
ational; erring, errant, **aberrant;
heretical,** unorthodox, heterodox; perverted, **distorted; delusive,** deceptive, **illusory**

17 **inaccurate, incorrect, inexact,**
unfactual, **unprecise,** imprecise,
unrigorous; **vague;** approximate;
out of line, out of plumb, out of
true, out of square

18 **mistaken, in error, erring,
wrong, all wet** <nonformal>, full
of bull or shit or hot air or it or
prunes or crap or beans <all non-
formal>; in the right church but
the wrong pew

19 **unauthentic** or **inauthentic,
unauthoritative, unreliable**
970.20; **misstated,** misquoted,
garbled; unfounded 935.13; spurious

ADVS **20 erroneously, falsely,** fallaciously; faultily; untruly; **wrong,**
wrongly; **mistakenly;** on the
wrong track

21 **inaccurately, incorrectly,** inexactly, unprecisely

975 ILLUSION

NOUNS **1 illusion, delusion; deception** 356, **trick;** self-
deception, self-delusion; **misconception, misbelief,** warped or
distorted conception; **bubble,
chimera;** will-o'-the-wisp;
dream; dreamworld; dreamland;
daydream; pipe dream and trip
<nonformal>; fool's paradise

2 **illusoriness;** delusiveness;
falseness, fallaciousness; **unreality;** unsubstantiality, imma-

teriality; **idealization** 985.7;
seeming, semblance, simulacrum, **appearance,** false
show, false light; **magic, sorcery**
690, illusionism, sleight of hand,
prestidigitation; magician, **sorcerer** 690.5, illusionist

3 **fancy, phantasy, imagination**
985

4 **phantom, phantasm,** wraith,
specter; shadow, shade; phan-
tasmagoria; **fantasy,** wildest
dream; **figment of the imagination** 985.5; **apparition, appearance; vision,** waking dream;
shape, form, figure, presence

5 **optical illusion, trick of eyesight;** afterimage

6 **mirage,** fata morgana, will-o'-
the-wisp, looming

7 **hallucination;** tripping <non-
formal>, mind-expansion;
consciousness-expansion

VERBS **8 go on a trip** and **blow
one's mind** <both nonformal>,
freak out <nonformal>; **halluci-
nate;** expand one's consciousness

ADJS **9 illusory,** illusive; illusional,
illusionary; **delusory,** delusive;
delusional, deluding; autistic;
**dreamy, dreamlike; visionary;
imaginary** 985.19; **erroneous**
974.16; **deceptive; chimeric,
chimerical, fantastic; unreal,**
unsubstantial 763.5, airy; unfounded 935.13; **false,** fallacious,
misleading; **specious, seeming,**
ostensible, supposititious; spectral, apparitional, phantasmal;
phantasmagoric, surreal

10 **hallucinatory,** hallucinative;
hallucinogenic, psychedelic,
consciousness-expanding, mind-
expanding, mind-blowing <non-
formal>

976 DISILLUSIONMENT

NOUNS **1 disillusionment,** disillusion, **disenchantment,** loss of innocence, cold light of reality, enlightenment; rude awakening,
bringing back to earth; debunk-
ing <nonformal>

VERBS **2 disillusion; disenchant,**
break the spell or charm; **dis-**

abuse, undeceive; **set right** *or* **straight,** put straight, enlighten, let in on, put one wise <nonformal>; open one's eyes, awaken, wake up; rob *or* strip one of one's illusions; bring one back to earth, let down easy <nonformal>; **burst** *or* **prick the bubble**; let the air out of; knock the props out from under; debunk <nonformal>; expose

3 be disillusioned, be disenchanted, have one's eyes opened, embrace reality; have another thing *or* guess coming <nonformal>

ADJS 4 **disillusioning, disenchanting,** disabusing, undeceiving, enlightening

5 **disillusioned, disenchanted, disabused,** stripped *or* robbed of illusion, enlightened, put straight; sophisticated, **blasé;** disappointed 132.5

977 MENTAL ATTITUDE

NOUNS 1 **attitude,** mental attitude; psychology; **position, posture,** stance; **way of thinking; feeling, sentiment,** the way one feels; opinion 952.6

2 **outlook,** mental outlook; **point of view, viewpoint, standpoint, perspective;** where one is *or* sits *or* stands; **view;** slant, way of looking at things, slant on things, where one is coming from <nonformal>; **frame of reference,** framework, arena, world, universe

3 **disposition, character, nature, temper, temperament,** mettle, makeup, stamp, type, stripe, kidney, make, mold; **turn of mind, inclination, tendency,** vein, mindset, **leaning,** animus, propensity, proclivity, predilection, predisposition; **bent, turn, bias,** slant, cast; idiosyncrasy, eccentricity

4 **mood, humor, feeling, feelings, temper, frame of mind, state of mind, morale, vein; mind**

5 <pervading attitudes> **climate,**

mental *or* intellectual climate, spiritual climate, moral climate, **ethos,** ideology, world view

VERBS 6 **take the attitude,** look at in the light of; **be disposed to,** incline toward, prefer

ADJS 7 **attitudinal; temperamental, dispositional,** inclinational; emotional, affective; mental, intellectual, ideational, ideological; spiritual; characteristic 864.13; innate

8 **disposed, predisposed, prone, inclined, given,** bent on, apt, **minded**

ADVS 9 **attitudinally; temperamentally, dispositionally,** constitutionally; **by temperament** *or* **disposition;** from where one stands *or* sits, from where one is; within the frame of reference *or* framework

978 BROAD-MINDEDNESS

NOUNS 1 **broad-mindedness; breadth,** broadness, broad gauge, latitude; **unbigotedness,** unprovincialism, cosmopolitanism; ecumenicalism, ecumenism

2 **liberalness, liberality,** catholicity, **liberalmindedness;** liberalism, libertarianism

3 **open-mindedness, openness,** receptiveness, receptivity; open mind

4 **tolerance,** toleration; **indulgence, leniency** 427, lenity; **forbearance, patience; permissiveness; charitableness,** charity, **generousness, magnanimity** 652.2; **compassion** 427.1, sympathy

5 **unprejudicedness, unbiasedness; impartiality** 649.4, evenhandedness, **justice** 649, **fairness** 649.3, **objectivity, detachment, dispassionateness, disinterestedness;** neutrality

6 **liberal;** libertarian; freethinker, ecumenicist; bleeding-heart liberal

VERBS 7 **keep an open mind,** judge not, suspend judgment, listen to reason, open one's mind to, judge on the merits; **live and let**

live; tolerate 134.5; accept, view
with indulgence, condone,
brook, be content with; live with
<nonformal>; shut one's eyes to,
look the other way, overlook,
disregard, ignore

ADJS 8 broad-minded, broad,
wide, wide-ranging, broad-
gauged, catholic; unbigoted, un-
hidebound, unprovincial, cosmopolitan; ecumenical

9 liberal, liberal-minded; freethinking

10 open-minded, open, receptive,
rational, admissive; persuadable, persuasible; unopinion-
ated, unwedded to an opinion

11 tolerant 134.9, tolerating; indulgent, lenient 427.7, condoning; forbearing, patient, long-
suffering; charitable, generous,
magnanimous 652.6; compassionate 427.7

12 unprejudiced, unbiased, un-
prepossessed, unjaundiced;
impartial, fair, just 649.8, objective, dispassionate, impersonal, detached, disinterested;
unswayed, uninfluenced

13 liberalizing, liberating, broadening, enlightening

979 NARROW-MINDEDNESS

NOUNS 1 narrow-mindedness, illiberality, uncatholicity; small-
mindedness, smallness, littleness, meanness, pettiness; bigotry, fanaticism; insularity, provincialism, parochialism; hideboundness, stuffiness <nonfor-
mal>; shortsightedness,
nearsightedness; closed mind,
mean mind, petty mind, shut
mind

2 intolerance; uncharitableness,
ungenerousness;

3 prejudice, prejudgment, predilection, prepossession, precon-
ception; bias, bent, inclination;
jaundice, jaundiced eye; partiality, partisanship, favoritism

4 discrimination; xenophobia,
know-nothingism; chauvinism,
superpatriotism; class consciousness, class prejudice, class

hatred; anti-Semitism; redbaiting
<nonformal>; racism, race prej-
udice, racial discrimination;
white or black supremacy, white
or black power; color line, color
bar; social barrier; segregation,
apartheid

5 bigot; racist, white or black supremacist; chauvinist, ultrana-
tionalist, superpatriot; sexist,
male chauvinist, female chauvinist, dogmatist, doctrinaire
969.7

VERBS 6 close one's mind, put on
blinders, blind oneself, have a
blind spot, have tunnel vision; not
see beyond one's nose; view with
a jaundiced eye, see but one side
of the question

7 prejudge, precondemn, accede
to prejudice

8 discriminate against, draw the
line, draw the color line; bait,
bash; red-bait

9 prejudice, jaundice, influence,
sway, bias; warp, twist, bend, distort

ADJS 10 narrow-minded, narrow,
closed, cramped, small-minded,
mean-minded, mean-spirited;
small, little, mean, petty; uncharitable, ungenerous; bigoted,
fanatical; illiberal; provincial, insular, parochial; hidebound,
straitlaced, stuffy <nonformal>;
authoritarian; shortsighted,
nearsighted; deaf, deaf to reason

11 intolerant, untolerating, unin-
dulgent

12 discriminatory; prejudiced, biased, jaundiced, colored; partial, one-sided, partisan; interested, nonobjective, undetached,
undispassionate; xenophobic,
know-nothing; chauvinistic, ul-
tranationalist, superpatriotic;
racist, opinionated 969.22

980 CURIOSITY

NOUNS 1 curiosity, inquisitive-
ness; interest, lively interest;
thirst or desire or lust or itch for
knowledge, inquiring or curious
mind; attention 982; alertness,
watchfulness, vigilance; nosi-

ness and snoopiness <both non-
formal>, prying; officiousness,
meddlesomeness 214.2; **morbid
curiosity, ghoulishness;** voyeurism, prurience

2 inquisitive person, quidnunc;
inquirer, inquisitor; **busybody,**
gossip, **snoop,** snooper; eavesdropper; sightseer; rubbernecker
or rubberneck <nonformal>;
Peeping Tom, voyeur

VERBS **3 be curious, want to
know, take an interest in,** burn
with curiosity; be watchful, be
vigilant; prick up one's ears, keep
one's ear to the ground; eavesdrop; keep one's eyes open, stare,
gape, peer, gawk, rubberneck
<nonformal>; nose out, nose
around for

  4 pry, snoop, peek, spy, nose, nose
into, poke *or* stick one's nose in;
meddle 214.7

ADJS **5 curious, inquisitive,** inquiring, quizzical; **alert, attentive**
982.15; burning with curiosity;
agape, openmouthed; morbidly
curious, **morbid, ghoulish; prurient,** voyeuristic

  6 prying, snooping; meddlesome
214.9

981 INCURIOSITY

NOUNS **1 incuriosity, uninquisi-
tiveness;** boredom; **inattention**
983; **uninterestedness, unconcern,** uninvolvement, **indifference** 102, **apathy,** passivity,
impassivity, listlessness, stolidity,
lack of interest; carelessness,
heedlessness, insouciance; aloofness, detachment, withdrawal,
reclusiveness

VERBS **2 take no interest in, not
care;** mind one's own business,
keep one's nose out; be indifferent

ADJS **3 incurious, uninquisitive,**
uninquiring; **inattentive** 983.6;
uninterested, unconcerned, uninvolved, **indifferent, apathetic,**
passive, impassive, stolid, phlegmatic, listless; aloof, detached,
distant, withdrawn, reclusive,
sequestered, eremitic

982 ATTENTION

NOUNS **1 attention, attentiveness;
attention span; heed,** ear;
**awareness, consciousness,
alertness** 339.5; **observation,**
advertence, advertency, **note, notice, regard,** respect; **intentness,**
concentration; diligence, assiduity, assiduousness, earnestness; **care** 339.1; **curiosity**
980

  2 interest, concern; curiosity
980; **enthusiasm,** passion, ardor,
zeal

  **3 engrossment, absorption, in-
tentness,** single-mindedness,
concentration, application, studiousness, **preoccupation, involvement, immersion;** obsession, monomania; contemplation, meditation

  4 close attention, scrutiny, rapt
attention, total *or* undivided attention; attention to detail, finickiness; harping, strict attention

VERBS **5 attend to,** look to, **see to;
pay attention to,** spare a thought
for, **give heed to; turn to,** give
thought to; direct one's attention
to, turn *or* bend *or* set the mind
to; **devote oneself to,** fix *or* rivet
or focus the mind *or* thoughts on,
apply oneself to, **occupy oneself
with, concern oneself with,** be
absorbed *or* engrossed in, be into
<nonformal>; take an interest in,
take hold of; **have a lot on one's
mind;** be preoccupied with; **lose
oneself in**

  6 heed, attend, be heedful, tend,
mind, watch, observe, regard,
look, see, view, mark, **note, notice,** get a load of <nonformal>

  7 hearken to, listen, hear; give
ear to, lend an ear to; prick up the
ears, **keep one's ears open,** keep
an ear to the ground, listen with
both ears, **be all ears**

  8 pay attention *or* **heed, take
heed,** give heed, **look out, watch
out** <nonformal>, **take care**
339.7; look lively *or* alive, **look
sharp,** sit up and take notice;
keep one's eye on the ball *or* not

miss a trick *or* not overlook a bet
<all nonformal>, keep a weather
eye out; mind one's business; give
one's undivided attention, give
special attention to; keep uppermost in one's thought; **concentrate on,** focus *or* fix on; **study,**
scrutinize

9 **take cognizance of, take note**
or **notice of,** take heed of, **take
account of, take into consideration** *or* **account, bear in mind,**
keep in sight *or* view, not lose
sight of

10 **call attention to, bring to one's
notice,** bring to attention, **mention,** mention in passing, touch
on; **single out,** call *or* bring to notice, direct to the attention, **feature,** highlight; **direct to,** address
to; **mention,** specify, touch on,
cite, **refer to,** allude to; **alert one,**
call to one's attention; **point out,
point to,** point at; **excite attention**

11 **meet with attention; catch the
attention,** strike one, draw *or*
hold *or* focus the attention, meet
or strike the eye, get one's ear, attract notice *or* attention, **excite
notice,** arouse notice, invite attention

12 **interest, concern,** involve in *or*
with, give pause; **pique, titillate,**
tantalize, tickle one's fancy, **attract, fascinate, provoke, stimulate, arouse, excite,** excite *or*
whet one's interest, arouse one's
enthusiasm, turn one on <non-
formal>

13 **engross, absorb, occupy, preoccupy, engage,** involve, take up;
**obsess; grip, hold, arrest, hold
the interest, fascinate, enthrall,**
spellbind, **hold spellbound,** mesmerize, hypnotize, catch

14 come to attention, stand at attention

ADJS 15 **attentive, heedful, mindful, regardful;** intent, diligent,
assiduous, intense, earnest, concentrated; **careful** 339.10; **ob-
serving,** observant; **curious**
980.5; agog, openmouthed; **all
eyes, all ears;** on the ball *and*

Johnny-on-the-spot <both non-
formal>; **meticulous** 339.12

16 **interested,** concerned; **alert to,
sensitive to, on the watch; curious** 980.5; **attracted,** fascinated, excited, turned-on <non-
formal>; keen on *or* about, enthusiastic, passionate

17 **engrossed, absorbed,** single-
minded, **occupied, preoccupied, engaged,** intent, intent
on, obsessed, taken up with, **involved, caught up in, wrapped
up in,** engrossed in, **absorbed in,
lost in, immersed in,** buried in;
head over heels in <nonformal>,
up to one's elbows in, up to one's
ears in

18 **gripped, held, fascinated, enthralled, rapt, spellbound,** mesmerized, **hypnotized,** fixed, riv-
eted, **arrested**

19 **interesting, stimulating, provocative,** thought-provoking,
thought-inspiring; **titillating,**
tickling, **tantalizing, inviting,
exciting; piquant,** lively, racy,
juicy; readable

20 **engrossing, absorbing,** consuming, **gripping,** riveting, **ar-
resting,** engaging, **fascinating,
enthralling, spellbinding,** enchanting, magnetic, hypnotic,
mesmerizing

ADVS 21 **attentively; heedfully,**
mindfully; **interestedly; raptly,**
with rapt attention; engrossedly,
absorbedly; devotedly, **intently,**
without distraction, **with undivided attention**

983 INATTENTION

NOUNS 1 **inattention,** inattentiveness, **heedlessness, unheedfulness, unmindfulness,
thoughtlessness; indifference**
102; disregard, disregardfulness,
regardlessness; **flightiness** 984.5,
giddiness 984.4, lightminded-
ness, dizziness <nonformal>; levity, frivolousness, flippancy; shallowness, superficiality; **inobser-
vance; unalertness,** unwariness,
unwatchfulness; **obliviousness,**
unawareness; **carelessness,** neg-

ligence 340.1; **absentmindedness, woolgathering, day-
dreaming** 984.2

VERBS **2 be inattentive, pay no attention,** pay no mind <nonfor-
mal>, **take no note** or **notice of,**
take no account of, miss, give no
heed, not hear a word; **disregard,
overlook, ignore**; think little of,
think nothing of, **slight,** make
light of; **close** or **shut one's eyes
to,** turn a blind eye, **look the
other way, blink at, wink at**;
hide one's head in the sand; **turn
a deaf ear to,** tune out <nonfor-
mal>; not trouble one's head with
or about; **be unwary,** be off one's
guard

3 wander, stray, divagate, ramble;
have a short attention span, let
one's attention wander, get off the
track <nonformal>; **fall asleep
at the switch** <nonformal>,
woolgather, **daydream** 984.9

4 dismiss, dismiss or drive from
one's thoughts; **put out of mind,
think no more of, forget, forget
it, let it go** <nonformal>, not give
it another or a second thought,
drop the subject, give it no more
thought; put or set or lay aside;
put on the back
burner or on hold <nonformal>;
turn up one's nose at, sneeze at;
shrug off, brush off or **aside** or
away, dismiss with a laugh;
slight 157.6

5 escape notice or **attention,** not
enter one's head, never occur to
one, fall on deaf ears, go over
one's head

ADJS **6 inattentive, unmindful,** inadvertent, **incurious** 981.3, **indifferent** 102.6; **heedless,** unheedful, **disregardful; unobserving,**
unobservant; **distracted** 984.10;
careless, negligent 340.10; **scatterbrained, giddy** 984.16, flighty

7 oblivious, unconscious, dead
to the world, out of it and not
with it <both nonformal>; **preoccupied** 984.11

**8 unalert, unwary, unwatchful,
unvigilant,** uncautious; **unprepared,** unready; unguarded,

off one's guard; **asleep,** nodding, napping, **asleep at the
switch** and asleep on the job and
goofing off <all nonformal>; daydreaming, woolgathering

984 DISTRACTION,
CONFUSION

NOUNS **1 distraction,** distracted-
ness, **diversion,** divided attention; too much on one's mind;
inattention 983

**2 abstractedness, abstraction,
preoccupation, absorption,** engrossment; **absentmindedness,
absence of mind; bemusement,**
musing; **woolgathering,** stargazing, **dreaming, daydreaming,**
pipe-dreaming <nonformal>,
castle-building; **brown study,**
reverie, trance; dream, **daydream,** fantasy, pipe dream
<nonformal>; daydreamer

3 confusion, fluster, flutter, ruffle; disorientation, **muddle,
muddlement,** befuddlement,
muddleheadedness; disorganization, **disorder,** chaos, **mess** and
mix-up and snafu <all nonfor-
mal>, jumble, **discomfiture, discomposure, disconcertion,** dis-
combobulation <nonformal>,
**bewilderment, embarrass-
ment, disturbance,** perturbation, **upset,** frenzy, bother; sweat
<nonformal>; **perplexity** 970.3

4 dizziness, vertigo, vertiginous-
ness, **giddiness,** wooziness
<nonformal>, **lightheadedness;
drunkenness** 88.1,3

5 flightiness, giddiness, volatility,
mercuriality; **thoughtlessness,**
witlessness, empty-headedness,
frivolousness, dizziness <nonfor-
mal>, foolishness 922; **scatterbrain, flibbertigibbet** 923.7

VERBS **6 distract, divert,** detract,
draw off the attention, take the
mind off of, cause the mind to
wander, lead the mind astray,
beguile; throw off one's guard,
put off one's stride, trip up

7 confuse, throw into confusion
or chaos, entangle, **mix up, fluster; flutter, flurry, rattle, ruffle**;

muddle, befuddle, addle, addle the wits, daze, maze, dazzle, bedazzle; upset, unsettle; throw into a tizzy; disconcert, discomfit, discompose, discombobulate <nonformal>, disorient, bewilder, embarrass, put out, disturb, perturb, bother, bug <nonformal>; perplex 970.13

8 dizzy, make one's head swim, make one's head reel or spin, go to one's head; intoxicate 88.22

9 muse, moon <nonformal>, dream, daydream, pipe-dream <nonformal>, fantasy; be lost in thought, let one's attention wander, dream of other things; wander, stray, ramble, divagate, let one's thoughts or mind wander, woolgather, go woolgathering, be in a brown study, stargaze, be out of it and be not with it <both nonformal>

ADJS 10 distracted, distraught; wandering, rambling; wild, frantic, beside oneself

11 abstracted, bemused, musing, preoccupied, absorbed, engrossed; absentminded, absent, faraway, not there; pensive, meditative; lost in thought, wrapped in thought, rapt, transported, ecstatic; unconscious, oblivious; dreaming, dreamy, drowsing, dozing, nodding, half-awake, napping; daydreaming, pipe-dreaming <nonformal>; woolgathering, castle-building, in a reverie

12 confused, mixed-up; flustered, ruffled, rattled; upset, unsettled, off one's stride; disorganized, disordered, disoriented, chaotic, jumbled; shaken, disconcerted, discomposed, embarrassed, put-out, disturbed, perturbed, all hot and bothered <nonformal>; in a stew <nonformal>; in a tizzy or sweat <nonformal>; perplexed

13 muddled, in a muddle; befuddled; muddleheaded; addled, addlepated, addlebrained; at sea, in a fog, hazy

14 dazed, dazzled, in a daze; silly,

knocked silly; groggy <nonformal>, dopey <nonformal>, woozy <nonformal>; punch-drunk and punchy and slap-happy <all nonformal>

15 dizzy, giddy, vertiginous, spinning, swimming, going around in circles; lightheaded, drunk, drunken 88.31

16 scatterbrained, rattlebrained, harebrained, giddy, dizzy <nonformal>, frivolous, feather-brained, featherheaded; thoughtless, witless, brainless, empty-headed 921.19

17 flighty, volatile, mercurial

985 IMAGINATION

NOUNS 1 imagination, imaginativeness, fancy, fantasy; mind's eye, flight of fancy

2 creative thought, conception; creative imagination, creative power or ability; inspiration, muse; genius 919.8

3 invention, inventiveness, originality, creativity, fabrication, creativeness, ingenuity; productivity, fertility, fecundity; fertile or pregnant imagination, seminal imagination, fertile mind; fiction, fictionalization

4 lively imagination, vivid imagination, highly colored or lurid imagination, excited imagination; verve

5 figment of the imagination, creature of the imagination, fiction of the mind, whim, whimsy, figment, imagination, invention; brainchild; imagining, fancy, idle fancy, imagery; fantasy, make-believe; phantom, vision, apparition, phantasm 975.4; fiction, myth, romance; wildest dreams, stretch of the imagination; chimera, bubble, illusion 975; hallucination, delirium; trip or drug trip <both nonformal>

6 visualization, envisioning, envisaging, imaging, calling to or before the mind's eye, representing in the mind; depicting in the imagination; conceptualization; picture, vision, image, mental

image, eidetic image, concept, **conception; imagery,** word-painting

7 **idealism, idealization; ideal**; rose-colored glasses; **utopianism;** flight of fancy; **romanticism,** romanticizing, romance; **quixotism,** quixotry; **impracticality, unrealism,** unreality; **wishful thinking,** wish-fulfillment fantasy, dream come true; autistic thinking, autism

8 **dreaminess,** pensiveness; **dreaming, musing; daydreaming,** pipe-dreaming <nonformal>, castlebuilding

9 **dream; reverie, daydream, pipe dream** <nonformal>; **brown study** 984.2; **vision; nightmare,** incubus, bad dream

10 **air castle, castle in the air,** castle in Spain

11 **utopia, paradise, heaven** 681, **heaven on earth;** millennium, kingdom come; lotus land, land of dreams, land of enchantment, land of heart's desire; Eden, Garden of Eden; the Promised Land, land of promise, land of plenty, land of milk and honey, Canaan, Goshen

12 **imaginer, fancier;** fantasist; mythmaker, mythicizer; **creative artist,** poet

13 **visionary, idealist;** prophet, **seer; dreamer, daydreamer,** castle-builder, lotus-eater, **wishful thinker; romantic,** romanticist, romancer; Quixote, Don Quixote; utopian; escapist; enthusiast, rhapsodist

VERBS 14 **imagine, fancy, conceive,** conceptualize, ideate; **invent, create, originate, make,** think up, hatch, concoct, fabricate, produce; **suppose** 950.10; **fantasize;** give free rein to the imagination, let one's imagination run riot or run wild, allow one's imagination to run away with one

15 **visualize, envision, envisage, picture, image,** objectify; **view with the mind's eye,** form a mental picture of, **see,** have a pic-

ture of; **call up,** summon up, **call to mind**

16 **idealize,** rhapsodize; **romanticize,** romance; paint in bright colors; see through rose-colored glasses; **build castles in the air or Spain**

17 **dream; daydream,** pipe-dream <nonformal>, have stars in one's eyes, have one's head in the clouds; fantasy, conjure up a vision; blow one's mind and go on a trip and trip and freak out <all nonformal>

ADJS 18 **imaginative,** conceptual, conceptive, ideational, ideative, notional; **inventive, original, creative, ingenious; productive, fertile,** fecund, prolific, seminal, pregnant; **inspired**

19 **imaginary,** notional; **imagined, fancied; unreal,** unrealistic, nonexistent, never-never; **all in the mind; illusory**

20 **fanciful, notional,** whimsical; **fantastic, fantastical,** preposterous, outlandish, baroque, rococo, florid; bizarre, grotesque, Gothic

21 **fictitious, make-believe, figmental,** fictional, fictive, fabricated, fictionalized; **fabulous, mythic, mythical,** legendary; mythified, mythicized

22 **chimeric, chimerical, aerial, ethereal,** phantasmal; gossamer; cloud-built, cloud-born

23 **ideal, idealized;** utopian, Arcadian, Edenic; pie in the sky <nonformal>; celestial

24 **visionary, idealistic, quixotic; romantic, romanticized;** storybook; **impractical, unpractical, unrealistic;** starry-eyed, dewy-eyed; with one's head in the clouds; **otherworldly,** transmundane

25 **dreamy, dreamful; dreamy-eyed;** dreamlike; **dreaming, daydreaming,** pipe-dreaming <nonformal>; **entranced,** in a trance, enchanted, spellbound, charmed

26 **imaginable, fanciable, conceivable, thinkable,** cogitable; **supposable** 950.15

986 UNIMAGINATIVENESS

NOUNS **1 unimaginativeness; prosaicness**, prosiness, prosaism; **staidness, stuffiness** <nonformal>; stolidity; **dullness, dryness**; aridity, barrenness, infertility, infecundity; **unoriginality**, uncreativeness

2 <practical attitude> **realism, practicalness, practicality, practical-mindedness**, sobermindedness, **hardheadedness, matter-of-factness**; earthiness, worldliness, secularism; the here and now; nuts and bolts, no nonsense, no frills; **pragmatism**; unsentimentality; reasonableness, rationality; lack of sentimentality; lack of feelings 94

3 realist, pragmatist, practical person, hardhead

VERBS **4 keep both feet on the ground**, call a spade a spade; **come down to earth**, come down out of the clouds

ADJS **5 unimaginative, unfanciful;** unromanticized; **prosaic**, prosy, unpoetic; **literal**, literal-minded; earthbound, mundane; **staid, stuffy** <nonformal>; stolid; **dull, dry**; arid, barren, infertile, infecund; **unoriginal**, uninspired; unaspiring, **uninventive** 890.5

6 realistic, practical; pragmatic, scientific; **unidealistic, unromantic, unsentimental, practical-minded**, soberminded, **hardheaded, matter-of-fact, down-to-earth, with both feet on the ground**; worldly, secular; sensible, sane, reasonable, rational, sound

987 SPECTER

NOUNS **1 specter, ghost, spook** <nonformal>, **phantom**, phantasm, **wraith, shade**, shadow, **apparition**, appearance, presence, shape, revenant; **spirit;** sprite, disembodied spirit, restless or wandering spirit or soul, dybbuk; unsubstantiality, immateriality, incorporeal being or entity; zombie; vision, theophany; haunt or hant <both nonformal>; banshee; poltergeist; grateful dead

2 White Lady

3 double, *Doppelgänger* <Ger>, doubleganger

4 eeriness, ghostliness, weirdness, uncanniness, spookiness <nonformal>

5 possession, spirit control; obsession

VERBS **6 haunt,** spook <nonformal>; **possess**

ADJS **7 spectral,** specterlike; **ghostly**, ghostlike; **spiritual, psychic**, psychical; **phantomlike**, phantom, phantasmal, **wraithlike**, shadowy; ectoplasmic, astral, ethereal 763.6; incorporeal 1051.7; **occult, supernatural** 869.15

8 disembodied, bodiless, immaterial 1051.7

9 weird, eerie, eldritch, **uncanny**, macabre

10 haunted, spooked and spooky <both nonformal>, spirit-haunted, ghost-haunted, specter-haunted; **possessed**, ghost-ridden; obsessed

988 MEMORY

NOUNS **1 memory, remembrance, recollection**, mind; engram; mind's eye, eye of the mind, mirror of the mind; inmost recesses of the memory; group memory, collective memory, race memory; atavism

2 tablets of the memory; corner or recess of the memory

3 retention, retentiveness, retentivity, memory span; eidetic memory or imagery, photographic memory, total recall

4 remembering, remembrance, recollection, recollecting, **recall**, recalling; **retrospect**, retrospection, hindsight; flashback, **reminiscence**, review, review of things past; **memoir; memorization**, memorizing, **rote**, rote memory, rote learning

5 recognition, identification, reidentification

6 **reminder, remembrance**;
prompt, prompter, tickler; *aide-mémoire* <Fr>, **memorandum**
549.4

7 **memento, remembrance, token, trophy, souvenir, keep-
sake, relic,** favor; *memento mori*
<L>; **memories, memorabilia**

8 memorability, rememberability

9 mnemonics, memory training;
mnemonic, mnemonic device

VERBS 10 **remember, recall, rec-
ollect**; remember as if it were
yesterday; have total recall, remember everything; reflect;
think of; call or **bring to mind,**
conjure up, evoke, recapture,
bring back; **think back, look
back,** carry one's thoughts back,
look back upon things past, **see
in retrospect,** hark back, retrace

11 **reminisce,** rake or dig up the
past

12 **recognize, know, tell, distinguish, make out; identify,
place,** have; **reidentify,** know
again; realize 927.12

13 **keep in memory, bear in mind,
keep in view,** hold or carry or retain in one's thoughts, store in the
mind, **retain, keep; treasure,
cherish,** enshrine or embalm in
the memory, cherish the memory
of; keep the memory alive, keep
alive in one's thoughts; brood
over, dwell on or upon, let rankle
in the breast

14 **be remembered,** sink in, penetrate, make an impression; live or
dwell in one's memory, be green
or fresh in one's memory, stick in
the mind, be stamped on one's
memory, **never be forgotten;
haunt one's thoughts,** obsess, be
on one's mind; be burnt into one's
memory; **rankle,** fester in the
mind

15 **recur,** return to mind, resurface

16 **come to mind,** pop into one's
head, come into one's head, flash
on the mind, pass in review

17 **memorize, commit to memory; learn by heart,** learn or get
by rote, get letter-perfect, learn
verbatim; know by heart or from

memory, have at one's fingers'
tips; give word for word, recite,
repeat, parrot, rattle or reel off;
be a quick study

18 **fix in the mind** or memory, infix,
inculcate, impress, imprint, etch,
engrave; **impress on the mind,
get into one's head,** hammer
into one's head, get across, get
into one's thick head or skull
<nonformal>; **burden the mind
with,** stuff or cram the mind
with; rivet in the memory, etch
indelibly in the mind

19 **refresh the memory, review,** re-
study, **brush up, rub up,** polish
up *and* bone up <both nonfor-
mal>, get up on; **cram** <nonfor-
mal>

20 **remind, put in mind,** remember, refresh the memory of; **remind one of, recall,** suggest, **put
one in mind of; take one back;
jog the memory,** awaken the
memory, give a hint or suggestion; **prompt,** give the cue;
nudge, nag

21 **try to recall,** rack one's brains,
cudgel one's brains; have on the
tip of one's tongue

ADJS 22 **recollective, memoried;**
mnemonic; retentive; **retrospective; reminiscent, mindful, re-
mindful, suggestive,** redolent,
evocative

23 **remembered, recollected,
recalled; retained,** kept in remembrance, enduring, lasting,
unforgotten; lodged in one's
mind, stamped on the memory;
vivid, eidetic

24 **remembering, mindful,** keeping or bearing in mind; **haunted,**
plagued, obsessed

25 **memorable, rememberable,
recollectable;** notable

26 **unforgettable, never to be forgotten, indelible,** indelibly impressed on the mind, fixed in the
mind; haunting, persistent, recurrent, nagging, plaguing, rankling, festering; obsessing, obsessive

27 **memorial, commemorative**

ADVS 28 **by heart, by rote, by** or

from memory; memorably; re-
memberingly
29 **in memory of,** *in memoriam*
<L>; in perpetual remembrance

989 FORGETFULNESS

NOUNS 1 **forgetfulness,** unmindfulness, absentmindedness,
memorylessness; mind *or* memory like a sieve; fuzzy memory,
dim *or* hazy recollection; **lapse of
memory; obliviousness, oblivion,** nirvana; nepenthe; **forgetting;** heedlessness 340.2
2 **loss of memory, memory loss,
amnesia; memory gap,** blackout
<nonformal>; fugue
3 **block,** blocking, **mental block;**
repression, suppression, defense
mechanism, sublimation
VERBS 4 **be forgetful,** suffer memory loss, be absentminded, have a
short memory, have a mind *or*
memory like a sieve, have a short
memory span
5 **forget,** clean forget <nonfor-
mal>; **not remember,** fail to remember, forget to remember,
have no remembrance *or* **recollection of,** draw a blank <nonfor-
mal>; lose one's train of thought,
lose track of what one was saying;
have on the tip of the tongue;
blow *or* go up in *or* fluff one's
lines
6 efface *or* erase from the memory,
obliterate, **dismiss from one's
thoughts** 983.4
7 **be forgotten, escape one, slip
one's mind,** fade from memory;
go in one ear and out the other
ADJS 8 **forgotten, unremembered,
unrecollected, unretained, un-
recalled,** past recall, out of the
mind, lost, erased, effaced, oblit-
erated, consigned to oblivion; out
of sight out of mind
9 **forgetful, forgetting,** inclined
to forget, **memoryless, unre-
membering, unmindful,** absentminded, **oblivious,** with a mind
like a sieve; suffering from *or*
stricken with amnesia; blocked,
repressed, suppressed, subli-
mated

10 **forgettable;** effaceable, erasable
ADVS 11 **forgetfully,** unmindfully,
absentmindedly

990 SUFFICIENCY

NOUNS 1 **sufficiency, adequacy,**
adequateness, **enough;** satisfaction, enough to go around; right
amount, no more and no less;
bare minimum, just enough,
enough to get by on
2 **plenty,** plenitude, plenteousness; myriad, myriads; **amplitude,** ampleness; substantialness; **abundance, copiousness;**
exuberance, riotousness; **bountifulness,** bounteousness, **liberality,** generousness, **generosity;**
lavishness, extravagance, **prodigality;** luxuriance, productiveness 889; **wealth, opulence** *or*
opulency, affluence; more than
enough; **fullness,** full measure,
repleteness; **overflow, outpouring,** flood, inundation, flow, avalanche; landslide; **prevalence,**
profuseness, **profusion,** riot; **superabundance** 992.2; **overkill;**
great abundance, as much as one
could wish, lots, a fistful <nonfor-
mal>, **scads** 247.4; bumper crop,
rich harvest; rich vein, bonanza;
enough and to spare; fat of the
land
3 cornucopia, horn of plenty, endless supply, bottomless well
VERBS 4 **suffice, do,** serve, **answer;** work, **avail;** answer *or*
serve the purpose, do the trick
<nonformal>, **suit; satisfy,** meet
requirements; **pass muster,**
make the grade *or* the cut *and*
hack it *and* cut the mustard *and*
fill the bill <all nonformal>; get
by *and* scrape by <both nonfor-
mal>, do in a pinch, **pass;** stretch
<nonformal>, reach, go around
5 **abound,** teem, **teem with,** crawl
with, swarm with, be lousy with
<nonformal>; proliferate 889.7;
overflow, flood; flow, **pour,**
shower
ADJS 6 **sufficient,** sufficing;
enough, ample, substantial,
plenty, satisfactory, adequate;

competent, up to the mark; suitable, fit 787.10; good, **good enough**; barely sufficient, minimal, minimum

7 **plentiful,** plenty, **plenteous,** plenitudinous; **galore** *and* up the gazoo *or* kazoo *and* up to the ass in <all nonformal>; numerous 883.6; **ample**; wholesale; abundant, abounding, **copious**; flush; **bountiful,** bounteous, **lavish, generous, liberal, extravagant, prodigal; luxuriant,** fertile, productive 889.9, **rich,** fat, **wealthy, opulent, affluent;** maximal; **full,** replete, overflowing; inexhaustible, bottomless; **profuse,** profusive; **prevalent,** rife, rampant, epidemic; lousy with <nonformal>, teeming 883.9; **superabundant** 992.19; a dime a dozen

ADVS 8 **sufficiently, amply,** substantially, **satisfactorily, enough;** competently, **adequately**

9 **plentifully,** plenteously, **aplenty** <nonformal>, **in plenty,** in good supply; **abundantly,** in abundance, copiously; **superabundantly** 992.24; **bountifully,** bounteously, **lavishly, generously, liberally, extravagantly, prodigally; fully,** in full measure, overflowingly; inexhaustibly, bottomlessly; exuberantly, luxuriantly, riotously; richly, opulently, affluently; **profusely;** beyond one's wildest dreams

991 INSUFFICIENCY

NOUNS 1 **insufficiency, inadequacy**; short supply; none to spare; falling short *or* shy; **undercommitment;** too little too late; a band-aid <nonformal>, a drop in the bucket, a cosmetic measure; **incompetence,** incompetency

2 **meagerness,** exiguousness, skimpiness, scantiness, spareness; meanness, miserliness, niggardliness, stinginess, parsimony; slim pickings <nonformal>, scrawniness, jejuneness, jejunity; austerity

3 **scarcity,** scarceness; **sparsity,** sparseness; **scantiness; dearth,**

paucity, poverty; **rarity,** rareness, uncommonness

4 **want, lack, need, deficiency, deficit, shortage, shortfall, incompleteness,** shortcoming 910; **absence** 222, omission; **destitution,** impoverishment, deprivation; starvation, famine, drought

5 **pittance,** dole; drop in the bucket; **mite,** bit 248.2; half rations; mere subsistence, starvation wages; widow's mite

6 **dietary deficiency,** vitamin deficiency; undernourishment, undernutrition, **malnutrition**

VERBS 7 **want, lack, need, require;** miss, feel the want of, be sent away empty-handed; run short of

8 **be insufficient,** be found wanting, leave a lot to be desired, not make it *and* not hack it *and* not make the cut *and* not cut it *and* not cut the mustard <all nonformal>, be in over one's head, **fall short,** fall shy, not come up to; run short

ADJS 9 **insufficient, inadequate;** found wanting, defective, wanting; **too few,** undersupplied; **too little,** precious little, a trickle *or* mere trickle; **unsatisfactory,** unsatisfying; cosmetic, superficial, symptomatic; **incompetent,** unqualified, not up to snuff, beyond one's depth *or* over one's head; understaffed, short-handed

10 **meager, slight,** skimpy, exiguous; scant, **scanty,** spare; miserly, niggardly, stingy, parsimonious; austere, abstemious, ascetic; frugal, sparing, impoverished; paltry; thin, scrawny, stunted; straitened, limited; jejune, unnourishing, unnutritious; subsistence, starvation

11 **scarce, sparse, scanty; in short supply,** at a premium; **rare,** uncommon; scarcer than hen's teeth <nonformal>; not to be had for love or money; not to be had at any price

12 **ill-provided,** ill-equipped; **unprovided,** unsupplied; undernourished; shorthanded, under-

manned; **empty-handed, poor,** impoverished; starved, half-starved, famished

13 **wanting, lacking, needing, missing, in want of; short of; out of,** clean *or* fresh out of <nonformal>, destitute of, devoid of, bereft of, deprived of, unblessed with; at the end of one's rope *or* tether

ADVS 14 **insufficiently; inadequately,** unsubstantially

15 **meagerly, slightly,** sparely, scantily, sparingly

16 **scarcely, sparsely, scantily;** uncommonly

992 EXCESS

NOUNS 1 **excess, excessiveness,** inordinateness, nimiety, **immoderateness, extravagance** *or* extravagancy, overindulgence, **intemperance** 669; unrestrainedness, abandon; gluttony 672; **extreme,** extremity, **extremes; boundlessness** 822.1; monstrousness, enormousness 247.1; **overmuch,** too much; **exorbitance** *or* exorbitancy, **outrageousness,** unconscionableness, **unreasonableness;** egregiousness; hyperbole, **exaggeration** 355

2 **superabundance,** overabundance, **plethora,** redundancy, too much of a good thing, **overplentifulness, oversupply, oversufficiency;** lavishness, **extravagance, prodigality; plenty** 990.2; **more than enough, enough and to spare; overdose,** overmeasure; too much of a good thing, egg in one's beer <nonformal>; drug on the market; spate, avalanche, landslide, deluge, flood, inundation; money to burn <nonformal>

3 **overfullness,** plethora, **surfeit, glut;** satiety 993; **saturation,** supersaturation; **overload,** overweight; **overflow; insatiability,** insatiableness

4 **superfluity,** superfluousness, fat; **redundancy;** fifth wheel <nonformal>; featherbedding,

payroll padding; duplication, overlap; **luxury,** extravagance, **frills** *and* bells and whistles *and* gimcrackery <all nonformal>; frippery, froufrou, gingerbread; **ornamentation, embellishment** 498.1; expletive, **padding, filling;** pleonasm, tautology; verbosity, prolixity 538.2

5 **surplus,** leftovers, overstock, **overage,** overrun, **overmeasure, oversupply; remainder, balance, leftover,** something extra *or* to spare; bonus, dividend; lagniappe <nonformal>; gratuity

6 **overdoing, overreaching; overkill;** overreaction; **overwork, overexertion,** overexpenditure, overtaxing, strain; too much on one's plate, too many irons in the fire; **overachievement**

7 **overextension, overdrawing,** spreading too thin, **overstretching,** overstrain, snapping *or* breaking point; **overexpansion;** inflation, distension, edema, turgidity, swelling, bloating 259.2

VERBS 8 **superabound,** overabound, **know no bounds, swarm,** pullulate, **teem;** overflow, spill over, overrun, overspread, overswarm, overgrow

9 **exceed, surpass, pass, top, transcend, go beyond;** overstep, **overreach,** overshoot the mark

10 **overdo, go too far,** pass all bounds, know no bounds, overact, **carry too far, go to extremes,** go overboard, go off the deep end; **run** *or* **drive into the ground; make a big deal of** *and* **make a Federal case of** <both nonformal>; overemphasize, overstress; overplay one's hand <nonformal>; **overreact; overtax,** exhaust, overexpend, overuse; **overwork;** overdevelop, tell more than one wants to know; overstudy; burn the candle at both ends; **spread oneself too thin, take on too much,** have too much on one's plate, have too many irons in the fire, do too many things at once; **exaggerate** 355.3; **overindulge** 669.5

11 pile it on, lay it on thick, lay it on with a trowel <nonformal>

12 carry coals to Newcastle, teach one's grandmother to suck eggs, flog a dead horse, labor the obvious, preach to the converted, gild the lily

13 overextend, overdraw, overstretch, overstrain; reach the breaking point; **overexpand,** overdistend, overdevelop, inflate, swell 259.4

14 oversupply, overprovide, overequip; **overstock;** overdose; flood the market; **flood, deluge,** inundate, engulf, swamp, overwhelm; be prodigal with

15 overload, overburden, overcharge, overfill, stuff, crowd, jam-pack, **congest,** choke; **overstuff,** overfeed; **surfeit, glut, gorge,** satiate 993.4; **saturate**

ADJS **16 excessive, inordinate, immoderate,** overweening, hubristic, **intemperate, extravagant;** unrestrained, unbridled; **extreme; overlarge, overgreat,** larger than life, elephantine, gigantic 247.7; overgrown, overdeveloped, hypertrophied; **overmuch,** a bit much, de trop; **exorbitant, undue, outrageous,** unconscionable, **unreasonable; out of bounds** or **all bounds,** out of sight *and* out of this world <both nonformal>, **boundless** 822.3; egregious; fabulous, **exaggerated** 355.4

17 superfluous, redundant; excess, in excess; unnecessary, unessential, expendable, **needless,** gratuitous, uncalled-for; pleonastic, tautologous, tautological; verbose, prolix 538.12; spare, to spare

18 surplus; remaining, unused, **leftover; over and above; extra, spare,** supernumerary

19 superabundant, plethoric, **overplentiful, oversufficient, overmuch; lavish, prodigal,** overlavish, overgenerous, overliberal; **swarming,** pullulating, **teeming,** overpopulous; plentiful 990.7

20 overfull, overloaded, overladen, overburdened, overcharged, saturated, drenched, soaked; **surfeited, glutted,** gorged, bloated, swollen, **satiated** 993.6, **stuffed,** overstuffed, **crammed, overcrowded,** jam-packed, bumper-to-bumper <nonformal>; choked, **congested; overstocked, oversupplied; overflowing,** filled to overflowing; plethoric; **bursting,** bursting at the seams, at the bursting point, distended

21 overdone, overwrought; overdrawn

ADVS **22 excessively, inordinately, immoderately, intemperately,** overweeningly, **overly, overmuch,** too much; **exorbitantly, unduly, unreasonably,** unconscionably, **outrageously**

23 in or **to excess, to extremes,** all out <nonformal>, to a fault, out of all proportion

24 superabundantly, overabundantly, **lavishly, prodigally, extravagantly;** beyond measure

25 superfluously, redundantly; tautologously; unnecessarily, needlessly, to a fare-thee-well <nonformal>

993 SATIETY

NOUNS **1 satiety, satiation, satisfaction, fullness, surfeit, glut;** contentment; **fill, belly**ful *and* skinful <both nonformal>; **saturation,** oversaturation; saturation point; more than enough, all one can stand or take; too much of a good thing

2 satedness, cloyedness, jadedness; **overfullness**

3 cloyer, surfeiter, sickener; **overdose**

VERBS **4 satiate, sate, satisfy,** slake, allay; **surfeit, glut, gorge; cloy,** jade, pall; **fill,** fill up; saturate; **stuff,** cram; **overfill,** overdose

5 have enough, have quite enough, **have one's fill;** have too much of a good thing, **have a bellyful** or skinful <nonformal>,

be fed up <nonformal>, have all one can take *or* stand, have had it

ADJS **6 satiated, sated, satisfied; surfeited, gorged,** replete, **glutted; cloyed,** jaded; **full,** full of, **overfull,** saturated; **stuffed,** overstuffed, crammed; **fed up** *and* fed to the gills *or* fed to the teeth <all nonformal>; **with a bellyful** *or* skinful <nonformal>; disgusted, **sick of,** sick and tired of

7 satiating, sating, satisfying; surfeiting; jading, **cloying**

994 EXPEDIENCE

NOUNS **1 expedience** *or* **expediency, advisability, desirability; fitness, fittingness, appropriateness,** propriety, seemliness, **suitability,** feasibility, **convenience;** timeliness, **opportuneness; usefulness** 387.3; **advantage, advantageousness, profit,** profitability, worthwhileness, fruitfulness; wisdom, prudence 919.7

2 expedient, means, means to an end, **provision, measure, step, action,** effort, **stroke, move,** countermove, **maneuver,** demarche; tactic, **device,** artifice, stratagem, **shift; gimmick** *and* dodge *and* trick <all nonformal>; **resort,** resource; working hypothesis; **temporary expedient, improvisation,** ad hoc measure; **fix** *and* **quick fix** <both nonformal>, **makeshift,** stopgap, jury-rig; **last resort** *or* resource, trump

VERBS **3 expedite one's affair,** work to one's advantage, come in handy, be just what the doctor ordered <nonformal>, fit like a glove; forward, advance, promote, profit, advantage, benefit; **work, serve,** answer *or* serve one's purpose, fill the bill *and* do the trick <both nonformal>

4 make shift, make do, make out <nonformal>, get along on, get by on, do with; use a last resort, scrape the bottom of the barrel

ADJS **5 expedient, desirable,** to be desired, **advisable, politic;** ap-

propriate, meet, fit, fitting, befitting, **right, proper, becoming,** seemly, **suitable,** feasible, doable, **convenient,** heaven-sent, felicitous; timely, seasonable, opportune; **useful** 387.18; **advantageous; profitable,** fructuous, worthwhile; **wise** 919.17

6 practical, practicable, pragmatic; feasible, workable, operable; **efficient,** effective, **effectual**

7 makeshift, stopgap, band-aid <nonformal>, improvised, **jury-rigged; last-ditch; ad hoc;** quick and dirty <nonformal>

ADVS **8 expediently, fittingly, appropriately, suitably,** congruously, rightly, properly, conveniently; practically; seasonably, opportunely; desirably, advisably; advantageously; as a last resort

995 INEXPEDIENCE

NOUNS **1 inexpedience, undesirability, inadvisability,** impoliticness; **unwiseness** 922.2; **unfitness, inappropriateness, unsuitability,** incongruity, **unmeetness,** unseemliness; **inconvenience,** awkwardness; ineptitude; untimeliness, inopportuneness; infelicity; disadvantageousness, worthlessness, futility

2 disadvantage, drawback, liability; detriment, impairment, mischief, injury; **a step back** *or* **backward; handicap** 1011.6, disability; millstone around one's neck

3 inconvenience, trouble, bother; unhandiness, awkwardness, clumsiness, unwieldiness; gaucheness, gaucherie

VERBS **4 inconvenience, put out, discommode,** incommode, disoblige, **burden, embarrass; trouble, bother,** put to the trouble of, **impose upon;** disadvantage 999.6

ADJS **5 inexpedient, undesirable, inadvisable, counterproductive,** impolitic, unpolitic, contraindicated; **impractical, impracticable,** dysfunctional; **ill-**

advised, **ill-considered, unwise; unfit, unfitting,** unbefitting, **inappropriate, unsuitable,** inept, unseemly, **improper, wrong,** out of place, out of order, incongruous; malapropos, inopportune, untimely, unseasonable; infelicitous, unfortunate, unhappy; futile 391.13

6 **disadvantageous, unfavorable;** unprofitable, unrewarding, worthless; **detrimental,** deleterious, prejudicial

7 **inconvenient, incommodious,** discommodious; **unhandy, awkward,** unwieldy; gauche

ADVS 8 **inexpediently, inadvisably,** impolitically, **undesirably; unfittingly, inappropriately, unsuitably,** ineptly, incongruously; inopportunely, unseasonably; infelicitously

9 **disadvantageously,** unprofitably, unrewardingly; **inconveniently,** unhandily

996 IMPORTANCE

NOUNS 1 **importance, significance, consequence, import, moment, weight, gravity;** materiality; concern, concernment, interest; **priority,** primacy, precedence, preeminence, **supremacy;** value, worth, merit

2 **notability, noteworthiness,** salience, memorability; **prominence, eminence, greatness,** distinction; **fame** 662.1; **stardom,** celebrity

3 **gravity, graveness, seriousness,** weightiness; no laughing matter, hardball <nonformal>

4 **urgency,** imperativeness, exigency; **momentousness, crucialness, cruciality; press,** high pressure, **stress,** tension, **pinch; crisis, emergency;** moment of truth, turning point, defining moment

5 **matter of importance** or **consequence,** one for the book and something to write home about <both nonformal>, something special; vital interest, matter of life or death; memorabilia

6 **salient point,** high point; **the point, main point, essence,** the name of the game and the bottom line and what it's all about and where it's at <all nonformal>, substance, gravamen, frontburner issue <nonformal>; **essential,** fundamental, substantive point; **gist, nub** <nonformal>, **heart,** meat, pith, kernel, **core; crux,** crucial or pivotal or critical point; turning point, **climax, cusp, crisis;** milestone, bench mark; linchpin

7 **feature, highlight,** high spot, centerpiece, pièce de résistance

8 **personage, important person,** person of consequence, **great man** or **woman, somebody, notable,** figure; **celebrity,** person of renown, personality; name, big name, nabob, **mogul,** panjandrum, very important person; sachem; mover and shaker; **worthy,** pillar of society; **dignitary,** dignity; **magnate;** tycoon <nonformal>, baron; power elite, Establishment; brass, top brass; ruling circle, lords of creation

9 <nonformal terms> **big shot, big wheel,** big fish, big shot, big cheese, big-time operator, **bigwig,** big gun, high-muckety-muck, lion, **VIP,** brass hat; sacred cow, tin god; big man on campus or BMOC

10 **chief, principal,** chief executive officer or CEO, overlord, **king;** leading light, luminary, **star,** superstar, prima donna, lead 707.6

11 <nonformal terms> **boss, honcho,** big enchilada, biggest frog in the pond, top dog, Mr Big, his nibs, himself

VERBS 12 **matter,** signify, **count, tell, weigh, carry weight,** cut some ice <nonformal>, stand out, mean much; be something, be somebody; be featured, star, get top billing

13 **value, esteem, treasure, prize,** appreciate, **rate highly,** think highly of, **think much of,** set store by; make much of, make a fuss about, make much ado about

14 emphasize, stress, lay emphasis or stress upon, feature, highlight, place emphasis on, **accent, accentuate, punctuate, point up; highlight,** spotlight; **star, underline, underscore;** overemphasize, overstress, overaccentuate; harp on; dwell on; make a big deal or Federal case of <nonformal>, make a mountain out of a molehill

15 feature; star, give top billing to

16 dramatize, play up <nonformal>, make a production of

ADJS **17 important, major, consequential, momentous, significant, considerable,** substantial, material, **great;** earthshaking; big-time and big-league and major-league and heavyweight <all nonformal>; high-powered <nonformal>; name and big-name <both nonformal>, self-important 140.8

18 of importance, of significance, of consequence, of note, of moment, of weight; not to be overlooked or despised, not to be sneezed at <nonformal>; viable

19 notable, noteworthy, celebrated, remarkable, marked, standout <nonformal>, signal; **memorable,** unforgettable, never to be forgotten; striking, salient; **eminent, prominent,** conspicuous, **outstanding, distinguished;** prestigious, esteemed, estimable; **extraordinary,** out of the ordinary, **exceptional, special,** rare

20 weighty, grave, sober, sobering, **solemn, serious,** earnest; portentous, fateful; formidable, awe-inspiring, larger than life

21 emphatic, decided, positive, forceful, forcible; **emphasized, stressed,** accentuated, punctuated; underlined, underscored; red-letter

22 urgent, imperative, imperious, **compelling, pressing,** high-priority, clamorous, insistent, exigent; crucial, critical, pivotal

23 vital, all-important, crucial, of vital importance, life-and-death; earth-shattering, epoch-making; **essential,** fundamental, indispensable, substantive, bedrock; **central,** focal

24 paramount, principal, leading, foremost, main, chief, premier, **prime, primary,** preeminent, **supreme,** cardinal; toprank, of the first rank, world-class, **dominant,** predominant, **overruling,** overriding

ADVS **25 importantly, significantly,** materially, momentously, prominently, conspicuously, signally, notably, markedly

26 at the decisive moment, in the clutch and when the chips are down and when push comes to shove <all nonformal>

997 UNIMPORTANCE

NOUNS **1 unimportance, insignificance,** inconsequentiality, **immateriality;** ineffectuality; inferiority, secondariness, low priority, expendability, marginality; **smallness,** negligibility; irrelevancy, meaninglessness; **pettiness,** picayunishness; irrelevance 775.1

2 paltriness, meanness, pitifulness, contemptibleness, pitiableness, despicableness, wretchedness, vileness, shabbiness, shoddiness, cheapness, worthlessness, unworthiness; tawdriness, meretriciousness, gaudiness 501.3

3 triviality, trivialness, nugacity, nugaciousness; **superficiality,** shallowness; slightness, flimsiness; **frivolity,** frivolousness, levity; **foolishness,** silliness, inanity, vacuity; triteness, vapidity; **much ado about nothing,** tempest in a teapot, big deal <nonformal>

4 trivia, trifles; trumpery, gimcrackery, bric-a-brac; **rubbish,** trash, chaff; peanuts and chicken feed and chickenshit and Mickey Mouse <all nonformal>, small change; minutiae, details

5 trifle, triviality, oddment, bagatelle, gimcrack, gewgaw, frippery, **trinket,** bibelot, curio, **bauble, knickknack,** knickknackery, folderol; hill of beans <nonformal>, molehill; a curse, a continental, a hoot *and* a damn *and* a darn <all nonformal>, a tinker's damn; picayune, red cent, two cents; drop in the ocean *or* the bucket; pinprick; mockery, child's play

6 an insignificancy, a marginal matter *or* affair, a trivial *or* paltry affair, a small *or* trifling *or* minor matter, **no great matter;** a little thing, matter of no importance *or* consequence, matter of indifference; **a nothing, a big nothing, a naught,** a mere nothing, nothing to speak *or* worth speaking of, nothing to write home about, nullity, nihility; **technicality**

7 a nobody, insignificancy, hollow man, **nonentity,** nebbish <nonformal>, a nothing, cipher; lightweight, mediocrity; whippersnapper *and* pip-squeak *and* squirt *and* shrimp *and* runt <all nonformal>; punk <nonformal>; small potatoes; **the little fellow,** the little guy <nonformal>, **the man in the street;** common man 863.3; figurehead; **small fry**

8 trifling, dallying, **dalliance,** flirtation, coquetry; fiddling, **puttering,** tinkering, piddling; dabbling; loitering, idling 331.4

9 <nonformal terms> **monkeying, monkeying around,** fiddling around, horsing around, fooling around, kidding around, playing around, screwing around

10 trifler, dallier; putterer, tinkerer, dabbler; amateur, dilettante, Sunday painter; **flirt, coquet**

VERBS **11 be unimportant,** be of no importance, **not matter,** not count, signify nothing, **not make any difference; cut no ice, not amount to anything,** not amount to a hill of beans *or* a damn <nonformal>

12 attach little importance to, give little weight to; make little of, deemphasize, downplay, **minimize, make light of, make** *or*

think nothing of, take no account of, set no store by; snap one's fingers at; not give a shit *or* a hoot *or* two hoots for <nonformal>, not give a damn about; bad-mouth <nonformal>, deprecate, depreciate 512.8; **trivialize**

13 make much ado about nothing, make mountains out of molehills

14 trifle, dally; flirt, coquet; toy, play, fool, play at, **putter,** tinker, **piddle; dabble;** toy with, fiddle with, fool with; nickel-and-dime <nonformal>

15 <nonformal terms> **monkey, monkey around,** fiddle, fiddle around, horse around, fool around, play around, **screw around,** muck around, piss around, mess around

ADJS **16 unimportant, of no importance,** of no great importance, **of no account,** of no significance, of no concern, of little *or* no consequence, no great shakes <nonformal>; no skin off one's nose *or* elbow *or* ass <nonformal>; secondary, of a low order of importance, low-priority, expendable; marginal

17 insignificant 248.6, **inconsequential, immaterial;** unessential, **not vital,** back-burner <nonformal>, dispensable; **inconsiderable,** inappreciable, negligible; **small, little,** minor, inferior; irrelevant

18 <nonformal terms> **measly, small-time, two-bit,** Mickey Mouse, chickenshit, nickel-and-dime, tinhorn, punk; not worth a dime *or* a red cent *or* a hill of beans; **one-horse, two-by-four,** jerkwater

19 trivial, trifling; nugacious, nugatory; **slight,** slender, flimsy; **superficial, shallow; frivolous, light,** frothy; futile, vain, otiose; **foolish,** fatuous, asinine; **silly; inane,** empty, vacuous; trite, vapid

20 petty, puny, piddling, piffling, niggling, pettifogging, picayune, picayunish; small-beer

21 paltry, poor, mean, sorry, sad, pitiful, pathetic, **despicable, contemptible,** beneath contempt, **miserable, wretched,** vile, **shabby,** scruffy, shoddy, scurvy, **crummy** *and* cheesy <both nonformal>, **trashy,** rubbishy; tinpot <nonformal>; **cheap,** worthless, valueless, dime-a-dozen; tawdry, meretricious, gaudy 501.20

22 unworthy, worthless, beneath notice

ADVS **23 unimportantly, insignificantly, inconsequentially; pettily; trivially,** triflingly; superficially, shallowly; frivolously

998 GOODNESS
<good quality or effect>

NOUNS **1 goodness, excellence, quality,** class <nonformal>; **virtue,** grace; **merit; value, worth; fineness,** niceness; **superiority, skillfulness** 413.1; wholeness, **soundness,** healthiness 81.1; **virtuousness** 653.1; **kindness, benevolence,** benignity 143.1; helpfulness 449.10; favorableness, auspiciousness 133.9; expedience, advantageousness 994.1; **usefulness** 387.3; cogency, validity

2 superexcellence, preeminence, supremacy, primacy, peerlessness, matchlessness; **superbness, magnificence,** splendidness, marvelousness

3 tolerableness, tolerability, **adequateness, satisfactoriness,** acceptability, admissibility

4 good, welfare, well-being, **benefit; interest, advantage; behalf;** blessing, benison, boon; **profit,** gain

5 good thing, a thing to be desired; **treasure,** gem, jewel, diamond, pearl; **pride and joy;** prize, trophy, plum; nothing to sneeze at <nonformal>; catch, find <nonformal>; godsend, windfall

6 first-rater, world-beater; wonder, prodigy, genius, virtu-

oso, **star, superstar;** luminary, leading light

7 <nonformal terms> **dandy, jim dandy, dilly, humdinger, pip, peach,** beaut, **lulu, daisy,** sweetheart, dream, crackerjack, pistol, corker, whiz, knockout, something else, something else again, killer-diller, the cat's pajamas *or* meow, whizbang, wow

8 the best, the very best, the best ever, the top of the line <nonformal>; **quintessence,** superlative; **choice, pick, select, elect, elite,** chosen; **cream, flower,** fat; cream of the crop, salt of the earth; nonesuch, paragon, nonpareil

9 harmlessness, innocuousness, benignity; inoffensiveness; innocence; heart of gold, milk of human kindness

VERBS **10 do good, profit,** avail; do a world of good; **benefit, help, serve,** be of service, advance, advantage; be the making of; do no harm

11 excel, surpass, outdo, go one better; do with a vengeance; be as good as, equal, emulate, go one-on-one with <nonformal>; **make the most of, optimize;** skim off the cream

ADJS **12 good, excellent, fine, nice,** fair; **splendid, capital, grand,** famous <nonformal>, noble; fit for a king; commendable, laudable, **estimable** 509.20; **sound,** healthy 81.5; virtuous; benevolent 143.15; beneficial; favorable, auspicious 133.18; expedient, advantageous 994.5; cogent, valid 972.13

13 <nonformal terms> **great,** swell, dandy, jim dandy, neat, cool, super, super-duper, mean, heavy, bad, groovy, out of sight, something else, dynamite, keen, killer, nifty, sexy, peachy, scrumptious, out of this world, hunky-dory, crackerjack, boss, smashing, solid, all wool and a yard wide; bang-up, ace-high, fine and dandy, OK, okay

14 superior, head and shoulders

above, **crack** <nonformal>; **high-grade, high-class,** high-quality, **world-class**

15 superb, superfine; **exquisite; magnificent,** splendid, splendiferous, **marvelous, wonderful,** heavenly, terrific, sensational; gilt-edged *and* gilt-edge, blue-chip; of the first water, as good as they come, out of this world <nonformal>

16 best, top-of-the-line <nonformal>, **prime,** optimum, optimal; **choice, select, elect,** elite, hand-picked; **prize, champion; supreme,** paramount, **unsurpassed,** unparalleled, unmatched, matchless; **peerless;** quintessential

17 first-rate, first-class, in a class by itself; unmatched, matchless; record-breaking

18 <nonformal terms> **A-1, A number one,** tip-top, top-notch, top-flight, top-drawer, tops

19 up to par, up to snuff <nonformal>; **up to the mark, up to scratch** <nonformal>

20 tolerable, goodish, fair, fairish, moderate, **decent,** presentable, **pretty good, not bad,** not half bad, not so bad, **adequate, satisfactory, all right,** OK *or* okay <nonformal>; better than nothing; **acceptable, passable,** unobjectionable, unexceptionable

21 harmless, unhurtful; well-meaning, well-meant; **uninjurious, innocuous,** innocent; inoffensive; **benign;** nontoxic, nonvenomous

ADVS **22 excellently, nicely,** finely, **capitally, splendidly, famously,** royally; **well,** very well, **fine** <nonformal>, aright

23 superbly, exquisitely, **magnificently,** tremendously, immensely, terrifically, **marvelously, wonderfully,** gloriously, divinely

24 tolerably, fairly, respectably, **adequately, satisfactorily,** passably, **acceptably,** unexceptionably, decently; **rather, pretty**

999 BADNESS
<bad quality or effect>

NOUNS **1 badness, evil,** viciousness, reprehensibility; dereliction, peccancy, iniquity; unwholesomeness, unhealthiness 82.1; unkindness, malevolence 144; inauspiciousness, unfavorableness 133.8; inexpedience 995; invalidity 19.3; improperness 638.1

2 terribleness, dreadfulness, direness; **atrociousness, outrageousness,** heinousness, nefariousness; **notoriousness, egregiousness, infamousness; abominableness,** odiousness, **loathsomeness, detestableness,** despicableness, contemptibleness; **offensiveness,** obnoxiousness; squalor, squalidness, sordidness, **wretchedness, vileness,** fulsomeness, **nastiness,** rankness, **foulness,** noisomeness; beastliness, bestiality, brutality; the pits <nonformal>; shoddiness, shabbiness; scurviness, **baseness** 661.3

3 evil, bad, wrong, ill; harm, hurt, injury, damage, detriment; **destruction** 395; despoliation; abomination, grievance, vexation, woe; blight, venom, toxin, bane 1000; **corruption,** pollution, defilement; fly in the ointment, worm in the apple; skeleton in the closet; snake in the grass

4 bad influence, malevolent influence, **ill wind;** evil genius, **hoodoo** *and* **jinx** <both nonformal>, **Jonah; curse,** whammy *and* double *or* triple whammy <all nonformal>, spell, hex, voodoo; **evil eye**

5 harmfulness, hurtfulness, banefulness, balefulness, deleteriousness, noxiousness, venomousness, toxicity, virulence, noisomeness, **malignance** *or* **malignancy, malignity, viciousness**

VERBS **6 harm, hurt; injure,** scathe, wound, **damage; destroy** 395.10; despoil, disadvantage, impair, distress; **wrong,** do wrong by, aggrieve, do evil; **molest,** afflict; **abuse,** bash <nonformal>, batter, outrage, violate, maltreat, mistreat 389.5; torment, **harass,** hassle <nonformal>, persecute, savage, crucify, torture 96.18; play havoc with, wreak havoc on, play hob with <nonformal>; **corrupt,** deprave, taint, pollute, infect, befoul, defile; **curse,** put a whammy on <nonformal>, give the evil eye; spell trouble, menace 514.2

ADJS **7 bad, evil, ill,** untoward, sinister; **wicked, wrong,** peccant, iniquitous, **vicious; sinful** 654.16; **inferior** 1004.9; malevolent 144.19; inauspicious, unfavorable 133.17; inexpedient 995.5

8 <nonformal terms> **lousy,** punk, bum, crappy, cruddy, cheesy, gross, raunchy, piss-poor, **crummy,** grim, putrid, barfy, stinking, stinky, creepy, hairy, god-awful, gosh-awful

9 terrible, dreadful, awful <nonformal>, dire, horrible, horrid; heinous, villainous, nefarious; **deplorable,** lamentable, regrettable, pitiful, pitiable, woeful, grievous, sad 98.20; flagrant, **scandalous,** shameful, **shocking,** infamous, **notorious,** arrant, **egregious;** shoddy, schlocky <nonformal>, shabby, scurvy, **base** 661.12; **odious, obnoxious,** offensive, **disgusting,** repulsive, loathsome, **abominable, detestable, despicable, contemptible,** beneath contempt; blameworthy, **reprehensible;** rank, fetid, foul, filthy, vile, fulsome, noisome, **nasty,** squalid, sordid, **wretched;** as bad as they come, as bad as they make 'em <nonformal>; below par, subpar, not up to scratch *or* snuff *or* the mark

10 execrable, damnable; accursed; infernal, fiendish, satanic, ghoulish, demoniac, demonic, diabolical

11 evil-fashioned, ill-fashioned

12 harmful, hurtful, baneful, baleful, **injurious, damaging,** **detrimental,** deleterious, **pernicious**; noxious, mephitic, venomous, poisonous, venenous, toxic, virulent, noisome; **malignant,** malign, malevolent, malefic; corruptive, corrupting, corrosive, corroding

ADVS **13 badly, ill,** evilly, wrong, wrongly, amiss

14 terribly, dreadfully, horribly, horridly, **atrociously, outrageously;** flagrantly, scandalously, infamously, notoriously, egregiously, nauseatingly, fulsomely, odiously, **vilely,** obnoxiously, **disgustingly**; wretchedly, sordidly, abominably, despicably, contemptibly, foully

15 harmfully, hurtfully, banefully, balefully, **injuriously, damagingly, detrimentally,** deleteriously, **perniciously**; noxiously, venomously, poisonously, virulently; **malignantly,** malevolently, malefically, **viciously;** corrosively, corrodingly

1000 BANE

NOUNS **1 bane, curse, affliction,** visitation, **plague, pestilence,** calamity, scourge, **torment,** open wound, crushing burden; death 307; destruction 395; vexation 96.2; thorn in the flesh *or* side; bugbear, **bête noire,** nemesis

2 blight, canker, cancer; mold, fungus, mildew, smut, must, rust; rot, dry rot; **pest**

3 poison, venom, toxin; **pesticide; insecticide; herbicide,** defoliant, Agent Orange, **weed killer;** fungicide

4 miasma, mephitis; effluvium, exhaust

5 sting, stinger, dart; fang

1001 PERFECTION

NOUNS **1 perfection, flawlessness,** impeccability, absoluteness; infallibility; spotlessness, stainlessness, immaculateness; chastity 664

2 soundness, integrity, intactness, wholeness, completeness; **fullness,** plenitude; finish

3 **acme of perfection, culmina-tion,** acme, ultimate, summit, pinnacle, peak, climax, consum-mation, **the last word,** a dream come true

4 pattern *or* standard of perfec-tion, quintessence; archetype, prototype, exemplar, **epitome; classic,** masterwork, master-piece, showpiece; **ideal** 785.4; **paragon** 659.4

VERBS 5 **perfect,** develop, flesh out, ripen, mature; crown, culmi-nate; whip into shape, fine-tune; do to perfection 407.7

ADJS 6 **perfect, ideal, faultless, flawless,** unflawed, **impeccable,** absolute; **just right;** spotless, stainless, taintless, unblemished, immaculate, **pure,** uncontami-nated, unadulterated; sinless; chaste 664.4; infallible; beyond all praise, irreproachable, **match-less, peerless** 249.15

7 **sound, intact, whole, entire, complete,** integral; **full;** total, ut-ter, unqualified 959.2

8 **undamaged, unharmed, un-hurt, uninjured,** unscathed, **un-spoiled,** virgin, inviolate, **unim-paired; unmarred,** unmarked, unscarred, unbruised; **unbroken,** unshattered; unmutilated, un-mangled, unmaimed; unfaded, unworn, unwithered, bright, fresh, pristine, mint

9 **perfected, finished,** polished, refined; done to a turn; **classic, classical,** masterly, masterful, ex-pert, proficient; thorough-going; **consummate,** quintessential, ar-chetypical, exemplary

ADVS 10 **perfectly; faultlessly, flawlessly, impeccably;** spot-lessly; immaculately; **wholly, en-tirely, completely, fully,** abso-lutely 793.15

11 **to perfection, to a turn, to a T;** to a fare-thee-well <nonformal>

1002 IMPERFECTION

NOUNS 1 **imperfection; faulti-ness, defectiveness; shortcom-ing, deficiency, inadequacy;** er-roneousness, **fallibility; un-**soundness, unevenness; **impair-ment** 393; **mediocrity** 1004

2 **fault, defect, deficiency, inade-quacy,** imperfection; **flaw,** bug <nonformal>; fly in the ointment, problem, snag, drawback; **crack,** rift; **weakness,** frailty, infirmity, **failing, foible, shortcoming;** weak point, Achilles' heel, chink in one's armor, weak link; **blem-ish; malfunction,** glitch <non-formal>

VERBS 3 **fall short,** miss the mark, miss by a mile <nonformal>, **not measure up,** not come up to the mark, not come up to scratch *or* to snuff <nonformal>, not pass muster, not hack it *and* not make it *and* not cut it <all nonformal>; not make the grade

ADJS 4 **imperfect,** not perfect; **de-fective, faulty, inadequate, de-ficient,** not all it's cracked up to be <nonformal>, found wanting; erroneous, **fallible;** inaccurate, inexact, imprecise 974.17; **un-sound, incomplete,** partial, patchy, sketchy; makeshift 994.7; **damaged, impaired** 393.27; **blemished** 1003.8; half-baked <nonformal>, undeveloped 406.12; impure, adulterated

ADVS 5 **imperfectly, inadequately; incompletely,** partially

1003 BLEMISH

NOUNS 1 **blemish, disfigurement,** disfiguration, **defacement;** scar, cicatrix; scratch; scab; blister, vesicle; port-wine stain *or* mark, hemangioma, strawberry mark; pock, pustule; **crack,** craze, check, rift, split; **deformity,** de-formation, warp, twist, kink, **dis-tortion**

2 discoloration, discolorment

3 **stain, taint, tarnish; stigma;** macula; **spot, blot, blotch,** patch, speck, fleck; **smirch, smudge, smear;** splotch, splash, splatter, spatter

VERBS 4 **blemish, disfigure,** de-face, **flaw, mar;** scar, cicatrize, scarify; **deform, distort**

5 **spot, blot, blotch, speckle;**

freckle; **spatter, splatter,** splash, splotch

6 **stain, discolor,** smirch, besmirch, **taint, tarnish; mark, stigmatize,** brand; smear; daub; **darken, blacken;** scorch, singe, sear; dirty, **soil** 80.16

7 **bloodstain, bloody,** ensanguine

ADJS 8 **blemished, disfigured,** defaced, **marred,** scarred, scarified, scabbed, scabby; cracked, crazed, checked, split; deformed, warped, twisted, distorted; **faulty, flawed, defective** 1002.4

9 **spotted, spotty,** maculate, macular, blotched, **blotchy,** splotchy; **speckled,** bespeckled; freckled; spattered, splattered, splashed

10 **stained, discolored,** foxed, **tainted, tarnished,** besmirched; stigmatized; **soiled** 80.21

11 **bloodstained,** blood-spattered, **bloody,** sanguinary, **gory,** ensanguined

1004 MEDIOCRITY

NOUNS 1 **mediocrity,** modestness, moderateness, middlingness, **indifference;** passableness, **tolerableness** 998.3; **dullness,** tediousness 117.1

2 **ordinariness, commonness, commonplaceness;** unexceptionality, unremarkableness; conventionality

3 **inferiority, poorness,** humbleness, **baseness, meanness, commonness,** coarseness, tackiness

4 **low grade,** low class, low quality, poor quality

5 **mediocrity, second-rater,** thirdrater, nothing *or* nobody special, no great shakes <nonformal>, no brain surgeon, no rocket scientist; tinhorn <nonformal>; **nobody, nonentity** 997.7

6 **irregular,** second, third; schlock <nonformal>

ADJS 7 **mediocre, middling, indifferent, fair, fairish, fair to middling** <nonformal>; respectable, passable, **tolerable; so-so;** of sorts <nonformal>; nothing to brag about, nothing to write home about; bush-league; dull,

lackluster, tedious 117.6; insipid, vapid, wishy-washy

8 **ordinary, average, common, commonplace,** garden-variety <nonformal>, run-of-the-mill; **unexceptional, unremarkable, unnoteworthy,** nothing *or* nobody special *and* no great shakes <all nonformal>, no prize package, no brain surgeon, no rocket scientist; conventional

9 **inferior, poor, base, mean, common,** cheesy *and* tacky <both nonformal>, tinny; shabby, seedy; irregular; second-best; **second-rate,** third-rate, fourthrate; **second-class,** third-class, fourth-class, etc; **low-grade, lowclass**

10 **below par,** below standard, **below the mark** <nonformal>, substandard, **not up to scratch** *or* snuff *or* the mark <nonformal>

ADVS 11 **mediocrely, middlingly,** fairly, fair to middling <nonformal>, moderately, **indifferently, so-so;** passably, **tolerably**

12 **inferiorly, poorly,** basely, meanly, commonly

1005 DANGER

NOUNS 1 **danger, peril, endangerment, imperilment, jeopardy, hazard, risk,** cause for alarm, **menace, threat** 514; **crisis, emergency,** hot spot, strait, plight, predicament 1012.4; powder keg; time bomb; loose cannon <nonformal>; gathering clouds, storm clouds; yawning *or* gaping chasm, quicksand, thin ice; hornet's nest

2 **dangerousness, hazardousness, riskiness, precariousness** 970.6, diceyness <nonformal>, **perilousness; unsafeness,** unhealthiness <nonformal>; **ticklishness,** touchiness, ticklish business *and* shaky ground <both nonformal>; **insecurity,** instability, unsteadiness, shakiness; sword of Damocles; **unreliability,** untrustworthiness 970.6; **unsureness,** unpredictability, **uncertainty**

3 **exposure, openness,** liability; **unprotectedness, defenselessness,** nakedness

4 **vulnerability,** pregnability, vincibility; weakness 16; **weak link, weak point, soft spot,** heel of Achilles, chink in one's armor

5 <hidden danger> snags, rocks, reefs; shoals; sandbank, sandbar; quicksands; crevasses; undertow, undercurrent; **pitfall;** snake in the grass; booby trap, snare, tripwire, pitfall

VERBS 6 **endanger, imperil; risk, hazard, gamble, gamble with; jeopardize,** compromise, **put in jeopardy,** put on the spot <nonformal>; **expose**

7 **take chances, take a chance, chance, risk, gamble,** hazard, push one's luck, **run the risk or hazard;** risk one's neck, go out on a limb, stick one's neck out<nonformal>, **expose oneself,** lower one's guard, **lay oneself open to,** leave oneself wide open, let oneself in for; **tempt Providence or fate,** skate on thin ice, go in harm's way, stand on a volcano, sit on a barrel of gunpowder, put one's head in the lion's mouth, play with fire, go through fire and water, sail too near the wind; throw caution to the wind, **take one's life in one's hand, dare, face up to, brave** 492.11

8 **be in danger,** have the odds against one, have one's back to the wall; hang by a thread; totter on the brink; be on the spot or in a bind <both nonformal>

ADJS 9 **dangerous, perilous,** bad, ugly, serious, critical, explosive, beset or fraught with danger; too close for comfort, **menacing, threatening** 514.3

10 **hazardous, risky, chancy,** dicey <nonformal>, aleatory, full of risk; **adventurous,** venturesome; **speculative,** wildcat

11 **unsafe; unreliable, undependable, untrustworthy,** treacherous, **insecure, unsound,** unstable, unsteady, rocky; **unsure, uncertain,** dubious

12 **precarious, ticklish, touchy,** touch-and-go, **critical, delicate;** on thin ice; hanging by a thread

13 **in danger, in jeopardy, in peril, at risk; endangered, imperiled, jeopardized,** at the last extremity, in deadly peril; threatened, on the spot and on or in the hot seat <both nonformal>; sitting on a powder keg; between Scylla and Charybdis, between the devil and the deep blue sea, between a rock and a hard place <nonformal>; cornered

14 **unprotected, unshielded, unsheltered, unguarded, undefended,** unfortified; **unarmed,** bare-handed; **defenseless, helpless**

15 **exposed, open,** out in the open, naked; out on a limb <nonformal>

16 **vulnerable, pregnable,** penetrable, expugnable; conquerable, beatable <nonformal>, vincible

ADVS 17 **dangerously, perilously, hazardously, riskily; precariously,** ticklishly

1006 SAFETY

NOUNS 1 **safety, security,** assurance; immunity, clear sailing; **protection,** safeguard 1007.3; airworthiness, crashworthiness, roadworthiness, seaworthiness; invulnerability 15.4

VERBS 2 **be safe, be on the safe side; keep safe, come through;** ride out, weather the storm; land on one's feet; save one's neck; lead a charmed life, have nine lives

3 **play safe** <nonformal>, **keep on the safe side,** watch out, take precautions 494.6; keep an eye or a weather eye out, look before one leaps; **save, protect** 1007.18

ADJS 4 **safe, secure, safe and sound; protected** 1007.21; on the safe side; unthreatened, unmolested; intact, untouched, with a whole skin

5 **unhazardous, undangerous, unperilous,** riskless, **unprecarious;** dependable, reliable, trustworthy, sound, stable, steady,

firm 969.17; harmless; invulnerable

6 in safety, out of danger, out of
the woods *or* over the hump *or*
home free <all nonformal>, **in
the clear, out of harm's reach** *or*
way; under lock and key; in shelter, in the shadow of a rock; on
solid ground, high and dry

7 snug, cozy; roadworthy, airworthy, seaworthy

ADVS **8 safely, securely,** reliably,
dependably

1007 PROTECTION

NOUNS **1 protection, guard,
shielding, safekeeping;** polic-
ing, **law enforcement; patrol,
patroling;** eye, protectiveness,
vigilance, watchful eye; protective custody; **safeguarding, security,** public safety, **safety** 1006;
shelter, cover, windbreak, lee;
refuge 1008; preservation 397;
defense 460

2 protectorship, guardianship,
stewardship, custodianship;
**care, charge, keeping, nurture,
nurturing, nurturance, custody,
fostering; hands,** safe hands,
wing; **auspices, patronage,
tutelage, guidance; ward,** watch
and ward; pastorate; **oversight,**
jurisdiction, ministry, governance; **child care,** day-care

**3 safeguard, guard; shield,
screen,** aegis; **bulwark** 460.4;
fender, mudguard, **bumper,
buffer, cushion;** seat *or* safety
belt; life preserver 397.6; lifeline,
guardrail, handrail; **anchor,** sea
anchor, drogue; **parachute;
safety net**

**4 insurance; annuity; social se-
curity** 611.7; **insurance company; insurance policy**

5 protector, keeper, safekeeper;
tower, pillar, tower of strength,
rock; **defender** 460.7

6 guardian, warden; custodian,
steward, **keeper, caretaker,** attendant; **curator,** conservator;
shepherd, cowherd; **game warden,** gamekeeper; **ranger,** forest
ranger; lifeguard

7 chaperon, duenna; **governess;**
escort

8 nurse, nursemaid, nursery-
maid, nanny <chiefly Brit>,
mammy <nonformal>; dry nurse,
wet nurse; **baby-sitter,** sitter
<nonformal>

**9 guard; outguard, outpost;
picket,** outrider; advance guard,
vanguard; rear guard; jailer
429.10; bank guard; railway *or*
train guard

10 watchman, watch; lookout;
sentinel, picket, **sentry; scout;
point,** forward observer, spotter;
patrol, patrolman

11 watchdog, guard dog, attack
dog; sheep dog

**12 doorkeeper, doorman, gate-
keeper, porter, janitor,** *concierge*
<Fr>, usher; receptionist

13 picket, picketer, demonstrator,
picket line

14 bodyguard, safeguard; **convoy,
escort;** guards, praetorian guard;
guardsman

**15 policeman, constable, officer,
police officer;** peace officer, arm
of the law; **trooper; sheriff, marshal;** deputy sheriff, deputy

16 <nonformal terms> cop, copper,
bluecoat, flatfoot, gumshoe,
shamus, dick; the cops, the law,
the fuzz; New York's finest

**17 police, police force; constabu-
lary;** state police, troopers *or*
state troopers, highway patrol,
county police, provincial police;
security force; special police;
posse, *posse comitatus* <L>; **vig-
ilantes,** vigilance committee

VERBS **18 protect, guard, safeguard, secure, keep, police, enforce the law;** keep from harm;
ensure, guarantee 438.9; **cushion;** champion, go to bat for
<nonformal>; ride shotgun
<nonformal>, fend, defend 460.8;
shelter, shield, screen, cover,
cloak; **harbor, haven;** nestle

19 care for, take care of; provide
for, support; take charge of, **take
under one's wing; look after, attend to, minister to,** look *or* see
to, look *or* watch out for <nonfor-

mal>, keep an eye on, **watch over,** keep watch over, **watch, mind, tend;** keep tabs on <nonformal>; **shepherd,** ride herd on <nonformal>; **chaperon;** babysit <nonformal>; **foster, nurture, cherish, nurse; mother**

20 **watch, keep watch, keep guard,** keep watch over; stand guard; be on the lookout 339.8; mount guard; **police,** patrol, pound a beat <nonformal>

ADJS 21 **protected, guarded,** safeguarded, defended; safe 1006.4–6; patented, copyrighted; **sheltered, shielded,** screened, covered, cloaked

22 **under the protection of,** under the auspices of, **under one's wing,** under the wing of

23 **protective, custodial,** guardian, tutelary; curatorial; vigilant, watchful; protecting, guarding, safeguarding, sheltering, **shielding,** screening, covering; fostering, parental

1008 REFUGE

NOUNS 1 **refuge, sanctuary, asylum, haven, port, harbor;** port in a storm, snug harbor, safe haven; stronghold 460.6

2 **recourse, resource, resort;** last resort; **hope; expedient** 994.2

3 **shelter, cover, covert**; concealment 346; foxhole; **bunker;** trench; storm cellar, cyclone cellar; air-raid shelter, bomb shelter, fallout shelter

4 **asylum, home,** retreat; **poorhouse; orphanage; hospice;** old folks' home, rest home, nursing home; foster home; halfway house; retirement home *or* village *or* community

5 **retreat,** recess, hiding place, **hideaway,** hideout; **sanctum, inner sanctum, sanctum sanctorum,** holy of holies; **den,** lair, mew; safe house; **cloister,** hermitage, ashram, cell; **ivory tower**

6 **harbor, haven, port, seaport,** port of call, home port; harborage, **anchorage,** moorage, moorings; **roadstead,** road,

roads; berth, slip; **dock,** dockage, marina, basin; **wharf, pier,** quay; jetty; breakwater, groin; seawall

VERBS 7 **take refuge, take shelter, claim sanctuary,** claim refugee status; throw oneself into the arms of; lock *or* bolt the door; take cover 346.8

8 **find refuge** *or* sanctuary, make port, reach safety; sequester oneself, dwell in an ivory tower

1009 PROSPERITY

NOUNS 1 **prosperity,** prosperousness; **success** 409; **welfare, well-being,** felicity; quality of life; comfortable *or* easy circumstances, **comfort, ease,** security; **life of ease,** the life of Riley <nonformal>, **the good life; bed of roses, luxury,** lap of luxury, Easy Street *and* Fat City *and* hog heaven <all nonformal>; fat of the land; fleshpots; milk and honey, loaves and fishes; a chicken in every pot; high standard of living; upward mobility; **affluence, wealth** 618

2 **good fortune** *or* **luck, fortune, luck,** the breaks <nonformal>; **fortunateness, luckiness;** blessing

3 **stroke of luck,** piece of good luck; blessing; **fluke** *and* lucky strike *and* scratch hit *and* **break** <all nonformal>

4 **good times,** palmy *or* halcyon days, days of wine and roses; heyday; golden era, **golden age;** age of Aquarius, millennium; **utopia** 985.11; **heaven** 681

5 **roaring trade, land-office business** <nonformal>, bullishness, bull market, seller's market; **boom**

6 **lucky dog** <nonformal>, fortune's child, destiny's darling

VERBS 7 **prosper, fare well,** get on well, do well, have it made <nonformal>, have a good thing going, go great guns <nonformal>; **turn out well, go well; succeed;** come a long way, get on <nonformal>; **advance,** progress, make progress, make headway, get ahead

<nonformal>, move up in the world, pull oneself up by one's own boot-straps

8 **thrive, flourish;** blossom, flower; batten, grow fat; be fat, dumb, and happy <nonformal>

9 **be prosperous, make good, make one's mark,** rise *or* get on in the world, do all right by oneself <nonformal>, **make one's fortune;** grow rich; do a land-office business <nonformal>

10 **live well, live in clover** *or* on velvet <nonformal>, **live a life of ease,** live *or* lead the life of Riley, **live high, live high on the hog** <nonformal>, live off the fat of the land, roll in the lap of luxury; have a fine time of it

11 **be fortunate, be lucky,** be in luck, luck out <nonformal>, have all the luck, **lead a charmed life; get a break** *and* get the breaks <both nonformal>; have a run of luck *and* hit a streak of luck <both nonformal>; strike it lucky *and* make a lucky strike *and* strike oil <all nonformal>, **strike it rich** <nonformal>, hit it big <nonformal>, come into money

ADJS 12 **prosperous; successful,** rags-to-riches; **well-paid, high-income,** well-heeled *and* upscale <both nonformal>; **affluent, wealthy; comfortable,** comfortably situated; on Easy Street *and* in Fat City *and* in hog heaven <all nonformal>, **in clover** *and* **on velvet** <both nonformal>, high on the hog <nonformal>

13 **thriving, flourishing, prospering, booming** <nonformal>; going strong <nonformal>; halcyon, palmy, balmy; fat, sleek; fat, dumb, and happy <nonformal>

14 **fortunate, lucky, providential; in luck; blessed,** favored; born under a lucky star, born with a silver spoon in one's mouth; **auspicious**

ADVS 15 **prosperously, thrivingly, flourishingly,** boomingly, swimmingly <nonformal>

16 **fortunately, luckily, providentially**

1010 ADVERSITY

NOUNS 1 **adversity,** difficulties, hard knocks *and* rough going <both nonformal>, **hardship, trouble,** troubles, **rigor,** vicissitude, stress of life; **hard life,** dog's life, vale of tears; tough row to hoe <nonformal>, ups and downs of life, things going against one; annoyance, irritation, aggravation; **difficulty** 1012; **trial,** tribulation, blight, **affliction** 96.8; plight, predicament 1012.4

2 **misfortune, mishap, misadventure, mischance,** grief; **disaster, calamity, catastrophe,** cataclysm, **tragedy; shock, blow,** nasty *or* staggering blow; **accident,** casualty, collision, crash; **wreck**

3 **reverse, reversal,** reversal of fortune, **setback; comedown,** descent

4 **unfortunateness, unluckiness,** lucklessness; starcrossed *or* ill-fated life; inauspiciousness 133.8

5 **bad luck,** ill luck, **hard luck, tough** *or* **rotten luck** <nonformal>, raw deal <nonformal>, tough *or* rotten break <nonformal>; **ill fortune,** bad fortune, ill wind

6 **hard times,** bad times, sad times; rainy day; stormy *or* heavy weather; **depression,** recession, **slump,** economic stagnation, **bust** <nonformal>

7 **unfortunate,** poor unfortunate, fortune's fool; **loser** *and* sure loser *and* non-starter <all nonformal>; hard case *and* sad sack *and* hard-luck guy <all nonformal>; the underclass, the dispossessed, the homeless, the wretched of the earth; victim 96.11

VERBS 8 **go hard with,** go ill with; **oppress, weigh on** *or* **upon,** weigh heavy on, weigh down, **burden,** overload, bear hard upon, lie heavy upon; try one, put one out

9 **have trouble;** be born to trouble; **have a hard time of it,** be up against it <nonformal>, lead *or*

live a dog's life; bear more than one's share; not know which way to turn; **be unlucky, have bad** *or* **rotten luck,** get the short *or* shitty end of the stick <nonformal>

10 come to grief, be stricken, be shattered, be poleaxed, be clobbered <nonformal>; run aground, go on the rocks *or* shoals; sink, drown; **founder**

11 fall on evil days, go *or* **come down in the world,** be on the skids <nonformal>, fall from one's high estate; **deteriorate,** degenerate, go to seed, decline; **go to pot** <nonformal>, go to the dogs; touch bottom, hit rock bottom; have seen better days

12 bring bad luck; hoodoo *and* hex *and* put the jinx on <all nonformal>; put the evil eye on

ADJS **13 adverse, untoward, detrimental, unfavorable;** hostile, antagonistic, inimical; contrary, opposing, in opposition; **difficult, troublesome, troublous, hard,** trying, rigorous, stressful; **not easy;** harmful 999.12

14 unfortunate, unlucky, unprovidential, unprosperous, sad, unhappy, hapless, luckless; **out of luck; down on one's luck** <nonformal>, down in the world, in adverse circumstances; underprivileged, depressed; born under an evil star, star-crossed; fatal, dire, **ominous, inauspicious** 133.17; **in a jam** *and* in a pickle *and* in a tight spot *and* between a rock and a hard place <all nonformal>, between the devil and the deep blue sea; up a tree *and* up the creek *or* up shit creek without a paddle <all nonformal>

15 disastrous, calamitous, catastrophic, cataclysmic, cataclysmal, **tragic,** ruinous, fatal, dire, baneful, grievous; **life-threatening, terminal**

ADVS **16 adversely, untowardly,** detrimentally, **unfavorably;** contrarily, conflictingly

17 unfortunately, unluckily, unprovidentially, sadly, unhappily; by ill luck; in adverse circumstances

18 disastrously, calamitously, catastrophically, cataclysmically, grievously, woefully, sorely, banefully, tragically, crushingly, shatteringly

1011 HINDRANCE

NOUNS **1 hindrance, hampering; check, arrest; impediment,** holdback; **resistance, opposition** 451; suppression, **repression, restriction, restraint** 428; **obstruction,** blockage, clogging, occlusion; **bottleneck,** gridlock; **interruption,** interference; **retardation, detention, delay,** setback; **inhibition; closure,** closing up *or* off; obstructionism, negativism, foot-dragging <nonformal>

2 prevention, stop, stoppage, stopping; prohibition, forbiddance; debarment; **determent; deterrence, discouragement; forestalling, preclusion, obviation,** foreclosure

3 frustration, thwarting, balking, foiling; discomfiture, disconcertion, confounding; **defeat**

4 obstacle, obstruction; hang-up <nonformal>; **block,** blockade, cordon, curtain; **difficulty,** hazard; **deterrent; drawback; stumbling block,** stumbling stone; fly in the ointment, **hitch, catch,** joker <nonformal>

5 barrier, bar; fence, wall, impenetrable wall; **bulwark, rampart,** defense, buffer, bulkhead, parapet, breastwork, work, earthwork, mound; logjam; roadblock; backstop; iron curtain, bamboo curtain

6 impediment, embarrassment, hamper; encumbrance; **trouble,** difficulty 1012; **handicap,** disadvantage, inconvenience; **burden,** imposition, onus, ball and chain, millstone around one's neck; **load**

7 curb, check, arrest, **stay, stop,** damper; **brake,** clog, drag, drogue; doorstop; shackle, chain, fetter, trammel 428.4

8 hinderer, obstructer; thwarter; obstructionist; filibuster, filibusterer

9 spoilsport, wet blanket, **killjoy,** grouch, malcontent, **dog in the manger** <nonformal>

VERBS **10 hinder, impede, inhibit, arrest, check, curb,** snub; **resist, oppose** 451.3; stonewall <nonformal>, stall off; **suppress, repress** 428.8; **interrupt**; intervene, interfere, meddle 214.7; damp, dampen, throw cold water; **retard,** slacken, **delay,** detain, **hold back, keep back,** set back, hold up <nonformal>; **restrain** 428.7

11 hamper, impede, cramp, embarrass; trammel, enmesh, entangle, ensnarl, entwine, tangle, snarl; fetter, shackle; **handcuff,** tie one's hands; **encumber, burden, saddle with,** weigh *or* weight down, press down; hang like a millstone round one's neck; **handicap,** put at a disadvantage; hobble, hamstring

12 obstruct, get *or* **stand in the way; dog; block,** put up a roadblock, occlude; **jam,** crowd, pack; **bar,** barricade, bolt, lock; **debar,** shut out; **close,** close off *or* up, shut tight; constrict, squeeze, **strangle,** strangulate, **stifle,** suffocate, **choke**

13 stop, stay, halt, bring to a stop, bring to a shuddering *or* screeching halt <nonformal>; **brake,** put on the brakes, hit the brakes <nonformal>; **block, stall, stymie,** deadlock; nip in the bud

14 prevent, prohibit, forbid; bar; keep from; deter, discourage, dishearten; **avert, parry, keep off, ward off, stave off, fend off,** fend, repel, deflect, turn aside; **forestall,** foreclose, **preclude,** exclude, debar, **obviate**

15 thwart, frustrate, foil, cross, balk; scotch, checkmate; **counter,** contravene, counteract; stand in the way of, confront, brave, defy, challenge; **defeat** 412.6,8,9; **discomfit,** upset, **disrupt, confound, disconcert, baffle,** nonplus, perplex; trip one up, throw

one for a loss <nonformal>; **circumvent,** elude; sabotage, **spoil, ruin,** blast; **destroy** 395.10; **throw a monkey wrench into the works** <nonformal>; put one's nose out of joint <nonformal>, upset one's applecart; **derail;** take the wind out of one's sails, steal one's thunder, cut the ground from under one; tie one's hands, clip one's wings

16 <nonformal terms> **queer, crab, foul up, louse up,** snafu, bollix up, gum up the works; **put a crimp in,** cramp one's style; cook one's goose; give one a hard time

ADJS **17 hindering,** troublesome; **inhibitive,** inhibiting, repressive; constrictive, strangling, stifling; restrictive 428.12; **obstructive;** cantankerous <nonformal>, contrary, crosswise; in the way

18 hampering, impeding, counterproductive; onerous, oppressive, burdensome, cumbersome, encumbering

19 preventive, prophylactic; **prohibitive, forbidding; deterrent,** discouraging

20 frustrating, confounding, disconcerting, baffling

ADVS **21** at a disadvantage, with everything against one

1012 DIFFICULTY

NOUNS **1 difficulty; hardness, toughness** <nonformal>, the hard way <nonformal>, **rigor,** rigorousness, ruggedness; **arduousness,** laboriousness, strenuousness, toilsomeness; **troublesomeness;** onerousness, oppressiveness, burdensomeness; complication, intricacy, **complexity** 798

2 hard job, tough job *and* heavy lift <both nonformal>, backbreaker, ballbuster <nonformal>, **chore,** man-sized job; Herculean task, Augean task; **uphill work** *or* **going,** rough go <nonformal>, **heavy sledding;** hard road to travel; hard *or* tough nut to crack *and* hard *or* tough row to hoe <all

nonformal>; bitch <nonformal>; **handful** <nonformal>

3 trouble, the matter; headache <nonformal>, problem, **inconvenience,** disadvantage; **ado,** great ado; hornet's nest, Pandora's box, can of worms 999.3; **bother, annoyance** 98.7; **anxiety, worry** 126.2

4 predicament, plight, strait, straits; **pinch, bind,** pass, clutch, situation, emergency; pretty pass, pretty *or* fine state of affairs, **sorry plight;** slough, quagmire, morass, swamp, quicksand; **embarrassment; complication,** imbroglio

5 <nonformal terms> **pickle,** crunch, fine kettle of fish, fine how-do-you-do; **spot, tight spot; squeeze, tight squeeze,** ticklish *or* tricky spot, hot spot, hot seat; **scrape, jam, hot water; mess,** holy *or* unholy mess, stew; hell to pay

6 impasse, corner *and* **box** *and* **hole** <all nonformal>; **cul-desac, blind alley, dead end,** deadend street; **extremity, end of one's rope** *or* **tether,** wit's end; **stalemate,** deadlock; standoff, standstill

7 dilemma, horns of a dilemma, double bind, no-win situation, **quandary,** nonplus; **vexed question,** thorny problem, Gordian knot, poser, teaser, enigma 522.8; paradox, oxymoron

8 crux, hitch, pinch, rub, snag, catch, joker <nonformal>, where the shoe pinches

9 unwieldiness, unmanageability; unhandiness; awkwardness, clumsiness; cumbersomeness

VERBS **10 be difficult, present difficulties**

11 have difficulty, have trouble, have a hard time of it, have one's hands full; be hard put; labor under a disadvantage, have the cards stacked against one *and* have two strikes against one <both nonformal>; struggle, **flounder;** have one's back to the wall, not know whether one is coming or going, go around in circles

12 get into trouble, plunge into difficulties; **let oneself in for, put one's foot in it** <nonformal>; **get in a jam** *or* **hot water** <nonformal>, **get into a scrape** <nonformal>, **get in a mess** *or* **hole** *or* **box** *or* **bind** <nonformal>; paint oneself into a corner <nonformal>, put oneself in a spot <nonformal>, put one's foot in one's mouth; have a tiger by the tail

13 trouble, beset; **bother,** get one down, <nonformal>, **disturb, perturb,** irk, plague, **torment,** drive one up the wall <nonformal>, make one lose sleep; **harass, vex, distress** 96.16; inconvenience, **put out,** discommode 995.4; **concern, worry** 126.3; **puzzle, perplex** 970.13; give one trouble; give one a hard time <nonformal>

14 cause trouble, bring trouble; ask for trouble, ask for it <nonformal>, bring down upon one's head, bring down around one's ears; **stir up a hornet's nest,** kick up a fuss *or* storm *or* row <nonformal>; open Pandora's box, open a can of worms <nonformal>

15 put in a hole <nonformal>, put in a spot <nonformal>; **embarrass; involve,** enmesh

16 corner, drive into a corner <nonformal>, **tree** <nonformal>, chase up a tree <nonformal>, force to the wall, push one to the wall, have one on the ropes <nonformal>

ADJS **17 difficult; not easy,** no picnic; **hard, tough** *and* **rough** *and* **rugged** <all nonformal>, rigorous, severe; wicked *and* mean *and* hairy <all nonformal>, **formidable; arduous, strenuous, toilsome, laborious,** Herculean; exacting, demanding; intricate, complex 798.4; abstruse 522.16

18 troublesome, besetting; **bothersome,** irksome, vexatious, painful, annoying 98.22; **burden-**

some, oppressive, onerous, back-breaking; **trying,** grueling

19 unwieldy, unmanageable, unhandy; inconvenient, impractical; **awkward, clumsy, cumbersome,** unmaneuverable; ponderous, bulky

20 troubled, sore beset; **bothered, vexed,** irked, annoyed 96.21; plagued, **harassed** 96.24; distressed, perturbed 96.22; ; **worried, anxious** 126.6,7; puzzled

21 in trouble, in deep trouble, in a predicament, in a sorry plight, in a pretty pass; out of one's depth

22 <nonformal terms> in deep shit *or* doo-doo, in a jam, in a pickle, in a spot, in a tight spot, in a fix, in a hole, in a bind, in a box; in a mess, in a scrape, in hot water, in the soup; up a tree, up the creek, up shit creek without a paddle, in Dutch, on the spot, behind the eight ball, on Queer Street, out on a limb

23 in a dilemma, on the horns of a dilemma, **in a quandary;** between Scylla and Charybdis, between the devil and the deep blue sea, between a rock and a hard place <nonformal>

24 at an impasse, at one's wit's end, at a loss, at a standstill; **nonplussed,** **baffled, perplexed, bewildered,** mystified, stumped <nonformal>, stymied

25 cornered, in a corner, with one's back to the wall

26 straitened, in desperate straits, **pinched,** sore pressed, **hard-pressed, hard up** <nonformal>, **up against it** <nonformal>; driven from pillar to post; **desperate, in extremities, at the end of one's rope** *or* **tether**

27 stranded, grounded, aground, **on the rocks,** high and dry; **stuck;** foundered, swamped; castaway, shipwrecked

ADVS **28 with difficulty,** with much ado; painfully; **arduously, strenuously, laboriously**

29 unwieldily, unmanageably, unhandily, inconveniently; **awkwardly, clumsily, cumbersomely;** ponderously

1013 FACILITY

NOUNS **1 facility, ease, easiness,** fac'leness, **effortlessness;** lack of hindrance, **smoothness,** freedom; easy going, smooth sailing; clarity, intelligibility 521; uncomplexity, uncomplicatedness, **simplicity** 797

2 handiness, wieldiness, manageability, maneuverability; **convenience,** practicality; **flexibility,** pliancy, **pliability,** malleability; adaptability

3 easy thing, mere child's play, simple matter, mere twist of the wrist

4 <nonformal terms> cinch, snap, pushover, breeze, waltz, duck soup, velvet, picnic, cherry pie, apple pie, cakewalk, , kid stuff, setup

5 facilitation, facilitating, easing, smoothing, smoothing the way; **speeding,** expediting, expedition, quickening, hastening; streamlining

6 disembarrassment, disentanglement, disencumbrance, uncomplicating, unhampering; **extrication,** disengagement, **freeing,** clearing; **simplification** 797.2

VERBS **7 facilitate, ease;** grease the wheels <nonformal>; **smooth, pave the way,** ease the way, **clear the way,** make way for; run interference for <nonformal>, open the door to; **open up, unclog,** unblock, unjam, unbar, loose 431.6; **lubricate; speed, expedite,** quicken, hasten; **help along,** help on its way; **aid** 449.11; **explain,** make clear 521.6; **simplify** 797.4

8 do easily, make short work of, do with one's hands tied behind one's back, do hands down, sail *or* dance *or* waltz through, wing it <nonformal>

9 disembarrass, disencumber, unload, relieve, disburden, unhamper, get out from under; **dis-**

entangle, disembroil, disinvolve;
extricate, disengage, **free**; liberate 431.4

10 **go easily, run smoothly**; present no difficulties, be effortless

11 **have it easy, have it soft** <nonformal>, have it all one's own way; breeze in <nonformal>, win in a walk *or* hands down <nonformal>

12 **take it easy** *and* **go easy** <both nonformal>, drift with the current, go with the tide; take it in one's stride, make little *or* light of, think nothing of

ADJS 13 **easy, facile, effortless,** smooth, painless; uncomplicated, straightforward, **simple** 797.6, Mickey Mouse <nonformal>, simple as ABC <nonformal>, easy as pie *and* easy as falling off a log <both nonformal>, like shooting fish in a barrel, like taking candy from a baby; **clear;** glib; **light**

14 **smooth-running,** frictionless, easy-flowing; well-lubricated, well-oiled, well-greased

15 **handy, wieldy;** tractable; **manageable,** maneuverable; **convenient,** foolproof, untroublesome, user-friendly; adaptable, feasible

ADVS 16 **easily,** facilely, **effortlessly, readily, simply,** lightly, swimmingly <nonformal>, without difficulty; hands down <nonformal>, with one hand tied behind one's back, standing on one's head; like a duck takes to water; **smoothly,** like clockwork

1014 UGLINESS

NOUNS 1 **ugliness, unsightliness, unattractiveness,** uncomeliness, unprepossessingness, inelegance; **homeliness,** plainness; shapelessness; clumsiness, ungainliness 414.3; **uglification, uglifying, disfigurement,** defacement

2 **hideousness,** horridness, horribleness, frightfulness, dreadfulness, terribleness, awfulness

<nonformal>; **repulsiveness** 98.2, repugnance, repugnancy, offensiveness, forbiddingness, loathsomeness; **deformity,** misshapenness

3 forbidding countenance, vinegar aspect

4 **eyesore,** blot, blemish, **sight** <nonformal>, **fright, horror, mess,** no beauty, no beauty queen, ugly duckling; **scarecrow,** gargoyle, monster, **monstrosity,** teratism; **hag,** harridan

VERBS 5 **offend,** offend the eye, **look bad;** look something terrible *and* look like hell *and* look like the devil *and* look like something the cat dragged in <all nonformal>; **uglify, disfigure,** deface, blot, blemish

ADJS 6 **ugly, unsightly, unattractive, unhandsome, unpretty, unlovely,** uncomely, **inelegant; unbeautiful,** unpleasing 98.17; **homely, plain;** not much to look at, hard on the eyes <nonformal>; ugly as sin, homely enough to stop a clock, not fit to be seen; **uglified, disfigured,** defaced, blotted, blemished, marred, spoiled

7 **unprepossessing, ill-favored;** hatchet-faced, horse-faced

8 **unshapely,** shapeless, **ill-shaped,** ill-made, ill-proportioned; **deformed,** misshapen, misproportioned, malformed, misbegotten

9 **ungraceful,** graceless; clumsy, **ungainly** 414.20

10 **inartistic,** unartistic, **unaesthetic; undecorative**

11 **hideous, horrid, horrible,** frightful, dreadful, terrible, awful <nonformal>; **repulsive** 98.18, repellent, repelling, **repugnant,** forbidding, loathsome, revolting; **ghastly,** gruesome

ADVS 12 **unattractively, unhandsomely, unbeautifully, unprettily**

13 **hideously, horridly, horribly,** frightfully, dreadfully, terribly, awfully <nonformal>; **repulsively, repugnantly,** offensively,

forbiddingly, loathsomely, revoltingly; gruesomely, ghastly

1015 BEAUTY

NOUNS **1 beauty, beautifulness,
prettiness, handsomeness, attractiveness** 97.2, **loveliness,
pulchritude, charm,** exquisiteness; beauty unadorned

2 grace, elegance

3 comeliness, fairness, per-
sonableness, pleasingness 97.1,
bonniness, agreeableness

4 good looks, good appearance,
good effect; **shapeliness,** nice
body, lovely build, physical or
bodily charm, curvaceousness,
sexy body; bodily grace, **gracefulness; beauties, charms, de-
lights,** good features

5 daintiness, delicacy, delicate-
ness

6 gorgeousness; gloriousness,
heavenliness, sublimity; **splendor,** splendidness, resplendence;
brilliance, brightness, radiance,
luster; **glamour** 377.1

7 thing of beauty, vision, picture
<nonformal>, **sight or treat for
sore eyes** <nonformal>

8 beauty, charmer; beauty queen,
beauty contest winner, Miss
America, bathing beauty; **glamor
girl,** cover girl, model; sex goddess; **belle;** beau ideal, paragon;
enchantress

9 <nonformal terms> **doll, dish,
cutie,** angel, angelface, babyface,
beaut, honey, dream, looker,
good-looker, stunner, dazzler,
dreamboat, peach, knockout,
raving beauty, pinup girl, pinup, bunny, pussycat, sex kitten,
ten

10 <famous beauties> Venus, Venus de Milo; Aphrodite, Hebe;
Adonis, Apollo

11 beautification, adornment;
decoration 498.1; **beauty care,**
beauty treatment, cosmetology

**12 makeup, cosmetics, beauty
products, beauty-care products;** war paint and drugstore
complexion <both nonformal>;
lipstick; nail polish

13 beautician, cosmetologist; hair-
dresser; barber; manicurist

14 beauty parlor or salon or shop;
barbershop

VERBS **15 beautify, prettify,** pretty
up or gussy up or doll up <all
nonformal>, grace, **adorn; decorate** 498.8; **glamorize; make up,**
paint and put on one's face <both
nonformal>

16 look good; look like a million
and knock dead and knock one's
eyes out <all nonformal>; take
the breath away; shine, beam,
bloom, glow

ADJS **17 beautiful, beauteous,** endowed with beauty; **pretty, handsome, attractive** 97.7, pulchritu-
dinous, **lovely, graceful;** elegant;
cute; pretty as a picture; tall dark
and handsome

**18 comely, fair, good-looking,
nice-looking, personable,** presentable, becoming, pleasing
97.6, **sightly;** pleasing to the eye,
lovely to behold; **shapely,** well-
built, well-shaped, well-
proportioned, stacked or well-
stacked <both nonformal>, curvaceous, curvy <nonformal>,
buxom, callipygian, callipygous;
Junoesque, statuesque

19 fine, exquisite, flowerlike,
dainty, delicate

20 gorgeous, ravishing; glorious,
heavenly, divine, sublime; **resplendent,** splendiferous, **splendid; brilliant,** radiant, shining,
beaming, glowing, blooming,
dazzling; glamorous

21 <nonformal terms> **eye-filling,
easy on the eyes,** not hard to
look at; **raving,** devastating,
stunning, killing

22 beautifying, cosmetic; decorative 498.10; beautified, made-up,
mascaraed

ADVS **23 beautifully,** beauteously,
**prettily, handsomely, attrac-
tively, becomingly;** elegantly, exquisitely; charmingly, enchantingly

24 daintily, delicately

25 gorgeously, ravishingly; rav-
ingly and devastatingly and stun-

ningly <all nonformal>; **gloriously,** divinely, sublimely; **resplendently,** splendidly, splendorously, splendrously; **brilliantly,** brightly, radiantly, glowingly, **dazzlingly**

1016 MATHEMATICS

NOUNS **1 mathematics, numbers, figures;** pure mathematics, abstract mathematics, applied mathematics, higher mathematics

2 <mathematical operations> notation, addition 253, subtraction 255, multiplication, division

3 number, numeral, digit, binary digit *or* bit, **cipher,** character, symbol, sign, notation

4 <number systems> **Arabic numerals,** algorithm, Roman numerals; **decimal system,** binary system, octal system, duodecimal system, hexadecimal system

5 large number, astronomical number, zillion *and* jillion <both nonformal>; googol, googolplex; infinity, infinitude 822.1; billion, trillion, etc 881.13

6 sum, summation, difference, product, **number, count, score, reckoning, tally,** the story *and* whole story *and* all she wrote <all nonformal>, the bottom line <nonformal>, **aggregate, amount,** quantity 244; **whole** 791, **total** 791.2

7 ratio, rate, proportion; quota; percentage, percent; **fraction**

8 series, progression; arithmetical progression, geometrical progression, harmonic progression

9 numeration, enumeration, numbering, counting, accounting, census, inventorying, telling, tallying; counting on the fingers, dactylonomy; **measurement** 300; quantification, quantization

10 calculation, computation, estimation, reckoning, calculus; totaling, toting <nonformal>

11 summation, summary, summing, summing up, recount, recounting, rehearsal, capitulation, **recapitulation,** recap *and* rehash

<both nonformal>, statement, **reckoning, count,** census, inventory, head count, nose count, body count

12 account of, count of, tab *or* **tabs of** <nonformal>, track of

13 figures, statistics, indexes *or* indices

14 calculator, computer 1041.2, estimator, reckoner; statistician, actuary

15 mathematician, arithmetician; geometrician; algebraist, trigonometrician, statistician

VERBS **16 number,** numerate, **enumerate, count, tell, tally;** count noses *or* heads <nonformal>; census, poll; **measure** 300.11; quantify, quantize

17 calculate, compute, estimate, reckon, figure, reckon at, tally, score; **figure out,** work out, dope out <nonformal>; **add, subtract, multiply, divide;** factor; **measure** 300.11

18 sum up, sum, say it all <nonformal>; **figure up,** reckon up, **count up, add up, tally up; total,** total up, tote up <nonformal>; **summarize, recapitulate,** recap *and* rehash <both nonformal>, **recount,** recite, relate; detail, itemize, inventory

19 keep account of, keep count of, **keep track of, keep tab** *or* **tabs** <nonformal>, keep tally

20 check, verify 969.12, doublecheck; **prove,** demonstrate; balance, balance the books; **audit,** overhaul; take stock, inventory

ADJS **21 mathematical,** numerical, numerary, arithmetic *or* arithmetical, algebraic *or* algebraical, geometric *or* geometrical, trigonometric *or* trigonometrical

22 numerical, numerary, numerative; **odd, even**; arithmetical, algorithmic; **cardinal, ordinal; digital; reciprocal,** prime, decimal, exponential, **logarithmic,** integral; positive, negative; rational, irrational, transcendental

23 numerative, enumerative; calculative, computative, estimative; **calculating,** computing, computational, estimating; statistical; quantifying, quantizing

1017 PHYSICS

NOUNS **1 physics;** natural *or* physical science; physical theory, quantum theory, relativity theory, special relativity theory, general relativity theory, unified field theory

2 physicist, aerophysicist, astrophysicist, biophysicist, etc

ADJS **3 physical;** aerophysical, astrophysical, biophysical, etc

1018 HEAT

NOUNS **1 heat, hotness**; superheat, superheatedness; **warmth,** warmness; incalescence; radiant heat, thermal radiation, induction heat, convector *or* convected heat, solar heat, atomic heat, molecular heat

2 <metaphors> **ardor,** ardency, **fervor,** fervency, fervidness, fervidity; eagerness 101; excitement 105; **anger** 152.5,8,9; **sexual desire** 75.5; love 104

3 temperature; room temperature, comfortable temperature; flash point; boiling point; melting point, freezing point; dew point

4 lukewarmness, tepidness, tepidity; tepidarium

5 torridness, torridity; extreme heat, intense heat, torrid heat; **hot wind** 318.7

6 sultriness, stuffiness, closeness, oppressiveness; **humidity, humidness, mugginess**

7 hot weather, sunny weather; sultry weather, stuffy weather, humid weather, muggy weather; summer, high summer; Indian Summer, **dog days; heat wave**

8 hot day, summer day; **scorcher** *and* **roaster** *and* broiler *and* sizzler *and* swelterer <all nonformal>

9 hot air, superheated air; thermal; firestorm

10 hot water, boiling water; **steam,** vapor; hot *or* warm *or* thermal spring; geyser

11 <hot place> **oven, furnace,** fiery furnace, inferno

12 glow, incandescence, fieriness; **flush, blush, bloom,** redness 41, rubicundity, rosiness

13 fire; blaze, flame; combustion, ignition, ignition temperature *or* point, flash point; **conflagration;** flicker 1024.8, wavering *or* flickering flame; smoldering fire; marshfire, ignis fatuus, will-o'-the-wisp; St Elmo's fire; **roaring fire; raging fire,** sea of flames; bonfire, balefire; wildfire, prairie fire, forest fire; backfire; brushfire

14 flare, flare-up, **flash,** flash fire, **blaze,** burst, outburst; deflagration

15 spark, sparkle; **scintillation,** scintilla; ignescence

16 coal, live coal, brand, firebrand, **ember; cinder**

17 fireworks, pyrotechnics *or* pyrotechny

18 <perviousness to heat> transcalency

19 thermal unit; British thermal unit *or* BTU

20 thermometer, thermal detector

21 <science of heat> thermochemistry, thermology

VERBS **22** <be hot> **burn** 1019.24, **scorch,** parch, scald, **swelter, roast,** toast, cook, bake, fry, broil, boil, seethe, simmer, stew; **be in heat; blaze,** combust, spark, **catch fire, flame** 1019.23, flame up, **flare,** flare up; **flicker** 1024.25; **glow,** incandesce; smolder; steam; sweat 12.16; gasp, pant; **suffocate, stifle,** smother, choke

23 smoke, fume, reek; smudge

ADJS **24 warm, thermal,** thermic; warm as toast; **sunny;** summery, aestival; **temperate,** warmish; **tropical,** equatorial, subtropical; semitropical; **tepid, lukewarm**

25 hot, heated, torrid; sweltering, sweltry; **burning,** parching, scorching, searing, scalding, blistering, baking, roasting, toasting, broiling, grilling, simmering; **boiling,** seething, ebullient; **red-hot,** white-hot; ardent; flushed, sweaty, sudorific; so hot you can fry eggs on the sidewalk <nonformal>, like a furnace or an oven; feverish

26 **fiery,** igneous, firelike, pyric; combustive

27 **burning, ignited,** kindled, enkindled, **blazing,** ablaze, ardent, flaming, **afire, on fire,** in flames; **glowing,** aglow, incandescent, candescent; sparking, scintillating, scintillant, ignescent; **flickering,** aflicker, guttering; **smoldering; smoking,** fuming, reeking

28 **sultry, stifling, suffocating, stuffy, close,** oppressive; **humid, sticky** <nonformal>, **muggy**

29 warm-blooded, hot-blooded

30 isothermal, isotheric

31 diathermic, diathermal, transcalent

1019 HEATING

NOUNS 1 **heating, warming,** calefaction, torrefaction; decalescence, recalescence; solar radiation, insolation; dielectric heating; induction heating; heat exchange

2 **boiling,** seething, **stewing,** ebullition, ebullience or ebulliency; decoction; **simmering; boil**

3 **melting, fusion,** liquefaction, liquescence, running; **thawing,** thaw; liquation

4 **ignition, lighting, kindling,** firing; reaching flash point or flashing point

5 **burning, combustion,** blazing, flaming; **scorching,** parching, singeing; **searing,** branding; **blistering,** vesication; **cauterization,** cautery; **incineration; cremation;** suttee, self-cremation, self-immolation; burning at the stake, auto da fé <Pg>

6 **burn,** scald, scorch, singe; sear; brand; sunburn, sunscald; windburn

7 **incendiarism, arson,** torch job <nonformal>; **pyromania;** pyrolatry

8 **incendiary, arsonist;** pyromaniac, firebug <nonformal>; fire buff <nonformal>

9 **flammability, inflammability,** combustibility

10 **heater, warmer; stove, furnace; cooker,** cookery; firebox

11 **fireplace, hearth,** ingle; **fireside,** hearthside, ingleside, inglenook, chimney corner; chimney, chimney piece, chimney-pot, chimney-stack, flue

12 **fire iron; andiron,** firedog; tongs, fire tongs; poker, salamander, fire hook; pothook, crook, crane, chain; trivet, tripod; spit, turnspit; grate, grating; gridiron, grid, griddle, grill, griller; damper

13 **incinerator,** burner; solid-waste incinerator, garbage incinerator; **crematory,** crematorium

14 **blowtorch,** alcohol torch, butane torch; blowpipe; **burner; welder;** acetylene torch or welder

15 cauterizer, cautery; **branding iron,** brand; **caustic, corrosive,** mordant; acid

16 <products of combustion> scoria, sullage, slag, dross; **ashes,** ash; **cinder,** clinker, coal; coke, charcoal, brand, lava, carbon, calx; **soot,** smut; **smoke,** smudge, fume, reek

VERBS 17 **heat,** raise or increase the temperature, **warm,** warm up, fire up, stoke up; chafe; take the chill off; overheat; preheat; **reheat,** recook, warm over

18 <metaphors> excite, inflame; incite

19 insolate, sun-dry; **sun,** bask, bask in the sun, sun oneself, sunbathe

20 **boil, stew, simmer, seethe;** distill

21 **melt,** melt down, liquefy; **run, fuse,** flux; refine, smelt; render; **thaw**

22 **ignite, set fire to, fire, set on fire, kindle,** enkindle, inflame, **light,** light up, strike a light, touch off, **burn,** conflagrate; **build a fire;** rekindle, relume; feed, feed the fire, **stoke,** stoke the fire, add fuel to the flame;

bank; poke *or* stir the fire, blow up the fire, fan the flame
23 **catch fire,** catch on fire, catch, take fire, **burn, flame,** combust, blaze, **blaze up, burst into flame**
24 **burn, scorch, parch, sear; singe; blister,** vesicate; **cauterize,** burn in; **char,** carbonize; solder, weld; vulcanize; oxidize; deflagrate
25 **burn up,** incendiarize, **incinerate, cremate,** consume, reduce to ashes, **burn to a crisp,** burn to a cinder; **burn down, go up in smoke**
ADJS 26 **heating, warming,** chafing, calorific; calefactory, calefacient; fiery, burning 1018.25,27
27 **inflammatory,** inflammative, **inflaming, kindling,** lighting; **incendiary**
28 **flammable, inflammable, combustible,** burnable
29 **heated, warmed,** warmed up; superheated; overheated; **reheated,** recooked, **warmed-over**
30 **burned, burnt,** burned to the ground, incendiarized, torched <nonformal>, burned-out, gutted; **scorched, blistered, parched, singed, seared, charred; burnt-up,** incinerated, cremated, consumed, consumed by fire; carbonized, pyrolyzed
31 **molten, melted,** fused, liquefied; meltable

1020 FUEL

NOUNS 1 **fuel,** energy source; heat source, combustible, inflammable, flammable; nonrenewable energy *or* fuel source; alternative energy source, renewable energy *or* fuel source; solar energy; wind energy; geothermal energy; synthetic fuels *or* synfuels
2 slack, coal dust
3 **firewood,** stovewood, wood; woodpile; **kindling;** brush, brushwood; log, backlog, yule log
4 **lighter,** light, igniter; **torch,** taper; brand, **firebrand**
5 **match,** matchstick; friction match; safety match
6 **tinder; punk,** spunk; tinderbox

VERBS 7 **fuel,** fuel up; fill up, top off; refuel; **stoke, feed,** add fuel to the flame; detonate, explode
ADJS 8 **fuel,** energy, heat; fossil-fuel; alternative-energy; carboniferous; clean-burning; high-sulfur

1021 INCOMBUSTIBILITY

NOUNS 1 **incombustibility, uninflammability, nonflammability;** fire resistance
2 **extinguishing,** extinction, **quenching,** dousing <nonformal>, **snuffing,** putting out; **choking, damping, stifling, smothering;** fire fighting
3 **extinguisher,** fire extinguisher; **foam,** carbon-dioxide foam, foam extinguisher
4 **fire fighter, fireman,** fire-eater <nonformal>; forest fire fighter, fire warden, smokejumper; volunteer fireman
5 **fireproofing;** fire resistance; fireproof *or* fire-resistant *or* fire-resisting *or* fire-resistive *or* fire-retardant material
VERBS 6 **fireproof,** flameproof
7 **fight fire; extinguish, put out, quench,** out, douse <nonformal>, **snuff,** snuff out, blow out, stamp out; stub out; **choke, damp, smother, stifle**
8 **burn out, go out, die; fizzle out** <nonformal>; flame out
ADJS 9 **incombustible, noncombustible, uninflammable, noninflammable, nonflammable,** unburnable
10 **fireproof, flameproof,** fireproofed, fire-retarded, fire-retardant
11 **extinguished,** quenched, snuffed, **out;** contained

1022 COLD

NOUNS 1 **cold, coldness; coolness;** low temperature, drop *or* decrease in temperature; **chilliness,** nippiness, crispness, briskness, sharpness, bite; **chill, nip,** sharp air; **frigidity, iciness,** frostiness; **rawness,** bleakness, keenness, sharpness, bitterness, severity, inclemency, rigor

2 <sensation of cold> **chill,** chilliness, chilling; shivering, **shivers,** shakes, dithers, chattering of the teeth; creeps, **cold creeps** <nonformal>; **gooseflesh, goose pimples,** goose bumps <nonformal>; **frostbite, chilblains**

3 cold weather, bleak weather, raw weather, bitter weather, wintry weather, arctic weather, **freezing weather; cold wave, cold snap; freeze,** frost, hard frost, deep freeze, arctic frost

4 <cold place> Siberia, Hell, Novaya Zemlya, Alaska

5 ice, frozen water; **icicle; floe, ice floe; iceberg,** berg, growler; **icecap;** ice pinnacle, serac, nieve penitente; **glacier,** glacieret, glaciation, ice dike; **sleet;** snow ice; névé, granular snow, firn

6 hail, hailstone; snow pellets; **hailstorm**

7 frost; hoarfrost, hoar, rime frost, white frost; killing frost; frost line

8 snow; granular snow, powder snow, tapioca snow; **snowfall, snowstorm,** snow squall, snow flurry; **snowflake,** crystal; **snowdrift,** driven snow; avalanche; **slush,** slosh

VERBS **9** freeze, grow cold, lose heat; **shiver, quiver,** quake, shake, tremble, shudder, dither; **chatter; chill; freeze,** freeze to death, perish with the cold, have goose pimples, have goose bumps <nonformal>; have chilblains

10 <make cold> **freeze, chill,** chill to the bone or marrow, make one's teeth chatter; **nip,** bite, cut, **pierce,** penetrate, go through or right through; **freeze** 1023.11; frost, frostbite; numb, benumb

11 hail, sleet, snow; frost, ice up, ice over, glaze over

ADJS **12 cool,** temperate; chill, **chilly; fresh,** brisk, crisp, bracing, **invigorating**

13 unheated, unwarmed

14 cold, freezing, crisp, brisk, nippy, snappy <nonformal>, **raw, bleak, keen, sharp,** bitter, biting, pinching, cutting, **piercing,** penetrating; inclement, severe, rigorous; **icy,** icelike, **ice-cold,** glacial, ice-encrusted; **frigid,** bitter or bitterly cold; numbing; **wintry,** brumal, hibernal; **arctic,** Siberian; stone-cold, cold as death

15 <nonformal terms> **cold as hell,** cold as a witch's tit or kiss, colder than hell or the deuce or the devil

16 <feeling cold> **cold, freezing, cool, chilly; shivering,** shivery, shaky, dithery; chattering, with chattering teeth; **frozen** 1023.14, half-frozen, frozen to death, chilled to the bone, blue with cold

17 frosty; frosted, rimed, **hoary,** hoar-frosted

18 snowy, snowlike, niveous; **snow-covered,** snow-robed, snow-blanketed; **snow-capped,** snow-tipped

19 snowbound, snowed-in, **ice-bound**

20 cold-blooded, hypothermic

1023 REFRIGERATION
<reduction of temperature>

NOUNS **1 refrigeration; cooling, chilling; freezing,** glaciation, congelation; adiabatic expansion, adiabatic absorption, adiabatic demagnetization; cryogenics; **air conditioning,** air cooling

2 refrigeration anesthesia, cryomoanesthesia

3 cooler, chiller; water cooler, air cooler; **ventilator; fan;** surface cooler

4 refrigerator, icebox, ice chest; refrigerator car, refrigerator truck, reefer <nonformal>

5 freezer, deep freeze, deep-freezer; ice-cream freezer; ice machine; **ice plant,** icehouse, refrigerating plant

6 cold storage; frozen-food locker, locker, freezer locker

7 <cooling agent> **coolant; refrigerant;** cryogen; ice, ice cubes; liquid air, ammonia, carbon dioxide, ether; ethyl chloride; liquid air, liquid oxygen *or* lox, liquid nitrogen, liquid helium, etc

8 antifreeze, coolant, alcohol, ethylene glycol

9 refrigerating engineering

VERBS **10 refrigerate; cool, chill;** water-cool, air-cool; **air-condition;** ventilate

11 freeze 1022.9,10, ice, glaciate, congeal; **deep-freeze,** quick-freeze, freeze solid; freeze-dry

ADJS **12 refrigerative,** refrigerant, frigorific; **cooling, chilling; freezing,** congealing; quick-freezing, deep-freezing

13 cooled, chilled; air-conditioned; air-cooled, water-cooled

14 frozen, frozen solid, congealed; **icy,** ice-cold, icy-cold, icelike; deep-frozen, quick-frozen

15 antifreeze

1024 LIGHT

NOUNS **1 light,** radiant *or* luminous energy, visible radiation, **illumination, radiation, radiance** *or* radiancy, irradiation, emanation; highlight; sidelight; photosensitivity; light source 1025; **invisible light,** black light, infrared light, ultraviolet light

2 shine, shininess, **luster, sheen, gloss,** glint; **glow, gleam,** flush, sunset glow; lambency; **incandescence,** candescence; shining light; afterglow; skylight, twilight glow

3 lightness, luminousness, luminosity; **lucidity,** translucence *or* translucency

4 brightness, brilliance *or* brilliancy, **splendor,** radiant splendor, **glory, radiance** *or* radiancy, resplendence *or* resplendency, **vividness,** flamboyance *or* flamboyancy; effulgence, refulgence *or* refulgency; **glare,** blare, blaze

5 ray, radiation 1036, **beam, gleam, stream, streak, pencil, patch,** ray of light, beam of light; ribbon of light, streamer, stream of light

6 flash, blaze, flare, flame, gleam, glint, glance; blaze *or* flash *or* gleam of light

7 glitter, glimmer, shimmer, twinkle, blink; sparkle, spark; **scintillation,** scintilla; coruscation; **glisten,** glister, spangle, tinsel, glittering, glimmering, shimmering, twinkling

8 flicker, flutter, dance, quiver; flickering, fluttering, bickering, guttering, dancing, quivering, lambency

9 reflection; reflected *or* incident light; reflectance

10 daylight, dayshine, day glow, light of day; day, daytime, daytide; **natural light; sunlight, sunshine,** shine; noonlight, white light, midday sun, noonday *or* noontide light; dusk, twilight 315.3; the crack of dawn, cockcrow, dawn 314.4; **sunbeam**

11 moonlight, moonshine, moonglow; **moonbeam**

12 starlight, starshine; earthshine

13 luminescence; phosphor, luminophor; **ignis fatuus, will-o'-the-wisp,** jack-o'-lantern, marshfire; fata morgana; fox fire; St Elmo's light *or* fire, wild fire, witch fire

14 halo, nimbus, aura, **aureole,** circle, ring, glory; **rainbow,** ring around the sun *or* moon; **corona,** solar corona, lunar corona

15 <nebulous light> nebula 1070.7; zodiacal light, gegenschein, counterglow

16 polar lights, **aurora; northern lights, aurora borealis;** southern lights, **aurora australis;** aurora polaris

17 lightning, flash *or* **stroke of lightning,** fulmination, bolt, lightning strike, **bolt of lightning,** bolt from the blue, **thunderbolt,** thunderball, fireball

18 iridescence, opalescence, nacreousness, pearliness; **rainbow;** nacre, mother-of-pearl

19 lighting, illumination, artificial light *or* lighting; tonality; light and shade, black and white, chiaroscuro, clairobscure, contrast, highlights

20 illuminant, luminant; electricity; oil, petroleum, benzine; gasoline; kerosene, coal oil; light source 1025

21 <measurement of light> **candle power,** luminous intensity, luminous power, luminous flux, flux, intensity, light; quantum; **light quantum, photon**

22 <science of light> photics, photology, photometry

VERBS 23 **shine,** shine forth, **burn, give light,** incandesce; **glow, beam, gleam,** glint, luster, glance; **flash, flare, blaze, flame,** fulgurate; **radiate,** send out rays; spread or diffuse light; **glare;** daze, dazzle, bedazzle

24 **glitter, glimmer, shimmer, twinkle, blink,** tinsel, coruscate; **sparkle,** spark, **scintillate; glisten**

25 **flicker,** bicker, gutter, **flutter, waver, dance,** play

26 **luminesce,** phosphoresce, fluoresce; iridesce

27 **grow light,** grow bright, **lighten,** brighten; dawn

28 **illuminate,** illumine, **light, light up, lighten,** enlighten, brighten, irradiate; bathe or flood with light; **shed light upon,** cast or throw light upon, shine upon; spotlight, highlight; floodlight

29 **strike a light, turn or switch on the light,** shine a light

ADJS 30 **luminous,** luminiferous, illuminant; **incandescent,** candescent; **lustrous,** orient; **radiant,** irradiative; **shining,** burning, streaming; **beaming; gleaming,** glinting; **glowing,** aglow, suffused, blushing, flushing; **sunny, sunshiny,** bright and sunny, light as day

31 **light,** lightsome; **lucid,** lucent, translucent, translucid, pellucid, diaphanous, transparent; **clear,** serene; **cloudless,** unclouded, unobscured

32 **bright, brilliant, vivid, splendid, resplendent,** bright and shining; fulgent, effulgent, refulgent; **flamboyant,** flaming; **glaring,** garish; **dazzling,** bedazzling, blinding, pitiless

33 **shiny,** shining, **lustrous, glossy,** glassy, **polished,** burnished

34 **flashing,** flashy, **blazing, flaming, flaring, burning,** fulgurant

35 **glittering, glimmering, shimmering, twinkling, blinking, glistening;** glittery, shimmery, twinkly, tinselly; **sparkling, scintillating,** scintillant, coruscating, coruscant

36 **flickering, fluttering, wavering, dancing,** quivering, lambent; flickery, fluttery, quivery; blinking, flashing, stroboscopic

37 **iridescent,** opalescent, nacreous, pearly, pearl-like

38 **luminescent;** autoluminescent, bioluminescent

39 **illuminated,** luminous, **lightened, lighted,** lit, **lit up,** flooded or bathed with light; irradiated; **alight, glowing,** aglow, lambent, suffused with light; sunlit, moonlit, starlit; spangled, bespangled, tinseled, studded; star-spangled, star-studded

40 **illuminating,** illumining, **lighting, lightening**

41 **luminary,** photic, luminal

42 photosensitive; photophobic; phototropic

1025 LIGHT SOURCE

NOUNS 1 **light source, luminary,** illuminant, incandescent body or point, **light,** glim; **lamp,** light bulb, lantern, candle, taper, torch, flame; match; **fluorescent light, fluorescent tube,** fluorescent lamp

2 **candle,** taper; tallow candle; wax candle; votary candle

3 **torch,** flaming torch, flambeau; **flare,** signal flare; beacon

4 traffic light

5 **firefly,** lightning bug, **glowworm,** fireworm

6 **chandelier,** luster; candlestick

7 **wick,** taper; candlewick, lampwick

1026 DARKNESS, DIMNESS

NOUNS 1 **darkness, dark, lightlessness; obscurity,** tenebrousness; **night** 315.4, dead of night;

sunlessness, moonlessness, starlessness; **pitch-darkness,** pitch-blackness, utter *or* thick *or* total darkness, intense darkness, velvet darkness; **blackness,** swarthiness 38.2

2 **darkishness, duskiness; murkiness, murk; dimness,** dim; **semidarkness,** half-light; gloaming, crepuscular light, **dusk**

3 **shadow, shade, shadiness;** umbra, umbrage, umbrageousness; gloom; mere shadow; penumbra; silhouette

4 **gloom, gloominess, somberness;** lowering

5 **dullness, flatness,** lifelessness, **drabness, deadness,** somberness, **lackluster, lusterlessness**

6 **darkening, dimming, bedimming; obscuration;** obscurement, obfuscation; eclipsing, occulting; **shadowing, shading,** overshadowing, **clouding,** overclouding, gathering of the clouds, overcast; blackening 38.5

7 blackout, dimout, brownout

8 **eclipse,** occultation; total eclipse, partial eclipse; solar eclipse, lunar eclipse

VERBS 9 **darken,** bedarken; **obscure,** obfuscate; **eclipse,** occult, occultate; **black out,** brown out; **overcast,** darken over; **shadow, shade,** cast a shadow, spread a shadow over, overshadow; **cloud,** becloud, cloud over, overcloud; gloom, begloom, somber, cast a gloom over, murk; **dim, bedim,** dim out

10 **dull,** mat, deaden; **tone down**

11 turn or switch off the light

12 **grow dark, darken,** lower; **dim, grow dim**

ADJS 13 **dark, black,** darksome, darkling; **lightless,** rayless, unlighted, **unilluminated,** unlit; **obscure,** obscured, obfuscated, eclipsed, occulted, clothed *or* shrouded *or* veiled *or* cloaked *or* mantled in darkness; tenebrous, tenebrific, tenebrious, tenebrose; **pitch-dark,** pitch-black, dark as pitch; ebon, ebony; black as night; sunless, moonless, starless

14 **gloomy, somber;** lowering; **funereal;** stormy, cloudy, clouded, overcast

15 **darkish,** darksome, **semidark; dusky,** dusk; fuscous; **murky,** murksome; **dim,** dimmed, bedimmed

16 **shadowy, shady, shadowed, shaded,** darkling, umbrageous; overshadowed; penumbral

17 **lackluster, lusterless; dull, dead,** deadened, **lifeless,** somber, **drab,** wan, **flat,** mat

18 obscuring

ADVS 19 **in the dark,** darkling, in darkness; in the dark of night, in the dead of night

1027 SHADE

<a thing that shades>

NOUNS 1 **shade, screen, light shield, curtain,** drapery, blind, veil; **awning; sunshade,** parasol, **umbrella,** beach umbrella

2 **eyeshade,** eyeshield, visor; goggles, dark glasses, **sunglasses,** shades <nonformal>

3 **lamp shade;** moonshade; globe, light globe

4 **light filter,** filter, diffusing screen; frosted glass, ground glass; stained glass; gelatin filter, celluloid filter; frosted lens

VERBS 5 **shade, screen,** veil, curtain, shutter, draw the curtains, put up *or* close the shutters; cover 295.19; **shadow** 1026.9

ADJS 6 **shading, screening,** veiling, curtaining; shadowing; covering

7 **shaded, screened,** veiled, curtained; sunproof; visored; shadowed, shady 1026.16

1028 TRANSPARENCY

NOUNS 1 **transparency,** transpicuousness, transmission *or* admission of light; **lucidity,** pellucidity, **clearness, clarity,** limpidity; **crystallinity,** crystal-clearness; **glassiness,** vitreousness, vitrescence; **diaphanousness,** sheerness, thinness, **gossameriness,** filminess, gauziness

2 transparent substance, diaphane; **glass,** glassware, glass-

work; stemware; pane, win-
dowpane, light, windowlight,
shopwindow; vitrine
VERBS **3 be transparent,** show
through; pass light; vitrify
ADJS **4 transparent,** transpicuous,
light-pervious; **lucid,** pellucid,
clear, limpid; unclouded, **crystalline,** crystal, **crystal-clear,** clear
as crystal; **diaphanous,** sheer,
thin; **gossamer,** gossamery, filmy,
gauzy
  5 glass, glassy, glasslike, clear as
  glass, vitreous

1029 SEMITRANSPARENCY

NOUNS **1 semitransparency,** semi-
pellucidity, semidiaphaneity;
semiopacity
  2 translucence, translucency, lu-
  cence, lucency, translucidity, pellucidity, lucidity
VERBS **3 frost,** frost over
ADJS **4 semitransparent,** semi-
diaphanous, semiopaque; frosty,
frosted
  5 translucent, lucent, translucid,
  lucid, pellucid; semitranslucent,
  semipellucid

1030 OPAQUENESS

NOUNS **1 opaqueness,** opacity, imperviousness to light; turbidity,
turbidness; cloudiness; **darkness, obscurity, dimness** 1026
VERBS **2 darken, obscure** 1026.9;
cloud, becloud
ADJS **3 opaque,** intransparent, non-
translucent, impervious to light;
dark, obscure 1026.13, **cloudy,**
roiled, roily, turbid

1031 ELECTRICITY, MAGNETISM

NOUNS **1 electricity; electrical
science; electrical** or **electric
unit,** unit of measurement
  2 current, electric current, current flow, amperage, electric flow,
  juice <nonformal>
  3 electric or **electrical field,**
  static field, electrostatic field,
  field of electrical force; **magnetic
  field; electromagnetic field;**
  variable field

  4 circuit, electrical circuit, path
  5 charge, electric or **electrical
  charge,** positive charge, negative
  charge; live wire
  6 discharge, arc, electric discharge; **shock,** electroshock, galvanic shock
  7 magnetism, magnetic attraction; **electromagnetism;** magne-
  tization; ferromagnetism; magnetic remanence; magnetic memory, magnetic retentiveness; magnetic elements; magnetic dip or
  inclination, magnetic variation or
  declination; hysteresis, magnetic
  hysteresis, magnetic lag or retardation; permeability, magnetic
  conductivity; magnetic flux; magnetic potential; magnetic viscosity; magnetics
  8 polarity, polarization; **pole,
  positive pole, anode, negative
  pole, cathode,** magnetic pole,
  magnetic axis; north pole, N pole;
  south pole, S pole
  9 magnetic force or **intensity,**
  magnetic flux density, gauss,
  oersted; magnetic tube of force;
  line of force; **magnetic field,
  electromagnetic field**
 10 electroaffinity, electric attraction
 11 voltage, volt, **electromotive
  force** or EMF, potential difference; **potential, electric potential**
 12 resistance, ohms, ohmic resistance, electric resistance; **reluctance,** magnetic reluctance or
  resistance; specific reluctance, re-
  luctivity; **reactance,** inductive reactance, capacitive reactance; **im-
  pedance**
 13 conduction; conductance, conductivity, mho; superconduc-
  tivity; **conductor,** semiconductor,
  superconductor; **nonconductor,**
  dielectric, insulator
 14 induction; magnetic induction,
  electromagnetic induction; self-
  induction, mutual induction; **in-
  ductance,** inductivity, henry
 15 capacitance, capacity, farad;
  collector junction capacitance,
  emitter junction capacitance, resistance capacitance

16 gain, available gain, current gain, operational gain
17 electric power, wattage, watts; hydroelectric power, hydro-electricity
18 powerhouse, power station, power plant; hydroelectric plant; nuclear or atomic power plant; power grid, distribution system
19 blackout, power failure, power loss; **brownout,** voltage drop, voltage loss
20 electrical device, electrical appliance; **battery,** accumulator, storage battery, storage device; **electric meter,** meter; **wire, cable,** electric wire, electric cord, cord, power cord, power cable
21 electrician, electrotechnician; wireman; **lineman,** linesman; power worker
22 electrotechnologist, electro-biologist
23 electrification, electrifying, supplying electricity
24 electrolysis; ionization; electro-galvanization; electrocoating, electroplating, electroetching; ion, cation, anion; electrolyte; nonelectrolyte
VERBS **25 electrify, galvanize,** energize, **charge;** wire, wire up; shock; **generate,** step up, amplify; step down; switch on or off, turn on or off; short-circuit, short
26 magnetize; electromagnetize; demagnetize, degauss
27 electrolyze; ionize; electro-galvanize; electroplate
28 insulate, isolate; **ground**
ADJS **29 electric, electrical, electrifying;** galvanic, voltaic; static, electrostatic; electromotive; **electrified,** electric-powered, battery-powered, cordless; solar-powered
30 magnetic, electromagnetic; di-amagnetic, paramagnetic, fer-romagnetic; **polar**
31 electrolytic; hydrolytic; ionic, anionic, cationic
32 electrotechnical
33 charged, electrified, live, hot; high-tension
34 positive, electropositive; **negative,** electronegative

35 nonconducting, nonconduc-tive, insulating, dielectric

1032 ELECTRONICS

NOUNS **1 electronics,** radio-electronics; electron physics, electrophysics, electron dynamics; semiconductor physics, transistor physics; photo-electronics, photoelectricity; mi-croelectronics; electron micros-copy; nuclear physics 1037; radio 1033; television 1034; radar 1035; automation 1040
2 <electron theory> electron the-ory of atoms
3 electron, negatron, cathode par-ticle, beta particle
4 electronic effect; Edison effect, thermionic effect, photoelectric effect
5 electron emission; thermionic emission; photoelectric emis-sion, photoemission; field emis-sion; thermionic grid emission; electron beam, cathode ray, an-ode ray; glow discharge, cathode glow; electron diffraction
6 electron flow, electron stream, electron or **electronic current;** electric current 1031.2
7 electron volt; ionization poten-tial; input voltage, output voltage; base signal voltage, collector sig-nal voltage, emitter signal volt-age; battery supply voltage
8 electronic circuit, transistor circuit, semiconductor circuit; vacuum-tube circuit, thermionic tube circuit; **printed circuit, mi-crocircuit; chip, silicon chip,** microchip; **circuitry**
9 conductance, electronic con-ductance; **resistance,** electronic resistance
10 electron tube, vacuum tube, tube, thermionic tube; radio tube, television tube; **special-purpose tube; vacuum tube component**
11 photoelectric tube or **cell, pho-totube,** photocell; electron-ray tube, **electric eye;** photosen-sitivity, **photosensitive devices**
12 transistor, semiconductor or solid-state device

13 **electronic device, electronic meter,** electronic measuring device; **electronic tester,** electronic testing device
14 electronics engineer
ADJS 15 **electronic;** photoelectric, **photoelectric;** microelectric; thermoelectric; thermionic; anodic, cathodic; transistorized

1033 RADIO

NOUNS 1 **radio**; radiotelephony, radiotelegraphy; communications, telecommunication 347.1
2 radiotechnology, radio engineering, communication engineering; radio electronics, radioacoustics
3 **radio, radio receiver**; radio telescope; **radio set, receiver,** receiving set; chassis; receiver part
4 **radio transmitter**, **transmitter**; transmitter part; microphone 50.9, radiomicrophone; **antenna,** aerial
5 radiomobile, mobile transmitter
6 **radio station,** transmitting station, **studio**; AM station, FM station, shortwave station, ultrahigh-frequency station, clear-channel station
7 **control room,** mixing room, monitoring booth; **control desk,** console, master control desk, instrument panel, control panel or board, jack field, mixer <nonformal>
8 **network,** radio links, **hookup,** communications net, circuit, network stations, network affiliations, affiliated stations; coaxial network, circuit network, coast-to-coast hookup
9 **radio circuit,** radio-frequency circuit, audio-frequency circuit, superheterodyne circuit, amplifying circuit; electronic circuit 1032.8
10 **radio signal,** radio-frequency or RF signal, direct signal, shortwave signal, AM signal, FM signal; unidirectional signal, beam; signal-noise ratio; **radio-frequency** or **RF amplifier,** radio-frequency or RF stage

11 **radio wave,** electromagnetic wave, hertzian wave; shortwave, long wave, microwave, high-frequency wave, low-frequency wave; carrier wave; **wavelength**
12 **frequency;** radio frequency or RF, intermediate frequency or IF, audio frequency or AF; high frequency or HF; very high frequency or VHF; ultrahigh frequency or UHF; **carrier frequency;** frequency spectrum; cycles, CPS, hertz, Hz, **kilohertz, kilocycles; megahertz, megacycles**
13 **band,** frequency band, standard band, broadcast band, amateur band, citizens band, police band, shortwave band, FM band; **channel,** radio channel, broadcast channel
14 **modulation;** amplitude modulation or AM; frequency modulation or FM; phase modulation or PM; sideband, side frequency, single sideband, double sideband
15 amplification, radio-frequency or RF amplification
16 **radio broadcasting, broadcasting; airplay, airtime;** commercial radio, public radio; AM broadcasting, FM broadcasting, shortwave broadcasting; **transmission, radio transmission**
17 **pickup, remote pickup,** spot pickup
18 **radiobroadcast, broadcast, radio program;** rebroadcast, rerun; simulcast; broadcast news, newscast, newsbreak, newsflash; all-news radio or format; sportscast; **talk radio;** talk show, audience-participation show, call-in or phone-in show, interview show
19 **signature, station identification,** call letters; **station break,** pause for station identification
20 **commercial,** message, **spot announcement,** spot and plug <both nonformal>
21 **reception; fading,** fade-out; **drift; interference,** noise interference, station interference; **static,** atmospherics, noise; **jamming,** deliberate interference

22 radio listener; radio audience, listeners, **listenership**

23 broadcaster, radiobroadcaster; commentator; news commentator; anchor, news anchor, anchor man *or* woman; announcer; disk jockey *or* DJ <both nonformal>; master of ceremonies, MC *or* emcee <both nonformal>

24 radioman, radio technician, radio engineer; **radio operator;** control engineer; **amateur radio operator, ham** *and* ham operator <both nonformal>, radio amateur

VERBS **25 broadcast,** radiobroadcast, radiocast, simulcast, **radio,** radiate, **transmit,** send; narrowcast; shortwave; beam; newscast, sportscast, put *or* go on the air; go off the air

26 monitor, check

27 listen in, tune in

ADJS **28 radio;** radiosonic; superheterodyne; shortwave; radiofrequency, audio-frequency; highfrequency, low-frequency, etc

1034 TELEVISION

NOUNS **1 television, TV, video;** the tube <nonformal>, the boob tube <nonformal>; **network television,** subscription television, pay TV; cable television, cable TV; closed-circuit television *or* closed circuit TV; public-access television *or* public-access TV

2 television broadcast, telecast, TV show; direct broadcast, live show <nonformal>; taped show, canned show <nonformal>; prime time, prime-time show *or* attraction; miniseries; situation comedy *or* sitcom <nonformal>; **serial,** soap opera *or* soap <nonformal>; quiz show; giveaway show; panel show; electronic *or* broadcast journalism, broadcast news, newscast, news show; documentary, docudrama; simulcast; television *or* TV performer, television *or* TV personality; news anchor, anchor, anchor man, anchor woman, anchor person

3 televising, telecasting

4 <transmission> photoemission, audioemission

5 <reception> **picture, image; color television; black-and-white television;** HDTV *or* high-definition television

6 television studio, TV station

7 mobile unit, TV mobile; video truck, audio truck, transmitter truck

8 transmitter; audio transmitter, video transmitter

9 relay links, boosters, booster *or* **relay stations;** microwave link; communication satellite, satellite relay; Telstar, Intelsat, Syncom; Comsat

10 television camera, telecamera, pickup camera, pickup; **camera tube;** camcorder; mobile camera

11 television receiver, television *or* **TV set,** TV, boob tube *and* idiot box <both nonformal>; **picture tube;** portable television *or* TV set; **screen;** raster; **videocassette recorder** *or* **VCR,** videotape recorder; video tape, videocassette

12 televiewer, viewer

13 television technician, TV man *or* woman, television *or* TV repairman *or* repairwoman, television engineer; cameraman, camerawoman, sound man, sound woman

VERBS **14 televise, telecast;** colorcast; simulcast

15 teleview, watch television *or* TV; telerecord, record, tape

ADJS **16 televisional, video;** telegenic; in synchronization, in sync <nonformal>, locked in

1035 RADAR, RADIOLOCATORS

NOUNS **1 radar,** radio detection and ranging; **radar set,** radiolocator <Brit>; oscilloscope, radarscope; radar antenna; radar reflector

2 airborne radar, aviation radar; **navar,** navigation and ranging; **teleran,** television radar air navigation; radar dome, radome

3 **loran,** long range aid to navigation; **shoran,** short range aid to navigation

4 **radiolocator;** direction finder, radio direction finder *or* RDF; radio compass

5 **radar speed meter,** radar detector

6 **radar station,** control station; Combat Information Center *or* CIC; Air Route Traffic Control Center *or* ARTCC; beacon station, display station; direction-finder station, radio compass station

7 **radar beacon, racon;** transponder; radar beacon buoy, marker buoy

8 <radar operations> data transmission, scanning

9 <applications> detection, interception, ranging, ground control of aircraft, air-traffic control, blind flying, blind landing, storm tracking, hurricane tracking; radar fence *or* screen; radar astronomy

10 **pulse,** radio-frequency *or* RF pulse, high-frequency *or* HF pulse, intermediate-frequency *or* IF pulse, trigger pulse, echo pulse

11 **signal,** radar signal; transmitter signal, output signal; return signal, echo signal, video signal, reflection, picture, target image, display, signal display, trace, reading, return, **echo, bounces, blips, pips**

12 **radar interference,** deflection, refraction; atmospheric attenuation, blind spots, false echoes; clutter, ground clutter, sea clutter

13 <radar countermeasure> **jamming, radar jamming;** tinfoil, aluminum foil, chaff

14 **radar technician,** radar engineer, radarman; air-traffic controller; jammer

VERBS 15 **transmit, send,** radiate, beam; **jam**

16 **reflect,** return, echo, bounce back

17 **receive, tune in,** pick up, spot, home on; pinpoint; identify, trigger; lock on; sweep, scan; map

1036 RADIATION, RADIOACTIVITY

NOUNS 1 **radiation,** radiant energy; ionizing radiation; **radioactivity,** radioactive radiation *or* emanation, atomic *or* nuclear radiation; natural radioactivity, artificial radioactivity; radiosensitivity; half-life; radiocarbon dating; contamination, decontamination; fallout 1037.16

2 **radioluminescence, autoluminescence;** cathode luminescence; synchrotron radiation

3 **ray, radiation,** cosmic ray bombardment, electron shower; electron emission 1032.5

4 **radioactive particle;** alpha particle, beta particle; heavy particle; high-energy particle; meson, mesotron; cosmic particle, solar particle, aurora particle, V-particle

5 <radioactive substance> radiator; alpha radiator, beta radiator, gamma radiator

6 **counter, radioscope,** radiodetector, **atom-tagger;** ionization chamber; ionizing event; X-ray spectrograph, X-ray spectrometer

7 **radiation physics,** radiological physics; radiobiology, radiochemistry, radiometallography, radiography, radiopathology; radiology; radiotherapy; fluoroscopy; X-ray photometry, X-ray spectrometry; atom-tagging; exposure, dose, absorbed dose

8 **radiation physicist;** radiobiologist, radiometallographer, radiochemist, etc; radiologist

VERBS 9 **radioactivate,** activate, **irradiate,** charge; **contaminate,** poison, infect

ADJS 10 **radioactive,** irradiated, **hot; contaminated,** infected, poisoned; exposed

11 **radiable;** radiotransparent, radiolucent; radium-proof; radiosensitive

1037 NUCLEAR PHYSICS

NOUNS 1 **nuclear physics,** particle physics, atomic science; quantum mechanics, wave mechanics; molecular physics; thermionics; mass spectrometry, mass spectrography; radiology 1036.7

2 <atomic theory> quantum theory, Bohr theory

3 atomic scientist, nuclear physicist, particle physicist; radiologist 1036.8

4 atom; tracer, tracer atom, tagger atom; atomic model, nuclear atom; nuclide; **ion; shell,** subshell, planetary shell, valence shell; **atomic unit;** atomic constant

5 isotope; protium, deuterium *or* heavy hydrogen *and* tritium <all isotopes of hydrogen>; radioactive isotope, **radioisotope;** carbon 14, strontium 90, uranium 235; artificial isotope; isotone; isobar, isomer, nuclear isomer

6 elementary particle, atomic particle, **subatomic particle,** subnuclear particle; **atomic nucleus, nucleus; nuclear particle,** nucleon; proton, neutron; deuteron *or* deuterium nucleus, triton *or* tritium nucleus, alpha particle *or* helium nucleus; **nuclear force,** weak force *or* weak nuclear force, strong force *or* strong nuclear force; weak interaction, strong interaction; fifth force; nucleosynthesis; nuclear resonance, nuclear magnetic resonance *or* NMR; strangeness; charm

7 atomic cluster, molecule; radical, simple radical, compound radical, chain, straight chain, branched chain, side chain; ring, closed chain, cycle; benzene ring *or* nucleus; lattice, space-lattice

8 fission, nuclear fission, fission reaction; **atom-smashing, splitting the atom;** atomic reaction; atomic disintegration *or* decay, alpha decay, beta decay, gamma decay; stimulation, dissociation, photodisintegration, ionization, nucleization, cleavage; neutron reaction, proton reaction, etc; thermonuclear reaction; **chain reaction;** breeding; bullet, target; proton gun

9 fusion, nuclear fusion, fusion reaction, thermonuclear reaction, thermonuclear fusion, laser-induced fusion, cold fusion

10 fissionable material, nuclear fuel; **critical mass,** noncritical mass

11 accelerator, particle accelerator, atomic accelerator, atom smasher, atomic cannon

12 mass spectrometer, mass spectrograph

13 reactor, nuclear reactor, pile, atomic pile, reactor pile, chain reactor, **furnace,** atomic *or* nuclear furnace; lattice; bricks; rods; radioactive waste

14 atomic *or* **nuclear power plant,** reactor engine

15 atomic energy, nuclear energy *or* **power,** thermonuclear power; activation energy, binding energy, mass energy; energy level

16 atomic explosion; thermonuclear explosion; blast wave, Mach stem; Mach front; mushroom cloud; **fallout,** airborne radioactivity, fission particles, dust cloud, radioactive dust; **atom bomb** *or* **atomic bomb** *or* **A-bomb, hydrogen bomb,** thermonuclear bomb, nuke <nonformal>

VERBS **17 atomize,** nucleize; activate, accelerate; bombard; cleave, fission, **split** *or* **smash the atom**

ADJS **18 atomic;** atomistic; atomiferous; subatomic, subnuclear; dibasic, tribasic; cyclic, isocyclic; homocyclic, heterocyclic; isotopic, isobaric, isoteric

19 nuclear, thermonuclear, isonuclear, homonuclear, heteronuclear, extranuclear

20 fissionable, fissile, scissile

1038 MECHANICS

NOUNS **1 mechanics;** leverage 905; tools and machinery 1039

2 statics

3 dynamics, kinetics, energetics

4 hydraulics, fluid dynamics, hydromechanics, hydrokinetics, fluidics, hydrodynamics, hydrostatics; hydrology, hydrography, hydrometry, fluviology

5 pneumatics; aeromechanics, aerophysics, aerometry, aerography, aerotechnics, aerodynamics, aerostatics

6 engineering

ADJS **7 mechanical,** mechanistic; biomechanical, hydromechanical, etc

8 static; biostatic, electrostatic, geostatic, etc

9 dynamic, kinetic, kinematic; geodynamic, radiodynamic, electrodynamic, etc

10 pneumatic, pneumatological; aeromechanical

11 hydrologic, hydrometric, hydromechanical, hydrodynamic, hydrostatic, hydraulic

1039 TOOLS, MACHINERY

NOUNS **1 tool, instrument, implement, utensil; apparatus, device,** mechanical device, contrivance, contraption <nonformal>, gadget, gizmo, gimcrack, gimmick <nonformal>; gadgetry; **hand tool; power tool;** machine tool; precision tool *or* instrument; **mechanization**

2 cutlery; **knife, ax,** dagger, sword, blade, cutter; perforator, piercer, puncturer, point; sharpener; **saw;** trowel; shovel; plane; drill; valve 239.10

3 machinery; machine, mechanism, mechanical device; heavy machinery, earthmoving machinery, earthmover; mill; welder; pump; **engine,** motor; **power source,** drive, motive power, prime mover; **appliance,** convenience, facility, utility, home appliance

4 mechanism, movement, action, motion, works, workings, innards, what makes it tick; drive train, power train; clockworks, watchworks, servomechanism 1040.13

5 gear, gearing, gear train; gearwheel, cogwheel, rack; **gearshift;** differential, differential gear *or* gearing; **transmission,** gearbox;

automatic transmission; standard transmission, stick shift; synchronized shifting, synchromesh

6 clutch

7 tooling, tooling up; **retooling;** instrumentation, industrial instrumentation; servo instrumentation

8 mechanic; grease monkey <nonformal>; artisan, artificer; **machinist**

VERBS **9 tool,** tool up, instrument; retool; **machine,** mill; **mechanize,** motorize; sharpen

ADJS **10 mechanical;** powered, power-driven, motor-driven, motorized; **mechanized**

1040 AUTOMATION

NOUNS **1 automation**; robotization, cybernation; **self-action,** self-activity; self-movement, self-motion, **self-propulsion;** self-direction, self-determination, automatism, self-regulation; automatization; servo instrumentation; computerization

2 automation technology, automatic control engineering, servo engineering, **servomechanics,** system engineering, systems analysis, feedback system engineering; **cybernetics;** telemechanics; systems planning, systems design; circuit analysis; bionics; information theory

3 automatic control, cybernation, servo control, robot control, robotization; cybernetic control; feedback control, digital feedback control, analog feedback control; control action; derivative *or* rate action, reset action

4 semiautomatic control; **remote control,** push-button control, remote handling; radio control; telemechanism; telemetry, telemeter, telemetering; transponder

5 control system, **automatic control system,** servo system, robot system; closed-loop system; open-sequence system; linear system, nonlinear system; data system, data-handling system, data-reduction system, data-input system, data-interpreting system, digital data reducing system; process-control system, annunciator system, flow-control system, motor-speed control system; automated factory, automatic *or* robot factory, push-button plant; servo laboratory, servolab

6 feedback, closed sequence, feedback loop, closed loop; feedback circuit, current-control circuit, switching circuit, flip-flop circuit, peaking circuit; positive feedback, negative feedback; reversed feedback, degeneration

7 <functions> accounting, analysis, automatic electronic navigation, automatic guidance, braking

8 process control, bit-weight control, color control, density control, dimension control, diverse control, end-point control, flavor control, flow control, fragrance control, hold control, humidity control, light-intensity control, limit control, liquid-level control, load control, pressure control, precision-production control, proportional control, quality control, quantity control, revolution control, temperature control, time control, weight control

9 variable, process variable; simple variable, complex variable; manipulated variable; steady state, transient state

10 values, target values; set point; differential gap; proportional band; dead band, dead zone; neutral zone

11 time constants; time lead, gain

12 automatic device, automatic; semi-automatic; self-actor, selfmover; **robot, automation,** mechanical man; bionic man; bionic woman

13 servomechanism, servo; automatic machine; **servomotor;** synchronous motor, synchronous machine

14 system component; control mechanism; regulator, control, controller, **governor;** servo control, servo regulator; control element

15 automatic detector; automatic analyzer; automatic indicator

16 control panel, console; coordinated panel, graphic panel; panelboard, set-up board

17 computer, computer science 1041, electronic computer, electronic brain

18 control engineer, servo engineer, system engineer, systems analyst, robot specialist; computer engineer, computer technologist, computer technician, **computer programmer;** cybernetic technologist, cyberneticist

VERBS **19 automate,** automatize, robotize; robot-control, servocontrol; program; computerize

20 self-govern, self-control, **self-regulate**

ADJS **21 automated,** cybernated, robotized; **automatic, spontaneous; self-acting,** self-active; **self-operating,** self-operative; **self-regulating,** self-governing, self-directing; **self-regulated, self-controlled**; automanual; semiautomatic; computerized, computer-controlled

22 self-propelled; self-propelling, self-moving, self-propellent; **automotive,** automechanical; **locomotive**

23 servomechanical, servocontrolled; **cybernetic**

24 remote-control, remotecontrolled; telemetered; by remote control

1041 COMPUTER SCIENCE

NOUNS **1 computer science**, computer systems and applications, computer hardware and software, computers, digital computers, machine computation, number-crunching <nonformal>; **computerization,** digitization; **data processing,** electronic data processing *or* EDP, data storage and retrieval; data bank; **information science,** information processing; computer crime *or* fraud, computer virus *or* worm; hacking

2 computer, electronic data processor, information processor, digital computer, analog computer, hybrid computer, machine, **hardware,** computer hardware; **processor,** central processing unit *or* CPU, multiprocessor, microprocessor, mainframe computer *or* mainframe, work station, minicomputer, microcomputer, personal computer *or* PC, home computer, laptop computer, briefcase computer, pocket computer; neural net *or* network, semantic net *or* network

3 circuitry, integrated circuit, logic circuit, **chip,** semiconductor chip, hybrid chip, wafer chip, superchip, microchip, neural network chip, **board,** printed circuit board *or* PCB, motherboard; **peripheral,** peripheral device *or* unit, input device, output device; **port,** channel interface, serial interface, serial port; **read-write head**

4 input device, keyboard; reader, tape reader, scanner, optical scanner, optical character reader, light pen, mouse

5 drive, disk drive, floppy disk drive, hard disk drive *or* Winchester drive, tape drive

6 disk, magnetic disk, floppy disk *or* floppy <nonformal> *or* diskette, hard *or* fixed *or* Winchester disk, disk pack; magnetic tape *or* mag tape <nonformal>, magnetic tape unit

7 memory, storage, memory bank, memory chip; **main memory,** random access memory *or* RAM, core, core storage *or* store, disk pack, magnetic disk, primary storage, backing store, read/write memory, optical disk memory, bubble memory; read-only memory *or* ROM, programmable read-only memory *or* PROM

8 retrieval, access, random access, sequential access, direct access

9 output device, terminal, workstation, video terminal, visual display unit *or* VDU, graphics terminal, **monitor,** cathode ray tube *or* CRT, **printer, serial printer,** character printer, impact printer, dot-matrix printer, daisy-wheel *or* printwheel printer, drum printer, **line printer, page printer,** non-impact printer, laser printer, electronic printer, graphics printer, color graphics printer

10 forms, computer forms

11 software, program, computer program

12 systems program, operating system *or* **OS,** disk operating system *or* DOS; control program monitor *or* CPM; **word processor,** text editor, editor, print formatter; spreadsheet, electronic spreadsheet, desktop publishing program, database management system *or* DBMS; **computer application**

13 language, assembler language, programming language, machine language, machine-readable language, conventional programming language, computer language, high-level language, interpreter, low-level language; **computer** *or* **electronic virus,** computer worm, phantom bug, Trojan horse, logic bomb

14 bit, binary digit, infobit, kilobit, megabit, gigabit, terbit; **byte,** kilobyte, megabyte

15 data, information, database, database management, file, record, data bank, input, input-output *or* I/O; **file,** data set, record, data record, data file, text file

16 network, computer network, communications network, local area network *or* LAN, mesh; **online system,** on-line service

17 liveware, programmer, systems programmer, system software specialist, application programmer, systems analyst

VERBS 18 computerize, digitize; **program,** boot, boot up, initialize, log in, log out, run, load, download, **compute,** crunch numbers <nonformal>; **key-board,** key in, input

ADJS **19 computerized;** machine-usable, computer-usable; computer-aided, computer-assisted; computer-driven, computer-controlled

1042 FRICTION

NOUNS **1 friction, rubbing,** rub, frottage; **drag,** skin friction; **resistance,** frictional resistance

2 abrasion, attrition, erosion, wearing away, wear, detrition, ablation; **grinding, filing,** rasping; fretting, galling; **chafing, chafe; scraping,** grazing, scratching, scuffing; **scrape,** scratch, **scuff; polishing,** burnishing, sanding, smoothing, dressing, buffing, shining; sandblasting; abrasive

3 massage, massaging, stroking, kneading; **rubdown;** whirlpool bath, Jacuzzi <trademark>; facial massage

4 massager, **masseur, masseuse**

5 <mechanics> force of friction; force of viscosity

VERBS **6 rub; massage,** knead, rub down; stroke 73.8

7 abrade, gnaw away; **erode,** erode away, ablate, wear away; rub away or off or out; **grind, rasp, file, grate, chafe,** fret, gall; **scrape, graze, scuff,** bark, skin; **fray,** frazzle; **scrub, scour**

8 buff, burnish, polish, sand, smooth, dress, shine, sandblast

ADJS **9 frictional,** friction; fricative; **rubbing**

10 abrasive, attritive, gnawing, erosive, ablative; scraping; **grinding, rasping;** chafing, fretting, galling

1043 DENSITY

NOUNS **1 density,** denseness, **solidity, solidness,** firmness, **compactness, closeness; congestion,** congestedness, crowdedness; **impenetrability,** impermeability; hardness 1044; incompressibility; **consistency;** viscidity, viscosity, **viscousness, thickness**

2 indivisibility, inseparability, infrangibility; indissolubility; unity 791; insolubility

3 densification, condensation, compression, concentration, consolidation; hardening, **solidification** 1044.5; agglutination, clustering

4 thickening; congealment, coagulation, clotting, **setting,** concretion; **jelling,** gelling; **curdling,** clabbering; **distillation**

5 precipitation, deposit, sedimentation; precipitate

6 solid, body, mass; lump, clump, cluster; concrete, concretion; conglomerate, conglomeration

7 clot, coagulate; **coagulant,** coagulator, thromboplastin or coagulin; casein, legumin; **curd,** clabber, clotted cream

8 <instruments> densimeter, densitometer; aerometer

VERBS **9 densify,** inspissate; **condense, compress,** compact, **consolidate, concentrate,** come to a head; **congest; squeeze, press, crowd,** cram, jam; pack or jam in; **solidify** 1044.8

10 thicken; congeal, coagulate, clot, set, concrete; gelatinize, gelatinate, jellify, **jell,** gel; **curdle,** curd, clabber

11 precipitate, deposit, sediment, sedimentate

ADJS **12 dense, compact, close; thick, heavy,** thickset, thick-packed, thick-growing, thick-spreading; **condensed, compressed,** compacted, concrete, consolidated, concentrated; **crowded, jammed,** packed, jam-packed, packed or jammed in; **congested,** crammed, crammed full; **solid,** firm, substantial, massive; incompressible; viscid, viscous, ropy, gluey

13 indivisible, undividable, **inseparable,** impartible, infrangible, indissoluble; cohesive, coherent 802.10; unified

14 thickened, inspissate or inspissated; **congealed, coagulated, clotted; curdled,** clabbered; **jel-**

lied, jelled, gelatinized; coagulant, coagulating

ADVS **15 densely,** compactly, **close,** closely, **thick, thickly,** heavily; solidly, firmly

1044 HARDNESS, RIGIDITY

NOUNS **1 hardness,** induration; **callousness,** callosity; rock-hardness, flintiness, steeliness; **strength, toughness** 1047; solidity, impenetrability, density 1043; obduracy 361.1

2 rigidity, rigidness; firmness, incompressibility; nonresilience or nonresiliency, inelasticity; **tension, tenseness,** tautness, tightness

3 stiffness, inflexibility, unpliability, unmalleability, intractability, unbendingness, starchiness; **stubbornness,** unyieldingness 361.2; **unalterability,** immutability; inelasticity

4 temper, tempering

5 hardening, toughening, induration, firming; **strengthening; tempering,** case hardening, steeling, seasoning; **stiffening,** starching; **solidification, setting,** curing, caking, concretion; callusing; sclerosis, arteriosclerosis, atherosclerosis; **petrification,** fossilization, ossification; calcification; vitrification, vitrifaction

6 <comparisons> stone, rock 1057, adamant

VERBS **7 harden,** indurate, firm, **toughen** 1047.3; **callous; temper,** anneal, **case-harden,** steel; season; **petrify,** fossilize; calcify; ossify; cornify, hornify

8 solidify, concrete, **set,** cure, cake; condense, thicken 1043.10; **crystallize,** granulate, candy

9 stiffen, rigidify, starch; **strengthen, toughen** 1047.3; back, brace, reinforce, shore up; **tense, tighten,** tense up

ADJS **10 hard, solid, tough** 1047.4; resistive, resistant, steely, iron-like; **stony,** rocky, rock-hard, rocklike, lithoid or lithoidal; adamant, adamantine; flinty, flintlike; concrete, cement; bony, osseous; hard-boiled; hard as nails or a rock, etc 1044.6; dense 1043.12; obdurate 361.10; hardhearted 94.12

11 rigid, stiff, firm, renitent, incompressible; **tense, taut, tight,** unrelaxed; **rodlike;** ramrod-stiff; stiff as a poker or rod; starched, starchy

12 inflexible, unflexible, **unpliable, unpliant, unmalleable, intractable,** untractable, **unbending, unyielding** 361.9, ungiving, **stubborn, unalterable,** immutable; **immovable** 854.15; **adamant,** adamantine; **inelastic**

13 hardened, toughened, steeled, indurate, indurated; **callous,** calloused; **solidified,** set; petrified, fossilized; vitrified; sclerotic; ossified; cornified, hornified; calcified; **stiffened, strengthened,** reinforced

14 hardening, toughening, indurative; petrifying

15 tempered, case-hardened, heat-treated, **annealed,** oil-tempered, heat-tempered; seasoned

1045 SOFTNESS, PLIANCY

NOUNS **1 softness,** give; **gentleness,** easiness, delicacy, tenderness; lenity, leniency 427; mellowness; fluffiness, flossiness, downiness, featheriness; velvetiness, silkiness

2 pliancy, pliability, plasticity, flexibility, ductility, tensility, **tractability,** amenability, adaptability, facility, give, **suppleness,** willowiness, **litheness, limberness; elasticity** 1046, **resilience,** springiness, resiliency; malleability, **impressionability,** susceptibility, responsiveness, receptiveness, sensibility, sensitiveness; agreeability 324.1; submissiveness 433.3

3 flaccidity, flaccidness, **flabbiness, limpness,** rubberiness, floppiness; **looseness,** laxness, laxity, relaxedness, relaxation

4 <comparisons> putty, clay, dough

5 **softening; easing,** cushioning; mollifying; **relaxation;** mellowing; tenderizing

VERBS 6 **soften,** soften up; **ease,** cushion; mollify; **subdue,** tone down; mellow; tenderize; **relax,** loosen; **limber,** limber up; massage, knead, plump up, fluff up

7 **yield, give,** relent, relax, bend, unbend, give way

ADJS 8 **soft;** mild, **gentle, easy, delicate, tender; softened,** mollified; soft as a kiss *or* a sigh *or* a baby's bottom

9 **pliant, pliable, flexible, plastic, elastic** 1046.7, **ductile,** tractile, **tractable, yielding,** giving, bending; adaptable, **malleable,** moldable; compliant 324.5, submissive 433.12; **impressionable,** susceptible, responsive, receptive, sensitive; **formable,** formative; **bendable; supple,** willowy, **limber; lithe,** lithesome, lissome, loose-limbed; **elastic,** resilient, springy; like putty *or* wax *or* dough, etc

10 **flaccid, flabby, limp,** rubbery, flimsy; **loose,** lax

11 **spongy,** pulpy, pithy

12 **pasty, doughy;** loamy, clayey

13 **squashy,** squishy, squushy, squelchy

14 **fluffy,** flossy, **downy,** pubescent, feathery; fleecy, woolly, lanate; furry

15 **velvety,** velvetlike; plush; **satiny,** satinlike; cottony; **silky,** silken, silklike, soft as silk

16 **softening, easing;** mollifying, emollient; demulcent; **relaxing,** loosening

ADVS 17 **softly, gently,** easily, delicately, tenderly; compliantly 324.9, submissively 433.17

1046 ELASTICITY

NOUNS 1 **elasticity, resilience** *or* resiliency, **give;** snap, **bounce,** bounciness; **stretch, stretchiness;** tone, tonus, tonicity; **spring, springiness;** rebound 902.2; **flexibility** 1045.2;

adaptability, responsiveness; **buoyancy** *or* buoyance; **liveliness** 330.2

2 **stretching;** extension; distension 259.2; **stretch, tension, strain**

3 **elastic;** elastomer; **rubber;** stretch fabric, spandex; whalebone, baleen; springboard; trampoline

VERBS 4 **stretch;** extend; distend 259.4

5 **give,** yield 1045.7; **bounce,** spring back 902.6

6 **elasticize;** rubberize, rubber; vulcanize

ADJS 7 **elastic, resilient, springy,** bouncy; **stretchable, stretchy,** stretch; extensile; **flexible** 1045.9; flexile; **adaptable,** adaptive, responsive; buoyant; lively 330.17

8 rubber, **rubbery,** rubberlike; rubberized

1047 TOUGHNESS

NOUNS 1 **toughness, resistance; strength, hardiness, vitality, stamina** 15.1; stubbornness, **stiffness; unbreakableness** *or* **unbreakability;** cohesiveness, **tenacity,** viscidity 802.3; **durability,** lastingness 826.1; **hardness** 1044; **leatheriness**

2 <comparisons> leather; gristle

VERBS 3 **toughen,** harden, stiffen, **temper,** strengthen; season; **endure, hang tough** <nonformal>

ADJS 4 **tough, resistant;** shockproof, impact-resistant; stubborn, stiff; **heavy-duty;** hard *or* tough as nails; **strong, hardy,** vigorous; cohesive, **tenacious,** viscid; **durable,** lasting 826.10; leathery, leatherlike, tough as leather; sinewy, wiry

5 **unbreakable,** nonbreakable, infrangible, shatterproof, fractureproof

6 **toughened,** hardened, tempered, annealed

1048 BRITTLENESS, FRAGILITY

NOUNS 1 **brittleness, crispness; fragility, frailty,** delicacy 16.2,

flimsiness, **breakability,**
crushability; lacerability;
friability, crumbliness 1049;
vulnerableness, **vulnerability**
1005.4

2 <comparisons> eggshell, matchwood, glass, china

VERBS **3 break, shatter,** fragment,
fragmentize, fall to pieces, shard,
disintegrate 805

ADJS **4 brittle, crisp; fragile, frail,**
delicate 16.14, flimsy, **breakable,**
frangible, fracturable; lacerable;
shatterable, splintery; friable,
crumbly 1049.13; fissile, scissile;
vulnerable 1005.16

1049 POWDERINESS, CRUMBLINESS

NOUNS **1 powderiness,** pulverulence, **dustiness; mealiness,**
flouriness, branniness; efflorescence

2 granularity, graininess, granulation; **sandiness, grittiness,**
sabulosity

3 friability, crispness, crumbliness; brittleness 1048

4 pulverization, comminution,
attrition, detrition; reduction to
powder *or* dust; fragmentation,
sharding; atomization; **powdering, crumbling;** abrasion 1042.2;
grinding, milling, shredding;
beating, pounding, shattering,
flailing, mashing, smashing,
crushing; disintegration 805

5 powder, dust; lint; efflorescence; **crumb,** crumble; **meal,**
bran, flour, farina; grits, groats;
filings, raspings, sawdust; soot,
smut; **particle, particulate,** particulates, airborne particles

6 grain, granule; **grit, sand;
gravel,** shingle

7 pulverizer, comminutor;
**crusher; mill; grinder; grater;
shredder;** pestle, **mortar and
pestle; masher;** millstone

8 koniology

VERBS **9 pulverize, powder,** comminute, triturate, pestle, disintegrate, reduce to powder *or* dust,
grind to powder *or* dust, grind up;
fragment, shard, shatter; atom-

ize; **crumble,** crumb; **granulate;
grind, grate, shred,** abrade
1042.7; **mill,** flour; **beat, pound,
mash, smash, crush,** crunch,
flail, squash, scrunch <nonformal>

10 <be reduced to powder> **powder,** come *or* fall to dust, **crumble, disintegrate** 805, break up;
effloresce; granulate

ADJS **11 powdery, dusty,** pulverulent, pulverous; **pulverized,**
pulverant, powdered, disintegrated, comminute, reduced to
powder; **particulate; ground,
grated,** pestled, milled, stoneground, comminuted, triturated,
levigated; sharded, **crushed;
fragmented; shredded; fine,** impalpable; **chalky,** chalklike;
mealy, floury, farinaceous; flaky
296.7; detrited; efflorescent

**12 granular, grainy, granulated;
sandy, gritty,** sabulous; shingly,
shingled, pebbled, pebbly; **gravelly**

13 pulverable, pulverizable, pulverulent, triturable; **friable,**
crumbly

1050 MATERIALITY

NOUNS **1 materiality; corporeity,**
corporality, embodiment; **substantiality** 762, concreteness
762.1; **physicalness,** physicality

2 matter, material, substance
762, **stuff; primal matter,** initial
substance, xylem; **element;**
chemical element 1058.1; elementary particle, fundamental
particle; constituent, component;
atom 1037.4; **molecule**

3 body, physical body, material
body, corpus <nonformal>, anatomy <nonformal>, person, **figure, form,** frame, **physique,**
bones, flesh, clay, hulk; soma;
torso, trunk

4 object, article, thing, material
thing, affair, something; artifact

5 <nonformal terms> **gadget**
1039.1; **thingumabob,** thingy,
thingumajig, doodad, dohickey, gimmick, gizmo, dingus,
widget

6 materialism, epiphenomenal-
ism, identity theory of mind, at-
omism, mechanism; physicalism,
behaviorism, instrumentalism,
pragmatism; dialectical materialism, Marxism; **positivism,** logical positivism, empiricism, **naturalism;** realism; worldliness,
earthliness, animalism, secularism, temporality

7 materialist, physicist, atomist;
dialectical materialist, Marxist;
naturalist; realist

8 materialization; substantiation;
embodiment, incorporation,
personification, **incarnation; reincarnation,** transmigration,
metempsychosis

VERBS **9 materialize** 762.5, corpo-
ralize; substantialize; **embody**
762.5, **incorporate,** personify, **incarnate; reincarnate,** reembody,
transmigrate

ADJS **10 material, substantial**
762.6; **corporeal,** corporal,
bodily; physical, somatic;
fleshly; earthly, **secular,** temporal, **unspiritual,** nonspiritual

11 embodied, bodied, **incorporated, incarnate**

12 materialist or **materialistic,** atomistic, mechanistic; Marxian,
Marxist; **naturalist, naturalistic,
positivist, positivistic; realist,**
realistic

1051 IMMATERIALITY

NOUNS **1 immateriality,** imma-
terialness; incorporealness, **bodi-
lessness; unsubstantiality** 763,
unsubstantialness; **intangibility,**
impalpability, imponderability;
**unearthliness, unworldliness;
supernaturalism** 689.2; **spirituality,** spiritualness, otherworldliness, shadowiness; occultism
689, occult phenomena; psychic
or psychical research; spirit
world, astral plane

2 incorporeal, incorporeity, immateriality, unsubstantiality 763

3 immaterialism, idealism

4 immaterialist, **idealist; spiritualist;** psychist, panpsychist, animist; **occultist** 689.11; medium;

ghost-raiser, ghost-hunter, ghost-
buster <nonformal>

5 dematerialization; **disembodiment,** disincarnation; **spiritualization**

VERBS **6** dematerialize, immaterialize, insubstantialize, **disembody,** disincarnate; **spiritualize,**
spiritize

ADJS **7 immaterial,** nonmaterial;
unsubstantial 763.5, insubstantial, **intangible,** impalpable, imponderable; **incorporeal; bodiless,** unembodied; **disembodied,**
discarnate; **unphysical,** non-
physical; **unfleshly;** spectral,
phantom, shadowy, ethereal;
spiritual, astral, psychic or psychical; **unearthly, unworldly,
otherworldly,** extramundane,
transmundane; supernatural; **occult**

8 idealist, idealistic, immaterialist, immaterialistic; solipsistic;
spiritualist, spiritualistic; panpsychist, panpsychistic; animist,
animistic

1052 MATERIALS

NOUNS **1 materials,** substances,
stuff; **raw material, staple,
stock;** material resources or
means; store, supply 386; strategic materials; matériel

2 <building materials> lath and
plaster, bricks and mortar; **roofing,** tiles, shingles; walling, siding; **flooring,** pavement, paving
material, paving, paving stone;
masonry, stonework, flag, flag-
stone, stone 1057.1; mortar, plas-
ters; **cement, concrete,** pre-
stressed concrete, reinforced concrete; brick, firebrick; cinder
block, concrete block; clinker,
adobe; **tile,** tiling

3 wood, lumber, timber; hardwood, softwood; **board,** plank;
deal; slab, puncheon; slat, lath;
boarding, timbering, timber-
work, planking; lathing, lath-
work; sheeting; paneling, panelboard; plywood, plyboard;
sheathing; siding; weatherboard,
clapboard; shingle, shake; log;

driftwood; firewood, stovewood; cordwood; cord

4 cane, bamboo, rattan

5 **paper**; sheet, leaf, page; quire, ream, stationery

6 **plastic**; thermoplastic; thermosetting plastic; molded plastic, extruded plastic; molding compounds; laminate; adhesive; plasticizer; polymer; **synthetic;** synthetic fabric *or* textile *or* cloth

VERBS 7 gather *or* procure materials; **store, stock,** stock up 386.11, lay in, restock; **process,** utilize

1053 INORGANIC MATTER

NOUNS 1 **inorganic matter**; inanimate matter, unorganized matter, inert matter, dead matter, **brute matter;** matter

2 **inanimateness, lifelessness,** inertness; **insensibility,** insensateness, senselessness, unconsciousness, unfeelingness

3 inorganic chemistry; chemicals 1058

ADJS 4 **inorganic,** nonorganic; **mineral,** nonbiological; unorganized; material 1050.9

5 **inanimate,** unanimated, examinate, dead, **lifeless,** soulless; inert; insentient, unconscious, **insensible,** insensate, senseless, unfeeling

1054 OILS, LUBRICANTS

NOUNS 1 **oil; fat,** lipid, **grease;** sebum, tallow, vegetable oil, animal oil; **ester;** essential oil; saturated fat, hydrogenated fat, unsaturated fat, polyunsaturated fat

2 **lubricant,** lubricating oil, lubricating agent; graphite, plumbago; silicone; mucus, synovia; petroleum jelly

3 **ointment, balm, salve, lotion, cream, unguent,** unction, chrism; lenitive, embrocation, demulcent, emollient; balsam; **pomade,** pomatum, brilliantine

4 **petroleum; fuel;** fuel oil; mineral oil; crude oil, crude

5 **oiliness, greasiness, unctuousness; fattiness,** fatness; richness; sebaceousness; adiposity; **soapiness,** saponaceousness; smoothness, slickness, sleekness, **slipperiness,** lubricity

6 **lubrication,** lubricating, **oiling, greasing**; grease *or* lube job <nonformal>; **anointment,** unction; chrismatory, chrismation

7 lubritorium; grease rack

VERBS 8 oil, grease; **lubricate; anoint,** salve, unguent, embrocate, dress; smear, daub; pomade; lard; smooth the way <nonformal>

ADJS 9 **oily, greasy; unctuous, oleaginous,** oleic; **unguent**; chrismal, chrismatory; **fat, fatty,** adipose; pinguid, pinguescent; rich; sebaceous; blubbery, tallowy, suety; lardy, lardaceous; buttery; soapy, saponaceous; mucoid; smooth, slick, sleek, **slippery**

10 **lubricant,** lubricating, **lubricative,** lubricatory; lenitive, emollient, soothing

1055 RESINS, GUMS

NOUNS 1 **resin; gum,** gum resin; oleoresin; synthetic resin, plastic; **rosin,** colophony, resinate

VERBS 2 resin, resinize, resinate; rosin

ADJS 3 **resinous,** resinic, resiny; resinoid; rosiny; **gummy,** gumlike; pitchy

1056 MINERALS, METALS

NOUNS 1 **mineral**; inorganic substance; extracted matter *or* material; **mineral world** *or* **kingdom;** mineral resources

2 **ore,** mineral; mineral-bearing material; natural *or* native mineral

3 **metal,** elementary metal; metallics; native metals, alkali metals, earth metals, noble metals, precious metals, base metals, rare metals, rare-earth metals *or* elements; gold *or* silver bullion; gold dust; metalwork, metalware

4 **alloy,** fusion, compound; **amalgam**

5 **cast, casting; ingot, bullion;** pig, sow; sheet metal

6 mine, pit; **quarry; diggings, workings;** coal mine, colliery; strip mine

7 deposit, mineral deposit, pay dirt; **vein, lode,** seam, dike; chimney; stock; placer, placer deposit, placer gravel; lodestuff, veinstone

8 mining; coal mining, gold mining, etc

9 miner, mineworker, pitman; coal miner; gold miner, gold digger; gold panner; placer miner; quarry miner; **prospector,** sourdough; wildcatter; **forty-niner**

10 mineralogy; crystallography; **petrology,** petrography; **geology**

11 metallurgy; physical metallurgy, powder metallurgy, electrometallurgy, hydrometallurgy, pyrometallurgy

12 mineralogist; metallurgist, electrometallurgist, metallurgical engineer; **petrologist,** petrographer; **geologist;** mining engineer

VERBS **13** mineralize; petrify 1044.7

14 mine; quarry; pan, pan for gold; prospect; hit pay dirt; mine out

ADJS **15** mineral; inorganic 1053.4

16 metal, metallic, metalloid *or* metalloidal; semimetallic; nonmetallic; bimetallic, trimetallic; metalliferous, metalbearing

17 brass, brassy, brazen; bronze, bronzy; copper, coppery, cuprous, cupreous; gold, golden, gilt, aureate; nickel, nickelic; silver, silvery; iron, ironlike, ferric, ferrous, ferruginous; steel, steely; tin, tinny; lead, leaden; pewter, pewtery; mercurial, mercurous, quicksilver

18 mineralogical, metallurgical, petrological, crystallographic

1057 ROCK

NOUNS **1 rock, stone;** living rock; **igneous rock,** plutonic *or* abyssal rock; volcanic rock, extrusive rock, scoria; magma, intrusive rock; granite, basalt, porphyry, **lava**<Hawaiian>; **sedimentary rock;** limestone, sandstone; **metamorphic rock,** schist,

gneiss; conglomerate, rubblestone, scree, talus, tufa; druid stone; monolith; crag; bedrock; mantlerock, regolith; saprolite, laterite

2 sand; grain of sand; sand pile, sand dune, sand hill; sand reef, sandbar

3 gravel, shingle

4 pebble, pebblestone, gravelstone; fingerstone; slingstone; spall

5 boulder, river boulder, shore boulder, glacial boulder

6 precious stone, gem, gemstone; stone: crystal; semiprecious stone; birthstone

7 petrification, petrifaction, lithification, crystallization

8 geology, petrology, crystallography; petrochemistry

VERBS **9** petrify, lithify, crystallize, turn to stone

ADJS **10 stone, rock,** lithic; petrified; adamant, adamantine; flinty, flintlike; marblelike; granitic; slaty, slatelike

11 stony, rocky; stonelike, rocklike, lithoid; sandy, gritty 1049.12; gravelly, shingled; pebbly, pebbled; porphyritic, trachytic; crystal, crystalline; bouldery, rockribbed; craggy; monolithic

1058 CHEMISTRY, CHEMICALS

NOUNS **1 chemistry,** chemical science, science of substances, science of matter

2 element, chemical element; table of elements, periodic table; rare earth element, rare gas element; **radical** group; **ion,** anion, cation; atom 1037.4; **molecule;** trace element, microelement, micronutrient, minor element; **chemical, chemical compound;** organic chemical, biochemical, inorganic chemical; fine chemicals, heavy chemicals; agent, **reagent**

3 acid; hydracid, oxyacid, sulfacid

4 valence, positive valence, negative valence; monovalence, uni-

valence, bivalence, trivalence, etc,
multivalence, polyvalence

5 atomic weight, atomic mass,
atomic volume, mass number;
molecular weight, molecular
mass, molecular volume; atomic
number, valence number

6 chemicalization, chemical
action; **chemical apparatus,**
beaker, Bunsen burner, burette,
centrifuge, condenser, crucible,
graduated cylinder *or* graduate,
pipette, test tube

VERBS **7 chemicalize;** alkalize, al-
kalify; acidify, acidulate, acetify;
isomerize, metamerize, polymer-
ize, copolymerize, homopolymer-
ize; ferment, work; catalyze
805.4; electrolyze

ADJS **8** chemical; biochemical,
chemicobiologic

9 valent; univalent, monovalent,
monatomic

1059 LIQUIDITY

NOUNS **1 liquidity, fluidity,** fluid-
ness, liquidness, liquefaction
1062; wateriness; **juiciness,** succulence; milkiness, lactescence;
lactation; suppuration; **moisture,
wetness** 1063.1; **fluency,** flow,
flux; **circulation;** turbulence, turbidity

2 fluid, liquid; liquor 10.47, drink,
beverage; **juice, sap,** latex; milk,
whey; **body fluid, blood;** semiliquid 1060.5

3 flowmeter, fluidmeter, hydrome-
ter

ADJS **4 fluid,** fluidic, **fluent, flowing,** fluxional, fluxionary, runny;
circulatory, turbid; **liquid;** watery 1063.16; **juicy,** sappy, succulent; **wet** 1063.15

5 milky, lacteal, **lactic;** lactifer-
ous; milk, milch

1060 SEMILIQUIDITY

NOUNS **1 semiliquidity,** semi-
fluidity; creaminess

2 viscosity, viscidity, viscousness;
thickness, heaviness, stodginess;
stickiness, tackiness, glutinous-
ness, toughness, tenacity, **adhesiveness, gumminess; ropiness,**

stringiness; clamminess, sliminess, mucilaginousness; **glui-
ness;** syrupiness; gelatinousness,
jellylikeness; colloidality; pastiness; **thickening,** curdling, clotting, coagulation, jellification

3 mucosity, mucousness, snottiness <nonformal>; **sliminess**

4 muddiness, muckiness, **slushi-
ness,** sloshiness, sludginess,
sloppiness, slobbiness, **oozi-
ness; turbidity,** turbidness, dirtiness

5 semiliquid, semifluid; **goo** *and*
goop *and* **gook** *and* **gunk** *and* **glop**
<all nonformal>, sticky mess;
paste, pap, putty, **butter; pulp**
1061.2; **jelly,** gelatin, gel; **glue;**
size; **gluten;** mucilage; mucus;
dough, batter; **syrup,** molasses;
egg white, albumen; cornstarch;
curd, clabber; gruel, porridge;
soup, gumbo, purée

6 gum 1055, chewing gum, bubble
gum; chicle

7 emulsion; emulsification; emul-
sifier; **colloid**

8 mud, muck, mire, slush, slosh,
sludge, squash, swill, **slime; slop,
ooze, mire;** clay, slip; gumbo

9 mud puddle, puddle, slop;
mudhole, slough, muckhole,
chuckhole

VERBS **10 emulsify;** colloid, col-
loidize; cream; churn, whip, beat
up; **thicken,** curdle, clot, coagulate, clabber <nonformal>; jell,
jelly, jellify

ADJS **11 semiliquid,** semifluid,
semifluidic; buttery; creamy;
emulsive, colloidal; **pulpy**
1061.6

12 viscous, viscid, viscose; **thick,**
heavy, stodgy, soupy, thickened;
curdled, clotted, coagulated, clabbered <nonformal>; **sticky,
tacky,** tenacious, adhesive, clingy,
clinging, tough; gluelike, glutinous; **gummy,** gumlike, **syrupy;**
ropy, stringy; mucilaginous;
clammy, slimy, slithery; gooey
and **gunky** *and* **gloppy** *and* **goopy**
and gooky <all nonformal>; **gel-
atinous,** jellylike, jellied, jelled;
doughy, pasty; starchy

13 mucous, mucoid, phlegmy, snotty <nonformal>; muciferous

14 slimy; muddy, miry, mucky, **slushy, sloshy,** sludgy, **sloppy,** slobby, splashy, **squashy,** squishy, **squelchy, oozy,** soft, sloughy, plashy; **turbid, dirty**

1061 PULPINESS

NOUNS **1 pulpiness; softness** 1045; flabbiness; **mushiness,** squashiness; **pastiness,** doughiness; **sponginess,** pithiness; fleshiness, succulence

2 pulp, paste, mash, mush, smash, squash, crush; pudding, porridge, sponge; sauce, butter; poultice, plaster; pith; pulpwood; dental *or* tooth pulp

3 pulping, pulpefaction; blending; digestion; **maceration,** mastication

4 pulper, pulpifier, macerator, digester; **masher,** smasher, potato masher, beetle

VERBS **5 pulp,** pulpify; **macerate,** masticate, chew; regurgitate; **mash,** smash, squash, crush

ADJS **6 pulpy,** pulpous, pulplike, pulped; **pasty,** doughy; **mushy;** macerated, masticated, chewed; regurgitated; **squashy,** squelchy, squishy; soft, flabby; fleshy, succulent; **spongy,** pithy

1062 LIQUEFACTION

NOUNS **1 liquefaction,** liquefying, liquidizing, fluidization; liquescence, deliquescence; **solution,** dissolution, dissolving; **infusion,** soaking, steeping, brewing; **melting,** thawing, running, fusing, fusion; unclotting; percolation, leaching

2 solubility, solubleness, dissolvability, dissolubility; meltability, fusibility

3 solution; decoction, infusion, mixture; chemical solution; lixivium, leach, leachate; **suspension,** colloidal suspension; **emulsion,** gel, aerosol

4 solvent, dissolvent, dissolver, dissolving agent, resolvent, reso-

lutive, **thinner,** diluent; anticoagulant; liquefier, liquefacient

VERBS **5 liquefy,** fluidize; **melt, run,** thaw; melt down; fuse, flux; deliquesce; **dissolve,** solve; thin, cut; hold in solution; unclot, decoagulate; leach, percolate; **infuse,** decoct, steep, soak, brew

ADJS **6 liquefied, melted, molten,** thawed; unclotted; in solution, in suspension; colloidal

7 liquefying, liquefactive; **melting,** fusing, thawing; **dissolving**

8 solvent, dissolvent, thinning, cutting, diluent

9 meltable, fusible, thawable; **soluble, dissolvable,** dissoluble; water-soluble

1063 MOISTURE

NOUNS **1 moisture,** damp, wet; **dampness, moistness, wetness, wateriness;** soddenness, soppiness, sogginess; swampiness, bogginess, marshiness; dewiness; mistiness, fogginess 319.3; rainfall; exudation 190.6; secretion 13

2 humidity, humidness, **dankness,** dankishness, **mugginess,** stickiness, sweatiness; dew point; humidification

3 water; hard water, soft water; heavy water; drinking water, tap water; **groundwater,** underground water; water table, aquifer; spring water, well water; seawater, salt water; water vapor; hydrosphere; head, hydrostatic head; hydrothermal water; wetting agent, liquidizer, moisturizer; humidifier

4 dew, dewdrops, morning dew, night dew

5 sprinkle, spray, sparge, shower; spindrift, spume, froth, foam; **splash,** plash, swash, slosh; **splatter,** spatter

6 wetting, moistening, dampening, damping; humidification; **watering, irrigation;** hosing, wetting *or* hosing down; **sprinkling, spraying,** sparging; **splashing,** splattering, spattering; baptism; bath, bathing, rinsing, laving; **flooding,** inundation,

deluge; **immersion, submersion**
367.2

7 soaking, sopping, **drenching,**
sousing; ducking, dunking <non-
formal>; **saturation,** permeation; waterlogging; **steeping,**
maceration, infusion, brewing,
imbuement; infiltration, percolation, leaching, lixiviation

8 sprinkler, sparger, sparge,
sprayer, spray can, atomizer,
aerosol; nozzle; **shower,** shower
bath, shower head, needle bath;
syringe, douche, enema, clyster;
sprinkling *or* watering can; lawn
sprinkler; sprinkling system,
sprinkler head

9 <science of humidity> hygrol-
ogy, hygrometry

10 <instruments> hygrometer, hair
hygrometer, hygrograph

VERBS **11** be damp; **drip,** weep;
seep, ooze, percolate; exude
190.15; sweat; secrete 13.5

12 moisten, dampen, moisturize,
damp, **wet,** wet down; humidify;
water, irrigate; dew, bedew;
sprinkle, besprinkle, **spray,**
spritz <nonformal>, sparge;
splash, dash, **swash, slosh,
splatter, spatter,** bespatter; dabble, paddle; slop, slobber; hose,
hose down; syringe, douche;
sponge

13 soak, drench, imbrue, **souse,
sop,** sodden; **saturate,** permeate;
bathe, lave, wash, rinse, douche,
flush; **steep,** macerate, infuse,
imbue, brew, impregnate, inject;
infiltrate, percolate, leach, lixiviate

14 flood, float, **inundate, deluge,**
turn to a lake, swamp, over-
whelm, drown; dip, dunk <non-
formal>; **submerge** 367.7; sluice,
pour on, flow on

ADJS **15 moist; damp,** dampish;
wet, wettish; undried; **humid,
dank, muggy, sticky;** rainy
316.10; marshy, swampy, fenny,
boggy

16 watery, aqueous, aquatic; liquid; **splashy,** plashy, sloppy; hydraulic

17 soaked, drenched, soused,

bathed, steeped, macerated; **saturated,** permeated; **watersoaked,
waterlogged; soaking, sopping;
wringing wet,** soaking wet, sopping wet, wet to the skin, like a
drowned rat; **sodden,** soppy,
soggy, soaky; dripping, **dripping
wet;** flooded, swamped, inundated, deluged, drowned, submerged, immersed, dipped,
dunked <nonformal>

18 wetting, dampening, moistening, watering; **drenching, soaking,** sopping; **irrigational**

1064 DRYNESS

NOUNS **1 dryness, aridness,** aridity, waterlessness; **drought;
thirst,** thirstiness; watertightness

2 <comparisons> desert, dust,
bone

3 drying, desiccation, drying up;
dehydration; evaporation; air-
drying; insolation; withering,
mummification; dehumidifica-
tion

4 drier, desiccator, desiccative,
siccative, **dehydrator,** dehydrant;
dehumidifier; evaporator

VERBS **5** thirst; drink up, soak up,
sponge up

6 dry, desiccate, dry up, **dehy-
drate;** evaporate; dehumidify;
air-dry; insolate, sun-dry; cure;
torrefy, **bake, parch,** scorch,
sear; **wither, shrivel;** wizen,
weazen; mummify; **wipe,** rub,
swab, brush

ADJS **7 dry, arid; waterless,** un-
watered, anhydrous; **bone-dry,**
dry as dust, dry as a bone; like
parchment; sapless; **thirsty,**
thirsting, athirst; high and dry

8 rainless, fine, fair, bright and
fair, pleasant

**9 dried, dehydrated, desic-
cated,** dried-up; evaporated;
parched, baked, sunbaked,
burnt, scorched, **seared,** sere,
sun-dried, adust; **withered,
shriveled,** wizened, weazened

**10 drying, dehydrating, desicca-
tive,** desiccant

11 watertight, waterproof, rainproof, showerproof

1065 VAPOR, GAS

NOUNS **1 vapor,** volatile; **fume, reek,** exhalation, breath, effluvium; **miasma,** mephitis, fetid air; **smoke,** smudge; wisp *or* plume *or* puff of smoke; **damp,** chokedamp, blackdamp, firedamp

2 gas; rare *or* noble *or* inert gas; fluid; **atmosphere, air** 317

3 vaporousness; vapor pressure; **ethereality; gaseousness,** gaseous state; **gas,** stomach gas, gassiness, flatulence, flatus, windiness, farting <nonformal>

4 volatility, vaporability, vaporizability

5 vaporization, evaporation, volatilization, gasification; sublimation; distillation, fractionation; atomization; exhalation; fumigation

6 vaporizer, evaporator; atomizer, aerosol, spray

7 vaporimeter, manometer, pressure gauge

VERBS **8 vaporize, evaporate,** volatilize, **gasify;** sublimate; distill, fractionate; **aerate;** atomize, spray; fluidize; **reek, fume;** exhale, give off, emit; **smoke; steam;** fumigate; **etherize**

ADJS **9 vaporous,** vaporlike; **airy, aerial, ethereal; gaseous,** gasified, gassy, gaslike; vaporing; **reeking;** miasmic, mephitic; **fuming,** fumy; smoky, smoking; steamy, steaming

10 volatile; vaporable, vaporizable; **evaporative,** evaporable

1066 BIOLOGY

NOUNS **1 biology,** biological science, life science, the science of life; **botany,** plant science; **plant kingdom,** vegetable kingdom; **plants** 310; **zoology,** animal biology, animal science; **animal kingdom,** phylum, class, order, family, genus, species

2 biologist, naturalist, life scientist; **botanist,** plant scientist; **zoologist,** animal biologist, animal scientist

ADJS **3 biological,** biologic; **botanical,** botanic, plant; **zoological,** zoologic

1067 AGRICULTURE

NOUNS **1 agriculture, farming,** husbandry; cultivation, culture, geoponics, tillage, tilth; green revolution; agricultural engineering; agricultural economics; agrarian economy *or* economics, agrarianism; agribusiness

2 horticulture, gardening; landscape gardening, landscape architecture; truck gardening, market gardening; flower gardening, floriculture; viniculture, viticulture; orcharding, pomiculture, citriculture

3 forestry, arboriculture, silviculture, forest management; Christmas tree farming; forestation, reforestation; deforestation

4 <agricultural deities> vegetation spirit *or* daemon, fertility god *or* spirit

5 agriculturist, agriculturalist; agronomist; **farmer, yeoman,** cultivator, sodbuster, **tiller of the soil;** crop-farmer, dirt farmer <nonformal>, etc; gentleman-farmer; **peasant,** countryman, rustic; **planter,** tea-planter, coffee-planter, etc; tenant farmer; sharecropper; **agricultural worker, farm worker,** farmhand, farm laborer, migrant *or* migratory worker *or* laborer; planter, sower; reaper, harvester

6 horticulturist, nurseryman, gardener; landscape gardener, landscape architect; **florist;** vinegrower, viniculturist, viticulturist; orchardist

7 forester; arboriculturist, silviculturist, tree farmer; **ranger,** forest ranger; woodsman; **logger, lumberman,** lumberjack

8 farm, grange; boutique farm, dirt farm, tree farm, etc; **plantation,** cotton plantation, etc; **homestead; barnyard,** farmyard; collective farm; farmland, cropland, arable land, plowland, fallow

9 field, tract, plot, patch; cultivated land; clearing; hayfield, corn field, etc; **paddy, paddy field,** rice paddy

10 garden; flower bed, border; **vineyard**

11 nursery; conservatory, greenhouse, lathhouse, **hothouse**; potting shed; forcing bed, **hotbed,** cold frame; seedbed

12 growing, raising, cultivation; **green thumb**

13 cultivation, culture, **tilling,** dressing, working; harrowing, plowing, furrowing, weeding, hoeing, pruning, thinning; irrigation

14 planting; sowing, seeding, insemination; breeding, hydridizing; **dissemination,** broadcasting

15 harvest, harvesting, **reaping, gleaning,** gathering

VERBS **16 farm, ranch; grow, raise,** rear; crop; dryfarm; sharecrop; **garden; have a green thumb**

17 cultivate, dress, work, till, dig, spade; mulch; **plow,** plow under, plow up, fallow; **harrow,** rake; **weed,** hoe, cut, prune, thin; slash and burn; fertilize 889.8

18 plant, set, put in; **sow, seed,** inseminate; **disseminate,** broadcast, scatter seed; drill; dibble; **transplant,** reset, pot; **forest,** afforest

19 harvest, reap, crop, **glean, gather,** gather in, bring in; **pick,** pluck; mow, cut; hay; nut

ADJS **20 agricultural, agrarian,** geoponic, agronomic; farm, **farming;** arable; **rural** 233.6

21 horticultural; viticultural; arboricultural, silvicultural

1068 ANIMAL HUSBANDRY

NOUNS **1 animal husbandry,** animal rearing or raising or culture, stock raising, **ranching;** herding, grazing, keeping flocks and herds, running livestock; breeding, stockbreeding, stirpiculture; pisciculture, fish culture; apiculture, bee culture, beekeeping; cattle raising; sheepherding; stock farming, fur farming; pigkeeping; dairy-farming, chicken-farming, pig-farming, etc; cattle-ranching, mink-ranching, etc

2 stockman, stock raiser; breeder, stockbreeder, sheepman; cattleman; **rancher,** ranchman; dairy farmer; **stableman, groom; blacksmith,** horseshoer, farrier

3 herder, drover, herdsman; shepherd, shepherdess, **sheepherder;** goatherd; swineherd; **cowboy,** cowgirl, cowhand, puncher and **cowpuncher** and cowpoke <all nonformal>; **wrangler,** horse wrangler

4 apiarist, apiculturist, **beekeeper,** beeherd

5 farm, stock farm, animal farm; **ranch;** horse farm, stable, stud farm; **cattle ranch;** pig farm, piggery; chicken farm or ranch, turkey farm, duck farm, poultry farm; sheep farm or ranch; fur farm or ranch, mink farm or ranch; **dairy farm**

VERBS **6 raise, breed,** rear, grow, hatch, feed, nurture, fatten; keep, run; ranch, farm; culture; backbreed

7 tend; groom, rub down, brush, curry, currycomb; water, drench, feed, fodder; bed, bed down, litter; milk; harness, saddle, hitch, bridle, yoke

8 drive, herd, punch cattle, **shepherd,** ride herd on; spur, goad, prick, lash, whip; wrangle, round up

1069 EARTH SCIENCE

NOUNS **1 earth science, earth sciences;** geoscience; geography, geology, geological science, oceanography, oceanographic science, meteorology, atmospheric science, planetary science, space science

2 earth scientist, geoscientist; **geologist, geographer, oceanographer, astronomer, meteorologist,** weather man

1070 THE UNIVERSE, ASTRONOMY

NOUNS **1 universe, world, cosmos; all creation,** totality of being, sum of things; nature, system; wide world, whole wide world; **macrocosm;** metagalaxy; open universe, closed universe, oscillating universe, steady-state universe, expanding universe, pulsating universe; sidereal universe

2 the heavens, heaven, **sky, firmament;** empyrean; **the blue,** azure, cerulean, the blue serene; **ether, air;** vault, cope, canopy, vault *or* canopy of heaven, starry sphere, celestial sphere, starry heaven *or* heavens

3 space, outer space, cosmic space, empty space, ether space, pressureless space, celestial spaces, interplanetary *or* interstellar *or* intergalactic *or* intercosmic space, metagalactic space, **the void,** the void above, ocean of emptiness; chaos; outermost reaches of space; astronomical unit, light-year, parsec; interstellar medium

4 stars, fixed stars, starry host; music *or* harmony of the spheres; orb, sphere; **heavenly body,** celestial body *or* sphere; **comet; comet cloud; morning star,** daystar; **evening star; North Star,** polar star, lodestar, Polaris

5 constellation, configuration; star cluster, galactic cluster, open cluster, globular cluster, stellar association, supercluster

6 galaxy, island universe, galactic nebula; spiral galaxy *or* nebula; barred spiral galaxy *or* nebula; elliptical *or* spheroidal galaxy; disk galaxy; irregular galaxy; radio galaxy; **the Local Group; the Galaxy, the Milky Way**

7 nebula, nebulosity; gaseous nebula; hydrogen cloud; dark nebula; dust cloud; dark matter; planetary nebula; whirlpool nebula

8 star; quasar, quasi-stellar radio source; **pulsar,** pulsating star, eclipsing binary X-ray pulsar; **black hole,** gravitational collapse, giant black hole, white hole, active galactic nucleus; **magnitude,** stellar magnitude, visual magnitude; relative magnitude, absolute magnitude

9 planet, wanderer, terrestrial planet, inferior planet, superior planet, secondary planet, major planet; minor planet, planetoid, asteroid; asteroid belt

10 Earth, the world; globe, terrestrial globe, the blue planet; geosphere, biosphere, magnetosphere

11 moon, satellite; orb of night, queen of heaven, queen of night; silvery moon; **new moon,** wet moon; **crescent moon,** crescent, waxing moon, waxing crescent moon; decrescent moon, decrescent, waning moon, waning crescent moon; gibbous moon; **half-moon,** demilune; **full moon, harvest moon,** hunter's moon; **eclipse**

12 <moon goddess, the moon personified> Diana, Phoebe, Cynthia, Artemis

13 sun; orb of day, daystar; photosphere, chromosphere, corona; sunspot; sunspot cycle; solar flare, solar prominence; solar wind; **eclipse,** eclipse of the sun, solar eclipse

14 <sun god or goddess, the sun personified> Sol, Helios, Hyperion, Titan

15 meteor; falling *or* shooting star, meteoroid, fireball, bolide; **meteorite;** micrometeorite; siderolite; tektite; meteor dust, cosmic dust; meteor trail, meteor train; meteor swarm; meteor shower

16 orbit, circle, trajectory; circle of the sphere, great circle, small circle; **ecliptic; zodiac;** zone; meridian, celestial meridian; equator, celestial equator, equinoctial; equinox, vernal equinox, autumnal equinox; apogee, perigee; aphelion, perihelion; period

17 observatory, astronomical observatory; radio observatory, orbiting astronomical observatory *or* OAO, orbiting solar observatory *or* OSO; **planetarium; telescope,** astronomical telescope; reflector, refractor; **radio telescope; spectroscope,** spectrograph; **observation;** bright time, dark time

18 cosmology, cosmography, **cosmogony;** nebular hypothesis; **big bang** *or* expanding universe theory, oscillating *or* pulsating universe theory, steady state *or* continuous creation theory, plasma theory; creationism, creation science

19 astronomy, stargazing; astrophotography, stellar photometry; spectrography, spectroscopy, radio astronomy, radar astronomy, X-ray astronomy; **astrophysics,** solar physics; celestial mechanics, gravitational astronomy

20 astrology, horoscopy; judicial *or* mundane astrology; **horoscope,** nativity; zodiac, **signs of the zodiac; house,** mansion; house of life, mundane house, planetary house *or* mansion; aspect

21 cosmologist; cosmogonist; cosmographer, cosmographist

22 astronomer, stargazer, astrographer, astrophotographer; radio astronomer, radar astronomer; **astrophysicist,** solar physicist

23 astrologer, astromancer, stargazer, horoscoper, horoscopist

ADJS **24 cosmic, universal;** cosmological, cosmogonal, cosmogonical, cosmographical

25 celestial, heavenly, empyrean; astral, starry, stellar; star-spangled, star-studded; side-real; zodiacal; equinoctial; **astronomic** *or* **astronomical,** astrophysical, **planetary,** circumplanetary; planetoidal, planetesimal, asteroidal; **solar,** heliacal; terrestrial; **lunar,** lunate, lunary, cislunar, translunar; meteoric, meteoritic; extragalactic, anagalactic; galactic; nebular, nebu-

lous, nebulose; interstellar, intersidereal; interplanetary; intercosmic

26 extraterrestrial, exterrestrial, extramundane, space; **transmundane, otherworldly,** transcendental

ADVS **27 universally,** everywhere

1071 THE ENVIRONMENT

NOUNS **1 the environment,** the natural world, global ecology, ecosystem, global ecosystem, the biosphere, the ecosphere, the balance of nature, macroecology, microecology; **ecology,** bioregion; **environmental protection; environmental control,** environmental management; environmental assessment, environmental impact analysis; emission control; **environmental science**

2 environmental destruction, ecocide; environmental pollution; **air pollution,** atmospheric pollution, air quality; **water pollution,** groundwater pollution, pollution of the aquifer; **environmental pollutant;** eutrophication; **biodegradation**

3 environmentalist, conservationist, preservationist, environmental activist, ecofreak *and* treehugger *and* eagle freak <all nonformal>

1072 ROCKETRY, MISSILERY

NOUNS **1 rocketry,** rocket science *or* technology; **missilery,** missile science *or* technology; rocket *or* missile testing; rocket *or* missile project *or* program; instrumentation; telemetry

2 rocket, rocket engine *or* **motor,** reaction engine *or* motor; rocket thruster; retrorocket; rocket exhaust; plasma jet, plasma engine; ion engine; jetavator

3 rocket, missile, ballistic missile, guided missile; torpedo; bird <nonformal>; **payload; warhead,** nuclear *or* thermonuclear warhead, atomic warhead; multiple *or* multiple-missile warhead

4 rocket bomb, flying bomb *or* torpedo, cruising missile; **robot bomb; buzzbomb**

5 multistage rocket, step rocket; two- *or* three-stage rocket; **booster,** booster unit, booster rocket, takeoff booster *or* rocket; piggyback rocket

6 test rocket, research rocket

7 proving ground, testing ground; firing area; impact area; control center, mission control, bunker; radar tracking station, tracking station, visual tracking station; meteorological tower

8 rocket propulsion, reaction propulsion, jet propulsion, blast propulsion; **fuel, propellant,** solid fuel, liquid fuel, hydrazine, liquid oxygen *or* lox; **thrust,** constant thrust; **exhaust,** jet blast, backflash

9 rocket launching *or* **firing,** ignition, launch, shot, shoot; countdown; **lift-off,** blast-off; flight, trajectory; **burn; burnout,** end of burning; velocity peak; altitude peak, ceiling; descent; airburst; impact

10 rocket launcher; launching *or* **launch pad,** launching platform, firing table; **silo;** takeoff ramp; tower projector, launching tower; rocket gun, bazooka, antitank rocket; multiple projector, calliope, Katusha

11 rocket scientist *or* technician, rocketeer *or* rocketer, rocket *or* missile engineer

VERBS **12 rocket, skyrocket**

13 launch, project, **shoot, fire,** blast off; abort

1073 SPACE TRAVEL

NOUNS **1 space travel, astronautics,** cosmonautics, **space flight;** interplanetary travel, space exploration; space walk; **space science,** space technology *or* engineering; **aerospace science,** aerospace technology *or* engineering; space *or* aerospace research; multistage flight, step flight, shuttle flights; trip to the moon, trip to Mars, grand tour;

space terminal, target planet; science fiction

2 spacecraft, spaceship, space rocket, rocket ship, manned rocket, interplanetary rocket; **rocket** 1072.2; orbiter; **shuttle,** space shuttle; **capsule, space capsule,** ballistic capsule; **nose cone, heat shield,** heat barrier, thermal barrier; command module, lunar excursion module *or* LEM, lunar module *or* LM; moon ship, Mars ship, etc; reconnaissance rocket; **multistage rocket** 1072.5, retrorocket, rocket thruster, attitude-control rocket, main rocket; **burn;** space docking, docking, docking maneuver; **orbit,** parking orbit, geostationary orbit; earth orbit, apogee, perigee; lunar *or* moon orbit; **guidance system,** terrestrial guidance; soft landing, hard landing; injection, insertion, lunar insertion, Earth insertion; **reentry, splashdown**

3 flying saucer, unidentified flying object *or* UFO

4 rocket engine 1072.2; atomic power plant; solar battery; power cell

5 space station, space island, island base, halfway station, advance base; manned station; space airport, **spaceport,** spaceport station, space dock, launching base, research station, space laboratory, space observatory; radio relay station, radio mirror; space mirror, solar mirror; moon station, moon base, lunar base

6 artificial satellite, satellite, unmanned satellite, sputnik; communications satellite, active communications satellite, communications relay satellite, orbiting observatory, geophysical satellite, navigational satellite; **probe, space probe,** interplanetary explorer

7 <satellite telemetered recorders> micro-instrumentation

8 astronaut, cosmonaut, **spaceman, spacewoman,** shuttle crew member, space traveler; planetary colony, lunar colony; extraterrestrial visitor, alien, man from Mars, Martian, little green man

9 rocket society

10 <space hazards> cosmic particles, intergalactic matter, aurora particles, radiation, cosmic ray bombardment; rocket *or* satellite debris, space junk <nonformal>; meteors, meteorites; asteroids; meteor dust impacts, meteoric particles, space bullets; extreme temperatures; the bends, blackout, weightlessness

11 space suit, pressure suit, G suit, anti-G suit

VERBS **12** travel in space, go into outer space; orbit the earth, go into orbit, orbit the moon, etc; navigate in space; escape earth, leave the atmosphere, shoot into space; rocket to the moon, park in space, hang *or* float in space, space-walk

ADJS **13 astronautical,** cosmonautical, spacetraveling, spacefaring; rocketborne

Index

How to Use This Index

Numbers after index entries refer to categories and paragraphs in the front section of this book, not to page numbers. The part of the number before the decimal point refers to the category in which synonyms and related words to the word you are looking up are found. The part of the number after the decimal point refers to the paragraph or paragraphs within the category. Look at the index entry for **ability** on the next page:

ability 18.2

This entry listing tells you that you can find words related to **ability** in paragraph 2 of category 18.

Words, of course, frequently have more than one meaning. Each of those meanings may have synonyms or associated related words. Look at the entry for **absorb**:

absorb 187.13, 570.7

This tells you that you will find synonyms for **absorb** in category 187, paragraph 13. It also tells you that you will find synonyms for **absorb** in category 570, paragraph 7.

Words that appear in all capital letters are the names of categories.

Not all words in the main part of the book are included in the index. Many adverbs ending with **-ly** have been left out of the index; but you will find the common adverbs ending in **-ly** here, such as **eagerly** or **easily**. If you can't find the adverb ending in **-ly** that you are looking for, look up the word in its adjective form and go to that category.

To make it easier to find phrases, we have indexed them according to their first word, unless that first word is an article such as **a**, **the** or **an**. You do not have to guess what the main word of the phrase is to find it in the index. Simply look up the first word in the phrase. For example, **give birth** will be found in the Gs, **INORGANIC MATTER** in the Is and **let out** in the Ls.

abandon, 370.5
abandoned, 370.8
ABANDONMENT, 370
abase, 137.5
abate, 252.8
abbreviation, 537.4
abduct, 482.20
abduction, 482.9
abductor, 483.10
abet, 449.14
ability, 18.2
able, 18.14
able-bodied, 15.16
ably, 18.16
abnormal, 869.9
ABNORMALITY, 869
ABODE, 228
abolish, 395.13
abomination, 638.2
abortion, 410.5
abound, 990.5
about, 223.26
about-face, 163.10
about to, 838.13
abrade, 1042.7
abrasion, 1042.2
abrasive, 1042.10
abridge, 557.5
abridged, 557.6
ABRIDGMENT, 557
abroad, 773.6
ABSENCE, 222, 222.4
absent, 222.11, 222.19
absentee, 222.5
absently, 222.16
absolutely, 793.15
absorb, 187.13, 570.7
absorption, 570.2
abstain, 668.7
abstainer, 668.4
abstinence, 668.2
abstinent, 668.10
abstract idea, 931.3
abstracted, 984.11
absurd, 922.11
absurdity, 922.3
abundant, 883.8
abysmal, 275.11
accelerate, 174.10
acceleration, 174.4
accelerator, 1037.11
accent, 524.11, 524.9,
709.25
accept, 123.2, 134.7
acceptable, 107.12
accepted, 332.14
accessibility, 965.3
accessible, 965.8
accession, 417.12
accommodate, 385.10
accommodations, 385.3
accompanier, 768.4
ACCOMPANIMENT, 768

accompany, 768.7
accompanying, 768.9
accomplice, 616.3
accomplish, 407.4
accomplished, 407.10
ACCOMPLISHMENT, 407,
413.8
ACCORD, 455
accordingly, 765.11
account, 349.3, 622.2,
628.2
account book, 628.4
account of, 1016.12
accountant, 628.7
accounting, 1040.7, 628.12,
628.6
ACCOUNTS, 628
accumulation, 769.9
accuracy, 972.5
accurate, 972.16
accurately, 972.20
ACCUSATION, 599
accuse, 599.7
accused, 599.15, 599.6
accuser, 599.5
accusing, 599.13
accustom, 373.9
accustomed, 373.16
aceldama, 308.11
ache, 26.5
aching, 26.12
acid, 67.6, 1058.3
acknowledge, 332.11
acknowledgment, 332.3,
887.2
acoustic, 50.17
acoustics, 50.5
acquaintance, 587.4
acquiesce, 441.3
acquire, 472.8
ACQUISITION, 472
acquisitive, 472.15
acquit, 601.4
ACQUITTAL, 601
acrimonious, 17.14
acrimony, 17.5
acrobatic maneuvers,
184.13
act, 328.3, 328.4, 704.29,
704.7
acting, 328.10, 704.8
ACTION, 328
activate, 17.12
activation, 17.9
active, 330.17
actively, 330.25
ACTIVITY, 330
actor, 707.2
add, 253.4
add to, 253.5
addict, 87.20
addicted, 87.24
adding, 253.3

ADDITION, 253
additional, 253.10
additive, 253.8
address, 524.27, 553.13,
553.9
adhesive, 802.4, 802.12
adjacent, 223.16
adjoin, 223.9
ADJUNCT, 254
adjustment, 92.27, 465.4,
787.4
administer, 573.11, 643.6
administration, 573.3,
643.2
administrative, 573.14
admission, 187.2
admonish, 422.6
adolescence, 301.6
adolescent, 301.13
adopt, 371.15, 621.4
adoption, 371.4, 621.2
adrift, 182.61
adult, 303.12, 304.1
adulterate, 796.12
adulteration, 796.3
adulterer, 665.13
adultery, 665.7
advance, 162.5
advantage, 249.2
advantageously, 249.19
advent, 838.5
adventure, 404.2)
adverse, 1010.13
adversely, 1010.16
ADVERSITY, 1010
advertisement, 352.6
advertising matter, 352.8
ADVICE, 422
advise, 422.5
advisee, 422.4
adviser, 422.3
advisory, 422.8
aesthete, 496.6
affair, 830.3
affairs, 830.4
affect, 500.12, 93.14
AFFECTATION, 500, 533.3
affected, 93.23, 500.15,
533.9
affectedly, 500.20
affecting, 93.22
affiliation, 450.2
affirm, 334.5
AFFIRMATION, 334
affirmatively, 332.2, 334.8
affirmatively, 332.16,
334.10
affirmed, 334.9
afflict, 85.49
affliction, 96.8
afford, 626.7
afoot, 405.23
afoul, 182.72

attractor, 906.2
attributable, 887.6
attribute, 887.3
attribute to, 887.4
ATTRIBUTION, 887
auction, 734.4, 734.11
auctioneer, 730.8
audible, 50.16
audibly, 50.18
audience, 48.6
audition, 48.2
auditorium, 704.15
auditory, 48.13
augur, 133.12
augured, 133.15
auspicious, 133.18
author, 547.15, 718.4, 885.4
authoritative, 417.15, 969.18
authoritatively, 417.18
authoritativeness, 417.2, 417.3
authorities, 575.15
AUTHORITY, 417
authorization, 443.3
authorize, 443.11
authorized, 443.17
authorship, 547.2, 718.2
autograph, 337.3
automate, 1040.19
automated, 1040.21
AUTOMATION, 1040.
automobile, 179.9
AUTOMOBILE RACING, 756
autopsy, 307.18
autumn, 313.4
avail, 387.17
avail oneself of, 387.14
available, 222.15
avenger, 507.3
average, 246.2, 863.3
averse, 99.8
AVIATION, 184, 184.49
AVIATOR, 185
aviatrix, 185.2
avocation, 724.7
avocational, 724.17
avoid, 164.6, 157.7, 368.6
AVOIDANCE, 368, 368.14
await, 130.8
awake, 23.4, 23.8
awaken, 23.5
awakening, 23.2
award, 646.2
away 188.21, 222.18
awesome, 122.11
awn, 3.9
axiom, 973.2
axle, 914.5
baby carriage, 179.6
bachelor, 565.3

back, 217.3, 449.13, 836.12
backslider, 394.3
backsliding, 394.2
backswept, 217.12
backward, 163.12
backwards, 163.13
backwater, 182.34
bad, 999.7
bad influence, 999.4
bad luck, 1010.5
BADNESS, 999
BAD PERSON, 660
badly, 999.13
bag, 195.2
bagpipe, 711.9
bah!, 157.10
balanced, 789.9
balcony, 197.22
balk, 361.7
ball, 282.7
ballistics, 462.3
balloonist, 185.7
ballot, 609.19
ballroom, 705.4
balm, 86.11
band, 280.3, 1033.13
bandit, 483.4
BANE, 1000
bang!, 56.13
banging, 56.11
banish, 908.17
banishment, 908.4
bank, 729.13
banker, 729.10
banking, 729.4
bankroll, 728.17
bankrupt, 625.8
bantamweight, 297.3
BANTER, 490, 490.5
banterer, 490.4
bantering, 490.2, 490.7
baptism, 701.6
baptize, 701.16
bar, 88.20, 597.4
barbarian, 497.7
barbarism, 526.6
barefoot, 6.15
bargain, 633.3, 731.5, 731.17
barn, 228.20
barrier, 1011.5
base, 199.2, 274.4, 661.12, 900.8
BASEBALL, 745
baseball team, 745.2
baseless, 763.8, 935.13
baseness, 661.3
base on, 199.6
basic, 199.8
basics, 817.6
BASKETBALL, 747
bastard, 561.5
bath, 79.8

bathing, 79.7
bathos, 488.3
bathroom, 197.26
battlefield, 463.2
battle flag, 458.12
battlement, 289.3
battleship, 180.7
beady, 282.10
beam, 273.3
bear, 161.7, 311.23, 737.12, 891.13
beard, 3.8
bearded, 3.25
bearing, 889.10, 891.6, 914.7
beast of burden, 176.8
beast, 144.14, 660.7
beat, 709.26
beat time, 708.44
beau, 104.13
beautician, 1015.13
beautification, 1015.11
beautiful, 1015.17
beautifully, 1015.23
beautify, 1015.15
beautifying, 1015.22
BEAUTY, 1015, 1015.8
beauty parlor, 1015.14
becalm, 173.11
becalmed, 173.17
because, 887.10
because of, 887.9
become, 760.12
bed, 199.4
bedding, 900.20
bedroom, 197.7
bee, 311.33, 582.14
beef, 10.13
Beelzebub, 680.7
beer, 88.16
before, 165.4, 216.12, 813.6
befriend, 587.10
beg, 440.15
beggar, 440.8
begin, 817.7
beginner, 817.2
BEGINNING, 817, 817.15
behave, 321.4
behave oneself, 321.5
BEHAVIOR, 321
behavioral, 321.7
behaviorism, 321.3
behemoth, 257.14
behind, 166.6, 217.13, 449.27, 910.6
behoove, 641.4
belch, 908.9, 908.28
BELIEF, 952, 952.2, 952.21
believability, 952.8
believable, 952.24
believe, 952.10
believed, 952.23
believer, 692.4, 952.9

believe in, 952.15
believing, 692.5
bell, 54.4
belong to, 469.7
belong, 617.15
belongings, 471.2
beloved, 104.24
below, 274.10, 274.11
bend, 279.3
benediction, 696.5
BENEFACTOR, 592
benefice, 698.9
beneficiary, 479.4
benefit, 387.4, 478.7, 592.3
benefitting, 592.4
BENEVOLENCE, 143
benevolences, 143.6
benevolent, 143.15
benevolently, 143.20
benighted, 315.10, 929.16
bequeath, 478.18
bequest, 478.10
berate, 510.19
berating, 510.7
bereave, 307.28
bereaved, 307.35
bereavement 473.1
bereft, 473.8
berserk, 671.9
beside, 218.11
besiege, 459.19
best, 249.5, 249.7, 998.8,
  998.16
bet, 759.3, 759.25
betray, 351.6, 645.14
betrayal, 645.8
betrothal, 436.3
better, 392.14
betting system, 759.4
between, 213.12
beverage, 10.47
beware, 494.7
bewilder, 970.12
bewildered, 970.24
bewildering, 970.27
bewitch, 691.9
bewitched, 691.13
bewitcher, 690.9
bewitching, 691.11
beyond one, 19.20
beyond, 261.21, 522.26
bias, 204.3
Bible, 683.2
bibliography, 558.4
bibliological, 554.20
bibulous, 88.35
bid, 439.6, 733.9
bier, 309.13
bigot, 979.5
bill, 613.9, 628.11, 870.5
billion, 881.12
billow, 238.22
bind, 428.10, 799.9

bingo, 759.15
biological classification,
  305.3
biological, 1066.3
biologist, 1066.2
BIOLOGY, 1066
biosphere, 306.6
bird, 311.28
birdhouse, 228.23
birdlike, 311.47
birds, 769.6
BIRTH, 1, 78.6
birthplace, 885.8
biscuit, 10.29
bisect, 874.4
BISECTION, 874
bisector, 874.3
bit, 1041.14
bite, 8.2, 68.5
bitter, 64.6
bitterness, 152.3
black, 38.8
blacken, 38.7
blackening, 38.5
black-haired, 38.13
blacking, 38.6
blackjack, 759.11
black magic, 690.2
BLACKNESS, 38
blackout, 184.21, 1026.7
black out, 184.46
blame, 599.8
blameworthy, 510.25
blanket, 295.10, 295.12
blare, 53.5, 53.10
blaspheme, 694.5
blast, 56.8
bleach, 36.4
bleached, 36.8
bleed, 12.17, 91.27
bleeding, 12.23
BLEMISH, 1003, 1003.4
blemished, 1003.8
bless, 696.13
blight, 1000.2
blighted, 393.42
blind, 30.4, 30.7, 30.9
blinded, 30.10
blindfold, 30.5
BLINDNESS, 30
bliss, 681.5
blissful, 97.9
block, 230.7, 989.3
blond, 37.9
blood, 2.23
bloodletting, 91.20
blood relationship, 559.1
bloodstain, 1003.7
bloodstained, 1003.11
bloodsucker, 311.36
blow, 318.20
blower, 318.18
blowtorch, 1019.14

blow up, 395.18
blue, 45.2, 45.3
blues, 112.6
blunder, 974.5, 974.14
blunt, 286.2, 286.3
BLUNTNESS, 286
blur, 32.4
blush, 139.8
blushing, 139.5, 139.13
BLUSTER, 503, 503.3
blusterer, 503.2
blustering, 503.4
boast, 502.6
boastful, 502.10
boastfully, 502.14
BOASTING, 502
BOAT, 180
boatman, 183.5
bodily, 14.1
BODILY DEVELOPMENT,
  14
BODY, 2, 1050.3
bodyguard, 1007.14
boil, 1019.20
boiling, 1019.2
boisterous, 671.20
bomb, 459.23, 462.20
bombardment, 459.7
bombast, 545.2
bombastic, 545.9
bond, 738.5
bone of contention, 456.7
bonus, 624.6
boo, 508.3, 508.10
BOOK, 554, 554.3
bookbinding, 554.14
bookholder, 554.17
book-learned, 927.22
booklet, 554.11
booklover, 554.18
bookmaker, 759.20
bookstore, 554.16
bookworm, 928.1
boom, 56.4, 56.9
boon companion, 588.5
boorish, 497.13
boorishness, 497.4
booth, 736.3
bootleg liquor, 88.18
booty, 482.11
border, 211.4, 211.10
bordered, 211.12
bordering, 211.11
bore, 118.4, 118.7
bored, 118.12
born, 1.4
borrow, 621.3
BORROWING, 621
boss, 610.7
botanical classifications,
  808.5
botched, 414.21
both, 872.7

circuit, 913.2, 1031.4
circuitous, 913.7
circuitously, 913.9
CIRCUITOUSNESS, 913
circuitry, 1041.3
circular, 280.11
CIRCULARITY, 280
circulatory, 2.31
circumscribe, 210.4
circumscribed, 210.6
CIRCUMSCRIPTION, 210
CIRCUMSTANCE, 765
circumstances, 765.2
circumstantial, 765.7
circumvention, 415.5
circus artist, 707.3
citation, 646.4, 956.5
cite, 956.13
citizen, 227.4
citizenship, 226.2
CITY, 230
city planning, 230.10
claim, 376.2, 421.6
claimed, 421.10
clairvoyant, 689.14
clap, 159.13
clash, 35.14, 61.2
clashing, 61.5
class, 572.11, 607.1, 808.2
classical music, 708.6
classification, 800.3
CLASSIFICATION, 808
classified, 808.8
classify, 800.8, 808.6, 807.11
clay, 742.3
clean, 79.18, 79.25
cleaned, 79.26
cleaner, 79.14
cleanly, 79.29
CLEANNESS, 79
cleanser, 79.17
cleansing, 79.2, 79.28
cleanup, 807.6
clear, 521.11
clear-sighted, 27.21
clear-witted, 919.13
cleave, 224.4
clef, 709.13
cleft, 224.7
CLERGY, 699
clergyman, 699.2
clerical, 547.28
clicking, 55.2
climate, 977.5
climax, 75.23
climb, 193.11
climber, 193.6
clique, 617.6
cliquish, 617.18
cloak, 5.12, 5.39
clockwise, 161.24
cloister, 703.6

close, 293.6, 293.12, 819.3
close attention, 982.4
closed, 293.9
closet, 197.15
CLOSURE, 293
clot, 1043.7
clothe, 5.38
clothier, 5.32
CLOTHING, 5, 5.44
cloture, 856.5
CLOUD, 319, 319.6
cloudiness, 319.3
cloudy, 319.7
clownish, 489.16
club, 901.20
clue, 517.9
clumsily, 414.24
clumsiness, 414.3
clutch, 1039.6
clutches, 474.4
coal, 1018.16
coarse, 497.11
coarsen, 294.4
coarseness, 497.2
coast, 182.39
coastal, 234.7
coastward, 182.67
coat, 295.24
cock, 76.8
code, 345.10, 673.5
coded, 345.16
codex, 547.11
codify, 673.9
coerce, 424.7
coercion, 424.3
coercive, 424.12
coffin, 309.11
cognitive, 930.21
cognizance, 927.2
cognizant of, 927.16
cohabit, 563.17
cohere, 802.6
COHESION, 802
cohesive, 802.10
coil, 281.2
coiled, 281.7
coin, 728.28
coincide, 777.4, 835.4
coinciding, 777.8
coiner, 728.25
coining, 728.24
COLD, 1022, 1022.14, 1022.16
cold-blooded, 1022.20
cold weather, 1022.3
collaborator, 616.4
collapse, 85.8, 260.4, 260.10, 410.3
collate, 942.5
collateral, 438.3
collation, 942.2
collect, 472.11
collection, 472.2, 769.11

collector, 769.15
college, 567.5
college student, 572.5
collide, 901.13
COLOR, 35, 35.8, 35.13
color blindness, 30.3
colored, 35.16
colorful, 35.18
coloring, 35.11
colorless, 36.7
COLORLESSNESS, 36
comb, 79.21
COMBATANT, 461
COMBINATION, 804
combine, 804.3
combined, 804.5
combining, 804.7
come, 838.6
come across, 940.3
comedian, 707.9
comedy, 704.6
comeliness, 1015.3
comely, 1015.18
come out, 348.6, 352.16
COMFORT, 121, 121.6
comfortable, 121.11
comfortably, 121.14
comforter, 121.5
comforting, 121.13
comic, 488.6, 704.35
comicalness, 488.2
COMMAND, 420, 420.8
commanding, 420.13
commend, 509.11
commendation, 509.3
commender, 509.8
comment, 341.5
commentary, 556.2
commentator, 556.4
comment upon, 341.11
COMMERCE, 731
commercial, 731.21, 1033.20
commercialism, 731.12
commercialization, 731.13
COMMISSION, 615, 615.10
commissioned, 615.19
commissioned officer, 575.18
commit, 429.17, 436.5, 478.16
commitment, 429.4, 478.2
commit suicide, 308.21
committee, 423.2
commodity, 735.2
common, 497.14
commoner, 572.7
common man, 606.5
commonness, 497.5
commotion, 809.4
communal, 476.9
communicability, 343.4

communicable, 343.11
communicate, 343.6, 343.7
communicate with, 343.8
COMMUNICATION, 343
COMMUNICATIONS, 343.5, 347
communicative, 343.10
communion, 476.2
communism, 611.5
Communist, 611.13, 611.21
community, 617.2
communize, 476.7
COMPACT, 437
companion, 588.3
company, 617.9, 768.2, 769.3
comparability, 942.3
comparative, 942.8
comparatively, 942.10
compare, 942.4
compared to, 942.11
compare notes, 942.6
COMPARISON, 942
compartment, 197.2
compass, 574.9
compel, 424.4
compensate, 338.4
compensating, 338.6
COMPENSATION, 338
compete, 457.18
competent, 413.24
competition, 457.2
competitive, 457.23
competitor, 452.2
compilation, 554.7
complacency, 107.2
complacent, 107.10
complain, 115.15
complaint, 115.4
complete, 407.6, 407.12, 793.6, 793.9, 819.7
completed, 407.11
completely, 793.14
COMPLETENESS, 793
completing, 407.9, 793.10
completion, 407.2, 793.4
complex, 92.22, 798.2, 798.4
COMPLEXITY, 798
compliance, 427.2
complicate, 798.3
compliment, 509.6, 509.14
complimentary ticket, 634.2
component, 795.2, 795.5
compose, 548.16, 708.46, 795.3
composed, 106.13
composed of, 795.4
composer, 710.20
COMPOSITION, 548.2, 795
composure, 106.2

compound, 796.5
comprehensive, 771.7
COMPROMISE, 468, 468.2
COMPULSION, 424
compulsively, 424.13
compulsory, 424.10
compunction, 113.2
compute, 253.6
computer, 1040.17, 1041.2
COMPUTER SCIENCE, 1041
computerize, 1041.18
computerized, 1041.19
concave, 284.16
CONCAVITY, 284
conceal, 346.6
concealed, 346.11
concealing, 346.15
CONCEALMENT, 346
conceit, 140.4
conceited, 140.11
conceive, 78.11
concentrate, 930.10
concentric, 208.14
conception, 78.4
concern, 126.4
concertmaster, 710.19
conciliar, 423.5
concise, 537.6
concisely, 537.7
CONCISENESS, 537
conclude, 945.10
conclusion, 934.8, 945.4
concoction, 405.3
concur, 332.9, 898.2
CONCURRENCE, 898
concurrent, 898.4
concurrently, 898.5
concussive, 901.24
condemn, 602.3
condemn to death, 308.19
CONDEMNATION, 602
condemnatory, 510.22, 602.5
condescend, 137.8
condescension, 137.3
condition, 958.2
conditional, 764.6, 958.8
conditionally, 958.11
conditioning, 92.26
CONDOLENCE, 147
condone, 134.7, 148.4
conduct, 708.45
conductance, 1032.9
conduction, 1031.13
conductor, 710.17
cone, 282.5
confer, 541.11
conference, 541.6
confess, 351.7, 701.17
confession, 351.3
confessional, 351.11
confidence, 969.5

confidence game, 356.10
confident, 969.21
confidential, 345.14
confidentially, 345.20
confine, 212.6, 429.12
confined, 429.19
CONFINEMENT, 429
confirm, 956.11
confirmation, 956.4
confirmed, 373.19
confirming, 956.18
conform, 579.4, 866.3
conformist, 866.2, 866.6
CONFORMITY, 866
confound, 944.3
confront, 216.8, 451.5
confuse, 810.3, 984.7
confused, 809.16, 984.12
CONFUSION, 809.2, 984, 984.3
conglomeration, 802.5
congratulate, 149.2
CONGRATULATION, 149
congratulations!, 149.4
congratulatory, 149.3
conical, 282.12
conjecture, 950.11
conjure, 690.11
connoisseur, 496.7
conquer, 412.10
conquered, 412.17
conscience, 636.5
conscientious, 644.15
conscientiousness, 644.2
consecutive, 811.9
consecutively, 811.11
consensus, 787.3
CONSENT, 441, 441.2
consenting, 441.4
consentingly, 441.5
consequently, 886.7
conservatism, 611.1, 852.3
conservative, 611.9, 611.17, 852.4, 852.8
consider, 930.12
considerate, 143.16
considerately, 143.21
considerateness, 143.3
consideration, 930.2
consistency 787.1, 802.2
consistent 787.9, 802.11
consolation, 121.4
conspicuous, 348.12
conspicuously, 348.16
conspicuousness, 348.4
constancy, 846.2
constant, 846.5
constantly, 846.7
constellation, 1070.5
constitution, 673.6
construct, 266.5
constructional, 891.15
consumable, 388.2, 388.6

dirt, 80.6
dirty, 80.15, 80.22
disable, 19.9
disabled, 19.16
DISACCORD, 456, 589.2
disadvantage, 995.2
disadvantageous, 995.6
disagree, 456.8, 788.5
disagree with, 82.4
disagreeing, 788.6
DISAGREEMENT, 456.2, 788
disappear, 34.2
DISAPPEARANCE, 34
disappoint, 132.2
disappointed, 132.5
disappointing, 132.6
DISAPPOINTMENT, 132
DISAPPROVAL, 510
disapprove, 510.10
disapproving, 510.21
disarm, 465.11
disarmament, 465.6
disarrange, 810.2
disarranged 809.13, 810.5
DISARRANGEMENT, 810
disassemble, 801.15
disastrous, 1010.15
disastrously, 1010.18
disband, 770.8
disbelieve, 695.14, 954.5
discard, 390.3, 390.7
discarded, 390.11
discerning, 943.8
discernment, 943.2
discharge, 1031.6
disciple, 572.2
disclose, 351.4
DISCLOSURE, 351
disconsolate, 112.28
DISCONTENT, 108
discontented, 108.7
discontinue, 812.3
discontinuous, 812.4
DISCORD, 61
DISCOUNT, 631, 631.2, 728.27
discourteous, 505.4
discourteously, 505.8
DISCOURTESY, 505
discover, 940.2
DISCOVERY, 940
discriminate, 943.4
discriminate against, 979.8
discriminating, 943.7
DISCRIMINATION, 943, 979.4
discriminatory, 979.12
discursive, 538.13
discuss, 541.12
discussion, 541.7
disdain, 157.3
disdainful, 141.13

DISEASE, 85
diseased, 85.59
disembodied, 987.8
disgorge, 908.25
disgrace, 661.5, 661.8
disgraceful, 661.11
disgracefully, 661.16
disguise, 786.3
disguised, 346.13
disgust, 64.4
dish 11.1, 10.7
dishabille, 5.20
disheveled, 809.14
dishonest, 645.16
dishonestly, 645.24
disillusion, 976.2
disillusioned, 976.5
disillusioning, 976.4
DISILLUSIONMENT, 976
disincline, 379.4
disintegrate, 805.3
DISINTEGRATION, 805
disjointedly, 801.28
disk, 1041.6
DISLIKE, 99, 99.3, 103.6
disliked, 99.9
dislocate, 160.5
dislocated, 160.9
dislocation, 160.1
dislodge, 160.6
dismay, 127.19
dismiss, 908.18, 908.19, 983.4
dismissal, 908.5
DISOBEDIENCE, 327
disobedient, 327.8
disobediently, 327.12
disobey, 327.6
DISORDER, 809, 809.9
disorderly, 809.13
disparage, 512.8
DISPARAGEMENT, 512
disparager, 512.6
disparaging, 512.13
disperse, 770.4
dispersed, 770.9
DISPERSION, 770
displaced person, 160.4
DISPLACEMENT, 160
display, 348.2, 501.4
dispose, 807.9
disposed, 977.8
disposition, 977.3
dispossess, 480.23
DISPROOF, 957
disprove, 957.4
disproved, 957.7
dispute, 457.21
disqualify, 19.11
disregard, 435.3
disreputable, 661.10
disreputably, 661.15
DISREPUTE, 661

DISRESPECT, 156, 156.4, 505.2
disrespectful, 156.7
disrobing, 6.2
disruption, 801.3
dissatisfy, 108.5
dissect, 801.17
dissection, 801.5
dissension, 456.3
DISSENT, 333, 333.4
dissenter, 333.3
dissenting, 333.6
dissimilar, 786.4
DISSIMILARITY, 786
dissipate, 669.6, 770.5
dissipation, 669.2
dissociate, 805.4
dissociation, 92.20, 805.2
dissonant, 61.4
dissuade, 379.3
DISSUASION, 379
dissuasive, 379.5
DISTANCE, 261, 261.3
distant, 261.8
distended, 259.13
distension, 259.2
distill, 88.30
distillery, 88.21
distinct, 31.7
distinction, 662.5, 943.3
distinctness, 31.2
distinguish between, 943.6
distinguished, 662.16
distort, 265.5
distorted, 265.10
DISTORTION, 265
distract, 984.6
distracted, 984.10
DISTRACTION, 984
distress, 96.16, 98.14
distressed, 96.22
distressing, 98.20
distressingly, 98.28, 247.21
distribution, 477.2
dither, 105.6
dive, 184.41
diver, 367.4
diverge, 171.5
DIVERGENCE, 171
diverging, 171.8
diversified, 782.4
diversify, 781.2, 782.2
divest, 6.5
divested, 6.12
dividend, 624.7, 738.7
divination, 689.10, 961.2
divine, 677.16, 678.16
diviner 689.16
diving, 367.3
DIVORCE, 566, 566.5
divorcé, 566.2
divulge, 351.5
divulgence, 351.2

dizziness, 984.4
dizzy, 984.15, 984.8
do, 328.6
docile, 433.13
doctor, 90.4
doctrinal, 952.27
doctrine, 676.2
document, 549.5
documentary, 549.18
dodge, 368.8
DOER, 726
dog, 311.17
dogmatic, 969.22
domesticate, 432.11
domesticated, 228.34
domesticity, 228.3
dominance, 417.6
dominate, 612.15
domineer, 612.16
don, 5.42
donation, 478.6
done, 11.7
doomsday, 838.3
doorkeeper, 1007.12
dose, 86.6, 87.19, 792.5
double, 872.5, 873.4, 987.3
DOUBLENESS, 872
doubly, 873.5
doubt, 954.2, 954.6
doubted, 954.12
doubter, 954.4
doubtful, 970.17
doubting, 954.9
down, 3.19, 194.13
downcast, 194.12
downhill, 204.16
downright, 247.12
downtrodden, 432.16
dowsing, 961.3
draft, 275.6
drag, 184.27
draggle, 80.19
drain, 239.5
dramatic, 704.33
dramatics, 704.2
dramatist, 704.22
dramatize, 704.28, 996.16
draw in, 187.12
drawing, 192.3, 712.13, 712.5
draw off, 192.12
dreadfulness, 98.3
dream, 985.9, 985.17
dreamy, 985.25
dregs, 256.2
dress, 5.16
dressed up, 5.45
dressing, 86.33
dressmaker, 5.35
dress up, 5.41
drier, 1064.4, 1064.9
drift, 184.28
drink, 8.4, 8.29, 88.7, 88.9

drinkable, 8.34
drinker, 88.11
drinking, 8.3, 88.4
drink to, 88.29
drive, 756.4, 1041.5, 1068.8
driver, 178.9, 178.10
drive out, 908.14
drollery, 489.3
drooping, 202.10
drop, 282.3, 912.7
drowned, 307.32
drown out, 53.8
drudge, 725.14, 726.3
drug, 86.5, 87.2
drugstore, 86.36
drum, 55.4
drummer, 710.10
dry, 1064.6, 1064.7
dry goods, 735.3
drying, 1064.3, 1064.10
DRYNESS, 1064
duct, 2.21
dudgeon, 152.7
due, 623.10, 639.2, 639.7, 639.10
duel, 457.7
DUENESS, 639
dull, 94.7, 117.6, 921.16, 1026.10
DULLNESS, 117, 1026.5
dully, 117.10
duly, 639.11
DUPE, 358
duplicate, 784.3, 873.3
DUPLICATION, 873
durability, 826.1
durable, 826.10
DURATION, 826
during, 820.14
dusk, 315.3
dutiful, 641.13
dutifully, 641.18
DUTY, 641
dwarf, 258.5, 258.13
dwell on, 848.9
dying, 307.33
dynamic, 1038.9
dynamics, 18.7
each, 864.19
eager, 101.8
eagerly, 101.13
EAGERNESS, 101
ear, 2.10, 48.7, 310.27
eared, 48.15
earlier, 844.10
EARLINESS, 844
early, 844.7, 844.11
early bird, 844.4
early death, 307.5
earshot, 48.4
EARTH SCIENCE, 1069
Earth, 1070.10
earthy, 234.5

easily, 1013.16
east, 161.17
easy, 1013.13
eat, 8.20
eater, 8.16
EATING, 8, 8.31
eccentric, 160.12, 926.3, 926.5
ECCENTRICITY, 926
ecclesiastic, 698.13
ECCLESIASTICAL
   ATTIRE, 702
eclipse, 1026.8
economic, 731.22
economical, 635.6
economically, 635.7
ECONOMICS, 731, 731.10
economist, 731.11
economize, 635.4
economizer, 635.3
economizing, 635.2
economy, 731.7
eddy, 238.12, 238.21
edge, 285.2
edging, 211.7
edible, 8.33
edition, 554.5
educated, 570.16
educational, 568.18
eeriness, 987.4
EFFECT, 886
effectual, 387.21
effeminate, 77.14
egotist, 140.5
egress, 190.2
eject, 908.13
EJECTION, 908
elaborate, 860.6
elapse, 820.5
elastic, 1046.3, 1046.7
ELASTICITY, 1046
elate, 109.8
elect, 371.12, 371.20
election, 371.9, 609.15
electioneering, 609.12
elective, 371.22
electorate, 609.22
electric, 1031.29
ELECTRICITY, 1031
electrify, 1031.25
electronic, 1032.15
ELECTRONICS, 1032
ELEGANCE, 533
elegant, 496.9, 533.6
element, 209.4, 1058.2
elemental, 678.6
elementary education, 568.5
elementary school, 567.3
elephantlike, 311.45
elevate, 911.5
elevating, 911.10
ELEVATION, 911

elevator, 911.4
eleventh hour, 315.5
elicit, 192.14
eligibility, 371.11
eligible, 371.24
eliminate, 772.5
elimination, 772.2
ELOQUENCE, 544
eloquent, 544.8
eloquently, 544.15
emaciation, 270.6
emasculation, 19.5
embalming, 397.3
embark, 188.15
embarkation, 182.5, 188.3
embattled, 458.23
embodied, 1050.11
embodiment, 762.4
embody, 762.5
emboss, 283.12
embrace, 562.3, 562.18
embryo, 305.14
embryonic, 305.22
emerge, 190.11
EMERGENCE, 190
emerging, 190.18
emetic, 86.18, 86.49
emigrate, 190.16
emigration, 190.7
eminent, 247.9, 662.18
emotional, 93.17
emphasize, 996.14
emphatic, 996.21
employ, 615.14
employed, 615.20
EMPLOYEE, 577, 577.3
empower, 18.10
empowerment, 18.8
empty-headedness, 921.6
emulate, 336.7
emulsify, 1060.10
emulsion, 1060.7
enact, 704.30
enamor, 104.23
enamored, 104.28
enchanted, 691.12
encircle, 209.7
encircled, 209.11
enclose, 212.5
enclosed, 212.10
enclosing, 212.11
ENCLOSURE, 196.6, 212, 212.3
encore, 848.6
encore!, 848.18
encounter, 457.15
encourage, 375.21, 492.16
encouragement, 492.9
END, 395.2, 819, 819.5
endanger, 1005.6
endearing, 104.25
ENDEARMENT, 562, 562.5

ENDEAVOR, 403, 403.5
ended, 819.8
ending, 819.10
endorser, 332.7
endow, 478.17
endowed, 478.26
endowment, 478.9
endure, 134.5, 826.6
enemy, 589.6
energetic, 17.13
energetically, 17.16
energize, 17.10
energizer, 17.6
energizing, 17.15, 17.8
ENERGY, 17
engage, 457.16
engagement, 615.4, 704.11
engender, 817.14
engineer, 178.12, 461.14, 726.7
engineering, 1038.6
engrave, 713.9
engraved, 713.11
engraving, 713.2
engross, 982.13
engrossed, 982.17
engrossing, 982.20
enigma, 522.8
enigmatic, 522.17
enjoy, 95.12
enjoy oneself, 95.13
enlarge, 259.4, 259.5
enlist, 615.17
enlisted man, 461.8
enlistment, 615.7
ENMITY, 103.2, 589
enough!, 993.8
enrage, 152.25
enrich, 618.9
ensuring, 969.8
entail, 771.4
entailment, 771.2
enter, 189.7, 817.9
entering, 189.12
enterprise, 330.7
enterprising, 330.23, 404.8
entertain, 585.8
ENTERTAINER, 707
entertainment, 743.13
enthusiast, 101.4
enthusiastic, 101.10
ENTRANCE, 189, 189.5
entreat, 440.11
entreaty, 440.2
entree, 187.3
entrenchment, 460.5
entry, 628.5
envious, 154.4
ENVIRONMENT, 209, 1071
environmental, 209.9, 765.8

environmental disease, 85.32
environmentalist, 1071.3
ENVY, 154, 154.3
ephemeron, 827.5
epidemic, 85.5
epitaph, 309.18
equable, 670.13
equal, 789.4, 789.5, 789.7
EQUALITY, 789
equalize, 789.6
equally, 789.11
equanimity, 106.3
equating, 789.2
equinox, 313.7
equip, 385.8
EQUIPMENT, 385, 385.4
equivalent, 789.8
equivocate, 539.3
era, 823.5
eradicator, 395.9
erect, 200.9
erection, 200.4
err, 974.9
errand boy, 353.4
erroneous, 974.16
erroneously, 974.20
ERROR, 974
erupt, 671.13
ESCAPE, 369, 369.6
escaped, 369.11
escapee, 369.5
escort, 768.5, 768.8
espouse, 509.13
essence, 766.2
essential, 192.18, 766.9
essentially, 766.11
establish, 159.16, 891.10
established, 854.13
establishment, 159.7, 891.4
estate, 228.7, 471.4
esteem, 662.3
estimate, 945.3, 945.9
et cetera, 253.14
etch, 713.10
ethical, 636.6
ETHICS, 636
etiquette, 580.3
etymology, 526.15
eureka!, 940.11
evacuate, 908.22
evacuation, 908.6
evade, 368.7
evangelist, 684.2, 699.6
evasive, 368.15
EVENING, 315, 315.2, 315.8
EVENT, 830, 830.2
eventful, 830.10, 830.11
eventually, 830.12
every, 863.15
everywhere, 158.12
evict, 908.15

fallibility, 970.7
fallible, 970.22
falling-out, 456.4
fall out, 456.10
fallow, 406.14
fall through, 910.3
false, 354.25
false alarm, 400.2
falsehearted, 354.31
falsely, 354.35
FALSENESS, 354
falsified, 265.11
falsify, 354.16
familiar, 587.19
familiar spirit, 678.12
familiarity, 587.5
family, 559.5
famously, 662.21
fan, 318.19
fanatic, 925.18, 925.32
fanaticism, 925.11
fanciful, 985.20
fancy, 975.3
fantastic, 869.12
far, 261.15
far and wide, 261.16
farewell!, 188.22
farfetched, 775.8
farm, 1068.5, 1067.8, 1067.16
farmstead, 228.6
farsightedness, 28.4
farthest, 261.12
fascinate, 377.7
FASHION, 578
fashionable, 578.11
fashionably, 578.17
fast, 174.15, 515.2, 515.4, 708.25, 799.14
fast day, 515.3
fasten, 799.7
fastening, 799.3
fastidious, 495.9
fastidiously, 495.14
FASTIDIOUSNESS, 495
FASTING, 515, 515.5
fat, 7.7
fatality, 308.7
fate, 963.2
Fates, 963.3
father, 560.9
fatherland, 232.2
FATIGUE, 21, 21.4
fatiguing, 21.13
fatten, 259.8
fault, 1002.2
faultfinder, 510.9
favor, 650.8, 893.2
favorable, 449.22
favorite, 104.16
fawn, 138.7
FEAR, 127, 127.10
fearful, 127.23

fearfully, 127.32
fearlessness, 492.3
feast, 8.9, 8.24
feather, 3.16, 3.21
feathered, 3.28
feathery, 3.27
feature, 996.7, 996.15
feces, 12.4
FEE, 624.5, 630, 630.6
feebleminded, 921.21
feed, 8.18, 8.28, 10.4
feedback, 1040.6
feel, 93.10
feeler, 73.4, 941.4
FEELING, 93
feline, 311.41
fell, 912.5
fellowship, 587.2, 617.3
female, 77.4
feminine, 77.13
FEMININITY, 77
feminization, 77.11
feminize, 77.12
fence, 212.4, 212.7, 732.6
fencing, 457.8
fend off, 460.10
fertilization, 78.3, 889.3
fertilize, 78.10, 889.8
fertilizer, 889.4
fertilizing, 889.11
fervent, 93.18
fervently, 93.26
fester, 12.15
festering, 12.21
festival, 743.4
festive, 743.28
festivity, 743.3
fetch, 176.16
fever, 85.7
feverish, 85.57
few, 884.2, 884.4
fewer, 884.6
FEWNESS, 884
fiancé, 104.17
fiasco, 410.6
fickle, 364.6
FICTION, 722
fictional, 722.7
fictitious, 985.21
fidelity, 644.7
fidget, 128.6
fiducial, 952.25
field, 724.4, 1067.9
fiery, 671.22, 1018.26
fifth, 881.17
fight, 457.4, 754.3, 754.4
figment of the imagination, 985.5
figurative, 536.3
figuratively, 536.4
figure, 262.4, 349.6, 498.9
figurehead, 575.5
FIGURE OF SPEECH, 536

figures, 1016.13
FILAMENT, 271
file, 811.7
filial, 561.7
fill, 196.7, 793.7
film, 706.7, 714.10
filth, 80.7
filthy, 80.23
final, 819.11
finally, 819.12
FINANCE, 729, 729.15
financer, 729.9
FINANCIAL CREDIT, 622
financial district, 737.8
financing, 729.2
find, 472.6
find fault, 510.15
fine, 603.3, 603.5, 1015.19
finery, 5.10, 498.3
finger, 73.5
finical, 495.10
finishing touch, 407.3
fire, 1018.13
fire fighter, 1021.4
fireplace, 1019.11
fireproof, 1021.6, 1021.10
fireworks, 1018.17
firm, 15.18, 359.12, 425.7
firmly, 425.9
firmness, 15.3, 359.2, 425.2
first, 817.3, 817.17, 817.18
first name, 527.4
first-rate, 998.17
fish, 10.23, 382.10
fisher, 382.6
fishing, 382.3
fishlike, 311.48
fission, 1037.8
fist, 462.4
fit, 152.8, 405.8
FITNESS, 84, 787.5
fitted, 405.17
fitting, 405.2
fix, 854.9
fixation, 92.21
fixed, 854.14
flaccid, 1045.10
flag, 647.6
flake, 296.3
flaky, 296.7
flammable, 1019.28
flare, 1018.14
flare up, 152.19
flash, 1024.6
flashing, 1024.34
flatter, 511.5
flatter oneself, 502.8
flatterer, 511.4
flattering, 511.8
FLATTERY, 511
flaunt, 501.17
flavor, 63.7
flavored, 62.9

flavorful, 63.9
flavoring, 63.3
fledgling, 302.10
flee, 368.10
flicker, 1024.8, 1024.25
flickering, 1024.36
flight, 184.9, 368.4
flighty, 984.17
flinch, 127.13
fling out, 188.11
flirt, 562.11, 562.20
flirtation, 562.9
flit, 827.6
float, 180.11, 182.54
floating, 182.60
flock, 769.5
flood, 1063.14
flooded, 238.25
floodgate, 239.11
floor, 197.23, 295.22
floral, 310.35
flounder, 916.8, 916.15
flout, 454.4
flow, 184.29, 238.4, 238.16
flow in, 189.9
flower, 310.22, 310.32
flowering, 310.24
flowing, 172.8, 238.24
fluency, 544.2
fluent, 544.9
fluffy, 1045.14
fluid, 1059.2, 1059.4
flunk, 410.17
flutter, 916.4, 916.12
fluttering, 916.18
fly, 184.36
flying, 184.50
flying saucer, 1073.3
foam, 320.2, 320.5
foamy, 320.7
focal, 208.13
focus, 208.10
focus on, 936.3
fog, 319.2
foggy, 319.9
foist, 775.5
FOLD, 291, 291.5
folded, 291.7
folding, 291.4
foliage, 310.16
folk music, 708.11
follow, 166.3
follower, 166.2
follower, 616.8
FOLLOWING, 166, 166.5
folly, 922.4
fond of, 104.30
FOOD, 10
FOOL, 356.15, 923
foolable, 922.12
foolhardy, 493.9
foolish, 922.8
foolishly, 922.13

FOOLISHNESS, 922
foot, 199.5
FOOTBALL, 746
footing, 900.5
footwear, 5.27
foppery, 500.4
foppish, 500.17
for, 449.26
force, 424.2
forcibly, 424.14
forebode, 133.11
foreboding, 133.2
foregoing, 836.11
foreknowledge, 960.3
foresee, 960.5
foreseeable 960.8
foreshow, 133.10
FORESIGHT, 960
forest god, 678.11
forestry, 1067.3
foretaste, 960.4
forethought, 960.2
forever, 828.2, 828.12
forewarn, 399.6
forewarning, 399.2, 399.8
forget, 148.5, 989.5
forgetful, 989.9
forgettable, 989.10
forgive, 148.3
forgiven, 148.7
forgiving, 148.6
forgotten, 989.8
fork, 171.4, 171.7
forked, 171.10
forlorn, 584.12
FORM, 262, 262.6, 262.7,
   262.8, 709.11, 806.5
formal, 580.7
formalism, 580.2
FORMALITY, 580
formalize, 580.5
formally, 580.11
formative, 262.9
former, 813.5, 836.10
formerly, 836.13
formless, 263.4
forms, 1041.10
formula, 419.3
forth, 190.21
fortification, 460.4
fortified, 460.12
fortify, 460.9
fortitude, 492.6
fortunate, 1009.14
fortunately, 1009.16
forum, 423.3
forward, 162.8
foster, 449.16
foundation, 900.6
foundry, 739.4
fountainhead, 885.6
fox, 311.20
fragile, 763.7

FRAGILITY, 1048
FRAGRANCE, 70
fragrant, 70.9
frail, 16.14
frailty, 16.2
frame, 266.4, 900.10
fraud, 356.8
fraught, 793.12
freak, 926.4
freakish, 869.13
free, 430.21
free agent, 430.12
free and clear, 469.12
FREEDOM, 430
free-for-all, 457.5
freehold, 471.5, 471.10
freeloader, 634.3
freely, 430.32
freeman, 430.11
freethinker, 695.13
free will, 430.6
freeze, 1022.9, 1022.10,
   1023.11
freezer, 1023.5
freight, 176.6
frenzied, 105.25
frenzy, 925.7
FREQUENCY, 846,
   1033.12
frequent, 221.10, 846.4
frequently, 846.6
fresh, 83.13, 840.8
friability, 1049.3
FRICTION, 1042
FRIEND, 588
friendly, 587.15
friends with, 587.17
FRIENDSHIP, 587
frighten, 127.15
frightened, 127.25
frightener, 127.9
frightening, 127.6, 127.28
frighten off, 127.21
frightfully, 127.34
fritter away, 486.5
frolic, 743.5
from, 188.21
FRONT, 216, 216.10,
   609.33
front on, 216.9
frontier, 211.5
fronting, 216.11
frost, 1022.7, 1029.3
frosty, 1022.17
frozen, 1023.14
frozen out, 1022.19
fruit, 10.36
fruitless, 391.12
frustrating, 1011.20
frustration, 1011.3
FUEL, 1020, 1020.7,
   1020.8
fugitive, 368.5, 368.16

full, 793.11
fullness, 793.2
full size, 257.3
full-sized, 257.22
fully, 765.13
fun, 743.2
function, 387.5, 724.3
function as, 888.8
funds, 728.14
funeral, 309.5
fur, 4.2
furnish, 478.15
FURNITURE, 229, 735.5
FURROW, 290, 290.3
furrowed, 290.4
furtherance, 449.5
fury, 105.8, 680.10
fuse, 462.15
fusion, 1037.9
fussbudget, 495.7
futile, 125.13
futility, 391.2
FUTURE, 838, 838.8
futurity, 838.4
gaiety, 109.4
gaily, 109.18
gain, 472.3, 1031.16
gainful, 472.16
gains, 251.3
gait, 177.12
galaxy, 1070.6
gallant, 504.9, 504.15
gallantry, 504.2
gamble, 759.2, 759.23,
  970.8
gambler, 759.21
GAMBLING, 759
game, 743.9, 745.3, 746.3,
  748.2, 749.3, 749.6,
  750.2, 752.3
gape, 292.16
gaping, 292.2, 292.18
garage, 197.27
garden, 1067.10
garish, 35.19
garment, 5.3
garmentmaker, 5.33
garment making, 5.31
garner, 386.7
GAS, 1065, 1065.2
gate, 239.4
gaudy, 501.20
gay, 109.14
gaze, 27.5, 27.15
gear, 1039.5
gender, 530.10
genealogy, 549.9, 560.5
general, 863.11
GENERALITY, 863
generalization, 863.8
generalize, 863.9
generally, 863.17
genesis, 860.3

genetic, 78.16
genetic disease, 85.12
genetic material, 305.9
genital, 2.27
genitals, 2.11
genius, 919.8
gentile, 688.6
GENTRY, 608, 608.3
genuine, 972.15
genuinely, 972.19
geriatrics, 303.8
germ, 85.41
gestalt, 92.32
gesture, 517.14, 517.21
GI, 461.7
giant, 272.16
giantess, 257.13
gibe, 508.2
gift, 478.4
girl, 302.6
give, 478.12, 634.4
giveable, 478.23
give birth 1.3, 78.13
given, 478.24
giver, 478.11
give up, 370.7
GIVING, 478
gladden, 95.8
glance, 27.4, 27.17
glandular, 13.8
glare, 27.16
glass, 1028.5
glide, 177.35
glider, 181.12
gliding, 177.16
glitter, 1024.7, 1024.24
glittering, 1024.35
gloom, 112.7, 1026.4
gloomy, 112.24, 1026.14
glorification, 662.8, 696.2
glorify, 662.13, 696.11
glory, 247.2
glow, 1018.12
glum, 112.25
glumly, 112.35
glutton, 672.3
GLUTTONY, 672
gnarled, 288.8
go, 177.19
go away!, 908.31
goad, 375.8, 375.15
gobble, 8.23
go-between, 576.4
goblin, 680.8
God, 677.2, 678.2, 678.4
Godhead, 677.9
godliness, 692.2
godly, 692.9
gods, 678.1
godsend, 472.7
goer, 190.10
go for, 349.10
GOLF, 751

golfer, 751.2
gone, 34.4
good, 998.4, 998.12
GOOD PERSON, 659
GOODNESS, 998
goody!, 95.20
gore, 459.26
gorgeous, 1015.20
gossip, 552.7, 552.12
govern, 612.12, 893.8
governing, 612.18
GOVERNMENT, 612,
  612.3
GOVERNMENT
  ORGANIZATION, 613
governor, 575.6, 575.13
gradation, 245.3
gradual, 245.5
gradually, 175.14
graduate, 245.4, 572.8
graft, 191.6, 609.34
grain, 1049.6
GRAMMAR, 530
grammatical, 530.17
grandeur, 501.5
grandfather, 560.13
grandiloquent, 545.8
grandiose, 501.21
grandmother, 560.15
grant, 443.5
granular, 1049.12
grapevine, 552.10
GRAPHIC ARTS, 713
grass, 310.5
grassland, 310.8
grate, 58.10
grate on, 58.11
grateful, 150.5
gratify, 95.7
grating, 58.16
GRATITUDE, 150
gratuitous, 634.5
gratuitously, 634.6
gratuity, 478.5
gravel, 1057.3
graveyard, 309.15
gravitate, 297.15
gravity, 297.5, 996.3
gray, 39.3, 39.4
gray hair, 3.3
gray-haired, 39.5
great, 247.6
greatly, 247.15
GREATNESS, 247
greed, 100.8
greedily, 100.32
greedy, 100.27
Greek, 522.7
green, 44.3, 44.4, 310.7
greet, 585.10
greeting, 585.4
greetings, 585.3
greetings!, 585.15

grieve, 112.17
grill, 937.22
grilling, 937.13
grimace, 265.4, 265.8
grind, 287.8
groom, 79.20
grope, 937.32
grouping, 807.3
grove, 310.12
grow, 14.2, 251.6, 259.7, 272.12
growing, 1067.12
growl, 60.4
grown, 14.3, 259.12
GROWTH, 85.38, 259, 259.3, 310.2
grudge, 589.5
gruff, 505.7
gruffly, 505.9
grunt, 60.3
guarantor, 438.6
guard, 1007.9
guardian, 1007.6
guess, 950.4
guest, 585.6
guide, 573.9, 574.7
GUILT, 656
guilty, 656.3, 656.5
GULF, 242
gullible, 953.9
gum 1055, 1060.6
gun, 462.10
gunfire, 459.8
gust, 318.6
gustatory, 62.8
gutter, 239.3
HABIT, 373, 373.4
habitable, 225.15
HABITAT, 228, 228.18
HABITATION, 225
habitual, 373.15
habitually, 373.21
habituated, 373.18
hack writer, 547.16, 718.5
Hades, 682.3
haggard, 270.20
hail, 1022.6, 1022.11
hail!, 509.23
hair, 3.2
hairdo, 3.15
hairless, 6.17
hairlike, 3.23
hairy, 3.24
hale, 83.12
half, 874.2, 874.5
hall, 197.4
hallelujah!, 696.16
hallucination, 975.7
hallucinatory, 975.10
halo, 1024.14
halved, 874.6
hamper, 1011.11
hampering, 1011.18

hand, 183.6
handbook, 554.8
handcar, 179.16
handicap, 603.2
handle, 900.11
handwriting, 547.3
handy, 387.20, 1013.15
hang, 202.2, 202.6, 604.18
hangar, 184.24
hanger-on, 138.6
haphazard, 971.4
haphazardly, 809.18
happening, 830.9, 971.6
happily, 95.18
happiness, 95.2
happy, 95.15
harbinger, 133.5
harbor, 1008.6
hard, 1044.10
harden, 1044.7
hardened, 654.17, 1044.13
hardening, 1044.5, 1044.14
HARDNESS, 1044
hard times, 1010.6
hard work, 725.5
hare, 311.24
harem, 563.10
hark!, 48.16
harmful, 999.12
harmfully, 999.15
harmless, 998.21
harmonic, 709.16
HARMONICS, 709
harmonious, 533.8, 708.49
harmonize, 787.7, 708.35
harmony, 533.2, 708.3
harness, 385.5
harp, 711.3
harp on, 118.8
harsh, 144.24
harshly, 144.33
harshness, 98.4, 98.8, 144.9
harvest, 1067.15, 1067.19
HASTE, 401
hasten, 401.4
hastening, 401.3
hastily, 401.12
hasty, 401.9
HATE, 103, 103.5
hateful, 103.8
hater, 103.4
hating, 103.7
haul, 176.13
haunt, 987.6
haunted, 987.10
hazardous, 1005.10
head, 198.4, 198.6
headquarters, 208.6
heal, 396.21
healer, 90.9
HEALTH, 83
HEALTH CARE, 83.5, 90

health-care professional, 90.8
healthful, 81.5
healthiness, 83.2
health resort, 91.23
healthy, 83.8
hear, 48.11
HEARING, 48
hearken to, 982.7
hearse, 309.10
heart, 93.3
heartache, 112.9
heartless, 144.25
heartlessly, 144.34
heart-shaped, 279.15
HEAT, 1018, 1019.17
heated, 105.22, 1019.29
heater, 1019.10
HEATING, 1019, 1019.26
HEAVEN, 681
heavenly, 681.12
heavens, 1070.2
heavily, 297.21
heavy, 297.16
heavyweight, 257.12
heed, 982.6
HEIGHT, 272, 272.2
heighten, 272.13
heir, 479.5
HELL, 682
hellfire, 682.2
hellish, 682.8
helm, 573.5
helper, 449.7
helpful, 449.21
helpfully, 449.24
helpfulness, 449.10
helping, 449.20
helpless, 19.18
helplessness, 19.4
hemorrhage, 12.8
hence, 188.20, 887.7
henchman, 610.8
henpecked, 326.5
herald, 133.14, 353.2, 575.21
heraldic device, 647.2
herculean, 15.17
herder, 1068.3
here, 159.23, 221.16
hereafter, 681.2
hereditary, 560.19
heredity, 560.6
heresy, 688.2
heretic, 688.5
hermaphrodite, 75.30
hero, 492.8, 659.5
hesitant, 362.11
hesitate, 362.7
hesitation, 362.3
heterosexual, 75.13
hey!, 982.23
hibernate, 22.15

hide, 346.8
hideous, 1014.11
hideously, 1014.13
hierarchy, 698.7, 808.4
high, 58.13, 272.14
higher, 272.19
HIGHLANDS, 237, 272.3
hill, 237.4
hilly, 237.8, 272.18
hinder, 1011.10
hindering, 1011.17
HINDRANCE, 1011
hint, 248.4, 551.4, 551.9
hinterland, 233.2, 233.9
historian, 719.4
historical, 719.7
historically, 719.9
HISTORY, 719
hit, 901.4, 901.14
hitchhike, 177.31
hive, 739.2
ho hum!, 118.15
hoax, 356.7
HOCKEY, 749
hodgepodge, 796.6
hoggish, 80.24
hold, 474.2, 474.6, 474.7
hole, 292.3
holiday, 20.4
hollow, 284.13
Holy City, 681.3
holy day, 701.11
holy man, 659.6
holy orders, 698.10, 699.4
home, 228.2
homeless person, 331.10
homelike, 228.33
homicide, 308.2
homosexual, 75.14, 75.29
honest, 644.13, 644.16
honestly, 644.21
honesty, 644.3
honeymoon, 563.16
HONOR, 646, 646.8,
   662.12
honorary, 646.10
honored, 646.9
hoodwink, 356.17
hook, 799.8
hooked, 279.8
HOPE, 124, 124.7
hopeful, 124.11
hopefully, 124.14
hopeless, 125.12
hopelessly, 125.17
HOPELESSNESS, 125
horizon, 201.4
horizontal, 201.3, 201.7
horizontally, 201.9
horrid, 98.19
horridly, 98.27
horse, 311.10
HORSE RACING, 757

horticultural, 1067.21
horticulture, 1067.2
hosiery, 5.28
hospitable, 585.11
hospitably, 585.13
hospital room, 197.25
hospital, 91.21
HOSPITALITY, 585
host, 585.5
hostile, 589.10
hostility, 451.2, 589.3, 99.2
hot, 1018.25
hot-tempered, 110.25
hot water, 1018.10
hot weather, 1018.7
hot wind, 318.7
house, 225.10, 228.5
housed, 225.14
householder, 227.7
housing, 225.3
hovel, 228.11
how, 384.9
howling, 60.6
huge, 257.20
hugeness, 257.7
hull, 295.16
hum, 52.7, 52.13
human, 312.13
humanism, 312.11
humanize, 312.12
HUMANKIND, 312
humanly, 312.17
human nature, 312.6
human rights, 642.3
humble, 137.10
humbled, 137.13
humbly, 137.16
humbug, 354.14
humidity, 1063.2
humiliate, 137.4
humiliated, 137.14
humiliating, 137.15
humiliation, 137.2
HUMILITY, 137
humming, 52.20
HUMOR, 489
humorist, 489.12
humorous, 488.4
humpbacked, 265.13
hunch, 933.3
hunger, 100.19
hungry, 100.25
hunt, 382.9
hunter, 311.13, 382.5
hunting, 382.2
hurdy-gurdy, 711.14
hurl at, 459.28
hurried, 401.11
husband, 563.7
husk, 6.9
hustle, 330.13
hut, 228.9
hybrid, 796.8, 796.15

hybridize, 796.13
hygiene, 81.2
hygienist, 81.3
hypnosis, 22.7
hypnotic, 22.24
hypnotism, 22.8
hypnotist, 22.9
hypochondria, 112.4
hypocrisy, 354.6
hypocrite, 357.8
hypocritic, 354.33
ice, 10.45, 1022.5
iconoclasm, 695.9
IDEA, 931
ideal, 785.4, 985.23
idealism, 985.7
idealist, 1051.8
idealize, 985.16
identical, 777.7
identically, 777.9
identification, 517.11,
   777.2
identify, 777.5
ideology, 931.8
idiomatic, 523.20
idiot, 923.8
idle, 331.12, 331.18
idleness, 331.2
idler, 331.8
idling, 331.4
idol, 697.3
idolatrize, 697.5
idolatrous, 697.7
IDOLATRY, 697
if, 958.14
ignite, 1019.22
ignition, 1019.4
ignoramus, 929.8
IGNORANCE, 929
ignorant, 929.12
ill, 85.55
illegal, 674.6
illegally, 674.8
illegible, 522.19
illegitimacy, 674.2
illegitimate, 674.7
ill humor, 110.1
ill-humored, 110.18
illogical, 935.11
illogically, 935.15
ill-time, 843.3
illuminate, 1024.28
illuminated, 1024.39
illuminating, 1024.40
ILLUSION, 975
illusory, 975.9
illustrious, 662.19
image, 349.5, 349.11
imaginable, 985.26
imaginary, 985.19
IMAGINATION, 985
imaginative, 985.18
imagine, 985.14

nobleman, 608.4
noblewoman, 608.6
nobody, 222.6, 997.7
nocturnal, 315.9
node, 283.5
noise, 53.3
noisemaker, 53.6
noisy, 53.13
nomad, 178.4
NOMENCLATURE, 527
nominal, 527.15
nominate, 371.19
nomination, 371.8, 609.11
nonchalance, 106.5
nonchalant, 106.15
noncombatant, 464.5
nonconformist, 788.9,
   867.3
NONCONFORMITY, 867
none, 761.4, 761.12
nonessential, 767.2
nonexistent, 761.8
nonobservant, 435.5
nonpartisan, 609.28,
   609.45
nonresident, 222.12
nonrestrictive, 430.25
nonsectarian, 675.27
nonsense, 520.2
nonsensical, 520.7
noodles, 10.32
nook, 197.3
NOON, 314, 314.5, 314.7
normal, 868.3, 868.8
NORMALITY, 868
normalization, 868.5
normalize, 868.6
normally, 868.10
north, 161.15
north wind, 318.9
nose, 283.8
nostrum, 86.2
notable, 996.19
notation, 709.12, 1016.2
NOTCH, 289, 289.4
note, 709.14
notebook, 549.11
nothing, 761.2
notions, 735.6
noun, 530.5
nourish, 7.15, 8.19
novel, 840.11
novelty, 840.2
novice, 572.9
now, 837.3, 840.16
noway, 248.11
nowhere, 222.17
nozzle, 239.9
nuclear, 208.12, 305.7,
   305.21, 1037.19
NUCLEAR PHYSICS, 1037
nudity, 6.3
numb, 94.8

number, 530.8, 883.2,
   1016.16, 1016.3
numeration, 1016.9
numeric, 1016.22
numerous, 883.4
numerously, 883.12
numismatics, 728.22
nun, 699.17
nurse, 90.10, 1007.8
nursery, 1067.11
nut, 10.37
nutrient, 7.3
nutriment, 10.3
NUTRITION, 7
nutritionist, 7.13
nutritious, 7.19
nymph, 678.9
oaf, 923.5
oar, 180.15
oath, 334.4, 513.4
obdurate, 361.10
OBEDIENCE, 326
obedient, 326.3
obediently, 326.6
obeisance, 155.2
obey, 326.2
obituary, 307.14
object, 333.5, 1050.4
objection, 333.2
objective, 380.2
obligate, 641.12
obligation, 436.2
obligatory, 424.11, 641.15
oblige, 424.5, 449.19
obliged, 641.16
oblique, 204.9, 204.13
obliquely, 204.21
obliterate, 395.16
oblivious, 983.7
oblong, 267.9
obscene, 666.9
obscenity, 666.4
obscure, 522.15
obscuring, 1026.18
obscurity, 522.3
obsequious, 138.14
OBSERVANCE, 434
observant, 434.4
observation, 27.2
observation post, 27.8
observatory, 1070.17
observe, 434.2
obsess, 925.25
obsessed, 925.33
obsession, 925.13
obsessive, 925.34
obsolesce, 390.9
obsolete, 841.15
obstacle, 1011.4
OBSTINACY, 361
obstinate, 361.8
obstinately, 361.14
obstruct, 1011.12

obstruction, 293.3
obtainable, 472.14
obvious, 969.15
occasional, 847.3
occasionally, 847.5
o'clock, 831.16
occult, 689.23
OCCULTISM, 689
OCCUPATION, 724
occupational, 724.16
occupied, 724.15
occupy, 724.10
cccur, 830.5
occur to, 930.18
OCEAN, 240, 240.3
oceanic, 240.8
oceanography, 240.6
octave, 709.9
odd, 869.11
oddity, 869.3, 869.4, 869.5
oddly, 869.19
ODOR, 69
odorize, 69.7
odorless, 72.5
odorous, 69.9
off, 255.14
off-color, 35.20
offal, 80.9
offend, 152.21, 156.5,
   1014.5
offense, 152.2, 674.4
offensive, 98.18, 459.30
offensiveness, 98.2
OFFER, 439, 439.4
office, 739.7
officeholder, 610.11
official, 575.16
officiate, 724.13
offset, 338.2, 338.5, 778.4
offshoot, 561.4
oh!, 122.20
oil, 1054.1, 1054.8
oiliness, 1054.5
oily, 1054.9
ointment, 1054.3
old, 841.10
old age, 303.5
older, 841.19
old-fashioned, 841.16
old-fogyish, 841.17
old man, 304.2
OLDNESS, 841
old woman, 304.3
olfactory, 69.12
omen, 133.3
ominous, 133.17, 961.12
ominously, 133.19
omnipotence, 18.3
omnipotent, 18.13
omnipresent, 221.13
on, 295.37, 900.25
once, 836.14, 847.6
one, 871.3, 871.7

precautionary, 494.10
precede, 813.2
PRECEDENCE, 813
preceding, 813.4, 815.4
PRECEPT, 419
preceptive, 419.4
precious, 632.10
precious stone, 1057.6
precipice, 200.3
precipitate, 401.10, 1043.11
precipitation, 1043.5
PRECURSOR, 815
PREDETERMINATION, 963
predetermine, 963.6
predicament, 1012.4
predict, 961.9
predictable, 961.13
predicted, 961.14
PREDICTION, 961
predictor, 961.4
prefer, 371.17
preferable, 371.25
preferably, 371.28
preference, 371.5
prefix, 813.3
pregnancy, 78.5
pregnant, 78.18
prehensile, 474.9
prejudge, 946.2, 979.7
prejudged, 946.3
prejudice, 979.3, 979.9
preliminary, 817.16
premature, 844.8
prematurely, 844.13
premeditated, 380.9
premise, 934.7
PREMONITION, 133
PREPARATION, 405
preparatory, 405.20
prepare, 405.6
prepared, 405.16
prepare to, 405.10
PREROGATIVE, 642
preschool, 567.2
prescribe, 420.9
PRESENCE, 221
PRESENT, 221.12, 837, 837.2
PRESERVATION, 397
preservative, 397.4, 397.12
preserve, 397.7, 397.8, 397.9
preserved, 397.13
press, 287.6, 424.6, 548.11, 555.3
pressure group, 609.31
prestige, 417.4, 662.4
presto, 708.55, 851.13
presume, 640.6
presume on, 640.7
presumption, 640.2

presumptuous, 141.10
presumptuously, 141.16
pretensions, 501.2
PRETEXT, 376, 376.3
prevail, 863.10
prevalence, 863.2
prevalent, 863.12
prevaricate, 344.7
prevaricating, 344.11
prevent, 1011.14
prevention, 1011.2
preventive, 1011.19
previous, 833.4
previously, 833.6
prewar, 833.5
PRICE, 630, 630.11, 738.9
priced, 630.14
prickly, 285.10
PRIDE, 136, 140.2
priest, 699.5
prime, 405.9
primitive, 841.11
prince, 608.7
princess, 608.8
principal, 571.8
print, 517.7, 548.14, 548.3, 713.5, 714.5, 784.5
printed, 548.19
printed matter, 548.10
printer, 548.12
PRINTING, 548
prior to, 833.7
prison, 429.8
prisoner, 429.11
privacy, 345.2
private, 345.13, 584.9
privately, 345.19
privilege, 642.2
PROBABILITY, 967
probable, 967.6
probably, 967.8
probationary, 572.13
PROBITY, 644
process, 714.15, 888.2, 891.9
procession, 811.3
proclaim, 352.13
procrastinate, 845.11
procrastination, 845.5
procreate, 78.8
PROCREATION, 78, 78.2
procurer, 665.18
prodigal, 486.2, 486.8
produce, 889.7, 891.8
produced, 891.17
producer, 891.7
PRODUCT, 892
PRODUCTION, 704.13, 891, 891.2, 892.2
productive, 889.9
profane, 686.2
profession, 952.7
professional, 726.4

professionalism, 724.8
professionally, 724.18
professor, 571.3
profit, 472.12
profitably, 472.17
profligate, 665.25
prognosis, 91.13
program, 609.6
progress, 162.2
PROGRESSION, 162
progressive, 162.6
prohibit, 444.3
prohibited, 444.7
PROHIBITION, 444, 668.3
prohibitionist, 668.5, 668.11
prohibitive, 444.6
project, 381.2, 714.16, 903.11
projectile, 903.5, 903.15
projection, 285.4
projector, 714.12
proliferation, 889.2
prominent, 662.7
promise, 133.13, 436, 436.4
promised, 436.8
promising, 124.13
promissory, 436.7
promote, 446.2
PROMOTION, 352.5, 446
prompt, 375.13, 844.9
prompter, 375.10
promptly, 844.15
PROOF, 15.14, 548.5, 713.7, 956, 956.3
propaganda, 569.2
propagandize, 569.4
propeller, 903.6
propertied, 471.8
PROPERTY, 471, 704.17
prophet 961.4, 684.1
PROPHETS, 684
prophylactic, 86.20, 86.42
propitiate, 696.14
proportion, 477.7
proportionate, 477.13
proportionately, 477.14
proposal, 439.2, 562.8
propose, 439.5, 562.22
proprietor, 470.2
propriety, 637.2
propulsive, 903.14
prosaic, 117.8, 721.5
PROSE, 117.5, 721, 721.3, 721.4
prosper, 1009.7
PROSPERITY, 1009
prosperous, 1009.12
prostitute, 665.16, 665.28
prostitution, 665.8
protect, 1007.18
protected, 1007.21
PROTECTION, 1007

reach out, 261.5
react, 902.5
REACTION, 902
reactionary, 902.4
reactive, 902.9
reactor, 1037.13
read my lips, 535.5
ready-made, 405.19
ready-mades, 5.4
real, 471.9, 760.15
real estate, 471.6
realism, 986.2
realist, 986.3
realistic, 986.6
reality, 760.2
really, 760.16
REAR, 217, 217.9
rearrange, 807.13
rearrangement, 807.7
reason, 885.2, 934.15
reasonably, 934.24
reasoned, 934.21
REASONING, 934
rebel, 327.5
rebellious, 327.11
rebuttal, 938.2
recant, 363.8
recede, 168.2
receding, 168.5
receipt, 627.2
RECEIPTS, 627
receive, 187.10, 479.6,
　585.7, 627.3, 1035.17
received, 479.10
RECEIVING, 479
recent, 840.12
RECEPTION, 187,
　1033.21
receptive, 187.16
receptivity, 187.9
recess, 284.7
RECESSION, 168
recessive, 168.4
recipient, 479.3
reciprocal, 776.10
reciprocally, 776.12
reciprocate, 776.7
reckless, 493.8
recklessly, 493.11
recklessness, 493.2
reclamation, 396.2
recluse, 584.5, 584.10
recognition, 988.5
recognize, 988.12
recoil, 902.2, 902.6
recommendation, 509.4
recompense, 624.3
reconcile, 465.8
reconciliation, 465.3
reconnaissance, 937.8
reconnoiter, 937.28
reconsider, 930.15
reconstruction, 396.5

RECORD, 50.12, 549,
　549.15
recorded, 549.17
RECORDER, 549.13, 550
recording, 549.16
recourse, 1008.2
recover, 396.20, 481.6
recovery, 396.8, 481.3
recrimination, 599.3
recruit, 461.18
recumbent, 201.8
recuperate, 396.19
recuperative, 396.23
recur, 849.5, 988.15
recurrent, 848.13
red, 41.6
redden, 41.4, 41.5, 152.14
redeem, 396.12, 685.6
redeemed, 685.9
redemption, 685.4
red-handed, 656.4
redheaded, 41.10
reduce, 252.7
reduced, 252.10, 633.9
reducing, 270.9
reduction, 255.2
redundancy, 848.3
reel in, 905.9
referendum, 613.8
refer to, 956.14
refine, 79.22
refinement, 79.4
refinery, 79.13
reflect, 1035.16
reflection, 784.7, 1024.9
reform, 392.5
reformer, 392.6
reform school, 567.9
refrain, 329.3
refresh, 9.2
refreshed, 9.4
refreshing, 9.3
REFRESHMENT, 9
refrigerate, 1023.10
REFUGE, 1008
REFUSAL, 325.1, 442
refuse, 325.3, 391.4, 442.3
refutable, 957.10
refute, 957.5
refuting, 957.6
regalia, 647.3
regards, 504.8
regenerate, 692.10
regent, 575.12
REGION, 231
regional, 231.8
registration, 549.14
registry, 549.3
regress, 163.5
REGRESSION, 163
regressive, 163.11
REGRET, 113, 113.6
regretful, 113.8

regretfully, 113.11
regrettable, 113.10
regular, 849.6
regularity, 780.2, 849.1
regularly, 780.8, 849.9
rehabilitate, 857.14
rehabilitation, 857.4
rehearse, 704.32
reimbursement, 624.2
reinforcements, 449.8
reject, 372.2
rejected, 372.3
REJECTION, 372
rejoice, 116.5
REJOICING, 116, 116.10
RELAPSE, 394, 394.4
relate, 774.6
related, 559.6, 774.9
relate to, 774.5
RELATION, 774
RELATIONSHIP BY
　BLOOD, 559
RELATIONSHIP BY
　MARRIAGE, 564
relative, 774.7
relatively, 774.12
relativity, 774.2
relax, 20.7, 670.9
release, 120.2, 120.6, 431.2,
　431.5, 475.4
relevance, 774.4
relevant, 774.11
reliability, 969.4
reliable, 969.17
RELIEF, 120, 715.3
relieve, 120.5
relieved, 120.10
RELIGIONS, 675
religious, 675.25,
　699.15
RELIGIOUS BUILDINGS,
　703
RELIGIOUS FOUNDERS,
　684
religious orders, 699.16
RELIGIOUS RITES, 701
religious school, 567.8
relinquish, 475.3
relinquished, 475.5
reluctant, 325.6
reluctantly, 325.9
rely on, 952.16
remain, 256.5, 852.5
REMAINDER, 256
remaining, 256.7
remake, 396.18
remark, 524.25, 524.4
remarkable, 247.10
remedial, 86.39
REMEDY, 86, 86.38,
　396.13
remember, 988.10
remembered, 988.23

shrinking violet, 139.6
shrubbery, 310.9
shrunk, 260.13
shudder at, 99.5
shuffle, 758.4
shut out, 412.16
shy, 139.12
shyly, 139.15
shyness, 139.4
Siberia, 1022.4
sibilant, 57.3
sibilate, 57.2
sibyl, 961.6
SIDE, 218, 218.4, 218.6,
  934.14
side with, 450.4
siege, 459.5
sigh, 52.8, 52.14, 318.21
sight, 29.5
sight-see, 917.6
sight-seeing, 917.4
sightseer, 917.3
sign, 437.7, 517.1, 518.6
signal, 182.52, 517.15,
  517.22, 1035.11
signature, 527.10, 1033.19
signify, 517.17
signing, 437.3
SILENCE, 51, 51.8
silence!, 51.14
silencer, 51.4
silent, 51.10
silently, 51.13
sill, 900.9
silly, 923.6
similar, 783.10
SIMILARITY, 783
similarly, 783.18
simple, 499.6, 797.6
SIMPLICITY, 797
simplification, 797.2
simplified, 797.9
simplify, 499.5, 797.4
simply, 797.11
simultaneous, 835.5
simultaneously, 835.7
since, 836.17
sing, 708.38
singer, 710.13
singly, 871.13
sink, 80.12, 194.6, 284.12,
  367.8, 410.11
sinkage, 194.2
sip, 62.2
Sir, 648.3
sit, 173.10
sit down, 912.10
SIZE, 257, 257.15
skeleton, 2.2, 2.24
ski, 753.4
skier, 753.2
SKIING, 753
SKILL, 413

skilled, 413.26
skilled in, 413.27
skilled worker, 726.6
skillful, 413.22
skillfully, 413.31
skin, 2.4, 295.3
skoal!, 88.38
skull, 198.7
skyscraping, 272.15
slack, 1020.2
slander, 512.3, 512.11
slap, 604.3, 604.12, 901.8,
  901.19
slaughter, 308.16
sled, 179.20
sleek, 287.10
SLEEP, 22, 22.2, 22.13
sleeper, 22.12
sleep-inducing, 22.23
sleeplessly, 23.9
sleepy, 22.21
slenderize, 270.13
slenderizing, 270.21
slide, 194.4, 194.9
slight, 157.6, 340.8
slim, 270.8
slime, 80.8
slimy, 1060.14
sling, 462.9
slip, 974.4
slip away, 368.12, 369.9
slippery, 287.11
slipshod, 340.12
slob, 809.7
slope, 237.2
slough, 2.5
slovenly, 809.15
slow, 175.9, 175.10
slowing, 175.4
slowly, 175.3
slow motion, 175.2
SLOWNESS, 175
small, 258.16
smart, 26.3, 919.14
smartly, 578.18
smell, 69.6, 69.8
smelling, 69.3
smile, 116.3, 116.7
smith, 726.8
smoke, 89.14, 1018.23
smoking, 89.10
smooth, 287.3, 287.5,
  287.9, 294.8
smoother, 287.4
smoothly, 287.12
smuggle, 732.8
smuggler, 732.5
smuggling, 732.2
snags, 1005.5
snap, 56.2, 56.7
snapping, 56.10
snare, 356.13
snob, 141.7

snobbery, 141.6
snobbish, 141.14
snow, 1022.8
snowy, 1022.18
snub, 157.2, 157.5
snuff, 89.8
snug, 121.9, 1006.7
snuggle, 121.10
so, 958.15
soak, 1063.13
soaked, 1063.17
soaking, 1063.7
so be it, 332.20
sober, 516.3
sober up, 516.2
SOBRIETY, 516
SOCCER, 752
sociable, 582.22
sociably, 582.25
social circle, 582.5
SOCIAL CLASS, 607
SOCIAL CONVENTION,
  579
social gathering, 582.10
social life, 582.4
socialism, 611.6
socialist, 611.14, 611.22
SOCIAL STATUS, 607
society, 578.6
sofa, 900.19
soft, 1045.8
soften, 1045.6
softening, 1045.5, 1045.16
softly, 1045.17
SOFTNESS, 1045, 35.3
software, 1041.11
soil, 80.5, 80.16
soiled, 80.21
sojourn, 225.5, 225.8
sole, 871.9
solecism, 531.2
solely, 871.14
solemn, 111.3
SOLEMNITY, 111
solemnly, 111.4
solicit, 440.14
solicitation, 440.5
solicitor, 730.6
solid, 1043.6
solidify, 1044.8
SOLILOQUY, 542
solitary, 584.11
solitude, 584.3
solo, 708.15
Solomon, 920.2
solubility, 1062.2
SOLUTION, 939, 1062.3
solvable, 939.3
solve, 939.2
solvent, 729.17, 1062.4,
  1062.8
some, 244.3
somehow, 384.11

stinker, 71.3
stint, 484.5
stipulate, 421.7
stipulation, 421.2
stir, 330.11
stock, 738.2
STOCK MARKET, 737
stoic, 134.3
stolen, 482.23
stone, 1057.10
stony, 1057.11
stop, 293.7, 856.2, 856.7, 1011.13
stopped, 293.11
stopper, 293.4
stopping, 293.5
storage, 386.5
STORE, 386, 386.10
stored, 386.14
storehouse, 386.6
storm, 459.6, 671.4
stormy, 318.23
story, 719.3, 722.3
straight, 277.6, 277.7, 644.14
straighten, 277.5
strain, 725.2, 725.10
straitened, 1012.26
stranded, 1012.27
strangle, 308.18
stratagem, 415.3
strategist, 415.7, 610.6
stratification, 296.4
stray, 164.4
STREAM, 238
streetcar, 179.17
streets, 383.11
STRENGTH, 15, 68.3
strengthen, 15.13
strengthening, 15.5
stretch, 1046.4
stretching, 1046.2
strict, 425.6, 687.8
strictly, 425.8
strident, 58.12
strike, 727.5, 727.10
strikebreaker, 727.8
striker, 727.6
strike up, 708.37
string, 711.20
string instrument, 711.2
strip, 271.4, 480.24
stripe, 47.5
striped, 47.15
stroke, 73.8
stroll, 177.28
strong, 15.15, 68.8, 69.10
stronghold, 460.6
strongly, 15.23
strong man, 15.6
strong-willed, 359.15
structural, 266.6
STRUCTURE, 266, 266.2

struggle, 725.3, 725.11
strum, 708.40
strumpet, 665.14
strut, 501.15
strutting, 501.23
stubby, 268.10
stuck, 854.16
studded, 283.17
STUDENT, 572
studio, 712.17
studious, 570.17
study, 568.8, 570.12, 570.3
stuff, 8.25
stuffed shirt, 501.9
stuffing, 10.26
stuffy, 173.16
stultify, 922.7
stupefied, 25.7
stupid, 921.15
stupidity, 921.3
stupid person, 923.2
stupor, 22.6
sturdy, 762.7
sty, 80.11
style, 532.2, 712.8
stylish, 578.12
stylist, 532.3
Styx, 682.4
suave, 504.18
subconscious, 92.41
subdue, 432.9
subdued, 432.15
subject, 432.7, 432.13, 941.7
SUBJECTION, 432
subjugate, 432.8
subjugated, 432.14
submarine, 180.9
submerge, 367.7
submersible, 367.9
SUBMISSION, 433
submissive, 433.12
submit, 433.6
submit to, 433.9
subordinate, 432.5
subsequent, 834.4
subsequently, 834.6
subservience, 432.2
subsidize, 478.19
subsidy, 478.8
substance, 196.5, 762.2
SUBSTANCE ABUSE, 87
substantial, 762.6
substantially, 762.8
substitute, 861.2, 861.4, 861.8
substitute for, 861.5
SUBSTITUTION, 861
subtract, 255.9
SUBTRACTION, 255
subversive, 357.11
succeed, 409.7, 814.2, 816.5

succeeding, 814.4
succeed with, 409.11
SUCCESS, 409
successful, 409.14
successfully, 409.15
successor, 816.4
such as, 783.12
suction, 187.5
sudden, 829.5
suddenly, 829.9
suddenness, 829.2
sue, 598.12
suffer, 26.8, 96.19, 443.10
sufferance, 443.2
sufferer, 96.11
suffice, 990.4
SUFFICIENCY, 990
sufficient, 990.6
sufficiently, 990.8
suffocation, 308.6
suffrage, 609.17
suggestion, 950.5
suggestive, 519.6
suicide, 308.5
suit, 5.6, 787.8
sulk, 110.14
sulks, 110.10
sullen, 110.24
sullenly, 110.30
sultan, 575.10
sultry, 1018.28
sum, 728.13, 1016.6
sum up, 1016.18
summary, 557.2
summation, 1016.11
summer, 313.3, 313.8
summerhouse, 228.12
summit, 198.2
summon, 420.11
summons, 420.5, 598.13, 598.2
sun, 1070.13
sun god, 1070.14
superb, 998.15
superbly, 998.23
superficial, 921.20
superfluous, 992.17
superintendent, 574.2
superior, 249.12, 249.4, 998.14
SUPERIORITY, 249
superlative, 249.13
superlatively, 249.16
supernatural, 869.15
supersonic, 174.16
superstition, 953.3
supervise, 573.10
supervising, 573.13
supervision, 573.2
supplicatory, 440.16
SUPPLY, 386, 386.2
SUPPORT, 449.12, 449.3, 609.41, 900, 900.21

supported, 900.24
supporter, 616.9, 900.2
supporting, 900.23
suppose, 950.10
supposed, 950.14
supposedly, 950.17
supposing, 950.19
SUPPOSITION, 950, 950.3
suppress, 106.8, 428.8
suppressed, 428.14
suppression, 92.24, 428.2
supremacy, 249.3
surely, 969.24
surface, 182.47
surfacing, 182.8
surgeon, 90.5
surgery, 90.2, 91.19
surname, 527.5
surplus, 992.5, 992.18
surprise, 131.2, 131.7
surprised, 131.12
surprising, 131.11
surprisingly, 131.15
surrender, 433.2, 433.8
surreptitiously, 345.18
surrogate, 92.31
surround, 209.6
surrounded, 209.10
surrounding, 209.5
surveillance, 937.9
survivor, 256.3
susceptibility, 896.2
suspend, 202.8
suspender, 202.5
suspense, 130.3
suspiciousness, 153.2
sustain, 855.4
swagger, 501.8
swan song, 307.10
swear off, 668.8
sweat, 12.7, 12.16
sweaty, 12.22
sweep, 79.23
sweeper, 79.16
sweet, 66.4
sweeten, 66.3
sweetening, 66.2
sweetheart, 104.10
sweets, 10.38
swelling, 283.4
swiftly, 174.17
SWIFTNESS, 174
swim, 182.56
swimmer, 182.12
swimwear, 5.29
swine, 311.9
swing, 915.6
swinging, 915.17
sword, 462.5
swordlike, 285.13
sycophant, 138.3
syllogism, 934.6
sylvan, 310.37

symbol, 92.30, 517.2
symbolic, 519.10
symmetric, 264.4
SYMMETRY, 264
sympathy, 93.5
synchronous, 835.6
syncopate, 708.43
syncopated, 709.29
table, 807.4, 870.2, 900.15
tableware, 8.12
tacit, 51.11, 519.8
tacitly, 519.13
taciturn, 344.9
tackle, 905.6
tactile process, 3.10
tactile, 73.10
tail, 217.6, 217.11
tailor, 5.34
tailored, 5.47
tainted, 393.41
take, 134.8, 480.10, 480.13
takeoff, 184.8
TAKING, 480, 480.25
take it easy, 331.15,
1013.12
take off, 6.6, 184.38, 193.10
talent, 413.4
talented, 413.29
talk, 541.3
talkative, 540.9
talker, 524.18
tamper with, 354.17
tap, 901.7, 901.18
tapered, 270.15
task, 724.2, 725.16
TASTE, 62, 62.7, 496
tasteful, 496.8
tastefully, 496.11
tasting, 62.6
tasty, 63.8
tax, 630.9
tax collector, 630.10
tea, 582.13
teach, 568.10
teachable, 570.18
TEACHER, 571
TEACHING, 568
team, 617.7, 749.5, 752.2
tear apart, 801.14
tearful, 115.21
tedious, 118.9
TEDIUM, 118
teeming, 883.9
teem with, 883.5
teen-age, 301.14
teens, 301.7
telegram, 347.14
telegraph, 347.2, 347.19
telepathy, 689.9
telephone, 347.4, 347.18
televise, 1034.14
TELEVISION, 1034
telltale, 551.19

temper, 152.6, 1044.4
TEMPERANCE, 668
temperate, 668.9
temperature, 1018.3
tempered, 1044.15
temple, 703.2
tempo, 709.24
temporal, 820.7
temporarily, 827.9
tempter, 377.4
ten, 881.6
tenacity, 802.3
tenant, 470.4
tend, 895.3, 1068.7
TENDENCY, 895
tenderness, 93.6
tending, 895.4
tending to, 895.5
TENNIS, 748
tense, 128.13, 530.12
tension, 128.3
tent, 295.8
term, 823.3, 824.4
terminal, 210.10
terrestrial, 234.4
terrible, 127.30, 999.9
terribly, 999.14
terrified, 127.26
terrify, 127.17
terrifying, 127.29
test, 941.2
testify, 956.9
testimony, 598.8, 956.2
textural, 294.5
TEXTURE, 294
thank, 150.4
thanks!, 150.6
THEATER, 704, 704.14
theatrical, 501.24
THEFT, 482, 482.3
then, 820.11
theologian, 676.3
theological, 676.4
THEOLOGY, 676
theoretical, 950.13
theoretically, 950.16
theorist, 950.7
theorize, 950.9
THEORY, 950, 950.2
THERAPY, 91
there, 159.24
thick, 269.8
thicken, 269.5, 1043.10
thickened, 1043.14
thickening, 1043.4
thicket, 310.13
THIEF, 483
thievish, 482.21
thin, 763.6, 270.12, 270.16
think, 930.8, 952.11
think over, 930.13
thirst, 1064.5
thirsty, 100.26

wicked, 654.16, 660.12
wickedly, 654.19
wickedness, 654.4
wide, 261.19
widow, 566.4, 566.6
wife, 563.8
wig, 3.14
wigged, 3.26
wiggle, 916.7, 916.14
wigwam, 228.10
WILL, 323, 323.2
willing, 324.5
willingly, 324.8
WILLINGNESS, 324
will power, 359.4
WIND, 318
windblown, 318.24
wind instrument, 711.6
window, 292.7
windy, 318.22
wine, 88.17
wing, 254.3
wink, 28.10
winner, 409.6
winning, 757.6
winter, 313.6
WISDOM, 919, 919.5
wise, 919.17, 920.3
wiseacre, 920.6
wise man, 920.1
WISE PERSON, 920
WISE SAYING, 973
wish for, 100.16
wishy-washy, 16.17
wistful, 100.23
wistfulness, 100.4
WIT, 489
witch, 593.7
with, 253.12, 450.8, 768.12
withhold, 484.6

with honor, 646.11
without, 991.17
witness, 956.6
wits, 918.2
witticism, 489.7
witty, 489.15
woman, 77.5
womankind, 77.3
women's rights, 642.4
WONDER, 122, 122.5
wonderful, 122.10
wonderfully, 122.14
wondering, 122.9
wood, 1052.3
woodland, 310.11
woodwind, 711.8
WORD, 526, 677.11
wordplay, 489.8
wordy, 538.12
work, 724.12, 725.4, 725.12
workable, 888.10
WORKER, 607.9, 726,
   726.2
work force, 18.9
work of art, 712.10
WORKPLACE, 739
worm, 311.37
wormlike, 311.51
worn, 393.31
worn-out, 393.36
worried, 126.8
worrier, 126.3
worry, 126.2, 126.5, 126.6
worsen, 119.3
WORSHIP, 696, 696.10
worshiper, 696.9
worth, 630.2
worthless, 391.11
woven, 740.7
wrap, 295.20

wrapper, 295.18
wreck, 393.8
wrest, 480.22
wrestler, 461.3
wrestling, 457.10
wretch, 660.2
wretched, 96.26
wriggly, 916.21
wrinkle, 291.3, 291.6
wrinkled, 291.8
write, 547.18, 547.21, 718.6
writer, 547.13, 718.3
WRITING, 547, 547.10,
   547.22
WRONG, 638, 638.3
wrongdoer, 660.9
WRONGDOING, 655,
   655.5
wrongly, 638.4
X-ray, 91.9
yearning, 100.5
yellow, 43.3, 43.4
yes, 332.18
yield, 433.7, 472.5, 627.4,
   1045.7
yoke, 799.10
yonder, 261.13
young, 301.9, 561.2
young people, 302.2
YOUNGSTER, 302
YOUTH, 301
zeal, 101.2, 692.3
zealous, 101.9,
   692.11
zero hour, 459.13
zest, 68.2
zestful, 68.7
zigzag, 204.8, 204.12
zone, 231.3
zoo, 228.19